lonely planet

France

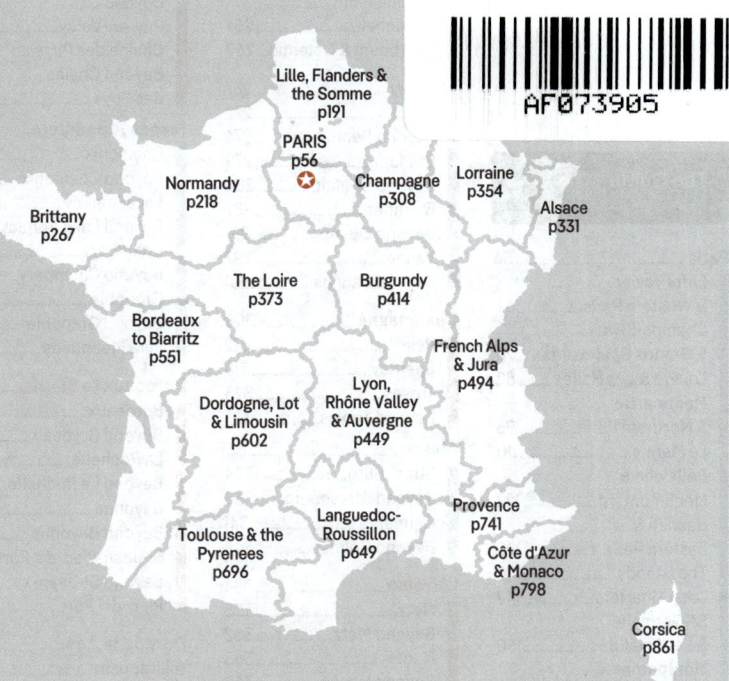

Lille, Flanders & the Somme p191

PARIS p56

Normandy p218

Brittany p267

Champagne p308

Lorraine p354

Alsace p331

The Loire p373

Burgundy p414

Bordeaux to Biarritz p551

Dordogne, Lot & Limousin p602

Lyon, Rhône Valley & Auvergne p449

French Alps & Jura p494

Toulouse & the Pyrenees p696

Languedoc-Roussillon p649

Provence p741

Côte d'Azur & Monaco p798

Corsica p861

Nicola Williams, Jean-Bernard Carillet, Cyrena Lee, Daphné Leprince-Ringuet, Chrissie McClatchie, Anna Richards, Daniel Robinson, Madeleine Rothery, Paul Stafford, Ryan Ver Berkmoes, Mary Winston Nicklin

CONTENTS

Plan Your Trip

The Journey Begins Here 4
France Map 8
Our Picks 10
Regions & Cities 24
Itineraries 28
When to Go 38
Get Prepared 40
Tasting French Wine 42
Exploring France by Bike 44
The Food Scene 46
The Outdoors 50

The Guide

Paris 56
Eiffel Tower
& Western Paris 62
Champs-Élysées
& Grands Boulevards 76
Louvre & Les Halles 82
Montmartre
& Northern Paris 96
Le Marais 110
Belleville &
Ménilmontant 122
Bastille &
Eastern Paris 129
The Islands 140
Latin Quarter 149
St-Germain
& Les Invalides 160
Montparnasse
& Southern Paris 174

Lille, Flanders
& the Somme 191
Lille 194
Beyond Lille 200
Amiens 202
Beyond Amiens 205
Boulogne-sur-Mer 212
Beyond Boulogne-
sur-Mer 214

Normandy 218
Rouen & Giverny 224
Beyond Rouen
& Giverny 229
Côte d'Albâtre
& Le Havre 232
Côte Fleurie 238
D-Day Landing Beaches,
Caen & Bayeux 246
Mont St-Michel 253
Beyond Mont
St-Michel 257
Cherbourg & Cotentin 260

Brittany 267
Rennes 272
Beyond Rennes 276
St-Malo 279
Beyond St-Malo 284
Quimper 287
Beyond Quimper 291
Vannes 297
Beyond Vannes 301

Champagne 308
Reims 312
Épernay 318
Troyes 323
Beyond Troyes 327

Alsace 331
Strasbourg 334
Beyond Strasbourg 338
Colmar 341
Beyond Colmar 344

Lorraine 354
Metz 358
Beyond Metz 362
Nancy 365
Beyond Nancy 369

The Loire 373
Blésois 378
Touraine 385
Anjou 397
Nantes 406

Burgundy 414
Dijon 420
Beyond Dijon 426
Beaune 430
Beyond Beaune 436
Auxerre 442
Beyond Auxerre 445

Lyon, Rhône Valley
& Auvergne 449
Lyon 454
Beyond Lyon 463
Gorges de l'Ardèche 467
Beyond Gorges
de l'Ardèche 473
Le Puy-en-Velay 476
Beyond Le
Puy-en-Velay 479
Chaîne des Puys 482
Beyond Chaîne
des Puys 489

French Alps & Jura 494
Chamonix 500
Beyond Chamonix 510
Lake Annecy 514
Beyond Lake Annecy 521
Chambéry 524
Beyond Chambéry 528
Grenoble 534
Beyond Grenoble 538
Jura Mountains 541

Bordeaux to Biarritz 551
Bordeaux 556
Beyond Bordeaux 566
La Rochelle 573
Beyond La Rochelle 578
Bayonne 583
Beyond Bayonne 588
St-Jean-Pied-de-Port 594
Beyond St-Jean-
Pied-de-Port 598

Dordogne, Lot
& Limousin 602
Périgueux 610
Beyond Périgueux 614
Vézère Valley 622
Cahors 628
Beyond Cahors 633
Limoges 639
Beyond Limoges 643

Languedoc-Roussillon ... 649
Nîmes 654

Beyond Nîmes	660
Montpellier	663
Beyond Montpellier	669
Causses et Cévennes	675
Beyond Causses et Cévennes	679
Carcassonne	682
Perpignan	686
Beyond Perpignan	689

Toulouse & the Pyrenees ... 696
Toulouse	702
Beyond Toulouse	712
Parc Naturel Régional des Pyrénées Ariégeoises	721
Parc National des Pyrénées	727
Beyond Parc National des Pyrénées	734

Provence ... 741
Marseille	746
Beyond Marseille	755
Arles	762
Beyond Arles	766
Avignon	769
Beyond Avignon	774
Luberon	781
Gorges du Verdon	790

Côte d'Azur & Monaco ... 798
Nice	806
Beyond Nice	815
Cannes	823
Beyond Cannes	829
St-Tropez	835
Beyond St-Tropez	842
Monaco	850

Corsica ... 861
Bastia	866
Beyond Bastia	869
Calvi & La Balagne	873
Beyond Calvi	876
Corte	879
Beyond Corte	882
Ajaccio	884
Beyond Ajaccio	888
Bonifacio	892
Beyond Bonifacio	895

Astronomical clock (p336), Cathédrale Notre-Dame, Strasbourg

Toolkit

Arriving	902
Getting Around	903
Money	904
Accommodation	905
Family Travel	906
Health & Safe Travel	907
Food, Drink & Nightlife	908
Responsible Travel	910
LGBTIQ+ Travellers	912
Accessible Travel	913
How to Shop at the Food Market	914
Nuts & Bolts	915
Language	916

Storybook

A History of France in 15 Places	920
Meet the French	924
How to Make a French Girl	926
Pavement Politics	929
Who Owns the Côte d'Or: The Cost of Continuity	932

Grand Balcon Nord (p506), Chamonix

FRANCE
THE JOURNEY BEGINS HERE

Despite living over half my life in France, I still can't shake off the uncanny feeling I'm on holiday. Renovating a 19th-century *canut's* (silk weaver's) apartment in Lyon while raising two out of three children thrust me no-holds-barred into French life. Now at home by Lake Geneva in Haute-Savoie, weekends of endless possibilities punctuate rural village life: skiing and trail running and wild swimming in ice-cold alpine lakes, cycling around Europe's cleanest lake, cultural flits to Paris, trips to regions so different each could honestly be a different country. That I clocked up 12,715km by train in 2024 (download the SNCF Connect app and create an account to bag your own annual count) is testament to the ease with which this extraordinary country can be explored. Do it. The sheer diversity of landscapes veined with ancestral *art de vivre* is bewitching.

Nicola Williams
@tripalong

When Nicola isn't running up a mountain or catching a train somewhere for Lonely Planet, she writes about France, Italy and Switzerland for the Telegraph, National Geographic and BBC. Nicola researched the French Alps and Bordeaux to Biarritz chapters.

My favourite experience is tuning into earth's heartbeat on a hike from alpine pasture to apocalyptic field of ancient glacial till on Chamonix's **Grand Balcon Nord** (p506).

WHO GOES WHERE

Our writers and experts choose the places which, for them, define France.

Exploring the World War I battlefields of Flanders and the **Somme** (p191) is endlessly moving. The museums explain what happened in these lands 100 years ago. Huge memorials capture the scope of the carnage. But I find the tiny and little-visited cemeteries the most heartbreaking and the perfect places to contemplate our responsibility for the horrors others endure in our names.

Ryan Ver Berkmoes
Bluesky: ryanvb

Ryan Ver Berkmoes has contributed to over 170 Lonely Planet guidebooks. He divides his time between Europe and California. Ryan researched the Lille, Flanders & The Somme and Champagne chapters.

There's nothing more relaxing than a day at the beach on the coast of **Cotentin** (p260), either walking along the dunes and beach huts at Gouville-sur-Mer (pictured) or bathing in the fresh waters of St-Germain-sur-Ay. A long stretch of beach and massive tidal changes has the capacity to make us feel awe. And during *moussettes*, or spider crab season, there's nothing better to eat – savouring the gifts of the seas you're admiring.

Cyrena Lee
@cyrenaly

Cyrena Lee is a writer based in the forest of Fontainebleau. She is the author of A Little Bit of Lucid Dreaming. Cyrena researched the Normandy chapter.

Aiguilles de Port-Coton in **Belle-Île-en-Mer** (p305) may sound somewhat underwhelming at first – but don't let the pitch discourage you. The site, where the coast breaks up into rocky spurs dramatically emerging from the water, lashed by the ocean's waves, inspired some of Claude Monet's most famous paintings. Watch it from above whether it rains or shines – it is without doubt one of the most epic spots in Brittany.

Daphné Leprince-Ringuet
@daphneleprince

Daphné Leprince-Ringuet is a journalist and writer based in Paris, but escapes at every opportunity to explore France. Daphné researched the Brittany chapter.

There's something special about the **Cap Corse** (p870). This northern tip of Corsica, the nearest to mainland Europe, does feel special and unique. The coastal route that hugs the shoreline and the inland secondary roads lend themselves perfectly to a road trip. And what a road trip! Gobsmacking sea views, gorgeous villages, intimate bays, seductive beaches, massive Genoese towers (pictured)... This is Corsica at its finest.

Jean-Bernard Carillet
@jb.carillet_photography

Jean-Bernard Carillet is a writer, photographer and videographer focused on travel, nature and culture. Jean-Bernard researched the Alsace, Lorraine and Corsica chapters and contributed to the Paris chapter.

If the past is a foreign country, as the novelist LP Hartley (who was not named for Lonely Planet) put it, then it's a particularly hard one to visit. Fortunately, the Loire Valley city of **Angers** (p397) offers a rare portal back to the late 1300s thanks to the Tapestry of the Apocalypse (pictured). In 71 vivid, action-packed scenes, spear-wielding angels skewer seven-headed dragons, demons lay waste to walled cities and the innocent are barbecued, offering a peek at our ancestors' profoundest fears and most fervent longings.

Daniel Robinson

Daniel Robinson has been writing about France for Lonely Planet for over 30 years, and has also written travel guides to Vietnam, Germany, Tunisia, Israel and Singapore. Daniel researched the Loire chapter.

Beaune (p430) will never cease to amaze me – with its mythical history and rich viticulture, I always discover something new each time I visit. I'm particularly impressed with how the vignerons are responding to climate change. They approach it with curiosity, as though it's a new opportunity to learn more about the region's infamous *terroir* (land).

Madeleine Rothery

@mad.e.leiner

Madeleine is an Australian writer based in France. She puts her love for storytelling into uncovering the diverse personalities and experiences that make up France's food and wine landscape. Madeleine researched the Burgundy chapter.

Cantal (p486) must be the most underrated place in France. It's well watered – you wouldn't get such electric green hills without that – and the weather in the valleys is no indication of how it will be at the top of a volcano. You can be basking in bright sunshine below and find yourself in thick cloud or even snow at the summit. And the food…a fondue made from all five of Auvergne's PDO cheeses means no regular fondue will ever compare.

Anna Richards

*Instagram: annahrichards_*

Anna Richards is a writer living in Lyon, writing about all things French. She's the author of Paddling France *for Bradt Guides. Anna researched the Lyon, Rhône Valley & Auvergne chapter.*

Cirque de Navacelles (p679) yawns open like a portal to a lost world. I always enjoy sitting on the cliff edge – the river valley unfurling before me with Navacelles village on the valley floor below – and listening to visitors react when they see it for the first time. That awe is the wonder of travel encapsulated in a single sound. I still say 'wow' every time I see the Cirque de Navacelles.

Paul Stafford

@paulrstafford

Paul Stafford is based in Birmingham, UK, but can usually be found anywhere that is not at all like Birmingham. When not entangled in a web of words, he is making music as one half of the alternative indie rock duo PHWOAR. Paul researched the Languedoc-Roussillon and Pyrenees & Toulouse chapters.

The **Jardin des Plantes** (p154) in Paris isn't just a botanical extravaganza with historical roots as Louis XIII's medicinal herb garden, it's a veritable treasure trove waiting to be discovered. The red panda in the menagerie is a heart stealer, but I also find myself gawking at the greenhouse orchids, the 300-year-old cedar of Lebanon and the crazy cool fossils in the Galerie de Paléontologie (pictured). The garden's bounty of secrets reminds me of Paris itself, peppered with surprising, serendipitous delights at every turn.

Mary Winston Nicklin

marywinstonnicklin.com

Mary Winston Nicklin is a Franco-American writer and editor based on the Left Bank of Paris. She researched the Paris chapter.

It might not be the most scenic nor joyful experience in the Dordogne-Lot-Limousin region, but if there's one site not to miss it's the WWII martyr village, **Oradour-sur-Glane** (p643). More than ever, it's essential that the horrors of war aren't forgotten and this village, frozen in time the day the Germans invaded in 1944, killing all but five of the 600-plus inhabitants, is the most stirring and significant place I've ever visited in almost 20 years of living in France.

Chrissie McClatchie

@chrissie_mcclatchie

Chrissie McClatchie is a French Australian travel writer who splits her time between the Côte d'Azur and the Lot. She researched the Dordogne, Lot & Limousin, Provence and Côte d'Azur & Monaco chapters.

CONTRIBUTING WRITERS

Alexis Averbuck

alexisaverbuck.com

Alexis paints and writes about her adventures – from living in Antarctica for a year to crossing the Pacific by sailboat. Alexis contributed to the Paris and Côte d'Azur & Monaco chapters.

Fabienne Fong Yan

@a.fab.journey

Fabienne is a writer and content creator about food, travel and culture. Fabienne contributed to the Paris chapter.

Michael Frankel

Michael is a Marseille-based freelance writer who lives for the slow doors of a hotel room clicking behind him as he makes his way down to the street. Michael contributed to the Provence chapter.

Rooksana Hossenally

@roxy.inparis

Rooksana is a travel and culture writer – and the author of the monthly newsletter about hyperlocal places in Paris: What's Up, Paris? Rooksana contributed to the Paris chapter.

Ashley Parsons

@jailoo.studio

Ashley is a travel and adventure writer splitting her time these days between Provence and the French Alps. Ashley contributed to the Provence chapter.

Nicola Leigh Stewart

@nicolaleighstewart

Nicola is a travel, food and drinks writer based in Paris. Nicola contributed to the Paris chapter.

Rowan Twine

@rowan.rt instagram

Rowan is a writer and photographer who's always hungry for a story or a meal. Rowan contributed to the Paris chapter.

Peter Yeung

@ptr_yeung

Peter is a Paris-based journalist and photographer who writes human-centred stories about culture, food and the arts. Peter contributed to the Paris chapter.

Lorraine
Unearth northeastern France's great industrial heritage (p354)

Route des Vins d'Alsace
Admire half-timbered villages, castles and stork nests (p349)

Chamonix
Journey across snow-white seracs into Italy (p500)

Lyon
Tap into the city's vibrant food scene and nightlife (p454)

Aubrac
Taste yesteryear cheese cuisine in a *buron* (shepherd's hut) (p681)

Gorges du Loup
Trade the Riviera crowd for unsung *villages perchés* inland (p832)

Bonifacio
Find your paradise on a Corsican beach (p892)

SUMPTUOUS CHÂTEAUX

No place on earth does châteaux like *la belle* France. Best up, countrywide, many are thrillingly accessible, be it over sightseeing, wine-tasting, hopelessly romantic dining or a sublime night's sleep in a four-poster. For architectural splendour, set your sights on the Renaissance jewels of the Loire Valley or sumptuous châteaux built for wealthy winemakers around Bordeaux and Burgundy. For wild châteaux *sans* crowds, set your soul loose amid ruined, sun-sizzled Cathar castles smacking of 13th-century persecution in Languedoc-Roussillon.

Showtime

Book tickets in advance online for Loire Valley châteaux summer shows (including nighttime musical strolls at Azay-le-Rideau, p393) and Versailles' magical 'dancing fountain' extravaganzas (p184).

Bike It

In the château-littered Loire (p373) and Bordeaux's Médoc (p566), steer off the busy tourist-trodden route along backstage cycling trails. Rent wheels to bike between châteaux stops.

Escape Games

Challenge kids to uncover treasure in vines or escape historical villains against a ticking clock: games at **Château Nestuby** (p847) in the Côte d'Azur and **Château de Bourdeilles** (p614) in Dordogne are family gold.

Hall of Mirrors (p185), Château de Versailles

BEST CHÂTEAUX

Spell-binding fountain displays, equestrian shows and 700-odd rooms make the UNESCO-listed king of French castles ❶ **Château de Versailles** (p184) a spectacular bucket-list experience.

During the autumnal rutting season, observe deer in the stillness of dawn on the forested estate of ❷ **Château de Chambord** (p381).

Follow in the footsteps of illustrious fashion designer Coco Chanel around ❸ **Château de Crémât** (p812) in Nice.

Gawp at no-holds-barred contemporary luxury accompanied by footmen dressed in rococo gowns at 17th-century ❹ **Château du Champ de Bataille** (p229).

Indulge your French fantasy of a boozy château dinner and overnight, fuelled with homemade Armagnac, at 13th-century ❺ **Château de Mons** (p720).

ARTIST PORTFOLIO

From world-class prehistoric cave art to Mona Lisa, France's illustrious art portfolio spans all eras and genres. Normandy's light spawned Impressionism, the 'wild cat' Fauvists broke with 19th-century realism in sun-scorched Roussillon, and Provence and the Côte d'Azur inspired a flush of 20th-century 'isms'. Every city and town has a *musée des beaux-arts* (fine arts museum), but it's the experiential art trails and festivals, and the house-museums and gardens where artists lived and worked, that make France's art journey so *beau*.

For Free

Spurn the museum crowd for a church. Many are free to enter and richly decorated with spectacular frescoes, sculptures and decorative arts.

On the Street

Blek Le Rat brought spray-paint rats to Paris in the 1980s and French street art hasn't looked back. Watch for street-art festivals with artists at work. Hunt for Invader mosaics.

Digital Art

Shift perspective: swap conventional art museums for digital art galleries where a WWII submarine pen in Bordeaux (p562) morph into modern-art canvas.

Jardin du Palais (p715), Musée Toulouse-Lautrec, Albi

BEST ARTISTIC ENCOUNTERS

Pair period art at Paris' packed ❶ **Musée du Louvre** (p86) with provocative contemporary art at Bourse de Commerce – Pinault Collection and the Fondation Cartier in dazzling new digs.

Discover the humanity and fragility of Henri de Toulouse-Lautrec's portraits at Albi's ❷ **Musée Toulouse-Lautrec** (p715), in a UNESCO-prized palace no less.

View Le Corbusier murals at ❸ **Villa E-1027** (p820) and the architect's Côte d'Azur 'château' with celestial sea views during a seaside stroll along the high-drama Sentier du Cap Martin.

Follow Impressionist footsteps around the canvas-worthy rural idyll of France's little-known Creuse. Monet devotees: don't miss the ❹ **Lot nursery** (p638) that gave the world his famous water lilies.

Join the dots between sardine-fishing villages and quaint streets in ❺ **Roussillon** (p788) to see where Matisse, Picasso et al collectively changed the course of art history.

Passerelle de Mazamet (p712), Hautpoul

PERCHED IN THE CLOUDS

There's no avoiding hilltop villages – known as *villages perchés* (perched villages) in Provence and *bastides* in the Dordogne where many were fortified. Practically sitting in the clouds, they were built atop a hillock or rocky crag from the 10th century so villagers from the plains could better defend themselves against Saracen attacks.

Festivals & Fairs

Every village celebrates its patron saint or commemorates a historic event with a *fête* – think dancing, drinking, much food and merriment alfresco.

Lunch Date

End your old-world village ramble around gold stone, pink granite or whitewash with lunch in the village *auberge* (country inn) – invariably overlooking a fountain-clad square or wrapped in wisteria.

BEST HILLTOP VILLAGE EXPERIENCES

In sun-baked Provence, tackle the lavish cluster of hilltop villages in the ❶ **Luberon** (p786) *à vélo* – e-wheels fully justified.

It takes nerves of steel to cross the quivering 140m-long suspension footbridge from Mazamet to the high-drama village of ❷ **Hautpoul** (p712), clinging to a mountainside beyond Toulouse.

Ditch the Côte d'Azur crowd for a scenic drive around unsung *villages perchés*, crashing waterfalls and storied forest in the ❸ **Gorges du Loup** (p832) – break for lunch in pretty Tourrettes-sur-Loup.

It's a gruelling plod up to the heady heights of cobbled rue de l'Horloge in medieval ❹ **Cordes-sur-Ciel** (p715), but the artisan craft workshops are a fine reward.

Revel in Corsican beauty beaded with soul-soaring sea and mountains views. Motor from hilltop village to hilltop village on a ❺ **Balagne** treasure tour. (p873)

THE BEACH SCENE

France's 3427km-long coastline is dramatically diverse – and raises the curtain on so much more than flopping on sun-kissed sands or sipping cocktails beachside. Hike along a *sentier du littoral* (coastal footpath) perfumed with sea salt and herbal scrub, admire picture-postcard surroundings afloat, or marry the old-school 'sun, sand and sea' formula with one of France's incredible top sights.

BEST BEACHY EXPERIENCES

On the western coast of Normandy's blissfully unspoiled ❶ **Cotentin Peninsula** (p260), walk endless stretches of beach and watch the tide – among Europe's biggest – race in.

Beach in the City

Paris Plages in the capital might be France's celebrity urban *plage,* with summer swimming in the Seine since 2025, but beaches pop up in other French cities too: around Grenoble (p537), Toulouse...

Safe Swimming

When a yellow or red flag is flying, skip the dip. On the Atlantic Coast, check the *marée* (tide) and watch for dangerous currents.

On the glitzy Riviera, the only way to access beach club **La Guérite** (p804) on ❷ **Île Ste-Marguerite** is by boat. Expect a glam crowd and the odd celeb.

Embark on a two-day **kayaking adventure** (p470) along the ❸ **Ardèche River**, breaking on pebble beaches for picnics and setting up bivouac camp overnight.

Embrace your inner beach bum in ❹ **Bonifacio** (p892). Nudist, snorkelling, kite-surfing, spectacular sunset, a boat to a paradise island – whatever you want, there's a beach with your name on it in.

Boat it to ❺ **Cap Ferret** (p571) then bike it to L'Herbe for oysters at a farm overlooking its tiny golden-sand beach and an overnight with the friendly ghosts of 1860s pine resin workers.

FROM LEFT: SERFF79/SHUTTERSTOCK, ANTOINE2K/SHUTTERSTOCK

Pont du Gard (p660)

HISTORY AT LARGE

France's historic repertoire is staggering – in volume and diversity. From relics left behind by the country's oldest human inhabitants to emotive reminders of modern French history, sightseeing in the land of the Gauls is gargantuan and enriching. Museums and monuments abound countrywide, and some of the most fascinating historical sights are at large in the open countryside.

Crowd Busters

Visit big sites early morning or late afternoon to avoid the worst crowds. Arrive by bike or e-bike to dodge car-park queues.

Guided Tours

Reserve a guided tour to get the most out of sights. Look for *visites insolites* (unusual tours) raising the curtain on hidden spaces and secrets.

BEST HISTORY JOURNEYS

Pair ❶ **Carnac** (p303) with less-visited megalithic menhirs and cairns in Morbihan, ending with a walk on Carnac beach at low tide.

Learn about Roman engineering at ❷ **Pont du Gard** (p660) near Nîmes – paddle under the 52-arch aqueduct in a canoe to experience a different viewpoint.

Head out of town from ❸ **Amiens** on an emotive and extraordinary road trip (p208) – by bike or car – to understand the true human cost of WWI's awful Battle of the Somme.

Remember WWII on Normandy's ❹ **D-Day Landing Beaches** (p246) where endless stretches of gold sand bear silent testimony to the human price of France's liberation.

Unearth northeastern France's great industrial heritage with a night walk round retired ironworks ❺ **Parc du Haut-Fourneau U4** (p364), illuminated until midnight.

BONNES AFFAIRES

Such is the diversity and magnitude of *la belle France* that you really don't need a fortune to have a good time. Saving money and spending wisely is the driver behind the country's wealth of *bonnes affaires* – good-value deals that represent excellent value for money, and don't cost an arm and a leg.

BEST GOOD-VALUE EXPERIENCES

In ❶ **Cancale** (p286) swap seafood fine-diners for oysters at the town's oyster farmers market. Bonus: big views of hallowed Mont St-Michel.

Take a train along ❷ **Corsica**'s handsome coast between Calvi and L'Île-Rousse (p876). With such priceless sea views, the cost is peanuts.

Your ticket to ❸ **Abbaye de Flaran** (p720) near Condom doesn't just cover the 12th-century Cistercian abbey's cloisters and buildings. It also includes an unsung art collection starring Picasso, Dalí, Rodin and Courbet.

Walk across the bay of ❹ **Mont St-Michel** (p253) with local guide Romain Pilon and learn how to not get trapped in quicksand. Paired with unparalleled dusk or dawn views of the Gothic icon, the €20 guide fee is a steal.

Fuel a fun night out in ❺ **Caen** with a cocktail mixing beer, white wine and calvados at **Ecto Bar** (p252) and free dancing at **L'Écume des Nuits** (p251). Or hit a summer *guinguette (outdoor tavern)* – ditto for other river cities.

Bargain Dining

Almost every restaurant under the French sun serves a two- or three-course weekday lunch menu – for a snip of its regular dinner price. In Paris, stand in line for a table at a trendy, yesteryear *bouillon* (p102).

Santé!

Wineries offer cellar tours with tastings – free or for a nominal fee. Trust us, €25 to explore 5km of cellars and taste six wines at Beaune's Patriarche Père et Fils (p433) is a *très très bonne affaire*.

FROM LEFT: LILLISPHOTOGRAPHY/GETTY IMAGES, LABELLEPATINE/SHUTTERSTOCK

PLAN YOUR TRIP · OUR PICKS

CAFE LIFE

Lounging over *un café* or early-evening apéritif on a cafe pavement terrace is one of France's great sensual delights. Cornerstones of local life and prime people-watching terrain, French cafes range from vintage *café tabac* (selling newspapers, cigarettes and drinks) to fashionista hangouts with craft coffee, cocktails and live music after dark.

BEST CAFE TERRACES

❶ **Le Marais** (p121) is Parisian people-watching 'hood supreme: over wine at funky **Café La Perle**, under striped awning at **Le Progrès** or in the afternoon sun at **Le Saint-Gervais**.

Lap up ❷ **Chamonix'** energising, high-octane vibe and full frontal views of Mont Blanc at **Rose du Pont** (p503), a stunning 'Belle Époque Paris meets Cham' cafe-bar.

In ❸ **Marseille**, watch local life in African Noailles unfold around the market: **Cafe Prinder** (p750) has served cups of strong coffee since 1925.

❹ **Bordeaux** (p557) spoils for choice with atmospheric, cafe-filled squares: start with car-free place Camille Jullian ('place Ca-Ju' to locals) and place du Palais.

Market squares always sport a cafe terrace overlooking the action. Bayonne's riverside ❺ **Les Halles** (p587) is a buzzy Basque classic.

Drinks

Coffee comes with a small glass of tap water. Order *un citron pressé* (iced water with fresh lemon juice), *kir* (white wine and blackcurrant liqueur) or – down south – aniseed-flavoured pastis.

FROM LEFT: MARIA SBYTOVA/SHUTTERSTOCK, THOMAS DUTOUR/SHUTTERSTOCK

Le Zinc

Paris' emblematic zinc bar has never gone out of fashion. All the rage in the 19th century, many cafes countrywide still sport an original or new zinc-topped bar.

Opening Hours

Cafes generally open from 7am until 11pm, morphing come dusk into a bar; some are shut by 7pm and others rock until 2am.

Citadel (p873), Corsica

BEST SCENIC ROAD TRIPS

Driving doesn't get more dazzling than along the trio of corniches corkscrewing dramatically from ❶ **Nice to Monaco** (p818).

It's a sensory thrill cycling through one of the world's most famous vineyards along ❷ **La Voie des Vignes** from wine town Beaune (p440).

Spot vultures wheeling overhead and break for an icy river dip between panoramic viewpoints in the ❸ **Gorges de l'Ardèche** (p469).

Journeys are measured in hours, not kilometres, in ❹ **Corsica** (p861) – road-trip the entire island, it's so devilishly handsome.

Enjoy the Alsatian difference over wine along the ❺ **Route des Vins d'Alsace** (p349) or Vosges peaks and *ballons* on the unsung ❺ **Route des Crêtes** (p845).

OPEN ROAD ESCAPES

With its smorgasbord of mountains, valleys, gorges and rivers – not to mention those lofty châteaux, coquette villages and lavish spread of vineyards – France was clearly created with road tripping in mind. Hit the open road by car, camper van, motorcycle or e-bike – take your foot off the pedal to savour every vista.

Themed Motoring

Flowering mimosas (Côte d'Azur), Cathar castles (Languedoc), D-Day beaches (Normandy), *grands crus* wines (Burgundy), châteaux (Loire), volcanoes (Auvergne). Signposted driving itineraries are diverse and endless.

Cols & Belvédères

Roads up to *cols* (mountains passes) can be perilously narrow, steep and sinuous. Pull over at signposted *belvédères* (panoramic viewpoints) to swoon safely.

WILD WAYS

France's kaleidoscope of natural landscapes, some more *sauvage* (wild) than others, invites sensory overload and a mountain of outdoor escapades. There are gentle, serene landscapes where wildlife is rich and time slows; razor-sharp alpine peaks and ice-blue glaciers screaming a call to action and mountains to climb by old-school train. Whichever green swathe of the hexagon you end up in, move with care and preferably on foot or bike to hear the call of the wild.

GR Walking Trails

France sports some 120,000km of *sentiers*. Long-distance *grande randonnée* or GR trails, marked by red-and-white-striped indicators, are easy to access as half- or full-day walks.

Shrinking Wetlands

Learn about these incredibly productive ecosystems – essential for the survival of birds, reptiles, fish and amphibians – in wetland nature reserves managed by the Conservatoire du Littoral *(conservatoire-du-littoral.fr)*.

Wildlife Watch

Observe flamingoes in the Camargue, vultures in Languedoc and the Pyrenees, storks in Alsace, bottlenose dolphins and whales in the Côte d'Azur, ibex at altitude in the Alps, and migratory birds in the far north.

Télécabine Panoramic Mont Blanc (p505)

PLAN YOUR TRIP — OUR PICKS

BEST WILDERNESS EXPERIENCES

Find Pyrenean highs at ❶ **Cirque de Gavarnie** (p732) – hike in October when beech forests glow gold, snow sparkles on summits and the summer crowd is gone.

Climb a mountain or cruise a protected nature park by train – aboard Pays Basque's **Train de la Rhune** (p600), the Pyrenees' **Petit Train d'Artouste** (p730) or by steam power in the ❷ **Cévennes** (p678).

Make a vertiginous journey to remember at high altitude across ice fields and seracs from ❸ **Chamonix** into Italy aboard the **Télécabine Panoramic Mont Blanc** (p505).

Tuck into cheesy *aligot* (cheese and potato dish) around a shared table in a *buron* (stone hut) once reserved for shepherds in ❹ **L'Aubrac region** (p680).

Ditch Corsica's Corte crowd for a hike through maquis into the remote depths of ❺ **Vallée du Tavignanu** (p883) – explore the deep car-free gorge on foot or horseback. Swim in natural green pools.

Horse riding (p767), Camargue

ROMANTIC LIAISONS

It's no coincidence that Renaissance gardens at the Loire Valley's Château de Villandry are planted with pink, white and red springtime tulips, summer begonias and chiselled boxwoods to portray tender, passionate, flighty and tragic love: the French are masters of romance. Almost every town and weekly market has a flower shop/stall, should you wish to say it with *fleurs*.

Exchanging Kisses

Unless it's your lover, *la bise* – cheek-skimming kisses, two to four, between any gender – is the standard greeting for casual acquaintances and friends. Desiring more? French oysters are said to be an aphrodisiac.

Lavender Fields

French fields of sunflowers, poppies, mustard seed and golden wheat are all eminently romantic. Provence in June seduces with sweetly scented swathes of purple lavender.

BEST DATES FOR ROMANCE

Grand boulevards, elegant parks, Seine-side strolls, a river cruise awash with monumental views: *flânerie* in ❶ **Paris** (p56) is the essence of French romance.

Drift over the ancient village of ❷ **Rocamadour** (p633), stuck to a cliff above the Lot's Alzou Gorge, in a hot air balloon. Soak up every hue of green and gold.

In ❸ **Biarritz**, watch the day's last rays cast France's most sought-after waves in soft pink over sunset drinks at a fashionable bar overlooking surf beach **Plage de la Côte des Basques** (p589).

Idle along the north bank of the ❹ **Maine** (p400), linger on the grass, and gaze up at Anjou's château and cathedral.

Gallop across vast golden sands on a white horse in an end-of-the-earth wetland odyssey in Provence's gloriously untamed ❺ **Camargue** (p767).

Paris 2024 Cauldron (p88), created by Mathieu Lehanneur

BEST NEW EXPERIENCES

Gazing at the ❶ **Paris 2024 Cauldron** (p88), floating like a hot-air balloon above Jardin des Tuileries, is Paris' hot new summer date. After dark is bewitching.

Mosey around ❷ **Mareterra** (p856), the newest neighbourhood to rise spectacularly from the sea in swanky Monaco.

A trio of world-class art 'musts' have reopened after remodelling: Toulouse's ❸ **Musée des Augustins** (p709), Bayonne's ❸ **Musée Bonnat-Helleu** (p585) and Cézanne's pad in ❸ **Aix-en-Provence** (p758).

Go virtual diving, real-life snorkelling or simply bone up on marine-life protection at Cap d'Antibes' interactive ❹ **Posidonia – Espace Mer et Littoral** (p830).

Fancy learning a new craft? Artisanal broom-making has never been so cool. Craft your own fly swatter or keyboard brush at ❺ **La Balaiterie** (p234) in Normandy.

WHEN YOU'VE SEEN IT ALL

In true French fashion, the country's creatives and innovators never keep still, ensuring perpetual inspiration for well-travelled Francophiles. New openings aside, shake things up with off-season travel to experience something different: the opening of Nice's sea-urchin fishing season, the blaze of sweetly scented mimosas in bloom...

Forward Planning

Chamonix hosted the first ever Winter Olympics in 1924, making it all the more fitting that Savoie, Haute-Savoie and Isère should host the next Games in 2030 (p503). Watch plans unfold in Nice, Lyon and the French Alps.

Beyond the Obvious

Think out of the box to unearth nature in the most unexpected of places: take the surprising biodiversity in Paris' monumental cemeteries and clandestine Petite Ceinture (p183).

REGIONS & CITIES

Find the places that tick all your boxes.

Paris

HERCULEAN CULTURE, HISTORY AND JOIE DE VIVRE

The French capital might be one of the world's most visited cities, yet there is always something new to inspire, seduce and wildly entertain (Seine swimming, anyone?). Take time out from the iconic sights to uncover extraordinary art and architecture, neighbourhood parks, scenic bike rides and artisan shopping through a local lens.

Normandy

HISTORIC BATTLEFIELDS AND FAT OF THE LAND

Venture beyond the dizzying, often-overwhelmed icons – Mont St-Michel, D-Day Landing Beaches, Bayeux Tapestry, Rouen Cathedral and the Étretat cliffs – to find the yin to Normandy's yang: a dreamy Impressionist canvas of pebbly beaches, sleepy farming villages, green fields speckled with cows and a profusion of blossom-pink fruit orchards.

PARIS p56

Normandy p218

Brittany p267

The Loire p373

Brittany

THE LAND OF LEGENDS

Wild, windswept and awash with old-fashioned adventure, Brittany fuses the call of nature with swashbuckling history. Once an independent kingdom, a Celtic heartbeat pulsates fiercely through handsome medieval towns, ocean scapes and *très belle* islands. Standing stones predating Stonehenge, a moonlit *fest-noz* (Breton dance festival), pirate beaches galore: it's endlessly captivating.

The Loire

DAZZLING CASTLES, VINEYARDS AND CUISINE

The Loire's emblematic Renaissance châteaux were built for supremely refined living, but drive or cycle a short distance and you can explore castles and dungeons that plunge you into the Middle Ages. Beyond, France's longest river nurtures fruit orchards, vineyards, towns offering superb cuisine and the region's signature *douceur* (gentle living).

Lille, Flanders & the Somme

BEAUTY TARNISHED WITH HISTORY'S REALITIES

Sea views, Flemish cuisine and artisan beers: Hauts-de-France merits more attention. It's a fascinatingly historic place, with outstanding museums in Lille, Gothic treasures in Amiens, and grand, intimate, WWI cemeteries and monuments that dominate with their immense beauty and heartbreak.

Champagne

SOAKED IN HISTORY AND BUBBLY

Learn how grapes become the world's most fabled bubbles on cellar visits and vineyard tours in this UNESCO-listed region. But it's not just fizz. Reims cathedral is a waltz through regal French history, while you'll need a full day to walk the medieval streets of extraordinary half-timbered Troyes.

Lille, Flanders & The Somme p191

Champagne p308

Lorraine p354

Alsace p331

Burgundy p414

Lorraine

UNDERRATED CULTURAL TREASURES AND GREEN ESCAPES

Few linger in Lorraine. But this industrial underdog, once powered by coal and iron, is sporting a lighter, brighter coat. Historic cities Metz and Nancy lure architecture and modern-art aficionados (Centre Pompidou-Metz is a stunner), while history buffs gravitate to Verdun's WWI battlefields. When fresh air beckons, hit the Vosges Mountains.

Alsace

A FRENCH REGION WITH A GERMAN TWIST

Proudly unique and fiercely Alsatian, this northeast chunk of France steals urbanite hearts with its student-fuelled capital Strasbourg – an appealing mashup of half-timbered architecture, museums and staunchly local cuisine – and riverside Colmar. Slow is the only pace along Alsace's cherished Route des Vins. Ditto for the Vosges – mountains few visitors have even heard of.

Burgundy

EPICUREAN DELIGHTS AND DIVINE NATURE

A heartfelt joie de vivre and indecent obsession with exceedingly fine wine and food pulsates through this rolling green wedge of France. It's a tapestry of canals, mustard fields and some of the world's most celebrated vineyards, all peppered with dashing capital Dijon and a smorgasbord of architecturally resplendent small towns.

Dordogne, Lot & Limousin

VINEYARDS, CHÂTEAUX AND PREHISTORIC CAVES

Market stalls overflow with truffles, duck products and red malbec wines in this rural region, carved by the course of the Dordogne River. Find some of Europe's most spectacular prehistoric rock art hidden in its ancient, cliff- and cave-hewed midst. Castle aficionados, take note: this is France's medieval château hub.

Bordeaux to Biarritz

AN EPIC TALE OF WINE, SEA AND SURF

The wave-crashing Atlantic is omnipresent in this naturally glamorous, southwest stretch. Bordeaux, cradled by historic châteaux and vineyards, is wine central, while it's surf bum meets seaside fashionista on the Côte d'Argent. When the glitz overwhelms, leg it to ancient pilgrim towns and Basque villages near Spain.

Pyrenees & Toulouse

ASTOUNDING MOUNTAINS, ADVENTURES AND ARTISANAL WONDERS

Exploring the Pyrenees is akin to gatecrashing the party of France's last wilderness. Crowding the horizon are snowcapped peaks, thundering waterfalls, vulture-specked skies and mountain lakes so crystal clear you could cry – and it all leaves you wanting more. Caves safeguard prehistoric art, pilgrims gravitate to sacred Lourdes, and medieval villages hem in the 'pink city' of Toulouse.

Lyon, Rhône Valley & Auvergne p449

Dordogne, Lot & Limousin p602

Bordeaux to Biarritz p551

Languedoc-Roussillon p649

Toulouse & the Pyrenees p696

Languedoc-Roussillon

LAYERED HISTORY, MOUNTAIN ADVENTURE AND CATALAN CULTURE

Curling around the Med from Provence to the Pyrenees, this coastal region in the hot south screams sand, seafood and debonair modern living. Inland, crumbling hilltop castles, gorges, caves and sparsely populated plateaux unfurl around the Cévennes mountains, promising outdoor thrills in spades. Then there's feisty Roussillon, a captivating Catalonia-France-Spain cocktail.

Lyon, Rhône Valley & Auvergne

VOLCANOES, VINEYARDS AND ANCIENT HISTORY

The country's rich past bubbles up in Roman Lyon, with an unprecedented gastronomic heritage, a vibrant cultural scene and party-fuelled river life. Downstream, it's all about prized Côtes du Rhône reds and gorge escapades in the rock-chiselled Ardèche. In rural, silent Auvergne, the pace deliciously slows.

French Alps & Jura

ONE OF EUROPE'S TRUE MOUNTAIN EPICS

In France's celebrated alpine playground, buckle up for heart-thumping skiing, soul-soaring mountain hikes and a nourishing dose of time-honoured pastoral charm – cheese crafted in ancestral chalets! High-octane Chamonix sits as queen at the foot of snowy Mont Blanc. The antidote? Rolling hills, vineyards and cultural quirk in the off-beat Jura.

French Alps & Jura p494

Côte d'Azur & Monaco

WHERE THE MOUNTAINS MEET THE MED

Synonymous with hedonism and glamour since the 19th century, the Côte d'Azur, or French Riviera, never goes out of fashion. Urban cool, old-world opulence and groundbreaking art meet in coastal queen Nice, while the jet set turns heads in movie star Cannes, mythical St-Tropez and megalomaniacal Monaco.

Provence p741

Côte d'Azur & Monaco p798

Corsica p861

Corsica

ISLAND OF BEAUTY, MARVELS AND SURPRISES

Though part of France for 200-plus years, Corsica is proudly different. A microcosm of island beauty if ever there was one, expect untouched diverse landscapes, time-forgotten hilltop villages, hair-raising motoring along serpentine coastal roads and adrenaline-infused outdoor action in spades. Untamed and beautiful, Corsican beaches assure the ultimate detox.

Provence

THE EPITOME OF THE FRENCH COUNTRY DREAM

There's far more to Provence than pastis, *pétanque* and hilltop villages glinting gold in the afternoon sun. Roman amphitheatres, modern art, bull-herding cowboys and white Camargue horses, vineyards, lavender fields and black truffles: the hues, scents and sights are electrifying. Then there's Marseille. Oh, and outdoor-action HQ Gorges du Verdon.

ITINERARIES

Iconic France

Allow: 10–14 days   **Distance:** 1200km

If you're in town to catch the best of *la belle France*, this highlight-studded trip is for you. Expect world-class museums and châteaux, Roman relics and a dizzying dose of urban action by the sea. With more time, each stop can easily be extended to a few days.

PARIS ⏱ 2 DAYS

The bird's-eye city view from the **Eiffel Tower** (p56) is a breathtaking introduction to the capital that doesn't tire. Experience it at night, or gorge on the Paris panorama unfurling atop **Arc de Triomphe** (p78) instead. Don't miss a concert in the soul-soaring **Sainte-Chapelle** (p140) and **Versailles** (p184). Factor in ample time for cafe lounging, bistro lunches and Seine-side strolls.

BLOIS ⏱ 1 DAY

Four centuries of French history come alive in small town **Blois** (p378), one-time feudal seat of the powerful counts of Blois. Play the French *flâneur* in its old-town tangle of tufa mansions and half-timbered houses, then plunge into Château de Blois' bloody history. Rent a bicycle or e-bike to devote the afternoon to Renaissance celebrity **Château de Chambord** (p381), 16km east.

VÉZÈRE VALLEY ⏱ 1 DAY

Descending into caves painted by prehistoric artists is the subterranean thrill of this rural valley in the **Dordogne** (p602). Learn the back story at the Musée National de Préhistoire in the pretty riverside village of **Les Eyzies** (p627) before plunging into nearby Grotte de Font-de-Gaume and later Lascaux in **Montignac** (p625). Buy tickets for both in advance online.

🚗 **Detour** *Break the journey in* **Toulouse** (p702) *to explore the* **Canal du Midi** (p709). 🚌 *1 day*

❹ CARCASSONNE ⏱ 1 DAY

The drive south through honey-coloured **Sarlat-la-Canéda** (p618) and cliff-hanging **Rocamadour** (p633) is beautiful. Along the way stop at a farm to buy a round of goat's cheese. After the wilderness of the southern Lot's UNESCO-listed Causses de Quercy, crowded **Carcassonne** (p682) can be jarring – linger over a late lunch of *cassoulet* (rich bean, pork and duck stew) and save the citadel for sunset.

Champs-Élysées (p76), Paris

5
PONT DU GARD ⏱ 1 DAY

Roman history buffs will have a field day. Stop in **Narbonne** (p689) to pore over Roman history at the city's world-class museum before continuing along the A9 to the awe-inspiring UNESCO World Heritage Roman aqueduct. Bring your swimming kit for daredevil diving and high jumping from the rocks nearby after exploring **Pont du Gard** (p660).

6
ARLES ⏱ 1 DAY

Camargue capital **Arles** (p762) is a sultry southern showstopper. Stroll golden-hued streets and riverside greenways, sit in the stalls in the town's amphitheatre, and shop for Provençal produce at the Saturday-morning market. Arles' contemporary antidote: the sensational, Frank Gehry-designed Fondation Luma.

↪ **Detour** Visit the Musée de la Romanité, amphitheatre and the Maison Carrée in **Nîmes** (p654). 🚗 5 hours

7
MARSEILLE ⏱ 2 DAY

Embrace the high-octane energy of Provence's sprawling metropolis, stitched from an eclectic portfolio of museums and 111 wildly diverse 'villages'. To get under its salty, weathered, mistral-kissed skin, begin your DIY tour of **Marseille** (p746) with fishermen at the Vieux Port. Don't forget the beaches along the coast and **Les Goudes** (p753), old-world launchpad for hikes and sea kayaks in **Les Calanques** (p755; pictured).

FROM LEFT: STEVANZZ/SHUTTERSTOCK, ERIC LAUDONIEN/SHUTTERSTOCK, DMITRI T/SHUTTERSTOCK

ITINERARIES

Atlantic Coast Cruiser

Allow: 1 week   **Distance:** 565km

Pea-green vineyards, open-sea oyster farms and the golden contours of Europe's largest sand dune shimmering in the sun – France's wind-whipped Atlantic coast is one long parade of postcard views and tantalising culinary stops. Driving allows you to motor off-track between villages and vines, but this highly appealing train-and-bike combo is the greener route.

Tour St-Nicolas (p575), Rochelle

① NANTES ⏱ 1 DAY

Atlantic Ocean and Loire River vibes mix in the old Breton capital **Nantes** (p406). Catch mechanical bestiary at Les Machines de l'Île on urban island Île de Nantes (pictured), visit its château, and track the city's edgy urban scene along the walking trail Le Voyage à Nantes. Grab lunchtime oysters at the city's covered market and sunset drinks at **Le Bateau-Lavoir** (p410).

② LA ROCHELLE ⏱ 2 DAYS

This prominent French sea port from the 14th to 17th centuries remains one of France's most attractive seafaring cities. Scale the sturdy stone heights of the maritime towers (pictured) in **La Rochelle** (p573) for bird's-eye city and coastal views. Scoff spectacular seafood, enjoy an afternoon stroll to Cap Horn's curious 16-sided lighthouse, and spend one day cycling around **Île de Ré** (p580).

FROM LEFT: JEANLUCICHARD/SHUTTERSTOCK, DENNIS VAN DE WATER/SHUTTERSTOCK, ALBERTORP/SHUTTERSTOCK

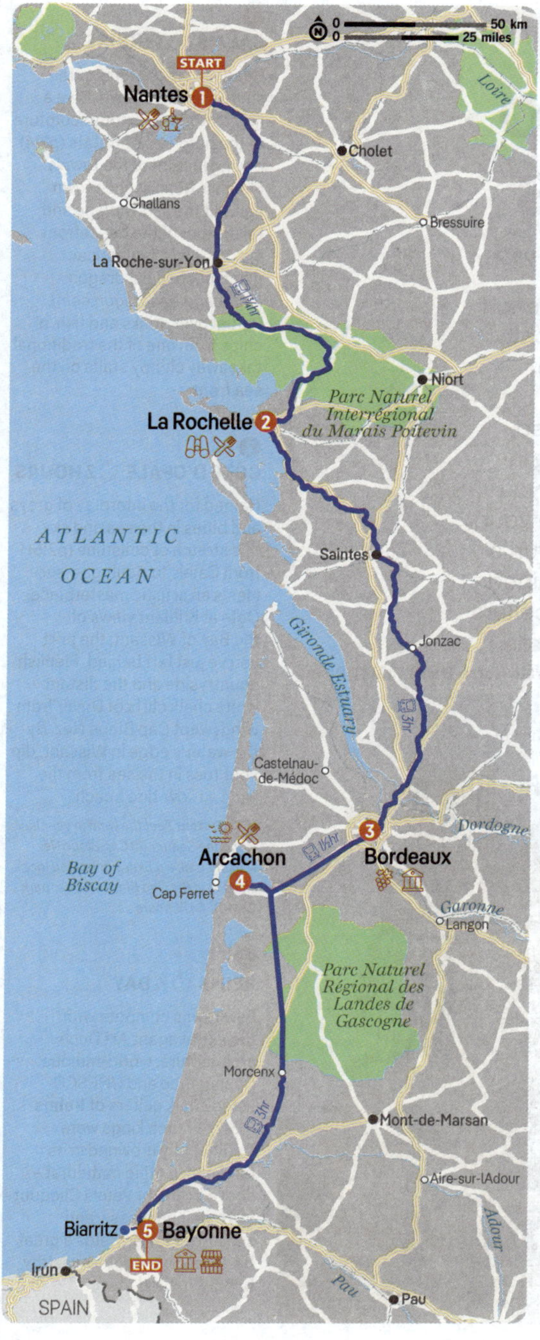

③ BORDEAUX ⏱ 1 DAY

A day spent feasting on exceedingly fine architecture, art, food and some of the country's most prestigious wines in **Bordeaux** (p556) is a day well spent. The historic part of the city forms the world's largest urban UNESCO World Heritage Site, but Bordeaux's flush of contemporary museums and edgy art spaces are equally captivating.

④ ARCACHON ⏱ 2 DAYS

Old-fashioned seaside charm rules the roost in palm- and pine-tree scented **Arcachon** (p569). Whittle away a blissful day flopping on the pristine golden-sand beach, seafood-lunching with sea views and riding boats across the bay to oyster-rich **Cap Ferret** (p571) and **Île aux Oiseaux** (p570). The bike ride to **Dune du Pilat** (p570) is as exhilarating as the colossal sand dune.

⑤ BAYONNE ⏱ 1 DAY

Seriously good chocolate, ham (pictured) and Basque buzz make the small but larger-than-life French Basque capital **Bayonne** (p583) well worth lingering in. Delve into its rainbow of half-timbered houses to unravel Basque culture at the **Musée Basque et de l'Histoire de Bayonne** (p583), overdose on France's finest hot chocolate and market shop.

➤ **Detour** The glitzy seaside resort and surf capital of **Biarritz** (p588) is a bus ride away. 🚌 5 hours

ITINERARIES

Calais to the Alps

Allow: 3 days   **Distance:** 985km

Skiers en route to the French Alps from England typically drive this route from the trans-Channel port of Calais in eight hours or so, sometimes overnighting in Reims or Troyes. When you have time to spare, take your foot off the pedal to unfurl a kaleidoscope of cabin-lined beaches, Champagne cellars and world-class vineyards.

Cathédrale Notre-Dame (p312), Reims

❶ CALAIS ⏱ 3 HOURS

Head off the car ferry or rail shuttle and into town. Give a nod to Rodin's famous sculpture of the burghers of **Calais** (p214) posing in front of the town's Flemish-Renaissance town hall. Hit the sandy *plage* and take a tour of the beachfront inside Calais' fantastical, giant mechanical dragon (compagniedudragon.com). Refuel over drinks and fish 'n' chips from one of the traditional takeaway chippy stalls on the sea front.

❷ CÔTE D'OPALE ⏱ 2 HOURS

Named for the interplay of greys and blues in the sea and sky, this stretch of coastline (p215) from Calais to Boulogne-sur-Mer is an artistic masterpiece. Ogle at brilliant views of the Bay of Wissant, the port you've just left behind, Flemish countryside and the distant white chalk cliffs of Dover from windswept Cap Blanc Nez. By the water's edge in Wissant, dip your toes in the sea from the wide-at-low-tide beach.

Detour *Feel the wind in your hair along the Sentier du Cap Blanc Nez walking trail, a 6.5km signposted loop starting in the Cap Blanc Nez car park (D940). 🚶 1½ hours*

❸ REIMS ⏱ ½ DAY

Few towns compete with the extravagant Art Deco architecture, world-famous Champagne and UNESCO-listed chalk cellars of **Reims** (p312). French kings were traditionally crowned in its landmark Gothic cathedral – spot a bottle of Veuve Clicquot in its stained glass – and scaling its tower yields a great bird's-eye view of the wealthy, bubbly-fuelled town.

ROSSHELEN/SHUTTERSTOCK

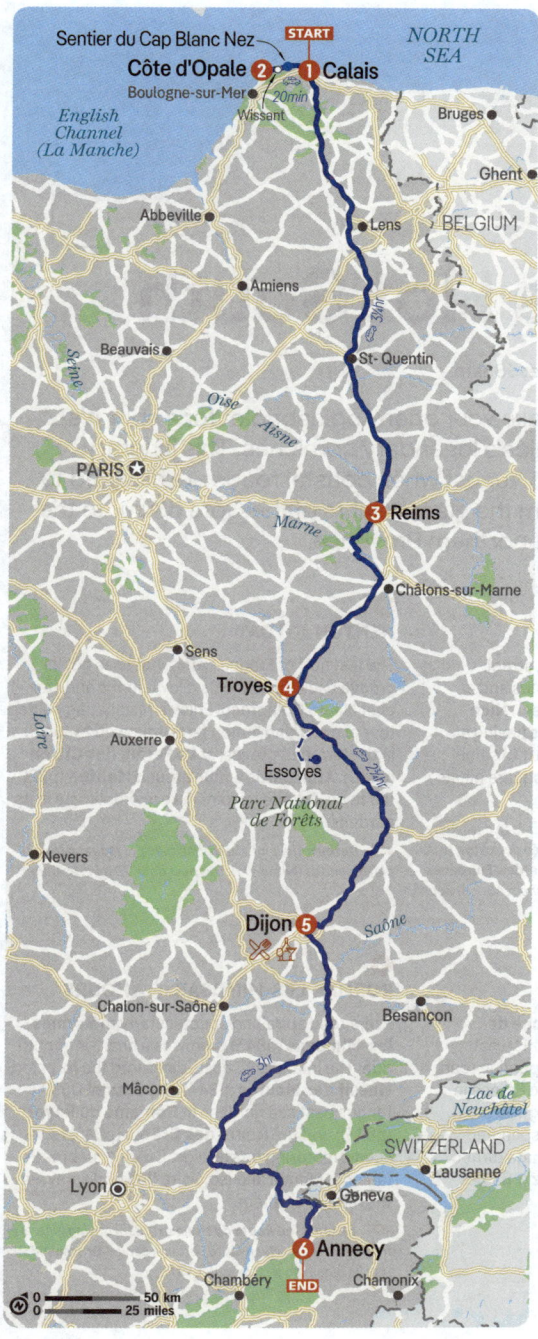

④ TROYES ½ DAY

A splendid mirage of half-timbered medieval houses, some so close they're almost caught in an embrace, awaits you in handsome **Troyes** (p323). Its cobbled streets were made for slow, romantic meandering.

🚗 *Detour:* Art lovers won't be able to resist visiting the home, glorious flower garden and studio of Renoir in the village of **Essoyes** (p327).
🚌 *3 hours*

⑤ DIJON 1 DAY

The **Cité International de la Gastronomie et du Vin** (p423) is reason alone to linger in **Dijon** (p420), seat of the Duchy of Burgundy and modern Burgundy's gastronomic powerhouse. Food-themed exhibitions, a food court, and a cooking and wine school at La Cité cook up ample entertainment and eating. Tasting Bourgogne wine is non-negotiable (spitting allowed for drivers). Families with younger children might prefer following the trail of bronze owls in town along the **Parcours de la Chouette** (p422).

⑥ ANNECY 2 HOURS

Depending where you're heading in the Alps, you're not far away now – count an hour to **Chamonix** (p500). Get in the alpine mood in **Annecy** (p514) with a chestnut, *génépi*- or pine-flavoured ice cream from vintage ice-cream parlour **Glacier des Alpes** (p515), buried in Annecy's romantic Venetian-style old town. Savour magnificent lake views from the vast lawn tumbling down to the water.

🚗 *Detour:* With more time on your hands, shake out your legs with a spin around **Lake Annecy** by bike (p518).
🚲 *½ day*

ITINERARIES

France's Hot South

Allow: 7–10 days **Distance:** 385km

If there's one region to take your open-top cabriolet for a spin, it's the flashy Riviera with Nice's legendary corniches. This itinerary, best avoided in July and August when coastal roads are clogged to bursting, whisks you from the glam heights of the Côte d'Azur to the wild, untamed gorges of northern Provence.

❶ NICE ⏱ 2 DAYS

Exceptional modern-art museums, street markets, emblematic pebble beaches and a rabbit-warren old town: Riviera queen **Nice** (p806) sizzles. Traditional cuisine is having a moment as the city's chefs elevate it to semi-gastronomic status. Pack in three square meals a day.

Detour: Cast aside the coastal crowds for a dip in Côte d'Azur backcountry, along the sinuous Vallée de la Roya to La Brigue's frescoed **Sanctuaire Notre-Dame-des-Fontaines** (p822). Think the Sistine Chapel of the southern Alps. 1½ hours by car

❷ MENTON ⏱ 1 DAY

The last huff of France before Italy has got its groove back thanks to its juicy lemons and star chef Mauro Colagreco. Enjoy a fascinating guided tour of a working lemon farm, followed by lunch in the terraced groves, at **La Ferme des Citron** (p820). Afterwards amble around **Menton** (p820) old town. Admire its miniature microclimate in its gardens.

Detour: The pint-sized principality of **Monaco** (p850), playground of the super rich, is next door. 20 mins by train

❸ ST-TROPEZ ⏱ 1 DAY

The drive along the coastal **Corniche de l'Estérel** (p833) towards St-Tropez is what Riviera motoring is all about: a serpentine road, inaugurated by the Touring Club de France in 1903, weaving between the flaming-red rock of Massif de l'Estérel and the sun-spangled turquoise sea. Mythical fishing village turned over-touristed celebrity **St-Tropez** (p835) is equally glam.

❹ BORMES-LES-MIMOSAS ⏱ 4 HOURS

Every road spiralling spectacularly to **Bormes-les-Mimosas** (p843) promises a heart-in-mouth ride. The inland D98 nose-dives into the forested **Massif des Maures** (p844); the coastal D559 tangos past sea gardens in **Domaine du Rayol** (p843); and the **Route des Crêtes** (p845) is scenic motoring on steroids. Catch your breath later over lunch and exquisite flower displays in the medieval village.

Detour: The **Route du Mimosa** (p833) driving itinerary from Bormes-les-Mimosas to perfume capital **Grasse** (p831) is at its blooming best in winter. 🚗 1 day

5
AIX-EN-PROVENCE ⏱ 1 DAY

With its grandiose architecture, elegant avenues, cafes spilling onto sun-baked streets and art portfolio of sculpted stone fountains, **Aix-en-Provence** (p758) encapsulates the classic Provençal vibe. Admire art in the Musée Granet and shop at the market; don't miss the newly reopened **Jas de Bouffan** (p758) where painter Paul Cézanne lived with his family.

6
REILLANNE ⏱ 4 HOURS

Chic hilltop villages in the **Luberon** (p781) delight. Perched at 600m, lesser known **Reillanne** (p785; pictured) is a classic Provençal *village perché*. Meander narrow lanes, taking in centurion limestone houses, its château, central fountain and hub of local life **Café du Cours** (p785). Expect music, dancing and party vibes. If it's Sunday, Reillanne's produce market is gold.

7
GORGES DU VERDON ⏱ 1 DAY

Get set for heart palpitations. Home to eagles, vultures and wild boar, Provence's **Gorges du Verdon** (p790) is France's most spectacular canyon. Drive snail-slow from **Moustiers Ste-Marie** (p790) to take in the canyon panorama from the vertigo-inducing cliffside D952. The walls of the deep ravine rise to a dizzying 700m – twice the height of the Eiffel Tower – in places.

FROM LEFT: JEAN-LUC ICHARD/GETTY IMAGES, RICHARD SEMIK/SHUTTERSTOCK, SERGE GOUJON/SHUTTERSTOCK

St-Malo (p279)

ITINERARIES

Breton Oysters & Norman Cheese

Allow: 1 week   **Distance:** 500km

Buckle your seat belt and loosen your belt in anticipation of the copious amounts of oysters and cheese you'll end up devouring on this epicurean road trip through Brittany and Normandy. Tranquil beaches and mythical islands provide a perfect 'exhilarating sea air' pairing. If you have extra time, shoals more tantalising distractions tempt.

❶ CARNAC ⏱ 3 HOURS

Begin where it all began – at the standing stones of **Carnac** (p303). Take your time. They date to the 5th century BCE and form the world's highest concentration of menhirs. Guided tours shine light on myths and legends surrounding the mystifying megaliths, and off trail, you can hike through surrounding woods to soak up Carnac's primordial energy.

❷ BELLE ÎLE ⏱ 2 DAYS

Catch a ferry from Quiberon on the 4km-long Presqu'île de Quiberon to **Belle Île** (p305). This ravishing Breton island lives up to its *belle* (beautiful) name: wild coastline, sandy beaches, traditional fishing villages and a fun dining-drinking scene in main settlement Le Palais (pictured).

🚗 ***Detour:*** *Break the drive to St-Malo with a 2–4km walk in the thick, myth-drenched Paimpont Forest – well worth it if you have kids in tow (p276).* 🚙 *3 hours*

❸ ST-MALO ⏱ 1 DAY

The enthralling mast-filled port town of **St-Malo** (p279) is a dramatic sight. With one of the world's greatest tidal ranges, brewing storms see waves lash the ramparts ringing this walled city. Privateers ruled here in the 17th century and their ghosts linger in the old city's cobbled lanes and private mansions.

🚗 ***Detour:*** *Rent a bike and cycle along the Rance River to quaint village **St-Suliac** for a crêpe (p284).* 🚙 *3 hours*

④ MONT ST-MICHEL ⏱ ½ DAY

Celtic mythology claims **Mont St-Michel** (p253) to be a sea tomb to which souls of the dead were sent. Keenly feel its history as you approach; barefoot across rippled sand with a hiking guide is best. Stay late to see the abbey at sunset. Dine on local foraged produce and sleep over at **Auberge Sauvage** (p255).

🚗 *Detour: Oyster fiends, head to the famous oyster market in **Cancale** (p286), a 45-minute motor west.*

⑤ CABOURG ⏱ 1 DAY

Holiday like Proust in this seaside town on Normandy's art-strewn Côte Fleurie. **Cabourg** (p243) delivers with its immersive museum plunging visitors into the Belle Époque. End the day with a boardwalk stroll from Cap Cabourg to Plage Le Home Varaville.

🚗 *Detour: Drive 30 minutes west to Ouistreham, gateway to Normandy's powerfully emotive **D-Day Landing Beaches** (p246). 🚗 1 day*

⑥ PAYS D'AUGE ⏱ 2 DAYS

Motoring inland ushers in a different Normandy – a fertile tapestry of green apple orchards, half-timbered villages and fields dotted with cows (pictured). Spend two days in **Pays d'Auge** (p244) pottering along peaceful country lanes. Learn how Calvados is made at a farm distillery, taste Normandy's four prized AOP cheeses, visit Camembert and dine exceedingly well.

FROM LEFT: BLUEJAYPHOTO/GETTY IMAGES, JULIEN JEAN ZAYATZ/SHUTTERSTOCK, BARMALINI/SHUTTERSTOCK

WHEN TO GO

Anytime. Beach-lounge in the hot south well beyond summer, rip down alpine ski slopes in winter, or opt for slower rhythms out of season.

Ever since French nobles paid peasants a pittance to walk the medieval pilgrimage to Santiago de Compostela in Spain on their behalf and English alpinists conquered mountain peaks to unveil tourism in the Alps, France has been a highly desirable place to go.

France consistently hits the headlines as 'the world's top tourist destination', notching up 100 million annual visitors in 2024. Making it even easier to get around responsibly, greening public transport and encouraging longer sojourns are top priorities for a country whose new 'dream big, live slow' road map has one overriding goal: becoming the global benchmark for sustainable tourism by 2030.

Play your part. Explore a lesser-known region. Stay longer in one place. Rejig your French fiesta to a quieter time of year. If you can, avoid July and August.

Accommodation Reservations

In inland cities, there are no strictly prescribed seasonal rates; rather, hotels are often pricier Monday to Thursday. On the coast, higher summer rates apply. Increasingly, across the board, flexible rates reflect occupancy: just like airlines, the fewer rooms left, the higher the price.

⊕ I LIVE HERE

BORDEAUX WINE COUNTRY

An international marketing exec working between the Médoc and Cognac, **Tristane de La Presle** shares her favourite moments in the vines.

September offers good weather conditions, a variety of colours and harvest excitement, especially when hand-picking occurs. In Cognac, distillation begins in October, providing a unique atmosphere. The second-best season is coming out of winter during pruning. I love to see the winemakers fostering the vines at dusk under winter skies. There's something magical about this handcrafted process, the respect for landscape and soil.

WEATHER WARNINGS

Download the Météo France app to check weather forecasts and pertinent weather warnings, issued twice daily (meteofrance.com). Alerts are coloured green, yellow, orange or red – the highest – to reflect the severity of an impending heatwave, storm, destructive wind or rainfall.

St-Émilion (p566)

Weather through the Year: Paris

JANUARY	FEBRUARY	MARCH	APRIL	MAY	JUNE
Avg. daytime max: 6.9°C	Avg. daytime max: 8.1°C	Avg. daytime max: 11.6°C	Avg. daytime max: 15.2°C	Avg. daytime max: 18.6°C	Avg. daytime max: 22.1°C
Days of rainfall: 9	Days of rainfall: 8	Days of rainfall: 8	Days of rainfall: 9	Days of rainfall: 9	Days of rainfall: 8

THE MISTRAL

The legendary mistral is a cold, dry, northwesterly wind that whips across Provence for days at a time. Folklore claims it drives people crazy. Its furious gusts, reaching over 100km/h, can destroy crops, rip off roofs, and drive tempers around the bend.

Arts Festivals

Village, town and city, the nation takes to the streets for celebrating **Fête de la Musique** (fetedelamusique.culture.gouv.fr), a national music festival marking summer solstice. All sounds, all venues – staged and impromptu. **21 June**

The setting alone for France's largest jazz festival, **Jazz à Vienne** (p463) is utterly spellbinding: a fortnight of open-air performances in Vienne's remarkable Roman amphitheatre. **late June and early July**

Rouse your inner thespian with Avignon's world-famous performing-arts festival, **Festival d'Avignon** (p771), raising the curtain on three weeks of performances by French and international theatre companies. Catch street acts in its fringe fest. **July**

Traditional Celtic music fills the Breton town of Quimper during its landmark summer festival, **Festival de Cornouaille** (p288) – Brittany's biggest celebration of Breton dance, music and traditional costume. **July**

Larger-than-Life Spectacles

Just how creative can you can get with 140 tonnes of lemons? See for yourself at Menton's **Fête du Citron** (p820) when floats parade through town decorated with lemon sculptures. **February**

Shepherds walk their sheep up to summer pastures during St-Rémy-de-Provence's **Fête de la Transhumance**. In the French Alps, it's goats and cows (p730). **May or June**

Espadrille throwing, tugs-of-war and stone-lifting *festivals de force basque* (strongman competitions) are wilder Basque traditions celebrated during Bayonne's **Fêtes de Bayonne** (p585), essentially five days of all-nighters. **July or August**

Géants (giants) – wickerwork body masks, up to 8.5m tall and animated by a person walking inside – come out of the woodwork for pre-Lenten carnivals, street parades and summer festivals in Lille, Arras and other northern French towns. **May to September**

TRAIL RUNNING IN THE ALPS

Doug Mayer of Run the Alps (*runthealps.com*) shares his trail-running passion on guided and self-guided trail running tours around Chamonix.

September is a bit of a secret among Alps residents. There are fewer people on the trails, the weather is cooler and, generally speaking, more stable. I also love June. One of the treats of Alps trail running is getting up high and crossing a late-season snowfield. It brings a high-mountain experience to your run.

Trail running, Chamonix (p500)

CHANGING CLIMATE

France has endured some of the hottest, driest summers on record in recent years, and suffered wildfires on an unprecedented scale. Flash floods, storms raining hail stones the size of golf balls and other violent 'unseasonal' extremes are now the norm. Winter snowfall is no longer predictable.

JULY	AUGUST	SEPTEMBER	OCTOBER	NOVEMBER	DECEMBER
Avg. daytime max: 24.2°C	Avg. daytime max: 24°C	Avg. daytime max: 20.9°C	Avg. daytime max: 16.4°C	Avg. daytime max: 10.7°C	Avg. daytime max: 7.5°C
Days of rainfall: 8	Days of rainfall: 7	Days of rainfall: 6	Days of rainfall: 8	Days of rainfall: 9	Days of rainfall: 10

Lyon (p454)

GET PREPARED FOR FRANCE

Useful things to load in your bag, your ears and your brain.

Clothes

Smart-casual outfits Cities are a catwalk of mixed styles; aim for smart casual. Pack at least one smarter outfit – a dress or smart trousers, no jeans or sneakers – for dining in midrange to upmarket restaurants and evenings out.

Rain-proof jacket Increasingly unpredictable weather patterns make an easy-to-stash waterproof shell – much-appreciated windbreaker too – in a day-bag essential.

Light scarf or sarong Cover bare shoulders when visiting churches, your head from the sun or your face when sunbathing. A sarong doubles as beach wrap, dressing gown, picnic rug, sheet...

Sturdy hiking sandals or shoes Hilltop village with cobbled streets, vineyard or riverside walk, châteaux with labyrinthine steps and passages or lighthouse with spiralling staircase: wherever you go in France, you'll be forever grateful for a flat, comfy robust pair of sandals or shoes.

Manners

Always say bonjour (or *bonsoir* after 5pm) when entering a business or passing a fellow hiker.

Exchange bisous (cheek-skimming kisses) – at least two, but in some parts of France it can be up to four – with casual acquaintances and friends.

Use the formal vous when speaking to anyone unknown or older than you; reserve informal *tu* for close friends, family and children.

📖 READ

And Their Children After Them (Nicolas Mathieu; 2018) Goncourt Prize–winning 'coming of age' novel set in a post-industrial town.

Amuse Bouche (Carolyn Boyd; 2024) A celebratory study in how to eat your way around every region in France.

The Insolents (Ann Scott; 2023) A woman leaves Paris post-pandemic to reinvent her life. Scott astutely depicts modern French life.

Granite Island: A Portrait of Corsica (Dorothy Carrington; 1971) A definitive portrait of Corsica and a travel writing classic.

Words

Bonjour (bon-zhoor) How you say 'good morning' or 'hello'. Come late afternoon, switch to **bonsoir** ('good evening') to greet anyone, be it a shopkeeper, bartender, bus driver or hiker on a trail.
Salut (sa-loo) The more casual, informal way of saying 'hello' or 'hi' to friends and family, and can be used any time of day. It also means 'bye', 'ciao' and 'cheers'.
Comment allez-vous?' (ko-mon ta-lay-voo) Used to ask how someone is. If the person you are asking is a close friend or child, switch from the formal form of 'you' (*vous*) to the more casual *'Comment vas-tu?'* (ko-mon va-too).
S'il vous plaît' (seel voo play) The same rule applies to 'please' for people you don't know; use *'s'il te plaît'* (seel ter play) for friends, kids and anyone who invites you to use the less-formal 'tu' form by saying *'Tu peux me tutoyer'* (too per mer too-twa-yay).
Merci (mair-see) Thank you
De rien (der ree-en) 'You're welcome' or 'It's nothing'.
Garçon! Never use this to beckon waiting staff in restaurants. Attract their attention by saying *'Monsieur!'* (mess-yer) for men and *'Madame!'* (ma-dam) for women. The French tradition of addressing young or single women as *'Mademoiselle'* is dated.
Un café (un ka-fay) If you simply ask for 'a coffee' in cafes, bars and restaurants, you'll automatically get a short, strong espresso. To order a longer black or milky coffee, cappuccino etc, you must specify.

WATCH

The Count of Monte Cristo (Matthieu Delaporte and Alexandre de La Patellière; 2024; pictured) Big-screen adaptation of Alexandre Dumas' classic adventure novel from 1846.

Vingt Dieux (*Holy Cow*; Louise Courvoisier; 2024) Living the ultimate French cheese dream: a teen's quest to make a wheel of Comté in rural Jura.

Simone Veil, A Woman of the Century (Olivier Dahan; 2022) Emotive biography of the Nice-born Holocaust survivor and women's activist.

L'Amour Ouf (*Beating Hearts*; Gilles Lellouche; 2024) French comedy based in northern France in the 1980s and '90s.

LISTEN

Talking France (thelocal.fr) Podcast dissecting current affairs, cultural issues and hot topics of the day by The Local's clued-in news team.

Resonate (Papooz; 2024) Cult Paris-based duo, Ulysse Cottin and Armand Penicaut, elevate spirits with their upbeat mix of French folk, pop and rock.

Way Back Home (Saint DX; 2024) 'When I'm feeling romantic despair, I listen to Saint DX' says one of our writers. The seductive, Sade-esque vibe of Aurélien Hamm's voice is indisputable.

Famille (Ben Mazué; 2025) Charismatic singer-songwriter-rapper Ben Mazué searches for beauty in daily life in music inspired by African music and American soul.

White wine, Pouilly-Fumé

TRIP PLANNER

TASTING FRENCH WINE

The French thirst for wine dates to Roman times when oenophiles identified fertile pockets of Gaul to plant *vignobles* (vineyards) to spawn France's most celebrated wine regions: Burgundy, Bordeaux, Champagne, Alsace, the Loire and Rhône valleys, Provence and Languedoc. Needless to say, *dégustation* (tasting) – including heaps of non-alcoholic vintages these days – is an essential part of French wine culture.

Terroir & AOCs

Modern winemakers have survived crop-decimating disease and devastating frosts to hone techniques, safeguard tradition, diversify and seal their reputation as custodians of a Herculean wine legacy unmatched elsewhere on the globe. Now they are battling climate change and global economic turmoil.

France is the world's largest producer of wine after Italy, and its wildly varied *terroir* (land) assures diverse, exciting and sometimes complex wines – increasingly organic, biodynamic or natural.

Quality wines in France are Appellation d'Origine Contrôlée (AOC) or Appellation d'Origine Protégée (AOP): the wine has met stringent regulations governing where, how and under what conditions it was grown and bottled. Some regions have a single AOC (like Alsace); others dozens. Bordeaux has 65, including iconic names like Médoc, St-Émilion and Graves.

Red

France's most respected reds hail from Burgundy, Bordeaux and the Rhône Valley (notably strong-bodied Châteauneuf-du-Pape, bequeathed by the Avignon popes). The ability of Bandol reds, produced from dark-berried mourvèdre grapes, to mature at sea ensured they travelled far beyond home shores in the 16th and 17th centuries.

BUYING & TASTING TIPS

Bordeaux and Provence Many estates run guided tours with tasting; reserve in advance.

Burgundy Wineries are almost impossible to visit; buy from *négociants* (wine merchants) in specialist wine shops instead.

Provence Many *vignerons* (growers) open their doors to visitors; taste two or three vintages before buying. In Provence fill your own container with cheap *vin de table* (table wine) at the local wine cooperatives.

More options Tourist offices and *maisons des vins* have lists of *domaines* (estates), châteaux, *caves* (wine cellars) and cooperatives that offer tasting and sales.

Drive safely Don't drink and drive – ask for a spittoon.

Monks in Burgundy began making wine in the 8th century, believing divine spirits in the soil spoke to them through wine. Burgundy vineyards remain small and are divided into *climats* – a viticultural patrimony UNESCO-listed since 2015. Winegrowers in Côte d'Or, Chablis, Châtillon and Mâcon produce small quantities of excellent reds from pinot noir grapes. The best Bourgogne vintages demand 10 to 20 years to age.

White

Vines were planted by the Greeks in Massilia (Marseille) around 600 BCE and crisp Cassis whites remain the perfect companions to coastal shellfish and seafood. The Loire Valley produces France's greatest variety of wines, some in troglodyte caves. Light delicate whites from Pouilly-Fumé, Vouvray, Sancerre, Bourgueil and Chinon are excellent. Muscadet, cabernet franc and chenin blanc grapes contrast with chardonnay grapes that go into Burgundy's great whites.

Wines from Alsace are almost exclusively white – mostly varieties produced nowhere else in France. Known for their clean, fresh taste, fruity Alsatian whites pair well with red meat. Alsace's four most important wines are riesling (known for its subtlety), gewürztraminer (pungent and highly regarded), pinot gris (robust) and muscat d'Alsace (less sweet than southern France muscats).

Rosé

Chilled, fresh pink rosé wines are synonymous with the hot south. Côtes de Provence, with 20 hectares of vineyards between Nice and Aix-en-Provence, is France's sixth-largest appellation. Look for rosés from Bandol, Coteaux d'Aix-en-Provence, Palette and Coteaux Varois.

TASTING WINE 2.0

There is so much more to tasting wine in France than a simple swill, smell, sip and swallow or spit. *Dégustation* (tasting) is as much about location and the sharing of ancestral knowledge by winemakers.

Cahors Taste big Argentinian-style reds crafted from malbec grapes on a road trip through under-the-radar Cahors AOC vineyards. Linger late to catch live music in the vines (p630).

Château Lynch-Bages Tour Médoc (p568) cellars designed by Chinese architect Chien Chung Pei – his father dreamt up the Louvre's head-turning glass pyramid in Paris (p86).

Cité Internationale de la Gastronomie et du Vin Open your viticultural foray through Bourgogne greats with a 'tasting package' in the cellar of Dijon's landmark gastronomy and wine HQ. With 250 wines by the glass and 3000+ bottles, you need to be selective (p432).

Fête des Vendanges de Montmartre Paris' urban vineyard in Montmartre celebrates its October grape harvest with five days of wine-fuelled festivities (p101).

Route des Vins d'Alsace Taste organic wine at a 16th-century winery, play vintner for a day or sample sweet wines made with overripe grapes along France's oldest wine route from 1953 (p349).

Boutique Champagne Visit a lesser-known bubbly house like Épernay's Champagne Leclerc Briant. It ages one cuvée at sea and ferments another in a gold-lined oak barrel (p322).

Finistère (p291), Brittany

TRIP PLANNER

EXPLORING FRANCE BY BIKE

Never has cycling around France been so popular. The French have typically slipped in their saddle for a Sunday afternoon spin since the 1960s. But as electric bikes dominate the mainstream, and dedicated cycling paths and themed cycling itineraries boom (in cities and countryside), everyone's doing it. Cut carbon and join the peloton.

Renting Wheels

Most towns have at least one bike rental shop, stocked with regular city bikes, touring bikes, mountain bikes (VTT), kids' bikes and trailers. Electric-assisted bikes (*vélo à assistance électrique*) with maximum speeds of 25km/h are everywhere; verify battery duration before pedalling off. Rental shops require a copy of your ID or passport and a deposit (usually a credit-card slip of €250) that you forfeit if the bike is damaged or stolen. Reserve wheels in advance in high season. Some places, typically in busy riding hub Lake Annecy (p518) in the French Alps, don't accept reservations; in July, August and at weekends, arrive dot on 9am to ensure wheels.

Accueil Vélo

Some hotels offer enclosed bicycle parking. For a warm welcome and safe stowing of you and your wheels overnight, stay in a hotel, B&B, campground or self-catering accommodation accredited with an 'Accueil Vélo' label – some 7000 bike-friendly sites (also museums and monuments) countrywide are listed on en.francevelotourisme.com.

Transporting Bikes & Luggage

Travel to the start of your cycling route by train, or mix-and-match day rides with train trips in different regions. Bicycles can be taken along on virtually all intraregional TER trains and most long-distance intercity trains, without a reservation but

TOOLKIT: APPS, MAPS & TOURS

Apps Plot trips with GPS route planner Komoot; locate spots to pitch tents with Park4night; find walks and hikes to weave into longer rides with MaRando and Visorando, and search for cycling itineraries by bike type on Cirkwi.

France Vélo Tourisme Definitive guide to cycling in and around France; download GPX files for GPS itineraries. *en.francevelotourisme.com*

Freewheeling France Comprehensive cycling guide, with handy list of rental shops that deliver bikes – useful for routes starting and ending in different places. *freewheelingfrance.com*

Tours Pay €80 to €160 for a full-day, guided tour by e-bike; tourist offices have info.

---

subject to space availability. Look for the special bike carriage, equipped with bike racks to stow your bike.

Transporting bikes on regional TER trains is free. OUIGO, Intercités and TGV trains command a €10 fee; select the '+ un vélo' or 'add bikes' tab when buying tickets on sncf-connect.com or the SNCF Connect app. On the Atlantic Coast, bikes require their own ticket aboard boats to/from Cap Ferret.

In the Loire Valley (p393), dozens of private companies transport baggage for cyclists; find details on loireavelo.fr.

Road Rules

Helmets are only legally required for children under 12, but most adults wear them. If a rental shop doesn't automatically offer you a helmet (common on the coast) ask for one. Helmets are included in the rental price.

Use dedicated bike paths or delineated cycling lanes – riding bikes on sidewalks is forbidden.

The legal speed limit is 25km/h, including for e-bikes (45km/h for s-pedelecs with number plate).

It's illegal to cycle on roads while using headphones or ear-pods.

SUGGESTED ROUTES

All these long-distance routes divide into neat, half- or full-day chunks – ideal for bike-packers and casual riders seeking a scenic day out.

La Loire à Vélo Join the dots between châteaux in the Loire Valley with this 900km network of cycling lanes. The 82km weekend ride from Blois, taking in five châteaux and returning by train from Onzain, is a highlight. *loirebybike.co.uk*

Route des Grands Crus Burgundy sports a circular 800km 'grand tour' of the region, but its tour de force for wine buffs on wheels is this 60km ride from Dijon to Côte de Nuits vineyards, châteaux and tasting cellars. *bourgogne-tourisme.com*

ViaRhôna This reasonably flat, 815km route meanders south through eastern France to the Med. A vineyard- and river-stitched 70km leg (p465) from Vienne to Tournon-sur-Rhône pairs bike with train from Lyon. *viarhona.com*

La Vélodyssée Ocean hounds, this breathtaking coastal odyssey (p570) along France's Atlantic Coast is for you. Expect exhilarating sea views and wind on the 1250km pedal from Roscoff (Brittany) to Hendaye (Pays Basque). *lavelodyssee.com*

La Vélomaritime Approach over-touristed Mont St-Michel by slow road from Roscoff, 430km west, via a flush of Breton seaside towns and the pink-hued Côte de Granit Rose. Of Brittany's nine cycling routes, inland La Régalante freewheels 275km south from Mont St-Michel to Nantes. *lavelomaritime.fr*

'Accueil Vélo' label

Choucroute garnie (sauerkraut topped with meat or fish)

THE FOOD SCENE

Above all else, French cuisine reflects the culinary beauty of the season – an uncompromising snapshot of the land.

Lunch on a shaded terrace framed by lemon groves on a Riviera farm. Learn how to cook freshwater river eels with a Loire chef or shop for the morning's catch from Monaco's last fisherman. Peep into the pungent cellars of a fourth-generation *fromager-affineur* (cheese ripener) in the Alps. Taste vintages aged on glaciers, on the sea bed or in chalk caves carved by Gallo-Romans. The depth and diversity of France's food scene is dizzying.

No Western cuisine is so seminal – or such an open invitation to indulge your taste buds around a well-dressed table, zinc-topped bistro bar or picnic rug. Renaissance kitchens in the Loire Valley refined the bedrock of French cooking as we know it, and from the 17th century the nation's emblematic gastronomy was codified by early celebrity chefs in a litany of cookbooks. Contemporary makers and creators continue the quest for epicurean excellence and experiment while staying faithful to French cuisine's unshakeable holy trinity: signature cooking methods, fresh ingredients and regional variety of phenomenal proportion.

The French Pantry

The recent British trend in 'scratch cooking' didn't happen in France – it has simply always been that way. Pantries in French homes burst with nut, olive and vegetable oils and vinegars to make a dressing for the habitual green salad served after the main course. Dried herbs and spices jostle for shelf

---

Best French Dishes

BŒUF BOURGUIGNON
Beef and red-wine stew – Burgundy is the best place on earth to experience it.

QUICHE LORRAINE
Eggs, milk or cream and bacon bits baked in a pastry shell; traditionally has no cheese.

CHOUCROUTE GARNIE
Alsatian sauerkraut, piled high with sausages, bacon and ham knuckle; a brasserie staple countrywide.

space with dry ingredients to bake cakes and loaves. Croissants and *pains au chocolat* (*chocolatines* in southwest France), *baguettes,* macarons and jewel-like patisserie (cakes) are among the few items the French systematically buy in – often on Sunday and always at the local *boulangerie* (bakery).

Forget junk food. France is a country where vending machines spit out AOP cheese, ready-grated fondue kits, oysters with knife and lemon ready to be shucked...

Regional Kitchens

From Hauts-de-France in the north to the Pyrenees on the sun-blazed Franco-Spanish border, France takes no culinary prisoners when it comes to enjoying food. Climatic and geographical factors contribute to its spectacular diversity: the hot south favours olive oil, garlic and tomatoes, while cooler pastoral regions north prefer cream and butter. Coastal regions feast on mussels, oysters and saltwater fish; those near lakes and rivers cook up freshwater fish.

Couple natural geographical diversity with the insatiable pride each region has in its own traditions and culture – festivals, harvest feasts, centurion dishes, local dairy or goat farm cheese, wine from the village château – and the regional differences in cuisine become gargantuan. Go to Burgundy and Bordeaux for wine-based cooking; Normandy for cream, apples and cider; Brittany and the Atlantic Coast for seafood; Lyon for offal; Corsica for earthy dishes smacking of the herbal maquis; Languedoc-Roussillon for Catalan cuisine; and Pays Basque for a slice of Spanish spice.

Moules-frites **(mussels and fries), Braderie de Lille**

FOOD & WINE FESTIVALS

Fête de la Truffe (p616) Prized black truffles are the star turn of Sorges' January truffle festival.

Fête des Fraises (carpentras.fr) Carpentras' strawberry festival makes April an extra-sweet month to visit this Provençal market town.

Lyon Street Food Festival (p461) Not just street food: live cooking and workshops by 100-plus chefs, concerts and DJ sets in a former Lyonnais factory in June.

Fête de la Coquille et de la Pêche (p223) Good reason to visit summer-crowded Honfleur in October: to feast on a fabulous frenzy of Norman seafood.

Vin et Hip Hop (vinhiphop.com) A wild October harvest party at Clos de Vougeot; sip young winemakers' wines while dancing to hip-hop DJ sets in a 16th-century château.

Braderie de Lille (p197) Europe's largest outdoor flea market is as much about overdosing on mussels as bargain hunting.

Pain au chocolat **(pastry with chocolate)**

STEAK FRITES	**MOULES FRITES**	**COQ AU VIN**	**MOULES À LA CRÈME**	**SOUPE À L'OIGNON**
Beef steak, cooked *saignant* (rare) unless you specify otherwise, and skinny fries.	Bowl of mussels in their shells, cooked in broth and served with skinny fries.	Chicken cooked in white wine.	Mussels cooked in a wine or cider and cream sauce.	French onion soup is traditionally served with cheesy toast on top.

CHEESE TALK

There is no single official number of *fromages* in France – there are simply too many. At food markets, seek out a *fromage d'auteur* (boutique cheese) unique to a local farm or play safe with one of the country's 46 AOP cheeses. Chefs in cheesemaking regions meanwhile transform the local cheese into an experiential dish to remember:

Aligot Essentially cheesy mashed potato – the stickiest, stringiest you're ever likely to encounter – cooked up in parts of Auvergne, the Cévennes and Pyrenees.

Plaisir au Chablis Creamy cheese from Burgundy, washed once a week in local white Chablis to give it a distinctive wine flavour (p446).

Reblochon The Holy Grail of Savoyard cheeses and the secret behind *tartiflette*, best sourced direct from a mountain cheesemaker (p523).

Matouille Savoyarde Oven-baked potatoes, garlic and white wine smothered in melted Tome des Bauges cheese; at its finest on a terrace overlooking Europe's largest glacier (p507).

The true joy of regional cuisine is unveiled in situ: slurping oysters at home compared to fresh from an Étang de Thau oyster farm with glass of Picpoul de Pinet in hand in Languedoc is night and day. Ditto for a slice of blue-veined Roquefort, plastic-wrapped from the supermarket or with sheep farmers in the eponymous town. To get under the skin of authentic French cuisine, eat Corsican *stufatu* (stew) in Corsica, Marseillaise bouillabaisse in Marseille, Breton *kouign amann* (butter cake) in Brittany, Alsatian *choucroute* in a *winstub* (traditional tavern) and a traditional *repas marcaire* (cowherd's meal) with locals in the Vosges Mountains.

Vegetarian & Vegan

Vegetarians and vegans make up a small but flourishing minority in a country where *viande* (meat) once meant 'food' and where many waiters still believe quiche Lorraine or scallops served in a creamy chorizo sauce are vegetarian. In cities and larger towns, dedicated vegetarian restaurants cover the gambit of French dining, fast food to gastronomic, with ample *végétarien* (vegetarian) and *végétalien* (plant-based) dishes; food-driven Lyon even has a veggie wine bar (p462). In rural France, vegan dining remains challenging.

Be aware that *frites* (chips) in northern France are traditionally double-fried in animal fat (suet or beef lard). Most French cheeses are made with rennet, an enzyme derived from the stomach of a calf or young goat. Some red wines are clarified with the albumin of egg whites.

Market Gastronomy

There is so much more to the French *marché* (market) than everyday food shopping. It is also a place to taste old-school dishes that are hard to find outside your grandma's kitchen: creamy *teurgoule* (rice pudding) at the weekly open-air market in Pont l'Évêque (p244), *galette-saucisse* (sausage wrapped in a savoury crêpe) at Rennes' **Marché des Lices** (p272), and battered courgette flowers deep-fried before your eyes at Cannes' **Marché Forville** (p828) spring to mind.

At the other end of the spectrum, covered markets – often with kitchen-clad stalls, pop-ups and restaurants serving lunch – reflect trends in the contemporary food scene. The Pourcel brothers push the boundaries of traditional cuisine at their gourmet bistro Terminal #1 (p667) at Montpellier's Marché du Lez. Chef Alexandre Serre's *soupe de poisson* (fish soup; p828) at Cannes' Marché Forville is legendary.

Bouillabaisse

Local Specialities

Dare to Try

Canard à la presse Rouen's ghoulish 'n' glorious pressed duck.
Pied de cochon à la Ste-Ménéhould Boiled breaded pig's trotters – the bones are meant to melt in your mouth.
Tripes à la mode de Caen Tripe from Caen, slow-cooked in a clay pot, is France's most prized.
Lewerknepfle Liver, shallot and parsley *quenelles* (dumplings) from Alsace.
Gras doubles à la basquaise Calf stomach, head and Bayonne ham stew with tomatoes, white wine and Espelette pepper.

Cheap Eats

Crêpes & galettes Sweet and savoury, large, round, thin pancakes with toppings.
Pissaladière Niçoise 'pizza' topped with salty anchovies and caramelised onions.
Teurgoule Normandy's old-school rice pudding, best at a market.
Flammekueche Alsatian thin-crust pizza dough topped with sour cream, onions and bacon bits.

Pissaladière

Croque monsieur Toasted ham-and-cheese sandwich; *croque madames* are egg-topped.

Street Food

Frites Best from a chip van in Nord-Pas-de-Calais.
Socca Chickpea-flour pancake from Nice on the Côte d'Azur.
Pan bagnat Tuna and salad bap, dripping in fruity green olive oil, ideally from a food truck on the French Riviera.
Panisse Chickpea fritters, traditionally associated with Marseille but Nice-hot too.
Agneau rôti Roast lamb, from street carts on Sunday in towns and villages on the Presqu'île Cotentin in Brittany.

MEALS OF A LIFETIME

Le Jules Verne (p67) Michelin-starred fine dining restaurant on the 2nd floor of the Eiffel Tower.
Le Mirazur (p821) Italian-Argentinian chef Maura Colagreco cooks up a triple-starred storm at this 1930s restaurant bejewelling a Riviera hillside in Menton.
Le Petit Léon (p624) Bucolic garden dining in the insanely foodie Dordogne.
Auberge Sauvage (p255) The fruits of the land and sea, in a 16th-century Norman presbytery.
Racine (p313) Assuming money's no option, your choice of 250 Champagnes with Japanese-accented cuisine in Reims.
Circle (p455) Sublime proof that there's far more to France's 'gastronomic capital', Lyon, than tripe and *tête de veau* (rolled calf's head).

THE YEAR IN FOOD

SPRING

Markets burst with green asparagus, tiny tender *violets de Provence* (baby purple artichokes), tangy watercress and fresh goat cheese. Easter cooks up lamb for lunch. The first strawberries are handpicked.

SUMMER

Melons, cherries, peaches, apricots, figs, garlic and tomatoes brighten markets. Breton shallots are dug up and laid out to air-dry in the sun. On the coast, foodies gorge on buckets of seafood and shellfish.

AUTUMN

The *vendange* (grape harvest) begins and nutty red rice in the Camargue is harvested. Normandy apples go into cider. Chestnuts fall in the Ardèche, Cévennes and Corsica. Mushrooming and game season begin.

WINTER

Nets catch olives in silvery groves in Provence and Corsica. Dordogne and Provençal markets sell black truffles. In the Alps, skiers dip into cheese fondue. Christmas means Champagne and oysters.

Paragliding (p520), Lake Annecy

THE OUTDOORS

From Alpine glaciers, whitewater rivers and precipitous canyons to the pea-green rollercoaster of the volcanic Massif Central and the southwest's blue surf, French landscapes scream outdoor escape.

However steely your nerves might be, France's physical diversity is dizzying. A coastline stretching for 3427km, from Italy to Spain and the Basque country to the Straits of Dover, inspires seafarers to embrace all sorts of nautical hijinks – at sea and on dry land. Inland emerald-green lakes and ice-white rivers deliver go-slow recharge and fast-paced buzz in buckets, while in the snowy Alps, skiers burn fresh lines. Countrywide, walkers set their sights on the next iconic GR (*grande randonnée*, or long-distance trail) or *puy* (hill) to bag.

Walking & Hiking

The French have been die-hard hikers for centuries, due no doubt to the sheer variety of their country's landscape – alpine mountains, flamingo-pink wetlands, cliff-crusted coastal paths, cavernous gorges and mythical forests.

Hikes range from blockbuster legends of snow axe- and crampon-proportion (the 10-day Tour de Mont Blanc in the French Alps, for example) to pilgrim trails along fields and country lanes (Chemins de St-Jacques de Compostelle to Santiago de Compostela in Spain). Lower alpine trails follow ancient shepherd routes, Breton *sentiers du littoral* (coastal paths) mirror smuggler paths, and modern-day routes mix old-school walking with zip lines and canyoning.

No hiking permits are needed. In southern France and Corsica, paths in forested areas – including in Marseille's Massif des Calanques – may be closed between 1 June and 30 September due to forest fire risk.

Road Cycling & Mountain Biking

Be it spinning with local cyclists on their Sunday ride or slogging up a steep mountain face, two wheeling in France has no limits for exploring France by bicycle (p44).

The road cycling season runs from June to September. July and August mean moun-

---

More Outdoors

SNORKELLING
Eyeball spectacular rock formations and waters teeming with sea life from several entry points along the dive-rich Côte d'Azur. (p804)

CLIMBING
Pit your head for heights against the Devil's Bridge (p473). Or scamper up a 1950s grain silo – France's highest urban climbing wall (p563).

PARAGLIDING
It requires no skill – just guts or the dream to fly with birds – to paraglide in tandem above Lake Annecy (p559).

FAMILY ADVENTURES

Form a family team to race against the clock in the world's largest ski area, **Enduro 3 Vallées** (p530).

Snorkel with teens around 2m-tall busts in **Écomusée Sous-Marin** (p827), an underwater art gallery offshore from Cannes' Île Ste-Marguerite.

Harness the wind to sand-yacht across Norman beach **Char à voile** (p263). Or scare mum silly coasteering.

Watch dolphins waltz with waves in the Med afloat a replica 16th-century schooner in **St-Jean-Cap-Ferrat** (p817).

Hobnob with Mont Blanc and Europe's largest glacier on a hike along Chamonix' **Grand Balcon Nord** (p506).

Take your pick of five rivers in the Dordogne (p608) and canoe past castles, cliffs and caves. Cycle back along a railway track.

---

tain biking – VTT or *vélo tout-terrain* – in the French Alps, Pyrenees and other mountainous areas. Wheel rental is widespread, with electric-assisted road and mountain bikes widely available. Les Gets and Morzine in Les Portes du Soleil (p523) have world-class bike parks with carved descents, jumps and cable cars to cart bikes and riders up the mountain.

Skiing & Snowboarding

Whisper the words 'French Alps' to any skier and watch their eyes light up. With 200-plus resorts and Mont Blanc (4805m) at its helm, this Herculean wedge of mountains cradles some of Europe's best downhill skiing and snowboarding. Limited winter skiing is possible in the Pyrenees and lower-altitude Massif Central. France's ski season runs late December to early April.

Alpine resorts range from powerhouses for hardcore pow adventurers (Chamonix, p500) to low-octane alpine villages (St-Nicolas de Véroce, p513) with gentle beginner and family-friendly runs. With increasingly erratic snowfall, snow-sure resorts at higher altitudes – Val Thorens, Avoriaz, Tignes, Val d'Isère – are more popular than ever. Ditto for snow touring, which allows skiers to ski well away from relentlessly crowd-packed pistes in resorts, often in virgin snows. To help pick the right resort for you, see p546.

Forget summer skiing; Les Deux Alpes, the last remaining resort to open for no more than a handful of weeks in June and July, is strictly reserved for race clubs and pros.

Buy/recharge lift passes (*forfaits de ski*) online to save euros; pay €35 to €85 per day, depending on resort size and prestige. Children up to the age of five and over 75s generally ski for free but still need a physical pass to access lifts; bring passport or ID as proof of age.

ACTION AREAS
For the best outdoor spots and routes, see the map on p52

Vallée Blanche (p500), Chamonix

FAT BIKING
Speed down fresh corduroy on snow bicycles with ultra-fat tyres in La Plagne (p530).

SEA KAYAKING
Paddle the Atlantic: to a cinematic island fortress from La Rochelle or an extraordinary chameleon of a bird island from Arcachon (p569).

VIA FERRATA
Cling to steel cables on a high-up climbing route in the Gorges du Gard (p661).

SAILING
Sail like a jet setter aboard a catamaran from St-Tropez (p828). Or speed out to sea in a Zodiac to swim along the Corniche d'Or (p841).

ACTION AREAS

Where to find France's best outdoor activities.

Sea Kayaking/Surfing
1. Golfe du Morbihan (p299)
2. Côte d'Albâtre (p233)
3. La Rochelle (p577)
4. Arcachon (p569)
5. Parc National des Calanques (p755)
6. Biarritz (p564)
7. Cap Ferret (p571)
8. Sète (p589)
9. Campomoro (p889)

Walking/Hiking
1. Grand Balcon Nord (p506)
2. Chemin de Stevenson (GR70; p678)
3. Puys de Sancy, Dôme & Mary (p484)
4. GR20 (p864)
5. GR34 (p291)
6. GR10 (p727)

FRANCE

THE GUIDE

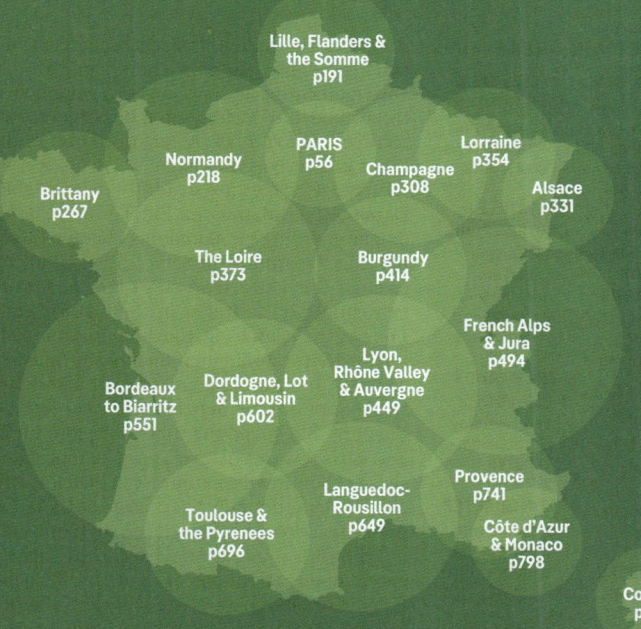

- Lille, Flanders & the Somme p191
- Normandy p218
- PARIS p56
- Champagne p308
- Lorraine p354
- Alsace p331
- Brittany p267
- The Loire p373
- Burgundy p414
- French Alps & Jura p494
- Bordeaux to Biarritz p551
- Dordogne, Lot & Limousin p602
- Lyon, Rhône Valley & Auvergne p449
- Toulouse & the Pyrenees p696
- Languedoc-Rousillon p649
- Provence p741
- Côte d'Azur & Monaco p798
- Corsica p861

Chapters in this section are organised by hubs and their surrounding areas. We see the hub as your base in the destination, where you'll find unique experiences, local insights, insider tips and expert recommendations. It's also your gateway to the surrounding area, where you'll see what and how much you can do from there.

Louis XII statue, Château Royal de Blois (p378), Blésois
PATRICK73/SHUTTERSTOCK

Researched by Mary Winston Nicklin, Nicola Leigh Stewart, Fabienne Fong Yan, Rooksana Hossenally, Rowan Twine, Peter Yeung, Alexis Averbuck & Jean-Bernard Carillet

Paris

CULTURE, HISTORY AND JOIE DE VIVRE

Embrace riverside palaces, art-laden museums, palate-pleasing cuisine, dynamic neighbourhoods and a pleasure-loving way of life in Paris, contender for World's Best City.

THE MAIN AREAS

EIFFEL TOWER & WESTERN PARIS
Elegant and iconic, bejewelled by treasures. **p62**

CHAMPS-ÉLYSÉES & GRANDS BOULEVARDS
Grand monuments and great shopping. **p76**

LOUVRE & LES HALLES
Famed palace museum, garden and city centre. **p82**

MONTMARTRE & NORTHERN PARIS
Historic hilltop village above fascinating neighbourhoods. **p96**

LE MARAIS
Fashionable bars, dining and boutiques. **p110**

BELLEVILLE & MÉNILMONTANT
Arts, views and multicultural walks. **p122**

BASTILLE & EASTERN PARIS
Fabulous markets, drinking and entertainmentt. **p129**

THE ISLANDS
Chic historic heart featuring Notre Dame. **p140**

LATIN QUARTER
Busy hub with ancient marvels and literary life. **p149**

ST-GERMAIN & LES INVALIDES
Fashion, design and cafe culture. **p160**

MONTPARNASSE & SOUTHERN PARIS
Brasseries, eclectic life and street art. **p174**

A visit to the seductive French capital is a timeless experience. Be it sipping Champagne atop the Eiffel Tower, lunching cheek by jowl in a neighbourhood bistro, or people-watching on a buzzing cafe pavement terrace, the *art de vivre* (art of living) in the City of Light is utterly contagious.

Paris' cityscapes are instantly recognisable – Notre Dame cathedral, the iron Eiffel Tower, the Arc de Triomphe guarding the glamorous Champs-Élysées, lamp-lit bridges spanning the Seine, cafes spilling onto wicker-chair-lined streets. A short stay or first-time visit can entice you to linger in the historic centre – the Louvre, the islands, St-Germain and the Latin Quarter – with its myriad monuments and 'must-sees'. And constant innovation means facelifts and new attractions sprouting up across town (*bonjour*, Fondation Cartier!). But spend the time to explore further afield and Paris rewards in its micro-neighbourhoods with a sense of home and community in districts where more city residents actually live – Bastille, Canal St-Martin, Belleville, Montparnasse, Passy, to name just a few.

Dining is a quintessential part of any Parisian experience, whether at intimate restaurants, Michelin-starred temples of gastronomy, *boulangeries* (bakeries) or lively street markets filled with fresh produce, perfect for a picnic. Shopping is also a key draw in this stylish city, from vintage fashion through to emerging designers and *haute couture* houses. Or join Parisians playing in one of the many verdant oases – former royal hunting grounds like the Bois de Boulogne or more central gardens like Luxembourg or the Seine-side Tuileries.

Paris is one of the world's great art repositories, and its priceless treasures are showcased in palatial museums (art lovers should check out the Paris Museum Pass and the Passlib'), contemporary galleries and innovative multimedia spaces. Plus, Parisians know how to have a good time: venture out into its ubiquitous and widely varied bars, clubs and entertainment venues to enjoy a night out in one of the world's best cities.

For places to stay in Paris, see p188

Montmartre (p96)

Find Your Way

Become fluent in local transit and the sprawling, varied French capital becomes easy to traverse. The convenient metro covers the city, while buses allow sightseeing while travelling. A surge in new bike lanes and infrastructure has prompted a cycling revolution. Though, for many, walking the beautiful streets is *the* way to go.

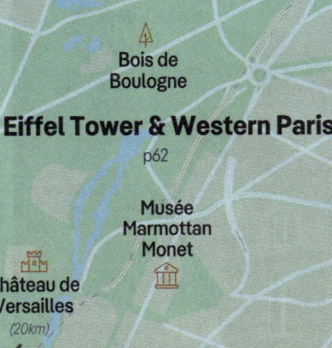

Bois de Boulogne

Arc de Triomphe

Champs-Élysées & Grands Boulevards
p76

Eiffel Tower & Western Paris
p62

Place de la Concorde

Musée Marmottan Monet

Jardin des Tuileries

Château de Versailles
(20km)

Eiffel Tower

Hôtel des Invalides

Musée d'Orsay

St-Germain & Les Invalides
p160

Montparnasse & Southern Paris
p174

METRO & RER
The fastest way to get around, metros are a reliable staple, and RER express trains save time crossing the city and serve the suburbs and airports. It's usually quicker to walk than to take the metro for only one or two stops.

BUS
With no stairs, buses are widely accessible and are good for parents with prams/strollers and people with limited mobility. Bus lines complement the metro: for some journeys a bus is the more direct – and scenic – way to go. Bus stops and RATP or IDF Mobilités apps show schedules, routes and wait times.

Montmartre & Northern Paris
p96

🛕 Basilique du Sacré-Cœur

ARRIVING IN PARIS
Most international airlines fly to **Aéroport de Charles de Gaulle**, 28km northeast of central Paris, or **Aéroport d'Orly**, 19km south of central Paris. Paris also has five major train stations with international service, and trains are the easiest public transport into the city.

Belleville & Ménilmontant
p122

Louvre & Les Halles
p82

🌿 Musée du Louvre

Le Marais
p110

🪦 Cimetière du Père Lachaise

The Islands
p140

🛕 Cathédrale Notre Dame de Paris

Bastille & Eastern Paris
p129

🌿 Jardin du Luxembourg

🏛 Panthéon

Latin Quarter
p149

🌿 Jardin des Plantes

🪦 Les Catacombes

WALKING
The best way to explore Paris is on foot. In central Paris the views are unparalleled, with historic architecture and glittering waterways. Further afield it's a chance to soak up neighbourhood life. Wear comfortable shoes and watch for slippery/uneven cobblestones.

🏰 Château de Fontainebleau
(65km)

THE GUIDE

PARIS

59

Plan Your Days

Paris is a compact city; it's easy to travel between neighbourhoods. These itineraries cover key sights and offbeat wonders. But always leave time for wandering and noticing – this is a city for the *flâneur*.

Basilique du Sacré-Cœur (p97)

Day 1

Morning
- Start on the Île de la Cité, site of **Notre Dame** (p142), restored after the 2019 fire. Continue into the Latin Quarter to see the Roman amphitheatre **Arènes de Lutèce** (p153) and the market delights of **rue Mouffetard** (p153).

Afternoon
- Laze in the **Jardin du Luxembourg** (p162) or pop by a storied cafe like **La Palette** (p165). Swoon over impressionist masterpieces in the **Musée d'Orsay** (p166), admire Delacroix murals in the **Église St-Sulpice** (p169) and explore the backstreet boutiques of St-Germain.

Evening
- Catch a concert at one of the jazz clubs along rue des Lombards, such as **Sunset/Sunside** (p95), **Duc des Lombards** (p95) or **Le Baiser Salé** (p95).

You'll Also Want to...
Leave Paris' big sights behind and explore its rich neighbourhoods to catch the vibe of the capital's dynamic everyday life.

GO UNDERGROUND
Beneath the cobblestone streets and elegant boulevards of Paris, there's a sprawling underground realm. Explore the labyrinthine tunnels of the **Catacombs** (p176), one of the world's largest ossuaries.

EXPLORE THE ART SCENE
With illustrious museums like the Louvre, Paris is one of the world's great art cities. Even walls serve as canvases for pioneering street artists. Discover magnificent murals on a walking tour (p179).

CRUISE THE WATERWAYS
Flanked by famous monuments, the Seine River is the city's lifeblood. Hop on a cruise (p69) to admire Paris from the water, or explore the canal tributaries by boat (p105).

Day 2

Morning
- IM Pei's glass pyramid is your compass point to enter the **Louvre** (p86). Afterwards, stroll through the **Jardin des Tuileries** (p88) or the **Jardin du Palais Royal** (p82). Tap into the soul of the former Les Halles market on **rue Montorgueil** (p91).

Afternoon
- Scope out Victor Hugo's house in the city's prettiest square, the **Place des Vosges** (p110), then wander through the Marais to uncover gardens, museums and boutiques.

Evening
- The Bastille neighbourhood calls for a cafe crawl: try **L'Atelier Saisonnier** (p132) on nightlife strip rue de Lappe. Catch live music at **Les Disquaires** (p134), samba nights at **Café de la Plage** (p134) or an eclectic musical mix at **Café de la Danse** (p134).

Day 3

Morning
- Montmartre's slinking streets and steep staircases are enchanting, especially in the early morning when tourists are few. Head to the hilltop **Sacré-Cœur basilica** (p97), and also take a gander at the **vineyard** (p101). Then head to the **Canal St-Martin** (p104), spanned by wrought-iron bridges.

Afternoon
- Culture-packed Western Paris is home to the world's largest Monet collection at the **Musée Marmottan Monet** (p63), contemporary art at the **Palais de Tokyo** (p70) and Asian masterpieces at the **Musée Guimet** (p73).

Evening
- Ascend the **Eiffel Tower** (p66), to experience glittering *la ville lumière* (City of Light) by night.

DINE ON PARISIAN CUISINE

From charming neighbourhood bistros to fine-dining destinations like **Le Jules Verne** (p67), from historic *bouillons* to Asian cantines, the Paris food scene has never been better.

PLAY IN THE GREAT WIDE OPEN

Join joggers, families, horse-race aficionados and art lovers in the former royal hunting grounds, the **Bois de Boulogne** (p74) in western Paris, or **Bois de Vincennes in the east** (p138).

REVEL IN CHÂTEAU LIFE

The Paris region is home to some of Europe's most mind-blowing châteaux. Plan a day trip to **Versailles** (p184) or **Fontainebleau** (p186) to the stunning palaces that housed French monarchs for centuries.

PARTY LIKE A PARISIAN

Nothing beats a sultry, Seine-side party. Check out the floating bars, concert venues and nightclubs moored near **Invalides** (p160) or in the 13e near France's national library, the **Bibliothèque Nationale de France** (p180).

Eiffel Tower & Western Paris

ELEGANT | ICONIC | BEJEWELLED BY TREASURES

GETTING AROUND

To reach the Eiffel Tower, take the metro line 6 to Bir-Hakeim, or RER C to Champ-de-Mars Tour Eiffel. The 16e is served by metro lines 2, 6, 9, 10 and RER C. Traverse the 16e from north to south on line 9 (Trocadéro to Exelmans).

Walking is the easiest way to appreciate the 16e's village ambience. Plus, you can admire the architecture as you stroll.

Numerous bike lanes, plus the Vélib' bike-share scheme, make cycling easy and convenient in the 16e; travel from Trocadéro to Auteuil in just 10 minutes.

☑ TOP TIP

Though excellent top-end restaurants dot the 16e, it's more affordable to picnic in one of the many green spaces. Build a feast with goodies from bakeries, markets and shops.

Ascend the Eiffel Tower to find all of Paris at your *pieds*. To your west, the panoramas unfurl past the Trocadéro to the elegant 16e *arrondissement*, flanked by the Seine and the glorious green Bois de Boulogne. In centuries past, Passy village was home to luminaries such as Benjamin Franklin and Balzac, before it was annexed to the city in 1860. Nowadays, must-try restaurants and food markets vie for your attention alongside standout museums – the most of any Paris district. The 16e's architecture is another draw, with nature-inspired art nouveau residences, art deco buildings, and modernist villas commissioned by well-heeled residents. Above it all, the scene-stealing tower sets even the most hardened hearts aflutter.

A Tale of Two Hamlets

Village vibes in Passy and Auteuil

Swing by the **Cimetière de Passy**, just opposite the Trocadéro, to get a sense of the illustrious residents who've called Passy home. Among the elaborate tombs carved by sculptors like Rodin and Zadkine, you'll find artist Edouard Manet, composer Claude Debussy, perfumer Guerlain and industrialist Renault. The boutique-lined rue de Passy is the central artery – look for treasures at the antiques store **Passy Brocante** at the end of the impasse des Carrières, a cobbled lane named for the quarries that once provided stone for construction. Passy's beating heart is the vibrant **Marché Couvert de Passy** – at this covered market browse stinky cheese at Androuet, lunch at the fishmonger's counter, admire the *cave de maturation* where the butcher ages prime cuts of meat, then head to the pedestrian market street rue de l'Annunciation to pick up dessert at **Philippe Conticini**.

In adjacent Auteuil, go gaga for Guimard (some of the art nouveau pioneer's buildings are clustered on rue Jean de La Fontaine, including cocktail bar **Cravan**), or ease into local life by taking a seat at a *café terrasse* in front of the Église d'Auteuil. A market pops up on Wednesday and Saturday mornings in the middle of the village – the charming square

Cimetière de Passy

WATER & WINE

Before the 16e was a chic Parisian neighbourhood, this swathe of countryside was covered with vineyards and agricultural fields. Wine production really flourished in the Middle Ages, when the Auteuil vineyards, cultivated by monks, produced wines that were prized as far away as Denmark. (Locals also loved the libations because they were outside the city limits, hence tax-free.) In Passy, the wine museum M **Musée du Vin** occupies the vaulted cellars of the Couvent des Minimes de Chaillot, whose medieval monks tended grapes. Nearby, the narrow rue des Eaux recalls another claim to fame: Passy was renowned for its springs in the 18th century, and cure-seeking visitors would imbibe this therapeutic elixir at a dedicated thermal establishment.

on the rue d'Auteuil faces Hôtel de Verrières, the mansion that hosted 18th-century literary salons and glittering soirées for the royal court. American president John Adams resided here when he served as an ambassador.

Monet Mania
A sublime setting for art

Housed in the duc de Valmy's former hunting lodge (well, let's call it a mansion), the **Musée Marmottan Monet** (*marmottan .fr/en; adult/child €14/free*) is home to the world's largest Claude Monet collection. Take this unique chance to immerse in a real cross-section of the artist's work, beginning with paintings such as the seminal *Impression, soleil levant* (1873) and *En promenade près d'Argenteuil* (1875), passing through numerous water-lily studies, before moving on to considerably more abstract pieces dating to the early 1900s. Masterpieces to look out for include *La barque* (1887), *Cathédrale de Rouen* (1892), *Londres, le Parlement* (1901) and the various *Nymphéas* – many of these were smaller studies for the works now on display in the **Musée de l'Orangerie** (p89). This varied collection – a bequest by Monet's last direct descendant – is showcased in a dedicated downstairs gallery designed for that purpose.

continued on p70

 EATING IN THE 16E: CLASSIC FRENCH

Les Coltineurs: This bistro's name is a nod to the workers who once loaded heavy goods onto Seine boats when there was a port nearby. *hours vary Wed-Sun* €€

La Rotonde de la Muette: Lauded brasserie with velvet banquettes, wood panelling and brass light fixtures. Try the Grand Marnier soufflé. *7am-midnight* €€

Le Petit Rétro: An art nouveau time capsule from 1904, classified as a historic monument, serving traditional treats like steak-frites. *noon-2.30pm & 7.30-10.30pm* €€

Les Marches: Red-chequered tablecloths on bistro tables at this classic joint beneath the Palais de Tokyo, with a €20 lunch menu. *noon-2.30pm & 7.30-10.30pm* €€

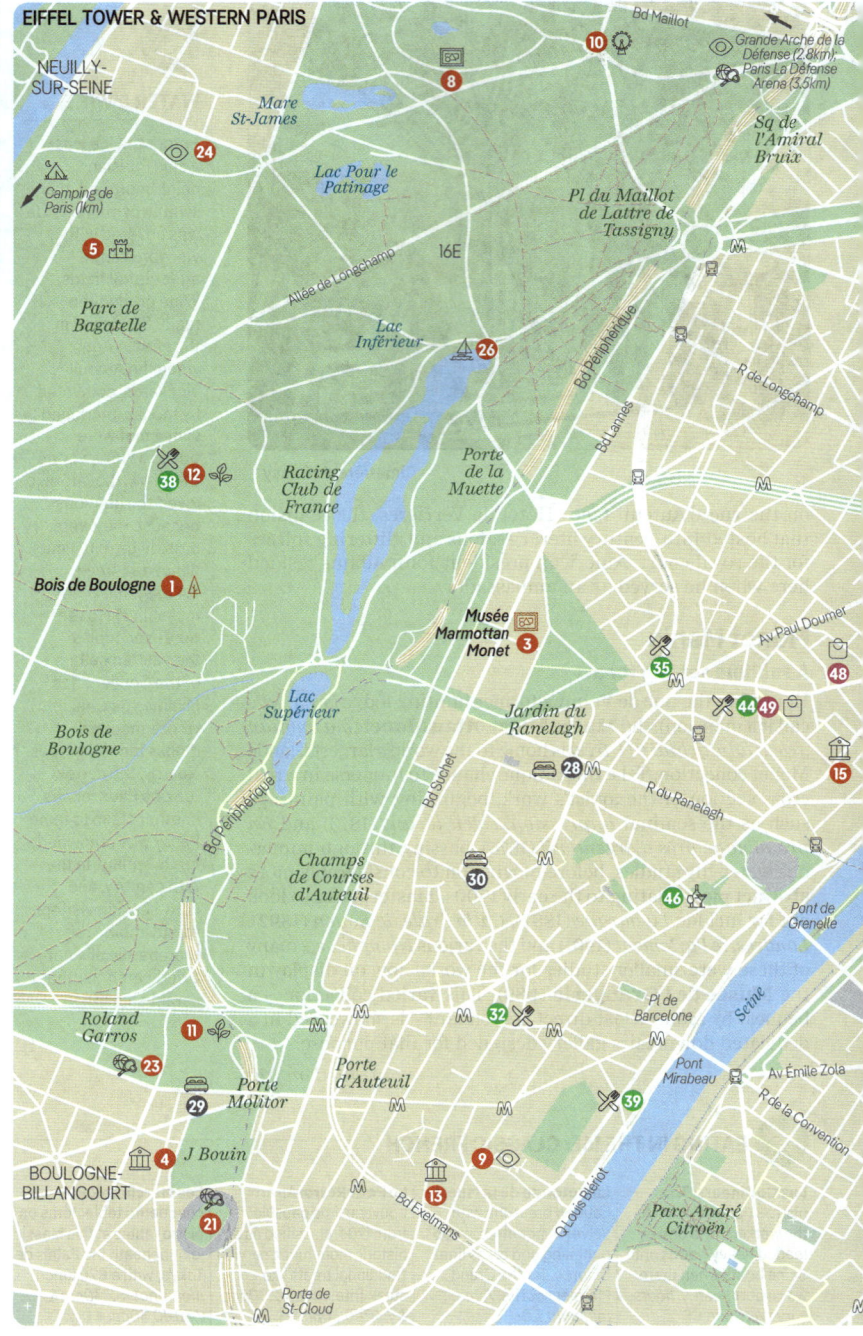

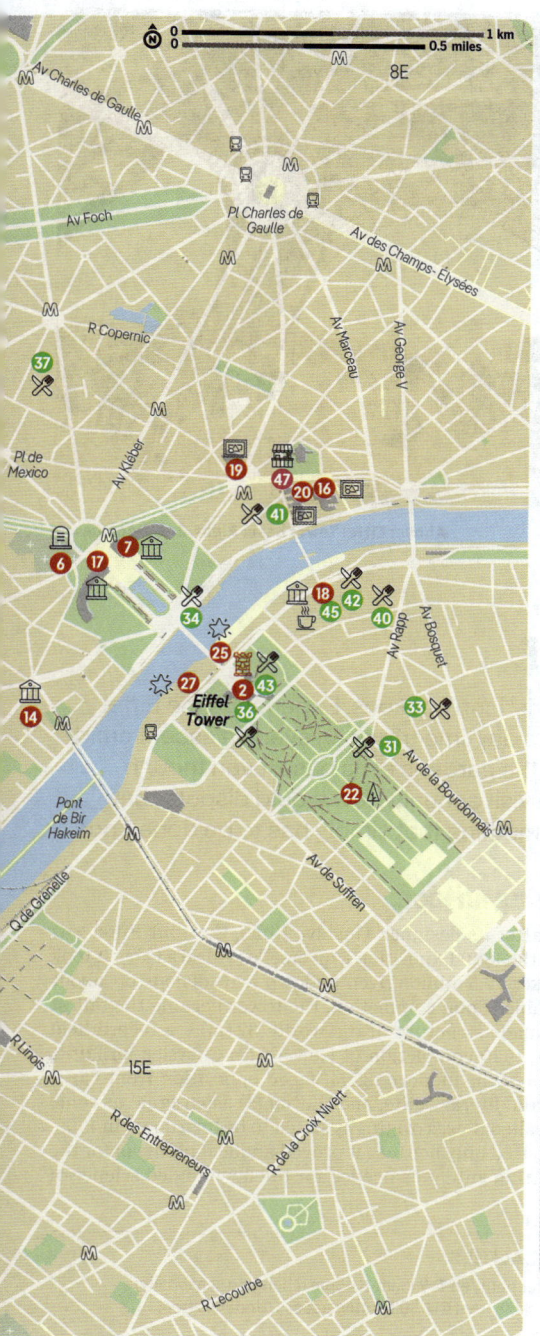

✪ HIGHLIGHTS
1. Bois de Boulogne
2. Eiffel Tower
3. Musée Marmottan Monet

● SIGHTS
4. Appartement-atelier de Le Corbusier
5. Château de Bagatelle
6. Cimetière de Passy
7. Cité de l'Architecture et du Patrimoine
8. Fondation Louis Vuitton
9. Hôtel Jassedé
10. Jardin d'Acclimatation
11. Jardin des Serres d'Auteuil
12. Jardin Shakespeare
13. Laboratoire Aérodynamique Eiffel
14. M Musée du Vin
15. Maison de Balzac
16. Musée d'Art Moderne de Paris
17. Musée de l'Homme
18. Musée du Quai Branly – Jacques Chirac

see 17. Musée National de la Marine

19. Musée National des Arts Asiatiques Guimet
20. Palais de Tokyo
21. Parc des Princes
22. Parc du Champ de Mars
23. Stade Roland Garros
24. Villa Windsor

● ACTIVITIES
25. Bateaux Parisiens
26. Lac Inférieur Boat Hire
27. Vedettes de Paris

● SLEEPING
28. Hôtel Beauséjour Ranelagh
29. Hôtel Molitor
30. Villa du Square

● EATING
31. Arnaud Nicolas
32. Auberge du Mouton Blanc
33. Bistrot des Fables
34. Ducasse sur Seine

see 27. Francette

35. La Rotonde de la Muette
36. Le Jules Verne
37. Le Petit Rétro
38. Le Pré Catelan
39. Les Coltineurs
40. Les Deux Abeilles
41. Les Marches
42. Les Ombres
43. Madame Brasserie
44. Marché Couvert de Passy

● DRINKING & NIGHTLIFE
45. Café Jacques
46. Cravan

● ENTERTAINMENT
see 7. Théâtre National de Chaillot

● SHOPPING
47. Marché Président Wilson
48. Passy Brocante
49. Philippe Conticini

● TRANSPORT
see 25. Batobus Stop

THE GUIDE

PARIS EIFFEL TOWER & WESTERN PARIS

65

Above: Eiffel Tower base; Right: 2nd-floor view

TOP EXPERIENCE

Eiffel Tower

Piercing the city skyline, Paris' icon beckons. Experience the Eiffel Tower in myriad ways, from a daytime trip or an evening ascent amid twinkling lights to a stroll in the gardens at its base. Even though nearly seven million people visit annually, few would dispute that each time is unique – it's something that simply has to be done once.

DON'T MISS

- 2nd-floor panorama
- Top-floor Champagne bar
- 1st-floor Pavillon Ferrié
- Tactile stair descent
- Gardens under the tower
- Nightly twinkle-show

Exploring an Icon

Named after its designer, Gustave Eiffel, the Tour Eiffel was built for the 1889 Exposition Universelle (World's Fair). It took 300 workers, 2.5 million rivets and two years of nonstop labour to assemble. Upon completion, the tower became the tallest human-made structure in the world (324m) – a record held until the 1930 completion of New York's Chrysler Building. A symbol of the modern age, it faced opposition from Paris' artistic and literary elite, and the 'metal asparagus', as some snidely called it, was originally slated to be torn down in 1909. It was spared only because it proved an ideal platform for the transmitting antennas needed for the newfangled science of

PRACTICALITIES

- toureiffel.paris/en
- 9.15am-11.45pm (changing seasonally)
- Adult tickets from €14.50 for stair access. Under 4s free.

PAINT JOB

Painting the Eiffel Tower is a herculean task. Every seven years, a 50-person crew works at night to strip the old paint and then repaint the entire structure. The tower has sported six different colours throughout its lifetime. The most recent golden hue, unveiled for the 2024 Olympics, was the yellow-brown shade originally conceived by Gustave Eiffel.

radiotelegraphy. Now a local nickname for the tower is *La dame de fer* (Iron Lady).

1st Floor

Of the tower's three floors, the 1st (57m) has the most space, with a broad wooden deck for lounging, but the least impressive views. The glass-enclosed **Pavillon Ferrié** houses an immersion film along with a small **cafe, pizza bar** and **souvenir shop.** On the outer walkway, follow a discovery circuit to learn more about the tower's ingenious design and history. Check out the sections of glass flooring that offer a dizzying view of the antlike people walking on the ground far below. This level also hosts the restaurant **Madame Brasserie**.

2nd Floor

Views from the 2nd floor (115m) are grand – impressively high but still close enough to see the details of the city below. Pinpoint locations in Paris and beyond using telescopes and panoramic maps placed around this level. Story windows give an overview of the lifts' mechanics, and the vision well allows you to gaze through glass panels to the ground. Also up here are toilets, **souvenir shops**, a **macaron bar**, and Michelin-starred restaurant **Le Jules Verne** (accessible by a dedicated lift in the south pillar).

Top Floor (Summit!)

Views from the wind-buffeted top floor (276m) stretch up to 60km on a clear day. At this height the sweeping panoramas are more thrilling than detailed. You'll exit the lift onto a glass-enclosed level with directional panels orienting many of the world's cities. Then take one of the two small sets of

TOP TIPS

● Book tickets well in advance.

● Ascend as far as the 2nd floor (on foot or by lift), where a separate lift on the 2nd-floor mezzanine serves the top floor (closed during heavy winds).

● The top floor and stairs aren't accessible to people with limited mobility.

● The stairs to the very top are closed to the public. You must book (or buy at the tower base) a lift ticket.

● Minimise queuing for lifts by descending via the stairs from the 1st or 2nd levels.

● Bring a jacket, as it can be breezy at the top.

NIGHTLY SPARKLES

Every hour on the hour, the entire tower sparkles for five minutes with 20,000 6-watt lights. They were first installed for Paris' millennium celebration in 2000 – it took 25 mountain climbers five months to install the current bulbs and 40km of electrical cords.
For the best view of the light show, head across the Seine to the Jardins du Trocadéro.

metal stairs to the highest tier, which is open-air. Celebrate your ascent with a glass of bubbly from the **Champagne bar** at this topmost level – or opt for mineral water, lemonade and macarons. Afterwards, peep into Gustave Eiffel's restored top-level **office** where wax models of Eiffel and his daughter Claire greet Thomas Edison. Somewhat unbelievably, there are also toilets up here.

Guide

The Eiffel Tower's online visitor's guide *(guide.toureiffel.paris)* can be accessed by the tower's wi-fi network. There's also an information booth at the base, near the west pillar, which has brochures and information on guided tours and activities for kids.

Ticket Purchases & Queueing Strategies

Even on a good day the base of the Eiffel Tower can be a chaotic scrum of confused travellers. A bit of preparation can save time waiting in often atrocious queues, especially in high season (June to September) and during holidays like Easter. Generally attendance is lowest on Tuesdays, Wednesdays and Thursdays.

External Security

Nowadays, bulletproof glass barriers surround the tower's base. Visitors must pass through external security at one of the two entrances to the glass enclosure on av Gustave Eiffel. The two exits are on quai Branly. The security lines are divided

Siene river cruise

between walk-in visitors, people with prebooked tickets, and people with reservations at the restaurants. You are allowed through this point without a ticket if you just want to stroll the gardens directly under the tower itself.

Tickets

Once inside, there are ticket booths (with long queues) at the south pillar. It is well worth prebooking online to reduce waiting. And, at certain times, only people with prebooked lift tickets to the top will be allowed up there (ie sometimes there are no tickets available on the day). But most days you can buy a stairs ticket or a stairs-plus-ticket-to-the-top. If you can't reserve your tickets ahead of time, expect lengthy waits both for tickets and for lifts.

Pre-purchasing tickets online gives you an allocated timeslot and means you enter straight away to go through a second security check just before the lift or stairs. Print your ticket or show it on your phone.

Taking the Stairs

The climb consists of 327 steps to the 1st floor and another 347 steps to the 2nd floor. The stairs to the top are not open to the public for safety reasons. You must buy a lift ticket at the base or online (there are no ticket sales for the top on the 2nd floor). Plan for 10 to 20 minutes between floors, depending on your fitness level.

Top-Floor Lift

Ascend as far as the 2nd floor (either on foot or by lift), and from there a separate lift goes up to the top floor (closed during heavy winds). This lift to the top is only accessible by walking up a small flight of stairs to the 2nd-floor mezzanine where the lift is located. Note that the top floor and stairs aren't accessible to people with limited mobility. Pushchairs must be folded in lifts, and bags or backpacks larger than aeroplane-cabin size aren't allowed. You will need your ticket to access the lift, after, once again, waiting in a queue.

Seine River Cruises

Taking to the Seine on a river cruise is an idyllic way to view the Eiffel Tower. **Bateaux Parisiens** runs hourlong circuits with audioguides in 14 languages and themed lunch and dinner cruises. **Vedettes de Paris** offers one-hour cruises from its base at the foot of the Eiffel Tower. The hop-on-hop-off **Batobus** stops at the Eiffel Tower. **Green River Cruises** has pontoon boats you can privatise. Chef Alain Ducasse oversees the floating restaurant **Ducasse sur Seine** on a luxurious electric boat, where both lunch and dinner are served. The only Michelin-starred cruise is aboard the *Don Juan II*, an art deco–style yacht kitted out with a fireplace, wooden panelling and brass fixtures. The multicourse dinner menu is by chef Frédéric Anton of Le Jules Verne fame.

PARC DU CHAMP DE MARS

Running southeast from the Eiffel Tower, the grassy green jewel of the **Parc du Champ de Mars** – an ideal summer picnic spot – was originally used as a parade ground for the cadets of the 18th-century École Militaire (Military Academy). This school in the vast French-classical building commissioned by Louis XV at the southeastern end of the park counts Napoléon Bonaparte among its illustrious graduates.

WHY I LOVE THE 16E

Mary Winston Nicklin, Lonely Planet writer

Stubborn stereotypes cling to this refined western district; it's often neglected by Parisians from across town who assume it's bourgeois and boring. (A long-time Left Banker, I was guilty as charged!) *Au contraire*. The 16e is far from sleepy. There are so many museums, it's almost criminal. Top chefs open gastro destinations next to bistro institutions **(Auberge du Mouton Blanc** fed the likes of Molière). But what I love most is the village vibe, far from the tourist crowds. Whether slurping oysters in the Passy market or admiring art nouveau architecture in Auteuil, I find the 16e has retained the spirit of the country villages that once populated the scenic hillsides above the Seine.

continued from p63

With acres of gilt and plush Empire-style furnishings, the mansion almost eclipses the art collection. Head-turning decor includes a bed that once belonged to Napoléon, an enormous wood desk sculpted with winged lions and a splendid geographic clock by porcelain powerhouse the Manufacture de Sèvres. Upstairs, don't miss the ensemble of paintings by Berthe Morisot, the famed female impressionist. The illuminated manuscripts are also worth a gander, though the room is (understandably) dim. Temporary exhibitions, included in the admission price, are usually superb.

Prose in Passy
Revel in the life of a literary icon

Transport yourself back in time at the pretty, three-storey house where realist novelist Honoré de Balzac (1799–1850) hid from his creditors to live and work from 1840 to 1847. (He used a pseudonym, and visitors had to pronounce a special password.) This is a small pocket of old-school Passy streets, and you can look over the wall at the rue Berton, a cobbled lane that served as Balzac's secret exit. The **Maison de Balzac** *(maisondebalzac.paris.fr/en; adult/child €9/free)* is perfect for fans of literature and letters – you can peruse rooms of memorabilia, correspondence and prints. Decorated with an ornamental wood fireplace, the study contains the armchair and table where Balzac conceived the *Comédie Humaine*. You'll also spy the porcelain coffeepot, painted with his initials, that famously fuelled his all-nighters. The app (there's wi-fi on-site for downloading) is crammed with audio commentary, including fascinating details about how Balzac maintained his manically intense work habits. Settle in at the on-site **Rose Bakery cafe** for fresh-baked treats, soups and quiche – garden tables with the Eiffel Tower high in the distance make for the perfect setting to contemplate your next great work.

Modern Art Fest
Play at Palais de Tokyo and Paris' modern-art museum

Soaring columns, art deco friezes... what exactly is that palace on the Seine? **Palais de Tokyo** was created for the 1937 Exposition Internationale des Arts et Techniques dans la Vie

Parisians cross town for the lemon meringue pie.

 EATING NEAR THE EIFFEL TOWER: OUR PICKS

Les Deux Abeilles: Homemade delights await at this old-fashioned tearoom that's adored by regulars. *9am-7pm Tue-Sat* €

Bistrot des Fables: A zinc bar contributes to the old-world charm, along with traditional classics like herring potato salad, devilled eggs and beef stew. *hours vary* €€

Francette: Toast the tower from the deck of this floating restaurant moored right on the quay. For the best views, reserve an outside table. *noon-1am* €€

Arnaud Nicolas: The charcuterie maestro stocks a boutique and runs this restaurant with a lunch menu changing every two weeks. *noon-2.30pm & 7-10pm Tue-Sat* €€

Palais de Tokyo

WORLD'S FAIR LEGACY

Starting in the 19th century, World's Fairs drew massive crowds to gape at exhibitions designed to showcase the latest in technology, culture and industry. Paris played host to seven such events, for which staggering architectural monuments were constructed – many later dismantled. Taking its place for the 1937 International Expo was the Palais de Chaillot, perched above fountain-bedecked gardens facing the Eiffel Tower. Today the eastern wing houses the **Cité de l'Architecture et du Patrimoine**, devoted to French architecture, as well as the **Théâtre National de Chaillot**, staging dance and theatre. The **Musée National de la Marine** and the **Musée de l'Homme** (tracing human evolution) are housed in the western wing.

Moderne (International Exposition of Art and Technology in Modern Life). Nowadays the western wing, also called Palais de Tokyo *(palaisdetokyo.com; adult/child €13/free)*, is Europe's largest contemporary-arts centre. The concrete-and-steel interior is a slick host for interactive exhibitions and installations. (There's no permanent collection.) Eating, drinking and entertainment options are fun: Bambini and Forest, with tables in the central courtyard over a reflecting pool with the Eiffel Tower in the distance, and basement nightclub Yoyo.

In the east wing, the **Musée d'Art Moderne de Paris** *(mam.paris.fr/en)* displays a vast collection representative of just about every major artistic movement of the 20th and 21st centuries, with works by Modigliani, Braque, Chagall and Soutine. The real jewels, though, are monumental installations: an entire room of murals by Henri Matisse, and Raoul Dufy's *La Fée électricité*, a fresco depicting the history of electricity. The room is so dazzling that visitors sit on stools, transfixed, losing themselves in the effervescent colours. These permanent exhibitions are all – somewhat unbelievably – completely free. And superbly peaceful compared to the slammed Orsay and Louvre. Look out for excellent temporary exhibitions (not free), such as 'The Atomic Age', a past hit. Download the free multilingual app online.

To Market, To Market
Feast on fresh delicacies

Stroll the open-air **Marché Président Wilson** across from Palais de Tokyo, where fresh-cut flowers crowd vendors of heirloom vegetables, fish and artisanal charcuterie. Adored by the city's top chefs, this lively market brims with the highest-quality products: poultry from Maison Priolet, Normandy-grown fruit from Moulin de l'Abbaye and cheese from Les Fromages de Sophie. Looking for lunch? You'll also find food

CELEBRATE ARCHITECTURE

Take a walk around the Passy and Auteuil areas of the 16e *arrondissement*, a festival of gorgeous art nouveau, art deco and modernist masterpieces.

START	END	LENGTH
Porte Dauphine metro	Le Corbusier studio apartment	7km; 2½hrs

Start a study of art nouveau designs by famed Hector Guimard (1867–1942) at ❶ **Porte Dauphine metro** with its fanning entrance. Stately, treelined ❷ **av Georges Mandel** was opera star Maria Callas' last home (No 36), and look for No 59 with its elaborate glass awning and ironwork balconies. Continue on to ❸ **39 rue Scheffer**, an art nouveau stunner from 1911.

Then, get your architecture orientation at ❹ **Cité de l'Architecture et du Patrimoine** (p71). Upstairs in the museum, find the maquette of ❺ **25bis rue Benjamin Franklin** (named for the fellow who lived at 66 rue Reynard) – it's just down the street with an elaborate inlaid floral façade. Guimard's glory, ❻ **Castel-Béranger** at 16 rue Jean de la Fontaine, won the award for Paris' best façade in 1898. Guimard built his home and studio, an asymmetrical celebration, in 1909 at ❼ **122 av Mozart**. His ❽ **Hôtel Jassedé** at 41 rue Chardon Lagache showcases elaborate brickwork.

Swing by the ❾ **Laboratoire Aérodynamique Eiffel**, Gustave Eiffel's 1912 aerodynamic lab at 67 rue Boileau, the first of its kind. Pop into the ❿ **Hôtel Molitor pool complex**, an art deco icon built in 1929. If you've timed it correctly, visit UNESCO-listed ⓫ **Appartement-atelier de Le Corbusier**. Designed between 1931 and 1934, the world's first glass-fronted apartment building was the renowned architect's home.

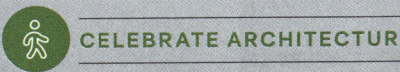

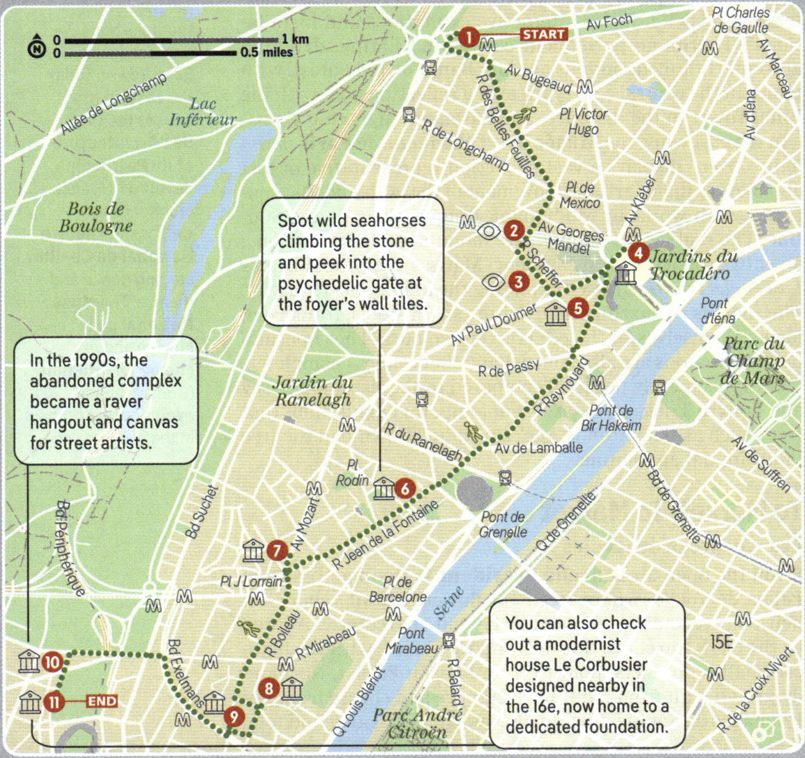

stands with readymade meals you can pack up for a picnic, including Japanese street food, spice-topped Lebanese flatbread, crêpes and Turkish sandwiches. The many temptations are available Wednesday and Saturday mornings, and it's one of the most convenient options to reach in the 16e.

A Trip Around the World
Transport yourself to faraway lands

On the banks of the Seine, the **Musée du Quai Branly – Jacques Chirac** *(quaibranly.fr/en; adult/child €14/ free)* provides boundless inspiration for travellers, armchair anthropologists and those who simply appreciate traditional craftwork. Presenting indigenous art from around the world, it's a tribute to the incredible diversity of human culture. The museum's layout adds to the feeling that you're embarking on a voyage – to access the collections, ascend a spiral ramp illuminated with a visual 'river' of words calling out the collection's people and places. Unique interiors don't have rooms or high walls.

Highlights include remarkable carvings from Papua New Guinea (Oceania); clothing, jewellery and textiles from India to Vietnam (Asia); an excellent collection of masks (Africa); and art from great American civilisations – the Mayas, Aztecs and Incas. Numerous aids on hand help you navigate the vast collection and delve deeper. Multimedia touchscreens provide context, while tailored walks (available online and upon request at the entrance) focus on specific themes. Temporary exhibits and performances are also generally excellent. **Café Jacques** is pleasantly set in the gardens (check out the enormous 'green wall'), while fine-dining restaurant **Les Ombres** offers Eiffel Tower views from the rooftop.

Across the river, **Musée National des Arts Asiatiques Guimet** *(guimet.fr/en; adult/child €13/free)* is a sublime portal to Asia. France's foremost Asian arts museum entices with a superb collection from all corners of the continent. In fact, it's possible to observe the gradual transmission of both Buddhism and artistic styles along the Silk Road in some of the museum's pieces, from the 1st-century Gandhara Buddhas from Afghanistan and Pakistan to the later Central Asian, Chinese and Japanese sculptures. Above all, it's a place where you'll want to get lost in beauty – from the neoclassical rotunda in the historic library to the Khmer courtyard. In this elegant space there are delights at every turn. Keep an eye out for Tibetan mandalas, centuries-old terracotta horses from China and the world's largest collection of Khmer artefacts outside Cambodia.

THE CITY'S BIGGEST GARDEN

Under Mayor Anne Hidalgo, who took office in 2014, city hall has been on a mission to reinvent Paris as a green capital with myriad environmental initiatives. One of the most emblematic is the transformation of the Trocadéro–Pont d'Iéna axis into the city's largest garden. The idea is to add greenery to the place du Trocadéro, prioritising pedestrians and bikes – essentially extending the park through the Jardins du Trocadéro, across the Pont d'Iéna (the bridge will become pedestrianised), to the Eiffel Tower and the Champ de Mars beyond. Construction began after the 2024 Summer Olympics.

Jardin des Serres d'Auteuil

TOP EXPERIENCE

Bois de Boulogne

On the western edge of Paris, vast Bois de Boulogne, the remnant of a royal hunting preserve, was once the province of kings. Now it welcomes one and all for verdant strolls and picnics, rowboat rides on ponds, an array of formal gardens and greenhouses, plus a famous art foundation, a children's amusement park and the clay courts of Stade Roland Garros.

DON'T MISS

Parc de Bagatelle

Fondation Louis Vuitton

Jardin des Serres d'Auteuil

Jardin d'Acclimatation

French Open

Lac Inférieur rowboats

Jardin Shakespeare historical plantings

Playground for All

The 845-hectare Bois de Boulogne (Forest of Boulogne) was at times the home of castles and a convent, at other times a haunt of brigands and the site of battles. The British and Russian armies camped here after the defeat of Napoléon.

The park as you see it now owes its informal layout to Baron Haussmann, who, inspired by London's Hyde Park, planted 400,000 trees here in the 19th century. Along with its myriad gardens and other sights, the park has 15km of cyclepaths and 28km of bridle paths through 125 hectares of forested land.

Fondation Louis Vuitton

Designed by Frank Gehry, this striking contemporary-art centre in the northwestern corner of the park opened its doors

PRACTICALITIES

- paris.fr/lieux/bois-de-boulogne-2779 ● free entry ● open 24hr
- sites within park may have seasonal opening hours/entry fees

in late 2014. It's next to the Jardin d'Acclimatation, and the soaring glass-panelled building hosts one or two temporary shows at a time, from pop art to Basquiat × Warhol. A shuttle runs between the Arc de Triomphe and the museum during opening hours.

Jardin d'Acclimatation

Inaugurated by Emperor Napoléon III as France's first leisure park, the Jardin d'Acclimatation is a longtime family favourite, with a host of attractions including a petting zoo and trampolines. It was fully renovated in 2018 but it's still delightfully old school, with rides like the Enchanted River (1928) still in service.

Parc de Bagatelle

Few Parisian parks are as romantic as this one, punctuated with waterfalls and a Chinese-style pagoda. The newly restored **château**, slated to open to the public for the first time in 2026, was built as the result of a 1775 wager between Marie Antoinette and her brother-in-law, the Count of Artois. Part of Paris' Botanical Gardens, the park blooms with irises, peonies and the famous 10,000 roses in summer.

Villa Windsor

Home to Charles de Gaulle and his family after WWII, this legendary mansion was where the Duke and Duchess of Windsor lived after Edward VIII abdicated the British throne. Fans of TV series *The Crown* will recognise the pad later owned by Mohamed Al-Fayed. At the time of research, the villa was undergoing restoration to open to the public.

Le Pré Catelan

In this area of the Bois de Boulogne, the **Jardin Shakespeare** is lush with plants, flowers and trees mentioned in Shakespeare's plays. Watch for summer performances in the attached **open-air theatre**. The three-Michelin-star restaurant here, also called Le Pré Catelan, is helmed by Frédéric Anton.

Lac Inférieur

On the eastern side of the park, rent an old-fashioned **rowboat** to explore Lac Inférieur, the largest of Bois de Boulogne's lakes – romance guaranteed.

Jardin des Serres d'Auteuil

It's worth the pilgrimage to the southeastern end of the Bois de Boulogne for this manicured garden with impressive conservatories, which opened in 1898. Browse the rare tropical plants – there's even an aviary and carp-filled pool in the *palmarium*. Complementing the historic edifices are six contemporary greenhouses, flanking the Simonne-Mathieu tennis court (part of the Stade Roland Garros).

FRENCH OPEN TENNIS & LOCAL SPORTS

The park's **Stade Roland Garros** is the home of the sizzling clay-court French Open (held late May to early June). At other times, the tennis museum – inaugurated as the Tenniseum in 2024 – traces the history of the sport and the tournament. Nearby **Parc des Princes** hosts Paris St-Germain (PSG) football and **Paris La Défense Arena** hosts rugby.

TOP TIPS

● Dogs must be kept on a leash.

● Buy picnic supplies outside of the park and bring them with you. Amenities are thin on the ground inside.

● Vélib' bike-share stations are near most park entrances, but not within the park itself.

● Metro lines 1 (Porte Maillot, Les Sablons), 2 (Porte Dauphine), 9 (Michel-Ange-Auteuil) and 10 (Michel-Ange-Auteuil, Porte d'Auteuil), and the RER C (Avenue Foch, Avenue Henri Martin) serve the park.

● Be warned that the area can be a distinctly adult playground day and night, especially along allée de Longchamp and allée de la Reine Marguerite, where sex workers cruise for clients.

Champs-Élysées & Grands Boulevards

GRAND MONUMENTS | GREAT SHOPPING

GETTING AROUND

Paris is an easy city to walk around, and strolling up the famed Champs-Élysées is the best way to see it.

There are a few key metro stations along the Champs-Élysées, and the Grands Boulevards stop is right on, as the name suggests, Grands Boulevards.

If you're visiting some of the fancier addresses around the Champs-Élysées you might want to arrive by taxi (or Uber or Bolt). It might even include a drive around the manic Place de l'Étoile which sits around the Arc de Triomphe.

☑ TOP TIP

Motorised traffic is banned from the Champs-Élysées once a month, usually the first Sunday, making a delightful car-free experience for pedestrians.

The world's most famous avenue, home to designer shops and surrounded by palace hotels, sits quite at home in the prestigious 8e *arrondissement* while next door in the 9e, the streets around Grands Boulevards offer a more down-to-earth slice of Parisian life.

What both have in common is they are home to some of the city's most historic and majestic monuments – the Arc de Triomphe, the Petit Palais, La Madeleine to name just a few – which tell some of Paris' most fascinating stories; tales of various kings, both Napoléons, and one very big and bloody revolution. You'll also find two of Paris' top shopping destinations here, thanks to *haute couture* boutiques and the Printemps and Galeries Lafayette department stores, as well as a great place for ending your day with a drink, a film, or a grandiose night at the opera.

Meander the Avenue des Champs-Élysées
The world's most famous avenue

Often called the most beautiful avenue in the world, the **Avenue des Champs-Élysées** is now largely avoided by Parisians, other than those who work in the area, but its worldwide fame often makes it a bucket-list sight for tourists, particularly for first-time visitors to Paris.

Most people come to shop, even if you can find the same stores back home. Beyond its shopping street reputation, the avenue has some beautiful architecture and a richer history than the high-street shops would lead you to believe. If you're in the area it's worth strolling up the famed Champs-Élysées for yourself, although to get the most out of the experience avoid the chain stores and try and find somewhere more French. The historic **Guerlain** store is particularly beautiful, you can pick up beauty products from cult French brand Biologique Recherche, or stop by department store **Galeries Lafayette** (p81). Another tip is to skip the overpriced touristy restaurants, there are better places to eat in the area, and just stop somewhere for coffee.

CHAMPS-ÉLYSÉES & GRANDS BOULEVARDS

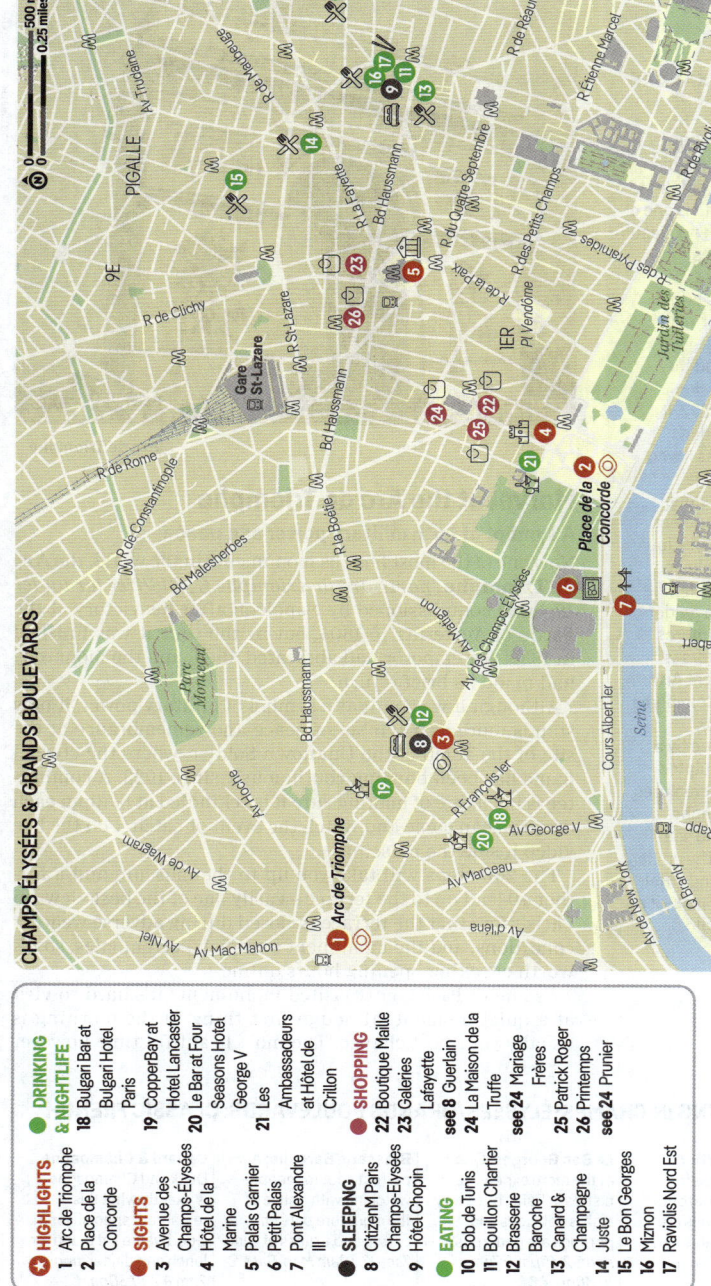

★ HIGHLIGHTS
1. Arc de Triomphe
2. Place de la Concorde

● SIGHTS
3. Avenue des Champs-Élysées
4. Hôtel de la Marine
5. Palais Garnier
6. Petit Palais
7. Pont Alexandre III

● SLEEPING
8. CitizenM Paris Champs-Élysées
9. Hôtel Chopin

● EATING
10. Bob de Tunis
11. Bouillon Chartier
12. Brasserie Baroche
13. Canard & Champagne
14. Juste
15. Le Bon Georges
16. Miznon
17. Raviolis Nord Est

● DRINKING & NIGHTLIFE
18. Bulgari Bar at Bulgari Hotel Paris
19. CopperBay at Hotel Lancaster
20. Le Bar at Four Seasons Hotel George V
21. Les Ambassadeurs at Hôtel de Crillon

● SHOPPING
22. Boutique Maille
23. Galeries Lafayette
see 8 Guerlain
24. La Maison de la Truffe
see 24 Mariage Frères
25. Patrick Roger
26. Printemps
see 24 Prunier

77

PONT ALEXANDRE III

Built for the 1900 Universal Exhibition, the gilded gold **Pont Alexandre III** is one of the city's art nouveau masterpieces and Paris' most emblematic bridge. Named after Tsar Alexander III, who finalised the Franco-Russian alliance in 1892, it was Alexander's son Nicholas II who laid the bridge's foundation stone in 1896. Its opulent design features four imposing columns, two at each end, topped with golden bronze sculptures of winged horses that represent Arts, Sciences, Commerce and Industry, accompanied by a series of sculpted fantastical creatures such as nymphs, cherubs, and sea monsters. The opulent backdrop and Eiffel Tower view make it a popular photo op.

Arc de Triomphe

Marvel at the Arc de Triomphe
A symbol of both military power and peace

Now one of the most famous monuments in the world, the **Arc de Triomphe** *(paris-arc-de-triomphe.fr; €16/free for under 18s)* was commissioned by Napoléon after his victory at the Battle of Austerlitz in 1805, but by the time it was finished in 1836, the emperor had abdicated, died, and the monarchy had made its brief return.

Although it was built as a symbol of military power, it now stands more as a symbol of peace and remembrance at the site of the Tomb of the Unknown Soldier, where the eternal flame has been burning continuously since 1923. A committee is in charge of making sure it is rekindled at 6.30pm each day; you can come and watch the event or catch it on the live video inside the museum.

The 200 steps will take you up to the museum and a further 40 lead up to the terrace – easily one of the best views in Paris. Note that the terrace is closed during adverse weather conditions, and the monument for official ceremonies, so it's worth checking opening hours online.

As one of Paris' most visited monuments it's hard to visit at a quiet moment, although first thing in the morning is usually your best chance. The most beautiful time however

EATING IN CHAMPS-ÉLYSÉES/GRANDS BOULEVARDS: CLASSIC FRENCH

Bouillon Chartier: Expect to queue for an hour (or more) but the classic dishes are great value at this Paris institution. *11.30am-midnight* €

Le Bon Georges: One of the more expensive bistros in Paris, but every dish is delicious and portions are generous. *noon-2.30pm & 7pm-10.30pm* €€€

Brasserie Baroche: A perfect spot for people-watching with a slice of the signature *paté en croute* and a glass of wine. *7am-12.30am Mon-Sat* €€

Canard & Champagne: Duck and Champagne is exactly what this restaurant specialises in. Good-value set menu for lunch and dinner. *noon-2pm & 7-10.30pm* €

is sunset, and although you're likely to be caught up in an even bigger crowd of tourists, it's worth it to catch the view at its prettiest. Two days a year, you can even see the sun fall right through the arc's centre, usually on or around 10 May and 1 August (this year's exact date isn't posted on the website but you can find it through a Google search). To get the ultimate shot, don't stand at the arch itself, you need to be on the Champs-Élysées, or even as far back as **Jardin des Tuileries** (p88).

Crowning Glory at Hôtel de la Marine
An architectural masterpiece reborn

The beautiful **Hôtel de la Marine** *(hotel-de-la-marine.paris; from €9)* museum tells the story of the building's former life as the home of Le Garde-Meuble de la Couronne (Royal Furniture Depository), which was responsible for conserving the crown's collection of furniture, tapestries, arts, jewels, and weapons, as well as crafting new furnishings on demand. Following the abolition of the monarchy, some of the most important events in French history took place in this building, including the signing of Marie Antoinette's death warrant (she was executed just outside on place de la Concorde) and the signing of the bill to abolish slavery in France. Get an audioguide when purchasing your ticket for English-language explanations as you move through the rooms, which were once the gilded apartments of Marc Antoine Thierry de Ville d'Avray, La Garde-Meuble's last intendant (high official). In a separate part of the building, two rooms are dedicated to the Al Thani Foundation, a nonprofit organisation that brings together incredible works of art from antiquity to the modern day. The signs aren't in English, so again, it really is worth paying for the audioguide, which provides some fascinating information. The final room will host a series of two temporary exhibitions each year in collaboration with world-class institutions, such as London's Victoria and Albert Museum.

Magnificent Fine Arts at Petit Palais
The museum of Paris

Commissioned by the city of Paris to showcase fine arts at the 1900 Exposition Universelle (World Fair), the **Petit Palais** *(petitpalais.paris.fr; permanent collection free/temporary exhibitions from €12)* was one of the purpose-built monuments

OFF WITH THEIR HEADS!

Created in 1772, **place de la Concorde** sits on what was once a dry moat and fields surrounding the Jardin des Tuileries and the former royal palace. It's famously where Louis XVI and Marie-Antoinette were guillotined in 1793 during the French Revolution, along with many others, gaining the square the name place de la Révolution. Renamed place de la Concorde in 1795, it was redesigned between 1836 and 1846 to add the two fountains, Fontaine des Mers and Fontaine des Fleuves, and the statues representing various French cities that sit around the edge of the square. But its most famous monument is the 3300-year-old Egyptian Luxor Obelisk, erected in 1836 after France received it as a gift from Egypt's ruler.

There's a DJ playing vinyls on Thursday nights.

 DRINKING NEAR THE CHAMPS-ÉLYSÉES: BEST HOTEL BARS

| **Le Bar at Four Seasons Hotel George V**: Cocktails crafted with latest techniques at elegant and cosy gentlemen's club-style bar. *5pm-1am* | **Bulgari Bar at Bulgari Hotel Paris**: Sleek black bar hidden at the back of Bulgari Hotel: a cool and sexy setting for after-dark cocktails. *10am-midnight* | **Les Ambassadeurs at Hôtel de Crillon**: One of Paris' most palatial hotels of course has an equally opulent bar: the gilded gold Les Ambassadeurs. *5pm-1am* | **CopperBay at Hotel Lancaster**: Cool 10e *arrondissement* cocktail bar has opened up a third outpost inside the historic Hotel Lancaster. *5pm-1.30am* |

GRAND PALAIS

Erected for the 1900 Exposition Universelle (World Fair), the glass-roofed monument reopened in 2025 after a painstaking restoration that returned it to its original art nouveau splendour. The four-year project enlarged the exhibition space and capacity, while adding a buzzy brasserie, called the GrandCafé, with one of the prettiest terraces in Paris. Bedecked in cast iron and glass, the soaring Nef (nave) hosts major events, art shows, and even DJ-led soirées throughout the year. In the winter, there's even a massive ice-skating rink set up — considered the world's largest such temporary rink — with glittering disco balls adding to the party vibes.

which, for the first time, was designed to remain a permanent fixture after the world fair had ended.

Designed by architect Charles Girault, the idea was to create a crowd-pleasing monument (think marble and moulding) but which also drew inspiration from Greek classical influences (note the grand columns) and the fashionable art nouveau style. Girault's previous life as an ironmonger also influenced the design, as seen in the gold ironwork entrance and the main curved staircase with floral motifs.

Outside, Girault added a central garden to offer a moment of tranquillity away from the city's crowds, especially during the hugely popular Exposition Universelle. It's now a lovely spot to stop for a coffee from the museum's cafe.

Notable works include *Les Halles* by Léon Lhermitte; *The Sleepers* by Gustave Courbet, a commission from a Turkish diplomat who then kept it hidden behind a curtain due to its racy subject matter (and who also commissioned Courbet's most famous work, *Origin of the World,* now in the **Musée d'Orsay**, p166), and the recently restored *Portrait de l'Artiste en Costume Oriental (Self-Portrait in Oriental Attire)* by Rembrandt, who added the dog later to his only full-length self-portrait to hide his legs, as he wasn't happy with the final result.

Downstairs you'll find an Arts and Crafts collection intended to shine a light on the works as an art form in their own right, a collection of art nouveau treasures, including Hector Guimard's (the man behind the now iconic Paris metro entrances) entire dining room, and a collection of Monets. The information is all in French but excellent guided tours are available with an English-speaking guide, or you can find more about the works on the website.

Napoléon III's Great Palais Garnier

Garnier's sumptuous celebration of music and dance

In an emperor power move, Napoléon III commissioned a new Paris **opera house** *(operadeparis.fr; adult/concession/children under 12 €15/10/free)* after an assassination attempt at the former opera house on nearby rue Le Peletier. Charles Garnier was just 35 years old, and as yet unknown, when he won the commission. He surprised everyone, including Empress Eugénie, who was less than impressed when Garnier presented his designs. Napoléon III died before he ever got to see it and it's now visitors who use what would've been his private entrance to protect him from would-be attackers.

EATING NEAR GRANDS BOULEVARDS: AFFORDABLE EATS

Miznon: A Middle Eastern restaurant with some of the best falafel in town. The meze plates are great for sharing. *11am-11pm* €

Juste: Well-priced and good oysters. The lunchtime prix fixe menu of *moules frites* also comes with a bonus glass of wine. *hours vary* €

Raviolis Nord Est: This down-to-earth restaurant is known for its tasty dumplings (ravioli in French) and noodles. *hours vary* €

Bob de Tunis: Octogenarian Bob is still making Tunisian sandwiches at this tiny sandwich shop/lunchtime restaurant (only four tables). *8am-6pm* €

Once inside, the 'show' starts not in the auditorium but on another stage: the grand staircase. With its sweeping steps and numerous observational balconies, Garnier purposefully designed it for posing. In the auditorium, he flattered high society by choosing red velvet seating to complement the gilded gold, saying that the pink tinge reflected on women's faces helped them look 'more youthful and radiant'. Crowning the space is a fresco ceiling by Marc Chagall, a recent design addition, and the opera house's impressive chandelier, which inspired an event in Gaston Leroux's *The Phantom of the Opera* when it fell from the ceiling in 1896.

Aside from the auditorium, one of the Palais Garnier's most prestigious rooms is the Grand Foyer, inspired by the Hall of Mirrors at Versailles and recently restored to its full splendour. You can wander around just admiring all of this grandeur but it's worth taking a tour of some kind: the audio tour is excellent and cheaper than taking a private group tour (bookable on the website), but with the latter you'll be able to actually sit in the auditorium, unless it's in use for practice. And make sure to reserve a ticket in advance online; due to the high number of visitors, it's not guaranteed you'll get a ticket on the day at the box office.

Browse Les Grands Magasins
Paris' monuments to commerce

In true Paris style, the city's *grands magasins* (department stores) are more than simply a shopping destination, they're also architectural monuments. The 9e *arrondissement* is home to two of the grandest: the flagships of **Galeries Lafayette** *(haussmann.galerieslafayette.com)* and **Printemps** *(printemps.com)*, which sit nearly side by side as neighbours (and competitors) on bd Haussmann. Both specialise in high-end luxury, whether you're looking for womenswear or kitchenware.

If you're not here to shop, it's worth a visit for the architecture alone. The stained-glass art nouveau *coupole* (cupola) is the most famous sight of the 19th-century Galeries Lafayette Haussmann, and all of Paris at Christmas when it crowns the store's annual festive installation.

Printemps has its own *coupoles* to match, shimmering with gold and mosaics on the outside and housing cafes and a fantastic vintage section on the inside. If you're interested in its history, Printemps offers tours booked through the Cultival website. Galeries Lafayette also has fashion shows, cooking and pastry classes. Avoid going on weekends if you want to dodge the crowds. And if you can't decide on something to buy, a drink from one of the panoramic terraces or bars admittedly costs more than what you'd pay on the ground, but it's worth the splurge for the view.

FOOD SHOPS NEAR PLACE DE LA MADELEINE

Patrick Roger: Minimalist boutique mirrors the pared-back collection of chocolates, which focuses on the purity of chocolate and praline.

La Maison de la Truffe: Luxurious truffle-infused range runs from truffle crisps to whole white and black truffles.

Mariage Frères: With more than 800 tea references from 36 countries, Mariage Frères has one of the largest tea selections in the world.

Boutique Maille: You can buy jars of France's most famous brand of Dijon mustard in the supermarket, but the mustard-obsessed will love the choice at this boutique.

Prunier: Pick up French caviar, blinis, smoked salmon and more at Chef Yannick Alléno's fabulous boutique.

Louvre & Les Halles

FAMED PALACE MUSEUM | GARDEN | CITY CENTRE

☑ TOP TIP

If you have limited time and wish to make the most of it, plan your days in advance and prioritise booking tickets to the main museums, as they attract crowds. Then arrange your itineraries accordingly, including restaurant reservations.

Stretching over the 1e and 2e *arrondissements,* this quarter might have the highest concentration of historical landmarks and architectural wonders in the city. Once the residence of kings, with the most visited museum in the world at its heart, it perfectly embodies Paris' urban evolution through the ages. While Baron Haussmann's urban planning largely defines its present-day layout – with vast squares and high-end venues – the district's essence is also found in its narrow cobblestone streets and well-preserved 19th-century covered passages, offering glimpses into the past. Near former palaces, Les Halles and its surroundings – once described as 'the womb of Paris' by French writer Émile Zola – remain a vibrant hub of movement and commerce, stretching all the way up to Sentier.

Historical Cradle of Culture

MAP P83

Stroll in the Palais Royal

A serene haven adored by locals, the **Jardin du Palais Royal** *(domaine-palais-royal.fr)* is tucked between the Louvre and the busy av de l'Opéra. It is one of those historical places in Paris where tourists and Parisians seamlessly merge, both enjoying the magnificence of centuries-old architecture in their own way. It is true that there's something mesmerising about strolling beneath its impeccably trimmed trees and

GETTING AROUND

The area has many cultural attractions, activities, and food venues. Therefore, it is easiest and best explored on foot to navigate all the landmarks.

It is easily accessible by metro, with Châtelet as Paris' most central hub for metro and suburban train lines. Other convenient stations include Palais Royal – Musée du Louvre (Line 7) and Sentier (Line 3).

Cycling is increasingly convenient in the area, as car traffic becomes more restricted and cycle lanes are better implemented. Rental bike stations are common around the main landmarks.

LOUVRE & PALAIS ROYAL

- ⭐ **HIGHLIGHTS**
- 1 Jardin des Tuileries
- 2 Musée du Louvre
- 🔴 **SIGHTS**
- 3 Colonne Vendôme
- 4 Fondation Cartier pour l'Art Contemporain
- 5 Jardin du Carrousel
- 6 Jardin du Palais Royal
- 7 Jeu de Paume
- 8 Musée de la BNF (Bibliothèque Nationale de France)
- 9 Musée de l'Orangerie
- 10 Musée des Arts Décoratifs
- 🟢 **EATING**
- 11 19 SAINT ROCH
- 12 Aki Boulangerie
- 13 Au Petit Bar
- 14 Chez Miki
- 15 Comme un bouillon
- 16 Jantchi
- 17 Kodawari Ramen Tsukiji
- 18 La Cordonnerie – Chez Yvette & Claude
- 19 Le Grand Véfour
- 20 Le Soufflé
- 21 Matin des Oliviers
- 22 Michi
- 23 Nodaïwa
- 24 Public House
- 25 Tomo
- 26 Udon Jubey
- 🔴 **ENTERTAINMENT**
- 27 Comédie Française
- 🔴 **SHOPPING**
- 28 Au Nain Bleu
- 29 Book Off
- 30 Brigitte Tanaka
- 31 Junku
- 32 Kure Bazaar
- 33 Maison Wa
- 34 Merci #2
- see 33 Nishikidori – Le Comptoir des Poivres

long arcaded galleries – their depth and symmetry creating an illusion of infinity.

Built in 1624 by Cardinal de Richelieu, King Louis XIII's prime minister, Palais Royal has long been at the heart of Paris' political and cultural life. However, its characteristic galleries date back to the late 18th century, initiated by Louis-Philippe d'Orléans. By then, they had become home to shops, cabarets and residences.

continued on p88

WALKING TOUR

A Sheltered Walk Back in Time

The area's covered galleries were inspired by the success of those at the Palais Royal, where shops, cabarets, and other businesses thrived in the late 18th century. Landlords soon started constructing their own covered passages. They quickly gained popularity, as they offered the revolutionary experience of shopping indoors, sheltered and in a comfortable environment. Some passages in residential areas may be closed on weekends.

❶ Galerie Beaujolais & Passage du Perron

The northern gallery of the Palais Royal, housing a few luxury shops, is connected to Passage du Perron, which used to be a meeting place for speculators, due to its proximity to the stock exchange.

The Walk: Exit north and look for stairs on your right.

❷ Passage des Deux Pavillons

Check out Olympia Le Tan's shop, famous for her original 'book clutch' concept. Exiting the passage, you'll be right across from Galerie Vivienne. Its owner bought and rebuilt Passage des Deux Pavillons, directing people from Palais Royal into his gallery, much to the annoyance of his rival, the owner of Galerie Colbert next door.

The Walk: Walk a few steps left and enter Galerie Colbert.

Passage des Panoramas

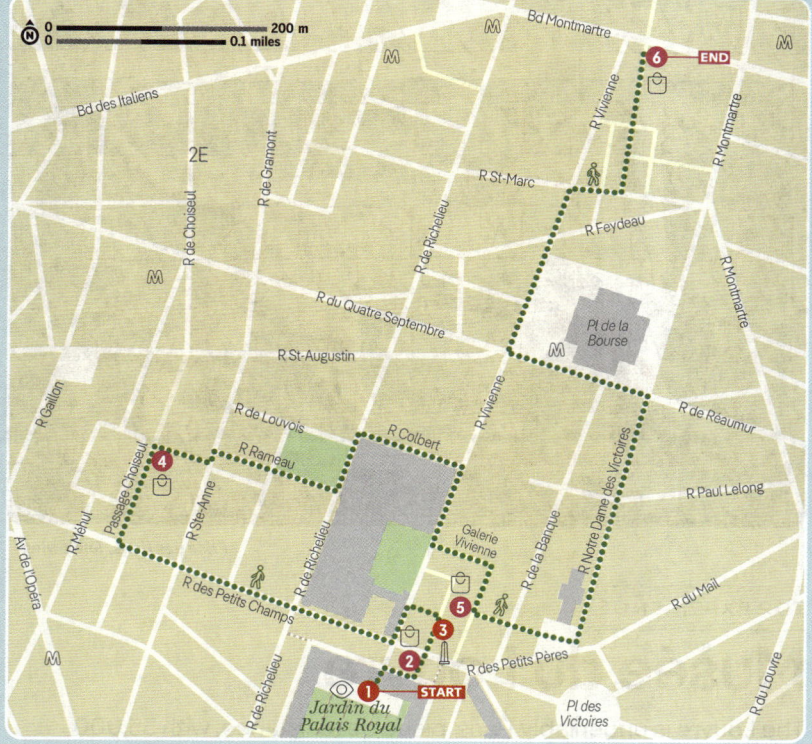

3 Galerie Colbert
At the heart of Galerie Colbert's rotunda stands a statue depicting the nymph Eurydice being bitten by a snake. Stop for lunch at Le Grand Colbert.

The Walk: Head left onto Rue des Petits Champs, then right towards the entrance of passage Choiseul.

4 Passage Choiseul
Restored in 2007, this passage is one of the longest in Paris and used to have strong associations with literature and theatre. This heritage is still evident at Lavrut, a magnificent stationery store.

The Walk: Exit at the north end of passage Choiseul. Enjoy square Louvois and its ornamental fountain as you head to 6 rue Vivienne.

5 Galerie Vivienne
One of the most stunning covered galleries in the area, Galerie Vivienne is bathed in light and adorned with a mosaic floor, beautifully decorated shopfronts and illuminated windows. Treat yourself to coffee and cake at Le Valentin Vivienne, appreciate the fine fabrics at Wolff and Descourtis, discover vintage postcards at Librairie Jousseaume and find a gift at the pretty Si tu Veux toy store.

The Walk: Leave through the rue de la Banque exit and walk up north towards Palais Brongniart. Make a detour to the charming place des Petits-Pères before continuing to rue St-Marc.

6 Passage des Panoramas
Opposite 7 rue St-Marc, this **passage** is interconnected with other galleries. Despite being a bit darker, it has its own picturesque charm, filled with vintage shop signs hanging overhead. Visit Culottées cafe near the entrance for a quick takeaway. With more time, sit at Caffè Stern, housed in the former workshop of renowned engraver Stern. Finish here or continue further north through Passage Jouffroy and Passage Verdeau.

Frise des lions, **Sully wing**

TOP EXPERIENCE

Musée du Louvre

The Louvre is undeniably Paris' pièce de résistance, with 35,000 works of art on display, including iconic masterpieces, spread across four floors. Glancing at each piece for one minute would take 24 days without sleeping, not to mention the time needed to appreciate the museum's grand surroundings. Therefore, careful planning is essential to fully experience the world's largest art museum.

DON'T MISS
- Mona Lisa
- Winged Victory of Samothrace
- Venus de Milo
- The Sphinx's Crypt
- Le Salon Carré
- Cour Marly and Cour Puget

First Time at the Louvre?

Entering the museum for the first time can be intimidating. The key to approaching the vast collections of the Louvre is to consider them from two significant perspectives: Western Art spanning from the Middle Ages to the mid-19th century, and the art and crafts of five ancient civilisations that preceded and influenced it. Simultaneously, immerse yourself in the museum's captivating architecture shaped by multiple sovereigns. To navigate the museum, just remember that it is

PRACTICALITIES
- louvre.fr/en ● €22 general admission, free under 18s
- Closed Tuesdays

made of three wings: the parallel Richelieu (North), Denon (South) and Sully (East).

The Louvre can be both awe-inspiring and overwhelming. Possibly the best way to visit it is to allow yourself to choose, explore and be pleasantly surprised. Don't worry about seeing every masterpiece – enjoy the journey itself!

Guided by Ancient Civilisations

The antiquities department showcases pieces dating from the Neolithic period to the decline of the Roman Empire. Exploring chronologically, the treasures of ancient civilisations will primarily lead you through the ground floor, with an additional area dedicated to Egyptian antiquities on level 1. Begin your journey in the Richelieu wing, exploring the Mesopotamian art (considered the earliest human civilisation). Continue to the Sully wing to descend into the Sphinx's Crypt and uncover Egyptian art. Proceed to the Denon wing to see Greek, Etruscan and Roman art.

Gardens of Sculptures

Sculpture enthusiasts should not miss the atmospheric Cour Marly and Cour Puget, on level -1 of the Richelieu wing. These indoor courtyards bathed in natural light house French masterpieces created under Louis XIV. The Cour Marly provides an atmospheric setting reminiscent of its original location in one of the king's residences. Interestingly, in an arrangement that may seem counterintuitive, ascending to the upper level will transport you back in time to medieval French sculpture. Moving through the Richelieu wing on the ground floor, you'll then encounter more sculptures from the 17th to 19th centuries.

A European Tour of Masterpieces

The top floors showcase European paintings and decorative arts from the Middle Ages to the mid-19th century. Many visitors explore these floors towards the end of their visit, following the sequential order of the rooms. If you're a painting enthusiast, you should prioritise these floors during your visit. They are must-visit areas for iconic artworks like the *Mona Lisa*, as well as monumental paintings such as the *Wedding at Cana* and the *Raft of the Medusa*. In addition, don't miss the impressive Great Gallery, the historic Salon Carré (the precursor to exhibition salons), and the opulent Galerie d'Apollon adorned with stunning murals and golden embellishments.

Around the Louvre, Around the World

As no ordinary museum, the Louvre takes you on a journey to different eras and continents. Don't miss the apartments of Napoléon III, almost untouched for nearly 150 years, at the end of the Richelieu wing on the first level. For a broader cultural experience, explore the small section dedicated to American, African, Asian and Oceanic arts, situated in a remote part of the Denon wing (access through level 1).

ANTIQUE MYSTERY

The oldest displayed piece is the statue of Aïn Ghazal (Room 303, Sully Wing), unearthed in the 1980s in Jordan and dating to about 7000 BCE. Its subject is still a mystery: was it a man, a child, a god? In comparison, the Winged Victory of Samothrace and the Venus de Milo both date back to the 2nd century BCE, which means more than 6000 years separates them from the enigmatic statue!

TOP TIPS

● Make sure to book your ticket online in advance, as you won't need to line up at the museum desk and there may be special offers available.

● The website is a valuable resource for finding inspiration and planning your visit, with thematic itinerary ideas.

● Arriving early will give you the opportunity to explore the galleries with fewer crowds.

● Wear comfortable shoes – you'll be walking through 403 halls and nearly 15km of corridors!

● If you're visiting with children, take a break at the Studio (Richelieu wing, level -1), which provides creative materials for them to enjoy.

Jardin des Tuileries and Musée du Louvre (p86)

PERFECT BACKDROP FOR THE PARIS 2024 CAULDRON

For two months in 2024, the rise of the flying Paris 2024 Cauldron was a spectacular rendezvous in Paris' sky. Watching the hot-air balloon cradling the Olympic Flame soar every evening had become a ritual, and looking for the best viewing spots, a real sport. We admired not only the cauldron's original design, but also the perfect illusion of fire created by electricity and vapour, 'burning' against the sunset.

Seeing the cauldron go at the end of the summer was heart-wrenching, so much so that the city of Paris announced that it would be back every summer until the opening of the 2028 Los Angeles Games. View from two spots: the **Jardin du Carrousel** and from rue du 29 Juillet, on the Tuileries' northern side.

continued from p83

Some landmarks have endured the test of time. Beneath the Galerie de Beaujolais for instance, a 200-year-old restaurant still stands: it is said that Napoléon Bonaparte and his wife Joséphine used to lunch at **Le Grand Véfour**, as did artists such as Victor Hugo.

The building also houses the Conseil Constitutionnel and part of the Ministry of Culture's offices, but it is best known as the home of the **Comédie Française**, France's National Theatre (entrance located on Pl Colette), and most notably, for the contemporary artworks displayed in the southern part of the garden – such as an open-air museum.

The Splendour of a French Garden   MAP P83

Wander through Jardin des Tuileries

It's the sense of infinite perspective that first meets the eye when walking into the **Jardin des Tuileries**. We owe its design to royal gardener André Le Nôtre, hence some resemblance with Versailles. Structured like a traditional French garden, the first part made of flowerbeds is best enjoyed from the windows of the Louvre. In the middle, lines of perfectly trimmed trees offer some shade to joggers. Contemporary and classical sculptures play hide-and-seek in the garden's

EATING NEAR PALAIS ROYAL: OUR PICKS

Daroco: Enjoy pizza in this chic Italian restaurant in the romantic covered passage Galerie Vivienne. *noon-3pm & 7-11.30pm Tue-Sat, to 11pm Sun-Mon* €€

Jantchi: Try bulgogi, kimchi soup or *yukkaejang* (vermicelli soup) at this Korean restaurant. *noon-2.45pm & 6.30-10.15pm Mon-Fri, 11.45am-10.30pm Sat* €€

Eats Thyme: Lebanese restaurant with vegan, vegetarian and meat options. Don't miss the *manoush* flatbread. *11am-10.30pm Mon-Sat, to 4.30pm Sun* €€

Comme un bouillon: Small venue serving French popular classics, including traditional *steak-frites* and *oeufs-mayonnaise*. *11.45am-10pm Mon-Fri, noon-10pm Sat* €

alleyways, surprising strollers at times. The two long, stone-washed 19th-century buildings spotted at the Concorde end now host renowned museums: **Musée de l'Orangerie** and the **Jeu de Paume** gallery.

During summer and winter holidays, the garden hosts one of the most popular Parisian fairs, with dozens of rides and food stalls. A 70m-high big wheel offers a chance for a bird's eye view of Paris on clear days.

Watch a Play à La Française
Theatre night at the Comédie Française

MAP P83

Housed in the front building of Palais Royal, the **Comédie Française** theatre *(comedie-francaise.fr)* usually showcases plays by classical playwrights, such as Molière – considered the historical patron of the place – Racine, Tchekov, Shakespeare... It is the only theatre in France with its own company.

Theatre enthusiasts will love catching a performance in the Richelieu room, if only to admire the Italian-style horseshoe-shaped auditorium and richly decorated ceiling. Seated in the red velvet seats, Parisians from two centuries ago were ready for the show, waiting for the three blows on the stage. This convention in classical French theatre signals that the actors are about to enter the stage.

If you simply wish to visit, book a weekly guided tour, but don't forget to check if they're available in your preferred language.

Museum Marvels Near the Louvre
A visual-art museum trip

MAP P83

Modern- and contemporary-art enthusiasts should not miss **Musée de l'Orangerie** *(musee-orangerie.fr; adult/child €12.50/8.50)* and the **Jeu de Paume** *(jeudepaume.org; adult/child €12/free)*, both in the Jardin des Tuileries, as well as **Musée des Arts Décoratifs** *(madparis.fr; adult/under 26 years €15/free)* in the Louvre's northern wing. They offer complementary approaches, allowing art-lovers to dig deeper into specific periods or media, perhaps in a slightly less overwhelming atmosphere than at the Louvre.

For those interested in impressionism, the Musée de l'Orangerie provides a unique immersive experience into Monet's water lilies, the culmination of the painter's life work. Housed in specially designed oval rooms, the immense canvases completely draw the viewer in. Arriving early usually allows for a more tranquil viewing.

BEST CONCEPT STORES FOR SOUVENIRS

Brigitte Tanaka: One French and one Japanese designer's tiny shop, where you will find only delicately embroidered organza bags, all inspired by Paris.

Au Nain Bleu: Traditional toy shop with beautiful selection of quality plush toys.

Kure Bazaar: Following a French manicure at its relaxing beauty salon facing av de l'Opéra, don't leave without your selection of nail polish in a Paris-themed box.

Merci #2: Paris-themed books, fruit-shaped candles, designer accessories and homewares you didn't know you needed.

Junku: Not just a Japanese bookstore. People interested in this culture will love shopping for stationery, tableware items, small toys and accessories.

 EATING NEAR THE LOUVRE: OUR PICKS

Nodaïwa: Japanese restaurant specialising in *unagi* (traditional grilled eel) served in various refined preparations. *noon-2.30pm & 7-10pm Wed-Sat* €€€

Matin des Oliviers: Great for a tasty Mediterranean brunch/snack. Choose from Turkish eggs to avocado toast. *9am-6pm Mon-Thu, to 8pm Fri, 8am-8pm Sat-Sun* €€

Public House: British food comes to Paris: have a Scotch egg and meat pie, or quality fish and chips in an elegant pub atmosphere. *8am-2am* €€

Boutique Yam'Tcha: Hong-Kongese tearoom has soft bao buns with original fillings (Stilton and cherry jelly). *noon-7pm Tue, Thu & Sat, to 4pm Wed, noon-6pm & 7-10pm Fri* €€

PLACE VENDÔME: HIGH-FASHION IN THE CITY

At the centre of Pl Vendôme, the 44m-high **Colonne Vendôme** – a Napoleonic commemorative monument – resembles a gem in a jewel case. One of the five royal places in Paris, Pl Vendôme is famous for its classical architecture and is home to high-end jewellery houses like Cartier, Van Cleef & Arpels, Boucheron and Chaumet. The place has long been associated with elegance and fashion. The stopper of the Chanel N°5 perfume bottle, for instance, is inspired by the square's distinctive octagonal shape. It pays tribute to Coco Chanel, who resided here for decades. During Paris Fashion Weeks (twice a year), Pl Vendôme becomes a show of fashionistas and celebrities invited to the haute-couture catwalks.

Jeu de Paume stands in contrast with its impressionist counterpart: it primarily focuses on contemporary photography and the exploration of new media.

Last but not least, the Musée des Arts Décoratifs provides a rich testament to the French *art de vivre* and history of decorative arts. Its extensive collection pays tribute to artists and craftspeople who have brought beauty and functionality into our daily lives, through the art of furniture making, glassware, ceramics, jewellery, fashion, graphic design and even advertising. Don't miss the museum shop, adored by design lovers.

More Than a Historical Reading Room   MAP P83
Inside the national library's collections

Initiated by Cardinal de Richelieu, the **Musée de la BNF (Bibliothèque Nationale de France)** *(bnf.fr/en/the-bnf-museum; €24)* is also the house of the Depot Légal (legal depot), where any published work in France is registered. Therefore, a staggering 40 million documents are preserved here and across a few other Parisian sites. We are not only talking about books: they include all sorts of objects, manuscripts, photographs and even costumes. Each catalogued piece must serve a purpose in advancing human knowledge.

To make this extensive archive more accessible, the Richelieu site was ingeniously transformed into a museum. The Galerie Mazarin, featuring an Italian-style painted ceiling, sets the stage for rotating exhibits or rare objects and manuscripts. It's like a constantly changing mini-Louvre.

Note that the National Library is also renowned for its breathtaking reading rooms dating back to the 19th century: the Oval Room, open to the public *(bnf.fr/en/richelieu)*, and the beautiful Salle Labrouste, for researchers only. You can still catch a glimpse of the latter as long as you don't disturb the readers.

Eat & Shop Like in Tokyo   MAP P83 & P92
Explore Paris' Japanese quarter

Just a stone's throw away from the Palais Royal, Paris' Japanese quarter has thrived on rue Ste-Anne and the surrounding streets since the 1980s, forming today a vibrant neighbourhood beloved by Parisians who appreciate Japanese, and more recently Korean, cultures.

Foodies will love wandering around, trying a *matcha melonpan* (bun) from **Aki Boulangerie** *(akiparis.fr)* or the *anko dorayaki* (red-bean paste-filled pancake) from **Tomo**

EATING NEAR THE LOUVRE: FRENCH MEALS   MAP P83

Au Petit Bar: Quaint tiny bar still serving traditional Parisian ham-and-butter baguette sandwiches, which is a surprisingly rare find in this high-end area. *7am-9.30pm Mon-Sat* €

19 SAINT ROCH: Near the Tuileries, creative restaurant offers refined French dishes with seasonal products. *12.15-2pm & 7-11pm Tue-Fri* €€€

Le Soufflé: Traditional soufflé cake has been this house's successful speciality for years. Sweet or savoury, enjoy it in a convivial setting. *noon-4pm & 7-10pm Tue-Sat* €€

La Cordonnerie – Chez Yvette & Claude: French home-style dishes, such as pepper steak, *andouille* (Breton sausage) and creamy scallops. *noon-2pm & 7.30-10pm Mon-Fri* €€

Musée de la BNF (Bibliothèque Nationale de France)

(patisserietomo.fr), one of the first Japanese tearooms in the area. Beyond these well-established spots, now there are all sorts of Japanese food concepts: from the traditional *okonomiyaki* (seafood omelette) to matcha-only tearooms, and yuzu cheese tarts or crêpes served in cones like in Harajuku, a popular area in Tokyo.

If you're more into finding souvenirs for a Japan-enthusiast and less about eating, stop by **Nishikidori – Le Comptoir des Poivres** *(nishikidori.com)*, a high-end delicatessen shop specialising in pepper; and **Maison Wa** *(maisonwa.com)*, where you'll find a tasteful selection of Japanese ceramics and decoration. Book lovers will enjoy **Book Off** *(lingonbook.fr)*, one of the largest Japan-devoted bookshops, where you're sure to find any manga you like.

For the most passionate foodies, don't miss **iRASSHAI** *(irasshai.co)*, although it is a bit further away towards Les Halles. Paris' biggest concept store dedicated to Japanese food, it offers a well-stocked grocery store, a cafe and a restaurant.

Montorgueil's Food Delights

MAP P92

A historical market-street food tour

Vintage shop signs hanging overhead remind us of **rue Montorgueil**'s past as the main supply lane to Les Halles' food

WHY I LOVE THE LOUVRE & PALAIS ROYAL AREA

Fabienne Fong Yan, Lonely Planet writer

After moving to Paris as a young adult, I immediately developed the habit of strolling in the centre of the city, from Palais Royal to the Tuileries, to take in all the beauty of this quarter. I started to notice little details: sculptures in gardens, engravings on frontispieces, hidden fountains… they sparked my curiosity and led me to uncover the various layers of Paris' history. But what charms me the most, even today, is how as Parisians, we seamlessly integrate all this beauty and art into our daily lives: I worked in a heritage-listed edifice, and ate countless takeaways from the Japanese quarter seated on one of the Palais Royal benches, and never once got tired of it at all.

🍽 EATING NEAR THE LOUVRE-PALAIS ROYAL: JAPANESE MEALS — MAP P83

Kodawari Ramen Tsukiji: One of the most popular ramen venues in the quarter, for its original immersive fish-market decor and its fusion recipes. *11.45am-11pm* €	**Udon Jubey**: Sit at the counter or in the underground vault, to enjoy light udon noodles served in extra creamy broth or cold refreshing dishes. *11.30am-9.45pm* €	**Michi**: Here, the chef serves high-quality delicate sushi, in the style of tiny Tokyoite venues. You can sit at the counter to admire his skills. *noon-2pm & 7-10pm Tue-Sat* €€	**Chez Miki**: Elegant Japanese canteen with small bites to share as well as more hearty rice bowls topped with grilled or freshly sliced fish. *noon-2.30pm & 6-10pm Thu-Mon* €€

MONTORGUEIL, LES HALLES & SENTIER

- ● **SIGHTS**
- 1 Bourse de Commerce
- 2 Église St-Eustache
- 3 Forum des Halles
- 4 Rue Montorgueil
- 5 Tour St-Jacques

- ● **SLEEPING**
- 6 123 Sebastopol
- 7 Edgar & Achille
- 8 Hôtel Odyssey

- ● **EATING**
- 9 Au Pied de Cochon
- 10 Au Rocher de Cancale
- 11 Baltis
- 12 Boutique Yam'Tcha
- 13 BrEAThe
- 14 Cloud Cakes
- 15 Daroco
- 16 Eats Thyme
- 17 Eric & Lydie
- 18 Kitchen Izakaya
- 19 L'Escargot Montorgueil
- 20 Maslow
- 21 PLAQ Chocolat
- 22 Stohrer
- 23 Tartelettes

- ● **ENTERTAINMENT**
- 24 Duc des Lombards
- see 3 Forum des Images
- 25 Le Baiser Salé

- see 25 Sunset/Sunside
- ● **SHOPPING**
- 26 À La Mère de Famille
- 27 Cul de Cochon
- 28 iRASSHAI
- see 26 La Fermette
- 29 Passage des Panoramas

Stohrer

market. Now a pedestrian area, it is a busy market street, on which many establishments have an old story to tell.

Don't miss the oldest bakery in Paris, **Stohrer** *(stohrer.fr)* – open since 1730 – renowned for its rum baba and mirrored walls; and buy some chocolate at **À La Mère de Famille** *(lameredefamille.com)*. Cheese lovers will adore **La Fermette's** *(la-fermette-paris.com)* selection, and you will find the tastiest *saucissons* (dried sausages) at **Cul de Cochon** *(culdecochon.com)*.

Au Rocher de Cancale *(instagram.com/aurocherdecancale)* has been serving oysters since the early 1800s, and **L'Escargot Montorgueil** *(escargotmontorgueil.com)* specialises in buttered snails. For a hearty meal, don't hesitate to enjoy a pig's trotter at the famed brasserie **Au Pied de Cochon** *(pieddecochon.com)*, open overnight. It made its name when Les Halles was still the city's main market, serving affordable meals to salespeople working late at night (or early in the morning), using less noble, but still tasty, parts of the pig.

On Thursdays and Sundays, get your fresh groceries from the outdoor market around **Église St-Eustache** (p94).

Mesmerising Rotunda of Art MAP P92
Explore the Bourse de Commerce

The circular walls, the glass roof and dome ceiling create a vertiginous impression upon entering the **Bourse de Commerce** *(pinaultcollection.com; adult/child €15/free)*. It's hard to imagine that this place was once a busy hub for commercial trades or even a wheat warehouse.

It is now a contemporary art gallery showcasing the collection of its patron, French billionaire François Pinault. But beyond his already impressive

---

THE NEW FONDATION CARTIER POUR L'ART CONTEMPORAIN

At the time of research, **Fondation Cartier pour l'Art Contemporain** was about to move into new premises on Pl du Palais Royal. The new location is rather legendary: a Haussmannian landmark, formerly the Louvre des Antiquaires – a 1970s antique department store. Jean Nouvel, who had already designed the much-admired former (modern) building, has remained the Fondation's architect and worked on the long-awaited renovation of the new building's interior.

The contemporary art exhibitions commissioned by the Fondation will take place on three levels, some parts being designed as mobile platforms to be able to modify the exhibition spaces at will.

OLD SHOP SIGNS MAKING HISTORY

Rue Montorgueil is known for its preserved 19th-century shop signs. Visit the **Musée Carnavalet** (p115) in Le Marais, dedicated to the history of Paris, to see a collection of these nostalgic signs.

UNDER THE CANOPY

Once described as 'the belly of Paris', Les Halles underwent significant redevelopment after the relocation of the fresh-food market to Rungis in the 1970s. Today, it remains a gathering place as the central transport hub in the city, with a vast green space welcoming people from all walks of life.

The remarkable metal 'canopy' now sheltering the **Forum des Halles** is an architectural tour de force. It houses a popular underground mall, along with cultural venues such as the **Forum des Images**, a multimedia centre dedicated to the art of cinema, quite popular with Parisians. Among notable shops on the ground floor, the flagship **Lego store** has displays of monumental brick constructions, including representations of Paris monuments.

Église St-Eustache

collection, the Bourse du Commerce welcomes well-established and emerging contemporary artists alike to create temporary exhibitions in situ. Its central room is therefore usually dedicated to an installation, while more traditional exhibitions are hosted on the floors above.

When visiting this unique space, have a look at the compelling circular mural, depicting international trade during an era of extensive colonial expansion: it deserves both an admiring and a critical eye. Daily guided tours in English are available (no additional charge), providing insightful commentary on the site's heritage.

Awe-inspiring Organ Recitals MAP P92
Music by stained-glass light

Known for its impressive Gothic architecture, **Église St-Eustache** *(saint-eustache.org)* attracts visitors for its breathtaking stained-glass windows. However, the church's true masterpiece is its organ. With 8000 pipes and a unique design allowing the organist to play in the nave (close to the audience), it is considered one of France's most beautiful

EATING NEAR MONTORGUEIL-LES HALLES: OUR VEGETARIAN PICKS MAP P92

BrEAThe: Creative vegan kitchen: a great variety of sushi/Japanese-style dishes. Try the 'Discovery' plate to share. *noon-2.30pm & 6.30-10pm Mon-Sat, from 11.30am Sun* €€

Kitchen Izakaya: Don't be afraid to order three/four small plates among the refined 'tapas-style' options at this charming canteen. *noon-3pm & 7-11pm Tue-Sat, noon-2.30pm Mon* €€

Maslow: Large, welcoming vegetarian restaurant by the river, advocating for hearty, creative meals and slow living. *noon-11pm Mon-Sat, 11.15am-9pm Sun* €€

Eric & Lydie: In this hybrid place in Passage du Grand Cerf, locals like the vegetarian bento box (meat options available). *11.30am-7pm Wed-Fri, to 6pm Sat, from 1pm Tue* €-€€

instruments. St-Eustache's musical tradition dates back centuries. During Sunday services, you can listen to the glorious sound of the organ. Additionally, on Sunday afternoons, organists present public auditions, and the church regularly hosts larger concerts.

Jazz Your Night Out
MAP P92
One street, many jazz bars
Whether you're an ardent jazz enthusiast or simply seeking an evening of soul-stirring melodies, the jazz bars along rue des Lombards are your gateway to an unforgettable night out. Step into **Le Baiser Salé** (*lebaisersale.com; prices vary*) to listen to contemporary or fusion jazz, with Afro-Caribbean influences. For a contrasting ambience, head to the spacious and sophisticated atmosphere of **Duc des Lombards** (*ducdeslombards.com; €29-41*), where you can savour the sounds of classical jazz, swing or even Latin jazz with two concerts per night. At **Sunset/Sunside** (*sunset-sunside.com; €20, prices can vary*), get a taste of two clubs in one. Sunset highlights acoustic and traditional jazz styles, while Sunside showcases more contemporary jazz and improvisation. There's something to satisfy every jazz lover along this street.

Take 300 Steps to Heaven
MAP P92
A panoramic embrace of Paris
Who would suspect that the most incredible, panoramic view in Paris is also the starting point of the St-Jacques de Compostelle pilgrimage? Just steps away from Châtelet, in a small patch of green, the **Tour St-Jacques** (*boutique.toursaintjacques.fr; €12*) looms above the city. However, few people, including locals, are aware that it opens seasonally to the public, giving visitors the unique opportunity to discover the history of what was once part of the Church of St-Jacques-de-la-Boucherie, dating back to the 16th century. Following your guide, you will ascend 300 steps on a narrow spiral staircase to finally marvel at a breathtaking 360-degree view of Paris and hear stories about the tower's intriguing connections to alchemist Nicolas Flamel. Try to book in advance, online or at the kiosk at the foot of the tower, and wear comfortable shoes for the climb.

CENTRE POMPIDOU 2026–2030

Until 2030, Centre Pompidou, and the iconic building lined with giant coloured pipes towering above the centre of Paris that has been hosting some of the most avant-garde exhibitions for the past 48 years, will be closed to the public. The renovation addresses safety, accessibility and sustainability issues – but also aims at rethinking the space for new generations of art enthusiasts.

During this time, travelling exhibitions will take place not only in various places in Paris but also in other cities. By the end of 2026, a gallery curated by Centre Pompidou, dedicated to creation and conservation, will be opened in Massy, a 40-minute train ride from Paris.

It always has two seasonal must-try flavours.

 EATING NEAR MONTORGUEIL-LES HALLES: SWEET TREATS MAP P92

| **Tartelettes**: Intimate tearoom creating indulgent fruit tarts and other cakes – perfect for enjoying on cold winter days. *9am-7pm Mon-Fri, from 10am Sat & Sun* € | **PLAQ Chocolat**: Specialised shop, where the chocolate is made right before your eyes. Try its no-milk hot chocolate. *11am-7.30pm Mon-Fri, from 10am Sat, 10am-6.30pm Sun* €€ | **Cloud Cakes**: A vegan bakery with colourful mouthwatering cupcakes and pastries. Savoury plant-based options are also available for brunch. *9am-7pm Mon-Sat* € | **Baltis**: Lebanese ice-cream parlour. Taste traditional *halwa* with crushed pistachios, and creative flavours like olive oil and basil. *12.30-7.30pm Sun-Fri, to 11pm Sat* € |

Montmartre & Northern Paris

HISTORIC HILLTOP VILLAGE | FASCINATING NEIGHBOURHOODS

☑ TOP TIP

Although gritty, the neighbourhoods in the north and northeast of Paris are fairly safe as far as big cities go. If it's one place you need to stay on your guard, it's at the foot of the hill that leads up to Sacré-Cœur. It's not unusual for pickpockets and con artists to work the crowds here.

Perched on a hill in the 18e *arrondissement,* Montmartre has long stood apart, first as a rural village, then as a bohemian stomping ground for artists like Picasso and Toulouse-Lautrec. Its winding streets, once home to windmills and cabarets, drew creatives seeking inspiration and escape from central Paris. Meanwhile, the surrounding northern neighbourhoods evolved as working-class enclaves, shaped by waves of immigration and cultural fusion. Over time, gentrification, artistic revival, and a renewed interest in authentic, local experiences have transformed the area. Today, this corner of Paris blends grit and charm, and is the most exciting place to get under the surface of the city.

Take a Deep Dive into Montmartre   MAP P98
The village's arty hangouts live on

Visitors are often busy admiring the standalone houses and quaint cafes that look like they are stuck in a time past, but look beyond and you'll see that Montmartre's arty side still lives on in the form of **street art**–splashed walls, small artist **ateliers and galleries**, a handful of caricature artists on the very top of the hill on pl du Tertre, as well as more formal venues like the **Théâtre des Abbesses** *(theatredelaville-paris.com/fr/lieux/les-abbesses)*, which puts on plays and contemporary ballets. There is also a small **Dalí Museum** *(daliparis.com)* with more than 300 of his artworks, from

continued on p100

GETTING AROUND

Your best bet is taking Metro Line 2 (Anvers, Barbès-Rochechouart), Line 4 (Château Rouge, Porte de Clignancourt), and Line 12 (Abbesses, Jules Joffrin), covering Montmartre and beyond.

Walking is essential here, as it's the only way to soak up Montmartre's hills, hidden stairways and cobblestone lanes. Wear good shoes and bring a rain jacket.

Bus/tram offers a slower, scenic ride: try Bus 85 or 31 for local hops, or Tram T3b to reach the Saint-Ouen flea market and La Villette with ease.

TOP EXPERIENCE

Basilique du Sacré-Cœur

Rising above Montmartre (the hill of martyrs), the Basilique du Sacré-Cœur, dedicated to the Sacred Heart of Jesus is a vantage point, a sanctuary, a Parisian rite of passage, and one of the city's most visited landmarks. From its gleaming domes to one of the world's largest mosaics, its grandeur stuns. Below, the streets buzz with artists and cafes, but up here, the sweeping views and quiet reverence are a moment apart.

Christ in Majesty mosaic

Get Behind the History

Perched at the highest point in Paris, Montmartre officially became part of the city's 18e *arrondissement* in 1860. The Basilique du Sacré-Cœur, its luminous white dome hovering above Paris like a celestial apparition, was built later, rising as close to the heavens as possible to atone for the city's sins, particularly after the Revolution, making it a politically charged monument many locals disagree with.

See One of the World's Biggest Mosaics

Designed in a striking Roman-Byzantine style, the basilica took five architects over four decades to complete (1875–1919). Its brilliant white façade comes from calcite-rich stone that naturally cleans itself with rain. Inside, the apse features Christ in Majesty, one of the world's largest mosaics, while the Blessed Sacrament, positioned above the high altar, remains the heart of the basilica's spiritual devotion.

Climb Up for Sweeping City Views

Visitors can climb the 300 steps to the dome for breathtaking panoramic views of Paris, while inside, chapels, stained-glass windows, and a crypt bathed in natural light create a contemplative atmosphere. The basilica's perpetual adoration prayer cycle, which began in 1885, continues uninterrupted, and on Sundays, the grand organ resonates through the sacred space during mass and vespers.

TOP TIPS

● You can spend the night at the Basilica from 11pm to 7am if you pray for at least an hour, as part of the continuous prayer cycle, unbroken since 1885 (sign up on the Basilica website).

● Arrive early; as it's a sunset spot, it gets overcrowded around then.

● Visit on weekdays to avoid the crowds

PRACTICALITIES

● sacre-coeur-montmartre.com (email for guided visits) ● 10am-7pm, but check the site before your visit, as times may vary according to Basilica events ● adult/child/groups €8/5/6, tickets available on-site only

MONTMARTRE, PIGALLE & BATIGNOLLES

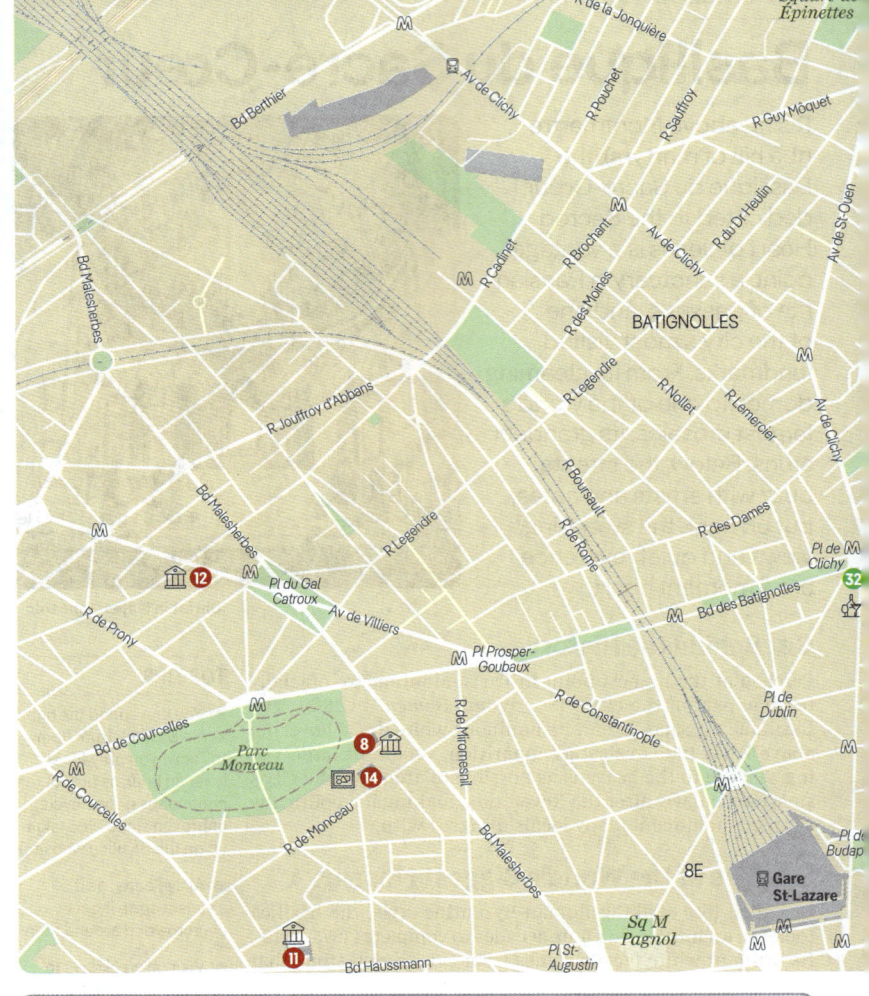

- ⭐ **HIGHLIGHTS**
  1. Basilique du Sacré-Cœur
- 🔴 **SIGHTS**
  2. Cité des Arts de Montmartre
  3. Dalí Museum
  4. Halle St-Pierre
  5. Le Bateau-Lavoir
  6. Le Mur des je t'aime
  7. Maison de Dalida
  8. Musée Cernuschi
  9. Musée de la Vie Romantique
  10. Musée de Montmartre
  11. Musée Jacquemart-André
  12. Musée Jean-Jacques Henner
  13. Musée National Gustave Moreau
  14. Musée Nissim de Camondo
  15. Parc de la Turlure
  16. Place du Tertre
- ⚫ **SLEEPING**
  17. Hotel Élysée Montmartre
  18. Hôtel HoY
  19. Le Village Montmartre by Hiphostels

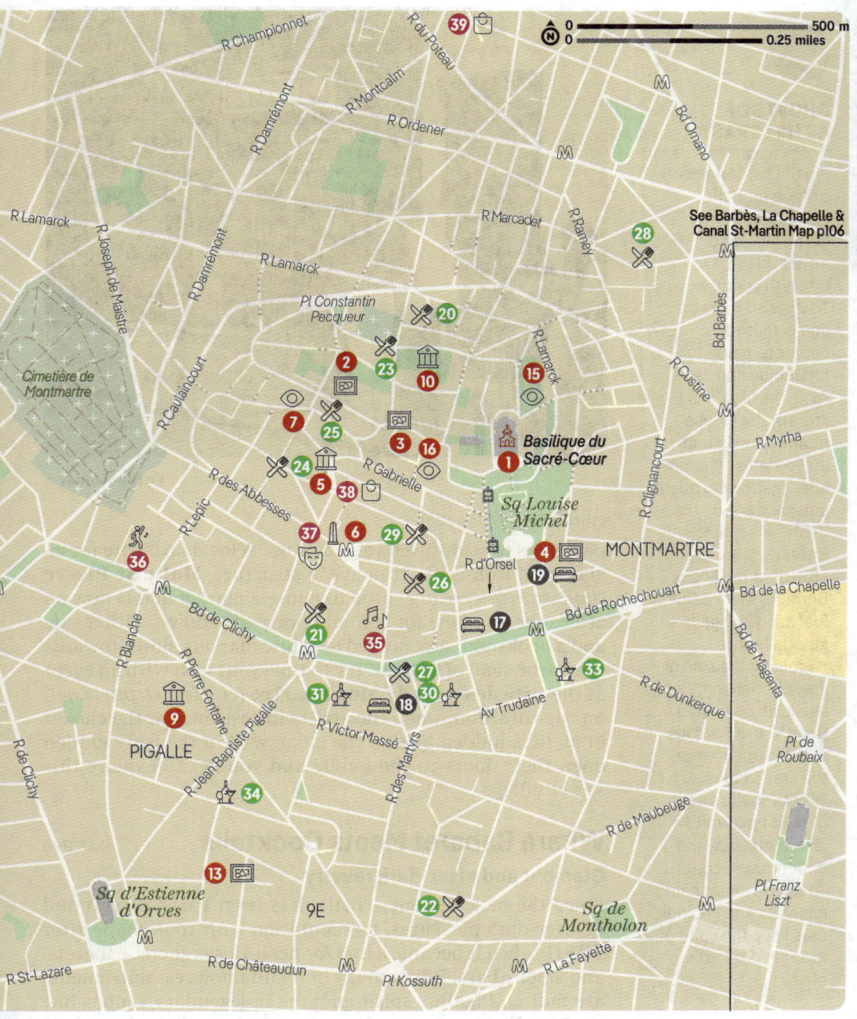

● EATING	27 Maggie	32 La Fête	● SHOPPING
20 Aléa	see 18 mesa de HOY	33 Minore	38 Au Marché de la Butte
21 Bouillon Pigalle	28 Pantobaguette	see 30 Sister Midnight	39 Dizonord
22 Caillebotte	29 Spree Café Galerie	34 Stéréo	
23 La Maison Rose			
24 La Part des Anges	● DRINKING	● ENTERTAINMENT	
25 Le Bon, La Butte	& NIGHTLIFE	35 Madame Arthur	
26 Le Progrès	30 Classique	36 Moulin Rouge	
	31 Dirty Dick	37 Théâtre des Abbesses	

Fotoautomat

GHOSTS OF ARTISTS PAST

Pigalle has long been a stage for Paris' most electrifying performers and artists. In the late 19th century, Toulouse-Lautrec immortalised its cabarets, painting La Goulue and Jane Avril, the high-kicking stars of the Moulin Rouge. The district pulsed with bohemian energy, drawing poets and painters. By the 1920s, Josephine Baker mesmerised crowds at the Folies Bergère, while Édith Piaf sang in Pigalle's streets before becoming the soul of French chanson. Jazz musician and writer Boris Vian added his avant-garde flair to the area's clubs. After WWII, Pigalle's neon glow lit up a world of jazz, burlesque and underground culture. Today, its music halls, cabarets and cocktail bars keep the spirit of its legendary artists alive.

continued from p96

paintings to sculptures and etchings. A local favourite for its glass and iron-clad art nouveau structure, **Halle St-Pierre** *(hallesaintpierre.org)* used to house a market and is now an atmospheric venue for contemporary art shows, with a cafe and a bookshop, surrounded by fabric markets, down towards the Barbès end of the hill. Try to time your visit with an event at the **Cité des Arts de Montmartre** *(citedesartsparis.net)* on rue Girardon, when the artists in residency at the cluster of ateliers hidden behind the stone wall in the leafy garden open their doors to the public and you get to explore this secret village.

Where Cabaret Meets Cocktails MAP P98
Glamour and after-dark revelry

Since the belle époque, Pigalle has been Paris' playground of after-dark pleasures. Its reputation truly took shape after WWII, when it became a hub for neon-lit sex shops, cabarets, and smoky bars. While many of its infamous establishments are fading, Pigalle's spirit endures in legendary venues like the **Moulin Rouge** *(moulinrouge.fr; adult €103)*, where since 1889, high-kicking dancers and extravagant have been bringing

 EATING IN MONTMARTRE: OUR PICKS ──────── MAP P98

Le Bon, La Butte: Cosy bistro serving French staples with a contemporary twist. *7pm-midnight Tue-Thu, noon-3pm & 7pm-midnight Fri-Sat, noon-4pm & 7-11pm Sun* €€

Aléa: Terrific, simple market-led cuisine in a spot locals love. *noon-1.30pm & 7.30-9.30pm Wed-Thu, noon-1.30pm & 7.30-10pm Fri, noon-2pm & 7.30-10pm Sat, 12.30-2pm Sun* €€

La Part des Anges: Laid-back local spot with great traditional food like magret de canard (duck breast). *7pm-10.30pm Tue-Thu, 7pm-10.45pm Fri, noon-2.30pm & 7-11pm Sat* €€

Le Progrès: A typical Parisian cafe open all day for coffee and wine, and the day's specials, as well as snails and steak tartare à la carte. *9am-2am* €€

ESSENTIAL MONTMARTRE ON FOOT

Discover Montmartre's main sights and delve into its history with this walking tour.

START	END	LENGTH
Pigalle	Halle St-Pierre	2.3km, 1½hrs

Start on ① **rue des Abbesses**, with its shops and cafes, and head to rue des Trois Frères. Pass the ② **Mur des je t'aime** (Wall of 'I Love Yous') and ③ **Spree Café Galerie** and the ④ **Fotoautomat**, which usually has a queue but takes great snaps. At rue Androuet you'll pass ⑤ **Au Marché de la Butte**, featured in the film *Amélie*, and then on to place Emile Goudeau and ⑥ **Le Bateau-Lavoir** artist studios, where artists like Picasso once lived. Take rue d'Orchampt, passing singer Dalida's former home, ⑦ **Maison de Dalida**, then walk to ⑧ **rue de l'Abreuvoir**, one of the most scenic streets in the city. Pass by ⑨ **La Maison Rose**, ivy-clad houses and the vineyard, continue along rue des Saules, and on to rue St-Vincent to ⑩ **Parc de la Turlure**, for a magnificent view of the back of the Sacré-Cœur. To reach the front of the basilica take ⑪ **rue du Cardinal Guibert** and admire the dome and panoramic rooftop views. Make a detour west to the ⑫ **place du Tertre** to see the crowded square of artists and restaurants. Back at Sacré-Cœur, walk left down the stairs through the ⑬ **square Louise Michel** to the ⑭ **Halle St-Pierre** in the area's textile neighbourhood, where you can see the basilica from the bottom of its pedestal.

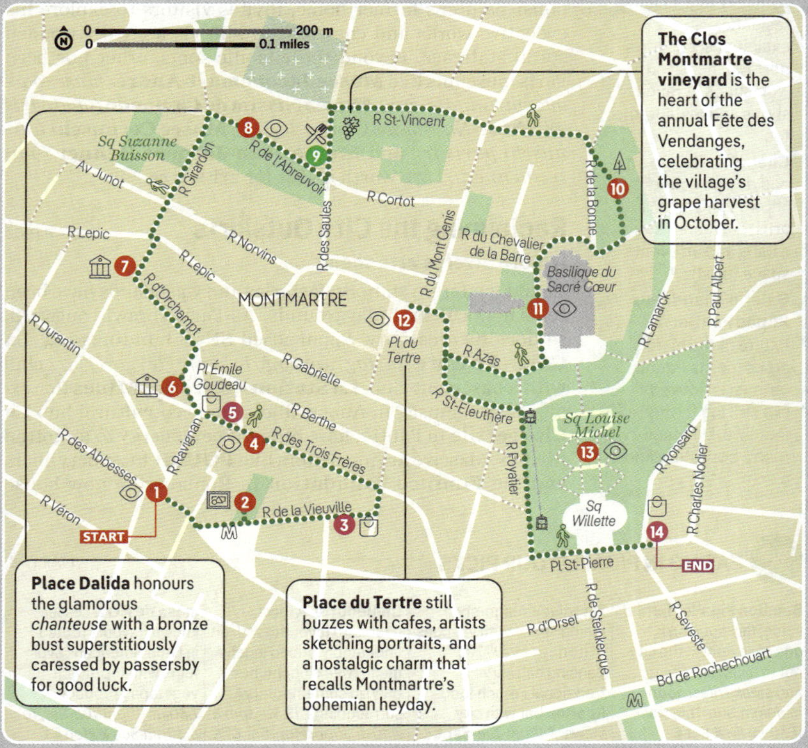

The Clos Montmartre vineyard is the heart of the annual Fête des Vendanges, celebrating the village's grape harvest in October.

Place Dalida honours the glamorous *chanteuse* with a bronze bust superstitiously caressed by passersby for good luck.

Place du Tertre still buzzes with cafes, artists sketching portraits, and a nostalgic charm that recalls Montmartre's bohemian heyday.

ART-WORLD INSIDER

Alexandra Weinress *(@theseenparis)* helps visitors navigate Paris' offbeat art scene through bespoke tours.

Le 19M: Chanel's 25,500-sq-m hub brings together top artisans specialised in embroidery to feather work. Also a gallery, a bookstore and a cafe.

Le 104: A publicly run, multipurpose space with diverse cultural programming, residencies, exhibitions, concerts, performances and workshops. A range of shops and restaurants too.

Chapelle XIV: An art and design gallery showcasing emerging artists, a record store, a cafe, and an event space (p104).

Galerie Thaddaeus Ropac Pantin: A fixture of the Marais art scene, its Pantin outpost is housed in a striking former metalworking factory. Also a bookstore and a cafe.

the cancan to life in nightly shows at 9pm and 11pm. Cabaret **Madame Arthur** *(madamearthur.fr)* is a fun evening out of live music and gender-bending performances, keeping Pigalle's legacy of spectacle and seduction alive. Beyond the show lights, Pigalle's warren of small spaces has always been central to its illicit charm, once home to shadowy dens, opium-fuelled escapades, and whispered rendezvous. Today, these tight quarters have found a new life as cocktail bars, where locals and visitors mingle over expertly crafted drinks. Spots like **Sister Midnight**, **Dirty Dick**, **Minore** and **Classique** shake up inventive cocktails, blending Pigalle's hedonistic past with a squeakier-clean present.

Artist Ateliers & Villa Museums   MAP P98
Artists' homes turned hidden museums

In Montmartre, the **Musée de Montmartre** *(museedemontmartre.fr; adult/child €15/free)* occupies a 17th-century house that once housed Renoir, immersing visitors in the area's vibrant artistic past. Down the hill in Pigalle, the **Musée de la Vie Romantique** *(museevieromantique.paris.fr)* offers a glimpse into the life of Dutch painter Ary Scheffer and his illustrious guests, including Dickens and Chopin. Nearby, the **Musée National Gustave Moreau**, housed in the symbolist painter's former home, invites visitors to explore his evocative works and charming studio via a creaky wooden spiral staircase. Beyond these iconic spots, other northern Paris museums like **Musée Jacquemart-André** *(musee-jacquemart-andre.com)*, **Musée Nissim de Camondo** *(madparis.fr/Musee-Nissim-de-Camondo-125)*, **Musée Cernuschi** *(cernuschi.paris.fr)*, and **Musée Jean-Jacques Henner** *(musee-henner.fr)* are worth a visit for art lovers.

Reclaiming the City Outskirts   MAP P103
A more diverse arts scene

Abandoned train stations, factories and wastelands have been reborn as cultural playgrounds. As Paris sprawls outward, so does its creativity. Repurposed SNCF buildings like **La Gare – Le Gore** *(instagram.com/la_gare_le_gore)* jazz club with a basement club, **La Station – Gare des Mines** (for experimental music) in Aubervilliers, and eco-cultural hub **La Cité Fertile** in Pantin, have brought new energy to forgotten corners. Massive art incubators like **POUSH** in Aubervilliers and the **Fiminco Foundation** in Romainville now house

---

 EATING IN PIGALLE: OUR PICKS ———————————————— MAP P98

Bouillon Pigalle	Maggie	Caillebotte	mesa de HOY
Bouillon Pigalle: Terrific value, this *bouillon* is one of several in the city not to miss for escargot and *steak-frites*. *noon-midnight Sun-Thu, from 11.30am Fri & Sat* €	**Maggie**: Vintage-style dining space with vestiges of its days as a 1920s dancing hall serves traditional French food. Rooftop bar with city views. *7-10pm Tue-Sat* €€	**Caillebotte**: A local neobistro favourite with an unbeatably priced lunch menu (week lunchtimes only) in contemporary surroundings. *12.30-3pm & 7.30-11.30pm Mon-Sat* €€€	**mesa de HOY**: Lesser-known flavours rooted in Latin American savoir-faire, with top-notch vegetarian produce. *7.30am-10pm Tue-Sat, to 6.30pm Sun & Mon* €€

THE AFRICA CONNECTION

Paris' African heritage is complex, runs deep and is rooted in its former colonies – Senegal, Mali, Ivory Coast, Algeria and the Democratic Republic of Congo, among others, were once part of the French colonial empire – especially in neighbourhoods like Château Rouge and La Goutte d'Or in Barbès. These areas pulse with life, from the scent of grilled meat and *bissap* juice to the colourful stalls of Marché Dejean selling spices, fabrics and beauty products from across the continent. Institutions like the Musée Dapper and La Colonie (now closed but influential) have spotlighted African art and thought. Music venues like **Le 360** and **New Morning** showcase musical talent from all over Africa.

international artists. Even former universities and factories, like Césure in the Latin Quarter and an old airship hangar in Meudon, are now cultural spaces, blending performance, community and creativity.

Paris After Dark

MAP P92, P103 & P106

Party all night in the City of Light

After a sleepy spell, Paris' nightlife is roaring back to life, especially its electronic music scene. New clubs are opening at a dizzying pace, from the cavernous 3000-sq-m **Mia Mao** (p107) in La Villette to gritty, genre-blending nights at **Essaim** *(instagram.com/essaimparis)* near Gare du Nord. Over in Place de Clichy, **La Fête** *(instagram.com/paris.lafete)* is drawing stylish crowds, while **Fawa Wafa** *(fawa-wafa.org)*, tucked under a 19e-*arrondissement* flyover (formerly Le Péripate), offers a raw, DIY energy. Across the city, underground parties and pop-up sets are multiplying, with lineups spanning house, techno, Afrobeat, and experimental sounds. It's a good time to be a night owl in Paris, if you can keep up.

Record Revival

MAP P98 & P106

Paris loves vinyl

Vinyl is having a serious moment in Paris, and the city's revival is best felt in its old and new generation of record shops. **Yoyaku** in La Chapelle is one of Paris' top independent record stores and labels, known for its tightly curated selection of vinyl, spanning house, techno, minimal, electro and acid. It also distributes music for over 500 labels and 500 shops worldwide. In 2020, the team opened **Chapelle XIV**, a sleek cultural space in the 20e *arrondissement* that blends a record shop, a cafe, an art gallery and creative workshop under one roof. Open daily, it's a great spot to browse records or catch an art show. **Dizonord**, near Montmartre, is a playful, eclectic space with new and secondhand vinyl, books, tapes and kid-friendly events. Over by Canal St-Martin, **Record Station** is a crate-digger's dream, packed with original pressings and imports spanning soul, funk, punk, jazz, reggae and more. There are lots of other spots across the city though.

Canal Strolls

MAP P106

Bohemian-chic Paris by the water

A short walk from Gare de l'Est, **Canal St-Martin** offers a slower, stylish side of Paris. The treelined waterway, spanned by iron footbridges and flanked by cobblestone pavements comes to life in warmer months when locals settle along the banks with wine, snacks and portable speakers. It's the kind of place where picnics stretch into impromptu dinners at a nearby restaurant. It's a favourite area with locals because its cluster of street-art-covered thoroughfares are packed with creative boutiques, trendy bars and restaurants. Browse the beautiful Indian homewares at **Jamini** *(jaminidesign.com);* the carefully curated homewares at **La Trésorerie** *(latresorerie.fr);* and the

Canal St-Martin

treasures at thrift store **Thanx God I'm a V.I.P.** *(thanxgod.com)*, where you might be able to dig out a Dior sports jacket or designer dress at a bargain price. If you're here to work and you want to work out, then the glass-roof **La Montgolfière** *(lamontgolfiereclub.com)*, inside an old hot-air-balloon workshop, should be your go-to. Pop into bookshop **Artazart** *(artazart.com)* to leaf through the fantastic children's books and design magazines from all over the globe.

Aquatic Adventure

MAP P103 & P106

Exploring northern Paris on the water

As well as a cruise along the River Seine, it's also possible to explore northern Paris on a canal cruise. Make a booking to explore the Canal St-Martin and Parc de la Villette and watch the locals sitting canal-side enjoying drinks, and pass through swing bridges and banks covered in street art. Several companies provide cruises, such as **Canauxrama** *(canauxrama.com)* in Jaurès; **Paris Canal Croisières** *(pariscanal.com)* from Porte de Pantin; and **Akwa Experience** *(akwa-experience.com/en)*, where you can hire a self-drive boat with a group of people and putter along the Canal de l'Ourcq, bookended by Jaurès and La Villette.

The Creative Edge of Paris

MAP P106

Music, art, clubs and culture

This last pocket of Paris, just before the *Périphérique* (ring road) spills into the suburbs, is an eldorado for night owls and culture seekers. Along the canal between Stalingrad and Jaurès, legendary venues like **La Rotonde** (p182), housed in a grand 18th-century rotunda; and **Point Ephémère** *(pointephemere.org)*, a hub for alternative music and visual arts, pulse

LISTENING BARS

The concept of listening bars, originally popularised in Japan, has inspired the opening of new bars that play vinyl records. Gone are the days of music merely as background noise, as bars put listening to music on vinyl back in the spotlight.

Favourite bars in the north of Paris include wine bar **Stéréo** *(stereoparis.com)* near Pigalle, and tapas bar **Pantobaguette** *(pantobaguette.fr)* close to Montmartre. Elsewhere in town, check out Le Discobar, Montezuma Café, Bambino, Fréquence and original vinyl bar Les Disquaires, among others.

BARBÈS, LA CHAPELLE & CANAL ST-MARTIN

● **SIGHTS**
1 Canal St-Martin
2 Chapelle XIV
3 Le 104

● **ACTIVITIES**
4 Akwa Experience
5 Canauxrama

6 La Montgolfière

● **SLEEPING**
7 Generator Hostel

● **DRINKING & NIGHTLIFE**
8 Essaim

● **ENTERTAINMENT**
see 3 Le 104
9 Le 360
10 New Morning
11 Point Éphémère

● **SHOPPING**
12 Artazart
13 Jamini
see 13 La Trésorerie
14 Thanx God I'm a V.I.P.
15 Yoyaku

with activity year-round. Keep walking towards Riquet and you'll find **Le 104** *(104.fr)*, a multidisciplinary space that's part gallery, part community center, and part dance-floor for the city's youth. If you're there in summer, then plan an evening at the **Cinéma en Plein air**, an annual open-air film festival in the Parc de la Villette, which is a beloved summer tradition; just bring a blanket and some snacks and you're set. **Festival 100%** in spring is also worth popping by for the cutting-edge performances, installations, and art by emerging talents. Another festival worth adding to your diary is the **Mondial du Tatouage** (the World Tattoo Convention), which brings together tattoo artists from all over the world under one roof at the Grande Halle; there are a number of talks, exhibitions and events too.

Science, Sound & Silver Spheres MAP P103
Family fun and futuristic vibes

The city opens up at **Parc de la Villette** *(lavillette.com)*, a green sprawl anchored by the **Cité des Sciences et de l'Industrie** *(cite-sciences.fr)*, one of Paris' best museums for immersive, kid-friendly learning. Don't miss the refurbished **La Géode** *(lageode.fr)*, reopened in spring of 2025: a huge mirrored dome and 3-D cinema that catches the sky in its curves. By night, nearby venues like **Le Zénith** *(le-zenith.com)*, **Le Trabendo** *(letrabendo.net)*, **Cabaret Sauvage** *(cabaretsauvage.com)*, and newcomer **Mia Mao** *(miamao.fr)* take over, with everything from indie gigs to global club nights. On the water, **La Péniche Cinéma** *(penichecinema.com)*, a floating club–bar, and the **Grande Halle de la Villette** *(lavillette.com)*, a former abattoir turned events hall, complete the vibrant scene.

LA VILLETTE: PARIS' PLAYGROUND

Spanning 55 hectares in northeast Paris, **La Villette** is the city's largest park and a bold example of urban redevelopment. A vast industrial wasteland that was once occupied by slaughterhouses is now home to myriad cultural venues and 20 themed gardens and open lawns. When the government launched an international competition for the project in 1983, it was Swiss-French architect Bernard Tschumi who won the bid, over big names like Zaha Hadid. His plan called for 26 'follies', red enameled steel structures that he likened to a 'deconstructed building'. The 15-year redevelopment resulted in a culture-centric playground for Parisians.

 EATING & DRINKING IN LA VILLETTE: OUR PICKS ——— MAP P103

Le Pavillon des Canaux: Whimsical cafe–bar styled like a cosy home. Enjoy coffee in the 'bathtub' or work from the 'bedroom'. *hours vary* €€

Paname Brewing Company: Canal-side microbrewery attracts a lively crowd. House-made beers, expansive deck overlooking the water. *11am–1pm* €€

Les Bancs Publics: Straightforward, charming bistro with tables along the canal during warmer months. Classic French dishes. *8am-2am Mon-Sat, 9am-6pm Sun* €

Au Boeuf Couronné: The last vestige of the old Villette meat halls, this belle époque gem serves top-quality steaks in a chic, throwback dining room. *noon–midnight* €€

Antique kitchen utensils for sale

TOP EXPERIENCE

Marché aux Puces de St-Ouen

Founded in 1885, the Marché aux Puces de St-Ouen is the world's largest antiques market, located just beyond Paris' northern edge. It spans 12 distinct markets, with antiques, vintage furniture, rare collectibles, fashion and curiosities. For serious collectors or curious wanderers, there is endless inspiration and irresistible old-world charm.

DON'T MISS

Marché Paul Bert Serpette

Marché de L'Entrepôt

Marché Vernaison

Marché Dauphine

Mob Hotel

Mains d'Oeuvres

A Storied Legacy of Treasure Hunting

Les Puces unfolds like a village within a village, equal parts treasures and time capsules. What began as an informal sprawl of rag pickers selling secondhand wares has evolved into the largest antiques market in the world, a labyrinthine network of more than a dozen markets spread across seven hectares. On weekends, some 180,000 visitors descend upon its narrow alleys, hunting for everything from gilded mirrors and art deco light fixtures to vinyl records and timeworn furniture. With its mix of museum-grade galleries and showrooms, dusty bric-a-brac stalls and discreet ateliers, it presents more than shopping: it's a window into the layered, eclectic soul of Paris.

A Maze of Markets

The allure of Les Puces lies in the diversity and distinct rhythm and charm of each market. **Marché Vernaison**, the oldest, is a warren of open-air lanes lined with vintage postcards,

PRACTICALITIES

● pucesdeparissaintouen.com ● 11am-5pm Mon, 8am-noon Fri, 10am-6pm Sat & Sun

HAGGLING

Haggling is part of the charm at Les Puces. Approach vendors with a smile, and you might knock 10–20% off the price. While some accept cards, cash is often preferred for smaller items or better deals. Vendors are relaxed, often found reading, napping, or chatting, and expect you to take your time, happily sharing details about their goods.

embroidered linens and costume jewellery. **Marché Paul Bert Serpette**, the crown jewel, draws a discerning crowd of interior designers and collectors who come for 20th-century design icons, museum-worthy antiques and impeccably curated vignettes. Inside the vaulted glass pavilion of **Marché Dauphine**, the atmosphere is more freewheeling: vinyl records, retro cameras, tribal artefacts and the occasional taxidermied bird. **L'Entrepôt** is one of the smallest markets but it's mighty and has a bunch of old zinc-top brasserie bars and spiral staircases from houses all over the country. The joy, of course, is in the serendipity: a meandering stroll, a spontaneous chat with a vendor, and a find you never knew you needed.

A Weekend Ritual of Culture, Food & People-Watching

A visit here is as much about ambiance as it is about the hunt. Open Fridays, Saturdays, Sundays and Mondays, the market comes alive with a mix of locals, designers, tourists and curious *flâneurs*. Live music often spills out of cafes, while dealers chat with regulars over espresso and wine. You'll find locals tucking into couscous at Le Coq d'Or on rue des Rosiers, or enjoying a hearty bistro meal at a bargain price at nearby Le Bouillon du Coq, opened by top chef Thierry Marx. There's also the stylish **Mob Hotel** designed by Philippe Starck (not Mob House, which is a little drab), a cult favourite for pizza and cocktails. The flea market isn't just a shopping destination, it's a cultural experience of history, art and everyday Parisian life, regardless of whether you're buying or just browsing. In fact, La Chope des Puces, an old bistro that puts on jazz concerts, is an ode to the unique spirit of this sprawling village of stalls and showrooms. And if you have time, take in a show or a DJ night at indie arts hub **Mains d'Oeuvres**, nearby.

TOP TIPS

● The easiest way to reach the market, without having to wade through tens of stalls pedalling cheap designer knockoffs, is to get metro line 4 to Porte de Clignancourt. Don't be put off by the unpolished surroundings. Cross the ring road and enter the market on rue des Rosiers. Maps and lots of background information to help you plan your trip here are available on the Puces website.

● Sunday morning is the best time to visit. Vendors are all open, the crowds are manageable, and there's a lively local buzz.

Le Marais

FASHIONABLE BARS | DINING | BOUTIQUES

☑ TOP TIP

The Marais' pavements can get uncomfortably crowded on weekends, as shoppers descend on the boutiques. Weekdays are more breathable, though Mondays see shop and museum closures, including the Musée National Picasso-Paris. The Musée des Archives Nationales is a haven of peace, with its lovely hidden gardens.

The 4e is the only district in Paris that escaped the Haussmannian redesign of Paris, with almost all of its narrow streets and occasionally crooked buildings from the pre-Revolutionary era. Today Le Marais also has a plethora of activities. Admire stunning 17th- and 18th-century *hôtels particuliers* (private mansions) as you explore, or while visiting the museums, which many *hôtels particuliers* now house. Enjoy falafel in a historically Jewish district, then stretch your budget in trendy boutiques, designer stores and art galleries. An LGBTIQ-friendly attitude welcomes the community to rainbow-hued bars and clubs. Le Marais invites exploration of its winding lanes and never fails to satisfy.

An Enduring Royal Square

MAP P111

Relax in the place des Vosges

Place des Vosges is the vision of King Henry IV, who wanted a grand square in Paris. This landmark was constructed in 1605 and has remained a social hub and one of the most elegant squares in the city throughout the centuries.

Today visitors and locals still converge upon the spacious lawns beneath the shade of trees. The square is ideal for picnicking, so consider stopping into **Brigat'** *(brigat.paris)* to buy a tiramisu patisserie to enjoy on the grass. Later, stroll the arcades to admire art galleries and *hôtels particuliers*, including the former residence of writer Victor Hugo, or have coffee at one of the traditional French restaurants tucked under the arcades.

 GETTING AROUND

Le Marais is best explored on foot to navigate the crowds, browse boutiques and admire the architecture. Don't underestimate how long it can take to explore all the side streets.

Cycling down the rue Rivoli bike lanes is a great way to access Le Marais, but weekend crowds can be frustrating, so it's easiest to save the bike for larger streets.

For the lower Marais, the best underground stop is St-Paul, but it can get crowded on weekends. Metro stations Filles du Calvaire and Arts et Métiers are both good alternatives.

LE MARAIS SOUTH

● SIGHTS
1. Agoudas Hakehilos Synagogue
2. Hôtel de Sully
3. Hôtel de Ville
4. MAIF Social Club
5. Maison de Victor Hugo
6. Maison Européenne de la Photographie
7. Mémorial de la Shoah
8. Musée Carnavalet
9. Place des Vosges
10. Polka Galerie

● SLEEPING
11. Hôtel Jeanne d'Arc le Marais
12. MIJE Fourcy
13. People Marais

● EATING
14. Brigat'
15. Brutus
16. Capitaine
17. La Collective Parisienne
18. Notre Café Marais

● DRINKING & NIGHTLIFE
19. Artesano
20. Les Souffleurs

● SHOPPING
21. Candora
22. Frederic Malle
23. Maruis Fabre
24. Système Solaire

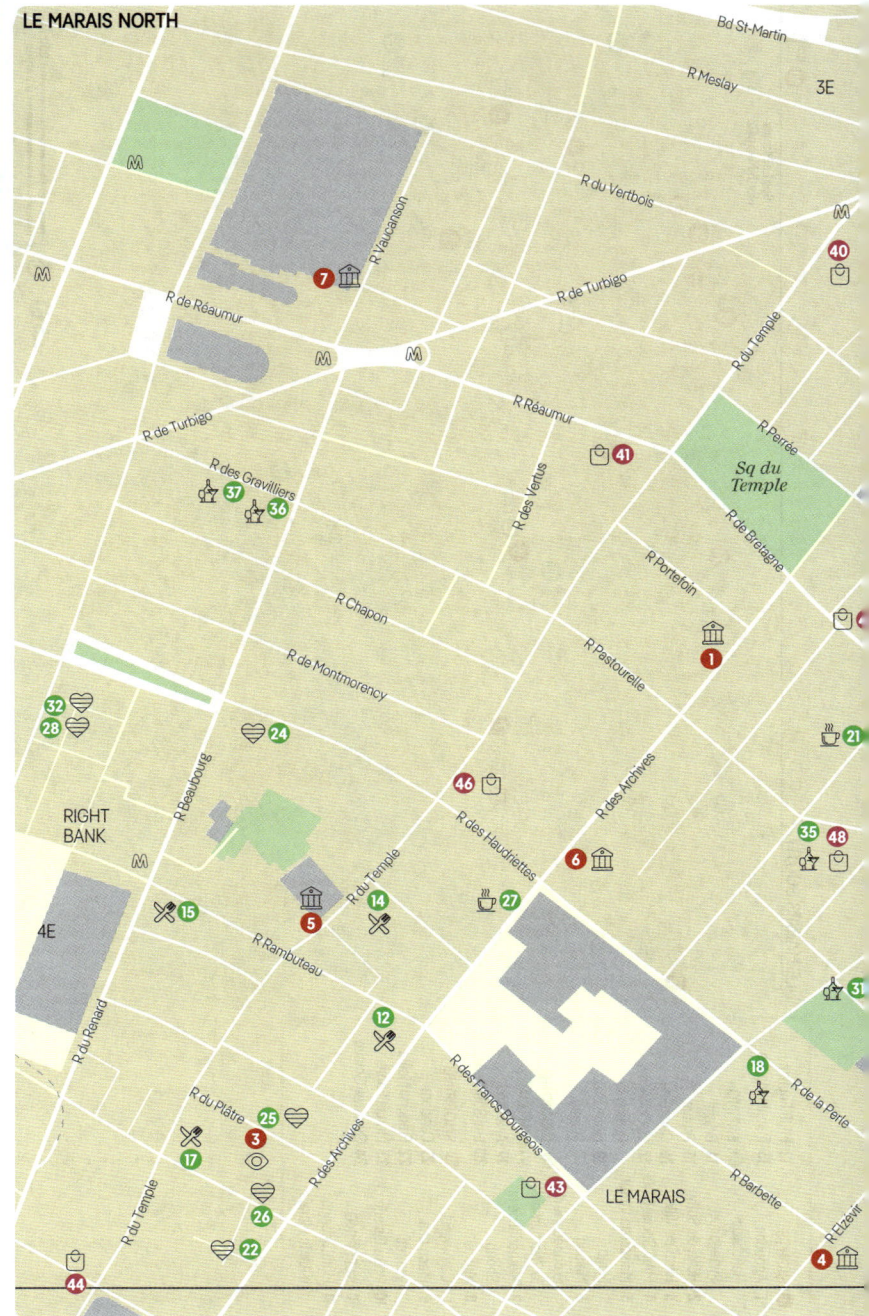

● SIGHTS
1. Fondation Henri Cartier-Bresson
2. Galerie Emmanuel Perrotin
3. Lafayette Anticipations
4. Musée Cognacq-Jay
5. Musée d'Art et d'Histoire du Judaïsme
6. Musée de la Chasse et de la Nature
7. Musée des Arts et Métiers
8. Musée National Picasso-Paris
9. Place de la République

● SLEEPING
10. Suzie Blue

● EATING
11. Bistrot Instinct
12. Carré Pain de Mie
13. Le Marché des Enfants Rouges
14. Le Reflet
15. Legay Choc
16. Pontochoux
17. Tata Burger

● DRINKING & NIGHTLIFE
18. Café La Perle
19. Candelaria
20. Causeries
21. Cortado
22. Cox
23. Delicatessen Place
24. Duplex Bar
25. Elles Bar
26. freedj
27. Ha Noi 1988 Flowers & Archives
28. La Mutinerie
29. Le Barav
30. Le Progrès
31. Le Saint-Gervais
32. Les Aimant·e·s
33. Little Red Door
34. Martin
35. Sotto
36. Spootnik Bar
37. Terra bar à vins

● SHOPPING
38. Alix D. Reynis
39. BIS Boutique Solidaire
40. Bobby
41. BRUT
42. Empreintes
43. Fragonard
44. Free 'P Star
45. Liquides Bar à Parfums
46. Praline
47. RSVP
48. Sabre
49. The Room

THE GUIDE

PARIS LE MARAIS

MARIANNE

In the centre of place de la République you're greeted by a woman standing tall atop a richly decorated plinth. This triumphant statue depicts Marianne, the personification of the French Republic. She has been its emblem since the First Republic in 1792, but this statue was created in 1883 by sculptor Léopold Morice. In this depiction she holds aloft an olive branch in her right hand, symbolising peace, and rests her left hand on a tablet inscribed with *les droits d'hommes*, human rights. Encircling the plinth at her feet are three stone statues that represent *La Liberté*, *La Fraternité* and *L'Égalité* – liberty, brotherhood and equality – the values of the French motto. The lion proudly guards an urn labelled *suffrage universel* (universal suffrage).

Hôtel de Ville

The Intersection of History & Politics   MAP P112
Admire place de la République

Place de la République has become one of Paris' most renowned squares, largely due to the years of social unrest that have marked recent decades in France. Symbolising democracy and the collective spirit of the people, the square serves as a gathering point for demonstrations and marches, with groups often gathering around the statue of Marianne in the centre. Crisscrossed by commuters during the week, at the weekend this expansive square becomes a space frequented by skateboarders, dancing clubs, street performers and locals who come together to socialise and participate in civic activities.

Admire Paris' Old Institutional Heart   MAP P111
Visit the Hôtel de Ville

The intricate neoclassical façade of Paris' town hall can evoke a sense of awe. The Hôtel de Ville features numerous statues representing notable figures from Paris' history, including politicians, scientists, artists and industry pioneers, as well as allegories of the arts.

The esplanade, now known as place de la Libération, was called place de Grève until President Charles de Gaulle

Get bottles from its sister location, Delicatessen Cave!

 DRINKING IN LE MARAIS: BUZZING WINE BARS   MAP P112

Le Barav: The perfect neighbourhood bar for great prices and an excellent playlist. If the terrace is full, get your name on the waitlist. *5pm-midnight Tue-Sat*

Martin: Sprawling terrace always full of conversation and cigarette smoke. Serves fresh small plates with a lengthy natural-wine list. *4pm-2am Tue-Sat*

Terra bar à vins: A modern wine bar where well-dressed patrons enjoy wine and a bite to eat in minimalist surroundings. *7pm-1am Tue-Sat*

Delicatessen Place: Get comfy in this wine bar decorated straight from a vintage market and enjoy glasses of wine served only by recommendation. *5-10pm*

delivered his 'liberation of Paris' speech at the Hôtel de Ville in 1944. It now regularly welcomes cultural events and street performers, but these kinds of shows replaced another – for five centuries it had been the site where criminals were executed.

Journey Through Paris' History
Discover the Musée Carnavalet

MAP P111

At the **Musée Carnavalet** *(carnavalet.paris.fr; free)*, you're first welcomed by a grand hall adorned with old shop signs, reminders of Paris' vibrant commercial life throughout the centuries. As you wander through the museum's spacious rooms, you'll encounter artworks, artefacts and historical finds that recount the layered history of Paris.

The city is showcased in all its forms and across all eras through numerous scale models, paintings, architectural remnants and modern masterpieces. Murals, entire shops and even a hotel ballroom were all moved to the Hotel Carnavalet to testify to their enduring magnificence. Our favourite floor is dedicated to the French Revolution and includes a pair of guillotine earrings, complete with dangling severed heads.

Embrace Parisian Style
Go vintage shopping in the fashion capital

MAP P111 & P112

Every year Paris Fashion Week brings hordes of stylishly attired attendees to Le Marais, but the cost of buying a new Parisian wardrobe can add up quickly. Fortunately, Le Marais has a range of vintage and secondhand boutiques to suit all manner of budgets and styles. Wander in and out of boutiques along rue Turenne. Less curated are **BIS Boutique Solidaire** *(bisboutiquesolidaire.fr)* and the boutiques of **Free 'P Star** *(instagram.com/freepstar_officiel)* on rue Verrière; **Bobby** *(bobby-boutiques.com)* stocks more current styles; **Système Solaire** *(systeme-solere.com)* and **The Room** *(theroom.fr)* focus on luxury items with matching prices. Finally, **BRUT** *(brut-clothing.com)* has military deadstock and reworked original designs.

Be Inspired By Human Ingenuity
Explore Musée des Arts et Métiers

MAP P112

The immersive collection of the **Musée des Arts et Métiers** *(arts-et-metiers.net; adult/child €12/free)* includes scientific instruments, mechanical devices, vehicles, communication equipment and much more. It features notable inventions,

PARTICULIER MUSEUMS

Musée Cognacq-Jay: Housed in the Hôtel Donon are the collections of Ernest Cognacq and Marie-Louise Jay, founders of La Samaritaine department store.

Musée National Picasso-Paris: Dating to the 17th century, the Hôtel Salé's classic architecture contrasts with 5000 artworks by Picasso.

Maison de Victor Hugo: The famous author's residence (1832–48) showcases furnishings, manuscripts and memorabilia.

Musée de la Chasse et de la Nature: Unusual museum explores historical relationship of humans and animals with a focus on the hunt.

Musée Carnavalet: Vast museum spans Paris' history in centuries-old mansions.

 EATING IN LE MARAIS: MODERN FRENCH RESTAURANTS — MAP P111, P112

Brutus: Enjoy crisp *galettes* and artisanal cider on a sun-soaked *terrasse*. Leave room for the house speciality, the chocolate hazelnut galette. *hours vary* €€

Le Reflet: A convivial French 'bistronomy' restaurant that employs people living with Down syndrome. *hours vary* €€

Bistrot Instinct: Creative seasonal menus from Chef Maximilian Wollek; his *œuf mayonnaise* is a permanent fixture. *noon-2pm & 6.30-9.30pm Mon-Sat* €€€

Capitaine: This cosy modern brasserie has a regularly changing menu with a seafood focus. *noon-2pm & 7.30-10.30pm Wed-Sat, 7.30-10.30pm Tue* €€€

EXPLORING JEWISH TRADITIONS & HISTORY

Le Marais has been home to Jewish communities since the Middle Ages; explore its Jewish history in places where this heritage is still visible today.

START	END	LENGTH
Musée d'Art et d'Histoire du Judaïsme	Mémorial de la Shoah	1.4km; 2½hrs

Discover Jewish history and practices in ❶ **Musée d'Art et d'Histoire du Judaïsme**, housed in the historic Hôtel de St-Aignan. Established in 1948 by Holocaust survivors, this institution showcases a diverse collection of artworks depicting Jewish history and culture, encompassing European and Maghreb communities. Exit along rue des Archives and head to ❷ **rue des Rosiers**, renowned for its culinary delights and cultural importance. Visit ❸ **Librairie du Temple**, a bookshop dedicated to Jewish books and culture. The most curious will take a peek at ❹ **Joseph Migneret Garden**. Named after a professor who played a vital role in rescuing Jewish children during WWII, this hidden garden is a peaceful sanctuary. Continue to rue Pavée, where you'll find a striking ❺ **synagogue** designed by Hector Guimard, famous for his art nouveau metro station entrances. Guimard created this synagogue as a tribute to his Jewish wife. You're now at the former location of the Pletzel ('small square' in Yiddish).

Conclude your tour at the ❻ **Mémorial de la Shoah**, accessible via the Allée des Justes de France. The memorial comprises a museum and document centre dedicated to the Shoah, providing a solemn and contemplative setting, including the Tomb of the Unknown Jewish Martyr in the crypt.

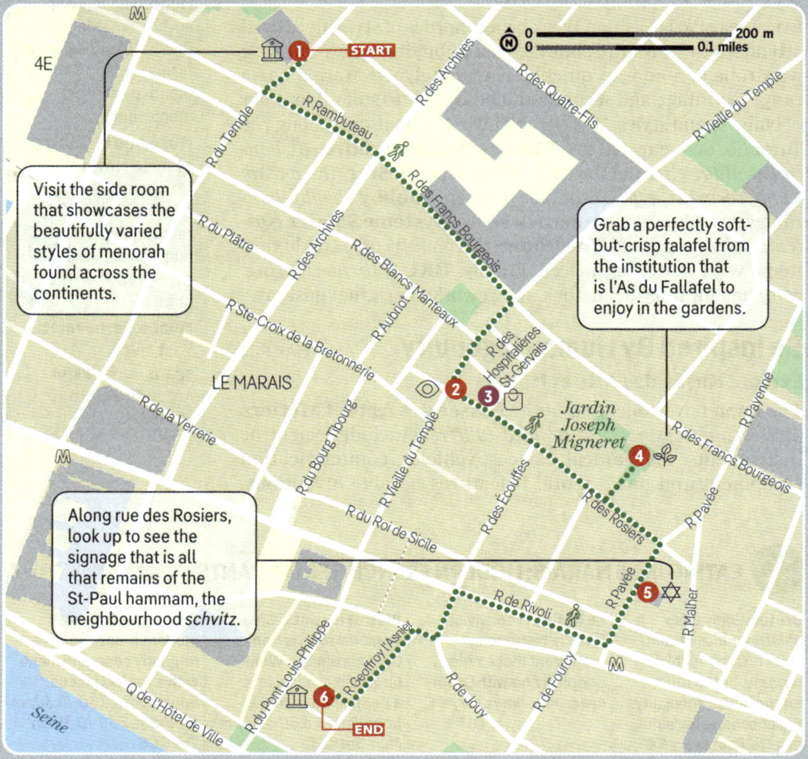

> Visit the side room that showcases the beautifully varied styles of menorah found across the continents.

> Grab a perfectly soft-but-crisp falafel from the institution that is l'As du Fallafel to enjoy in the gardens.

> Along rue des Rosiers, look up to see the signage that is all that remains of the St-Paul hammam, the neighbourhood *schvitz*.

such as Blaise Pascal's Pascaline (an early mechanical calculator), the original model of the *Statue of Liberty* designed by Bartholdi, Foucault's pendulum (with daily demonstrations at noon and 5pm), and even a reconstruction of the laboratory of chemist Antoine Lavoisier. There is even a disconcerting darkened room dedicated to automata, which includes videos of their movements complete with discordant music. Additionally, it offers educational opportunities for children through regular workshops that familiarise them with the spirit of invention and pioneering innovation. Visit on a weekday morning to enjoy having the museum largely to yourself.

Brunch from the Stalls
Dine in the oldest Parisian covered market

MAP P112

Le Marché des Enfants Rouges, dating back to the 17th century, still exudes plenty of charm after undergoing renovations in the 1990s. It has become a vibrant gathering place for both locals and visitors. The market is home to a diverse array of food stalls and small dining places. Immerse yourself in the lively atmosphere and explore the generous, typically French market stalls offering fresh food, fruit, flowers, cheese and charcuterie products. As the market is open on Sundays as well, one of the best experiences is to indulge in brunch at one of the numerous local or international food stalls surrounding the market. Enjoy vegetarian delights at **Au Coin Bio** *(aucoinbio-restaurant.fr)*, order a Japanese bento at **Chez Taeko**, or tuck into Levantine pitas at **Chez Jeanphi** *(instagram.com/chez_jeanphi)*.

Savour French Savoir-Faire
Buy the best products made in France

MAP P111 & P112

Dining has always been an important part of French culture, which is why creating your own set of cutlery at **Sabre** *(sabre.fr)* is a perfect way to bring Paris home to your table. **Empreintes** *(empreintes-paris.com)* showcases some of the best French designers, with a focus on artisanal decorative objects, jewellery and home goods. **Alix D. Reynis** *(alixdreynis.com)* designs elegant ranges of porcelain goods that are handmade in Limoges. For traditional cubes of green Marseille soap, try **Maruis Fabre** *(marius-fabre.com)*. Finally, if you need something to fit all your goodies, stop into **RSVP** *(rsvp-paris.com)* to pick out a handmade leather bag, or **Praline** *(pralineparis.com)* for bags stitched in Paris using sofa material from Strasbourg.

PARISIAN POP-UP MARKETS

The food markets, *brocantes* (flea markets) and *vide-greniers* (garage sales) of Paris present a wide range of products, from vegetables to antique mirrors. *Brocantes* tend to have higher-quality items, while *vide-greniers* can be more of a mix, with a better chance of finding a well-priced treasure. They often reflect the tastes of their *arrondissement*, so expect more high-quality goods in Le Marais, especially around rue de Bretagne, and lots of clothing. Find fresh-food markets along the bd Beaumarchais and in place Baudoyer. The dates and locations for all markets are listed online and most happen at weekends. Arrive early and bring cash to get the widest choice, and take your time strolling between stalls.

DRINKING IN LE MARAIS: HIDDEN BARS

MAP P112

Sotto: This cellar-like bar hidden underneath Italian restaurant Carboni's is the ideal spot for a fruity cocktail and a tiramisu. *7pm-2am*

Little Red Door: A speakeasy with talented mixologists, accessible through a small, discreet entrance. Expect queues. *5pm-1.30am*

Candelaria: A hidden cocktail bar accessed through a taco restaurant, it's one of Paris' original speakeasies and still highly regarded. *4pm-2am*

Spootnik Bar: If a futuristic cosmonaut met an audiophile in Berlin this is the delicious cocktail bar that they would open. *7pm-2am Tue-Sat*

WALKING TOUR

Walking Through Time in Le Marais

One of the few areas to have remained untouched by Baron Haussmann's reconstructions, Le Marais contains layers of history dating as far back as the Middle Ages. Its evolutions from marsh to aristocratic hub to insalubrious shambles are still peeking out between its present-day luxury. Discover the remains of medieval life and the tranquillity of 17th-century mansions and hidden courtyards.

❶ Medieval Houses on rue François-Miron

At Nos 11 and 13 are two of the oldest houses in Paris; they date from the 14th century, although their current appearances include 16th-century additions. Further up the street at No 46 is the **Association pour la Sauvegarde et la Mise en Valeur du Paris Historique** *(1-6pm Mon-Fri, to 7pm Sat, 2-6pm Sun)*. Tours *(adult/child €5/2)* are offered in English on Wednesdays.

The Walk: Head east along rue de Jouy, then south along rue des Nonnains-d'Hyères before walking east on rue de l'Hotel de Ville.

❷ Hôtel de Sens

This remarkable Gothic mansion from the 15th century was once a residence for Sens' archbishops. Try to spot the Revolution-era cannonball lodged above a window.

The Walk: Take rue de l'Ave Maria and reach the entrance to Village St-Paul's courtyards.

❸ Village St-Paul

Try to picture domestic servants of wealthy families that once washed clothes while live chickens clucked in the courtyards of this neighbourhood that now house, fashionable boutiques and restaurants.

Hôtel de Sens

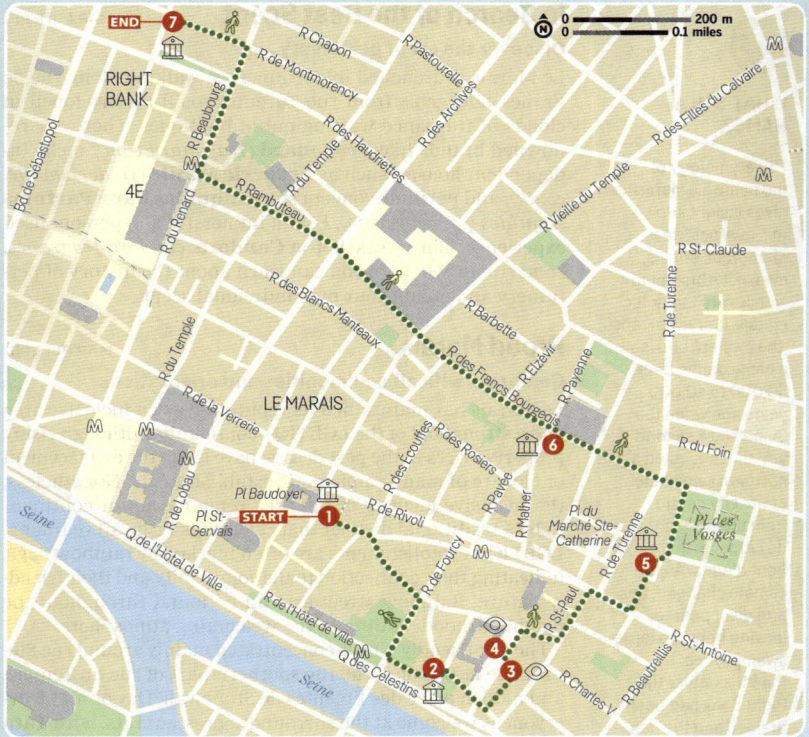

The Walk: Exit through rue des Jardins St-Paul.

④ King Philippe Auguste's Wall
You're across from the largest remnants of King Philippe Auguste's Wall, a defensive fortification built at the end of the 12th century to protect Paris from potential attacks.

The Walk: Head north to rue St-Antoine and enter the courtyard of Hôtel de Sully.

⑤ Hôtel de Sully
Built in 1624, this **magnificent** *hôtel particulier* represents the characteristic mansions of Le Marais during its fashionable era and features a passageway leading to place des Vosges.

The Walk: Exit through the passageway to place des Vosges, then head north along its western side. At the corner, turn west onto rue Francs-Bourgeois.

⑥ Hôtel de Lamoignon
In 1759 the last resident of this mansion bequeathed 14,000 books to the city of Paris upon his death. Four years later, this *hôtel particulier* became the first public library in Paris, open to all. Today it houses the **Historical Library of Paris** (*10am-6pm Mon-Sat*).

The Walk: Continue along rue Francs-Bourgeois towards metro Rambuteau, then turn right onto rue Beaubourg and look for rue de Montmorency, the second street on the left.

⑦ Nicolas Flamel's House
This is believed to be the oldest house in the city. It was built by the scribe Nicolas Flamel; the detailed inscription on the façade dates its construction to 1407.

In Search of the Best Scent

MAP P111 & P112

Discover the art of perfumery

Le Marais is drenched in perfumeries; walking along rue de Francs Bourgeois from rue Turenne you'll be enveloped in clouds of fragrance wafting out of boutiques. There are renowned brands like **Fragonard** *(fragonard.com);* niche independent houses, such as **Frederic Maille** *(fredericmalle.co.uk);* and perfume concept store **Liquides Bar à Parfums** *(liquides-parfums.com).* For an immersive and personalised experience, join a workshop at **Candora** *(candora-fragrance.com; from €98):* here you can learn about the history of perfumery and create your own individual scent.

Proud Marais

MAP P111 & P112

Celebrate with all communities and orientations

Le Marais has maintained its reputation as an inclusive area and a stronghold of the LGBTIQ+ community, although rising property prices in the past decade have led to the displacement or closure of many emblematic establishments. Nonetheless, the inclusive identity of the area remains, and it continues to be a traditional district that celebrates Pride all year long. LGBTIQ+ establishments are often marked by rainbow flags, indicating their connection to the community and their friendly nature. Rainbow street art can be found throughout the neighbourhood, adding to the welcoming atmosphere.

The gay-friendly vibe is concentrated mainly around rue Ste-Croix de la Bretonnerie, the southern part of rue du Temple, and hidden place des Émeutes de Stonewall. Day or night, everyone is welcome at the surrounding restaurants, with **Tata Burger** *(instagram.com/tataburger_restaurant)* number one for a suggestive burger, and **Legay Choc** *(instagram.com/legaychoc)* selling phallic sweet treats.

The real excitement begins when night falls, **freedj** *(freedj.fr),* **Cox** *(cox.fr),* **Duplex Bar** *(instagram.com/duplex_bar_paris)* and **Les Souffleurs** *(instagram.com/lessouffleuses)* are all vibrant bars that attract a diverse crowd. **Elles Bar** *(instagram.com/elles_bar_paris)* provides a venue for lesbians. Slightly further away on rue St-Martin are feminist venue **La Mutinerie** *(lamutinerie.eu)* and **Les Aimant·e·s** *(instagram.com/barlesaimantes).*

WHAT'S IN A NAME?

The etymology of the name 'Le Marais' gives insight into this *quartier*'s less glamorous origins, even if it's brimming with luxury today. 'Le Marais' literally means 'the swamp', and is a name dating back 30,000 to 40,000 years ago when the Seine had a second arm that encircled a northern semicircle of the city centre from the Bassin de l'Arsenal to the Pont d'Alma. As the climate changed, this arm disappeared, leaving behind a large swampy area. By the 9th century the Right Bank had been drained and the rich, swampy land was a fertile resource for agriculture. The area came to be known for its pastures, market gardens, and *maraîchers* (vegetable growers), before becoming a more desirable area during the Renaissance.

 EATING IN LE MARAIS: QUICK BITES ──── MAP P111, P112

Pontochoux: Enjoy a warming platter of Japanese curry made from scratch; even the marinated vegetables are homemade. *11.30am-7pm* €

Notre Café Marais: Bright cafe with a sunny terrace. Serves simple, classic fare while employing and supporting people with Down syndrome. *8.30am-3pm Tue-Fri* €

Carré Pain de Mie: Combining the best of Japan and France, these cloudlike sandwiches include fillings like *tonkotsu* and croque monsieur. *10am-8pm* €€

La Collective Parisienne: This social-enterprise cafe serves wholesome seasonal lunches from a four-item menu plus a dessert. *noon-3pm Mon-Fri* €

Find Your Inspiration

MAP P111 & P112

Explore art in Le Marais

The **Maison Européenne de la Photographie** (*MEP; mep-fr.org; adult/child €13/free*) is dedicated to contemporary photography, and through temporary exhibitions features cutting-edge international photographers. In a different vein, the **Fondation Henri Cartier-Bresson** (*henricartierbresson.org; adult/child €10/6*) preserves and promotes the work of the renowned French photographer, considered a pioneer of modern photojournalism. The foundation exhibits highlights from the archives and work by contemporary photographers. Finally, **Polka Galerie** (*polkagalerie.com*) exhibits and sells fine-art photography, both by established contemporary artists and emerging photographers.

The artistic exploration of Le Marais would not be complete without its numerous art galleries. **Lafayette Anticipations** (*lafayetteanticipations.com*) has cultural events, temporary exhibitions of contemporary designers, a trendy bookshop and a cafe. **Galerie Emmanuel Perrotin** (*perrotin.com*) exhibits artists from around the world in its spacious gallery, runs cultural events and sells art-inspired items, including books and clothing. The area also supports art communities, with venues like **MAIF Social Club** (*maifsocialclub.fr; free*) running a programme of exhibitions, workshops, a cafe and an ethical concept store. There are information cards in English and it's always buzzing with visitors, from school groups to drawing clubs.

People-Watching Hot Spots

MAP P112

Sit and absorb Parisian life

Le Marais is a place to see and be seen, and by far the best way to do this is while sipping a glass of wine or a cup of coffee. For these more traditional spots, be sure to have cash, as many have minimum spends for cards. It can be competitive getting a seat under the striped awnings of **Le Progrès** (*leprogresmarais.fr*), so arrive for your morning coffee and settle in. **Le Saint-Gervais** (*lesaintgervais.fr*) is an afternoon suntrap and conveniently around the corner from the Musée National Picasso-Paris. For the evening, **Café La Perle** (*cafelaperle.com*) is a fashion and artsy hot spot. While you're here, look across the street for the regularly changing murals by Le Mur.

MARCHE DES FIERTÉS

Running in Paris since 1981, the **Marche des Fiertés** has its origins in the Gay Pride marches that began in New York. In Paris the annual parade is attended by over 500,000 people and includes support from more than 200 volunteers. Organisation of the event is led by the group Inter-LGBT, who bring together around 90 organisations. Their shared mission is to 'combat discrimination based on sexual orientation or gender identity, as part of the promotion of human rights and fundamental freedoms'. Open to all, whether you identify as an ally or part of the community, the event is a celebratory and political day filled with music, costumes, placards, floats, a final concert and dance-filled afterparties.

Look for a copy of Arturo's self-produced newspaper!

 DRINKING IN LE MARAIS: SPECIALIST COFFEE SHOPS — MAP P111, P112

Causeries: A delicate oasis of Danish coffee and natural wine with elegant decor and a gentle vinyl soundtrack. *hours vary* €

Ha Noi 1988 Flowers & Archives: Discover salted-cream or egg-yolk coffee at this florally perfumed Vietnamese cafe and flower shop. *10am-7pm* €€

Cortado: Step briefly into Spain at this buzzing coffee shop that serves Spanish nibbles and excellent cortados. *hours vary* €

Artesano: Arturo Valentino roasts his Mexican coffee every week for this cafe filled with music and photography. *9am-1.30pm & 2.30-5.30pm* €€

Belleville & Ménilmontant

ARTS | VIEWS | MULTICULTURAL WALKS

GETTING AROUND

Although it may be more challenging than other areas because of the sometimes steep streets, walking remains the best way to stumble upon the details holding the soul of Belleville.

Choose your metro station wisely, considering they can be far apart from each other and either bottom or top of the hill. Useful stations are Belleville (Lines 2 and 11) and Philippe Auguste (Line 2).

Buses and electric bikes can help bridge the distance between your metro station and final destination, in this less central – slightly underserved – quarter.

Stretching over the 19e and 20e down to some of the neighbouring streets of the 10e and 11e, Belleville used to be a separate town outside Paris, and Ménilmontant one of its boroughs. Incorporated into the city in 1860, they maintained a strong identity, with a vibrant artistic spirit, multicultural quarters, and a somewhat rebellious nature, inherited from the historical popular movements born on their streets. Day or night, these quarters offer a dynamic scene where people seem to easily connect with each other despite a variety of backgrounds. Many locals proudly claim that Belleville is not Paris, it is Belleville! Walk its hills, explore its urban art and diverse food scene: come and discover what they mean.

Festive Belleville

A lively quarter by day and night

With many bars, cafes and live music venues, the northeastern area of Paris, from Popincourt to Belleville and Ménilmontant, has a festive reputation. Belleville's in particular dates back to the 14th century, when the village began welcoming its first taverns and *guinguettes* (outdoor taverns) – where you could drink and dance. Why Belleville? Monks produced wine on the slopes of what is now Parc de Belleville, so supply was easy.

One of the most famous local celebrations was the 19th-century Descente de la Courtille – a lively procession ('down Courtille Street') that marked the Paris Carnival.

Don't miss a night at **Aux Folies**, a former cabaret turned cinema and now a beloved bar, open since 1872. Édith Piaf sang on stage here during her teenage years. On the other side of the boulevard, **Le Zèbre de Belleville** *(lezebre.com)* has unique cabaret-dinner shows. **La Bellevilloise** *(labellevilloise.com),* a former cooperative hall created by workers, has transformed into one of the favourite music and dancing venues for Parisians. Its weekend jazz brunch is particularly appreciated.

BELLEVILLE & MÉNILMONTANT

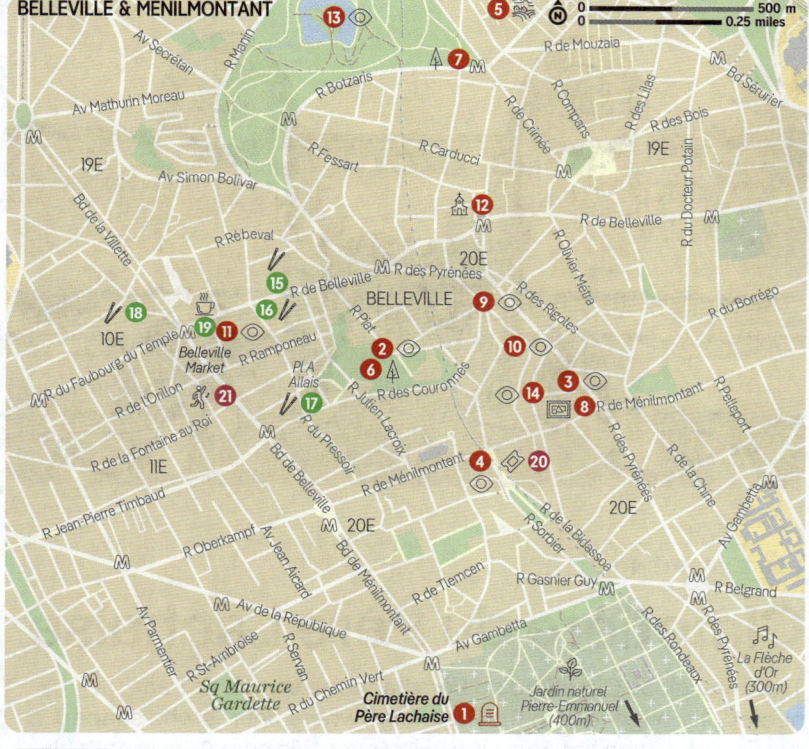

- ★ **HIGHLIGHTS**
- 1 Cimetière du Père Lachaise
- ● **SIGHTS**
- 2 Belvédère de Belleville
- 3 Cité Leroy
- 4 Jérôme Mesnager's art
- 5 La Mouzaia
- 6 Parc de Belleville
- 7 Parc des Buttes-Chaumont
- 8 Pavillon Carré de Baudouin
- 9 Place Henri Krasucki
- 10 Rue de Savies
- 11 Rue Dénoyez
- 12 Saint-Jean-Baptiste de Belleville
- 13 Sybille's Temple
- 14 Villa de l'Ermitage
- ● **EATING**
- 15 Lao Siam
- 16 Mian Guan
- 17 Pavillon aux Pivoines
- 18 Raviolis Nord Est
- ● **DRINKING & NIGHTLIFE**
- 19 Aux Folies
- ● **ENTERTAINMENT**
- 20 La Bellevilloise
- 21 Le Zèbre de Belleville

Prettiest Sunset
Panoramic Paris

Take your time wandering along **Parc de Belleville's** terraced slopes, hearing a waterfall trickle between the meandering trails. Spot the vines, a reminder of Belleville's history as a winemaking village since the Middle Ages.

Going up, you'll reach the **Belvédère de Belleville**, a meeting point for street artists but also the second-highest summit in Paris, with a view stretching from Montparnasse to the Eiffel Tower. As you're facing west, you're arguably standing on the best sunset spot in the entire city.

☑ TOP TIP

Belleville's streets can be winding and steep, and the landmarks are a bit spread out, so wear good shoes and take your time to explore. Cemetery lovers will appreciate themed guided tours of Père Lachaise led by entertaining cemetery historian Thierry Le Roi (necro-romantiques.fr).

TOP EXPERIENCE

Cimetière du Père Lachaise

The prestigious Cimetière du Père Lachaise serves as Paris' necropolis, aligned with the Panthéon, where figures who shaped the French nation are honoured. However, this cemetery is not only a resting place for the renowned. Today it stands as an otherworldly space where extraordinary funerary monuments coexist with the graves of both famous and lesser-known individuals.

DON'T MISS

- The Monument to the Dead
- Lovers Héloïse and Abélard
- Oscar Wilde
- Jim Morrison
- Édith Piaf
- Victor Noir
- Molière and La Fontaine

An Eternal English Garden

When commissioned to design the new Parisian cemetery in the early 19th century, architect Alexandre-Théodore Brongniart envisioned a space that would embody nobility without grandiosity, simplicity without neglect, and invoke religious sentiments without fear. He aimed to create a place of peaceful remembrance, with a melancholic charm based on a combination of nature and monuments. Inspired by English gardens, the cemetery was meticulously planned, with winding paths and a significant portion dedicated to nature. Today, as you

PRACTICALITIES

● paris.fr/dossiers/bienvenue-au-cimetiere-du-pere-lachaise-47 ● 8am-6pm Mon-Fri, from 8.30am Sat, from 9am Sun ● Main entrance: rue du Repos (metro: Philippe Auguste, Line 2) ● Visitors must leave 30 minutes before closing

enter, the cacophony of the city fades away and the graves seamlessly blend into the undulating landscape, creating a feeling of beautiful strangeness, as if you were suspended between two worlds.

The Construction of a Legendary Place

Overlooked at the time of its inauguration, the cemetery faced challenges in gaining popularity due to its location far from the city. However, to enhance its appeal, the city of Paris relocated the graves of famous figures like Molière and La Fontaine (Division 25), and had an impressive sepulchre erected for the mythical medieval lovers Héloïse and Abélard (Division 7). Over time, politicians, scientists, artists and writers followed, solidifying Père Lachaise's reputation as the eternal resting place of the renowned.

Funerary Art for Posterity

The entire site is recognised for its historical heritage, with all funerary steles dating to before 1900 listed as Historical Monuments. Additionally, 14 monuments are classified – the classification is reserved for works that hold public interest from a historical or an artistic perspective. Among them: the Wall of the Federates, Godde's chapel on the former Jesuit house site, bd Ménilmontant's monumental gate, the Monument to the Dead and 10 sepulchres. These include Héloïse and Abélard, Molière and La Fontaine, Oscar Wilde (Division 89), Frédéric Chopin (Division 11), Antoine de Guillaume-Lagrange (Division 29), Montanier-Delille (Division 11), Cartellier-Heim (Division 53), Georges Guët (Division 19) and Yakovleff (Division 82).

Rituals & Superstitions of Père Lachaise

Like all cemeteries, where the boundaries between worlds blur, Père Lachaise has its own superstitions and esoteric rituals associated with its iconic graves. Couples renew their vows in front of Héloïse and Abélard's tomb, seeking eternal love. Oscar Wilde's tomb has long been the object of passionate kisses believed to bring luck in love. Journalist Victor Noir's effigy (Division 92) is central to erotic morbid fertility rituals. Laying hands on the dolmen of medium Allan Kardec (Division 44) is believed to grant wishes. Lastly, the ritual offerings left on Jim Morrison's grave (Division 6) perpetuate a cult (mainly based on alcohol).

A RURAL GARDEN IN THE CITY

Below Père Lachaise, **Jardin naturel Pierre-Emmanuel** hosts native plant species from the Parisian region and offers a glimpse into Paris' nature when it was still rural. With minimal mowing to respect natural cycles, the meadows allow vegetation to thrive. This true biodiversity reserve provides a habitat for frogs, newts and water lilies, and contrasts radically with the usual meticulously arranged parks of Paris.

TOP TIPS

● Download the cemetery map from a QR code at the entrance: this will help you locate specific graves and landmarks.

● Choose the right entrance: there are five different ones, but only three of them are near metro stations.

● Wear comfortable shoes: the cemetery is vast, with uneven terrain and stairs. Be prepared for walking and stay hydrated.

● Show respect: remember that this is a graveyard where people come to pay their respects to their loved ones. Don't climb on tombs and keep noise levels low.

● Plan ahead: if you have limited time or specific graves you want to visit, plan your itinerary in advance.

WALKING TOUR

Exploring Belleville's Villages: a Patch of Countryside

With its rolling hills and winding streets, Belleville has a history as both a festive and idyllic area. Its slopes were covered in vineyards, and waterfalls ran down its hills. Wandering through former workers' courtyards, now picturesque passages, step back in time to discover Belleville's pastoral legacy. Wear good shoes for this tour, as this 3km-long walk will constantly take you up and down!

❶ La Mouzaïa

Begin your tour among the colourful houses and gardens of Villa Paul Verlaine and Villa des Boers. This now enchanting housing estate dating from the 1880s was built on the slopes of a former gypsum quarry – now the Parc des Buttes-Chaumont – and was initially created to house working-class families.

The Walk: Make for rue du Général Brunet and walk all the way down to Botzaris metro.

❷ Parc des Buttes-Chaumont

Try and get a glimpse of Montmartre from the highest slopes of the park (p128).

The Walk: Exit the same way you came from. Walk along the park's railings on rue Botzaris. Turn left on rue des Alouettes, left again on rue Fressart and finally right on rue Lassus.

❸ Saint-Jean-Baptiste de Belleville

It is one of the first Neogothic **churches** in Paris. Besides its two steeples, the 19m-high nave is particularly impressive.

Place Henri Krasucki

The Walk: Walk on rue de Jourdain towards Pl des Grandes Rigoles and take the flight of stairs leading to rue Levert.

❹ Place Henri Krasucki

A French resistant, union worker and active member of the French communist party, Henri Krasucki was a freedom activist until his last breath. The square named after him is among the most beloved among Belleville residents.

The Walk: Continue west on rue des Envierges.

❺ Belvédère de Belleville

On clear days, a beautiful panoramic view of Paris opens up. Street art enthusiasts shouldn't miss the Belvédère de Belleville (p123).

The Walk: Turn left on Passage Piat, walk down the stairs. Turn left on rue des Couronnes and right on rue Henri Chevreau. Make a left on rue de la Mare.

❻ Rue de Savies

Covered in colourful murals, this street bears the name of the original farm that gave birth to the entire city of Belleville during the Middle Ages, 'la Ferme Savies'.

The Walk: Take the stairs up, then right on rue de l'Ermitage.

❼ Villa de l'Ermitage & Cité Leroy

A narrow yet picturesque vegetation-covered passage will appear on your left: it's Villa de l'Ermitage, and at the end of the cobblestoned way, another hidden passage, Cité Leroy, both vestiges of Ménilmontant's village history.

The Walk: Exit on rue des Pyrénées and turn right onto rue de Ménilmontant.

❽ Pavillon Carré de Baudoin

Conclude with a cultural pause. This **18th-century building**, formerly a venue for parties, has been repurposed as a contemporary arts centre.

A MULTICULTURAL & REBELLIOUS SPIRIT

Ali Lair *(@alifrompariss)*, a local food tour guide, shares his approach to Belleville.

Festive, welcoming, and affordable – Belleville has been shaped by its history of cultural diversity, following the arrival of various communities: Jewish, Tunisian, Chinese, Vietnamese, and more. But Belleville is also, by nature, an artistic, working-class and rebellious area. The Paris Commune took place on Belleville's hill! I love stopping by Le Monte-en-l'Air, a fantastic feminist bookshop. And you shouldn't miss the many murals: they bring life to the walls and are an integral part of Belleville, where street art was born. Don't miss Belleville's **Belvédère** (p123), **rue Dénoyez** and **Mesnager's dancing figures** (rue de Ménilmontant), which capture the neighbourhood's revolutionary spirit.

Parc des Buttes-Chaumont

Food on the Hill

Picnic in Buttes-Chaumont

With its undulating terrain, **Parc des Buttes-Chaumont** has excellent picnic areas, highly appreciated by locals in summer. Yet this charming backdrop hides a more sombre story. A former landfill and then a gypsum quarry, it was finally abandoned in 1860, leaving the area neglected and prone to crime. Only under Napoleon III was it transformed to become today's peaceful hilly refuge.

With a bit of stamina, don't hesitate to climb the artificial hill standing in the middle of the lake: you'll discover characteristic elements of English gardens, including bridges, grottoes and a replica of a Greek ruin, **Sybille's Temple**.

Cultural events around Chinese food also take place here.

EATING IN BELLEVILLE: ASIAN MEALS

Lao Siam: This popular Thai restaurant in Belleville has been a local favourite for years. It's easier to get a table for lunch. *noon-3pm & 7-11pm Thu-Mon, 7-11pm Wed* €€

Mian Guan: Tiny restaurant specialising in Chinese handmade noodles served in savoury soups. Spicy/non-spicy options. *noon-3pm & 6-10.45pm Wed-Mon* €

Raviolis Nord Est: This small discreet restaurant specialises in dumplings, in the style of northeastern Chinese cuisine. *11am-11pm* €

Pavillon aux Pivoines: Recreated traditional Chinese house. Former chef's daughters revisit classic Chinese dishes. *noon-2.30pm & 7.30-10.30pm Tue-Sat, noon-3pm Sun* €€

Bastille & Eastern Paris

FABULOUS MARKETS | DRINKING | ENTERTAINMENT

This lesser-known, more typically local area, which spans parts of the 11e, 12e and 20e *arrondissements*, has key historical sites and a compelling industrial heritage to complement an increasingly cool, youthful scene. Near Bastille, craft workshops that were buzzing in the 19th and early 20th centuries are today home to vibrant arts venues, hip cafes, independent shops and creative restaurants. Going east, the landscape transforms. Past Nation's broad residential avenues and the city limits lies the Bois de Vincennes, one of Paris' green lungs. These neighbourhoods are distinct but most retain a village-like charm, thanks to their history as *faubourgs* (small boroughs), representing a different, more relaxed and lived-in side of Paris.

> ☑ **TOP TIP**
> Often overlooked by tourists, this area presents a captivating blend of experiences – from a local-loved market to the elevated promenade atop a former railway viaduct – that will reward those who enjoy travelling off the beaten path.

Time for Revolution
MAP P130
Visit a Parisian symbol of liberty

On 14 July 1789, the inhabitants of Faubourg St-Antoine, sick of prolonged food shortages due to an ongoing siege of Paris, stormed Bastille prison. But when the guards refused to surrender, the situation escalated. Rebels seized 250 barrels of gunpowder, freed prisoners and put the military governor's head on a pike. This was the first episode of the French Revolution.

The **place de la Bastille** is a powerful symbol of the 1789 events, but it also broadly represents the freedom of the French

GETTING AROUND

Walking is the best way to explore and it's eminently possible, thanks to the area's density and surfeit of green paths. But beware that, unless you're keen for an urban hike, the distance between Bastille and Vincennes is large.

The area is well served by the municipal Vélib' bikes and there are many cycling lanes, even if busier streets near Bastille are trickier to navigate.

Metro lines 1 and 8 will likely be the most helpful if you want to save time and energy (or if the weather isn't great).

BASTILLE & EASTERN PARIS

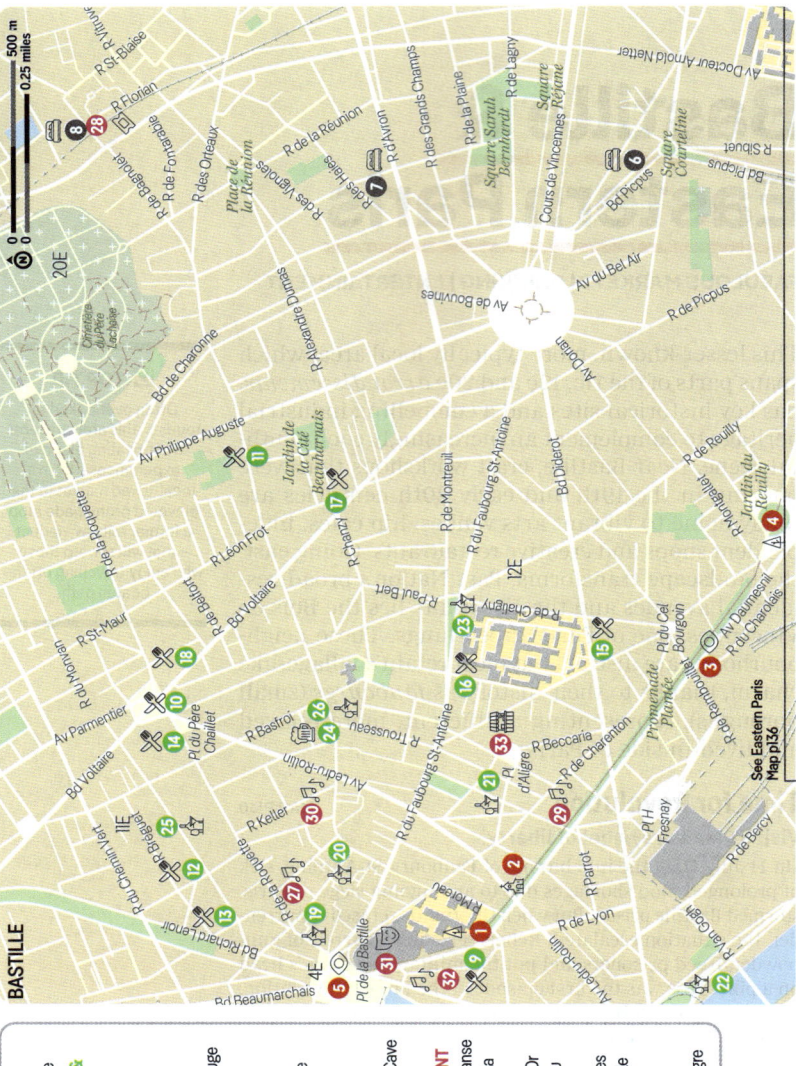

SIGHTS
1. Coulée Verte René-Dumont
2. Église St-Antoine des Quinze Vingts
3. Ground Control
4. Jardin de Reuilly
5. Place de la Bastille

SLEEPING
6. Hôtel du Printemps
7. JO&JOE Paris – Nation
8. Mama Shelter Paris East

EATING
9. Amarante
10. Aux Bons Crus
11. Boulangerie Manobaké
12. Boulangerie MieMie
13. Café de l'Industrie
14. Chez Aline
15. La Cantine Diderot
16. L'Ébauchoir
17. Pépite
18. VG Pâtisserie

DRINKING & NIGHTLIFE
19. Bar des Ferrailleurs
20. L'Atelier Saisonnier
21. Le Baron Rouge
22. Le Mazette
23. Les Blouses Blanches
24. Les Cuves de Fauve
25. Les Mauvais Joueurs
26. Septime La Cave

ENTERTAINMENT
27. Café de la Danse
see 24 Café de la Plage
28. La Flèche d'Or
29. Le POPUP du Label
30. Les Disquaires
31. Opéra Bastille
32. Supersonic

SHOPPING
33. Marché d'Aligre

Place de la Bastille

people. The central column commemorates the *Trois Glorieuses*, the three-day July Revolution of 1830, topped by the winged statue of the *Génie de la Liberté* (Genius of Liberty). At its base are two funerary stones: one commemorating the fallen during the 1830 revolution, with 500 individuals buried underneath; the second honouring those who died in the 1848 revolution, which brought an end to the monarchy.

This symbolic political history means that Bastille, like the nearby place de la République, draws frequent protests (practically every weekend in the afternoon), so if you're in the mood for marching, join in for a quintessential Parisian experience. Otherwise, there's usually a more relaxed atmosphere, so grab a coffee at one of the many surrounding cafe terraces and gaze at this famous symbol of liberty.

A Night at the Opera

MAP P130

See a show at one of Europe's largest opera houses

With its striking glass and steel façade, the **Opéra Bastille** (operadeparis.fr/en) was inaugurated on 13 July 1989 to commemorate the bicentenary of the storming of the Bastille. Featuring one of Europe's largest performance stages, the 2745-seat venue hosts bold modern music and dance shows

BASTILLE'S ANCIENT FORTRESS

Nothing remains of Bastille's fortress, originally constructed in the 14th century to defend the eastern flank of Paris against the English during the Hundred Years' War. By 1417 the royal castle took on an unusual new aspect: it formally became a state prison, housing inmates for centuries until it was destroyed during the 1789 revolution. Today, only a small sign on a building near bd Henri IV indicates the boundaries of the former stronghold, once with eight towers and surrounded by a 24m-wide moat. Over the centuries, various urban designs have been proposed to update the place de la Bastille, such as placing a monumental, elephant-shaped fountain at its centre, though this was never realised.

 EATING NEAR BASTILLE: OUR BAKERY PICKS — MAP P130

Boulangerie MieMie: Baked goods include cream puffs and an 'anti-waste' croissant cake made with pastry scraps. *8am-8pm Tue-Sat, 8am-1pm Sun* €

Boulangerie Manobaké: Rising star in the Paris bakery scene. Charming mosaic interior, quality cinnamon rolls, apple tarts and carrot cake. *hours vary* €

VG Pâtisserie: Vegan croissants and *pains au chocolat* made with organic wheat grown 80km from Paris. *1-7pm Tue, 9am-7pm Wed-Sat, 9am-6pm Sun* €

Pépite: Social-media posters come for the decadent black sesame-filled croissants, but the broader pastry selection is seriously good too. *7am-8pm Tue-Sun* €

Passage L'homme

FÊTE DE LA MUSIQUE

If you are in Paris on 21 June, the longest day of the year, get ready for the **Fête de la Musique** (Festival of Music). During this jovial annual celebration, which was launched in 1982 by the French government to encourage and support amateur music, the city's streets are filled all day and night with every kind of music genre imaginable. Concerts include big-hitter names, and are even held in unique venues including the Louvre, but one of the best ways to experience the festival is to just stroll around by foot in neighbourhoods like Bastille, encountering concerts by chance.

and is part of a broader effort to promote contemporary arts, in contrast with its traditional counterpart, the Palais Garnier.

Guided tours on Saturdays *(adult/child €20/13, only in French)* are the chance to learn about the modernist architecture – still divisive among Parisians – designed by Uruguayan-Canadian architect Carlos Ott. Last-minute deals are available at the ticket office an hour before shows, and *avant-premiere* nights for people under 28 offer tickets for just €10, but usually require booking far in advance.

Bottoms Up

MAP P130

A bar for every mood

The Bastille area comes alive at night and it is one of the best areas in Paris to have a merry night of drinking. Rue de la Roquette and rue de Lappe are lined with bars and clubs, so if you're looking for a rowdy time you'll inevitably end up here. Look out for **Bar des Ferrailleurs**, which has a cosy ambience and creative cocktails, and **L'Atelier Saisonnier**, which is perfect for a few glasses of wine and cheese. Further afield, **Les Mauvais Joueurs** is a fun board-game bar to spend a chill evening with friends, while the minimalist, industrial-style **Les Cuves de Fauve** is one of the best places in the city to drink craft beer and **Septime La Cave** is a hip spot that specialises in natural wine.

 EATING NEAR BASTILLE: OUR PICKS — MAP P130

Café de l'Industrie: Fake rhino heads, plastic pink flamingos and portraits of film stars fill this fun, retro bistro delivering classics. *8.30am-2am Mon-Sun* €

Chez Aline: Former butcher's shop selling lunch fare: *jambon beurre* baguettes and *oeufs mimosa* (devilled eggs) on its daily blackboard. *11.30am-3.30pm Mon-Fri* €

Amarante: Pork and veal specialities sitting along classic bistro staples. Understated decor, impeccable service. *12.30-1.30pm & 7.30-9.30pm Thu-Tue* €€

Aux Bons Crus: In the style of a French *relais routier* (truck stop), with red-and-white chequered tablecloths; one for gourmands. *noon-2.30pm & 7.30-10.30pm Mon-Sun* €€

EXPLORE THE ARTISANS' COURTS

Strolling around the picturesque passages that dot Faubourg St-Antoine provides a glimpse into its past as a centre of artisanship.

START	END	LENGTH
Cour Damoye	Passage du Chantier	1.5km; 1hr

As far back as the 15th century there's been a proud tradition of artisanship among Faubourg St-Antoine's inhabitants, including woodworkers, furniture makers and potters, with their workshops lining the area's picturesque, tranquil courtyards and passages. A stroll will immerse you in the historic atmosphere, even if the area is quickly modernising.

Start at ❶ **cour Damoye**, a site founded by an ironmonger that was previously home to ragpickers and scrap dealers, but is now a courtyard filled with charming townhouses. Exit via rue Daval and head along frantic rue de Lappe, known for its nightlife, for a few minutes.

Turn left to ❷ **passage L'homme**, surrounded by nostalgic, peeling storefronts, a cute antique games shop and a furniture shop with the sign of a chair hanging out front. Follow the street's curve onto ❸ **passage Josset**, past colourful street murals, perhaps have a coffee at Passager, before turning right onto busy rue de Charonne. Continue to ❹ **passage de la Main d'Or**, once again cobblestoned and calm, before traversing the narrow passage on the southern end. Turn right and walk to ❺ **74 rue du Faubourg St-Antoine**, formerly a 19th-century furniture factory, where you can admire its 32m brick chimney, then make a final detour through ❻ **passage du Chantier**, a tunnel-like route still home to artisans.

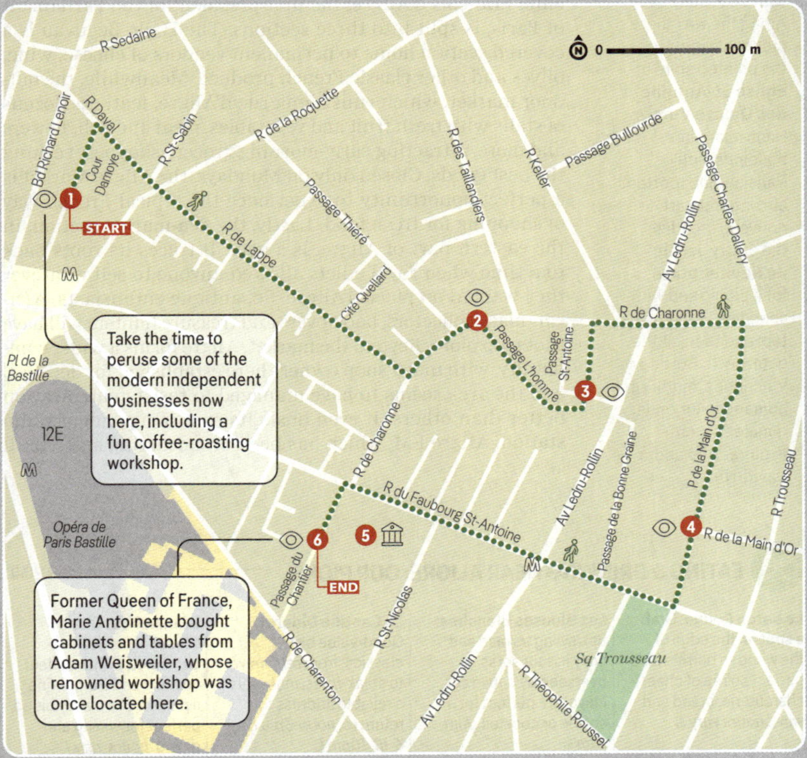

> Take the time to peruse some of the modern independent businesses now here, including a fun coffee-roasting workshop.

> Former Queen of France, Marie Antoinette bought cabinets and tables from Adam Weisweiler, whose renowned workshop was once located here.

WHY I LOVE THE COULÉE VERTE RENÉ-DUMONT

Peter Yeung, Lonely Planet writer

The **Coulée Verte René-Dumont** is a 4.5km elevated green walkway in Paris that inspired New York City's High Line. I usually prefer to go eastward on the flower-filled route along former train tracks, since the city gradually becomes greener and calmer with each step. Along the way there's plenty of sights: the pointed spire of **Église St-Antoine des Quinze Vingts**; Haussmannian buildings with Parisian zinc rooftops and intricate art nouveau façades; the pretty **Jardin de Reuilly**, prime for a picnic and with sparkling water on tap; and then, at the gateway to Bois de Vincennes, murals in homage to legendary female French explorer Alexandra David-Néel.

Live Music

MAP P130

Intimate venues with great bands

Bastille is a great place to see live music in a smaller, more intimate setting. **Les Disquaires** (lesdisquaires.com) is a cafe–concert venue with an eclectic programme, but largely focusing on rock and pop, before turning into a nightclub open until 5am on weekends. The Brazilian samba nights on Fridays at **Café de la Plage** (lecafedelaplage-paris.com), which also holds *forró* dance classes, are a joy. Meanwhile, the 500-seat **Café de la Danse** (cafedeladanse.com) welcomes mid-tier acts from around the world. Elsewhere, don't miss the Tuesday jazz nights at **Le POPUP du Label** (popup.paris), which hosts all kinds of emerging artists throughout the week, and **Supersonic** (supersonic-club.fr), another platform for young talent, with shows every day that often have free entry.

Market Day

MAP P130

See the district's living soul

Locals and tourists adore the vibrant **Marché d'Aligre**, without doubt one of the best of the more than 70 open-air fresh-produce markets in Paris. The Aligre Market, which was built in 1843 and later named after local resident Etienne François d'Aligre, the first president of the Parliament of Paris, is split into three sections. The Halle Beauvau is a covered section home to permanent vendors of cheese, wine, olives and other classic French produce. Meanwhile, the outdoor market, which runs along rue d'Aligre, features dozens of stalls with fresh fruit and vegetables, meat and fish, flowers and more, attracting early-morning grocery shoppers seeking the best goods. Closed only on Mondays, the Aligre Market is a perfect opportunity to experience the typical French way of shopping for fresh food. Lastly, the flea-market section, in the eastern part of Aligre, is a gem. It traces its roots back to a time when royal edicts allowed anyone to sell whatever they wanted on place d'Aligre. So, antique enthusiasts, African-mask collectors, booklovers and treasure hunters will have a lot to explore. Beyond the market, Aligre forms a wider community, with many shop owners here established for decades, and the area seems to have managed to resist gentrification better than others. It even hosts its own independent radio station, Aligre FM, which has been broadcasting since 1981.

EATING & DRINKING NEAR ALIGRE: OUR PICKS

MAP P130

Le Baron Rouge: Grab a spot on the edge of the wooden barrels for a perfect soirée of cheese, charcuterie, bread and wine. *hours vary* €

Les Blouses Blanches: Sprawling terrace and cosy indoor sofas, overseen by house cat Maya, are perfect for a coffee or cocktail. *7am-2am* €

La Cantine Diderot: Good-value bistro classics, from *œuf mayo* to *steak-frites*, make this a reliable address to return to. *noon-3pm & 6-10.30pm* €

L'Ébauchoir: Quality seasonal produce combined with excellent cooking and a long wine list make this classy bistro perfect for wining and dining. *hours vary* €€

Marché d'Aligre

End of Empire

MAP P136

Learn about France's complicated colonial past

Set in a grandiose art deco building, the **Palais de la Porte Dorée** (Palace of the Golden Gate) is an underrated destination on the edge of Paris. Constructed for the Colonial Exhibition of 1931, a dark chapter in France's history during which racist stereotypes were perpetuated in a celebration of the French Empire, the building is nonetheless an architectural curio lined with massive columns, sprawling murals and glorious mosaics (especially those in the Marie-Curie Hall on the ground floor). Since 2007, the building has been home to the **Musée de l'Histoire de l'Immigration** (*histoire-immigration.fr/en; adult/child €12/free*), a fascinating museum that covers the often painful history of immigration in France – from the transatlantic slavery trade, in which France transported over a million enslaved Africans to the Caribbean, to the immigration linked to the World Wars, France's colonisation of Algeria, xenophobia under former president Valéry Giscard d'Estaing, and, more recently, the emergence of refugee camps in Calais. Scant space is usually given to these stories in France, yet they are more relevant than ever.

LA FLÈCHE D'OR

Set in the former Charonne train station, **La Flèche d'Or** *(flechedor.org)*, or The Golden Arrow, is a vibrant alternative arts venue named after the train–boat service that ran between Paris and London via Calais and Dover from 1926 to 1972. In the 1990s, students from the École des Beaux-Arts de Paris turned the decommissioned station into a concert space, which in 2024 was the subject of urgent repairs by Paris city hall. Today, the venue remains markedly left wing, hosting concerts, cinema screenings, fundraisers, drag shows and poetry nights, often with a focus on climate issues, politics and LGBTIQ+ rights.

Don't miss the heavenly homemade millefeuille.

 EATING NEAR BERCY: OUR PICKS

MAP P136

Au Vinyle Gourmand: Part vinyl store, part canteen run by a Franco-Vietnamese couple serving simple Viet food – bo buns, banh mis. *hours vary* €

L'Auberge Aveyronnaise: Specialises in trad cuisine of France's southern Aveyron region, notably *aligot* (cheese and potato dish). *12.30-3.30pm & 7-11pm Tue-Sat* €€

Au Trou Gascon: New owner has blown fresh life into this emblematic Parisian address with stylish mod European dishes. *noon-2pm & 7-10.30pm Tue-Sat* €€€

Alexa Cafe: Simple, delicious French classics and generic international staples like burgers and pizzas, delivered with warm service. *hours vary* €

BASTILLE & EASTERN PARIS PARIS

THE GUIDE

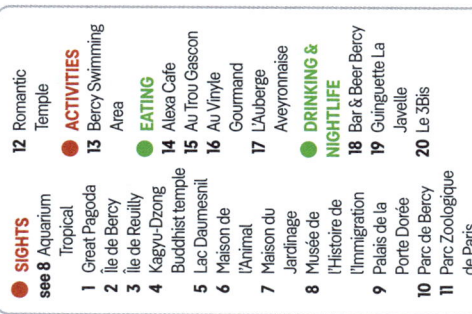

● SIGHTS
- see 8 Aquarium Tropical
- 1 Great Pagoda
- 2 Île de Bercy
- 3 Île de Reuilly
- 4 Kagyu-Dzong Buddhist temple
- 5 Lac Daumesnil
- 6 Maison de l'Animal
- 7 Maison du Jardinage
- 8 Musée de l'Histoire de l'Immigration
- 9 Palais de la Porte Dorée
- 10 Parc de Bercy
- 11 Parc Zoologique de Paris
- 12 Romantic Temple

● ACTIVITIES
- 13 Bercy Swimming Area

● EATING
- 14 Alexa Cafe
- 15 Au Trou Gascon
- 16 Au Vinyle
- 17 L'Auberge Gourmand
- Aveyronnaise

● DRINKING & NIGHTLIFE
- 18 Bar & Beer Bercy
- 19 Guinguette La Javelle
- 20 Le 3Bis

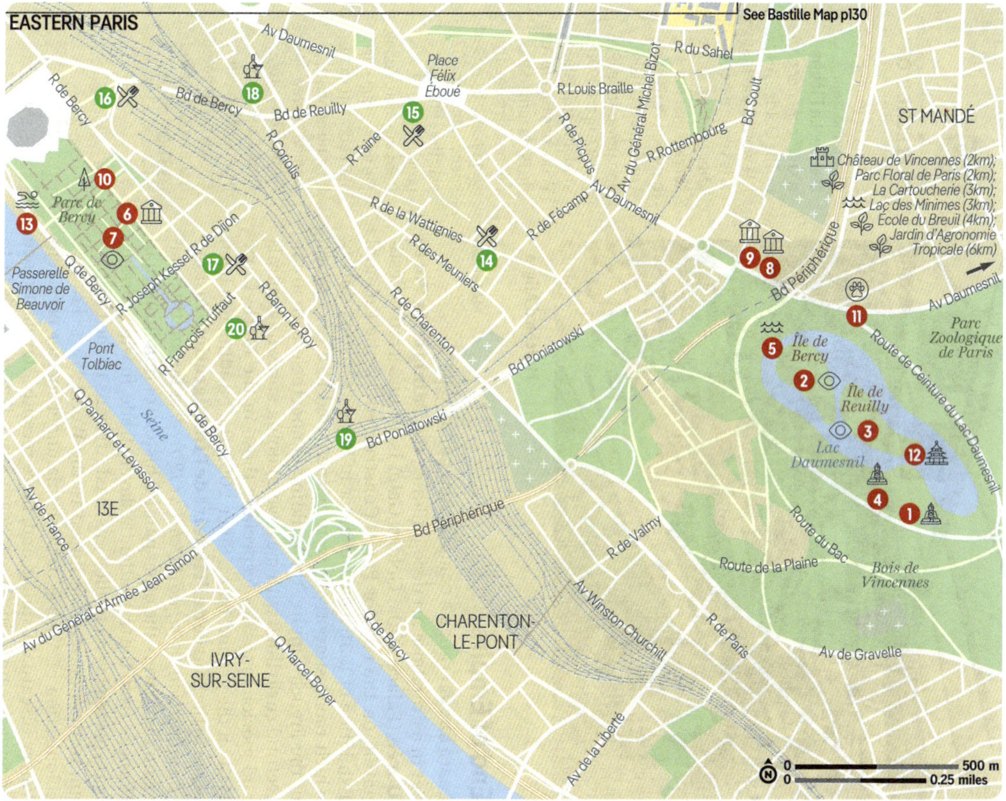

The palace also hosts the diverting **Aquarium Tropical** *(combined entry with museum €15)*, part of the initial museum a century ago and home to 400 species, including small crocodiles, seahorses and stingrays, with detailed panels in English. When your legs tire, pause at the airy cafe terrace.

Unique Green Space
From urban vineyards to gardening

MAP P136

Possibly the most underrated park in Paris, the rectangular **Parc de Bercy** houses a curious mishmash of styles. In the western area, large lawns are great for picnicking. The central area, Jardin Yitzhak Rabin, includes a pretty rose garden. This central zone, full of little secluded areas to sit, also contains the **Maison du Jardinage**, an educational place in a quaint house where gardening experts are often on hand to give advice, and the 2025-opened **Maison de l'Animal**, an events and exhibition space dedicated to urban biodiversity in Paris. To the east, across some footbridges, is the Romantic garden, which has turtle-filled ponds lined with oaks, sweet gums and willows.

The park has a curious link with winemaking: during the 19th century it was the site of enormous wine warehouses, when Paris was the world's largest hub for the wine and spirits trade. This vinicultural history, dating as far back as the Middle Ages, persisted until the 1950s when bottling on vineyards was preferred. Even today it endures through the park's 400 grapevines, still harvested annually, and you can see the train tracks that were once used to transport wine.

Urban Swimming
Go for a dip in the Seine

MAP P136

In 1900, during the first edition of the Olympic Games in Paris, swimming races took place in the River Seine. Decades of industrialisation polluted the waters until a nadir was reached in the 1970s. After a mass clean-up operation, including the construction of water-treatment plants and rainwater-storage basins, swimming was possible once again for the 2024 Games. Since the summer of 2025, the public has also been able to bathe in the famous river, including at the **Bercy swimming area** by the Simone de Beauvoir footbridge. The area is supervised, marked with buoys and equipped with showers and lockers.

GROUND CONTROL

Located in a former mail-sorting hall, **Ground Control** *(groundcontrolparis.com)* is a sprawling 6000-sq-metre culture and events space. While this isn't a place of great tradition and charm, it's modern and lively, filled with repurposed train station decor and colourful murals. There's a packed schedule, including dance and yoga classes, sports screenings, DJ sets and even an urban agriculture-awareness workshop run by a local nonprofit (one of several that are based here). It's a great place to grab a drink with snacks from the many food stands, particularly during the summer at the large outdoor terrace.

DRINKING NEAR BERCY: OUR PICKS

MAP P130, P136

Guinguette La Javelle: *Guinguette* with rowdy atmosphere on industrial edge of Paris. Open spring and summer. *5pm-midnight Mon-Fri, from noon Sat & Sun*

Le Mazette: Watch sunset with a cocktail on this multistorey boat, which has concerts and club nights. *6.30pm-midnight Wed-Fri, to 6am Sat & Sun*

Bar & Beer Bercy: Cheerful service and several craft beers on tap, including tasting flights, make this a cosy local watering hole. *4pm-2am*

Le 3Bis: This board-game/karaoke bar has playful decor and a themed room inspired by the TV show *Friends*. *hours vary*

Lac Daumesnil

TOP EXPERIENCE
Bois de Vincennes

The wonderful Bois de Vincennes is one of the capital's two 'green lungs' along with the Bois de Boulogne (p74). Parisians flock to this 995-hectare forest for a breath of fresh air but also for the myriad things to see and do, from boat rides on lakes to restorative nature walks, floral gardens, a zoo, a racecourse, a circus and a historic château.

DON'T MISS

Boating on the lakes

Parc Floral de Paris

Château de Vincennes

Parc Zoologique de Paris

Jardin d'Agronomie Tropicale

La Cartoucherie

Boating on the Lakes

Most rent rowboats at **Lac Daumesnil**, artificially built in 1860, to the west of the park. One-hour rides costs €15 for up to four people. The isles at the lake's centre, **Île de Reuilly** and **Île de Bercy**, can be accessed by a footbridge to the south. Don't miss the pretty, Greek-inspired **Romantic Temple** and the grotto below with waterfalls. Here and the surroundings are prime – and popular – for picnics and sunbathing. Just south, the **Kagyu-Dzong Buddhist temple** and the towering **Great Pagoda**, open on weekends, make for a peaceful visit. Boats can also be rented *(up to four, per hour €12)* at the north edge of the smaller, lesser-known **Lac des Minimes**, in the forest's northeast. Drinks and snacks are available nearby at

PRACTICALITIES
● parisjetaime.com/eng/culture/bois-de-vincennes-p1017 ● 24hr; free to enter (some activities/sites have fees and limited opening times)

the **Confiserie Du Lac**, or, on Friday and Saturday nights, at **Rosa Bonheur à l'Est**, which hosts live music and DJs on an island in the lake until 1am.

Fun-Packed Flower Park

Inaugurated in 1969, the 28-hectare **Parc Floral de Paris** is one of the city's best places to admire flowers, from bonsai gardens to tropical greenhouses. Come between April and September *(adult/child €2.70/1.55)* for the best sights. There's also family-centred activities, including an 18-hole mini-golf course, zip lines, an escape game, a children's theatre and a butterfly garden. Majestic blue peacocks frequent the park and are easier to spot late morning or at lunchtime.

Château de Vincennes

To the north of the forest, Château de Vincennes attracts relatively few visitors. But this gleaming castle, which began in the 12th century as a hunting lodge before being transformed into a fortress, royal residence and prison, is worth an hour-long visit. Entry to the expansive courtyard is free, however a ticket *(adult/child €13/free)* is required for the site's dungeon, one of the tallest in Europe, allowing you to explore and ascend the tower for a panoramic view. A ticket also allows entry to Ste-Chapelle, a small version of its famed counterpart in central Paris, with its stained-glass windows and beautiful entrance door; one of the first masterpieces of the flamboyant Gothic style.

Parc Zoologique de Paris

The **Parc Zoologique de Paris** *(parczoologiquedeparis.fr/en; adult/child €22/17)* is a whole lot of fun and great for a change of pace. Divided into geographic zones, such as Patagonia, the Andes and Madagascar, this triangle-shaped zoo contains more than 3000 animals and 250 species. There are daily feeding sessions with animals, including giraffes, sea lions, ostriches and baboons.

Jardin d'Agronomie Tropicale

The lesser-known, tranquil Jardin d'Agronomie Tropicale is filled with lush vegetation and has remnants of the 1931 Colonial Exhibition, including a pretty Chinese gate and Cambodian stupa. Grab lunch/coffee at the lovely *cantine*.

École du Breuil

The municipal École du Breuil is yet another delightful green space to visit, with a wonderful lotus garden. The benches at this horticulture school are carved from tree trunks.

La Cartoucherie

This **cultural complex** of five theatres in the forest showcases theatre, dance and circus arts.

ECOLOGICAL FESTIVAL

We Love Green *(welovegreen.fr)*, held in Bois de Vincennes in June, is a festival that raises awareness about ecological issues through music and art. Hop on the metro, bus or a bike (coming by car is discouraged) to get to this three-day event, spread over five stages in the forest, including a dedicated Think Tank stage for environmental talks.

TOP TIPS

● Phone signal can be weak in parts, so bear that in mind when meeting friends. It's a good idea to download maps on your phone before you go.

● The forest is vast so it's worth considering using a bicycle to traverse it. There are a number of municipal Vélib' stations scattered throughout the forest.

● Rubbish bins are few and far between, so be prepared to carry out whatever you bring in.

● There are many water stations across the forest. Don't forget to bring your reusable drink bottle.

● Some sites are only open on the weekend, which will also be by far the busiest time to come, so choose wisely.

The Islands

CHIC HISTORIC HEART | NOTRE DAME

GETTING AROUND

The islands are easiest on foot, and the quays are a quick descent down stairs or ramps.

Cité (line 4) on Île de la Cité is the Islands' only metro station. Saint-Michel (line 4 and RER B and C) serves Notre Dame from the Left Bank, and Pont Marie (line 7) on the Right Bank is Île St-Louis' closest station. Buses serve the islands, too.

The hop-on, hop-off Batobus stops opposite Notre Dame on the Left Bank.

The Romans set up shop on these two inner-city islands and slowly the entire city radiated out. The larger of the two islands, Île de la Cité, is home to majestic Notre Dame, resplendent once again after its devastating 2019 fire, and Sainte-Chapelle, a symphony of kaleidoscopic 13th-century stained glass. It sits footsteps from today's functioning Palais de Justice and the dungeons in the French Revolution prison, Conciergerie. Cross Pont St-Louis to reach enchanting Île St-Louis, graced with charming boutiques and sun-bathed quays beckoning to picnickers. In the evening from Pont Neuf, with its dramatic busts of ogres and kings, appreciate the lights sparkling on the length of the Seine. Revel in it – you're in Paris.

Shimmering Stained Glass of Sainte-Chapelle

Glorious Gothic chapel bedazzlement

No sight in Paris is as dazzling as the radiant Holy Chapel called **Sainte-Chapelle** *(sainte-chapelle.fr; adult/child Jun-Sep €18/free, Oct-May €13, combined ticket with Conciergerie Jun-Sep/Oct-May €25/20)*, hidden away like a precious gem within the city's original, 13th-century Palais de Justice (Law Courts) and Palais de la Cité, the former royal residence. Paris' oldest, finest stained glass laces its sublime Gothic interior – best viewed on sunny days when light floods in, creating an entrancing rainbow of bold colours.

Sainte-Chapelle was built in just six years and consecrated in 1248. It was conceived by French king Louis IX to house his collection of holy relics, including the famous Ste-Couronne (Holy Crown, Jesus' wreath of thorns), which he acquired in 1239 from the Emperor of Constantinople for a sum easily exceeding the amount it cost to build the chapel. In reality, it was safeguarded at Notre Dame, as it is today (p145).

Enter through the lower chamber of the chapel, once used by palace staff, and mount a spiral stair signposted 'Chapelle

☑ TOP TIP

Reserve your entrance *(free)* for Notre Dame starting three days before your desired date. Tickets keep getting released, so check back if they're not available, and you could score a time slot and QR code that will let you use the reserved-entrance line.

continued on p146

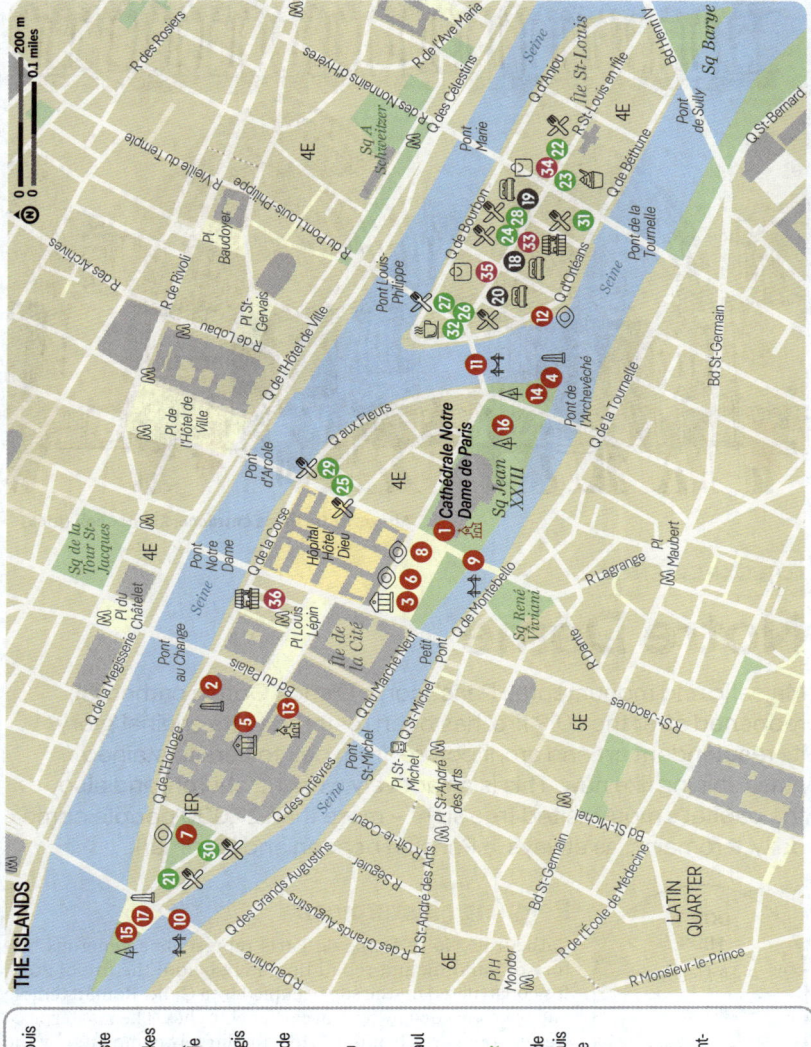

THE ISLANDS

⭐ **HIGHLIGHTS**
1 Cathédrale Notre Dame de Paris

🔴 **SIGHTS**
2 Conciergerie
3 Crypte Archéologique
4 Mémorial des Martyrs de la Déportation
5 Palais de Justice
6 Parvis Notre Dame
7 place Dauphine
8 Point Zéro des Routes de France
9 Pont au Double
10 Pont Neuf
11 Pont St-Louis
12 Quai d'Orléans
13 Sainte-Chapelle
14 Square de l'Île de France
15 Square du Vert-Galant
16 Square Jean XXIII
17 Statue of Henri IV

⚫ **SLEEPING**
18 Hôtel des Deux Îles
19 Hôtel du Jeu de Paume
20 Hôtel Saint-Louis en l'Isle

🟢 **EATING**
21 Atelier du Geste à l'Émotion
22 Aux Petits Cakes
23 Berthillon
24 Bouillon de l'Île
25 Café Leone
26 Café Saint Régis
see 24 Hadrien
see 25 La Dame de Paris
27 La Sarrasine
28 Le Mâche-dru
29 Les Deux Colombes
30 Restaurant Paul
31 Wonderland Brunchy

🟢 **DRINKING & NIGHTLIFE**
32 La Brasserie de l'Isle Saint-Louis
see 27 L'Étiquette

🔴 **SHOPPING**
33 Fleuryan
34 La Boucherie Gardil
35 La Ferme Saint-Aubin
36 Marché aux Fleurs Reine Elizabeth II

Above: Notre Dame entrance; Right: Choir (p145)

TOP EXPERIENCE

Notre Dame

Majestic and monumental, Paris' iconic French Gothic cathedral, reopened after the 2019 fire, has been restored to its original glory, its resplendent art and architecture, from bell towers to stained glass shining like new. This is an actively working church, and also the capital's most visited free sight – more than 29,000 people come daily. It remains, as always, a Parisian beacon and landmark.

DON'T MISS

Rose windows

Bell towers

Façade carvings

Flying buttresses

Treasury & Crown of Thorns

The Mays paintings

Underground ruins

Cathedral concerts

Reigning Masterpiece

Cathédrale Notre Dame de Paris represents a generous history of building and rebuilding, long before the fire of 2019. It's constructed on the site occupied by a Gallo-Roman temple and was preceded by several earlier churches. The masterpiece we see today was begun in 1163 and largely completed by the early 14th century. It was badly damaged during the Revolution, prompting architect Eugène-Emmanuel Viollet-le-Duc to oversee extensive renovations between 1845 and 1864. That's when many of the magnificent forest of ornate **flying buttresses** that encircle the cathedral chancel and support its walls and roof were added.

PRACTICALITIES

● notredamedeparis.fr ● 7.50am-7pm, to 10pm Thu, 8.15am-7.30pm Sat & Sun ● Admission free, treasury adult/child €12/6, towers extra

With the devastating 2019 fire, this French Gothic landmark, long considered the city's geographic and spiritual heart, went through a massive restoration and, amazingly, reopened its doors in December 2024. Because everything – including undamaged elements – was cleaned, the cathedral looks brand-new.

Grand Plan & Fabulous Façade

Notre Dame is known for its sublime balance, though if you look closely you'll see all sorts of minor asymmetrical elements introduced to avoid monotony, in accordance with standard Gothic practice. These include the slightly different shapes of each of the three main **portals**; its statues were once brightly coloured to make them more effective as a *Biblia pauperum* – a 'Bible of the poor' to help the illiterate faithful understand Old Testament stories, the Passion of the Christ and the lives of the saints.

Landmark Occasions

Henry VI of England was crowned here in 1431 as King of France. In 1558 Mary, Queen of Scots married the Dauphin Francis (later Francis II of France). At the unusual 1600 marriage of Marie de Médici to Henri of Navarre, he, as a Protestant who couldn't enter the church, stood outside. In 1804 Napoléon I was crowned by Pope Pius VII. And Joan of Arc was beatified in 1909 and canonised in 1920.

Towers

A constant queue marks the entrance to the **Tours de Notre Dame** (*tours-notre-dame-de-paris.fr*), the cathedral's bell towers. Climb the 422 spiralling steps to the 69m-high top

REBUILDING NOTRE DAME

On the evening of 15 April 2019, a blaze broke out under the cathedral's roof. Firefighters were able to control the fire and ultimately save the church, but the damage was catastrophic. The restoration involved over 1000 artists and not only repaired fire-damaged elements, but cleaned and restored everything to the untarnished condition of the era of Viollet-le-Duc. It cost about €900 million (via donations).

TOP TIPS

● Huge queues get longer through the day – arrive early; or late Thursday night.

● Reserve tickets online or through Notre Dame app (three days to two hours before your arrival).

● Fast track entrance for people with disabilities (no reservation needed).

● Collect an audioguide *(€5)* from the info desk inside, or download the app.

● Check online for free tours by volunteers.

● No public restrooms inside; paid ones on the Parvis (square) out front.

● Metro stops Cité (line 4) and Saint-Michel (line 4 and RER B and C) are each a five-minute walk away.

● Remember Notre Dame is an active place of worship.

SAVED BY THE HUNCHBACK OF NOTRE DAME

The damage inflicted on Notre Dame during the French Revolution saw it fall into ruin, and it was destined for demolition. Salvation came with the widespread popularity of Victor Hugo's 1831 novel *The Hunchback of Notre Dame*, which sparked a petition to save it. Much of the action – like when Quasimodo swings down a bell rope to save dancer Esmeralda from the gallows – takes place at the cathedral.

of the **South Tower** (the one on the right as you face the church). On your way up, you'll pass through a room with displays on the cathedral's history before you reach the **Galerie des Chimères** (Gargoyles Gallery). These grotesque statues divert rainwater from the roof to prevent masonry damage, with the water exiting through their elongated, open mouths. Although they appear medieval, they were installed by Viollet-le-Duc in the 19th century.

This route also brings you to Emmanuel, the cathedral's original 13-tonne bourdon **bell**. During the night of 24 August 1944, when the Île de la Cité was retaken by French, Allied and Resistance troops, the tolling of the Emmanuel announced Paris' approaching liberation. Emmanuel's peal purity apparently proceeds from the precious metals Parisian women threw into the pot when it was recast from copper and bronze in 1631.

Finish the climb at the top where there's a spectacular view over Paris. There's a 1000-visitor maximum per day, so book your timed-entry ticket in advance.

Rose Windows & Organ

Inside, behold the three masterpiece rose windows colouring the cathedral's vast 127m-long, 48m-wide interior. The 13m-wide southern window is the largest and depicts the theme of the Last Judgement. The window on the northern side of the transept remains virtually unchanged since the 13th century. Admire the 10m-wide window over the western façade, with the Virgin Mary in the centre, above the **organ**. The organ is

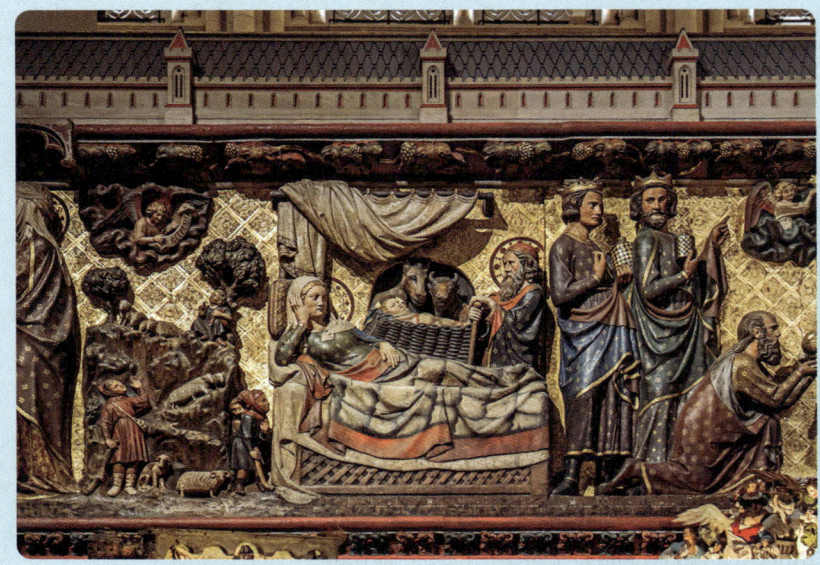

Choir screen carvings

one of the largest in the world, with 8000 pipes (900 of which have historical classification), 115 stops, five 56-key manuals and a 32-key pedalboard.

Controversially, some of the stained glass in Notre Dame's southern chapels has been commissioned to be replaced by French artist Claire Tabouret with an estimated installation of 2026. The idea is to take the originals, created by Viollet-le-Duc, and display them in a museum.

The Choir & Artwork

Don't miss the cathedral's grand wooden **choir**, with its carved stalls and statues representing the Passion of the Christ. The exterior is ornately decorated with scenes from the gospels.

Admire the 13 impressive paintings, called the **Mays**, in their nave chapels. From 1630 to 1707, city goldsmiths gave 76 of these as gifts commemorating one of the acts of the apostles. You'll also notice a collection of modern paintings and **tapestries**, including a Matisse, now hanging in place of a new collection of tapestries that's being woven.

Much of the art in the cathedral is now marked with clear signage in French, English and Spanish, making it easier to learn about each piece, sculpture or fresco.

Treasury

It is absolutely worth the fee *(adult/child €12/6)* to enter the *trésor* (treasury), which houses Notre Dame's dazzling sacred jewels and relics in the cathedral's southeastern transept. Check out the wonderful **Les Camées des Papes** (Papal cameos), sculpted with incredible finesse in shell and framed in silver. The 268 pieces depict every pope in miniature from St Pierre to Benoît XVI.

Crown of Thorns

The **Ste-Couronne** (Holy Crown), the wreath of thorns placed on Jesus' head before he was crucified, was given to Notre Dame in 1239 by the king St Louis (he acquired it from the Emperor in Constantinople). A gigantic golden reliquary in the axial chapel was made during the post-fire restoration to house the crown, a piece of the cross and a nail from the crucifixion.

The crown is offered for viewing between 3pm and 5pm on the first Friday of the month and Fridays during Lent, plus 10am to 5pm on Good Friday.

Centre of France

Distances from Paris to every part of metropolitan France are measured from a **bronze star** embedded in the cobbles of the cathedral's front square (called **Parvis Notre Dame** or place Jean-Paul II). The Parvis is undergoing a renovation that will include underground services, slated to open in 2027.

ANCIENT UNDERGROUND RUINS

Descend under the square in front of Notre Dame to the fascinating **Crypte Archéologique** *(crypte.paris.fr; adult/child incl exhibition €11/free)*, a 117m-long and 28m-wide cavity moodily displaying 4th-century Gallo-Roman ruins and other layers of Île de la Cité history. Cool computer simulations show the area as it was in Roman times, and exhibits delve into local Roman baths and artefacts, the success of Victor Hugo's *Hunchback of Notre Dame*, and the cathedral's past.

CATHEDRAL MUSIC

Music has always been a sacred part of Notre Dame's soul. Try to experience a Sunday Gregorian or polyphonic Mass or free organ recital. Or get a ticket for an evening concert *(musique-sacree-notredamedeparis.fr)*.

FEELING THE SEAT OF POWER

Palais de Justice stands on ground once occupied by the Romans' administrative buildings. Over time, they were replaced by other seats of power (Merovingian and Capetian kings ruled here). That ended when Charles V (1338–80) moved over to the Louvre and other palaces after he was forced to watch his trusted counsellors killed here. During the Revolution, new courts were installed here.

Its current façade dates from the latter half of the 19th and turn of the 20th century. You can walk its near-empty halls, though court proceedings are private. There is a dedicated security line (separate to the queue at Sainte-Chapelle, which lies in its central courtyard).

La Brasserie de l'Île Saint-Louis

continued from p140

Haute' to reach the glorious upper chapel where royals, such as Catherine de Médici, and their close friends worshipped.

Stir your soul at a classical music **evening concert** *(fnac. com)*.

There are discounts on entrance on Wednesdays from April to September.

Royal Palace Turned Brig at the Conciergerie
Prisons through the ages

A royal palace in the 14th century, the **Conciergerie** *(paris-conciergerie.fr; adult/child €13/free, combined ticket with Sainte-Chapelle Jun-Sep/Oct-May €25/20)* later became a prison. During the Reign of Terror (1793–94), alleged enemies of the Revolution were incarcerated here before being brought before the Revolutionary Tribunal next door in the 13th-century **Palais de Justice**; still a working courthouse *(free)*.

Almost 2800 prisoners were held in the Conciergerie's dungeons (in various 'classes' of cells) before being sent to the guillotine; the star prisoner was Queen Marie Antoinette. Seek out the display of some of her delicate personal items, like her camisole and cross. As the Revolution began to turn on its own, radicals Danton and Robespierre were locked up at the

EATING ON ÎLE DE LA CITÉ: OUR PICKS

Les Deux Colombes: Charmingly tucked into a quiet corner of Île de la Cité with friendly service and hearty classics. *noon-3pm & 5.30-10pm Tue-Sun* €€

Café Leone: Opt for a table on the back patio looking out on quieter rue de la Colombe for tasty pizzas and pastas. *9.30am-11pm* €€

La Dame de Paris: Pick up top-notch pastries, crêpes and sandwiches from the art deco shop, or sit at its adjacent cafe. *9am-10pm* €

Restaurant Paul: The best of the charming dining options on place Dauphine, with a good lunchtime *prix fixe menu*. *noon-2.30pm & 7-10pm* €€

Conciergerie and, finally, the judges of the tribunal themselves.

Rent a HistoPad *(tablet-device guide; €5)* to explore in augmented reality and take part in an interactive, 3D treasure hunt. There are often free guided tours at 11am and 3pm.

Rotating exhibitions (like displays on Paris' culinary history or travel writing and advertising) fill the beautiful Rayonnant Gothic **Salle des Gens d'Armes**.

Picnic on the Banks of the Seine
The sweet island life

Happy Parisians dot the **quays** and parks of the islands, relaxing, reading, romancing and, of course, picnicking. Join them! Gather provisions at the islands' lovely purveyors – from luxe sandwiches and tarts at **Atelier du Geste à l'Émotion** or **Le Mâche-dru** and excellent breads at **Aux Petits Cakes** *(aux-petits-cakes.eatbu.com)*. Buy *fromage* (cheese) from **La Ferme Saint-Aubin**, salami at **La Boucherie Gardil** or a little of everything at the small grocery store on rue St-Louis en l'Île or lovely **Fleuryan**. Pick up a bottle of wine at **L'Etiquette**. Dessert? Chocolate from **Hadrien** or ice cream from **Berthillon**.

Cafe Life
Lounge the day away in style

For excellent people-watching, head to the point where Pont St-Louis meets the island of the same name. There, you'll find one of the islands' best dining experiences: **Café Saint Régis** *(lesaintregis-paris.com)*. Waiters in long white aprons, a ceramic-tiled interior and retro vintage decor make this a deliciously Parisian hangout any time of the day. Or pop across the street to **La Brasserie de l'Îsle Saint-Louis** *(labrasserie-isl.fr)* for its broad patio with ace views.

Play on the Pont Neuf & Island Bridges
Enjoy gorgeous history, modern musicians

Start with the city's oldest bridge, confusingly named Pont Neuf, or 'New Bridge'. It has linked the western end of Île de la Cité with both riverbanks since 1607, when the king, Henri IV, inaugurated it by crossing the bridge on a white stallion. The bridge's epic arches (seven on the northern stretch and five on the southern span) are decorated with 381 *mascarons* (grotesque figures) depicting barbers, dentists, pickpockets,

ISLANDS THROUGH TIME

Île de la Cité was the site of the first settlement in Paris (c 3rd century BCE) and later the centre of Roman Lutetia. It remained the hub of royal and ecclesiastical power, even after the city spread to both banks of the Seine in the Middle Ages. Smaller Île St-Louis was actually two uninhabited islets called Île Notre Dame (Our Lady Isle) and Île aux Vaches (Cows Island) in the early 17th century – until a builder and two financiers cut a deal with Louis XIII to create one island and build two bridges to the mainland.

Nowadays, redevelopment of part of the hospital Hôtel Dieu into shops, dining establishments and offices, plus the redesign of the Parvis of Notre Dame and the flower market will change the islands again.

 EATING ON ÎLE ST-LOUIS: CASUAL FARE

Bouillon de l'Île: Smoothies, breakfasts and cheap-and-cheerful vegetarian lunches feature at this busy small cafe with excellent prices. *9am-3pm* €

Le Mâche-dru: Little more than a hole in the wall with two friendly guys dishing out fresh sandwiches made from top ingredients. *11.45am-5pm Tue-Sun* €

La Sarrasine: Get your crêpe fix, from buckwheat *galettes* to sugary delights, or opt for its *prix fixe menus* of classic French dishes. *11am-11pm* €

Wonderland Brunchy: All things brunch: waffles, avocado croissants and more. *10am-5pm Mon-Thu, to 1.30pm Fri, 9am-5pm Sat & Sun* €

> **WHY I LOVE PARIS' ISLANDS**
>
>
>
> **Alexis Averbuck**, Lonely Planet writer
>
> Every time I come to Paris I make a pilgrimage to the islands. By day, by night, the views offer the soaring romance and twinkling lights we all dream about when we think of the City of Light. There's great people-watching too, as locals and tourists alike cut through on their way elsewhere or seek a picnic spot on the quay. I also love thinking about how these islands are the very root of the original city, built layer upon layer of history, from pre-Roman to Notre Dame and Ste-Chappelle (with its heart-thrilling stained glass) and the busy brasseries of today. I almost feel like you haven't fully experienced Paris until you've come to its islands.

loiterers, and so on. If you can, come by at night, when they are illuminated.

As you amble onto the island, notice an equestrian **statue of Henri IV**, known to his subjects as the Vert Galant ('jolly rogue' or 'dirty old man', perspective depending) – it commemorates that inaugural crossing. From here, you can wander into the peaceful and tree-adorned **place Dauphine**.

You wouldn't imagine that it and Pont Neuf were used for public executions in the 18th century. In the last century, the bridge became an objet d'art in 1963, when School of Paris artist Nonda built, exhibited and lived in a huge Trojan horse of steel and wood on the bridge; in 1985, when Bulgarian-born 'environmental sculptor' Christo famously wrapped the bridge in beige fabric; and in 1994 when Japanese designer Kenzo covered it with flowers.

The islands' bridges are also top spots for buskers. Stroll down the quay and through the Parvis of Notre Dame to take in the street entertainment at **Pont au Double** (linking Notre Dame with the Left Bank) and **Pont St-Louis** (linking both islands), which buzz with performers, even in winter.

In fact, the current postcard-perfect Pont St-Louis dates from 1969. It is the seventh bridge built on this spot to link the two islands. The first – made from wood – was completed in the 1630s.

An Historic Flower Market
Stop and smell the roses

As you stroll the Île de la Cité, look out for the sweet **Marché aux Fleurs Reine Elizabeth II**. Blooms have been sold at this quaint covered flower market since 1808, making it the oldest market of any kind in Paris. Browse blooming orchids, garden statuary and lavender sachets. A renovation is underway, in stages, through to 2028.

Quiet Parks & River Vistas
Slip into verdant views

In all the beauty of central Paris it's easy to forget that the Seine is a living river (Hemingway used to fish here!) with a rich ecology. Get a glimpse of both wildlife and manicured gardens at the island's parks.

At the westernmost tip of the Île de la Cité, weeping willows grace the picturesque **Square du Vert-Galant**. Sitting at the islands' original level, 7m below their current height, the waterside park is reached by stairs leading down from the Pont Neuf. Especially romantic for drinks or a picnic at sunset, it can get crowded in summer evenings.

Behind Notre Dame, **Square Jean XXIII** is part of a massive redevelopment of Notre Dame's public spaces that will connect the **Parvis Notre Dame** (p145) with the **Square de l'Île de France** at the island's eastern tip. Rarely busy and with superb river views, this square is also home to **Mémorial des Martyrs de la Déportation** (*cheminsdememoire.gouv.fr; admission free*), commemorating the 200,000 French who were deported to Nazi concentration camps during WWII.

Latin Quarter

BUSY HUB | ANCIENT MARVELS | LITERARY LIFE

The Latin Quarter, one of Paris' oldest and most storied neighbourhoods, grew around the Sorbonne University in the Middle Ages, becoming a hub of scholarship, debate, and revolutionary ideas. Its name comes from the Latin once spoken in its medieval schools, echoes of which still shape the area's intellectual spirit. Spanning the 5e and 6e *arrondissements*, between the Jardin du Luxembourg and the Jardin des Plantes, it's crowned by the neoclassical Panthéon, resting place of France's great minds. Roman ruins, student bars, and bohemian haunts coexist with arthouse cinemas, the Natural History Museum, the Césure arts hub, and cultural landmarks like the Institut du Monde Arabe and the Grande Mosquée de Paris.

> ☑ **TOP TIP**
>
> As the Latin Quarter is one of the biggest neighbourhoods, save at least a day to visit. Avoid visiting at the height of summer (July and August), as overtourism here is real. Queues are long and you'll be hard pushed finding a free table at restaurants and bars – booking ahead is key.

Architecture Worship

Medieval vestiges and Paris' oldest wall

Stroll the Latin Quarter to catch glimpses of its impressive Roman and medieval roots. The star attraction on top of the **Ste Geneviève** hill is the **Panthéon** (p152), a regal Roman-inspired resting place for some of the country's greatest figures. Adjacent to the Panthéon, don't miss the magnificent **Église St-Étienne du Mont**, built between 1492 and 1655. In a chapel in the nave's southeastern corner, you'll find the

continued on p153

GETTING AROUND

The Latin Quarter has some good transport links like Metro lines 10 (Cluny–La Sorbonne), 4 (Saint-Michel), and RER B (Luxembourg), which offer quick access in and out of the area.

Hopping on a bus to the area, (bus 38 or 47), is a more scenic and less hurried way to see the city.

As there are more and more cycling lanes, cycling has become more pleasant. For short hops or spontaneous detours, grab a Vélib' city rental bike from one of the many docking stations nearby.

LATIN QUARTER

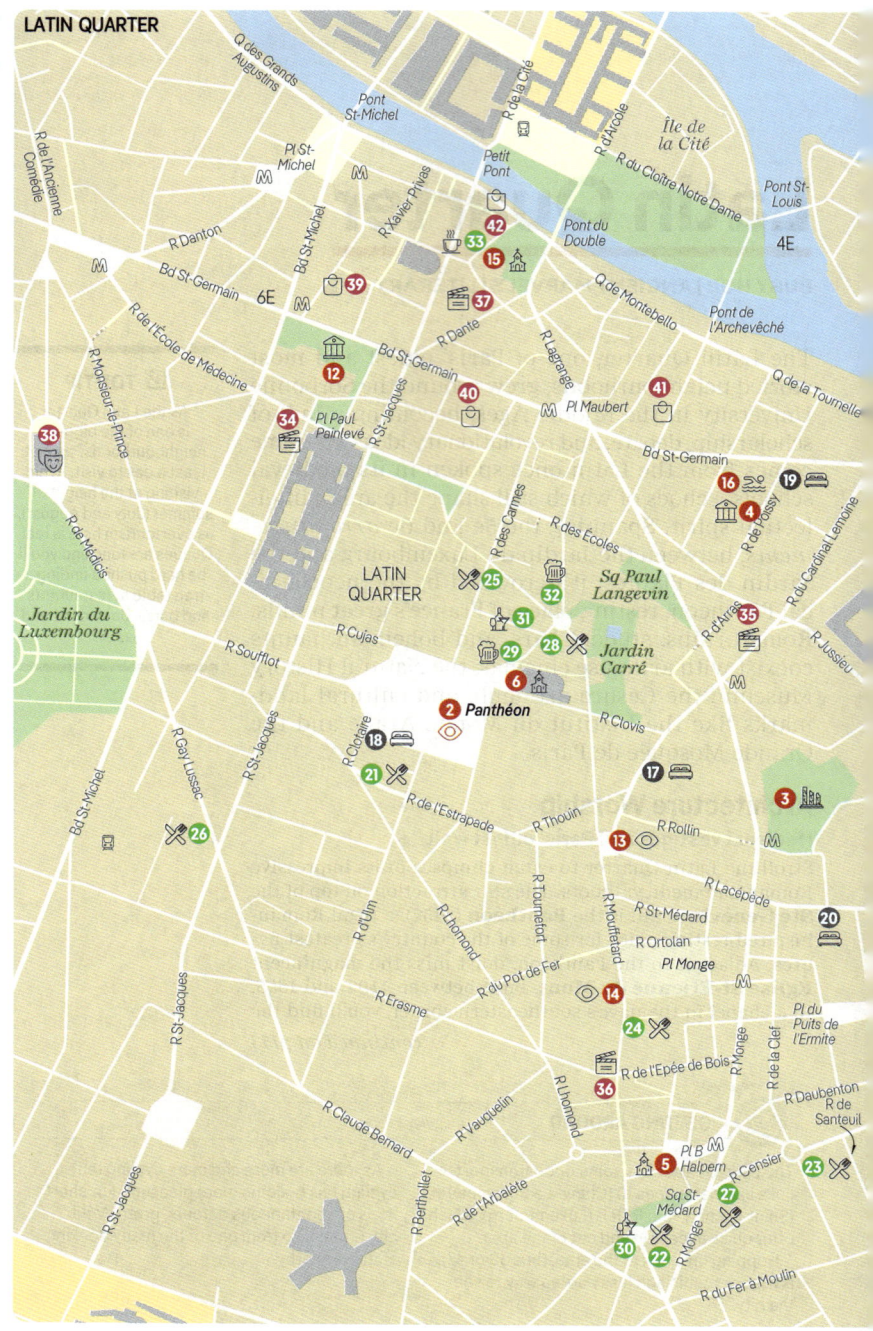

HIGHLIGHTS
1. Jardin des Plantes
2. Panthéon

SIGHTS
3. Arènes de Lutèce
4. Collège des Bernardins
5. Église Saint-Médard
6. Église St-Étienne du Mont
7. Galerie de Géologie et de Minéralogie
8. Grande Galerie de l'Évolution
9. Grande Mosquée de Paris
10. Institut du Monde Arabe
11. La Ménagerie
12. Musée de Cluny – Musée national du Moyen Âge
13. place de la Contrescarpe
14. rue Mouffetard
15. St-Julien-le-Pauvre

ACTIVITIES
16. Piscine Pontoise

SLEEPING
17. Hôtel des Grandes Écoles
18. Hotel Les Dames du Panthéon
19. Hôtel Pilgrim
20. Le Jardin de Verre by Locke

EATING
21. Café de la Nouvelle Mairie
22. Calice
23. Cantine de Césure
24. Dose
25. Jozi Brunch
26. Les Papilles
27. Pot O'Lait
28. TRAM

DRINKING & NIGHTLIFE
29. Bombardier
30. Cave La Bourgogne
31. Le Piano Vache
32. Le Violon Dingue
33. Tea Caddy

ENTERTAINMENT
34. Le Champo
35. Le Grand Action
36. L'Epée de Bois
37. Studio Galande
38. Théâtre de l'Odéon

SHOPPING
39. Abbey Bookshop
40. Librairie Eyrolles
41. Messy Nessy's Cabinet
42. Shakespeare & Company

THE GUIDE

PARIS LATIN QUARTER

TOP EXPERIENCE

Panthéon

The Panthéon, a neoclassical marvel, once held the title of Paris' tallest building. Today, it remains a prominent feature of the skyline, with stunning city views from its dome, accessible by 203 steps. Inside, it honours France's greatest thinkers, with a pediment depicting key figures of the Nation and Liberty: a symbol of intellectual and national pride.

Foucault's Pendulum

TOP TIPS

- Demand is high, particularly in summer (July and August). Book online as far in advance as possible.

- No cloakrooms or luggage storage on-site. Bags/luggage exceeding 20x40x40cm not permitted inside.

- Group tickets: reservations.pantheon@monuments-nationaux.fr

PRACTICALITIES

- paris-pantheon.fr/en
- 10am-6.30pm (Apr-Sep) & 10am-6pm (Oct-Mar)
- adult/child €13/free

Know the Backstory

The Panthéon was commissioned by King Louis XV around 1750 as an abbey dedicated to Ste Geneviève, Paris' patron saint, in gratitude for his recovery from illness. It wasn't until 1790, a year after the French Revolution, that it opened, when it played a secular role as the temple of the nation and mausoleum for the remains of key figures. But it did revert back to religious purposes several times.

Where France's Greatest Thinkers Rest

Two-time Nobel Prize–winner Marie Curie was the first woman to be interred based on achievement. In 2018, Auschwitz survivor, feminist icon and human-rights activist Simone Veil became the fifth woman to be interred. Other notable figures include Victor Hugo and Voltaire.

Foucault's Pendulum

Taking pride of place at the very heart of the Panthéon, Foucault's Pendulum is named after French physicist Léon Foucault. In 1851 he demonstrated the rotation of the Earth using laboratory apparatus rather than astronomical observations for the first time, by suspending the revolutionary device from the Panthéon's ceiling. The original pendulum is now housed at the **Musée des Arts et Métiers** (p115), while a working copy has been displayed at the Panthéon since 1995.

continued from p149

tomb of Ste Geneviève, the city's patron saint, who is said to have turned away Attila the Hun from Paris in 451 CE. Fans of the Woody Allen film *Midnight in Paris* will recognise the stone steps as the place where Owen Wilson's character is collected by a vintage car and transported back to the 1920s.

Don't miss the **Arènes de Lutèce**, a 2nd-century Roman amphitheatre that seated 10,000 people for gladiator fights. Found by accident in 1869 when rue Monge was under construction, it's now used by locals for playing football and boules.

Another architectural marvel is the **Collège des Bernardins** *(collegedesbernardins.fr; free)*. Dating back to 1248, this former Cistercian college originally served as the living quarters and place of study for novice monks. It's now an art gallery and Christian culture centre, with a range of events and free exhibits showcased under the stunning stone vaulted ceiling.

Medieval Market Street
Atmospheric shopping and lively student bars

Another remnant from the Middle Ages, **rue Mouffetard** slopes down from the Panthéon and narrows to just 7m in places. Once named after the foul-smelling *mouffette* (skunk) due to the polluted River Bièvre, this cobbled street has seen centuries of change. Though now lined with market stalls (except Mondays), casual dining venues and tourist-friendly restaurants, it still retains echoes of its past. The 16th-century **Église Saint-Médard**, with its beautiful stained-glass windows, stands as one of the few historical landmarks that survived the Revolution and Haussmann's redesign of Paris.

At the foot of rue Mouffetard lies **place de la Contrescarpe**, once called a 'cesspool' for its raucous goings-on by Hemingway but long favoured by literary icons. From Descartes to Simone de Beauvoir, and later Joyce and Hemingway himself, the area was a magnet for philosophers and writers drawn to its boisterous bars and dancehalls. While the wild nights of Parisian bohemia have faded, the square is still lively with people-watching and cafe terrace culture.

Beautiful Bookshops
English-language spots with Parisian soul

French literary giants and expatriate authors found creative refuge in both the city's cafes and bookshops, like the whimsical

continued on p156

FRANCE'S ACADEMIC CENTRE

The Latin Quarter has been the heart of French academia since the Middle Ages. Its honey-hued university buildings, including the Sorbonne and the beautiful Faculty of Medicine, echo centuries of intellectual life. The Sorbonne, restructured after the 1968 student protests, now comprises 10 autonomous universities with around 55,000 students. While most buildings are only open during the European Heritage Days each September, the Sorbonne Chapel welcomes visitors year-round. This historic neighbourhood blends scholarly prestige with a vibrant, lived-in atmosphere that continues to inspire students, writers and thinkers today.

 EATING IN THE LATIN QUARTER: OUR PICKS

TRAM: Restaurant serving homemade fare, from chia bowls in the morning to fresh ceviche, salads and cake. *9am-7pm Tue-Sat, 10am-5.30pm Sun* €

Calice: Retro bistro and wine bar that serves reliable staples like meaty *pâté en croûte* as well as lighter fish dishes and fancy desserts. *noon-2pm & 7-10pm Tue-Sun* €€

Café de la Nouvelle Mairie: Bistro food, around the corner from the Panthéon on a fountained square. Terrace in warmer months. *8am-midnight Mon-Fri* €€

Les Papilles: Pocket-size old-school bistro, wine bar and *épicerie* (specialist grocer) with excellent market-driven fare and natural wines. *noon-2pm & 6.30-10pm Tue-Sat* €€

TOP EXPERIENCE

Jardin des Plantes

A garden oasis with a wealth of museums – and even a dinosaur or two – the 24-hectare botanical garden lined by a double alley of plane trees, was originally created as a medicinal herb garden in 1626. There's plenty to see here, like the abundant exotic plants inside four elegant greenhouses (the Grandes Serres), each growing like mini-worlds of their own.

DON'T MISS

- The four greenhouses
- Paleontology & Compared Anatomy Gallery
- Gallery of Evolution
- Geology & Mineralogy Gallery
- Small zoo

Gardens & Four Greenhouses

Wander through the Jardin des Plantes and you'll find more than just a botanical garden – it's a living museum. Paths wind past centuries-old trees, seasonal blooms, and themed gardens, from medicinal plants to the tranquil Alpine Garden. Step into the soaring art deco greenhouses for a sensory journey through tropical rainforests and arid deserts. Inside, mist clings to lush leaves, orchids hang like jewels, and the air is thick with green. Open year-round, the gardens are free to enter, while the greenhouses require a ticket. Arrive early for a quiet stroll, or linger at golden hour when the light feels cinematic.

PRACTICALITIES

- jardindesplantesdeparis.fr/en
- garden: free; tickets required for museums/zoo/greenhouse
- hours vary seasonally, check website

Gallery of Paleontology & Compared Anatomy

The spectacle is striking: a majestic herd of large terrestrial and aquatic vertebrates stretches out before you in one of Paris' most transportive museums. The Gallery of Paleontology and Comparative Anatomy invites you to journey through 460 million years of evolution, with more than 2000 fossils – including 316 complete skeletons – on display. Marvel at the 25m-long diplodocus; a cast of a tyrannosaurus rex skull; cynthiacetus the whale ancestor; and even Sacabambaspis janvieri, one of the oldest known vertebrates. Upstairs on the balcony, more than 5000 fossils trace the delicate imprints of ancient life – from insect wings to the petals of the first flowers. It's worth taking your time here, as there is so much to see.

Gallery of Evolution

They don't speak, but they tell the story of life itself. In the **Grande Galerie de l'Évolution**, over 7000 preserved specimens trace the astonishing diversity of the natural world. Opened in 1994 within a soaring 19th-century hall designed by Jules André, the space marries history and science under a luminous 1000-sq-metre glass roof. On the ground floor, skeletons of marine giants – the southern right whale, blue whale, and sperm whale – greet visitors. Upper levels showcase land mammals and birds, with sweeping galleries providing views of the great 'procession of life' below. It's a theatrical, immersive celebration of Earth's biodiversity and evolution.

Geology & Mineralogy Gallery

The **Galerie de Géologie et de Minéralogie** dazzles with one of the world's oldest and most prestigious collections. Inside its elegant neoclassical hall, stretching 187m and framed by columned porticoes, visitors enter the spectacular 'Earth Treasures' room. Here, Martian meteorites, colossal crystals, rare rocks, and luminous minerals reveal the extraordinary story of our planet and solar system. Named after mineralogy pioneer René Just Haüy, the gallery is both a scientific and visual marvel. As you explore, learn to distinguish sulfur from quartz and cooking salt; though they have different chemical formulas, the same composition can create two distinct minerals, depending on their crystal structure. Carbon, for example, appears both as a pencil lead and as a diamond!

JARDIN DES PLANTES' ZOO

For a peaceful escape, visit the **Ménagerie** at the Jardin des Plantes, home to 500 animals across 150 species, many of which are endangered. One of the world's oldest zoos, it focuses on small and medium-sized species that thrive in its intimate enclosures. Wander through different habitats, from red pandas who stay in the trees to snow leopards perfectly adapted to snowy mountain environments, and witness the zoo's dedication to conservation and animal diversity. Designed for four-to-six-year-olds and seven-to-12-year-olds, the Ménagerie's web app lets children discover 15 species, including red pandas and Przewalski's horses, through fun challenges and quizzes.

TOP TIPS

● Go early in the morning or late in the afternoon to enjoy the gardens at their most peaceful, especially in spring (end of March to mid-April), when the cherry blossoms or peonies are in bloom.

● Don't miss the tucked-away Alpine Garden, often overlooked by tourists

● If you're with kids, the zoo, a conservation centre in a wide open space, is a delight.

Shakespeare & Company

LOCAL LATIN QUARTER

Audrey Demarre (@audreydemarre), a local multidisciplinary embroidery artist, lists some of her neighbourhood go-tos.

Messy Nessy's Cabinet: Run by Anglo-American Vanessa Grall, founder of the digital magazine *Messy Nessy Chic*. Her boutique is a charming, curious and witty selection of Parisian treasures.

Piscine Pontoise: The most beautiful swimming pool in Paris; an art deco gem. Countless films have been shot in this stunning setting, where swimming feels like pure pleasure.

Tea Caddy: A perfect spot for English-style teatime in a timeless Parisian cafe. Just steps from the River Seine, it feels almost like cosying up by a fireplace, and it hasn't changed in decades.

continued from p153

Shakespeare & Company *(shakespeareandcompany.com)*, a hub for expats since 1919. Originally it stood at 12 rue de l'Odéon, and regulars included Ernest Hemingway and F Scott Fitzgerald. When WWII broke out, it was forced to close. In 1951, new owner George Whitman reopened it in its current location at 37 rue de la Bûcherie. More than 70 years later, it's still a must-visit spot for its bewitching atmosphere and selection of works. There's also the cosy, Canadian-run **Abbey Bookshop** *(abbeybookshop.org)*, where towering stacks of books and regular readings invite lingering. The **Librairie Eyrolles** is a beloved Left Bank institution, known for its vast selection of art, design, and photography books. And along the Seine, the **bouquinistes** (p158) continue to sell vintage books, posters and magazines from green wooden stalls.

Calm at the Paris Mosque

A North African oasis for food and relaxation

One of the biggest mosques in France and Paris' central mosque, the **Grande Mosquée de Paris** *(grandemosqueedeparis.fr)* has a striking Moorish-style minaret, which peeks out from behind smooth white walls as you approach along the street. Visit the interior to see the intricate tile work

DRINKING IN THE LATIN QUARTER: OUR PICKS

Cave La Bourgogne: On pretty square St-Médard, it's perfect for soaking up the local vibes while sipping on a coffee or a glass of red. *7am-1am*

Le Violon Dingue: 'The crazy violin' is a studenty bar with sports showing on big screens upstairs and pub quizzes downstairs. *6pm-5am Tue-Sat*

Le Piano Vache: A 1970s rock den with live music on the weekends; it's a favourite on the student circuit. *5pm-2am Mon-Sat*

Bombardier: An old English pub with the best view of the Panthéon, located right across from the blockbuster monument that also serves food. *hours vary*

THE LATIN QUARTER'S ARCHITECTURE WALK

A compact tour that will give you a glimpse of the area's incredible history and essential stops.

START	END	LENGTH
St-Michel metro station	Grande Mosquée	1 day

Start at ❶ **St-Michel**, braving the crowds for a glimpse of Notre-Dame Cathedral across the River Seine. Peek at the medieval-style street ❷ **rue Galande** around the corner, and move on to the château-like ❸ **Cluny National Museum of the Middle Ages**, with its Roman thermal bath remains. As you edge closer to the grandiose Faculty of Medicine, you'll pass the art deco ❹ **Le Champo** (p158), one of a handful of arthouse cinemas in the area. Stop for a pastry at the near-century-old ❺ **Pâtisserie Viennoise**. Continue to the ❻ **Collège des Bernardins** (p153), a former 13th-century Cistercian college, and then to the Jean Nouvel–designed ❼ **Institut du Monde Arabe** (p158). Take a stroll around the 2nd-century ❽ **Arènes de Lutèce** (p153), a Roman-era amphitheatre, then head west on rue Clovis to see a section of the ❾ **wall of Philippe II Augustus**, the oldest city wall in Paris. Continue up the slight hill to see the ❿ **Église St-Étienne du Mont** (p149) and its marvellous façade, adjacent to the ⓫ **Panthéon** (p152), where the great thinkers of France rest. Across the square is the ⓬ **Panthéon-Sorbonne University**; this is one of the most famous buildings of the Sorbonne network. Walk southwards, past place de la Contrescarpe, and continue along ⓭ **rue Mouffetard** (p153) to see some of its medieval overhangs. Finish close to the Jardin des Plantes at the ⓮ **Grande Mosquée de Paris** for a steam bath.

THE BOUQUINISTES, THEN & NOW

Lining the top of the river banks at quai de la Tournelle, Pont Marie and quai du Louvre, faded boxes open to reveal *bouquinistes* (secondhand book stalls) selling out-of-print books, rare magazines, postcards and old posters.

In the 16th century, itinerant peddlers sold their wares on Parisian bridges. Sometimes their subversive (for example, Protestant) materials would get them into trouble with the authorities. By 1859 the city had wised up: official licences were issued and eventually the permanent boxes were installed.

and calligraphy. There is also a **North African hammam** (steam bathhouse) with timings for women and men, a pretty courtyard **restaurant** *(la-mosquee.com)* that serves delicious couscous, tagines and meat skewers, as well as a **tearoom** with sweet, fragrant mint tea and traditional cakes. There is also the possibility of smoking **shisha** in the front garden.

Arty Odéon
French film, history and Paris' oldest bas-relief

Named after the neoclassical Roman-inspired **Théâtre de l'Odéon** (inaugurated in 1782), one of the most famous in the city for its classic and contemporary plays, the Odéon area is at the crossroads of St-Germain des Prés and St-Michel. The metro is marked by an Odéon cinema and there is a clutch of arthouse cinemas scattered across the Latin Quarter that are popular with figures in the film industry. The art deco **Le Champo** *(cinema-lechampo.com)* opened in 1928 and is where director François Truffaut liked to go to see other directors' film retrospectives. Other notable independent cinemas include **Christine21** *(pariscinemaclub.com)*, owned by Oscar-winning actress Isabelle Huppert and her son; and **Cinéma St-André des Arts**, on the street of the same name. **Studio Galande** *(studiogalande.fr)* is another one to have on your list, especially if you want to see *The Rocky Horror Picture Show*, which has been shown every Friday and Saturday evening for the last four decades. When here, pay attention to the bas-relief above the door of **St-Julien-le-Pauvre** *(St Julian the Poor; sjlp-paris.org)* in a rowboat. It's a medieval sculpture from the 14th century, cited as being the oldest in Paris. Back toward rue Mouffetard, built in the 1970s, the pocket-sized arthouse cinema **L'Epée de Bois** *('the wooden sword'; cine-epeedebois.fr)* has two screens and shows recent (non-dubbed) French and other European flicks, and stands on the spot of a centuries-old theatre of the same name. The cinema **Le Grand Action**, 10 minutes away, shows cult international films too.

Must-Visit Museums
From the Middle Ages to the Arab World

The **Institut du Monde Arabe** *(Arab World Institute or IMA; imarabe.org; adult/child €10/free)* is an unsung museum with an extraordinary design by the French architect Jean Nouvel. It features a metallic screen of moving geometric motifs

EATING IN THE LATIN QUARTER: QUICK BITES

Pot O'Lait: Try tasty *galettes*, generously filled with goat's cheese and smoked salmon. *11.15am-2.30pm & 6.30-10pm Mon-Thu, 11.15am-2.30pm & 7-10.30pm Fri & Sat* €	**Dose**: Get your caffeine hit with artisan-roasted craft coffee and follow with a lunch of homemade quiche on rue Mouffetard. *8am-6pm Tue-Fri, 9am-6pm Sat & Sun* €	**Cantine de Césure**: Art hub Césure's canteen is a good-value, zero-waste spot with easy options like burgers and salads. *10am-11pm Tue-Sat* €	**Jozi Brunch**: Easy plates of avocado toast and fruit pancakes served most of the day. *8am-4pm Mon-Fri, 9am-5.30pm Sat & Sun* €

Théâtre de l'Odéon

designed to look like a *mashrabiya*, a window of ornate latticework in Islamic architecture, where the motifs are actually 240 light-sensitive shutters that automatically open to control the amount of light in the building. Founded by France and 18 Arab countries with the aim of creating a research hub about the Arab world, the IMA seeks to provide a secular location for the promotion of Arab civilisation, art, knowledge and aesthetics. There's a museum, library, auditorium, meeting rooms and a rooftop restaurant, Dar Mima, serving North African fare.

Another Latin Quarter standout is the **Musée de Cluny – Musée national du Moyen Âge** *(musee-moyenage.fr; adult/child €13/free)*, which showcases sublime medieval treasures, including the celebrated series of tapestries, the *Lady and the Unicorn* (1500). The buildings incorporate the 15th-century mansion Hotel de Cluny and the frigidarium (cold room) of a Roman-era bathhouse. Designed by architect Bernard Desmoulin, the contemporary entrance building houses the ticket office, bookshop, souvenir boutique and cloakroom. Following renovations, it now has enhanced explanatory panels and interactive displays. It is also possible to access the 1st-floor late-Gothic chapel, La Chapelle de l'Hôtel de Cluny, with rich carvings of Christ on the cross, 13 angels and floral and foliage ornaments. Make time to visit the little-known gardens too, restored in 2026. There's also a small cafe on site.

US JAZZ LEGENDS & PARIS

Ever since the end of WWI, France has provided US jazz musicians with both a stage and a measure of respect they were often denied at home – along with basic civil rights. The Latin Quarter, in particular, emerged after WWII as a sanctuary for jazz. In the 1940s and '50s, its smoky clubs welcomed talents like Bud Powell and Sidney Bechet, who found freedom and reverence in Paris' bohemian circles. Jean-Pierre Leloir's evocative book *Jazz Images* captures this deep French affection for the music and its makers. Paris wasn't paradise, but for many, it was a vital refuge and an inspiring one.

St-Germain & Les Invalides

FASHION | DESIGN | CAFE CULTURE

GETTING AROUND

Paris is a pretty compact city and easy to walk around, and St-Germain des Prés is one of the prettiest neighbourhoods for strolling.

The metro is quick, easy and cheap. The stations St-Germain des Prés (line 4) and Odéon (lines 4,10) will put you in the heart of the 6e *arrondissement*.

If you're comfortable cycling, you can pick up Vélib' bikes across the city. Sign up online for a one- or three-day ticket.

In the Middle Ages, the Left Bank was considered the countryside of Paris, dominated by open fields, known in French as *près* – hence the name St-Germain des Prés. But the development of the Abbey de St-Germain in the 6th century (where the Église St-Germain-des-Prés stands today) quickly turned the place into a spiritual and intellectual hot spot.

The area really came into its own at the turn of the 20th century when its lively cafe scene attracted creatives from across the globe with promises of rich intellectual banter over endless carafes of cheap table wine. Today St-Germain des Prés is home to some of the city's priciest real estate, and a few film stars, but reverberations of its colourful past still echo through its immaculately preserved cobblestone streets.

Go Shopping at Marché Biologique Raspail   MAP P165
Paris' largest organic food market

Every Sunday between 7.30am and 2.30pm on the bd Raspail (between rue de Sèvres and rue de Rennes), you'll find **Marché Biologique Raspail**, Paris' top organic food market. All the 50 or so stalls here must adhere to the national guidelines on organic produce. This, in turn, means that the prices are higher than at your usual neighbourhood market, but it's a great place for otherwise hard-to-find goods, such as freshly baked gluten-free bread, vegan curries and superfood powders like spirulina and maca.

Quiet Reading at Bibliothèque Mazarine   MAP P161
The oldest public library in France

Located within the Institute of France (the national body conceived to protect French culture) is the oldest public library in the country: **Bibliothèque Mazarine**. Once the private reading room of Cardinal Mazarin, today it is both a public workspace and national archive, containing a stunning

☑ TOP TIP

As you wander about, be sure to keep an eye out for plaques signposting the former abodes of creative titans. You'll quickly realise that almost every great thinker of the past 200 years once called this area home.

● HIGHLIGHTS
1. Jardin du Luxembourg

● SIGHTS
2. Église St-Germain-des-Prés
3. Église St-Sulpice
4. Le Bateau Ivre
5. Maison Gainsbourg
6. Monnaie de Paris
7. Musée National Eugène Delacroix
8. Square Laurent-Prache
9. Bibliothèque Mazarine

● SLEEPING
10. Hôtel Dame des Arts
11. Hôtel de l'Abbaye Saint-Germain
12. Hôtel St-André des Arts
13. L'Hôtel

● EATING
14. Boulangerie Liberté
15. Brasserie Lipp
16. Breizh Café Odéon
17. Café Pavane
18. Huîtrerie Regis
19. La Boissonnerie
20. Le Christine
21. Le Comptoir des Saints-Pères
22. Le Comptoir du Relais
23. Polidor

● DRINKING & NIGHTLIFE
24. Café de Flore
25. Café du Clown
26. Cafe Nuances
27. Castor Club
28. Cravan
29. La Balle au Bond
30. La Palette
31. Le Bar
32. Les Deux Magots
33. Maison Fleuret

● SHOPPING
34. Debauve & Gallais
35. Galerie Stéphane Olivier
36. Librairie François Chanut
see 7 Yvelines Antiques

collection of rare and ancient manuscripts. The resplendent reading room is open to the public from 10am to 6pm, Monday through Friday, but you must register on-site for an access card *(free for five days/annual pass €15).*

All visitors are then required to wash their hands before entering the room in absolute silence. As you are not allowed to simply thumb through the treasured volumes, the library organises free (and wonderfully informative) daily guided tours in both French and English.

TOP EXPERIENCE

Jardin du Luxembourg

A 22-hectare expanse along the southern edge of the Latin Quarter, the Jardin du Luxembourg is a beloved Parisian playground for children and adults alike. Today the former residence of Marie de' Médici houses the French Senate, and the flower- and orchard-filled gardens are its official property. Highlights include the 17th-century Médici Fountain, the Orangerie greenhouse, Musée du Luxembourg and lovely statues scattered among treelined paths.

TOP TIPS

● Timings vary depending on season, so check the site before making the trip.

● Be mindful of designated picnic spots, as not all lawns are permitted for use or you might get whistled off by the keeper.

PRACTICALITIES

● jardin.senat.fr
● 7.30/8.15am to 4.45/9.30pm season-depending ● free (except the Musée du Luxembourg; depends on the exhibition)

Thinking of Italy

Following the assassination of King Henri IV in 1610, Marie de' Médici became regent of France for her young son, Louis XIII. Feeling poorly housed at the Louvre and longing for the atmosphere of her native Italy, the queen decided to build an Italian-style palace of her own. In 1612, she acquired the Petit Luxembourg, a modest three-winged residence, which was lavishly transformed with gardens inspired by the Boboli Gardens in Florence.

Get Your Bearings

The focal point of the garden is the *grand bassin* (central pond) around which distinctive Fermob garden chairs are scattered – the perfect place to enjoy a picnic, read a book or simply rest weary legs. In the spring and summer months, the pond springs to life, as toy sailing boats race across its waters. There's a selection available to rent.

Leisure Pursuits

Tennis, pétanque courts, chess tables… There's a bevy of recreational activities, not to mention the delights for young children, including a playground and Paris' oldest merry-go-round, designed by Charles Garnier (the architect of the Palais Garnier, p80), and topped with an ancient ring-tilting game that's a rite of passage for Parisian kids.

A One-Stop Shop for French Luxury

MAP P165

The world's first department store

At the intersection of the ever-chic rue du Bac and rue de Sèvres stands **Le Bon Marché**, a shopping temple with elegant architecture that matches the luxurious fashion brands housed within. Founded in 1838, it's where shopping was transformed into an *art de vivre*.

In 1852, Le Bon Marché was taken over by husband-and-wife team Aristide and Marguerite Boucicaut, who drastically improved the customer experience with their department store vision. Before rich Parisians would shop in the *passages couverts* (covered passages) to protect them from the city's weather, while everyone else would go to shops specialised in selling just one thing, and they might not even be allowed to browse. The Boucicauts introduced a fixed-price system (haggling was still the norm) and installed amenities such as a reading room where people could wait while others shopped. The pair also improved the working conditions of the employees.

Although the eye-watering price tags of the goods for sale are no longer exactly 'a good deal' (the store's name translated into English), to wander Le Bon Marché is to experience the world of historic French luxury – without having to spend a euro. Take the central escalators, which were designed by Andrée Putman with now iconic square panels to mirror the original ceiling above. In fact, don't forget to always look up while you're browsing around the designer clothes and beauty brands; Gustave Eiffel designed many of the building's wrought-iron ceilings along with architect Louis-Charles Boileau. The Eiffel-designed ceiling in La Librarie, the store's bookshop, is said to hold more weight in the iron than the Eiffel Tower. And don't forget to stop in at the bathrooms (complete with an old-school powder room) – the Boucicauts were the first to innovate in-store separate-sex bathrooms. Now the store continues to innovate with a regular events programme that includes art exhibitions and dance and acrobatic performances.

If all the browsing has made you peckish, pop next door (or across one of the connecting bridges) to **La Grande Épicerie**

> **RIMBAUD'S THE DRUNKEN BOAT**
>
> Wander down quaint rue Férou (where Hemingway once lived) in the 6th arrondissement and you'll notice a wordy mural that's unlike any of the other graffiti scrawled across the city's façades. Take a step back from the wall and you can parse together the lengths of French poet Arthur Rimbaud's masterpiece **Le Bateau Ivre** (The Drunken Boat). Written when he was just a teenager, the symbolist ballad recounts a journey aboard a sinking ship at sea. The rue Férou mural was commissioned in 2012 by the French government, with support from a Dutch poetry society, as an homage to the poet. Local folklore has it that Rimbaud first recited it at a location nearby – hence the mural's peculiar setting.

 EATING IN ST-GERMAIN-DES-PRÉS: OUR PICKS — MAP P161

La Boissonnerie: Contemporary bistro serving seasonal dishes alongside a great wine list. Friendly, lively setting. *12.30-2.30pm & 7-10.30pm* €€

Café Pavane: Run by the daughter of chocolatier Jean-Paul Hévin, the menu features Russian-inspired dishes. *11am-7.30pm Wed-Sun* €

Le Christine: Gastronomic creations (and plant-based options) in unpretentious setting. Fantastic wines. *noon-2pm & 7-10pm* €€€

Breizh Café Odéon: Paris-wide crêperie serves the best *galettes* and crêpes. Great for dining in groups/with kids. *10am-11pm* €

Huîtrerie Régis: Best oysters in Paris. Can quickly get booked out. *noon-2.30pm & 6.30-10.30pm Mon-Fri, 2-10pm Sat & Sun* €€€

Le Comptoir des Saints-Pères: Classic bistro with a very local crowd. Hemingway and Picasso also used to pop by. *7am-11pm* €€

Polidor: Historic bistro, frequented by the likes of Rimbaud, James Joyce and Ernest Hemingway. *noon-3pm and 7pm-midnight* €€

Le Comptoir du Relais: Classic French dishes served nonstop, which is hard to find in Paris, with a selection of natural wines. *noon-11pm* €€

Café de Flore

THE LADIES' PARADISE

Le Bon Marché was the inspiration for the novel *Au Bonheur des Dames* (The Ladies' Paradise) by French author Émile Zola. Published in 1883, the book detailed the innovations of the department store but also its role in destroying local boutiques, as all goods were now gathered under one roof.

But more pertinently for Zola, Le Bon Marché represented a step towards women's emancipation. Over half of the store's workforce were women – unheard of at the time – and unmarried women were provided accommodation in dormitories located in the store, and even classes in singing, art and so on, giving them a sense of independence and the opportunity to work in public-facing roles outside the home or factories.

de Paris, Le Bon Marché's gourmet food store. The selection is staggering, with breads and pastries made fresh on-site each morning.

Literary Libations

MAP P161

Raising a glass to Hemingway

St-Germain is home to some of the most famous dining establishments beloved by the 20th century's greatest writers, artists and philosophers.

Les Deux Magots, located on place St-Germain des Près, is considered by many to be the 1930s birthplace of surrealism, as the likes of André Breton, Man Ray and Max Ernst gathered here to plan out the movement's manifesto. Lost Generation writers James Joyce and Ernest Hemingway were also regulars – it is believed that the latter penned his great novel *The Sun Also Rises* at one of the back tables.

Across the road is rival literary haunt **Café de Flore**. Although creative people were known to flit between each cafe, Flore had one great advantage: a fireplace-heated upper floor where writers came to work during the frosty winter months. It was here that great existentialist philosophers like Simone de Beauvoir, Jean-Paul Sartre and Albert Camus would write their defining oeuvres.

DRINKING IN ST-GERMAIN-DES-PRÉS: BEST COFFEE SHOPS — MAP P161, P165

Ten Belles: The Left Bank outpost of beloved British Franco bakery Ten Belles, famed for delicious sourdough loaves. *8.30am-4.30pm Mon-Fri, 9am-5pm Sat & Sun*

Café du Clown: Great coffee, good spot for people-watching from the terrace outside the Marché St-Germain. Note that the toilet is inside the market. *8am-6pm*

Cafe Nuances: Hole-in-the-wall for freshly baked pastries and coffee to go. Beans in reusable cloth bags make great gifts. *8am-7pm Mon-Fri, from 9am Sat & Sun*

Maison Fleuret: Cute coffee shop inside historic former bookshop. Plant-based dishes and pastries from Maison Fleuret's baking school. *9am-6.30pm Wed-Sun*

★ HIGHLIGHTS
1 Hôtel des Invalides
2 Musée d'Orsay

● SIGHTS
3 Dôme des Invalides
4 Jardin Catherine-Labouré
5 Musée de l'Armée
6 Musée Rodin
7 Square Boucicaut
8 Square Roger-Stéphane

● EATING
9 Café Central
see 9 Café du Marché
10 Davoli
11 Maison Bergeron
12 Poilâne
13 Tapisserie

● DRINKING & NIGHTLIFE
14 Bar Joséphine
15 Le Flow

see 9 Petitbon
16 Rosa Bonheur sur Seine
17 Ten Belles

● SHOPPING
18 Chapon
19 Jacques Genin
20 Kaviari
21 La Grande Épicerie de Paris
22 La Sablaise
23 Le Bon Marché

see 20 Le Chocolat Alain Ducasse
24 Le Repaire de Bacchus
25 Marché Biologique Raspail
see 20 Mariage Frères
26 Marie-Anne Cantin
27 Patrick Roger

Today, it comes down to personal preference, but be warned that you might be queuing for a while for a seat. Ask for a terrace table if you want to people-watch over a coffee, or go in the early evening for an aperitif.

Down the road on rue de Seine is **La Palette**, a lesser-known but equally storied bar that was frequented by artists such as Picasso and Cézanne. Today, its creative vibe lives on, as it's the local hangout spot for students from the nearby fine-arts school L'École des Beaux-Arts.

continued on p168

TOP EXPERIENCE

Musée d'Orsay

The second-most-visited museum in France after the Louvre, the Musée d'Orsay is housed in a former railway station and contains one of the most important collections of impressionist and postimpressionist works in the world. There's sublime architecture and masterpieces from Monet and Cézanne; plan on spending at least half a day here immersing yourself in modern French art history.

DON'T MISS

Édouard Manet's *Le Déjeuner sur l'herbe*

Vincent Van Gogh's *Starry Night Over the Rhône*

Edgar Degas' *La Petite Danseuse de Quatorze Ans*

Claude Monet's *Londres, le Parlement*

A Living History of Architecture

As you enter the Musée d'Orsay, take a pause to notice the layout of the ground floor, with sculptures in two straight rows, and small galleries annexed along the outer edges of the space. It was organised to mimic the layout of the original railway station within which it is housed. Given the sheer significance of the encasing building, it was decided from the outset that the Musée d'Orsay would elevate the history of architecture to the same revered rung as that of the history of art. Accordingly, galleries dedicated to the museum's impressive collection of architectural drawings by the likes of Gustave Eiffel and Viollet-le-Duc interject those allocated to fine art.

PRACTICALITIES

● musee-orsay.fr ● adult/concession €16/13 ● 9.30am-6pm Tue-Sun, to 9.45pm Thu

At the end of the ground floor is a space dedicated to the history of Paris' urban development. Look below you and you'll notice an intricate scaled model of the city as it stood in 1914 when the museum first opened.

The Impressionists

Most people visit the Musée d'Orsay for its collection of impressionist works and rightly so: the 5th floor of the museum is largely dedicated to the movement. By tracing the galleries in a clockwise direction you'll get a fairly comprehensive overview of the development of the movement from impressionism to postimpressionism to neo-impressionism. Here is where the movement's masterpieces, such as Monet's *Londres, le Parlement*, Van Gogh's *Starry Night Over the Rhône*, and Edgar Degas' sculpture *La Petite Danseuse de Quatorze Ans* are exhibited alongside other fabled modern works, such as Cézanne's *Nature morte* series.

Cinema as Art

Few people know that, from its beginnings, the Musée d'Orsay has devoted one of its sections to the history of cinema and cinematography, innovating an approach that considers film as art, and not simply as technique or entertainment. On the 5th floor, tucked away alongside the impressionist collection, is a gallery tracing the medium's history and technical developments, with projections of short clips from pivotal films in the medium's history. To complement this venture, the Musée d'Orsay often holds screenings in its auditorium of some of the most important works of cinema from the early 20th century. Check the official website for a schedule.

History Through a Contemporary Lens

Although the focus of the Musée d'Orsay is modern art from the period between 1848 and 1914, several times a year the museum invites the biggest names in today's contemporary art scene, such as Jean-Philippe Delhomme, Marlene Dumas and Peter Doig, to curate exhibitions featuring their own works interwoven with selections from the permanent collection. By placing contemporary art in direct dialogue with historical masterpieces, it urges us to consider the works with a fresh perspective while emphasising their enduring importance. On one Thursday evening per month, the museum also hosts 'Curious Thursdays', when young artists from other creative worlds (like dance and music) are invited to perform among the art. Check the website for schedule details.

THEMED TOURS

It's impossible to view the entire collection in one day – instead it's advisable to pick one or two of the themes mentioned as entry points to discover the collection. Alternatively, take one of the museum's themed guided tours. Held daily in English, French and Italian, the 1½-hour tours are centred around fun themes such as masterpieces, animals and parties. Check the museum's website for departure times.

TOP TIPS

● Book your ticket online in advance so that you can skip the snaking queues to enter.

● The best time to visit is when it opens at 9.30am or on Thursday evenings when the museum is open until 9.45pm.

● Rent an audioguide, which provides commentary from the museum's curators on over 300 works.

● Entry to the museum is free on the first Sunday of every month, but you'll have to reserve a time slot in advance via the museum's website.

● Break up your visit with a pause in the museum's gilded tearoom, which was formerly the railway station's dining room.

SECRET GARDENS

For leafy respite from the city, seek out one of the St-Germain des Prés' gardens.

Jardin Catherine-Labouré: This little-known garden is located just a stone's throw from Le Bon Marché on the grounds of a former 17th-century convent.

Square Roger-Stéphane: Another green oasis, which you can find at the end of the pedestrian street rue Juliette Récamier, off rue de Sèvres.

Square Laurent-Prache: It's easy to miss this little square, even though it's hidden in plain sight right next to the Benedictine abbey of St-Germain des Prés.

Square Boucicaut: This large square behind St-Sulpice metro station is great for kids, or for enjoying an ice cream from the nearby Le Bac à Glaces.

Chapel of the Holy Angels, Église St-Sulpice

continued from p165

Although literary folklore would make it seem like artists subsisted entirely on coffee and dry sherry, à la Ernest Hemingway, even the most starved of them had to eat at some point – which is why they'd head to **Brasserie Lipp**, the favourite of French poets Paul Verlaine and Guillaume Apollinaire. While it's still popular with writers today, it also pulls in France's most high-profile politicians. Jacques Chirac's favourite table was on the left of the entrance if you are looking into the restaurant.

Finish off your literary tour with an after-dinner drink at **L'Hôtel**, where Oscar Wilde died in 1900 of meningitis. Wilde had made what was then known as L'Hotel d'Alsace his home and famously declared in his final days, 'My wallpaper and I are fighting a duel to the death. One of us has got to go'. Although the building – and its wallpaper – have since been given a luxurious renovation, the bar remains open for guests wishing to pay homage to the illustrious writer.

Serge Gainsbourg's Legacy   MAP P161
Paris' most personal 'museum'

Until September 2023, the heavily graffitied former abode of French singer Serge Gainsbourg, located at 5bis rue de Verneil,

 DRINKING IN ST-GERMAIN-DES-PRÉS: BEST COCKTAIL BARS   — MAP P161, P165

Cravan: The big sister to the original Cravan in the 16e. Expect cool design and excellent cocktails and, as a bonus, you can even book. *5pm-1am Tue-Fri, from noon Sat*

Castor Club: Look for an unnamed wood-panelled door to find this hunting lodge-inspired bar with a soundtrack of country music. *7pm-2am Tue & Wed, to 4am Thu-Sat*

Bar Joséphine: Once frequented by Picasso and Josephine Baker, this palace hotel bar serves up excellent cocktails and draws a local (sometimes celeb) crowd. *5pm-1am*

Le Bar: Chef Cyril Lignac's sexy cocktail bar (not to be confused with restaurant Bar des Prés across the road) is great for starting/ending the evening. *7pm-1am Wed-Sat*

had never been open to the public – despite being a site of pilgrimage for the singer's massive fan base.

Now, **Maison Gainsbourg** (*maisongainsbourg.fr; adult/ concession €12/6, house & museum from €16*) has been opened to all by his daughter Charlotte Gainsbourg, who has personally narrated the 30-minute audioguide to give visitors an intimate and rather poignant glimpse into his private life and her childhood. After you've finished your tour of the house, you head across the street to the museum, which showcases 450 personal objects across eight chapters of Gainsbourg's life and musical career. It's all in French, so make sure to pick up the English-language booklet that accompanies it at the entrance. There's also a cafe and cocktail bar (named Le Gainsbarre) as an homage to the late-night venues the musician was so fond of, and it's free to pop by for a drink even if you're not visiting the house or museum. Bear in mind that as the house is small, and to keep the personal feel of the visit, only a few people are allowed in at a time, meaning that tickets sell out well in advance. If you don't manage to get any, you can still book for just the museum so you don't miss out completely.

Majestic Masterpieces in St-Sulpice   MAP P161
Divine Delacroix and pious Pigalle

Despite being just 1 sq metre smaller than the Notre Dame de Paris, the **Église St-Sulpice** has long lived in its shadow – until Dan Brown's *The Da Vinci Code* drew crowds to the monumental Roman Catholic church in search of the hidden treasures detailed in his epic novel.

Construction of the current church began in 1642, but it passed through the hands of several different architects – which accounts for its unique mishmash of baroque and neoclassical references – until work was halted entirely by the French Revolution. In fact, the right tower on the church's western façade (designed by Italian architect Servandoni, who drew inspiration from London's St Paul's Cathedral) remains unfinished to this day.

But what's so special about Église St-Sulpice is the artworks contained within. Immediately to your right after entering, in the Chapel of the Holy Angels, are three well-preserved wax murals painted by French artist Eugène Delacroix between 1855 and 1861. Also look out for the peculiar pair of holy water fonts, located on either side of the nave and the giant clamshells, which were gifted to King Francis I by the

ÉGLISE ST-GERMAIN-DES-PRÉS

Before Notre Dame de Paris was completed, **Église St-Germain-des-Prés**, located at place St-Germain, was the central church of worship for Parisians. The church in its current form was built in the 11th century, yet it had been the site of a Benedictine abbey since 558. In the 8th century, it was renamed in honour of St-Germain, a former bishop of the city. The church has since undergone many transformations, including the addition of the flying buttresses, but the bell tower on the western façade remains practically unchanged since 990. Don't forget to visit the adjoining Chapelle de St-Symphorien, left over from the original abbey, under which St-Germanus is believed to be buried.

There's indoor seating here to eat in.

 EATING IN ST-GERMAIN-DES-PRÉS: BEST BAKERIES   MAP P161, P165

| **Maison Bergeron**: Consistently voted as having one of the top 10 croissants by the Greater Paris Bakers' Union. *7am-8.15pm Mon-Sun* € | **Poilâne**: Perhaps France's most famous *boulangerie* (bakery): sourdough *miches* (big round country loaves), *punitions* (butter cookies), apple tarts. *7.15am-8pm Mon-Sat* € | **Boulangerie Liberté**: Chic, new-wave *boulangerie* with buttery croissants made on-site. Locations around Paris. *7.30am-8pm Mon-Sat, 8.30am-5pm Sun* € | **Tâpisserie**: Delicious creations from team behind seafood restaurant Clamato and one-Michelin-star Septime. *8.30am-7pm Wed-Fri, 9.30am-9pm Sat, 9.30am-5pm Sun* € |

THE ROYAL HISTORY OF CHOCOLATE

In 1779 when Sulpice Debauve was appointed Louis XVI and Marie-Antoinette's pharmacist, the Versailles court had already adopted a chocolate habit. At the time chocolate was always drunk, not eaten, but when Marie-Antoinette began to complain about the bitterness of her migraine medicine, Debauve had the idea to sweeten the remedy with cacao and almond milk and presented the Queen with the first solid chocolate. These round chocolate medallions, which were shaped like ancient coins, instantly won royal approval and Marie-Antoinette's pistoles, as she called them, can still be found in the **Debauve & Gallais** shop today.

Venetian Republic, that sit atop stone bases hand-carved with sea motifs by Jean-Baptiste Pigalle. The white marble statue of Mary, located at the far end of the church, was also sculpted by the prolific artist.

Throughout the year, classical-music recitals are held at the church, with tickets available online from L'Officiel des Spectacles or directly on-site before each performance.

Péniche Party

MAP P161 & P165

Aperitifs to float your boat

Where the 6e and 7e *arrondissements* meet the Seine are several *péniches* – houseboats docked permanently along the riverbanks. Some are still private homes, while others have been converted into restaurants, bars and clubs – they're a great way to experience the city's most famous waterway.

Rosa Bonheur sur Seine is the most popular *péniche*, known for its club nights and live music (with everything from salsa to jazz). Be sure to check out its official Facebook page for a complete schedule. Tickets are required for certain events and often sell out in advance. Purchase drinks and food on board and enjoy on the nearby riverside benches.

If you want a more ambient aperitif, then **La Balle au Bond** will be your pick of the *péniches*. The plant-lined rooftop terrace makes the perfect place to relax, drink in hand, while watching the sunset over the Seine. It's open daily for aperitifs and dinner, and on Saturdays and Sundays for brunch.

If you're ready to dance the night away, head to **Le Flow**, a *péniche* with views of the glorious Pont Alexandre III. It regularly hosts live DJ sets on its rooftop and stays open until the early hours on Saturdays and Sundays.

A Cabinet of Military Curiosities

MAP P165

Les Invalides and Musée de L'Armée

At the end of the sprawling Esplanade des Invalides stands the **Hôtel des Invalides**, the hospital commissioned by Louis XIV for wounded soldiers (partially in operation today) and from which some 32,000 weapons were pillaged by revolutionaries before the storming of the Bastille prison on 14 July 1789.

Today, the Hôtel also houses various museums, the main one being **Musée de L'Armée** *(musee-armee.fr; adult/concession/under 26 years €17/12/free)*, France's national military museum. With over 500,000 artefacts, it has the third-largest collection of weapons and armour in the world. Don't be

 EATING IN ST-GERMAIN-DES-PRÉS: BEST CHOCOLATE SHOPS — MAP P165

Jacques Genin: Some of the silkiest, smoothest chocolates in Paris. The caramels and *pâtes de fruits* might be the best in the city. *10.30am-7pm Tue-Sat* €€

Chapon: There are a few outlets across Paris but try to find ones with a Bar à Mousse aux Chocolats for a cone of absolutely delicious, thick chocolate mousse. *hours vary* €

Jean-Paul Hévin: Fabulous chocolate desserts as well as chocolate boxes. Pick up a box of the excellent macarons too. *10am-7.30pm Tue-Sat* €

Patrick Roger: Minimalist interiors highlight the purity of the high-quality chocolates. Three locations in the 6th *arrondissement*. *hours vary* €€

EAT YOUR WAY THROUGH RUE CLER

The pedestrian-only rue Cler is perhaps the most famous market street in Paris – plan on spending half a day discovering the street's gastronomical goodies.

START	END	LENGTH
Petitbon	Le Chocolat Alain Ducasse	650m; 1hr

As it's never a good idea to shop on an empty stomach, begin at 1 **Petitbon** for sandwiches and the best coffee in the neighbourhood. Before continuing down rue Cler, take a slight detour west along rue du Champ de Mars to stock up on cheese from local legend fromager 2 **Marie-Anne Cantin**.

Trace your steps back to rue Cler and continue north along the street. As no French meal can begin without an aperitif, stop at 3 **Davoli** for nibbles. Yes, it is an Italian *épicerie* but it sells the finest charcuterie on the street. Alternatively, order a glass of wine at 4 **Café du Marché** and 5 **Café Central**, which have the biggest terraces for people-watching.

If oysters are in season, stop by 6 **La Sablaise**, located just two doors down the street, where the staff will happily prepare a platter to go. Pop across the road to 7 **Le Repaire de Bacchus** and pick up a bottle of Petit Chablis to wash the oysters down with.

For foodie souvenirs, head to 8 **Kaviari** for caviar, and 9 **Mariage Frères** for some of Paris' best teas, packaged up in its signature beautiful black canisters. Saving the best until last, finish up at 10 **Le Chocolat Alain Ducasse**, the chocolate shop from the giant of French gastronomy, Alain Ducasse.

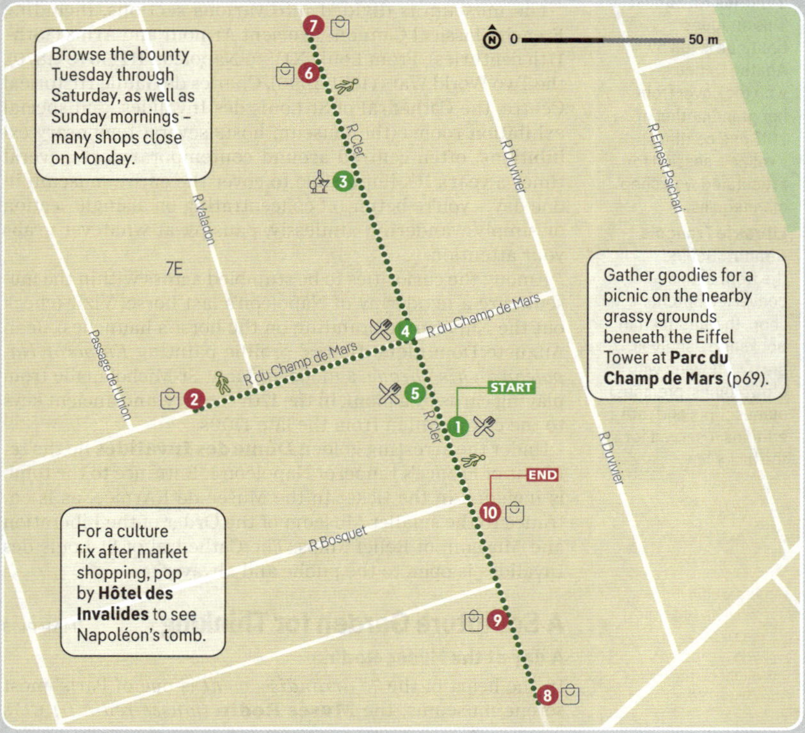
Browse the bounty Tuesday through Saturday, as well as Sunday mornings – many shops close on Monday.
0
50 m
R Cler
R Duvivier
R Ernest Psichari
R Valadon
7E
Gather goodies for a picnic on the nearby grassy grounds beneath the Eiffel Tower at **Parc du Champ de Mars** (p69).
R du Champ de Mars
Passage de l'Union
START
END
R Bosquet
For a culture fix after market shopping, pop by **Hôtel des Invalides** to see Napoléon's tomb.
1
2
3
4
5
6
7
8
9
10

ANTIQUE HUNTING

Marin Montagut (@marinmontagut), illustrator, designer and author, shares his favourite places.

Galerie Stéphane Olivier: Olivier exhibits a mix of Scandinavian furniture from the '50s to the '70s and works by contemporary designers. I love immersing myself in his timeless selection, which echoes nature and inspires harmony and poetry.

Yvelines Antiques: This antiques boutique is run by Agathe Derieux, who took over from her grandmother in 2013 and continues Yveline's passion for articulated workshop mannequins.

Librairie François Chanut: Behind the front of this converted butcher's shop, this antiquarian bookshop's shelves are overflowing with old volumes, precious manuscripts and rare editions reserved for the lucky few.

Musée Rodin

deterred from visiting if warfare and military paraphernalia are not your thing – the 8000-sq-metre complex is more of a gigantesque cabinet of curiosities with something to pique everyone's interest.

The museum is divided into various sections, including French Classical Cannons, Ancient Armour and Arms (13th–17th centuries), From Louis XIV to Napoléon III (1643–1870), the Two World Wars (1871–1990), Charles de Gaulle Historical Centre, the Cathedral of St-Louis des Invalides, and special exhibition rooms (the museum hosts several temporary exhibitions, often centred around contemporary art, several times a year). It's impossible to cover the entire museum in one day – you're better off concentrating on a single section or simply wandering aimlessly, pausing at whatever grabs your attention.

Among the curiosities to be stumbled across within the museum are a taxidermy of Napoléon's last horse, Vizir (check out the Napoléonic branding on the horse's haunches), Jean Auguste Dominique Ingres' prolific painting *Emperor Napoléon on his Throne*, a model of Mont St-Michel made from playing cards by a monk in the 17th century, and ancient keys to the city of Milan from the late 1700s.

Under the arresting golden **Dôme des Invalides** lie the remains of France's Emperor Napoléon I. Entrance to the tomb is included in the ticket to the Musée de L'Armée, as is entrance to the smaller Museum of the Order of the Liberation and Museum of Relief Maps. The Cathedral of St-Louis des Invalides is open to the public and always free.

A Sculpture Garden for Thinking

MAP P165

A day at the Musée Rodin

In the heart of the 7e *arrondissement* is one of Paris' most serene museums, the **Musée Rodin** *(musee-rodin.fr; €15)*, dedicated to the prolific oeuvre of French sculptor Auguste Rodin. The museum is housed within the 19th-century Hôtel Biron, a former aristocratic mansion where Rodin had two showrooms and which was chosen by the sculptor himself to become a museum after his death. It now contains some 6000 sculptures and 8000 drawings by Rodin (though not all are on display!), including 30 of Rodin's most famous artworks, plus a room dedicated to sculptor Camille Claudel, who was at various points also Rodin's collaborator, muse and lover.

Rodin is considered by many an art historian to be the founder of modern sculpture, known for his unparalleled talent to translate the complexities of human emotion into meticulously sculpted clay, bronze and plaster works. Among his most famous sculptures are *The Thinker*, *The Kiss* and *The Gates of Hell* – all of which are on show at the museum. But what makes this museum so special is its tranquil sculpture garden, which is used to present some of Rodin's works. Although it's a beautiful space all year round, and it's interesting to see how the sculptures catch the light in different seasons, the months of April and May are particularly lovely when the garden's Rodin roses – of course named after the sculptor – are in full bloom. There's also a cafe with an outdoor terrace, which is a particularly lovely spot to stop for a coffee and enjoy the gardens. Also look out for two temporary exhibitions a year, one of which, Atelier Rodin, is designed for children aged six months to 10 years to learn about sculpture in a fun, hands-on way.

The Musée Rodin is open from Tuesday, a particularly busy day after being closed on Monday, through to Sunday. An entry ticket provides you with access to both the museum and the garden, and guided tours are also available, but only in French.

An Intimate Look at Delacroix   MAP P161
The painter's works and apartment

Tucked away in the charming place Furstemberg is a small museum dedicated to Delacroix, **Musée National Eugène Delacroix** *(musee-delacroix.fr; adult/under 18 years €9/free)*, housed in the painter's former apartment. Delacroix chose the location to be close to the nearby St-Sulpice church while he was working there on three large-scale murals, which you can still see today. It's also where Delacroix ended up spending the last few years of his life with his loyal housekeeper, whose former room is now where the museum's lift is. The rest of the rooms have been transformed into the museum, including Delacroix's atelier in the garden, although none of his possessions remain, as they were all sold after his death. For Delacroix fans, seeing the smaller paintings here is a nice complement to viewing his more famous and much larger works in the Louvre, and as you can imagine, a much quieter place to enjoy the artist's work. Note that although the museum is wheelchair accessible, Delacroix's atelier in the garden at the back isn't. If you'd like a guided tour in English, email the museum, which can organise a visit with an external guide.

FRANCE'S OLDEST BUSINESS

The **Monnaie de Paris** (The Paris Mint) is the oldest enterprise in France, created in 864 by King Charles II. It's been in continuous operation ever since, although not always in the same majestic building that you see now. When King Louis XV realised that the 14th-century workshop on rue de la Monnaie was no longer suitable for minting royal coins, he commissioned a bigger and better building on the other side of the Seine. Designed in the fashionable neoclassical style, the mint was finished in 1775: the year after Louis XV died. Minting coins was serious business; forgers were boiled alive until the French Revolution came along. When it did, the building was surprisingly left untouched: even the Revolutionists understood and respected how important coins were for daily life.

Montparnasse & Southern Paris

BRASSERIES | ECLECTIC LIFE | STREET ART

☑ TOP TIP

Take a lift to the 27th floor of the **TOO** (p182) luxury hotel for sensational views from the rooftop bar. The distinctive skyscraper **Tour Montparnasse** (p182) also has views of Paris from the indoor observatory.

If you're in search of a Paris that few visitors take time to explore, southern Paris will appeal to you. You can start with fabled Montparnasse and its legendary brasseries before delving into the huge 15e *arrondissement*. This is a very tranquil part of Paris, with lots of greenified areas, wonderful local parks and atmospheric squares. In the 14e *arrondissement*, you'll find yet-to-be-discovered micro-neighbourhoods and great picnic-friendly parks. And then, to the east, there's the fast-evolving 13e, with Paris' largest Chinatown, pocket-sized districts that scream village life, some striking street art and even more stunning contemporary architecture, including the fabulous Duo Towers – a recent landmark in the city. Who said southern Paris was boring?

Feel the Pulse of La Butte Aux Cailles   MAP P181
A mix of village life and urban vibes

Much less touristy and congested than other Parisian villages such as Montmartre or Mouffetard, **La Butte aux Cailles** extends on a gently sloping hill immediately west of place d'Italie. Wandering its cobblestone streets bordered by low-rise buildings, you'll feel teleported to another era in rural France. Its main thoroughfare is rue de la Butte aux Cailles, lined with

continued on p178

GETTING AROUND

Use metro line 6 to get from one *arrondissement* to the next. Montparnasse Bienvenüe is the metro hub for Montparnasse and the 15e. Bibliothèque François-Mitterrand and place d'Italie are convenient 13e stops.

Buses fill the gap in areas lacking comprehensive metro coverage. Bus 62 travels from Bibliothèque François-Mitterrand to Javel via the southern quartiers. Bus 39 links Balard with Gare du Nord via Gare Montparnasse.

For cycling, handy Vélib' Métropole stations include 5-7 rue d'Odessa, 14e; 13 bd Edgar Quinet, 14e; 2 av René Coty, 14e; and two facing place d'Italie, 13e.

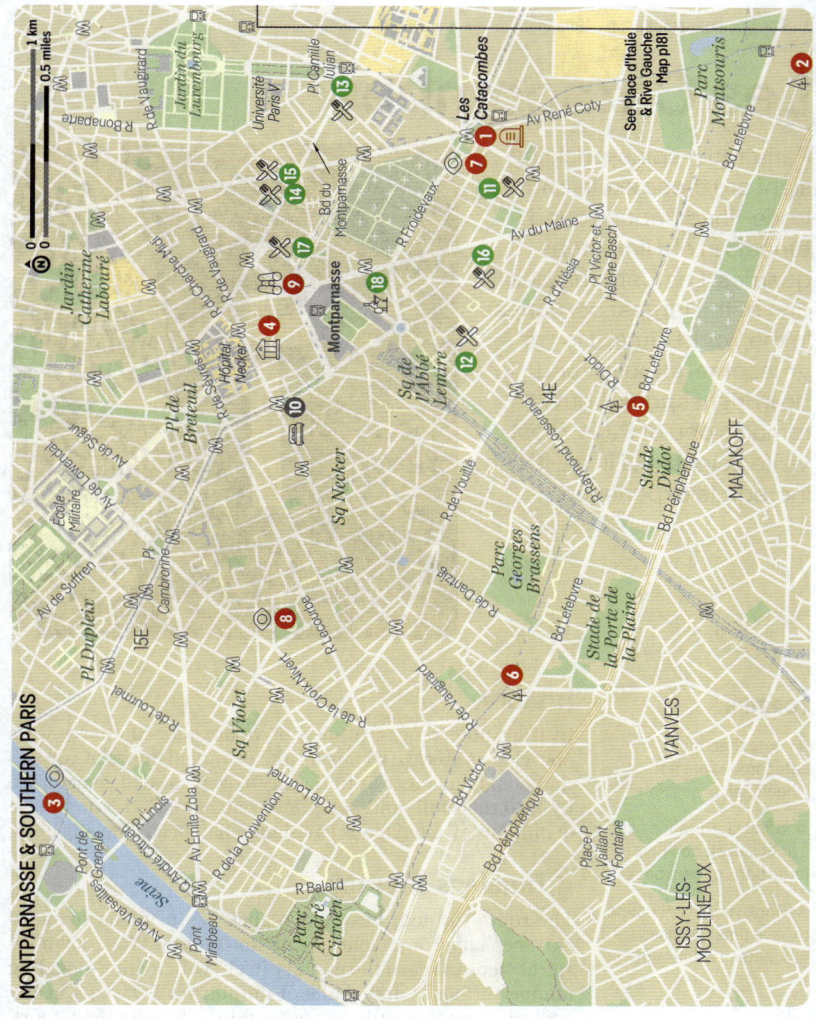

MONTPARNASSE & SOUTHERN PARIS

★ HIGHLIGHTS
1. Les Catacombes

● SIGHTS
2. Cité Universitaire
3. Île aux Cygnes
4. Musée Bourdelle
5. Petite Ceinture du 14e
6. Petite Ceinture du 15e
7. Rue Daguerre
8. Square St-Lambert
9. Tour Montparnasse

● SLEEPING
10. Villa M

● EATING
11. A Mi-Chemin
12. La Cantine du Troquet Pernety
13. La Closerie des Lilas
14. La Coupole
15. La Rotonde
16. L'Assiette
   see 15 Le Dôme
17. L'Opportun
   see 4 Rhodia

● DRINKING & NIGHTLIFE
18. Food Society

TOP EXPERIENCE

Les Catacombes

Paris' most spine-prickling sight are these skull- and bone-lined underground tunnels in old limestone quarries. Les Catacombes is one of the largest ossuaries in the world. Sure, it is gruesome, ghoulish and downright spooky, but it remains one of Paris' most visited sights. All in all, it's an incredible experience.

TOP TIPS

- Note that the catacombes are not wheelchair accessible.
- Bring sturdy shoes and a light jacket; don't carry large bags or backpacks.
- Book your ticket online to save time and hassle – it guarantees a time slot.

PRACTICALITIES

- catacombes.paris.fr
- adult/child €31/12
- 9.45am-7.15pm Tue-Sun

History

In 1785 subterranean tunnels of an abandoned quarry were upcycled as storage rooms for the exhumed bones of corpses that could no longer fit in the city's overcrowded cemeteries. By 1810 the skull- and bone-lined catacombs – resting place of millions of anonymous Parisians – had been officially born.

A Timeless Journey

The route through Les Catacombes begins at its spacious entrance on av du Colonel Henri Rol-Tanguy. Walk down 131 spiral steps to reach the ossuary itself, with a mind-boggling number of bones and skulls of millions of Parisians neatly packed along the walls. 'Arrête, c'est ici l'empire de la mort' ('Stop, here is the empire of death') – this inscription at the entrance to the ossuary inspires fear and respect. But there's much more than skulls and bones. The site is also of great interest from a geological, philosophical, architectural and archaeological perspective. Visits cover about 1.5km of tunnels in all, at a cool 14°C. The exit is up 112 steps via a minimalist all-white 'transition space' with giftshop at 21bis av René Coty, 14e.

People with claustrophobia may experience some anxiety in the confined environment.

THE HEART & SOUL OF THE 14E

The 14e has lots of hidden corners and off-the-beaten-track areas that are worth exploring on foot for their laid-back and bohemian atmosphere.

START	END	LENGTH
rue Daguerre	jardin François Héritier	3.2km; 2½hrs

Begin on lively ❶ **rue Daguerre** (p182), which is chock-a-block with restaurants, groceries and delis. Head southeast to ❷ **square Ferdinand Brunot** and the adjacent square de l'Aspirant Dunand. Both are playing grounds for kids living nearby when the sun is out. Walk east to ❸ **rue Hallé**. At No 12, there's a lovely half-moon-shaped square flanked with houses reminiscent of a French provincial town. Back on av du Général Leclerc, walk south and turn right onto passage Rimbaut, a narrow lane that leads to av du Maine. Take rue du Moulin Vert and turn onto ❹ **impasse du Moulin Vert**, flanked with houses that have façades covered with ivy and vines – you couldn't wish for a more picturesque street. It's a five-minute stroll westwards to ❺ **place Flora Tristan**, a bijou *placette* (small square) with pavement terraces. Continue south to ❻ **rue des Thermopyles**, arguably the most photogenic street south of the Seine. With its small houses equipped with colourful shutters, flowery gardens and serene ambiance, this paved street that screams rural France is a gem to wander. You'll then emerge on busy ❼ **rue Raymond Losserand**, which has plenty of dining options, bakeries, bars and shops. Walk north and turn right onto allée du Château Ouvrier, which ushers in ❽ **jardin François Héritier**, an intimate garden where you can picnic.

WHY I LOVE SOUTHERN PARIS

Jean-Bernard Carillet, Lonely Planet writer

Originally from Metz (Lorraine), I came to Paris as a student to complete a master's degree at La Sorbonne. I was happy to live at the Cité Universitaire de Paris in the 14e and, since then, I've called southern Paris home. I love the serenity, discretion and peacefulness of southern Paris and its numerous little gems, especially La Butte aux Cailles and its village-y atmosphere, but I also like the modern vibes and bold architecture in Paris Rive Gauche, near Bibliothèque Nationale de France – see you in TOO Tac Tac Sky Bar, one of my favourite drinking spots. In the 14e, I love hanging around Pernety, which feels so Parisian (and is totally untouristy).

---

continued from p174

numerous laid-back bars, shops and restaurants, but all the adjacent streets are well worth a look, as is the super relaxing Parc Brassaï. A few jewel streets to stroll include passage Boiton; rue des Cinq Diamants; rue Samson; rue Alphand; passage Sigaud; passage Barrault and rue Michal; as well as the adorable rue Daviel with the Petite Alsace (Little Alsace) enclave, complete with brick and timbered houses; and Villa Daviel, which is lined with superb houses and gardens. Plan half a day to explore the area.

And there's the superb **Piscine de la Butte aux Cailles** *(paris.fr/lieux/piscine-de-la-butte-aux-cailles-2927; €3.50)*. Built in 1924, this art deco swimming complex – a historical monument – has a spectacular vaulted indoor pool and, since 2017, Paris' only Nordic pool. In the depths of winter, we Parisians of the 13e head here to swim 25m laps in a five-lane outdoor pool, heated to a toasty 27°C.

Asian Appeal
MAP P181

Immerse yourself in Chinatown

Southeast of place d'Italie and near rue de Tolbiac is Paris' largest Chinatown. Don't let the massive tower blocks dating from the 1960s deter you from exploring this district. It's a fascinating piece of Southeast Asia, with plenty of surprises, including culinary delights, colourful festivals and art. It's easy to spend an afternoon in this neighbourhood.

If you're a fan of underground cultures, head to **La Dalle des Olympiades**, off rue de Tolbiac. This vast concrete esplanade with platformed pedestrian zones surrounded by towers has become the focal point for local K-pop dancers and skateboarders. On rue Paul Klee, **La Danse de la Fontaine Émergente** ('Dance of the Emerging Fountain') is a large fountain built of stainless steel, plastic and glass, designed by French Chinese sculptor Chen Zhen. Completed in 2008, it looks like a giant stylised dragon winding its way across the square, emerging and submerging from the concrete pavement. High-pressure water flows inside the sculpture. The most unusual sacred site in Paris must be the **Autel du Culte de Bouddha** (37 rue du Disque) – this small yet colourful Buddhist temple is hidden in an underground car park beneath a tower block.

For any Asian food you can imagine, as well as many decorative and household items, shop at **Tang Frères** (48 av d'Ivry), the biggest Asian store in Paris (and possibly Europe).

 EATING IN THE 13E: BISTRO FARE — MAP P181

La Butte aux Piafs: Hearty bistro fare and a congenial atmosphere. Near La Butte aux Cailles. *noon-2pm & 7-10pm* €

Simone Le Resto: Pavement-terrace tables at vibrant neobistro. Inventive menus created from high-quality products. *noon-2pm & 7-10pm Mon-Fri, 7-10pm Sat* €€

Comme Promis: Seasonal ingredients are used to prepare dishes both classic and contemporary at this gem of a bistro. *hours vary* €€

Marso & Co: This modern bistro has gorgeous fish and meat dishes, and the banana cake is a dessert delight. *noon-2pm & 7.15-10pm Mon-Fri* €€

EXPLORE A GIANT ART SCENE

Over 30 murals enliven streets and thoroughfares between av de France, rue de Tolbiac and bd Vincent Auriol, with more added every year.

START	END	LENGTH
Chevaleret metro station	13 rue Lahire	1.6km; 1hr

Start from the 1 **Chevaleret metro station**. Nearby you can enjoy the poignant 2 **Embrace and Fight** (85 bd Vincent Auriol), by Conor Harrington, *La Madone* (81 bd Vincent Auriol), a masterpiece created by famous artist Inti, and *Les Oiseaux* (The Birds; 91 bd Vincent Auriol), by Pantonio. Continue west along bd Vincent Auriol to see the monochromatic 3 **Le Visage** (The Face; 6 rue Jenner), also by Pantonio, on your right. Then the stunning 4 **Rise Above Level** (cnr bd Vincent Auriol and rue Jeanne d'Arc) comes into view, a massive mural by Shepard Fairey. On the opposite side of bd Vincent Auriol, don't miss the awesome 5 **Dancer** (98 bd Vincent Auriol), by the collective Faile.

Other great works to look for further west include 6 **Le Chat** (cnr bd Vincent Auriol and rue Nationale), monumental *La Marianne* (186 rue Nationale), by Shepard Fairey, which represents the symbol of the French Republic, and the strikingly expressive *Turncoat* (190 rue Nationale), by D*Face (who is from London). Be awed by the elaborate 7 **Sun Daze** (167 bd Vincent Auriol), created by the talented twins How and Nosm and, on an adjacent building, a splendid portrait of a geisha-like woman (169 bd Vincent Auriol), by British artist Hush. Further south, marvel at 8 **Bach** (57 rue Clisson) and the nearby 9 **colourful fresco** (13 rue Lahire) by Inti.

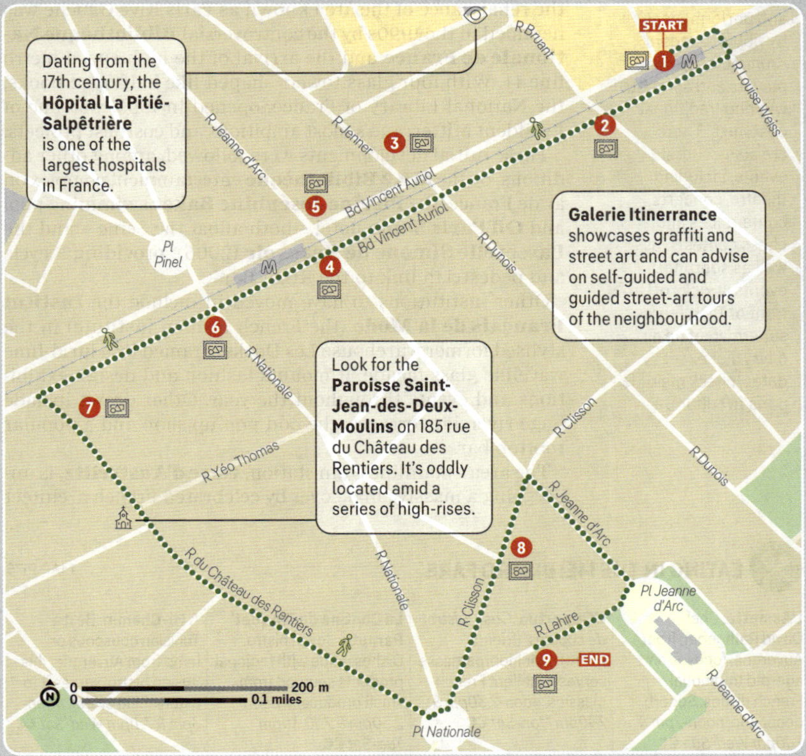
Dating from the 17th century, the **Hôpital La Pitié-Salpêtrière** is one of the largest hospitals in France.
START
R Bruant
R Louise Weiss
R Jeanne d'Arc
R Jenner
Bd Vincent Auriol
Bd Vincent Auriol
R Dunois
Pl Pinel
Galerie Itinerrance showcases graffiti and street art and can advise on self-guided and guided street-art tours of the neighbourhood.
R Nationale
Look for the **Paroisse Saint-Jean-des-Deux-Moulins** on 185 rue du Château des Rentiers. It's oddly located amid a series of high-rises.
R Clisson
R Yéo Thomas
R Dunois
R Jeanne d'Arc
R du Château des Rentiers
R Nationale
R Clisson
Pl Jeanne d'Arc
R Lahire
END
R Jeanne d'Arc
Pl Nationale
200 m
0.1 miles

CHINESE NEW YEAR IN THE 13E

If you happen to be here in late January or February, don't miss Chinese New Year (also known as Spring Festival). With about 2000 participants and more than 200,000 spectators, it's one of the most spectacular events in the city. Celebrations typically last about two weeks and feature colourful parades as well as lion and dragon dances. Expect brightly lit red lanterns, firecrackers and performances by ribbon dancers, drummers, cymbal players and acrobats wearing traditional costumes. There are also cultural events, including theatre, concerts, conferences and chess contests, as well as sporting events. It kicks off in front of Tang Frères supermarket on av d'Ivry. For exact dates, check mairie13.paris.fr/culture.

Other atmospheric shops well worth visiting include **Exo Store**, a department store on av de Choisy; as well as **Aux Merveilles d'Asie** (great for unusual gifts) and **Kim Than**; both on av d'Ivry.

Tucked beneath the towers on av d'Ivry and av de Choisy you'll find great Vietnamese pho noodle bars and family-run restaurants serving homemade dumplings and spicy soups. If, like us, you're a pastry lover, fall for **Pâtisserie de Choisy** on av de Choisy or trendy **Fu Pâtisserie** (its brunches are also excellent). See you there!

If you happen to be here in September, consider joining the crowds at **RICE – Le Marché Treiz'Asiatique** on bd Auguste Blanqui. This recent festival features plenty of Asian street food stalls as well as cultural workshops and live performances. Check the Instagram @ricemarche.paris for dates.

Explore Paris Rive Gauche   MAP P181

Paris' most innovative district

Paris' largest urban redevelopment since Haussmann's 19th-century reformation continues apace in the 13e *arrondissement*. Plan at least three hours to get a feel for the area.

Centred on a once-nondescript area south of the Latin Quarter spiralling out from the big busy traffic hub of place d'Italie, the renaissance of the area known as Paris Rive Gauche was heralded in the 1990s by the controversial **Bibliothèque Nationale de France** and the arrival of the high-speed metro line 14. With four glass towers shaped like half-open books, the National Library of France, opened in 1995, was one of President Mitterrand's most ambitious and costliest projects.

These initial developments were followed, among other additions, by the **MK2 Bibliothèque** entertainment complex on av de France, the **Piscine Joséphine Baker** swimming pool and **Off Paris Seine** hotel – both afloat the Seine – and the **Passerelle Simone de Beauvoir** (2006), providing a cycle and pedestrian link to the Right Bank.

Other institutions to have moved in include the **Institut Français de la Mode** (the French fashion institute) in the stylised former warehouse Les Docks. Framed by a lurid-lime wavelike glass façade, it mounts fashion and design exhibitions and events throughout the year. Other draws include huge riverside terraces, the odd pop-up shop and a popular rooftop bar.

The area's mainline train station, **Gare d'Austerlitz**, is undergoing a massive makeover by celebrated French architect

EATING IN THE 14E: BISTRO FARE   MAP P175

L'Assiette: Chef David Rathgeber, from Auvergne, focuses on age-old traditional French dishes. Superb decor, too. *noon-2pm & 7-10pm Wed-Sun* €€

L'Opportun: Cosy *'bistrot de copains'* (friends' bistro) near Montparnasse serves excellent French classics. *noon-2.30pm & 7-10pm Mon-Sat* €€

La Cantine du Troquet Pernety: Jovial bistro. Dishes made with regional products sourced from small producers. *noon-2.30pm & 7-10.30pm Tue-Sat* €€

A Mi-Chemin: Be it a Tunisian couscous or lamb from Auvergne, this 'fusion bistro' serves it to astonishing effect. *noon-3pm & 7-11pm Wed-Sat* €€

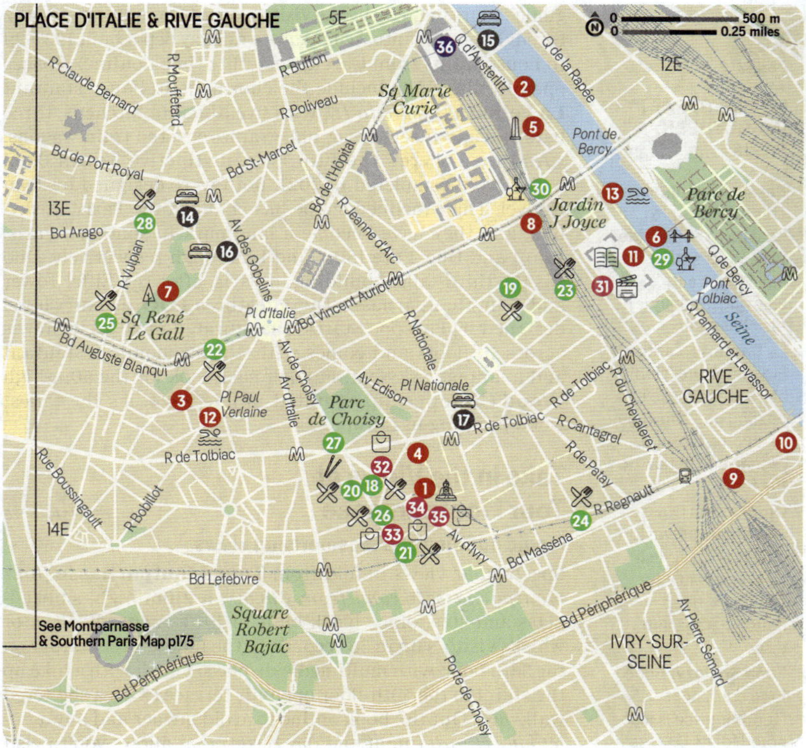

PLACE D'ITALIE & RIVE GAUCHE

● SIGHTS
1. Autel du Culte de Bouddha
2. Institut Français de la Mode
3. La Butte aux Cailles
4. La Dalle des Olympiades
5. La Danse de la Fontaine Émergente
6. Passerelle Simone de Beauvoir
7. Square René Le Gall
8. Station F
9. Tours Duo
10. Wood Up

● ACTIVITIES
11. Bibliothèque Nationale de France
12. Piscine de la Butte aux Cailles
13. Piscine Joséphine Baker

● SLEEPING
14. Hôtel Henriette
15. Off Paris Seine
16. Oops
see 9 TOO Hotel
17. Urban Bivouac Hotel

● EATING
18. Basilic & Spice
19. Comme Promis
20. Fu Pâtisserie
21. Impérial Choisy
22. La Butte aux Piafs
23. La Felicità
24. Lao Viet
25. Marso & Co
26. Pâtisserie de Choisy
27. Pho Bành Cúon 14
28. Simone Le Resto

● DRINKING & NIGHTLIFE
29. Bateau El Alamein
30. Djoon Club
see 29 La Dame de Canton

● ENTERTAINMENT
31. MK2 Bibliothèque

● SHOPPING
32. Aux Merveilles d'Asie
33. Exo Store
34. Kim Than
35. Tang Frères

● TRANSPORT
36. Gare d'Austerlitz

Jean Nouvel. The station itself will be overhauled, and new shops, cafes and green spaces will open up in the surrounding streets. The renovation is due to wrap up in late 2027.

Another notable rehabilitation is **Station F** *(stationf.co)*, the world's largest start-up campus, where 1000 entrepreneurs from all over the globe dream up groundbreaking new projects and businesses. Each Wednesday or Thursday at 11.30am,

WHERE TO PARTY IN SOUTHERN PARIS

Bateau El Alamein: This deep-purple boat has a Seine-side terrace for sitting amid tulips and enjoying live bands. Also has a bar.

La Dame de Canton: Floating *boîte* (club) aboard a Chinese junk hosting pop and indie to electro, hip-hop, reggae and rock. Skip the food.

Djoon Club: Glass-and-steel bar and loft club that's a stylish weekend venue for soul, funk, deep house, garage and disco.

Food Society: Huge food court near Montparnasse is also noted for its DJ sets and themed soirées (evenings) featuring salsa and *kizomba*.

guided tours in English take visitors on a 45-minute *(free)* waltz through the gargantuan hangar – a railway depot built 1927–29 to house trains from Gare d'Austerlitz (book online). Spaces open to the public include the enormous Italian restaurant **La Felicità** *(lafelicita.fr)*, with five different kitchens, three bars and a twinset of original, graffiti-covered train wagons.

And then there's the futuristic, distinctive **Tours Duo**, which were completed in 2021. Both were designed by Jean Nouvel. Their inclined shape has changed the Parisian skyline, and they have become a landmark in southern Paris. Duo 1 and Duo 2 are 180m and 122m high respectively. Duo 1 is the third-tallest building in Paris, after the Eiffel Tower and Tour Montparnasse. Duo 2 features **TOO**, a luxury hotel designed by Philippe Starck. Inaugurated in 2022, it ranges across 10 floors and comes with a gastronomic restaurant and a fantastic sky-bar. Further east, look for the 50m-high **Wood Up** tower. Inaugurated in late 2024, it's the tallest wood building in Europe.

Take in the Views at Tour Montparnasse

MAP P175

Iconic building and mesmerising views

Spectacular views unfold from **Tour Montparnasse** *(tourmontparnasse56.com; from €18.50)*, a 210m-high, smoked-glass-and-steel office block built in 1973. A speedy elevator whisks visitors up in 38 seconds to the indoor observatory on the 56th floor, with multimedia displays. Finish with a hike up the stairs to the 59th-floor open-air terrace (with a sheltered walkway). Our tip: book online to avoid queues and buy a *billet jour et nuit* (night and day ticket) that allows you to visit twice – thus you can savour the views early in the morning and at sunset when the light is at its finest.

Ramble Down Rue Daguerre

MAP P175

Enjoy an authentic slice of Parisian life

Paris' traditional village atmosphere thrives along rue Daguerre, 14e. Tucked just southwest of the Denfert-Rochereau metro and RER stations, this narrow street – pedestrianised between av du Général-Leclerc and rue Boulard – is lined with florists, *fromageries* (cheese shops), *boulangeries*, patisseries, greengrocers, delis (including Greek, Asian and Italian) and classic cafes where you can watch the local goings on. Shops set up market stalls on the pavement; Sunday mornings are

DRINKING IN MONTPARNASSE: HISTORICAL BRASSERIES ——— MAP P175

La Closerie des Lilas: Brass plaques reveal where Hemingway and others stood/sat/fell at the 'Lilac Enclosure' (opened 1847). *noon-2.15pm & 7-10.15pm* €€

Le Dôme: A 1930s art deco extravaganza, monumental Le Dôme is famous for its shellfish platters. *noon-2.45pm & 7-10.30pm* €€

La Rotonde: Around since 1911, elegant La Rotonde is renowned for its superior food. *7.30am-midnight* €€

La Coupole: Opened in 1927, famous for its mural-covered columns, dark wood panelling, soft lighting. Great seafood. *8am-midnight Tue-Sat, to 11pm Sun & Mon* €€

especially lively. It's a great option for lunch before or after visiting **Les Catacombes** (p176), or packing a picnic to take to one of the area's parks or squares.

Walk along the Petite Ceinture
MAP P175
Paris' most unusual trail

This little marvel of a walking path is not to be missed if you want to see Paris from a different perspective – it really feels like entering another world. In the 15e, the **Petite Ceinture du 15e** stretches for 1.3km, with biodiverse habitats including forest, grassland and prairies supporting 220 species of flora and fauna. In addition to the endpoints, there are three elevator-enabled access points along its route: 397ter rue de Vaugirard; opposite 82 rue Desnouettes; and place Robert Guillemard. On the eastern side of Parc Georges Brassens, a promenade *plantée* (planted walkway) travels atop a stretch of the Petite Ceinture's tracks by Porte de Vanves.

Not enough for you? From there, get to 96bis rue Didot in the 14e, which is the access point for the 750m-long **Petite Ceinture du 14e**, which goes to Porte d'Orléans – another delightful section.

Find more information at petiteceinture.org.

See Quirky Sculptures at Musée Bourdelle
MAP P175
Off-the-radar cultural gem

You won't find many great cultural institutions in southern Paris, but there are a couple of relatively unknown yet not-to-be-missed museums, and **Musée Bourdelle** *(bourdelle.paris.fr; free)* in the 15e, is one of them. Monumental bronzes fill the house and workshop where sculptor Antoine Bourdelle (1861–1929), a pupil of Rodin, lived and worked. The Hall des Plâtres room, with its peculiar layout and architecture, is our favourite. We also love the three oh-so-peaceful sculpture gardens, with a flavour of belle époque and post-WWI Montparnasse. The museum usually has a temporary exhibition *(adult/child €10/8)* going on alongside its free permanent collection.

Don't leave the museum without a stop at **Rhodia**. This cafe–restaurant on the 1st floor serves delectable light meals and exquisite cakes.

HISTORY OF THE PETITE CEINTURE

Long before the tramway or the metro, the 35km Petite Ceinture (Little Belt) steam railway encircled the city of Paris. Constructed during the reign of Napoléon III between 1852 and 1869 as a way to move troops and goods around the city's fortifications, it became a thriving passenger service until the metro arrived in 1900. Most passenger services ceased in 1934 and goods services in 1993, and the line became an overgrown wilderness. Until recently, access was forbidden (although that didn't stop maverick urban explorers).

Of the line's original 29 stations, 17 survive (in various states of disrepair). Petite Ceinture railway corridor is being regenerated, with the opening of several sections with walkways alongside the tracks.

 EATING IN THE 13E: ASIAN RESTAURANTS — MAP P181

| **Pho Bành Cúon 14**: This buzzy restaurant is wildly popular with in-the-know locals for its super-fresh pho (soup). *11.30am-10pm Wed-Mon* € | **Impérial Choisy**: Renowned for its Cantonese cuisine and its top-quality Peking duck. *noon-11pm* € | **Lao Viet**: This unpretentious venue serves up some of the 13e's best Vietnamese and Laotian cuisine in a cosy interior. *noon-2.30pm & 6.30-10.30pm Wed-Mon* € | **Basilic & Spice**: This highly praised venue serves Khmer and Thai dishes, such as *pad kra pao* (chicken with basil and fried egg). *noon-2.30pm & 7-10.30pm Tue-Sun* €€ |

TOP EXPERIENCE

Versailles

Sprawling over 900 hectares, the monumental, 400-year-old Château de Versailles is France's most famous and grand palace. It's situated in the leafy, bourgeois suburb of Versailles, 22km southwest of central Paris. The estate is divided into three main sections: the 580m-long palace; the gardens, canals and pools to the west of the palace; and the Trianon Estate to the northwest.

DON'T MISS

- The Palace
- Hall of Mirrors
- King's & Queen's State Apartments
- Formal gardens and fountains
- Lunch near the Grand Canal

History

The estate began in 1623 as a hunting lodge for Louis XIII. Subsequently, Louis XIV transformed it into a vast, baroque château. Some 30,000 workers and soldiers toiled on the property, the bills for which all but emptied the kingdom's coffers.

The Château de Versailles was the kingdom's political capital and the seat of the royal court from 1682 up until the fateful events of 1789 when revolutionaries massacred the palace guard. Louis XVI and Marie Antoinette were ultimately dragged back to Paris, where they were ingloriously guillotined. In the 19th century, Napoléon and Josephine lived on the estate, as did Charles de Gaulle in the 1940s.

PRACTICALITIES

- en.chateauversailles.fr ● adult/child from €21/free ● 9am-5.30pm Tue-Sun

The Palace

Work on the palace began in 1661 under the guidance of architect Louis Le Vau (Jules Hardouin-Mansart took over from Le Vau in the mid-1670s); painter and interior designer Charles Le Brun; and landscape artist André Le Nôtre, whose workers flattened hills, drained marshes and relocated forests as they laid out the seemingly endless gardens, ponds and fountains.

Le Brun and his hundreds of artisans decorated every moulding, cornice, ceiling and door of the interior with the most luxurious and ostentatious of appointments: frescoes, marble, gilt and woodcarvings, many with themes and symbols drawn from Greek and Roman mythology.

Few alterations have been made to the château since its construction, apart from most of the interior furnishings disappearing during the Revolution and many of the rooms being redecorated by Louis-Philippe (r 1830–48), who opened part of the château to the public in 1837. The château is in the final stages of a lavish €400 million restoration.

Hall of Mirrors

The palace's opulence peaks in its shimmering Galerie des Glaces (Hall of Mirrors). This 75m-long ballroom shines with 17 sparkling mirrored features comprising 357 individual mirrors on one side and an equal number of windows overlooking the gardens and the setting sun on the other.

King's & Queen's State Apartments

Luxurious, ostentatious appointments adorn every feature of the palace's Grands Appartements du Roi et de la Reine (the King's and Queen's State Apartments). Rooms are dedicated to Hercules, Venus, Diana, Mars and Mercury.

Other Notable Rooms

The **Galerie des Batailles** (Battle Gallery) is longer than the Hall of Mirrors and features 33 huge paintings that recall mostly forgotten French military victories. Savour the thematic decor in the **Salon de la Guerre** (War Room) and the **Salon de la Paix** (Peace Room), which bookend the Hall of Mirrors.

Gardens, Estate & Equestrian Academy

A walk through the sprawling and artful formal gardens, natural areas, huge Grand Canal and the Trianon palaces is a highlight. Or take in a horse show at the **National Equestrian Academy of Versailles**.

Getting There & Away

Versailles is best reached by the RER C line, which ends at Versailles Château Rive Gauche (some trains go elsewhere). Other stations with Versailles in their names are a much longer walk from the château and town centre.

HISTORIC VERSAILLES

Don't miss the historic centre of Versailles town. Build a superb picnic at the market stalls of **Les Halles de Versailles** on the **place du Marché**. In the old St-Louis quarter, next to the **Cathédrale St-Louis**, the **Potager du Roi** (King's Kitchen Garden) dates from the time of gourmand Louis XIV.

TOP TIPS

● Prepurchase tickets on the château's website for a dedicated time slot – otherwise admission is not guaranteed.

● Official group guided tours, such as the King's Private Apartments, are worthwhile.

● Consider getting tickets for a concert in the Royal Chapel or Royal Opera for a unique palace experience.

● Download the official Château de Versailles app, which is loaded with audio tours and info for the entire estate.

● The four-person rental electric carts are limited to a set route covering a fraction of the estate. Rental bikes and e-bikes allow the most freedom. Explore the Grand Canal with a rowboat. The shuttle train is very slow.

Salle du Trône (Throne Room)

TOP EXPERIENCE

Château de Fontainebleau

The classy town of Fontainebleau grew up around its magnificent château, one of the most beautifully decorated and furnished in France. Although vast in scale, its size pales in comparison to the ridiculous scope of Versailles – and that's for the good. Many people find Fontainebleau to be a much more immersive experience as there is time to savour the château, gardens and grounds.

DON'T MISS

Chapelle de la Trinité

Galerie François Ier

Salle de Bal

Boudoir de la Reine

Chambre de Napoléon

Horseshoe staircase

Cour Ovale

History

The resplendent, 1900-room Château de Fontainebleau's list of former tenants and guests reads like a who's who of French royalty and aristocracy. Every square centimetre of wall and ceiling space is richly adorned with wood panelling, gilded carvings, frescoes, tapestries and paintings.

The first château on this site was built in the early 12th century and enlarged by Louis IX a century later. Only a single medieval tower survived the energetic Renaissance-style reconstruction undertaken by François I (r 1515–47). The *Mona Lisa* once hung here amid other fine works of art in the royal collection.

PRACTICALITIES

● chateaudefontainebleau.fr/en ● adult/child €14/free ● 9.30am-6pm Apr-Sep, to 5pm Oct-Mar

During the latter half of the 16th century, the château was further enlarged by Henri II (r 1547–59), Catherine de Médici and Henri IV (r 1589–1610). Even Louis XIV got in on the act: it was he who hired landscape artist André Le Nôtre, celebrated for his work at Versailles, to redesign the gardens.

Fontainebleau was beloved by Napoléon Bonaparte. Napoléon III was another frequent visitor. During WWII the château was turned into a German headquarters. Later, it served as the Allied and then NATO headquarters from 1945 to 1965.

Grands Appartements

The spectacular **Chapelle de la Trinité** (Trinity Chapel), the ornamentation of which dates from the first half of the 17th century, is where Napoléon III was christened in 1810. Note how the murals play with perspective.

Galerie François 1er, a jewel of Renaissance architecture, was decorated from 1533 to 1540 by Il Rosso, a Florentine follower of Michelangelo. In the seeming acres of carved-wood panelling, François I's monogram appears repeatedly along with his emblem, a dragonlike salamander.

A top sight, the **Salle de Bal**, a 30m-long ballroom dating from the mid-16th century, is renowned for its mythological frescoes, marquetry floor and Italian-inspired coffered ceiling. Its large windows afford views of the **Cour Ovale** (Oval Courtyard) and the gardens. The gilded bed in the 17th- and 18th-century **Chambre de l'Impératrice** (Empress' Bedroom) was never used by Marie Antoinette, for whom it was built in 1787. She actually favoured the **Boudoir de la Reine** (Queen's Bedroom), which attests to her under-appreciated design sensibilities. Note the lovely sunrise on the ceiling.

The gilding in the **Salle du Trône** (Throne Room), which was the royal bedroom before the Napoléonic period, is decorated in a rich tableau of golds, greens and yellows.

The **Musée Chinois de l'Impératice Eugénie** (Chinese Museum of Empress Eugénie) offers a change from all the carved wood. It was created in 1863 for the Asian art and curios collected by Napoléon III's wife.

Echoes of Napoléon

Napoléon Bonaparte preferred Fontainebleau to Versailles because he found it more 'intimate'. The **Musée Napoléon I** presents the family history of the emperor, right down to his favourite articles of clothing. A suite of rooms recalls his time in the château: the **Chambre de Napoléon** preserves the decidedly non-minimalist decor of his bedroom. (Don't miss the great man's bathroom, complete with a very short tub.) The **Salon de l'Abdication** is where he called it quits in 1814.

HORSESHOE STAIRCASE

The couples taking wedding photos in front of the château's emblematic staircase are following in royal footsteps. Back in the day, it was where princesses like Marie Leszczyńska were greeted in pomp and circumstance before their nuptials. Commissioned by Louis XIII in the 17th century, it was widely copied across Europe. Later it was immortalised by Napoléon's farewell speech to his troops gathered in the courtyard before his exile to Elba.

TOP TIPS

- Refreshment and lunch options within the complex are limited. Outside the gates in town, you'll find good choices for picnics and meals around rue des Sablons.

- Preserve your flexibility by not buying château tickets in advance, as it draws a fraction of the crowds at Versailles.

- There are dozens of daily trains between Paris' Gare de Lyon and the Fontainebleau Avon station.

- You can easily ride the bus from the station to Fontainebleau's town centre and the château's entrance and walk all the way back as part of a tour of the gardens and grounds.

Places We Love to Stay

€ Budget €€ Midrange €€€ Top End

Eiffel Tower & Western Paris   MAP p64

Camping de Paris € On the Bois de Boulogne's western edge by the banks of the Seine, this year-round campground has 290 sites for tents or camper vans, along with kitchen-equipped wood caravans and static tents made of canvas and wood.

Hotel Beauséjour Ranelagh €€ A melange of museum-worthy art and designer furniture creates the feel of an elegant Parisian home at this family-run hotel that's deeply connected to the neighbourhood.

Villa du Square €€ Elegant townhouse next to Le Corbusier Foundation. Five guest rooms show off an eclectic mix of antiques and designer decor.

Champs-Élysées & Grands Boulevards   MAP p77

Hôtel Chopin € A rare budget hotel in Paris, and in the unique location of one of the city's historical *passages couverts*. This historic hotel originally opened in 1846 and features classic, period-inspired rooms overlooking the Paris rooftops.

CitizenM Paris Champs-Elysées € A budget place to stay in the upmarket 8e. Rooms are basic but cleverly and comfortably designed, and there's an Eiffel Tower view from the rooftop bar.

Rayz Eiffel €€ This contemporary chic hotel has a rooftop hangout overlooking the nearby Eiffel Tower. The 25 rooms come with kitchenettes – some have furnished balconies with views.

Louvre & Les Halles   MAPS p83, p92

Edgar & Achille €€ An intimate hotel in the heart of Sentier, overlooking a quiet square. Each room has a distinct decoration, from a wooden cabin style to a rock 'n' roll–themed decor.

123 Sebastopol €€ A cinema-themed hotel where each floor is dedicated to a film director or film-music composer, with an entertaining atmosphere. It is family-friendly and conveniently located between Sentier and Le Marais.

Hôtel Odyssey €€ Tucked behind Palais Royal, this small hotel is designed like a wooden boat. It has intimate rooms where you can feel like you're in a cocoon once you've drawn the curtains on your bed cubicle.

Montmartre & Northern Paris   MAPS p98, p103, p106

Le Village Montmartre by Hiphostels € A well-priced hostel at the bottom of Montmartre and close to Pigalle's restaurants and bars. There's an outdoor patio, dorm beds and private rooms, some of which have views of the Sacré Coeur Basilica.

Generator Hostel € A buzzy, design hostel with a fun rooftop bar strung with lights, a lively social scene, and industrial-chic interiors near bohemian Canal St-Martin, with its stylish boutiques and dining venues.

Hôtel HoY €€ One of the most restful places to stay; there's a yoga studio and in-room mats. The highlight is the ground-floor flower shop and the excellent MESA, serving up creative plant-based dishes steeped in Latin American flavours.

Hotel Élysée Montmartre €€ This airy, light-filled boutique stay with soothing hues, is slotted between legendary music halls Elysée Montmartre and Le Trianon – steps from Pigalle.

Le Marais, Ménilmontant & Belleville   MAPS p111, p112, p123

People Marais € This modern hostel is built for community, with well-equipped dorms, communal kitchens, and a light-filled sociable cafe and restaurant.

MIJE Fourcy € This winding 17th-century *hôtel particulier* has basic, clean rooms in an incredibly central location steeped in history. It only offers wi-fi on the ground floor, but rates do include a French breakfast.

Hôtel Jeanne d'Arc le Marais €€ Modernised rooms retain timber beams or exposed stone walls, while others have feature walls with patterned wallpaper. The pièce de résistance: the 6th-floor attic room with a sweeping Paris rooftop view.

Suzie Blue €€ Certified green-key former convent. Its eco-conscious offerings include toiletries Terre de Mars and organic refreshments. Its coffee shop is the perfect space to brunch or work.

Bastille & Eastern Paris
MAPS p130, p136

JO&JOE Paris – Nation € Modern, lively hostel has a busy schedule of events, comfy bunks with privacy curtains, and a 100-sq-metre rooftop that serves homemade pizzas.

Hôtel du Printemps €€ The 38-room Spring Hotel, a stone's throw from place de la Nation, offers excellent value for Paris. Set on a treelined boulevard in an untouristy area, it's compact and comfortable, even if a little far from the action.

Mama Shelter Paris East €€ This hip Philippe Starck–designed, 170-room hotel draws a younger, creative crowd to its off-grid location, thanks to its bold industrial decor, rooftop bar and playful touches such as cartoon-mask lampshades.

The Islands
MAP p141

Hôtel du Jeu de Paume €€€ Contemporary hotel in a former royal tennis court on Île St-Louis' main street, with rooms inspired by modern artists.

Hôtel des Deux Îles €€€ Elegantly floral decor with top-floor rooms peeping out over Parisian rooftops and chimney pots.

Hôtel Saint-Louis en l'Isle €€€ Swank and subtle, this stellar abode includes a 17th-century stone-cellar breakfast room.

Latin Quarter
MAP p150

Hôtel des Grandes Écoles €€ Hidden in a closed-off alleyway next door to writer James Joyce's former Latin Quarter abode, this charming three-star hotel has tables out in a leafy courtyard for breakfast in the sun.

Hotel Les Dames du Panthéon €€ Killer views of the Panthéon. Tucked into a building just next to it, the zany, beamed rooms here overlook the landmark.

Le Jardin de Verre by Locke €€ A bright and breezy apartment hotel with attractive contemporary interiors. Rooms are simple but functional and the bold hues bring a cheerful twist.

Hôtel Pilgrim €€ A comfortable hotel where beds have fabric headboards. There's a rooftop terrace and a pool, as well as a small gym. It's just a few minutes' walk to the River Seine and Notre Dame Cathedral.

St-Germain & Les Invalides
MAPS p161, p165

Hôtel St-André des Arts €€ This 30-room boutique address is part of a small group of Left Bank Hotels, but this one feels the youngest and freshest, with its bright '60s-inspired decor.

Hôtel de l'Abbaye Saint-Germain €€ This hotel is right in the heart of St-Germain-des-Prés, but quietly tucked away with its own leafy private courtyard. Rooms are just as pretty, dressed in a classic floral French style.

Hôtel Dame des Arts €€ This hip hotel is one of St-Germain-des-Prés coolest addresses, with design-led rooms and a rooftop terrace with fantastic views that pulls in locals as well as guests.

Hôtel des Académies et des Arts €€ An effortlessly cool design hotel housed in the building where Modigliani once had his studio (it's now room 52). The hotel also has its own art atelier downstairs.

Montparnasse & Southern Paris
MAPS p175, p181

Oops € This colourful design hostel has four- to six-bed dorms and doubles with bathrooms, as well as a wide range of facilities.

Urban Bivouac Hotel € A great base if you want to explore the Paris Rive Gauche area and the Butte aux Cailles neighbourhood.

Hôtel Henriette €€ One of the Left Bank's most stunning boutique addresses, with designer chairs, 1950s lighting and vintage pieces.

Villa M €€€ From its façade covered with plants to its colourful rooms with a Starck-inspired decor, the Villa M makes a perfect Montparnasse base. Also has a great restaurant and a fantastic rooftop bar.

Hôtel Jeanne d'Arc le Marais

For places to stay in Lille, Flanders & the Somme, see p217

THE GUIDE

LILLE, FLANDERS & THE SOMME

Above: Place du Général de Gaulle (p194), Lille; Right: Thiepval Memorial (p207), Thiepval

Researched by
Ryan Ver Berkmoes

Lille, Flanders & the Somme

BEAUTY TARNISHED WITH HISTORY'S REALITIES

The 20th century was not kind to Hauts-de-France, but its inherent qualities of resilient culture, natural beauty and indomitable hospitality nevertheless shine through.

'Lest we forget' is an oft-quoted phrase, and one particularly relevant to Hauts-de-France – it has been through the mill. The site of the most severe fighting of WWI, the front lines between Allied and German forces on the Western Front sat at a violent stalemate for years, leaving millions dead.

But even over 100 years later, this nightmare still resonates through modern movies like *1917* and *All Quiet on the Western Front*, and in the enduring prose and poetry of the war. More importantly, visiting the WWI battlefields is a timeless and contemplative journey. With time, the human stories have come to dominate the experience, whether you're in one of the many well-funded, high-concept museums and memorials or a tiny cemetery down a seemingly forgotten country lane. And then there's Dunkirk and WWII.

When walking around the handsome squares of Arras or Lille or watching fat seals sliding down the tidal flats in the Baie de Somme, it's easy to forget how fresh these wartime scars are. The Hauts-de-France has been picked up and put back together too many times over the last 100-odd years, but that hasn't crushed the region's spirit. Visit for Dunkirk's carnival, Lille's irrepressible sense of fun, the beer, the food, the sheer energy on the beaches and, yes, the beauty you will discover amid the harsh history.

JON NICHOLLS PHOTOGRAPHY/SHUTTERSTOCK

THE MAIN AREAS

LILLE
Beer, neighbourhoods to explore and nightlife.
p194

AMIENS
Incomparable cathedral and waterfront pleasures.
p202

BOULOGNE-SUR-MER
Huge aquarium and Côte d'Opale.
p212

Find Your Way

The largely flat terrain was made for railroads, although the network is more of a tangle than it is logical. Cyclists will also value the terrain, though ultimately drivers will be most rewarded with flexibility.

Lille, p194
This historic city has lively, vintage neighbourhoods and a gilded clock tower that chimes Beethoven's 'Ode to Joy' each hour.

Boulogne-sur-Mer, p212
Whether in the old upper town or down at the docks, it's a city to walk and enjoy.

Amiens, p202
France's largest Gothic cathedral steals the visual thunder, but the real action day and night is near the water.

CAR
Brits can bring their car via ferry or Eurotunnel to Calais. A car is essential for exploring the WWI battlefields and for visiting the coast. You can rent one at Lille and Amiens train stations.

TRAIN
Eurostar services run from London to Lille. TGV trains from Paris speed to Lille. Other main cities have direct Paris services. The local network requires careful planning. Use the SNCF Connect app.

Palais des Beaux Arts (p196), Lille

Plan Your Time

Hauts-de-France doesn't require detailed itineraries. Start your day and see where it takes you, whether it's wandering Lille, visiting the WWI battlefields or exploring the coast.

Short Stay

● **Lille** (p194), capital of the north, knows how to party: the student population ensures that its plethora of bars and restaurants are always lively. Don't miss the magnificent and surprising art museum, the **Palais des Beaux Arts** (p196). Head south to Vimy, where the **Canadian National Vimy Memorial** (p210) provides a gentle yet monumental opening to WWI. Then, ponder the 580,000 names at the nearby **Ring of Remembrance** (p211).

With More Time

● Visit the superb **Historial de la Grande Guerre** (p206) museum in Péronne, which starts to make WWI personal. Follow the **Seeing the Human Side of WWI** driving tour (p208) to understand the Battle of the Somme beyond the statistics. Visit **Arras** (p201) or **Amiens** (p202) to see how the region rebuilt its past. Then make for **Boulogne-sur-Mer** (p212) and the **Côte d'Opale** (Opal Coast; p215) for blustery beauty.

Seasonal Highlights

SPRING
Raucous parades take place during Dunkirk's Carnaval season (p215) and flowers bloom in Amiens' *hortillonnages* (floating gardens).

SUMMER
The Côte d'Opale heaves with families settling in for long, languid stays. Iconic red poppies bloom along the Somme through June.

AUTUMN
Lille kicks off with its famous *braderie* (p197). Armistice Day sees remembrance ceremonies across the region.

WINTER
Christmas markets in Lille and Arras add extra sparkle to the decorative Flemish façades. Amiens' cathedral lights up after hours.

Lille

WALKABLE METROPOLIS | ARTISAN BREWERIES | ART COLLECTION

☑ TOP TIP

If you're in Lille on Tuesday, Thursday or Sunday (the biggest day), don't miss the Marché de Wazemmes, the enormous international street market in the culturally diverse district of the same name. Note: it's all over by 2pm.

Lille may be France's most underrated metropolis. Recent decades have seen the country's fourth-largest city transform from an industrial centre into a glittering cultural and commercial hub. Highlights include its intriguing old town with ornamental French and Flemish architecture, renowned art museums, stylish shopping, outstanding cuisine, a nightlife scene enlivened by 80,000 university students, and some 1600 designers in its environs.

The Lillois have a well-deserved reputation for friendliness, and they're so proud of being friendly that they often mention it, usually over one of the superb beers brewed at one of the many artisan breweries, which, like *frites,* show the Belgian influence.

Thanks to the Eurostar and the TGV, Lille makes an easy weekend destination from London, Paris, Brussels and beyond. A recent phenomenon is visitors arriving by *péniches* (barges) from Belgium and the Netherlands – the waterways around Lille's old citadel are often filled with barges heavily laden with bikes.

Lille's Gilded Centre
Pick an avenue, any avenue

Stand on **Place du Général de Gaulle** (the former Grand' Place) and spin around. To the north, beyond the **Cathédrale**

GETTING AROUND

Central Lille is easily walked. Lille's public transport *(ilevia.fr)* has two metro lines (use the Gambetta stop for Wazemmes). There's also an extensive network of trams and buses, and pay-per-use bicycle hire on almost every corner – download the V'lille app.

Paris is only 65 minutes by TGV. Note that Lille has two train stations 500m apart: **Gare Lille-Flandres** (local trains and some TGVs) and **Gare Lille-Europe** (Eurostar and some TGVs). Double-check which station your train is using as tracks are switched right up to departure.

HIGHLIGHTS
1 Palais des Beaux Arts

SIGHTS
2 Cathédrale Notre-Dame-de-la-Treille
3 Chambre de Commerce
4 Citadelle de Lille
5 Opéra
6 Parc de la Citadelle
7 Place du Général de Gaulle
8 Vieille Bourse

SLEEPING
9 Clarance Hotel
10 Grand Hôtel Bellevue
11 L'Hermitage Gantois
12 Mama Shelter Lille
13 OKKO Hotels Lille Centre
14 People Lille
15 Rosa Hotel

EATING
16 Café de Paris – Chez Boubier 1930
17 Chez Raoul Estaminet
18 Coffee Makers
19 Estaminet ch'tite Brigitte
20 Les Compagnons de la Grappe
21 Lucky Panda
22 Meert
23 Paddo Café

DRINKING & NIGHTLIFE
24 Au Boudin Bar
see 21 Bierbuik
25 HEIN l'estaminet
26 La Capsule

SHOPPING
see 22 Fromagerie Philippe Olivier
27 Les Halles de Wazemmes
28 Quentin Bailly
see 8 Vieille Bourse Book Market

TRANSPORT
29 Gare Lille-Europe
30 Gare Lille-Flandres
31 Le Grand Huit

Notre-Dame-de-la-Treille, are great nightlife districts. Before you is the Flemish Renaissance extravaganza, the 1653 **Vieille Bourse**: peek around the back side and take in the Louis XVI–style **Opéra** (1923) and the neo-Flemish **Chambre de Commerce** and its 76m-high spire adorned with a gilded clock. Now, choose an avenue and explore!

LILLE'S BEST SHOPS

Les Halles de Wazemmes: This sprawling covered food market has it all from Thai and Argentinian to French patisseries. *8am-8pm Tue-Sun*

Meert: This chocolate shop with 1839 jewellery-box interior is famed for *gaufres* (waffles) served to royalty since 1761. Has a tearoom. *10am-7.30pm*

Fromagerie Philippe Olivier: Hauts-de-France cheeses including Crémet du Cap Blanc Nez, Rollot, Vieux Samer and orange-crusted Maroilles. *10am-4.30pm Mon-Sat*

Vieille Bourse Book Market: The old stock exchange's courtyard hosts a book market with maps, posters, chess games and live music, too. *1-7pm Tue-Sun*

Quentin Bailly: The Lille native makes artful pralines, truffles and more. Handmade ice cream in summer. *10am-7pm Tue-Sat*

Lille Braderie

Artful Surprises
France's best regional museum

Lille's luminous **Palais des Beaux Arts** *(pba-lille.fr; adult/child €7/free)* exhibits France's second-largest collection after the Louvre. Its cache of sublime 15th- to 20th-century paintings includes works by Rubens, Van Dyck and Manet. In just two hours, visitors can get a survey of all the major themes of European art.

Brilliant curatorial sleight of hand lets viewers discover thematic and compositional similarities between seemingly unrelated works simply by the proximity with which they're hung. A fine example is Marc Chagall's *L'Apparition de la famille de l'artiste* (*The Appearance of the Artist's Family*; 1935-1947), which takes on a whole new meaning when seen in context with the nearby *Jésus au Jardin des Oliviers* (*Jesus in the Garden of Olive Trees*; 1600-1610) by El Greco.

More whimsically, but equally effective, is the contrast of Van Gogh's *Les Vaches* (*The Cows*; 1890) with *Cinq Études de Vaches* (*Five Studies of Cows*; 1620) by Jacob Jordaens.

 DRINKING BEER IN LILLE: TOP CHOICES

Au Boudin Bar: A student favourite which serves largely Belgian beer at rock-bottom prices and shows major (and minor) sports matches. Tree-shaded terrace. *5pm-1am Mon-Sat*

HEIN l'estaminet: Run by the city's coolest brewery, with over 20 different beers on tap. Three levels of colourful decor and lively terrace. *noon-11.30pm*

Bierbuik: Regular live music, fine Flanders beers and dishes that come with generous portions of frites. In the heart of vibrant nightlife. *noon-midnight*

La Capsule: Spread across three levels, Lille's best craft-beer bar is renowned for serving up 300 different brews over the course of a year. *5pm-1am*

On the lower level, don't miss the extraordinary displays of enormous 18th-century **scale models of fortified cities** in northern France and Belgium. Minutely detailed, these are works of art in their own right (they were used to plan military campaigns). Note that the model of Ypres was used as a guide for the reconstruction of that Renaissance city after it was pulverised in WWI.

The Braderie Hoopla
Join the huge festivities

Early every September, Lille hosts one of Europe's largest flea markets (and spectacles), the **Lille Braderie** (braderie-de-lille.fr). It's a sight to behold: over 100km of stalls across the city centre, which attract around two million visitors over a long weekend.

Culture with a Splash
Lille's most innovative museum

The building is the exhibition at the **La Piscine – Musée d'Art et d'Industrie** (roubaix-lapiscine.com; adult/child €9/free). In an old art deco public swimming pool in the Lillois suburb of Roubaix (metro Roubaix Grand Place), this show-stopper of a museum now literally and figuratively echoes its past. Galleries celebrate art and industry, largely from the 19th and 20th centuries, with sculptures reflecting off areas where water still stands. Both temporary and permanent exhibitions rarely disappoint.

> **L'ISLE TO LILLE**
>
> Lille owes its name – once spelled L'Isle – to its 11th-century beginnings as an island in the Deûle River – traces of which you can still see in the centre.
>
> Various powers fought over this important trading city until it came under Habsburg control in 1477. Later, Charles V of Spain took charge. Lille enjoyed its 'Golden Century' when it expanded in the early 17th century.
>
> In 1667, the city was captured by French forces led personally by Louis XIV, who promptly set about fortifying his prize, creating the Vauban-designed Citadelle.
>
> In the 19th century, Lille was the centre of the industrialised textile industry. Writer Victor Hugo exposed the appalling living conditions of the city's working class in the 1850s.

 EATING & DRINKING IN LILLE: OUR PICKS

Estaminet ch'tite Brigitte: Working-class Flanders dishes are served with creative flair. Hearty fare rarely found outside the region, in a fun setting. noon-10.30pm €€

Chez Raoul Estaminet: Bistro that's a top choice for mussels, served three ways on checkered tablecloths in a cosy dining room. noon-2.30pm, 6.30-10.30pm Tue-Sun €€

Café de Paris – Chez Boubier 1930: Beloved classic serves one thing: succulent ribeye steak under a Béarnaise-like sauce with unlimited perfectly crisp frites. 11.30am-9pm €€

Les Compagnons de la Grappe: Seems touristy, but this temple of Flanders cuisine is locally beloved for its well-crafted specialities, served in a lovely courtyard. noon-10pm €€

Lucky Panda: Lille's best Vietnamese. Dishes are often a nod to traditional French cuisine, with unusual fusions that span Europe and Asia. noon-2pm, 7-10pm Tue-Sat €€

Paddo Café: Full-on breakfasts. Serves eggs any way you like them, filled brioche baps and ricotta pancakes; come later for sandwiches, salads etc. 8am-5pm €

Friterie des Lilas: It's worth the minor trek beyond Gare Lille-Europe for the city's best frites (and there's a lot of competition). 11.30am-2pm, 6.30-9pm €

Coffee Makers: Organic foods to start your day, fine pastries plus sandwiches for lunch; coffee roasted in-house. 10am-6pm €

CYCLING TOUR

Riding a Riverside Beer Trail

The Deûle River begins its journey in Douai, just south of Lille, before merging with the River Lys at the Belgian border. A flat cycle lane stretches along the shady banks of the river, much of the trail following old railway tracks. Along the way are numerous *guinguettes* – waterside bars with space to dance – where, in Lille – as opposed to other parts of France – cheap beer is the drink of choice.

❶ Parc de la Citadelle

Hire a well-loved Dutch-style bike from **Le Grand Huit** *(legrandhuit.eu)* and begin with a short circuit of Parc de la Citadelle. You'll have to pay if you want to see exotic fauna at the zoo, but anyone can see the grazing sheep around the walls of the 17th-century **Citadelle de Lille** (now a NATO base).

The Cycle: Stay on the lower bank of the Deûle, and with Parc de la Citadelle behind you, follow the well-marked greenway running east towards Belgium.

❷ Guinguette de la Madeleine

This part of the route is the most urban, passing old factories, scrap yards and Lille's suburbs. If you're thirsty, the first *guinguette* you reach is **Guinguette de la Madeleine** *(hours vary)*, but pace yourself – you're only 2km in.

The Cycle: Keep cycling east, leaving the city behind you.

❸ Wambrechies

The first town worth stopping at is Wambrechies, on the west bank of the river.

Deûle River, Lille

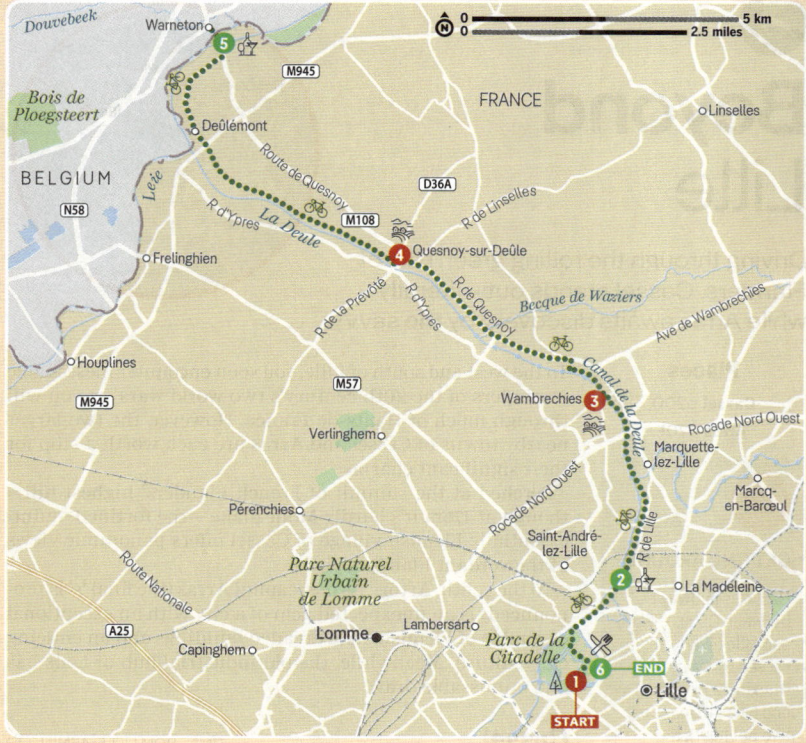

Cross the Pont de Wambrechies to reach **Le Cap** (*10am-8pm*), a former *guinguette* gone upscale and now serving good food.

The Cycle: It's simple: keep heading the same way! Quesnoy-sur-Deûle is around 6km away.

4 Quesnoy-sur-Deûle & Deûlémont

Quesnoy-sur-Deûle is on the east bank of the river, with a beautiful red-brick church. You've left the railway tracks behind by this point. The landscape becomes greener and more pastoral. A modern *guinguette*, **Station Troquet** (*11am-7pm Wed-Sun*) is in a serene little park. Several *péniches* (private barges) are moored here.

The Cycle: It's 8.5km to Warneton, the first town in Belgium, but there are stops on the way.

5 Guinguette de la Marine & Warneton

Belgium awaits, but speed up as you go past a large, frozen-foods factory that kicks up a stink. After the air clears, bear right to join the Route de Quesnoy, which takes you onto a bridge over the River Lys. The island in the middle holds your last *guinguette* in France, **Guinguette de la Marine** (*10am-10pm*). After a drink, cross into Belgium. There isn't loads to do in Warneton, but riverside bar **La Bascule** (*10am-11pm*) is cheery and has cheap Belgian beers.

The Cycle: Turn around and ride back to Lille, criss-crossing the river to stop at as many *guinguettes* as take your fancy. It's 20km back.

6 Péniche Archimède

Once you reach Parc de la Citadelle, you can return your bike. Walk about 150m west through the waterfront Jardin Vauban for a final drink at Guinguette de la Marine. Sate that hunger with burgers, charcuterie plates, veggie specialities and more.

Beyond Lille

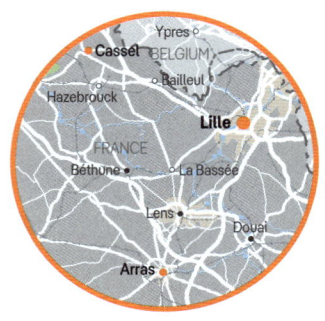

Driving through the rolling green hills of Flanders, Cassel stands out – literally – while Arras awaits discovery by the savvy.

Places
Cassel p200
Arras p201

GETTING AROUND

Cassel is midway between Calais (59km) and Lille (49km). It's served by trains from Dunkirk (25 minutes) and Lille (40 minutes, two per hour); the station is 2.5km downhill from the centre. Buses link the pair, or you can take a taxi.

Arras' train station is 750m southeast of the main squares. Service includes Amiens (40 minutes), Lille (40 minutes) and Paris (50 minutes by TGV). The old centre is easily explored on foot.

To the west and south of Lille, you soon encounter inescapable reminders of the 20th century's two world wars, as you will through much of Hauts-de-France. However, the two larger nearby towns of Cassel and Arras are each worth a stop for their significant charms.

Perched at the summit of French Flanders' highest hill – though at 176m it's hardly Mont Blanc – the fortified, quintessentially Flemish village of Cassel offers panoramic views of the verdant Flanders plain.

To the south, Artois' former capital Arras (the final 's' is pronounced) is an unexpected gem of a city with an exceptional ensemble of Flemish-style arcaded buildings and an enticing cafe culture. Meanwhile, the old industrial hub of Lens has one unmissable draw.

Cassel

TIME FROM LILLE: **45MIN**

See a town above it all

Sitting 176m above the plains, Cassel has been prominent in Flanders affairs for centuries. From the train or car park (if it's a busy summer weekend and you can't drive close), the **walk** up follows winding trails up the hill and affords broad views of the region.

In the centre, the long, cobblestoned **Grand' Place** is the town's focal point. It's ringed by austere 16th- to 18th-century red-brick buildings with steep slate roofs. Cafes, bars, good restaurants and shops serve the busy day-tripping trade. **Le Passage** hosts a collection of stalls run by local artisans. Nearby, the **Musée de Flandre** *(museedeflandre.fr; adult/child €8/free)*

 EATING & DRINKING IN CASSEL: OUR PICKS

Haut Bonheur de la Table: Exceptional fine French restaurant with well-priced changing menus created from local ingredients. Terrace with views. *lunch Thu-Mon, dinner Thu-Sat* €€

Estaminet Kasteelhof: At the highest *estaminet* (traditional Flemish restaurant) in Flanders, quaff Flemish beer while enjoying the views. Terrace tables in summer. *11am-10pm Thu-Sun* €€

Estaminet La Taverne Flamande: Broad terrace with broader views; enjoy the hearty fare at this trad tavern with lashings of style. *noon-2pm, 7-9.30pm Thu-Sun* €€

Entrance Cafe au Trois Moulins: Right at the main entrance to the old town, enjoy the action at the outdoor tables or partake of the nearly 100-year-old interior. *9am-8pm* €

Arras

has a worthwhile, well-presented collection of Flemish art, both old and modern, including canvases in the 15th-century Flemish primitive style and explorations of the local carnival culture.

Arras

TIME FROM LILLE: **45MIN**

Savour a masterpiece

Arras has two extraordinary ancient market squares: the **Grand' Place** and the almost adjacent, smaller, cafe-lined **Place des Héros**. Both are surrounded by 155 harmonious 17th- and 18th-century Flemish Baroque houses topped by curvaceous gables. Although the structures vary in decorative detail, their 345 sandstone columns form a common arcade unique in France. Like 80% of Arras, both squares – especially handsome at night – were heavily damaged during WWI and then rebuilt with flair.

The Flemish Gothic **Hôtel de Ville** (city hall) dates from the 16th century but was completely rebuilt after WWI. It's the location of the **tourist office** *(arraspaysdartois.com)*, which has info on the various ways to tour the building. For a panoramic view, take the lift (plus 43 stairs) up the 75m-high, UNESCO-listed gilded **belfry** *(adult/child €3.50/2.40)*. Or, for a subterranean perspective, head down into the *souterrains* (cellars), also known as *boves*, which were turned into British command posts, hospitals and barracks during WWI.

Don't miss the **Marché à Arras** *(8am-1pm, Wed & Sat)*, one of northern France's best markets. The quality of the produce and the prepared foods is superb.

LOUVRE AT THE COALFACE

Destroyed in WWI and battered in WWII, Lens was once entirely dependent on coal mining. Millions of tons of the black stuff were pulled from the earth here in the 19th and the first half of the 20th century, fueling French industry and warming French hearths.

Today, Lens' industrial legacy is on the same slag heaps still looming around the countryside, even as the coal residue has been scrubbed off French monuments and cities over the last several decades.

To bring a new facet of life to Lens, in 2012, a branch of the Louvre Museum was opened on the site of one of the old coal pits. The **Musée du Louvre-Lens** *(louvrelens.fr; free)* does not have permanent displays but rather stages two major exhibitions a year.

EATING & DRINKING IN ARRAS: OUR PICKS

La Cave des Saveurs: Flemish dishes and the local speciality *andouillette d'Arras* (finely ground chitterling sausage) served in a vaulted cellar. *noon-2pm, 7-10pm Mon-Sat* €€

Carpe Diem: Casual bistro with Flemish fare. Inspired regional beer and wine list; good outdoor tables on a quiet street. *noon-2pm, 7-10pm Tue-Sun* €€

La Dame Jeanne Bar à Vin: Intimate wine bar in atmospheric vaulted cellar. Menu changes with the seasons; offers wine courses. *6-11pm Tue-Sat* €€

Chunkies Bakery: Corner shop sells cookies and treats in myriad variations. Not a place for healthy breakfast, but a place to get happy. *noon-6pm* €

Amiens

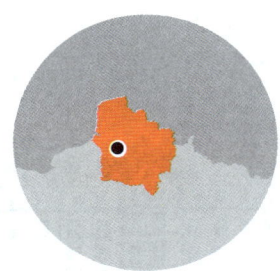

GOTHIC CATHEDRAL | TOURING BY LAND & WATER | VIBRANT NIGHTLIFE

☑ TOP TIP

Parking is always at a premium in the centre of Amiens. If saddled with a car, there are large underground garages by the train station. Don't bother trying to find something closer to the cathedral; leave your car at the train station and enjoy seeing the city on foot.

Synonymous with a larger-than-life cathedral, Amiens makes an ideal way station in the region and a base for visits to the myriad WWI sites to the north and west. The pedestrianised streets in the shadow of the 13th-century spire of France's largest Gothic cathedral are home to good restaurants and make for good walking amid other centuries-old survivors.

The River Somme scenically bisects the city and along its banks are green spaces and the red-brick streets of Amiens' preserved former working-class neighbourhood, *le quartier* St-Leu. Its canals and half-timbered buildings give it an appealing old feel, but it's entirely contemporary, with riverside bookshops, lively bars, and restaurants serving everything from Japanese to Senegalese cuisine.

Nearby, the *hortillonnages* are a network of waterways that wind through urban vegetable gardens within sight of the cathedral. You can serenely navigate these waters, escaping to a land of vibrant floral displays and verdant community gardens.

GETTING AROUND

Amiens' train station is in the centre and the cathedral, museums, St-Leu and *hortillonnages* are all accessible on foot.

Amiens is a regional train hub, with services to the towns and cities of the coast, as well as Arras and Lille. Paris is 70 minutes away.

Amiens' Crowning Glory

France's largest cathedral

The so-big-you-can't-comprehend-it **Cathédrale Notre-Dame** *(cathedrale-amiens.fr)* has drawn pilgrims and visitors to Amiens for centuries, and its UNESCO-recognised details astound (p204). Inside, don't miss the stained-glass windows, which dapple the cathedral floor with kaleidoscopic colours. While looking down, find and follow the octagonal, 234m-long labyrinth on the black-and-white floor of the nave, which evokes the quest towards salvation.

Treasury visits *(adult/child €5/free)* feature medieval masterpieces in gold. Climbing the North Tower *(adult/child €7/free)* can be unforgettable, and not just for the exertion – it's 302 steps to the top. Midway, there's a respite where you can appreciate the gargoyle waterspouts up close – a spectacle on a rainy day! Once up top, the region is all around you.

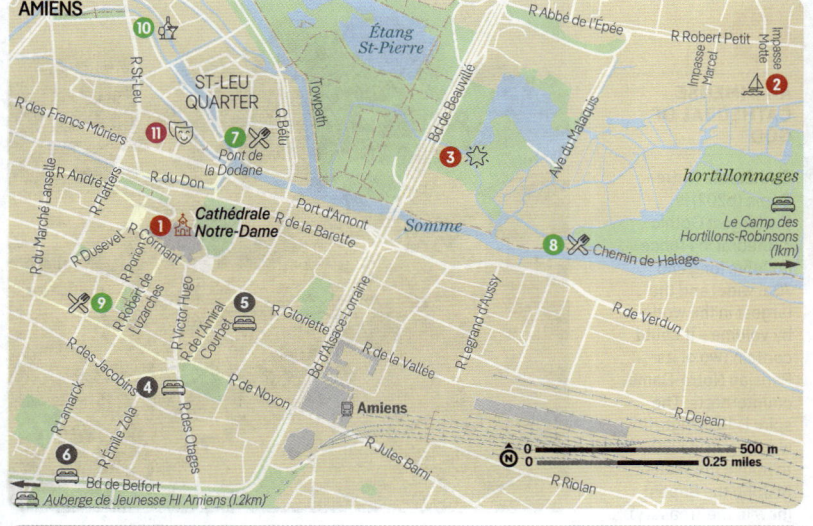

- **HIGHLIGHTS**
  1 Cathédrale Notre-Dame
- **ACTIVITIES**
  2 Club Nautique de Rivery
  3 Hortillonnages Cruises
- **SLEEPING**
  4 Hôtel Spa Marotte
  5 Hôtel Victor Hugo
  6 Une Maison en Ville
- **EATING**
  7 Le Dos d'Âne
  8 Ô'Jardin
  9 Querelle
- **DRINKING & NIGHTLIFE**
  10 Delirium Café Amiens
- **ENTERTAINMENT**
  11 Chés Cabotans d'Amiens

Voyage in the Gardens

The ultimate floating urban escape

Amiens' *hortillonnages* (vegetable gardens) span some 300 hectares of colourful gardens, which spill down to meet a warren of rivers and 65km of little channels. Sunflowers, bougainvillea, scarecrows, windmills and even flocks of sheep enliven the scene, which includes actual produce farms that supply local restaurants.

Floating along this watery idyll is delightful on a balmy day. The riverside restaurant **Ô'Jardin** *(o-jardin-amiens. fr; adult/child €7/free)* hires out rowboats for short paddles

EATING & DRINKING IN AMIENS: OUR PICKS

Querelle: One of the best, run by a gracious family in an antique-filled parlour. Excellent cocktails and wine list; order off the chalkboard. Book ahead. *7pm–midnight Tue-Sat* €€

Ô'Jardin: Fresh fare and a lovely, shady garden that reflects its *hortillonnage* location; long menu of seasonal specials and brasserie standards. On-site boat rental. *9am–11pm* €€

Le Dos d'Âne: A St-Leu fixture, crêperie with traditional decor, outdoor seating and locally made Maroilles cheese on just about everything. *noon–9pm* €

Delirium Café Amiens: Anchors a row of bars on a St-Leu canal, named for the high-octane Belgian beer. Regular live music. *5pm–1am*

AN IMMENSE CATHEDRAL OF GOD

Cathédrale Notre-Dame (p202) is the largest Gothic cathedral in France (at 145m long and 70m wide) and the largest in the world by volume – it could contain two of its Parisian Notre-Dame counterparts. The spire is 112m high. It was begun in 1220 to house the skull of St John the Baptist (now in the Treasury). Architecturally, the cathedral is renowned for its soaring Gothic arches (42.3m high over the transept), unity of style and immense interior. Centuries of artwork have been accumulated here; look for the 17th-century statue *L'Ange Pleureur* (The Crying Angel) behind the Baroque high altar. Bronze and stone plaques in the south transept honour American, Australian, British, Canadian and New Zealand soldiers who perished in WWI.

Hortillonnages (p203)

around a set circuit, or for longer adventures **Club Nautique de Rivery** *(hortillonnages-canoe.com; adult/child from €13/7)* hires out kayaks. It's also worth checking to see if **Hortillonnages Cruises** *(hortillonnages-amiens.fr)* is operating its guided boat tours.

Amiens & Puppets
800 years of entertainment

Supported by the city, the beloved puppet theatre **Chés Cabotans d'Amiens** *(ches-cabotans-damiens.com; adult/child €10/5)* has its roots in local traditions as old as the cathedral. Kids (and the rest of the family) love the traditional shows – even if they're not fluent in French or local dialects.

Beyond Amiens

The Western Front in WWI passed right through Hauts-de-France; today, moving memorials and compelling museums recall the sacrifices.

Travelling the green hills, verdant farmland and thick forests between Amiens and Lille, you soon notice old concrete structures in fields, perfectly manicured cemeteries in remote locations, soaring memorials appearing out of the blue and well-funded museums in tiny villages.

All are the legacy of WWI, which left its mark here like in few other places in four years of constant trench warfare, which included landmark battles like the Somme. The frontlines are one long band of sights across the landscape and as the years have passed, the focus has turned from the militaristic aspects to the human costs.

Visits here are fascinating *and* affecting, even if you didn't think a war fought over 100 years ago would interest you.

Places
Albert p205
Villers-Bretonneux p206
Péronne p206
Longueval p207
Thiepval p207
Cambrai p210
Bullecourt p210
Vimy p210
Compiègne p211

Albert
TIME FROM AMIENS: **35MIN**

Monument to realism
On the frontlines for most of WWI, Albert was constantly bombarded, mostly by the Germans. In 1915, shells hit the iconic gilded statue of the Virgin Mary atop the **Basilique Notre-Dame de Brebières**, causing it to lean down as if to toss the baby Jesus. Few of the Allied troops who passed by forgot the shocking sight, which lasted through the war.

Today, the church and statue are reconstructed. Underneath is the **Somme 1916 Museum** *(musee-somme-1916.eu; adult/child €8/5)*, which recreates a long wartime trench to give a realistic account of the conditions faced by the troops.

Outside, there are cafes on the square. Albert is on the **No 32 Memory Route Cycling Tour** from Arras to Amiens.

GETTING AROUND
Exploring the Hauts-de-France region's towns, battlefields and memorials for WWI requires the flexibility of your own vehicle. Numerous tour companies offer tours of varying durations. Bikes are good on the back roads and allow for more contemplative travel, but sourcing rentals is only possible in regional centres such as Lille and Amiens.

Trains are a limited option; Albert is on the Amiens–Arras–Lille line, while Cambrai and Compiègne are on the Paris–Lille line.

HOW TO VISIT THE WWI SIGHTS

Amiens makes an excellent hub for visiting the sites along the Western Front. It has many good accommodation options. Arras (p201) is also good, although the selection is smaller. Sleeping and dining options are more limited elsewhere. During the day, you may not find lunch options in the smaller villages. Either bring a picnic or plan on stopping in larger towns. If a particular museum or memorial is important to your visit, always confirm the hours, as they vary by season. Cemeteries tend to be accessible 24/7. While driving around, an informative and engaging WWI podcast is *Not So Quiet on the Western Front*. Good audiobooks include Paul Fussell's slow burn, *The Great War and Modern Memory*.

Australian National War Memorial

Villers-Bretonneux

TIME FROM AMIENS: **30MIN**

Australia's place of remembrance

On a gentle ridge, the main place of remembrance for the over 295,000 Australians who fought on the Western Front is an important stop. The **Australian National War Memorial** *(sjmc.gov.au; free)* is centred on a 30.5m **tower**, which overlooks a battlefield where Australian and British troops repelled the Germans in April 1918. Walls are carved with the names of over 10,700 soldiers missing in France. Like many monuments built in the 1920s and 1930s in the region, the memorial bears scars from fighting in WWII.

Behind the tower, the **Sir John Monash Centre** is a flashy, modern museum that starts with a 360-degree video about WWI that's long on stunts and special effects but short on historical context. Much more affecting are the simple photos later in the exhibits showing veterans returning to Australia surrounded by deliriously happy relatives. Their 1000-yard stares amid the celebrations only hint at what they've survived.

Péronne

TIME FROM AMIENS: **1HR**

The first museum to visit

For historical and cultural context, the best place to start a visit to the WWI battlefields is the outstanding **Historial de la Grande Guerre** *(historial.org)* inside Péronne's fortified medieval château. This award-winning museum tells the story of the war chronologically, with equal space given to the German, French and British perspectives on what happened, how and why. Displays show how propaganda was used to whip populations into pro-war frenzies.

The visually engaging material includes the bone-chilling engravings of German artist Otto Dix, which capture the naive patriotism and unimaginable horror of the war. The light-filled galleries detail the experiences of soldiers.

Longueval

TIME FROM AMIENS: 45MIN

South Africa's memorial

The **Mémorial Sud-Africain Delville Wood** (1926; *delville wood.com; free*) stands where the 1st South African Infantry Brigade was nearly wiped out in hand-to-hand fighting in July 1916 (of the 3153 men at the start of the battle, only 143 were alive and unhurt five days later).

The complex reflects the transformation of South Africa over the decades – in WWI, black South Africans were banned from combat roles but supplied labour, and many died. Monumental apartheid-era bronzes reflect old racial attitudes; newer displays in the museum do not. In 2016, the names of all the South Africans who died in WWI were inscribed on a memorial wall and the complex was rededicated.

In the town, there is a small memorial to the village's dead in several wars. Take note of the Dobel family: fighting killed members in 1870, during WWI and at the start of WWII. Then the entire family was killed. They were Jewish.

Thiepval

TIME FROM AMIENS: 45MIN

The first and last day

Its silhouette recognisable from afar, the 45m-high **Thiepval Memorial** (*cwgc.org; free*) honours the missing of the Somme and is inscribed with the names of more than 72,000 British and South African soldiers whose remains were never recovered or identified. Designed by Edwin Lutyens, the memorial was built from 1928 to 1932 on the site of a German stronghold that was stormed on 1 July 1916, the bloody first day of the Battle of the Somme.

The on-site **Thiepval Museum** (*historial.org; adult/child €6/3*) is run by Péronne's outstanding **Historial de la Grande Guerre**. It pulls no punches, providing a 60m-long illustrated walk-through of the events of the first day. A room dedicated to the photos and actual last letters home of the dead may prove unbearable for some.

The surrounding lands are dotted by small cemeteries and memorials that stretch to the horizon of the now pastoral rolling green hills.

BATTLE OF THE SOMME

The Battle of the Somme is a bloody exclamation mark on the overall slaughter of the Western Front. Fought between 1 July and 18 November 1916 along a nearly 40km front north and south of the River Somme, it was one of the deadliest of WWI, with nearly 60,000 casualties on the first day alone. In 141 days, over one million casualties were suffered on both sides; territorial gains were minor.

A joint British and French action, it was an attempt to break German lines and relieve the pressure on French forces fighting at Verdun. Mistakes and hubris on the part of commanders contributed to the failure, while the troops fought for their lives on the ground.

EATING & DRINKING BEYOND AMIENS: TOP CHOICES

Le Canberra: Friendly pub shows Bullecourt's affection for all things Australia. Displays highlight experiences from the war. Good coffee, cold beer. *hours vary* €

Le Hygge Café: On a leafy Albert square, brasserie near the church and museum has a casual menu. Good breakfast and lunch. *10.30am-midnight* €€

Le Bistrot D'Antoine: Delicious bistro on a square with a fountain overlooking the château and museum in Péronne. Good-value lunch menu. *noon-2pm, 7-9pm Tue-Sat* €€

Le Bistrot Dit Vin: Artful all-day bistro serves a wide range of French dishes, from *choucroute* to salads. Attractive presentation, good desserts. *9am-10pm Tue-Sat* €€

ROAD TRIP

Seeing the Human Side of WWI

Appropriately dotted with random patches of red poppies, the fields of northern France have been smoothed by decades of farming and carpeted with crops like sugar beets, potatoes and yellow-flowered rapeseed. But WWI remains everywhere. The verdant expanses are punctuated by countless decaying concrete pillboxes and tiny cemeteries.

❶ 38th Welsh Division Memorial

The Western Front's most surprising memorial, the bright, red animated **38th Welsh Division Memorial** dragon (1986) is everything a cold stone cenotaph is not. Walk 700m north to **Flatiron Copse Cemetery**, a typically British Commonwealth War Graves Commission (CWGC) cemetery in an isolated spot, built where the soldiers died. Look for the sets of brothers (Philby, Hardwidge and Tregaskis).

The Drive: Narrow lanes lead to Contalmaison and the next stop. Watch for **Bell's Redoubt**, a memorial to an English football player who died here and won the Victoria Cross.

❷ Lochnagar Crater

On the morning of 1 July 1916, the German trenches ran along here until the British detonated 27 tonnes of explosives, leaving a 30m-deep and 100m-wide crater. Today, the **Lochnagar Crater** is a privately held memorial *(lochnagarcrater.org; free)* with a pastoral bent. Signage tells the compelling stories of those who lived and died, including John Scollen, Vera Brittain and Alfred Moxham.

The Drive: Head north on country lanes via Authuille. Fierce Somme fighting occurred here, and there are many monuments, including the **Thiepval Memorial** (p207).

Lochnagar Crater

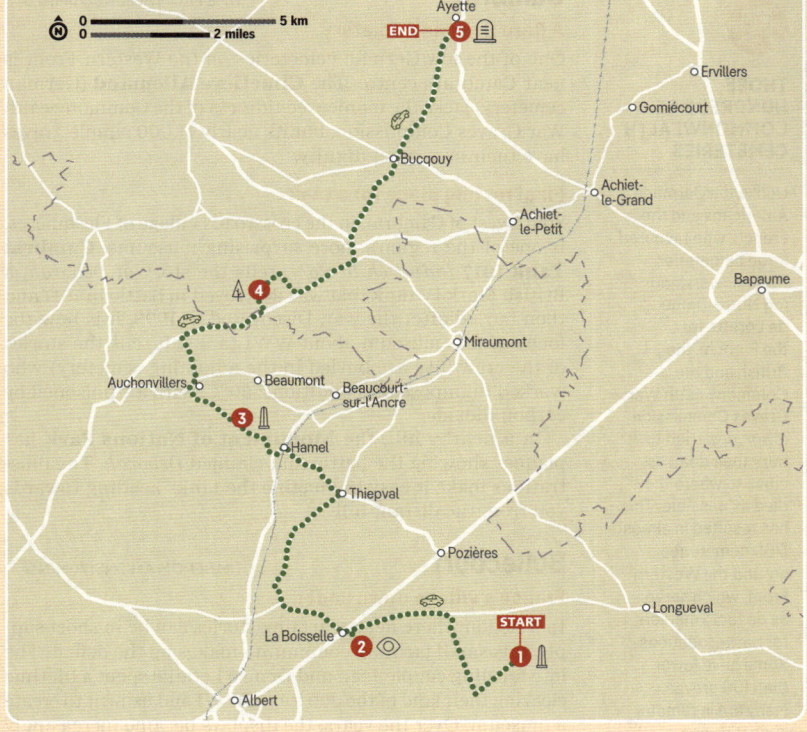

3 Beaumont-Hamel Newfoundland Memorial

The Newfoundland Regiment attacked the Germans here on 1 July 1916 and suffered 86% casualties in 30 minutes. The battlefield, with its **Beaumont-Hamel Newfoundland Memorial** *(veterans.gc.ca; free)*, is well preserved. A small museum gives an overview. The bronze caribou, like the Welsh dragon, is one of the region's most uplifting monuments.

The Drive: Drive on farming roads via barely there Auchonvillers to a cluster of cemeteries. You'll spot some of the CWGC's least accessible and smallest cemeteries.

4 Sheffield Memorial Park

Look for a copse of trees at **Sheffield Memorial Park** in a hollow amid lonely fields. Before the draft, the British military encouraged people to volunteer in units of 'pals' as a way to get recruits. But when battles went wrong, like the Somme, entire neighbourhoods, companies and clans were wiped out. Walk through the trees to the poignant **Railway Hollow Cemetery**.

The Drive: Country roads take you away from the Somme battle area to Ayette village.

5 Ayette Indian & Chinese Cemetery

By 1918, the Western Front was a hellscape of millions of dead soldiers. The British recruited tens of thousands of Chinese labourers to toil in Europe, giving them the gruesome task of recovering and burying Allied war dead. Some 80 of these *travailleurs chinois* (Chinese labourers) are buried in this secluded CWGC **Ayette Indian & Chinese Cemetery**, along with people of other nationalities. Further north, the **Neuve-Chapelle Memorial** is a moving tribute to Indian soldiers, including one unit of 1000, entirely wiped out in one night's battle.

THOSE HUNDREDS OF COMMONWEALTH CEMETERIES

Unlike the Germans, Americans and the French, who favoured large cemeteries for their war dead (eg Notre-Dame de Lorette for the French), the British and the Commonwealth War Graves Commission *(cwgc.org)* tried to bury their dead as close to where they died as possible. This has resulted in almost 1700 cemeteries around the Western Front, which serve as de facto markers for battle locations. Some have fewer than 100 graves. Many are in remote, evocative spots; all are meticulously maintained. Usually, a brass door near the entrance will protect an index of graves, a visitors' log and possibly a description of the battle. You'll likely see mementoes left by relatives at the base of some markers.

Cambrai

TIME FROM AMIENS: **70MIN**

A Rare German Cemetery

One of the few German cemeteries on the Western Front is near Cambrai's centre. The **Cimetière Allemand** (German cemetery) lacks the manicured tidiness of the Commonwealth War Graves Commission, but its nearly 11,000 simple graves have their own quiet dignity.

Final resting place for a tank

Southwest of Cambrai, in the crossroads village of Flesquières, is one of the region's more surprising museums. **Cambrai Tank 1917** *(adult/child €6/4)* tells the story of *Deborah*, a British Mark IV tank that was destroyed in battle in 1917 and then buried after the war. Discovered in 1998, it is now the focus of this museum about WWI tanks. It tells the stories of the crew (five are buried in the adjoining cemetery) who worked in impossible conditions: 50°C, with air poisoned by carbon dioxide.

On a nearby hill, the **Monument of Nations Park** has plaques showing the battle that claimed *Deborah*. The illustrations make it easy to imagine the tanks heading towards you from the distant hills.

Bullecourt

TIME FROM AMIENS: **70MIN**

France's village down under

In a region where heartwarming stories can be in short supply, this small farming community makes up the deficit. The late farming couple Jean and Denise Letaille spent a lifetime clearing their land of the detritus of WWI and using it to create a museum. Over the years, the displays became increasingly professional and today the **Jean & Denise Letaille Bullecourt 1917 Museum** *(adult/child €5/free)* tells the story of the Battle of Arras, which raged all around here.

And the story doesn't end there. Australian troops did much of the fighting against the Germans here. Over the decades, Bullecourt has forged close ties Down Under, such that the cafe is named Le Canberra, Oz-themed murals decorate buildings, and every 25 April (Anzac Day), the town switches to Australian time.

Vimy

TIME FROM AMIENS: **1¼HR**

Canada's heartfelt memorial

After the war, the French attempted to erase signs of battle and return northern France to agriculture and normalcy. Conversely, the Canadians remembered their fallen by preserving part of the crater-pocked battlefield at the **Canadian National Vimy Memorial** *(veterans.gc.ca; free)* as it was when the guns fell silent. The resulting chilling, eerie moonscape of Vimy is a poignant place to comprehend the hell of the Western Front.

Visitors can hike the grounds to the soaring white limestone **WWI Memorial** with its allegorical figures and names of the nearly 11,300 missing Canadians carved into its base.

Elsewhere, there are recreated trenches sans any of the distasteful elements. A small **museum** gives a useful abbreviated summary of the war and is a tonal shift from others: it shows German and Canadian troops coexisting peacefully.

Countless names

On a ridge overlooking the WWI ruins of the village of **Ablain-Saint-Nazaire**, the monumental **Ring of Remembrance** *(memorial1418.com)* overwhelms visitors with the waste and folly of the Western Front. You walk past panel after panel engraved with 579,606 tiny names: WWI dead from both sides are listed alphabetically, without reference to nationality, rank or religion. Across the road from the memorial is the vast French military cemetery, **Notre-Dame de Lorette**; 6000 unidentified French soldiers are interred in the base of the **Lantern Tower** (1921).

Trails with signs detailing the wartime fighting lace the surrounding hills.

Compiègne

TIME FROM AMIENS: 1¼HR

Where WWI ended

The site of the official armistice in WWI is today recalled at the **Mémorial de l'Armistice** *(armistice-museum.com; adult/child €7/5)*, which has a replica of the railcar where the papers were signed (Hitler destroyed the original site in 1940; the carriage was burned in 1945).

Horrors of the next war

Often overlooked, the **Mémorial de l'Internement et de la Déportation – Camp de Royallieu** *(memorial-compiegne.fr; €4)* memorialises the atrocities of another war. This former French military base was used as a Nazi transit and internment camp from 1941 to 1944. Three surviving barracks house a moving museum that follows the fate of the 54,000 people held here. Many were marched to the train station (where today a WWII-era boxcar continues the chilling theme) and then on to Auschwitz.

WHY FROMELLES IS MEANINGFUL TO ME

Ryan Ver Berkmoes, Lonely Planet writer

The once-forgotten Battle of Fromelles encapsulates the futility and waste of WWI. On 19 July 1916, 1917 Australians and 519 Britons were killed in just one day of a poorly planned assault on German lines. The commander was told the night before that the attack was unnecessary. However, he declared that men would be depressed if they didn't get to fight. The sordid tale is laid out in a 30-minute visit to the **Musée de la Bataille de Fromelles** *(musee-bataille-fromelles.fr; adult/child €5/free)*. You can also get a walking guide to battle sights around the village. One stop is an old concrete pillbox in a farmer's field where a young Austrian corporal was stationed. His name: Adolf Hitler.

 EATING BEYOND AMIENS: OUR PICKS

Le Poppy Bar: Near the Lochnagar Crater (p208); looks basic from the outside, but it serves good, traditional dishes that draw residents from afar. *noon-2pm, 7-9pm Mon-Fri* €

Le Tommy Cafe: In Pozières; definitely mention the war – it has a small museum and sandbag decor. Serves English pub food. *10am-5pm Tue-Sun* €

Bistrot du Terroir: Genteel little bistro in Compiègne; classic menu of well-prepared dishes presented with care. Warm welcome; good wine list. *noon-2pm, 7-10pm Mon-Sat* €€

Les Halles du Grenier à Sel: Fruit, veggies, cheeses, wines and prepared dishes sold inside a Compiègne store built in 1784. Picnics! *8am-7pm Tue-Sat* €

Boulogne-sur-Mer

SEASIDE STROLLS | SEAFOOD EATS | SEE THE AQUARIUM

Once a port bustling with ferries and freighters (it still sees some traffic), Boulogne (the sur-Mer is dropped for non-formal occasions) today has a waterfront devoted to pleasure that's best enjoyed on foot. On the delightful 1.5km stroll from the Marché aux Poissons (fish market) out to the made-for-selfies little red lighthouse at the end of the breakwater, enjoy harbour and ocean views while passing Boulogne's star attraction, Nausicaá, one of the world's largest aquariums. Nearby is the city's large white-sand beach, backed by cafes.

Meanwhile, Boulogne's double-threat plays out up the hill. The Haute-Ville (Upper City) is perched high above the rest of town and girded by a 13th-century wall. It oozes medieval charm.

Centred on the Grande Rue and rue Adolphe Thiers, the Basse-Ville (Lower City) may not have the same architectural heritage, but it is close to the water and is good for nightlife.

Lofty Charm

Walk up to old Boulogne

Boulogne's hilltop Upper City (Haute-Ville) is an island of centuries-old buildings and cobblestone streets. You can walk around the top of the ancient stone defensive walls – look for signs for the Promenade des Remparts.

Enter through the **Porte Neuve**, a 13th-century gate, modified in the 17th and 19th centuries. It's at the northeastern end of the rue de Lille. You can't miss the 19th-century **Basilique Notre Dame**. Its towering 101m-high dome is visible from all over town. At 128m long, the vast, partly Romanesque crypt is believed to be the longest in France.

The real pleasure of the old town is simply strolling. Look for **Hôtel Desandrouin**, built between 1777 and 1780 as a private mansion, and the **Hôtel de Ville**, with a medieval 37m-high square belfry dating from the 12th century.

GETTING AROUND

The Upper and Lower Cities are both walkable; the walk between them is not far, but it is steep. If you prefer to take a bus, take bus L. Cycléco *(cycleco-boulogne-sur-mer.fr)* rents bikes.

The main train station, Gare Boulogne-Ville, is 1.2km southeast of the Basse-Ville (take bus F). The following have direct services: Amiens (1½ hours), Calais-Ville (40 minutes), Lille (one hour) and Paris (2½ hours).

☑ TOP TIP

Have lunch at the Marché aux Poissons (fish market) where over a dozen vendors sell seafood just unloaded from fishing boats docked alongside. Look for *cabillaud* (Atlantic cod), *carrelet* (plaice) and *sole* (sole) – Boulogne's most important commercial fish. You'll also find *homard* (lobster), *crabe* (crab) and *huîtres* (oysters) in season.

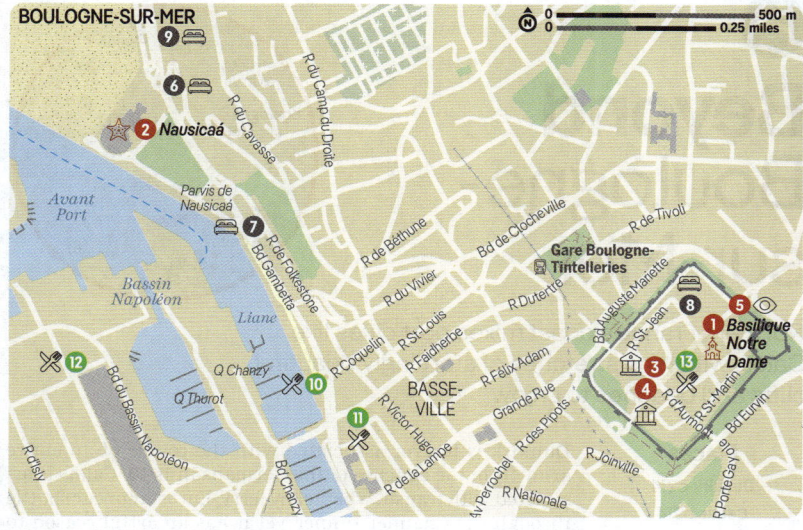

BOULOGNE-SUR-MER

- 🔴 **HIGHLIGHTS**
  1. Basilique Notre Dame
  2. Nausicaá
- 🔴 **SIGHTS**
  3. Hôtel de Ville
  4. Hôtel Desandrouin
  5. Porte Neuve
- ⚫ **SLEEPING**
  6. Hôtel La Matelote
  7. Hôtel Monsieur Georges
  8. L'Enclos de l'Evêché
  9. Opal'Inn
- 🟢 **EATING**
  10. Chez Sandrine La Poissonnerie
  11. L'Aurore
  12. Le Châtillon
  13. L'Îlot Vert

Europe's Largest Fish Tank
One of the world's great aquariums

At ginormous **Nausicaá** *(nausicaa.fr; adult/child €30/23)*, which has Europe's largest tank, you feel as though you're swimming with the sharks or some of the other 60,000 creatures living here. Sea turtles, California sea lions and African penguins are just a few of the residents – some of whom were born right here. Star attractions include a 21m-long underwater viewing window, an underwater tunnel (good for watching the manta rays glide by overhead) and a balcony providing bird's-eye views.

Kids of all ages can engage with ecologically conscious exhibits and activities, including fish petting, feeding sessions and sea-lion shows throughout the day. One of the most popular sessions is about how to eat responsibly from the sea – a fitting topic here in Boulogne, France's most important fishing port.

 WHERE TO EAT IN BOULOGNE: OUR PICKS

Le Châtillon: 1950 bar-restaurant with red banquettes and brass maritime lanterns; famous seafood platters must be booked ahead. *5.30am-4.30pm Mon-Sat* €€

L'Îlot Vert: Haute-Ville bistro with style and a changing menu based on what's in season. Book the cobbled, ivy-draped rear courtyard. *noon-1.30pm, 7-9pm Tue-Sat* €€

L'Aurore: Busy Basse-Ville brasserie, good for a drink or meal. Simple menu features the regionally popular 'Welsh', the cheesy take on Welsh rarebit. *noon-1am* €

Chez Sandrine La Poissonnerie: Namesake chef prepares array of fresh seafood dishes at the fish market. Raw oysters, cooked treats, sandwiches etc. *7.30am-1pm Tue-Sun* €

Beyond Boulogne-sur-Mer

Northern France's coast mixes port cities like Calais with long stretches of startlingly beautiful cliffs and beaches to enjoy.

Places

Dunkirk p214
Calais p214
Côte d'Opale p215
Le Crotoy p216
St-Valery-sur-Somme p216

Dunkirk is forever associated with the rescue of an entire army from the clutches of the Germans in 1940. Calais is associated with transit, whether by ferry, Eurostar or car shuttle through the Channel Tunnel, yet it has an artful reason to pause. Boulogne-sur-Mer is the place to stay longer, mixing an extraordinary aquarium with a beach, incredible seafood and an alluring old town.

All along the English Channel, the Côte d'Opale dazzles with natural beauty and activities that take advantage of the typically blustery days. Tops among its seaside villages is St-Valery-sur-Somme on the Baie de Somme (Bay of Somme), which mixes history, natural beauty and a wily sense of hospitality.

GETTING AROUND

Train service along the coast can be frustrating, requiring various changes as there is not one line along the entire length. Dunkirk, Calais and Boulogne are all linked to Paris (1–2½ hours). Dunkirk is linked to Lille and Calais. Calais is linked to Lille, Boulogne and Amiens. The southern Côte d'Opale has no train service. Buses *(trans80.hautsdefrance.fr)* connect to trains at Berck and Abbeville.

Dunkirk

TIME FROM BOULOGNE-SUR-MER: **1HR**

A city not to escape

In 1940, Dunkirk (French: Dunkerque) gained lasting fame thanks to the remarkable evacuation of 338,000 Allied troops. Destroyed by German attacks, post-war rebuilding did the city no favours. Today, its profile is bolstered by the 2017 Christopher Nolan film *Dunkirk*.

Walk out on the **Malo Pier** *(Jetée de Malo)*, a key location in the movie where Kenneth Branagh goes pacing on 'the mole' and the Red Cross ship gets sunk. Get the real story at the **Museum Dunkerque 1940** *(dynamo-dunkerque.com; adult/child €8/free)*. Get the whole view from the 15th-century **Le Beffroi** *(beffroi-dunkerque.fr; adult/child €5/3.50)*, the landmark 58m-high lift-equipped bell tower.

Calais

TIME FROM BOULOGNE-SUR-MER: **35MIN**

Feast on the burghers

Only 34km from the English port of Dover, Calais has always buzzed with cross-channel traffic.

The reason to visit is Rodin's monumental statue, **Les Bourgeois de Calais** *(The Burghers of Calais*; 1889). With the flamboyant **Hôtel de Ville** as a backdrop, the work stands proud

Les Bourgeois de Calais in front of Hôtel de Ville

on a flower-filled square. It portrays six local leaders (burghers) in 1347 as they surrender to besieging English forces, knowing that they will soon be executed – but hoping that their sacrifice will mean their fellow Calaisiens will be spared.

The resigned expressions of the burghers and their bleak, far-off gazes presage those of countless troops who passed through here going to the Western Front, and of the ongoing groups of asylum seekers trying to reach the UK in hopes of a better life.

Côte d'Opale TIME FROM BOULOGNE-SUR-MER: **10-30MIN**

Tour the magnificent coast

The most spectacular section of the **Côte d'Opale** is between Calais and Boulogne-sur-Mer. This 40km stretch is a mirror image of the White Cliffs of Dover. You can tour it by car, bike or on foot over long-distance trails.

Just past Sangatte, the coastal dunes give way to cliffs that culminate in windswept, 134m-high **Cap Blanc-Nez**, which affords breathtaking views of the Bay of Wissant, the port of Calais, the Flemish countryside (pockmarked by Allied bomb craters, such as those on the slopes of Mont d'Hubert) and the distant English coast. Paths lead to several massive WWII German bunkers.

CARNAVAL DE DUNKERQUE

The Carnaval de Dunkerque originated in 1676 as a feast for the fishing fleet before it set sail on six-month trips to harvest cod around Iceland, a trip many would not return from. Over the centuries, the feasting merged with carnival partying, resulting in a celebration that now runs from January to March. Different Dunkirk districts celebrate each weekend and festival-goers dress up in brightly coloured nautical themes, often with accents of historical figures or pop-culture characters. Umbrellas are big. A highlight is herring tossing, where carnival participants throw the notoriously smelly fish from floats into the crowd to celebrate the town's maritime history. The climax is Trois Joyeuses, the Sunday, Monday and Tuesday before Ash Wednesday.

 EATING & DRINKING NORTHWEST OF BOULOGNE: OUR PICKS

La Marie Galante: All local seafood in Audresselles; piled-high seafood platters are house speciality, but other briny mains star. Book. *lunch & dinner Tue-Sun* €€

Histoire Ancienne: Bistro-style dishes served in a classic central Calais dining room with a zinc bar. Traditional service. *noon-1.30pm, 7-10.30pm Tue-Sat* €€

Café du Minck: Traditional cafe-bar; big terrace near old Calais waterfront. Nautical caps hang from the ceiling. Fresh fish dishes and charcuterie plates. *8.30am-9.30pm Tue-Sun* €

Bommel Bar: Old-fashioned beer bar by Dunkirk's waterfront has huge bunches of local hops hanging from the ceiling and an array of regional brews. *6-pm-1am Wed-Sat*

Le Crotoy

TIME FROM BOULOGNE-SUR-MER: **1HR**

Chill out in a bayside beach town

Occupying a picturesque spot on the northern bank of the Baie de Somme, laid-back Le Crotoy is a lovely place to relax. Its broad, sandy beach is uncrowded and its southerly exposure gives it plenty of sunshine.

Over 300 bird species have been sighted at **Parc du Marquenterre** *(parcdumarquenterre.fr; adult/child €12/9)*, a bird sanctuary that's an important migratory stopover between northern Europe and West Africa. Marked walking circuits (2km to 6km) take you to marshes, dunes, meadows, a brackish lagoon and observation posts.

St-Valery-sur-Somme

TIME FROM BOULOGNE-SUR-MER: **1½HR**

Port town with a past

A cargo and fishing port as late as the 1980s, St-Valery-sur-Somme is a tidy visitor magnet on the south side of the bay. It's got a charming maritime quarter, a pocket-sized **17th-century walled town** with cobbled streets, a white-sand **beach** and a scenic **promenade** that stretches along the seafront. Like an impressionist seascape, the deep brick reds of St-Valery's houses are complemented by sea hues that range from sparkling blue to overcast grey, and are accented by dashes of red, white and blue from flapping French flags.

The grey and harbour **seals** found off Pointe du Hourdel, 8km northwest of town, draw a steady stream of seal-spotting boats from several operators. Nature excursions with **Rando-Nature en Somme** *(randonature-baiedesomme.com; guided walks adult/child €15/7)* around the wide, flat bay are justifiably popular.

Chemin de Fer de la Baie de Somme *(chemindefer-baie desomme.fr; adult/child €14.50/10)* runs historic trains for the 14km scenic trip around the bay to Le Crotoy. Suggestion: hike one-way, ride the train the other. Indeed, the web of regional trails are made for hiking and cycling. The **tourist office** *(tourisme-baiedesomme.fr; 10am-5.30pm)* can help with oodles of maps, bike rental sources and more. The bayside trip to **Pointe du Hourdel** is popular, as is the onward 20km coastal trip south to Mers-les-Bains.

BEST ACTIVITIES TO CATCH THE WIND

Sand-Yachting: *Char à voile* is synonymous with the north of France. It's like sailing on land using a three-wheeled go-kart which speeds over the beaches around the Baie de Somme and Côte d'Opale.

Wingfoil: The wind elevates the rider (holding an inflatable sail) above the water – often the rudder barely skims the surface. **École de Voile** *(voile-cayeux-surmer.fr; from €100)* in Cayeux-sur-Mer has two-hour lessons.

Windsurfing: Glisse Sensations Mers *(surf-paddle-mers.fr)* in Mers-les-Bains rents gear (from €25 per hour) and offers lessons.

Kitesurfing: Surf the waves and capture the wind at once with **Opal Kitesurfing School** *(opale-kite.fr; lessons from €110)* in Berck-sur-Mer.

WHERE TO EAT SOUTH OF BOULOGNE: OUR PICKS

La Pêcherie: Beautifully presented dishes change weekly at St-Valery-sur-Somme bar-brasserie; seafood is the mainstay. Terrace tables have river views. Book. *10am-2pm, 6-8pm Tue-Sun* €€

Le Jardin: St-Valery-sur-Somme fine dining and carefully curated wine list; 'What the Phoque' (What the Seal) pairs wine to your chosen wildlife. *noon-2pm, 7-9pm Wed-Sun* €€

Amazone: Gracious St-Valery-sur-Somme coffee shop with delicious baked goods and avocado toast. Good smoothies. Sit inside with antiques or along the street. *9.30am-6pm Thu-Sun* €

Le Carré Gourmand: Changing menu at this intimate Le Crotoy restaurant with a shady terrace. Artistically presented dishes with local ingredients. *noon-2.30pm, 7-9.30pm Thu-Mon* €€

Places We Love to Stay

€ Budget €€ Midrange €€€ Top End

Lille MAP p195

People Lille € A cracking bar, outdoor spaces, and pleasingly private dorm bunks with curtains. Activities include art lessons and dance parties.

Mama Shelter Lille € Vibes galore, with regular DJ sets and concerts held in the restaurant-bar. Rooms have plenty of character.

Rosa Hotel €€ Great-value hotel mere steps from the train station. Stylish rooms and great service with lively cafes right out the door.

Grand Hôtel Bellevue €€ Richly decorated, spacious rooms in a historic hotel overlooking the Grand' Place. Gracious, full service.

OKKO Hotels Lille Centre €€ Bang in the city centre, with complimentary snacks and refreshments available 24/7; contemporary style, like a deluxe IKEA.

L'Hermitage Gantois €€ Enchanting, harmonious spaces behind a Flemish-Gothic façade; rooms have a refined modern style with sumptuous details. In-house chapel dates from 1637.

Clarance Hotel €€€ The most beautiful rooms in the city. In an 18th-century mansion with a formal grey-stone façade and garden; has a Michelin-starred restaurant.

Cassel

L'Art Doize € Spacious rooms, some with views of the Grand' Place; all have antique-style furnishings mixed with art-forward modern design.

Châtellerie de Schoebeque €€ Elegant 18th-century hotel. During WWI, it was used by Marshal Ferdinand Foch, the French general who ultimately won the war.

Arras

La Cour des Grands €€ Chic common spaces with leather armchairs, plenty of reading material and a lively bar. Neutral decor and huge freestanding tubs in some rooms.

Les Clés des Places €€ Comfortable rooms and a small courtyard in a 17th-century building which shows its roots as an old residence. Decor is minimalist.

Entre Cour et Jardin €€ This majestic manor with opulent interior is close to the town centre. Gardens provide a laid-back place to meet friends or relax.

Amiens MAP p203

Auberge de Jeunesse HI Amiens € The most affordable option, with large dormitory rooms, non-central location and a simple buffet-style breakfast.

Le Camp des Hortillons-Robinsons € Eco-camp in the heart of the *hortillonnages*, equipped with tents hidden among the trees. Book ahead to arrange access.

Hôtel Victor Hugo € Bargain-priced, family-run hotel has simple but comfortable rooms. The best rooms are on the top floor, offering views and natural light.

Une Maison en Ville €€ Four beautifully decorated rooms and a spa with a pool, massage room and hammam in the vaults.

Hôtel Spa Marotte €€ Boutique hotel with modern luxury at its most romantic; 12 light-drenched rooms are huge. Good, central location.

Boulogne-sur-Mer MAP p213

Opal'Inn € Across from the beach. Good-value rooms are small but comfy and decorated in pastels. Sea views and balconies are worth the extra.

L'Enclos de l'Evêché €€ Imposing 19th-century mansion next to the basilica is an elegant seven-room B&B with a cobbled courtyard. Trad furnishings, great breakfast.

Hôtel Monsieur Georges €€ Harbourside hotel with stylish modern rooms in a trad package. Splurge for the front ones with small balconies and great views.

Hôtel La Matelote €€ Plush modern hotel; rooms are decorated in rich colours and have modern wooden furnishings. Better rooms have views and balconies.

St-Valery-sur-Somme & Around

Logis Hôtel le Relais Guillaume de Normandy €€ On the waterfront, mock-Tudor mansion from the early 1900s with period touches, such as a mosaic entryway and creaky wooden stairs. Book ahead in summer.

Château du Romerel €€ Four forested hectares envelop this 1870-built château with elegant, beautifully furnished rooms. Shaded outdoor pool opens in summer.

Le Piloti €€ Modern eco-lodge outside of Le Crotoy on a pond; offers rental bikes and simple cabins, with cooking facilities hidden among the reed grass.

Researched by
Cyrena Lee

Normandy

HISTORIC BATTLEGROUNDS AND FAT OF THE LAND

Impossibly long stretches of beach, dizzying rock cliffs, wild *bocage, calvados,* cider and Norman cows – France's northwest region is worth tucking into and getting lost in for days on end.

Normandy's breathtaking landscapes singlehandedly inspired the Impressionist art movement; painter Claude Monet obsessively painted the Rouen cathedral, sunrise at Le Havre and his backyard water lilies in Giverny. From the world-famous and epically surreal Mont St-Michel abbey, all the way to the cliffs of Étretat, the Normandy coast is littered with iconic destinations.

But dig a bit deeper to appreciate Normandy's immensity and diversity – as one Norman described it to me, 'everything that's good about France, you can find in Normandy'. Acres and acres of apple orchards are lovingly transmogrified into cider and brandy, cows' milk is churned into four kinds of AOP cheese, and the rich cream and butter of the land are used to make tarts, pies and rice puddings.

History buffs can immerse themselves in reenactments, like of Operation Overlord, when the Allied Forces invaded France in 1944, or spin even further back in time with the Bayeux Tapestry that recounts the Norman conquest of England. Poetic souls can lose themselves on literary walks, like in Proust's Cabourg, or mingle with the many working artists and artisans of the region today. Those who dare to venture into the off-beaten tracks (once for tractors, now suitable for cars) will be rewarded with scenes of serenity and unique goods found nowhere else.

JUSTIN FOULKES/LONELY PLANET

THE MAIN AREAS

ROUEN & GIVERNY
Normandy's historic cultural capital and Monet's dreamscape. **p224**

CÔTE D'ALBÂTRE & LE HAVRE
Coastal treasures and concrete architectural inspiration.
p232

CÔTE FLEURIE
Appreciate and embody art.
p238

For places to stay in Normandy, see p265

Above: Mont St-Michel (p253); Right: *Calvados* (apple brandy)

D-DAY LANDING BEACHES, CAEN & BAYEUX
Unravel in time. **p246**

MONT ST-MICHEL
Feast on the ecodiverse Bay.
p253

CHERBOURG & COTENTIN
Go off the grid up north.
p260

Find Your Way

Normandy consists of five *départements*: Seine-Maritime up north, Eure to the south, Calvados to the west where the D-Day beaches are, forestial Orne below, and La Manche – the sleeve along the English Channel.

D-Day Landing Beaches, Caen & Bayeux, p246
Relive WWII history at beaches where the Allied Forces landed. At Bayeux, go further back in time to see the epic tapestry of William the Conqueror.

TRAIN
Various cities, like luxurious beach town Deauville (also known as Paris' 21st *arrondissement*), Rouen, Caen, Le Havre and Étretat are easily accessible by direct trains from Paris. More isolated areas require more planning with buses to get to, say, the D-Day beaches or Mont St-Michel; service is sparser.

CAR
A car is most convenient to explore every nook and cranny of the less touristy areas. Up further north, many old tractor routes have been turned into zigzagging roads that lead to unexpected surprises, like a handmade straw broom *atelier* or a fourth-generation linen farm with fields of golden flax.

BIKE
Cyclists have over 480km of bike routes to spin over. The GR-21 offers 180km of glorious white cliffs and port cities on the Côte d'Albâtre. The Veloscenic route offers a tour of Normandy's southern region, from Paris to Mont St-Michel. A VéloWest route provides roads from the D-Day Landing Beaches south.

Mont St-Michel, p253
The iconic Gothic abbey floats upon a bay rich with wildlife and a prime setting for birdwatching, while the surrounding lands offer adrenaline doses and forage feasting.

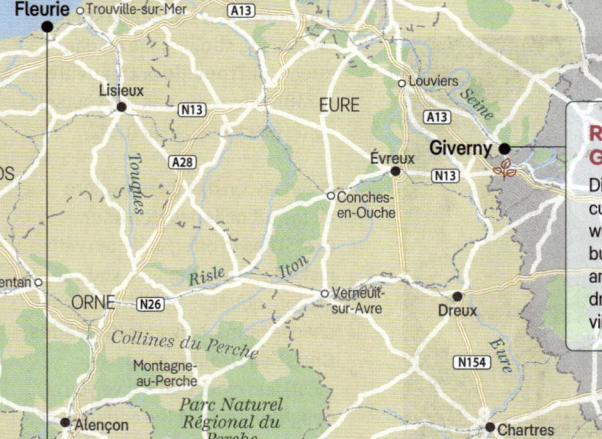

Cherbourg & Cotentin, p260
Located at the northern tip of La Manche, or the 'sleeve', Cotentin includes the historic port city of Cherbourg and endless farms and fishing villages to explore.

Côte d'Albâtre & Le Havre, p232
Stroll in architect Auguste Perret's iconic, concrete post-WWII re-imagining of a port city. On the Côte d'Albâtre, walk in Impressionist footsteps alongside staggering cliffs.

Rouen & Giverny, p224
Dive into Normandy's cultural capital Rouen, where Joan of Arc was burned at the stake, and wander Monet's dreamy, picturesque village of Giverny.

Côte Fleurie, p238
Late 19th-century Belle Époque joie de vivre collides with modern-day glamour at the well-heeled beach resorts of Deauville, Trouville and postcard-perfect port city Honfleur.

Plan Your Days

With such a vibrant diversity of land, sea, city, forest, cheese and *calvados,* a few days in Normandy doesn't cut it. Aim to stick to one area for short trips, but ideally, stay a while.

Cliffs of Étretat (p232)

Just a Few Days

● From Paris, just over an hour's drive will get you to Monet's **Giverny** (p224). Spend a day soaking in the master of Impressionism's home, then drive straight to the **Côte Fleurie** (p238) to walk in Proust's footsteps in **Cabourg** (p243).

● On day two, relax sore feet with seawater therapy at **Thalassotherapy Thalazur Cabourg** (p239), and then spend an evening strolling the elegant streets of **Trouville** or **Deauville** (p238), where you can get yourself some fancy headwear (p242).

● Finally, on day three explore all the art galleries **Honfleur** (p243) has to offer, and then with just a short drive inland, you can explore quintessential Normandy cheese farms, *calvados* (**Calvados Christian Drouin** , p244, is a must) and cider that'll give you a delightful taste of the countryside.

Seasonal Highlights

Many businesses hit the snooze button in low season. However, the region can be enjoyed without crowds during winter months.

FEBRUARY
The five-day Mardi Gras pre-party takes place yearly at the UNESCO-listed **Carnival de Granville**; a parade of outrageous floats, music and joy.

APRIL
Kick off summer season with the **Fête du Cresson** (watercress festival) at Veules-les-Roses. Early tourist birds get more of the metaphorical worm.

JUNE
History buffs, pay homage to WWII events with the annual **D-Day Festival Normandy**.

Historic Highlights in a Week

- Set up base in charming **Bayeux** (p246) to admire the 11th-century tapestry. From there, most **D-Day Landing Beaches** (p246) attractions are a short drive away; spend a day in contemplation of WWII.

- On day three, explore castles, museums, nightlife and famed tripe in **Caen** (p246). Then, drive south at dawn to the iconic **Mont-St-Michel** (p253) and stay until sunset to see the floating abbey at dusk. Head to **Auberge Sauvage** (p255) for a mind-blowing meal, and then to **Avranches** (p257) for coffee, a book and a different perspective.

- Spend the last few days further up the coast in **Granville** (p258) to visit Christian Dior's childhood home or take a day-trip to the Îles Chausey. Finish at **Villedieu-les-Poeles** (p258) for a copper and bell crafts tour, and take home cookware from **Mauviel 1830** (p259).

The Ultimate Deep Dive

- Explore off-the-map delights like Bois Guilbert's **Jardins des Sculptures** (p230) and spend a night in a historic Norman estate turned poetic wonderland, where you can take a sculpture workshop. Then retrace Joan of Arc's footsteps in **Rouen** (p224) before going antiquing. On the northern coast, explore the **Côte d'Albâtre** (p232), starting with **Veules-les-Roses** (p235) for oysters. Visit a linen farm or a broom factory, then head to **Fécamp** (p235) for cod washed down with a fancy herbal liqueur cocktail at the **Palais Bénédictine** (p237). Contemplate nature at the cliffs of **Étretat** (p232), then enjoy the contrasts of the concrete architecture of **Le Havre** (p232).

- If you have more time, explore the treasures of northern **Cotentin** (p260), where you can spend days getting lost in the wilderness of **La Hague** (p264).

JULY
During the hottest month of the region, escape north to **Cotentin** for relaxing beach time, or catching the **Festival du Lin** in Seine-Maritime.

AUGUST
Cheese connoisseurs, rendezvous at the **Foire aux Fromages à Livarot** which takes place every first weekend of the month.

SEPTEMBER
Dance at the **Offcourts Festival** in Trouville or ogle stars at the **American Film Festival** (p239) in Deauville.

OCTOBER
Head to Honfleur for a seafood-frenzy at the **Fête de la Coquille et de la Pêche** and a costume parade.

Rouen & Giverny

HISTORIC WALKS | INSPIRED GARDENS | UNIQUE ART

☑ TOP TIP

Late May to early October are the best times to visit Rouen, as the capital tends to skew rainy and grey. Pack an umbrella and comfortable walking shoes. For the best views, hike up Ste-Catherine hill, about half an hour from the cathedral and a 500-stair climb.

Rouen, Normandy's official capital, is an open-air museum with moments of history to relive at every corner: see where Simone de Beauvoir and Albert Camus lived, walk along the macabre skullbones at the 15th-century ossuary Aître St-Maclou and stand on the very spot where the patron saint of France, Joan of Arc, was burned at the stake for hearsay.

The Gros Horloge, an intricate Renaissance clock, connects the past to the present. As you admire the gilded hands, stroll along the cobblestone streets of the Old Town to take in the historic monuments still in dialogue with artists today, like the 15th-century Gothic Palais de Justice, whose WWII bullet scars have been filled in with Lego donated by locals.

Just an hour away lies Giverny, Monet's private sanctuary immortalised by the world-famous *Water Lilies*. But nestled all around you'll find surrealist castles, sculpture gardens and villages preserved from the time of *Madame Bovary*.

Quiet Contemplation on Saintly Death MAP P225
Stand where Joan of Arc gasped her last breath

Ironically, there's something overwhelmingly monumental about standing in a monument-less spot at **Place du Vieux Marché**, where a 19-year-old girl who'd saved France from English invasion was tied and burned at the stake. You can climb up the vestiges of a 13th-century castle, the **Donjon de**

GETTING AROUND

Trains run frequently from Paris St-Lazare to Rouen and Giverny, which are both explored and enjoyed best on foot. In Rouen, electric bikes are easily hired with the app Lovélo, while public transport (bus, metro, TEOR) is easy to access and free on Saturdays. If driving, note that tolls from A13 and A14 have become automatic; pay online at sanef.com within 72 hours. Giverny is a hotspot with limited accessibility and no luggage storage; pack light and bring a baby carrier.

ROUEN

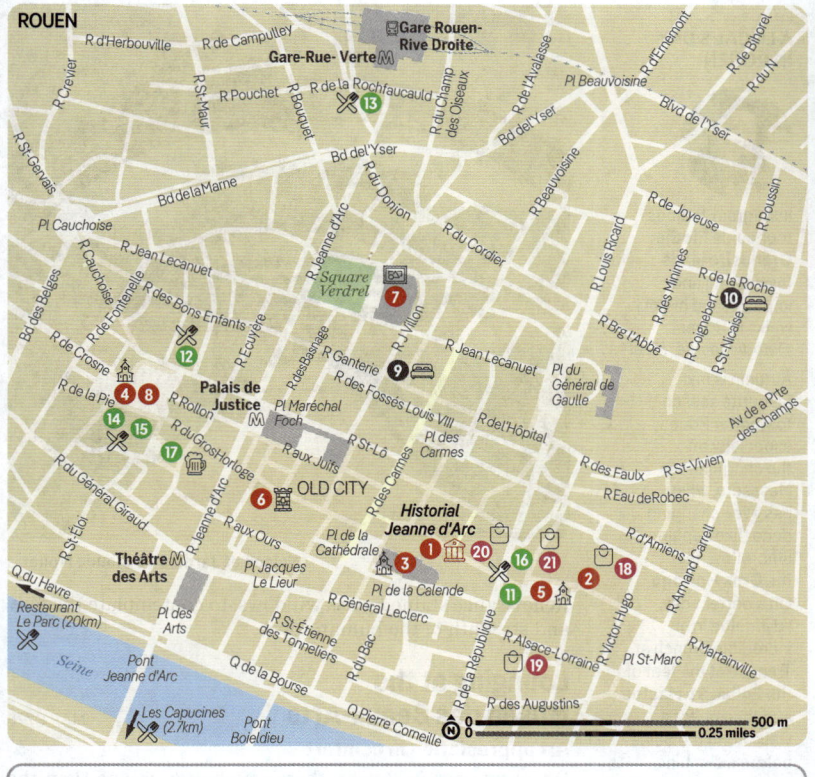

- ★ **HIGHLIGHTS**
  1. Historial Jeanne d'Arc
- ● **SIGHTS**
  2. Aître St-Maclou
  3. Cathédrale Notre Dame
  4. Église Ste-Jeanne-d'Arc
  5. Église St-Maclou
  6. Gros Horloge
  see 2 La Galerie des Arts du Feu
  7. Musée des Beaux-Arts
  8. Place du Vieux Marché
- ● **SLEEPING**
  9. Hôtel Le Vieux Carré
  10. La Boulangerie
- ● **EATING**
  11. Artefact
  12. Gill Côté Bistro
  13. Hôtel de Dieppe
  14. La Couronne
  15. Paul-Arthur
  16. Tandem
- ● **DRINKING & NIGHTLIFE**
  17. Public
- ● **SHOPPING**
  18. ABN Antiquités
  19. Dalala Vintage
  20. Hera Vintage
  21. La Galerie de L'Astrée

Rouen *(donjonderouen.com)* – free on weekends or book an escape game – where she was tried. The ruins of her place of imprisonment are at 102 rue Jeanne d'Arc.

To better grasp the magnitude of the Maid of Orleans' impact, head to the **Historial Jeanne d'Arc** *(historial-jeannedarc.fr; adult/child €12/9, closed Mon)* museum for a multimedia presentation on her trials and influence. At the **Cathédrale Notre Dame** *(cathedrale-rouen.net; free)*, find a breathtaking stained-glass depiction of her life and a sculpture of Joan's final moments at the stake. Afterwards, you can head inside the upside-down Viking boat-shaped **Église Ste-Jeanne-d'Arc** *(cathorouen.org/leglise-sainte-jeanne-darc)*, which is an aesthetically pleasing contrast of 1970s architecture and

A LOCAL'S DAY IN ROUEN

Instagram-famous tour guide **Elodie Grandsire** leads fascinating and impassioned history walks in Rouen. @elodie_guide_local

Autumn is my favourite season to wander Rouen, especially on the charming rue Massacre, which has ever-changing decor like hanging umbrellas, near the **Gros Horloge**. On a perfect day, I'd indulge in an incredible brunch at Tranché at the feet of the **Église St-Maclou**, and then go for a walk along the Seine before a climbing session at Arkose. To wrap up the day, I'd head to place de la Pucelle for a drink on the terrace as the sun sets, and then pop into **Public** where comedians pop up to try out their jokes for some free laughs on Saturday evenings. I love Rouen for its convivial, laid-back spirit and Norman charm.

Maison et Jardins de Claude Monet

Renaissance stained glass windows, to contemplate the folly and strength of the human spirit.

Lounging at the Musée des Beaux-Arts

MAP P225

Art appreciation in comfort

On rainy days in Rouen, there's no better escape than the **Musée des Beaux-Arts** *(mbarouen.fr; 10am-6pm Wed-Mon; general admission/temporary exhibitions free/from €17)*, which offers the most elegant and relaxing shelter and a stunning collection to admire without the crowds. Amid the ample rooms with vaulted ceilings, it's a delightful change of pace to admire masterpieces by masters the likes of Caravaggio, Vêlazquez and Poussin from the comfort of an array of floor bean bags or a living room couch arrangement. When I visited on a Friday afternoon, I was lucky enough to be serenaded by a stranger who'd decided to tickle the ivories of the grand piano.

Treasure Hunt for a Genuine Artefact of History

MAP P225

Antiquing, vintage goods, homewares and jewels

For object lovers and collectors, a stroll on the charming and winding rue Damiette is a must, as it crosses a concentration of antique dealers. Run now for three generations, **La Galerie de L'Astrée** has three boutiques of carefully curated heirloom art pieces and decorations to furnish your home. To embellish your body, head to **Hera Vintage** for a delightful selection of jewellery that spans decades from art deco to retro, with options at every budget. **ABN Antiquités** offers a bit of everything, from vintage Tintin statues to dusty 20-year-old bottles of wine. Fans of mid-century design: don't miss **Dalala Vintage** for a touch of modernity. Many shops are closed Sundays through Tuesdays, so Saturdays are ideal for splurging.

Dine with a Duck Ceremony Master

MAP P225

Duck à la rouennaise

There is perhaps no other dish that epitomises the French penchant for snobbery, refinement and grandness than pressed duck, a Rouen delicacy. To experience this sumptuous meal, reserve at least three days in advance, because only a certified Duck Master can make this elaborate dish, also called *canard du sang* or blood duck.

Conceived as a way to use ducks that perished in transport, the bird is ceremonially and laboriously pressed through a special and rare contraption until all of the blood leaks out into a silver sauce cup. From that, along with wine and shallots, a sauce is made, as well as the rest of the dish. Watch the Duck Master deftly manipulate the dish with a medal adorning his neck, signifying membership to the *Ordre des Canardiers* (Order of the Duck Birds), founded in 1986.

Warning: the plate is more pomp and circumstance and may disappoint foodies, but for those who want to experience highfalutin dining at its Frenchest and have the spare cash to spend, do so now (the tradition is slowly petering out). Four restaurants of the region still proudly carry on the tradition: **Hôtel de Dieppe**, **La Couronne**, **Restaurant Le Parc** and **Les Capucines**.

Skip the Crowds at Monet's Secret Island

MAP P228

Île aux Orties at Giverny

Monet's residence of over four decades, **Maison et Jardins de Claude Monet** *(claudemonetgiverny.fr; adult/child/under-7 €12/6.50/free)* is a powerful testament to the lasting legacy of a visionary artist: his world-famous waterlilies and his eccentric, brightly coloured home dotted with his collection of Japanese block prints are flocked to by thousands of tourists each year. The queue for the waterlilies tour, which tears through the house at a frenetic pace, can be intimidating – but

FINDING THE MUMMIFIED CAT

Rouen's population was decimated by the Black Plague in the 14th century. Testament to its victims is the **Aître St-Maclou**, an ossuary to wander among the dead, now also a home to the art gallery **La Galerie des Arts du Feu** *(galeriedesarts dufeu.fr)*; you can also catch ceramicists at work. As you ponder your destiny to dance with death as you admire the *danse macabre*, carvings of skulls, bones and instruments of death, look out for the tiny mummified cat that's on display in a window. Legend has it that a black cat, symbolising the devil, was interred in the walls to protect the living. But rumours contend that the cat is merely a hoax concocted by local Beaux-Arts university students.

 EATING IN ROUEN: OUR PICKS — MAP P225

Paul-Arthur: Run by a former Top Chef contestant, this innovative bistro offers a six-course tasting menu at lunch. *noon-2pm & 7-10pm Tue-Sat* €€€

Artefact: A minimalist cafe and canteen that offers creative bites and latte art with a terrace overlooking the church St-Maclou. *9am-6.30pm Tue-Sat* €

Tandem: A seasonal menu with playful plating in a warm and friendly atmosphere. It's gastronomy without any fussy pretentiousness. *12.15-1.30pm & 7.30-9.30pm Wed-Sat* €€

Gill Côté Bistro: On the corner of the Old Market, this modern bistro offers simple dishes prepared by famed chef Gilles Tournadre. *noon-2.30pm & 7-9.30pm* €€€

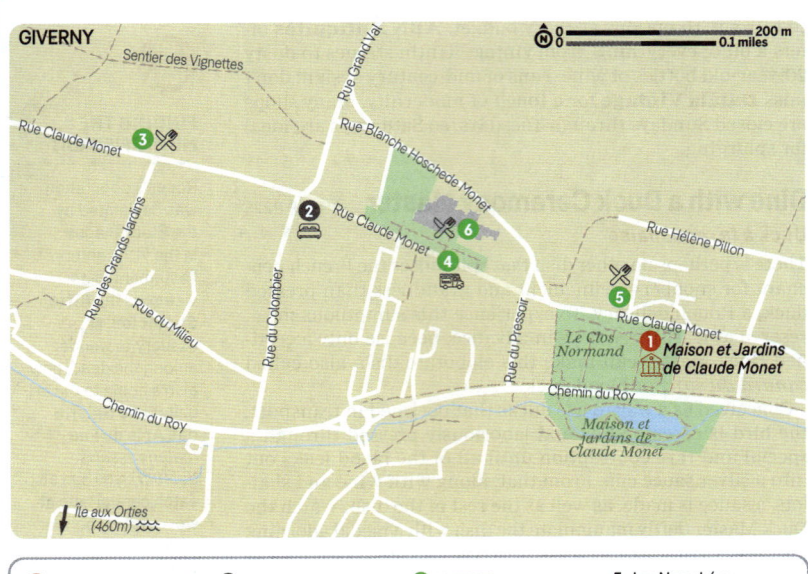

HIGHLIGHTS
1 Maison et Jardins de Claude Monet

SLEEPING
2 Au Bon Maréchal

EATING
3 Au Coin du Pain'tre
4 Cocorico
5 Les Nymphéas
6 Oscar

if you pause and gaze out of the window and focus on a flower, you'll surely be left with an impression of the painter's life. Reservations are strongly recommended (weekdays are slightly less crowded than the weekend) and beware of big holiday weekend crowds.

To contemplate his life with more breathing room, walk up to his humble grave and contrast it with the greatness of his legacy. Better yet, picnic at the lesser-known **Île aux Orties**, a patch of land Monet owned at the confluence of where the Epte River meets the Seine, that once turned into an island during a heavy rain period. To get there, walk past the windmill near the car parks until you reach the small rue des Batards until you reach the river for a more isolated experience of one of his rarer, inspired landscapes.

 EATING IN GIVERNY: OUR PICKS

Tucked away inside the Musée des Impressionismes

MAP P228

Au Coin du Pain'tre: Simple plates like quiches and baguette sandwiches. The highlight: relaxing over breakfast or lunch with a garden view. *9am-7pm* €

Cocorico: Pop-up food truck with fresh sandwiches, burgers and desserts at reasonable prices for a takeaway picnic, when the sun's out. *Apr-Oct. hours vary* €

Les Nymphéas: Family-friendly garden restaurant with crowd-pleasing staples like crêpes, fondue, raclette, burgers and salads. *12.15-2.30pm Mon-Fri, 7-10pm Mon-Thu, to 11pm Fri & Sat* €€

Oscar: This recently opened gourmet bistro offers refined plates in a stylish setting by Michelin-starred chef David Gallienne. *10am-6pm Mon-Thu, to 9pm Fri & Sat* €€€

Beyond Rouen & Giverny

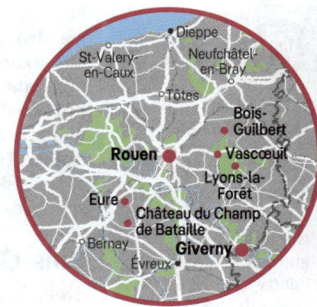

Just south of Rouen, the Eure *département* where Giverny sits, one can explore quaint villages, fascinating sculpture gardens and art-filled castles.

Places

Château du Champ de Bataille p229
Bois-Guilbert p230
Vascœuil p230
Lyons-La-Forêt p231

Explore the lush and untrampled countryside, with natural wonders like the ancient beech groves and cathedral forests near Lyons-la-Forêt, where Claude Chabrol chose to film *Madame Bovary*. Eure is also home to impressive castles, from the ruins of Richard the Lionheart's Château Gaillard to the lavishly renovated Château du Champ de Bataille. In just less than an hour's drive from Rouen, there are ample options for day trips and encounters with many locals who have continued the traditional Norman way of life: making art, cider, *calvados*, sculptures, art, beer and more. But if you opt for a day longer, you can take the time to soak up all the stunning medieval architecture and nature's bounty.

Château du Champ de Bataille

TIME FROM ROUEN: **50MIN**

The charmed world and gardens of designer Jacques Garcia

Forget the crowds of Versailles. Experience modern luxury at the baroque 17th-century **Château du Champ de Bataille** *(chateauduchampdebataille.com; Apr-Sep, hours vary; admission from €13)*, bought and refurbished by famed interior designer Jacques Garcia, known for his work in furnishing some of Paris' fanciest hotels. After a storm ravaged the gardens in the '90s, Garcia completely reconstructed the formal French gardens (the largest private park in Europe, funded independently by his deep pockets). Take a full afternoon to explore the delightfully rich grounds, with features like a row of sphinx-shaped hedges, an antique Greek temple studded with crystals, maximalist sitting rooms with lush carpeting and intricate fabrics next to a greenhouse of massive ferns, an outdoor theatre, fountains with gilded fish sculptures and an opulent grotto lined with deities.

Opt for the château visit, where you'll be greeted by employees in the era's formal wear; footmen are dressed in royal

GETTING AROUND

Driving is best to explore the hidden gems beyond Rouen and Giverny, though public transportation is possible to get to popular tourist destiations for those who don't mind transfers and waits. An hour's ride on bus 218 gets you to one of the most beautiful villages, Lyons-la-Forêt; check nomad.normandie.fr/lignes-de-cars for schedules and routes. Other destinations aren't accessible by public transport, so it's best to hire a car for the most freedom and flexibility.

A TASTE OF NORMAN BEER

Beer and whisky lovers, rejoice – there is more to imbibe in Normandy than cider and *calvados* at the hearty and stout-y, viking-themed **Ferme Brasserie Northmaen**. Founded by Normandy native Dominique Camus in 1997, this bustling farm and brewery produces over 17 varieties of beer, from homegrown blondes to IPAs and even a selection of five different whiskies from the surrounding golden wheat fields. A trip is worth the taste of the humble, single-malt 'farm' whisky named Thor Boyo, and free tastings and guided visits are available on Saturdays at 3.30pm if reserved in advance. If your French is rusty, bring a translator or just go to soak up the popular Lagertha beer.

blue and rococo gowns. In the cabinet of curiosities, admire a jaw-dropping collection of rare specimens like baby elephants and tigers of yesteryear, sitting rooms and bedrooms worthy of royals, and a faithful reproduction of servant quarters and kitchens in the basement. Once a year, during the Journées du Patrimoine, lucky visitors can step inside **Le Palais Moghol**, an Indian-style palace dripping with lavish furnishings of tiger skins, torana arches and an azure indoor pool, which serves as Garcia's private residence.

Bois-Guilbert

TIME FROM ROUEN: **30MIN**

Sleep in an artist's poetic garden

Enter the magical world of sculptor and artist Jean-Marc de Pas, who has transformed his family château in Bois-Guilbert, built in 1620, into the waking dream that is now his evolving sculpture garden, **Les Jardins des Sculptures** *(lejardindessculptures.addock.co; admission from €12)*. The car park is diagonal from the entrance. With over 17 acres to explore, the artist invites you to contemplate the cosmos and the depth of nature, and a small room pays homage to the academics, astronomers and economists of the de Pas family.

Spend a night in the stunning château, which boasts original detailing like wood parquet floors and exposed brick, in one of the comfortable and well-equipped rooms upstairs. You can also interact with the earth directly with a clay modelling workshop; if you're lucky, the artist himself will be around, and on Sunday evenings during the summer, you can enjoy slow sunsets accompanied by classical music. Jean-Marc and his wife Stéphanie are living examples of Norman hospitality, creativity and discreet pride in their region, which has plenty to discover – like the **Jardin de Valérianes**, the **Musée des Traditions et Arts Normands**, Château de Vascœuil and a pony club next door.

Vascœuil

TIME FROM ROUEN: **30MIN**

A 17th-century castle and Salvador Dalí

Find striking contrasts of centuries-old Norman architecture paired with surrealist art and yearly contemporary art exhibitions at the meticulously renovated 17th-century **Château de Vascœuil** *(chateauvascoeuil.com; Apr-Oct, hours vary; admission from €9)*. You can explore a unique octagonal tower

Set menus that will dazzle.

EATING BEYOND ROUEN & GIVERNY: OUR PICKS

Le Champêtre: This welcoming spot near the château has good wine, set menus with fair prices and French cuisine home-cooked with love. *11am-2pm Mon-Sat, 7-11pm Fri & Sat* €

Délice Pizza: For a quick, easy and cheesy bite in Buchy, these takeaway pizzas hit the spot after a long day on the road. *5.30-10.30pm Sat-Mon, Wed & Thu, from 11.30am Fri, 12.30-10.30pm Tue* €

Auberge Bucheoise: Refined gastronomic restaurant offering amuse-bouches to kick off artful plates worthy of Instagram. *11am-9.30pm Thu-Sat & Mon, 11am-4pm Sun* €€€

Chez Ch'Rystophe: Brick-wall dining space, vivacious terrace and classics like burgers and healthier poke bowls. *noon-1.30pm Tue-Sun, 7-9.30pm Fri & Sat* €€

Lyons-La-Forêt

EURE'S BEST CIDER MILLS & CHEESE

Manoir du Val: Next to 17th-century Château de Beaumesnil, taste some of the finest ciders (the rosé variety deserves a special mention).

La Quesne, Ferme et Fromagerie: Family-friendly guided visits to an organic farm where you can see the cheese-making process from A-Z.

Le Pressoir d'Or: Stroll over 40 heaven-scented hectares of apple orchards and taste a wide variety of ciders and juices.

La Ferm'entente: Quench any thirst with your choice of raw ciders, organic beers, apple juices and spirits.

La Chèvre Rit à Marcouville: An idyllic goat cheese farm open for visits on Wednesdays, Fridays and Saturdays.

that dates back to the 12th century, and wander through either a manicured French garden that's been restored faithfully to the original 1774 plans or a wild, untamed English garden. There's also France's only museum dedicated to writer Jules Michelet (you can even visit the tower where he wrote *The History of France*), plus over 60 sculptures from international artists like Erró and Salvador Dalí. Americans may appreciate the surrealist's *The Victory of Liberty* sculpture, a spin on the Statue of Liberty with two torches instead of one.

Lyons-La-Forêt

TIME FROM ROUEN: **45MIN**

Walk in Madame Bovary's footsteps

Classed as one of the most beautiful villages in France, Lyons-La-Forêt is a prime example of medieval Normandy, tucked near the biggest beech forest in the country, Forêt Domaniale de Lyons.

Wander around a town that hasn't changed much since the mid-19th century and admire the half-timbered houses and a great outdoor market hall where Claude Chabrol's *Madame Bovary* was filmed (though the real adulterous scandal, which inspired Flaubert's literary masterpiece, is said to have taken place in Ry, just 10 miles north). Without going into debt like the tragic heroine, you can take home egg-shaped candles as a souvenir from **L'Empreinte** *(lempreinte-decoration. fr; 10am-12.30pm & 2.30-6pm Thu-Sun)* or a vintage find from **Jan Brocante** *(10am-12.30pm & 2.30-6pm, Thu-Mon)*.

At the bakery **Aux Délices de Lyons** across from the outdoor hall, get La Normande, a decadent and filling tart made with flan, apples, almonds and a butter crust. When asked if the recipe was typical of Normandy, the baker shrugged: 'My wife made it'.

Côte d'Albâtre & Le Havre

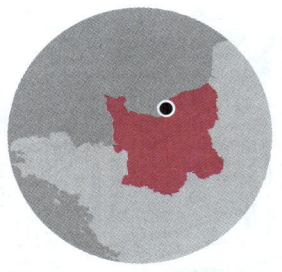

POST-WAR ARCHITECTURE | SEASIDE CLIFFS | CHARMING VILLAGES

GETTING AROUND

Le Havre is easily accessible by daily trains from Paris (2½ hours) and Rouen (50 minutes). A cheap bus ride on Ligne 13 will get you from Le Havre (Grand Hameau station) to the cliffs at Étretat (Le Grandval). To explore smaller towns like Veules-les-Roses or to go inshore, a car is quickest and most convenient. Cyclists will enjoy the Vélomaritime, 43km of cycling routes between Le Havre and Étretat.

☑ TOP TIP

If you're driving to Étretat, parking in the city itself is limited and can be a nightmare even during the low season. Parking near the train station (Parking de la Gare) will cost €7.50, but it gets you easy access to the cliffs without the hassle of finding a spot in town.

Wade into the seductive waters of the stunning Côte d'Albâtre (Alabaster Coast), 130km of coast along the English Channel, which runs up to the northern small fishing village Le Tréport. Along the coast, ripe for water sports like sailing and windsurfing, hiking and fishing, you'll also find jaw-dropping cliffs at Étretat, as well as tranquil and charming villages like Veules-les-Roses with juicy oysters, bustling and historic port cities like Fécamp, and various treasures just inland.

At the southernmost point, Le Havre, you'll find a striking city that begs the question: what would a modern French city look like built from a blank canvas? Find the answer in architect Auguste Perret's re-imagining of the port city through modular grid urban planning and concrete architecture. The city is a breath of fresh air (literally: winds gust through the wide avenues) crowned with other feats of design, from the impressive Bibliothèque Oscar Niemeyer to the distinctive geometric cut of the Église St-Joseph.

Coast Along the Iconic Alabaster Cliffs

Hiking the cliffs of Étretat

France's famous cliffs, Étretat's staggering arches have been sculpted over millennia by winds and the whims of the sea, and immortalised by Monet over 80 times. More recently, the cliffs have also unfortunately been the cause of deaths due to reckless photos – skip the selfies at the top and don't stray off established paths.

Falaise d'Aval and the adjacent Aiguille are the most iconic, featuring a needle shooting from the water alongside an arch, and the **Falaise d'Amont** offers a bird's-eye view of Étretat. Hikes here are choose-your-own-adventure: opt for the steep steps to the neo-Gothic stone church, **Chapelle Notre-Dame-de-la-Garde**, for a peaceful (yet windy) picnic – the view from the church is better than a visit inside. Hardcore hikers, head to the intensive and rewarding five-hour Roc Vaudieu Loop. If

you're short on time, take the Porte d'Amont Loop that starts at Chemin de Criquetot.

Waterside & Poetic Contemplations
Literary and kayaking adventures in Étretat

It's best to move slowly and observe. Local naturalist guide **Cyriaque Lethuillier** *(natterra.fr; tours from €30)* narrates poetic walking tours, sprinkled with Guy de Maupassant quotes and existential thoughts on deep geological time. Book a twilight stroll with Cyriaque for dusk magic or a fishing expedition for sea life encounters.

A CHEF'S IDYLLIC DAY

Chef Louis Vatelier, owner of **La Source de Veules-les-Roses**, shares his ideal day in the village. @louisvat

I've always wanted to be a chef in my hometown, where life unfolds with the seasons and tides. A perfect day would kick off with strolling the low tide at the Veules-les-Roses beach, headed towards Sotteville-sur-Mer for coffee. After lunch, I'd spend the afternoon browsing **Les Mondes de Zulma** for books and **Le Relais des Artistes**, the sublime home decor boutique run by Wyndham Follet for vintage gems nestled inside a typical Norman house that his parents built, opposite the church. To end the day, I'd meander through the narrow streets before having a drink at the beach hut **L'Optimiste**, to savour oysters harvested just a few metres away.

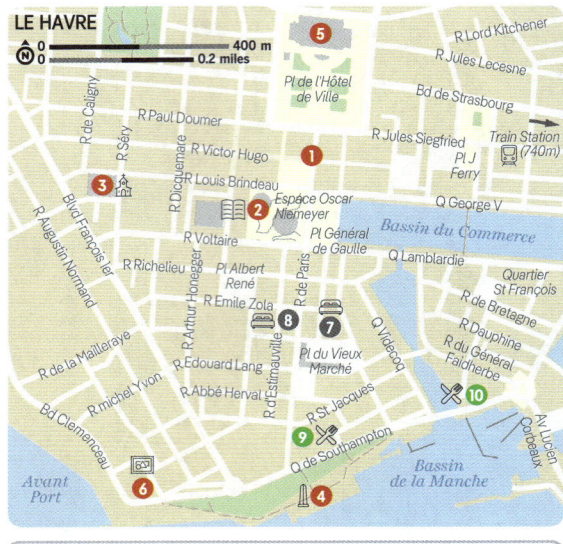

SIGHTS
1 Appartement Témoin Perret
2 Église St-Joseph
3 Esplanade Nelson Mandela
4 Hôtel de Ville
5 Musée d'Art Moderne André Malraux
6 Bibliothèque Oscar Niemeyer

SLEEPING
7 Hôtel Lilybloom
8 ibis Styles Le Havre Centre Auguste Perret

EATING
9 Calice et Mandibule
10 Chez Lili

To wade deeper into the waters, head to **Voiles et Galets** (*voilesetgalets.com; rentals from €15*) for an unforgettable kayak or paddleboard ride under some epic scenery; no reservations as rentals depend on weather conditions. Don't miss a paddle out to the **Plage du Fourquet** to enjoy a secluded beach.

Make a Broom, Get Swept Off Your Feet
A modern broom-making factory of yesteryear

Discover the art of artisanal broom-making at **La Balaiterie** (*labalaiterie.fr; tours 10am, 2pm & 4pm Mon-Sat, by reservation Sun; from €16*), just 20 minutes from charming Veules-les-Roses. It's run by Marie-Laure and Arnaud Gabriel, a couple who are reviving the lost art of handmade brooms using replicas of centuries-old machines. The in-depth tour explains the process from cultivating sorghum to harvesting, dyeing and fabricating. It also includes a visit to see the life's work of another Norman artist, Gilbert Housset, whose more than 50 mind-blowing wood sculptures include impressively faithful replicas of denim jackets and a Jeep (you can even open the hood).

The craft-inclined can try their hand at making a tiny *balayette* (brush) for sweeping a fireplace, a charming sorghum fly swatter or a keyboard brush; reserve online ahead or simply take a piece of utility art home with you to keep your floors clean and impress guests. Brides and grooms-to-be can also get a custom-designed *voiture balai* (a broom attached to the last car of a wedding procession) to add a quirky French tradition to their wedding.

The Softness of Farm-to-Bed Linens
Spend a day at a fourth-generation linen farm

Walk among the dreamy fields of flax that bloom a delicate shade of indigo – June is the best month to catch the ephemeral flowering – and learn how linen sheets are produced from fibre to textile at sustainable and eco-friendly **La Maison Embrin** (*embrin.fr; Apr-Aug, hours vary*). Run by Camille and Alexis Ménager, you can tour their fields and farmhouse (allow about an hour) for an in-depth look at the process of growing, harvesting, and transformation of flax plant to fabric (done by nearby local cooperation Terre de Lin) – you can even visit the *atelier* (workshop) where their sheets are designed and sewn. Over half of the world's linen textiles are made in Normandy and at the Embrin farm, you can find yourself at the heart of linen production.

Take home custom-embroidered sheets (or have them shipped) or elegant table linens from their showroom. The real stars of the show are the *courtepoints*, quilt bed covers – a nostalgic heirloom item commonly found in Norman houses. Embrin's designs often feature artistic nods to the sweeping Côte d'Albâtre landscapes and eye-catching flora.

360-Degree Views & Deep Dives into History
A museum and marvellous port views

The history of Fécamp, France's first cod port, traces back well over 1000 years to the time of the Duke of Normandy and Viking descendant Richard II. Head to the **Fisheries Museum** (*musee-fecamp.fr; adult/student/child €9/6/free*) to soak

IN THE PATH OF RUSSIAN PAINTERS

Stretching just 1.1km, France's shortest river runs through **Veules-les-Roses**, a tiny village of idyllic windmills and thatched-roof cottages where Russian Impressionist painters found endless inspiration during the 1850s. Along the river you can see the mill and watering hole, and beachside you can see the same sea as immortalised by painters Alexei Petrovitch Bogolyubov and Vassily Dmitrievich Polenov. Close to the stone bridge near the source of the river, there's a watercress mill (also painted by Polenov), and today the watercress is still enjoyed by locals with an annual festival.

EATING ON THE CÔTE D'ALBÂTRE: RESTAURANTS LOVED BY LOCALS

Calice et Mandibule: Extensive tea menu, soups, salads and stews at a community restaurant that also hosts creative workshops. *noon-2pm Tue-Thu, 11am-10pm Fri, 11am-6pm Sat, to 2pm Sun* €	**Chez Lili**: Enjoy a fancy cappuccino or rosé on the vibrant terrace and chase it with oysters. Le Havre. *9am-10pm Mon-Wed, to midnight Thu-Sat, 10am-10pm Sun* €	**Le Romain d'Étretat**: Each pizza on the extensive menu is delicious and well-priced. Ever-popular and good for kids. *noon-2pm Sat-Fri, 7-9.30pm Sun-Thu, to 10pm Fri & Sat* €	**O4saisons**: A mere five-minute drive out of Étretat will get you out of tourist traps and to delicious and fresh homestyle cooking. *noon-2pm daily, 7-9pm Fri-Tue, to 9.30pm Wed & Thu* €€
Le Barbican: Unassuming spot with locally sourced produce. A fine show of French cooking and British fish and chips that hit the spot. Fécamp. *noon-1.30pm Mon-Sat, 7.30-9pm Fri, Sat & Tue* €	**Le Bateau**: Inventive crêpes (try with scallops) and surprisingly good cocktails. Garden dining and a large fireplace for chilly nights. Varengeville-sur-Mer. *noon-2pm Wed-Sun, 7-9pm Tue-Sat* €€	**La Source de Veules-les-Roses**: Local gastronomy and produce at its finest in a cosy and chic atmosphere. *noon-2pm Sat-Tue, 7-9pm Sun-Tue, 8.30am-11am Wed, 7-10pm Fri & Sat* €€€	**L'Optimiste**: A beachside food truck with mouth-watering lobster rolls served up with crispy, golden fries. Veules-les-Roses. *hours vary* €

STROLL INTO THE 1950S IN LE HAVRE

Explore post-WWII architecture on foot with this city centre walking tour.

START	END	LENGTH
Hôtel de Ville	Bibliothèque Oscar Niemeyer	4.2km; 4hrs

Begin at ❶ **Hôtel de Ville**, the imposing, geometric town hall rebuilt in 1958, considered emblematic of Auguste Perret's architectural style. It acts as the city's focal point.

Post-visit, head south across the square to the ❷ **Appartement Témoin Perret**; it's open daily during peak season but make sure to reserve in advance and arrive 15 minutes early. This meticulously restored five-room apartment is typical of Perret's style. Clean lines, typical of the Reconstruction period, dominate this post-war home. It allows you to imagine an alternate universe, where France's buildings and interior design are conceived from scratch in the 1950s.

Afterwards, head a few blocks west to see Perret's final work: ❸ **Église St-Joseph**, built in memory of WWII bombing victims. The unusual combination of concrete walls accented with abstract, geometric stained glass, along with an octagonal tower, creates an intriguing beauty – you can't help but feel moved to a higher state.

Wander south (opt for the scenic route on bd Clemenceau) to ❹ **Musée d'Art Moderne André Malraux** *(muma-lehavre.fr; full price/ under-26 €10/free)*, a modern building filled with Impressionist works, redesigned by Perret's pupil, Guy Lagneau.

Finish the day back in the town centre at the sweeping and vast ❺ **Bibliothèque Oscar Niemeyer**, designed by the famed Brazilian architect, where you'll be spoiled for choice for comfy seats to recline in and books to browse.

Distinctly 1950s **Appartement Témoin Perret** is furnished with works by designer René Gabriel and outfitted with retro kitchen gadgets and books.

Peckish? Pop into **Calice Et Mandibule** (p235), an eco- and veg-friendly cafe and community space, for special tea blends, dessert or a hearty lunch.

Find the colourful shipping container sculpture by designer Vincent Ganivet on the **Esplanade Nelson Mandela**, constructed for the city's 500th anniversary.

Palais Bénédictine

it all in, for a 360-degree view of the port and surrounding cliffs, and an in-depth view of humanity's evolution through a fascinating curation of historic objects like old-time bathing suits, furniture, pirate jewellery and Impressionist paintings. Marvel at the massive, prehistoric mammoth tusks found in the port, walk among dories and admire relics of an 18th-century Masonic lodge. The museum is open daily (though closed on Tuesdays from mid-September to end of April).

Feast on the Sea & Drink Like a Fish
Oysters, herring and an elegant herbal liqueur

For direct contact with the sea, head to **Le Marché aux Poissons** *(open Tue, Fri & Sat)* for straight-from-the-ocean oysters washed down with white wine, or house-smoked salmon. Herring lovers should head to the bustling and cosy **Chez Nounoute**. As evening falls, freshen up and quench your thirst at the neo-Gothic 19th-century **Palais Bénédictine** *(benedictinedom.com; tours from €23; book in advance)*, where you can either take a cocktail workshop and tour or head straight to the upscale, glass-vaulted-ceiling bar **La Verrière** for a taste of the herbal Bénédictine liqueur, concocted from 27 flowers, berries, herbs, roots and spices.

Breath of Fresh Air Over a Concrete City
A revamped old military fort

For a bit of greenery, head to **Les Jardins Suspendus** *(free; open daily April-Sep)* for the best views of the city and ocean, perfumed with the scent of roses. The 19th-century Vauban-style military fortress, once used for defensive firepower battles, is now a place where over 6000 types of plant life blossom.

Tropical greenhouses harbour cactuses, orchids, water lilies, begonias and more, and the flowers' scents harmonise into a delightful bouquet. Rest tired feet afterwards at **L'Orangeraie** tea house for an affogato or a freshly pressed juice.

ART DECO REVIVAL: LE NORMANDY

Originally opened in 1934 and designed by Le Havre native Henri Daigue, this palatial art deco cinema with a stunning glass façade miraculously survived WWII in Le Havre, and hosted famed performers like Duke Ellington, Benny Goodman and Charles Aznavour. In 1991, due to a failure to keep up-to-date with safety norms, the theatre closed and was abandoned to the ravages of time. Luckily, after three years of intensive restoration, **Le Normandy** was set to reopen at the end of 2025 as a theatre with all its original period details, like a 6m-long quartz-topped bar, lush carpeting and crystal chandeliers. It's worth peeking inside just to see the love and care put into the fastidious restoration.

Côte Fleurie

ART GALLERIES | SOPHISTICATION | MARCEL PROUST

☑ TOP TIP
Deciding between Deauville and Trouville? The latter is more laid-back and family friendly, whereas Deauville caters to the celebrity jet set, with luxury shopping and high-end restaurants. Around the streets of Trouville, keep an eye out for the street art of famed late artist **Miss. Tic**, known for poetic lines graffitied next to dark-haired women.

One of Normandy's most famous coastlines bears the nickname of the 'Flowery Coast' for good reason: during France's Belle Époque, writers and artists like Marcel Proust and Eugène Boudin, as well as the upper-class bourgeois, flocked to these dreamy shorelines, which inspired them and were believed to restore health. The mid-19th-century sea-bathing craze led to the construction of stunning seaside villas along the beautiful, blooming shore between the D-Day Landing Beaches and the mouth of the Seine at Le Havre.

Today, seaside resort towns Deauville and Trouville-sur-Mer are still favoured by the well-heeled set, while Honfleur remains popular for history and art, and Cabourg for Marcel Proust sights. Thalassotherapy, using seawater for well-being, is still a popular activity, but the main draw of the Côte Fleurie is the art. Here, one can bloom artistically, see and be seen, and bask blissfully in the culture of aesthetes.

Browse Bookshelves in Refined Elegance
A cultural centre oozing with style by Moatti-Rivière architects

Deauville's **Les Franciscaines** *(lesfranciscaines.fr; special exhibitions adult/student/under-16 €16/9/free)*, a hybrid media centre featuring a museum, theatre, auditorium and library, and a striking modern design set in antiquity: a jaw-dropping

GETTING AROUND

From Paris St-Lazare, you can easily get to Deauville by train in just over two hours. Deauville is fairly flat but the cycling lanes are rather lacking. Rent a bike in Trouville at **Les Trouvillaises** and you can get around the Flowery Coast in style – or even in tandem with a partner. To get between Deauville and Trouville, take a long and leisurely walk along the harbour. During high tide, you can opt for an inexpensive, quick and bumpy boat ride. During low tide, a third option reveals itself: a footbridge that connects the two cities. Just bring pocket change with you: the toll per person is €1.20.

Les Franciscaines

chandelier that spans over 400 sq metres hangs over the ancient courtyard, adorning the rows of arched windows. Tuck yourself into a corner and prop your feet on footstools in the form of cactus trompe l'oeil while browsing the ample book collection. In the chapel, modern theatre seating and stage lighting next to the original stained glass results in an unbelievably harmonious discord that hits the perfect note for soaking up culture in style.

Originally built in 1875 as a hospital for sailors and an orphanage, the building also held WWI and WWII soldiers, a school for girls and a convent, and was acquired by the city of Deauville in 2012. Moatti-Rivière architects secured a competition to redesign the site, which opened in 2021. It's a near-spiritual devotion to culture, the arts, and the range and depth of human imagination.

Best of all, access to this cultural cachet is free: the main parts of the building are open to any visitors who want to lounge and flick through the collection of books and magazines in the mezzanine, vast inner courtyard or sunny backyard garden. Paid entry gives you access to the curated exhibitions, and, in the evenings, you can snag tickets to a show in the adjoining chapel.

Indulge in Seawater Therapy
Thalassotherapy in modernity

In 1865, French doctor Jacques de la Bonnardière wrote a thesis on the healing benefits of seawater, dubbing the concept thalassotherapy. Thalassotherapy centres quickly sprang up all over France and have remained a staple of seaside resorts. Tired travellers can rest their feet and float their bodies at the modern and clean **Thalassotherapy Thalazur Cabourg** *(thalazur.fr/cabourg)* that overlooks Proust's promenade.

continued on p242

BEST ANNUAL FÊTES & FESTIVALS

Dîner sur la Digue: Join thousands of guests at this highly anticipated dinner party alongside the boardwalk in Cabourg. Reserve, pack your picnic or grab a meal from vendors. Dress up in Belle Époque fashion!

Cabourg Mon Amour Festival: Groove during this annual three-day, open-air music festival, with music styles from electro to rap. *cabourgmonamour.fr*

Fête des Marins: Every Pentecost weekend (the 7th Sunday after Easter), get suited in sailor stripes in Honfleur for parades, concerts, photos and more.

Offcourts Festival: September festival celebrating French & Québécois short films. Free screenings, concerts and festivities.

American Film Festival: Each September, stars gather in Deauville to celebrate American cinema. *festival-deauville.com*

CÔTE FLEURIE

HIGHLIGHTS
1. Les Franciscaines
2. Marché aux Poissons
3. Villa du Temps Retrouvé

SIGHTS
4. Beuvron-en-Auge
5. Domaine Familial Louis Dupont
6. Dunes de Cabourg
7. Le Hôme-Varaville
8. Les Planches de Deauville
9. Luc-sur-Mer
10. Promenade Marcel Proust

ACTIVITIES
11. Calvados Christian Drouin
12. Thalassotherapy Thalazur Cabourg

SLEEPING
13. Hôtel Flaubert
14. Hotel Le Trouville
15. Le Grand Hôtel de Cabourg
16. Les Sources Du Val
17. Logis Hôtel Ferme de la Grande Cour
18. Thalazur Cabourg

EATING
19. Belle Époque

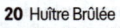

20 Huître Brûlée	26 Margaux à La Mangeoire
see 4 La Colomb'auge	27 Pollen
21 Laurence Salon de Thé	28 SaQuaNa
22 Le Cyrano Deauville	
see 1 Le Réfectoire	● DRINKING & NIGHTLIFE
23 Le Square	
24 Les Etiquettes	29 Bar à Vin Les Affiches
25 L'Étoile des Mers	

● SHOPPING
31 Atelier Julien Schuster
32 Atelier Philippe Géraud
33 Entre Tissu et Papier
34 Galeries Bartoux Normandy
35 Maison Laurette
36 Maître Tailleur Elia B
37 Poterie du Mesnil de Bavent
38 Varvara Bracho Contemporary

● ENTERTAINMENT
30 Casino Barrière Trouville

● TRANSPORT
39 Les Trouvillaises

continued from p239

Swim between waterfall massages and waterjet lounge chairs in the large indoor pool and stretch out your limbs in the hammam. Among many treatments based on harnessing marine powers, the classic massage while a delicate shower of seawater gently falls on your back is a unique experience. However, those who enjoy more aggressive massages may be disappointed. After a treatment, sip on herbal tea made with meadowsweet flower, organic licorice and red fucus seaweed while you gaze out at the rippling grass framing an endless ocean.

Immerse Yourself in the Art of Headwear
An afternoon with a milliner and custom-made hats

Fancy a fancy hat? Enter the elegant world of artisanal milliner Laure Fessard of **Maison Laurette** *(maisonlaurette.com; 10.30am-6.30pm Thu-Sat & Mon, 2.30-6.30pm Tue & Wed)*, who creates some of the finest head accessories for every occasion: a fascinator for a horse race at the Deauville-La-Touques racecourse *(francegalop-live.com/hippodromes/deauville)*, a wedding hair comb, a traditional *canotier* (straw hat) for a French picnic, or even a customised design worthy of a royal wedding. More masculine-leaning styles can pick up a classy fedora or Panama hat. Either way, your head is in good hands with Laure, who'll help you decide on a style and then take measurements of your noggin to ensure the perfect fit.

Bespoke hats can be picked up or shipped (plan for at least two weeks to make them) but there are also plenty of premade choices from headbands to miniature fascinator hats – perhaps for a night at the historic gambling house **Casino Barrière Trouville** *(casinosbarriere.com/trouville)* or an upscale dinner at **Belle Époque**. To go the whole nine yards, head across the street from Maison Laurette to **Maître Tailleur Elia B** *(10.30am-7.30pm Tue-Sat)* for custom couture dresses (rentals also available) and suits; it's best to call in advance to catch the master seamstress Elia Baron herself.

> **THE ROARING TWENTIES IN DEAUVILLE**
>
> Many casinos in France – including the baroque-styled Casino de Deauville restored by Jacques Garcia and the glamorous, sprawling Trouville-sur-Mer Casino, which was constructed in 1912 and modelled on the Versailles Opera House – are near the seashores and in spa towns. This stems from a law Napoleon set in place in 1806 to curb gambling and draw tourism to other regions in the country. During the 1920s, famous figures like Coco Chanel (in 1913 she opened her first store ever on rue Gontaut-Biron, now rue Lucien Barriere) and Pierre Fresnay could be spotted in the glitzy resort town scene. Literary characters Tom Buchanan and Daisy of *The Great Gatsby* honeymooned in Deauville too.

 EATING IN DEAUVILLE & TROUVILLE: OUR PICKS

Le Cyrano Deauville: A classic brasserie where all the Deauville locals can be found. *7am-8.30pm Mon-Fri, 7am-7.30pm Sat* €€

Le Réfectoire: Don't miss the all-you-can-eat brunch on the terrace of Les Franciscaines. *10.30am-6.30pm Tue-Sun* €€

L'Étoile des Mers: Stylish setting and seafood like the signature Viennese langoustine. *9am-7pm Wed-Mon* €€

Le Square: Local and homemade fare with photo-worthy trompe d'oeil desserts in cubist shapes. *9.15am-10.30pm Fri-Tue* €

Marché aux Poissons: In the heart of Trouville, pick your plucked-from-the-sea morsels and have 'em cooked on the spot. *9am-7pm Tue-Sun, 10am-7pm Mon* €€

Margaux à La Mangeoire: Family-friendly terrace with solid burgers and views of the next-door horse riding school. *9am-6pm* €

Les Étiquettes: A modern bistro and cosy wine bar off the tourist street in Trouville – order the ravioli. *noon-2pm daily, 7-10pm Mon-Fri, 5-10pm Sat & Sun* €€

Bar à Vin Les Affiches: A cheery, light and airy beachside tapas spot with a seafood emphasis. *noon-2.30pm & 6.30-10pm Thu-Mon* €€

Le Grand Hôtel de Cabourg

Holiday like Proust in Cabourg
Go in search of lost time

How we experience time is relative to our perception. A visit to the **Villa du Temps Retrouvé** *(villadutempsretrouve.com; adult/student/child €9/7/free)* is a thoughtfully curated and ever-changing frame of reference that transports you to the Belle Époque era through the eyes and life of Marcel Proust. Furniture and paintings from the period between the two World Wars rotate in and out, as well as films, costumes and photographs. The charm of the Villa du Temps Retrouvé lies in its immersive nature: pick up a telephone to hear an anecdote of the era or stroll up to the piano to serenade guests with some Claude Debussy.

Afterwards, stroll the streets that make up Cabourg's unique fan-shaped layout and head to the centre, where you'll find **Le Grand Hôtel de Cabourg** *(grand-hotel-cabourg.com)*, an embodiment of Belle Époque grandeur. Proust famously slept in room 414 and wrote parts of his masterpiece *À la Recherche du Temps Perdu* (*In Search of Lost Time*) here. Pause for lunch at the Le Balbec inside the hotel for delicate service in a poetic and elegant setting. Dishes are pricey, but the quality and attention to presentation, combined with the seaside views, are worth it. Next, head to the **Promenade Marcel Proust** with comfortable walking shoes for the long boardwalk stroll to enjoy the villa views that stretch from the **Dunes de Cabourg** to **Le Hôme-Varaville**.

Meet the Artists of Honfleur
Galleries and ateliers galore

The port city of Honfleur, where the Seine meets the English Channel, is famous for its idyllic and extremely photogenic harbour, cobblestones and half-timbered houses. Art collectors

---

COUNTRYSIDE THROUGH AN ARTIST'S EYES

Carole Leprevost's oil paintings capture the easy nature of Normandy living: Norman cows – recognisable by the spots around their eyes – seascapes, starfish and portraits of beloved pets. Based in Dives-sur-Mer, Leprevost's love of the region has her constantly on the move. *@leprevost carole; leprevost-art.fr*

There are endless places I love – like the Ferme de la Grande Cour in Honfleur for a relaxing break, the Villa du Temps Retrouvé and the Grand Hôtel where Proust wrote *In Search of Lost Time*, in Cabourg. I always urge my friends to dare to go just a little further, to visit villages like **Beuvron-en-Auge**, **Luc-sur-Mer**, and **Ver-sur-Mer**. Most of all, I love visiting **La Poterie du Mesnil de Bavent,** a world of ceramic workshops and wonder.

AN AOP CHEESE & CALVADOS ROAD TRIP

Stop at cheese farms around Pays d'Auge to sample four AOP cheeses. Wash it down on an apple-scented stretch with family-run cideries and distilleries.

START	END	LENGTH
Sarl Villiers	La Fromagerie d'Isigny	310km; 8hrs

Start with a taste of Neufchâtel-en-Bray, a cute heart-shaped creamy cheese made by Middle Ages dairymaids who gifted it to English soldiers, at the long-time family-run ❶ **Sarl Villiers**. (In town, Earl Monnier Fromagerie has its own excellent Neufchâtel).

Head west for under two hours on A29 to the family-run ❷ **Calvados Christian Drouin** distillery, a paradisiacal 17th-century Augeronne farmhouse. The two-hour rare *calvados* tasting tour takes place in private cellars, with sips siphoned from barrels dating back to the 1960s.

Just south, the ❸ **E Graindorge Fromagerie** factory tour explains in detail how Livarot and Pont-l'Évêque are made. Pick some up from nearby farmers like **Fromagerie Durand** and **Fromagerie Clos de Beaumoncel**.

Loop back north for a refined cider and *calvados* experience at the elegant ❹ **Domaine Familial Louis Dupont** estate. Find original combinations like a cider mixed with quince fruit, and a Cidre Triple that's produced like a dark beer.

For a final stop, head an hour east to sample Crème d'Isigny straight from the factory at ❺ **La Fromagerie d'Isigny**, which makes the richest, thickest and creamiest of creams in Isigny-sur-Mer. Walt Disney's ancestors were also from the region, pronounced *'d'is-zee-nee'*. Pick up butter, cream, cheese, yogurt and – during summer season – the best ice cream you'll ever taste.

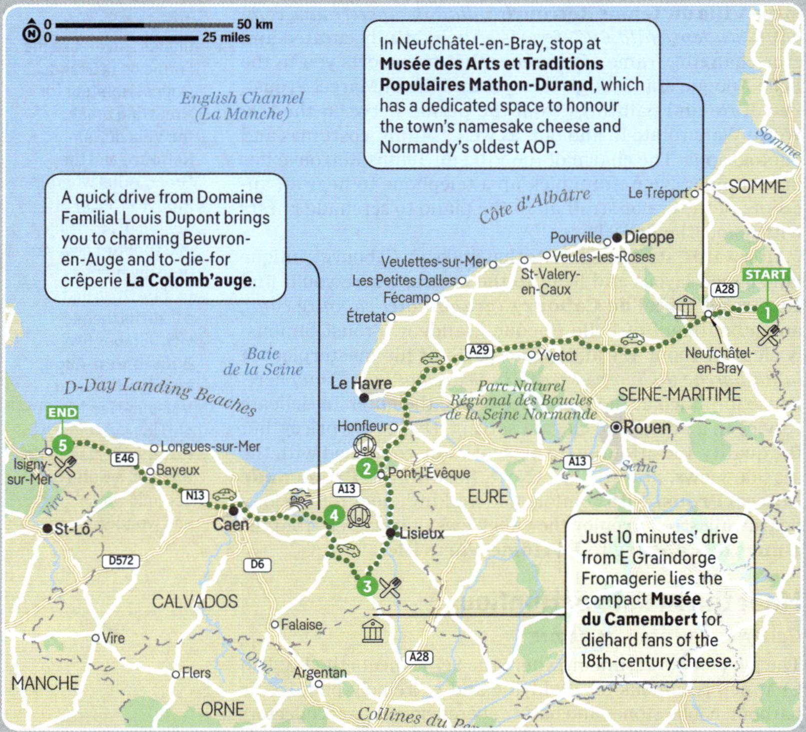

> In Neufchâtel-en-Bray, stop at **Musée des Arts et Traditions Populaires Mathon-Durand**, which has a dedicated space to honour the town's namesake cheese and Normandy's oldest AOP.

> A quick drive from Domaine Familial Louis Dupont brings you to charming Beuvron-en-Auge and to-die-for crêperie **La Colomb'auge**.

> Just 10 minutes' drive from E Graindorge Fromagerie lies the compact **Musée du Camembert** for diehard fans of the 18th-century cheese.

Camembert, Fromagerie Durand

and admirers can do more than snap a picture: with over 100 art galleries dotting the storefronts, where beaver fur sellers once hawked their goods taken from the New World, there's something for every budget. Start with the famous **Galeries Bartoux Normandy** or the non-profit art gallery **Entre Tissu et Papier**, which specialises in delicate paper creations, handmade goods and upcycled crafts made from vintage fabrics.

Even better, skip the middleman and visit artists' workshops. Linogravure fans should pop into the snug brick-walled **Atelier Julien Schuster** *(instagram.com/julienschuster)*, at the edge of the Old Bassin, for whimsical prints of Norman cows, fish, cats, the moon and Honfleur architecture. Watercolour fans will love **Varvara Bracho Contemporary** *(varvara-bracho.com)* and can take home work by this Russian-born artist who finds inspiration in the port city and Parisian cafes. Dada and surrealist enthusiasts should not miss **Atelier Philippe Géraud** *(instagram.com/geraud.philippe)*, with seriously fun works by an unserious, self-proclaimed painter, photographer and jokester. Call ahead, as hours vary per the whims and schedule of the artist.

HOLLYWOOD IN DEAUVILLE

At the height of seaside resort fashion during the 19th century, Deauville – known by some as the 21e *arrondissement* of Paris – was the place to see and be seen for high society and celebrities. Architect Charles Adda built an art deco–style Pompeian bathhouse and renovated the promenade with the infamous **Les Planches de Deauville** that run alongside the sea for 643m. Each wooden plank bears the name of a Hollywood star, in homage to the creation of the American Film Festival (p239), which began in 1975, including big names like Clint Eastwood, Robin Wright Penn, Nicole Kidman and more.

EATING IN HONFLEUR: OUR PICKS

Pollen: Carb fans, do not miss this cute bakery for delectable pastries, Sunday brunch and top-notch coffee. Get there early. *8am-7pm Thu-Sun, 8am-1.30pm Mon, 8.30am-7pm Wed* €

SaQuaNa: A rotating, seasonal menu fused with inspired flavours like yuzu, paired with the freshest breads. Don't skip the homemade dessert platter. *7.30am-3.30pm & 7pm-midnight Wed-Sun* €€

Laurence Salon de Thé: Cosy, kitschy spot with fresh and colourful salads, excellent iced tea and a charming host, Laurence. *10.30am-5pm* €

Huître Brûlée: Sustainably sourced oysters and biting cider, with a nice pork loin for the seafood averse. *12.15-1.30pm & 7.15-9.30pm* €

D-Day Landing Beaches, Caen & Bayeux

WORLD WAR II | WILLIAM THE CONQUEROR | COCKTAILS & TRIPE

GETTING AROUND

Renting a car is ideal to tour the D-Day Landing Beaches yourself – Caen has more options than Bayeux – but many guided tours will shuttle you around in Jeeps or vans. Local transportation, like buses, is available, but is far less reliable, so plan accordingly.

When US soldiers landed on Normandy's Omaha Beach on the morning of 6 June 1944, the ensuing crescendo to WWII left indelible scars on the French countryside. From west to east, the 80km stretch of sand comprises the American landing beaches of Utah and Omaha; Gold Beach, where the British landed; Juno Beach for the Canadians, and then another American landing destination, Sword Beach. Decades later, D-Day remains a monolithic legend that has left countless memorial and military sites, cemeteries, museums and remains of what was once the largest harbour in the world.

WWII obsessives could spend a lifetime diving into history, but even pacifists will find a distinct tranquillity in the wake of a world war.

The fields beyond the shores are flush for discovery, and a quick drive south will bring you to historical Bayeux or the vibrant capital of *calvados*, Caen.

A Night at a WWII Museum
History fanatics and personal collections

The wife and husband team behind guesthouse **D-Day Aviators Le Manoir** *(ddayaviatorslemanoir.fr)*, Anne Florence and Paul Hontang, are both pilots with passions. Paul is a history expert, constantly on the hunt to add to their impressive collection of war detritus: a plane cockpit adorns the living room, and guests breakfast on a table made from a German plane engine. Anne Florence has a personal collection of over 500 *dentelles*, traditional lace bonnets and hats worn to signify the different life stages of a woman. Ask her for a peek in the garage next door. Situated in **Arromanches-les-Bains**, where the world's largest artificial harbour was assembled by the Allied Forces, the manor house is centrally placed for visiting all along the D-Day Landing Beaches and right next to the newly renovated **Musée du Debarquement** *(musee-arromanches.fr; adult/child €12.90/8.30)*, a stunningly detailed presentation of why and how the critical events of 6 June 1944 took place.

☑ TOP TIP

Set up basecamp in either Caen (for student nightlife vibes), Bayeux (for historic, quiet charm) or Arromanches-les-Bains for a central location on the D-Day Landing Beaches. If you plan to visit many museums, the Explore Normandie Day Pass *(explorenormandypass.com)* for €1 offers discounts at over 70 museums and sites.

Artificial harbour remains, Arromanches-les-Bains

For a wilder ride, head to the family-friendly **La Batterie du Holdy Guesthouse** *(batterie-du-holdy.com)*, run by owner and local historian Jean Férollier, just south of Utah Beach. He'll transport you back to the events of 6 June 1944, with his cinematic and immersive reenactments in the very buildings where WWII action took place. Different storylines are available, but book in advance for the biggest show. Booking a night here is well worth it – an impassioned Jeep tour is included without steep prices. The real gold mine is the treasure trove of anecdotes Jean generously shares with his guests, and the delight of breakfast served in a 1940s-era grocery store.

Immersive History
All-sensory war reenactments and ghosts

For a bird's-eye point of view, head to **D-Day Experience** *(dday-experience.com; adult/child from €9/7)* where you can

continued on p250

THE FORGOTTEN BATTLE AT HOLDY BATTERY

In the early morning of 6 June 1944, a battle took place at the Batterie du Holdy, located near Ste-Marie-du-Mont. Its significance is equal to Richard Winters' 'Easy' Company – the 506th Parachute Infantry Regiment of the 101st Airborne Division – attack on a German battery, immortalised in the drama *Band of Brothers* (2001).

Occupied by Germans during WWII, US Airborne paratroopers dropped in on German soldiers, and Captain Lloyd E Patch of the 502nd Division used the nearby farm (now a guesthouse you can stay in) to fire on the enemy, which allowed the Americans to take control of the battery before playing a key role in the critical capture of Ste-Marie-du-Mont.

 EATING AROUND THE D-DAY LANDING SITES: BEST BEACHSIDE GRUB

L'Embusqué: Quality burgers and fries in a kitschy WWII setting. You can even eat inside the bus with heightened views. *noon-5pm Tue-Sun* €	**L'Overlord**: Top-notch pizzas with a variety of toppings and a very respectable Caesar salad. *11.30-2.30pm & 6.30-10.30pm, Thu-Mon & Tue, 12.30-2.30pm Tue & Wed, 7.30-10.30pm Wed* €	**A10 Canteen**: Next to the Victory Museum, dine in post-war style on comfort foods like pizza, burgers and cocktails. *12.30-2.30pm Tue-Sun, 7-10pm Tue-Sat* €	**Restaurant L'Ephémère**: Delicious homemade tapas on a sunny terrace nestled inside a castle. *12.30-2pm Thu-Sun, 7-8.30pm Thu-Sat* €€
Les Sablés d'Asnelles: The best shortbread you'll ever taste and other sweet-toothed treats. *9.30-12.30pm & 2-6pm Tue-Sat* €€	**L'Armoire Gourmande**: A fancy *épicerie* bursting with goodies all made in Normandy. Pick up *saucisson* for a picnic. *9.30am-12.30pm Mon-Fri, 2-7pm Mon-Sat, 3-7pm Sun* €	**Bleu Banane**: Outstanding fish and chips, burgers and tacos with chill vibes next to a tiny and pleasant port. *9am-7pm Tue & Wed, to 6pm Thu, to 9pm Fri, to 5pm Sat, 10am-6pm Sun* €	**L'inéLucTable**: Seaside views on Luc-Sur-Mer serving up classic French comfort foods like melted Camembert, steak tartare, plus wine and cocktails. *8.30am-9.30pm* €€

D-DAY LANDING BEACHES, CAEN & BAYEAUX

⭐ HIGHLIGHTS
1. Bayeux Tapestry

● SIGHTS
2. Airborne Museum
3. Batterie d'Azeville
4. Batterie de Crisbecq
5. Château de Caen
6. Conservatoire de la Dentelle de Bayeux
7. D-Day Experience
see 7 Dead Man's Corner Museum
8. La Pointe du Hoc
9. Mémorial de Caen
10. Memorial Museum of Omaha Beach
11. Musée de Normandie
12. Musée des Beaux-Arts
13. Musée du Débarquement
14. Overlord Museum
15. Radar Museum 1944
16. Utah Beach Landing Museum

● SLEEPING
17. Camping de Ste-Mère-Église
18. D-Day Aviators Le Manoir
19. Domaine Airborne
20. Ferme Hay Day
21. Hôtel François d'O

22 La Batterie du Holdy Guesthouse	28 La Normande	● **DRINKING & NIGHTLIFE**
23 Le Declic Hotel	29 L'Armoire Gourmande	36 Au Chef Raide
● **EATING**	30 L'Embusqué	37 Boumbap
24 A10 Canteen	31 Les Sablés d'Asnelles	38 Ecto Bar
25 Au Louis d'Or	32 L'inéLucTable	39 La Rhumba
26 Bleu Banane	33 L'Overlord	40 L'Antirouille
27 Chez Paulette	34 Patanella	41 L'Écume des Nuits
	35 Restaurant L'Éphémère	42 L'Hydropathe
		● **SHOPPING**
		43 Morgane Thomassin Céramiste

Batterie de Crisbecq

continued from p247

board a real 1943 C-47 aircraft to relive the day soldiers of the 101st Airborne flew over the English Channel and descended upon Normandy. After the 4D flight simulation, you hop next door to the **Dead Man's Corner Museum** *(dday-experience.com/en/dead-mans-corner-museum)*, a compact house that served as the German paratroopers' headquarters and an aid station for wounded soldiers, now brimming with original artefacts. The immersion here is more ethereal: it's rumoured to be haunted by the commander of a bombed reinforcement tank who lay dead for several days in front of the house the morning after D-Day.

Go Behind Enemy Lines
German batteries and underground radars

On the coast along the English Channel, known as La Manche, near Utah Beach, there are a few German artillery batteries to visit. The **Batterie de Crisbecq** *(batteriedecrisbecq.fr; adult/child €12.50/8.50)*, also known as the Battery of St Marcouf, is the largest and most spectacular. Built in 1941 by the German military engineering group Todt, the bunker today lets you walk in German soldiers' footsteps – the former trenches have been excavated and now serve as walking paths between the 22 blockhouses. View up close battle scars, grenade traps and visible damage. The **Batterie d'Azeville** *(batterie-azeville.manche.fr; adult/child €8/4)* is smaller in scale, but stands intact today due to a one-in-a-million chance: on D-Day, an American destroyer successfully shot a shell through the opening of the blockhouses. The shell miraculously didn't explode but crossed through the blockhouse and ended up a dud behind the fields.

If you *literally* want to go underground in WWII sites, head to the under-the-radar **Radar Museum 1944** *(musee-radar.fr; adult/under-10 €7.50/free)*, a former German listening station that has preserved its original state. Run by friendly and impassioned volunteers, the guided visits at this lesser-known museum are well worth reserving in advance.

BEST WWII MUSEUMS & MEMORIALS

Memorial Museum of Omaha Beach: The memorial of steel shooting out of the sand stops the breath, while the well-curated museum pays tribute to fallen soldiers.

Utah Beach Landing Museum: The westernmost beach hosts one of the biggest museums built on German fortifications. Inside, get a rare glimpse of an original B-26 bomber.

La Pointe du Hoc: View the ravages of a battlefield and old bunkers at this powerfully sobering memorial point. Plan for many stairs.

Overlord Museum: A collectors' paradise, with restored trucks, vehicles, dioramas and veteran tributes, with attention to detail down to the mood lighting.

Airborne Museum: Near the historic Ste-Mère-Église church, this museum focuses on the airborne troops and hosts an original glider and a C-47 plane.

Fingerwork Lace Intricacy
Learning the art of needlework

Lacemaking is a craft that dates back to the Renaissance. At one point, Bayeux had over 35,000 lace factories, filled with hundreds of young women producing intricate lace shawls, bonnets and more. The Bayeux Chantilly style of lacemaking uses fine thread and a thick cord for embellishment and is usually done in black lace, following the fashion of the time. For a sense of the amount of labour needed to produce just one shawl, count at least 10,000 hours. Unsurprisingly, machines have since rendered the hand-lacemaking industry a dying art.

But in Bayeux's 15th-century Maison d'Adam et Ève building, you can find Cécile Roquier and Véronique Thomazo, who run the **Conservatoire de la Dentelle de Bayeux** (dentellesbayeux.com; workshops from €26) and keep the art of lacemaking alive. Day workshops are available with the pair – Cécile specialises in bobbin lacemaking and Véronique in needlework – where you can learn how to fastidiously make a small lace keychain in a day. If you're looking to simply appreciate the beauty of lace and to soak in the relaxed and peaceful atmosphere, don't miss a visit.

Medieval Conquests & Mythical Beasts
The Bayeux Tapestry and ceramics

In the medieval town that was largely spared during the WWII bombardments despite its proximity to the D-Day Landing Beaches, there is no shortage of intricate architectural details and remnants of history that will fascinate visitors. Bayeux's most prized treasure? The 11th-century hand-embroidered wool thread **Bayeux Tapestry** (bayeuxmuseum.com/la-tapisserie-de-bayeux; adult/under-10 €12/free), coveted by Hitler himself – he had plotted to steal the immense 230ft scroll to take back to Germany. The pilgrimage to contemplate the complex piece of art that commemorates William the Conqueror's Conquest of England demands absolute attention: in a darkened room, the tapestry is carefully presented in a loop that will send you on a dizzying spin back to mythical times, complete with dragons and griffins.

Today, Bayeux continues its tradition of object storytelling: head to **Morgane Thomassin Céramiste** (morganeceramique.com) to admire the local artist's studio and shop full of delicate ceramics painted with inspiration drawn from her archaeological, mythological and historical studies. Her functional and

CAEN'S NIGHTLIFE & MUSIC SCENE

Théo Le Vigoureux, Caen native and electronic music producer, shares his cultural highlights. @fakearmusic

What's special about Norman culture and music is that it has an English influence – there's an appetite for rock and an indie scene. Head to rue Écuyère, where all the student hangout spots and bars are located. A few of my favourites include **Au Chef Raide**, **La Rhumba** and the emblematic nightclub **L'Écume des Nuits**.

Beer lovers should try this Norman beer, Kékette (a slang word for sex) which is brewed locally. Get some with friends and hang out on the lawns of the **Château de Caen** (p252) at night.

For the festival scene in Normandy, I like Festival Beauregard at Hérouville-St-Claire and the NDK Festival in Caen.

🍴 EATING IN BAYEUX: OUR PICKS

Au Louis d'Or: Inexpensive but solid crêpes in Bayeux; reserve in advance. *noon-2pm Sun & Mon, to 9pm Tue, Wed, Fri & Sat* €

Patanella: A newer Italian spot in Bayeux favoured by locals with well-priced and delicious pizzas and pastas. *11am-10pm Tue-Sat, 11.30am-10pm Mon* €€

Chez Paulette: Quirky, funky retro decor with healthy bites like bagels, quiches, salads and an ample tea selection. *noon-3pm Mon-Sat, 6-9pm Thu, 6.30-9pm Fri & Sat* €

La Normande: Local dishes with a star of the show: medal-winning tripe, cooked Caen style. *noon-1.45pm Thu-Mon, 6.45-9pm Mon-Sat* €€

CAEN SPECIALITIES

L'Embuscade Cocktail: Caen's most famous cocktail, *l'embuscade* – aptly named 'the ambush' – consists of a mix of blonde beer, white wine, *calvados*, blackcurrant syrup and lemon juice and will knock you off your feet. Students drink it to kick off a night and continue through the wee hours on rue Écuyère, nicknamed 'thirsty street' for the number of bars to ambush yourself with.

Tripe à la Caen: Famous for being William the Conqueror's favourite dish, tripe done Caen-style is a good gateway to consuming animal stomach. Stewed in spices, onion, garlic and a bouquet of French herbs along with carrots and celery, the tripe is tender, satisfyingly chewy, and bursting with flavour. Wash it all down with apple juice (like William) or some *calvados*.

beautiful pieces, like a teacup adorned with a phoenix, are delightful mashups of ancient myths and modernity.

Pilgrimage to the Pacifist's Museum of War
A sobering memorial to keeping peace

Travelling offers a disconnect from the day-to-day, and it can also be an opportunity to remind ourselves of the urgency to remain steadfast in keeping peace. The **Mémorial de Caen** (*memorial-caen.fr; adult/under-10 €20.80/free*) presents the reality of war without the glorification of victorious battles. In addition to WWI, learn about its aftereffects, the Cold War and the rise of Hitler – there's also a newly opened room dedicated to victims of the Holocaust.

The museum is heavy in symbolism. The narrow doorway is reminiscent of the crack in the iron Atlantic Wall and gives way to a massive hall where a British Typhoon aircraft looms overhead before a hellish spiral downwards. Detailed and dense, plan at least a full day to truly take in the sobering scope of war. Anti-gun pacifists will appreciate Swedish artist Carl Fredrik Reuterswärd's sculpture of a gun with its barrel twisted into a knot, simply titled *Non-Violence*.

Museum Hop in Castle Ruins
Norman history and fine art

Viking descendant William the Conqueror built the **Château de Caen** in 1066. Used as barracks during WWII, it was bombed heavily but is now home to the **Musée des Beaux-Arts de Caen** and the **Museé de Normandie** (*mba.caen.fr; pass for both adult/under-26 €10/free*), and was the site of the recent 1000-year celebration of the city. High up on the edges of the ramparts, you'll find one of the best views of Caen, where you can marvel at how time has changed the face of the city from medieval to modern.

At the Beaux-Arts museum, admire fine oil paintings from centuries ago, such as the gruesomely captivating *Judith Beheading Holofernes* by Caravaggio. Across the road, the Musée de Normandie recounts the rise of human civilisation with the Normans at the centre of the story. A glimpse of prehistoric life all the way to the present day is offered, along with cultural objects crucial to Norman culture, like the hats women would wear, the cabinetry, and books detailing Norman dance and song.

DRINKING IN CAEN: OUR PICKS

Boumbap: A convivial spot with home cooking and Asian-fusion flavours, with grooving DJ sets amd cocktails at night. *noon-1am Wed-Sun, 11.30am-3pm Sun*

Ecto Bar: Located on the thirsty rue Écuyère, find cheap beers and shots, homemade rum, espresso martinis, friendly service and good music. *3pm-1am Mon-Sat*

L'Hydropathe: A charming and laid-back wine bar aptly named for waterphobes with a variety of delicious tapas and outdoor seating. *noon-1am Tue-Sat*

L'Antirouille: A hip and retro neighbourhood bar outfitted with cassette tapes and kitschy decor. *4pm-1am Tue-Sat, 4-11pm Sun*

Mont St-Michel

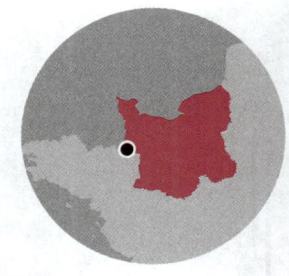

BIODIVERSE BAY | TIDE-WALKING | WONDROUS ABBEY

For a millennium, Mont St-Michel has entranced visitors with majestic views that metamorphose with the tides. When the seas rise, a 1000-year-old Gothic abbey crowns the top of an island of craggy rock. Conceptualised from a dream in which an archangel bids a bishop to build a place of devotion in an impossible place, Mont St-Michel captures the imagination of anyone who crosses its sandy paths. The sometimes-island itself changes as quickly as the sea; only a handful of inhabitants live there in comparison to the millions of annual tourists who crowd the winding streets that ascend to the pointed top.

Once you've snapped your photo of the jaw-dropping sight and have heard the bells ring in the abbey, the next best step is to immerse yourself in the incredible biodiversity of the bay. With slow and careful observation and turning off the tourist paths, you can find yourself in a vivid, waking dream full of flora, fauna and culinary delights.

Nocturnal Visits & High-Tide Thrills
A night visit to the bay

The traditional approach to the **Abbaye du Mont St-Michel** (*abbaye-mont-saint-michel.fr; adult/child €16/free*) is an established, elevated wood-plank path with guardrails, next to the road where shuttles ferry visitors back and forth all day. But in the spirit of Robert Frost: the road less travelled makes all the difference. If you're pressed for time, try to go as early as possible to avoid the crowds, and plan on eating and sleeping off the almost-island to avoid handing over a lot of cash for mediocre tourist traps.

Instead, take the unconventional route and sink your toes in the sometimes-moving quicksand with local guide **Romain Pilon** (*labaiecderomain.fr; tours per person from €15*), native of the bay and a guide for over two decades. Fishing enthusiasts can go shrimping with Romain during select windows throughout the year, usually mid-September through October

GETTING AROUND

The nearest train stop is Pontorson (just short of five hours from Paris), where buses will take you 350m from the entrance of Mont St-Michel. But a car is your best bet to get around the bay and surrounding villages, though parking near Mont St-Michel is pricey. Getting to the island of Mont St-Michel itself is fairly straightforward: you can walk or queue up for a free shuttle bus that runs all day. If you plan on walking across the bay, it's best to hire a guide and check tide changes here: ot-montsaintmichel.com/marees.

☑ TOP TIP

Avoid the summer months (July and August) for the best views and fewer crowds. If you find yourself here during high season, try to go at dusk or dawn to beat the rush.

MONT ST-MICHEL NORMANDY

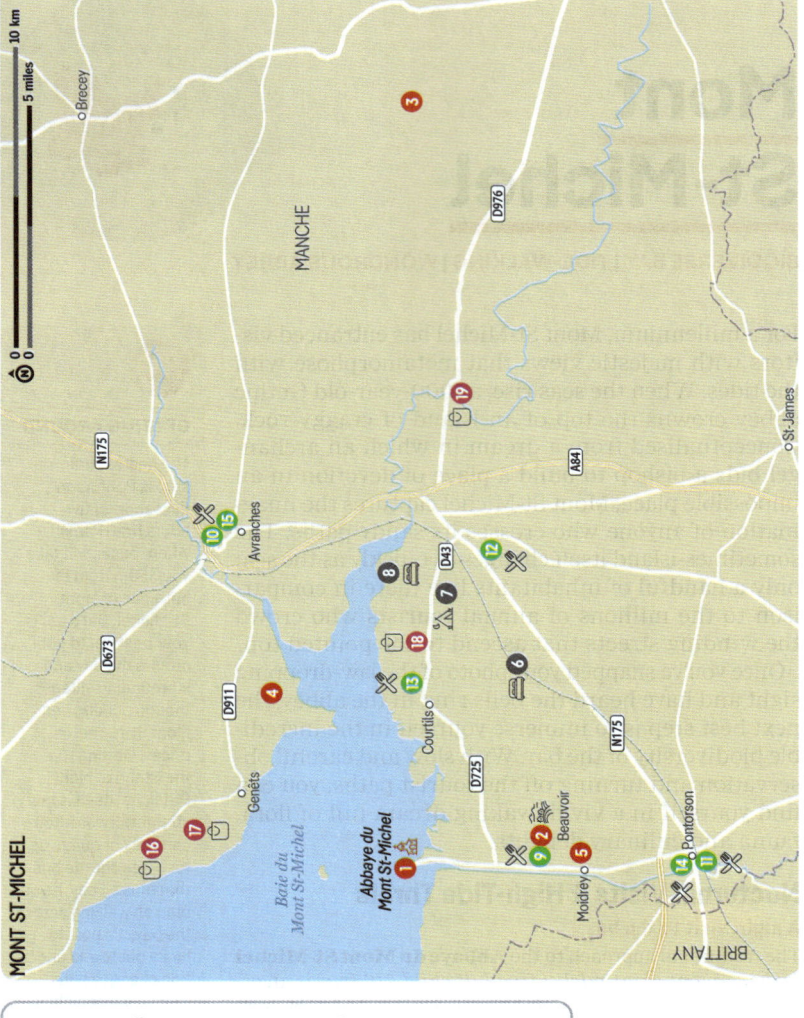

MONT ST-MICHEL

HIGHLIGHTS
1. Abbaye du Mont St-Michel

SIGHTS
2. Beauvoir
3. Jardin du Trèfle
4. La Ferme des Cara-Meuh
5. Moulin de Moidrey

SLEEPING
6. Auberge Sauvage
7. Camping La Baie du Mont St-Michel
8. Chambres d'Hôte Les Bruyères du Mont
9. Boulangerie Mont Moulin
10. Crèmerie-Fromagerie Caseus
11. Crêperie Univers Sarrasin
12. La Brocante
13. La Parenthèse de la Baie
14. Le Grillon

see 1 Le Logis Sainte Catherine

15. Maison Montagu

SHOPPING
16. Chez Mimile
17. L'Atelier Sea Frais
18. Le Grange de Courtils
19. Ô Fil des Saisons

EATING
see 6 Auberge Sauvage

254

and a short window in April. But year-round, the best way to see Mont St-Michel is with his 'Sortie Nocturnes'.

Night owls will meet at 7.30pm and then skulk around the bay as night falls. Enter a hidden world over the next few hours, bathed in the light of the spectacular sunset and surrounded by the cries of geese and migratory birds – identified by your guide – and the moving waters and sound of the shifting shores. The visit ends at 11.30pm, cloaked in the mystical magic of night where you'll emerge with uncovered secrets and views of the bay. Early birds may prefer Romain's adrenaline-pumping visits that end in synchronicity with the high tide. As the sea can rise at the speed of a galloping horse, it's thrilling to witness it so closely – but be warned, only true experts who know the area and whims of the oceans can handle the tide safely.

Go Birding, or Become a Bird
Birdwatching and paragliding

If you're travelling with a group, flock together and book the **Birding Bus** (birding-msm.com; from €10), run by ornithologist and biologist-by-training Sébastian Provost, who showcases bird-watching as a fascinating artform that brings to life hidden worlds. At various points along the bay, you'll encounter birds, seals and even dolphins, from the coast towards Granville, the *marais* (marsh) of Claire-Douve at Dragey-Ronthon, the viewpoint of Mont-Manet at Genêts and much, much more. Like the birds, your movements on his itinerary reflect the changing seasons and tides, and adapt accordingly. The fleeting close encounters will, however, leave an indelible mark on your memories of the bay.

For those who like to fly solo, jump for a bird's-eye view of Mont St-Michel and its surroundings – literally. With experienced and competition-winning paraglider **Leo Hamard** (parapenteenbaie.fr; flights from €80), you can float above the abbey and the bay like a bird. Watch your feet dangle and

BEST SHOPS

L'Atelier Sea Frais: Top-notch quality, artisanal smoked salmon in oak, apple and cherry woods.

Chez Mimile: A vintage goldmine for clothing, furniture and homewares.

La Ferme des Cara-Meuh: Quaint farm with the best caramels you'll ever taste, cute pigs, deer and cows.

Le Grange de Courtils: Renovated garage for cider, *calvados*, pommeau, cookies and more local treats.

Jardin du Trèfle: A delightful, small family-run cheese farm with fresh products and friendly smiles.

Ô Fil des Saisons: A one-stop shop for cheese, local goods and treats.

EATING NEAR MONT ST-MICHEL: OUR PICKS

Auberge Sauvage: A Michelin-starred haven set in a 16th-century presbytery, where local produce and foraged delicacies dominate the menu. *7.30pm-midnight Thu-Mon* €€€

La Brocante: Enjoy simple snacks, sandwiches, crêpes, coffees and wines in this retrofitted old autoshop. *10am-6pm Mon, Thu & Fri, 11am-6pm Sat & Sun* €

La Parenthèse de la Baie: Roadside crêperie with filling burgers, crêpes and a heaping pile of mussels; well worth the stop. *noon-2pm & 7-9pm Wed-Sun* €

Le Grillon: Unpretentious and unfussy spot to taste lamb chops made from the sheep that graze the salty fields. *12.30-1.30pm Sat-Wed, 7-8.30pm Fri-Tue* €€

Crèmerie-Fromagerie Caseus: A delightful fromagerie in Avranches with takeaway *casse-croûte* sandwiches. *9.30am-3pm & 5-7pm Tue-Fri, 8.30am-1pm & 3-6pm Sat* €

Le Logis Sainte Catherine: A rotating menu with innovative plates like *moussette rillettes*, plus a dazzling terrace and elegant deco. Book online. *hours vary* €€€

Crêperie Univers Sarrasin: A quick stop for quality buckwheat crêpes. *noon-1.30pm & 7-8.30pm Thu-Tue* €

Maison Montagu: Satisfy any urges for fresh and crisp salads at this mostly organic spot. *10am-4pm Tue-Sat* €

MAD FOR MOUSSETTES IN MAY

Crab lovers, take note of *moussettes*, the nickname of a variety of young spider crab that's found all over fish markets in La Manche from April to June, and are especially bountiful during the month of May. Known for their sweet, subtle and abundant flesh, enjoy them without any condiments needed (my advice: wear a bib and gloves to avoid the mess). You can buy them precooked or boil in water for 20 minutes. As a bonus, eating *moussettes* also helps out the local ecosystem since the spider crabs have infiltrated the Normandy region and pose a threat to mussel producers.

Moulin de Moidrey

be dazzled by the singular feeling of lightness and freedom flying on the winds. Adrenaline junkies and first-timers alike can spring for the 'acrobatic' flight option (weather contingent) for a truly head-spinning flight. Reserve a date in advance online, but the jumping-off point is a choose-your-own adventure dictated by the winds – the cliffs at Champeaux are magical, however, with birds flying overhead, honeycomb reefs, golden gorse and lilac heath plants.

Visit a Working Windmill Built in 1806
Flours and tours at the Moulin de Moidrey

To see how flour was made in simpler times, head to **Moulin de Moidrey** *(guided visits from €1.50; hours vary, closed Dec)*, a magnificently restored stone windmill and one of the last operating ones in Europe. Declared a UNESCO World Heritage Site in 2007, the windmill today produces buckwheat, rye and flours for bread made the traditional way.

Depending on the season, the surrounding fields blaze gold or blue and frame an epic view of Mont St-Michel. There's a car park on site, but I recommend parking in the nearby village Beauvoir, where you can make a pit stop at the **Boulangerie Mont Moulin** for an apple tart to fuel the 17-minute walk to the windmill. After the visit, you can take home local goods and flour from the store inside the windmill.

Beyond Mont St-Michel

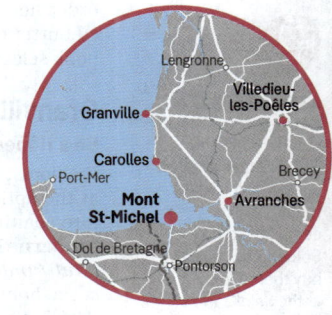

Sometimes the best experiences aren't from up-close, but from a panoramic distance in one of Mont St-Michel's nearby towns, islands or cliffsides.

Places
Avranches p257
Granville p258
Villedieu-les-Poêles p258

Within the radius of Mont St-Michel lie a few worthy destinations to visit – including an operating stone windmill, the Saint James Atelier and more. To the north, the city of Avranches offers a stunning panoramic view of Mont St-Michel along with historical treasures like medieval manuscripts. Further up the coast, you can have tea in Christian Dior's childhood garden at Granville or enjoy tranquil sights and local art at one of the many historical and beachside towns, like Genêts. A bit further inland, bell and copper enthusiasts will adore the artisanal savoir-faire in the scenic town of Villedieu-les-Poêles. The further you stray away from Mont St-Michel, the less touristy it gets and the more you'll stumble upon authentic examples of good Normandy-style living infused with the fresh ocean air or the fruits of the land. So wander away.

Avranches

TIME FROM MONT ST-MICHEL: **25MIN**

Revel in the magic of old books

Despite the magnitude of effort spent to construct Mont St-Michel, the pursuit of intellectual vigour persisted inside the abbey walls. The material proof remains at the **Scriptorial** *(scriptorial.fr; entry from €3)*, a museum built on medieval fortifications in Avranches, which complements the abbey visit with a close-up look at over 200 manuscripts filled with centuries-old hand-calligraphy and hand-bound masterpieces of monks, and a look at their daily lives. Kids have plenty to explore on a tactile level, like parchment paper and well-curated temporary exhibits.

After a visit, you can pick up a novel (a small English language selection is available) from **Librairie Mille et Une Pages** *(closed Sun & Mon)*, stroll past the ruins of **Donjon d'Avranches,** admire a view of the abbey from afar, and then head to the ultra-cosy secondhand bookstore and coffee shop **Prose Café** *(instagram.com/prosecafe_avranches)*, run by bibliophile Catherine Muller. Open daily except for Mondays,

GETTING AROUND

Both Granville and Villedieu-les-Poêles are under an hour's drive away from Mont St-Michel, and both towns have accessible parking and are best experienced on foot. Don't be afraid to drive up and down the coastline and turn into any one of the seaside villages – the area is bustling and alive, and you never know what you might find.

ATELIERS, BIG & SMALL

Saint James Atelier: Life doesn't always require you to earn your stripes. Sometimes you can buy them. Do so at the Saint James Atelier (*fr.saint-james. com/pages/visite- de-l-atelier; tours €5*), which makes iconic horizontally striped sweaters and shirts. Located in the eponymous village of St-James, the factory tour gives an inside look at the evolution of the original sweaters – plan for an hour. Email ahead to book: visite@ saint-james.fr.

Atelier Galerie Gravure Mathilde Loisel: At the far end of St-Jean-le- Thomas, there's a shoreside compound that houses several workshops – aptly titled 'The Workshops at the End of the Sea' (*Les Ateliers du Bout de la Mer*) – which include the ceramic workshop of artist Célline Faille, Marie Blanche Pron's graphic design studio and Mathilde Loisel's engraving workshop.

order her special latte doused with a spoonful of local salted butter caramel, a slice of carrot cake and then peruse the book selection while the coffee brews.

Granville

TIME FROM MONT ST-MICHEL: **50MIN**

Be a flâneur in Granville

Fashionistas, spend the morning shopping for high-end threads at the aptly named **Flâneurs Granville** (*flaneurs.net*), before soaking up the eclectic collection at the **Musée d'Art Moderne Richard Anacréon** (*museesdegranville.fr/mamra; adult/under-26 €5.50/free*). Granville native, bookseller and social hobnobber Richard Anacréon was friends with famous Parisian artists of the 1940s, such as writer Colette and poet Paul Valéry.

For lunch, linger over a fine three-course meal of locally sourced seafood at **Loca Café** without a steep price tag, and then take a digestive walk along the **Plage du Plat Gousset** towards the **Musée Christian Dior** (*musee-dior-granville. com; adult/under-18/under-12 €10/7/free*). Spend an afternoon lazing about in the gardens of the famed designer's childhood home and enjoying his privileged views of the beach, and then make your way back to town to see the ships at the port. If you have the luxury of time, take an hour-long ferry operated by **Vedettes des Îles Chausey** (*resa.vedettesjo- liefrance.com; adult/under-14/under-3 €34/22.50/11.50*) to the **Îles Chausey**, which are 18km offshore. Plan for at least six hours to amble around the wild paradise of sand, craggy rocks and rising tides.

Villedieu- les-Poêles

TIME FROM MONT ST-MICHEL: **40MIN**

Copper, bells and craftsmanship

We often hear church bells ringing in the distance without a second thought. But there is an entire art and operation behind the creation of large bells, which you can witness at the living, breathing, grunting bell foundry **Fonderie de Cloches Cornille Havard** (*cornille-havard.com; adult/child/under- 6 €10/8.50/free*). This tour hits all the right notes: it kicks off with a rather startling ringing of the bell before diving into the intricate and ingenious process of making bells, from making a mould, to a cast, to the nitty-gritty details of how

Go early to this tiny but mighty bakery.

 EATING IN GRANVILLE: OUR PICKS

Loca Café: Aesthetically pleasing, gourmet seafood with reasonable prices and set menus. *11am-11.30pm, Fri-Tue* €€

La Table de Louis: Classic French brasserie with a terrace, top- notch meat dishes and oysters. *noon-2.30pm daily, 7-10pm Sun-Thu, 7-10.30pm Fri & Sat* €€

La Fabbrica: Tucked- away Italian spot with inventive pasta shapes near the port. Large menu, generous portions. *noon-2.30pm Tue-Sat, 7-10.30pm Thu-Sat* €€

Boulangerie Champs Libres: Churns out dishes of the day, impeccable breads, sandwiches and even *teurgole* (rice pudding). *9.30am-2pm & 3.30-7pm Tue-Fri, 9am-4pm Sat* €

Musée Christian Dior

they become embossed and personalised, and the musical notes that can be produced.

At the other end of town, the dusty and dark **Atelier du Cuivre** *(atelierducuivre-shop.com; adult/child €9.20/7.80)*, founded in 1850, offers equally fascinating tours – barring the language barrier, though there is a 15-minute introductory film in English – demonstrating the savoir-faire of making copper cookware from cauldrons to large jam jars. According to the tour, the benefits of copper are not just in the even heat distribution when cooking: at the gift shop, you can pick up a copper cup that boasts a 'copper cure' benefit, which claims a host of health benefits from drinking an occasional glass of copper-infused water. For more cookware, the French brand **Mauviel 1830** *(mauviel-boutique.com, tours from €8)*, with prestige and prices to match, also has an open factory nearby, which offers more established tours in better lighting.

A PERFECT DAY IN CAROLLES

Tips from **Antoine LeFranc**, local guide, baker and children's book author. *antoinelefranc.fr; @explorons_carolles*

A perfect day for me would be dictated by the tides – it's better to swim during the high tide, and a day at the **Carolles-Plage** is a must, especially followed by a coffee at one of the three beachside restaurants. I would go to one of the local markets to enjoy the products of the land – Thursdays in Carolles, Fridays in Juloville and Saturdays in Champeaux. In the afternoon, I'd go hike in the **Vallée du Lude** or walk in the **Vallée des Peintres**, and then finish with a drink, listening to some music, at **L'Almartia** bar, which is found in the courtyard of the old school.

Cherbourg & Cotentin

ISOLATED WILDERNESS | UNCROWDED BEACHES | FISHING VILLAGES

GETTING AROUND

The appeal of Cotentin is that the roads are less travelled and the landscapes are more wild. From Paris Saint-Lazare, you can catch a 3½-hour train ride to Cherbourg, but a car is the most convenient option to get around the region. The sporty will delight in the plethora of hiking and biking trails in La Hague to appreciate unspoiled nature on foot or on two wheels.

A proper visit to the Cotentin peninsula would take weeks. This haven of unspoiled wilderness is a mosaic of colours from different landscapes of *bocage* (subdivided farmland), cliffsides and beaches. A good entryway is the Val-de-Saire region, which includes the port city of Cherbourg and waters brimming with juicy oysters, pulled out at the serene fishing villages of Barfleur and St-Vaast-la-Hougue.

Westward, the increasingly isolated countryside grows wilder at La Hague – oft compared to Ireland – and on the southwest coast lies the Côte de Isles, made of fine-sand beaches and warmer waters from the Gulf Stream. Eastward are the better-known D-Day Landing Beaches (p246), but the real joy of this region is going off the popular track. Get lost in the old zigzagging tractor paths-turned-roads in fertile pastures that stretch for miles, and discover local delicacies straight from the land and sea.

Relive the Last Moments of the Titanic
Aquarium and museum in art deco architecture

Before the *Titanic* sank into the ocean, the ship made its last call to the ferry port of Cherbourg, which sits at the northernmost point of Cotentin. Head to **Cité de la Mer** *(citedelamer. com; adult/child/under-5 €21/15/free)*, a major maritime museum set in an emblematic art deco transatlantic terminal building (Gare Maritime) where ocean liner passengers embarked and disembarked. Most thrillingly, you can relive the *Titanic*'s final moments: walk through a first-class cabin and admire recovered artefacts from the ship herself, before experiencing a rumbling, fatal iceberg collision with sound effects.

Descent into the aquarium gives close encounters with deep-sea creatures like miniature seahorses, jellyfish and countless fish species that you can discover with a 'fishipedia' app. In the third section of the massive museum there's **Le Redoutable**, where you can take a mind-blowing and slightly claustrophobic tour in an actual nuclear submarine: squeeze your way

☑ TOP TIP

All over the Cotentin peninsula, there's a weekly roast meat tradition. In nearly every town and village streetside, on Sunday mornings you'll see carts full of juicy rotisserie chickens and massive lamb legs – get in line for your lunch and take it to the nearest beach for a seaside picnic.

CHERBOURG & COTENTIN

★ HIGHLIGHTS
1. Cité de la Mer

● SIGHTS
2. Baie d'Écalgrain
3. Cidrerie Claids
4. Cidrerie Distillerie Le Père Mahieu
5. Cidrerie Théo Capelle
6. Île Tatihou
7. Jardins Maritimes de l'île de Tatihou
8. Maison Herout
9. Musée de la Libération
10. Musée Maritime de l'Île de Tatihou
11. Omonville-la-Rogue
12. Phare de Gatteville
13. Tour Vauban de Tatihou

● ACTIVITIES
14. Club Nautique de Coutainville

● SLEEPING
15. Ambassadeur Hôtel
16. Camping les Carolins
17. Domaine du Mont Roulet
18. Hôtel les Fuchsias
19. Hôtel Restaurant le Landemer

● EATING
20. Boa Coffee and Food
21. Café de France
22. Gibon
23. Le P'ti Wan
24. L'Entre Deux Tours

● SHOPPING
25. Biscuiterie de Quineville
26. Le Parapluie de Cherbourg
27. Les Kabosses
see 25 Maison Gosselin

BEST OF ÎLE DE TATIHOU

When you purchase a ticket to board the amphibious boat that brings you to the island, you get free access to the attractions.

Jardins Maritimes de l'île de Tatihou: Bask in the sunshine framed by exotic plants for a mini-tropical vacation.

Musée Maritime de l'île de Tatihou: Learn about naval battles under the reign of Louis XIV and the local ecosystem. Bonus: you can climb onto an old fishing boat.

Tour Vauban de Tatihou: Constructed in 1694 after a French loss at the Battle of La Hougue, you can explore the grounds that include a chapel, remnants of war, and the scent of blackberries come summer.

Le Parapluie de Cherbourg

around the small world that was created for life deep under water, including cramped cafeteria quarters, a games room with cards, the bathroom and stacked dormitory beds.

The Romance of The Umbrellas of Cherbourg
An inside look at luxury umbrella fabrication

French cinephiles will also recognise the city from the 1964 hit starring Catherine Deneuve. Today, anchored on the docks, you can visit **Le Parapluie de Cherbourg** *(parapluiedecherbourg.com/la-boutique)*, founded by Jean-Pierre Yvon, who decided to create the namesake brand to extend his family's tannery business, founded in 1800. Step into a living museum to observe umbrellas of yesteryear and the craftsmanship that goes into luxury umbrellas carefully designed to withstand the strongest of Normandy winds. A warning: they come with eye-watering price tags (the cheaper end starts at €160).

A Glimpse of German Occupation
Liberation Museum in Cherbourg

Located inside the 19th-century Fort du Roule, the **Musée de la Libération** *(cherbourg.fr/culture-et-loisirs/musees/musee-de-la-liberation; entry €5)*, established in 1954, was one of the first memorials to WWII. With period clothing, propaganda and fascinating posters, you can get a feel of what life was like in Cherbourg during the German occupation and what went on during the Liberation. For those who haven't brushed up on their French lessons, the explanations may be lacking. Admission is free on Wednesdays.

Walk to an Island at Low Tide
Local oysters and culinary treats at Île Tatihou

The world is your oyster – literally – at **St-Vaast-la-Hougue**, an emblematic fishing village of Cotentin where sailing boats bob in serenity on the harbour. You can walk among its overflowing oyster beds at low tide and even reach the nearby **Île**

Tatihou on foot. It's about half an hour to walk to the island; if the tides aren't in your favour, you can catch the amphibious boat *(tatihou.manche.fr; adult/child/under-3 €16/6.50/free)*.

Grab a sandwich and some sweets for a picnic on this island of green serenity. Sugar fiends will love 'Les Roches de Tatihou' from the local **Gibon** bakery – a delightful cream puff that melts in your mouth. For more sweetness, peruse the infamous **Maison Gosselin** *(maison-gosselin.fr)* speciality grocery store, open year-round, whose retro decor harks back to simpler times. Note: there are no garbage cans on the island, so plan ahead.

When you're back from island hopping, snag even more gourmet treats at the **Biscuiterie de Quineville**, which is open daily during July and August – they even sell *teurgoule* (a sweet, cinnamon-flavoured rice pudding...taste-tested and approved by my Norman father-in-law). When the sugar high crashes, make a beeline to the portside **L'Entre Deux Tours** for the best lunch deal in town: six oysters and a glass of Muscadet served with fresh bread, butter and all the vinegared shallot trimmings.

Stairmaster Your Way to Deep Blue Views
The lighthouse's 365 steps

Barfleur, otherwise known as the pearl of the Val-de-Saire region, is a beautiful port city where dukes and kings of Normandy departed to conquer English territory during medieval times. In the mid-14th century, Edward III burned the village to the ground – but despite its volatile history, the beauty of Barfleur persists in its mesmerising, ever-changing sea colours. Eat your pick of seafood at the port (**Café de France** is reliable), but if you need respite from French fare, the little Thai food truck **Le P'ti Wan** is delicious.

For the best view from Barfleur, head to the **Phare de Gatteville** *(phare-de-gatteville.fr; entry €3.50)*, composed of 11,000 granite stones – it opens at 10am year-round, so get there early to avoid crowds. Built between 1829 and 1834, the lighthouse is an engineering marvel that looms overhead at 75m high. At the entrance, a small exhibition illuminates the history of the lighthouse and its role in guiding seafarers along the precarious Raz de Barfleur (a nefarious sea current).

The best part is the panoramic observation deck at the top. Climb 365 steps up – the workout also gives you an inside look at the lights and mechanics of the lighthouse – and be rewarded with incredible views of the *bocage* of the northern Cotentin countryside, the edges of Calvados and the vast, deep blue English Channel waters.

Harness Wind Power and Chill Beachside
Sand yachting, sailboarding and beach huts

One of the best ways to enjoy the vast stretches of beaches is to do so at a hair-raising speed. Enter sand yachting at the **Club Nautique de Coutainville** *(club-nautique-coutainville.fr)*. Sit in a triangular-shaped go-kart with sails attached, pop on a helmet and go for a wild, wind-propelled and adrenaline-pumped

NORMANDY'S BOCAGE

Bocage is used to describe the particular and distinctive patchwork-esque landscape common to Normandy. It consists of a mix of hedgerows that line square plots of green pastures and copses, or small groups of trees. The most beautiful and well-preserved *bocages* can be found on D577, a route between villages Vire and Villers-Bocage.

During WWII, this landscape posed logistical challenges to the soldiers, since traversing this type of land with thick groves of trees and vegetation was difficult. In certain areas, you can still see the traces of the metal wiring used to allow the war tanks to traverse the lands, which is now used by local farmers as fences or for reinforcing chicken coops.

A TIDE-Y EXPLANATION

On the western coast of the Cotentin peninsula, you'll find some of the biggest tides in all of Europe. The biggest one is found at Mont St-Michel, with a height difference of up to 15m. To best appreciate the disappearing and reappearing act of sandy beaches, unadorned shores are best. Check with the local tourist office for a tide calendar for the tidal coefficients. These numbers, between 20 and 120, indicate the amplitudes of the tides. The larger the number, the more sandy beach at low tide. St-Germain-sur-Ay is a particularly spectacular spot to walk the endless stretches of beach out into the horizon and watch it all become engulfed by the waters.

ride. A rental gets you all the gear, a full run-down and how-to, and two hours where you can let loose. Email or call ahead to reserve a spot in summer. Do note it's best when the sands aren't too damp, otherwise you'll end up with a harsh facial scrub. You can also harness the power of the winds on the sea by sailboarding, or kayak for a calmer experience.

After your adrenaline rush, head north 15 minutes to **Gouville-sur-Mer**. Take a walk alongside the picturesque changing cabins with roofs painted in primary colours that pop among the long tufts of sun-yellowed grass. Then, roll up to **Boa Coffee and Food** to enjoy a cocktail, beer or casual meal in a fun, open-air beachside ambience – they're open daily through the high season until the end of August. Before day's end, swing by **Les Kabosses** for some of the best artisanal chocolate that'll ever melt in your mouth; check online, their summer hours vary.

Cliff-Jump into Ocean Waters in La Hague
Coasteering in La Hague

Coasteering is the ultimate sport based on play. First, you dress up in a full-body wetsuit, topped with a life jacket. Finish with a pair of old sneakers and then follow your professional lifeguard and guide with **Coasteering ASES Cotentin** (*secourisme50.fr/coasteering*) into the **Baie d'Écalgrain** or **Omonville-la-Rogue**, in the heart of La Hague.

Part and parcel of the fun is the anticipation. The wind whips your hair as it flaps beneath your helmet, there's nervous anticipation as you scramble over the waves on the shore, then you climb up for a view of the unruly ocean's edge, walking a narrow path placed between high craggy, black rocks. As you stand on the edge near the water, have faith in your guide's knowledge of the terrain and their professional lifeguarding skills...and leap!

The water hits – a cold shock to the system that pumps up the adrenaline in the best way possible. Others jump with you, and the group melds together, down into caves and then back out again, and to the pebble beaches with the help of a wave.

Though you'll need a base level of fitness to go coasteering, the best part about the sport is the communal aspect: everyone sticks together, and nearly everyone can participate. Coasteering is possible all year but it's more inviting during warmer months – book online ahead and plan for at least three hours of water adventures.

DRINKING IN CHERBOURG & COTENTIN: BEST FARMS & CIDRERIES

Cidrerie Distillerie Le Père Mahieu: An organic cider farm with fine *calvados* that ages in oak barrels tucked in their 16th-century basement. *10am-noon & 2-6.30pm Mon-Sat*

Cidrerie Théo Capelle: A modernised and brightly lit cider mill with a special local apéritif, Cotentinoix, for fans of bitter flavours. *9am-12.30pm & 2-7pm Mon-Sat*

Maison Herout: Top-notch ciders and a to-die-for *pommeau* with sleek branding. *9am-5pm Mon-Fri*

Cidrerie Claids: A small, bucolic farm that has delicious ciders, Norman whisky and a friendly host. *hours vary, call ahead*

Places We Love to Stay

€ Budget €€ Midrange €€€ Top End

Rouen & Giverny
p225, p228

Hôtel Le Vieux Carré € A cosy family-run guest house and tearoom in Rouen city centre. The decor feels like walking into a Norman countryside house.

La Boulangerie B&B €€ A quirky Rouen-based guesthouse with a private terrace with the smell of fresh bread wafting into the guest rooms.

Au Bon Maréchal €€ This quaint family-run hotel was frequented by Monet himself. Best for easy access to the museums, and it has a little garden to enjoy.

Côte d'Albâtre & Le Havre
p234

ibis Styles Le Havre Centre Auguste Perret € A reliable budget option, if not a bit worn, and keeps in theme with the 1950s decor of the French architect.

Hôtel Lilybloom €€ Tiny-house style hotel rooms that embody cosy glamping (there's a sauna on site) with breakfast delivery to your door.

Dormy House €€€ Overlooking the cliffs of Étretat, this upscale hotel has the best breakfast views, ultra-comfortable beds, and best of all free parking (you'll be thankful for it).

Côte Fleurie
p240

Logis Hôtel Ferme de la Grande Cour € A welcoming farmhouse turned bed and breakfast with top-notch dining. Honfleur is visitable by foot.

Hôtel Le Trouville €€ Clean and convenient, with charm to boot. Easy access to the beach and town.

Les Sources Du Val €€€ Just outside of Honfleur, this quaint and modern guesthouse is pure serenity, situated next to a natural spring and a river.

Hôtel Flaubert €€€ Cosy comfort in four-star luxury with a literary flair, plus easy access to the Trouville beach.

Thalazur Cabourg €€€ Thalassotherapy on the shore with spacious rooms.

D-Day Landing Beaches, Caen & Bayeux
p248

Camping de Ste-Mère-Église € A three-star campground next to Airborne Museum for longer stays or even a night in a military truck.

La Batterie du Holdy Guesthouse € Simple furnishings set in a historic WWII building, chock-full of anecdotes from the hosts, and an interactive experience on site (p247).

Ferme Hay Day € No-frills farmhouse B&B and camping grounds with country breakfast, fresh eggs and bike rentals.

Hôtel François d'O € Plenty of charm and clean comfort conveniently located in Caen city centre.

Le Declic Hotel € In the heart of old Bayeux, this clean and welcoming hotel has hearty breakfasts and free parking.

Domaine Airborne €€ A comfortable 17th-century farmhouse that was invaded by paratroopers during WWII, located next to a nature reserve.

Mont St-Michel
p254

Chambres d'Hôte Les Bruyères du Mont € Find an enchanted garden and gracious host Nadine in this guesthouse near Mont St-Michel.

Camping La Baie du Mont St-Michel €€ A well-maintained, no-frills campsite with friendly hosts and plenty of hot water for showers.

Auberge Sauvage €€€ Farmhouse chic aesthetic with a garden and tennis courtyards – and a Michelin-starred restaurant (p255).

Cherbourg & Cotentin
p260

Ambassadeur Hôtel € Comfortable rooms with options for solo travellers, conveniently located right next to the harbour.

Hôtel les Fuchsias €€ Overflowing with charm and hospitality, this former coach house now has a heavenly garden.

Domaine du Mont Roulet €€ A cosy luxury B&B base in La Hague, complete with a Nordic bath to decompress after long hikes.

Hôtel Restaurant le Landemer €€ A three-star stay atop a rocky cliff in Cherbourg, in an old farmhouse with a quality restaurant.

Camping les Carolins €€ A clean and pleasant campground with mobile homes or tents, a pool and grill bar.

Above: St-Malo (p279); Right: Traditional dance festival, Vannes (p297)

*Researched by
Daphné Leprince-Ringuet*

Brittany

THE LAND OF LEGENDS

Extraordinary natural wonders, historical heritage and hearty food: Brittany is a breath of fresh air away from the crowds.

La Bretagne, ça vous gagne! This French maxim, translating as 'Brittany wins you over', says it all. Those who venture to France's westernmost region rarely leave without promising they'll be back.

It's hard not to fall for the charm of Brittany, which offers some of nature's most wonderful sights with unspoiled rawness. Over 2000km of coastline, the ocean's mystical draw and mesmerising landscapes never fail to enchant visitors. But it is also worth exploring the region's rich history, from its Celtic roots, which are still ubiquitous, to its countless postcard-perfect medieval villages. It will soon feel as if you are in a place suspended in time, swaying between myth and reality. This is when Brittany's nickname, 'the land of legends', truly comes alive.

Brittany likes to set itself apart, as if challenging strangers to get to know it. Until the 16th century, it was independent of the Kingdom of France. Five centuries later, despite attempts to dilute the region's identity – Breton language was banned in schools until the mid-20th century – Breton culture is experiencing a revival. Crêperies line the main street in every town. Traditional dance and music festivals are flourishing. Breton costumes come out at every opportunity. Bilingual Breton-French schools are opening all over the place.

It might seem a little intimidating, but to those who make the effort, Brittany will give the warmest welcome. That's got to be worth braving the rain.

THE MAIN AREAS

RENNES
Rock and roll and medieval heritage.
p272

ST-MALO
Pirate city between land and sea.
p279

QUIMPER
Breton roots near an epic coastline.
p287

VANNES
Slow life and beautiful beaches.
p297

Find Your Way

Brittany's main towns and cities can usually be reached by train or bus and explored on foot. Much of the region, however, is remote – which is also where you will find the most wonderful sights. Driving, cycling and hiking will let you see more.

Quimper, p287
A place where Breton culture comes alive in dance and music – right next to a mystical coastline staring into the Atlantic Ocean.

Vannes, p297
A bon vivant and relaxed city with lots to offer, from peaceful beaches to water sports and panoramic bike rides.

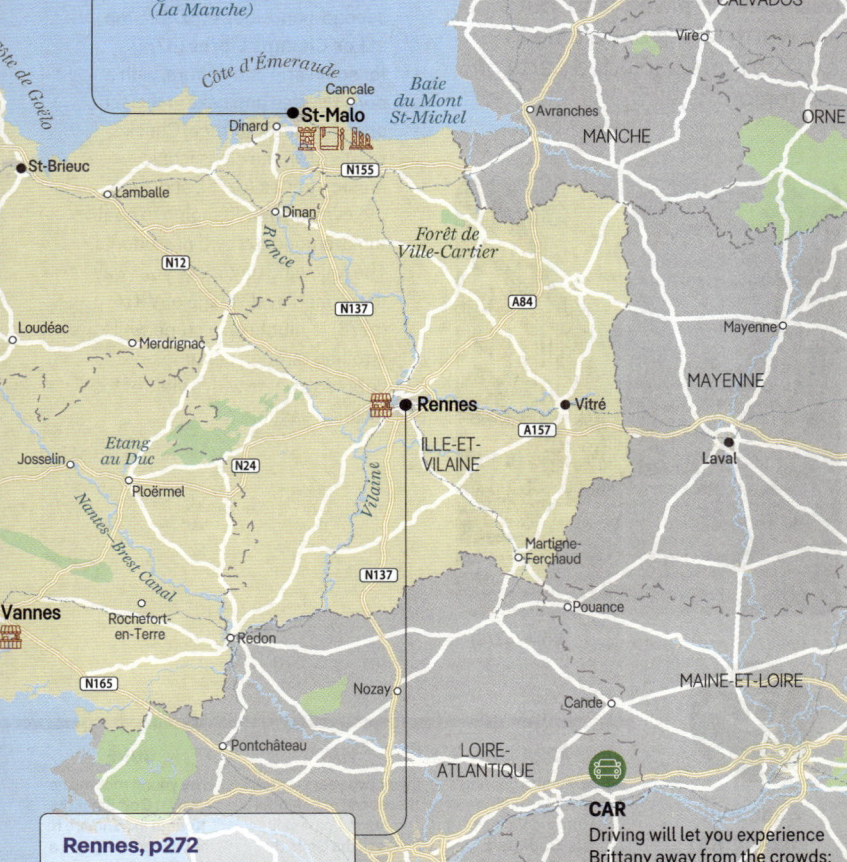

St-Malo, p279
Imposing fortifications quietly watch over a city of famous privateers and explorers, at the intersection of beautiful seascapes and tranquil riverside walks.

CYCLING & WALKING
Hiking and cycling are the best ways to take in the scenery. The gorgeous GR34 footpath follows the entire coast over more than 2000km, while cycling routes abound across the region, with nine notable cycling itineraries that span the whole of Brittany.

BUS & TRAIN
There are direct trains from Paris to Rennes, Vannes, Quimper and St-Malo. Regional trains also run to the main hubs; book on the SNCF website. Local buses link to smaller towns, but can be infrequent. Plan on the Korrigo app *(korrigo.bzh)*, which aggregates train and bus information.

Rennes, p272
A medieval city loaded with history and now taken over by lively student bars; a great entry point to the region.

CAR
Driving will let you experience Brittany away from the crowds: you'll be able to stay on the coast far from urban life, or drive to the starting point for a hike that no one else has done. Plus, Breton highways are toll-free.

Plan Your Time

Brittany is packed with pretty towns and cities that you can easily visit in a weekend, but it is worth taking extra time to explore more secluded parts of the region.

Vitré (p278)

A City Break

● If you've only got a couple of nights, keep things easy: jump on a train to **Rennes** (p272), grab a *galette-saucisse* for lunch at **Marché des Lices** (p272) and spend the afternoon strolling through the centre and browsing second-hand shops (p274). Stop at **Les Champs Libres** (p274) for some arts and culture, with a bonus coffee and cake in the sun on the centre's terrace. Check what's on in the city's iconic **music venues** (p275), and spend the evening headbanging to cool tunes among a crowd of students. The following day, make your way to the medieval village of **Vitré** (p278) to nibble on a crêpe while strolling through centuries-old cobbled streets with a view of the fortified castle.

Seasonal Highlights

Winters are tough in Brittany, with unforgiving weather and few open attractions. Many more tourists visit in the spring and summer.

APRIL
Brittany starts gearing up for the high season and Vannes hosts **Tradi'Deiz**, a huge traditional dance festival during which thousands of professional dancers and musicians parade in the city streets.

MAY
Every two years, watch thousands of beautiful vintage boats sail across the Golfe du Morbihan during the **Semaine du Golfe**. Expect regattas, parades, music, shows, and of course food and drink.

JUNE
The young rock music festival **God Save the Kouign** in Penmarc'h has already become a must-see, attracting high-profile artists in an intimate setting at the heart of Le Pays Bigouden.

Five-Day Getaway

● If you have a car, book accommodation with a nice view on the coast between St-Malo and Cancale. Spend your first day in **St-Malo** (p279) walking around the city's fortifications and historical centre. Sit on **Plage du Sillon** (p281) for sunset and book yourself a **panoramic dinner** (p283).

● The following day, explore the **Côte d'Emeraude** (p284). Pick an alluring beach, like **Plage des Chevrets** (p286) or **Anse du Guesclin** (p286), or plan a hike to **Pointe du Grouin** (p286).

● Stop in **Cancale** (p286) for a few hours to snack on some fresh oysters facing Mont-St-Michel, and make time for a day trip to the medieval town of **Dinan** (p285) to stock up on handcrafted goodies.

If You Have More Time

● From Quimper, rent a car and head to **Crozon Peninsula** (p291). Stay 2–3 nights to make time for hikes along the wonderful coast and ocean activities like a **boat trip** (p292).

● Drive down the coast over the next few days, stopping for surf sessions in **Pointe du Raz** (p292) and **Plage de la Torche** (p294). On the way, you can take a lunch detour through the medieval village of **Locronan** (p296).

● Stop in **Le Guilvinec** (p293) for some fresh langoustines and head back to **Quimper** (p287). Take the train to **Vannes** (p297) for a couple of nights, then jump on a ferry to **Belle-Île-en-Mer** (p305). Stay for a few days to explore the island, walk the coastal footpath, discover picturesque Breton villages and grab a drink with sailors in **Le Palais** (p305).

JULY
A fun time to travel as the tourist season peaks and dozens of summer music festivals kick off around Brittany. Quimper's **Festival de Cornouaille** (p288) pays tribute to Breton music, dance, costume and food.

AUGUST
An iconic festival happening for the past 25 years in Crozon Peninsula, **Festival du Bout du Monde** ('at the world's end') is dedicated to world music. Cities and towns across Brittany come alive with local festivals to celebrate summer.

NOVEMBER
Join Brittany's biggest ***fest-noz*** (p289; a traditional party) **Yaouank** (p275), a typical Rennes festival that mixes Breton, world and contemporary music.

DECEMBER
A great time to visit Brittany's medieval villages such as Locronan or Rochefort-en-Terre as they put on magical Christmas lights. In Rennes, the famous **Trans Musicales** music festival (p275) takes over the city.

Rennes

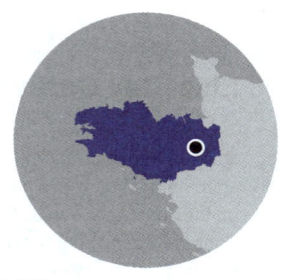

ARTS & CULTURE | MEDIEVAL VILLAGES | STUDENT LIFE

GETTING AROUND

You can easily get around the historical centre by foot and you're unlikely to walk any more than 15 minutes to reach any destination – but be aware that much of the medieval part of the city is cobbled. Rennes is also well served by public transport links through the STAR network *(star.fr)*, including two metro lines, buses and a bike share service.

Both the historical and administrative capital of the region, Rennes stands proudly at the entrance of Brittany. From its beloved speciality, the *galette-saucisse* (sausage wrapped in a savoury crêpe, or *galette*), to the highly symbolic Parlement de Bretagne (Parliament of Brittany), there is little room for doubt: this is a city that is firmly *bretonne*. But just like the historical centre, where medieval half-timbered houses mingle with 18th-century classical stone dwellings – the result of restoration work undertaken after a fire destroyed a significant part of the city centre in 1720 – Rennes is a place where tradition meets modernity. Home to popular universities and shaped by its large student population, Rennes is also undoubtedly contemporary. Expect new takes on Breton cuisine, a vibrant cultural scene and an abundance of art collectives and community organisations – all in a city that does not overwhelm and where everything can still be reached on foot.

A Taste of Rennes

Marché des Lices' *galette-saucisse*

On a Saturday morning in Rennes, there's only one place to be: the **Marché des Lices** on place des Lices, France's second-largest market with over 250 producers selling everything from fresh fruits and vegetables to world foods through local delicacies. It's also one of the oldest in the country, having recently celebrated its 400th anniversary. Head to one of the terraces lining the market for an *apéro* and some serious people-watching, featuring restaurant chefs shopping for the week, hungover students and seasoned Rennais fast filling their shopping carts. Make sure you grab yourself a *galette-saucisse*, a Rennes must-have, from one of the food trucks – purists will frown on mustard and onions, although it is delicious – but keep in mind that past 1pm, you're likely to be informed that they are all sold out.

☑ **TOP TIP**

The permanent collections of some of Rennes' museums, like the **Musée de Bretagne** (p274) and the **Musée des Beaux-Arts**, are free. On the first Sunday of every month, both permanent collections and temporary exhibitions in museums across the city are free as well.

RENNES

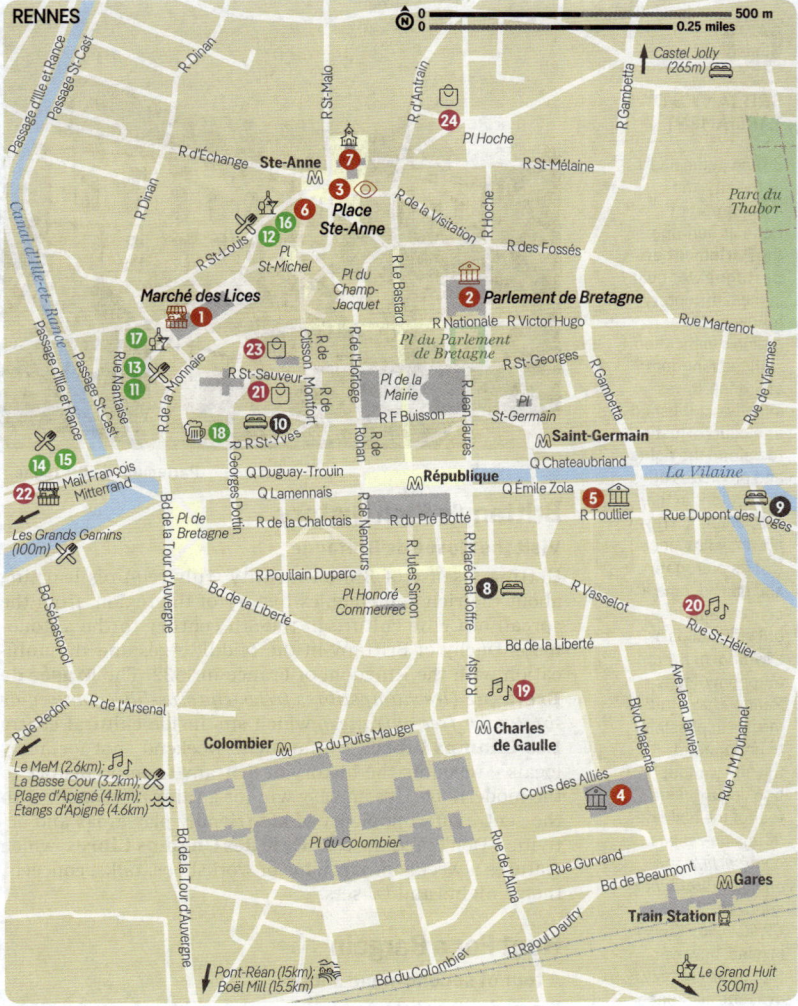

- **HIGHLIGHTS**
  1. Marché des Lices
  2. Parlement de Bretagne
  3. Place Ste-Anne
- **SIGHTS**
  4. Musée de Bretagne
  5. Musée des Beaux-Arts
  6. Rue St-Michel
  7. St-Aubin Basilica
- **ACTIVITIES**
  see 4 Les Champs Libres
- **SLEEPING**
  8. Balthazar Hôtel & Spa
  9. Hostel Les Chouettes
  10. Marnie & Mister H
- **EATING**
  11. Café Breton
  see 4 Café des Champs Libres
  12. Chez P'tit Louis
  13. Coquille
  14. Oh My Biche
  15. Superkraft
- **DRINKING & NIGHTLIFE**
  16. Le Bistrot de La Cité
  17. Le Gazoline Bar-Concerts
  18. Oan's Pub
- **ENTERTAINMENT**
  19. Le Liberté
  20. Ubu
- **SHOPPING**
  21. Confidentiel
  22. Les Puces de Rennes
  23. Soleil Noir
  24. Vacarme

Parlement de Bretagne

BRITTANY'S OWN PARLIAMENT

Sitting at the heart of the city and a major part of Rennais heritage, the **Parlement de Bretagne** was built in the 17th century following the region's unification with the Kingdom of France. It was initially established as a court of justice to defend the rights and privileges of the Bretons in the face of French royal power. It has since lost its prerogatives and has become a court of appeal – but still stands as a symbol of Breton autonomy. Many Rennais have told me it is impossible to understand the city without booking a guided tour of the building *(tourisme-rennes.com/sortir/parlement-de-bretagne; adult/child €9.50/6.50)*. Keep in mind, however, that tours are only available in French.

Brittany's Rich History
Visit the Musée de Bretagne

Getting a sense of Breton identity truly requires learning about the rich and complex history of the region, from the spread of Celtic culture in the 5th century to the autonomous Duchy of Brittany in the Middle Ages and the unification with the Kingdom of France in 1532. The **Musée de Bretagne** *(leschampslibres.fr/les-champs-libres/musee-de-bretagne; free entrance)*, which sits inside cultural centre **Les Champs Libres** – a favourite weekend spot for many locals – recounts the history of Brittany from prehistory to the modern age. It's an easy win for a rainy afternoon, with the centre offering plenty of kid-friendly play areas and activities. Don't miss the cosy **Café des Champs Libres**, which features a weekly programme of workshops, talks, concerts, theme nights and DJ sets.

Hunt For a Bargain
A tour of second-hand shops

From vintage Gucci to stylish century-old wooden furniture carved in Breton style, the streets of Rennes' historical centre are hiding troves of second-hand gems waiting to be found in

---

 EATING IN RENNES: OUR PICKS

Café Breton: A no-fuss cosy restaurant with stylish vintage decor and welcoming service from the owners. *noon-2pm & 7.30-10pm Tue-Sat* €€

Chez P'tit Louis: A cute restaurant and terrace tucked in a corner of the historical centre. Creative dishes and a tasteful selection of wines. *hours vary* €€

Coquille: Fresh and colourful dishes based on local, seasonal produce. A modern take on Breton cuisine in a slick, contemporary bistro. *noon-2pm & 7-10pm Mon-Sat* €€

Les Grands Gamins: Hearty meals and a weekend brunch in a cool cafe that works just as well for afterwork drinks. *hours vary* €

multitudes of *friperies*, *brocantes* and *dépôts-ventes*. **Confidentiel**, **Soleil Noir** and **Vacarme** are three good spots to start bargain-hunting.

Every second Sunday of the month, a huge flea market, **Les Puces de Rennes**, takes over **Mail François Mitterrand** in the southwest of the city. A perfect excuse to treat yourself to brunch on the sun-soaked terrace of one of the many cafes lining the street, such as **Les Grands Gamins**, **Superkraft** and **Oh My Biche**. Booking is advised.

Vilaine, Only by Name
Cycle to Étangs d'Apigné

On a sunny summer day, the Rennais go for a dip at **Étangs d'Apigné**, a set of idyllic ponds located just a few kilometres outside of the city. Rent a bike and head south on the V42, a greenlane that stretches along the Vilaine River all the way to the English Channel. You'll find **Plage d'Apigné** about 20 minutes later, where you can set up for the afternoon. Grab lunch at **La Basse Cour** (*labassecour.org*), just a five-minute ride away – a bar, restaurant and cultural hub established in an old farmyard and dedicated to sustainable eating, with a bustling programme of concerts, jam sessions, exhibitions and workshops.

Feeling up for a challenge? You can continue on the V42 through the picturesque village of **Pont-Réan** and all the way to the scenic **Boël Mill**, 25km away from Rennes. The round trip back to the city will take three hours, featuring peaceful riverbank scenery bordered by lush forests.

A Night Out in Rennes
Dive into the *soirées rennaises*

Rennes lives at the pace of the tens of thousands of students who populate it, and the best spot to indulge in a cheap drink is on **Place Ste-Anne**, which surrounds the majestic **St-Aubin Basilica** with student bars aplenty lodged in colourful half-timbered buildings. It is also the starting point of **rue St-Michel**, evocatively nicknamed the 'road of thirst'. You'll find across Rennes an abundance of bars with gigs and DJ sets, but if you're in the market for a serious boogie, keep an eye on the programmes of Rennes' most famous concert halls like **Le Liberté** (*leliberte.fr*), **Ubu** (*lestrans.com*) and **Le MeM** (*lemem.fr*). At the time of writing, Le MeM was expected to re-open in 2026.

ROCK'N'ROLL RENNES

Rennes emerged as a major hub for rock bands in France in the late 1970s and '80s, thanks to influential artists like Marquis de Sade and Niagara. In 1979, the **Trans Musicales** festival launched, initially focusing on local artists but quickly growing throughout the years into an international event encompassing a variety of genres. Trans Musicales has remained hugely popular and still happens every December, alongside a number of other music festivals happening throughout the year. They include **Yaouank** in the autumn, which mixes Breton, world and contemporary genres, and **Rock'n'Solex** in May, a student festival dedicated to music and mopeds. A match made in heaven.

Try the homemade rhum arrangé (in moderation)

 DRINKING IN RENNES: BEST LIVE MUSIC BARS

Le Gazoline Bar-Concerts: Rock, punk and beer. Local student hangout with maximalist decor and lots of outdoor seating. *hours vary*	**Oan's Pub**: DJ sets are regularly hosted in this lively pub located in the historical centre. *5pm-1am Sun-Fri, noon-1am Sat*	**Le Bistrot de la Cité**: A hidden, cosy neighbourhood bar that puts on concerts by local musicians. *noon-1am Tue-Sat, 4pm-1am Sun*	**Le Grand Huit**: Concerts and DJ sets in a huge venue dedicated to funfairs, featuring merry-go-rounds and games. *hours vary*

Beyond Rennes

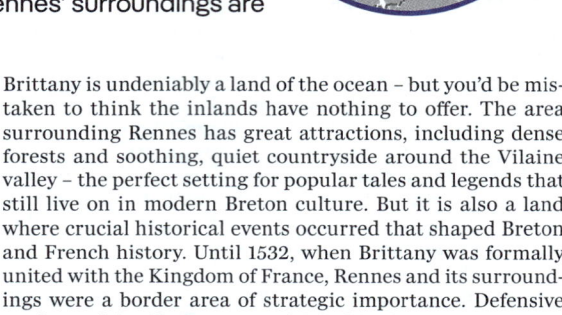

The stage of plenty of medieval action, both mythical and real, Rennes' surroundings are loaded with history.

Places
Forêt de Paimpont p276
Vitré p278
Fougères p278

Brittany is undeniably a land of the ocean – but you'd be mistaken to think the inlands have nothing to offer. The area surrounding Rennes has great attractions, including dense forests and soothing, quiet countryside around the Vilaine valley – the perfect setting for popular tales and legends that still live on in modern Breton culture. But it is also a land where crucial historical events occurred that shaped Breton and French history. Until 1532, when Brittany was formally united with the Kingdom of France, Rennes and its surroundings were a border area of strategic importance. Defensive castles and fortified towns multiplied in the region, many of which are impeccably preserved and can still be visited. A must-see for any medieval history amateur.

GETTING AROUND

With some planning, you can get to Vitré by **train** and Fougères by **bus** from Rennes thanks to multiple connections daily, and you won't need more than a day trip to make the most of each. A car is preferable, however, to make your way to and around Forêt de Paimpont. You'll likely be completing several walking routes departing from different points, some of which are up to 20km apart. Once on site, you can also opt to cycle between departure points by renting bikes, including electric ones, from Paimpont.

Forêt de Paimpont

TIME FROM RENNES: **45MIN**

Walk in the footsteps of King Arthur

A great destination if you love tales and legends, and certain to be a big hit with children, is **Forêt de Paimpont** *(Paimpont Forest; destination-broceliande.com/decouvrir/incontournables/foret-broceliande; free)* – a mysterious woodland that inspired 12th-century writer Chrétien de Troyes' Arthurian legends, which is named in his poems as the 'Brocéliande forest'. Forêt de Paimpont is home to some of the mythical sites mentioned in the legend of King Arthur, such as the Fountain of Youth and Merlin's Tomb. The woods cover 110 sq km and are largely private property, meaning they can only be visited by foot and using dedicated trails. Seven walking routes exist to cover key highlights, ranging between 2km and 4km and departing from parking lots dotted across the forest.

Find out more about the itineraries by visiting the tourist office in one of the three main departure points – **Paimpont**, **Tréhorenteuc** or **Iffendic** tourist office. When planning your trip, keep in mind that the forest is a hunting ground from September to March, meaning that access is strictly regulated in the winter months. Prioritise a visit in the spring and summer, when all the sites are open.

Jump aboard a horse-drawn carriage

Fancy a slower pace? At the heart of the forest in the hamlet of Folle Pensée, a 15-minute drive from Paimpont, **Les Calèches**

Forêt de Paimpont

de Barenton *(tourisme-broceliande.bzh/en/activite/carriage-ride-around-barenton; carriage of 1-4 people from €65)* offer daily 45-minute rides through dedicated trails on board carriages drawn by a typically Breton draught horse. Call or email ahead to book, especially if you're keen to make it extra – for instance making it longer or departing at a specific time. You can also request that a professional storyteller join the ride to add a touch of magic with tales, legends and secrets from the forest. Tours are available in English.

The Gate of Secrets

For an immersive experience that is certain to be a big hit with children, book 'The Gate of Secrets' *(tourisme-broceliande.bzh/en/activite/la-porte-des-secrets/; adult/child €7.50/5)* – an hour-long tour and show set inside the **Abbaye de Paimpont**, in which a virtual forest warden, Pierre, will take you through the legends of Brocéliande forest. With magical decor and interactive elements, you will explore the forest's myths, flora and fauna, popular tales and creatures, making for a great introduction to the woodland's mysteries. Suitable for children aged five years and over, with audio guides available in multiple languages; make sure you book ahead.

KING ARTHUR'S NATIONALITIES

You may think that the legend of King Arthur is unquestionably British. With reason: Arthur and Guinevere, Excalibur and the Knights of the Round Table are all part of medieval retellings of the legendary history of British kings, notably in the work of 12th-century Welsh writer Geoffrey of Monmouth. But around the same time, Arthurian legends travelled to Europe and were picked up by French poet Chrétien de Troyes. Building on the character of King Arthur, Chrétien de Troyes added ingredients of his own – which is how Camelot, Lancelot and the Holy Grail, for example, came to have French origins.

EATING NEAR FORÊT DE PAIMPONT: OUR PICKS

La Fée Gourmande: Sitting by Paimpont Lake, a charming crêperie with a view and a sunny terrace. *hours vary* €

L'Atelier: Elegant restaurant in the centre of Paimpont, offering traditional French food and a lunchtime menu. *hours vary* €€

Les Forges de Paimpont: A few kilometres outside of Paimpont, hearty food and generous portions in a traditional stone house. *noon-2pm & 7-9.30pm Wed-Sun* €€

La Grande Vallée: Friendly crêperie with a huge garden and a *guinguette* (tavern) atmosphere in Tréhorenteuc. *hours vary* €

LES MARCHES DE BRETAGNE

Until the 16th century, Brittany was an autonomous region – and its easternmost part, which bordered the Kingdom of France, was of particular strategic and military importance. This is why the region is known as the **Marches de Bretagne** (the border of Brittany), and is dotted with fortified towns and castles that formed a robust defence and protection system against enemy incursions into the region. It was also a hub for commerce and trade with neighbouring countries. Today many of these towns have kept their medieval architecture and charm, and attract tourists interested to see where some of Brittany's history was made. While Vitré and Fougères are two of the most famous sites, there are many more, including **Châteaugiron**, **La Guerche de Bretagne** and **Dol-de-Bretagne**.

Vitré

TIME FROM RENNES: **20MIN**

Take a stroll in the Middle Ages

Walking in Vitré is like taking a step back in time: the town is packed with adorable half-timbered houses, tiny cobbled streets and, as a key strategic site in the Middle Ages, the mandatory fortifications and castle, **Château de Vitré**. For a short stroll with a view of the town's walls, walk along **Promenade du Val** until you reach the Vilaine River, and then along the riverside to the **Pré des Lavandières**. Walking up **Chemin des Tertres Noirs**, you will catch a view of the whole town and castle sitting in the surrounding countryside. Don't forget to stop at one of the many bars, cafes and restaurants lining **Rue d'En-Bas** for a snack or a treat before you go.

Fougères

TIME FROM RENNES: **1HR 10MIN**

Visit a 1000-year-old castle

The first traces of a castle in the town of Fougères go back to the 11th century, and due to its strategic location the site remained a stronghold throughout the centuries. Today it is one of the largest and best-preserved medieval fortresses in Europe, and a must-see for military history enthusiasts. Make sure you ask for the audio guide, which is included in the entrance to **Château de Fougères** *(chateau-fougeres.com/en; adult/child €10/5)*. And keep an eye out for the castle's events programme in the summer, which includes medieval re-enactment performances, atmospheric nocturnal openings and every Thursday evening, a free show including musicians, dancers, equestrians and circus artists.

 EATING IN VITRÉ & FOUGÈRES: BEST CRÊPERIES

La Broustal: Cute stone-house crêperie near the castle in Fougères with a lovely sunny terrace. *hours vary* €

Tivabro: Nestled in a medieval stone house in Fougères, offering a classic menu of crêpes and *galettes* in a cosy setting. *hours vary* €

La Crêperie du P'tit Léon: Located in the picturesque rue d'En-Bas in Vitré, with a mouthwatering menu prioritising local produce. *noon-2pm & 7-9.30pm Tue-Thu, to 10pm Fri-Sat* €

Place aux Crêpes: A warm welcome always awaits in this small crêperie in Vitré. A rich menu and an easy-going, friendly atmosphere. *hours vary* €

St-Malo

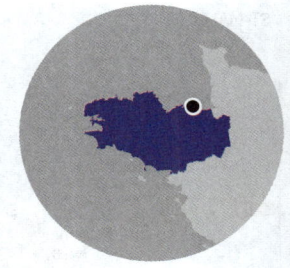

FAMOUS PIRATES | EMERALD COAST | DIVINE OYSTERS

'Not French, not Breton, I am Malouin.' St-Malo's slogan sets the tone. Circled and protected by its commanding ramparts yet resolutely open to the sea, it takes great pride in its very distinctive identity. One of the most prosperous ports in France from the 15th century onwards, it became home to great seafarers such as Jacques Cartier, the first European to make his way to Canada in the 16th century. But St-Malo is most famous for the high number of privateers who enriched the city in the 17th and 18th centuries. Commissioned by the King of France to pillage enemy boats during war times, privateers owned hundreds of armed ships in the port of St-Malo towards the end of the 18th century. The city walls, which date back to the 12th century, were expanded and fortified to better defend these accumulated treasures, and quickly became emblematic of the city. St-Malo has remained a vibrant city to this day, bustling with life, flavoured with sea breeze and popular with tourists, and as ever defiantly facing the sea – as if the spectres of famous corsairs like René Duguay-Trouin and Robert Surcouf were still haunting the town's windy streets.

> ☑ **TOP TIP**
>
> The picturesque *intra-muros* is contained within the ramparts, but the city also includes less crowded areas such as St-Servan, Sillon-Courtoisville or Rothéneuf, where you will find more local restaurants, cheaper hotels and easier parking spots.

 GETTING AROUND

To visit St-Malo *intra-muros* (the historic centre contained within the ramparts) you'll be better off by foot: it can be crossed in 15 minutes and is near-impossible to drive around. If you are coming by car, you can use a paid parking just outside the city walls, or use free parking further out. You can also opt for the **Paul Féval Park & Ride**, which has a day fee and regular bus links to the city. St-Malo's bus network MAT *(reseau-mat.fr)* links to the **city walls** and **train station**, and to neighbouring districts.

⭐ **HIGHLIGHTS**	11 Grand'Porte
1 Fort National	12 Môle des Noires
2 Mémorial 39–45	13 Petit Bé
3 Porte St-Thomas	14 Plage de Bon-Secours
🔴 **SIGHTS**	15 Plage de l'Eventail
4 Anse des Sablons	16 Plage du Môle
5 Bastion de la Hollande	17 Plage du Sillon
6 Bastion St-Louis	18 Porte de Dinan
7 Bastion St-Philippe	19 Porte St-Vincent
8 Cathédrale St-Vincent	20 Quai Solidor
9 Château de St-Malo	21 Statue of Jacques Cartier
10 Grand Bé	22 Tour Bidouane
⚫ **SLEEPING**	
23 Grand Hôtel des Thermes	
24 Hôtel France & Chateaubriand	
25 Hôtel Quic en Groigne	
26 Le Beaufort	
27 Villa Ellersie	
🟢 **EATING**	
28 Bouliche	
29 Doma	
30 La Cale Solidor	
31 La Touline	
32 L'Amiral St-Malo	
see 23 Le Cap Horn	
33 Le Corps de Garde	
34 Les Flibustiers	
🔵 **TRANSPORT**	
35 City Walls Bus Stop	
36 St-Malo Train Station	

Three Centuries of Military History

Visit the Fort National

Standing imperiously on a rocky island facing the sea, St-Malo's **Fort National** (fortnational.com; adult/child €5/3) was built in 1689 and was originally intended to protect the city's port. It has been the stage throughout the centuries of legendary attacks and epic battles – and has also known darker days during World War II, when it was used as a prison by

Fort National

the Germans. The site is now open to visits every day in the summer, and during some school and bank holidays. Opening hours depend on the time of the day: you'll need to wait for the tide to be low to walk across **Plage de l'Éventail** to reach the fort. You can book a 35-minute guided tour in English by email, with written translations also available in a number of other languages.

Sunset by the Sea

Pop a beer at Plage du Sillon

Just outside of the *intra-muros*, the sandy **Plage du Sillon** extends over 3km to the north of St-Malo, lined with glamorous 19th-century villas. It's a prime spot for a long walk along the promenade and a sit-down, particularly at sunset. Watch the golden hour lights take over the city in the distance and the sky elegantly reflecting against the tall windows of the Belle Époque buildings facing the sea. The beach makes for a

---

FOR THE FISHING ENTHUSIASTS

Benjamin Glais, fishing guide and instructor with Fish'in Bretagne in St-Malo, shares his best tips for fishing on the city's beaches. *fishinbretagne.fr*

Fishing is practised at low tide on the foreshore, in front of the city walls, where you can look for many different species. The long sandbank of **Plage du Môle** is where you will find bivalve molluscs such as clams or oysters. Rocky sites, like **Grand Bé**, **Petit Bé** and **Fort National**, offer plenty of crustaceans (crabs and lobsters) and more molluscs (shellfish, abalone). Make sure you release anything you won't consume, and read the rules on size, quotas and protected species before you go.

Make sure you leave room for dessert

🍴 EATING IN ST-MALO: OUR PICKS

Doma: A cosy room and a short, tasty menu based on seasonal produce that is reasonably priced. *noon-1.30pm Wed-Sat, 7.30-9.30pm Tue-Sat* €€

La Touline: Classic crêperie with high-quality ingredients at the heart of the *intra-muros*. *hours vary* €

Les Flibustiers: A warm spot with a terrace in the centre offering no-fuss *planches* (platters), salads, tartines, quiches and soups. *hours vary* €

Bouliche: Away from the crowds near to Cité d'Alet, a local gem with creative plates. *noon-2pm Tue, 7-10pm Wed, noon-2pm & 7-10pm Thu-Sat* €€

WALK ST-MALO'S RAMPARTS

Circle St-Malo's historic centre by walking the 12th-century walls that have become the symbol of the corsair city.

START	END	LENGTH
Porte St-Thomas	Porte St-Vincent	2km; 1hr

The fortified walls that surround St-Malo's old town form a walkable loop and are the best way to grasp the military and strategic importance of the site – while catching sights of the historic centre and the beautiful seascape it faces. You can climb to the pathway using the stairs in one of the eight gates (or *portes*) dotted along the way, or thanks to three access ramps. One itinerary starts at ❶ **Porte St-Thomas**. Climb the stairs and see **Plage du Sillon** (p281) spreading to the north, with **Fort National** (p280), a 17th-century military bastion, standing right in front of you. Make your way towards ❷ **Tour Bidouane**, from where you'll catch a clear view of the surrounding coastline, and of the nearby islands **Grand Bé** (p281) – where French writer François-René de Chateaubriand was buried – and **Petit Bé** (p281). Walking alongside **Plage de Bon-Secours** (p286), you'll reach ❸ **Bastion de la Hollande** and its ornamental cannons. Continue to ❹ **Bastion St-Philippe**, which overlooks **Môle des Noires**, a 500m-long pier indicating the entrance to the port of St-Malo. As you head towards ❺ **Bastion St-Louis**, look to your left towards the city: you'll walk past restored corsair houses, one of which, near ❻ **Porte de Dinan**, was occupied by Robert Surcouf. Continue to ❼ **Grand'Porte**, the city's oldest gate, and finish at ❽ **Porte St-Vincent**, where you can observe St-Malo's busy main street rue St-Vincent to one side and **Château de St-Malo** to the other.

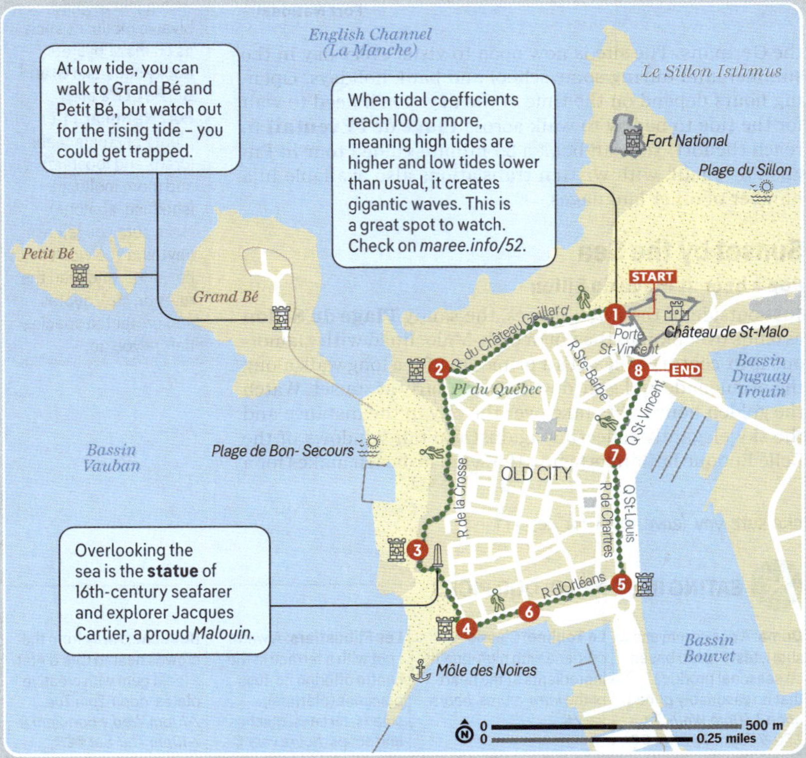

> At low tide, you can walk to Grand Bé and Petit Bé, but watch out for the rising tide – you could get trapped.

> When tidal coefficients reach 100 or more, meaning high tides are higher and low tides lower than usual, it creates gigantic waves. This is a great spot to watch. Check on maree.info/52.

> Overlooking the sea is the **statue** of 16th-century seafarer and explorer Jacques Cartier, a proud *Malouin*.

great picnic spot, but the promenade is also lined with fancy bars and restaurants.

Hike to Pointe de la Varde
Cliffs dropping into the bay

A few kilometres away from the historical centre, in St-Malo's northern district of Rothéneuf, Pointe de la Varde is a protected natural site culminating 32m above sea level, offering an unobstructed view of the surrounding bay. Park near **Plage du Pont**, where you'll be able to catch the GR34 footpath that will take you around the coast and all the way to the site. Once there, you'll recognise the shape of St-Malo's historic town in the distance, as well as the **Plage du Sillon** (p281). Continue on the GR34 past **Plage de la Varde** and along the coast to **Plage du Nicet**. You can either go back the same way you came, or take a more direct route through Rothéneuf along av de la Varde and rue des Petits Ports; account for about 1½ hours walking in total.

Around the Cité d'Alet
Find some quieter local hangouts

Once you have passed the port of St-Malo, walk the footpath running along **Anse des Sablons** to the peninsula located south of town. Cité d'Alet, as it is named, is where the first traces of the city of St-Malo were found, as early as the 4th century. Gallo-Roman remnants now sit next to **Mémorial 39–45**, a memorial to the violent bombings Alet was subjected to during World War II. Follow signs for the *chemin de ronde*, which runs around the peninsula with lovely views of St-Malo's walls and of the coastline to **Dinard**. Indulge in a drink with the locals at one of the bars and cafes lining **Quai Solidor** and soak up the quieter atmosphere away from the crowded town centre.

THE PRICE OF LIBERATION

The old town of St-Malo as we know it today came very close to not surviving at all. In August 1944, after four years of German occupation, St-Malo and its surroundings were relentlessly bombed by the Allies. When the city was liberated on 17 August 1944, 80% of the old town was destroyed. The ramparts, miraculously, were still standing. Instead of razing everything left to the ground and rebuilding afresh, however, it was decided to reconstruct everything just as it was. A colossal, complex project that took years, including 18 months just to clear out the 500,000 cu metres of ruins. In 1972, when **Cathédrale St-Vincent** was inaugurated, St-Malo was officially completely restored.

EATING IN ST-MALO: DINNER WITH A VIEW

L'Amiral St-Malo: At the heart of the port of St-Malo, expect a breathtaking view of the bay and elegant, traditional cuisine based on local fish and meats. *noon-2pm & 7-10pm* €€

Le Corps de Garde: An unmissable spot when walking along the ramparts. Crêpes and *galettes* are served in this prime *intra-muros* location overlooking the sea. *9am-10pm* €

Le Cap Horn: Special-treat yourself in this fancy restaurant overlooking Plage du Sillon, which is part of the emblematic Grand Hôtel des Thermes. *noon-2pm & 7.30-9pm* €€€

La Cale Solidor: Local cuisine focusing on seafood in a relaxed spot on Quai Solidor in the Cité d'Alet. *12.15-1.30pm & 7.15-8.30pm Wed-Sun* €€

Beyond St-Malo

Quiet, unspoiled riverside or beautiful, windswept coastal path? You can't go wrong when visiting St-Malo's surroundings.

Places
Cap Fréhel p284
Vallée de la Rance p284
Cancale p286

Although St-Malo is typically defined by its maritime history, it truly sits at the intersection of land and sea. Don't miss out on the beautiful landscapes you can find in the surrounding areas when you follow the Rance River into the valley. You will be met with breathtaking sights of untouched nature and the quiet, still atmosphere that is so characteristic of the riverside. You can also choose to stay near the sea and discover the Côte d'Emeraude (Emerald Coast), which stretches from Cancale to Cap Fréhel and owes its name to the water's wonderful colours. Expect plenty of heavenly sandy beaches, spectacular cliffs and, of course, the ever-changing, temperamental and unpredictable sea.

GETTING AROUND

With some organisation, you will be able to reach most of the towns and villages surrounding St-Malo by bus and train. Note that you will need extra planning if you are travelling on a Sunday or on a public holiday. A car will let you travel stress-free, while enabling you to see more remote sites such as Cap Fréhel – which, particularly on the coast, tend to be far from any public transport.

Cap Fréhel

TIME FROM ST-MALO: **1HR**

Hike the Côte d'Emeraude

Lined by the GR34 footpath, the Emerald Coast won't let you down: pretty much any itinerary will deliver incredible sights. The panoramic view from Cap Fréhel, however, is particularly reputable – in fact, the parking fee next to **Phare du Cap Fréhel** and large summer crowds speak for themselves. To make the most of your day trip, use the free parking next to **Fort la Latte** instead, which is 5km away, and hike your way to Cap Fréhel. The walk features plenty of rocky cliffs, delightful coves and superb flora. If you make it within opening hours, you can also visit the lighthouse in Cap Fréhel to enjoy a stunning view of the coast *(dinan-capfrehel.com/sit/phare-du-cap-frehel; adult/child €3/1.5)*. Accounting for frequent photo stops, it will take you between 3 hours and half a day to get there and back.

Vallée de la Rance

TIME FROM ST-MALO: **40MIN**

Cycle from St-Malo to St-Suliac

Rent a bike from St-Malo and jump on the marked cycle route EV4 heading for the small and beautiful village of **St-Suliac**, which sits further south on the banks of the Rance River. The ride, over 15km, will take about an hour and offer plenty of panoramic views of the river, including intimate coves, pine forests and small, peaceful beaches lining the estuary. In

Phare du Cap Fréhel

St-Suliac, you will be greeted by adorable stone houses, flowery window sills and cute **Port de St-Suliac**, alongside plenty of restaurant and crêperie options for a break before you return.

Tour artists' galleries in Dinan

Sitting further down the Rance River, the medieval town of Dinan was known for its prolific weaving and tanning activity between the 14th and 18th centuries. Nowadays, it provides the perfect setting for the dozens of artists who have chosen to establish their galleries along the winding, cobbled streets of the town centre.

Painters, sculptors, ceramicists, jewellers, photographers and glassmakers abound, particularly concentrated in **Rue du Jerzual**, a long and narrow street that links the upper town to the **Port de Dinan**, which is located 78m lower. It's a tough climb back, but totally worth snapping a pic under the flowery balconies lining the street's colourful half-timbered houses. Visit the website of Dinan's artists' collective Art'Dinan *(art-dinan.com)* to select your favourite creators, and keep an eye on upcoming events and exhibitions.

DINAN'S BEST CRAFT SHOPS

Deewi: One of Dinan's most famous shops, Deewi is managed by an arts collective and displays the work of dozens of Breton artists, from jewellery to ceramics to cosmetics and fashion.

Tartine de Laine: Translated as 'Toast of Wool', Tartine de Laine is owned by two sisters who specialise in handcrafted clothing.

Katell Leclaire: Contemporary jewellery created with ethically sourced and traceable materials, including recycled silver and safely mined gold and stones.

Poirier Cuir: Beautifully made leather handbags, wallets and belts in a family-owned shop that has specialised in leatherwork for several generations.

L'Atelier de Mona: A colourful, intimate workshop where you'll discover Mona's world of oil paintings, watercolours and jewellery.

 EATING IN DINAN: BEST CRÊPERIES

| **La Cour St-Sauveur:** Generously garnished crêpes and *galettes* in the upper part of town, with a cute back garden. *noon-2pm & 7-9pm Thu-Mon* € | **Crêperie Ahna:** A central crêperie and terrace that also offers stone-grilled meats. *noon-2pm & 7-10pm Tue-Sat* € | **La Fontaine du Jerzual:** A sunny spot overlooking the famous rue du Jerzual to stop for lunch or a snack. *noon-2pm & 7-9pm Mon-Fri, noon-9pm Sat & Sun* € | **Crêperie Luun:** A tasty menu based on local produce in a stone house with great views of the port. *hours vary* € |

BEST BEACHES ON THE CÔTE D'EMERAUDE

Denise Louaisil, now retired after running two guesthouses on her family's dairy farm, offers her favourite beaches in the region.

Plage de Port-Mer in Cancale is a perfect spot for families to discover the town, just like **Plage de Bon-Secours** at the foot of St-Malo's walls, which is also protected from the wind. I would advise going for a dip in the evening, when the crowds have left Bon-Secours almost deserted but the sun is still shining. East of St-Malo, near St-Coulomb, there is the beautiful, dune-bordered **Plage des Chevrets**, as well as one of the most coveted spots on the Côte d'Emeraude, the sandy **Anse du Guesclin**, whose turquoise waters are particularly inviting.

Cancale

TIME FROM ST-MALO: **30MIN**

World-famous oysters

If you drive to Cancale, make sure that you arrive through the one-way **Route Panoramique**. The view of the fishing port will give you instant cravings for fresh seafood which, as it turns out, is what the town does best. Head to the **Marché aux Huîtres** (oyster market) on port de la Houle, where local farmers sell their produce, and enjoy a taste of the famous Cancale oyster with a glass of white wine. Sitting on the seafront, if the tide is low, you will be able to see the oyster farms that produce the delicacies – and weather permitting, you might even discern Mont St-Michel (p253) on the horizon.

Secrets of oyster farming

Not sure how to differentiate between a cupped and a flat oyster? Book yourself in for a guided tour with **Ostreïka** (ost reika.com; adult/under-7 €12/ free). For about an hour, you'll be taken for a stroll – low tide permitting – through Cancale's oyster farms and taught everything you need to know about oyster farming. Tours run from February to November, are available in English and must be booked online. Mud-proof boots can be rented for free.

A digestive walk

Shake off all that seafood and wine with a stroll along the GR34 footpath, which runs through Cancale, and no more than 15 minutes will take you to **Pointe du Hock**, where you'll catch lovely views of the town. If you are after a proper hike, you can push all the way to **Pointe du Grouin**, which is almost 7km away but will reward you with exhilarating views of the Côte d'Emeraude, the bay of Mont St-Michel and the Normandy coastline. Bus line 9 on the MAT network will take you back to the centre in Cancale, but note that it does not run every day of the week, especially in low season.

EATING IN CANCALE: BEST SEAFOOD

Marché aux Huîtres: Buy platters direct from producers at Cancale's oyster market, and savour them sitting down facing the sea. *9am-7pm, to 8pm Jul & Aug* €

L'Atelier de l'Huître: A sit-down restaurant and producer on the port offering the freshest seafood platters. *9am-7pm Tue-Sat* €€

À Contre-Courant: A friendly, cosy restaurant offering reasonably priced dishes with a focus on seafood. *hours vary* €

Côté Mer: Treat yourself to an exceptional view of the seafront in this restaurant specialising in seafood. *hours vary* €€

Quimper

DRAMATIC SEASCAPES | BRETON CULTURE | WATER SPORTS

Quimper may at first seem like just another pretty medieval town, but it holds a significant place in Celtic and Breton identity. Its origins are a characteristic mix of myth and reality, with archaeological evidence of activity dating back to antiquity in the district of Locmaria. This was followed by the legendary establishment of the current town centre in the 4th century by the Celtic King Gradlon, whose mythical Kingdom of Cornouaille eventually became a real region of which Quimper was the capital. Today Cornouaille is no longer officially a regional division, but it is very much still alive in the pride that Quimper takes from its Celtic roots. The town is a hub for traditional dance, music and costume, which are remarkably celebrated during the annual Festival de Cornouaille (p288), and have contributed to making Quimper the unofficial capital of Breton culture.

Soak up Breton Culture
Myths, arts and traditions

It is said that the legendary King Gradlon of Cornouaille, a key figure in Celtic mythology, made Quimper the capital of his kingdom between the 4th and 5th centuries. He asked Corentin, a hermit who had shown him a prodigious fish that regenerated itself after it had been eaten, to build a cathedral on the town's grounds. Corentin thus became the first of many future bishops of Quimper. Quimper's attachment to these myths and legends truly comes to life in the city: visit **Cathédrale St-Corentin** and you'll notice the statue of King Gradlon on horseback standing between the spires.

For more on the region's history, arts and traditions, stop next door, where you'll find the **Musée Départemental Breton** (musee-breton.finistere.fr; adult/child €7/free). The museum, established in 1846 in the imposing walls of what used to be the episcopal palace, is dedicated to Breton heritage. It recounts the history of the region from prehistoric times to the modern age, and looks at the importance of

GETTING AROUND

Don't burden yourself with a car: Quimper's historic centre is small and partly pedestrianised. You'll find free parking for up to 12 hours near the **train station** in **Michel-Gloaguen Car Park,** from where it's a 15-minute walk to the town centre. Locmaria district, which is further out, requires walking another 15 minutes by the river.

☑ TOP TIP

Quimper is a small town and you will only need one or two nights to see it all. If you are planning to stay for longer and would like more food and drink options, it is worth looking for accommodation in surrounding towns and cities.

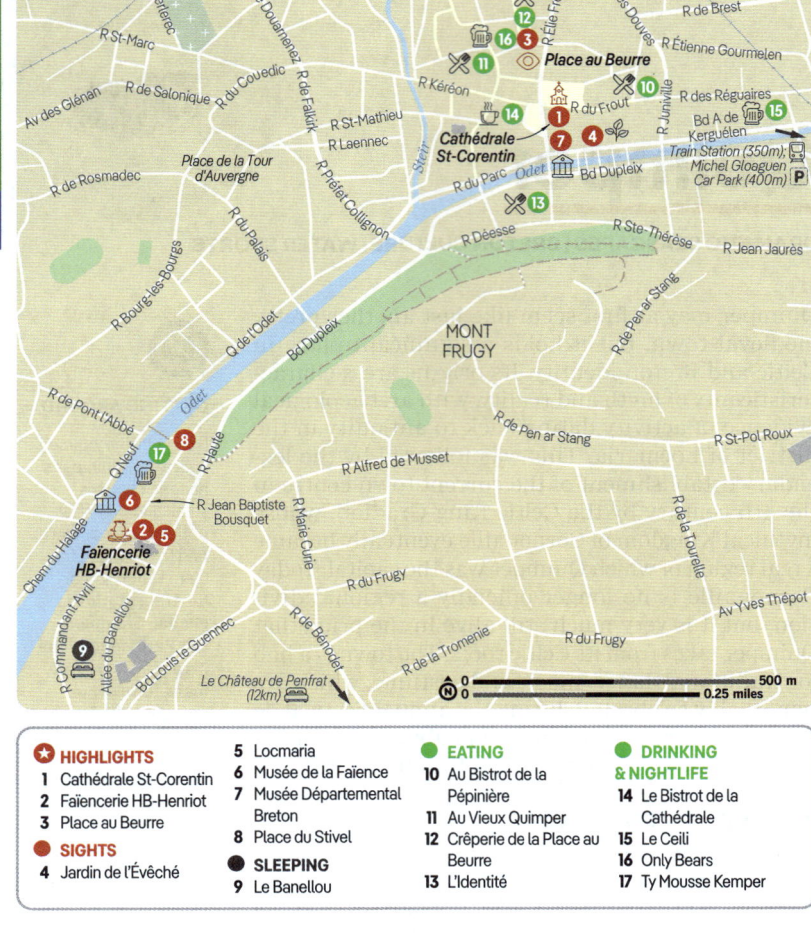

	HIGHLIGHTS	5	Locmaria		EATING		DRINKING
1	Cathédrale St-Corentin	6	Musée de la Faïence	10	Au Bistrot de la		& NIGHTLIFE
2	Faïencerie HB-Henriot	7	Musée Départemental Breton		Pépinière	14	Le Bistrot de la Cathédrale
3	Place au Beurre	8	Place du Stivel	11	Au Vieux Quimper	15	Le Ceili
	SIGHTS		SLEEPING	12	Crêperie de la Place au Beurre	16	Only Bears
4	Jardin de l'Évêché	9	Le Banellou	13	L'Identité	17	Ty Mousse Kemper

traditional costume, furniture and ceramics in strengthening Breton identity.

A Century-Old Festival

Dance and eat in Breton style

A stroll around the medieval streets of Quimper, stopping for a mandatory crêpe on the famous **Place au Beurre** (translated as Butter Square), is pleasant year-round – but if you can, visit Quimper during the **Festival de Cornouaille**. The yearly event has enlivened the winding streets of the town almost every month of July since 1923 and is a joyful celebration of Breton identity. It was the first ever festival dedicated to the region's culture, putting on traditional dance

Festival de Cornouaille

and music performances, with participants proudly wearing Breton costumes, complete with lace headdresses and colourful aprons. Nowadays, more than 150,000 visitors attend over the course of several days, together with 2000 musicians and dancers. The event culminates with the election of the Queen of Cornouaille, who is tasked with representing the region for the year, and is selected on the basis of a thesis she has written about Breton culture, her costume and a traditional dance performance.

There are also plenty of kid-friendly activities: a whole day is dedicated to children, during which they can enjoy their own shows, parades and workshops. The festival gathers people of all ages and is widely seen as a festive and friendly event – and it will be an immediate submersion into the heart of what Brittany is all about. All of this to be enjoyed, of course, while eating and drinking delicious Breton specialities.

Stock Up on Breton Tableware

The ceramics of Locmaria

The **Locmaria** district is where the first traces of a Gallo-Roman port-city were found in Quimper. As early as the 15th century, pottery workshops started developing in the area, but

FESTIVAL MUST-DO: FEST-NOZ

Igor Gardes, the director of Breton cultural centre **Le Triskell** and previously director of the Festival de Cornouaille, explains how to get initiated in traditional Breton dancing.

Like the barn dance or ceilidh, *fest-noz* comes straight from folklore and tradition. It is the dance of parties, of weddings, of 'let's help the neighbour tamp down the garden soil'. For someone on the outside, of course, it can be a little intimidating to get involved while everyone holds hands and stamps their feet. So, if you only do one thing during the festival, it must be to attend some of the free Breton dance classes that are organised throughout the week. You'll learn simple, basic steps over a couple of hours, and put it all into practice at the evening *fest-noz*. Don't be self-conscious – no one's judging you!

Fine dining at reasonable prices.

EATING IN QUIMPER: OUR PICKS

Crêperie de la Place au Beurre: A crêpe here is a Quimper must-do. This iconic crêperie serves a classic menu with outside dining. *noon-9.30pm* €

Au Vieux Quimper: A half-century-old authentic crêperie in Quimper's historical centre. *11.45am-2pm & 7.45-9.30pm Tue-Sat* €

Au Bistrot de la Pépinière: Cosy restaurant with a tasty menu mixing traditional cuisine and modernity. *noon-1.30pm & 7-9.20pm Tue-Sat* €€

L'Identité: A local spot away from the crowds of the centre, with friendly owners. *noon-1.15pm & 7-9pm Tue-Thu, to 9.15pm Fri & Sat* €€

Faïencerie HB-Henriot

BAGADOÙ & CELTIC DANCE CIRCLES

Celebrating Breton tradition more formally, *bagadoù* and Celtic dance circles abound in Quimper. *Bagadoù* (the plural of *bagad*) are groups inspired by Scottish pipe bands. Quimper is home to one of Brittany's most famous *bagadoù*, Bagad Kemper. The region's Celtic dance circles are also well-established. Eostiged Ar Stangala circle, for instance, has been the sacred national Breton dance champion more than a dozen times. Note that every Thursday evening throughout July and August in Quimper, a free performance called *Derrière les Remparts* is put on by a *bagad* and a circle, starting outside the cathedral and continuing in **Jardin de l'Evêché** – if you are in town, don't miss it.

it was in the 17th century that the area saw the explosion of ceramics manufacturing, a trade that continues to this day and is now mostly carried out by manufacturer HB-Henriot. From April to September, you can book a 30-minute guided workshop tour of the **Faïencerie HB-Henriot** *(henriot-quimper. com; adult/child €5/free)* or simply visit the shop to purchase some beautiful hand-painted *faïences* (ceramics). This is where you can find the original Breton bowl, also known as the *bol à oreilles* (bowl with ears), which is typically painted with the name of its owner – a great souvenir or gift to bring back. You'll notice the *bol à oreilles* is now reproduced *en masse* and sold in many shops across the region; in most cases you can place an order for a specific name if you can't find it readily available. For more, you can stop by the **Musée de la Faïence** *(Pottery Museum; musee-faience-quimper.com; adult/child €5/3)*, also open April to September, before finishing off with a relaxed drink at one of the riverside bars on **Place du Stivel**.

DRINKING IN QUIMPER: OUR PICKS

Le Ceili: Dark but cosy Breton pub and a local favourite, with bar games and a programme of evening events. *11am-1am Mon-Fri, from 5pm Sat & Sun*

Only Bears: Vibey beer hall on place au Beurre offering a large selection of drinks and some options to snack. *hours vary*

Le Bistrot de la Cathédrale: Unpretentious spot for simple food and drinks, and a large terrace with a fantastic view of Quimper's cathedral. *7.30am-11pm Mon-Sat*

Ty Mousse Kempe: Relaxed spot to hang out with the locals in Locmaria, with a sunny terrace overlooking the river. *hours vary*

Beyond Quimper

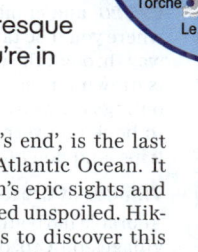

Stunning hikes by the ocean, picturesque villages and delicious seafood: you're in good hands, Finistère has it all.

Finistère, which literally means 'the land's end', is the last stop before facing the immensity of the Atlantic Ocean. It is an evocative name that teases the region's epic sights and rugged coastline, which has largely remained unspoiled. Hiking enthusiasts will find countless options to discover this beautiful landscape, without ever tiring of its theatrical panoramas that, particularly on a stormy day, give out an end-of-the-world atmosphere.

That is not to say, however, that you cannot find a diversity of sights and experiences in the region. From the fishing ports of Le Pays Bigouden (Bigouden Country) to visiting artists' galleries in Pont-Aven and learning about the neo-druidic movement in Locronan – there is a huge variety of day trips and longer stays on offer in Quimper's surroundings.

Places
Crozon Peninsula p291
Pointe du Raz p292
Le Guilvinec p293
Pointe de la Torche p294
Pont-Aven p296
Locronan p296

Crozon Peninsula
TIME FROM QUIMPER: 1HR 10MIN

Hike the GR34

The section of the GR34 footpath that runs along Crozon Peninsula is one of the most sought-after in Brittany – well-deserved fame that can be attributed to the jaw-dropping scenery it offers, featuring dizzying cliffs, sandy beaches, pine forests, mysterious grottos and colourful heathland. Walking is by far the best way to make the most of the area and you can simply hike the peninsula's entire coastal path, which takes about a week.

There are plenty of other options if you have less time, since you can hop in and out of the GR34 at pretty much any point. South of the peninsula, for instance, you can start at the famous **Cap de la Chèvre**, with its 80m-high windswept cliffs and 180-degree view of the sea. Walk up towards **Plage de la Palue** on the Atlantic-facing coast, before crossing through the hamlet of **Kerroux** to catch the GR34 on the eastern side, back to your starting point. Where the coast faces the immense **Baie de Douarnenez**, it puts on Mediterranean colours – with dense pine forests and plenty of emerald creeks. It's a similar atmosphere on the popular **Ty ar C'huré walk** from **Morgat** to the idyllic **Plage de l'Île Vierge**. Expect crowds in the summer, and keep in mind that the beach had to shut recently due to safety issues incurred by overtourism. There

GETTING AROUND

Quimper is ideally located at the heart of southern Finistère, meaning that it is geographically close to most other points you might want to explore in the region. Bus links exist to some towns and villages like Le Guilvinec and Locronan, but are not practical if you are hoping to get around remote areas like Crozon Peninsula and Pointe du Raz. Driving around will let you discover a lot more, more easily.

TOP SPOTS ON THE GR34

Sandrine Péron is an artist and engraver based in Brest, who spends every summer in the Cité d'Artistes in Camaret-sur-Mer. These are her favourite spots on the GR34 footpath. *sandrineperon.com*

Le Sillon des Anglais ('the furrow of the English') is a strip of stones between the forest and the harbour; peculiar atmosphere and aesthetic.

Pointe de Cornouaille offers a leap into military defence history, set against a scenery that invites you to conquer the harbour.

Anse de Pen Hat leaves you speechless, facing its unspoiled beauty; both soft and raw, loud and peaceful, it is a real mix of emotions.

Plage de Lostmarc'h, between sand and heath, is a must-see for any nature lover and for surfers.

are many alternatives that are less busy, such as **Pointe du Grand Grouin**, **Pointe du Toulinguet**, **Pointe de Pen-Hir** and **Plage de Veryac'h**, all some of the peninsula's most remarkable spots.

Crozon from the sea

Always dreamt of learning how to set the sails and steer a boat? In **Camaret-sur-Mer**, one of the main villages on Crozon Peninsula, you can book a boat trip from April to October with **Le Grand Bleu** *(legrandbleu.bzh; adult/child from €25/20)* and climb aboard a traditional wooden sailing boat where you'll be taught how to manoeuvre while making your way through the waters north of the peninsula. The itinerary is drawn on the day, depending on weather conditions, and outings range from 1½ hours to seven hours, with the option to book an overnight stay. Check the website for upcoming trips, and don't forget to bring sun cream.

Villages of Crozon

Adorable harbours and a slower pace of life await in the small villages on Crozon Peninsula. Stroll around the **Cité d'Artistes** (the artists' district) in colourful **Camaret-sur-Mer** to the north, where dozens of artists, inspired by the beautiful nature around, have established galleries. Photographers, painters, jewellers and sculptors abound, providing plenty of opportunities to bring back a unique souvenir. In **Morgat** (p291) in the south, a lively seafront awaits, filled with bars and restaurants overlooking the beach. A short walk will take you to **Plage du Kador**, another atmospheric, intimate beach just outside the town centre. Even the tiny port village **Le Fret** has a small selection of cool bars and restaurants sitting on the harbour. And of course, no village in Crozon has any shortage of delicious food options, with most restaurants focusing on fresh local produce.

Pointe du Raz

TIME FROM QUIMPER: 1HR

Stand at the world's end

One can only feel small when contemplating the immensity of the Atlantic Ocean from the famous Pointe du Raz. **Phare de la Vieille** stands in the distance – a worldly symbol for the dangerous environment surrounding the lighthouse. As one of Brittany's westernmost points, this is a prime location for glorious sunset views. Walk along the coast to **Pointe du Van**,

---

 EATING IN CROZON PENINSULA: RESTAURANTS WITH A VIEW

Chez Germaine: Lively crêperie and bar facing Plage de Veryac'h for a drink and a relaxed meal. Probably one of the most remote spots in Crozon. *noon-10pm Wed-Sun* €

Le Korrigan: Salads, burgers, local fish and meats, and homemade desserts in a postcard-worthy restaurant on top of Plage de Postolonnec. *noon-2pm & 7-10.30pm Thu-Mon* €

Les Yeux dans l'Eau: Cosy restaurant and wine bar offering pizzas and Breton-inspired dishes on the small port of Le Fret. *noon-2pm & 7-9pm Fri & Sat, noon-3pm Sun* €

Bar Restaurant de la Cale: An authentic menu and hearty portions in a peaceful setting facing the sea, with a sunny terrace. *9.30am-2.30pm Thu-Tue; 6-11pm Thu-Sun* €€

Fishing boats, Le Guilvinec

about 1½ hours away, to take in the scenery. Or you can get stuck right in: **Baie des Trépassés**, which sits between Raz and Van, is a local surfing and bodyboarding spot. You can easily rent equipment and organise a class with **ESB Surf School** (esb-audierne.com) in July and August, but make sure you call ahead outside of the high season.

Le Guilvinec
Return from the sea

TIME FROM QUIMPER: **35MIN**

Almost every day between 4pm and 5pm in Le Guilvinec, France's third-largest fishing port, dozens of fishing boats return after spending about 12 hours at sea. Watch this fascinating ballet from the rooftop terrace of **Haliotika**, a centre dedicated to the town's fishing industry, where you'll find the best view of the port entrance and of the fishermen unloading their catch. The fish are immediately auctioned at the *criée* underneath the terrace, which you can tour in real-time with a Haliotika guide *(haliotika.com; adult/child €14.90/9.90)*.

Tours are in French but a leaflet can be provided in different languages. The tour ticket includes entrance to Haliotika's

WHY I LOVE FINISTÈRE

Daphné Leprince-Ringuet, Lonely Planet writer

Finistère is where Brittany's reputation as the land of legends truly comes alive. It is easy to picture why it has inspired so many myths when walking on the coast, facing thousands of kilometres of mysterious, dangerous, unpredictable ocean waters. Perhaps thanks to the awe and wonder inspired by its rugged cliffs, dramatic waves and occasionally furious skies, the region remains mostly untouched – meaning that you truly get the chance to soak up the spectacle. Granted, the water's not so warm, and you may need to pack a few jumpers on top of your swimming costume. But the exhilarating sights and experiences you will get here are worth the extra layers.

Don't miss the homemade salted caramel

🍴 EATING IN CROZON PENINSULA: OUR PICKS

Crêperie de la Marine: Simple but delicious crêpes and *galettes* in a cosy restaurant with a terrace facing the port of Camaret-sur-Mer. *10.30am-10pm* €

La Terrible Bistro-Librairie: Artsy bistro and bookshop in Camaret-sur-Mer offering tasty food and putting on regular events throughout the year. *hours vary* €

Cantine et Canons: Refined dishes based on local produce and organic ingredients, with an extensive wine menu. *noon-1.30pm Fri-Tue, 7-9pm Fri-Tue & Thu* €€

Sovaj: A welcoming bar and restaurant with a homemade lunch menu and tasty snacking options throughout the rest of the day. *noon-midnight Sun-Thu, to 1am Fri & Sat* €

SEAL SPOTTING

Annette Lahaye-Collomb, a sailor, writer and artist based in Finistère, shares one of her favourite sea trips. *anetteproductions.fr*

Out at sea in front of Penmarc'h, there is a rock formation called *étocs*. Make your way to the **Port du Guilvinec** to climb aboard the **Soizen** boats *(soizen.fr; adult/child €22/16)*, which offer a discovery tour of the grey seal colony inhabiting this rocky archipelago. The tour is respectful of the gentleness of the spot: the motor runs idle as you glide over transparent waters – perfectly described by the Breton word *glaz*, which means blue or green. The seals are only a few metres from the boat, sheepishly poking out of the water. You will find yourself moved by the quiet beauty, where sunlight plays with the ocean blues.

Plage de la Torche

museum, which has recreated the inside of a trawler, and where you'll learn about the tough day-to-day life of fishermen. Once your seafood cravings start kicking in, indulge in some ultra-local produce at the terrace's bar **L'Hannexe**, which specialises in langoustines, a local delicacy in Le Guilvinec.

Pointe de la Torche

TIME FROM QUIMPER: **35MIN**

World-famous surfing spot

Pointe de la Torche, a rocky spur that stands at the southern tip of **Baie d'Audierne**, separates the 2km-long, ocean-facing **Plage de la Torche** from the more sheltered **Plage de Pors Carn**. Visit in the summer and you will find yourself among campers and vans featuring plate numbers from around the world. Exposed to the ocean waves, the area's beaches attract surfers year-round and are particularly popular on sunny days. You'll find plenty of options on site to rent surfing equipment and book classes, but be mindful that strict safety rules are in place due to the frequently dangerous conditions, and that swimming is regulated.

EATING IN PAYS BIGOUDEN: OUR PICKS

Le Poisson d'Avril: Creative takes on fresh products in this unpretentious restaurant sitting on the Port du Guilvinec. *noon-2pm Wed-Sun, 7-9.30pm Wed-Sat* €€

An Atoll: Lobster and (practically) only lobster in a dreamy location overlooking the beach. *noon-1.30pm Tue-Sun, 7-9pm Tue-Sat* €€

Restaurant Les Rochers: Huge windows facing the famous rocks of St-Guénolé, plus an inventive menu largely focused on local seafood. *noon-2pm & 7-9pm Thu-Tue* €€

Chez Marie-Cath: Hearty menu portions featuring the famous *kouign bigouden* (pancakes) in a relaxed atmosphere near Plage de Pors Carn. *11am-midnight* €€

FISHING TOWN HOPPING BY BIKE

Pays Bigouden makes for a lovely cycle through sandy beaches, romantic dunes and small port villages – while never straying far from the best seafood.

START	END	LENGTH
Le Guilvinec	Le Guilvinec	28km; 2½hrs

Start in ❶ **Le Guilvinec** (p293). From ❷ **Haliotika** (p293), follow the signs for the *plages* in **rue de Men-Meur** and keep going until you reach the start of **chemin des Communaux** on your left, a bike lane that runs along ❸ **Plage de la Grève Blanche**. When you reach the end of the path (after about 800m), take a left then right to stay on the car-free trail. You'll see signs indicating the road is shared with pedestrians. You'll be cycling uninterrupted through the dunes along the beautiful ❹ **Plage du Stêr** until you reach the small port of ❺ **Kerity**. From there, you'll see signs for the V45 cycle route; follow them along **rue de la Corniche**.

See the tall lighthouse in the distance? It's the ❻ **Phare d'Eckmühl**, which you're aiming for. Start noticing how sandy beaches are giving way to a rocky coastline. After you've passed the lighthouse, follow the V45 along the coast heading for the port town of ❼ **St-Guénolé**. It's worth pushing an extra 2km on the V45 to ❽ **Plage de Pors Carn**, to mingle with the surfers at ❾ **Chez Marie-Cath** and watch Pointe de la Torche making its way into the ocean in the distance. Head back towards St-Guénolé where, at the end of rue des Jonquilles, you'll find the start of a 7.5km green lane taking you directly back to Le Guilvinec.

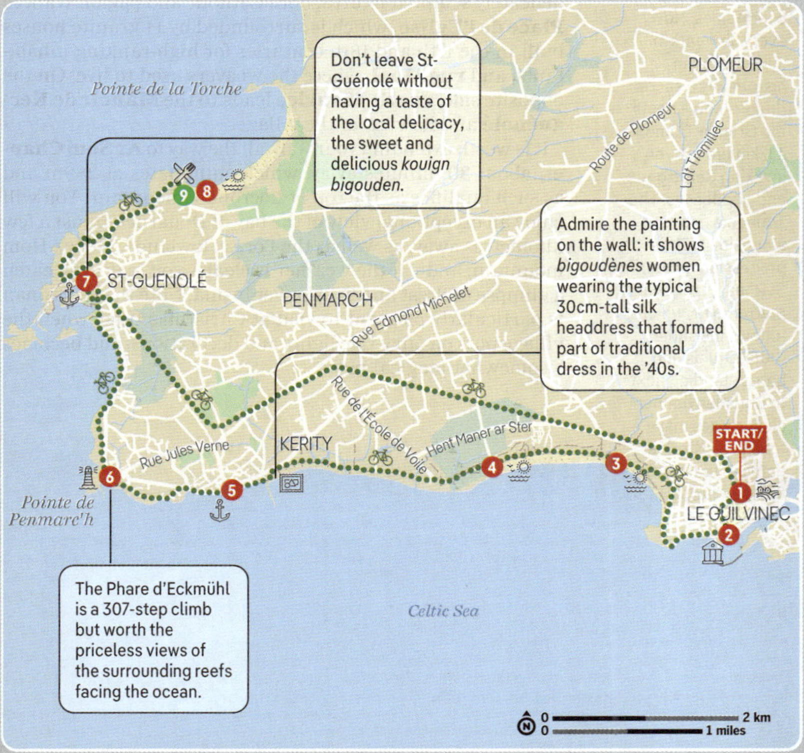

Don't leave St-Guénolé without having a taste of the local delicacy, the sweet and delicious *kouign bigouden*.

Admire the painting on the wall: it shows *bigoudènes* women wearing the typical 30cm-tall silk headdress that formed part of traditional dress in the '40s.

The Phare d'Eckmühl is a 307-step climb but worth the priceless views of the surrounding reefs facing the ocean.

BRITTANY'S DRUIDIC REVIVAL

Like its Celtic neighbours, Brittany was a land of druids before it was Christianised. At the start of the 20th century, inspired by Welsh neo-druidic movements, the Gorsedd of Brittany was created as an organisation bringing together druidic devotees under the authority of the Grand Druid of Brittany. The Gorsedd established and re-established many rituals and ceremonies. Now, every six years in July, Locronan – historically a sacred druidic land – hosts the Grande Troménie, a 12km procession invoking Celtic gods and goddesses. The Troménie happens alongside a Christian procession honouring St Ronan, Locronan's patron saint, which follows the same route. Druids and bards standing next to Christian banners and crosses make for a live historical timeline that attracts thousands of visitors.

Pont-Aven

TIME FROM QUIMPER: **30MIN**

A real-life Gauguin painting

At the end of the 19th century, suffocated and uninspired by Paris, Paul Gauguin settled in the small village of Pont-Aven, which quickly became the place to be for young painters such as Émile Bernard, Paul Sérusier and Henry Moret. It is easy to see, while walking through the village's streets listening to the nearby Aven River's soft hum and smelling the fragrant wisteria, why Pont-Aven was so inspiring. The town is now packed with artists' galleries and the reputable **Musée de Pont-Aven** is well worth a visit. Wander around *flâneur*-style to soak up the atmosphere and don't leave without a few boxes of *galettes* and *palets*, Pont-Aven's famous butter biscuits (not to be confused with Brittany's quintessential buckwheat-based *galettes*).

Locronan

TIME FROM QUIMPER: **25MIN**

Take a step back in time

The village of Locronan seems to have remained untouched since the 16th century, when it gained fame and prosperity thanks to the production of sailcloth. You will be greeted by magnificent, dark granite houses, many of which display delicately sculpted figures, both Catholic and pagan. Walk to **Place de l'Église**, which is surrounded by 14 granite houses built in the 17th and 18th centuries for high-ranking inhabitants, and **rue Moal**, where the weavers used to live. On the opposite side, **rue St-Maurice** leads to the **Manoir de Kerguénolé** and its view of the village.

It is worth extending your walk all the way to **Ar Sonj Chapel,** about 30 minutes away, which culminates at 289m and as such qualifies as the top of Locronan 'mountain'. You will enjoy an exceptional view of the bay of Douarnenez just a few kilometres away, as well as the Porzay lowlands, Ménez-Hom mountain, and – if the weather is clear – you may even catch a glimpse of Brest and Crozon Peninsula. Note that Locronan is particularly pleasant to visit at Christmas time, when the village puts on fairy-tale lights and decorations, and becomes a somewhat magical place.

Vannes

UNSPOILED ISLANDS | SLOWER PACE | SANDY BEACHES

Unassumingly overlooking the Golfe du Morbihan, Vannes sits on centuries of palpitating history, a rich heritage that comes alive in its winding streets lined by half-timbered houses and mansions, its charming cobbled squares and its imposing fortifications proudly resisting the passage of time. A major town in the Middle Ages, Vannes was particularly prized by the Dukes of Brittany, witnessing one of the most significant turning points in the history of the region in 1532 as the treaty uniting Brittany to the Kingdom of France was signed – also unofficially known as the end of Breton freedom.

Today Vannes has become a hearty, friendly city, adored by its inhabitants whose tranquil enjoyment of life is contagious. You will find students, young professionals, families and older people who are always willing to give Vannes' many visitors a warm welcome, while not losing a trace of their irreducible attachment to Breton identity.

Creative Takes on Breton Food
Lunch at Halles des Lices

Open Tuesday to Sunday until 2pm, Vannes' **Halles des Lices** food court is the place to see and be seen. Located on place des Lices, a large public square in the centre that is always busy with cafes and restaurants, the *halles* offer appetising produce from local farms, street-food vendors, creative takes on traditional food – think sausage-stuffed samosas made with *galettes* – and plenty of seating areas to grab a glass of wine while you try a bit of everything. Once you have satisfactorily gorged on cheeses, charcuteries and organic wines, order a coffee to take away and go for a digestive walk in the nearby **Jardins des Remparts** – a lovely flowery garden from where you'll catch the best view of the city walls.

GETTING AROUND

Most parts of Vannes' centre are pedestrianised, meaning that if you are driving, you'll be better off using one of the car parks dotted around the surrounding areas. Walking distances outside of the centre can get long – the **train station** is a 20-minute walk away and the **Gare Maritime** (ferry terminal) is another 30 minutes – but Vannes has an excellent bus network operated by Kicéo (*kiceo.fr*) with lines running regularly every day.

☑ TOP TIP

There aren't many hotels in Vannes' historic centre. If you like being at the heart of the action, it's worth checking alternative options on Airbnb.

- ⭐ **HIGHLIGHTS**
- 1 Halles des Lices
- 2 Port de Vannes
- 3 Vannes et Sa Femme
- 🔴 **SIGHTS**
- 4 Eglise St-Patern
- 5 Jardins des Remparts
- 6 Porte St-Vincent
- 7 St-Patern
- ⚫ **SLEEPING**
- 8 Hôtel Le Bretagne
- 9 Le Roscanvec
- 10 Maison de la Garenne & Spa
- 🟢 **EATING**
- 11 Boulangerie Pain Grillé
- 12 Chez François
- 13 Crêperie St-Guenhaël
- 14 Derrière
- 15 Gourmandise et Sucre Grain
- 16 L'Antidote
- 17 L'Atelier Bistrot
- see 1 Tous Dans le Pétrin
- 🟢 **DRINKING & NIGHTLIFE**
- 18 Bar Chez Fred
- 19 Bar les Z'oubliettes
- 20 Les Valseuses
- 🔴 **SHOPPING**
- 21 Brûlerie St-Patern
- 22 La Yamouna

The Montmartre of Vannes

Hang out in St-Patern

North-east of Vannes' medieval centre is where you'll find **St-Patern**, technically the oldest part of town, a district located where the Romans first founded a city in the 1st century BCE. Nowadays St-Patern is a popular local hangout, filled with bars and restaurants lining hilly streets around the main church **Église St-Patern** – which has caused some to nickname the area the 'Montmartre of Vannes'. Pay a visit to some of the iconic shops in the district, such as **Brûlerie St-Patern**, a coffee roaster and cafe, and second-hand bookshop **La Yamouna**, also known as 'Chez Stéphane' after the owner. In the evening, St-Patern truly comes alive as it fills up

Half-timbered houses, Vannes

with *vannetais* coming out for a drink – a great stop to soak up the relaxed and laid-back lifestyle of the city.

A Day Trip to the Beach
Sunbathe at Conleau Peninsula

Although the city centre is slightly further inland, Vannes stretches all the way to the top of the Golfe du Morbihan, where you'll find **Conleau Peninsula** and its beach. From **Pointe des Emigrés**, you can catch the start of promenade Paul Chapel – a 45-minute walk to the peninsula featuring dense pine tree forests on the right and lovely views of the river on the left. With its cafes and restaurants, seawater swimming pool and beach, Conleau is popular with local residents in the summer months, so expect some crowds if you are visiting in the high season. The coastal footpath goes all the way around the peninsula, with views of the small port of **Port-Anna** in Séné on the other side of the river, and – for a taster of Breton culture – past the famous street-art piece *Breton un jour, Français jamais* ('once a Breton, never a Frenchman') that decorates the wall opposite the seawater pool.

BRETON PASTRIES

Brittany is mostly known for its crêpes and *galettes*, but pastries are not to be outdone. And they are not for the faint-hearted, typically requiring heaps of salted butter – another Breton speciality and a matter of regional pride and identity. As one B&B host once put it to me: 'Frankly, I don't see the point of unsalted butter.' Among the must-have desserts you should try, you'll find *kouign amann*, a warm pastry made with laminated dough that is caramelised, which contains equal parts sugar, flour and butter. *Far breton* is a flan-like cake that you can have on its own or stuffed with prunes. *Gâteau breton*, for its part, is a generous shortbread biscuit that is best enjoyed when filled with salted caramel.

 EATING IN VANNES: BEST BRETON PASTRIES

Chez François: A small but hugely popular stall on place des Lices serving *kouign amann* and various Breton cakes to take away. *10am-7pm Tue-Sun €*

Boulangerie Pain Grillé: Off-the-beaten-track bakery and coffee shop in St-Patern district offering modern takes on traditional pastries. *8am-2pm & 4-7pm Tue-Fri, 8am-6pm Sat €*

Tous Dans le Pétrin: One of a few bakeries in Halle des Lices, which boasts an award-winning *kouign amann*. *8am-2pm Tue-Sun €*

Gourmandise et Sucre Grain: A traditional bakery near the port that is famous across Vannes for its *kouign amann*. *8am-7pm Tue-Sun €*

VANNES ET SA FEMME

As you wander through Vannes' historic centre, don't miss **Vannes et Sa Femme** (Vannes and his wife) – one of the most emblematic representations of the city. Poking out of a medieval house at the intersection of rue Bienheureux-Pierre-René-Rogue and rue Noë, the granite sculpture shows a man and a woman happily greeting visitors, and is thought to go back to the 16th century. Multiple theories exist regarding its origins: some theorise the sculpture used to mark the entrance of a cabaret, others that it belonged to a local family, the Vennes, who were known to have lived in the area, and who may with time have become the Vannes.

Vannes et Sa Femme

Golden Hour on the Port
Apéro with the *vannetais*

Cross **Porte St-Vincent**, the main entrance to the city that was originally built in the 16th century, and you will immediately be met with the hustle and bustle of the **Port de Vannes**. Bars, cafes and restaurants abound, lining both sides of the Marle River over a few hundred metres. You'll find the port buzzing with activity at most times of the day, but it's when the sun starts setting that the real action begins. For some serious *apéro* time, head to **La Traverse** *(linktr.ee/latraverserivegauche)*, a bar and cultural centre on the left bank with a huge terrace overlooking the river, which has become a staple of Vannes' artistic scene over the past few years.

 EATING & DRINKING IN VANNES: OUR PICKS

L'Antidote: Beautiful setting and chic eating with a reasonably priced lunch menu and evening plates to share. *10am-11pm Tue-Sun* €€

L'Atelier Bistrot: Mains for lunch and *apéro*-style tapas and *planches* (platters) in the evening. A friendly spot with a terrace in the historic centre. *hours vary* €

Crêperie St-Guenhaël: A classic crêperie also offering Breton tapas, tucked in a medieval house with a dark, atmospheric room downstairs. *noon-2.30pm & 7-9pm Tue-Sat* €

Derrière: A refined menu with modern twists on Breton ingredients, with friendly and welcoming service. *10am-2.30pm & 6pm-midnight Tue-Sat* €€

La Traverse: A cultural space supporting emerging artists doubling as a bar, making for a quirky spot for a drink at the port. *4pm-midnight Wed-Sun, to 1am Sat*

Les Valseuses: A local favourite. Karaoke nights, live music, bar service and an enthusiastic student crowd. *4pm-2am Tue-Sun*

Bar Chez Fred: Wine bar with a terrace on place des Lices, offering meat and fish *planches* (platters) made with local produce. *hours vary*

Bar les Z'oubliettes: No-fuss bar beautifully nestled in the city walls with a simple food menu and weekend events. *hours vary*

Beyond Vannes

The sea-facing Morbihan region lives at the pace of winds and tides. Expect salty hair and seafood aplenty.

'Mor' (Breton for 'sea') and *'bihan'* (small). The region's very name refers to the 'small sea' enclosed in the gulf, which often takes the spotlight. It's easy to see why: within a 20km stretch of water, you'll find countless islands, medieval port villages, quiet beaches and salt marshes. Protected from the Atlantic Ocean, the gulf is a place of tranquil waters and peaceful coastlines – but as with everywhere in Brittany, you're never far from dramatic scenery. Outside of the gulf to the west, Quiberon Peninsula stares directly at the Atlantic, offering dazzling views of the windswept coast. To the east on the ocean side, Rhuys Peninsula is lined with interminable sandy beaches inviting you in for a walk.

Places
Île-aux-Moines p301
Auray p302
St-Armel p302
St-Gildas-de-Rhuys p303
Carnac p303
Rochefort-en-Terre p304
Quiberon Peninsula p306

Île-aux-Moines
TIME FROM VANNES: **50MIN** 🚌 + ⛴

Tour the 'Pearl of the Gulf'
The 7km-long Île-aux-Moines, also known as the 'Pearl of the Gulf', is the largest island in the Golfe du Morbihan and a pleasant destination for a day trip. Make your way to the **ferry terminal** in the small village of Port-Blanc, where you'll catch a five-minute boat ride to the island. Boats depart daily every 30 minutes and don't need to be booked in advance *(izenah-croisieres.com/liaisons-regulieres; adult/child €6.60/4.20)*.

When you arrive, follow the road signs for the green path, a 2km walk that will take you to **Le Bourg**, the island's main town; on the way, you can stop on the popular **Plage du Dréhen** with its multicoloured cabins. You'll find restaurants, crêperies and cafes in town, which is also the start of several itineraries signposted based on different colours.

GETTING AROUND

With buses and trains, you'll be able to reach most towns around the Golfe du Morbihan from Vannes. The city's **Gare Maritime** (p297) (ferry terminal) also has links to many islands – including Belle-Île-en-Mer – although they are much more frequent in the summer months.

Venturing further, however, could quickly cause some scheduling headaches. Driving will let you explore places like Quiberon Peninsula, Carnac, Rhuys Peninsula and Rochefort-en-Terre in more depth and with less stress.

Following the blue itinerary will take you to the southern tip of the island. Enjoy the dense vegetation of pine trees, palm trees and eucalyptus, and colourful camellias and mimosas, as you walk past millennia-old megaliths, small beaches and quiet coves. After 1½ hours of walking, you'll reach **Pointe de Nioul**, where you'll find an unobstructed view of the gulf. Return using the coastal footpath – it isn't signposted but the trail runs around the whole island. Make sure you check how late boat transfers back to Port-Blanc run, as this can change through the year.

Auray
TIME FROM VANNES: **20MIN**
Unwind in the cutest medieval port
In Auray, a small village nestled on the river of the same name, the impeccably preserved 15th-century **Port de St-Goustan** reveals itself at the bottom of rue du Château, a narrow cobbled street lined with flowery stone houses and artisan shops, which links to the upper side of town. Cross the vaulted stone bridge to place St-Sauveur and sit down at one of the many cafes to soak up the surreal atmosphere of a place suspended in time.

St-Armel
TIME FROM VANNES: **15MIN**
Salt marshes and a near-desert island
Salt farming in the region can be traced back to the 15th century, and the **Marais Salants de Lasné** (salt marshes) next to the town of St-Armel were built in the 17th century. Today, a section of the marshes is owned by salt worker Nathalie Krone; another part is used for oyster farming, and a third one has been kept as a quiet zone for the multitudes of migratory birds that can be spotted year-round across the site. Krone organises guided tours in French throughout the year to explain the fascinating and complex process of salt farming *(lapaludieredugolfe.fr/la-paludiere-du-golfe-visite; adult/child €7.50/6.50)*.

You can also walk through the marshes yourself, staying on the dedicated roads, to take in the tranquil atmosphere of the site – perhaps even spotting some lapwings, brant geese and spoonbills. If the tide is low, walk to **Île Tascon**, a small island you can tour in about one hour, which counts only eight residents, one farm and plenty of stunning views of the gulf. When you're back in St-Armel, reward yourself at **Le Moulin**

THE ISLANDS OF MORBIHAN

Old Breton legends say that the fairies of Brocéliande forest, chased from their home, cried so many tears that they created the Golfe du Morbihan. They threw flower wreaths in the gulf and created as many islands as there are days in the year. Official counts – between 40 and 60 islands – contradict the original version, but there is plenty to explore. **Île-aux-Moines** (p301) is the largest, but from Vannes you can also jump on a ferry direct to **Île d'Arz**. **Île Tascon** and **Île Berder** can be accessed when the tide is low. Feeling more adventurous? **Varec'h Kayak** in Baden offers two- and three-hour tours around nearby islets, so you can take it all in from the sea.

 EATING IN AURAY: OUR PICKS

Crêperie St-Sauveur: A crêperie tucked in a medieval house hidden behind the port, with an original menu and a small shop with local delicacies. *noon-1.30pm & 7-8.30pm Thu-Mon* €

Billig Café: A self-described 'modern crêperie' on the quieter side of the port, offering a no-fuss menu that also includes *planches* (platters). *hours vary* €

La Fromentine: Elegant restaurant with retro decor in the pedestrianised rue du Château serving classic French dishes. *hours vary* €

Merlot L'Enchanteur: Wine bar and bistro with a relaxed terrace on a cute medieval square in the upper side of town. *10am-9pm Tue-Sat* €€

Port de St-Goustan

à **Café** with a *gochtial* – a half-bread, half-brioche that was born in the town and has become a famous delicacy across the gulf. It's also one of the few spots where you can purchase a bag of salt produced in the marshes.

St-Gildas-de-Rhuys
TIME FROM VANNES: 30MIN

Beach day on the Atlantic side
Trade the peaceful stillness of the waters inside the Golfe du Morbihan for the sandy, windy, oceanic beaches and dunes spreading along the Atlantic side of Rhuys Peninsula. You'll be spoilt for choice, but a good place to start is near the village of **St-Gildas-de-Rhuys** on **Plage des Govelins**, where a good number of *vannetais* like to spend the day on a sunny weekend. Further east in the commune of **Sarzeau**, you'll find other big hits like **Plage du Beg Lann**, made of pebbles and crushed shells, and **Plage de St-Jacques**, one of the finest sandy beaches in the region.

Carnac
TIME FROM VANNES: 35MIN

A millennium-old enigma
About 3000 megaliths, the vast majority of which are standing stones (also known as menhirs), are found in Carnac over

BEST BEACHES IN RHUYS PENINSULA

Plage de Port-Navalo, Arzon: At the entrance of the gulf, a beautiful beach under the trees. Extremely popular in summer due to its proximity to Port-Navalo's bars and restaurants.

Plage du Fogeo, Arzon: Family-friendly sandy beach and turquoise waters, with a sailing school that offers rentals for the day.

Plage de Port-Maria, St-Gildas-de-Rhuys: Cosy, quiet beach that never gets too busy, even in summer. Note that swimming is not supervised.

Plage du Kerver, St-Gildas-de-Rhuys: Long sandy beach stretching all the way to Arzon facing west. Perfect for a long walk at sunset.

Plage de Suscinio, Sarzeau: Tricky to park but worth the effort. Huge, unspoiled beach facing the Atlantic and overlooked by a castle.

 EATING IN RHUYS PENINSULA: BEST OYSTERS

Les Viviers du Logeo: Oyster farm and bar with a sunny terrace overlooking the gulf, with a view of Île aux Moines. *hours vary* €

La Cabane à Milo: Fresh oysters, prawns, shellfish and fish *rillettes* (a paste-like spread) facing the sea, and a comprehensive white wine menu. *hours vary* €

Les Viviers du Ruault: Award-winning oysters to taste in the sun in the farm's relaxed eatery by the water. *9.30am-1pm & 4-7pm, Mon-Sat, 9.30am-1pm Sun* €

La Belle d'Ilur: Near Vannes, oyster tastings as well as seafood, fish soup and fish *rillettes*. Beautiful outside seating and a cosy inside room for rainy days. *11am-9pm* €

LAND OF MEGALITHS

Although the alignments in Carnac are particularly impressive, they are not the only megaliths around. In fact, the south of Morbihan is a renowned megalithic hot spot, with up to 550 sites registered so far. Get your hands on the *pass mégalithes*, which will give you discounted access to five key megalithic points of interest in the area. They include the **Carnac Alignments**, the **Musée de la Préhistoire** in Carnac, **Cairn de Petit Mont** in Arzon, **Cairn de Gavrinis** on the eponymous island and the **Locmariaquer Megaliths,** with its star 20m-high menhir which has now broken into four enormous pieces. You can ask for the pass at any of these locations upon payment of the full fee for your first visit.

Carnac megaliths

a distance of 4km – the highest concentration in the world, dating back to the 5th century BCE and an unmissable experience for any history enthusiast. Access to the dedicated footpaths that run alongside the alignments is free and you can wander autonomously, following one of the provided itineraries; it takes two hours to loop the entire site.

The **Maison des Mégalithes** at the entrance of the site provides useful context to start your visit, but it is worth booking a guided tour *(menhirs-carnac.fr; adult/child €13/6)*, which will take you through a small section inside the alignments with explanations about the historical background and techniques employed to lift the stones, as well as the different hypotheses that could explain this as-yet unresolved mystery. Note that tours are a lot more frequent in the summer months, and from May to September can be booked in English.

Rochefort-en-Terre

TIME FROM VANNES: **35MIN**

Lunch in a picture-perfect village

The 12th-century village of Rochefort-en-Terre sits proudly at the top of a hill with adorably flowered half-timbered houses lining slopey streets. Behind the stone façades brightened by colourful geraniums and climbing ivy, you'll often find the

EATING IN ROCHEFORT-EN-TERRE: OUR PICKS

Café Breton: A rustic bistro in a 16th-century building offering seasonal crêpes and *galettes*, as well as a small food menu. *9am-9pm* €€

L'Art Gourmand: Retro cafe (p306) offering savoury snacks but mostly known for its extensive choice of homemade cakes and biscuits. *9am-7pm Tue-Sun, 2pm-7pm Mon* €

Café Crêperie La Terrasse: Delicious *galettes* and friendly service in a small restaurant with a hidden garden at the back. *hours vary* €

Maison Cachée: Bistronomy and ultra-local eating at a reasonable price in one of the most sought-after restaurants in the region. *12.15pm-1.15pm & 7.15-9.30pm Thu-Sat; 12.15pm-1.30pm Sun* €€

TOP EXPERIENCE

Belle-Île-en-Mer

Aptly named 'beautiful island', Belle-Île-en-Mer boasts some of Brittany's most renowned landscapes: peaceful countryside fields and chaotic rocky coastlines, interspersed with picturesque port villages. The island seduced famous artists like Claude Monet, who in 1886 stayed for 10 weeks and relentlessly painted the island's galvanising scenery. Watch out for familiar seascapes like *Les Rochers de Belle-Île* and *Les Pyramides de Port-Coton*.

Aiguilles de Port Coton

Breathtaking Coastline

Belle-Île offers 85km of spectacular coastline – picture dark shredded rocks dramatically withstanding ocean waves – that is walkable in four to five days on the GR340 footpath. There are also dedicated cycling routes across the island and main roads for cars. Hop on and off your vehicle to reach the footpath, where you'll be sure to witness some wonderful sights.

Famous Spots

To find the most jaw-dropping spots, follow the famous people. The mystical **Pointe des Poulains**, a solitary lighthouse overlooking the cliffs, offers one of the most epic panoramas on the island. It's also where French actress Sarah Bernhardt acquired a military **fort**. **Aiguilles de Port Coton**, a stack of pointed rocks stunningly emerging from the ocean, was painted by Monet. Not far, **Plage de Donnant** makes for a mesmerising spectacle of huge waves crashing into the sandy beach.

Villages of Belle-Île

Belle-Île's main town **Le Palais** is an archetypal sailor's den that turns enjoyably rowdy in the summer evenings. But it's also worth making your way to the colourful port of **Sauzon**, a 10-minute drive away, to bask in its peaceful atmosphere and delicious seafood.

TOP TIPS

● Schedule at least one night in Belle-Île to explore all its wonders.

● Pay extra to bring your car or bike on the ferry, or use one of the rental options in Le Palais.

● Steep hills and strong winds make for a tough cycle. Rent an electric bike or moped.

PRACTICALITIES

● oceane.breizhgo.bzh/line/belle-ile-en-mer ● return ticket adult/child €40.70/23.20
● year-round from **Gare Maritime de Quiberon**; Apr-Oct to Vannes, Port Navalo, Le Croisic and La Turballe

BEST BEACHES IN QUIBERON PENINSULA

Plage du Conguel: At the far end of the peninsula, with beautiful views of Quiberon Bay. You can swim on the northern side.

Plage du Porigo: Perfect sandy beach for families, protected from wind and sunny from the morning hours. Swimming is supervised in summer.

Plage du Petit Rohu: Sandy beach on the bay side of the peninsula; doesn't get too busy even in high season.

Plage de Port Rhu: On the *côte sauvage*, this beach is hard to access but famous for unspoiled beauty. Swimming is not allowed.

Plage de Port Blanc: Another must-see on the *côte sauvage*, nestled between windswept dunes and steep cliffs. Swimming is not allowed.

workshops of artists and artisans ranging from painters to glassmakers and wood workers. The two streets that make up the centre are lined with appetising restaurants and sun-soaked terraces that quickly fill at lunchtime. Make sure you leave space for dessert: you won't resist stopping by **L'Art Gourmand**, a heavenly shop located in a 16th-century coaching inn that offers a never-ending range of cakes, chocolates, biscuits and ice cream.

Quiberon Peninsula

TIME FROM VANNES: **50MIN**

From bay to ocean

Quiberon Peninsula is divided between its Atlantic-facing western flank and its east coast, which lines Quiberon Bay, making for a range of wildly different landscapes. Sandy beaches abound on the bayside, but the opposing *côte sauvage* (wild coast) footpath is particularly prized for hiking. Head to **Quiberon**, the main town on the peninsula, and make your way to **Château Turpault**, which marks the beginning of the *côte sauvage*. The walk northward along the coastal footpath stretches for up to 12km until reaching the fishing village of Portivy. Expect rugged cliffs lashed by emerald waters, commanding *pointes* eating into the Atlantic and local wonders like **La Roche Percée** (the 'pierced rock'). From Portivy, you can return to Quiberon by bus and – only in the summer months – by train. Check timetables before you go.

Dinner with a view

As you look into the ocean from Quiberon's *côte sauvage*, you'll be pretty much facing thousands of kilometres of unobstructed Atlantic waters – meaning some of the best sunsets in the region. Sit down for a beer and a relaxed dinner in Portivy to watch the spectacle, or enjoy a gourmet dinner with a view back in Quiberon.

EATING IN QUIBERON PENINSULA: BEST SUNSETS

Le Bateau Ivre: Unpretentious restaurant practically sitting on the beach in Portivy, offering fresh seafood, crêpes, salads and *moules frites* (mussels and chips). *9.30am-1am Wed-Mon* €

Rivage: Beautiful restaurant with huge windows on Portivy, with an elegant, creative menu focusing on local seafood. *7.30-9.30pm Wed, 12.30-2.30pm & 7.30-9.30pm Thu-Mon* €€

Le Vivier: Relaxed seafood restaurant with a stunning view and terrace in the middle of the *côte sauvage*. *10.30am-10pm* €€

La Mer à Boire: Slightly outside of the hustle and bustle of Quiberon, a fancy spot with an elaborate menu facing the sea. *10am-3pm Tue, to midnight Thu-Mon* €€

Places We Love to Stay

€ Budget €€ Midrange €€€ Top End

Rennes
MAP p273

Hostel Les Chouettes € No-fuss hostel in the city centre offering private and shared rooms with views of the Vilaine, and a '100% Breton' breakfast.

Marnie & Mister H €€ A 16th-century building in the heart of the historic centre, offering five rooms tastefully decorated in British dandy style.

Castel Jolly €€ In a quieter part of town, this private mansion converted into a guesthouse sits right next to the Thabor Gardens.

Balthazar Hôtel & Spa €€ Halfway between the train station and the historical centre, a luxury experience in a boutique hotel and spa overlooking the city.

St-Malo
MAP p280

Hôtel Quic en Groigne € Quiet rooms at the heart of the historic centre, with a simple, cosy atmosphere.

Hôtel France et Chateaubriand €€ Sea-facing rooms and a panoramic restaurant, in the building where Chateaubriand was born.

Villa Ellersie €€ Tasteful decor in a historical building. Breakfast comes with an exceptional view of the sea.

Le Beaufort €€ Comfortable rooms, including some with a terrace overlooking the sea, in an elegant hotel on Plage du Sillon.

Grand Hôtel des Thermes €€€ St-Malo's most famous hotel, built in the 19th century and now offering a five-star experience with a spa and wellness centre.

Dinan

Le Logis du Jerzual €€ Rooms with a view in an old tannery located on the famous rue du Jerzual.

La Maison Pavie €€ Take a step back in time in this 15th-century mansion converted into a guest house opposite St-Sauveur basilica.

Quimper
MAP p288

Le Banellou €€ Cosy and welcoming guest house at the heart of Locmaria district in Quimper. Bookings only from two nights.

Le Château de Penfrat €€ A 20-minute drive from Quimper but worth the effort. Art deco rooms in a splendid 19th-century hunting house with a huge garden and park. Bookings only from two nights.

Crozon Peninsula

Kermaria € Elegant traditional guesthouse offering a sea view in every room and the sandy beach of Morgat at your feet.

Hôtel de France € A comfortable hotel and restaurant facing the sea, ideally located on the port of Camaret-sur-Mer.

Camping Plage de Goulien € Popular campsite just 100m from the sandy Plage de Goulien, with snacking options in the evenings and mornings.

Vannes
MAP p297

Hôtel le Bretagne € Great location for a reasonable price. Simple, quiet rooms, some with a view of the city walls.

Maison de la Garenne & Spa € Elegant and comfortable guesthouse and spa in a beautiful 19th-century mansion, with access to a flowery garden and pool.

Le Roscanvec €€€ One of the only hotels in Vannes' historic centre, Le Roscanvec offers five luxury rooms with views of the city in a 17th-century mansion.

Belle-Île-en-Mer

Grand Hôtel de Bretagne € Quiet and comfortable hotel despite sitting right on the seafront of the busy port in Le Palais.

Camping Les Grands Sables € Welcoming and pleasant campsite near the coast offering plenty of amenities including bike rentals.

Le Grand Large €€ Epic scenery from the seaview rooms in this hotel majestically facing the ocean near Aiguilles de Port-Coton.

Quiberon Peninsula

Sauvage € Open-air accommodation site right next to the beach on the bay side, offering glamping, mobile homes and camping options.

Rivage €€ Tasteful decor in a hotel and restaurant wonderfully located in the small harbour of Portivy.

Researched by
Ryan Ver Berkmoes

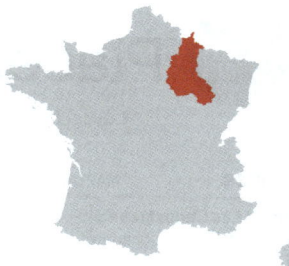

Champagne
REGION SOAKED IN HISTORY AND BUBBLY

Sprawling green vineyards, fascinating stories, compelling towns and – of course – plenty of sparkle continue to draw visitors to Champagne.

It's hard to believe now that Champagne's beloved bubbles were once thought to be a fault in the region's still wine. It wasn't until Dom Pierre Pérignon, a Benedictine monk at Hautvillers Abbey, started to master the art of winemaking that the sparkling wine began to be appreciated. 'Come quickly, I am tasting the stars!' is what he reportedly exclaimed upon tasting Champagne in 1693, and our love of the world's most famous sparkling wine has endured ever since.

For centuries, Champagne was the celebratory drink for French coronations and by the 18th century, bottles were popping at parties in British high society. Today, bubbly means 'celebration' the world over and legions of fans visit its namesake region each year to taste the magic. As F Scott Fitzgerald apparently said: 'Too much of anything is bad, but too much Champagne is just right.'

The famous Champagne houses welcome visitors to underground caverns, perfectly manicured vineyards and exquisite tasting rooms. And beyond the business of bubbly, visitors discover so much more, such as the storied city of Reims with its magnificent cathedral and culinary delights.

And even as Épernay sounds one luxurious Champagne note, other towns in the region show the diversity of the appeal. Impossibly beautiful country drives lead to places like the incomparable Troyes, an extraordinary medieval city unlike any other in France. With time, even more surprises await.

THE MAIN AREAS

REIMS
Art deco architecture and world-famous Champagne.
p312

ÉPERNAY
Home to Champagne's most famous avenue.
p318

TROYES
Lose yourself in a half-timbered wonderland.
p323

For places to stay in Champagne, see p329

THE GUIDE

CHAMPAGNE

Left: Veuve Clicquot vineyard (p317); Above: Cathédrale Notre-Dame (p312), Reims

Find Your Way

Trains link Reims and Épernay. Local services cover some smaller towns. Troyes and Langres are also linked. However, to enjoy the region, you'll need a vehicle for when you're not in a town or city.

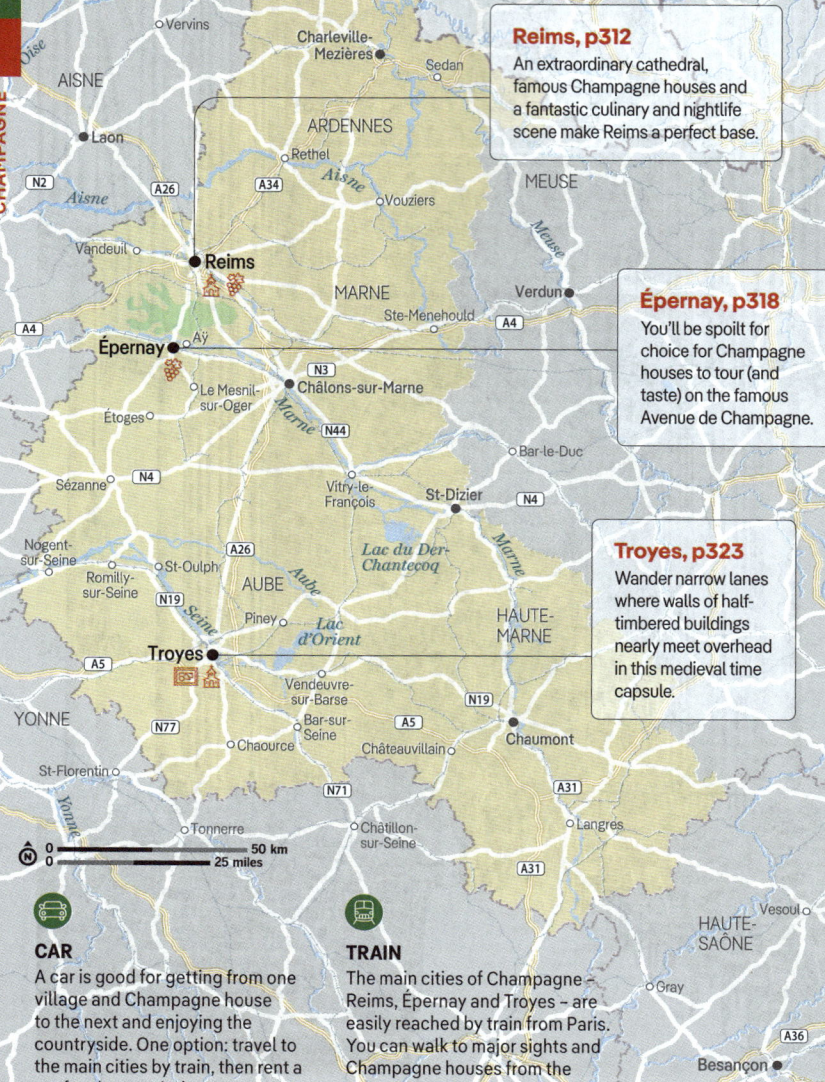

Reims, p312
An extraordinary cathedral, famous Champagne houses and a fantastic culinary and nightlife scene make Reims a perfect base.

Épernay, p318
You'll be spoilt for choice for Champagne houses to tour (and taste) on the famous Avenue de Champagne.

Troyes, p323
Wander narrow lanes where walls of half-timbered buildings nearly meet overhead in this medieval time capsule.

CAR
A car is good for getting from one village and Champagne house to the next and enjoying the countryside. One option: travel to the main cities by train, then rent a car for short periods.

TRAIN
The main cities of Champagne – Reims, Épernay and Troyes – are easily reached by train from Paris. You can walk to major sights and Champagne houses from the train stations – and avoid parking hassles.

Halles du Boulingrin (p316), Reims

Plan Your Time

Champagne's main cities make easy day trips from Paris, but to really discover its history, characterful towns, *terroir* (land) and many styles of the sparkling wine, you'll need more days.

A Day Trip to Reims

● Make your first stop the incredible **Cathédrale Notre-Dame** (p312) and step inside the 13th-century Gothic monument to marvel at the stained glass. Wander over to the area around the **Halles du Boulingrin** (p316), the city's food market, which anchors many fine restaurants. After, discover the *crayères* (chalk cellars) hidden underneath one of the **famous Champagne houses** (p317).

With More Time

● Enjoy Reims, then see what Épernay's **Avenue of Champagne** (p319) is all about. Get a vehicle and explore the immediate region, stopping at alluring villages such as **Châtillon-sur-Marne** (p320) with its views, artful **Aÿ** (p321) and charming **Aÿ** (p320). Explore the lanes of compellingly restored **Troyes** (p323). Discover Renoir's inspiration in **Essoyes** (p327) and gaze out on your own domain from **Langres** (p324).

Seasonal Highlights

SPRING
Champagne is lovely in spring, with warmer temps, lush vineyards and country meadows alive with wildflowers.

SUMMER
Reims hosts various music festivals in July, but the region falls quiet during the August holidays. September brings the busy harvest.

AUTUMN
Catch the vineyards now to see them turn from verdant green to beautiful autumnal shades of umber, orange and vermilion.

WINTER
Christmas celebrations and markets enliven Champagne, giving a festive air that helps offset the cold temps and frost.

Reims

REGAL HISTORY | WALKABLE CITY | FINE DINING

GETTING AROUND

As a small city, central Reims rewards walkers, but to reach sights such as Basilique St-Rémi and the Champagne houses you'll want to take the bus. The city bus follows a circular route serving most of the major sights (single ticket €1.80, all-day ticket *journée* €4.50). Full info at grandreims-mobilites.fr.

Reims is a train hub and regional services radiate out to cities like Épernay and Troyes. By TGV, Paris is only 45 minutes.

☑ TOP TIP

The **tourist office** (*reims-tourisme.com*), just west of the cathedral, has stacks of information on the Champagne region and Reims (plus free city maps), as well as cool giant cork stools where you can perch while using the free wi-fi. It also has lockers where you can leave your phone to charge.

Paris may be the capital, but Reims is the city of kings. After Clovis, the first king of France, was baptised in Reims in 496, every king after him until Charles X in 1825 made the journey from Paris and Versailles to be crowned in the city, and more specifically, in Reims Cathedral after it was completed in 1275. Wine flowed freely to celebrate the occasion and this is where Champagne got its reputation as being 'the wine of kings and the king of wines.'

These days, Reims is still famous for its centuries-old cathedral, its many fountains and its historic Champagne houses, but it's also a lively contemporary city which, as well as making an ideal base for visiting the region, also deserves a couple of days in its own right. Expect fantastic restaurants, buzzy bars and the expected cafe scene offering breaks from sightseeing around the strollable centre.

The Cathedral of Kings
Reims' Gothic masterpiece

One of France's finest examples of Gothic architecture, the 13th-century **Cathédrale Notre-Dame** (*Reims Cathedral; cathedrale-reims.fr*) is a significant French monument. After King Clovis was baptised on this site in 496, every King of France was crowned here using an oil that, according to legend, was sent from God.

Joan of Arc won points for bringing Charles VII safely here to be anointed with oil at his coronation during the English invasion; she now has a **chapel** dedicated to her inside (and a **statue** out front) while the famous oil is on show next door in the 17th-century **Palais du Tau**. It's due to reopen sometime in 2026 with the new **Musée des Sacres** (*Museum of Coronations; palais-du-tau.fr*).

The **main stained-glass rose window** in the western facade survived both world wars and is, amazingly, the 13th-century original. The smaller rose below it was completed in 1937 by

continued on p316

REIMS

CHAMPAGNE REIMS

★ HIGHLIGHTS
1. Cathédrale Notre-Dame

● SIGHTS
2. Immeuble Kodak
3. Joan of Arc statue
4. Palais du Tau
5. Porte de Mars

● ACTIVITIES
6. Bibliothèque Carnegie

● SLEEPING
7. Demeure Belle Epoque
8. Hôtel Azur
9. Hôtel Cecyl Reims
10. Hôtel Continental
11. Hôtel de la Paix
12. La Caserne Chanzy Hôtel & Spa
13. Le Clos des Roys

● EATING
14. Boulangerie Pâtisserie Paintagruélique
15. Kiosque à Huîtres & Coquillages
16. Le Bocal
17. L'ExtrA
18. Maison Fossier
19. Ö Double A
20. Pâtisserie Waïda
21. Racine

● DRINKING & NIGHTLIFE
22. Café du Palais
23. Glue Pot
24. Le Pavé
25. Le Wine Bar by Le Vintage

● ENTERTAINMENT
26. Opéraims

● SHOPPING
27. A l'Iris de Florence
28. Halles du Boulingrin

● INFORMATION
29. Tourist Office

🍽 WHERE TO EAT IN REIMS: TOP CHOICES

Ö Double A: On the buzzy place du Forum, small corner brasserie with a ring of outdoor tables and offering top local Champagnes by the glass. *9.30am-9.30pm* €€

Le Bocal: Excellent seafood bistro serving sublime oysters (from Maison Gillardeau) and desserts from Brittany's beloved butter maker, Bordier. Also, a fishmonger. *noon-1.30pm, 7-9.30pm Tue-Sat* €€

L'ExtrA: In the food-rich neighbourhood around Marché du Boulingrin, L'ExtrA combines social responsibility with an innovative menu of exquisite northern seafood and produce. *noon-2pm, 7-10pm Tue-Sat* €€

Racine: Chef Kazuyuki Tanaka creates Japanese-accented menus that sing with bright flavours and creative finesse; two Michelin stars, with 250 Champagnes. *noon-4pm Fri-Sun, 7pm-midnight Thu-Mon* €€€

Champagne Pommery (p317)

TOP EXPERIENCE

Champagne

Champagne's grapes are grown in four main winegrowing areas: Montagne de Reims, Marne Valley, Côte des Blancs and Côte des Bar. You'll find smaller producers – or houses – scattered about these beautiful lands as well as larger and more famous names in Reims and Épernay. Sampling the variations of this famous drink and indulging in the region's pleasures defines delight.

DON'T MISS

Veuve Clicquot (p317)

Champagne Pommery (p317)

Maison Ruinart (p317)

Atelier 1834: Champagne Boizel (p322)

Champagne De Castellane (p322)

Visiting Champagne Houses

Touring Champagne producers is the very reason many come to the region and time spent in the caves, tasting rooms and out in the vineyards can be magical. Know that the experiences are as varied as the wines themselves.

Large houses with famous names have well-honed visitor operations with a carefully designed menu of experiences. Most will have a basic visit that includes a tour and a tasting or two of popular vintages for €40 or under. From there, optional add-ons abound, from rare vintage tastings to chef-led lunches to vineyard excursions.

PRACTICALITIES

● Scan this code for searchable listings of nearly 500 Champagne producers.

One of the delights of the smaller producers is the more intimate experience, with perhaps only one level of tasting and which may be redeemable with a purchase. However, know that smaller producers may not have any dedicated staff for visits, so pre-planning and booking is essential.

Make sure to contact each producer in advance to make sure that they can welcome you, and remember that nearly every house will be open for either a morning (10am or 11am) or afternoon appointment (2pm or 2.30pm), sometimes both. Some producers do tastings only while others will take you through the cellars, and even out to vineyards. Prices vary and can range from free to up to €30 or €40.

Champagne 101

Like all wine regions in France, Champagne has its own specific rules for making its famous bubbles. Chardonnay, pinot noir and pinot meunier (often just called meunier) are the main grapes used to make Champagne, but arbane, petit meslier, pinot blanc and pinot gris are also permitted.

Champagne made from 100% chardonnay, a white grape, is called a *blanc de blancs* (literally, white of whites) and Champagne made from 100% pinot noir or meunier, both black grapes, is called a *blanc de noirs* (white of blacks).

Rosé is made by either the maceration method, when the skin of black grapes are left in contact with the juice to add colour, or by blending white and red wine together, a technique only allowed in Champagne.

Producing Bubbly

Vines are vigorously pruned to produce a small quantity of high-quality grapes. Indeed, to maintain exclusivity (and price), the designated areas where grapes used for Champagne can be grown and the amount of wine produced each year are limited.

Making Champagne according to the traditional method (*méthode champenoise*) is a complex procedure. Two fermentation processes are used, the first in casks and the second after the wine has been bottled and had sugar and yeast added. Bottles are then aged in cellars for two to five years, depending on the *cuvée* (vintage).

During the two months in early spring that the bottles are aged in cellars kept at 12°C, the wine turns effervescent. The sediment that forms in the bottle is removed by *remuage*, a slow process in which each bottle, stored horizontally, is rotated slightly every day for weeks until the sludge works its way to the cork. Next comes *dégorgement*: the neck of the bottle is frozen, creating a blob of solidified Champagne and sediment, which is then removed.

All of this time and labour contribute to the cost of each bottle.

CHAMPAGNE SAVINGS

You'll be overwhelmed with opportunities to buy bubbly in Reims and the Champagne region. But do yourself a favour and avoid the prices at the producers, *caves* and boutiques. Instead, search for *hypermarché* (hypermarket) in your map app and look for the huge French discount store brands such Auchan and Carrefour. In the Champagne region, they have hundreds of choices of local bubbly on offer at discount prices.

TOP TIPS

- If you like your Champagne dry, be sure to buy extra brut. Don't be fooled by Sec, which means 'dry' in English, it's pretty sweet. In fact, from sweetest to driest, here's the labels: doux, demi-sec, sec, extra sec, brut and extra brut.

- A 'grower Champagne producer' means that the house grows all its own grapes, which gives it maximum control over its own unique flavour as opposed to those blending grapes from others to produce a set taste.

- The Reims and Épernay tourist offices offer maps and apps with bike routes between Champagne producers and through the vineyards.

Sculpture, Basilique St-Rémi

FROM CHALK TO CHAMPAGNE

The highest profile Champagne houses are primarily split between Reims and Épernay. While the latter has the famous avenue de Champagne (p319), Reims has the *crayères*, translated to chalk cellars, chalk pits or even chalk cathedrals in English due to their pyramid shapes. Recognised as World Heritage Sites by UNESCO, the *crayères* were first dug around the 4th century by the Gallo-Romans, who used the chalk to construct buildings. Coincidentally, the resulting *'caves'* also perfectly complement the Champagne-making process thanks to their natural levels of humidity, temperature and darkness, which provide the ideal conditions for storing and ageing Champagne. When you see the Champagne vineyards south of the centre, look for decades-old skylights in the ground illuminating the cellars below.

continued from p312

master glassmaker Jacques Simon, whose family has been crafting glass in Reims since 1640.

Other notable windows include the 'Champagne window' featuring – of course! – Dom Pierre Pérignon, also made by Jacques Simon and paid for by the Champagne oligarchy; you can even spot a bottle of Veuve Clicquot in a form of stained-glass marketing. Marc Chagall created a window in the central axial chapel to the rear.

For sweeping views, climb the 250 steps up the **tower** *(adult/child €9/free)*. From the square, see how many of the 2300 exterior statues you can count. Better yet, don't! (The 13th-century *L'Ange au Sourire* – Smiling Angel – presiding beneficently above the central portal is worth seeking out.)

Art Deco Reims

It's not all Gothic statues

You can find 50 buildings around the centre of Reims with art deco accents. For example, **Pâtisserie Waïda** *(3-5 place Drouet d'Erlon)* may have a neon-lit exterior, but inside it hides an art deco tea room with stained-glass details. Of the 10 buildings that are purely art deco, the **Bibliothèque Carnegie** *(2 place Carnegie)* wows with art deco lights, ironwork and typography outside.

Other key examples include the 1930 **Immeuble Kodak** *(2 rue des Capucins)*, the last art deco building to go up during the city's reconstruction; the cinema **Opéraims** *(3 rue Théodore Dubois)*; the **Halles du Boulingrin** *(place du Boulingrin)*, home

CASUAL EATING IN REIMS: OUR PICKS

Boulangerie Pâtisserie Paintagruélique: One of the region's best bakeries, artful artisan loaves, croissants and pastries are luscious. Tables inside and on the square. *6.30am-1.30pm Wed-Sun* €

Kiosque à Huîtres & Coquillages: Fresh seafood truck with tables on a street corner; wines by the glass. Oysters, mussels and more. *10am-8pm Wed-Sun* €€

Boulangerie-Pâtisserie Julianne: Excellent bakery with prepared food and sandwiches near Basilique St-Rémi and the Champagne houses. Elaborate pastries and savoury treats. *6am-7pm* €

Maison Fossier: Powder-pink purveyor of the locally inescapable iconic biscuits, which recall a slightly sweet, crunchy loofah pads. Sold everywhere. *10am-7pm Mon-Sat* €

to Reims' unmissable food market; and the shop **A l'Iris de Florence** (*8 rue de Talleyrand*), celebrated for its mosaic façade.

Church of the Ages
With a museum about the ages

Battered and bruised, **Basilique St-Rémi** wears its 1000 years of history for all to see. It mixes Romanesque elements from the mid-11th century (the worn nave and transept) with early Gothic features from the latter half of the 12th century (the choir, with a large triforium gallery). Excellent illuminated signs detail the 121m-long former Benedictine abbey's history.

Part of the complex, the renovated **Musée St-Rémi** (*musees-reims.fr; adult/child €6/free*) is housed in a 17th- and 18th-century abbey with a serene cloister. The collection inside reveals itself in layers, starting with the history of Reims in Roman times. A large model of the city includes the **Porte de Mars**, which still stands today. Medieval times are a focus and stories of this often bleak period are told in art and artefacts. It's easy to lose two hours here.

Visit Champagne Houses
Names that sparkle

Champagne houses in Reims cluster south of the centre; you can walk between most. Tours always include the ancient chalk caverns, *crayères,* a highlight.

Veuve Clicquot (*veuveclicquot.com; tastings from €36*) has the longest *crayères*, with more than 24km hidden under Reims. Above ground, the house is one of the few big names to offer vineyard visits.

Champagne Pommery (*vrankenpommery.com; tastings from €27*) grew to prominence in the late 19th century under the legendary Mme Pommery. An art lover, she commissioned sculptor Gustave Navlet to carve bas-reliefs by candlelight in her 18km of *crayères*. The house now has rotating contemporary (and entertaining!) art shows above and below ground.

Champagne Taittinger (*taittinger.com; tastings from €40*) has a glam new visitor centre with a relaxing courtyard that balances out the shop, where you can get boxed sets of bubbly for €1000+. The storied *crayères* date to the 4th century.

Maison Ruinart (*ruinart.com; tours €85*) is the world's oldest Champagne house, dating back to 1729. It was the first to use *crayères* to age its precious bottles and arguably has the most impressive, with the cellars reaching as far as 40m underground.

ROMANESQUE CHURCHES NEAR REIMS

Quiet country villages northwest of Reims have 11th-century Romanesque churches.

Savigny-sur-Ardres: It sits on a knoll with plaques festooning the neighbouring garage where General de Gaulle implored the French on 28 May 1940 to resist the Nazis.

Courville: A castle once stood nearby and the evocative church is tall to repel invaders.

Église Saint-Pierre de Saint-Gilles: Surrounded by a large cemetery, it was once part of a sprawling priory.

Arcis-le-Ponsart: Its walls are part of a castle and partially enclose the church and the remains of a turret.

Lagery: A restored 18th-century market and washhouse are in the town square; nearby church has the original carving with the name 'St-Martin' by the door.

WHERE TO DRINK IN REIMS

Café du Palais: Family-run since 1930, this art deco cafe is the place to sip Champagne; extraordinary collection of bric-a-brac. *9am-9pm Tue-Sat*

Glue Pot: One of the city's most impressive Champagne and wine lists by the glass; plush red booths and a comfort-food menu (good fries). *noon-2am*

Le Pavé: Come *apéro* hour, long tables along this antique-shop-filled street fill with lively cocktail lovers. Live music many nights. *5.30pm-1.30am Tue-Sun*

Le Wine Bar by Le Vintage: Convivial spot for a glass of wine or Champagne (hundreds on offer) with charcuterie. Recommendations offered. *6pm-midnight Tue-Sat*

Épernay

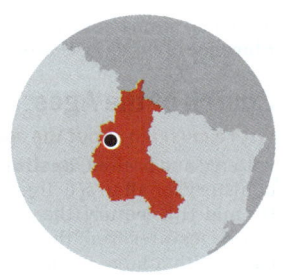

CHAMPAGNE | FAMOUS PRODUCERS | WALKING IT OFF

GETTING AROUND

Épernay is walkable and you can get to most places from the train station on foot. Hourly trains from Reims take 35 minutes. Trains to Paris take 80 minutes.
Near the station, **De la Selle au Guidon** *(delaselleauguidon.fr)* rents all types of bikes including e-bikes; it delivers within a 30km radius of Épernay.

Prosperous Épernay, the self-proclaimed *capitale du Champagne* and home to many of the world's most celebrated Champagne houses, is at its heart a tidy, walkable French regional town whose principal industry happens to be a French luxury product.

Not architecturally distinctive, this city of 22,000 is home to the renowned avenue de Champagne, where famous producers sit side by side. Most welcome visitors for cellar tours and tastings and some also have their own bars with shady terraces. Visitors can sit sipping Champagne on one of the most famous avenues in the world, knowing that beneath them are 110km of subterranean cellars with more than 200 million bottles of Champagne just waiting to be popped open.

You can stay here, although your experience would be distinctly one-note. Instead, many take the train from Reims or stay in one of the attractive villages out in the countryside.

 TOP TIP

Most, although not all, of Épernay's Champagne houses welcome visitors for tours and tastings. It's recommended to book in advance as spots easily sell out, particularly at popular houses such as Moët & Chandon.

Château Perrier

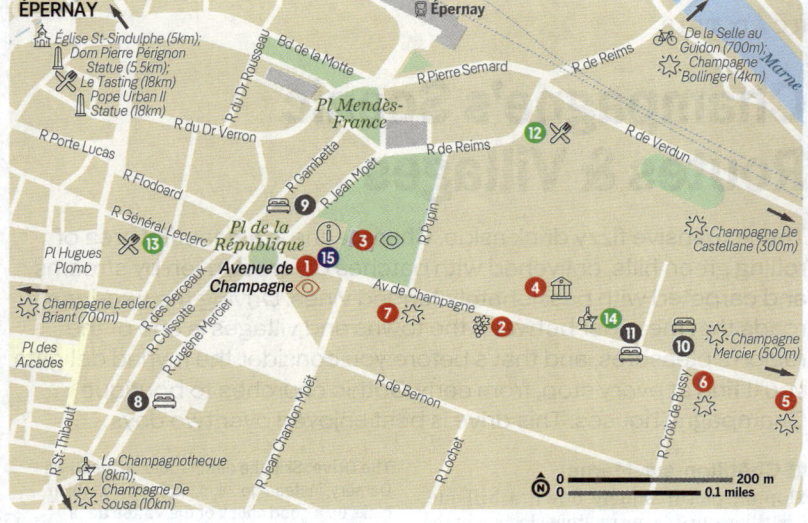

- **HIGHLIGHTS**
  1. Avenue de Champagne
- **SIGHTS**
  2. Champagne Perrier-Jouët
  3. Hôtel de Ville
  4. Musée du Vin de Champagne et d'Archéologie Régionale
- **ACTIVITIES**
  5. Atelier 1834: Champagne Boizel
  6. Champagne A Bergère
  7. Moët & Chandon
- **SLEEPING**
  8. Boutique-Hôtel de Champagne
  9. Hôtel Jean Moët
  10. Le 25bis by Leclerc Briant
  11. Parva Domus Chambres d'Hôtes
- **EATING**
  12. La Grillade Gourmande
  13. Maison Vincent Dallet
- **DRINKING & NIGHTLIFE**
  see 10 #Brut
  14. Le 19 Avenue de Champagne
- **INFORMATION**
  15. Tourist Office

Popping Up Champagne Ave

Touring caves and tasting

The storied **Avenue de Champagne** is the reason to visit Épernay, even if the streetscape itself is bland in an upmarket sort of way. It's what's inside that mix of architectural styles, which includes Gothic, Renaissance and classicism, that counts.

Start at the **Tourist Office** *(epernay-tourisme.com)* in front of the **Hôtel de Ville** (town hall; behind there's a lovely park for a break). Here, the uber-helpful staff will cheerfully fill your next year with Champagne-related activities if you allow them, otherwise they have maps, info, tours and much more.

Next, get the obligatory selfie with the fuzzy-edged statue of Dom Pérignon, the 17th-century monk who perfected the method for making mediocre wine sparkle.

Now, begin touring. Consider a stop at **Château Perrier**, the 1850s gilded home of the **Musée du Vin de Champagne et d'Archéologie Régionale**, or the Champagne Museum *(archeochampagne.epernay.fr; adult/child €10/free)*. The full museum is exhaustive and exhausting, however with some

continued on p322

ROAD TRIP

Champagne's Scenic Routes & Villages

That expensive fizzy drink aside, Champagne is a beautiful area of rolling green hills, enlivened with patches of forest, riven by streams and carpeted with passionately tended vines. Driving the two-lane roads that meander between the towns and villages is one of the region's pleasures, and that's before you consider the myriad delights you'll find at every stop, from early Gothic churches to boutique Champagne houses. This drive is best enjoyed over two days.

1 Châtillon-sur-Marne

Sloping picturesquely down a hillside, Châtillon-sur-Marne reclines sleepily in the Vallée de la Marne, one of the top Champagne-producing regions. Woven with narrow streets, it's a pretty base for vineyard walks and its cellars produce Champagnes worth lingering for.

It's easy to find, just look for the 25m-high **Pope Urban II Statue** (1042–99) at the town's peak. Views from the surrounding park are sweeping. The main square features **Le Tasting** *(10am-6pm Tue-Sun)*, a bar with a *terroir* menu and picnic supplies.

The Drive: Skip the direct route on the D1 via Damery, instead go 21km via Cuchery, which picks up a good chunk of the **Vallée de la Marne Champagne Route** and its pinot meunier vineyards.

2 Hautvillers

Perched above a sea of emerald vines and ablaze with forsythia and tulips in spring, Hautvillers is where **Dom Pierre Pérignon** (1638–1715) is popularly believed to have created Champagne – a somewhat tipsy-looking **statue** recalls this. His **tomb** is in the nearby **Église St-Sindulphe** and draws reverential bubbly drinkers

Vineyards around Hautvillers

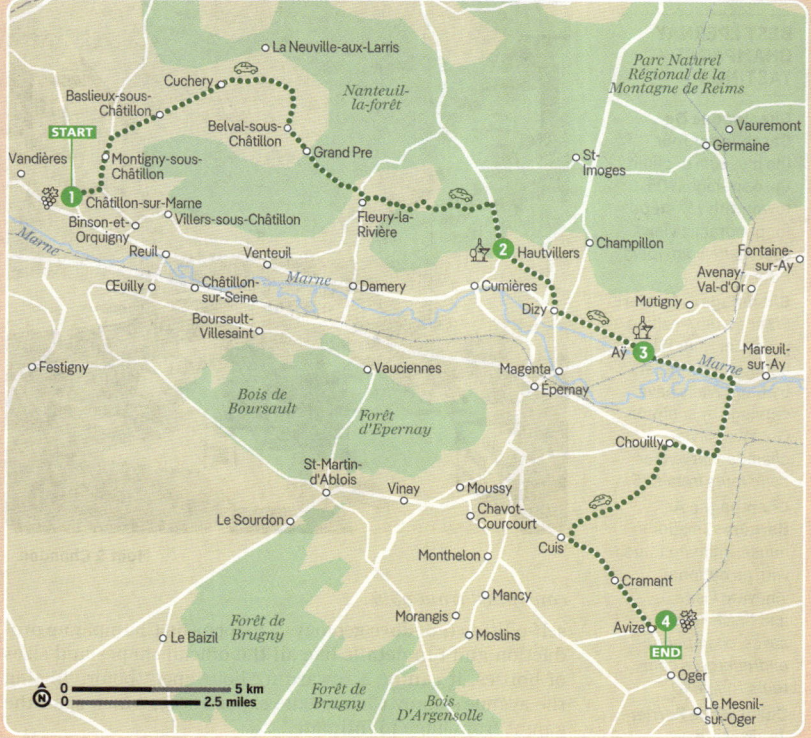

throughout the year. Producers have shops in town and there are plenty of hotels and restaurants. Walking routes radiate out in all directions.

The Drive: It's a short and beautiful 6km through the manicured vineyards to Aÿ. Look for the tombstone-shaped stones denoting ownership. You'll see many revered Champagne names.

3 Aÿ

The main reason to visit this busy market town is just northeast of the centre. Family-run **Champagne Bollinger** (*champagne-bollinger.com; tours from €100*) has a passionate worldwide following and that's only partially because it's the favourite fizz of James Bond. (One of the main buildings looks like Auric Goldfinger's Swiss headquarters in the classic 007 film that bears his name.)

Aÿ is also the birthplace of René Lalique, the famed glass and jewellery maker and key figure during the art nouveau movement. A **town walk** (*ay-champagne.com/visiter/rene-lalique*) recalls his work.

The Drive: Much of this 16.5km segment follows the fabled **Côte des Blancs Champagne Route**, which is planted almost exclusively with white Chardonnay grapes (the name means 'hillside of the whites').

4 Avize

Right in the heart of gently rolling *blanc de blancs* country and surrounded by rows of immaculately tended vines, Avize is lauded far and wide for its outstanding Champagnes. The town and the neighbouring village of **Cramant** (a beautiful walk 2.5km walk) have a dozen superb small producers like **Champagne De Sousa** (*champagnedesousa.com; tastings by appointment*). Enjoy the local bubblies on the terrace at **La Champagnothèque** (*11am-6pm Thu-Mon*) in Cramant.

BEST ÉPERNAY CHAMPAGNE TASTINGS

Champagne De Castellane: Tour the museum or climb the 66m-high 1905 tower with 237 steps for panoramic views. castellane.com; tours from €30

Champagne Mercier: France's best-selling producer; tour 18km of underground cellars by train. Walls have carvings by sculptor Gustave Navlet. champagnemercier.com; tours from €25

Champagne A Bergère: Smaller house. Intimate tours with an optional vineyard visit and finish in their *caves*. champagne-andrebergere.com; tours from €40

Champagne Perrier-Jouët: All-day, top-end restaurant-bar for sampling vintages in its art nouveau mansion and gardens. No tours. perrier-jouet.com

Champagne Leclerc Briant: Biodynamic and organic house with experimental production techniques. leclercbriant.fr; tours from €45

Moët & Chandon

continued from p319

self-editing (goodbye geology...) to focus on Champagne production and fun details like all the official shapes and sizes of bottles, it can be a rewarding hour spent before hitting the avenue's many Champagne experiences, which span the gamut from huge to intimate.

Moët & Chandon *(moet.com; tours from €45)* is the big dog of Épernay, with 28km of *caves*. Visit options within its bank-like exterior can be bewildering.

Atelier 1834: Champagne Boizel *(boizel.com; tours from €40)* is still personably run by the Boizel family, in a tradition dating to 1834. Unlike many of the *maisons*, these are still working cellars. Highly recommended.

BEST PLACES TO EAT & DRINK IN ÉPERNAY

La Grillade Gourmande: Helmed by Alain Ducasse alum Christophe Bernard. Lunchtime set menus are great value for the high quality. Presentation is flawless. *lunch & dinner Tue-Sat* €€€

Maison Vincent Dallet: *Chocolaterie*, patisserie and tearoom, with delectable pralines, macarons and pastries plus coffee and works of art crafted in chocolate. *7.30am-7.30pm Tue-Sun* €

#Brut: Trust manager Jules Parrour to personally guide you through his handpicked Champagne menu, which favours organic producers. *3-9.30pm Wed-Sun*

Le 19 Avenue de Champagne: Explore over 100 Champagne producers in a chilled setting, both inside and out; food trucks show up on weekends. *2-7pm*

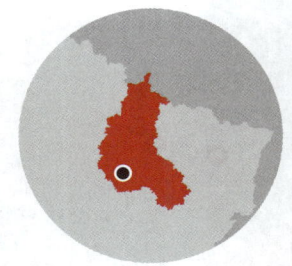

Troyes

WALKABLE CENTRE | MEDIEVAL BUILDINGS | UNMISSABLE MUSEUMS

In polls of France's most romantic towns, Troyes invariably makes the grade – and with good reason. It's astonishingly intact, ludicrously pretty historic centre wings you back to the Middle Ages, with its warren of cobbled streets, fine ensemble of half-timbered houses in pastel hues, once home to wealthy textile merchants, and uplifting Gothic churches. Shamefully overlooked, it's a superb place to get a sense of what Europe looked like back when Molière was penning his finest plays and the Three Musketeers were swashbuckling.

Beginning in the early 1960s, a concerted and ongoing preservation effort has saved medieval Troyes. Hundreds of buildings have had their 19th- and 20th-century modernised facades stripped away and their half-timbered souls uncovered.

Troyes punches well above its weight culturally too, with galleries and museums that are fascinating and unique. Exploring this intriguing city on foot (p326), where every turn yields a new surprise, is one of Champagne's great pleasures.

GETTING AROUND

Troyes is on the train line that links Mulhouse (three to six hours) in Alsace with Paris Gare de l'Est (1½ hours). Getting around Champagne is a challenge without taking some combination of trains and buses. Plot your connections with the SNCF Connect app.

Central Troyes is easily walkable.

Walls of Glowing Colour

Behold a grand cathedral

All at once imposing and delicate with its filigree stonework, Troyes' **Cathédrale St-Pierre et St-Paul** is a stellar example of champenois Gothic architecture. The flamboyant **west facade** dates from the mid-1500s, while the 114m-long interior is illuminated by a spectacular series of 180 **stained-glass windows** (13th to 17th centuries) that shine like jewels when it's sunny. Also notable is the fantastical **baroque organ** (1730s) sporting musical *putti* (cherubs), and a tiny **treasury** with enamels from the Meuse Valley.

Back in 1429, Joan of Arc and Charles VII stopped off here on their way to his coronation in Reims. Today, the large sunny **square** is a fine place to stop off for a drink at one of the cafes.

☑ TOP TIP

Stop by the excellent tourist office and get the free Tour of the Historic Centre map, which provides very good information about the city's wealth of old sights.

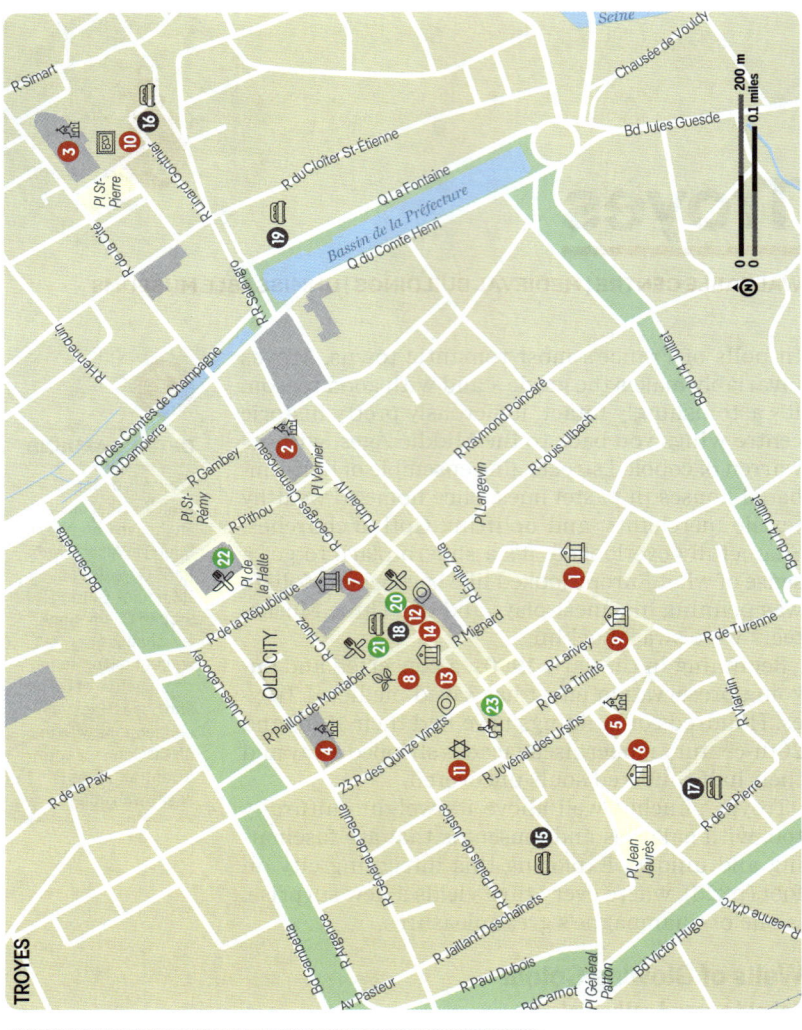

TROYES

SIGHTS
1. Angoiselles Mansion
2. Basilique St-Urbain
3. Cathédrale St-Pierre et St-Paul
4. Église Ste-Madeleine
5. Église St-Pantaléon
6. Hôtel de Vauluisant
7. Hôtel de Ville
8. Jardin Juvénal
9. Maison de l'Outil et de la Pensée Ouvrière
10. Musée d'Art Moderne
11. Rashi House and Synagogue
12. Rue Champeaux
13. Ruelle des Chats
14. Tourelle de l'Orfèvre

SLEEPING
15. Brit Hotel Les Comtes de Champagne
16. Hotel La Maison De Rhodes
17. Le Clos Guivet
18. Le Relais St-Jean
19. Maison M Troyes

EATING
20. Le Tablier
21. Le Valentino
22. Marché des Halles

DRINKING & NIGHTLIFE
23. Les Cabaretiers

Cathédrale St-Pierre et St-Paul (p323)

Toolin' Around
Using their hands in the Middle Ages

Worn to a sensuous lustre by generations of skilled hands, the 11,000 hand tools on display at the surprising **Maison de l'Outil et de la Pensée Ouvrière** *(House of Tools; mopo3.com; adult/child €8/free)* – each designed to perform a single, specialised task with exquisite efficiency – bring to life a world of manual skills made obsolete by the Industrial Revolution. The collection is housed in the magnificent Renaissance-style Hôtel de Mauroy, built in 1556. A **courtyard** with a fountain spans the block.

See Top Modern Art
Bold colours in an old palace

Housed in a 16th- to 18th-century bishop's palace, **Musée d'Art Moderne** *(musees-troyes.com/art-moderne; €8)* celebrates French art from 1850 onwards (especially the work of local glassmaker and painter Maurice Marinot). The sensational collection includes Degas, Rodin, Matisse, Modigliani, Picasso and Seurat. The bold, direct-from-the-tube colours of the Fauvists are a highlight.

FUN FACTS ABOUT TROYES

Beyond half-timbered intrigue, Troyes has other facets that may surprise you. If you've ever read or seen a story about Lancelot or the search for the Holy Grail (in Africa or Europe), you've enjoyed creations of the 12th-century poet and troubadour Chrétien de Troyes (1135–83), who was, as his name indicates, a local lad.

Not trusting crypto and thinking gold bullion might be a better hedge against uncertain times? Then you'll be buying using the troy ounce, a unit of measure derived from exchange standards established in Troyes in the 12th and 13th centuries.

Every time you've noticed a Lacoste shirt, Petit Bateau kidswear or cottony Dim underwear, you've recognised a brand name created in Troyes, France's historic knitwear capital.

 EATING & DRINKING IN TROYES: OUR PICKS

Le Tablier: Fine all-around brasserie with engaging staff, tasty locally sourced food and a spread of tables in the shadow of half-timbered confections. *noon-11pm* €€

Marché des Halles: Fruit, veggies, bread, charcuterie, fish and glorious cheese from top regional vendors. Stalls offer prepared foods and excellent breakfasts and lunches. *7am-7pm* €€

Le Valentino: Romantic rose-hued, modern French restaurant with a cobbled 17th-century courtyard. The chef skilfully creates market-driven and seasonal specialities. *noon-1.30pm, 7.30-9.30pm Tue-Sat* $$

Les Cabaretiers: Jazzy music makes this little wood-floored bar with medieval views from the terrace tables a fine place for an evening of cocktails. *5pm-1.30am Tue-Sun*

WANDERING OLD TROYES

Half-timbered houses – with lurching walls and off-beam floors – give Troyes its irresistible appeal. Return to the Middle Ages on this walking tour.

START	END	LENGTH
Hôtel de Ville	Cathédrale St-Pierre et St-Paul	1.6 km; 2hrs

The classical ❶ **Hôtel de Ville** is a good place to start. Follow the ❷ **Rue Champeaux** west into a dark thicket of half-timbered buildings with pickup sticks of exposed beams. Look for the 16th-century Tourelle de l'Orfèvre (Silversmith's Tower) at the corner with rue Paillot de Montabert. Turn down the foreboding ❸ **Ruelle des Chats** (Alley of the Cats), still as dark and narrow as it was four centuries ago – the upper floors almost touch. Find the namesake cat in the stonework. Go one street northeast to the early Gothic ❹ **Église Ste-Madeleine**. Highlights include the rare Flamboyant Gothic rood screen and the statue of a deadly serious Ste Marthe, a masterpiece of the 16th-century Troyes School.

Head south to rue Brunneval and the ❺ **Rashi House and Synagogue**. Troyes was home to the iconic 12th-century Jewish scholar Rashi. Follow rue Juvénal des Ursins to the faded-with-age ❻ **Église St-Pantaléon**. Filled with rich artistic works of the Troyes School, it sits on a little square facing the **Hôtel de Vauluisant**, a haunted-looking, Renaissance-style mansion. Walk west on rue Général Saussier, pausing at the 16th-century ❼ **Angoiselles Mansion**. Then admire the exuberantly Gothic ❽ **Basilique St-Urbain** with its fine 13th-century stained glass. Cross the channel off the Seine and finish at the luminous ❾ **Cathédrale St-Pierre et St-Paul** (p323).

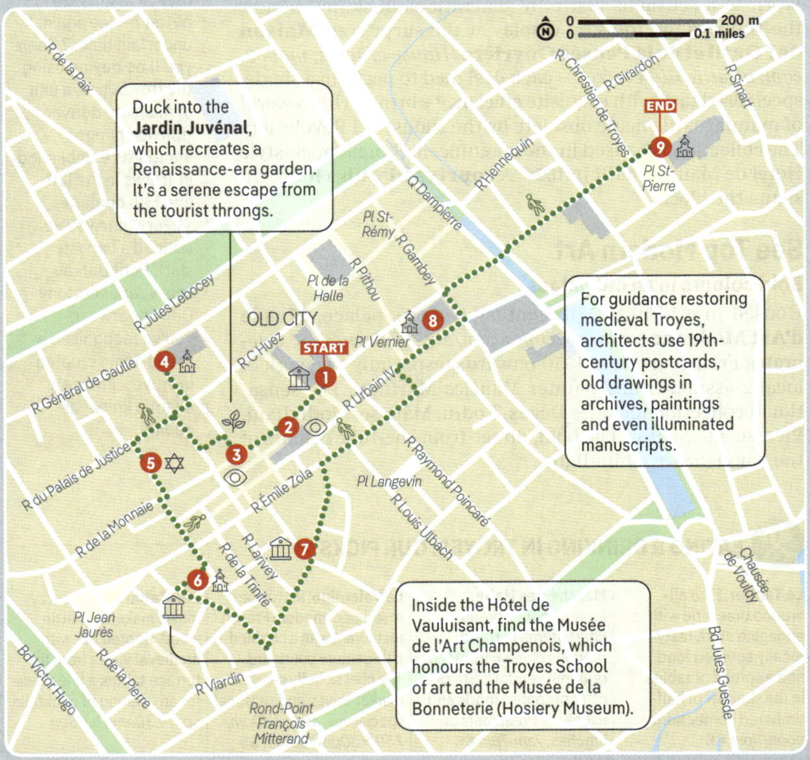

> Duck into the **Jardin Juvénal**, which recreates a Renaissance-era garden. It's a serene escape from the tourist throngs.

> For guidance restoring medieval Troyes, architects use 19th-century postcards, old drawings in archives, paintings and even illuminated manuscripts.

> Inside the Hôtel de Vauluisant, find the Musée de l'Art Champenois, which honours the Troyes School of art and the Musée de la Bonneterie (Hosiery Museum).

Beyond Troyes

Thoughts of fizzy drinks fade as you head southeast from Troyes into the verdant countryside filled with history and artful inspirations.

Spreading picturesquely across the southern half of the Champagne region, Aube is all the more alluring for being largely off the tourist radar. A fine place for slow touring, this pretty *département* (department or county) hides châteaux, quiet stone villages and fortified old redoubts like Langres. On a warm summer day, an amble along its rivers or through its sun-dappled woods and softly lit meadows could be straight out of an impressionist painting – and indeed compact and cute Essoyes is Renoir's old 'hood.

It's easy to see why Renoir loved this riverside village so much that he spent his last 25 summers here: its neat stone houses glow golden in the late afternoon sun amid vineyards and flower-flecked fields.

Places
Essoyes p327
Langres p328

Essoyes
Savouring Renoir's world

TIME FROM TROYES: 1HR

There's no doubt that you're in Renoir territory when you reach Essoyes, as murals of his work decorate the sides of many of the light beige sandstone buildings.

Begin your visit at the **Espace des Renoir**, which houses the useful **tourist office** *(renoir-essoyes.fr; combined ticket to all sights adult/child €12/free)* and an enjoyable small **museum**, which will give you a quick briefing on the great man's life, with – not surprisingly – a focus on his time spent in the area.

From here, follow the standout *circuit découverte*, a marked trail that loops around the village, taking in viewpoints that inspired the artist, the family home and the cemetery where he lies buried.

At **La Maison Familiale** you can see the family's tidy bourgeois home, which they bought in 1896 with the proceeds from his fame as a painter. Continue out back to the **Jardin Renoir**, perhaps the loveliest stop in Essoyes. In spring and summer, it bursts forth with tulips, anemones and roses. Compare its beauty to that shown in the reproductions of his works, which feature it.

The main stop is the **L'Atelier Renoir**, his studio, which has displays on the hallmarks of his work (the female form,

GETTING AROUND

Essoyes is 49km southeast of Troyes. Trains run frequently between Troyes and the nearest station in Bar-Sur-Aube, 30km away. Langres is well-connected by trains to Troyes (70 minutes), Reims (2¾ hours) and Paris (2½ hours).

The region is best explored, however, with your own vehicle because wandering its leafy back lanes and sinuous country roads is part of its great appeal.

Langres

RENOIR & ESSOYES

Pierre-Auguste Renoir (1841–1919) is one of the great impressionists. His use of dramatic light and vivid colours causes his works to burst forth at the viewer. During his peak years, he chronicled life in Paris, capturing scenes that resonate to this day.

Later, Renoir loved Essoyes so much that he spent his last 25 summers there, although his arthritis caused him to spend the colder months in the south of France near Nice (p806) during his final years.

In Essoyes, he grew more inwardly focused. His 1890 masterpiece, *Madame Renoir and her son Pierre*, shows his wife Aline Charigot (who was born in the village) with their son out in the garden, which continues to be open to visitors.

the striking use of colour and light), alongside original pieces such as his antiquated wheelchair and the box he used to carry his paintings to Paris. Note the beauty of his skylit space for painting.

Finally, his grave in the nearby **Le Cimetière** is marked by a contemplative bronze bust.

Langres

TIME FROM TROYES: 1½HR

Walking above it all

Sitting high on its own promontory, Langres' history as a fortified town goes back to the time of the Gauls, when the Romans watched over their domain from this lofty perch.

The present walls mostly encircle the old town and date back to the 15th century. Long **walkways** interspersed with **defensive towers** along the ramparts give you sweeping vistas.

Start a visit at the monumental 17th-century **Porte des Moulins** and wander the narrow streets at random. Look for surprising architectural details like a carved cow skull on a cornice or a hidden Flamboyant Renaissance façade.

The centrepiece of Langres is the 12th-century **Cathédrale Saint-Mammès de Langres**. Although frequently remodelled over the centuries, it still shows its roots in Burgundian Romanesque style, which emphasised height and angles over rounded shapes.

On the square outside, look for the **statue** and plaque honouring **Jeanne Mance** (1606–73), a local woman who lived an extraordinary life in service to others.

WHERE TO EAT & DRINK BEYOND TROYES

L'Union: Essoyes lacks top dining choices except for this small bistro, with an excellent seasonal menu of classic dishes. Tables outside. *noon–2pm, 7-9pm Thu-Mon* €€

Le Dépôt Gourmand: All the stunning land you can see from lofty Langres is prime territory for picnics; get top regional foods here. *10am-6pm Tue-Sat* €

Les Domaines Qui Montent: Good dining choices abound in Langres; this wine shop serves lovely cheeseboards and other simple meals at lunch. *10am-7pm Tue-Sat* €€

Bulle d'Osier: Fine dining in Langres. Enthusiastic young staff flex their culinary chops exploring their creative limits. Book ahead. *lunch & dinner Tue-Sat* €€€

Places We Love to Stay

€ Budget €€ Midrange €€€ Top End

Reims
MAP p313

Hôtel Cecyl Reims € Central good-value hotel combines an original 1920s facade with bold, contemporary style inside. Close to the train station.

Hôtel Azur € Down a side street, a petite, lift-free B&B with a warm welcome that extends to the cheery room decor. Breakfast outside in the sun.

Demeure Belle Epoque €€ Wildly eclectic interior varies from room to room at this period hotel but is always striking and attractive. Breakfast in the garden.

Hôtel de la Paix €€ A classy mid-range option, this contemporary hotel is just off cafe-lined place Drouet d'Erlon. Enjoy the pool and Zen courtyard garden.

Le Clos des Roys €€ Near the cathedral, a historic home turned B&B with a gracious welcome; quiet, countrified rooms.

Hôtel Continental €€€ This 19th-century mansion still has its original features and sits right on place Drouet-d'Erlon. Has the services of a grand hotel.

La Caserne Chanzy Hôtel & Spa €€€ Former fire station (*caserne* in French) turned sleek city-centre hotel. Rooms with a cathedral view are splurge-worthy.

Épernay
MAP p319

Boutique-Hôtel de Champagne € Light-filled rooms are quiet and comfortable and overseen by a team of helpful staff. Good-value choice.

Parva Domus Chambres d'Hôtes €€ This family-owned *chambre d'hôte* (B&B) is the oldest on the avenue de Champagne; it shares a pretty walled garden with #Brut bar.

Champagne A Bergère €€ The namesake boutique hotel of the noted Champagne house (p322). Traditional luxuries delivered with style – and bubbly.

Hôtel Jean Moët €€ Housed in a beautifully converted 18th-century mansion, this old-town hotel offers traditional yet stylish rooms.

Le 25bis by Leclerc Briant €€€ Champagne house Leclerc Briant has transformed this former solicitor's home into a beautiful guesthouse.

Aÿ

La Mongeardière €€ This pretty *chambre d'hôte* is housed in a historic 18th-century property. The pleasures of Champagne Bollinger are a short walk away.

Les Chambres Collery €€€ A charming *chambre d'hôte* owned by Champagne Collery. Restful nights in a traditional estate with a large garden.

Manoir Henri Giraud €€€ The family behind the Champagne Henri Giraud house owns this intimate luxury hotel with rooms overlooking vineyards and a pool.

Troyes
MAP p324

Brit Hotel Les Comtes de Champagne € Massive wooden beams have kept this lift-free trio of half-timbered houses vertical since the 16th century. Good value.

Le Clos Guivet €€ Restored B&B charms with four large, individually designed rooms, stylishly decorated in muted colour schemes. Superb fresh breakfast.

Le Relais St-Jean €€ On a narrow medieval street in the old city, combines half-timbered charm with 24 contemporary rooms.

Maison M Troyes €€ Boutique B&B with 19th-century charm plus modern style. Most of the spacious, sunny, wood-floored rooms face gardens.

Hotel La Maison De Rhodes €€€ Once home to the Knights Templar, this half-timbered medieval mansion sits atop 12th-century foundations. Creaking staircases lead to spacious rooms.

Essoyes

Hotel Restaurant Arts & Millésimes € Comfortable and good-value modern guesthouse on the edge of Renoir's village. Decent-sized pool.

Hôtel Restaurant Cœur des Bulles €€ In the midst of the Côte des Bar Champagne vineyards, a luxury retreat with a top restaurant and pool in Loches-sur-Ource.

Langres

Le Belvédère des Remparts €€ Family-owned charmer near the Porte des Moulins with a small pool in a garden. Bright rooms and close to everything.

Rooms Chapter €€ In a quiet part of the Old Town, a gracious B&B in a historic building with large rooms. Fine, renovated bathrooms.

For places to stay in Alsace, see p353

Above: La Petite France (p336), Strasbourg; Right: Maison des Têtes (p343), Colmar

Researched by
Jean-Bernard Carillet

Alsace

A FRENCH REGION WITH A GERMAN TWIST

With an intriguing mix of French and German influences, Alsace is a distinctive region that leaves you wondering exactly where you are.

Who doesn't fall in love with Alsace? This narrow strip of northeast France, which bumps into Germany to the east and Switzerland to the south, feels so different from the rest of the country and offers a wide array of attractions and surprises. So hard to nail in terms of its character, Alsace proudly guards its own distinct identity, language, cuisine, history and architecture – part French, part German, 100% Alsatian. Alsace is idiosyncratic and colourful at the same time, and that's why it's so appealing. With its splendiferous cathedral and irresistible backdrop of old half-timbered houses and canals, Strasbourg sets the tone. Further south, Colmar, the old centre of which is criss-crossed by romantic cobbled lanes and interlocking waterways, is another feast for the eyes.

No trip to Alsace is complete without a meander on the Route des Vins, one of France's most cherished wine roads. Here lusciously green vineyards cowering beneath hilltop castles unfold in a gentle, almost artistic way. Nature lovers and outdoor enthusiasts will find invigorating escapes by heading further up to the Massif des Vosges (Vosges Mountains). The misty rounded peaks, glacial lakes and thick forests are a haven for walking and biking, or simply a breath of fresh air.

Is Alsace a folk tale come to life? You be the judge.

THE MAIN AREAS

STRASBOURG
Culinary delights, art and culture. **p334**

COLMAR
Alsace's most charming city. **p341**

ROUTE DES VINS D'ALSACE
One of France's most iconic drives. **p349**

Find Your Way

Embracing only two *départements* (Bas-Rhin and Haut-Rhin), Alsace is fairly easy to navigate. It has an extensive road and train network, which makes it convenient to travel around. Strasbourg's international airport is 17km southwest of the city centre.

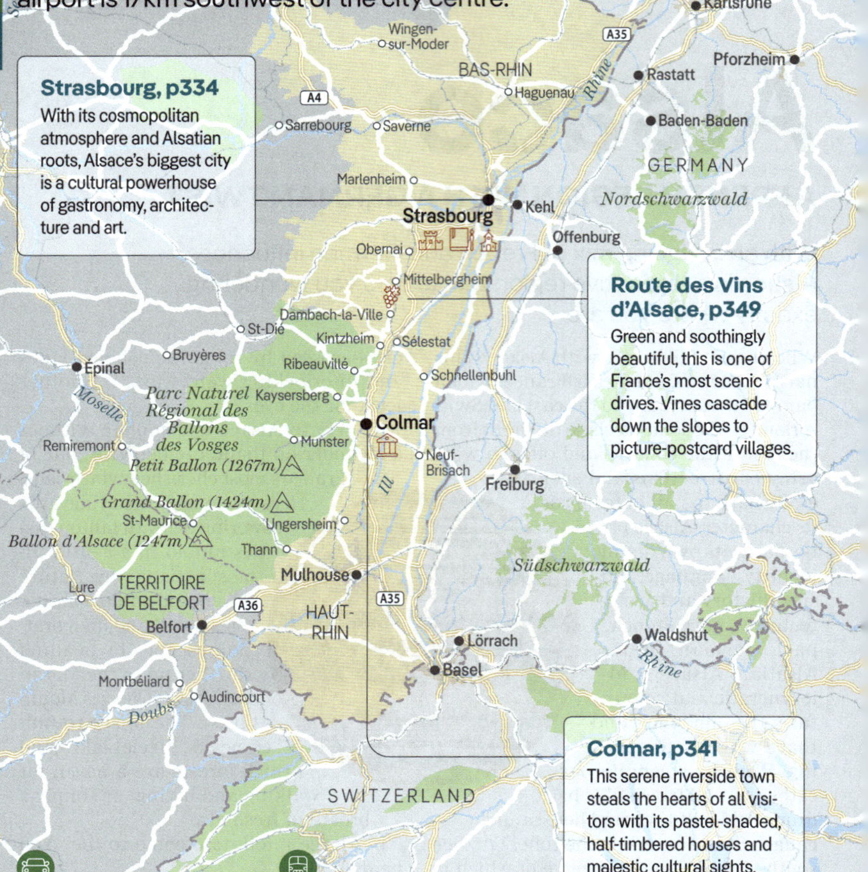

Strasbourg, p334
With its cosmopolitan atmosphere and Alsatian roots, Alsace's biggest city is a cultural powerhouse of gastronomy, architecture and art.

Route des Vins d'Alsace, p349
Green and soothingly beautiful, this is one of France's most scenic drives. Vines cascade down the slopes to picture-postcard villages.

Colmar, p341
This serene riverside town steals the hearts of all visitors with its pastel-shaded, half-timbered houses and majestic cultural sights.

CAR
From Strasbourg, the A35 heads south to Colmar and Mulhouse. For the Massif des Vosges, it's best to have a car – winter tyres are required in the cold months. The Route des Vins is also car-friendly.

TRAIN
Strasbourg and Mulhouse are major train hubs and have fast TGV connections to various cities in France, including Paris. Major towns and some villages are served by a number of regional TER trains.

Château de Fleckenstein (p339), Parc Naturel Régional des Vosges du Nord

Plan Your Time

Major cities can easily be visited in a weekend, but it is worth taking extra time to explore lesser-known, more secluded parts of the region.

A Long Weekend

● Start in **Strasbourg** (p334), Alsace's most iconic city. Marvel at the magnificent **cathedral** (p334) and rent an **electric boat** (p337) to see the historic centre from the water. From here, it's an easy drive to **Hunspach** (p338), one of the region's most appealing villages. Or, head straight to the **Parc Naturel Régional des Vosges du Nord** (p339) to visit the superb **Musée Lalique** (p339).

Five Days to Explore

● After a day in Strasbourg, speed south to pretty **Colmar** (p341), which will take your breath away. From there, the **Route des Vins** (p349) beckons – allow at least a day, preferably two, to saunter along this famous wine trail. Should you want to explore a more secluded area, drive to the **Sundgau** (p345), at the southern tip of Alsace.

Seasonal Highlights

SPRING
Alsace is lovely in the springtime, with warmer temperatures and lush green forests, especially in the Vosges.

SUMMER
The best season for outdoor activities, especially in the Parc Naturel Régional des Vosges du Nord.

AUTUMN
Explore the Route des Vins, when vines are heavy with grapes and colours are at their vibrant best.

WINTER
Christmas markets light up towns in December. Expect fairy-light-covered craft stalls, mulled wine and treats.

Strasbourg

ARCHITECTURE | FINE DINING | URBAN VIBES

☑ TOP TIP
Last-minute accommodation is tricky to find from Monday to Thursday when the European Parliament is in plenary session (see europarl.europa.eu for dates). Book ahead for December, when beds are at a premium because of the Christmas market.

Strasbourg is a city like no other in France, and not only because it's the seat of many European institutions. Situated only a few kilometres west of the Rhine and the German border, it has a unique character. Here, the Latin and German worlds collide, and this reflects in the city's culture, architecture and ambience. Walking a fine tightrope between France and Germany, and between a medieval past and a progressive future, Strasbourg pulls off its act in inimitable Alsatian style.

The impossibly photogenic city centre concentrates the best of Old Strasbourg, with a flurry of twisting backstreets lined with crooked half-timbered houses, scenic canals, flower-filled courts, opulent shops and inviting *winstubs* (traditional taverns), all cowering beneath the soaring magnificence of the cathedral – a medieval marvel in pink sandstone.

Awe-inspiring Cathédrale Notre-Dame
Gothic splendour and sensational views

Completed in all its Gothic grandeur in 1439, **Cathédrale Notre-Dame** *(cathedrale-strasbourg.fr; astronomical clock adult/child €4/2, platform €8/5)* is the unchallenged Strasbourg icon in the heart of the city. The lace-fine facade lifts the gaze little by little to flying buttresses, leering gargoyles and a 142m spire. The interior is exquisitely lit by 12th- to 14th-century stained-glass windows. We love the quirky Gothic-meets-Renaissance

GETTING AROUND

Leave the car. Since Strasbourg's centre is relatively small, it's easy to tackle it on foot – allowing you to appreciate the city's wonderful atmosphere at a slow pace. You can use public transport to reach more distant areas in the suburbs, but the best way to get around the city is by bike. Strasbourg has an extensive *réseau cyclable* (cycling network) and the city's self-rental **Vélhop** system *(velhop.strasbourg.eu)* can supply you with a bike. Pay by card and receive a code to unlock your bike. Taxis hover in front of the train station.

STRASBOURG

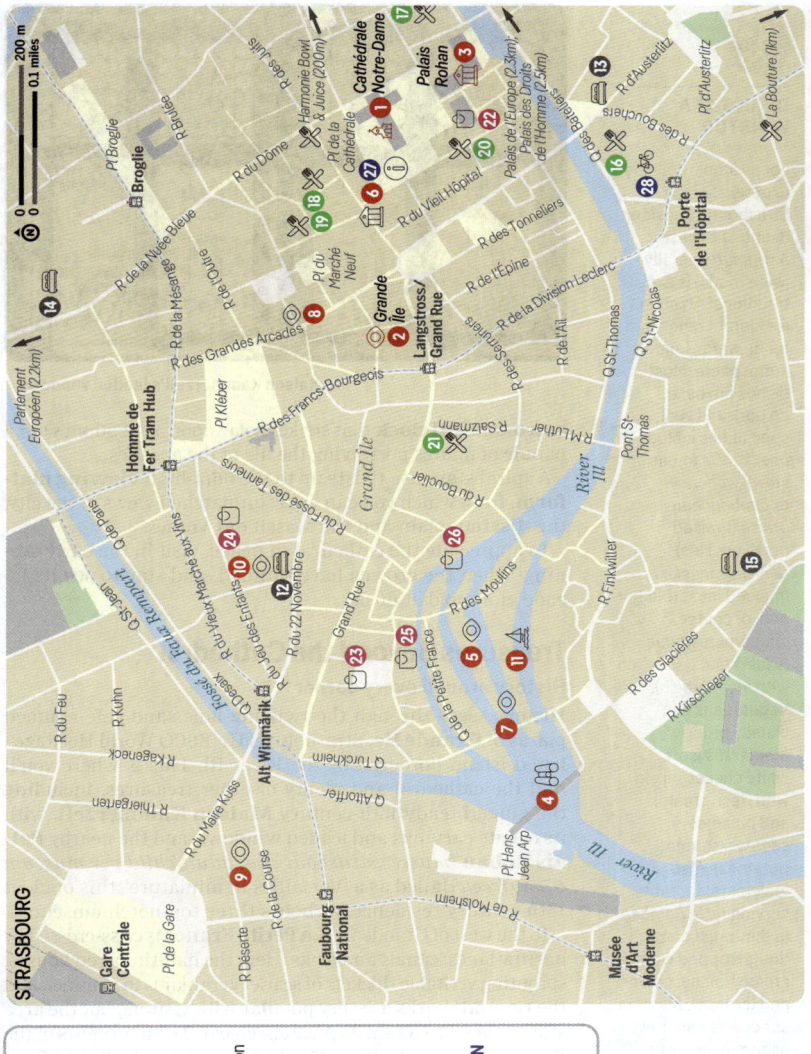

ALSACE STRASBOURG

⭐ HIGHLIGHTS
1. Cathédrale Notre-Dame
2. Grande Île
3. Palais Rohan

● SIGHTS
4. Barrage Vauban
5. La Petite France
6. Maison Kammerzell
7. Ponts Couverts
8. Rue des Grandes Arcades
9. Rue Déserte
10. Rue du Jeu-des-Enfants

● ACTIVITIES
11. Marin d'Eau Douce

● SLEEPING
12. Hôtel Boma
13. Hôtel Cour du Corbeau
14. Léonor Hôtel
15. Les Haras

● EATING
16. Au Pont Corbeau
17. Bistrot et Chocolat
18. Chez Yvonne
19. Le Clou
20. Le Tire-Bouchon
21. Origin

● SHOPPING
22. Alsatrucs
23. Le Terrier
24. Les Herbes Folles
25. Little Nuage
26. Un Noël en Alsace

● INFORMATION
27. Main Tourist Office

● TRANSPORT
28. Vélhop

Maison Kammerzell's leaded windows

DINING AT A WINSTUB

For an iconic culinary experience in Strasbourg, consider dining at a *winstub*. A *winstub* (literally 'wine room') is a traditional Alsatian restaurant renowned for its warm, homey atmosphere. Most dishes are based on pork and veal; specialities include *baeckeoffe* (meat stew), *wädele* or *jambonneau braisé* (braised pork knuckles), *fleischschnäcke* (minced meat rolls) and, of course, *choucroute garnie* (sauerkraut garnished with meat or fish). Vegetarians can usually order *bibelaskäs* (soft white cheese mixed with fresh cream) and *pommes sautées* (sautéed potatoes). Also look for restaurants serving *tarte flambée* (a thin-crust pizza dough topped with crème fraîche, onions and lardons). Alsatian specialities are best accompanied with Alsatian white wines.

astronomical clock that strikes solar noon at 12.30pm with a parade of figures portraying the life of the apostles.

A spiral staircase twists up to the 66m-high **viewing platform**, from which you can enjoy unmatched views of the city, the Alsatian plain and the Massif des Vosges.

To appreciate the cathedral in peace, visit in the early evening, when the crowds have thinned, and stay to see its facade glow gold at dusk.

Treasures Beyond the Cathedral

History around every corner

History seeps through the twisting lanes and cafe-rimmed plazas of **Grande Île**, Strasbourg's UNESCO World Heritage-listed island bordered by the River Ill. This is where you'll find the cathedral and plenty of other treasures, including the gingerbready 15th-century **Maison Kammerzell**, with its ornate carvings and leaded windows, and the nearby **Palais Rohan** *(musees.strasbourg.eu; adult/child per museum €7.50/free)*. Hailed as a 'Versailles in miniature', this opulent 18th-century residence harbours three top-notch museums.

To the west of Grande Île, **La Petite France** is criss-crossed by narrow lanes, canals and locks. Here the half-timbered houses, sprouting veritable thickets of scarlet geraniums in summer, and the riverside parks are very popular with visitors, but the area still manages to retain its Alsatian charm. Drink in views of the River Ill and the **Barrage Vauban** dam from the **Ponts Couverts** (Covered Bridges) and their trio of 13th-century towers.

VEGAN OPTIONS IN STRASBOURG: OUR PICKS

Harmonie Bowl & Juice: Excellent bowls, soups and curries inspired by fresh and comforting Asian flavours. *noon-2pm, 7-9.30pm Tue-Fri, noon-2pm Sat* €

Origin: New-generation coffee shop and veg canteen with an array of baked goods on display – try the chocolate-filled doughnut. *9am-6pm* €

La Bouture: Whips up an awesome selection of vegan treats at lunchtime. The brunch on Sunday is great. *hours vary* €

Bistrot et Chocolat: Be seduced by salads, burgers and more at this chilled-out bistro. The ultimate showstopper is the *forêt noire* (Black Forest) cake. *10am-7pm* €

Visit the European Quarter
Where Europe is being made

About 2km northeast of central Strasbourg, the European Quarter is a city within the city, with its own architecture and unique energy. In larger-than-life buildings, politics that shape the lives of 447 million European citizens are discussed, decided and implemented.

Overlooking the River Ill, the oval-shaped building of the **Parlement Européen** *(europarl.europa.eu)* is striking. You can take an audioguide tour or sit in on debates. Dates are available from the **tourist office** or on the website. For individuals, it's first come, first served (bring ID).

A futuristic glass crescent, the Council of Europe's **Palais de l'Europe** *(coe.int)* across the River Ill can be visited on free one-hour weekday tours (ask to join a group); see the website for reservations. You can also take a virtual tour at 70.coe.int/virtual-tour-en.html.

It's just a hop across the Canal de la Marne to the swirly silver **Palais des Droits de l'Homme** *(European Court of Human Rights; echr.coe.int)*, the most eye-catching of all the EU institutions. It ensures that 46 European states abide by the European Convention on Human Rights.

Strasbourg From the Water
A smooth exploration of the city

Instead of taking a boat cruise, rent a small electric boat (no license is required) to explore the River Ill and its waterways at your own pace – a great way to see the city from another perspective. Contact **Marin d'Eau Douce** *(marindeaudouce.fr; 1hr from €45)* in La Petite France.

Murals, Collages & Graffiti
Edgy street art around the city

Strasbourg doesn't limit itself to iconic monuments and picturesque neighbourhoods. Over the last few years, the city has emerged as a playground for renowned street artists and is a great open-air museum, with more than 500 works around different neighbourhoods. Our favourite streets include **rue du Jeu-des-Enfants**, **rue Déserte** and **rue des Grandes Arcades**. A map of the various murals can be found online; check strasbourg.streetartmap.eu.

BEST GIFT SHOPS IN STRASBOURG

Les Herbes Folles: This design shop is a great place for eco-shopping, with lots of quality jewellery, cosmetics and accessories made by local designers.

Un Noël en Alsace: Embrace the cosy (albeit a bit kitschy) charm of Alsatian Christmas decor at this lovely shop, which sells Christmas baubles, garlands and other well-crafted ornaments.

Alsatrucs: Sells a wide array of handcrafted gifts inspired by Alsatian culture and traditions.

Little Nuage: Here you'll find plenty of carefully selected, locally made accessories, jewellery, homewares and upcycled items.

Le Terrier: Half-gallery, half-cabinet of curiosities, Le Terrier features creations made of ceramic as well as paper and textile sculptures.

EATING IN A WINSTUB: OUR PICKS

Chez Yvonne: Near the cathedral, Chez Yvonne is an institution. Traditional decor and excellent Alsatian dishes. *11.45am-2pm & 6.30-10pm Tue-Sat* €

Le Tire-Bouchon: Arguably the best *choucroute* in Strasbourg is served at this snug, amiable *winstub*. *11.30am-9.30pm* €

Au Pont Corbeau: The essence of Alsace quaintness with dark timber, checked tablecloths and roll-me-out-the-door hearty grub. *noon-2pm & 7-9.30pm Mon-Fri, noon-2pm Sun* €

Le Clou: The menu is packed with classics – *wädele, bibelaskäs* – all of which marry nicely with a glass of local pinot noir. *11.45am-2.30pm & 6-10pm* €

Beyond Strasbourg

Unexpected treasures abound north of Strasbourg, an area that very few French people, let alone foreigners, consider visiting.

Places
Betschdorf & Soufflenheim p338
Hunspach p338
Sélestat p340

Keen to discover uncrowded, undervalued territories in Alsace? Head north! Forget all about time in this hauntingly beautiful part of Alsace, which conveys a sense of mystery. An hour's drive northwest of Strasbourg takes you to the Parc Naturel Régional des Vosges du Nord. This is a gentle, unhurried region of billowing hill country sprinkled with small lakes, carpeted with dense forests, laced by rivers and freckled with cute villages and hilltop castles. The scenery makes a perfect backdrop for myriad outdoor pursuits, including hiking and cycling. Back in the Alsatian plain, towards the Rhine, you can make a stop at cute-as-can-be Hunspach, before heading to Soufflenheim and Betschdorf, two villages renowned for their pottery workshops. To the southwest, Sélestat is well worth a detour.

GETTING AROUND

For Wingen-sur-Moder and Niederbronn-les-Bains in the Vosges du Nord, there are regular train services from Strasbourg (about 35 minutes). Nowhere in Alsace is having your own set of wheels going to enhance your experience as much as in northern Alsace, whose towns, villages and valleys are all best explored by car. For Betschdorf and Hunspach, you'll also need your own wheels. Sélestat is easily reached by train.

Betschdorf & Soufflenheim

TIME FROM STRASBOURG: **45MIN**

Meet potters at work

Alsace has a strong tradition of pottery making, and nowhere is that more clear than in the villages of Betschdorf and Soufflenheim, about 50km north of Strasbourg. Earthenware and crockery have been fashioned here for several centuries, and most Alsatian families still use a colourful Soufflenheim pot to cook *choucroute* (sauerkraut). One of the most reputable workshops in Soufflenheim is **Poterie Siegfried-Burger** *(siegfried-burger.fr)*. Betschdorf pottery is usually grey with cobalt blue motifs, and is primarily used for decorative or storage purposes.

Both villages have main streets dotted with pottery shops and potters' workshops, which welcome visitors. Potters produce dishes, pitchers, plates, flower pots, mugs and cooking pots. Much of the history of Betschdorf's pottery can also be seen in the town's small **Musée de la Poterie** *(betschdorf.com; adult/child €4/2.50)*, which is open from April to September.

Hunspach

TIME FROM STRASBOURG: **45MIN**

Chill out in a picturesque village

About 60km north of Strasbourg, Hunspach is not your average chocolate-box Alsatian village. Surrounded by fields and orchard trees, it's instantly recognisable due to its black and white

THE WONDERS OF PARC NATUREL RÉGIONAL DES VOSGES DU NORD

The lightly trafficked, scenic secondary roads that criss-cross the Parc Naturel Régional des Vosges du Nord (Northern Vosges Natural Park) are a treat.

START	END	LENGTH
Maison des Rochers de Graufthal	Chemin des Cimes	110km; 4hrs

Covering 1300 sq km of hills and woods, the Northern Vosges are the stuff of storybooks – very *à la Grimms*. Start your green escape from ① **Maison des Rochers de Graufthal**, which features a few quirky troglodyte dwellings painted in blue. A few kilometres to the north lies ② **La Petite Pierre**, a laid-back town amid a sea of greenery. Follow the D135 to the north until Wingen-sur-Moder where you can enjoy ③ **Musée Lalique**. This state-of-the-art museum harbours a collection assembling exquisite gem-encrusted and enamelled jewellery, perfume bottles and sculpture created by French art nouveau designer René Lalique. Head due north to ④ **Bitche**, which has a stunning citadel atop a hill. Take the D662 east to the spa town of ⑤ **Niederbronn-les-Bains**. Even if you're not here for a soak in the thermal pool, it's worth a stroll through the town's historic centre, which looks all the more striking against the hilly backdrop of the Vosges. Continue further northeast to ⑥ **Château de Fleckenstein**. Teetering at the top of a rocky spur near the German border, these red-sandstone medieval ruins proffer mind-blowing views from their ramparts.

For a unique experience, end your trip at ⑦ **Chemin des Cimes**, near Drachenbronn-Birlenbach; a 1050m-long treetop walk on a footbridge and impressive 29m-high spiralling observation tower to enjoy fantastic panoramas.

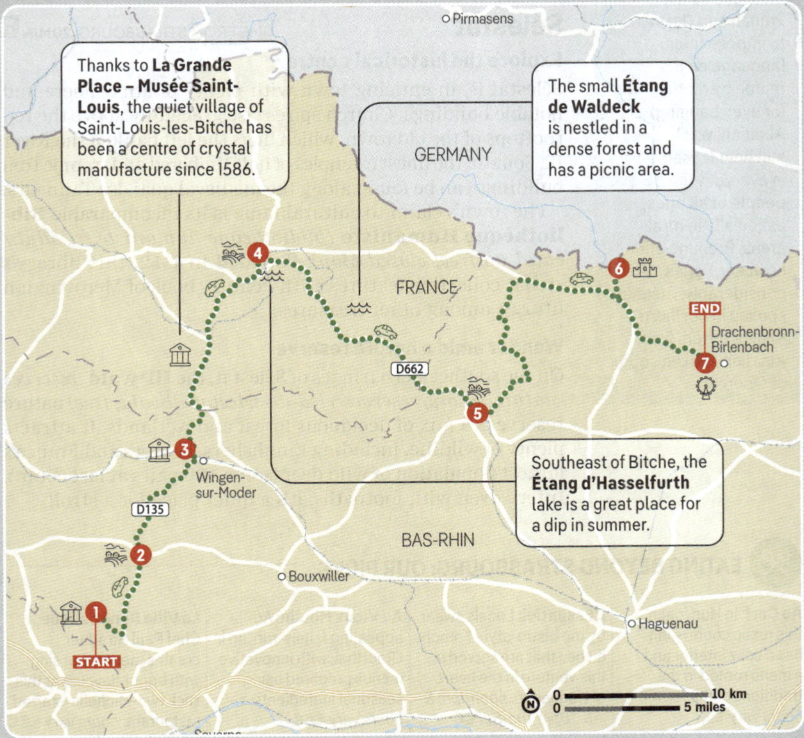

ALSACE BEYOND STRASBOURG

Thanks to **La Grande Place – Musée Saint-Louis**, the quiet village of Saint-Louis-lès-Bitche has been a centre of crystal manufacture since 1586.

The small **Étang de Waldeck** is nestled in a dense forest and has a picnic area.

Southeast of Bitche, the **Étang d'Hasselfurth** lake is a great place for a dip in summer.

Hunspach (p338)

LOCAL LINGO

The official language in Alsace is French, but Alsatian is also widely spoken. The roots of Alsatian (Elsässisch) go back to the 4th century, when Germanic Alemanni tribes assimilated the local Celts (Gauls) and Romans. Similar to the dialects spoken in nearby Germany and Switzerland, it has no official written form (spelling is something of a free-for-all). Yet despite heavy-handed attempts by the French and Germans to impose their language on the region by restricting (or even banning) Alsatian, you'll still hear it used in everyday life by people of all ages, especially in rural areas. Pronunciation, however, varies considerably. Alsatian spoken in northern Alsace differs from Alsatian spoken south of Obernai.

half-timbered 18th- and 19th-century houses. Unlike villages on the Route des Vins, you won't find any colourful facades here, for the natural white of lime was cheaper. Leave your car in a car park and walk around the peaceful streets. To soak up the atmosphere, it's well worth having lunch or dinner in the village.

Sélestat

TIME FROM STRASBOURG: **20MIN**

Explore the historical centre

Sélestat is an enticing town with plenty of atmosphere and notable buildings. Church spires rise gracefully above the red rooftops of the old town, which hugs the left bank of the River Ill. Some of the finest examples of half-timbered and trompe l'œil buildings can be found along the medieval quai des Tanneurs.

The town's claim to cultural fame is its incomparable **Bibliothèque Humaniste** (bibliotheque-humaniste.fr; adult/child €6/free; closed Mon). Founded in 1452, this library's stellar collection features a 7th-century book of Merovingian liturgy, among other treasures.

Wander amid a nature reserve

On the southeastern fringes of Sélestat, the **Ill*wald** (reserves-naturelles.org/reserves/ried-de-selestat-illwald; free) nature reserve is a mix of deciduous forest and wetlands. It attracts plenty of wildlife, including kingfishers, beavers and France's largest population of wild deer (some 400 pairs at last count). Interwoven with footpaths, it's a quiet place for a stroll.

EATING BEYOND STRASBOURG: OUR PICKS

Au Cerf: In Hunspach, this rustic country inn has a cosy interior and a menu rooted in the traditions of the terroir. hours vary €

L'Essentiel: Locals swear by the bistro-style French dishes that are served in this venture in the heart of Haguenau. noon-1pm & 7-8.30pm Tue-Sat €€

Au Vieux Moulin: An appealing family-run inn in Graufthal, with innovative menus prepared using seasonal ingredients. hours vary €€€

La Villa René Lalique: Chef Paul Stradner creates menus that sing with bright flavours at this slick two-Michelin-starred restaurant. hours vary €€€

Colmar

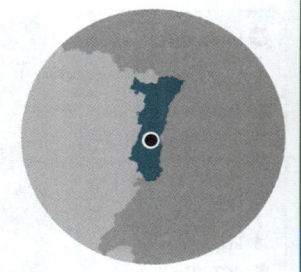

RICH HISTORY | DREAMY CITY CENTRE | VIBRANT STREETS

Colmar is a joy. More intimate, harmonious and easy-going than Strasbourg, 70km to the north, it looks as though it has been plucked from the pages of a medieval folk tale. Sure, it doesn't have such an iconic attraction such as Strasbourg's cathedral, but its centre is blessed with an array of scenic spots. Wandering along its streets is like seeing childhood fairy stories come to life. Candy-coloured buildings from the late Middle Ages and the Renaissance, sinuous cobbled lanes, cute boutique shops selling local produce and a flower-lined river that you can explore in a flat-bottom barge – it's all there. And the Route des Vins and the Massif des Vosges are right on its doorstep. Colmar is a great city in all seasons, but if you happen to be there in December, you'll enjoy its Christmas market, one of the most vibrant in eastern France.

GETTING AROUND

Daily direct train services connect Paris and Colmar. There are also direct train services to Metz, Nancy, Mulhouse and Strasbourg. The most convenient car park for the historic centre is on place Scheurer-Kestner just north of Musée Unterlinden. Once in the city, walking is the way to go. You can also rent a bike or an e-bike with **Colmar Vélo – Vélodocteurs** (velodocteurs.com; per day from €12).

Petite Venise (p342)

☑ TOP TIP

As you approach Colmar on the N83, 3km north of the old town, look for the spitting image of the **Statue of Liberty**. This 12m-high replica was erected to mark the centenary of the death of local lad Frédéric Auguste Bartholdi (1834–1904), creator of the NYC statue.

HIGHLIGHTS
1. Musée Unterlinden
2. Petite Venise

SIGHTS
3. Ancienne Douane
4. Grand' Rue
5. Maison des Têtes
6. Maison Pfister
7. Rue des Clefs
8. Rue des Marchands

ACTIVITIES
9. Colmar au Fil de l'Eau

SLEEPING
10. La Maison des Têtes
11. Le Colombier
12. L'Esquisse Hôtel & Spa

EATING
13. La Cocotte de Grand-Mère
14. La Soï
15. L'Artémise
16. Wistub de la Petite Venise

Feel the Pulse of Petite Venise
Canals, rowboats and candy-coloured houses

If you see just one thing in Colmar, make it the **Petite Venise** (Little Venice) quarter, at the southern edge of the old city. This is the beating heart of Colmar. Don't expect anything resembling Venice, though. It's a compact area, which runs along the scenic River Lauch – hence the nickname. The backstreets are punctuated by impeccably restored half-timbered houses in sugared-almond shades, many ablaze with geraniums in summer.

Petite Venise is best explored on foot or by rowboat. **Colmar au Fil de l'Eau** *(barques-colmar.fr; adult/child €9/4)* runs 25-minute guided tours on small rowboats, departing next to Pont St-Pierre.

Architectural Highlights in the Old Town
Eye-catching buildings galore

The historic centre of Colmar is a maze of pedestrian malls dotted with plenty of cultural highlights. Look for **rue des Clefs**, **Grand' Rue** and **rue des Marchands**, medieval streets

Maison Pfister

lined with dozens of restored, half-timbered houses. **Maison Pfister** (1537) is remarkable for its exterior decoration, including delicately painted panels and a carved wooden balcony. **Maison des Têtes** (House of the Heads) has a fantastic facade crowded with 106 grimacing stone faces and animal heads. At the southeastern tip of rue des Marchands is the **Ancienne Douane** (Koïfhus in Alsatian; Old Customs House), another medieval camera-friendly building, with loggia and a variegated tiled roof.

Cultural Immersion in Musée Unterlinden

A gem of a museum

Art lovers should make a beeline for **Musée Unterlinden** (*musee-unterlinden.com; adult/child €13/8*), if only for the late-Gothic **Retable d'Issenheim** (Issenheim Altarpiece), which is hailed as one of the most profound works of faith ever created. It illustrates with unrelenting realism scenes from the New Testament, including the Nativity and the Crucifixion. There's an English audioguide. The building itself, which is gathered around a superb Gothic-style Dominican cloister, is photogenic.

WHY I LOVE COLMAR

Jean-Bernard Carillet, Lonely Planet writer

Being from neighbouring Lorraine, I often travel to Alsace. I like the sense of opulence and prosperity that emanates from this region. In December, I never miss a chance to delve into Colmar's sparkly Marché de Noël (Christmas Market). It's colourful, festive and brimming with good cheer. I love the lights, the mood and, of course, the food and drink. Mulled wine, spicy *bredele* (biscuits), markets loaded with gifts, hand-crafted decorations and gingerbread hearts – it's all there. It's so special. There's a kind of magical atmosphere that can't be found anywhere else in France. And if I want a lesser-known Alsatian Christmas market, I go to nearby Turckheim.

EATING IN COLMAR: OUR PICKS

L'Artémise: This gourmet tearoom serves irresistible pastries in vintage surrounds. Great brunches too. *9am-6pm Thu-Mon* €

La Soï: Whips up fine *Flammekueche* (flambéed pie), cooked to thin, crisp perfection, in a cosy, wood-lined dining space. *noon-1.30pm & 7-9.30pm Fri-Tue* €

Wistub de la Petite Venise: This snug and inviting *winstub* serves a wide range of well-executed Alsatian classics. *hours vary* €€

La Cocotte de Grand-Mère: *Bistrorant* (half bistro, half restaurant) rustling up satisfying French cuisine with a creative twist, including chicken with truffle. *noon-1pm & 7-8pm Mon-Fri* €€

Beyond Colmar

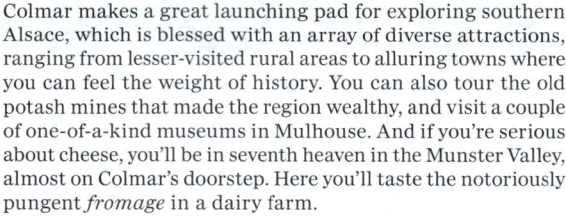

History, nature and culture are deeply intertwined around Colmar. Wherever you go, you'll find ample opportunities to get off the beaten track.

Places
Munster p344
Mulhouse p344
Neuf-Brisach p345
The Sundgau p345
Route de la Potasse p346

Colmar makes a great launching pad for exploring southern Alsace, which is blessed with an array of diverse attractions, ranging from lesser-visited rural areas to alluring towns where you can feel the weight of history. You can also tour the old potash mines that made the region wealthy, and visit a couple of one-of-a-kind museums in Mulhouse. And if you're serious about cheese, you'll be in seventh heaven in the Munster Valley, almost on Colmar's doorstep. Here you'll taste the notoriously pungent *fromage* in a dairy farm.

Often overlooked by mainstream tourist trails, southern Alsace packs a punch. You'll be positively surprised.

GETTING AROUND

With enough patience many towns in southern Alsace can be reached by bus or train from Colmar. Getting to Mulhouse is straightforward, with frequent train services from Colmar. There are regular bus services between Colmar and Neuf-Brisach. But to get to the more out-of-the-way places, including the Vosges Mountains and the villages of the Sundgau, you'll definitely need your own wheels.

Munster
TIME FROM COLMAR: **20MIN**
A gourmet adventure for cheese lovers
The quiet stream-side town of Munster, less than 10km west of Colmar in a lovely valley, is famed for its eponymous cheese. Rich, white and creamy, with a pungent, earthy aroma when ripe and a mild flavour when fresh, Munster cheese has been made in this valley to the time-honoured methods of the Benedictine monks since the 7th century. Only the milk of the cows that lazily graze the Vosges' highest pastures is good enough for this semisoft cheese, delicious with cumin seeds, rye bread and a glass of spicy gewürztraminer.

You'll find several dairy farms where you can taste and buy Munster. Look for **Ferme Versant du Soleil** (*ferme-versant-du-soleil.fr*) and **Ferme-Auberge du Christlesgut** (*christlesgut.com*).

Mulhouse
TIME FROM COLMAR: **20MIN**
Visit world-class industrial museums
The industrial city of Mulhouse, 43km south of Colmar, has none of the quaint Alsatian charm that you find further north, but we bet you'll love the city's industrial museums. An ode to the automobile, the striking glass-and-steel **Musée National de l'Automobile** (*musee-automobile.fr; adult/child €18/11*) showcases 400 rare and classic motors, from old-timers such as the Bugatti Royale to Formula 1 dream machines.

Neuf-Brisach

Trainspotters will be in their element at **Cité du Train** *(cite dutrain.com; adult/child €16/12)*, Europe's largest railway museum, displaying SNCF's (France's national rail network) prized collection of locomotives and carriages.

Neuf-Brisach

TIME FROM COLMAR: **20MIN**

Time travel in a UNESCO world treasure

About 16km southeast of Colmar, Neuf-Brisach has remarkably well-preserved red-sandstone fortifications, which were enshrined as a UNESCO World Heritage Site in 2008. Shaped like an eight-pointed star, the fortified town was commissioned by Louis XIV in 1697 to strengthen French defences and prevent the area from falling to the Habsburgs. It was conceived by French military architect Vauban (1633–1707).

The Sundgau

TIME FROM COLMAR: **1HR**

Immersion in a rural paradise

One of Alsace's best-kept secrets, the Sundgau offers a wonderful bucolic atmosphere with rolling pasturelands

MORE CHEESE TASTING

You can also sample cheese at a dairy farm in the **Alps** (p510) and the **Pyrénées** (p729). Other places that will appeal to cheese lovers include **Camembert** (p244) in Normandy, **Roquefort** (p678) in Languedoc and **Auvergne** (p484).

EATING BEYOND COLMAR: OUR PICKS

Zum Sauwadala: In Mulhouse, this place is known for its excellent, hearty Alsatian classics in a cosy setting. *11.30am-1.30pm Tue-Sun, 6.30-9.30pm Tue-Sat* €

L'Abbaye d'Anny: In Munster, this welcoming venue features salads, *galettes* (crêpes), *tartes flambées* and other treats in warm surroundings. *hours vary* €

Au Cheval Blanc: Laid-back restaurant in Ferrette with a menu of fresh seasonal produce in well-prepared dishes. *11.30am-1.30pm & 6-8.30pm Wed-Sat, 11.30am-3pm Sun* €

Restaurant Kastenwald: Reputable inn near Neuf-Brisach casting a modern spin on French and Alsatian staples. *noon-1.45pm & 7-8.30pm Wed-Sun* €€

A GRIM SIDE OF LOCAL HISTORY

About 60km north of Colmar, off the D130, stands **Natzweiler-Struthof** *(struthof.fr)*, the only Nazi concentration camp on French territory. Today the sombre remains of the camp are still surrounded by guard towers and concentric, once-electrified barbed-wire fences. The *four crématoire* (crematorium oven), the *salle d'autopsie* (autopsy room) and the *chambre à gaz* (gas chamber), 1.7km from the camp gate, bear grim witness to the atrocities committed here. In all, some 22,000 of the prisoners (40% of the total) interned here and at nearby annexe camps died; many were shot or hanged. In early September 1944, as US Army forces approached, the 5517 surviving inmates were sent to Dachau.

Pasturelands, the Sundgau

interspersed with ponds and time-forgotten villages. At the southernmost tip of Alsace, towards the Swiss border, this little morsel of paradise is a dream come true for those seeking to get well and truly off the beaten track. There are only secondary roads, and plenty of cycling paths. Villages worth exploring include **Friesen** and **Hirtzbach**, with their magnificent traditional farms, and charm-filled **Ferrette**, which has castle ruins. For the ultimate bijou fairy-tale castle, head to remote **Château du Landskron** in Leymen, which sits at the Swiss border. Gourmands, take note: the local speciality here is *carpe frite* (fried carp), which is served in a number of traditional inns around the area, including **Au Soleil** *(restaurant-au-soleil.fr; noon-2pm Sun-Fri, 7-9pm Wed-Sat)* in Liebsdorf.

Route de la Potasse

TIME FROM COLMAR: **30MIN**

Discover vestiges of Alsace's industrial heyday

This is certainly not your typical Alsatian destination, but the area around Ensisheim, north of Mulhouse, will appeal to travellers who are after something different. From 1910 to

EATING BEYOND COLMAR: OUR PICKS

Auberge du Tanet: In the Vosges Mountains, a great inn in which to sample tasty regional specialities in a cosy dining room. *noon-2pm Fri-Tue, 7.30-9pm Sat* €

Auberge Sundgovienne: Enticing inn in nearby Altkirch putting a spin on traditional dishes. *noon-1.45pm & 7-8.45pm Wed-Sat, noon-1.45pm Sun* €€

Au Vieux Porche: In oh-so-charming Eguisheim, this great venue does well-executed Alsatian dishes. *noon-2pm & 7-8.45pm Wed-Sat, noon-2pm Sun* €€

La Table d'Olivier Nasti – Le Chambard: Two-Michelin-starred restaurant famous for its creative menus and fabulous wine list. *noon-2pm Fri-Sun, 7-9pm Wed-Sun* €€€

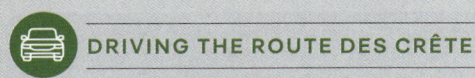

DRIVING THE ROUTE DES CRÊTES

Partly built during WWI, the Route des Crêtes (Ridge Road) takes you to the Vosges' highest *ballons* (rounded mountain peaks).

START	END	LENGTH
Col du Bonhomme	Cernay	80km; 3hrs

Start your mountain adventures at ❶ **Col du Bonhomme** (949m), about 30km west of Colmar. The first leg crosses dense conifer forests and leads to the bottle-green ❷ **Lac Vert** (Green Lake), just below the main road. The marked trail that loops around the Lac Vert (allow about one hour) is super scenic. The D61 continues to ❸ **Col de la Schlucht** (1139m), home to a small ski station in winter. You then enter the Massif du Hohneck, the wildest area of the whole Vosges range, with windswept *chaumes* (highland meadows) and craggy rock formations. You can drive up to ❹ **Le Hohneck** summit (1363m) for some sublime views over the Alsatian valleys. The D431 then reaches ❺ **Le Markstein**, a ski station that also offers plenty of activities in summer, especially paragliding, mountain biking and hiking. Be sure to have a *repas marcaire* (cowherd's meal) at the ❻ **Ferme-Auberge du Treh**, a farm restaurant that serves delicious Alsatian dishes. It's a short drive to the dramatic, wind-buffeted summit of ❼ **Grand Ballon**, the highest point in the Vosges at 1424m. Past the Grand Ballon, the D431G starts a swooping descent into the valley. Stop at ❽ **Monument du Hartmannswillerkopf**, a poignant WWI memorial that commemorates the sacrifice of more than 7000 soldiers, before reaching ❾ **Cernay**, which has a few historical buildings. From here, it's an easy drive to Mulhouse.

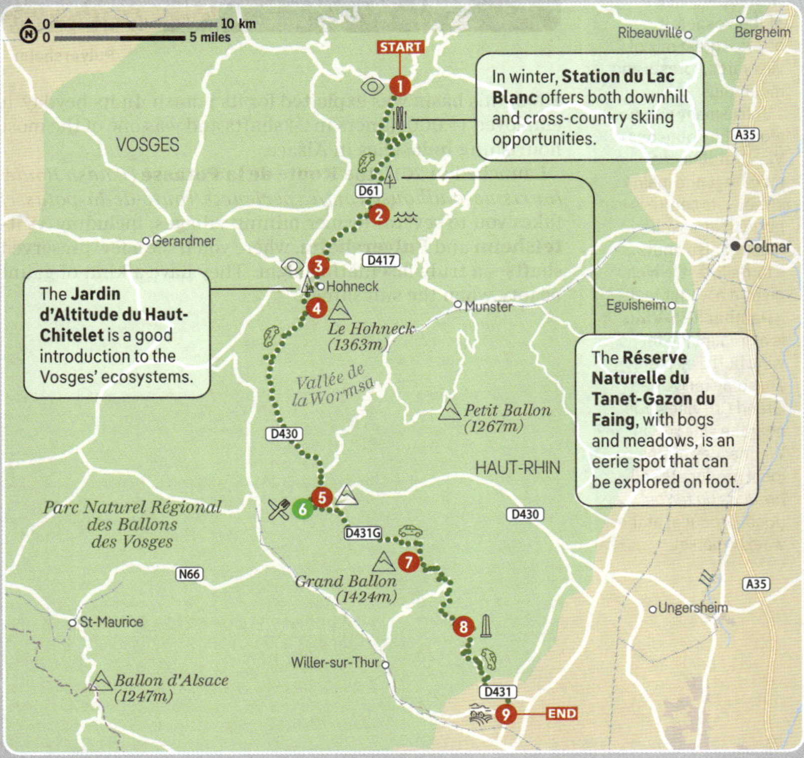

In winter, **Station du Lac Blanc** offers both downhill and cross-country skiing opportunities.

The **Jardin d'Altitude du Haut-Chitelet** is a good introduction to the Vosges' ecosystems.

The **Réserve Naturelle du Tanet-Gazon du Faing**, with bogs and meadows, is an eerie spot that can be explored on foot.

THE ROUTE DES VINS' MOST UNDERRATED VILLAGES

Angela Prado runs **Maison Moritz-Prado**, a winery in Albé. She names her favourite villages on the Route des Vins. *@maison-moritzprado*

Albé is an utterly peaceful, off-the-beaten track village with a distinct character. It's in a secluded valley with superb views of the Vosges. It offers a great mix of vineyards, forests and mountains.

Unlike many villages along the Route des Vins, **Andlau** has more that one main street – its centre is a maze of atmospheric lanes. It also abuts a large forest, which gives it a wilder feel.

Dambach-la-Ville is a great place for wine buffs, as there are some renowned Grand Cru vineyards near the village. On Wednesday morning, local producers sell *produits du terroir* (local produce) at the weekly market.

Pulversheim

2002, this basin was exploited for its potash. In its heyday, it employed 14,000 miners in 24 shafts and was one of the most flourishing industries in Alsace.

Launched in 2017, the **Route de la Potasse** *(Potash Route; tourisme-mulhouse.com/experiences/route-de-la-potasse)* takes you to several former mining villages, including **Wittelsheim** and **Pulversheim**, where you'll see a few preserved shafts – a truly fascinating sight. They have a kind of gaunt beauty when the sun shines.

Mittelbergheim vineyards

TOP EXPERIENCE

Route des Vins d'Alsace

This iconic wine route stretches 170km from Marlenheim, 21km west of Strasbourg, southwards to Thann, 46km southwest of Colmar. The road is like a 'greatest hits' of all things Alsatian. Vines march up the hillsides to castle-topped crags and the mist-shrouded Vosges, and every kilometre or so an exquisitely preserved medieval village invites you to stop and soak up the atmosphere.

DON'T MISS

- Eguisheim
- Château du Haut Koenigsbourg
- Riquewihr
- Kaysersberg
- Ribeauvillé
- Obernai
- Mittelbergheim

The Wine Route (Northern Part)

From **Marlenheim**, the gateway to the Route des Vins, a well-marked country lane wriggles through soothing beautiful scenery to medieval **Molsheim**, centred on a picture-perfect square. A vision of half-timbered, vine-draped, ring-walled loveliness, **Obernai**, 5km to the south, is one of the most alluring towns along the road. Life still revolves around the place du Marché, the market square where you'll find the 16th-century town hall and the bell-topped Halle aux Blés (Corn Exchange).

Next head to **Mittelbergheim**, a delightful peaches-and-cream jumble of houses lining slim, undulating streets. It's home to numerous cellars, each marked by a wrought-iron sign.

PRACTICALITIES

- routedesvins.alsace
- best season: April to October

TOP TIPS

- No appointment is usually needed for a cellar visit and tasting session, but check opening hours in advance.

- Pace yourself. Visit two to three wineries per day and set aside some time for cultural visits and activities.

- Tastings are free, but you're expected to buy at least one bottle.

- If you don't speak French, ask if there is anyone at the *domaine* who speaks English.

- If you're the one driving, you should spit your wine out like the pros do when tasting.

- September is harvest time – it's great for enjoying the buzz and atmosphere but winegrowers are very busy and may be less available.

A vineyard trail, the Sentier Viticole, wriggles across the slopes towards the perky twin-towered **Château du Haut-Andlau** (*chateaudandlau.com*) and the lushly forested Vosges.

Another camera-friendly stop is **Dambach-la-Ville**, a fortified town protected by ramparts and massive gateways. Here lots of houses are painted in ice-cream shades of pistachio, caramel and raspberry, and date from before 1500.

To the southwest, make a short detour to the **Château du Haut Kœnigsbourg** (*haut-koenigsbourg.fr; €12*), a turreted castle hovering above vineyards and hills. The wraparound panorama takes in the Vosges, the Black Forest and, on cloud-free days, the northern Alps.

The Wine Route (Southern Part)

The village of **Bergheim** is a joy to behold. The town is enclosed by a sturdy 14th-century ring-wall, overflowing with geraniums and enlivened by half-timbered houses in bright pastels.

Sitting snugly in a valley and presided over by a castle, medieval **Ribeauvillé**, 22km south, is a Route des Vins must. Along the main street, keep an eye out for the 17th-century

Pfifferhüs (Fifers' House), the **Hôtel de Ville** and the nearby clock-topped **Tour des Bouchers** (Butchers' Bell Tower).

In the quiet walled hamlet of **Hunawihr**, 1km south of Ribeauvillé, you're almost guaranteed to see storks. Almost next door, **Riquewihr** may be the most enchanting town on the itinerary. Medieval ramparts enclose a maze of twisting lanes, hidden courtyards and half-timbered houses, each brighter and lovelier than the next. Of course, its chocolate-box looks also make it popular, so arrive early morning or evening to appreciate the town at its peaceful best.

Just 10km northwest of Colmar, **Kaysersberg** is another instant heart-stealer with its backdrop of vines, castle and 16th-century bridge. Arrive before 10am or in the evening to have the streets to yourself. From there, travel south to close-to-nature **Katzenthal**, which is great for tiptoeing off the tourist trail for a while. *Grand cru* vines ensnare the hillside, topped by the medieval ruins of **Château du Wineck**. Then swing by **Eguisheim**, a quirkily laid-out village – it's circular in shape. The square place du Château St-Léon IX marks the heart of the old town. You can continue south to **Guebwiller** and **Thann** for more astonishing vineyards (and mountain) views.

Wine Tasting on the Route des Vins

Many of the independent AOC wine producers offer free tastings at their cellars. Some also offer unusual experiences, including yoga courses, picnics, *apéros* (predinner drinks) or treasure hunts in the vineyards.

GETTING AROUND

Driving is the easiest way to reach villages and small towns on the Route des Vins, and the meandering country roads make for a memorable road trip. Many towns and villages along the route are also served by train from Strasbourg or Colmar. Outdoorsy types will find plenty of opportunities to enjoy the Route des Vins at their own pace, whether by bike or on foot. Look for the Sentiers Viticoles footpaths. Bike hire is available in all the major towns.

Kaysersberg

ALSATIAN WINES

Forget about the fairly widespread preconception about 'fruity' Alsatian. Alsace wines are usually single variety wines, rather than blends. Key grape varieties include riesling, sylvaner, gewürztraminer, muscat and pinot gris. Make sure you sample all of them to appreciate the wide palette of aromatic nuances they offer. Some riesling can even smell of petrol!

In Dahlenheim near Marlenheim, stop at **Domaine Pfister** *(melaniepfister.fr)*, which is run by Mélanie Pfister. She specialises in high-calibre, organic *vins de gastronomie* (wines for gastronomic restaurants).

In Mittelbergheim, check **Domaine Gilg** *(domaine-gilg.com)*, a family-run winery that's won many awards for its sylvaner, pinot and riesling.

Domaine Marcel Deiss *(marceldeiss.com)* in Bergheim, near Ribeauvillé, has an original approach – it grows several grape varieties on the same vineyard plot. Try Schoenenbourg, its signature white.

In Hunawihr, you can visit **Domaine Mittnacht Frères** *(mittnachtfreres.fr)*. On top of all the typical Alsace wines, they also produce some more creative wines, including the Découvertes (a mix of grape varieties) and the quirky Solar, which has macerated orange.

After Ribeauvillé, pause at **Domaine Becker** *(vinsbecker.com)* in the village of Zellenberg. Ask for Martine Becker, who speaks English. The family has been making wine since the 16th century, so they are largely on top of the job. They produce an outstanding range of organic wines. In the same village, **Jean Huttard** *(alsace-jean-huttard.fr)* offers a unique 'winegrower for a day' experience in the cellars or in the vineyards as well as various workshops. In Kientzheim, there is no better address to sample stellar rieslings than **Domaine Paul Blanck** *(blanck.com)*. This forward-thinking vintner also offers qigong and geology classes in his vineyards.

In Riquewihr, **Hugel** *(m.hugel.com)* is your stop for a tasting session in a smart cellar right in the heart of town – try their selection of delectable *vendanges tardives* (sweet, late harvest wines made from overripe grapes)

After exploring the old town of Kaysersberg, make a beeline for the woman-run **Domaine Weinbach** *(domaineweinbach.com)*, a hallowed name among wine buffs.

In Eguisheim, call in at **Maison Émile Beyer** *(emile-beyer.fr)*, which has been run by the same family for 14 generations. Tastings take place in ancient cellars housed in what was once a medieval coach inn right by the main square.

# Places We Love to Stay

€ Budget €€ Midrange €€€ Top End

Strasbourg   MAP p335

Hôtel Boma € Sassy Boma ticks all the boxes: international chic interior, congenial atmosphere and splashes of colour.

Léonor Hôtel €€ Slick, spacious rooms dressed in soothing tones in a gorgeously restored 18th-century building.

Les Haras €€ Les Haras is a strikingly contemporary conversion of the former national stud farm. The contemporary rooms are all about understated elegance.

Hôtel Cour du Corbeau €€€ A 16th-century inn lovingly converted into a boutique hotel, with rustic-chic rooms and a lovely spa.

Beyond Strasbourg

Ferme Auberge du Moulin des 7 Fontaines € Oozing with atmosphere, this traditional inn is blessed with lovely views over the northern Vosges.

Maison Ungerer € In pretty Hunspach, this half-timbered house full of nooks and crannies is a great find.

Alsace Village € Set in a meadow near a forest, this venue offers plenty of bucolic charm. In Obersteinbach.

Hôtel Le Moulin €€ A haven of peace in Gundershoffen, with 12 tastefully decorated rooms and a reputable restaurant.

Gîtes de la Karlsmühle – Moulin 1846 €€ Four lovingly restored, spacious *gîtes* (flats) in a vast and quiet property west of Hunspach.

La Source des Sens €€ A great base to explore the Parc Naturel Régional des Vosges du Nord. It has a restaurant and a superb spa. In Morsbronn-les-Bains.

Colmar   MAP p342

Le Colombier €€ Behind the peach-hued, shuttered facade of a 16th-century townhouse in Petite Venise lies this truly welcoming hotel with elegant rooms.

La Maison des Têtes €€€ This hotel occupies a magnificent historic building. Each of its 21 rooms has rich wooden panelling, a marble bathroom and romantic views.

L'Esquisse Hôtel & Spa €€€ Comar's hottest design hotel, L'Esquisse is quaint on the outside and ubercool on the inside, with sleek rooms and a superb spa.

Beyond Colmar

Auberge Sundgovienne € This top-notch venture in the Sundgau offers neat rooms and a great in-house restaurant.

La Villa Estérel € A well-run B&B in a leafy property south of Mulhouse, near the Rhine.

La Maison Hotel € A boutique-hotel for less than €100 right in the heart of Mulhouse? Yes it's possible. No two rooms are alike.

Domaine de Haslach €€ North of Munster, this is a great spot to decompress. Has well-equipped rooms, ecolodges and a few wooden *cabanes* (huts) on stilts.

Hôtel & Spa Mont Champ du Feu €€ In a ski resort southwest of Obernai, this is a truly welcoming option with smart rooms overlooking the wooded peaks of the Vosges.

Route des Vins   MAP p350

Clos Froehn € A beautifully renovated farmhouse flanked by a medieval tower in Zellenberg. Vineyard views are stunning.

La Villa Haute Corniche €€ Four impeccable rooms in a superb villa above Obernai, with cardiac-arresting views of the vineyards.

Domaine La Commanderie €€ In Boersch, this atmospheric venue has four rooms in a recently refurbished 15th-century house.

Le Chambard €€ A splash of five-star luxury in the heart of Kaysersberg, Le Chambard offers elegantly contemporary rooms, a terrific spa, a cosy *winstub* (wine tavern) and a Michelin-starred restaurant.

Researched by
Jean-Bernard Carillet

Lorraine

UNDERRATED CULTURAL TREASURES AND GREEN ESCAPES

Sandwiched between Alsace and Champagne, Lorraine is one of France's lesser-known regions. Expect plenty of good surprises – without the crowds.

If you're in search of a region that nobody knows (even the French!), Lorraine will appeal to you, as it must be one of France's most underrated destinations. It doesn't have the reputation of its prestigious neighbours – Champagne to the west and Alsace to the east – and, although bordering Germany, Luxembourg and Belgium, it's often overlooked by visitors en route to more established holiday spots. Indeed, Lorraine has long suffered from an image problem and an inferiority complex. From the 19th to the 20th centuries, the region was the industrial powerhouse of eastern France and since the 1980s it has been associated with declining industries (think coal and steel).

With the worst of times now firmly behind it, Lorraine the underdog is emerging as a proper tourist destination by touting an astonishing – and quite unspoiled – array of assets. Its two main historic cities, majestic Metz and effortlessly glam Nancy, will satisfy a visitor's deepest craving for well-preserved old-world atmosphere, while its rolling countryside dotted with mirabelle plum orchards and appealing towns and villages has a strong photogenic appeal. For history buffs, the region's WWI battlefields around Verdun offer an exceptional opportunity to learn about the Great War. To the east, the Vosges Mountains, which straddle Lorraine and Alsace, offer plenty of experiences for nature lovers and outdoorsy types. One thing is sure: there's no overtourism here.

THE MAIN AREAS

METZ
Avant-garde art and a medieval atmosphere.
p358

THE MEUSE VALLEY
A bucolic, under-the-radar area.
p362

NANCY
One of eastern France's most appealing cities.
p365

For places to stay in Lorraine, see p371

Left: Ossuaire de Douaumont (p362), the Meuse Valley; Above: Arc Héré (p366), Nancy

Find Your Way

Encompassing four *départements* (Moselle, Meurthe-et-Moselle, Meuse and Vosges), this unheralded swath of eastern France harbours fascinating historic cities, stunning cultural sights and well-preserved natural wonders. Our picks reflect the region's travel hubs.

Meuse Valley, p362
This peaceful, rural region west of Metz seems little changed over the centuries and is a great place to decompress.

Metz, p358
Lorraine's graceful capital boasts a Gothic marvel of a cathedral, superlative art collections and a laid-back atmosphere.

Nancy, p365
A well-kept secret, this elegant city is home to one of the most grandiose 18th-century squares in Europe.

CAR
It's best to have a car to explore this region. Metz is on the A4, which links Paris and Reims with Strasbourg. Both Nancy and Metz are on the A31 from Dijon to Luxembourg.

TRAIN
It's easy to reach the major cities in Lorraine by train from Paris or Strasbourg. Take the TGV to Metz or Nancy, from where you'll find connections to a number of smaller towns around the region.

Cathédrale St-Étienne (p358), Metz

Plan Your Time

Lorraine is not a place that inspires rushing. From the Meuse *département* (to the west) to the Vosges Mountains (to the east), plenty of unusual experiences await.

Pressed for Time

● With a few days in hand put all your attention on the two main cities. Check out the sights in **Metz** (p358), including the architecturally innovative **Centre Pompidou-Metz** (p360) and marvellous Gothic **Cathédrale St-Étienne** (p358) before heading to **Nancy** (p365). Look for the best **art nouveau wonders** (p368) around the centre before heading to a cafe on gorgeous **place Stanislas** (p365).

A Five-Day Odyssey

● Spend a day in Metz then stop at the oh-so-photogenic **Uckange ironworks** (p364) before heading west to the **Meuse Valley** (p362). Visit the poignant **WWI battlefields** (p362) near Verdun before driving south along the scenic valley to **St-Mihiel** (p364). From there, head to **Nancy** (p365). On your last day, head to the **Hautes Vosges Mountains** (p369) to fill your lungs with fresh air.

Seasonal Highlights

SPRING
Spring brings sunshine, flowers and mild temperatures, ideal for visiting Metz or Nancy, or the WWI battlefields around Verdun.

SUMMER
Few crowds and lots of outdoor pursuits – hiking, cycling and swimming in lakes – make Lorraine a great summer destination.

AUTUMN
Lorraine's numerous forests is blanketed in a symphony of colour as trees become a riot of golden yellows and oranges.

WINTER
December is a good month to soak up festive vibes, especially in Nancy and Metz, where Christmas is a big thing.

Metz

STRIKING ARCHITECTURE | FINE DINING | RELAXED ATMOSPHERE

☑ TOP TIP

Don't underestimate Metz – it deserves at least a full day, preferably two, to do it justice. Before or after visiting the cathedral, pause at Metz' grand **Marché Couvert** *(closed Sun & Mon)*, just across the street. Once a bishop's palace, now a temple to fresh local produce, it's a fine spot for good picnic fare.

Traversed by the elegant Moselle river, Metz (pronounced 'mess') remains firmly off the beaten track. This city is proud of its origins, which go back to Roman times, when it stood astride major trade routes. Although lying quite close to the German border, it feels more like a southern city thanks to its stunning honey-coloured historic centre built from golden Jaumont limestone. The adjoining, more recent regal Quartier Impérial is also well worth a gander. Enchanting Metz' visual centrepiece is its Gothic marvel of a cathedral. Close to the railway station, the Centre Pompidou-Metz is another stunner, with superb art collections that draw crowds from afar.

Metz is not only about monuments and sights. It's an adorable, atmospheric city blessed with a lovely quality of life. Enjoy a flourishing dining scene, large and beautiful flower-lined public spaces and parks, a superb riverside setting and, in summer, buzzy pavement cafes. In all, a really pleasant surprise.

A Flamboyant Cathedral
Gothic marvel filled with stained-glass windows

Nothing can prepare you for that first skyward glimpse of the lofty Gothic **Cathédrale St-Étienne** *(cathedrale-metz.fr; free)*, dating from the 13th century, with its lacy golden spires towering above the heart of the old town. The interior

GETTING AROUND

Metz' historical centre is relatively compact, so you can comfortably do your urban exploration on foot. If you're driving, you'll find several car parks in the centre, including the vast **Parking de la République** and **Parking Metz Coislin**, from which it's an easy walk to most sights and restaurants. Some hotels have private parking as well. You can also rent a bike or an e-bike with **Velomet** *(lemet.fr; half day from €2)*, which has two main rental points, including one on place d'Armes next to the cathedral and one near Centre Pompidou-Metz. Taxis hover in front of the **train station** (p361).

METZ

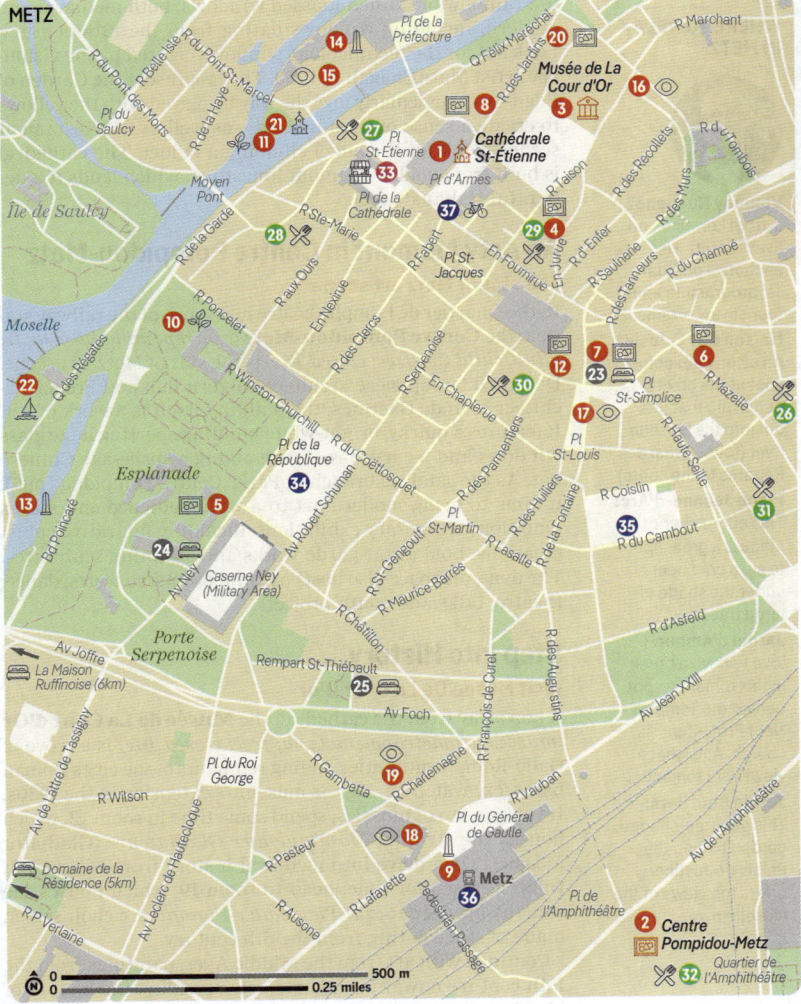

★ HIGHLIGHTS
1. Cathédrale St-Étienne
2. Centre Pompidou-Metz
3. Musée de La Cour d'Or

● SIGHTS
4. Atelier Sainte Croix des Arts
5. Galerie de l'Arsenal
6. Galerie Modulab
7. Galerie Octave Cowbell
8. Galerie PJ
9. Gare de Metz
10. Jardin Boufflers
11. Jardin d'Amour
12. La Vitrine Éphémère
13. Maison de l'Éclusier
14. Opéra-Théâtre
15. Place de la Comédie
16. Place Jeanne-d'Arc
17. Place St-Louis
18. Post Office
19. Quartier Impérial
20. Schmirlab
21. Temple Neuf

● ACTIVITIES
22. Bateau Solaire Solis

● SLEEPING
23. Hôtel de Fouquet
24. La Citadelle Metz – MGallery
25. Villa Camoufle

● EATING
26. 2'Moiselles
27. Au Cul d'Poule
28. Casa Ricci
see 24 La Réserve
29. Les Pas Sages
30. Restaurant Derrière
31. Timilia
32. Yozora

● SHOPPING
33. Marché Couvert

● TRANSPORT
34. Parking de la République
35. Parking Metz Coislin
36. Train Station
37. Velomet

WHERE TO RELAX IN METZ

Vianney Huguenot is from Lorraine and lives in Metz. He anchors a popular TV programme about tourism in Lorraine.

Maison de l'Éclusier: An utterly peaceful spot at the tip of a peninsula that juts out into the Moselle river (follow Quai des Régates to the south).

Place Jeanne-d'Arc: This atmospheric place is a great spot to sip a cold beer under the shade of large trees.

Jardin d'Amour: I love to have a break in this romantic spot behind the Temple Neuf Protestant church. And what a view! Very romantic.

Jardin Boufflers: This oak-tree-shaded garden behind the Palais de Justice offers top views of the Moselle river.

---

is a rainbow of stained-glassed windows, both medieval and modern, including windows dating from the 13th century. Look out for the technicolour windows created by the visionary artist Marc Chagall in 1963. They represent the Garden of Eden – we particularly love the way he played with the yellows to create a sense of illumination – as well as Old Testament scenes. Look for the angel climbing a ladder. The cathedral is built from golden Jaumont limestone, which lends it a delightful Italianate feel.

An Arty Moment in Centre Pompidou-Metz
The star of Metz art scene

In the Quartier de l'Amphithéâtre just south of the railway station, the **Centre Pompidou-Metz** *(centrepompidou-metz.fr; adult/child €14/free; closed Tue)* is the star of Metz' art scene. Designed by Japanese architect Shigeru Ban and French architect Jean de Gastines, the building itself is a work of art. It features a quirky, bright-white building sporting huge glass windows and a curved roof resembling a space-age Chinese hat. As the satellite branch of Paris' Centre Pompidou (p95), it aims to bring modern art to a wide audience and stages ambitious temporary exhibitions, including figurative cubist creations, bold avant-garde works and stunning sculptures. The dynamic space also hosts cultural events, concerts, dance, theatre, talks and youth projects.

Step into History
Visit Musée De La Cour D'or

A hop away from the cathedral, the **Musée de La Cour d'Or** *(musee.eurometropolemetz.eu; free; closed Tue)* is a trove of Gallo-Roman antiquities, hiding remnants of the city's Roman baths, excavated during the museum's extension in the 1930s. If you're a fan of mosaics, spend some time in room 12, which houses the striking *Mosaïque aux Gladiateurs* (Gladiator Mosaic). Then delve into medieval history from room 14. If you're pressed for time, head to room 19, which houses the superb *Chancel de Saint-Pierre-aux-Nonnains*, a choir screen made of stone dating from the 6th century.

Continue with art from the Middle Ages, paintings from the 15th century onwards and artefacts revealing the history of Metz' ancient Jewish community.

You can easily spend a few hours in this well-organised museum.

 EATING IN METZ: BEST BISTROTS

Les Pas Sages: Serves well-executed French dishes with a contemporary twist as well as tempting desserts. *noon-2pm Tue-Sat & 7-9pm Thu-Sat* €

Au Cul d'Poule: With its light-filled interior, imaginative food and excellent location, this is a top choice right near the cathedral. *noon-1.45pm & 7-9.30pm Tue-Sat* €€

Restaurant Derrière: Regional, seasonal cuisine is prepared with flair in this intimate restaurant occupying a historic building. *hours vary* €€

Timilia: Born in Lorraine, but of Italian descent, chef Olivier Parise serves the finest Italian cuisine in the region. *noon-1pm Fri & Sat, 7.30-8.30pm Tue-Sat* €€€

Imperial Metz
A unique ensemble of Wilhelmian architecture
Built under the German occupation after 1871, when Metz was integrated to the Second Reich, the German **Quartier Impérial** (Imperial Quarter) is a whimsical mix of art deco, neo-Romanesque and neo-Renaissance influences. Completed in 1908, the monumental Rhenish neo-Romanesque **Gare de Metz** (train station) sets the tone. Across the square lies the massive former **post office**, built in 1911 of red Vosges sandstone. Wander along rue Gambetta and av Foch, where you'll find lofty bourgeois villas reminiscent of that era.

Atmospheric Squares
Compelling townscapes
For some great photo ops, head to **place St-Louis**, a superb square surrounded by medieval arcades and merchants' houses dating from the 13th to 17th centuries. It's a popular drinking spot, especially in summer, with plenty of buzzy pavement cafes.

Not far from the cathedral, and bounded by one of the channels of the Moselle river, neo-classical **place de la Comédie** is home to the city's 18th-century **Opéra-Théâtre**, France's oldest theatre still in use, and the neo-Romanesque Protestant church **Temple Neuf**, which was built under the German occupation in 1904. It's especially photogenic at sunset.

View Metz from the River
A unique perspective on the city
Metz is a verdant city with a splendid riverside setting that's best enjoyed on a small solar-powered boat. **Bateau Solaire Solis** *(metz-bateau-solaire.com; from €16)* runs scenic one-hour tours, which glide along the Moselle river, taking in the place de la Comédie and, to the west, a wild area nicknamed 'Little Amazonia', where you'll spot beavers and various water birds. It departs from Quai des Régates.

METZ' BEST ART GALLERIES

Galerie Octave Cowbell: Features the works of local artists, with an emphasis on nature.

Galerie de l'Arsenal: Well-established venue housed in a historic building displays compelling contemporary art.

Galerie PJ: Stylish gallery that specialises in contemporary arts – mostly paintings.

Galerie Modulab: Well-regarded spot with an emphasis on contemporary art; mostly paintings and drawings.

Atelier Sainte Croix des Arts: With Montmartre-style decor, this gallery exhibits the sculptures of Philippe Buiatti and Jean-Marie Wunderlich, both from Metz.

Schmirlab: The place to go if you're a fan of screen printing. Also runs workshops.

La Vitrine Éphémère: Near place St-Louis, this eclectic gallery showcases works of about 30 local artists.

 EATING IN METZ: OUR PICKS

Casa Ricci: Prepare to battle the throngs of locals at his family-owned trattoria. The rich, homemade *suppli* (risotto-like dish) and arancini are memorable. *11.45am-2pm Tue-Sat* €

2'Moiselles: Market-driven venue where regional ingredients are creatively transformed, tucked away near place St-Louis. *noon-1pm & 7-9pm Thu-Mon* €€

Yozora: This chic restaurant inside Centre Pompidou-Metz serves fusion food. *7.30-9pm Wed-Sun* €€€

La Réserve: Set in an historic building on the edge of the city centre, La Réserve is known for its modern take on regional staples. *noon-1.30pm & 7-9pm* €€€

Beyond Metz

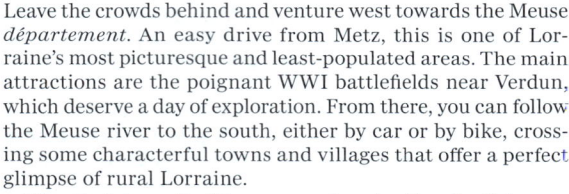

Metz' surroundings pack much more than you'd expect, from industrial heritage sites and WWI battlefields to serene valleys and quaint historical towns.

Places
The Meuse Valley p362
Uckange p364
Petite-Rosselle p364

Leave the crowds behind and venture west towards the Meuse *département*. An easy drive from Metz, this is one of Lorraine's most picturesque and least-populated areas. The main attractions are the poignant WWI battlefields near Verdun, which deserve a day of exploration. From there, you can follow the Meuse river to the south, either by car or by bike, crossing some characterful towns and villages that offer a perfect glimpse of rural Lorraine.

After that dose of wilderness, make a beeline for Uckange, north of Metz, to admire a sensational former industrial site, now a heritage monument open to visitors. Be ready to experience Lorraine from an unexpected perspective.

GETTING AROUND

Driving is a great way to explore the fairly hilly region surrounding Metz, especially if you are planning to take advantage of the many landscape photo opportunities found in the countryside and visit the lesser-known corners of this part of the region. Pick up a rental car at Metz train station. That said, train services from Metz can get you to Verdun and Uckange. There are also a few bicycle paths if you want to get around by bike.

The Meuse Valley

TIME FROM METZ: **1HR**

Drive or bike from Verdun to St-Mihiel

Flowing for over 1000km from its trickling source in the Vosges Mountains towards the North Sea, the serpentine Meuse traverses the Meuse *département* through lush green meadows and a gorgeous valley flanked by small forested hills and mirabelle orchards. The valley has pretty villages and towns, including **Verdun**. Don't miss a visit to the massive underground **Citadelle Souterraine** *(citadelle-souterraine-verdun. fr; adult/child €16/8, no kids under 8; closed Jan)*, which was turned into an impregnable command centre in 1916. Then head to the poignant **WWI battlefields** and vestiges that lie about 10km northeast of Verdun. Here the moonscape hills are scarred with trenches and shells, and there are several monuments to visit, including the 137m-long memorial **Ossuaire de Douaumont** *(verdun-douaumont.com; adult/child €7/3)* and the huge military cemetery out front. Also consider visiting the two massive **Fort de Vaux** *(memorial-verdun.fr; adult/child €14/9)* and **Fort de Douaumont** *(memorial-verdun.fr; adult/child €14/9)*. Also on the battlefields, the Mémorial de Verdun tells the story of '300 days, 300,000 dead, 400,000 wounded', with insightful displays of war artefacts and personal items, as well as a recreation of the battlefield. For a truly immersive experience, we suggest that you explore the battlefields (and the whole Meuse Valley) by bike following a well-maintained

WHERE FOUR COUNTRIES (ALMOST) MEET

Lorraine shares borders with Germany, Luxembourg and Belgium, which allows for an original multicountry driving tour.

START	END	LENGTH
Thionville	Longwy	98km; 2hrs

There are very few places in the world where four countries' borders meet. From northern Lorraine, you can claim to have visited all four in a couple of hours. Start from ❶ **Thionville**, about 30km north of Metz. Then head northeast for 17km to ❷ **Rodemack**, a delightful medieval village with a castle and ramparts. Continue towards ❸ **Contz-les-Bains**, another lovely village surrounded with emerald-green vineyard-lined hillsides that by autumn are groaning with grapes. Nearby ❹ **Sierck-les-Bains** sits in a bend of the Moselle and has a superb medieval castle that lords over the valley. Follow the D419 to Perl – you're now in Germany – and cross the bridge that leads to ❺ **Schengen** – you're now in the far south-east corner of Luxembourg. This is where the 1985 and 1990 treaties that led to the border-free travel agreement across large parts of Europe were signed. Drive west along the border with France until ❻ **Esch-sur-Alzette**, Luxembourg's second city. In the industrial Belval quarter, two gigantic blast furnaces have been very imaginatively preserved as the startling focus of an impressive new regeneration project. Take the A13 then the E44 westwards before going past the southern outskirts of Athus – you're now in Belgium. Not for long, because ❼ **Longwy**, 9km to the southwest, beckons, with its great fortifications. You're back in Lorraine!

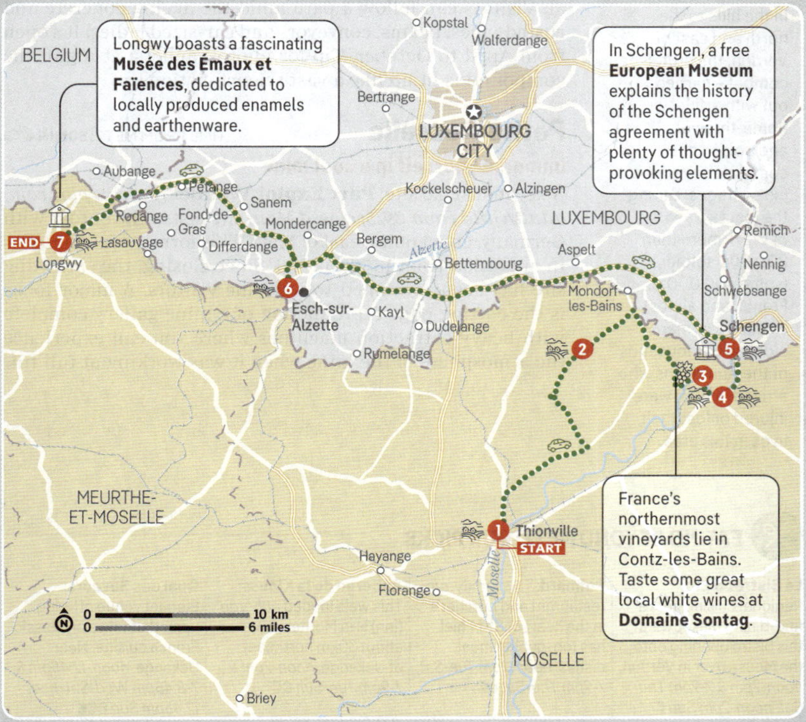

> Longwy boasts a fascinating **Musée des Émaux et Faïences**, dedicated to locally produced enamels and earthenware.

> In Schengen, a free **European Museum** explains the history of the Schengen agreement with plenty of thought-provoking elements.

> France's northernmost vineyards lie in Contz-les-Bains. Taste some great local white wines at **Domaine Sontag**.

THE GUIDE

LORRAINE BEYOND METZ

VERDUN DURING WWI

After the annexation of Lorraine's Moselle *département* and Alsace by Germany in 1871, Verdun became a front-line outpost. Over the next four decades it was turned into the most important and heavily fortified element in France's eastern defence line.

During WWI, Verdun itself was never taken by the Germans, but the evacuated town was almost totally destroyed by artillery bombardments. In the hills to the north and east of Verdun, the brutal combat – carried out with artillery, flame-throwers and poison gas – completely wiped out nine villages. During the last two years of WWI, more than 800,000 soldiers (some 400,000 French and almost as many Germans, along with thousands of the Americans who arrived in 1918) were injured or lost their lives in this area.

cycling path. The Verdun **tourist office** rents e-bikes *(half-/full day €20/30)* and has maps.

For a change of scene and atmosphere, head to **St-Mihiel**, about 35km to the south. This superb town retains a remarkably complete Renaissance core, with elaborate *hôtels particuliers* (grand townhouses).

Another lovely riverside town is **Commercy**, about 20km south of St-Mihiel. The town's main landmark is the majestic **Château de Commercy**, which Stanislas Leszczynski, the duke of Lorraine, used as a leisure palace to host grandiose receptions during the 18th century. The sweet-toothed will head to nearby **À La Cloche Lorraine** *(madeleine-commercy.com)* which sells delicious madeleines (a type of lemon-flavoured sponge cake baked in a shell-like-shaped mould), which are a speciality of Commercy.

Uckange
TIME FROM METZ: **20MIN**

Be awed by a one-of-a-kind industrial heritage site

Just 20km north of Metz, in Uckange, the hulking former ironworks of **Parc du Haut-Fourneau U4** *(hf-u4.com; adult/child from €4/3; closed Mon)* are one of Europe's great heavy-industrial relics. The plant blasted its last pig iron in 1991 and was declared a national heritage site in 2001. The view of the Herculean blast furnace and its annexes is exceptional. Visitors can follow a path amid the ageing concrete and rusted pipes, beams, conveyors and car-sized ladles. It's open from April to October. Tip for photographers: at night, the compound is lit up like a vast science-fiction set.

Petite-Rosselle
TIME FROM METZ: **50MIN**

Immerse yourself in a coal mine

A key industrial site, **Parc Explor Wendel** *(parc-explor.com; adult/child from €9/5; closed Mon)* sits just at the border with Germany, about 60km east of Metz. This former coal mine was in operation from 1856 to 1986. Since closing, the sprawling site has been revamped to welcome visitors. A major focus is the cutting-edge reproduction of a mine gallery complete with heavy extraction machines where you can experience the atmosphere of the mine when it was working at full tilt.

EATING BEYOND METZ: OUR PICKS

Le Bistrot d'Elo: Regional cuisine gets a fine-dining makeover at this bistro opening onto the Meuse river in Verdun. *noon-2pm & 7-9pm Thu-Sat, noon-2pm Sun* €

Polmard: This family-run restaurant and butcher's in the heart of St-Mihiel has top-quality meat dishes. *noon-2pm Tue-Sat, 7-9pm Thu-Sat* €€

Auberge de la Klauss: This well-lauded *auberge* (inn) is in Montenach, about 30km northeast of Uckange. *noon-2pm & 7-9pm Tue-Sun* €€

Quai des Saveurs: Elegant venue offering upmarket takes on classic French cuisine. Near Uckange. *noon-12.45pm & 7-8.45pm Wed-Sat, noon-12.45pm Sun* €€€

Nancy

ART DECO | FINE DINING | URBAN VIBES

Delightful Nancy will take your breath away. The former capital of the dukes of Lorraine catapults you back to the riches of the 18th century, when much of the city centre was built. It's hard not to fall for its air of refinement, stately elegance and sense of majesty. Nothing epitomises Nancy more than the impossibly photogenic place Stanislas, at the heart of the city – it simply ranks as one of the most harmonious and perfectly proportioned squares in the world. Architecture buffs or Instagram romantics, take note: if you're seeking unusually beautiful facades, you've come to the right place. Nancy is one of the founding centres of art nouveau in the late 19th century, and boasts some impressive examples of that artistic movement in and around the centre. And did we mention that Nancy is endowed with a flourishing fine-dining scene and trendy cafes and wine bars?

TOP TIP

If you happen to visit Nancy between late November and late December, be sure to attend the Fêtes de la St-Nicolas. Nicolas is the patron of Lorraine, and he is celebrated with much pomp in Nancy, with festive twinkle, carols, shows, carousels and handicrafts.

Take in Neoclassical Place Stanislas

Nancy's crowning glory

With its gleaming-white classical facades, gilded wrought-iron gateways and rococo fountains (look out for the one of a trident-bearing Neptune), the grand neoclassical place Stanislas and UNESCO World Heritage Site is Nancy's focal point and a true feast for they eyes.

Designed in the 1750s, the square is named after the enlightened, Polish-born Stanislas Leszczynski, the last duke of

GETTING AROUND

Driving around the city centre may be tricky, especially at peak hours. Your best bet is to leave your car in one of the car parks dotted around the centre – the most convenient one is the **Parking Stanislas**, just south of the eponymous square. There's no real need to use public transport as the part of Nancy you'll likely want to visit is easily negotiable on foot or by bicycle. **VelOstan'lib** *(velostanlib.fr)* has 34 rental points dotted around town, where you can hire bikes 24/7. Rental points can be seen on its online map.

★ **HIGHLIGHTS**	10 Shopping Mall	19 L'Éliceur	● **SHOPPING**
1 Musée des Beaux-Arts	11 Statue	20 L'Impromptu	24 Confiserie Lefèvre-Lemoine
● **SIGHTS**	● **SLEEPING**	● **DRINKING & NIGHTLIFE**	25 Maison des Sœurs Macarons
2 Arc Héré	12 Hôtel Crystal	21 Café du Commerce	● **TRANSPORT**
3 Chambre de Commerce	13 Hôtel d'Haussonville	22 Café Jean Lamour	26 Parking Stanislas
4 Graineterie Génin-Louis	14 Hôtel Littéraire Stendhal	see 21 Grand Café Foy	27 VelOstan'lib
5 Hôtel de Ville	15 Maison de Myon	see 22 Jojo	
6 LCL Crédit Lyonnais	● **EATING**	● **ENTERTAINMENT**	
7 Parc de la Pépinière	16 Brasserie L'Excelsior	23 Opéra National de Lorraine	
8 Pharmacie du Gingko	17 Brasserie Wallace		
9 Place de la Carrière	18 L'Arsenal		

Lorraine, who was offered the Duchy of Lorraine by his son-in-law Louis XV in 1736. He undertook major building programmes that transformed Nancy into one of Europe's most palatial cities. His **statue** stands in the middle of the square.

Among the opulent edifices overlooking the square are the **Hôtel de Ville** (town hall) and **Opéra National de Lorraine** (opera-national-lorraine.fr). To the north is the grandiose **Arc Héré**, a triumphal arch that honours Louis XV; look for the gods of war and peace that adorn the facade. Past Arc Héré, the 300m-long, tree-shaded **place de la Carrière** is a great place for a serene stroll. It was once a riding and jousting arena.

The entire square is an all-pedestrian zone. You'll find some cafes (great for a drink, less so for a meal) with terraces opening onto the square. Our favorite is **Grand Café Foy** (grand-cafefoy.com) but **Café du Commerce** (cafeducommercenancy.com) and **Café Jean Lamour** are also well worth considering. **Jojo** is known for its cocktails.

Visit Musée des Beaux-Arts
Nancy's standout gallery

Lodged in a regal 18th-century edifice, **Musée des Beaux-Arts** (musee-des-beaux-arts.nancy.fr; adult/child from €7.50/5; closed Tue) occupies art lovers for hours. A wrought-iron staircase curls gracefully up to the 2nd floor, where a chronological spin begins with 14th- to 17th-century paintings. The 1st floor spotlights 17th- to 19th-century masterpieces of the Rubens, Picasso and Caravaggio ilk. But as we're in Nancy, the city of art nouveau, we suggest that you spend time in the basement, which features the works of Nancy-born architect and designer Jean Prouvé (1901–84). You'll find a great selection of Prouvé's furniture, architectural elements, ironwork and graphic works.

Sweet Shopping
Pick up bergamotes and macarons

Nancy is famous in Lorraine for its sweet specialities, including macarons and *bergamotes* (bergamot boiled sweets). Tempted? Head to **Confiserie Lefèvre-Lemoine** (lefevre-lemoine.fr) on rue Poincaré, a delightfully old-fashioned sweet shop founded in 1840, which sells delectable *bergamotes de Nancy,* caramels, macarons, gingerbread and glazed mirabelles. Another treasure trove of sweet treats is **Maison des Sœurs Macarons** (macaron-de-nancy.com; closed Sun) on rue Gambetta. As the name suggests, this old-world confectioner specialises in macarons, but it also has *bergamotes* and other goodies made of *mirabelles de Lorraine*.

Relax in Parc de la Pépinière
Nancy's oasis of greenery

On a hot summer's day, do what the locals do: head to 'La Pep' (**Parc de la Pépinière**), a vast garden not far from place Stanislas. You'll find plenty of shade, peace and quiet. It also has ornamental fountains, a rose garden and a Rodin sculpture of Baroque landscape painter Claude Lorrain.

ART NOUVEAU & ÉCOLE DE NANCY

Art nouveau (1850–1910) is an artistic movement that flourished in various parts of Europe and the USA in the second half of the 19th century. It's an ornamental style of design that extended its reach to everyday wares, including glassware, jewellery, furniture and architecture. The style was characterised by sinuous curves and flowing asymmetrical forms reminiscent of creeping vines, water lilies, the patterns on insect wings and the flowering boughs of trees.

In France, one of its founding centres was Nancy, thanks to glassmaker and ceramist Émile Gallé, who launched the École de Nancy in 1900, joining creative forces with masters of decorative arts and architecture such as Jacques Grüber, Louis Majorelle and the Daum brothers.

 EATING IN NANCY: OUR PICKS

L'Impromptu: Inside the covered market, this excellent place features market-fresh mains and exquisite desserts. *noon-2.30pm Tue-Sat* €

Brasserie Wallace: The food – brasserie classics – looks as good as it tastes at this upbeat spot. *noon-2pm & 7-9.30pm Tue-Sat* €

L'Arsenal: Sleek venue featuring a season-driven menu of bright flavours in dishes such as beef fillet with braised mushrooms. *noon-2pm & 7-9pm Tue-Sat* €€

L'Éliceur: Near place Stanislas, this modern bistro draws on the best of seasonal, regional produce. *noon-2pm & 7.30-9.30pm Tue-Sat* €€

ART NOUVEAU TRAIL

Discover Nancy's most appealing art nouveau buildings and be sure to have your camera ready to capture superb architectural details.

START	END	LENGTH
Musée de l'École de Nancy	Brasserie L'Excelsior	2.7km; about 1½hrs

Being one of the birthplaces of art nouveau in Europe, Nancy is home to some impressive examples of this artistic movement. Wherever you wander around the city, you're bound to stumble across splendid art nouveau handiwork, from sinuous grillwork to curvaceous stained-glass windows and doorways that are a profusion of naturalistic ornament. You can learn all about it during a visit to ❶ **Musée de l'École de Nancy**, which brings together an exquisite collection of art nouveau interiors, curvaceous glass and landscaped gardens. Original works of art by local stars, including Émile Gallé, who founded the École de Nancy, are on display. It's housed in a splendid 19th-century villa about 2km southwest of the centre. Then head north to the ❷ **Villa Majorelle** (1901), a whimsical building featuring grand windows and sinuous metal supports on the balcony. Inside, the Les Blés dining room, with its vine-like stone fireplace, is Instagrammable to boot. Walk east until you get to the eye-popping ❸ **Graineterie Génin-Louis** on rue Bénit (corner of rue St-Jean), with a blue metal frame adorning the facade. From there, it's a short walk to the ❹ **Chambre de Commerce**, blessed with an elaborate canopy and windows enhanced by wrought iron. End up at nearby ❺ **Brasserie L'Excelsior** (1911), an atmospheric eatery with a superb fin-de-siècle decor.

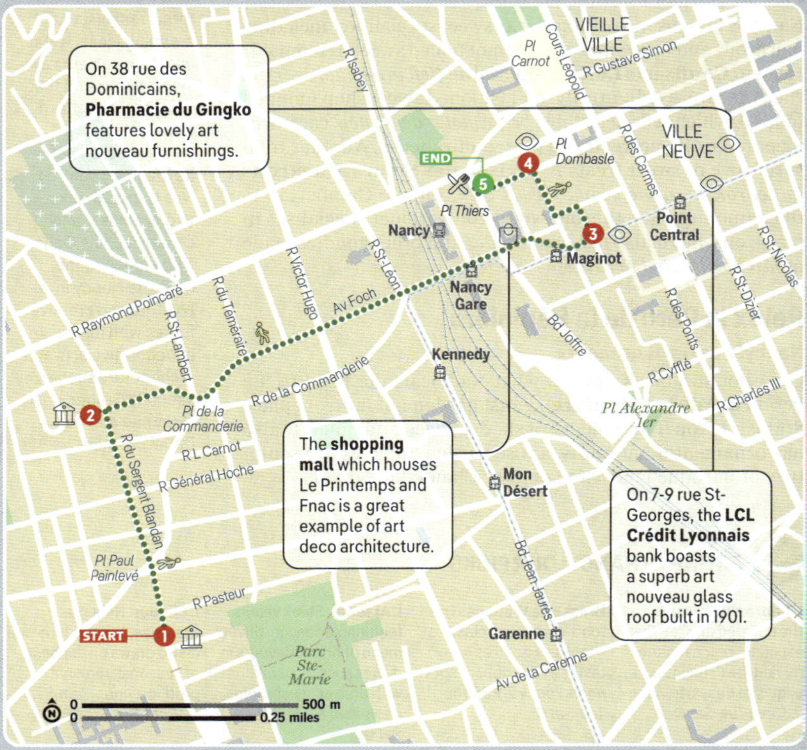

Beyond Nancy

The wildly picturesque Hautes Vosges Mountains and incredibly scenic vineyards around Toul make for great escapes from Nancy.

As you exit Nancy to explore its surroundings, it's easy to find places in which to mellow out. The Toulois area, a short drive west, is a well-kept secret in Lorraine, with picturesque villages as well as a patchwork of farm houses, vineyards and mirabelle plum trees that carpet the countryside.

About an hour's drive southeast of Nancy, the lushly forest-cloaked hills of the Hautes Vosges Mountains beckon. With its softly rounded heights, fragrant pastures, glacial lakes and dairy farms, the Lorraine side of the range feels wilder and more rustic than the Alsace side. If it's peace, tranquillity, outdoor activities and a true taste of humble mountain life you're seeking, the Hautes Vosges Mountains are your answer.

Places

The Toulois p369
Gérardmer p369

The Toulois

TIME FROM NANCY: **20MIN**

Discover a slice of bucolic Lorraine

In a bend of the Moselle river about 25km west of Nancy, **Toul** is an instant heart-stealer with its 18th-century fortifications and majestic Gothic cathedral complete with gargoyles, a striking portal and two massive twin bell towers.

The winemaking villages in the area are supremely picturesque; set in rolling hills and spring-blossoming plum orchards, **Bruley** and nearby **Lucey** are within easy reach. Explore and you'll find a smattering of *domaines* where you can sample *gris de Toul*, one of France's most underrated appellations. In Lucey, stop by **Maison Lelièvre** *(vins-lelievre.com)*, which also rents e-bikes to tour the vineyards. In Bruley, **Domaine Regina** *(domaineregina.com)* is run by Isabelle Mangeot, who organises tastings in a vaulted cellar, while **Maison Eulriet** *(maison-eulriet.com)* produces top-quality liqueurs, jams and other goodies made of mirabelles. Returning to Nancy, you can follow the D90 that crosses **Liverdun**, a hilltop village with sweeping panoramas of the Moselle valley.

If you want to explore the area by e-bike, contact **Velostation** *(velostation.com/-toul; from €10)* in Toul.

Gérardmer

TIME FROM NANCY: **1¼HRS**

Explore the Hautes Vosges Mountains

About 100km southwest of Nancy, Gérardmer is the jewel of the Hautes Vosges, with a mellow atmosphere and scenic setting.

GETTING AROUND

Toul can easily be reached by train from Nancy, while Gérardmer is harder to access by public transport (you'll need to take a train to Épinal then a connecting bus to Gérardmer). A car is strongly advised to visit the more remote corners and towns of this region. The Toulois area can also be negotiated by e-bike from Nancy following the Boucle de la Moselle cycling path, but you'll need two days.

THE HAUTES-VOSGES' MOST SCENIC ROADS

D417: Starting from Gérardmer, this road climbs to Col de la Schlucht (1139m), which marks the border with Alsace.

D486: A lovely road that connects Gérardmer and La Bresse, 12km to the south. It proffers superb mountain views.

D8: Between Xonrupt-Longemer (east of Gérardmer) and Anould (15km), this secondary road crosses great forests and pastures.

D34: From La Bresse, this road follows the Moselotte valley before climbing through the mountains to Col de Bramont (995m).

D44: Between Docelles and Bruyères, north of Gérardmer, the D44 meanders along the Vologne valley and crosses several villages.

Bol d'Air Tyrolean slide

It lies on the eastern shore of **Lac de Gérardmer**, a dark-blue mountain lake that lies cradled by thickly wooded hills. In summer you can rent an SUP or kayak to glide across the lake. When the sun is out, a couple of beaches fringing the lake beckon. Needless to say, Gérardmer and its surroundings are prime **hiking** and **mountain-biking** territory, with a good network of well-signposted trails for all levels (the **tourist office** has maps). For an easy walk, wander around the Lac de Gérardmer or the nearby **Lac de Longemer** – count on 1½ hours (each).

Adrenaline junkies can try **zip-lining** in **La Bresse**, another lovely town nestled in a valley south of Gérardmer. **Bol d'Air** *(bol-d-air.fr; adult/child €36/16)* has set up a 1.3km-long (yes!) Tyrolean slide in a sensational setting over the valley, with the Vosges Mountains forming a perfect backdrop. Kids over six are welcome. It also offers plenty of other family-friendly activities.

Trott' In Vosges *(trottinvosges.fr; from €40)* runs guided electric scooter tours in the forests south of Gérardmer. It's fun and environmentally friendly to explore the area while enjoying top-notch panoramas.

EATING BEYOND NANCY: OUR PICKS

Auberge du Pressoir: This *auberge de campagne* (countryside inn) is in Lucey, north of Toul. *noon-2pm Tue-Sat, 7-9pm Thu-Sat* €€

Le Lido: Overlooking Lac de Gérardmer, Le Lido is known for its traditional dishes with a contemporary twist. *noon-1.30pm Tue-Sun, 7-8.30pm Tue-Sat* €€

Anico: A foodie haven in La Bresse. Food follows the season. The smart decor, with wood and stone, is a winner. *noon-1.30pm Wed-Sun, 7-8.30pm Wed-Sat* €€

Chalet-Hôtel Le Collet: Savour excellent *vosgien* (from the Vosges) specialities amid an all-wood setting. Near Gérardmer. *7-9pm daily, noon-2pm Sun* €€

Places We Love to Stay

€ Budget €€ Midrange €€€ Top End

Metz
MAP p359

Hôtel de Fouquet €€ This classy, high-ceilinged B&B overlooking the medieval place St-Louis offers three stylish rooms.

La Citadelle Metz – MGallery €€ A slick conversion of a 16th-century military arsenal and barracks, La Citadelle sits in a tranquil park in the heart of the city.

La Maison Ruffinoise €€ An enticing little hideaway in the heart of Ste-Ruffine, a village west of Metz, with two exquisitely decorated suites.

Domaine de la Résidence €€ This venture offers a bucolic setting on the southwestern outskirts of Metz. There's an onsite restaurant.

Villa Camoufle €€€ A boutique B&B set in a stately late-19th-century mansion right in the German Imperial Quarter.

Meuse Valley

Savy Hôtel Flottant €€ This lovingly restored houseboat bobs on the Meuse river in the centre of Verdun. It has eight cosy rooms and a superb deck terrace.

Les Jardins du Mess €€ A classy hotel occupying an 19th-century building overlooking the Meuse river in Verdun.

La Maison Mirabeau €€ This three-room B&B, housed inside a tastefully restored house, is a haven of peace and quiet, a five-minute stroll from the centre.

Domaine de Sommedieue €€ A great out-of-town choice: a historical building, a vast park with a few ponds and a restaurant. About 15km south of Verdun.

Uckange

Domaine de la Klauss €€€ A fantastic *auberge* (inn) in a rural area about 30km northeast of Uckange. Top amenities include a spa and a gastronomic restaurant.

Nancy
MAP p366

Le Clos Jeannon € On the southern outskirts of Nancy, this peaceful B&B set in a verdant property has five modern rooms. There's an on-site restaurant.

Hôtel Littéraire Stendhal € Fully renovated in 2024, this venue occupies a 17th-century former bishop's palace. The 41 stylish rooms are all different.

Hôtel Crystal €€ A great four-star venture near the train station. Pluses include a superb spa and a rooftop bar.

Maison de Myon €€ An elegant B&B in a quiet 17th-century old-city townhouse with light-filled rooms and antique furnishings.

Hôtel d'Haussonville €€ Seven plush rooms in a splendid Renaissance mansion right in the heart of the city.

La Villa 1901 €€ This chic B&B combines art nouveau with contemporary design flourishes, boho flair and garden out back.

The Toulois

Château de Choloy €€ This B&B in a stately 19th-century mansion near Toul is a great base for exploring the winemaking villages in the area.

Hautes-Vosges

Les Jardins de Sophie €€ A wonderful, family-run hotel with a boutique feel nestled in a deep forest near Gérardmer.

Domaine de Montagne – Chalet Frère Joseph €€ An incredibly romantic venue with 28 rooms in a bucolic setting. It has a top-notch spa and a well-regarded restaurant. In Ventron, 30km south of Gérardmer.

Chalet-Hôtel Le Collet €€ Rooms fulfil every mountain chalet fantasy: wood-panelling, cosy atmosphere and great amenities, including a wonderful spa and a great restaurant. About 13km east of Gérardmer.

La Cabane du Breuil €€€ Every imaginable luxury is available at La Cabane du Breuil: chic chalet-style rooms, a delightful spa and a high-calibre restaurant. In La Bresse.

Domaine Les Terres Bleues €€€ Opened in 2025, this intimate venture features two exclusive, ultra comfortable chalets. In Xonrupt-Longemer.

Above: Château de Villandry (p391), Touraine; Right: Ste-Maure de Touraine goat's cheese (p389)

Researched by
Daniel Robinson

The Loire

RIVERSIDE CASTLES, VINEYARDS AND CUISINE

Exquisite architecture, compelling history, superb wines and the kind of restaurants you came to France for – plus horses in Saumur and mechanical monsters in Nantes.

If you're looking for French splendour, style and gastronomy, the Loire Valley will exceed your expectations, no matter how great. Poised on the crucial frontier between northern and southern France – and just a short train or autoroute ride from Paris – the region was once of immense strategic importance. Kings, queens, dukes and nobles came here to build feudal castles and, later on, sumptuous Renaissance pleasure palaces – that's why this fertile river valley is sprinkled with hundreds of France's most opulent aristocratic estates, many sporting crenellated towers, soaring cupolas and twinkling banquet halls.

The Loire, much of it a UNESCO World Heritage Site, is also known for its outstanding wines – reds, whites, rosés and sparkling – and vineyards stretch along both banks of the Loire from the Blésois, westward through Touraine and Anjou, to the Atlantic. A network of walking trails, bike paths and tertiary roads makes it easy to visit both glittering châteaux and vine-encircled *domaines* (wine-growing estates) in a single afternoon.

Fans of French urban life will find medium-sized cities that are renowned for their *douceur de vivre* (the gentle pleasures of life), with verve and energy added by tens of thousands of students. Tours, Angers and Nantes are graced with handsome avenues, historic quarters traversed by narrow medieval streets and excellent (and moderately-priced) dining as well as an abundance of lovely gardens and romantic riverside promenades.

THE MAIN AREAS

BLÉSOIS
Royal city near three sublime châteaux.
p378

TOURAINE
Art, gastronomy and dazzling castles.
p385

ANJOU
Dynamic university city with wine and horses nearby.
p397

NANTES
Promenades, parks, dining and a mechanical elephant.
p406

Find Your Way

With trains connecting cities and some towns and an extensive network of bike paths, bike-friendly backroads and walking trails, the Loire is an ideal slow-tourism destination even if you're travelling by car.

Nantes, p406

Brittany's historic capital is now a dynamic university city with grand avenues, waterfront promenades, innovative art and a sincere reckoning with its slave-trading history.

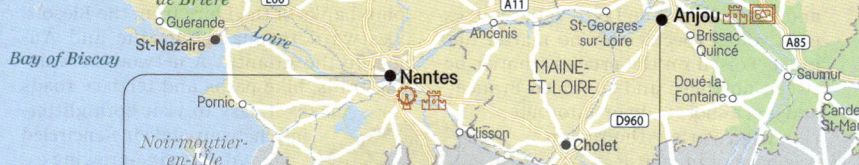

Anjou, p397

Angers has lively street life, a menacingly medieval château and two supremely moving tapestries. Head to Saumur for superior cuisine and wines and the crack Cadre Noir equestrians.

CAR

Having your own wheels is the easiest and quickest way to visit châteaux and vineyards. But if you stay in the city centre in Tours, Angers and Nantes, a car can be a liability as parking is in short supply and is time-limited and/or pricey.

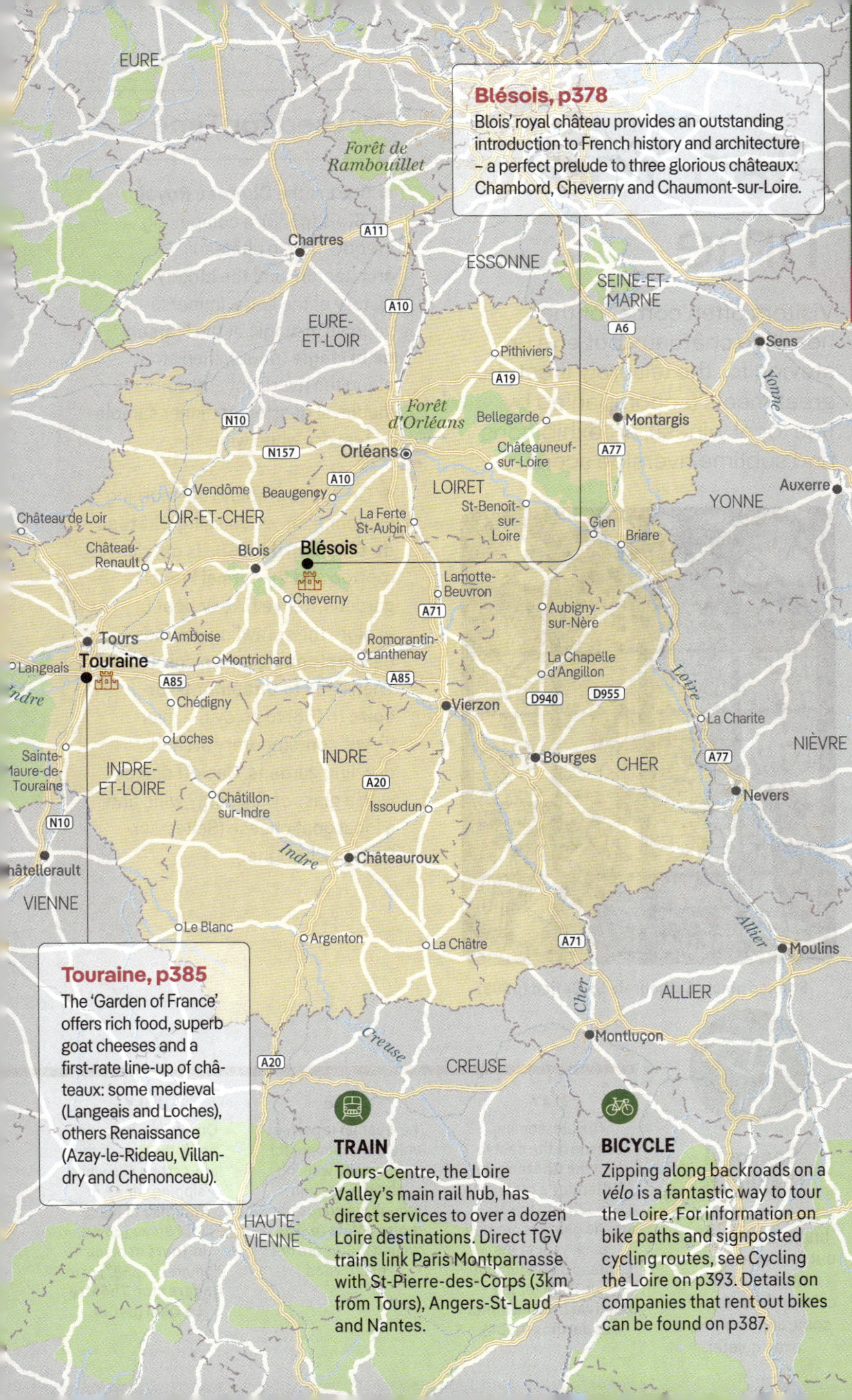

Blésois, p378

Blois' royal château provides an outstanding introduction to French history and architecture – a perfect prelude to three glorious châteaux: Chambord, Cheverny and Chaumont-sur-Loire.

Touraine, p385

The 'Garden of France' offers rich food, superb goat cheeses and a first-rate line-up of châteaux: some medieval (Langeais and Loches), others Renaissance (Azay-le-Rideau, Villandry and Chenonceau).

TRAIN

Tours-Centre, the Loire Valley's main rail hub, has direct services to over a dozen Loire destinations. Direct TGV trains link Paris Montparnasse with St-Pierre-des-Corps (3km from Tours), Angers-St-Laud and Nantes.

BICYCLE

Zipping along backroads on a *vélo* is a fantastic way to tour the Loire. For information on bike paths and signposted cycling routes, see Cycling the Loire on p393. Details on companies that rent out bikes can be found on p387.

THE GUIDE

THE LOIRE

Plan Your Time

Visitors often come for the headline châteaux but end up staying for the leisurely lifestyle, great meals (accompanied by fine local wines!), art exhibitions and sublime riverside scenery.

Stained glass, Cathédrale St-Gatien (p388)

Pressed for Time

● Start at the **Château Royal de Blois** (p378), a compelling introduction to château architecture and the bloody history of the Loire. Immerse yourself in magic at the **Maison de la Magie** (p380), then stroll along the riverfront and up to the medieval quarter. At dinner sample a local dry white wine.

● On day two, spend the morning exploring the astonishing **Château de Chambord** (p381), its dazzling rooftop and the formal French gardens. Rent a bike or boat to explore the sprawling grounds before stopping for a picnic lunch. Then head to **Chaumont-sur-Loire** (p388) to enjoy the river views, contemporary art and dazzling gardens. Cap off dinner with a glass of Cheverny wine and a local goat cheese (Selles-sur-Cher or Chavignol).

Seasonal Highlights

July and August bring warm weather, outdoor activities and crowds. Autumn is calm and winter, when some sights close, is even quieter.

MAY
The blossoming season is the best to visit the **Château de Villandry's** grounds (p391) and the 30 artistic gardens created each year at the Château de Chaumont-sur-Loire for the **Festival International des Jardins** (p384).

JUNE
The weather is perfect (unless it's raining) for cycling and walking along rivers and through vineyards; the **Loire a Vélo** (p393) cycling routes are not yet crowded.

JULY
On a balmy evening, enjoy the rays of the late-setting sun while sipping wine – in **Amboise** at place du Château (p390), in **Tours** at place Plumereau (p387) or in **Angers** atop **Théâtre Le Quai** (p400).

Five Days to Travel Around

● After taking in the glories of the Blésois, head west, stopping for the day either in **Loches** (p394), with its early-medieval fortress and dungeons, or **Amboise** (p389). If the latter, walk around the **Clos Lucé** (p390), Leonardo da Vinci's last home, and the **Château Gaillard** (p391).

● The next day, in **Tours** (p386), discover the extraordinary crafts skills of centuries past at the **Musée du Compagnonnage** (p387), then drop by **Cathédrale St-Gatien** (p388) and explore the medieval streets of **Vieux Tours** (p386).

● On your last day, pick up picnic supplies at the **Halles de Tours** (p386), then head out to the **Château de Villandry** (p391), famed for its Renaissance gardens, and the **Château de Langeais** (p392), suffused with the spirit of the late Middle Ages.

A Week-Long Stay

● After five days enjoying the delights of the Blésois and Touraine, head to **Angers** (p397). At the **Château d'Angers** (p397), peek into the 14th-century mind via the astonishing and mysterious Tapestry of the Apocalypse. Walk via **Cathédrale St-Maurice** (p399) to the riverside **Halles Cœur de Maine-Biltoki** (p400) for a hawker centre-style lunch. Cross the river to see another tapestry, the mid-20th-century **Le Chant du Monde** (p400).

● Spend your final day in **Nantes** (p406). At **Les Machines de l'Île** (p406), ride the Grand Éléphant and twirl on a three-level merry-go-round. In the afternoon, visit the city's riverside slavery monument, **Mémorial de l'Abolition de l'Esclavage** (p410), then learn about the history of the city, including its key role in the trade in enslaved people, at the **Château des Ducs de Bretagne** (p410).

AUGUST
To escape the heat, head to a troglodyte restaurant in **Turquant** (p403) or, in the Angers area, to a riverside *guinguette* (Belle Époque-style beer garden, p400) for drinks, cooked fish, music and merry crowds.

SEPTEMBER
Some towns, châteaux and vineyards, including Cheverny (p383) and Saumur (p401), celebrate the annual grape harvest by holding a **Fête des Vendanges**.

NOVEMBER
Blois' unique BD (graphic novel) museum, **Maison de la BD** (p381), holds its annual festival, a colourful blur of meetings with artists, book signings, scholarly lectures, concerts and an awards ceremony.

DECEMBER
Christmas spirit takes hold at châteaux including **Amboise, Azay-le-Rideau, Chaumont-sur-Loire, Chenonceau, Chinon, Loches** and **Villandry**. Some sights that are closed in winter open from mid-December to early January.

Blésois

MAGNIFICENT CHÂTEAUX | ROYAL HISTORY | EXQUISITE GARDENS

✓ TOP TIP

Check out the panoramic views from **Jardins de l'Évêché**, the peaceful gardens behind (east of) the cathedral, and from the top of the **Escalier Denis Papin**, the grand staircase that links rue Denis Papin and Blois' main commercial precinct with rue du Palais.

Towering above the northern bank of the Loire, Blois' royal château, one-time feudal seat of the powerful counts of Blois, offers a gripping introduction – the best in the region – to key periods in French history and architecture. Parts of the city still have a medieval vibe and several outstanding châteaux are right nearby, making Blois an ideal first stop in the Loire Valley and a superb base for exploring the region.

The peaceful, verdant countryside of the Blésois (the area around Blois) is home to some of France's most stunning châteaux, including graceful Cheverny; Chaumont-sur-Loire, famed for its captivating exhibitions of contemporary art and its gardens; and the cupola-capped *château extraordinaire* to top them all, Chambord.

In the centre of Blois, the partly pedestrianised commercial precinct – heavily damaged by German bombs in 1940 – is around rue Denis Papin and rue du Commerce. From there, the château is 400m to the southwest and the old city is up the slope to the north.

Royal Château with a Bloody History
French architecture from Gothic to Renaissance

Seven French kings lived in the **Château Royal de Blois** *(chateaudeblois.fr; adult/child €14.50/7.50)*, whose four grand

GETTING AROUND

Visiting châteaux and touring the countryside is easiest by car but you'll probably feel more in touch with your surroundings riding a bicycle (rentals available in Blois). Private companies offer minibus tours.

The Blois-Chambord train station, 600m west (up the hill) from Blois' château, has direct rail links with Amboise and Tours as well as services, via Orléans, to Paris Gare d'Austerlitz.

Blois' public transport company, Azalys *(bus. azalys.agglopolys.fr)*, runs two free electric **navettes centre-ville** (city-centre shuttles), N1 and N2, that take you all around the central parts of Blois, including along the river, three times an hour from Monday to Saturday.

BLOIS

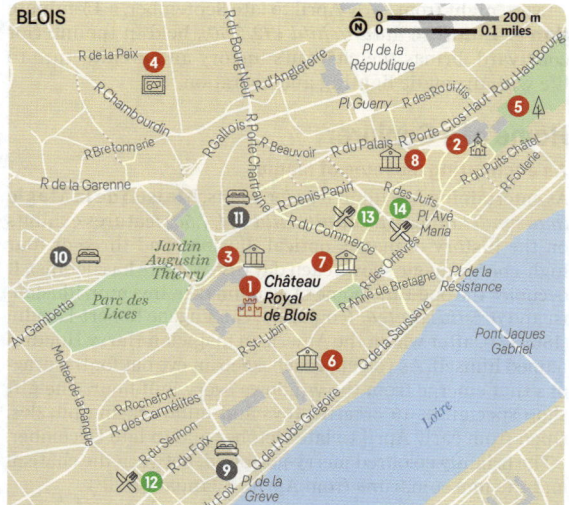

HIGHLIGHTS
1. Château Royal de Blois

SIGHTS
2. Cathédrale St-Louis
3. Centre de la Résistance, de la Déportation et de la Mémoire
4. Fondation du Doute
5. Jardins de l'Évêché
6. Maison de la BD
7. Maison de la Magie
8. Maison des Acrobates

SLEEPING
9. Côté Loire-Auberge Ligérienne
10. Hôtel Anne de Bretagne
11. Ibis Blois Centre Château

EATING
12. Au Rendez-Vous des Pêcheurs
13. L'Arboré Sens
14. Poivre et Sel

INFORMATION
see 3 Tourist Office

A DASTARDLY ASSASSINATION

The year was 1588 and France's blood-soaked Wars of Religion were raging, pitting Catholics and Protestants against each other in unspeakable acts of savagery. During a meeting of the Estates General in Blois' château – which brought together representatives of the clergy, the nobility and commoners – political conflicts, intrigue and personal frustration led France's Catholic king, Henri III, to have his arch-rival, Duke Henri I de Guise, a Catholic 'ultra' backed by Spain and the pope, murdered by royal bodyguards in his own private chamber. The king is said to have hidden behind a tapestry while the dastardly deed was done. He had the duke's brother, the Cardinal de Guise, killed the next day. The king himself was assassinated just eight months later by a vengeful friar.

---

wings were built during four distinct periods in French architecture: Gothic (13th century), Flamboyant Gothic (1498–1501), early Renaissance (1515–20) and classical (1630s). You can easily spend a half-day immersing yourself in the château's dramatic and bloody history and its extraordinary architecture. An informative audioguide costs €3; a HistoPad, offering augmented-reality views, can be picked up for free at the *consigne* (left-luggage facility).

The most sumptuous part of the **Gothic wing** is the richly painted **Estates General Room**, from the 13th century. In the **Renaissance wing** you'll find the extraordinary spiral **loggia staircase**, decorated with fierce salamanders and curly Fs, heraldic symbols of François I. The **King's Chamber** was the setting for one of the bloodiest episodes in the château's history, the assassination of Duke Henri I de Guise in 1588. Dramatic and very graphic oil paintings illustrate these gruesome events next door in the **Council Chamber**. In the Flamboyant Gothic **Louis XII wing** (look for his heraldic emblem, the porcupine), the **Musée des Beaux-Arts** (Fine Art Museum) – up the spiral staircase from the State Room – displays 300 16th- to 19th-century paintings, sculptures and tapestries.

Every night from early April to late September, a 45-minute **Son et Lumière** *(adult/child €12/7.50)*, held in the interior courtyard, brings the château's history and architecture to life with dramatic lighting and narration.

Home of a Conjurer
An enchanting museum of magic

As entertaining for children as for adults, **Maison de la Magie** *(maisondelamagie.fr; adult/child €14/7.50)* features exhibits on the history of magic, optical illusions and three or four high-energy magic shows each day (the website has details). It occupies the one-time home of watchmaker, inventor, illusionist and *prestidigitateur* (conjurer) Jean Eugène Robert-Houdin (1805–71), after whom the American magician Harry Houdini named himself. As you approach, keep an eye out for the dragons that emerge from the windows every half-hour. The gift shop specialises in creative toys and mind-teasing puzzles. Open from early April to late October and in late December.

The brightly coloured merry-go-round, between the château and the museum, runs from April to January *(€3)*.

Stroll Through the Centuries
The hillside alleyways of medieval Blois

Stretching east along the hillside from rue Porte Chartraine, Blois' medieval and Renaissance old town is well worth a stroll. Near the eastern end of rue du Palais, **Maison des Acrobates** at 3bis place St-Louis – one of Blois' few surviving 15th-century houses – has a facade decorated with wooden sculptures of figures from medieval farces.

The western façade of Gothic-style **Cathédrale St-Louis**, rebuilt after a terrible storm in 1678, mixes late-Gothic and neoclassical elements. Almost all the stained glass in the nave, bearing enigmatic Latin inscriptions, was created by Dutch artist Jan Dibbets in 2000. Near the entrance, you can pick up an English brochure with historical details.

The Foundation of Doubt
Discover the spirit of Fluxus

Avant-garde from the floorboards to the roof, the **Fondation du Doute** *(fondationdudoute.fr; adult/child €7.50/3.50)* showcases the art and 'state of mind' of the 1960s Fluxus movement, inspired in part by the American composer John Cage,

BEST AREAS TO DINE IN BLOIS

Rue St-Lubin, rue des Jacobins and rue Anne de Bretagne: Every Saturday from 8am to 1pm, market stalls sell ready-to-eat dishes, sausages, cheese, fruit and veggies.

Place Avé Maria: Surrounded by bars and restaurants with outdoor seating in the warm season. A block east of rue Denis Papin, at the bottom of rue des Juifs.

Rue St Martin: Home to a number of small restaurants with outdoor terraces. Just southwest of rue Denis Papin.

Rue Henry Drussy: This narrow street, stretching northeast from place de la Résistance, is lined with cheap eateries.

Place Victor Hugo, place du Château and the banks of the Loire: Perfect spots for a picnic!

 EATING IN BLOIS: OUR FRENCH PICKS

Poivre et Sel: Traditional French cuisine served on rustic tables, with old-style wood beams overhead. *noon-1.45pm & 7-9.30pm Mon-Sat €€*

L'Arboré Sens: A city-centre brasserie offering a pretty terrace, a good selection of salads, reasonable prices and, on some evenings, live music. *11am-midnight Mon-Sat €*

Côté Loire-Auberge Ligérienne: On the riverfront, French cuisine in an intimate, rustic dining room and, when it's warm, on a lovely terrace. *noon-1.30pm & 7.30-9pm Tue-Sat €€*

Au Rendez-Vous des Pêcheurs: An elegant bistro specialising in fish, including salmon, cod and zander, served on gorgeous ceramic plates. *12.15-1.15pm & 7.15-8.30pm Tue-Sat €€€*

which mocked the elitism of 'high art' and sought to bring art to the people, in part through humour. Works, on loan from collectors, 'invite visitors to call preconceptions into question' – as does the ironic commentary by Ben Vautier (whom everyone here calls just 'Ben') that decorates the building's façade. Situated 750m north of the château. The cafe serves light meals. Open 2pm to 6.30pm from Wednesday to Sunday; closed mid-December to early February.

Two Unique Museums
WWII history and graphic novels

The **Centre de la Résistance, de la Déportation et de la Mémoire** (blois.fr/crdm; adult/child €5/free), 100m down the hill from the tourist office, takes a sobering look at the history of Blois during WWII, including the demarcation line between German-occupied northern France and the Vichy-ruled south, which ran along the Cher River from June 1940 to November 1942. Ask at the ticket counter for an English translation. Open Sunday afternoon, Wednesday and Saturday (open daily except Monday during school holidays).

Graphic novels (bandes dessinées or BD), which have long had the status of art in France, are featured at **Maison de la BD** (maisondelabd.com; free), which offers a rare opportunity to see original drawings by some astonishingly talented BD artists. Visitors are welcome to consult the small library. Hosts a **BD festival** on the third weekend in November.

The Loire's Most Magnificent Château
Royal chambers and a double-helix staircase

One of the crowning achievements of French Renaissance architecture, the **Château de Chambord** (chambord.org;

> **VISITOR INFORMATION IN BLOIS**
>
> The friendly staff of Blois' **tourist office** (bloischambord.co.uk), across the square from the château, can supply town and cycling maps, a brochure detailing 15 rural cycling circuits, and information about hot-air balloon rides and bus and train transport to nearby châteaux. They also sell excellent city walking-tour brochures (€2), cycling guides, hiking maps, châteaux combo tickets and events tickets. The website offers a variety of self-guided walking tours – click on 'Tours and Activities' and then 'Self-Guided Tours'. Storing your luggage here costs €5 a day. Has a corner for kids to play and read books.

Château de Chambord

THE BIGGEST RENAISSANCE CHÂTEAU OF ALL

Begun in 1519 by François I (r 1515–47) as a weekend hunting retreat, the **Château de Chambord** (p381) quickly grew into one of the most ambitious – and expensive – building projects ever undertaken by a French monarch. Construction was repeatedly halted by financial problems, design setbacks and military commitments (not to mention the kidnapping of the king's two sons in Spain). Ironically, when Chambord was finally finished after three decades of work, François found his elaborate palace too draughty, preferring instead the royal apartments in Amboise and Blois. In the end he stayed here for a total of just 72 days.

adult/child €19/free) – with 426 rooms, 282 fireplaces and 77 staircases – is the largest, grandest and most visited château in the Loire Valley. Dress warmly in winter – the castle is no easier to heat now than it was five centuries ago.

Rising through the centre of the structure, the world-famous **double-helix staircase** – very possibly designed by the king's chum Leonardo da Vinci – ascends to the great lantern tower and the rooftop, where you can gaze out across the vast grounds and marvel at a mind-blowing skyline of cupolas, domes, turrets, chimneys and lightning rods.

The château's over-the-top magnificence really comes alive when you have a sense of how it fits into the sweep of French history. That's why it's worth checking out the film (subtitled in five languages) that's projected on loop on the ground floor. Nearby, you can visit exhibitions featuring François I, and 18th-century **kitchens**. Up on the 1st floor, you'll find a particularly impressive oil painting of Louis XIV, and the castle's most interesting rooms, including the splendid **State Bedchamber**, decorated with gilded wood panelling from the 18th century. As you would expect, the coffered ceilings are adorned with Francois I's heraldic salamanders and the letter F.

To add virtual-reality furnishings to some of the rooms, pick up – at the entrance to the château itself – a HistoPad tablet *(€6.50, 1½ hours)*, available in 12 languages. It also has versions for kids (including a treasure hunt, which some parents report is more of a distraction than a learning aid) and people in wheelchairs. In July and August, hour-long guided tours *(adult/child €7/4)* in English begin daily at 11.15am; reserve online or at the ticket counter.

The château is surrounded by Louis XIV-style **formal gardens** (château tickets required) and extensive grounds (open 24hr). The gardens are perfect for picnics; the map available at ticket counters shows the location of tables. At the

Embarcadère (boat dock), you can rent bicycles, quadracycles, electric golf carts and electric boats from early April to October. Places to eat, including several that serve crêpes and waffles, can be found just past the entrance pavilion, plus there's a restaurant in the château's inner courtyard.

Outdoor spectacles held in the warm season include a 45-minute **equestrian show** *(adult/child €18/14.30, adult incl château €32)* in which horses and colourfully clad riders take you through five centuries of Chambord's history. Show are held from early April to September and begin at 11.45am and/or 4pm from Tuesday to Sunday.

Crowning Glory of French Classical Architecture
Opulent furnishings – plus Tintin

Perhaps the Loire's most elegantly proportioned château, the **Château de Cheverny** *(chateau-cheverny.fr; adult/child €15/11)* is a perfect blend of symmetry, geometry and aesthetic order. Inside are some of the most sumptuous and elegantly furnished rooms anywhere in the region, virtually unchanged for generations because the same family has lived here, almost continuously, ever since the château's construction in the early 1600s. Known for its many family-friendly attractions, Cheverny is open 365 days a year.

Highlights on the ground floor include the formal **dining room**, with 34 painted wooden panels depicting the story of Don Quixote. In the **Galerie**, keep your eyes open for a certificate signed by US president George Washington (hint: it's hanging on the wall).

Upstairs are the **king's bedchamber**, with ceiling murals and tapestries illustrating stories from Greek mythology, and a **children's playroom** complete with toys from the time of Napoléon III. The **arms room** is full of pikestaffs, claymores, crossbows and suits of armour – including a tiny gilded one made to measure for a four-year-old duke – and a mid-17th-century Gobelins tapestry that's so well preserved you can still see the reds.

Behind the main château, the 18th-century **Orangerie** – where many priceless artworks, including (apparently) the *Mona Lisa*, were stashed during WWII – is now a **tearoom**. Nearby there's a **labyrinth** (maze). The gardens have a **picnic area**.

You can see some of the château's hunting dogs, a cross between Poitevins and English foxhounds in the **kennels**;

GOAT CHEESES OF THE BLÉSOIS & CHER

For lovers of *fromage de chèvre* (cheese made with goats' milk), the Loire is a paradise for the palate!

Selles-sur-Cher: Sold in disks that turn from white to blueish as they age, this harmonious cheese has a lemony tang, mineral notes and a flavour reminiscent of goats munching on freshly cut grass, with a hint of hazelnuts. The interior is often oozingly creamy.

Crottin de Chavignol: A dense cheese known for its earthy, tangy flavour and crumbly texture, Chavignol is sold in hard, knobbly little cylinders that are almost as tall as they are wide. As it ages, the cheese becomes firmer and acquires a fuller flavour.

EATING AT THE BLÉSOIS CHÂTEAUX: OUR PICKS

Café de l'Orangerie: The Château de Cheverny's cafe serves light meals, ice cream, desserts and drinks, including thick, creamy hot chocolate. *11am–château closing late Mar–mid-Nov* €

La Madeleine de Proust: Outstanding semi-*gastronomique* French cuisine near Chaumont-sur-Loire, reasonably priced and served with a smile. *noon–1.30pm & 7–8.30pm except Sun dinner, Tue dinner & Wed* €€

Café d'Orléans: Inside the Château de Chambord, this restaurant serves light meals made with local products, some from the castle's own estate. *10am–5.45pm* €€

Le Grand Chaume: At Chaumont-sur-Loire, fine French cuisine is served under an ultramodern dome topped with *chaume* (thatch). Reserve ahead. *7–9pm Fri–Wed* €€€

WINE TOURING IN THE LOIRE

Splendid scenery, meandering backroads, excellent bike routes and plenty of walking trails make the Loire an outstanding destination for *dégustation* (wine tasting). It's easy to put together a web of wonderful itineraries, drawing on 350 wine cellars producing reds, rosés, whites, dessert wines and *crémants* (sparkling wines).

A tourist office or *maison des vins* (wine visitor centre) can supply you with local options and – assuming it's reissued – *À la Découverte des Vins de Loire* (Discovering Loire Wines), a free map with an excellent, colour-coded presentation of the winegrowing areas that stretch from Blois to the Atlantic. It is produced by the region's winegrowers' association, **Vins de Loire** (vinsdeloire.fr), whose website has plenty of information in English and downloadable brochures under 'Tourist circuits'.

---

look for them about 50m beyond the giant sequoia, planted around 1870.

Fans of Tintin might find that the Château de Cheverny's facade looks oddly familiar. Turns out that Hergé used it as a model (minus the two end towers) for Moulinsart (Marlinspike Hall), the ancestral home of Captain Haddock. Devotees large and small may enjoy **Les Secrets de Moulinsart** *(adult/child incl the château €19.50/15)*, whose interactive exhibits explore the world of Tintin with recreated scenes, thunder and other special effects.

Contemporary Art Amid Innovative Gardens
A château that showcases dazzling creativity

Set on a strategic bluff with sweeping views along the Loire, the **Château de Chaumont-sur-Loire** *(domaine-chaumont.fr; adult/child €21/6, in winter €16/4)* has turned itself into one of the most engaging and exciting of the Loire castles. The main structure has a medieval exterior (cylindrical towers, a sturdy drawbridge) and an interior courtyard that is very much of the Renaissance, but far more enthralling are the 60 world-class installations of striking, nature-themed **contemporary art** (including exceptional photography); and, from late April to early November, the **Festival International des Jardins** (International Garden Festival), for which 30 magnificent gardens are created each year by jury-selected teams led by visual artists, architects, set designers and landscape gardeners.

A defensive château was built on this spot in the late 900s, but most of the present castle was constructed between 1468 and 1566. Following the death of Henri II in 1559, Catherine de' Médici (his widow) forced Diane de Poitiers (his mistress and her second cousin) to accept Chaumont in exchange for the grander surroundings of Chenonceau. Savvy Diane earned considerable sums from Chaumont's vast landholdings but stayed here only occasionally.

In the second half of the 18th century, the château was owned by Jacques-Donatien Le Ray, a supporter of the American Revolution and an intimate of Benjamin Franklin's (an exhibition dedicated to **Franco-American friendship** opened in 2024). In 1875, the château was purchased by the 17-year-old Princess de Broglie (pronounced 'broy'), heiress to the Say sugar fortune.

Out in the 32-hectare park, don't miss the brick **Écuries** (stables), an outbuilding constructed in 1877 to house the Broglies' horses in equine luxury. In addition to a fine collection of 19th-century equestrian gear and horse-drawn carriages of surprisingly varied design, there are installations of striking contemporary art. The website of the château, owned by the *région* of Centre-Val de Loire, has details on special events (eg for Christmas) and temporary exhibitions.

During the garden festival – when the **Prés du Goualoup** perennial gardens are also open – you can easily spend the whole day here. The château's four places to eat include a family-friendly buffet.

Touraine

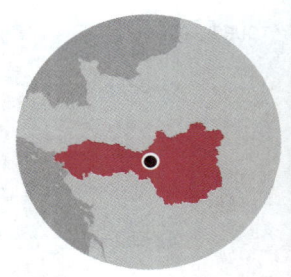

MEDIEVAL FORTRESSES | RENAISSANCE CHÂTEAUX | BUZZY URBAN LIFE

Often dubbed the 'Garden of France', the Touraine region is known for its rich food, fine wines, superb goat cheeses and famously pure French accent, as well as a first-rate line-up of glorious châteaux: some medieval (Langeais and Loches), others Renaissance (Azay-le-Rideau, Villandry and Chenonceau). Amboise is where the Renaissance established its first foothold in France thanks in part to Leonardo da Vinci, who spent his last years here at the invitation of François I.

Tours is a smart and vivacious city with an impressive medieval quarter, fine museums, well-tended parks and a university with over 30,000 students. Combining the sophisticated style of Paris with the sturdy traditionalism of central France, the city makes an ideal staging post for exploring the castles of Touraine. Tours' focal point is grand, semi-circular place Jean Jaurès, adorned with fountains, formal gardens and imposing public buildings (the town hall and the courthouse).

> ☑ **TOP TIP**
>
> Tours is lovely for daytime strolling but for an even more magical ramble, head out after dark, when the city's historic buildings are softly illuminated, bringing their architectural lines and delicate ornamentation into sharp relief.

 GETTING AROUND

Tours is the Loire Valley's main rail hub. Tours-Centre train station has direct services to Amboise, Angers-St-Laud, Azay-le-Rideau, Blois, Chenonceaux (yes, with an X), Chinon, Langeais, Loches, Nantes, Saumur and Tours. Bicycles – available to rent (p387) – can be taken aboard almost all trains, so you can train it out and pedal back or vice versa.

Most TGV trains from Paris Montparnasse stop at St-Pierre-des-Corps, 3km east of Tours-Centre; the two stations are linked by frequent shuttles. Avis and other car rental companies have counters (not always staffed) at one or both train stations.

Filbleu *(filbleu.fr)*, Tours' public transport company, runs two tram lines; bus services include the electric minibuses of Ligne C1 (Citadine), which link the cathedral with Halles de Tours via the city centre.

	SIGHTS	6 Tours American Monument	10 Hôtel Ronsard	● DRINKING & NIGHTLIFE
1	Cathédrale St-Gatien		11 Hôtel Val de Loire	15 The Pale
2	Cloître de la Psalette	● SLEEPING	● EATING	● INFORMATION
3	L'Artisan du Vitrail	7 Hôtel l'Adresse	12 Chez Gaster	16 Tourist Office
4	Musée des Beaux-Arts	8 Hôtel Mondial	13 Halles de Tours	
5	Musée du Compagnonnage	9 Hôtel Oceania L'Univers Tours	14 Tahina	

Half-Timbered Houses, Outdoor Cafes and Artisans

Tours' medieval quarter

Rue Nationale, with a sleek tram line running down the middle, is the city's grandest, most elegant shopping precinct. Strolling today, you'd never know that the entire area was destroyed in 1940 by German shelling. On the riverfront, a block to the east, stands the **Tours American Monument** *(abmc.gov)*, a gilded fountain commemorating the locally based logistics units of the WWI American Expeditionary Force.

A few hundred metres west of rue Nationale is **Vieux Tours** (the old city), a low-rise quarter with narrow streets lined with

  EATING & DRINKING IN TOURS: OUR PICKS

Halles de Tours: Thirty-eight market stalls sell everything for a picnic: cheese, bread, wine, fruit, veggies and scrumptious prepared dishes. *7am-7pm Mon-Sat, to 1pm Sun* €

Tahina: A '100% plant-based' restaurant serving hummus, falafel, burgers, cauliflower fritters and desserts. *11am-3pm Mon-Sat, 6.30pm-1.30am Thu & Fri* €

Chez Gaster: On rue Colbert, traditional, home-style French cuisine made with locally sourced ingredients. Gluten-free available. *noon-2pm & 7.30-10pm, closed Mon night, Tue & Wed* €€

The Pale: Authentically Irish pub on rue Colbert with 33 whiskies and 19 beers on tap. Hugely popular with locals of all ages and Anglophone students. *2pm-2am*

Place Plumereau

old stone and half-timbered houses. Its focal point is **place Plumereau** (known locally as place Plum'), which fills with cafe table when it's warm. A superb spot for a daytime coffee, an *apéro* or an after-dinner beer.

A few blocks further west, you come to the **Quartier des Arts** *(touraineloirevalley.co.uk/quartier-des-arts-tours)*, an arts district created by an association of local artisans. **L'Artisan du Vitrail** *(lartisanduvitrail.com)*, a stained-glass studio at 28 rue Eugène Sue, welcomes visitors when there's no sign in the doorway indicating Pascal Rieu's *'besoin de concentration'* (needs to concentrate on his work). Open Monday to Friday.

Pièces de Résistance from Centuries Past
Be amazed by astonishing artisanship

Tours' unique **Musée du Compagnonnage** *(museecompagnonnage.fr; adult/child €6.60/3.30)* spotlights France's renowned *compagnonnages*, guilds of skilled craftspeople who, over the centuries, have created everything from medieval cathedrals to the Statue of Liberty. Dozens of professions – ranging from carpentry to saddle-making to locksmithing – are celebrated here with masterpieces handmade from wood, wrought iron, bronze, stone, brick, clay, leather and even sugar. Standouts include exquisite wooden architectural models of elaborate towers and a miniature wrought-iron gate that took 14 years to make. Made fully wheelchair accessible in 2025. Closed Tuesday.

Fine Arts in the Archbishop's Palace
Paintings, sculptures and an elephant

Tours' **Musée des Beaux-Arts** *(mba.tours.fr; adult/child €8.40/4.20)* features paintings, sculpture, furniture and *objets d'art* from the 14th to 20th centuries. Highlights include

INFORMATION & DISCOUNTS

Tours' helpful and highly professional **tourist office** *(tours-tourisme.fr)*, a block north of the train station, offers abundant info in English. Drop by – or check out their excellent and comprehensive English-language website – for details on self-guided city walking tours, guided tours (including by bicycle, tuk-tuk and motorcycle sidecar), cultural events, activities, accommodation and local farm visits. Generally closed in the afternoon on Sunday and holidays.

Staff sell slightly reduced-price château tickets; the **Tours City Pass** *(24/48/72hr for €25/35/45)*, which gets you into all the city's museums; and, for cyclists, the **Pass Loire à Vélo**, which includes bike rental, lunches, wine tasting and museum and château visits *(24/48/72hr for €59/105/135)*.

canvases by Delacroix and Monet, a rare Rembrandt miniature and a Rubens *Madonna and Child*. Tickets are valid all day.

Outside in the courtyard, you can see a magnificent cedar of Lebanon planted in 1804 and, behind it, a flowery garden. To the right as you enter the compound, check out the taxidermied remains of Fritz, an Asian elephant who, during a 1902 visit to Tours by the Barnum & Bailey circus, escaped and, to the regret of many, was put down.

Gothic Meets Renaissance at the Cathedral
Buttresses, stained glass and a baroque organ

From the outside, **Cathédrale St-Gatien** *(visite-cathedrale-tours.fr)* wows passers-by with flying buttresses, gargoyles and twin Renaissance-style towers (69m). Inside, the 100m-long church dazzles with 29m-high Gothic vaulting in the nave, luminous stained glass and a towering baroque organ (in the south transept arm). English signs in the choir explicate the stained glass panels, some from the 13th century, others from the 21st (such as those in the north transept arm). Near the entrance, a rack has brochures on the structure's history.

From the north wall of the nave, you can access **Cloître de la Psalette** *(cloitre-de-la-psalette.fr; €5)*, an early Renaissance cloister, renovated in 2025, that features a spiral staircase and a scriptorium. Closed on Sunday morning and, from October to March, on Monday and Tuesday.

Elegant Arches & Delightful Gardens
A château that's also a bridge

Spanning the languid Cher River atop a graceful arched bridge, the **Château de Chenonceau** *(chenonceau.com; adult/child €18/15)* is one of France's most elegant castles. It's hard not to be moved and exhilarated by the glorious setting, the formal gardens, the magic of the architecture and the château's fascinating history. The interior is decorated with rare furnishings and an **art collection** that includes works by Tintoretto, Correggio, Rubens, Murillo, Van Dyck and Ribera (look for an extraordinary portrait of Louis XIV).

Chenonceau is largely the work of several remarkable women – hence its nickname, the Château des Dames. The distinctive arches and the eastern **formal garden** were added by Diane de Poitiers, mistress of Henri II. Following his death, Catherine de' Médici, the king's scheming widow, forced Diane (who happened to be her second cousin) to exchange Chenonceau for the rather less grand **Château de Chaumont-sur-Loire** (p384). Catherine completed the château's construction and added the **yew-tree maze** and the western **rose garden**. The most singular contribution of Louise of Lorraine's was her black-walled **mourning room** on the top floor, to which she retreated when her husband, Henri III, was assassinated in 1589.

The château's *pièce de résistance* is the 60m-long, chequerboard-floored **Grande Galerie** over the Cher River, scene of many an elegant party hosted by Catherine de Médici and Madame Dupin. Used as a military hospital during WWI, it

---

BEST AREAS FOR DINING & SIPPING IN TOURS

Drinking in Vieux Tours: Place Plumereau and adjacent rue du Commerce and rue du Grande Marché are lined with open-air cafes and pubs that attract big crowds on warm nights.

Eating in Vieux Tours: Mid-range restaurants (including French) can be found along or near rue du Grand Marché, rue de la Rôtisserie and recently upgraded rue de Châteauneuf.

Place du Grand Marché: Cheap student grub.

Rue Colbert: Stretching east from rue Nationale for 600m, this pedestrianised street has small, good-value French bistros and international cuisines (eg Indian, Lebanese, Ethiopian).

Place Jean Jaurès: Cafes and restaurants, with year-round outdoor seating, sit under the chestnut trees south of the fountains.

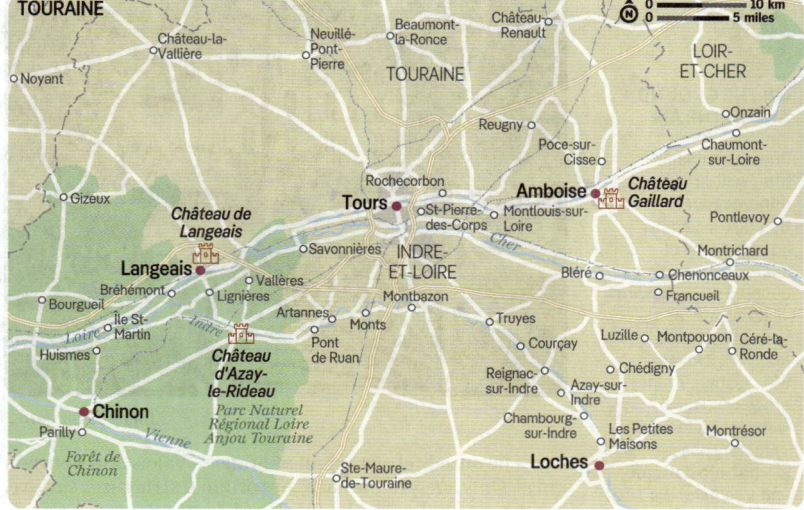

served from 1940 to 1942 as an escape route for *résistants*, Jews and other refugees fleeing from the German-occupied zone (north of the Cher) to the Vichy-controlled zone (south of the river).

The upper level of the gallery, the **Galerie Médicis**, has a well-presented exhibition (in French and English) on the château's colourful history and the women who moulded it. An outbuilding houses the **Apothicairerie de la Reine** (Queen's apothecary) and the **Cabinet des Sciences**, opened in 2024, which showcases 18th-century scientific instruments.

The excellent 1¼-hour audioguide *(€5)*, in 12 languages, has a nicely done version for kids aged seven to 12 (in French and English). There's a great deal to see, so plan on spending at least half a day here. Chenonceau's elegant restaurant, **L'Orangerie**, serves brunch-style French meals from noon to 3pm and becomes a *salon de thé* (tearoom) from 3pm to 4.30pm You can taste Touraine wines in the château's historic wine cellar, the **Cave des Dômes** (closed in November and January). Chenonceaux (the name of the village has an X at the end) is an easy train ride from Tours.

Riverside Town with a Commanding Castle
Amboise and its royal château

The elegant town of **Amboise**, final resting place of the incomparable Leonardo da Vinci, is situated on the gorgeous southern bank of the Loire, guarded by a soaring château. With excellent dining and one of France's most vivacious weekly markets (on Sunday morning), Amboise is a convivial base for exploring both the Loire countryside and nearby castles.

Towering above town, the massively fortified **Château Royal d'Amboise** *(chateau-amboise.com; adult/child €16.90/10.80)*

GOAT CHEESES OF TOURAINE

Ste-Maure de Touraine: Easy to spot because it's shaped like a log, this ash-coated cheese is tangy and even fruity, with a walnutty aroma. The rye straw running down the middle is laser-engraved with the cheesemaker's ID number.

Cœur de Touraine: Instantly identifiable because it's shaped like a *cœur* (heart), this cheese has an aromatic rind made blackish by ash and a thick, creamy interior that mingles tangy with goaty.

Couronne lochoise: Shaped like a bagel, this cheese has a delicate rind and a smooth, creamy interior, with a mild, goaty flavour and hints of grass and citrus.

Château Gaillard

ON THE GROUND AND IN THE AIR

Private companies offer well-organised **minibus tours** that take in various combinations of châteaux, sometimes coupled with vineyard visits, as well as specialised tours featuring cycling or wine tasting. Tourist offices and their websites have details.

Floating peacefully in a **hot-air-balloon** *(montgolfière)* is a gorgeously romantic way to see the Loire countryside. Operated by about a dozen companies, flights are generally possible from April to October, weather permitting, with departures early in the morning or in the evening. Tourist offices (eg Tours and Amboise) and their websites can provide contact information and help with reservations.

was a favoured retreat for all of France's Valois and Bourbon kings. Only a few of the château's original structures survive, but you can still visit the furnished **Logis** (Lodge) – Gothic except for the top half of one wing, which is Renaissance – and the Flamboyant Gothic **Chapelle St-Hubert** (1493), where Leonardo da Vinci's presumed remains have been buried since 1863. An exhibition opened in 2025 looks at France's conquest of Algeria in the 1830s and 1840s and at Abdelkader, the Sufi scholar who led Algerian opposition to French colonialism and who was imprisoned here from 1848 to 1852; 25 members of his entourage are buried on the grounds. The **ramparts** afford thrilling views of the town and Loire. Entry includes a virtual-reality HistoPad tablet in 12 languages.

At the base of the château walls (at place du Château), almost directly under the chapel, 10 local wine producers sell their wares by the glass *(€5-6)* or bottle at **Côt'é Chenin Vins d'Amboise**. Open March to mid-November; closed on Monday in the fall. A block southwest of the château, pedestrian-only rue Nationale is packed with attractive boutiques.

Leonardo Da Vinci's Last Home
Explore the world of history's greatest genius

It was at the invitation of François I that Leonardo da Vinci (1452–1519), aged 64, took up residence at **Le Clos Lucé**

Everything you'd want for a picnic

 EATING IN AMBOISE: OUR PICKS

Sunday Food Market: A riverside extravaganza with 200 to 300 stalls. *7.30am-1.30pm Sun, small market 7.30am-1pm Fri* €

Bigot: Founded in 1913, this classic *salon de thé* and *chocolaterie* serves puff pastries, *tarte tatin*, homemade ice cream and light meals. *9am-7pm Tue-Sun* €

L'Écluse: Next to an *écluse* (river lock), creative French cuisine is made using fresh seasonal products from the Loire area. *noon-1.30pm & 7-9pm Tue-Sat* €€

Auberge du Prieuré: Serves dishes popular during the Renaissance, with staff in period costumes. Reserve ahead. *noon-2pm Tue-Sun in French school holidays* €€

(vinci-closluce.com; adult/child €19.50/14.50), a grand manor house built in 1471. An admirer of the Italian Renaissance, the French monarch named Da Vinci 'first painter, engineer and king's architect', and the Italian spent his time here sketching, tinkering and dreaming up ingenious contraptions.

Fascinating scale models of 40 of Da Vinci's inventions are on display inside the house and around the lovely 7-hectare gardens. At the bottom of the gardens, in the immersive **Galeries Léonard de Vinci**, the master's greatest works are projected onto the walls; displays upstairs spotlight his mind-blowingly creative ideas in fields such as urban planning and civil and military architecture. Light meals (eg crêpes) are available on-site, or you can picnic at the tables near the entrance or on the grass.

As you walk up to Le Clos Lucé, keep an eye out for the **habitats troglodytiques** (cave houses, many now uninhabited) carved into the rock face overlooking rue Victor Hugo.

The Renaissance's First Foothold in France
A royal château with Da Vinci-era gardens

The earliest expression of the Italian Renaissance in France, the **Château Gaillard** (chateau-gaillard-amboise.fr; adult/child €16/13) was inspired by the refined lifestyle that Charles VIII fell in love with in Italy. The graceful château – its royal status indicated by four parallel rows of decorative elements just below the edge of the roof – is decorated with 16th-century-style furniture and modern stained-glass medallions inspired by medieval miniatures. In the rooms, QR codes connect you to YouTube videos in French and English.

Inside, beyond the 'cabinet of curiosities' – a glass case containing a 16th-century, horned 'mask of shame' from Germany and antique snuff bottles, among other oddities – are a vaulted **13th-century kitchen**, a medieval **courtyard** and a 17th-century **troglodyte kitchen**. The 3m-wide, medieval **spiral staircase** leads up to a room dedicated to Mary Stuart (Mary, Queen of Scots), who spent her honeymoon here – she had just married François II – in 1558. A film recounts her sad life.

The château's harmonious, Renaissance-style **gardens** were laid out by master gardener Dom Pacello de Mercogliano (1453–1534), an Italian Benedictine monk who established France's first *orangerie* (used to protect sensitive fruit trees during winter) in 1500. The château now grows more than 100 varieties of citrus, many of them quite rare (eg caviar lime and bizzarria of Florence), which spend the warm months out-of-doors.

Exquisite Gardens à la Française
The Renaissance is alive and flowering at Villandry

The gardens of the **Château de Villandry** (chateauvillandry.com; adult/child €14/8, gardens only €8.50/5.50, €2 in winter) are among France's most beautiful, with more than 6 hectares of cascading flowers, ornamental vines, manicured lime

GOAT CHEESES OF THE INDRE DÉPARTEMENT

Of the 15 French goat cheeses recognized by the EU with an AOP (Appellation d'Origine Protégée, 'protected designation of origin'), five are from the Loire Valley, including these two from the Indre Département:

Valençay: Shaped like a pyramid with the tip lopped off, the wrinkled, blackish rind is made up of natural mould coated with powdered vegetable ash. As it ages, the taste evolves from mild, with nutty undertones and a hint of sweetness, to robust and earthy. The texture is creamy and sometimes lightly gooey.

Pouligny St-Pierre: Resembling a yellowish, wrinkly, decapitated pyramid, the natural-mould rind hides a white and crumbly interior. Initial salty, tangy flavours are soon joined by overtones of sweetness.

VILLANDRY'S AMERICAN CONNECTION

The Château de Villandry was built in the early 1500s by Jean Le Breton, who served François I as finance minister and supervised the construction of the **Château de Chambord** (p381). While posted to Italy as the French ambassador, Le Breton became enamoured with the art of Italian Renaissance gardening, later creating his own ornamental masterpiece at Villandry.

The French government confiscated the château during the Revolution. In 1813, it was sold to Napoléon for use by his youngest brother Jérôme, who in 1803 had married a beautiful American heiress in Baltimore but cut contact with her and their son – founder of the Bonaparte family's illustrious American branch – after the French emperor, enraged at the union, forcibly annulled the marriage by imperial decree.

---

trees, razor-sharp box hedges and tinkling fountains. Try to visit when the gardens – all of them organic – are blooming, ie between April and October. Tickets are valid all day (get your hand stamped if you leave). The website has details on special events, eg Christmas decorations. An audioguide costs €4.

Wandering the pebbled walkways, you'll see the classical **Jardin d'Eau** (Water Garden), the hornbeam **Labyrinthe** (Maze) and the **Jardin d'Ornement** (Ornamental Garden), which depicts various aspects of love (fickle, passionate, tender and tragic) using geometrically pruned hedges and coloured flowerbeds. The **Jardin du Soleil** (Sun Garden) is a looser array of gorgeous multicoloured and multiscented perennials. But for many, the highlight is the 16th-century-style **Potager Décoratif** (Decorative Kitchen Garden), where cabbages, leeks and carrots create nine geometrical, colour-coordinated squares. Next to the **Jardin de Nuages** (Cloud Garden) there's a **playground** for under-10s. The gardens are tended by 10 full-time expert gardeners.

About 200m southwest of the château along the D16 you'll find a branch of Tours' **tourist office** (open from early April to late September), which rents bicycles (adult-size only) and sells tickets for Cher River **boat rides** *(bateliersducher.net)*; several restaurants, including a pizzeria; a *boulangerie*; and a number of places to stay.

The Loire's Most Medieval Château
Peek in on a secret royal wedding

No castle in the Loire is more authentically medieval in architecture, furnishings and spirit than the **Château de Langeais** *(chateau-de-langeais.com; adult/child €12/6)*. Built in the 1460s, it looks much as it did during the last decades of the Middle Ages, with crenellated ramparts and massive towers dominating the surrounding village. Original 15th-century furniture fills its flagstoned chambers, making it easy to imagine what aristocratic life in the Loire Valley was like six centuries ago.

Superbly preserved both inside and out, the château presents two faces to the world. From the town you see a fortified castle, nearly windowless, with machicolated walls rising forbiddingly from the **drawbridge**, which staff open and close by hand at the start and end of each workday. But the newer sections facing the courtyard, built on the cusp of the Renaissance, have large windows, ornate dormers and decorative stonework designed for more refined living.

In one room, an eerily realistic **wax-figure tableau** portrays the top-secret – and highly political – marriage of Charles VIII and 14-year-old Anne of Brittany, held right here on 6 December 1491, which brought about the historic union of France and Brittany. The story is dramatically narrated by Stéphane Bern.

Among the château's many fine, if faded, Flemish and Aubusson **tapestries**, look out for one from 1530 depicting astrological signs; three intricate panels with *millefleurs* ('thousand flowers') motifs; and seven panels from the famous

Bedroom, Château de Langeais

Les Neuf Preux series (woven 1525–40), whose nine 'worthy knights' – personages from the Old Testament, Greco-Roman antiquity and the Middle Ages – represent the epitome of medieval courtly honour. In each room, plasticised sheets in eight languages elucidate its history, architecture and furnishings. The **Chemin de Ronde** (Parapet Walk) gives you a knight's-eye view from the ramparts; gaps underfoot (machicolations) enabled boiling oil, rocks and excrement to be dumped on attackers.

Across the château's courtyard stand the remains of the oldest **keep** in France that's still standing, constructed by the great builder Foulques Nerra (Fulk III), count of Anjou, in the late 900s. In 2026 it may be possible to climb up the scaffolding for a view. Further up the hill you'll find picnic areas and two features that children will love, a wood-built **playground** and a **cabane suspendue** (tree house) constructed among the branches of an Atlas cedar.

The peaceful little Cher River town of Langeais has lovely walking streets, several excellent restaurants, a bustling Sunday morning **food market** and, facing the château's drawbridge, an excellent *fromagerie* (cheese shop).

Renaissance Castle Par Excellence
Splendidly elegant and perfectly proportioned

Romantic, moat-ringed **Château d'Azay-le-Rideau** *(azay-le-rideau.fr; adult/child €16/free)*, built almost exactly 500 years ago on a natural island in the middle of the Indre River, is wonderfully adorned with elegant turrets, exquisitely proportioned windows, delicate stonework and steep slate roofs. This is one of the Loire's loveliest Renaissance castles – Honoré de Balzac called it a 'multifaceted diamond set in the River Indre'. The famous, Italian-style **loggia staircase** overlooking the central courtyard is decorated with the salamanders

CYCLING THE LOIRE

The mostly flat Loire Valley is fabulous cycling country – there's nothing quite like pedalling through villages, vineyards and forests on your way from one château to the next. **La Loire à Vélo** *(Loire by Bike; loirebybike.co.uk)* maintains 900km of signposted routes from Nevers all the way to the Atlantic; pick up a free guide from a tourist office or access information (including details on route options and bike hire) from the website. Individual *départements*, including Indre-et-Loire (Touraine), Loir-et-Cher (Blésois) and Maine-et-Loire (Anjou), have their own cycling networks and brochures. **Les Châteaux à Vélo** *(chateauxavelo.co.uk)* maintains over 500km of marked bike routes in the Blésois. The **Geovelo** app can recommend routes that follow bike paths and avoid heavy traffic.

BICYCLE RENTAL IN THE LOIRE

Companies that rent out bicycles (classic, all-terrain, electric, tandem, kids', etc) and can arrange luggage transfer and self-guided bike tours include:

Détours de Loire: *(detoursdeloire.com)* Has offices in Blois, Tours and Nantes.

Les Vélos Verts: *(lesvelosverts.com)* Based in Blois, with departure points in Chaumont-sur-Loire, Tours, Amboise and Saumur.

Roue Lib: *(rouelib.com)* Based in Tours, with an office in Amboise that's open April to October.

In general, rental companies allow you to pick up and/or drop off bicycles at your hotel for a small surcharge; emergency repairs en route are free.

Château d'Azay-le-Rideau (p393)

and ermines of François I and Queen Claude. Audioguides *(1½ hours; €3)* are available in five languages.

The interior furnishings are mostly 19th-century, created by the Marquis Charles de Biencourt (who bought the château after the Revolution) and his heirs. The **English-style gardens** surrounding the château and the paths around the two ponds – actually a branch of the Indre – are great for a stroll or a picnic. Across the square from the ticket office, the **Jardin des Secrets** features heritage vegetables and flowers. From mid-July to late August, you can take a **flânerie nocturne** *(nighttime stroll; adult/child €8/4)* around the illuminated gardens, accompanied by ancient music, from nightfall until 11.15pm.

In the **Pressoir** (the outbuilding to the right as you exit the ticket-sales hall), there's a fascinating exhibition on the materials and methods used to repair the château and in the restoration of antique furnishings; the videos of expert artisans at work are riveting. Honey produced by 20 on-site beehives is on sale in the boutique.

A number of places to eat are located within a few hundred metres of the château, along rue Balzac around the village's main square, place de la République.

Ramparts, Towers, Dungeons & a Cage
Medieval castle on a hill

The sleepy town of **Loches** *(loches-valdeloire.com)*, on the Indre River, spirals picturesquely up from the modern town – through **Porte Picois** (15th century) and the forbidding **Porte Royale** (circa 1200) – to the **Cité Royale de Loches** *(citeroyaleloches.fr)*, a vast medieval bastion the size of a small town – a few lucky people even live here! It's a great destination for kids who are into knights, castles and dungeons. English signage is excellent.

The **Logis Royal** (adult/child incl Donjon €12.50/10.50), the royal residence of Charles VII and his successors, was originally built as a medieval fortress but later converted into a Renaissance-style hunting lodge. In May 1429, after her victory at Orléans, Joan of Arc famously met Charles VII here for the second time and nudged him towards coronation. The multimedia museum has rooms dedicated to some big personalities: Charles VII, Agnès Sorel (Charles VII's mistress, who is buried in an elaborate tomb in the nearby **Romanesque church**), Anne of Brittany and Joan of Arc. Kids age six to 10 can play a **memory game** using plasticised sheets with 14 photos.

At the southern end of the Cité Royale, the rectangular, 36m-high **Donjon** (defensive tower) – brought alive by a virtual-reality HistoPad, available at the entrance – was Loches' original medieval stronghold, built in the early 11th century by the cruel and feared Foulques Nerra, count of Anjou. Though the interior floors have fallen away, you can still see various architectural details, including the remnants of an 11th-century chapel and fireplaces. Climb dizzying catwalks for fantastic views.

Next door is the notorious **Tour Neuve** (New Tower), built in the 15th century by Charles VII; its rooftop **Terrasse à Feu** (Gun Terrace), once a platform for firing artillery, offers great views. In the basement, the circular **Cachots** (dungeons) are where the unfortunate Cardinal Balue was supposedly kept suspended from the ceiling in a wooden cage for betraying Louis XI. (In fact, this room was more likely a grain store, although you can see a replica of the cardinal's cage up the stairs next to the Donjon.)

Reached from the courtyard, the 15th-century **Martelet**, 27m deep, houses additional dungeons and 11th-century *tuffeau* (soft limestone) quarries.

Royal Lodgings, a Medieval Prison & Catapults

Hilltop fortress from the Middle Ages

Dominated by a massive medieval fortress, **Chinon** is etched into France's collective memory both as the favourite fortress of Henry II (1133–89), king of England, and as the venue for Joan of Arc's first meeting with Charles VII, in 1429. Below the château is an appealing **medieval quarter**, whose white *tuffeau* houses all have black slate roofs, conferring on the town its characteristic colour scheme. The narrow cobblestone streets and alleys present a cross-section of medieval architecture, best seen along rue Voltaire and its western continuation, rue Haute St-Maurice – both home to a number of French restaurants – and between there and the river. Restaurants can also be found along rue Rabelais, just east of the tourist office (p396).

Surrounded by colossal stone ramparts, the **Forteresse Royale de Chinon** (forteressechinon.fr; adult/child €12.50/ 10.50) – offering fabulous views across town, river and countryside – is split into three sections separated by dry moats.

CHINON WINES

The area surrounding Chinon is one of the Loire's main wine-producing areas. **Chinon AOP** (chinon.com) vineyards producing fine red wines, most made from cabernet franc grapes, stretch along both banks of the Vienne River. The soil here ranges from flinty clay to alluvial gravel, producing a wide variety of wines, some intense, others more refined. Most are aged in caves carved out of *tuffeau*, the soft local limestone, which offers the ideal temperature and humidity. The local tourist office has details on *domaines* that offer *dégustation* (wine tasting) and sales.

The Renaissance humanist and playwright François Rabelais (c 1494–1553), who was born in Chinon, was renowned for his outsized enthusiasm for life. Locals seems to believe that his *joie de vivre* lives on in the area's wines.

Forteresse Royale de Chinon (p395)

VISITOR INFORMATION IN CHINON

Chinon's **tourist office** (azay-chinon-valdeloire.com), conveniently situated on the main square, can provide you with a map of the town that suggests two walking tours and has details on bike and electric scooter rental, kayaking, boat trips and hot-air balloons. It also sells slightly reduced-price château tickets. There's a **summer kiosk**, open mid-June to mid-September, up near the château.

Except on market day (Thursday), free parking is available 500m east of the town centre at place Jeanne d'Arc. There are two more free parking lots above town at **Parking du Château**, across av François Mitterrand from the upper entrance to the château.

A free, glass-enclosed lift links the town centre with the château.

The ticket counter and shop are inside the 12th-century **Fort St-Georges**. Pass under the 14th-century **Tour de l'Horloge** (Clock Tower) and you'll come to the **Château du Milieu** (Middle Castle), vestige of a time when the Plantagenet court of Henry II and Eleanor of Aquitaine assembled here. Finally, **Fort du Coudray** sits on the tip of the promontory.

In the Château du Milieu, the restored south wing of the **Logis Royaux** (Royal Lodgings) has the royal chambers of Charles VII and Eleanor of Aquitaine, scale models of the castle, Joan of Arc memorabilia and archaeological finds. In the garden you can see scale models of a trebuchet and a bricole, used in the Middle Ages to catapult projectiles at the enemy. At the far end, the round, 13th-century **Tour du Coudray** was used to imprison Knights Templar in the early 1300s (look for their graffiti inside) and hosted Joan of Arc in 1429.

HistoPad virtual reality tablets (in nine languages) show various rooms as they might have looked in the Middle Ages and, for kids, present a treasure hunt. Kids can also get a little booklet, *On a tour with Bertille*, that takes them on a tour of the castle, with questions at each stop. The château lays on all sorts of special activities for children during French school holidays – the website has details.

The menu changes every few days

 EATING IN LOCHES & CHINON: OUR PICKS

Loches Food Market: Head to rue de la République and place de la Marne to find fruit, veggies, cheese and prepared dishes. *8am-12.30pm Wed & Sat* €

Chinon Food Market: Stalls sell fruit, vegetables, cheeses and other picnic supplies at place Jeanne d'Arc. *7am-1.30pm Thu* €

Le P'tit Restau: Impeccable, internationally inspired cuisine, made with fresh seasonal products, in Loches' Ville-Basse. *noon-2pm Fri-Tue, 7-9pm Fri & Sat* €€

Les Années 30: French classics, including venison (in season), served with exquisite attention to detail. In Chinon. *12.15-1.15pm & 7.30-8.30pm Thu-Mon* €€

Anjou

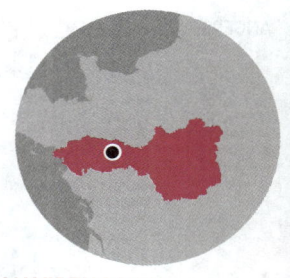

MEDIEVAL CASTLE | VIVID TAPESTRIES | EQUESTRIAN VIRTUOSITY

An intellectual centre in the 1400s and a lively university city today, Angers (pronounced ahn-*zhay*) – the historical seat of the Plantagenet dynasty and the dukes of Anjou – makes an engaging western gateway to the central Loire Valley. The mostly pedestrianised old town supports a thriving cafe culture, thanks in part to the dynamic presence of 46,000 students, and offers some excellent dining options. The city is famous for two sets of breathtaking tapestries, one – on display in the château – from the late 14th century, the other from the mid-20th.

Architectural gems in the region include the medieval Abbaye Royale de Fontevraud, delightful riverside villages such as Candes-St-Martin, and some charming châteaux. Europe's highest concentration of *habitations troglodytes* (cave dwellings) dots the banks of the Loire around cosmopolitan, equestrian Saumur, home of the crack Cadre Noire riding corps. Much of Anjou is covered with vineyards.

> ☑ **TOP TIP**
>
> For a truly spectacular vista across the Maine River, walk from the château's massive gate to the northern tip of **Promenade du Bout du Monde**. For a no less superb view in the other direction, take a lift up to the roof terrace of **Théâtre Le Quai** (p400), across the river in the Doutre Quarter.

Climb the Ramparts & Explore the Medieval Mind

A 14th-century tapestry in a 13th-century fortress

Looming above the river, the forbidding **Château d'Angers** (*chateau-angers.fr; adult €12 or €14, child free, €1 less online*),

GETTING AROUND

Angers-St-Laud train station, 600m south of the château (and the tourist office), has direct rail links to Saumur and Tours and, further afield, to Nantes and Paris Gare Montparnasse.

Local public transit services are run by Irigo *(irigo.fr)* and include three tram lines that bisect the city centre.

If you have a car, be aware that street parking is metered and strictly time-limited in the entire city centre, though a number of city-run parking garages are available. On many streets southwest of the château and south of the train station, you can park on the street for up to eight hours for €6.40. For details, see parking-angers.fr.

- **HIGHLIGHTS**
  1 Château d'Angers
  2 Musée Jean Lurçat de la Tapisserie Contemporaine

- **SIGHTS**
  3 Cale de la Savatte
  4 Cathédrale St-Maurice
  5 Galerie David d'Angers
  6 Maison d'Adam
  7 Montée St-Maurice
  8 Musée des Beaux-Arts
  9 Promenade du Bout du Monde
  10 Riverside Esplanade

- **SLEEPING**
  11 Hôtel Continental
  12 Hôtel du Mail
  13 Hôtel Marguerite d'Anjou

- **EATING**
  14 Brasserie de la Gare
  15 Chez Marguerite
  16 Crêperie La Boudeuse
  17 Grande Marché
  18 Gribiche
  19 Halles Cœur de Maine-Biltoki
  20 La Réserve
  21 La Soufflerie

- **ENTERTAINMENT**
  22 Les Quatre-Cents Coups
  23 Théâtre Le Quai

- **TRANSPORT**
  24 Angers-St-Laud Train Station

seat of power of the once-mighty dukes of Anjou, is ringed by moats, 2.5m-thick walls and 17 massive, menacing round towers. An audioguide *(€3)* is highly recommended.

As you enter the château, turn left and climb the stone stairs to reach the **Parapet Walk**. Perched atop of the castle's eastern and southern ramparts, it offers beautiful views of the city – and a tiny chenin blanc vineyard!

The château's artistic and historic highlight is the stunning, UNESCO-listed **Tapestry of the Apocalypse**, a 104m-long series of 71 scenes commissioned in 1375 to illustrate the story of the final bloody battle between good and evil as prophesied in the Bible's book of Revelation. The vivid, graphic novel-style scenes mix terror, pathos, extreme violence, humour and seven-headed dragons, giving visitors an extraordinary peek into the medieval mind, its dreams and its deepest fears. It also presents an incredibly vivid portrait of life and its sorrows in the 14th century, in France a time of plague (the Black Death) and political and social turmoil.

Medieval Streets, a Cathedral & Lots of Students

Stroll around Angers' hillside city centre

One of the earliest examples of Angevin (Plantagenet) architecture in France, the extraordinary, Gothic **Cathédrale St-Maurice** is distinguished by a striking Norman (mid-1100s) western portal decorated with extremely rare polychrome figures, a nave from the same period, 13th- to 15th-century **stained glass**, a towering **pipe organ** and an over-the-top, gilded baroque **baldachin** (1758) over the high altar. During construction of a new triple portal at the base of the west façade, enter through the south portal. From the square in front of the cathedral, a monumental staircase, **Montée St-Maurice**, leads down to the **riverside esplanade** and the eateries of **Halles Cœur de Maine-Biltoki** (p400).

Directly behind the cathedral stands the half-timbered **Maison d'Adam** (c 1500), one of the city's best-preserved medieval houses, which is decorated with a riot of carved, bawdy wooden sculptures. The carved-wood Tree of Life, on the corner, was once flanked by Adam and Eve; another loved-up couple can be seen nearby.

Angers' Art Scene

Paintings, sculptures and cinema

Central Angers has two worthwhile art museums. The **Musée des Beaux-Arts** (musees.angers.fr; adult/child €6/free) has an excellent 14th- to 20th-century collection (mainly paintings) that ranges from the French masters Ingres, Fragonard and Watteau to the Florentine Lorenzo Lippi to Flemish and Dutch Golden Age painters such as Jacob Jordaens. Don't miss the exuberant sculpture in the courtyard, *L'Arbre Serpents* (Serpent Tree) by Niki de Saint Phalle.

Across the museum gardens, **Galerie David d'Angers** (musees.angers.fr; adult/child €4/free) features plaster studio casts by Angers-born sculptor Pierre-Jean David (1788–1856), renowned for his lifelike sculptures, which adorn the

BEST DINING AREAS IN ANGERS

Rue St-Laud: This pedestrianised, city-centre street, heading northeast from rue Plantagenêt, is lined with cafes and restaurants, including gourmet hamburger joints and eateries selling Southeast Asian–style meals-in-a-bowl. Hugely popular with students.

Rue de la Roë: A number of restaurants look out on the trams that trundle up this sloping, city-centre street.

Place du Ralliement: At Angers' handsome central square, brasseries and cafes face the imposing stone façade of the 19th-century Grand Théâtre.

Place de la Gare and nearby avenues: A number of excellent restaurants and cafes can be found right around Angers' train station.

Specialities include pâté en croûte (pâté baked in pastry)

 EATING IN ANGERS: BEST FRENCH FOOD

| **Crêperie La Boudeuse:** Luscious savoury and sweet galettes and crêpes facing the Maison d'Adam. *noon-2pm & 7-9pm Thu-Mon* € | **Brasserie de la Gare:** A favourite of seafood lovers since 1912. Dine outdoors or in an Orient Express-themed salon. *11.30am-11pm* €€ | **La Réserve:** High atop Théâtre Le Quai, this bar-restaurant specialises in locally-grown beef. *10am-midnight or 1am Mon-Sat* €€ | **Gribiche:** Two young chefs give new life to classic, seasonal French cuisine. *noon-1pm Mon-Fri & 7.30-8.30pm Mon, Tue, Thu & Fri* €€ |

GUINGUETTES

A kind of pop-up riverbank restaurant with a beer garden vibe, *guinguettes* originated in Paris during the Belle Époque. Open only from spring to early autumn, they bring together wooden furniture, deck chairs, hanging fairy lights, local wine, tasty food and, often, live music. A century ago, the popular venues bustled with workers and members of the *petite bourgeoisie* (lower middle class) who came together to *guincher* – a dated way of saying dancing – to accordion melodies, and to enjoy hearty dishes paired with wines. These days, the focus is on good company and food, including zander with white butter sauce, Loire whitebait and melt-in-the-mouth *rillauds* (tender pork belly pieces). On summer days, *crêmet d'Anjou* (a yogurt-texture cream, but fresher and fluffier) is the perfect dessert.

Panthéon (p152) in Paris and can be seen in the Louvre (p86) and Paris' Père Lachaise cemetery (p124). A plaque in the front courtyard is dedicated to Thomas Jefferson.

Also in the city centre, **Les Quatre-Cents Coups**, an art cinema named after a 1959 film by François Truffaut, screens non-dubbed films on seven screens.

River Panoramas & a Modern Tapestry

Stroll along the north bank of the Maine

Across the river from the city centre, the **Doutre Quarter** is worth a wander. At **Cale de la Savatte**, a small marina where traditional wooden boats, called *toues*, mix with more modern ones, you can lounge on the grassy slope as you gaze across the river up to the château and the cathedral. For even more spectacular views of river and the old city, head to the 5th-floor patio atop **Théâtre Le Quai**, one of Angers' main performance venues; take the outside elevator directly to the roof. The bar-restaurant is open daily except Sunday.

About 700m northeast along the river, **Le Chant du Monde** (Song of the World; 1957-61) is an epic tapestry masterpiece – inspired by the Apocalypse Tapestry – created by Jean Lurçat (1892–1966) just over a decade after the slaughter of WWII. Housed in a vaulted, Plantagenet Gothic–style hospital hall (late 12th and early 13th centuries) in the **Musée Jean Lurçat de la Tapisserie Contemporaine** *(musees.angers.fr; adult/child €6/free)*, the 10 panels depict everything from the delights of Champagne to space exploration to nuclear holocaust; an excellent brochure in English explains the symbolism of each. A quintessentially mid-20th-century meditation on the human condition, it is exuberant but contemplative, and only guardedly optimistic. The museum also exhibits a changing kaleidoscope of extraordinarily beautiful 20th-century and 21st-century tapestries.

Where All the Cointreau in the World Is Made

Tour the Cointreau distillery

Drop by the **Cointreau Distillery** *(cointreau.com/fr/fr/distillerie-cointreau; 1¼-hr tour adult/child €12.50/4.50)*, 3km east of Angers' city centre, to sample and buy the bitter-orange liqueur just steps from where it's distilled. To discover (some of) Cointreau's production secrets, take a tour of the facilities; reserve ahead by phone or via the website (in French). Closed Sunday and Monday.

EATING IN ANGERS: BEST GOOD-VALUE MEALS

Halles Cœur de Maine-Biltoki: Angers' answer to Singapore's hawker centres, with 18 food vendors and picnic tables. *8am-10pm or 11pm Tue-Sat, 8am-3pm Sun* €

Grande Marché: This huge weekly market fills place du Général Leclerc with over 150 stalls selling fresh fruit, veg, clothes and bric-a-brac. *8am-1.30pm Sat* €

La Soufflerie: Soufflés, those notoriously finicky baked French specialities, and salads are served on tiny square tables. *noon-2pm & 7-10pm Tue-Sat* €

Chez Marguerite: This cosy *salon de thé* (tea room) serves tasty light dishes at lunch and delicious cakes. *noon-6pm Wed-Sat, 11.30am-3.30pm Sun* €

Place St-Pierre, Saumur

Medieval Streets, Liqueurs & Military History

Saumur, a garrison town with a long equestrian history

There's sparkly Parisian sophistication in **Saumur** but also an atmosphere of unhurried enjoyment. The local wines are world-famous, the restaurants may just be the Loire's best, and the spot is gorgeous. The **old town** is worth a wander – check out narrow **rue de la Tonnelle**, which links place de la République (along the river) with restaurant-filled **place St-Pierre** and its Plantagenet-style Gothic church, **Église St-Pierre**, adorned with a late 17th-century classical façade in a style typical of the Counter-Reformation. Saumur's **tourist office** has a brochure detailing historical walks.

About 500m west of place St-Pierre, you can sample absinthe and triple sec, and tour part of the production facilities, at **Distillerie Combier** (combier.fr; tours adult/child €6/free). Closed on Monday (open daily from June to September).

VISITOR INFORMATION IN SAUMUR

Saumur's **tourist office** (ot-saumur.fr), on the riverfront, can supply you with a city map, information on horse-riding options and flat-bottomed boat cruises, and a list of area sites that stay open in winter. It can also make reservations for Cadre Noir performances and has a free left-luggage service, especially useful for cyclists.

Almost next door, the **Maison des Vins** (House of Anjou and Saumur Wines), run by a winegrowers federation, is an excellent place to sample and purchase wines from 26 Saumur-area AOCs. It can also provide details on *domaines* offering tasting and tours. Closed on Sunday and Monday except in summer.

Anjou's oldest guinguette

 EATING ALONG THE ANJOU LOIRE: OUR PICKS

Guinguette de Port-Thibault: Shady Loireside *guinguette*, 8km southwest of Angers. Live music on Sundays and Fridays. *noon-10.30pm or 11.30pm Tue-Sun May–late Oct* €

Bistroglo: A troglodyte bistro in Turquant serving Loire favourites such as *galipettes* (stuffed mushrooms). *noon-2pm & 7-8.30pm except Sun dinner & Mon* €€

L'Hélianthe: Behind Turquant's town hall, this troglodyte restaurant has a hearty menu based on local products and classic French flavours. *noon-1.45pm & 7-8.45pm Fri-Tue* €€

La Guinguette à Jojo: Wicker chairs, playground and live music. It's 17km southeast of Angers. *7-11.30pm Wed, noon-5.30pm & 7-11.30pm Thu-Sun mid-May–mid-Sep* €€

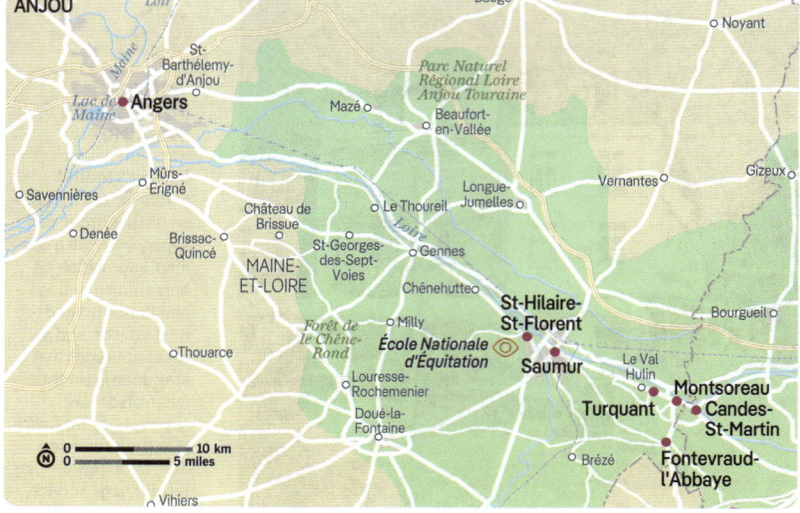

History buffs may want to head 2km south of the town centre to the **Musée des Blindés** *(museedesblindes.fr; adult/child €11/6)*, a tank museum that displays more than 200 *blindés* (tanks) and other 'armoured cavalry' vehicles from 17 countries, including all sides in WWI, WWII and the Cold War. Closed Thursday except in summer.

The Elite Cadre Noir & their Horses
Visit France's national horse-riding school

An equestrian centre since 1593, Saumur is renowned for the prestigious **École Nationale d'Équitation** *(ifce.fr/cadre-noir)*, one of the world's premier equestrian academies and home to the Cadre Noir, a world-class group of riding instructors that's also an equestrian display team. It is situated 4.5km due west of Saumur, just outside sleepy St-Hilaire-St-Florent.

Superb one-hour **tours** *(adult/child €8.50/6.50)* take visitors behind the scenes and around the spacious campus, built in 1980, stopping by the *manège* (riding arena), which has mirrors mounted on the walls, like a ballet studio. It's often possible to see horses and riders training (no photography); watch carefully and you'll get a sense of the incredibly intimate collaboration between horse and rider. Kids will love to pat the horses in their spacious stalls – several stomp their feet insistently if you don't stroke them! Commentary is in French, but written information is available in eight languages; call ahead for details on tours in English. It's a good idea to reserve a couple of days ahead during French school holidays, including in the summer. Offered from early February to October, tours generally begin at 10am, 11am, 2.30pm and 4pm except on Saturday afternoon, Sunday and Monday morning.

THE CADRE NOIR

The riders and horses of the Cadre Noir, founded in 1825, are famous for their astonishing discipline and acrobatic prowess, performed without stirrups. The school trains about 90 students, who are headed for careers as riding instructors, as well as 350 to 400 horses.

You can recognise members of the Cadre Noir by their distinctive black *(noir)* jackets and hats *(képis* for men, *bicornes* for women), gold spurs and the three golden wings on their whips. Look closely at their collar insignia and at the gold buttons of their tunics: a flaming grenade means they're members of the French military, a sun that they are civilians.

The **Cadre Noir equestrian display team** puts on two types of astonishingly graceful shows: **Matinales** *(adult/child €22/17)*, hour-long training demonstrations with commentary; and – this is what it's most famous for – ballet-like **Galas** *(adult/child from €37/17)* that showcase horses' and riders' extraordinary skills. Headsets provide simultaneous translation into English. Reserve by online or by phone, or via Saumur's tourist office. Galas are held on specific dates in April, June, September and October; tickets go on sale in mid-November of the previous year and usually sell out by the end of December.

Bluffs & Caves in Wine Country
Along the Loire East of Saumur
To take in the Anjou wine country by car, cross the Loire from Saumur and head either northwest along route D751 towards **Gennes**, or southeast on route D947 through **Souzay-Champigny** and **Parnay**.

Ten kilometres southeast of Saumur, the picturesque and easily strollable village of **Turquant** is one of the best places in the Loire to see troglodyte dwellings. Many have now been spruced up and converted into shops, galleries or restaurants.

The picturesque village of **Candes-St-Martin**, 4km southeast of Turquant (and 1.5 southeast of Montsoreau), occupies an idyllic spot where the Vienne and Loire rivers conflow. St Martin died here in 397, turning little Candes into a major pilgrimage destination. For great panoramas, climb the tiny streets above the **Collégiale St-Martin** church, past inhabited cave dwellings, or head down to the benches and path along the waterfront.

The Sign Says 'A Bad Place' – Don't Believe It!
Museum of the Art & Language movement
A surprising warning, written in gargantuan capital letters in the gravel of the courtyard, greets you as you approach Montsoreau's Renaissance-style **Château de Montsoreau-Musée d'Art Contemporain** *(chateau-montsoreau.com; adult/child €12/10)*, made famous in Alexandre Dumas *père*'s historical novel *La Dame de Monsoreau* and now a museum of conceptual art specialising in the UK- and US-based Art & Language movement. Many works feature words, often in English, with

WINE TASTING AROUND SAUMUR

The cabernet franc vineyards of the 16-sq-km **Saumur-Champigny winegrowing area**, south and southeast of Saumur on the south bank of the Loire, offer excellent winetasting opportunities amid exquisite scenery. Many of the renowned AOC producers here, both small and large, offer free tastings at their cellars from spring to early autumn; see saumur-champigny.com (click 'Vineyard and Winemakers', then 'The Winemakers' Directory') for details, including whether you need to reserve ahead. Note that winegrowers are especially busy during the *vendanges* (grape harvest) from late August to October. Many producers can be found on or near the picturesque D947, from which you can see *tuffeau* bluffs punctuated by cave houses.

 EATING & DRINKING IN SAUMUR: OUR PICKS

Halles St-Pierre: Food stalls set up on place St-Pierre, just outside the almost-moribund covered market, soon to be refurbished and revitalised. *7am-1pm Sat* €

Le Bœuf Noisette: Beloved for cuisine that's 'French, local and fresh', including Rouge des Prés *bœuf* (beef) and orange cake with triple sec. *noon-2pm & 7-9pm Tue-Sat* €€

L'Escargot: Traditional French dishes, including chicken with rosemary and, of course, stuffed snails, all beautifully presented. Excellent value. *noon-1.30pm & 7.30-9.15pm Tue-Sat* €€

Hôtel de Londres: The hotel's English gentleman's club-style bar, London Fizz, serves a spectacular Sunday brunch. *5-11pm Wed-Fri, 2-11pm Sat, 10am-3pm Sun* €€

THE WINES OF ANJOU-SAUMUR

In **Anjou-Saumur wine region**, which has 26 AOPs (appellations d'origine protégée, ie 'protected designations of origin'), the predominant red is cabernet franc, though you'll also find cabernet sauvignon, pinot noir and others. AOPs include Anjou, Saumur-Champigny, Bourgueil and Chinon. For touring route ideas, download the bilingual map-brochure *Je déguste l'Anjou* from anjou-tourisme.com.

One of the most densely packed stretches for wine tasting along the Loire River itself (as opposed to its tributaries) is around Saumur. Towns with multiple tasting rooms include **St-Hilaire-St-Florent**, where you'll find **Ackerman**, **Bouvet Ladubay**, **Langlois-Château** and **Veuve Amiot**; **Souzay Champigny**, home to **Château Villeneuve** and **Clos des Cordeliers**; and **Parnay**, where you'll find **Château de Parnay** and **Château de Targé**.

intellectual and theoretical pretensions that range from profound to silly. Temporary exhibitions change three times a year. For spectacular river views, climb to the roof of the tower.

Royal Abbey with Plantagenet Tombs
Medieval abbey with modern art

The charming, stone-built village of **Fontevraud-l'Abbaye** has been known since the Middle Ages for its illustrious abbey, burial place of some of France and England's most famous medieval royals.

The highlight of the **Abbaye Royale de Fontevraud** *(font evraud.fr; adult/child abbey & museum €17/10.50)*, founded in the 12th century, is the vast but movingly simple church, notable for its soaring pillars, Romanesque domes and polychrome *gisants* (funerary effigies) of four illustrious Plantagenets: Henry II, king of England (r 1154–89); his wife, Eleanor of Aquitaine (who retired to Fontevraud following Henry's death); their son Richard the Lionheart; and Richard's brother King John's wife Isabelle of Angoulême.

The cloister is surrounded by one-time dormitories, workrooms and prayer halls; the **Salle Capitulaire** (chapter room), with murals of the Passion of Christ by Thomas Pot; and a wonderful Gothic-vaulted **refectory**, where the nuns would eat in silence while being read the Scriptures. Both the nuns and the monks of Fontevraud were, exceptionally, governed by an abbess, generally a lady of noble birth who had retired from public life. Outside, there are medieval-style gardens and a **kitchen** with 21 chimneys and a conical roof, built entirely from stone to make it fireproof.

In 1804, by Napoleonic decree, Fontevraud was turned into a notoriously harsh prison, a role it played until 1963. Author

Château de Brissac

Jean Genet was imprisoned for stealing (but not here) and, based on that experience, wrote *Miracle de la Rose* (1946), which is set at Fontevraud.

The **Musée d'Art Moderne** displays the superb art collection of the textile magnate Léon Cligman (1920–2022) and his wife, the painter Martine Martine (Martine Lévy). Highlights include works by Degas, Derain, Georges Kars, Michel Kikoïne, Soutine, Toulouse-Lautrec, de Vlaminck and the sculptor Germaine Richier.

16th-Century Château with Luxurious Furnishings

Tapestries, chandeliers and vineyards

One of the Loire's most opulent castles, the seven-storey **Château de Brissac** *(brissac.net; adult/child €12.50/5, gardens only €6/free)* – France's tallest – has been owned by the Brissac family for 18 generations (since 1502). Many of the 204 rooms are sumptuously furnished with antique furniture, Flemish tapestries and twinkling chandeliers. A multimedia 'immersion' in the history of the château during the 16th-century Wars of Religion is set to open in late 2025. The serene 70-hectare grounds, whose vineyards boast four AOC vintages, can be visited on four themed paths. From May to September, one of the château's bedrooms turns into an opulent **B&B** *(double with breakfast from €585)* – ideal for a honeymoon! Situated 19km southeast of Angers. Closed on Tuesday and between noon and 2pm, except in July and August.

SAVENNIÈRES WINES

Grown on schist soils in a mild microclimate, the dry white wines of the Savennières AOC are known for being lively, aromatic and flinty, with overtones of beeswax, warm straw and chamomile. The chenin blanc vineyards that produce them stretch along the right (north) bank of the Loire between the villages of Bouchemaine – situated, as the name implies, near the spot where the Maine conflows with the Loire – and La Possonnière. Renowned for ageing well, the *appellation* derives its name from the village of Savennières, 15km southwest of Angers, and comprises only about 1.4 sq km of planted vineyards, which are subject to strict per-hectare production limits. Not only are Savennières wines highly sought after therefore, but the supply is very limited.

Nantes

EASYGOING LIFESTYLE | GREAT DINING | MECHANICAL MONSTERS

☑ TOP TIP

If you see a narrow, spring-green line painted on the pavement, follow it! It's part of **Le Voyage à Nantes** (*levoyageanantes.fr/en*; search for 'Permanent Voyage'), an 18km urban art trail that snakes around the city, passing by over 100 sculptures and art installations. The **tourist office** has a free map.

Nantes is where the Loire Valley ends and the river's estuary begins – you can almost smell the sea air. Animated by the presence of over 65,000 university students, the city offers visitors a lively mix of river and ocean vibes, with broad avenues, handsome riverside promenades and a château with deep Breton connections.

From the Middle Ages to the late 20th century, Nantes was one of France's foremost ports. But Nantes' maritime history has a dark side: in the 18th century, it was the country's main centre of the trade in enslaved people, a sinister aspect of the city's historic prosperity that is commemorated by a riverside memorial and museum exhibits. Following the abolition of slavery, Nantes became a centre of industry, shipbuilding and food processing, including the production of LU biscuits. In recent decades, this artsy city, ever spirited and innovative, has reinvented itself as a flourishing cultural crossroads and hub of higher education.

Ride on a Gargantuan Mechanical Elephant
Creativity meets hydraulics

Les Machines de l'Île de Nantes (*lesmachines-nantes.fr*), on the site of Nantes' old shipyard, is a serious and seriously

GETTING AROUND

To discourage vehicle use in the city centre, Nantes prioritises cyclists and public transport (run by Naolib; naolib.fr) and, locals say, makes driving and parking as inconvenient as possible. Save yourself hassle, time and money by ditching your car (if you have one) and taking buses, the three Navibus services (river shuttles on the Loire and Erdre) and the five tram lines, all of which are free on Saturday and Sunday. Or better yet, explore on foot. For details on bike rental, check out velo.naolib.fr.

Fun fact: the world's first public bus service, a horse-drawn omnibus, began operation in Nantes in 1826.

NANTES

⭐ HIGHLIGHTS
1. Château des Ducs de Bretagne
2. Les Machines de l'Île de Nantes
3. Mémorial de l'Abolition de l'Esclavage

🔴 SIGHTS
4. Cours Cambronne
5. Cours des 50 Otages
6. Île de Versailles
7. Jardin des Plantes
8. Maison des Hommes et des Techniques
9. Monument aux 50 Otages
10. Musée d'Arts de Nantes
11. Musée d'Histoire de Nantes
12. Musée Jules Verne
13. Musée Naval Maillé-Brézé
14. Place Graslin
15. Place Royale
16. Rue Crébillon
17. Tour Bretagne

⚫ SLEEPING
18. Hotel Duquesne
19. Okko Hôtels Nantes Centre Ville

🟢 EATING
20. Grazziana
see 14. La Cigale
21. Le Couscoussier
22. Magmaa Food Hall
23. Marché de Talensac
24. Pickles
25. Sepia
26. Vacarme

🟢 DRINKING & NIGHTLIFE
27. Le Bateau-Lavoir

🔴 ENTERTAINMENT
28. Le Lieu Unique
see 14. Théâtre Graslin

🔴 SHOPPING
29. Chocolatier Gautier-Debotté
30. Passage Pommeraye

🔵 INFORMATION
31. Tourist Office

---

wacky workshop that brings together Jules Verne's fecund imagination, Leonardo da Vinci's mechanical wizardry and the city's history of excellence in engineering. Kids will absolutely love the wondrous metal, wood and steel creatures that spring to life thanks to electricity and hydraulics. Closed on Monday except during French school holidays; open only in the afternoon in winter; closed early January to early February.

The **Galerie des Machines** (*adult/child €11/9*) is a mechanical bestiary whose 16 creatures 'come alive' and even fly, one

Musée Jules Verne

BEST MUSEUMS IN NANTES

Musée d'Histoire de Nantes: Presents a panoramic, multifaceted history of Nantes, including the dark era of the slave trade.

Maison des Hommes et des Techniques: Takes a fascinating look at Nantes in its ship-building heyday. Open weekdays. Free.

Musée d'Arts de Nantes: Art from the 13th to the 21st centuries fills both the historic Palais des Beaux-Arts (1890s) and ultramodern Le Cube.

Musée Naval Maille-Brézé: Tours of this French Navy destroyer escort (1950) take in the engine room, weapons systems, living areas and the *boulangerie*.

Musée Jules Verne: Showcases scale models, manuscripts, first editions and child-friendly interactive displays connected to Jules Verne, born on in Nantes on Île Feydeau in 1828.

at a time, when the guide flips the switches. The 50-minute tours are in French but that hardly matters when there's so much to see (a printed sheet in English is available). On the other side of the covered passage, you can peer down into the **Atelier** (workshop), where the site's wondrous creatures are built and repaired.

The highlight here is the **Grand Éléphant** *(adult/child €9.50/7.50)*, a 12m-tall, 48-tonne mechanical pachyderm that – and this is no exaggeration – has to be seen to be believed. Up to 12 times a day, it sets out on 'walks' around the site with up to 50 passengers aboard – but it's almost as much fun to watch the beast as it sprays water at shrieking kids as it is to ride it.

Across the cement expanses of the one-time dry dock, the **Carrousel des Mondes Marins** *(adult/child €9/7)*, a three-storey funfair merry-go-round, is a 'mechanical aquarium' filled with giant mechanical crabs, octopuses and other strange sea creatures. You can explore all three levels before choosing where to sit.

The massive concrete structure to the left as you approach Les Machines de l'Île is **Blockhaus DY10**, a WWII German

EATING IN NANTES: OUR INTERNATIONAL PICKS

Magmaa Food Hall: Has nine food stalls on the Île de Nantes offering international cuisines, a bar and plenty of tables. *11am-3pm Sun & Mon, to 11pm Tue-Sat* €

Le Couscoussier: Excellent Algerian (including Berber) couscous, served with all-you-can-eat vegetable stew, and tagines. *noon-2pm & 7-10.30pm except Tue & Wed lunch* €

Grazziana: Neapolitan pizza with puffy, super-fresh crust. A rue St-Léonard favourite. *noon-2pm & 7-10.30pm daily* €

Vacarme: Wine bar and restaurant that mixes French and Scandinavian influences – think Breton pork with kimchi. *noon-1.30pm & 7-9pm Tue-Sat* €€

EXPLORING NANTES' CENTRE ON FOOT

Discover Nantes' sprawling central market, grandest avenue, statue-adorned squares and a mid-19th-century shopping arcade.

START	END	LENGTH
Marché de Talensac	Cours Cambronne	1.6km- 2-3hrs

Start your stroll at Nantes' 160m-long main food market, the ❶ **Marché de Talensac** (p411), built in the mid-1930s, and pick up the fixings for a picnic. Then walk down the hill to the city's grandest avenue, ❷ **cours des 50 Otages**, which has a tram line and gardens with benches and picnic tables running down the middle. To the right, up the slope, stands the ❸ **Tour Bretagne**, an egregiously out-of-place, 37-storey office tower, built in the 1970s on the site of a medieval quarter damaged by American bombs in 1943.

At the late 18th-century ❹ **place Royale**, admire the classical buildings and the fountain (1865) before stopping off at ❺ **Chocolatier Gautier-Debotté**, a chocolate shop whose carved wood, murals and mirrors have hardly changed since 1860. Then walk up the slope through ❻ **Passage Pommeraye**, a delightful, tri-level shopping arcade built way back in 1843.

Pedestrianised ❼ **rue Crébillon**, the city centre's snazziest commercial thoroughfare, is lined with boutiques. At the top, ❽ **place Graslin** is graced by a fountain and presided over by the neoclassical, colonnaded ❾ **Théâtre Graslin** (built 1788), which faces the legendary brasserie ❿ **La Cigale**. End your walk – and sit down for a picnic (if any food from the market is left!) – at majestic ⓫ **cours Cambronne**, a tree-lined, neoclassical promenade that opened in 1791.

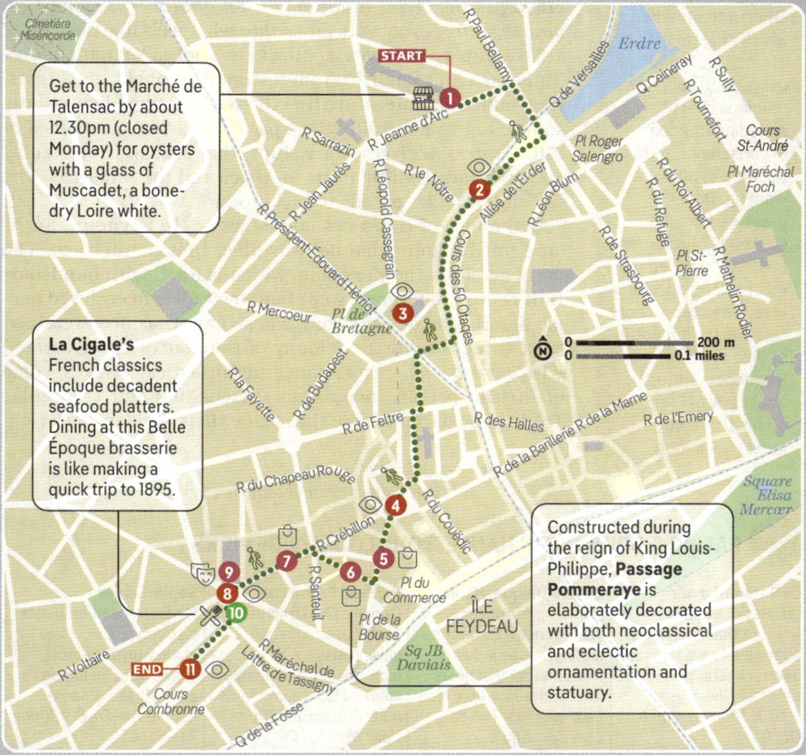

> Get to the Marché de Talensac by about 12.30pm (closed Monday) for oysters with a glass of Muscadet, a bone-dry Loire white.

> **La Cigale's** French classics include decadent seafood platters. Dining at this Belle Époque brasserie is like making a quick trip to 1895.

> Constructed during the reign of King Louis-Philippe, **Passage Pommeraye** is elaborately decorated with both neoclassical and eclectic ornamentation and statuary.

Nantes, France's Most Important Slave Port
A museum, a memorial and mascarons

Nantes is finally coming to terms with the huge role its port, ship-owners and grandees played in the Atlantic trade in enslaved people between the late 1600s and the early 1800s.

Inside the hulking, late 15th-century **Château des Ducs de Bretagne** (*chateaunantes.fr*), the 32 rooms of the innovative **Musée d'Histoire de Nantes** (*adult/child €9/free*) take an unvarnished look at the city's history, including sobering and evocative documentation of local participation in chattel slavery. In Room 11, mid-18th-century oil paintings depict rich Nantais being served by young enslaved African people, at the time an unsubtle if common way of flaunting one's elevated social status.

There is no charge to explore the château grounds, including the courtyard, surrounded by beautifully restored 15th- to 18th-century buildings and equipped with picnic tables; the ramparts walk; and the water-filled moat. Closed on Monday except in July and August.

To enter the moving **Mémorial de l'Abolition de l'Esclavage** (*Memorial to the Abolition of Slavery; memorial. nantes.fr; free*), you walk down into what feels like the hold of a slave ship, river waves lapping at the sides. Poignant quotes (in French and English) from testimonies, abolitionist texts, legal codes and literature line the walls. Embedded into the square above are 2000 glass panels bearing the names of 1710 *navires négriers* (slave ships) that set sail from Nantes and 290 slave-trading ports in Africa and the Americas. The website provides excellent background.

At the foot of cours des 50 Otages is **Île Feydeau**, an island until a Loire channel was filled in a century ago. The main artery is rue Kervégan, which is lined with handsome 18th-century buildings, some built by traders in enslaved people like Danyel de Kervégan, whose name has been retained 'as a witness to history'. Many of the houses are decorated with *mascarons* – grotesque and fantastical visages, some of African people, inspired by the colonial and Triangular Trade in enslaved people that made their builders very rich.

THE EDICT OF NANTES

Like much of the rest of France, the Loire was convulsed by the Wars of Religion (1562–98), a contest for religious and political primacy between Catholics and Calvinist Protestants that claimed the lives of at least 2 million people from violence, disease and starvation. The bloodletting played out in places such as Blois and Amboise, ending in 1598 with the signing of the Edict of Nantes, by which King Henri IV granted his Protestant (Huguenot) subjects religious liberty, including freedom of conscience and the right to public worship. Under pressure from the Catholic Church, Louis XIV revoked the edict in 1685, resulting in renewed repression that caused hundreds of thousands of Huguenots – the backbone of French commerce and industry – to flee.

Each menu has a vegetarian version

EATING & DRINKING IN NANTES: OUR LOCAL-VIBE PICKS

Le Bateau-Lavoir: Locals flock to this wooden shack, perched above the Erdre, for craft beers, cocktails, wine, tapas and live music. *5.30-11.30pm Apr–mid-Oct* €

Le Lieu Unique: Nantes' premier performance venue, once a LU biscuit factory, has an industrial-chic cafe-bar that hosts live bands. *11am-8pm Mon, 11am-midnight Tue-Sat, 3pm-8pm Sun* €

Pickles: British chef Dominic Quirke serves lively *gastronomique* cuisine made with high-quality, sustainably sourced local ingredients. *noon-2.30pm & 7.30pm-11pm Wed-Sat* €€

Sepia: Serves Mediterranean-influence *bistronomique* cuisine made with ultra-local ingredients, including edible flowers. *noon-1.30pm Tue-Fri, 8-9.30pm Tue-Sat* €€

Château des Ducs de Bretagne

Through Parks & Along Rivers
Explore waterfront promenades and public gardens

Lovely riverside promenades hug both banks of the Loire River, including on the Île de Nantes, and follow both sides of the Erdre River, which heads north from the northern end of cours des 50 Otages.

From the **Monument aux 50 Otages**, a memorial to French hostages executed in 1941 in revenge for the assassination of a German officer, walk 600m north along the Erdre to the **Île de Versailles**. An orange slice-shaped island that's accessible from both banks, it is home to a Japanese-style garden graced with azaleas and rhododendrons. Electric boats and kayaks can be rented from April to October.

At the **Jardin des Plantes**, botanical gardens established in the 1860s, magnolias, mulberry trees, Japanese maples, redwoods (sequoias) and magnificent cedars tower above rhododendrons, flower beds, duck ponds and fountains. For kids, there is a children's playground at the park's northern end and three pet-able goats at the southern end. Situated 700m east of the **Château des Ducs de Bretagne**, just north of the train station.

BEST AREAS TO EAT IN NANTES

West of Cours des 50 Otages: Your best budget bets in this area are the more than 150 food stalls that sell ready-to-eat dishes, cheese, bread, fruit and veggies at the **Marché de Talensac** (marche-talensac.fr). Open 7am or 8am to 1pm or 2pm except Monday.

Rue St-Léonard: Restaurants, cafes and pubs with outdoor seating line this pedestrianised street two blocks east of cours des 50 Otages. Head north to rue Léon Blum to find lively pubs and bars.

Between place du Bouffay and place du Pilori: Pedestrianised rue de la Bâclerie, rue des Échevins, rue de la Juiverie, rue des Chapeliers and rue du Château are lined with small, welcoming restaurants.

Île Feydeau: Rue Kervégan (at the eastern end), perpendicular rue Bon Secours and parallel quai Turenne are home to small restaurants, many serving international cuisines.

Places We Love to Stay

€ Budget €€ Midrange €€€ Top End

Blois (Blésois)   MAP p379

Hôtel Anne de Bretagne € Midway between Blois' château and the train station, this friendly, ivy-covered hotel has an airy breakfast room renovated in 2025. Excellent value.

Côté Loire-Auberge Ligérienne € Facing the river in Blois, this establishment – an inn since 1675 – has eight spotless rooms, some with 350-year-old beams and/or great Loire views (p380).

Ibis Blois Centre Château € Smack-dab in the centre of Blois. The early 20th-century lobby has a kids' play area; the rooms are modern and attractive. Belongs to the Ibis chain.

Chambord & Chaumont-sur-Loire (Blésois)

Relais de Chambord €€€ Chambord's former kennels are now a luxury hotel with an unbeatable château-adjacent location, country-chic rooms, a sensational bar, a spa and a bistronomique restaurant.

Le Bois des Chambres €€ A very classy 39-room/suite hotel, 300m from Chaumont-sur-Loire, that occupies a 19th-century barn and eco-friendly, modern pavilions surrounded by gardens.

Tours (Touraine)   p386

The People Hostel € Has spacious, cycling-themed public spaces and a kitchen – great for meeting people. Bunk beds are cramped. Lies 700m south of Tours' city centre.

Hôtel Val de Loire € Friendly staff welcome you to 14 upbeat rooms, many with (non-working) marble fireplaces. The charming breakfast room was redone in 2025. Facing Tours' tourist office.

Hôtel Ronsard € Built in 1920, with 20 quiet, brown-and-cream rooms. A favourite of actors and dancers performing at the nearby Grand Théâtre.

Hôtel Mondial € On the edge of Vieux Tours, near place Plumereau and lots of cafes and restaurants. Has 20 bright, magenta-accented rooms, including family rooms.

Hôtel l'Adresse € On a pedestrianised street in Tours' old quarter. The 17 boutique rooms have bright bedspreads, sparkling bathrooms and, on the 3rd floor, 17th-century rafters.

Hôtel Oceania L'Univers Tours €€ Check out the balcony mural in the lobby to spot famous guests who have stayed here since 1846, including Hemingway, Edison and Churchill. A classic.

Amboise (Touraine)

Éthic Étapes Île d'Or € A spartan but welcoming hostel on an island facing Amboise, with 114 beds in 30 rooms. Often full with school groups from March to June.

Camping Municipal de l'Île d'Or € City-run caravan and tent sites on an island facing Amboise, with outdoor activities for kids nearby. Open early Apr–mid-Nov.

Le Clos d'Amboise €€€ Built mostly in the 17th century, this posh pad offers stylish country living in the heart of Amboise, with a lovely garden and a heated pool.

Château de Pray €€€ A 16th-century château near Amboise whose 19 rooms are brimming with antique furnishings and old-fashioned charm.

Azay-le-Rideau

Hôtel de Biencourt € Just 150m from the entrance to Azay-le-Rideau, 17 charming rooms in a one-time school from the 17th and 18th centuries.

Hôtel Le Grand Monarque €€ An 18th-century coaching inn has been turned into a charming hotel just five minutes on foot from the château. Rooms are spacious, with a mix of 21st-century mod cons and antique touches.

Loches (Touraine)

La Demeure Saint-Ours €€ A B&B with five attractive, quiet rooms accessed via a 16th-century wooden staircase. In Loches, midway between Porte Picois and Porte Royale.

Hôtel de la Cité Royale €€€ Loches' imposingly neoclassical, mid-19th-century courthouse is now a four-star hotel, with a spa and indoor swimming pool.

Chinon (Touraine)

Hôtel Diderot € A gorgeous Chinon townhouse tucked away amid luscious rose-filled gardens and crammed with polished antiques. Owned by a mixed French and American couple.

Hôtel de France € An impeccable hotel right in the centre of Chinon. The 28 rooms, some with views of the château, were renovated in 2025.

Angers (Anjou) MAP p398

Hôtel Marguerite d'Anjou € A super-friendly hotel in a fantastic spot facing Angers' château. Has 19 modest but comfortable rooms and a ground-floor cafe that opened in 1962.

Hôtel Continental €€ An ecologically certified, metro-style hotel wedged into a triangular corner building (built 1890), smack in Angers' city centre.

Hôtel du Mail €€ Antique-style rooms are arrayed around a quiet courtyard in a one-time 17th-century convent, a few blocks east of Angers' city centre.

Saumur (Anjou)

Hôtel de Londres €€ Named in honour of the British capital in 1837, this historic, family-run hotel in Saumur has 30 spacious rooms decorated in jolly colours (p403).

Hôtel St-Pierre €€ Three houses from the 1600s meet smart, modern-day hotel comfort across the alley from the south portal of Saumur's most central church. Owned by the same family since 1991.

Château La Comtesse de Loire €€€ A Saumur classic in a splendid Belle Époque mansion built in 1896. Sumptuous throughout, with carved-wood and marble fireplaces, one with a picture window directly above the hearth.

Turquant & Montsoreau (Anjou)

Demeure de la Vignole €€ A swish hillside hotel just outside Turquant with five troglodytic rooms and a heated swimming pool carved into the rock face.

Hôtel La Marine de Loire €€€ Chic and romantic, with 11 country-style rooms, four guest houses, a spa, an outdoor pool and a bar. Facing the Loire in Montsoreau.

Nantes MAP p406

Hotel Duquesne € A comfortable, good-value hotel on Nantes' handsome main avenue, very near the city's main dining district.

Okko Hôtels Nantes Centre Ville €€ Central, design-driven Okko has 80 smart, functional rooms on six floors. Ground-floor 'Le Club' has sofas, all-day hot drinks and free nibblies daily from 6.30pm to 8pm.

Hôtel de la Cité Royale (Loches)

Researched by
Madeleine Rothery

Burgundy
EPICUREAN DELIGHTS AND DIVINE NATURE

In France's bucolic Burgundy region, viticulture, gastronomy and a patrician past converge among verdant landscapes and rustic villages.

'If Paris is France's head and Champagne her soul, then Burgundy is her stomach', write Masters of Wine Hugh Johnson and Jancis Robinson in *The Atlas of Wine*. With a wealth of gastronomical specialities – think mustard, bœuf bourguignon, *oeufs en meurette* – and as home to the most expensive vineyards in the world, Burgundy and its people are known for their hearty and heartfelt joie de vivre.

Since the settlement of the Romans, perhaps as far back as the 1st century CE, the region quickly flourished, in no small part because of the land's prosperous potential for viticulture. The rise of the puissant Duchy of Burgundy in the Middle Ages saw the region further develop as a hot spot for the arts and sciences, with its influence resounding across Europe. Architectural vestiges of this glorious era are still present today: from the colourful patchworked tiling to the half-timbered houses, Burgundian medieval architecture is some of the country's most iconic.

But for all the divine pomp and glory of its past, the region is charmingly rustic – one of the particularities of Burgundians is their absolute commitment to and care for the land. Beyond the vineyards lie lush forestland and a network of canals and rivers interwoven with spectacular hiking and cycling trails. A sojourn in Burgundy is a divine escape for epicures, history buffs and nature enthusiasts alike.

SERGII KOVAL/SHUTTERSTOCK

THE MAIN AREAS

DIJON
Gastronomy, art and history.
p420

BEAUNE
The spiritual home of wine.
p430

AUXERRE
Medieval monuments and riverside charm.
p442

> For places to stay in Burgundy, see p447

Left: *Oeufs en meurette* (poached eggs in red-wine sauce); Above: Clos de Vougeot (p427)

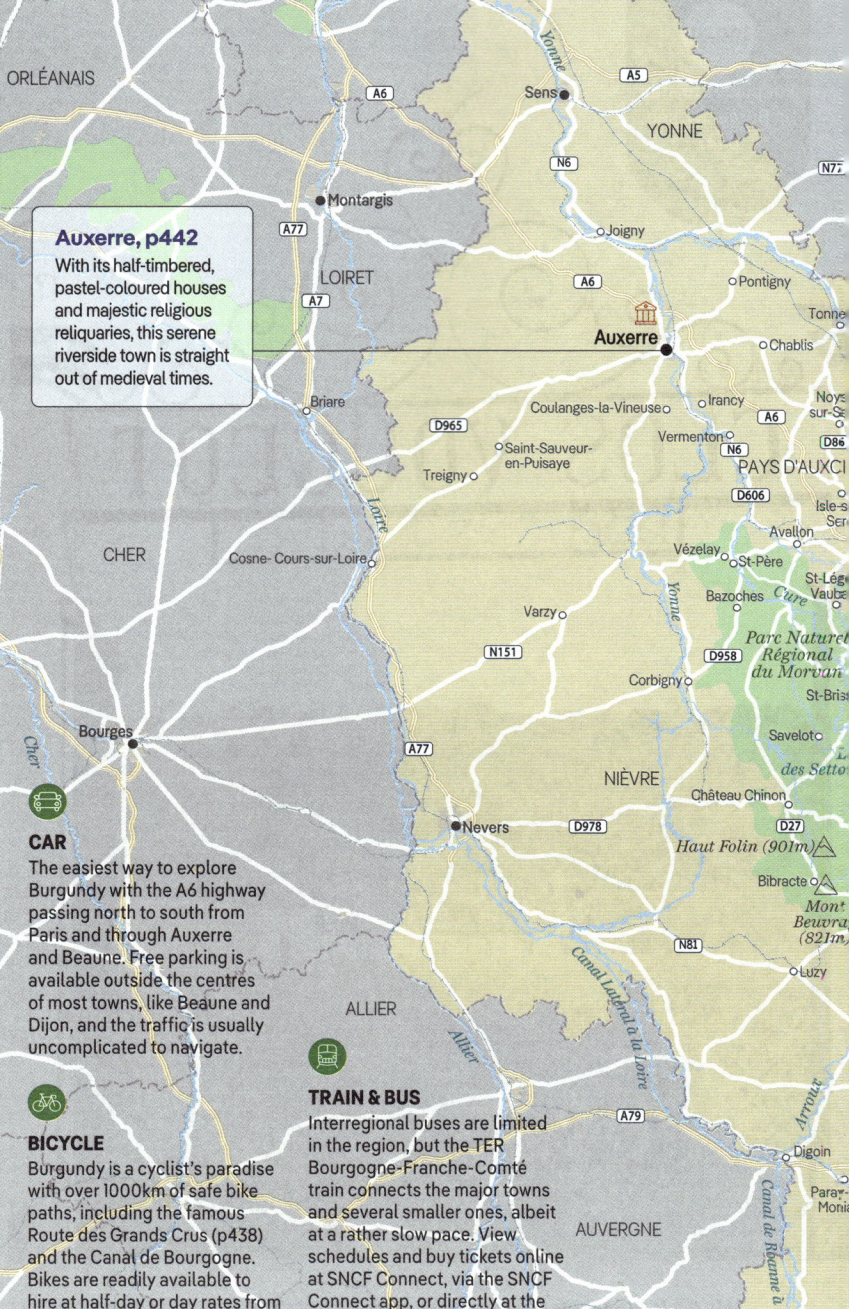

Auxerre, p442
With its half-timbered, pastel-coloured houses and majestic religious reliquaries, this serene riverside town is straight out of medieval times.

CAR
The easiest way to explore Burgundy with the A6 highway passing north to south from Paris and through Auxerre and Beaune. Free parking is available outside the centres of most towns, like Beaune and Dijon, and the traffic is usually uncomplicated to navigate.

BICYCLE
Burgundy is a cyclist's paradise with over 1000km of safe bike paths, including the famous Route des Grands Crus (p438) and the Canal de Bourgogne. Bikes are readily available to hire at half-day or day rates from most major towns.

TRAIN & BUS
Interregional buses are limited in the region, but the TER Bourgogne-Franche-Comté train connects the major towns and several smaller ones, albeit at a rather slow pace. View schedules and buy tickets online at SNCF Connect, via the SNCF Connect app, or directly at the station.

Find Your Way

Although all major Burgundian cities are accessible by train from Paris, a car is a must-have to zip from town to town. On the ground, swap four wheels for two and discover the countryside at your own leisurely pace.

BURGUNDY — THE GUIDE

Dijon, p420
The former seat of the wealthy Duchy of Burgundy, Burgundy's capital is still today a cultural powerhouse of gastronomy, architecture and art.

Beaune, p430
As the epicentre of one of the world's most prestigious viticulture regions, it's all about wine and its religious roots in Beaune.

Plan Your Days

Eat and drink to your heart's delight in Dijon and Beaune, but be sure to set aside time to venture outside the cities and explore the breathtaking Burgundian countryside and its historic villages.

Cathédrale St-Étienne (p443), Auxerre

A Dijon Day Trip

● As the region's capital, **Dijon** (p420) is a one-stop shop to discover the best of Burgundian culture. Start by following the **Parcours de la Chouette** (p442), a self-guided walking tour that winds past the historical highlights, like **Palais des Ducs** (p424).

● Spend the afternoon at the **Cité Internationale de la Gastronomie et du Vin** (p423), Dijon's epic exhibition space dedicated to French gastronomy where you can taste the best of the region's food and wine in one place. Stock up on local produce at the Cité, grab a bottle of wine and enjoy aperitif by the **Lac Kir** (p426).

Seasonal Highlights

Winter and summer can be difficult to weather with many regional businesses closing for August and from around November to March.

JANUARY
Pay homage to the patron saint of wine at **Le Festival de Saint-Vincent Tournante**, held at a different wine village each year.

MAY
It's Auxerre's **Fleur des Vignes**, a celebration of local wine and produce held along the banks of the Yonne River.

JUNE
Dijon Plage kicks off, a pop-up beach on Lac Kir with swimming, sunbeds, concerts and DJ sets all summer long.

Three Days to Travel Around

● Return to **Dijon** (p420) for the day before heading south to **Beaune** (p430) the following morning – an easy 45-minute drive or a 30-minute train ride. Begin the day exploring the medical menagerie of the **Hôtel-Dieu** (p430). See out the afternoon with a tasting and tour of one of **Beaune's historic wine négociants** (p432) or browsing the **Athenaeum de la Vigne et du Vin** (p433), a library dedicated to all things wine, from maps and books to rare bottle openers

● Spend your last day exploring the illustrious vineyards of the **Côte d'Or** by bike (p426) or by car (p427). If you're there on a Saturday, pick up food for a picnic from Beaune's farmers markets and **lunch among the vines** (p433).

If You Have More Time

● Meander slowly from Dijon to Beaune, spending time exploring the wild **Parc de la Combe à la Serpent** (p427) and the regal **Château du Clos de Vougeot** (p427).

● After two days (or more!) exploring Beaune and its surroundings, continue to the riverside town of **Auxerre** (p442). You could easily spend a day taking in the history of **Auxerre's old town** (p442) but be sure to also allow time to unwind by the serene **Yonne River** (p444). If you're not wined out, venture to the nearby mythical white-wine village of **Chablis** (p446). Otherwise, head to **Noyers-sur-Serein** (p445), one of France's most beautiful villages.

JULY	SEPTEMBER	OCTOBER	NOVEMBER
Beaune is the place to be for opera aficionados as it hosts the month-long **Festival International d'Opéra Baroque** (p432).	Harvest time for Burgundian winemakers! Vine workers flock from around the world to pick grapes and village parties are held to celebrate.	Grapes are pressed and the partially fermented juice enjoyed when Nuits-St-Georges hosts **La Fête du Vin Bourru** (p438).	**Les Trois Glorieuses** (p432) wine celebration takes place across the Côte d'Or and Noyers-Sur-Serein hosts its annual truffle fair.

Dijon

RICH GASTRONOMY | MEDIEVAL ARCHITECTURE | HERITAGE ART

☑ TOP TIP

Purchase a Dijon City Pass from the tourist office for free access to over 30 tourist attractions both in and around Dijon, plus free public transport, discounts on bike rentals, and exclusive guided tours. The pass is available in 24hr, 48hr and 72hr formats with prices starting from €25.

Once home to the industrious Dukes of Burgundy, the city of Dijon remains a cultural powerhouse of France for its contributions to the country's gastronomical scene. Now the capital of the Bourgogne-Franche-Comté region of France, Dijon was, between the 11th and 15th centuries, the seat of the wealthy Duchy of Burgundy and established itself as a European hot spot for the arts and sciences. As you traverse the city's historical centre, it's hard not to miss the vestiges of Dijon's golden past – from the regal Palais des Ducs et des États de Bourgogne to the iconic wood-thatched houses, echoes of its powerful past reverberate throughout.

But Dijon's glory days are far from over. In 2015 it was recognised as a UNESCO World Heritage Site for its role in Burgundian wine production and today it's synonymous with mustard, escargot, *oeufs en meurette* and other French gastronomical delights.

Follow the Owl's Trail
Dijon's old town by foot

A lesser-known fact about Dijon is that its unofficial symbol is a small owl, *la chouette*. No one quite knows why it was

GETTING AROUND

Dijon is a pedestrian-friendly city and easy to navigate by foot. If you arrive by car, your best bet is to leave your car outside of the city centre and make use of the great public transport system as parking within the centre is expensive and hard to come by.

Two tramlines connect the city, with trams arriving every five to 15 minutes. Tickets can be purchased with cash or card at the tram stop, but make sure you validate it (by holding it on the electronic reader within the tram until it beeps) each time you board – even when connecting.

The Divia City, a free electric shuttle bus, connects the city's two major tramlines. With stops at all major attractions, it also connects the centre to the SNCF train station. Shuttles leave every 11 minutes and operate Monday to Saturday, from 8am to 7.30pm (no service on Sunday). Alternatively, make use of the DiviaVélodi, city bikes available for rent at 40 stations located across the city.

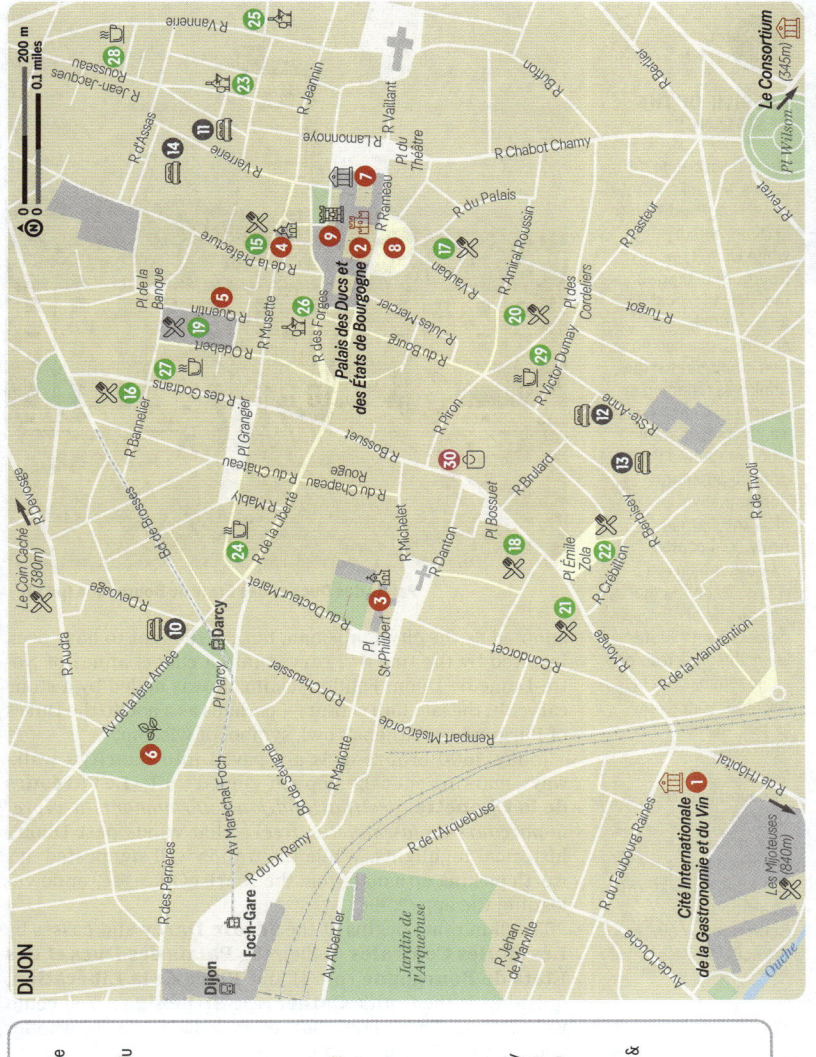

Palais des Ducs et des États de Bourgogne (p424)

APÉRITIF OF THE RESISTANCE

Made from *crème de cassis*, a blackcurrant-based liqueur distilled in Dijon, and dry white wine (typically Bourgogne Aligoté) the Kir is the local apéritif drink of choice. Once known as a *blanc-cassis*, the drink was renamed in honour of Canon Félix Kir, the mayor of Dijon who catapulted the drink to popularity during the 1950s after the German Army confiscated all Burgundian red wines. By paling the rich purple of *crème de cassis* with white wine, the drink took on a hue reminiscent of the stolen pinot noirs. Hence, its nickname: 'the resistance cocktail'.

Feeling fancy? Upgrade to a Kir Royal, where champagne or a local sparkling wine (known as a crémant de Bourgogne) replaces the usual white.

adopted as the city's talisman, but it's thought to have been inspired by the tiny owl carved into a chapel annex of Notre-Dame de Dijon. Folklore claims it was added by a stone carver in the late 15th century – perhaps as a nod to the Dukes of Burgundy or Athena's owl, symbol of wisdom.

Today, 1600 bronze owls are paved into the city's walkways, marking out a 22-stop self-guided trail – **Le Parcours de la Chouette** *(destinationdijon.com/moments-a-vivre/le-parcours-de-la-chouette; free)* – that winds past Dijon's historical highlights. While the trail is well signposted, it's worth picking up a map from the Tourist Office *(4€)* or downloading the app *(2.99€)*.

The 3km route begins at the **Jardin Darcy** and passes by **Les Halles Centrales** (p424), the **Palais des Ducs et des États de Bourgogne** (p424) and **Place de la Libération**, finishing at the Gothic **Cathédrale St-Bénigne**. You could walk it in under an hour, but set aside half a day to wander and dip into sites as you go.

 DRINKING IN DIJON: APÉRITIF HOUR

Chez Bruno: Let local legend Bruno guide you through his biblical wine list while teaching you the proper way to enjoy his artisanal charcuterie. *6-11pm Tue-Fri €*

La Cave Se Rebiffe: Cosy, laid-back wine bar with small plates and ever-knowledgeable staff who will happily demystify the extensive local wine selection. *6.30-11pm €*

Monsieur Moutarde: Chic cocktail bar by one of the world's top mixologists, set within a historic *hôtel particulier*, with plentiful non-alcoholic options. *5pm-2am, Tue-Sat €*

Tour Phillipe Le Bon: For an apéritif with a panoramic city view, Kir tastings atop the historic Tour Philippe Le Bon can be booked through the Dijon Tourist Office. *6.30 & 8.30pm Fri & Sat May-Oct €€*

The most important stop is the owl sculpture itself, hiding in the buttress of **Église Notre-Dame** (stop 9). Local superstition holds that if you rub it with your left hand and place your right hand on your heart, good fortune will follow for the rest of your day. If all that walking has you feeling peckish, **Aux Délices de la Chouette** *boulangerie* is nearby and serves up adorable owl-shaped pastries – and some of the best croissants in town.

The Art of Eating Well
Dive deep into French gastronomy

In 2010, French gastronomy was inscribed on UNESCO's Representative List of the Intangible Cultural Heritage of Humanity for its culinary traditions and the rituals of togetherness they inspire. Steeped in centuries of culture, it's a heady topic to explore – which is why Dijon opened the **Cité Internationale de la Gastronomie et du Vin** in 2022 *(citedelagastronomie-dijon.fr; free)*. Set on the grounds of a former hospital just a stone's throw from the Gare SNCF, this 1750 sq metre gastronomic temple includes a wine school, a campus of the prestigious École Ferrandi, interactive exhibitions, restaurants and specialist produce shops.

Plan to spend the best part of a day here. Begin at **Le Village Gastronomique** with a coffee and pastry at **La Gloriette**, one of eight boutiques spotlighting the best of French food culture (the others include a mustard bar, bakery, fishmonger, butcher, cheesemonger, bookshop and tableware store). Then potter over to the four themed pavilions: the five senses in cooking, the art of eating and drinking well, the traditions of patisserie and Burgundy's vineyard *climats* (p434).

When hunger inevitably strikes, **La Table des Climats**, directed by three-star Michelin chef Eric Pras, serves refined French cuisine paired with Burgundian wines. Next door, **La Cuisine Expérientielle** hosts a rotating roster of guest chefs, with an all-you-can-eat French-style brunch every Sunday *(11.20am-3.30pm; adult/child €32/12)*.

Budding oenophiles can head to **L'École des Vins**, which offers weekly English-language workshops *(from €27; reserve online)*, or test your tasting skills at **La Cave de la Cité**, with 250 wines by the glass and a library of more than 3000 references. In need of a break from all things grape? Head up to **Bamagotchi**, a cocktail bar and beer garden with a rooftop terrasse.

DIJON'S GINGERBREAD HOUSE

Although the original recipe for *pain d'épices* (which loosely translates to gingerbread) is believed to originate in China, Dijon quickly made it its own and has been the largest French producer of this honey-laced spiced cake since the 18th century. What makes Dijon's *pain d'épices* so special is the use of artisanal honey from the nearby Parc Naturel Régional du Morvan.

The only remaining artisanal producer in Dijon is **Maison Mulot et Petitjean**, which has been making the curious delicacy for over 200 years. You can visit its boutique and museum, located in the city's historic centre, to taste, what is arguably, the best *pain d'épices* in France as well as its crafty variations on the cake.

EATING IN DIJON: LOCAL CLASSICS

Le Bouchon du Palais: Old-school bistro serving classics like coq au vin and *escargots*, with excellent-value *formule* menus for lunch and dinner. *noon-1.30pm & 7-9pm Tue-Fri, noon-1.30pm Sat* €

Le Coin Caché: Tucked away on a quiet backstreet, this local favourite dishes up hearty, seasonal fare in a warm and unpretentious setting. *noon-2pm & 7-10pm, Mon-Fri* €€

Chez Léon: Home to perhaps the best bœuf bourguignon in Dijon. Rustic and familiar, with lively, friendly staff. *noon-2pm & 7-10.30pm, Tue-Sat* €

Monique: Female-run neo-bistro with a focus on reimagining regional fare using only seasonal, locally sourced produce. *noon-2pm & 7-9.30pm Thu & Fri, noon-2pm Tue, Wed & Sat* €€

DIJON'S EPICUREAN TEMPLE

Constructed between 1873 and 1874 on the site of a former Jacobin convent, the 4400m2 **Les Halles Centrales** houses Dijon's palatial covered farmers markets. The 13m-high epicurean temple bears a striking resemblance to another wrought-iron monument, the Eiffel Tower; Ballard, the mastermind behind the market, has confessed that he was inspired by the work of Dijon-born architect, Gustave Eiffel. On the ceiling's spandrels, ornate mythological motifs, including Hermès, the Greek god of commerce, and Ceres, the Roman goddess of harvest, keep watch over the 268 vendors below, symbolising prosperity, trade and seasonal abundance. In 1975, the building was listed as a national historic monument, a testament to Dijon's rich blend of culinary and architectural heritage.

Entry to the Cité is free; exhibition spaces are open Tuesday to Sunday, 10am to 6pm, with tickets required *(adult/child €9/5)*. A discovery pass includes all exhibitions and a 45-minute wine or juice tasting *(€11.50)*. For events, tastings and chef line-ups, check the Cité's website before you go.

Take a Walk on the Art Side
From tombs to Huyghes

You'd be mistaken to think Dijon's cultural significance ended with the fall of the Duchy of Burgundy in the 15th century. Today the city is home to some of France's most pioneering classical and contemporary art institutions.

No trip is complete without a visit to the **Palais des Ducs et des États de Bourgogne**, the former seat of the Dukes of Burgundy, located in the heart of the old town. While several architectural elements remain from the 14th and 15th centuries – such as the Tour Philippe le Bon, which rewards a 316-step climb with panoramic views – most of the edifice was completed in the 17th century. Admission is free; the Palais is open daily, except Tuesdays.

Within the Palais des Ducs sits the **Musée des Beaux-Arts** *(beaux-arts.dijon.fr; free)* France's second-largest museum after the Louvre (p86). Set aside an hour or two to explore its encyclopaedic collection spanning Antiquity to the 21st century, with a particularly impressive collection of Egyptian art. In addition to masterpieces by the likes of Rubens, Monet and Matisse, don't miss the Tombs of the Dukes of Burgundy, where Philip the Bold (Philippe le Hardi), John the Fearless and Margaret of Bavaria are laid to rest. Open every day except Tuesdays, the museum's permanent collections are free (€6/3 entry for temporary shows).

If contemporary art is more your speed, don't be fooled by the city's historic sheen. Dijon is home to one of France's leading contemporary art centres: **Le Consortium** *(leconsortium.fr; adult/child €5/free)*. Since its founding in 1977, it has hosted exhibitions by the likes of Cindy Sherman, Pierre Huyghe and Richard Prince, as well as the first shows in France by artists such as Christopher Wool, Wade Guyton and Joe Bradley.

Today, Le Consortium occupies a renovated cassis factory redesigned by Pritzker Prize–winning architect Shigeru Ban. The 350-piece permanent collection is paired with rotating exhibitions celebrating emerging talent as well as live music performances. It's open Wednesday to Sunday from 2pm to

---

 EATING IN DIJON: EXPERIMENTAL CUISINE

Le Chat Qui Pense: Home-cooked lunches served in Madame Sonnet's own home. Warm, welcoming and wonderfully old-school. *noon-2pm Mon-Fri* €€

U: Funky noodle bar serving Chinese noodles with globally inspired toppings, like kimchi, tahini, parmesan or chorizo. *noon-2pm & 7-10pm Wed-Sun* €

Parapluie: Let the chef surprise you with an elegant, ever-changing 'mystery' menu which is always seasonal, precise and artfully plated. *noon-1.30pm & 7.30-9.30pm, Mon-Fri* €€

Les Mijoteuses: Cosy, home-style vegetarian restaurant with hearty, flavourful dishes and a few vegan options. *noon-2pm Mon-Sat* €

Coq au vin (chicken cooked in wine)

6pm, with late closing on Friday evenings when entry is free of charge for all.

For local emerging talent, head to the **FRAC Bourgogne** *(frac-bourgogne.org; free)*, part of a series of regional art funds and centres opened in the 1980s as a national initiative to invest in the emerging art scene. Home to a collection of 700+ works from both local and international artists, FRAC Bourgogne regularly hosts temporary shows, workshops and artist talks. Take note of its obscure opening hours *(2.30-6.30pm Wed, Thu, Fri & Sun, 11am-1pm & 2-6pm Sat)*.

BURGUNDIAN FOOD EXPLAINED

Bœuf bourguignon: Burgundy's most iconic dish: a rich stew of slow-braised beef in red wine with carrots, onions, mushrooms and lardons.

Escargots à la bourguignonne: Baked in garlic, herb butter and parsley, and served with small tongs to clamp the shell while you pry the snail out.

Jambon persillé: A chilled terrine of ham and parsley set in gelatin, traditionally eaten as a starter with fresh bread and pickles.

Gougères: A classic apéritif snack: golden choux pastry puffs filled with melted local Gruyère cheese often enjoyed with crémant, a regional sparkling wine.

Coq au vin: Chicken braised in red wine with mushrooms, onions, and lardons – a lighter, yet equally as comforting, cousin to bœuf bourguignon.

 DRINKING IN DIJON: MORNING COFFEE

Espresso-T: Dijon's first third-wave coffee house, roasting beans on site and serving light bites like bagels. *10am-6.30pm Mon, Tue, Thu & Fri, 9am-7pm Sat* €

Morning Glory: Cosy cafe and beloved brunch spot serving pastries, homemade cakes and one of Dijon's best flat whites. *8am-7pm Tue-Sat, 9am-3pm Sun* €

WOLF Coffee and Toast: Korean-style speciality coffee and simple toasted sandwiches served in a calm, minimalist space. *8.30am-6pm Mon-Fri, 9am-6pm Sat & Sun* €

Nessy Coffee: Great coffee and even better food: think hearty portions, vibrant brunch plates and inventive juices. *9am-5pm Wed-Sun* €

Beyond Dijon

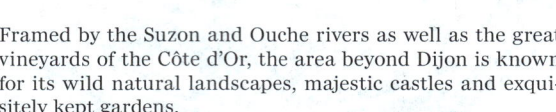

It's easy to get your dose of nature from Dijon as just beyond the centre are tranquil parklands and majestic gardens.

Places

Fontaine-d'Ouche p426
Vougeot p427
Bussy-Le-Grand p429

Framed by the Suzon and Ouche rivers as well as the great vineyards of the Côte d'Or, the area beyond Dijon is known for its wild natural landscapes, majestic castles and exquisitely kept gardens.

Until the 19th century, Dijon remained in close contact with the surrounding nature as it was the centre of wine, cassis and mustard production. But when the insect phylloxera destroyed France's vineyards, vines and agricultural land were sacrificed for the rapidly expanding urban centre.

In 1945, Mayor Félix Kir made a concerted effort to reconnect Dijon to its surroundings, cementing the city's place as a gateway not only to Burgundy's illustrious vineyards but also to some of the region's most cherished green spaces and cultural landmarks.

GETTING AROUND

Dijon's surrounding countryside is nearly impossible to explore without a car or bike. While the regional TER train does connect the city to several villages along the Côte d'Or, its schedule is unpredictable (and cancellations are common), and stations are often followed by a long, unremarkable walk to any point of interest. Taxis can be arranged from Dijon, but make sure to book in advance – and secure your return trip at the same time.

Fontaine-d'Ouche

TIME FROM DIJON: **20MIN**

Dijon's Favourite Watering Hole

On the western edge of Dijon lies **Lac Kir**, a manmade lake and greenbelt reserve crossed by the Ouche River. Completed in 1964, the Lac was named in honour of Dijon's beloved mayor Félix Kir (the same man after whom the apéritif was named; p422) who championed the space as a way for the local Dijionnais to reconnect with nature.

Just 15 minutes from the historic centre by bike or car, the lake hums with life all day: early walkers circle the 3.6km trail, while evening revellers picnic along the banks with a bottle of aligoté. The area also includes cycling paths, tennis and volleyball courts, and water sports rentals – kayaks, pedal boats and kiteboards are available when the weather permits. Fishing is also allowed year-round.

From June through August, part of the lake becomes **Dijon Plage**, a sandy beach complete with day beds, umbrellas and a beach bar, **La Plage Café**. It's the perfect place for a refreshing dip when temperatures soar in Dijon. In the evenings, the beach is turned into a performance venue with concerts, DJ sets and family-friendly programming *(destinationdijon.com/temps-forts/dijon-plage)*.

Clos de Vougeot

The Serpent's Trail

Just a 15-minute drive or 40-minute cycle from Dijon's historic centre (and a 10-minute walk from Lac Kir) lies the wild and wondrous **Parc de la Combe à la Serpent** (The Valley of the Snake). Spanning 333 hectares, the park is named after a 10th-century legend claiming the valley was haunted by a female snake and her kin – but rest assured, no serpents remain today.

From the Middle Ages to the 20th century, the valley was developed by monks and farmers: overgrown ruins of terraced vineyards, sheep-grazing pastures, orchards and pine tree plantations can still be seen today. Although largely abandoned in the first half of the 1900s, the area was declared a natural reserve in 1962. Since then, 28km of walking trails have been mapped out, along with picnic areas and a small animal reserve.

Park your car and then explore on foot or trail bike. Paths range from 4km (about an hour) to 12km (around three hours), and off-trail wandering is welcome. Just tread carefully: the park is a dedicated bee sanctuary and wild hives are hidden throughout the rocks and undergrowth.

Vougeot

TIME FROM DIJON: **30MIN**

Jamais En Vain, Toujours En Vin

Just a 30-minute drive south of Dijon, **Clos de Vougeot** *(closdevougeot.fr)* is a resplendent 16th-century Renaissance château

---

A BIRD-WATCHER'S DELIGHT

Since its creation in 1964, **Lac Kir** has been designated a protected nature zone. Several bird species rarely seen elsewhere in Burgundy can be spotted in and around the lake throughout the year. Keep your eyes (and ears) peeled for these.

Black-necked grebes: Tiny waterbirds often seen feeding on insects and fish during the winter months.

Red-throated loons: Also known as diving birds. Typically, only one is spotted each year.

Black-throated loons: Occasionally seen during their southward winter migration; sightings are rare and often years apart.

Eurasian wigeons: Known for their distinctive whistling calls, these sociable ducks migrate from Northern Europe and are most vocal in winter.

 EATING IN FONTAINE D'OUCHE: OUR PICKS

| **Au Maquis**: Artist residency with lively weekend BBQs, live music and drinks for passing cyclists. *5-10pm Fri, 11am-10pm Sat, 11am-6pm Sun* € | **La Plage Café**: Small cafe with lake views serving crêpes, waffles, croque monsieurs and drinks from morning coffee to evening apéritifs. *1-6pm Mon-Fri, 11am-6pm Sat, 10.30am-6pm Sun* € | **Le K**: Groovy lakeside cafe with a sprawling terrasse, great apéritif cocktails and easy-going fare like salads. *10.30am-10pm Wed-Sat, to 7pm Sun* €€ | **Café du Pont**: Cosy and cheerful, with a lovely terrasse and comfort food favourites like quiche and burgers. *9am-9pm Tue-Sun* € |

Salon des Devises, Château de Bussy-Rabutin

THE WORLD CHAMPIONSHIP OF OEUFS EN MEURETTE

On 14–15 October each year, chefs from around the globe descend upon **Clos de Vougeot** (p427) for the World Championship of Oeufs en Meurette, a cooking competition celebrating this iconic Burgundian dish. The plate consists of two poached eggs in a rich red wine sauce with bacon, onions and shallots. Visitors can watch the chefs at work, sample variations of the dish, and vote for their favourite in the public's prize.

It's only fitting that the championship is held at the château, as *oeufs en meurette* was adopted as its signature dish in 1953. To this day, it is served at every dinner of the Confrérie des Chevaliers du Tastevin. Head chef Alexandra Bouvret is famously able to prepare 1200 perfectly poached eggs in just five minutes flat!

set among Burgundy's most prestigious vineyards. While its past is illustrious – it was founded by Cistercian monks in the 12th century – it's now best known as a pilgrimage site for wine lovers. The château is the spiritual seat of the Confrérie des Chevaliers du Tastevin, a society devoted to celebrating and promoting Burgundy's great wines. Their motto says it all: *Jamais en vain, toujours en vin* ('Never in vain, always in wine').

The château is open to the public for self-guided visits *(adult/child €12/5)* or guided tours in English and French *(from €15)*. From the original Cistercian cellars and kitchen to the medieval vat houses and presses, it offers a rich and immersive walk through 900 years of intertwined winemaking and religious history.

Though Clos de Vougeot no longer produces wine, the 50-hectare *grand cru* vineyard surrounding it is divided among 80 owners – some with just a single row of vines. Tours and tastings, led by the château's sommelier, can be booked in advance and offer an ideal introduction to the complexity, mystique and reverence of Burgundian wine.

EATING IN VOUGEOT: OUR PICKS

La Table de Leonce: Four-course meal inside the Clos de Vougeot (p427) showcasing the best of Burgundian food and wine, including a private castle tour with the resident sommelier. *11.15am-3pm, Tue-Sun* €€€

Au Creux de Vougeot: Casual, family-friendly spot on the Vougeot riverbank, known for its excellent *oeufs en meurette*. *noon-1.30pm & 7-8.45pm Wed-Sun* €

La Table d'Eole: Fresh, seasonal dishes with a weekly changing menu, served in a historic stone house with vaulted cellar dining. *10.30am-3.30pm & 7.30-11.30pm Mon-Wed & Fri-Sat, 10.30am-3.30pm Sun* €€

La Friterie de la Piscine: This unassuming food truck with seating is a long-time local secret, known for some of the best pizza in the region. *11.30am-10pm Mon-Sun* €

Blackcurrant Fields Forever

Thirsty for something other than wine? Head to **Le Cassissium** (*cassissium.fr/en/home; adult/child €10.50/free*) in Nuits-St-Georges, an interactive museum dedicated to the local speciality, *crème de cassis* (blackcurrant liqueur). First crafted in the 16th century as a medicinal tonic (don't be put off – it's very sweet!), cassis remains a regional favourite.

The highlight of the visit is the tasting session, where you can sample various interpretations of the liqueur and learn how to mix it with your drink of choice.

Located a 20-minute drive from Dijon and just 10 minutes from Clos de Vougeot, all visits must be booked in advance. Guided tours in English are held daily at 2pm, though you're welcome to join a French-language tour with the help of an English booklet provided at the start.

Bussy-Le-Grand

TIME FROM DIJON: **45MIN**

Vanity, Vengeance and Very Fine Interiors

Château de Bussy-Rabutin (*chateau-bussy-rabutin.fr; adult/child €9/free*) makes for a delightfully offbeat day trip. Tucked into the hills near Bussy-le-Grand, the château is surrounded by formal French gardens, a tranquil moat and woodlands ideal for a picnic or wander.

Inside is a world of unexpected eccentricity. Start with the grand **Galerie des Hommes de Guerre**, where dozens of portraits of famous military men line the walls – chosen by Bussy not for admiration, but to reflect his own frustrations with court life. Don't miss the **Salon des Dames**, equally caustic in tone, and the unforgettable **Salon des Devises**, where allegorical frescoes and Latin mottos air Bussy's grievances with style.

Most rooms are open to explore, many retaining original 17th-century wood panelling and floors. Audioguides (available in English) bring each portrait and quote to life, offering juicy context behind the passive-aggressive decor. Outside, wander the manicured parterre gardens or climb to the wooded paths for sweeping valley views.

The château is open every day (*9.15am-noon & 2-5pm*). Although it is relatively compact, it is rich in personality so plan for about 90 minutes on site, with extra time for the gardens or nearby village. Tickets can be booked online or on site; check for seasonal events like open-air theatre or literary picnics in summer.

> **SCANDAL BEHIND THE STONES**
>
> Roger de Bussy-Rabutin, a 17th-century nobleman, military officer and cousin to Madame de Sévigné, fell from grace after circulating a satirical manuscript that mocked the court of Louis XIV. Exiled from Versailles in 1665, he retreated to his estate in Bussy-le-Grand, where he spent decades reshaping his château into a deeply personal reflection of loss, ambition and critique. Bussy covered the interiors with portraits of courtiers, military leaders and women of note – each accompanied by Latin inscriptions layered with subtle meaning. The château became both sanctuary and statement: an aristocratic memoir etched in oil and plaster. Rather than fade into obscurity, Bussy immortalised his exile, transforming Château de Bussy-Rabutin into a singular historical artefact of courtly life – seen through the eyes of a disgraced insider.

EATING NEAR BUSSY-LE-GRAND: OUR PICKS

Le Pause Rabutin: Just across from the château, this family-run lunch spot serves traditional fare with produce from their garden and red-checkered tablecloth charm. *noon-3pm Sat & Sun* €

Auberge du Cheval Blanc: This rustic *auberge* offers hearty, beautifully plated classics by the fireplace – think countryside comfort with a quiet touch of elegance. *7-9pm Fri & Sat, 12-2pm Sun* €

La Grange Ferme-Auberge de Flavigny: Communal, cafeteria-style spot in a stone barn, run by local farmers who cook hearty seasonal dishes using their own produce. *noon-5.30pm, Tue-Sun* €

Brasserie de Flavigny: Brewery serving its own beer alongside craft picks, with a menu of French classics and pub favourites like fish and chips. *11am-10pm Fri & Sat, 11am-7pm Sun* €

Beaune

MAJESTIC VINEYARDS | TILED ROOFTOPS | FOOD MARKETS

☑ TOP TIP

In recent years, Beaune and its surrounding villages have been hit hard by climate change with unseasonal frost and heatwaves significantly reducing grape yields. So be sure to indulge in a glass while in town, as the region's wines are becoming increasingly hard to get your hands on outside Burgundy.

As the capital of Burgundian wine, viticulture has been the beating heart of Beaune (pronounced 'bone') since its settlement by Romans around the 1st century CE. Although today the Côte d'Or's great wines are made in the villages surrounding Beaune, many winemakers and *négociants* (wine merchants) still have their cellars within the city. Wander around the walled historical centre – which is still encircled by ramparts dating from the 13th and 16th centuries – and you'll notice that every other shopfront is dedicated to wine and its gastronomical pairings. So monumental is the city's viticultural ancestry that it was inscribed as a UNESCO World Heritage Site in 2015 for its unique '*terroirs*' (p434) – a hard-to-translate term referring to a 'sense of place', the natural factors that hallmark the essence of a specific wine. But despite its illustrious past – and the eye-watering prices of its wines – Beaune remains a naturally rustic and welcoming village.

Medicinal Magic at the Hôtel-Dieu
Potions, lotions and Gothic delights

At the heart of Beaune's historic centre stands the **Hôtel-Dieu des Hospices Civils de Beaune**, the town's most iconic landmark. Founded in 1443 by Nicolas Rolin, Chancellor to the Duke of Burgundy, and his wife Guigone de Salins, the Hôtel-Dieu was established as a hospital and almshouse to care for

GETTING AROUND

Beaune is easily walkable, and you can meander from one end of town to the other in less than 20 minutes (although sturdy shoes are recommended to weather the cobbled stone pavements and explore the surrounding vineyards). Taxis are available to take you to the train station or to visit neighbouring villages, but book in advance where possible as numbers are limited. If you plan to drive, free parking is available outside of the historic centre.

- **HIGHLIGHTS**
  1. Boulangerie Marie Boucherot
  2. Hôtel-Dieu des Hospices Civils de Beaune
  3. Patriarche Père et Fils
- **SIGHTS**
  4. Bouchard Aîné & Fils
  5. Maison Louis Jadot
  6. Terroirs by Adeline
- **SLEEPING**
  7. Hostellerie Cèdre & Spa Beaune
  8. La Villa Fleurie
  9. Le Clos de l'Aigue
  10. L'Hôtel de Beaune
- **EATING**
  11. Anthocyane Wine Bistrot
  12. Crème
  13. Du Goût et Des Idées
  14. La Lune
  15. La Maison du Colombier
  16. Les Caves Madeleine
  17. Ma Cuisine
  18. Patisserie Fabien Berteau
  19. Samedi Café
- **DRINKING & NIGHTLIFE**
  20. La Dilettante
  21. Le Bout du Monde
  22. Publican Mister Brown
  23. St Romain Roasters
- **SHOPPING**
  24. Alain Hess Fromager
  25. Athenaeum de la Vigne et du Vin
  26. Avintures
  27. Épicerie Paysanne
  28. Maison Denis Perret
  29. Vivavin

the local population devastated by the Hundred Years' War. From receiving its first patient in 1452 to its closure in 1984, all care at the Hospices de Beaune was offered free of charge – many a local winemaker was even born here.

Step into the courtyard and look up: the glazed, polychrome roof tiles and carved wooden detailing offer one of the most vivid surviving examples of 15th-century flamboyant Gothic architecture. Inside, the complex is part art gallery, part medical time capsule (*musee.hospices-de-beaune.com; adult/child €12/4*). Wander through the Salle des Pôvres, the grand, bed-lined ward furnished with original crimson-curtained

Hôtel-Dieu des Hospices Civils de Beaune (p430)

WHERE WINE MEETS CULTURE

Alexandra Wilo, winemaker at Domaine Alussia, shares the lowdown on Burgundy's wine festivals – a chance to taste local wines (often with live music) in a region where wineries can be tricky to visit.

Montrachet Jazz Festival: Held the last weekend of May, a cosy festival that pairs the best white wines from Puligny-Montrachet, Chassagne-Montrachet and St-Aubin with live jazz.

Vin & Hip-Hop: In October, a fun harvest party held at **Clos de Vougeot** (p427). Sip young winemakers' wines while dancing alongside them to hip-hop DJ sets in a 16th-century château.

Atelier Escoffier at Moulin aux Moines: A food pop-up open in summer only in the **Clos du Moulin aux Moines** (moulinaux-moines.com). Many winemakers come here to relax as you can find interesting bottles from local wineries at great prices.

beds, then continue into the pharmacy and apothecary, where shelves still brim with elixirs and potions once administered to patients. Be sure to pause before the Polyptych of the Last Judgement, the Hospices' magnificent 15th-century altarpiece by Flemish master Rogier van der Weyden.

The Hospices also hosts cultural events throughout the year, including the month-long **Festival International d'Opéra Baroque** in November, which takes place in the courtyard.

Over the centuries, Hôtel-Dieu has received significant donations from benefactors, including more than 60 hectares of nearby vineyard land. Each year during **Les Trois Glorieuses** – a wine festival held on the third weekend of November – barrels produced from these vineyards are auctioned off to private collectors and wine professionals, with proceeds going to charity. If you're not in the market for a full barrel, bottles of the Hospices' wine are available year-round from the gift shop.

In Vino Veritas

An oenophile's paradise

Although the exact date is debated, the discovery of a 1st-century stoned-in vineyard just 30 minutes from Beaune

 DRINKING IN BEAUNE: WINE BARS

La Dilettante: Independent wines and craft beers accompanied by light tapas plates with a Japanese twist. *noon-3.30pm & 6-9pm, Mon, Tue, Thu & Fri, noon-4pm Wed* €

La Maison du Colombier: Exceptional wines by the glass and generous charcuterie plates served in a rustic, convivial setting with views of the basilica. *6pm-midnight Mon-Sat* €

Publican Mister Brown: Low-key pub-turned-wine bar with a leafy riverside terrasse overlooking the Bouzaise and hearty tapas plates to share. *5pm-1am Wed-Fri & Sun, 11am-2am Sat* €

Le Bout du Monde: Extensive by-the-glass list and local charcuterie (try the *jambon persillé*) in a moody, oak-lined room with leather armchairs. *6pm-midnight Tue & Wed, to 1am Thu, to 2am Fri & Sat* €€

suggests wine has been produced in the Côte d'Or since Roman times. The industry was formalised with the arrival of the Cistercian monks in the 5th century. Believing the land to be alive with spirits that 'spoke' through each vineyard, the monks planted only two grape varieties – pinot noir and chardonnay – to better understand the effect of *terroir*. By controlling the grape, they could isolate the voice of the soil.

Despite Burgundy's global fame (and the sky-high prices its wines now fetch), many winemakers remain modest – owner-operators who prune their own vines and consider themselves caretakers rather than creators. Because most plots are small and yields increasingly affected by climate change, cellar visits are rarely open to the public unless you're a trade professional.

Thankfully, Beaune is home to several renowned *négociants* (wine merchants) who open their doors to visitors. Of note is **Patriarche Père et Fils** *(patriarche.com/en/visit; €25)* which owns 5km of vaulted 13th-century cellars beneath the city, housing more than two million bottles. The self-guided tour, to be reserved online in advance, winds through tunnels lined with ageing wine, ending in a tasting of six wines. Private visits and candle-lit dinners can also be organised in advance.

Elsewhere in Beaune, **Bouchard Aîné et Fils** *(bouchard-aine.fr; €24)* one of the town's oldest *négociants*, offers tastings several times a day from Tuesday to Sunday. **Maison Louis Jadot** *(louisjadot.com/nous-trouver; €30)* also runs daily cellar tours and tastings at 3pm on weekdays and 10am on Saturdays – book ahead via email or phone.

For a more intimate experience – and the opportunity to taste premier and *grand cru* wines – head to **Terroirs by Adeline** *(terroirsbyadeline.com)*, a Beaune-based cooking school. Adeline leads hands-on workshops that teach you how to cook Burgundian dishes and pair them with the region's finest wines.

Dine & Wine Among the Vines

Picnic like a local

As any Burgundian will tell you, wine is best enjoyed with food – which is perhaps why the region's wine capital is also home to some of the finest speciality produce stores and farmers markets in France. And while tucking into bœuf bourguignon or *escargots* at a restaurant has its charms, it can get a little

WHY I LOVE BEAUNE

Madeleine Rothery, Lonely Planet writer

I've been visiting Beaune since I was four years old – the local way of life and its people are so intimately weaved into the fabric of my life. I am in constant awe of the vignerons' commitment to and respect of nature. Their work is relentless, but their passion infectious. Once you come to appreciate the finesse of their craft, wine takes on a whole new meaning.

Perhaps it's the belief in interconnectivity – with the land, with each other – which is sown into the heritage of the city that makes the locals so friendly and welcoming. Sometimes I'll find myself picnicking on a Saturday with people I'd met just the night before at the **Publican**!

DRINKING IN BEAUNE: WINE SHOPS

Fair prices and worldwide shipping

Athenaeum de la Vigne et du Vin: A vast wine library stocked with bottles, books, maps and all manner of wine-related miscellany. *10am-7pm Mon-Fri*

Avintures: Boutique wine shop specialising in small producers, most of whom the ever-friendly owner, Thomas Turner, knows personally. *10am-12.30pm & 2-7pm Mon, Wed & Sat, 10am-7pm Tue, Thu & Fri*

Maison Denis Perret: Excellent regional selection (including half bottles). Staff will happily decode Burgundy's wine regions and appellations. *9am-noon & 2-6pm Mon, 9am-7pm Tues-Sat*

Vivavin: A local institution for over 30 years, the friendly staff will be more than happy to guide you through a tasting of the wines. *9am-6pm Mon-Fri*

TALK OF THE TERROIR

There are a few words that you'll regularly hear in Beaune that cannot be easily translated. *Terroir* is the most complicated (yet the most used). Often described as 'somewhere-ness', it is the essence of a particular vineyard. It includes the soil, subsoil, drainage, aspect to the sun, susceptibility to weather conditions and meso-climate of the vineyard. The vigneron, therefore, interprets the *terroir* through the wine. Vineyards, or *terroirs*, are classified in terms of their potential to produce reputable wines. From lowest to highest, Burgundian wines are classified as regional, village, *premier cru* and *grand cru*. *Climat* does not refer to the climate but is a named area of vineyard containing *parcelles* (rows of vines), sometimes owned by different producers, each bringing their own interpretation of the *terroir*.

heavy meal after meal. So why not do as the locals do? Pack a picnic full of fresh, local fare, lace up your walking shoes and head to the vineyards.

Beaune hosts a region-renowned farmers market every Saturday morning, spread across Place Carnot and the covered marketplace of Les Halles, opposite the **Hospices de Beaune** (p430). Open from 8am to 1pm, it's the city's social hub – a mix of locals, chefs and visitors weaving through stalls of fresh produce, cheese, charcuterie, flowers and Burgundy's famous *pain d'épices*. There's also a smaller market on Wednesdays, though it lacks the full buzz. From March to November, the Saturday market is joined by a *brocante*, a flea and bric-a-brac market that's worth a wander even if you're just browsing.

Start your Saturday morning with a coffee from **St Romain Roasters**, a small-batch roastery from the nearby village of St-Romain who set up a cart within the market. If you're planning a picnic on another day, don't worry – Beaune is well-stocked with independent food shops. Head to **Alain Hess Fromager** on Place Carnot, your one-stop shop for artisan cheeses, cured meats and other gourmet finds. For fruit and vegetables, **Épicerie Paysanne** offers a carefully curated selection of organic produce from local farms. And for baguettes, croissants and sweet treats, **Du Goût et Des**

EATING IN BEAUNE: LOCAL FAVOURITES

Ma Cuisine: Family-style bistro, lined with old boxes and bottles, serving traditional Burgundian dishes with friendly, welcoming service. *noon-2pm & 7-9pm Mon, Tue, Thu & Fri* €€

Les Caves Madeleine: Fine food and wine in a laid-back setting with long shared tables – a go-to for local winemakers and industry folk. *noon-1.30pm & 7.15-9.45pm Wed-Sat, noon-1.30pm Tue* €€

La Lune: Japanese small plates and counter seating – perfect for when you're craving something other than classic French. *7.30pm-midnight Tue-Sat* €€

Anthocyane Wine Bistrot: Inventive, seasonal cooking in a quiet, understated setting. Excellent wines by the glass at refreshingly fair prices. *noon-1.30pm & 7-9pm Mon-Fri* €€

Beaune market produce

Idées is widely considered one of the best bakeries in town. Don't forget the essentials: a corkscrew, glasses, napkins and a knife for cheese.

Unlike Bordeaux and Champagne, there are very few *clos* (walled vineyards) in Burgundy which means that you are free to wander through the vineyards (including the most prestigious *grand cru* and *premier cru* vines!). That being said, there is an unspoken etiquette to be respected: remember the vines are the life's work and livelihood of local winemakers. Stick to the well-trodden walkways rather than meandering through the rows of vines. You may also encounter vine workers spraying the vines, which can be unpleasant to walk past, but it's not your place to complain – they are simply doing their job.

The closest vineyards are on the western edge of Beaune. For sweeping views over the vines and rooftops, climb toward the top of the hill, where ledgers and picnic spots await. Several benches are also scattered through the vines – the best known is the **picnic table** (*1 sur Roches, Volnay*) overlooking the *premier cru* vineyards of Pommard and Volnay. Once you're done, leave no trace: be sure to take all your rubbish with you.

A GLORIOUS NOVEMBER

On the third weekend of November each year, Beaune and its surroundings brim with festivities for *Les Trois Glorieuses*, a triumvirate of events marking the end of the wine-growing cycle in Burgundy. Celebrations kick off on the Saturday with a black-tie dinner organised by the Confrérie des Chevaliers du Tastevin de Bourgogne at **Le Clos de Vougeot** (p427). In Beaune, the city is closed to traffic and transforms into one giant street party – where everyone is invited. The following day is the Hospices de Beaune wine auction, with all proceeds benefiting local hospitals. The weekend closes with La Paulée de Meursault, a convivial lunch among winemakers, vineyard workers and other trade professionals.

Beaune's best patisserie

 EATING IN BEAUNE: PETIT DÉJEUNER

Crème: Third-wave coffee with beans from local roaster Saint Romain and simple breakfasts like egg rolls, served in a cool, laid-back space. *9am-8pm Tue & Thu, to 11pm Wed & Fri, to 4pm Sat* €

Boulangerie Marie Boucherot: Artisanal bakery known for what might be the best baguettes and sourdough in the region – plus croissants and classic pastries. *7.30am-7pm Wed-Sat, 7.30-2pm Sun* €

Patisserie Fabien Berteau: Berteau is known for his exotic-flavoured macarons (like lemon curd), creamy cheesecakes and perfect classic pastries. *9.30am-7pm Mon-Fri, 9am-7pm Sat, 9am-1pm Sun* €

Samedi Café: Tucked inside the covered market, this Saturday-only pop-up serves Beaune's best flat white and Korean vegan dishes. *9am-1pm Sat* €

Beyond Beaune

The villages surrounding Beaune are home to some of the most prestigious vineyards and cycling routes in the world.

Places

Hautes-Côtes de Beaune p436
Côte de Nuits p438

To the north and west of Beaune are the Côte de Nuits and the Côte de Beaune, respectively. Scattered among these stretches of vineyards are many a small winemaking village. Despite being surrounded by some of the most expensive parcels of vines in the world (a bottle of 1945 Domaine de la Romanée-Conti, located in Nuits-St-George, is the most expensive bottle of wine ever sold at US$558,000), the villages themselves remain quaint and rustic. Easy to access by both car and bike, spend a day village-hopping and exploring the vineyards.

Venture beyond the vineyards and you'll discover lush forests, full of beautiful hiking trails to walk off the indulgent Burgundian cuisine and wines.

GETTING AROUND

A car or bike (rentals are readily available in town) are essential to explore Beaune's surroundings, with most destinations around a 30-minute drive away. Roads in nearby villages are often narrow and winding, so are best navigated by confident drivers. Free parking is available in and around all villages. Although taxis are available to take you to and from neighbouring villages, they must be booked in advance and fares can rise very high, very quickly.

Hautes-Côtes de Beaune

TIME FROM BEAUNE: 30MIN

Chasing Waterfalls

Southwest of Beaune in the **Hautes-Côte-de-Beaune** is **Le Bout du Monde**, a limestone valley with caves to explore and a waterfall to chase. French novelist Alexandre Dumas declared that it was 'the Burgundy El Dorado, where the encircling rocks, high above, isolate it from the rest of the world'. It has been recognised as a European Natura 2000 zone for its unique biodiversity – keep your eyes peeled for peregrine falcons and white-breasted alpine swifts.

The easiest way to explore is to begin at Le Bout du Monde Grotte (the grotto). A free car park and picnic area are located 400m from the beginning of the walks. As you exit the car park, walk left until you hit a signpost indicating two walking trails. To the left is a very short walk alongside a stream towards the grotto (you can climb inside, if you have a torch). This walk, albeit short, can be slippery when the weather is damp or humid. To reach the waterfall, take the walking trail to the right. Although the sign indicates a 2.5km walk, it really is only 1km at most – and a very easy walk. Don't be disappointed if the waterfall isn't running, the canyon is still a sight to behold.

Although there are more complicated trails, these are reserved for experienced hikers only as they are steep and

Le Festival de St-Vincent Tournante

slippery. For a map of more complex trails around Le Bout du Monde, head to the **Beaune tourist office** or download the app AllTrails.

Pottering Around Town

It may be hard to believe that anything exists in this part of Burgundy beyond wine, but in the town of Sampigny-lès-Maranges lies a world of artisanal ceramics: **Poterie de Sampigny** *(poterie-sampigny.com)*. Housed in an ancient flour mill, the pottery was founded in 1984 by Sylvie Fresnais Didier, who is renowned worldwide for her unique glazing techniques in rustic ombrés and organic patterns. Today, Sylvie has transformed the mill into a living celebration of ceramics, hosting exhibitions and personally-led tours throughout the year. The boutique is open daily from 2pm to 6pm, but tours outside those hours can be arranged by contacting Sylvie directly via the website.

PATRON SAINT OF WINEMAKERS

St Vincent was chosen as the Patron Saint of Winemakers simply because 'Vincent', when pronounced in French, is a homophone for *vin-sang* (wine-blood). Since 1938, Burgundy has held a festival in his honour in a different wine village each year on the last weekend of January. The weekend-long festival, known as **Le Festival de St-Vincent Tournante**, attracts tens of thousands of visitors.

The weekend begins with an early morning procession of gloriously robed members of Burgundian wine societies throughout the vines, followed by a Catholic mass. The streets fill with concerts, performers and artisanal markets. Local wine cellars open their doors to the public for tastings, and the whole town is festooned with whimsical decorations crafted by volunteers.

 EATING IN THE HAUTES-CÔTES DE BEAUNE: OUR PICKS

Le Soleil: Cool neo-bistro serving market-fresh share plates and wines from small producers, just 10 min from Beaune in Savigny-lès-Beaune. *7-9pm Mon, Thu & Fri, 12.15-1.45pm Sat & Sun* €

Bistrot des Falaises: A St-Romain bistro beloved by winemakers, where the weekly changing menu depends entirely on what's fresh and local. *noon-1.30pm & 7.15-9pm Fri-Mon, 7.15-9pm Thu* €

Cave et Cuisine: Locally loved institution in Demigny serving high-quality regional fare with warm service and an extensive wine list. *noon-1pm & 7-8.30pm Thu-Sat, noon-1pm Sun* €

Auberge des Vignes: No-frills *auberge* with great-value fixed-price menus for lunch and dinner. Sit outside and dine beside the vines of Volnay. *noon-1.30pm & 7-9pm Thu-Mon* €

ROUGH WINES

On the third weekend of October each year, Nuits-St-Georges hosts **La Fête du Vin Bourru**. The literal translation of *vin bourru* is 'rough wines', but it isn't exactly a wine…it's somewhere between grape juice and wine, very sweet and rich in sugar as it's only partially fermented. Tens of thousands of visitors descend to watch the recently harvested grapes be pressed and taste the offshoot – often straight from the barrel or bottle.

It's also a spectacle of traditional Burgundian music and dance. During the Duchy of Burgundy, the region was the musical epicentre of Europe and, throughout the weekend, dances such as the energetic *bransle* (a sort of linedance) and the processional *pavane* are performed in full costume.

Château de Corton André

Côte de Nuits

TIME FROM BEAUNE: **25MIN**

Grand Cru-saders

To the north of Beaune runs the Côte de Nuits, home to no less than 24 *grand cru* vineyards and what many consider to be the best pinot noirs in the world. Although you can cycle the route, it gets quite hilly – best to hop in the car and cruise Burgundy's famous **Route des Grands Crus**. You can drive from Beaune to Gevrey-Chambertin, at the northern end of the Côte de Nuits, in 30 minutes, but set aside the best part of a day to explore the villages along the way.

The road is marked by brown signs bearing a white bunch of grapes, and free parking is available in every village. Another reason to drive? Most wine villages have a local *caveau* (wine shop), a sort of cooperative where you can stock up on locally produced wines at cellar-door prices – fill your boot, as you won't find these prices anywhere else.

Well-priced fixed menus

 EATING IN THE CÔTES-DE-NUIT: OUR PICKS

Le Grenier à Sel: In Nuits-St-Georges, this simple spot serves cheap set menus and ingredients sourced from local suppliers. *noon-2pm & 7-9pm Thu-Sat, noon-2pm Tue & Wed* €

Le Complexe: A quirky spot in Gevrey-Chambertin's sports complex, serving cheap fixed-price menus plus delicious burgers and pizza. *9.30am-10pm Tue-Sat, 9.30am-3pm & 5.30-10pm Mon* €

Le Chef Coq: An old hunting lodge in Nuits-St-Georges serving rich fare in a surprisingly light setting. In winter, enjoy an apéritif by the fire. *noon-1.30pm & 7-9pm Mon-Sat* €€

Bistro Lucien: A homey bistro in Gevrey-Chambertin, with pots and pans hanging from the ceiling, run by a lovely couple. *noon-2pm & 7-9.30pm Tue-Sat, noon-2pm Sun* €

There are many villages worth visiting along the Côte de Nuits, but these are perhaps the most important...

Technically part of the Côte de Beaune, **Aloxe-Corton** is the first stop as you head north of Beaune. Look out for the vine-covered Hill of Corton, topped with forest and home to the *grand cru* vineyards Corton and Corton-Charlemagne. In the centre of town stands the **Château de Corton André**, with its striking multicoloured Burgundian-tiled roof.

Fifteen minutes north lies **Nuits-St-Georges**, the village from which the Côte de Nuits takes its name. One of the largest villages on the route, it's also one of the most eventful. Each March, it hosts the auction of the **Hospice-de-Nuits-St-Georges**, a sister event to Beaune's better-known wine auction (p435). In October, it throws the **Festival des Vins Bourru**, where visitors flock to taste the just-pressed grape juice. While you're here, visit **L'Imaginarium** (*imaginarium-bourgogne.com; adult/child €10/free*), an interactive museum dedicated to *crémant de Bourgogne* – the region's sparkling wine, with its best bottles rivaling Champagne.

Home to only a few hundred residents, **Vosne-Romanée** is worth a stop to see the most expensive vineyards in the world: **Romanée-Conti** and **La Tâche**. These two *grand cru* monopoles – vineyards owned entirely by Domaine de la Romanée-Conti – may look unremarkable, but their wines regularly fetch upwards of €10,000.

In 2009, **Gevrey-Chambertin** was confirmed as one of the oldest winemaking villages in the Côte d'Or when traces of a 1st-century vineyard were found nearby. Locals are still known as Gibriaçois and Gibriaçoises in honour of the Roman village, Gibriacum, on which the town was founded.

BURGUNDY'S MONOPOLES EXPLAINED

A *monopole* refers to a vineyard exclusively owned and operated by a single estate – a rarity in a region where plots are typically divided among multiple producers.

The best-known example is **Domaine de la Romanée-Conti** (or 'DRC'), which owns the Romanée-Conti Grand Cru plot in Vosne-Romanée. The vineyard dates back to at least 1232, when it was acquired by the Abbey of St Vivant, but the estate was consolidated in 1869 by Jacques-Marie Duvault-Blochet.

DRC's philosophy of low yields and meticulous winemaking has cemented its reputation as one of the world's finest estates. In fact, the exclusivity and quality of its wines means they regularly fetch astronomical prices: a bottle of the 1945 vintage sold at auction in 2018 for US$558,000.

DRINKING IN THE CÔTES-DE-NUITS: TASTING WINE

La Cuverie de Vosne: Chic wine bar in Vosne-Romanée with over 2000 wines. Most of the profits go straight to the winemakers themselves. *11am-9.30pm Thu-Sat, to 8pm Mon & Tue*

Cave Moillard: Technically a *négociant*, this Nuits-St-Georges cellar offers relaxed tastings with owner Olivier, who's always more than happy to talk you through his wines. *10am-7pm*

La Cave de Monsieur Jean: Boutique shop in Gevrey-Chambertin where owner Jean shares his passion for Burgundy over tastings or a glass. *9.30am-noon & 2.30-6.30pm Mon & Wed-Sat, 10am-4.30pm Sun*

Café du Centre: No-frills local favourite in Nuits-St-Georges with a generous wine-by-the-glass list and copious charcuterie platters. *5.30am-11.30pm*

CYCLING TRIP

Cycle the Route of the Vines

La Voie des Vignes is one of France's most famous cycling routes. Following a 22km paved, cycle-only path from Beaune to Santenay, it winds through the prestigious vineyards of the Côte de Beaune. This demi-tour can be completed in around 2½ hours, but it's worth making a full day of it to rest and replenish in the villages along the way.

❶ Beaune

Begin in Beaune and rent a bike (electric is recommended, as there are hills along the route) from **Bourgogne Randonnées** *(bourgogne-randonnees.fr; adult/child €39/15 per day)* just 300m from the train station, or from **Bourgogne Évasion** *(bourgogne-evasion.fr; adult/child €45/15 per day)* located in the Parc de la Bouzaise. If you're riding between May and September, pack sun protection and a water bottle – there is very little shade en route. Most village restaurants only serve lunch between noon and 2pm, so consider picking up a picnic in Beaune (p430).

The Cycle: The route begins at the Porte des Avaux, just south of the Parc de la Bouzaise, and is signposted by a gate inscribed with Veloroute: La Voie des Vignes. Follow the path for 2.9km towards Pommard.

❷ Pommard

Pommard and its vineyards are famous for pinot noir. Visit the **Château de Pommard**

Cycling to Meursault

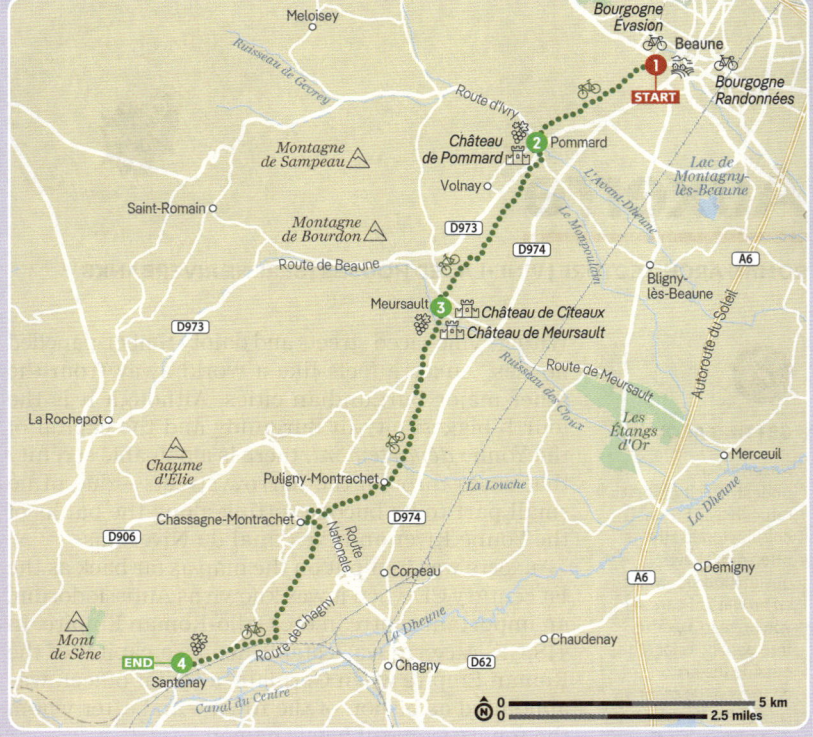

(*10.30am-6.30pm Mon-Sun*) a 17th-century castle with 20 hectares of gardens filled with sculptures by Rodin and others (advance booking required via telephone). Wine tastings can also be arranged ahead of time.

The Cycle: Rejoin the Voie des Vignes, marked by green signs with a white grape bunch dotted along the route, and cycle through the village of Volnay and its *premier cru* vineyards towards Meursault (5km).

③ Meursault

The largest village on the Côte de Beaune, Meursault is known for its white wines and five castles. Book a tour and tasting at the **Château de Meursault**, an 11th-century estate with 12th-century Cistercian-style cellars, or stop for lunch at Bistro de la Cueillette, a rustic restaurant set within the **Château de Cîteaux** in the centre of town (*noon-2pm Wed-Sun*).

The Cycle: Continue along the Voie des Vignes for 10km towards Santenay, passing through Puligny-Montrachet and Chassagne-Montrachet – home to some of the most celebrated white wine vineyards in the world.

④ Santenay

La Voie des Vignes finishes in Santenay, the last wine village on the Côte de Beaune, known for its red wines and 19th-century windmill. Take time to explore the relatively untouched upper village, Santenay-le-Haut, with its small chapel and the hamlet of St-Jean.

To return to Beaune, either cycle back along the Voie des Vignes or take the TER train from Santenay-les-Bains to Chagny, then transfer to a train bound for Beaune (around 25 minutes total; bikes are allowed onboard TER trains). Schedules can be unpredictable, so plan your return trip in advance.

Auxerre

ROMAN ARCHITECTURE | VINE-LACED HOUSES | SERENE RIVERBANKS

GETTING AROUND

Auxerre is a pedestrian city, albeit rather hilly. The small cobblestoned streets often don't have designated sidewalks so be wary of cars. If you drive to Auxerre, free parking is located outside the historic centre, on the other side of the Yonne River (where the Gare SNCF is). Taxis are far and few between (book well in advance if you need one), but Bus 1 connects the Gare SNCF to the historic centre *(€1.50 per trip)*.

☑ TOP TIP

For a self-guided walking tour of Auxerre, follow the Cadet Roussel Trail. With 67 stops traced out by tiny bronze arrows etched into the pavement, the trail weaves its way past every historical highlight. Pick up a map *(€2)* from the **tourist office** (p444) for detailed explanations of each site.

With its vine-laced streets and dainty timber-panelled houses, Auxerre feels like a world away from the other major Burgundian cities. Although it is the fourth-biggest city in Burgundy and the capital of the Yonne *département,* there is a palpable serenity that eases through the narrow streets – due in no small part to its bucolic setting along the banks of the Yonne River and the Canal du Nivernais.

Auxerre was first put on the map as far back as the 1st century CE when it was known as Autissiodorum, an important centre in the Gallo-Roman Empire. In 418 CE, Auxerre was established as a capital of the Roman Empire when Germain, a senior officer, was appointed as bishop of the town – and after whom the town's iconic abbey is named.

Today Auxerre rings with resonances of its past; it's an idyllic place to relax among nature and history.

Religious Reliquaries

A Roman religious hot spot

The town of Auxerre is encircled by a sprawl of modern buildings, but as soon as you cross the Yonne River into its old town, you'll feel as though you've travelled back in time. The hilly cobblestoned streets are, for the most part, still lined with small patchworked houses straight out of the Middle Ages. Nevertheless, the city's two historical touchstones – the Abbaye St-Germain and Cathédrale St-Étienne – loom protectively over the old town's skyline.

The **Abbaye St-Germain** *(abbayesaintgermain.fr)* is perhaps Auxerre's most defining monument. Nestled in the old town's southeastern corner, it was founded in 418 by the Roman Bishop Germain. Following his death in 448, Queen Clotilde, wife of Frankish King Clovis I, began expanding what was just a simple oratory in honour of its famous founder who was buried onsite. In 1277, monks began reconstructing the abbey in the Rayonnant Gothic style – the stately vaulted ribbed corridors still frame the courtyard today.

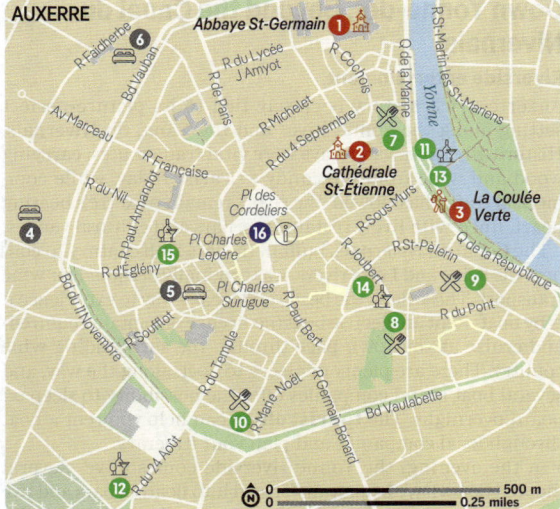

HIGHLIGHTS
1. Abbaye St-Germain
2. Cathédrale St-Étienne
3. La Coulée Verte

SLEEPING
4. Hôtel Les Maréchaux
5. Le Relais des Saints Pères
6. The Originals Boutique, Hotel Normandie

EATING
7. Cantina
8. L'Aspérule
9. Le Saint-Pèlerin
10. Restaurant à la Maison

DRINKING & NIGHTLIFE
11. La Péniche
12. La Petite Vitesse
13. La Scène des Quais
14. Le Bar du Théâtre
15. Le Galopin

INFORMATION
16. Tourist Office

The abbey is free to visit and open every day of the week, except Tuesdays during the winter months. To visit the meticulously preserved 9th-century crypt, it is necessary to join a guided tour *(€8)* but it is well worth it, if only to see the Carolingian painted wall frescoes, the oldest discovered in France. For a free guided tour in English, download the app Legendr which provides a commentated walk through of the abbey.

A five-minute walk from the abbey stands the arresting Roman Catholic **Cathédrale St-Étienne**, built between the 13th and 16th centuries on the grounds of an 11th-century Roman cathedral (the crypt of which still lies beneath the church). From the Roman crypt to the breathtaking stained-glass rose windows, the cathedral is a harmonious mix of various styles of Burgundian architecture. While it is open to the public every day of the week, the tourist office of Auxerre *(ot-auxerre.com; €8)* organises a daily tour at noon in English which provides an engaging explanation of the complex history of the cathedral.

 EATING IN AUXERRE: LOCAL FAVOURITES

Le Saint-Pèlerin: Quaint riverside spot known for its wood-fired cooking, where everything, right down to the fries, is made in house. *noon-1.30pm & 7.15-9.30pm Tue-Sat* €€

Cantina: Neo-bistro and wine bar with regular jazz concerts, natural wines and plenty of vegetarian options. *noon-1.30pm & 7.15-9pm Tue-Sat* €

L'Aspérule: Tiny, intimate gastronomic spot serving delicate, seasonal French dishes with a refined Japanese twist. *noon-1.30pm & 7.30-9pm Tue-Sat* €€€

Restaurant à la Maison: Warm and welcoming, with the feel of a private dining room, this spot serves inventive spins on classic French fare. *noon-1.30pm & 7.15-9.30pm Tue-Sat* €€

Down Yonne-der, Beyond the Canal du Nivernais

Riverside entertainment

Auxerre's rich history is closely tied to its picture-perfect setting along the Yonne River and the Canal du Nivernais. Historically, both waterways were vital trade routes, carrying wood and wine from Burgundy to Paris. Today, while commercial traffic has slowed, the rivers remain Auxerre's beating heart, lined with restaurants, bars and cultural venues.

The Canal du Nivernais, built in the late 18th century to connect the Seine and Loire rivers, was originally designed for wine transport. These days, the best – and local – way to experience it is by boat. Rent an electric boat (no licence or captain required) and cruise at your own pace through the surrounding wine country. There are plenty of places to dock along the way, and several boat rental companies offer the possibility to sleep on board overnight. The **tourist office** can help you rent a boat through local companies and plan your itinerary.

In the evening, the Yonne riverside comes alive. Several moored boats have been transformed into floating bars and live music venues. Start your night with an apéritif at **La Péniche Auxerre** then drift over to **La Scène des Quais**, a floating stage with live music and theatre performances most nights.

On the last weekend of May, the riverbanks are transformed into the annual **Festival Fleurs de Vigne**, as hundreds of local winemakers gather to share their wines with the public.

The Green Corridor

Walking the rails of the past

La Coulée Verte is a 9.5km walking trail that follows the path of a former railway connecting Auxerre to nearby St-Sauveur-en-Puisaye. Winding through the green outskirts of town, it offers a refreshing break from the urban bustle.

Starting at quai de la République, the trail runs alongside the Yonne River and then crosses into the forested Pays Auxerrois, ending at Gare SNCF Auxerre-St-Gervais. Along the way it reveals a quieter side of Auxerre, with cooling shade in summer and stunning views of the old-town skyline.

Best tackled on foot, the trail isn't ideal for cycling – metal track remnants make for a bumpy ride. Although it's easy to follow (simply look for the old railway tracks), the Auxerre tourist office can map out the route for you.

THE CLOWN ABOUT TOWN

The presence of a certain **Cadet Roussel** is felt everywhere throughout Auxerre: the self-guided walking tour (p442) is named after him, as is a main street, and a statue in the centre of town was erected in his honour.

Guillaume Joseph Roussel was the local court bailiff in the late 1700s, but he was more known for his eccentricity and absolute love of life. Unfortunately, he has not been remembered in history for his simple good nature. During the French Revolution, to which Roussel was opposed, his political enemy Gaspard de Chenu composed a song mocking his zany ways – which was adopted as the official marching anthem of the armies of the revolution.

 DRINKING IN AUXERRE: APÉRITIF O'CLOCK

La Péniche: Apéritif aboard a moored boat on the Yonne, with generous charcuterie platters and golden-hour views as the sun sets. *9am-8pm*

Le Galopin: Lively local favourite for craft beers and great cocktails. And after 10pm, it's where everyone ends up. *5pm-1am*

La Petite Vitesse: No-frills bar-tobacconist with a grand piano open to all to play – cheap drinks, lively locals and unbeatable ambience. *8am-7pm Mon-Sat*

Le Bar du Théâtre: Housed in a timber-panelled building, this cosy spot serves wine, snacks, bar games and live music in a warm, historic setting. *5pm-1am Tue-Sat*

Beyond
Auxerre

Dominated by vineyards and perfectly preserved medieval villages, to visit the countryside beyond Auxerre is to travel back in time.

Like other major Burgundian cities, the *pays auxerrois* is surrounded by vineyards but, aside from Chablis (the great town of chardonnay), these wine villages do not share the same shining reputation as those of the Côte d'Or.

The countryside beyond Auxerre is better known for its picturesque medieval villages. These towns rose to prominence during the Duchy of Burgundy and enjoyed several centuries of wealth as trading posts within the wine industry before the King of France, threatened by the Dukes' power, brought their industry to a halt. Nevertheless, many of these villages, like Noyers-sur-Serein, have been perfectly preserved: with their small wood-timbered houses and vine-covered streets, you'll feel as though you've stepped into a fairy tale.

Places
Noyers-Sur-Serein p445
Chablis p446

GETTING AROUND

The Yonne *département* is slightly better connected by TER train than the Côte d'Or, but exploring the surrounding countryside is still best done by car as train schedules are inconsistent and disruptions frequent. If you need a taxi, be sure to book several days in advance as drivers are few and in high demand. Free parking is available just outside most town centres.

Noyers-Sur-Serein   TIME FROM AUXERRE: 40MIN
A Perfectly Preserved Medieval Gem

Classified as one of the 'Most Beautiful Villages in France', Noyers-sur-Serein is a perfect example of Burgundy's medieval towns. Still the same size it was in the Middle Ages, it's encircled by remnants of its original city walls. Stroll its cobbled lanes, past timbered houses and flower boxes, and don't miss the **Lavoir de Noyers** – a stone washhouse built in 1802 where locals once did their laundry.

Creative Roots

In recent years, Noyers has attracted a wave of young artists, fuelling a flourishing local scene. Of note are leather specialists

 EATING IN NOYERS-SUR-SEREIN: OUR PICKS

Rouge et Blanc: A small, weekly-changing menu served in a cosy, timbered house. Reservations are essential. *6.30-9.30pm Thu-Sun* €

Restaurant de La Vielle Tour: Start with an apéritif in the fairy-lit courtyard, then enjoy a well-priced, seasonal menu made with local produce. *noon-2pm & 7.15-9pm, Fri-Tue* €€

Maison Paillot: Local butcher shop turned eatery serving charcuterie platters (don't miss the *jambon persillé*) with wines by the glass. *9am-12.30pm & 3-7pm Tue-Sat, 9am-12.30pm Sun* €

Les Millésimes: Tucked down a back alley, this cosy spot serves classic Burgundian fare and wines from the owner's own estate. *9.30am-5pm Mon, Thu & Sun, to 9pm Fri & Sat* €€

Chablis

CHABLIS' TERROIR

Chablis may only grow chardonnay, but don't let that fool you: there's nowhere else in the world that produces white wines quite like it. What sets Chablis apart is not the grape, but the ground beneath it. The vineyards sit atop Kimmeridgian soil, a unique blend of limestone, clay and prehistoric oyster shells from an ancient seabed that once covered the region. This fossil-rich *terroir* gives Chablis its hallmark flinty minerality and crisp salinity.

The sea salty taste of the wines is why Chablis pairs so naturally with oysters and other shellfish. Locals often say the best way to taste the *terroir* is with a dozen oysters on the half-shell and a chilled bottle of village Chablis.

Yazmhil et Brice Corman on the place de l'Hôtel de Ville, **Stéphanie Wahl**'s ceramics atelier and **La Poterie de la Maison des Sangliers**.

Be sure to pop in to the quirky **Musée des Arts Naïfs et Populaires** *(noyers-en-bourgogne.com/decouvrir/2429; adult/child €4/2)* jampacked with oddities and artworks by self-taught creators.

Ruins with a View

On the outskirts lie the ruins of the 10th-century **Château de Noyers**, dismantled by King of France in the 16th century and whose stones were repurposed to fortify the town's walls. Follow the Serein River north to find the trailhead; it's a 400-step climb with no handrail, but the panoramic views are well worth the effort.

Chablis

TIME FROM AUXERRE: 30MIN

Great Burgundian Whites

Chablis is Burgundy's great white wine village – and one of the few prestigious winemaking towns outside the Côte d'Or. Smaller and less touristy than its southern cousins, it's also friendlier to cellar visits. Within its centre, tastings can be booked at **Domaine Pinson**, **Laroche** and **Domaine Jean Collet et Fils**.

The best way to explore the vineyards is by bike: rent one from E-Bike Wine Tours *(e-bikewinetours.com; from €24)* and pack a vineyard picnic from **Les Jardins de Claude**, a charming *épicerie* known for regional cheeses and woven baskets. Don't miss the Plaisir au Chablis, a cow's cheese washed in Chablis wine and as *terroir*-driven as the wines themselves.

EATING IN CHABLIS: OUR PICKS

Le Maufoux: Traditional bistro in the town centre with a daily changing menu of local classics, based on what's freshest that day. *noon-1.30pm & 7-9pm Mon-Fri* €€

Au Fil du Zinc: Diners travel from afar for the gastronomic 5-7 course tasting menu showcasing seasonal creativity. *noon-1pm & 7.30-8.45pm Mon, Thu, Fri & Sat* €€€

Les Trois Bourgeons: Elegant, seasonal spot for traditional Burgundian fare like *oeufs en meurette* and bœuf bourguignon. *noon-1.30pm & 7.30-9.30pm Tue-Sat* €

Bistrot des Grands Crus: Convivial neo-bistro with playful takes on French classics and a gorgeous hidden courtyard. *noon-2pm & 7-9pm* €€

Places We Love to Stay

€ Budget €€ Midrange €€€ Top End

Dijon
MAP p421

Hotel Le Jacquemart € Ideally located just steps from the Palais des Ducs, this clean, modern hotel offers generously sized rooms and private parking – an excellent base for exploring the old town.

Le Petit Tertre € Charming family-run guesthouse with fully furnished apartments, each styled in lavish 18th-century decor. Home-cooked breakfast is delivered to your room each morning.

Hotel Maison Philippe Le Bon €€ Clean, comfortable rooms in a historic townhouse tucked away in a quiet corner of Dijon's old town, with warm, attentive staff happy to help with reservations.

La Cour Berbisey €€ Elegant boutique hotel in a beautifully restored 17th-century house near the city centre. Just five rooms, plus a heated indoor pool and sauna for ultimate relaxation.

Grand Hôtel La Cloche €€€ Dijon's only five-star stay, with chic modern rooms, secure overnight parking and an unbeatable location in the heart of the city.

Beaune
MAP p431

Burgundy Escape € Unique, well-equipped rental properties in and around Beaune, from cosy apartments to spacious homes for groups of all sizes. burgundyescape.com

Le Clos de l'Aigue €€ Cosy, family-run B&B just five minutes from the Hôtel-Dieu, with air-conditioned rooms, a sauna and a small pool.

L'Hôtel de Beaune €€€ A refined stay in a historic *hôtel particulier* and 16th-century cloister, with valet parking, a wine cellar and ever-knowledgeable staff.

Hostellerie Cèdre & Spa Beaune €€€ Luxury hotel set in a former mansion just outside the old town walls, with a full-service spa, romantic garden terrace and Michelin-starred restaurant.

La Villa Fleurie € Quaint, antique-furnished hotel just outside the centre, with warm, familial hosts who'll help you find your feet in town with restaurant reservations and local tips.

Auxerre
MAP p443

The Originals, Hotel Normandie €€ Fun, charming rooms in a playfully decorated bourgeois house, with parking just opposite and bikes available to rent.

Hôtel Les Maréchaux € Elegant 19th-century *hôtel particulier* set in tranquil private parklands, with a pool and free parking on site.

Le Relais des Saints Pères € Simple but charming guesthouse on the outskirts of the historic centre, set in a 400-year-old home with four cosy rooms, a homemade breakfast and warm, welcoming hosts.

Noyers-Sur-Serein

Côté Serein € Welcoming B&B in the heart of town with flexible room options for couples or groups, a seasonal pool and free use of kayaks and canoes on the peaceful Serein River.

La Vieille Tour € Charming guesthouse with rooms in a 13th-century tower, surrounded by a flower-filled garden. Homemade breakfast and views of the Serein.

Chablis

L'Hostellerie des Clos €€ A refined hotel in the heart of Chablis, with elegantly minimalist rooms, a tranquil spa, an exceptional local wine cellar and free parking

Hôtel du Vieux Moulin €€ Stylish boutique hotel in a converted 18th-century mill, with sleek modern rooms, exposed beams and a riverside terrace just steps from Chablis' main square

For places to stay in Lyon, Rhône Valley & Auvergne, see p492

Above: Pont d'Arc (p470), Gorges de l'Ardèche; Right: Beaujolais vineyards (p463)

Researched by
Anna Richards

Lyon, Rhône Valley & Auvergne

VOLCANOES, VINEYARDS AND ANCIENT HISTORY

Prehistoric caves, pilgrimages and some of the least explored parks in the country surround France's culinary capital, where every bistro is an epicurean adventure.

France's third city, Lyon, began life in the 1st century BCE as a Roman capital, Lugdunum, but that's recent history compared to its neighbours. To the west, the long-extinct volcanoes of Auvergne, some 11,000 years old, are a playground for hiking, mountain biking and even skiing. Just south, the towering limestone Gorges de l'Ardèche, the accumulation of billions of compressed fishbones, once lay under the sea and were formed some six million years ago. Labyrinthine caves also hide some of the oldest wall paintings in the country.

The relative inaccessibility is the region's charm, meaning Auvergne and the Rhône Valley haven't fallen victim to overtourism. Although often logistically complicated (and a car is invaluable!), here's where the intrepid can still enjoy panoramic mountain views in solitude in Cantal, sample wines at rock-bottom prices from pioneering young winemakers in Beaujolais and zip-line over gorges in the Ardèche hearing only birdsong.

At the heart of it all, Lyon still deservedly wears the crown as France's gastronomic capital. Sandwiched between two rivers and further watered by fine wines from Beaujolais to the north and the Rhône Valley to the south, it's a city where a day can start with breakfasting with *mâchon*, Lyon's offal and wine alternative to bottomless brunch, and finish dancing under moonlight in a 2000-year-old amphitheatre.

THE MAIN AREAS

LYON
Culinary capital with two rivers.
p454

GORGES DE L'ARDÈCHE
Adrenaline hive and ancient history. **p467**

LE PUY-EN-VELAY
Pilgrimages, medieval parties and religious history. **p476**

CHAÎNE DES PUYS
Explosive hikes and world-class cheeses.
p482

CAR

A car is invaluable for much of the rural Auvergne, where buses run infrequently. Ride-share platforms like BlaBlaCar are a great way of getting around if you don't drive, and car-rental apps such as Getaround are a practical way to cut rental costs.

BIKE

Hundreds of kilometres of bike lanes and Vélo'v stations make Lyon easy to explore from the saddle; electric Vélo'v speed up hilly sections (*€1.80/trip*). The city is intersected by the 815km ViaRhôna (p465), which runs from Geneva to the Mediterranean.

Chaîne des Puys, p482

Marmots frolic, rust-coloured cattle graze in pastures and cloud inversions form islands of volcanic peaks in a land where dinosaurs once roamed.

Le Puy-en-Velay, p476

The most important starting point on the French Camino de Santiago, Le Puy-en-Velay's cobbled streets, medieval festivals and volcanic stone churches give it a time-warp feel.

TRAIN

France's high-speed TGV network links major cities in the region to Paris, including Lyon (two hours), **Valence** (2½ hours) and **Montélimar** (three hours). Slower, scenic TER services link the capital with **Clermont-Ferrand** (3½ hours). Trains to Le Puy-en-Velay change at St-Etienne.

Find Your Way

On two wheels is the way to explore Lyon, where many of the bike lanes are as wide as roads. Auvergne rewards slow travellers with epic road trips, and the Ardèche's waterways beg to be kayaked.

Lyon, p454
Foodie capital Lyon has two thriving rivers home to floating restaurants, bars and clubs on *péniches* (barges), and tower block-sized murals filled with the city's history.

Gorges de l'Ardèche, p467
Limestone gorges sculpt a landscape equally fascinating above and below ground. Stalactite-laden labyrinths form the walls of France's incredible watery playground: the Ardèche River.

Plan Your Time

Don't underestimate distances: Auvergnat roads are slow, particularly when you're stuck behind a tractor. Skip typical to-do lists in Lyon – many of the city's treasures are reserved for travellers curious enough to *flâner* (stroll) the backstreets.

Train to Puy-de-Dôme (p484)

If You Only Do One Thing

● Loosen your waist belt and eat your way around **Lyon** (p454), France's culinary capital. Counterbalance visits to traditional *bouchons* (small bistros) with some of the city's veggie and fusion cuisine, make your own vintage at city wineries before dancing the night away on *péniche* clubs. Work up an appetite climbing up **Fourvière Hill** (p459) for views as far as Mont Blanc from the 19th-century basilica, and avoid the crowds by looking north over the Monts Lyonnais from **Cimetière de Loyasse** (p459). Unwind with a sundowner on the *terrasse* of bar-cum-bike repair shop **Velcroc** (p461) as the last rays hit the needle-like spires of **Basilica Notre-Dame de Fourvière** (p459).

Seasonal Highlights

Snow lingers on Auvergne peaks into late spring, summers are mild and rainfall high. Lyon, the Rhône Valley and the Ardèche are much drier.

JANUARY
Skiers hit the slopes in **Station du Mont-Dore**, **Le Lioran** and **Super Besse** (p488). Snowshoeing and nordic skiing are also popular throughout the Chaîne des Puys and Haute-Loire.

APRIL
The arrival of spring means Lyon's rivers come to life, with *péniche* (narrowboat) beer gardens spilling onto the banks. Water levels are high for kayaking the Ardèche River, although it's chilly for swimming.

MAY
Thousands of hikers embark on the Camino de Santiago from the 11th-century cathedral in **Le Puy-en-Velay** (p476). **Nuits Sonores** (p461), an electro festival running for five days and nights, transforms Lyon's former railway warehouses into giant parties.

A Few Days to Play With

● Hire a car to cruise around some of the most picturesque villages in Beaujolais, stopping to taste *crus* in châteaux and wineries as you go. Particularly picturesque are the *pierres dorées*, golden stone villages in southern Beaujolais. Stop for lunch at **La Table du Donjon** (p465) in Oingt with a view over the patchwork quilt of fields and vineyards stretching all the way to Lyon. Next, follow the Rhône south towards **Vallon-Pont-d'Arc** (p470) to spend a full day kayaking along the Ardèche River, passing under the 60m-high arch that gave the town its name. On the way back, stop in former Roman capital **Vienne** (p463) to admire mosaics at the **Musée et Sites de St-Romain-en-Gal** (p465) and the **Théâtre Antique** (p463).

If You Have More Time

● Drive out to the **Chaîne des Puys** (p482) to begin a road trip through France's volcanic heartland, a verdant and rural region where cows outnumber people. Catch the little train up to **Puy-de-Dôme** (p484) to find the ruins of the Gallo-Roman **Temple de Mercure** (p484) at the top. Squiggle-like roads wind south to **Mont-Dore** (p488), the base for summiting **Puy de Sancy** (p484), the highest peak in Auvergne. Follow the 'cheese route' south, dropping in at farms for tastings en route. Soak up the mountain views from **Chalet du Puy Mary** (p485), decorated with hundreds of cow bells. Sleep in a *buron* (shepherd's stone hut) before driving to **Le Puy-en-Velay** (p476) to learn about the history of the Camino and attend mass with hundreds of hikers.

JULY
Ancient amphitheatres reverberate with sound as **Nuits de Fourvière** (p461) in Lyon and **Jazz à Vienne** (p463) welcome acclaimed artists. Hiking season is in swing, particularly along the **Stevenson Trail** (p480), which many undertake with donkeys.

AUGUST
Ardèche's cool waters tempt tourists out of the cities, and Lyon becomes almost eerily quiet. At the end of the month, the *vendanges* (wine harvests) begin in Beaujolais and the Rhône Valley.

NOVEMBER
Gaudily dressed runners hydrate with wine as they tackle France's biggest boozy race during **Beaujolais Nouveau** (p465). The **Independent Winemakers' Showroom** arrives in Lyon, with tastings from small wine producers from all over the country.

DECEMBER
Lyon becomes a giant green screen for the **Fête des Lumières** (p461), the largest lights festival in the country, and mulled wine and roasted chestnuts are sold on every street corner.

Lyon

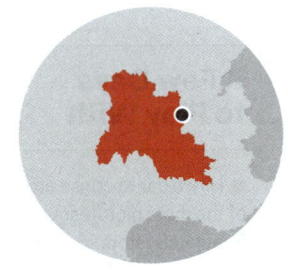

FINE WINE | UNPARALLELED DINING | VARIED HISTORY

☑ TOP TIP

Look down. Lyon has long been famous for giant murals designed as optical illusions which mimic building façades – but some of the best art installations are under your feet. Incognito street artist Ememem is Lyon's answer to Banksy, only they're solving the city's pothole problem by filling them in with mosaics.

First the Roman capital of the Gauls in the 1st century BCE, then European capital of the silk trade in the 16th century, Lyon's past has been multifaceted. As it industrialised and motorists began to pass through, it rose to prominence in the Michelin road guide, leading to the discovery of the city's unusual cuisine and *bouchon* restaurants. Eugénie Brazier, the first chef in the world to be awarded six Michelin stars (p458), was discovered here and had two Lyonnais restaurants.

Lyon today is wonderfully liveable. It has a sprinkling of everything: great food and wine, proximity to the mountains, immense parks, sugar factories turned clubs and architecture that yo-yos between Renaissance, baroque and art deco. In recent years, the city council has invested in all things green, meaning that bike paths are often as wide as car lanes, and footpaths and parks run along much of the riverbanks.

Before Lyon Came Lugdunum
Think about the Roman Empire

Until 43 BCE, Lyon was little more than a Gaulish village. Lucius Munatius Plancus, governor of Gaul, was sent to found a Roman colony by the senate, and Lugdunum was born. Under Emperor Augustus (27 BCE–14 CE) the city mushroomed, and many vestiges of its Roman origins are still standing

GETTING AROUND

Lyon's metro is comprehensive and reliable *(€2.10/journey)*. If doing multiple stops in a day, it's better value to get a day pass. A Lyon City Card *(€32/€44/€56/€68 for 24hr/48hr/72hr/96hr)*, available at **Only Lyon Tourist Office** on place Bellecour, includes entry into multiple museums, public transport, guided visits and certain boat trips. It's a bike-friendly city, so do as the Lyonnais do and travel on two wheels. Download the Vélo'v app for easy bike rental in the city.

Amphitheatre and Musée Gallo-Romain de Fourvière

today. The 1st-century-CE amphitheatre and **Musée Gallo-Romain de Fourvière**, home to summer concerts **Nuits de Fourvière** (p461) in June and July, is the largest. There's a great **museum** *(lugdunum.grandlyon.com; adult/child €7/3)* that thoroughly explores Lyon's origins and has plenty of interactive displays for kids, including one section where they can dress up as gladiators.

The 'other', smaller amphitheatre, the **Amphithéâtre Romain des Trois Gauls**, is free to visit. **Le Nid de Poule** *(le niddepoule.com)*, a performing arts festival with an open-air bar, takes place here from Tuesday to Saturday from late April to late June. Shows are largely in French.

Free to access and generally the domain of dog walkers and children hop-skipping over the ruins is the archaeological site behind **Cathédrale St-Jean-Baptiste**. The vestiges of the 4th-century Gaulish church at the **Jardin Archéologique** (behind the cathedral) were only discovered in the 1970s. Camp out on the terrasse of **Puzzle Café** to enjoy your morning coffee with a view over almost two millennia of history, backed by St-Jean-Baptiste's honey-coloured Gothic-Roman façade. On the front of the cathedral is France's only Muslim gargoyle, created in the sculptor's likeness in 2010.

WHAT'S A BOUCHON?

In other parts of the country, a *bouchon* is either a wine cork or a traffic jam. In Lyon, they're meat-heavy traditional restaurants formerly run by *Mères Lyonnaises* (Lyonnaise mothers), who'd feed workers cheap, cheerful and filling plates of offal, washed down with red wine. Restaurants sticking to tradition dish up *andouillette* (sausages made from pig intestines), kidney and tripe, and many of the upmarket *bouchons* have managed to make it quite palatable (though beware the tourist traps in Vieux Lyon). The truly traditional even serve *mâchon*: bottomless brunch with a Lyonnais twist. Instead of eggs and avocado, the menu includes *rognons de veau* (calf kidneys) and *tête de veau* (calf's head) all washed down with large quantities of wine…at 9am.

The spicy margaritas are incredibly moreish!

EATING IN LYON: PROPER GOOD GRUB

Circle: Six- or eight-course tasting menus where the quality of the simplest ingredients, like olive oil, shines through. *noon-1.15pm & 8-9.15pm Tue-Sat* €€€

Ayla: Franco-Lebanese sharing plates, as much of a feast for eyes as bellies. The tempura vine leaves stand out. *noon-2pm & 7.30-9.30pm Tue-Sat* €€

Astral: Classic French cuisine done well, managed by a young team. They also run wine tastings in the cellar. *noon-2pm & 7-9.30pm Thu-Mon* €€

Alebrije: Franco-Mexican fusion from one of Lyon's top female chefs, Carla Kirsch Lopez, who draws on inspiration from her two cultures. *7.30-9pm Tue-Sat* €€€

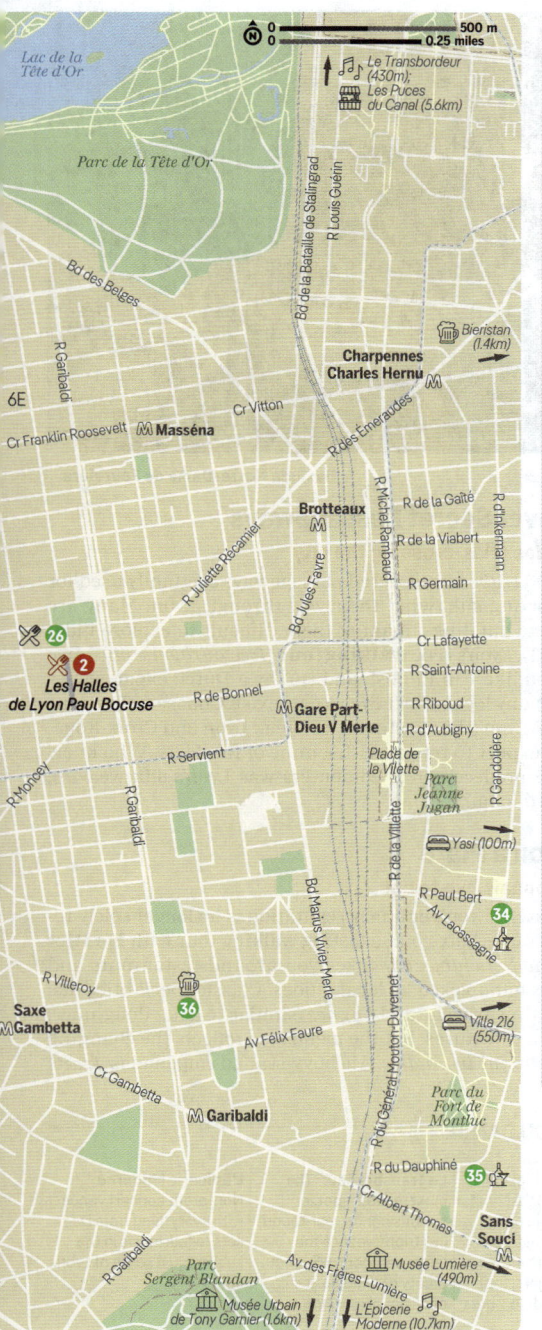

Basilica Notre-Dame de Fourvière

CELEBRATED CHEF EUGÉNIE BRAZIER

Eugénie Brazier (1895–1977) grew up in Ain, just outside Lyon, and had little education, but she began baking tarts with her mother as soon as she was old enough to hold a spoon. She worked as housekeeper to a wealthy Lyonnais family and honed her cooking skills from word-of-mouth recipes. She went on to work in several Lyonnais *bouchons*. Some years later, she opened La Mère Brazier and a sister restaurant-culinary school, where she trained some of the most celebrated chefs in the world, including Paul Bocuse. In 1933, Brazier became the first person ever to be awarded six Michelin stars, three for each restaurant. **La Mère Brazier** on rue Royale is still open and now holds two Michelin stars.

Discover Secret Passageways
Traboules criss-crossing the city

Over 400 *traboules*, covered passageways originally used for transporting silk, wind their way through Lyon. Many are in private buildings, making them difficult to explore independently. Lyon's **free walking tour** *(freetourlyon.com)* – give what you like – in English and run by a Dutch expat, shows places many locals don't even know exist. Choose from a tour of Vieux Lyon (the Old Town), or Vieux Lyon and Croix-Rousse, and expect to return with a mine of fun facts. Who knew that the predecessor to computers was Lyon's silk weaving Jacquard loom?

Lyon on a Plate
The Lyonnais live to eat

Fortunately, Lyon's culinary reputation is no longer solely reliant on offal. A six-course tasting walking tour with **No Diet Club** *(nodiet.club; €63)* takes you around restaurants and bakeries handpicked by local guides. Classic specialities like pink praline brioche and *bugnes* (similar to a flat doughnut), are regular features, but the menu also reflects the changing face of *cuisine lyonnaise*. Anchovy-stuffed empanadas, *fruits*

 DRINKING IN LYON: AS YOU DANCE

Hot Club: Regular jam nights in an atmospheric vaulted underground bar that has welcomed the likes of Louis Armstrong and Ella Fitzgerald. *7.30pm-midnight Wed-Sat*

Sonic: A dingy-looking *péniche* (barge) that hosts alternative music nights like darkwave post-punk. Sometimes there are noughties bangers, too, check the schedule. *hours vary*

Le Transbordeur: The most reliable spot for famous bands year-round, in a trippy yet not-too-large warehouse. Expect plenty of dancing and occasional moshing. *hours vary*

L'Épicerie Moderne: Non-profit concert venue with everything from DJ sets to folk music in the suburbs just south of Lyon. *hours vary*

de mer (seafood) and the quest to find Lyon's best pizza can all feature, although itineraries vary according to the guide you get and the day of the week. State any dietary requirements at the time of booking.

High on the Basilica Domes
A hill with history

It's difficult to imagine Lyon without **Basilica Notre-Dame de Fourvière** *(fourviere.org; free)* which dominates the skyline, but was only built at the end of the 19th century. The golden statue of the Virgin Mary predates the basilica: it was built by a local sculptor in 1852 and erected on the spires of the basilica to commemorate Lyon's liberation from the plague epidemic in 1643 (rumour has it that the disease never crossed the Rhône and stayed confined to the other side of Pont de la Guillotière).

Views from the top of Fourvière Hill are already impressive: they take in Lyon's twin rivers, the Saône and the Rhône, and (when you stand next to the basilica) the Alps. Around the back from **Cimetière de Loyasse** (about a five- to 10-minute walk away) you can also see the 'baby mountains', les Monts du Lyonnais.

The highest point, however, is from the basilica's domes. Inside the cathedral, stained-glass windows and ceilings adorned with golden stars and chandeliers of epic proportions create scenes straight out of a fairy-tale. Tours run daily from April to September *(booking.fourviere.org; adult/child €14/7)*. To get there, take the **funicular** from Vieux Lyon, or walk up through **Jardin du Rosaire**.

City Skiing
From sweating on dancefloors to slopes

Catch the metro at 5am in winter and you've got a curious mix. Students heading home after partying are to be expected, but the others are clad in salopettes, clutching skis and snowboards. **Skimania** *(skimania.com; from €57)* runs day trips to alpine ski resorts up to four times a week from December to mid-April, and the price of both your ski pass and return transfers from Lyon is often less than a ski pass purchased in station. Hire skis in Lyon or on-site with one of their partners for a discount.

Day trips range from some of the most famous ski resorts in the Alps (p546): Alpe d'Huez, Val Thorens and Courchevel,

LYON'S RESISTANCE HERO

During WWII, the *traboules* were the hideout of the French resistance. Jean Moulin, France's best-known freedom fighter, spent a considerable amount of the war in Lyon, and the resistance used the *traboules* to pass under the Gestapo's noses undetected, delivering messages. The secret passageways couldn't save Moulin though, and in 1943 he was captured by the infamous Klaus Barbie, an SS officer known as the 'Butcher of Lyon', and transferred to Montluc Prison, where he was brutally tortured. He died just days later. Recordings of Barbie's trial, and more on Lyon under the occupation, can be found at the **Centre d'Histoire de la Résistance et de la Déportation** *(chrd. lyon.fr; adult/child €6/free)*.

 EATING IN LYON: VEGGIE & VEGAN

Zoï: The butteriest tasting *pains au chocolat* in the city – and dairy-free. Prices are outrageously cheap. *8.30am-7pm Mon-Fri, from 10am Sat & Sun* €

Les Mauvaises Herbes: Inspired by his time onboard yachts, chef François Allemand draws influence from global cuisines. *7-11pm Tue-Sat, noon-3pm Thu-Sat* €€

Culina Hortus: Fine dining for herbivores in a majestic setting, with an extensive wine list. Dishes are works of art. *noon-3pm & 7.15-11pm Tue-Sat* €€€

Gustavo: Stomach-lining vegan fast food in party *quartier* La Guillotière, featuring seitan kebabs and falafel pittas. *11.45am-2.30pm & 7-10pm Tue-Sat* €

LYON'S ALTERNATIVE MUSEUMS

Lélia Withnell, Lyonnais illustrator who creates graphic designs of the city, shares her favourite museums. *@leliawithnell*

Musée Gadagne: A mash-up of Lyonnais history and puppetry with a fantastic hidden garden above street level. As enjoyable for adults as it is for kids.

Musée de l'Imprimerie et de la Communication Graphique: The museum tells you all about the history of books and graphic design techniques, but keeps it current with references to current design techniques.

Musée de l'Automobile Henri Malartre: This museum in Rochetaillée-sur-Saône, just north of Lyon, has the most spectacular setting – a château perched on a hill encircled by greenery. There's a very impressive collection of cars and bikes, too.

---

to smaller, family friendly stations like **Arêches-Beaufort**, **Chamrousse** and the **Sept Laux**. Buses leave between 5am and 7am from various points in the city. The rendezvous for the way back is religiously 4pm, and woe betide those who miss it – these buses don't wait. Transport-only passes for hikers are also available, as are weekend trips. Book as late as four days before to guarantee a bluebird day.

Open-Air Galleries
Frescoes, mosaics and Lyonnais history

Lyon's street art jumps out at you – this is a city with over 100 trompe l'oeils, optical illusions in the form of giant murals. The original was the **Mur des Canuts** in Croix-Rousse, the largest fresco in Europe when it was created. The 1200-sq-metre painting shows street scenes of the *quartier*: silk workshops, pedestrians and little nuggets of Lyonnais history, including the city's famous puppet, Guignol (similar to Punch and Judy).

Each one is a window into the history of different areas of the city, and artistic group CitéCreation works with residents to best depict their patrimony. In Lyon 1er, the **Fresque des Lyonnais** focuses on famous alumni, including the Lumière brothers, author Antoine de Saint-Exupéry and chef Paul Bocuse. It's always evolving and the community votes on who they'd most like to see on the wall. Occasionally, existing portraits are removed. In late 2024 Abbé Pierre, founder of a charity for the homeless, was blasted off the wall after being convicted of sex crimes.

Other frescoes particularly worth seeing are the **Fresque du Cinéma**, the **Fresque de Gerland** (celebrating success in the football World Cup) and and **Cité So'Coloc**, a leafy building painted like a window box on the walls of a social housing block for under 30s. For murals every which way you look, go to **Musée Urbain de Tony Garnier**, which has 25 murals planned by Lyonnais architect Tony Garnier, brought to life by artists all over the world. Download a full map at cm-tonygarnier.org to explore.

Lights, Camera, Action!
The birthplace of cinema

In 1870 the Lumière brothers Auguste and Louis moved to Lyon and studied at the city's technical school La Martinière. Twenty-five years later, they 'invented' cinema, showing the first presentation of projected film in Paris using their Cinématographe motion picture system.

The **Musée Lumière** *(institut-lumiere.org; adult/child €9.50/7.50)* in Lyon 3ème showcases the original cameras and video cameras used by the brothers, along with rotating exhibitions. In the same building, the **Institut Lumière** hosts regular cinematic screenings, including classic films, world cinema and animé, culminating in the Fête des Lumières in October, which attracts some of the biggest names in the industry (Tim Burton and Martin Scorsese have been previous guests, and night-long movie marathons feature).

Institut Lumière

In Vieux Lyon, the **Musée Cinéma et Miniature** *(musee miniatureetcinema.fr; adult/child €19.90/14.90)* provides a fascinating insight into the production and workings of more contemporary films, along with impossibly detailed miniature film sets. Costumes from the *Star Wars* series, scenery from *Alien vs. Predator* and props from the Harry Potter series make for a varied visit, although the ticket cost has increased astronomically.

Anarchistic Art
World news in pictures

La Demeure du Chaos *(demeureduchaos.com)*, in Lyonnais suburb St-Romain-au-Mont-d'Or, is a fascinating place. Catch one of several buses from Gare St-Paul in Vieux Lyon (40 minutes). The 'abode of chaos' is the collection of anarchist and artist Thierry Ehrmann, and the scrapyard-cum-dystopian film set makes you sit up and take notice. Far from pretty depictions of football match wins, here are nuclear disasters, Putin leering from walls, skulls bathing in blood and pasted headlines covering the shameful and distressing news of recent times. Open solely on Thursday afternoons on prior reservation, book online at least three weeks in advance.

BEST FESTIVALS

Nuits Sonores: Five day and night electro festival in May in the former SNCF warehouses. There are politically engaged workshops and talks when you're not raving.

Nuits de Fourvière: Nightly concerts held in the Roman amphitheatre in June and July, featuring all genres of music. Big names sell out with Glastonbury-esque speed.

La Fête des Lumières: France's largest lights festival with projections on buildings all over the city, including Cathédrale St-Jean. Held on and around 8 December.

Peinture Fraîche: Street art and graffiti interview with interactive displays and opportunities to create your own tags, held each October.

Lyon Street Food Festival: A bit pricey given the portion sizes, but a great opportunity to test small plates from top chefs. Runs for four days in June.

Try the chips with maroilles sauce, une tuerie!

 DRINKING IN LYON: BEST VIBES

Drôle d'Oiseau: The on-site microbrasserie makes for the ultimate short circuit, with draughts travelling one room from keg to glass. *5pm-midnight Tue-Wed, to 1am Thu-Sat*

Bieristan: The large beer garden and *Flammekueche* (Alsatian flatbread) make this a popular haunt in summer. A cooperative run by 20 people. *hours vary, closed Sun*

Canard de Rue: Duck themed, with a duck-heavy menu and rubber ducks, a nod to the owner's southwestern roots. *noon-1.30pm & 6.30-11.30pm Mon-Fri*

Velcroc: Former strip club turned bar-restaurant and bike repair workshop, with a sun-soaked terrasse. *5-11pm Sun-Wed, 5pm-midnight Thu-Fri, 3pm-midnight Sat*

On Canvas
Modern and classic art

Musée des Confluences *(museedesconfluences.fr; adult/child €12/free)* looks like a geometric, silver igloo at the confluence between Lyon's two rivers, the Rhône and Saône. The permanent exhibition is largely on anthropology and natural history, but it's the temporary exhibitions that lure people in, in recent years exploring everything from why we dream to why we fall in love.

Other galleries worthy of your time are the **Musée d'Art Contemporain** *(mac-lyon.com; adult/child €9/free)* for modern art or the **Musée des Beaux-Arts** *(mba-lyon.fr; adult/child €8/free)* for classical art and sculpture. The courtyard garden at the Beaux-Arts is free to visit and the shaded cloisters offer welcome respite from the summer end.

Lyon's Third River
Make your own vintage

Hemmed by Beaujolais to the north and the Rhône Valley to the south, it's little surprise that Lyon is often described as having three rivers: the Rhône, the Saône and an abundance of free flowing wine. **Chai Saint Olive** *(chaisaintolive.com)* buys its grapes from nearby wine growers and macerates them in the heart of the city. Visitors can book on for a tour and tasting, or learn to blend their own wine, coming away with a bottle of their homemade vintage at the end.

If you want to deep dive into the region's wines, unpack myth and snobbery around wine in general, and hear how many of our preconceptions around different types of wine come from history and politics, one person breaking down the jargon is Caroline Fazeli, who runs **Wine Dine Caroline** *(winedinecaroline.com; €100/€120 with lunch)* from a former silk weaver's studio in Croix-Rousse. An American – and what's more, a woman – she had to fight to build her reputation in France's male-dominated wine scene. Not your refined sip-and-spit affair; there's wine in abundance. Be prepared to unlearn everything you thought you knew – Beaujolais Nouveau (p465) isn't necessarily trash, chardonnay gets a bad rap and just because it's Bordeaux doesn't mean it's good.

FOOD & FLEA MARKETS

Les Puces du Canal: Vast flea market specialising in antiques. Go for Sunday lunch even if you're not shopping: it's cheap and a good spot for people watching.

Marché du Quai Augagneur: Weekends and Thursday afternoons from 2-8pm along the banks of the Rhône. Taco van is particularly good.

Quai St-Antoine: Lyon's largest food market on the banks of the Saône. Shoppers grab platters of oysters and perch on the riverbank.

Les Halles de Lyon Paul Bocuse: Covered market named after Lyon's legendary chef. Often expensive, but great for atmosphere, with French specialities like frogs' legs.

Marché de la Croix-Rousse: Neighbourhood food market with outsized veggies, excellent cheese stands and plenty of good cafes and brunch spots in the vicinity.

 DRINKING IN LYON: BEST WINE BARS

Les Assembleurs: Such a success they opened two; rue Mazenod is the original. Wines are quite literally on tap – mix your own combinations. *hours vary*

Odessa Comptoir: Largely organic and natural wines with a Middle Eastern tapas menu (excellent hummus). Try their orange wines. *6.30-11pm Mon-Wed, to midnight Thu-Sat*

BecBec: Friendly neighbourhood wine bar with an all-vegetarian menu. Extremely good value. *8am-11.30pm Wed-Fri, to 2.30pm Tue, 9.30am-11.30pm Sat*

Aromo: Cosy bar with wines from all over the world and date-vibe low lighting. Tapas, sharing boards and plenty of gin, too. *6pm-1am Tue-Sat*

Beyond Lyon

No one goes thirsty: vineyards abound in the Beaujolais hills and fertile Rhône Valley to the north and south of Lyon.

The golden stone villages of Beaujolais, quaint medieval towns like Beaujeu and more than 18,000 hectares of vineyards lend themselves to some of the most picturesque landscapes in the region, and with 10 *crus* (vineyards recognised as producing high-quality wine), it's a major player in wine production. To the south, the Rhône widens and is lined with hilltop vineyards sporting Hollywood-esque signs, among them E Guigal, Paul Jaboulet Aîné et Fils and Chapoutier. Some of the most prestigious wines in the country are grown here, and Condrieu, Tain and Crozes-Hermitage have become synonymous with high-end restaurants. These are regions best explored by bike – after all, four wheels are inadvisable after château-hopping and sampling the local tipples as you go.

Places
Beaujolais p463
Vienne p463
Rhône Valley p465
Hauterives p466

Beaujolais
TIME FROM LYON: **30MIN–1HR**
Cycle Through the Vines
Many wineries organise e-bike tours of their vineyards, but if you prefer to go under your own steam, tackle the 10km greenway between Belleville-en-Beaujolais and Beaujeu (find the map at velo-et-voie-vert-en-beaujolais.fr/fr). The tourist office rents electric bikes from Belleville's **Hôtel Dieu** *(beaujolais-tourisme.com; per half-day €25)*. Beaujeu is the former capital of Beaujolais and was the home of Anne of Beaujeu, princess and eldest daughter of Louis XI. An excellent wine tasting *(€2)* at community-run **Le Comptoir Beaujolais** offers great value for money. Servings are generous, the wines (all local) are delicious – many grown by female winemakers – and the service is friendly and informal.

Vienne
TIME FROM LYON: **20MIN**
Get Jazzy
The 1st-century **Théâtre Antique de Vienne** hosts the two-week jazz festival **Jazz à Vienne** *(jazzavienne.com; late June/early July)*. World-class artists and many of the biggest names in jazz perform in the ancient gladiator's arena. The sun sets directly behind the stage, making for two spectacles in one evening. Concerts last four or five hours, and before and after parties take place in town, too. Food and drinks are available,

GETTING AROUND
The main towns in Beaujolais, including Belleville-en-Beaujolais, Mâcon and Villefranche-sur-Saône, have regular trains to Lyon (all under half an hour on the speediest services). It's the same to the south: larger towns along the river including Vienne, Tournon-sur-Rhône and St-Clair-les-Roches are easy to reach. To get to most of the vineyards, which are in the countryside, it's a good idea to have a car, or at the very least a bike. Hire bikes in Lyon at **Lyon Vélo Location** (7ème).

463

ROAD TRIP THE MOST BEAUTIFUL VILLAGES IN BEAUJOLAIS

Drive past caramel-coloured stone houses, rows of vines that change with the season and turreted châteaux.

START	END	LENGTH
Oingt	Juliénas	53km; one day

Begin your road trip in the *pierres dorées*, Beaujolais' golden stone villages, which look lightly baked by sunlight even on rainy days. There are several Oingts a few kilometres apart, confusing for GPS. Aim for the small car park (paid) at **Parking rte du Bois d'Oingt**. The ruins of a medieval tower, the ❶ **Tour d'Oingt** are balanced like a cherry on top of the town's summit and views stretch to the Monts d'Or.

From here, drive north for 20km to ❷ **Vaux-en-Beaujolais** (D120/D504/D49E). Places regularly inspire stories; here the story inspired the place. Gabriel Chevallier's 1934 satirical novel *Clochemerle* explored a small village where petty problems like public urinals provoked arguments – and now murals all over town show scenes and characters from the book.

Another 24km north brings you to ❸ **Fleurie** (D43/D68E/D68), one of Beaujolais' *grand crus*, and the Beaujolais Wine Marathon's start point. Needle-like among the vines, Chapelle de la Madone crowns the landscape. You're in the heart of wine country, and the next stop, ❹ **Moulin-à-Vent**, (4km, D68/D68E1) is another *grand cru*. From the windmill there are 360-degree views over surrounding vineyards.

Finally, drive to ❺ **Juliénas** (5km, D68E1/D68/D17). Not officially a golden stone village, it's nonetheless toffee-coloured. The château is fairy-tale-like, with angular turrets, and there are heaps of wineries.

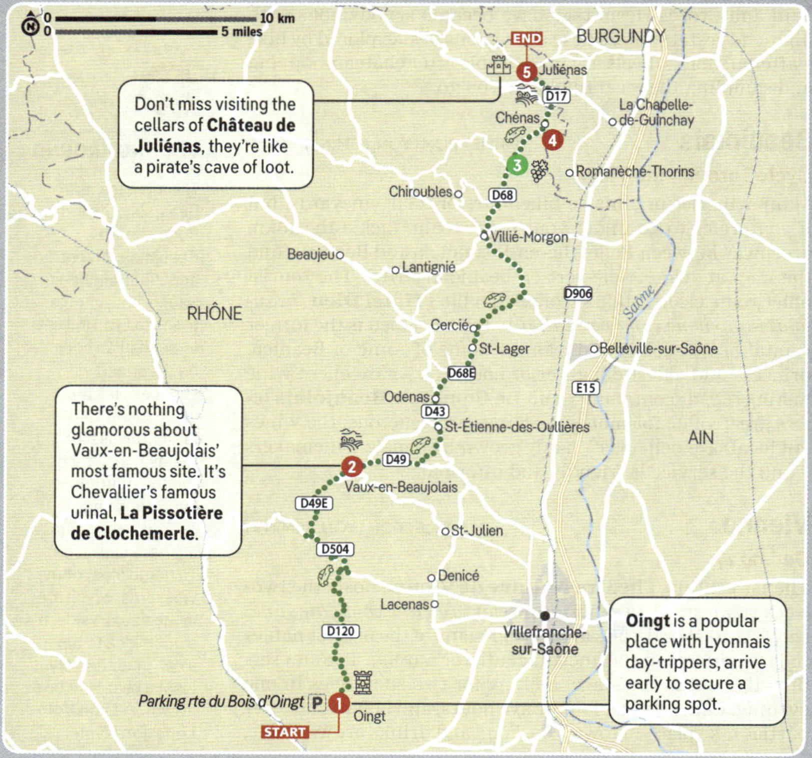

> Don't miss visiting the cellars of **Château de Juliénas**, they're like a pirate's cave of loot.

> There's nothing glamorous about Vaux-en-Beaujolais' most famous site. It's Chevallier's famous urinal, **La Pissotière de Clochemerle**.

> **Oingt** is a popular place with Lyonnais day-trippers, arrive early to secure a parking spot.

and trains and shuttle buses line up with concert schedules. Book transport spots a few days in advance. Outside of festival season, the **Quartier Latin Jazz Club** (quartierlatin-jazz-club.com), inside the Musée Gallo-Romain, hosts live Sunday afternoon jazz concerts at least twice a month. It's an intimate venue with views over the Rhône. Doors open from 5pm.

A Roman Holiday in Vienne

Rewind over 2000 years and Vienne, which now numbers fewer than 30,000 inhabitants, was more important than its neighbour Lyon – and one of the largest Roman strongholds in Gaul. The enormous mosaics at **Musée et Sites Archéologiques de St Romain-en-Gal** (musee-site.rhone.fr; adult/child €6/ free) are some of the finest you'll find anywhere, not just in France. The collection also features models of how the city was planned, pottery and other artefacts from the Roman period, mostly found on site. It's wonderfully comprehensive and entry is included with a Lyon City Card (p454).

Standing proudly in the town centre surrounded by cafes and residential buildings, like an escaped mini Pantheon, the **Temple d'Auguste et de Livie** is a multi-columned temple dating from at least 10 BCE. Grab a coffee and take a seat virtually underneath it.

Rhône Valley

TIME FROM LYON (VIENNE): **20MIN**

Cycling the ViaRhôna

The 815km cycling greenway linking Geneva to the Mediterranean follows the Rhône River all the way from source to sea; find route maps at viarhona.com. You'll need at least a week and strong calves if you want to tackle the whole route, but there are several sections that are easily accessible during a day. Vienne to Tournon-sur-Rhône, approximately 70km, is almost entirely flat, with some slight downhills. En route, you'll pass vineyards, châteaux, parks and fields on well-marked cycle paths which occasionally zigzag over one of the numerous bridges traversing the Rhône. Stop for tastings in Condrieu, fast becoming one of the most prestigious white wines in the country.

Once a year in May, the **ViaGusta** (vienne-condrieu.com; €46 without bike rental) turns a section of the ViaRhôna into an apéro-tour. Run by students at prestigious cooking school Lycée Hôtelier de l'Institution Robin, a ticket includes a five-course meal of amuse-bouche, starter, main, cheese and dessert, with wine pairings, served at intervals over a 9km

> **CELEBRATING BEAUJOLAIS NOUVEAU**
>
> Beaujolais Nouveau has gone viral. From California to Japan, the celebrations begin on the third Thursday of November, and the young wine from the same season's harvest is uncorked. It's little surprise that some of the biggest celebrations happen in Beaujolais. The **Beaujolais Wine Marathon**, held on the Saturday, attracts over 20,000 participants and finishes in Villefranche-sur-Saône. Fancy dress is the rule rather than the exception. There's a half marathon and 13km option for those keener on the wine tastings than the running aspect. Villefranche-sur-Saône has parties from Wednesday evening to Sunday, but the most traditional Beaujolais Nouveau celebrations are **Les Sarmentelles**, held in Beaujeu, also over the five days. Processions, flaming vine shoots stuck in barrels and open-door tastings all feature.

EATING IN BEAUJOLAIS: TOP PICKS

Ema: Deconstructed desserts and innovative mains like peanut-crusted polenta. Fantastic views. *noon-1.30pm Tue-Sat, 7.30-9.15pm Thu-Sat €€*

La Table du Donjon: Spectacular terrace enjoying views over the vineyards. Classic French cuisine, generous helpings. *noon-2pm & 6.30-8.30pm Wed-Sat, noon-2pm Sun €€*

L'USINE: An industrial chic smokehouse in an old factory. Buy some of their homemade bread to take with you. *noon-2pm & 7-9pm Thu-Sat €€*

Beurre Noisette: Menu changes weekly to focus on local, seasonal produce. Three-course lunches for €21. *noon-1.30pm Tue-Sat, 7.30-9pm Fri & Sat €€*

THE CONSCRITS

In 1880, Charles Hugand, local to Villefranche-sur-Saône, wanted to celebrate his 20 years since being called up for (then mandatory) military service. Ever since, and long after compulsory military service was abolished in France, anyone in Beaujolais celebrating a decennary birthday is considered a *conscrit* (conscripted). Each village celebrates their *conscrits* on a different weekend between January and May, and all participants wear a *gibus* (top hat) decorated with a ribbon in a colour denoting their age: green for 20-year-olds, yellow for 30-year-olds, a French tricolore for 80-year-olds, and so forth. Predictably for a wine region, parties are boozy and generally last several days.

Le Palais Idéal du Facteur Cheval

pedal. Portions feel on the small side, but perhaps that's because pedalling works up an appetite.

Hauterives

TIME FROM LYON: **90MIN**

The Postman's Dream Palace

Fuelled with social media feeds full of wanderlust, guidebooks and travel photography, most of us have a decent idea what a destination is going to look like before we arrive. Postman Joseph Cheval, delivering the mail in his rural community of Hauterives, La Drôme, never strayed far from home, but he regularly delivered the postcards of those who did. Inspired by the images of Hindu temples, Buddhist stupas and exotic wildlife, he began a project to satisfy his wanderlust – in his back garden.

In 1879 Postman Cheval began constructing his 'dream palace', **Le Palais Idéal du Facteur Cheval** *(facteurcheval.com; adult/child €9/5)*. Carved entirely by hand, the resulting building includes towers inspired by Babylon, shell grottos and surrealist columns distinctly reminiscent of Gaudí's Sagrada Família. The dream palace isn't large, and you can easily look around it in half an hour, but save time for the museum next door: it traces Postman Cheval's fascinating vision through the letters and postcards he delivered.

 DRINKING IN BEAUJOLAIS: TASTINGS TO TRY

| **Vignoble Perras**: An all-organic, family-run winery where the tasting cellar looks pulled from the pages of an interior design magazine. Basic tasting FOC. *noon-5pm Thu-Sat, 10am-noon Fri* | **Domaine Passot**: Come for the €5 tasting, stay for other activities including *mâchon* (brunch; 4 people minimum) among the vines. Campervan plots on site. *9am-noon & 2-6pm* | **Château de Pizay**: €10 tasting for 10 wines in spectacular surroundings, among Alice in Wonderland manicured gardens. *hours vary* | **Maison Jacoulot**: Liqueurs made with mint, lemon, plum and more in a distillery founded in 1891. Tastings are free. *8.30am-noon & 2-6pm Mon-Fri, from 10am Sat* |

Gorges de l'Ardèche

KAYAKING | GEOLOGY | NATURE

Limestone pillars higher than skyscrapers mask warrens of prehistoric caves, forests teem with wildlife (more than 500 species of plant and 100 species of animal), with the many twists and turns of the Ardèche River snaking through the middle: the Ardèche Gorges are wild, bold and a remarkable testimony to what can be created purely through the erosive power of water.

Millions of years ago, this part of France lay under the sea and the calcareous cliffs were formed from the bones of fish, crushed over time to create the porous, layered rock. Evidence of human habitation in the caves traces back some 300,000 years, when the area was home to prehistoric species: cave bears, cave lions and mammoths. Now the Ardèche River, gouging the limestone, creates a natural playground for thrillseekers, offering kayaking, paddle boarding, canyoning, climbing and mountain biking, and many other activities.

Prehistoric Cave Paintings
Upper Paleolithic Picassos

Grotte Chauvet 2 (*grottechauvet2ardeche.com; adult/age 10-17/child €18/9/free*) may be a replica of the original cave, which is closed to the public to avoid damaging the cave paintings, but it's a good one. The original, discovered in 1994, is a UNESCO World Heritage Site, and features cave paintings thought to be over 30,000 years old, composed of hand prints and sketches of cave bears, cave lions and mammoths. From the paintings it's possible to deduce incredible amounts of information, including the rough age and gender of the artists. The replica includes exceptionally informative guided visits and immersive sound and light shows.

Stick to the entry time on your ticket and go straight for the guided tour at the time stated when you arrive, as timings are strict. The visit of the cave replica itself lasts approximately one hour; factor in extra time for the sound and light show. Audio guides in English are available.

GETTING AROUND

It's difficult to get around Ardèche without a car, although your days will likely be spent outside, kayaking, paddle boarding, hiking and biking your way around. High-speed, TGV trains run to Montélimar, from where there are buses to Vallon Pont-d'Arc, taking one hour and 20 minutes. Hertz, Enterprise and Europcar all have car hire outlets in Montélimar.

☑ TOP TIP

If all roads lead to Rome, in Ardèche they all lead to Vallon-Pont-d'Arc, a tourist town teeming with water-sports rentals and souvenir shops. It's a necessary evil for kayak rentals, but sleep out of town if you've got a car.

THE GORGES OF THE ARDÈCHE

- **HIGHLIGHTS**
  1. Grotte Chauvet 2
- **SIGHTS**
  2. Belvédère des Templiers
  3. Belvédère du Serre de Tourre
  4. Pont d'Arc
- **ACTIVITIES**
  5. Aigue Vive
  6. Grotte Aven d'Orgnac
  7. Grotte St-Marcel
- **SLEEPING**
  8. Bivouac de Gaud
  9. Bivouac de Gournier
- **EATING**
  10. Le Petit Jardin
  11. Le Picourel
  12. Ô Tapas'oif

Take Blind Tasting Up a Level
Stalactites, stalagmites and sauvignon

Tasting wine underground feels a little like a Prohibition bar on steroids – except that here, you're dressed in a fetching red boiler suit, a hard hat and a headlight. 'Speleoenologie' is a combination of caving and wine tasting in the caverns and passageways of **Grotte St-Marcel** *(€78)*. Tours typically start at 9am Sundays. Yes, we're talking breakfast wine.

Accompanied by two guides (a speleologist and a sommelier), a visit includes awe-inspiring views of stalactites and stalagmites. Some of the caves, including a vast, hall-like cave named the cathedral, and another known as the organ, are immense. In other places, prepare to travel bent double, on all fours, or (this part is optional) on your belly like an earthworm. The wine tasting happens in the caves themselves, and when the headlights are extinguished, the dark and the silence are absolute, and all of the wines served are local. Get prepared to establish whether you can really tell a red from a white in sensory deprivation.

Other visits on offer at Grotte St-Marcel include ordinary speleology, or a sportier 'sensations' visit which includes rappelling through the caves and mud slides. There are also simple, walking visits to the illuminated, main sections of the caves *(available daily, €15)*.

Road Trip the Belvédères
The drive with a dozen panoramas

Oh OK, there are eleven *belvédères* (panoramic views), but that doesn't have quite the same ring to it. The 29km winding road between Vallon Pont d'Arc and St-Martin-d'Ardèche, meandering along the cornice of the gorges, has bird's-eye views over the river. Factor in at least an hour to account for plenty of photo stops and be prepared to drive slowly; the hairpin bends often hide cyclists.

Eyes to the sky, the *belvédères* are a fantastic place for spotting vultures, eagles and falcons. They nest in the limestone cliffs, pockmarked with caves that were also used by Resistance fighters as hideouts during WWII. **Belvédère du Serre de Tourre** is the best viewpoint for birdwatching, while **Belvédère des Templiers** has some of the best views of the river meanders.

Pimp Your Ride
Two wheels over four

Road tripping the Ardèche's belvédères is particularly popular with motorcyclists, with its twists and turns like loops in a roll of rope. **Good Motors** rents motorbikes from Avignon TGV, from where it's an hour's drive to St-Martin-d'Ardèche, at the southern end of the gorges. The deposit is steep (€1000, which tends to be debited from foreign bank cards and refunded a few days after the trip), and you might want to consider bringing your own helmet – they rarely have integrated jaw protection – but there's a great choice of bikes, from classic looking Royal Enfields to sporty and speedy Hondas, and service levels if you encounter problems are excellent. Book online in advance, it's done through an app and there are no staff on site.

The Cavernous Aven d'Orgnac
A limestone wonderland

The fact that no one deemed fit to paint a cave lion on the walls doesn't detract from the majesty of **Grotte Aven d'Orgnac** *(orgnac.com; adult/child €16/11)*, an 100-million-year-old network of caves. The site was only discovered in 1935 by Robert de Joly, and has largely been left as it was found, with a couple of dummies abseiling down from the hole in the cave roof to give an idea of scale. A walkway of 700 steps

A MARATHON BY WATER

Never jumped on the running hype? Ardèche's 'marathon' *(marathon-ardeche.com)* takes place on the water each year on the second weekend of November. Launched in 1985 (the same year as the Marathon du Médoc), it never reached Médoc levels of fame, but still attracts plenty of international competitors. It's shorter than a regular marathon, and participants race either 34km or 27km down the Ardèche River. Any waterborne mode of transport goes: kayak, paddleboard, dugout canoe or floating soapbox. Expect plenty of fancy dress, face paint and freezing rapids. Many people undertake it as a team.

EATING IN GORGES DE L'ARDÈCHE: OUR PICKS

Le Petit Jardin: Excellent river fish and a pretty garden with heaters and blankets. *noon-1.15pm & 7-8.30pm Wed-Sun, 7-8.30pm Tue* €€

Les Chevaliers: In the heart of Viviers, with inventive savoury crêpes (get creamy leek and river trout) and plenty of local wine. *noon-2pm & 7-10pm Tue-Sun* €€

Le Picourel: Hearty portions offering great value for money. Everything is homemade and they're one of the few places open year-round. *noon-2pm & 7-9pm* €

Ô Tapas'oif: Mexican, French and Spanish fusion with plenty of veggie options and an extensive cocktail menu. *hours vary, closed Tue* €€

KAYAK TRIP

Kayak the Gorges

Kayaking the Ardèche River is what climbing the Eiffel Tower is to Paris. It also reaches Parisian ring road levels of busy in high season, so much so that a website is in place to predict how busy the river will be. Canoë Malin can be consulted via the tourist office website *(gorges-ardeche-pontdarc.fr)*. The 32km descent is doable in one long day, or split over two. Shorter 7km and 13km routes are also possible.

❶ Vallon Pont-d'Arc

A little like a ski resort for kayaks, Vallon Pont-d'Arc is a sprawling mass of rental shops without a clearly defined centre. There's plenty of choice and so long as your kayak is seaworthy, rentals are much of a muchness, supplying laminated maps and a watertight tub for your belongings, and organising your return transfer at the end of whichever distance you choose to tackle. **Aigue Vive** *(aigue-vive.com)* are helpful and efficient.

The Route: Paddle south with the river for 4km, leaving civilisation behind you to reach the Pont d'Arc.

❷ Pont d'Arc

It doesn't take long to reach the showstopper, but what those who've taken the land route don't see are the caves inside the **Pont d'Arc** itself. By kayak, you can dip in and out of the caves and crane your neck to take in the 54m-high rock arch from the water.

Kayakers, Ardèche River

The Route: There's only one way to go on a river, and that's to keep following the current. The road deviates from the water to climb to the corniche at the top of the gorges, increasing the feeling of remoteness.

❸ Bivouac de Gaud

The first of two wild campsites, **Bivouac de Gaud** takes 12km of paddling to reach, and if you're tackling the full descent, don't stop for lunch before you get here. Some of the gnarliest rapids you'll encounter are between the Pont d'Arc and Gaud, but most are only Grade II with a couple of Grade IIIs.

The Route: A short 5km paddle takes you to the next camp spot, Bivouac de Gournier. The river flows quickly here.

❹ Bivouac de Gournier

Both of the **wild campsites** require you to obtain a permit from the tourist office in Vallon-Pont d'Arc to prevent overtourism (€16.50). They're typically open from April to September, but early season visitors would be wise to check. Some 17km into your trip, the rocky beach is the perfect place to picnic.

The Route: Right up until the final 4km, the cliffs of the Ardèche tower up around you, often reaching 300m high. Look out for vultures wheeling overhead, and goats coming down to drink at the river.

❺ Sauze

Sauze marks the end of the odyssey, and although it's tiny, it feels quite the metropolis after the wilderness. A large, flat car park is where you disembark, and there are several restaurant-bars by the river for thirsty kayakers. Keep a wide berth from the bank at the end to avoid getting tangled in fishing lines, it's a popular spot for fishermen.

BEST OF ARDÈCHE VILLAGES

Labeaume: Houses merge seamlessly with rock faces like something out of a fantasy film. The 'hanging gardens' are little more than a veg patch, but the views are wonderful.

Balazuc: Best viewed from the many-arched Balazuc Bridge crossing the Ardèche River, Balazuc's houses climb steeply uphill, squished together haphazardly, linked by narrow passageways.

Vogüé: The ruins of an old château languish in the river, with the castle that's still standing a few streets back from the water.

Salavas: World's apart from Vallon Pont-d'Arc across the river: one mushroomed, time stood still in the other.

Rochemaure: Crowned by the crumbling vestiges of a château, cobbled streets pass blue shuttered houses, window boxes overflowing with flowers and plenty of sunbathing cats.

Grotte Aven d'Orgnac (p469)

takes visitors down into the belly of the caves, where limestone stalactites and stalagmites create immense columns like dripped candle wax from floor to ceiling.

There's a short sound and light show at the end of the visit, and, fortunately, an elevator to take you back to the surface again. English language tours only run daily in July and August, with visits lasting roughly an hour. Group sizes are large, with 60 or so people in each time slot, which can make for an experience a little like herding cats; as a result the commentary can be a little hard to follow. But there are few places with such impressive natural rock formations.

A Time-Warp Town
It's still the 15th century here

Former seat of the bishopry of Vivarais, a historic region that covered most of Ardèche, and parts of neighbouring regions including Gard, Haute-Loire and Drôme-Provençale, **Viviers** began life in the 5th century. It stayed in the Renaissance, however: the biannual **Fête de la Renaissance** is the highlight of the town's calendar (at the time of writing, the next one was slated for 30–31 May 2026).

Refusal to leave the 15th century in the past is year-round. Walking through the medieval cobbled streets, many of the shop owners and residents have proudly stuck photos of their best Renaissance garb in their windows. After dark, when river cruises dock, there are often pantomime-esque medieval reenactments in town. Walk up to **Cathédrale St-Vincent**, which dominates the town to the point that the rest of the houses look like an extension of the castle walls; it's possible to drive, but wider cars won't pass through the stone arch. The oldest parts of the cathedral date from the 11th century, although the cathedral was added to, partially destroyed and rebuilt again during the 700 intervening years. Views from up the top take in vast swathes of the surrounding countryside and the Rhône River.

Beyond Gorges de l'Ardèche

There are few crowds here, just semi-ruined monasteries, farms, orchards and a delightfully slow pace of life.

An adventure playground for those looking for the road less travelled, the middle mountains of the Monts de l'Ardèche offer a plethora of mountain biking, hiking, climbing, via ferrata and kayaking in pristine surroundings with a fraction of the crowds that descend on the Pont d'Arc. Rocky hills made from sedimentary and volcanic stone mask remote little villages, waterfalls spring out at every turn, and chestnut trees flank footpaths and country roads, which plunge into valleys and wind up to hilltop peaks.

On its journey south from Vienne to Montélimar, the Rhône passes medieval towns with Gothic cathedrals and crumbling castles. Walled villages hide winding cobbled streets that climb past blue shuttered houses with stone walls to panoramic viewpoints.

Places
Monts de l'Ardèche p473
Drôme Provençale p475

Monts de l'Ardèche

TIME FROM GORGES DE L'ARDÈCHE: **FROM 1HR**

Soak at the Spa

Rainy days never looked better than at the **Thermes de Vals-les-Bains** *(thermesdevals.com; €27/31 weekdays/weekends)*. A sequoia redwood ceiling frames a spa circuit of 14 different stages, including Jacuzzis, cold water plunges, indoor and outdoor pools, a hammam and a sauna. In fine weather, the loungers around the outdoor pool are a real suntrap. There's also an extensive spa treatment selection (reserve treatments in advance to avoid disappointment).

Dangle at the Devil's Bridge

The Ardèche was made for climbing. Rivers slice through every available section of precipitous cliff, creating deep gorges. At **Pont du Diable** (Devil's Bridge) a route takes you up one side of the gorge before ziplining over and scaling the other side. It isn't particularly technical, but if it's your first time tackling a via ferrata, it's best to go with a guide. If experienced, hire your gear from **Location Via Ferrata Pont du Diable**.

GETTING AROUND

Car is your only option for much of the Monts de l'Ardèche and Drôme-Provençale, although TER train services link some of the Drôme's larger towns like Die and Nyons in Drôme-Provençale.

Lavender fields, Drôme Provençale

LES CASTAGNADES

The Ardèche's chestnut festivals last a full month between mid-October and mid-November, as different villages in the Monts take turns to host celebrations with music, parades, markets and fairs, tastings and, naturally, the scent of roasting chestnuts in the air. Giant skillets toast hundreds, if not thousands, of chestnuts at a time. There are 65 different types of chestnut grown in this region and it was a dietary staple in the Middle Ages, so expect plenty of period costume and frequent appearances from the Brotherhood of Chestnuts. For the full schedule (generally around eight villages participate) visit castagnades.fr.

The starting point is just above the Pont du Diable, and once you've got your harness, helmet and carabiners, a short scramble takes you to the start of the via ferrata. The first hundred metres or so are essentially a steep, woodland walk, before crossing a cable suspended above the river. There are two escape routes during the climb (which typically take around two hours) so keep an eye out for weather changes.

After roughly an hour, a zip line crosses the Ardèche River (which is much narrower here than further down in the gorges). Although you're already high up, the climb is far from done, and the next section of the via ferrata has some long climbs with small overhangs which you'll feel in your arms if you're not a habitual climber. There are also some steep descents on rungs. Views are wonderful, with trees and steep, rocky hills as far as the eye can see. The Devil's Bridge (the stone bridge, which gave the via ferrata its name) is crossed on foot just before arriving at base, where coffee and snacks are available at the hire centre.

 DRINKING AROUND GORGES DE L'ARDÈCHE

Domaine Eyguebelle: Liqueurs ranging from peach to pear in a former abbey surrounded by lavender fields, southeast of Montélimar. *10am-6pm Fri-Wed*

Brasserie DRAC: A lively little microbrasserie and taproom in the gorgeous riverside village of Jaujac. *4-9pm Tue-Sat*

Brasserie des Gorges de l'Ardèche: A large patio looks directly onto the Ardèche River in Ruoms. Hosts regular concerts. *11am-3pm & 5.30-11pm Jul & Aug*

Maison Jaillance: A cooperative in Die including some 200 winemakers, specialising in Clairette de Die AOC (sweet, sparkling white wine from muscat grapes). *10am-12.30pm & 2.30-6.30pm*

Cycle the Dolce Via

A 90km cycling greenway, the **Dolce Via** (dolce-via.com) is delightfully flat in contrast with the rest of the landscape, as it follows an old railway line. Shaped like a wonky forked tongue, it runs from St-Agrève to La Voulte, with a section branching off Lamastre, the start point for the current Train de l'Ardèche (trainardeche.fr) steam train. The largely gravel track goes over multiple viaducts, criss-crossing over the Eyrieux River. Much of the route follows the water and the many meanders of the river. There's less than 1500m of elevation gain across the whole 90km, with the 17km stretch between St-Martin-de-Valamas and St-Agrève being the hilliest. Many people choose to combine a section of the route with the steam train, riding the rails between Lamastre to St-Jean-de-Muzols, and cycling 28km back again. A one-way adult ticket plus bike costs €30, and bike spots are limited; don't leave booking to the last minute. There's no bike rental outlet in Lamastre or St-Jean-de-Muzols, but you can rent in Tournon-sur-Rhône from **Tournon Cycles** (tournon-cycles.fr) which has e-bikes, a quick pedal (2km) along a departmental road from the train station in St-Jean-de-Muzols.

Drôme Provençale

TIME FROM GORGES DE L'ARDÈCHE: 1HR

See France's Secret Lavender Fields

While the masses flock to Provence to see the lavender in bloom from mid-June to mid-July, in the Ardèche and the Drôme, they're laughing. The lavender fields might not be on the same scale, but the buzzing of bees is more prevalent than the click of camera shutters. The picture-perfect fortified village of Grignan draws the most crowds for aerial views over the lavender from the château. At **La Maison de la Lavande** (lamaisondelalavande.com; adult/child €10/free) in Ardèche, a little road train works a circuit around the lavender, where a fat sow is often roaming freely. There's also a little museum and a rather twee immersive film, in French with English subtitles. **Domaine de Saint-Paulet** (saintpaulet.com; by appointment only) in the Drôme is a triple whammy, producing wine, lavender and black truffles over 25 hectares. The canine truffle hunters are a highlight.

MONTÉLIMAR'S NOUGAT

The Ardéchois have a penchant for sugar, and it's not just crème de marrons (chestnut paste) that they're using to satisfy their sweet tooth. Montélimar is known for its nougat production, and the town has been producing the sweet for well over 300 years. A true Montélimar nougat contains at least 28% almonds, 25% lavender honey and 2% sugar, egg white, vanilla and pistachio nuts. It became particularly famous when motor travel took off after WWII and motorists heading for the French Riviera would stop off to buy snacks en route. There are still dozens of nougatiers in town but head to the **Arnaud Soubeyran Factory** just outside the centre to try multiple flavours.

Le Puy-en-Velay

CHURCHES | COBBLESTONES | THE CAMINO

GETTING AROUND

Parking in central Le Puy-en-Velay is a nightmare and traffic is greatly restricted, but cheap parking is available at Parking de Cluny, just a short walk from the old town. TER train services run regular links with St-Étienne, from where trains go all over the country.

It's as though time stood still after Le Puy-en-Velay reached the Middle Ages. Perhaps it's the relative absence of transport links, or the fact that many people arriving or leaving do so on foot, but the cobbled streets of Le Puy-en-Velay have remained firmly steeped in tradition. Sandwiched between two *puys* (basalt rocks), the town sits in a basin, presided over by an enormous statue of the Virgin Mary on one hill, and the needle-like Chapelle St-Michel d'Aiguilhe chapel on the other.

The main starting point for the Camino Francés, the French section of the Camino de Santiago, Le Puy-en-Velay is regularly humming with hikers and pilgrims. From here it's a 750km walk to St-Jean-Pied-de-Port on the Spanish border, which generally equates to over two months.

France's secularism seems somewhat obsolete here: a city dominated by a vast cathedral, whose entire past and present is wrapped up in Catholicism.

Get Lost in Time

Head to the city heights

You don't have to be attending a historic festival or walking an ancient pilgrimage to feel the centuries of history that have shaped Le Puy-en-Velay. Begin your visit by climbing up to the Virgin Mary, the **Statue de Notre-Dame de France**, for a 360-degree panorama from the crown (the final stage involves climbing up a ladder). Built in 1860, it was constructed using the metal from 213 Russian cannons taken by Napoleon III during the Crimean War. Locals will tell you that the sculptor killed himself after finishing the statue, when he realised he'd put the baby Jesus on the wrong side – but since this rumour is thought to have gone into circulation in the 1930s it's unlikely to be true.

Next, tackle the 268 steps up to the **Chapelle St-Michel d'Aiguilhe**. Built in 961 CE, there are faded remnants of centuries-old wall frescoes in the chapel. The 11th-century

☑ TOP TIP

Do your research before choosing a restaurant. As so many hungry pilgrims spend just a night or two in Le Puy-en-Velay, there's a glut of some of the very worst restaurants in the country, but the good ones are there if you're prepared to search for them.

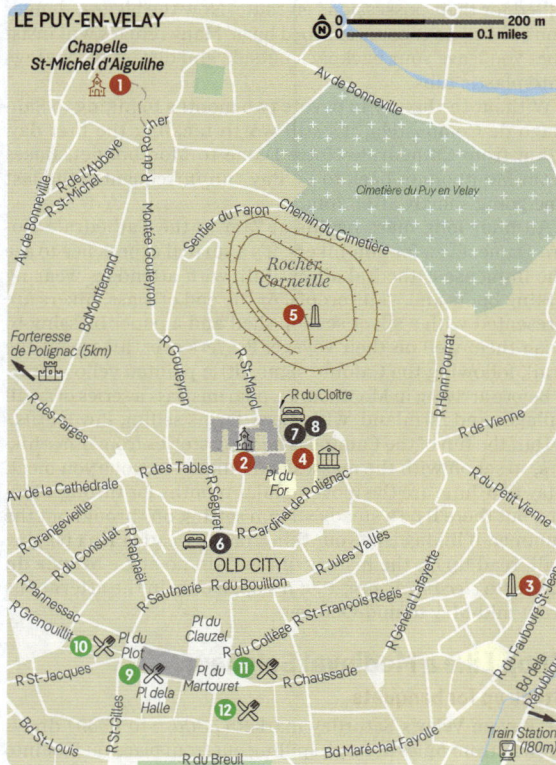

LE PUY-EN-VELAY

HIGHLIGHTS
1 Chapelle St-Michel d'Aiguilhe

SIGHTS
2 Cathédrale Notre Dame
3 La Fresque du Puy-en-Velay
4 Le Musée du Camino
5 Statue de Notre-Dame de France

SLEEPING
6 Demeure du Lac de Fugères
7 Gîte de la Prévôté
8 Les Cimes

EATING
9 Caulet-Flori
10 Chez Mon Pote
11 Coco & Rico
12 Merry & Pippin

PUY LENTILS

People who've never heard of Le Puy-en-Velay have still likely heard of the town's green lentils, which are on sale all over the world. They've been grown in the area for over 2000 years and are considered unique for their peppery flavour, and because they retain their shape when cooked. These lentils were brought over by the Romans and flourish here thanks to the volcanic soil. Now recognised with AOP (Appellation d'Origine Protégée) status, they're prepared in many restaurants in Le Puy-en-Velay, generally served mixed with meat and potatoes, or sold as a side dish or mixed into a salad.

Forteresse de Polignac is just a 10-minute drive from town (or over an hour on foot!), imposingly stationed on a rocky hill with some delightfully creepy dungeons.

A Pass'Card from the tourist office *(lepuyenvelay-tourisme.fr; €14)* grants entry to all three.

Embark on the Camino de Santiago
Mass and a pilgrimage

Hiked by over 300,000 people each year, the Camino de Santiago (or Chemin de St-Jacques as it's known in France), is one of the most popular long-distance hiking trails in the world. There are branches of the Camino all over Europe, but one of the most famous is the Camino Francés, which runs from Le Puy-en-Velay to St-Jean-Pied-de-Port on the France-Spain border. It first became a pilgrimage route in 951 CE when the bishop of Le Puy, Godescalc, embarked on his journey from Le Puy-en-Velay's **Cathédrale Notre-Dame**.

Throughout the Middle Ages, noblemen paid poorer members of society to undertake the pilgrimage on their behalf. The route was dangerous, and many pilgrims would be robbed or killed for their possessions en route. Now the biggest danger you're likely to encounter is bed bugs. Many refuges will insist that you leave your backpack outside and decant belongings into plastic tubs.

Without the luxury to devote two months to hiking to Santiago de Compostela, it's still worth tackling the first day, 17km from Cathédrale Notre-Dame to Montbonnet. Buses from Montbonnet back to Le Puy run infrequently, the last one going shortly after 2pm.

An hour-long mass begins at 7am in the Cathédrale Notre-Dame. Even for non-hikers, it's a surreal experience to see the immense cathedral all but full, with attendees wearing hiking boots and waterproofs. At the end of mass, hikers are presented with a silver scallop shell and a paper blessing to wish them well on their voyage. Prayers over, hikers hit the trail, following the Camino signs, little painted yellow suns.

Before arriving in Montbonnet, pilgrims pass a series of small villages and farmland, with many farms selling Puy lentils.

Half the fun of the Camino is hearing stories from other hikers, so set off with the masses and talk to everyone you meet. May and June are the most popular months for through-hikers, but there'll be a steady stream setting off throughout the summer. If hiking isn't your thing, or the weather isn't playing ball, read up on the history of the Camino at **Le Musée du Camino** *(lecamino.org; €7)*; it's open only in the afternoons from mid-May to mid-October.

Shop Like a Medieval Seigneur
Stock up for banquets

Le Puy-en-Velay's Saturday market *(7.30am to noon)* draws crowds from miles around, spilling out from place du Plot into the cobbled (and dare we say rather dingy) streets around. There's a wealth of produce from the surrounding countryside, including plenty of cheese stands, honey, mushrooms and meats. Walk for 10 minutes to the intersection of *faubourg* St-Jean and rue Droite to try to spot **La Fresque du Puy-en-Velay**, a street scene mural which covers the entire wall of a four-storey building. From afar, it looks like any other street in Le Puy, but as you approach you can see the people in the painting wearing pantaloons and holding bows and arrows, in homage to La Fête du Roi de l'Oiseau.

LA FÊTE DU ROI DE L'OISEAU

Each year, on the third weekend of September, the town plunges itself into the past with an enormous medieval festival, **La Fête du Roi de l'Oiseau**. With pomp, parades and puffy pantaloons, the inhabitants of Le Puy-en-Velay (and neighbouring communes) don full fancy dress and celebrate 'the good old days', setting up medieval encampments, jousting and dancing all over town. The festival culminates with an archery competition to crown the 'King of the Birds', which in centuries gone by entitled the winner to a year without paying taxes. Festival-goers consume *hypocras* (a medieval sweetened wine) in vast quantities and evenings are full of ruddy, wine-stained revellers looking like Henry VIII after a hunt.

EATING IN LE PUY-EN-VELAY: FOR HUNGRY HIKERS

Coco & Rico: Popular with a young crowd. Burgers, wraps and plenty of fried chicken. *noon-2pm & 6.30-10pm Mon-Sat, 6.30-9.30pm Sun* €

Merry & Pippin: Cheesy decor but good, hearty food and a warm atmosphere. *noon-1.45pm & 7-9.30pm Thu-Mon* €€

Chez Mon Pote: Largely meat dishes and burgers. Portions are generous and the food full of flavour. *8am-3pm Tue-Sat, 8am-3pm & 6.30-11pm Fri* €€

Caulet-Flori: Excellent little vegetarian joint which usually has a choice of just two dishes at lunch. Also does takeaway. *10am-6pm Mon-Sat, from 9am Sun* €

Beyond Le Puy-en-Velay

Forests and farmland hide centuries-old monasteries and churches in some of the least explored regions of France.

Tell friends you're off to Haute-Loire and you'll get blank looks, be they French or foreign – but this is a region full of history, unspoilt hiking trails and winter cross-country skiing, which rewards intrepid adventurers. Haute-Loire in general was once a very rich area, thriving on the lace trade. Now it's a sleepy sort of place, although it's certainly got character. In Livradois-Forez, the regional park northwest of Le Puy-en-Velay, cathedral town La Chaise-Dieu brings the hills alive with the sound of music during its annual classical music festival every August, now 60 years old. And where else would you see two prices at campsites: one for people and the other for donkeys?

The city of St-Étienne (or 'Sainté' as it's colloquially known) holds deep-rooted rivalry with Lyon, but it only really creates competition on the football pitch. Everything from St-Étienne's landscape, the railway line and even the football club itself stems from the mining trade.

Places
St-Étienne p479
Le Monastier-sur-Gazeille p480
La Chaise-Dieu p480

St-Étienne
TIME FROM LE PUY-EN-VELAY: **90MIN**

A Mine of Information
The **Musée de la Mine** *(musee-mine.saint-etienne.fr; adult/child €6.65/free)* gives not only a comprehensive history of Sainté's mining industry, but how the city evolved, and why it was the first place outside of Paris to get its own railway line. The **Musée d'Art et d'Industrie** *(mai.saint-etienne.fr; adult/child €6.65/free)* is all the more appealing whilst Lyon's textile museum remains closed for renovations, with a large collection of Jacquard looms and ribbons...and vintage firearms and bicycles.

Allez les Verts!
Dedicated to the football team AS St-Étienne, the **Musée des Verts** *(museedesverts.fr; with stadium visit adult/child €16/13; museum only €8/€6)* takes fans through the history of the club that has won 10 premiership leagues in France (at the time of writing). AS St-Étienne's heyday was 1967–76, when they won seven league titles in nine seasons.

GETTING AROUND
High-speed TGV services run from Paris Gare de Lyon to St-Étienne-Châteaucreux taking three hours. In the city, trams are the best way to get around. The simplest way to explore the countryside is by car. Check Blablacar *(blablacar.fr)* for rides, which tend to be in abundance to make up for the abysmal public transport.

KNIFE MAKING IN LIVRADOIS-FOREZ

The town of Thiers is famous for knife making, a trade that goes back 800 years here. In the past, knife makers would lie on their grinding stones and use the power of the Durelle River's rushing water to sharpen the blades lying down. The trade has far from disappeared, and there are still 78 cutlery-makers and 34 artisan knife-makers in the town, producing more than two-thirds of all French cutlery. It's not uncommon for children to learn how to make knives while still at primary school. Wecandoo (wecandoo.fr) has several workshops with local blacksmiths, ranging from a day to multiple days.

It's a bit of a schlep out of the city centre, but from Châteaucreux station it's either a 40-minute walk or a short hop on the T3 tramway to G Guichard.

Le Monastier-sur-Gazeille

TIME FROM LE PUY-EN-VELAY: **5HR**

Follow in the Footsteps of Stevenson and his Donkey

In September 1878, author Robert Louis Stevenson arrived in the little lace-making town of Le Monastier-sur-Gazeille in the Haute-Loire. Finding that the landscape – and variety of swear words used by the locals – reminded him of his native Scotland, he stayed for a month before purchasing a donkey named Modestine to walk all the way to St-Jean-du-Gard in the Cévennes. He documented his adventures in *Travels with a Donkey in the Cévennes*.

The GR70, as the Stevenson Trail is also known, now officially starts in Le Puy-en-Velay and finishes in Alès, presumably as they're easier to get to by public transport, bringing the distance to 270km, which generally takes 12 days. There are fewer road sections than the Camino and the footpath has more elevation gain and loss, leading many to choose it as a shorter but slightly more physically demanding alternative.

Many choose to emulate Stevenson's voyage and begin their trip in Le Monastier with a pack donkey to carry their belongings (rentals in Le Monastier-sur-Gazeille and St-Julien-Chapteuil). A donkey can be hired for however many days you want, and return transfers for yourself and your donkey are typically included in the rental price, but be aware of reviews from other customers and luggage weight limits to ensure the rental outlet isn't breaching animal welfare regulations. Donkeys are not supposed to carry more than 20% of their body weight (generally 27–30kg). Book accommodation in advance (a donkey is typically €5 extra). It's also perfectly possible to hike without a donkey, the trail passes numerous little villages so there's no need to be fully self-sufficient.

La Chaise-Dieu

TIME FROM LE PUY-EN-VELAY: **40MIN**

Hear the Echoes

La Chaise-Dieu, translating as 'seat of God', is a Benedictine abbey originally founded in 1043 by an abbot who was canonised after his death and became known as St Robert

Look out for them at local markets

EATING AROUND LE PUY-EN-VELAY: PERFECT PATISSERIES

Au Moine Gourmand: The monks made from chocolate, right next door to La Chaise-Dieu cathedral, are almost too pretty to eat. *8am-6pm Wed-Sat, 9am-7pm Sun* €€

Bruno Montcoudiol: Still riding off their 2006 world patisserie championships win, their cakes are nonetheless very good. There's another branch in Monistrol-sur-Loire. *hours vary* €€

Pascal Liotier: Also in Yssingeaux making exhibition-worthy sculptures from chocolate. *8.30am-6.30pm Wed-Sat, to 12.30pm Sun* €

École Nationale Supérieure de Pâtisserie: Training up tomorrow's finest pastry chefs in Yssingeaux, students regularly host cake sales. A far cry from Girl Scout cookies. *hours vary* €€

Église Abbatiale de St-Robert

of Turlande. The main building, the **Église Abbatiale de St-Robert**, built in the 14th century, forms the centre of La Chaise-Dieu's town, an architectural masterpiece of cloisters, arched windows and turrets.

The most curious room is the Echo Room, where people from other sides of the room can hear each other talking, without being overheard by those in between. It's thought to have been the pre-smartphone solution for monks to hear confessions from lepers without contracting the disease.

Other highlights include the immense 18th-century organ, many original wall frescoes – including the *Danse Macabre*, which stretches across three panels and four pillars – and the monastic choir room, with 144 stalls, still used by monks seven times each day to sing God's glory. The whole cathedral comes alive with music during the **Sacred Music Festival** (late August to early September), started by pianist Georges Cziffra in 1966, the most important event in the town's diary.

Outside the cathedral, don't miss stopping for coffee or a glass of wine at the superb bookshop-cafe **Dans la Forêt**, which has plenty of books on the surrounding region, as well as a good fiction section. They regularly host authors for talks.

COCO CHANEL'S SECRET HISTORY

If you thought you knew about Coco Chanel from the Audrey Tatou film *Coco Before Chanel*, you thought wrong. Before being sent to an orphanage, she grew up with her aunt in rural Livradois-Forez (the plaque is on her former home in Courpière). In her early 20s she worked as a water girl in Vichy. Many of the stories around her life came from Chanel herself. A compulsive liar, Chanel was a Nazi sympathiser during WWII. Towards the end of her life, she decided she wanted the real story of her childhood to be known, but her publicity team refused. To reveal where she'd really grown up would start unravelling a web of lies that linked to her activities during WWII – on the wrong side.

Chaîne des Puys

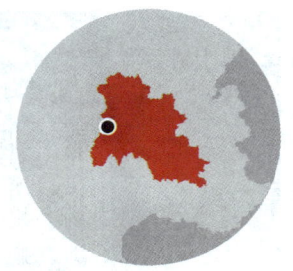

MOUNTAINS | HIKING | GEOLOGICAL MARVELS

☑ TOP TIP

Avoid visiting in April and early May. Local businesses tend to shut up shop between ski season and the start of summer hiking, so it's particularly difficult to find accommodation.

A mythical land of long dormant volcanoes, far from the typically trodden tourist trail, the *puys* of Auvergne (a string of 80 volcanic craters) stretch for more than 45km, forming a knobbly spine in the heart of France's Massif Central. One of the least populated parts of the country, it sits squarely in the middle of an area unofficially referred to as La Diagonale du Vide (the empty diagonal), and there's none of the crowds you'd get in the Alps or even the Pyrenees.

Travellers here are rewarded with vast panoramas from virtually untrodden mountain trails; warm, rural hospitality and traditions; and cheeses among the finest in France, often served up at atmospheric *burons* (stone huts formerly belonging to shepherds and cattle farmers). This is a place to strap on your hiking boots or unwind and marvel at the majesty of nature.

On Your Bike
Roll with the hills

Led by a young guide who swapped ski resort life to run mountain bike tours in the Auvergne, Joe Bike in Châtel-Guyon *(joebike.fr; two hours from €48 per person)* is no cycle in the park. Careening up and down dirt tracks, through forests and up and over boulders, you'll be glad of the suspension, and the fact that e-bikes are on offer to deal with all the elevation

GETTING AROUND

Chaîne des Puys is complicated without a car, as public transport in this area is few and far between. Service stations are also mostly limited to larger towns. Without a car, it's most practical to base yourself in one of the main urban hubs (Mont-Dore has several budget-friendly options, and infrequent buses to Clermont-Ferrand, 90 minutes away). Hitchhiking is widely accepted here and is generally easy but hitching is never entirely safe, and we don't recommend it. Travellers who hitch should understand that they are taking a small but potentially serious risk.

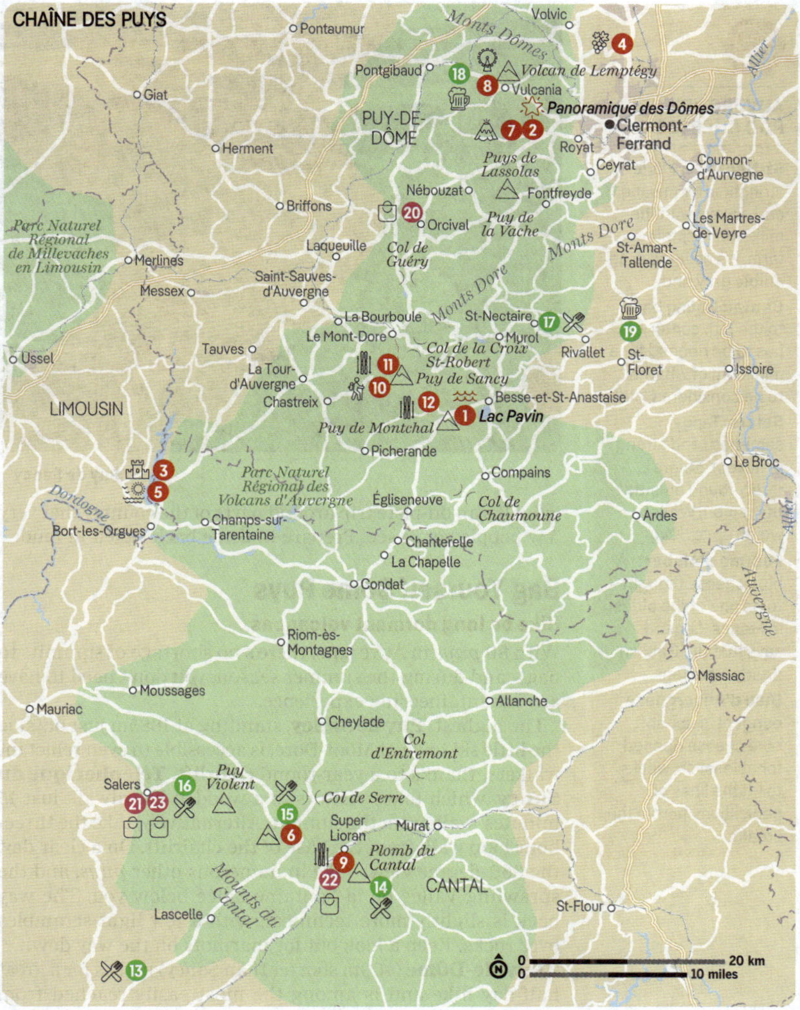

CHAÎNE DES PUYS

- ⭐ **HIGHLIGHTS**
- **1** Lac Pavin
- **2** Panoramique des Dômes
- 🔴 **SIGHTS**
- **3** Château de Val
- **4** Domaine Pierre Goigoux
- **5** Plage de la Siauve
- **6** Puy Mary
- **7** Puy-de-Dôme
- **see 7** Temple de Mercure
- **8** Vulcania
- 🔴 **ACTIVITIES**
- **9** Le Lioran
- **10** Puy de Sancy
- **11** Station du Mont-Dore
- **12** Super Besse
- 🔴 **EATING**
- **13** Bulle de Salers
- **14** Buron du Prat de Bouc
- **15** Chalet du Puy Mary
- **16** Les Burons de Salers
- **17** Les EpicurieuZ
- 🟢 **DRINKING & NIGHTLIFE**
- **18** Dark Lab
- **19** Le Beerarium
- 🟢 **SHOPPING**
- **20** Ajasserie d'Orcival
- **21** La Cave de Salers
- **22** La Ferme du Griou
- **23** La Petite Fabrik
- **see 17** L'Échoppe Romane
- **see 23** Tournicoti Tournicotou
- **see 23** Verre et Senteurs
- 🔵 **TRANSPORT**
- **see 11** Téléphérique du Sancy

AUVERGNE'S PDO CHEESES

St-Nectaire: Made straight after milking and always with the milk from a single farm, it's covered in an edible grey rind.

Cantal: Dating back to the 13th century, it has to be ripened for a minimum of 240 days to be considered 'old'.

Salers: Tangy, semi-hard and strong in flavour, Salers is rarely found outside the region. Wheels weigh up to 50kg.

Fourme d'Ambert: A blue cheese thought to be one of the oldest in France. Legend says that the Gaulish druids were fans.

Bleu d'Auvergne: A pungent, semi-soft blue cheese ripened for at least six weeks to let the lines of penicillium marble the cream.

Puy de Sancy

gain. It's an off-piste trip around parts of the country that very few people get to see. Prepare to come back caked in mud.

Bag Yourself Some Puys

Hike on long dormant volcanoes

With 80 *puys* in Auvergne, there's no shortage of summits to bag – and during the summer season, you don't need to have any mountaineering experience.

The highest, **Puy de Sancy**, standing at 1885m just outside the little ski town of Mont-Dore, is accessible to even reluctant walkers, thanks to a year-round chairlift, **Télépherique du Sancy**, which takes visitors to a wooden boardwalk just 15 minutes' walk from the summit. Alternatively, take the three-hour loop walk from the base of the chairlift. On a clear day, the 360-degree views take in numerous other *puys*, and the sprawling Vallée de la Fontaine Salée below you. The way back is slightly more technical, with a few light scrambles over rocks. Keep a look out for marmots on the way down.

Puy-de-Dôme (400m shorter than Sancy) makes for a great half-day hike and is among the most easily reached from Clermont-Ferrand (p489). Keep an eye out for the ruins of the **Temple de Mercure** near the top. A small on-site museum

EATING IN CHAÎNE DES PUYS: TAKEAWAY CHEESE

Ajasserie d'Orcival: Delicatessen with every imaginable cheese stuffed into sandwiches and quiches at rock bottom prices. *8.15am-7.15pm* €

La Ferme du Griou: Working farm producing vast wheels of Cantal, with plenty of soft cheese and St-Nectaire also sold on site. *9am-noon Mon-Sat, 4-6.30pm Mon-Tue & Thu-Sat* €

La Cave de Salers: Basement shop selling regional specialities, including the famous Salers cheese. The rind is particularly pungent. *9am-noon & 2-5.30pm Mon-Sat* €

L'Échoppe Romane: A small selection in St-Nectaire including little-known varieties like garlic and pepper-infused gaperon. *10am-6.30pm Thu-Mon* €

explains the history of the site, now almost 2000 years old. It's a three-hour round trip on foot from the car park, **Panoramique des Dômes**, or catch the cog railway train (15 minutes).

The most scenic is **Puy Mary**, at the south of the Chaîne des Puys, in Cantal. Standing at 1783m, much of the hiking route follows the crest of the mountain to reach the conical-shaped extinct volcano. Park at Pas de Peyrol to begin the hike (50 minutes there and back).

Geology Rocks
Journey to the centre of the earth

An educational theme park, **Vulcania** (*vulcania.com; adult/child €26.50/21.50*) has interactive exhibitions on how volcanoes are formed, 4D films and the largest planetarium in France. The rollercoaster, Namazu, is designed to mimic a seismic fault – it's not particularly scary for kids, but Lonely Planet writers have been known to test it out with their eyes closed. The building alone is worth a visit, looking like a gold-coated power station, but what's most fascinating is learning about the hardy seismologists who study volcanoes for a living.

The Youngest Volcano
A lake of superlatives

At a mere 7000 years old, **Lac Pavin**, which sits in a volcanic crater, is a spring chicken. It's also the deepest lake in Auvergne, and many would say the prettiest. A reasonably easy loop walk of 75 minutes (2.7km) takes you all around the lake perimeter on a trail that's largely tree-covered. It nonetheless gives views over the turquoise waters from every angle, often with fleeting glimpses of volcanic peaks in the background and Super Besse ski resort. Swimming in the lake isn't allowed, but you can hire a little boat to go out fishing – permits are available from Sancy tourist office online (*sancy.com; from €7*). There's on-road parking and a hotel-restaurant on the banks of the lake. It's nothing fancy, but service is friendly and there are always plenty of dogs.

Escape to the Château
If Dracula had Auvergnat roots

A 15th-century château-fort with fairytale turrets, **Château de Val** (*chateau-de-val.com; admission €8*) sits on a rocky

continued on p488

SHOPPING IN SALERS

Francesca and Arnaud Jalenques, owners of **Bulle de Salers** (*bulledesalers.fr*), share their favourite places to shop in Salers.

Everything at **La Petite Fabrik** is handmade by local artisans, who showcase their work on rotation. I particularly like the wooden toys, made by Fanny la Cocci in the Jordanne Valley.

Patrick Robin makes objects from animal horns – not from Salers cows, though, as their horns crumble! He's always got a story to tell when you go to his shop **Tournicoti Tournicotou**.

Glassblowers Pascal Philibert and Maryline Girardon, who run **Verre et Senteurs**, are so talented. Pascal has even been classed among the Meilleurs Ouvriers de France (best artisans in France).

The five-cheese Auvergnat fondue is award-winning

 EATING IN CHAÎNE DES PUYS: BURON RESTAURANTS

Bulle de Salers: In an old dairy shed surrounded by pastures, or feast-style dining in the fields when weather permits. *7-11.30pm Thu-Mon, 12.30-3.30pm Sat & Sun* €€

Chalet du Puy Mary: Atmospheric mountain chalet with wooden beams, strings of cowbells hung from the ceiling and plenty of blueberry tart. *9am-8pm* €

Les Burons de Salers: Cash only, with fabulous views and heart portions of *truffade* (p491) at lunch. *10am-7pm May-Sep, lunch by reservation* €

Buron du Prat de Bouc: At the crossover of numerous hiking trails, with local dishes like oven-baked St-Nectaire. *9am-6pm* €

ROAD TRIP

Cantal

Over 5700 sq km of verdant landscape – *puys*, rolling hills, rivers and picturesque stone villages – characterise the Cantal, one of the only regions in France where the population is in decline. An agricultural region, like much of Auvergne, it's a hot spot for hiking in summer and snow sports in the winter. With vast swathes of virgin countryside to be explored, if you want to see all Cantal has to offer, it's best tackled by car.

1 Aurillac

If you haven't already got your wheels, hire a car in **Aurillac**, the largest town in Cantal (and one of your only options for fuel). A former Gallo-Roman town, the tightly packed riverside houses are pretty, but it's a sleepy sort of place, save for each August when it hosts the performing arts Festival de Théâtre de Rue d'Aurillac. It attracts so many campers that the French government offers attendees free train tickets to get them to leave again.

The Drive: Follow the D17 through the valley to Lascelle.

2 Lascelle

Flanked by steep hills on either side, **Lascelle's** treasure is hidden by thick foliage. The **Gorges de la Jordanne** are a Lord of the Rings–esque tangle of trees, tiny waterfalls, wooden bridges and moss-covered stones; €5 grants entry to a 4km there-and-back hike.

The Drive: Continue along the D17 to Mandailles, where the D317 goes up and over a mountain

Salers

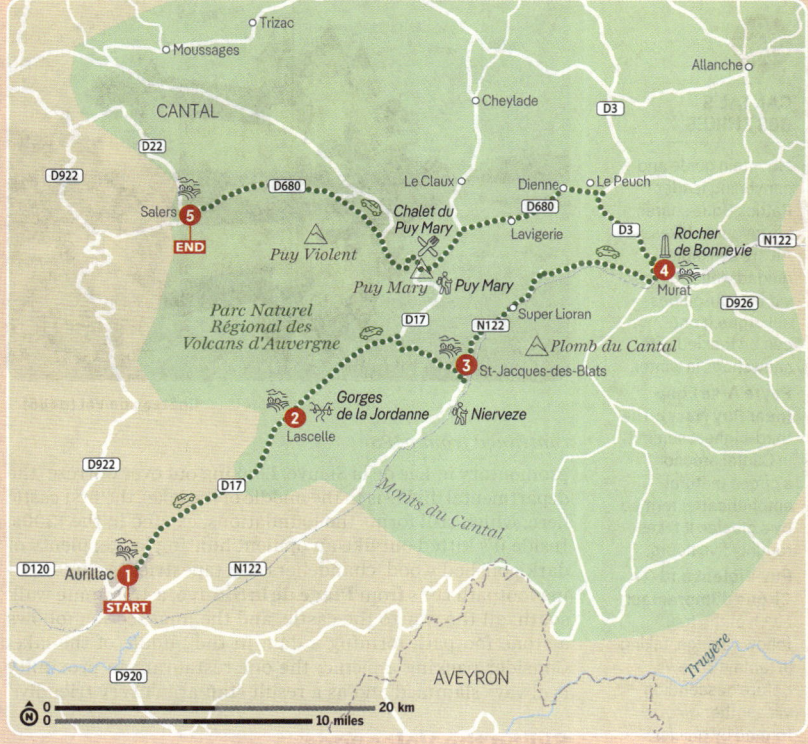

pass to your right, before zigzagging down to St-Jacques-des-Blats.

❸ St-Jacques-des-Blats

Either side of **St-Jacques-des-Blats** are fantastic walks. The little hamlet of **Nierveze** is particularly pretty, featuring stone houses with bright blue shutters, thatched roofs and an old flour mill. It's worth making the detour just to see the village, but consider making it an overnight trip and staying in a remote countryside *buron*. Don't take the hire car, owners will generally arrange jeep transfers.

The Drive: Take the N122 for 15 minutes to arrive in Murat.

❹ Murat

Don't judge **Murat** by its rather industrial, bleak-looking suburbs. It's an excellently preserved hotchpotch of twisting, medieval streets, with historic churches and a great viewpoint from the statue of the Virgin Mary on the hill (**Rocher de Bonnevie**) above town. During the school holidays, the tourist office runs *flambeau* (torch) lit night visits of the town.

The Drive: Take the D3 to Le Chaumeil, then the D680 to Salers. Stop at **Chalet du Puy Mary** (p485) to hike Puy Mary's summit (50 minutes there and back).

❺ Salers

A medieval stone town like Murat in miniature, with arguably even more charm, **Salers** was voted one of the prettiest towns in the country. Used as the backdrop for many films thanks to its beautifully preserved 15th-century ramparts and turreted little buildings, it's full of cheese shops and restaurants in cobbled streets. Stop for a *bourriol*, like a Breton galette only slightly thicker, filled with Cantal or Salers cheese.

CANTAL'S BEST HIKES

Mountain guide and canyoning leader Patrick Boue shares his favourite hikes. All are available guided walks to book via bureau-guides-auvergne.fr and can be tackled with snowshoes in winter.

Peyre Arse Loop (near Puy Mary): The third-highest summit in Cantal around a *cirque* (natural amphitheatre) formed by a glacier. It takes roughly five hours.

Puy Violent and Cirque d'Impramau: Much of the trail follows a ridge, taking in fantastic views, before descending via another *cirque* formed by glaciers. Count for 5½ hours.

Tour du Suc de Rond: A great summer hike for learning about the history of mountain life here, like cheese-making in the high pastures and *burons* (stone huts).

Château de Val (p485)

continued from p485

promontory in Lac de la Siauve. Looking out over Corrèze (the departmental divide is in the middle of the lake), the first castle here, which still forms the foundations, existed in the 1200s. Inside it's kitted out like an opulent hunting lodge; plenty of dark polished wood, chandeliers and tapestries. An undulating footpath runs from **Plage de la Siauve**, a 45-minute walk south, all the way to the castle, and the final section follows a stone footpath forming a dam in the middle of the lake. Consider packing a picnic; the one restaurant in proximity is always slammed and as a result staff aren't very friendly.

Skiing the Volcanoes
Wallet-friendly snowsports

The Chaîne des Puys has three ski resorts: **Station du Mont-Dore** (15 runs), **Super Besse** (33 runs) and **Le Lioran** (43 runs). The highest point at each of the resorts is over 1800m above sea level, but they're still considered low-altitude stations. Even in recent years, they've managed three-month seasons from Christmas to late March. They certainly don't rival the Alps in terms of snow quality, variety or even views, but it's some of the cheapest skiing you can do: a ski pass costs under €40 at Le Lioran, the largest of the resorts. In summer, Le Lioran's ski lift also runs up to Le Plomb du Cantal (1.5km walk to the summit), the highest peak in Cantal. Each resort also has a Nordic or cross-country ski area.

DRINKING IN CHAÎNE DES PUYS: LOCAL TIPPLES

Dark Lab: Microbrewery pouring equal quantities of craft beer and proper pub vibes. Regular events. *hours vary*

Les EpicurieuZ: Views over St-Nectaire and plenty of local wines and beers sold in the delicatessen. *9am-7pm*

Le Beerarium: Half-pint-sized microbrasserie with four classic beers and a rotating selection of guest brews. *3-7pm Thu, 9am-7pm Fri-Sat*

Domaine Pierre Goigoux: Winemaker growing gamay, chardonnay and pinot noir grapes on volcanic soil and running tastings and vineyard bike tours. *by reservation*

Beyond Chaîne des Puys

Towns and cities built from volcanic lava stone are not all they seem: they're shaking off industrial pasts to reveal surprising arts scenes.

Clermont-Ferrand is an oddity, a mix of industrial architecture and striking, Gothic buildings made from black, volcanic rock. With the reinstation of direct flights from the UK, this previously remote city may be starting to open up, although TGV trains still haven't made it here. The other towns in the region are similarly austere-looking at first glance. Riom and Volvic have a dark, witchy sort of charm – the architecture is handsome, but the volcanic stone means that on rainy days the cobbled streets are 50 shades of grey. Don't take them at face value: behind the stern exterior is a thriving artisanal crafts scene, excellent dining that doesn't break the bank, and plenty of ghost stories.

Places
Clermont-Ferrand p489
Randan p491
Volvic p491

Clermont-Ferrand

TIME FROM LE PUY-EN-VELAY: **2HR 15MIN**

Old Meets New in Clermont-Ferrand

Visitors often gloss over industrial Clermont-Ferrand. Geographically speaking, it's a curious city. There's no river, and the sprawling mass of black, volcanic stone sits in a basin between hills. It's now a thriving university town embracing an urban arts scene with vigour, with an impressive craft brewing scene.

To reveal the town's artistic side, start at the **Maison du Parcours Street Art Such'Art** in the heart of the old town, with the gleaming eyes of a black cat staring down the street from the double doors, and a kingfisher in flight on another door. From murals that cover the walls of entire buildings to the vibrantly decorated skatepark Philippe Marcombes, they've given the city a new burst of colour. Association End to End has transformed old buildings with colourful murals, including covering filled-in windows at the Fine Arts School with kaleidoscopic designs.

Between four walls, the art scene in Clermont-Ferrand is excellent, too. **FRAC Auvergne** *(fracauvergne.fr; free)* showcases contemporary art in light, airy exhibition rooms, and **Musée d'Art Roger Quilliot** *(MARQ; adult/child €5/free)*

GETTING AROUND

Ryanair runs direct flights to Clermont-Ferrand from London Stansted, and the city is well connected with long-distance buses, which are often more time efficient (and significantly more cost efficient) than the trains. There's still no TGV (high-speed) train service to Clermont-Ferrand. Flixbus *(flixbus.fr)* and Blablabus *(blablacar.fr/bus)* have direct services from Lyon (two hours), Bordeaux (five hours) and Paris (six hours). To get anywhere else in the region, a car is invaluable.

THE MICHELIN STORY

In 1889 the Michelin brothers, who ran a farming tools business in Clermont-Ferrand, helped a cyclist repair their pneumatic tyre. It was a lengthy process and failed just a few hundred metres later. The brothers decided to create a removable pneumatic tyre, creating a patent for it in 1891. They went on to become the second-largest producers of tyres in the world, known for iconic branding and the Michelin restaurant guide. The restaurant guide began as a sales ploy to sell more tyres, encouraging motorists to make more journeys around France by fuelling them with wanderlust, and recommending convenient hotels and restaurants along the route. Now coveted Michelin stars are the gold standard of the haute cuisine world over.

Cathédrale Notre-Dame-de-l'Assomption

has six floors filled with classical paintings and sculptures in Montferrand, one of the most historic parts of the city.

A Black Cathedral

Built in 1248, the twin, black-stone spires of Clermont-Ferrand's **Cathédrale Notre-Dame-de-l'Assomption** look like something from a particularly dark adaptation of *The Hunchback of Notre-Dame*. Each spire is 96.1m tall, and as this isn't a high-rise city, they tower over the other buildings. The origins of the first cathedral on this site date from as early as the 5th century CE, when then-bishop Namatius laid the foundation stones for the first cathedral. The 'new' cathedral in its present Gothic style began construction in 1248. Underneath the present-day cathedral is a vast network of labyrinths and catacombs – the catacombs here are larger than those in Paris, though sadly they are not currently open to the public. The tunnels were used by cheese makers to age cheeses right up until the latter half of the 20th century.

From 1350, work on the cathedral was put on pause for almost 500 years. The 100 Years' War and several outbreaks of plague had taken their toll on Clermont-Ferrand, financially as well as physically, and the cathedral wasn't completed in its present form until the 19th century. Now there are stained-glass windows of epic proportions, a crypt made from white marble, towering pillars and limestone statues of the Virgin Mary and other saints. If the stained glass seems extra

EATING & DRINKING IN CLERMONT-FERRAND: BUZZING SPOTS

Avenue: Classic French dishes with artistic flair, with some unusual plates too, such as bull stew. *noon-1.30pm & 7.30-8.30pm Tue-Fri, 7.30-9.30pm Sat* €€

La Bamboche: The place to go for evening vibes, with regular live-music events and karaoke nights. Plant bedecked ceilings and bar snacks. *5pm-1am Tue-Sat, to 10pm Sun, to midnight Mon* €

AIGO: Grab coffee and cake from inexpensive coworking-cum-cafe AIGO, with friendly service and super-fast wi-fi. *9am-6pm Mon-Thu, to 5pm Fri* €

Lard de Vivre: For world cuisine, hit up Lard de Vivre for tapas and the enormous carnivorous parrillas. *noon-1.30pm & 7-9pm Tue-Sat, 7-9pm Mon* €€

colourful, that's because all of the windows were completely redone by a local artist in the early 20th century.

The Ghosts of the Past

American expat and historian Dr Drew Manns has a love for all things dark and macabre, and Auvergne supplies witchiness in abundance. The **Haunted Clermont Experience** *(visitauvergne.org; €25)* is the city's first and only ghost tour, in English. Stops include an old school, in which took place attempts to summon demons, the vestiges of a prison where members of the Knights Templar were questioned and accused of sorcery, and a wayside building that once housed a poisoner's laboratory, and end at a pub.

Randan
TIME FROM CLERMONT-FERRAND: 40MIN

A Horror Film Holiday Home

Nobody knows exactly what happened to the **Domaine Royal de Randan** *(domaine-randan.fr; adult/child €7/free)*. Holiday home of Louis-Philippe, France's last monarch, and set amid 100 hectares of parkland, it would have once been spectacular.

In July 1925, the castle went up in flames. No one ever discovered the cause of the fire, and Randan was left a shell, abandoned. Although the building has been strengthened to make it safe and cleared of debris, it's still largely in ruins, giving it the air of a haunted house. Guided visits tour the house, which is an eclectic mix of a French stately home during the Industrial revolution and a vast taxidermy collection belonging to the last owner, Ferdinand d'Orléans. The ensemble is mysterious and rather sad, yet utterly fascinating. The estate itself has some 100 hectares of parkland, some of which is undergoing renovation work until 2027.

Volvic
TIME FROM CLERMONT-FERRAND: 20MIN

Painting on Lava

Volvic's water is famous, but once it was Volvic stone that stole the limelight: enormous grey volcanic slabs were used to construct many of the houses in the area. Coline Lespinasse runs enamel painting workshops in her intimate little studio, where participants paint directly onto little slabs of lava *(terravolcana.com; €38)*. You choose the design – views of Puy-de-Dôme and other Auvergnat *puys* are available to trace, if you prefer to stay on theme.

It takes a few days to dry, so book in for the start of your visit or pay extra to have your creation shipped.

TRUFFADE

It is a truth universally acknowledged that every Auvergnat culinary speciality must include lashings of Cantal cheese, and *truffade* is no exception. Auvergne's answer to a potato gratin, it's simply slices of potato in melted cheese with a little garlic, often served straight in the skillet. Call a spade a spade: *truffade* literally means 'potato', coming from the Auvergnat Occitan word 'trufla'.

Typically eaten by shepherds to sustain them during long days in the mountains, it's now a source of regional pride. Regular *truffade* eating contests take place across Auvergne, with winners capable of inhaling over 1.7kg of cheesy potato goodness in just 10 minutes. For perspective, a typical restaurant serving is 250g.

EATING BEYOND CHAÎNE DES PUYS: RURAL RIB STICKERS

En Attendant Louise: A true village institution, serving *truffade* that draws customers from miles around. *noon-1.30pm Tue-Sat, 7-8.30pm Fri & Sat* €

Ciboulette et Pain d'Épices: A friendly little vegetarian joint using organic and local produce. Good-value lunch menus. *noon-2.30pm Mon-Sat* €

Les Vinzelles: An events space, bookshop and cafe-restaurant with an on-site veggie garden, run by two sisters. *noon-7pm Thu-Sat, 11.30am-6.30pm Sun* €

Auberge de la Croix de Fer: A beautiful patio for fine weather days and an extensive wine list. *10.30am-10.30pm Wed-Sun* €€

Places We Love to Stay

€ Budget €€ Midrange €€€ Top End

Lyon MAP p456

Yasi € A colourful hostel with beer garden, hot tub and sauna, plus regular concerts, exhibitions and DJ sets. The bar is popular with locals.

Le Flâneur € Hostel in the heart of Lyon's buzzing 7th *arrondissement*. Rooms are sparse, communal spaces kaleidoscopic. Great for meeting people.

The People € Almost too stylish to be a hostel, with oodles of plants, Friday-night DJ sets alfresco, boules pitches and frequent visiting tattoo artists.

Mama Shelter € Quirky and moodily-lit, in keeping with the Mama Shelter brand, with an excellent bar-restaurant that also attracts locals. Enormous brunches.

Hotel de Verdun 1882 €€ Beautiful rooms in a historic building formerly belonging to the founders of Lyonnais institution Brasserie Georges.

Lyon Country House €€ A breath of fresh air just 15 minutes from the city centre with lodges, treehouses and suites.

Villa 216 €€ A 19th-century gated home hidden in the high-rise 3ème. Just two rooms, with a hot tub available for private use.

Fourvière Hôtel €€€ Chic, upmarket hotel in a former convent. The old altar and confessional booths spill over with houseplants.

InterContinental €€€ In the old Hôtel-Dieu (hospital) on the banks of the Rhône. High-ceilinged rooms with river views and a great cocktail bar.

Cour des Loges €€€ Lyonnais institution in the heart of the old town now run by the Radisson group. In its very own *traboule* (underground passage).

Beaujolais

Le Clos Zélie €€ Family-run property with five rooms set amid a vast park and vineyards. There's also a pool and wood-fired hot tub.

Demeures et Châteaux l'Abbaye Caladoise €€ Pretty rooms in an old abbey with a courtyard garden. Easy to reach with public transport, rather industrial surroundings.

Château de Pizay €€€ Ask for a room in the old part of the château for more atmosphere. There's also a spa and open-air pool (p466).

Rhône Valley

La Péniche €€ In both Vienne and Tournon-sur-Rhône, luxurious, floating barge accommodation with shipping containers for bikes. Each has five cabins.

La Pyramide €€€ 200-year-old property now run by Relais & Châteaux with a two Michelin-starred restaurant.

Gorges de l'Ardèche MAP p468

Camping les Trouillères € Small riverside campsite with plots, mobile homes and a couple of *roulottes* (wooden caravans on wheels), plus an outdoor pool.

Hôtel des Sites € Just far enough away from the bustle of Vallon Pont-d'Arc with warm service and spacious, good value rooms.

Bivouac de Gaud € Designated camping spot with no facilities along the banks of the Ardèche River, Bivouac de Gournier further downriver; book and pay via the tourist office (p471).

La Flor Azul € *Chambres d'hôte* run by a friendly, hands-on Dutch woman with plenty of local knowledge. Large rooms with plenty of character.

Prehistoric Lodge €€ Adults-only lodges and tents with every possible luxury. Each one is ringed by trees. Glamping at its finest.

Domaine Walbaum €€€ An opulent family estate with exquisite views over the vineyards and mountains, and plenty of activities on offer.

Hôtel du Couvent de Vagnas €€€ A beautiful building retaining all the character of the old convent. There's a pool and resident sheep and chickens.

Monts de l'Ardèche

Auberge les Grillons € Positively enormous self-catered apartments at rock-bottom prices in a sleepy little historic town. Breakfast is sumptuous.

Moulin de Montabonnel € *Chambres d'hôte* in a stone farmhouse with ceiling beams and enormous gardens, run by two sisters. There's even a hot tub.

Le Puy-en-Velay MAP p477

Gîte de la Prévôté € Atmospheric and historic budget accommodation attached to the cathedral. Popular with hikers. Shared bathrooms.

Les Cimes €€ On the floor above Gîte la Prévôté, this upmarket homestay-cum-hotel has just two rooms and the best views of the cathedral spires.

Demeure du Lac de Fugères €€ The most luxurious lodgings in Le Puy are in a 15th-century mansion with four-poster beds.

St-Étienne

La Maison Rouge € Community-run backpacker hostel. Basic dorms, but beds and pints are both very cheap. There's a small kitchen, too.

Haute-Loire

Camping Estela € Riverside campsite with plots, lodges and a field for donkeys, popular with hikers on the Stevenson Trail. Great value half-board option.

Maison Cha-Ri-Va-Ri € Colourful, world-inspired rooms furnished with impeccable taste. Always a warm welcome and generous breakfast spread.

Puy-de-Dôme

Le Chalet des Gentianes € Comfortable dorms, basic kitchen facilities and a bar downstairs serving a fantastic selection of local beers.

Archipel Volcans € Light, modern rooms which overlook the Puy-de-Dôme and a restaurant serving slap-up Sunday brunch and regional specialities.

Lodges de Lemptégy €€ Chic, squeaky clean, self-catered lodges on the slopes of a long dormant volcano. Generous baskets for breakfast.

Le Jas du Mas €€ Exquisitely designed rooms in the middle of the countryside, overlooking a small lake. Evening meals available.

Les Cabanes du Bois Basalte €€ Surrounded by trees, the view from these eco-cabins on stilts takes some beating. Breakfast baskets delivered to your room.

La Maison de la Monne €€ Inexpensive rooms geared towards hikers with great walking opportunities on the doorstep.

Cantal

Huttopia Lac de la Siauve € Glamping, chalets and plots in a magnificent multi-level campsite with lake views and e-bikes for hire.

Lac des Graves €€ Chalets and *roulottes* with modern, minimalistic interiors and an abundance of green space, set around a large lake. Resident horses, too.

Le Buron de Niercombe €€€ True remoteness in this old shepherd's hut, which is only accessible by jeep or on foot. Minimum two-night stay.

Clermont-Ferrand

Artyster € A renovated garage, with a factory-chic bar and social area. The best budget option in town.

Hotel Littéraire Alexandre Vialatte €€ A book-themed hotel with a bookshop in the bar and beautifully designed rooms.

InterContinental in former Hôtel-Dieu, Lyon

THE GUIDE

*Researched by
Nicola Williams*

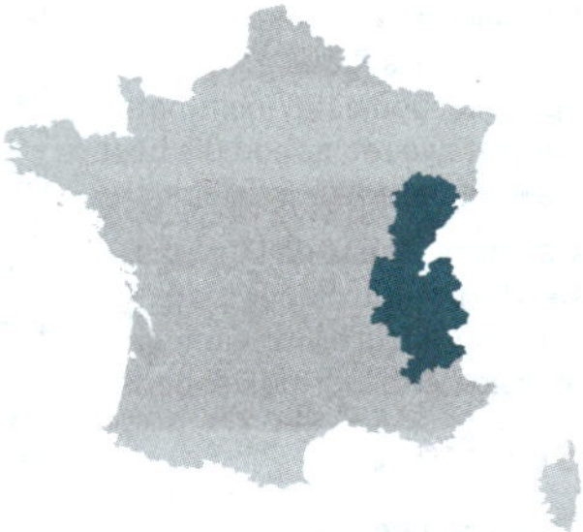

French Alps & Jura

ONE OF EUROPE'S TRUE MOUNTAIN EPICS

Heart-thumping adventure and pastoral tradition share the same starting gate in this high-octane playground, dedicated to safeguarding ancestral *savoir faire*.

The French Alps and Jura is where beauty of the most breathtaking nature and action collide. Glacier-carved national parks and shark-toothed mountain summits, ice-blue lakes and sky-high *cols*: the call of the wild is fierce in this eastern swathe of France, even more so for outdoor adventurers in town to bag the highest, longest – on skis, bike or simply your own two feet.

Rumbling across seven European countries, the Alps climax with western Europe's highest peak, Mont Blanc (4805m). The hypnotic snow-white crown of this storied mountain spirographs a kaleidoscope of magical shadows over the iconic ski and mountaineering town of Chamonix in Savoie (Savoy). South and southwest, from the Rhône River to the Italian border, romps Dauphiné, with student-powered Grenoble at its adrenalin-powered helm. In the less mountainous Jura region, rippling gently northwest along Savoie's border with Switzerland, life unfolds along slower rhythms: winemaking, cross-country skiing and bell-strung cows whose milk goes into some of France's tangiest, tastiest *fromage*.

Inhabited since prehistoric times, the French Alps have been fiercely contested since time immemorial. The desire to conquer that they arouse burns brighter than ever – the three-country Tour du Mont Blanc hiking and trail-running route around Mont Blanc, the Grand Route des Alpes driving itinerary, the GR5 hike and the Vallée Blanche ski descent have never been so wildly popular. Take time out to try for yourself.

THE MAIN AREAS

CHAMONIX
Bucket list
ski town. **p500**

LAKE ANNECY
Lake jewel of Haute-
Savoie. **p514**

CHAMBÉRY
Savoy's historical
capital. **p524**

GRENOBLE
Dauphiné's cultural
and action hub. **p534**

For places to stay in French Alps & Jura, see p549

THE GUIDE

FRENCH ALPS & JURA

Left: Beaufort cheese (p532); Above: Mer de Glace (p501), Chamonix

Find Your Way

Embracing the *départements* (departments) of Savoie, Haute-Savoie and Isère, the French Alps cover a vast area – not easy to navigate swiftly thanks to valleys and mountains blocking direct as-the-crow-flies routes. Our recommendations focus on four convenient bases.

CAR & MOTORBIKE

Roads to many ski stations are steep and serpentine. Snow clearing is frequent, but winter tyres or chains stowed in your trunk are obligatory November to March. Many *cols* (mountain passes) are snowbound and closed in winter; in early/late summer, check road conditions before setting out.

BUS & TRAIN

Buses link Moûtiers train station with Les Trois Vallées and Bourg-St-Maurice station with Val d'Isère/Tignes. Modane is the rail stop for the Vanoise, linked by bus to Bonneval-sur-Arc. For Chamonix, hop on the Mont Blanc Express train at TGV station St-Gervais-Le Fayet.

WALKING

The long-distance GR5 or Grande Traversée des Alpes walking trail (p532) crosses the entire French Alps en route from Lake Geneva to the Med (674km). Shorter trails tackle the entire region, and are the loveliest way of slow-hopping between remote hamlets, farms and mountain *refuges* (shelters).

Jura Mountains, p541

You can drive for hours without passing a soul in this deliciously rural neck of the woods, powered by gentle mountains, handsome wine-fuelled villages and cheese.

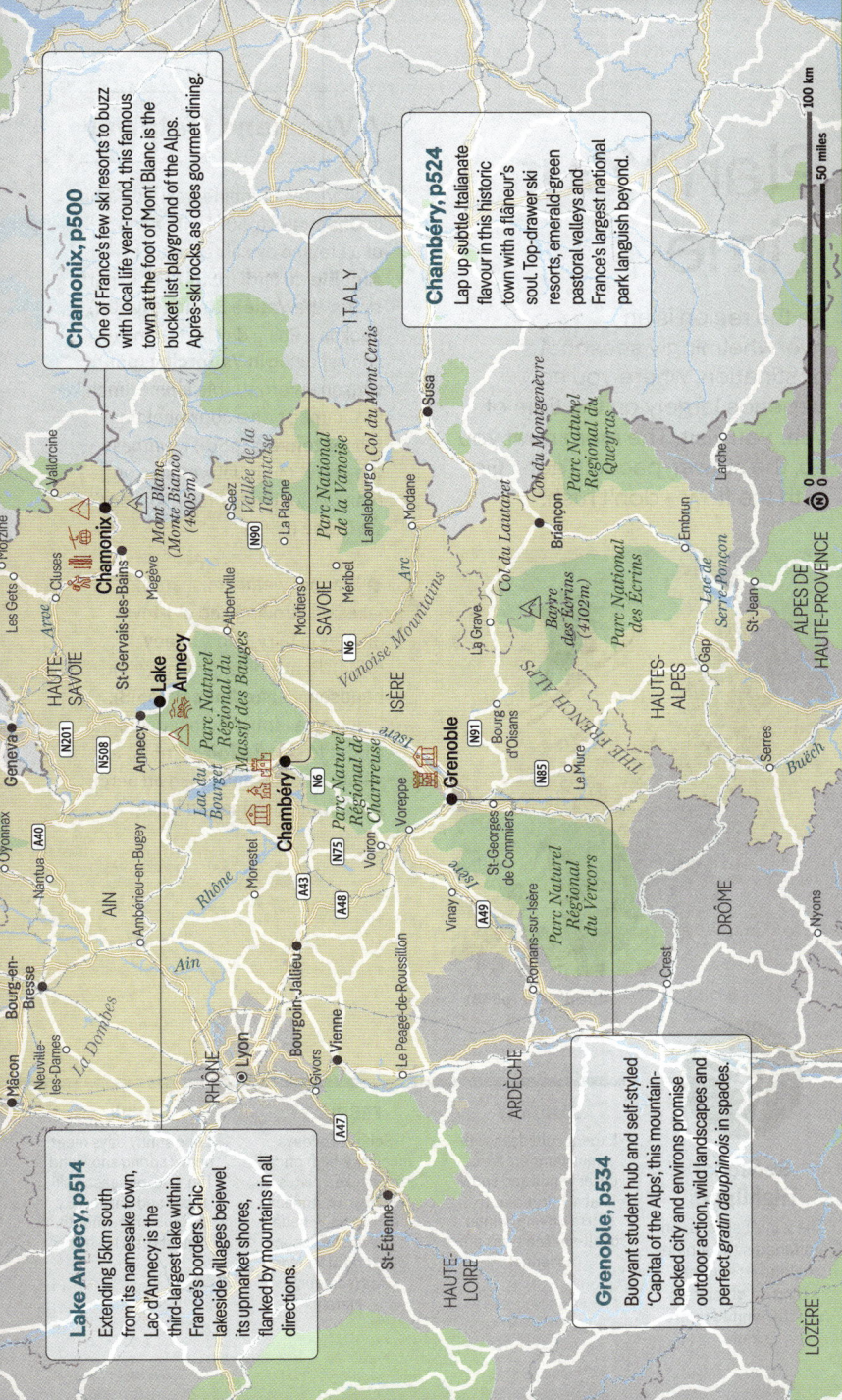

Plan Your Time

As the region is an overwhelmingly seasonal destination, where you go depends largely on the time of year you visit. The more rural you go, the slower-paced it gets. Go with the flow – don't rush.

Alpe d'Huez (p538)

A Weekend Getaway

● In winter, combine a ski weekend in **Chamonix** (p500) with a trip of a lifetime by cable car up to **Aiguille du Midi** (p504). For expert skiers, the **Vallée Blanche** (p500) beckons. Pair a day ski touring or snowshoeing in **Vallorcine** (p510) with an unforgettable alpine lunch. In summer, ride a cogwheel train to **Montenvers** (p501) to witness the effect of global warming on France's longest glacier, the **Mer de Glace** (p501).

● Warmer weather ushers in lakeside strolling and old-town ambles in fairy-tale **Annecy** (p514). Rent a bike to spin around handsome **Lake Annecy** (p518); lunch on a farm. Another day, catch a boat to chic **Talloires** (p515) to village-mooch and lunch on perch fresh from the emerald lake.

Seasonal Highlights

The winter ski season dominates the alpine calendar; summer skiing on glaciers is strictly limited to pro skiers.

JANUARY
Expect cold days with minus temperatures, bitter winds and snow at all altitudes. If you're driving, winter or all-season tyres are essential.

FEBRUARY
School holidays mean sky-high prices and packed pistes in ski resorts. Annecy celebrates Venetian carnival the second weekend after Mardi Gras (sometimes March).

APRIL
Long sunny days meet heavy spring snow and fun, end-of-season ski races and parties. By the end of the month, most resorts shut.

A Five-Day Odyssey

● Base yourself in **La Plagne** (p532), a winter wonderland action-packed on and off the ski slopes. Snowshoeing in a nature reserve, fat biking on snow, flying down an Olympic bobsled run and scaring yourself silly flying through the sky in an open-sided cable-car cabin are highlights. Recover afterwards in the deliciously languid, snow-blanketed **Parc National de la Vanoise** (p532).

● Embrace summer with mountain biking in **Les Portes du Soleil** (p521) – base yourself in **Les Gets** (p522), a top-drawer family destination. In **St-Gervais-les-Bains** (p512) ride the Tramway du Mont Blanc to the trailhead of a high-altitude glacier walk, visit a mountain gin distillery and a forgotten chapel loaded with world-class modern art (including a Matisse!). Stroll around alpine-chic **Megève** (p513).

More Time to Spare

● Detox with a winter foray in low-key **Jura** (p541), pairing cross-country skiing with wine in **Arbois** (p545) and cultural forays in the footsteps of Jean-Jacques Rousseau in **Besançon** (p541). Or devote time to urban **Grenoble** (p534), moving from the Dauphiné capital to a **Oisans** (p539) ski resort.

● June to September, road-trip along the **Route des Grandes Alpes** (p532) from Lake Geneva to Les Gets in **Les Portes du Soleil** (p521); stop en route at **Les Aigles du Léman** (p523). Marvel at **Lac de Roselend** (p531), taste cheese in **Beaufort** (p532), and navigate 21 hairpins up to **Alpe d'Huez** (p538). Catch your breath with scenic hiking and trailing eagles, orchids and blue cheese in the gloriously untouched **Vercors** (p540).

JUNE
Out come the walking boots and bicycles. Abondance cows head to flower-rich summer pastures; milk goes into prized Beaufort d'été cheese (until October).

JULY
Chair lifts and cable cars open to walkers and mountain bikers (until the end of August). Picnics and concerts beneath the stars unfold at **Saline Royale** (p544) during Les Nuits de Saline (May–Sep).

AUGUST
Summer in the Alps doesn't get busier than the first two weeks of August. Expect busy roads (especially Saturday) and occasional cable-car queues.

SEPTEMBER
Grapes are harvested in Savoie and Haute-Savoie. At the end of the month, purple crocuses bloom on saffron farms in the Massif des Chartreuse.

Chamonix

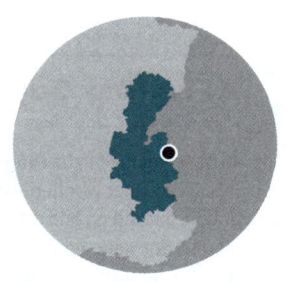

SKIING | HIKING | MOUNTAIN CULTURE

☑ TOP TIP

Pick the time of day and year that you embark on the ride of a lifetime up the Aiguille du Midi (p504). Early morning is best; in summer, the late-morning tourist crowd crammed into the gondola makes it feel like 'Disneyland at Altitude'. Advance ticket reservations are vital.

Free-rider king of the French Alps and springboard to some of Europe's most fêted mountain adventures, Chamonix has always been one ski spin ahead of the curve. The pioneering ski town and mountaineering base was discovered as a tourist destination by British explorers William Windham and Richard Pococke in 1741, and it hosted the first ever Winter Olympics in 1924. The Herculean task of saving its melting glaciers – not least France's longest, the serpentine Mer de Glace at the foot of Mont Blanc (4805m) – tops today's to-do list.

In winter and summer, high-altitude conquests on granite peaks and go-slow exploration through bucolic pastures strewn with wildflowers and traditional shepherd huts go hand in hand in this alpine town. Just walking down Chamonix' pedestrian main street rue du Docteur Paccard, loomed over by Mont Blanc's snow-white dome, it's impossible not to feel a sassy new spring in your step: the palpable buzz and anticipation of the next outdoor thrill around the corner.

Off-Piste Ride of a Lifetime

Bagging the Vallée Blanche

Tales of skiers cruising along and suddenly disappearing from sight are rife in La Vallée Blanche annals. Then again, skiing

GETTING AROUND

Moving between Chamonix' seven different ski areas – famously not linked by pistes – involves land transport, but the skiing is so good no one bats an eyelid. Buses in town and the Vallée de Chamonix (from Argentière or Col des Montets to Servoz and Les Houches) are free with a Carte d'Hôte (Guest Card) – get one free at your hotel or B&B. Check *www.chamonix-bus.com* for schedules. The same card covers free transport on the northbound Mont Blanc Express train.

Mer de Glace

MOUNTAIN TOOL KIT

Lift Passes: Find details of all passes at montblancnaturalresort.com.

Mountain Guides: Inside the Maison de la Montagne on place de l'Église, Compagnie des Guides de Chamonix has guides for every outdoor activity: snowshoeing, ice-climbing, off-piste skiing, summer mountaineering, climbing and canyoning.

Trail Access & Conditions: The **Office de Haute Montagne** *(chamoniarde.com)*, also in the Maison de la Montagne, provides practical information on hiking, climbing and ski-touring trails – including trail conditions.

Chamonix mobile app: Download the **tourist office** app *(en.chamonix.com)* to access weather forecasts, webcams, maps; purchase and top up lift passes, too.

across a snow bridge and tumbling metres like a rag doll into a dark ice-blue crevasse as the ruptured bridge collapses happens with surprising frequency.

This is just one reason why Europe's most legendary off-piste ski route – a jaw-dropping 2800m descent through a landscape of eerie, unearthly beauty – must be tackled with a certified guide. Starting at a dizzying 3800m, at the top cable-car station of the **Téléphérique de l'Aiguille du Midi** *(aiguille dumidi.montblancnaturalresort.com/en; adult/child return €78/66.30)*, the challenging 20km ski route follows three serpentine glaciers down to the lower, moraine-scarred reaches of France's longest glacier, the **Mer de Glace** ('Sea of ice').

Here, at around 1700m, the glass-sided **Télécabine de la Mer de Glace** – a state-of-the-art cable car directly above an ice cave – whisks Vallée Blanche skiers back up to **Gare du Montenvers** *(montenversmerdeglace.montblancnaturalresort.com; adult/child return incl train, cable car and ice cave €39.50/33.60)* at 1913m. From here Montenvers' cherry-red cogwheel train trundles down to Chamonix town in 20 minutes. This leg of the trip is also an exhilarating day trip for non-skiers year-round.

Late March to early April is the best time to tackle the Vallée Blanche, only suitable for confident skiers comfortable on black pistes and un-groomed terrain. Hook up with a guide from **Compagnie des Guides de Chamonix** *(chamonix-guides.com)* on a small-group expedition *(€155 per person,*

EATING IN CHAMONIX: QUICK BITES

Couloir: Homemade cakes, baguette sandwiches and inventive vegetarian dishes by the guys behind Chamonix-roasted Moody coffee. *8am-5pm Tue-Sun* €

Gaufres de Chamonix: The jumbo waffles cooked up in this tiny wooden chalet from 1965 are unmatched; join the queue outside 65 rue Whymper. *hours vary* €

Coopérative Fruitière du Val d'Arly: Picnic supplies: cheeses and *saucissons* (air-dried sausage) studded with Beaufort cheese or blueberries. *9am-7pm* €€

Cool Cats: Artisanal hot dogs, creative nachos and veggie bites on bar-clad rue des Moulins. *noon-midnight* €€

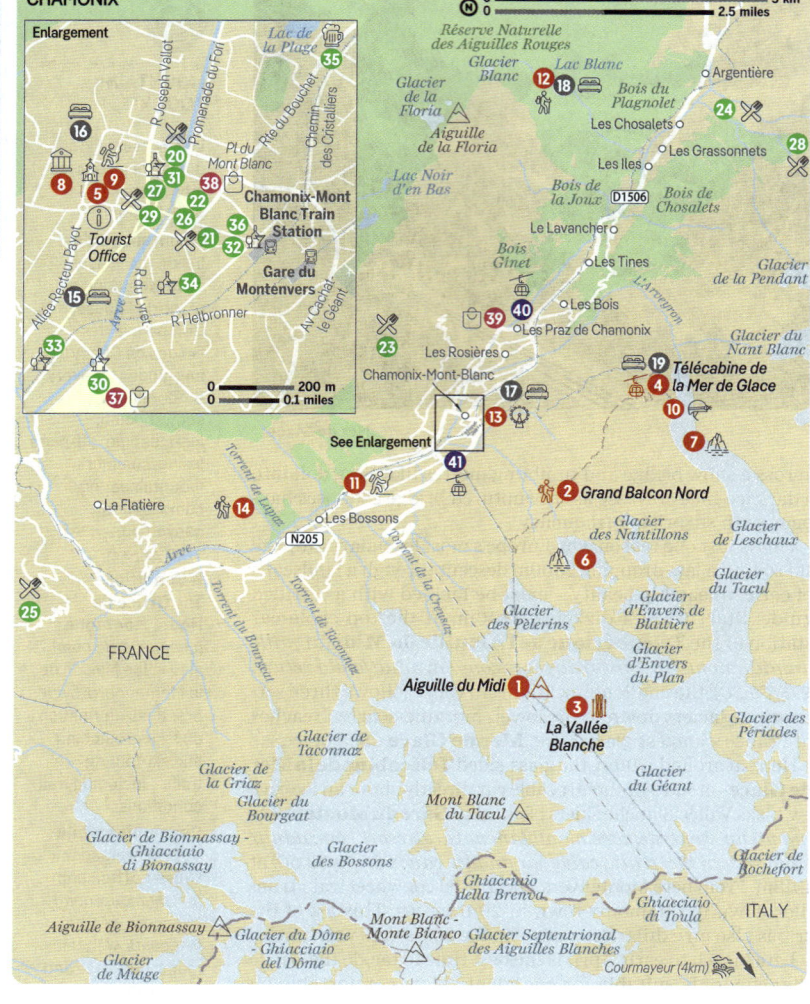

plus €90 in lift passes), with an overnight at 3613m at the Refuge des Cosmiques on the Col du Midi glacier (€425 incl lift pass) or – most magically of all – on a moonlight descent (€430 for two people).

Chasing Crystals

Admire glittering treasures in the Crystal Museum

The bittersweet silver lining to receding glaciers in the Alps is the glittering stash of richly coloured crystals the melting ice unveils. Red, pink and mint-green fluorites – unique to the Alps – jostle for the limelight with smoky black-quartz

★ HIGHLIGHTS
1. Aiguille du Midi
2. Grand Balcon Nord
3. La Vallée Blanche
4. Télécabine de la Mer de Glace

● SIGHTS
5. Église St-Michel
6. Glacier de Blaitière
7. Mer de Glace
8. Musée des Cristaux

● ACTIVITIES
9. Compagnie des Guides de Chamonix
10. Grotte de Glace
11. Koalagrimpe
12. Lac Blanc
13. Luge Alpine Coaster
see 9 Office de Haute Montagne
14. Parc de Merlet

● SLEEPING
15. Hôtel Richemond
16. La Folie Douce
17. Le Chamoniard Volant
18. Refuge du Lac Blanc
19. Refuge du Montenvers

● EATING
20. Cool Cats
21. Couloir
22. Gaufres de Chamonix
23. La Bergerie de Planpraz
24. La Crèmerie du Glacier
25. Les Vieilles Luges
26. MUMMA
27. Munchie
28. Refuge de Lognan
29. Rose du Pont

● DRINKING & NIGHTLIFE
30. Amnesia Club
31. Bar'd Up
32. Chambre Neuf
33. L'Hydromel
34. Maison des Artistes
35. MBC
36. Moö

● SHOPPING
37. Blackcrows
38. Cooperative Fruitière du Val d'Arly
39. Rabbit on the Roof

● TRANSPORT
40. Télécabine de la Flégère
41. Téléphérique de l'Aiguille du Midi

FRENCH ALPS 2030

All eyes are on Savoie, Haute-Savoie and Isère as the regions rev up for the XXVI Olympic Winter Games in February 2030. The operational HQ is in Lyon and both ice events and the closing ceremony are tipped to take centre stage in Nice, but the world's best athletes will compete for gold on ski slopes and in snow parks and snowy forest tracks in Courchevel, Val d'Isère, Serre Chevalier and La Clusaz, among others. Bobsledding will be in La Plagne (p531), evoking memories of the 1992 Albertville games that notably graced the region with cultural gems such as the Sentier du Baroque (p513). Chamonix hosted the world's first ever Winter Olympics in 1924.

gwindels, violet-brown axinites and purple amethyst in Chamonix' dazzling **Musée des Cristaux** (adult/child €8/free; closed Mon). It's located in the Espace Tairraz behind Chamonix' 18th-century baroque church **Église St-Michel**.

Many of the 1800 rock crystals displayed were unearthed by local rockhounds or *chasseurs des crystaux* ('crystal hunters') on climbing expeditions in the Massif du Mont Blanc. The oldest crystals were formed 25,000 years ago. From the 1800s until the 1950s, Chamonix' pink-fluorite dream lured crystal hunters from all over Europe.

Dirty Fries, Pine-Tree Mead & Amnesia

An après-ski bar crawl

Most Chamonix nights out begin in front of the **train station** on bar-busy **ave Michel Croz**, packed during après-ski 'hour', which roughly runs 4pm to 8pm. Line the stomach with Guinness at Swedish-run bar **Moö** (moobarcuisine.com), famous for cooking up the best dirty fries and burgers in town. Across the street at **Chambre Neuf** (instagram.com/chambreneuf), slam a plastic glass of Stella and dance on tables until 7.30pm when the live music ends.

continued on p508

EATING IN CHAMONIX: DINNER DATES

MBC: Burgers, ribs and wings, washed down with a locally made blonde, stout or mystery beer at Chamonix' much-loved microbrewery. *4pm-1am, from 10am Fri-Sun* €

Rose du Pont: Belle époque Paris meets Chamonix at this cafe-brasserie, with French cuisine and romantic river-facing balconies. *noon-midnight* €€

Munchie: Crispy artichoke, spicy tuna maki: fusion sharing plates, bursting with creativity and world flavours, on restaurant-lined rue des Moulins. *7pm-2am* €€

MUMMA: The bon vivant bistro in which to be seen over craft cocktails and gourmet Franco-Asian shared plates by chef David Lillieroth. €€

Bar Plan d'Aiguille

TOP EXPERIENCE
Aiguille du Midi

Its distinctive *aiguille* (needle) silhouette on the horizon make it easy to spot for miles around. This rocky tooth of an alpine peak (3842m) in the Massif du Mont Blanc ensnares France's highest cable-car station at 3777m, promising spine-tingling adventure for mountain enthusiasts and privileged access to a spectacular fairy-tale ice world for first-timers to high altitudes.

DON'T MISS
- Panoramic terraces
- Le Tube
- Pas dans le Vide
- Espace Mont Blanc
- Espace Histoire
- Pointe Helbronner
- Skyway Monte Bianco

Summiting

The giddy anticipation of new heights to be conquered is electric as you glide from Chamonix' bottom **Téléphérique de l'Aiguille du Midi** (p501) cable-car station to its top station at 3842m. The change of cabin at mid-station **Plan d'Aiguille du Midi** (2317m) is a prime opportunity to grab a coffee or *vin chaud* (hot wine) at mountain hut **Bar Plan d'Aiguille** and acquaint yourself with the numerous *aiguilles* sculpting Chamonix' distinctive skyline. An information panel in front of the mid-station hut identifies each rocky spur soaring overhead.

James Bond would have a field day at the futuristic top station, entwined around Aiguille du Midi's burnt-orange granite

PRACTICALITIES
- aiguilledumidi.montblancnaturalresort.com ● adult/child €88/68.90
- variable hours, also weather dependent

summit. Dimly lit tunnels spaghetti from the cable car, past wintertime skiers donning crampons to tackle the **Vallée Blanche** (p500) off-piste descent, to a succession of outdoor **panoramic terraces**. Information panels identify what's what in the surrounding breathtaking sea of snowy peaks.

The Pipe

Follow signs to **Le Tube** – a 34m-long metal pipe wrapped around part of the rocky spur. Take your time to traverse the cylindrical walkway, perforated with five slit windows overlooking ant-sized rock climbers in summer dangling on **Pointe Rébuffat**. Information boards impress with mind-blowing facts such as the 300 cu metres of concrete, 80 tons of steel and 500-plus helicopter trips it took to construct this wild, gravity-defying gallery.

Step in the Void

Ride the lift up to **Pas dans le Vide**, a glass-walled and -floored cabin overhanging a 1000m drop which, at 3830m sits just 12m short of the summit. This the highest point of the Aiguille du Midi tourist site and views down are predictably exhilarating or terrifying depending on your head for heights.

Onwards to Italy

'Once seen, never ever forgotten' accurately sums up the vertiginous summertime journey across a dazzling, neon-white sea of seracs, crevasses and ice fields aboard the **Télécabine Panoramic Mont Blanc** (*aiguilledumidi.montblancnaturalresort.com; adult/child €41/34.80*). Departing late May to late September from Aiguille du Midi's top station, this panoramic chain of cherry-red 'bubbles' carries summertime explorers across the Glacier des Géants to **Pointe Helbronner** (3466m) on the French–Italian border. The spellbinding, 360-degree panorama here of vast alpine peaks in the Massif de Mont Blanc and neighbouring Italian and Swiss Alps is unmatched. Little wonder that Pointe Helbronner is nicknamed '*le balcon sur les géants*' (the balcony over the giants).

Now in Italy, board **Skyway Monte Bianco** (*montebianco.com; adult/child €58/41*) to continue the magical ice odyssey by cable car another 4km to **Courmayeur** (1300m), one of Italy's glitziest ski resorts in the Val d'Aosta (Aosta Valley). The white semi-spherical cabins spin slowly at a full 360 degrees during the once-in-lifetime journey, ensuring peerless views of all the alpine greats: Mont Blanc, Monta Rosa, Gran Paradiso, the Matterhorn. Hop out at mid-station **Pavillon du Mont Fréty** (2200m) to learn about the cableway's history in its Hangar 2173 exhibition space and alpine flora in the botanical garden. End on an epicurean high with a tasting flute of sparkling Cuvée des Guides – produced at high-altitude from Pré Blanc grapes by experimental winemaker Blanc de Morgex et de La Salle – in its mountain wine cellar **Cave Mont Blanc**.

LEARNING AT ALTITUDE

One of Europe's highest museum complexes, Aiguille du Midi contains a rabbit warren of themed spaces at altitude. Fly over Mont Blanc, Aiguille Verte, Grandes Jorasses and other 4000m peaks in the Mont Blanc Massif with a 10-minute film in the **Espace Ascension**; learn how the site was engineered in the **Espace Histoire**; and marvel at the world of elite mountaineering and extreme winter sports in the **Espace Vertical**.

TOP TIPS

● Check the weather forecast – this pricey, high-altitude trip is only worth it on bluebird days.

● Advance reservations are obligatory; book day and time-slot online.

● Dress warmly, even in summer.

● Use hiking boots or snow boots with decent grip.

● Sunglasses and sunscreen are essential; binoculars are a bonus.

● Move slowly to avoid dizziness, nausea, vertigo, laboured breathing and other symptoms of mild altitude sickness.

● Aiguille du Midi is off-limits to those under three years and not recommended for under fives, pregnant women and anyone with respiratory troubles, flu or a heart condition.

HIKING TRIP

Grand Balcon Nord

With a cable car up to the trailhead, Montenvers' vintage cogwheel train down at the end and glaciers to gaze at in between, this scenic hike (6.75km, elevation gain 200m) is a family favourite. Views of Mont Blanc and Chamonix' 7km-long Mer de Glace ('Sea of Ice') are superlative. At the trail end, a cable car down to France's longest glacier and an ice cave morph a short walk into a memorable day out.

❶ Plan de l'Aiguille du Midi

Begin at the mid-station of the **Téléphérique de l'Aiguille du Midi** (p501), with spectacular peak views: north, a chain of rocky *aiguilles* (needles); above, Aiguille du Midi (3842m) capped by its rocket-esque cable-car station; and south, snow-white Dôme du Goûter (4304m) and Mont Blanc (4805m), 8.2km away as the crow flies.

The Hike: From the Plan de l'Aiguille du Midi *buvette* (snack bar), follow signs for Refuge du Plan de l'Aiguille du Midi. At the fork, bear right to start traversing the mountainside north.

❷ Glacier de Blaitière

The footpath undulates across streams and the unsettling grey rubble of the receded Glacier de Blaitière. Straight ahead, admire Aiguille de l'M(2844m) with its M-shaped summit, and the pale red-rose peak of Aiguille Verte (4122m; 'Green Needle'), conquered by English climber Edward Whymper in 1865. This is one of Chamonix' most revered mountaineering icons.

Refuge du Montenvers

The Hike: At the 4km marker, fork right sharply uphill to 'Le Signal'.

3 Viewpoint of Petit Dru

Across the valley, admire the flame-red rocks of the Aiguille Rouges nature reserve. As the trail reaches its highest point, the path morphs into a catwalk of rock slabs and boulders – some meticulously stacked, others flung by glacial flow thousands of moons ago. Round the final bend, admire razor-sharp Petit Dru (3733m) with its feared-and-revered, 1000m-high granite wall of a summit.

The Hike: Follow the stone path to 'Le Signal'.

4 Mer de Glace

An apocalyptic field of ancient glacial till and modern walkers' cairns heralds the first breathtaking glimpse of France's largest **glacier** (p501). The Signal Forbes (2204m) viewpoint is named after Scottish glaciologist James David Forbes (1809–68) who spent time here studying how glaciers move (about 90m a year or 1cm a minute in the case of the Mer de Glace). Picnic.

The Hike: From the Le Signal marker, follow the signed footpath 1.75km downhill.

5 Refuge du Montenvers

This 19th-century hotel Refuge du Montenvers (1853) was base camp for pioneering ascents of Les Drus, Grandes Jorasses and other mythical peaks in Chamonix. Behind, a pyramid marker celebrates famous visitors, including Napoleon III and the Empress Eugénie who trekked up here from Chamonix assisted by 60 mountain guides and several mules. Lunch on the hotel terrace – go for a fondue, *diots* (pork sausages) simmered in local white wine, or something with *matouille Savoyarde* (oven-baked potatoes, garlic and white wine smothered in melted Tome des Bauges cheese). End with blueberry tart or a decadent Mont Blanc (vanilla and chestnut ice-cream sundae).

FAMILY THRILLS

Grotte de Glace: This ice cave, accessed by Montenvers' Mer de Glace cable car then 170 steps, is sculpted in the ice-blue glacial flanks of the Mer de Glace.

Parc de Merlet: May to September, observe marmots, chamois and ibex in this wildlife park above Les Houches; visits must be reserved online (parcdemerlet.com; adult/child €9/6). Snowshoe here in winter.

Luge Alpine Coaster: Fly down 1.3km of hairpin turns on Chamonix' two-person 'luge on rails', open January to mid-November (planards.fr; 1/6 descents €9.50/47.50).

Koala Grimpe: Climbing lessons and multi-day courses for kids (four to 12 years). Teens can tackle a via ferrata (koalagrimpe.com).

continued from p503

Hit **rue des Moulins** next, a quaint riverside street peppered with bars – some with terraces overlooking the Arve's racing milky-green water. The drink deals are always a steal at Anglophone dive bar **Bar'd Up** *(bardup-chamonix.metro.bar)*. With pool table, sports screenings, live bands and a club vibe, it's easy to stay until closing at 2am. Too noisy? Try live jazz and boutique gin at sophisticated garden-bar **Maison des Artistes** *(maisondesartistes-chamonix.com)*, or mead made from pine forest honey and DJs at the deck at **L'Hydromel** *(hydromel-bar-chamonix.com)*.

On Friday and Saturday nights, arrive before 10pm to bag free entry to A-lister club nights at **La Folie Douce** *(lafoliedoucehotels.com; variable admission)*. Keep your wits about you at less tamed **Amnesia Club** *(facebook.com/amnesiaclubchamonix; variable admission)*, the town's long-standing party temple, where doors open around 1.30am (until 6am).

Marvel at Mont Blanc in Lac Blanc
Get up high on Chamonix' most popular hiking trail

Don trainers or sturdy walking shoes for the short but steep and rocky hike up to **Lac Blanc** (2352m). Despite horrific

 EATING IN CHAMONIX: BEST MOUNTAIN LUNCHES

Refuge de Lognan: The blueberry tart is a rite of passage at this mountain shelter on Argentière's Intégrale run. Cash only. *noon-2pm Jun-Sep & Dec-Apr* €

La Crèmerie du Glacier: 1920s forest cabin famed valley-wide for its gratins, fondues and *croûtes* (wine-soaked bread, oven-baked with toppings). *11.30am-3pm* €€

Les Vieilles Luges: A roaring fire welcomes skies at the Old Sledges, an 18th-century farmhouse on the slopes in Les Houches. *12.30-3pm Tue-Sun Dec-Apr* €€

La Bergerie de Planpraz: The cosy Sheepfold gazes seductively at Mont Blanc from its sunny terrace perched at 2000m. Order fire-grilled meat. *noon-3pm Dec-Apr* €€€

Lac Blanc

summertime crowds (avoid in July and August), marvelling at razor-sharp reflections of Europe's highest peak in the picture-postcard alpine lake is mind-blowing. Wild dipping in the crystalline water is prohibited.

Beat the crowds by hitting the trail at 8.30am when cable cars open; assume three to four hours to cover the 8.5km return-hike from the top of **Télécabine de la Flégère** *(adult/ child return €24/20.40)* at 1877m. Alternatively, overnight in Lac Blanc's lakeside mountain hut **Refuge du Lac Blanc** *(refuge-lac-blanc.fr; per person full board €85)* to gorge on sunrise views in splendid isolation. The WWII-era, 40-bed hut with basic cafe is open June to September.

Heartland of Ski Design

Shop for made-to-measure wooden skis

Learn how touring and freestyle skis are still made traditionally by hand at **Rabbit on the Roof** *(instagram.com/rabbitontheroof)*, the artisanal workshop of Peter Steltzner, who crafts bespoke wooden skis in ash in an old mill in Les Praz. His intricate marquetry inlays in walnut wood, engravings and paintings make each pair a unique work of art. Book atelier visits in advance.

Watch for test days – big mountain après-ski sessions, 'after work' gigs in the dark, ski-touring initiation parties – at **Blackcrows** *(black-crows. com)*; the 'Chamonix nest' of the famous Chamoniard freeride brand also rents skis. It's named after the alpine chough, one of the few birds able to fly at high altitudes above 4000m.

ICONIC SKI RUNS

If Chamonix' Vallée Blanche leaves you desperate for more once-in-a-lifetime descents, race down Les Houches' black, 3.3km-long Kandahar (officially called La Verte des Houches and host to Kandahar World Cup since 1928) or hit **Alpe d'Huez** (p538) to tackle famous black run La Sarenne.

Beyond Chamonix

Move from the cosmopolitan high life of high-octane Chamonix into a valley of baroque chapels, villages and hamlets where time scarcely moves.

Places

Vallorcine p510
St-Gervais-les-Bains p512
Combloux p513
Megève p513

It is fitting that a village where bread is still baked in the communal *four à pain* (bread oven) heralds the beginning of the **Vallée de Chamonix**. Wedged between the Massif du Mont Blanc and anchored by giant Mont Blanc and the lesser-known Chaîne des Fiz, this valley sports big mountain peaks and small mountain villages at every turn. It has its fair share of modern sprawl around St-Gervais and Sallanches, and sophisticated Megève throbs with A-listers during the winter ski season. But take time to ride a storybook mountain train to lesser-known pastures or seek out adventure stories in chapels loaded with priceless art, and you'll be finely rewarded.

Vallorcine

TIME FROM CHAMONIX: **30MIN**

A cinematic arrival

After the rush of action-packed Chamonix, the slower pace of rural life in old-world Vallorcine is refreshing. Chugging into the hamlet's toy-like station aboard the little red Mont Blanc Express train is picture-postcard stuff, and knowing Switzerland is just 2km north injects instant thrill.

Get a sense of just how tight-knit this small mountain community is at its linchpin the **Église Notre Dame de l'Assomption**, dating to the 13th century and rebuilt in 1755 after several avalanches. Inside, stained glass by contemporary South Korean artist Kim En Joong evokes the secular glass art depicting skiers in Chamonix' baroque Église St-Michel (p503).

Grassroots grazing

Gravitate to **La Ferme de Vallorcine** *(instagram.com/la_ferme_de_vallorcine)* where organic farmers Victorien and Melissa use milk from their 20-head herd of dairy cows to craft soft Vallorcin cheese (not unlike *Reblochon*), *Tomme de Savoie,* raclette, creamy *faisselles* (thick cream cheese) and yoghurts. Buy a round at the farm shop to later picnic on. In summer Victorien leads weekly guided farm visits and occasional *randonnées vaches* (guided walks with her cows) in lush summer pastures.

The ultimate grassroots graze? Lunching on gloriously golden puddles of gooey raclette on the sun-blazed winter terrace of **Le Café Comptoir** *(lecafecomptoir.com)*. Outdoor

GETTING AROUND

From the valley's **TGV station St-Gervais-Le Fayet**, 5km north of St-Gervais town centre, the **Mont Blanc Express** *(mont-blanc-express.ch)* has trundled north along the Vallée de Chamonix for over a century.

TGV arrivals can access the ski slopes via the 1909 railway **Tramway du Mont Blanc** (p512) to Bellevue above Les Houches or, since 2024, aboard the Le Valléen (linking St-Gervais-Le Fayet station with St-Gervais town) and L'Alpin cable cars to Le Bettex in St-Gevais' ski area.

Paragliding, Mont Blanc

barbecues, dances and concerts jazz up the summer season and – should you be unable to tear yourself away, – the cafe has rooms behind in a cluster of traditional *mazots* (irresistible, dollhouse-sized chalets).

Ski slow, fast or like it's 1966

In the middle of the village, on the riverbanks of L'Eau Noire, a cable car whisks winter skiers up to 21 gentle beginner-blue and intermediate-red runs in the unchallenging **Domaine de Balme–Le Tour** ski area. Beautiful views, of the Chamonix Valley and Swiss Alps to the north, give slower-paced ski touring and snowshoeing irresistible appeal.

If it's cheese and tranquility you're seeking, the steep, two-hour skin up to **Refuge de Loriaz** *(refuge-loriaz.com)* at 2020m for lunch is a ski-touring secret few locals like to share. Stay overnight in the former 1920s cheese dairy to dip into a cheese fondue for dinner.

Alternatively, rent an original pair of leather lace-up ski boots and wooden skis from the 1960s to hit the slopes during Vallorcine's slow-right-down, retro ski fest **Le Comptoir des Légéndes** *(comptoirdeslegendesduski.com; ski hire €10)* in March.

Expert skiers hungry for something new and fast can dabble in speed-riding with a mini-sail in Domaine de Balme's trademark open bowl of slopes. Paragliding school **Les Ailes du Mont Blanc** *(lesailesdumontblanc.com; from €210 per day)*, inside Chamonix' Maison de la Montagne, runs courses.

WHY I LOVE THE CHAMONIX VALLEY

Nicola Williams, Lonely Planet writer

Living locally, I'm eligible each year to run the MCC – a 40km stage of Chamonix' annual, iconic Ultra Trail du Mont Blanc (UTMB). Speed-hiking up unknown forest trails and scampering down unfamiliar mountainsides only confirms my deep love for a valley I've spent years exploring. I've canyoned white water in Vallorcine, and hiked up to La Junction (2589m) to be spellbound by the apocalyptic frenzy of seracs and crevasses where the Bossons and Taconnaz glaciers meet. I've snowshoed in forests around Servoz to cold-plunge in wild fairy pools and skinny-dip in waterfalls. The natural discoveries in this valley are endless, as are the myriad different crazy ways you can dig in and get your knees properly dirty.

 EATING BEYOND CHAMONIX: FONDUE WITH VIEW

Chez Mireille – Le Debarlin: Exceptional, semi-gastronomic Savoyard cuisine in Cordon village, in a chalet with Mont Blanc views. *hours vary* €€

Le Café Comptoir: Alpine cuisine with quirk in Vallorcine: try Armagnac-flambéed fondue and salted-caramel mousse. *9am-11pm, to 5pm Sun* €€

La Ferme des Trois Ours: Cheesy specialities in Vallorcine, in a farm restaurant strung with cow bells. *noon-2pm & 7-10pm Dec-May & Jun-Sep* €€

Le Refuge: Megève's go-to address for decadent truffle-laced cheese fondue in the mountain hamlet of Leutaz. *noon-2pm & 7-10.30pm Dec-Apr & Jun-Sep* €€€

TRAMWAY DU MONT BLANC

In service since 1913, this mountain train's four racing-green carriages – pulled by steam locomotive until 1956, now electric – are named after the daughters of the farmer whose land the historic cogwheel train crossed: Anne, Jeanne, Marie and Marguerite. Incredibly, when construction work began on the line in 1906 the plan was to extend the line to the top of Mont Blanc, but the outbreak of WWI intervened. To this day, alpinists attempting summit climbs up Mont Blanc continue to the end of the TMB line at Nid d'Aigle (2380m), from where they climb on foot to the Tête Rousse and Le Goûter *refuges* – starting points for bagging Europe's biggest mountain.

Combloux

St-Gervais-les-Bains TIME FROM CHAMONIX: **45MIN**

Ride France's highest cogwheel train

You almost want to stick your hand out the window and caress the bulbous, virgin-white heights of Dôme du Goûter, Mont Blanc and Dômes de Miage, so close do these iconic peaks feel from the **Tramway du Mont Blanc** *(tramwaydumontblanc. montblancnaturalresort.com; adult/child return €34/28.90)*. Boarding in **St-Gervais-Le Fayet**, sit on the right-hand side to bag the best views on the 49-minute journey up to **Plateau de Bellevue** (1800m). Ticket reservations are essential; upon arrival at Bellevue, book your return train.

A summer hiking trail (5.8km, 2½ hours) climbs from Bellevue to Nid d'Aigle (2380m). Views of Glacier de Bionnassay from this 'Eagle's Nest' are mind-blowing. Vertiginous in spots, with metal ladders and cables, the walk is not suitable for children or inexperienced walkers. Bring poles to traverse snowy patches, and lunch or overnight at spectacular 1930s mountain hut **Refuge du Nid d'Aigle** (2372m; *montblanc. ffcam.fr*); open mid-June to late September, online reservations obligatory.

Learn how alpine gin is made

Genépi (herbal liqueur) might be the Alps' ancestral spirit of choice (and only respectable way to end a fondue or other cheesy meal), but new-gen distillers are turning their skills

DRINKING IN MEGÈVE: PARTY SPOTS

La Folie Douce: Wild nights out begin on the snow at this piste-side icon between Megève and St-Gervais. *9.30am-4.30pm*

La Ferme St-Amour: Glamorous hostesses lead the drinking into the wee hours at this glitzy A-lister restaurant-bar. Dress the part. *7pm-3am*

Les 5 Rues: Pair Savoie wine or Moët & Chandon with live jazz, blues and DJs at this 1950s music club. *7pm-3am*

Cocoon Club: Fiery cocktails, shots and chasers well into the wee hours at Megève's veteran nightclub. *5pm-3am, to 5am Thu-Sun*

to gin. Discover how at **Distillerie St-Gervais** (*distillerie saintgervais.com*). In a solar-powered alpine hut built from recycled materials at 1430m, Scotsman James Abbott produces 135 bottles of small-batch Gin du Mont Blanc from each distillation. He sticks recycled-paper labels on glass bottles with a milk-based glue, and – with an advance reservation – is happy to show gin curios around his artisanal mountain distillery.

Combloux

TIME FROM CHAMONIX: **35MIN**

Uncover art along the Sentier du Baroque

Tear your eyes off those hypnotic mountains and focus on the artistic treasures that village chapels, built for 18th-century Catholics, squirrel away instead. Relatively flat, from Combloux, the **Sentier du Baroque** ribbons 20km (count on a seven-hour walk) to **Les Contamines-Montjoie**, where 14 oratories from 1728 frame the final path to **Chapelle Notre-Dame de la Gorge**. All along the trail, Baroque chapels are awash with ornamentation, trompe l'oeil frescoes and bold colour – lots of neoclassical sky blue.

In pretty **St-Nicolas de Véroce** (1180m), 10km into the walk, learn about *colporteurs* – young men from this remote hamlet who headed east on foot across the Alps between the 15th and 18th centuries to make their fortune peddling haberdashery. The money they sent home funded St-Nicolas' jewel of a baroque church and filled the **Musée d'Art Sacré** (*free*) in the neighbouring presbytery with artistic riches from all over Europe.

Megève

TIME FROM CHAMONIX: **45MIN**

Hobnob with the Parisian jet set

It's terribly upmarket in Megève, an all-season Parisian favourite where well-heeled tourists clatter along cobbled streets in horse-drawn carriages and pooches in bags are taken out for lunch. The village gained its glad rags in the 1920s when Baroness de Rothschild developed it as a ski resort: think designer fashion boutiques, Michelin-starred gastronomic temples, an outdoor ice rink and the onion bulb bell tower of 13th- to 19th-century **Église St-Jean Baptiste**. All cradled by 400km of downhill runs and the Massif de Mont Blanc as a backdrop. At après-ski hour, hobnob on the snow at jet-set central **La Folie Douce** (*lafoliedouce.com*) or Asian-flavoured **Le Tigrr Princesse** (*tigrr.fr*).

MODERN SACRED ART IN THE ALPS

Now recognised as a major milestone in the development of modern sacred art in France, the **Église de Plateau d'Assy** (*Église Notre-Dame-de-Toute-Grâce*), a 15-minute drive from St-Gervais in Plateau d'Assy, caused quite the furore when it was consecrated in 1950. Both its decoration and raison d'être – to serve care personnel working in local sanatoriums as well as the tuberculosis sufferers they treated – were reactionary. Artists of the day were commissioned for their skill rather than religious leaning, hence the priceless portfolio of early-modernist paintings, ceramics and mosaics by Henri Matisse, Marc Chagall, Georges Braque, Fernand Léger etc on display inside the church today.

 EATING IN MEGÈVE: DOWN-TO-EARTH DINES

Pizza d'Ici par Fred: Five-star sourdough pizzas, panini and waffles to take away from Fred's van on rue Charles Feige. *6-9.30pm Wed-Sun* €

Le River: When a late breakfast or brunch beckons, this tea room by the river hits the sweet spot. *9.30am-3.30pm Tue-Sun* €

Snack de la Petite Fontaine: The evening-only pots of cheese fondue at Justine and Édouard's snack bar are legendary. *9am-5pm, to 10pm Wed, Fri & Sat* €€

Alpage de Prè Rosset: Cheesy cuisine without pretension in a rustic shepherd's hut from 1853, on the slopes at 1893m. Rooms too. *noon-2.30pm Dec-Apr & Jul-Aug* €€

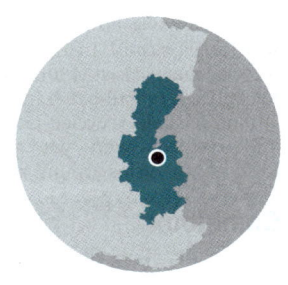

Lake Annecy

MOUNTAIN VIEWS | CHIC VILLAGES | BOATING

☑ TOP TIP

Annecy was designed for endless *flânerie*. Download the **Annecy Paysage** *(annecy-paysages.com)* app, designed by students, to explore Annecy through contemporary sculptures and public art installations decorating its lakefront and gardens. Grab digital or paper maps at the **tourist office** *(en.lac-annecy.com)*.

A chic weekend flit for Parisians, France's third-largest lake (Lac d'Annecy in French) promises lake lounging between mountain peaks. Chic restaurants and boutiques pepper wealthy Annecy, the lake's main town, which was made great by the medieval counts of Geneva and subsequent dukes of Savoy.

Colourful facades and flower-fringed canals characterise Annecy's old town, nicknamed 'Venice of the Alps'. Picnic-friendly lawns front the lake shore, ribboned with cycling and foot paths. The iron-arched footbridge of Pont des Amours (Lovers' Bridge), crossing from here into tree-shaded Jardins de l'Europe, exudes romance. Ditto for rowing boats moored beneath trees along Promenade Jacquet. Beyond Annecy town, wooden jetties protruding from grassy lakeside verges and metal ladders plunging into the water inspire wild dipping.

Annecy celebrates Mardi Gras with a Venetian masked carnival; August's Fête du Lac (fireworks, music and special effects) is equally thrilling. There's no 'right way' to explore here. Bike, boat, SUP or paraglider: pick your means to level up with Savoie's outdoor-action set.

Timeless Romance in a Handsome Old Town
French *flânerie* in Annecy Vieille Ville

Commanding views across ochre rooftops and flower-festooned canals to the lake and burly Massif des Bauges beyond,

 GETTING AROUND

Altibus *(altibus.com)* operates lake buses and **Compagnie des Bateaux** *(bateaux-annecy.com)* runs seasonal Navibus boats to the main villages. Bicycles can be taken on board for €4; rent classic and e-wheels at **Cyclable** *(velo-annecy.fr; per day from €24)*.

Find **Vélonecy** *(velonecy.com)* bike-share stations at Annecy **train station**, 15 minutes' walk from the lake, and by the Tour du Lac cycling path next to Park & Ride car parks in Duingt and St-Jorioz.

Château d'Annecy (musees.annecy.fr; adult/under 12yr €7/free) is the crowning glory of Annecy's romantic **Vielle Ville** (old town). Residence to the Counts of Geneva in the 13th and 14th centuries, it was abandoned three centuries on. The striking white castle cradles fine arts, natural history, archaeology and ethnology exhibitions today.

From the chateau, drop steeply down along stone-paved **Rampe du Château** to prison-turned-history museum **Palais de l'Isle** (adult/child €5/2.50). The best views of this eye-catching stone building, squatting on a triangular islet in the **Canal du Thiou** since 1325, are from **Pont Perrière**, the old town's iconic canal bridge safeguarded by Baroque **Église St-François de Salès**. Venetian vibes here are undeniable. Lap them up over a candied chestnut or génépi cone from 1960s ice-cream parlour **Glacier des Alpes** (glacierdesalpes.fr; 1/2/3 balls €3.50/6/7.50) on people-busy rue Perrière.

Feasting on Fresh Féra
Fishy fine dining in Talloires

To know Lake Annecy is celebrated for the purity of its waters only heightens the epicurean joy of devouring féra (whitefish) and écrivisses (crayfish), caught in the quiet of the night by one of Lake Annecy's two remaining professional fishermen.

In picture-postcard **Talloires**, 12km south of Annecy, **Le 1903** (perebise.com/restaurant-le-1903; menus from €80) is the razor-sharp, more affordable, modern bistro of the legendary, double Michelin-starred **Auberge du Père Bise** (perebise.com; menu from €260) – and the hot spot to feast on the highly sought-after catch of St-Jorioz fisherman Florent Capretti. Tables in the Scandi-styled dining room peer through floor-to-ceiling windows at the water and, depending on the season, you might find your lake fish laced with locally foraged or harvested wild garlic, morels or pea-green asparagus.

Lake Panoramas & Spectacular Sunsets
Fly with the birds above Col de la Forclaz

It requires no skill – just guts or the dream to fly with birds – to paraglide over Lake Annecy. April to November, tandem flights take off from the **Site de Montmin** (1276m) up high near the **Col de la Forclaz** (1150m) at the lake's southern tip. They land 10 to 20 minutes later at official landing zones

continued on p520

BEST SOUVENIR SHOPPING IN ANNECY

Établi 65: Chopping boards, ceramics, soap and fashion accessories in a boutique showcasing unique gifts by local artists and craftspeople.

La Bouchonnerie: Savoie wines with stories and craft beer in a specialist wine cellar on rue Président Favre.

Babeth: DIY génépi home kits, candles, soaps, vases and funky homewares. Grab a coffee too at this rue des Glières design boutique.

Marché de l'Art et des des Créateurs: Unique souvenirs and chit-chat with artists and creators are a cert at this day-long market filling quai de Vicenza and rue St-Maurice; last Saturday of each month.

Pierre Gay: Take home a round of Reblochon or chunk of Tomme de Bauges; this third-generation fromagerie vacuum-packs.

 EATING IN ANNECY: OUR PICKS

| Marché de la Vieille Ville: Open-air street market in the old town, stalls brimming with Savoyard cheeses, charcuterie and food to go. 7am-1pm Tue, Fri & Sun € | Les Baigneurs Café: Breakfast, brunch, specialist coffee and lunchtime tartines on a sun-soaked terrace. 8.30am-5.30pm Wed-Fri, from 9am Sat & Sun € | Bon Pain Bon Vin: Local produce fuels this old-school buvette with 1960s interior, traditional cuisine and specials chalked on the board. 10-1am €€ | Saba: Feast on creative French-Japanese fusion with local foodies at this sassy old-town bistro. noon-1.30pm & 7-9pm Mon, Tue, Thu & Fri, 7-9pm Wed €€€ |

LAKE ANNECY FRENCH ALPS & JURA

🟠 HIGHLIGHTS
1 Col de la Forclaz
2 Talloires
3 Vieille Ville

🔴 SIGHTS
4 Abbaye de Talloires
5 Château d'Annecy
6 Château de Duingt
7 Château de Menthon-St-Bernard
8 Doussard Plage
9 Église St-François de Sales
10 Palais de l'Isle
11 Plage d'Angon
12 Plage de la Brune
13 Plage de l'Impérial
14 Plage de St-Jorioz
15 Plage des Choseaux–Clos Berthet
16 Plage des Marquisats
17 Pont Perrière
18 Réserve Naturelle du Bout-du-Monde
19 Tour de Brauvivier

🟢 ACTIVITIES
20 Compagnie des Bateaux
21 Grotte de Notre Dame du Lac
22 Site de Montmin
23 SkiWake74
24 Takamaka

⚫ SLEEPING
25 Hôtel de Savoie
26 Hôtel du Château
27 Hôtel-Restaurant Les Tilleuls
28 Imperial Palace
29 Le Boutik

- **EATING**
- 30 Auberge de Montmin
- 31 Auberge du Père Bise
- 32 Bon Pain Bon Vin
- 33 Boulangerie du Lac
- 34 Glacier des Alpes
- 35 Le 1903
- 36 Le Balcon du Lac
- 37 Le Cadre
- 38 Le Roc
- 39 Les Baigneurs Café
- 40 Les Jardins du Taillefer
- 41 Marché de la Vieille Ville
- 42 Saba

- **DRINKING & NIGHTLIFE**
- 43 Café de la Place

- **SHOPPING**
- 44 Babeth
- 45 Etabli 65
- 46 La Bouchonnerie
- 47 Marché de l'Art et des Créateurs
- 48 Pierre Gay

- **INFORMATION**
- 49 Tourist Office

- **TRANSPORT**
- 50 Cyclable
- 51 Train Station

CYCLING TOUR

Tour du Lac by Bike

Lap up big mountain views and bijou villages on this 42km lake loop ride, best tackled clockwise (elevation gain 300m). The more scenic, eastern-shore bike path often skirts the water's edge, while the busier western-shore path is an inland spin along an abandoned 1930s train line. The route should take three to four hours excluding stops.

❶ Veyrier du Lac

Pick up the two-way cycling path in front of Cyclable (p514) and cruise 6km alongside the D909, past serrated Mont Veyrier (1291m) on your left. Break for coffee in Veyrier du Lac at Le Pêcheur, on grassy **Plage de la Brune**.

The Ride: Follow green signs for Menthon-St-Bernard along a quiet, residential back street.

❷ Menthon-St-Bernard

Climb up to place de l'Église in Menthon-St-Bernard, 3km south; its fairy-tale **Château de Menthon-St-Bernard** is a 2km detour uphill. At **Café de la Place** by the village fountain, refuel on coffee and a *tarte écureuil* (caramelised walnut tart) from the bakery.

The Ride: Stick to low gear for the climb along the traffic-busy D909A to Écharvines. Stay alert on the steep downhill swoop to Talloires.

❸ Talloires

It was in this pretty lakefront village cradling 17th-century **Abbaye de Talloires** that Cézanne painted in 1896. Admire the limestone hulk of Roc de Chère (601m) and, across the water, Château de Duingt. This is the lake's narrowest point where the built-up *'grand lac'* (north) spills into the wilder *'petit lac'* (south).

The Ride: Count 30 minutes (8.7km) on a dedicated cycling path to the lake's southern tip.

Château de Menthon-St-Bernard

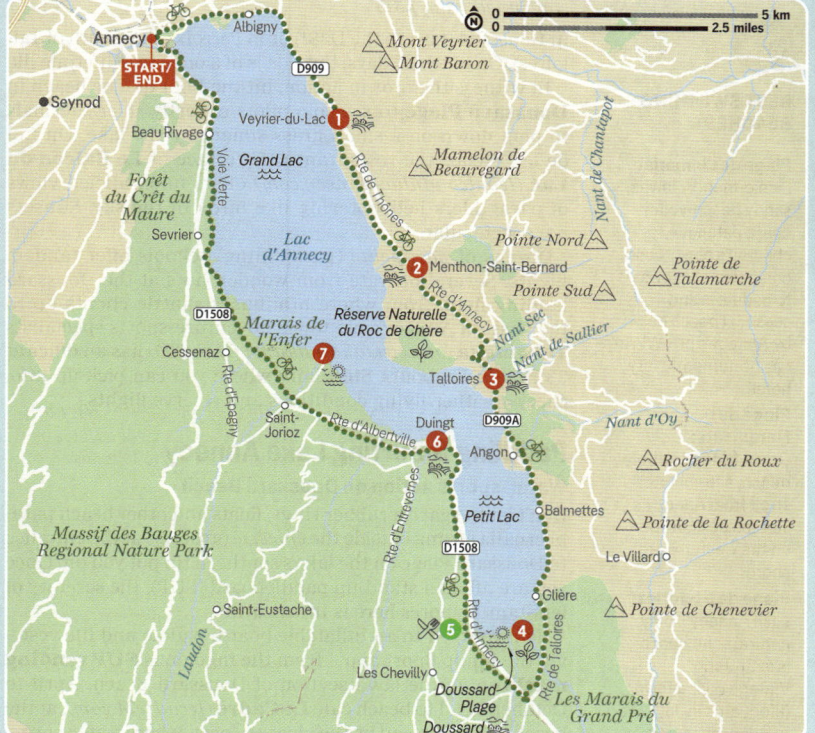

④ Réserve Naturelle du Bout-du-Monde

Doussard is the springboard for walks in the Réserve Naturelle du Bout-du-Monde, protecting reed beds. Along the reserve's circular boardwalk (3km), keep your eyes peeled for beavers. Climb medieval **Tour de Brauvivier** to watch paragliders dropping over rocky Dents de Lanfon (1824m) and Lanfonnet (1793m).

The Ride: After the 'Doussard Plage' turning, look for Les Jardins du Taillefer signposted on your left. Follow the gravel track 300m to the farm.

⑤ Les Jardins du Taillefer

Hemmed in by a turquoise lake and the fertile pastures of Massif des Bauges, the organic farm Les Jardins du Taillefer (jardins-du-taillefer.fr) is well placed for an idyllic garden lunch with a seasonal, vegetarian menu. Don't skimp on the cheese course.

The Ride: You're now on the Voie Verte, a greenway linking Annecy town with Val de Chaise, 13km south of Doussard.

⑥ Duingt

Pedalling through a defunct railway tunnel heralds your arrival in quaint Duignt (amazing village bakery alert!). Park and follow the footpath 10 minutes to hillside **Grotte de Notre Dame du Lac** for breathtaking lake views. Lakefront **Château de Duingt** hosts seasonal exhibitions.

The Ride: Cruise 3.5km cruise to your next stop. After **Hôtel-Restaurant Les Tilleuls**, look for signs on your right pointing to *le plage*.

⑦ St-Jorioz

Locals have been dipping in their lake's crystalline waters from the municipal beach here since 1929. Join the summertime throngs for a swim before your return to Annecy (8km, 25 minutes). Kudos for the retro *plongeoir* (diving tower).

BEST SWIMMING BEACHES

Plage de l'Impérial: Picnic-friendly lawns, sandy beach-volley court, pétanque, children's playground, concreted shallows to paddle in and seasonal beach bar – by Annecy's pre-WWI casino-turned-luxury hotel.

Plage des Marquisats: Grass-fringed pebble beach, a 15-minutes stroll from Annecy's Jardins de l'Europe on the western lake shore.

Plage de St-Jorioz: Lake Annecy's only natural sand beach is in St-Jorioz. Vintage diving tower (lifeguards in July and August), changing cabins, showers, snack bar.

Plage d'Angon: A spot to be seen, 2km south of Talloires, with beach volleyball and pétanque.

Plage des Choseaux–Clos Berthet: Untamed grass and pebbles in Sévrier, a 10-minute walk south from the busy municipal beach.

continued from p515

in Doussard (next to the D281) or in Perroix (2km south of Talloires). On bluebird days, the ride is of a once-in-a-lifetime ilk.

To witness the pros in action, hit the Bout du Lac beach in **Doussard Plage** to see solo pilots expertly steer thermals to plop down on a small grass square by the lake. On Col de la Forclaz, the restaurant-cafe terrace of **Le Balcon du Lac** *(lebalcondulac-annecy.com)* offers unparalleled views of paragliders helicoptering like birds in the sky. Sunsets are spectacular.

Dozens of *parapente* (paragliding) schools offer tandem flights. Several operate from wooden huts at the Doussard landing field, from where minibuses shuttle clients up to the pass. In Annecy's old town, adventure-sports specialists **Takamaka** *(annecy.takamaka.fr; from €95)* has an office at 23 rue du Faubourg Ste-Claire where you can pick up info, check weather/flying conditions and reserve flights.

Paddling & Surfing Lake Annecy

Water-sports action on Doussard Beach

Don't let the garish rubber rings, floats and other beach paraphernalia strung outside the *épicerie* (grocery) at the entrance to Doussard Plage on the lake's southern tip put you off. Once you are afloat a stand-up paddleboard (SUP), the serenity of less-tamed shores here is intoxicating.

Help yourself to an inflatable board, paddle and life vest – via the Equip Sport app – from the ingenious **SUP vending machine** on the lawn section of Doussard Beach. April to October, head to beach cafe **Le Cadre** *(lecadre74.com)*, at the beach's opposite end by the pleasure port, where water-sports school **SkiWake74** *(skiwake74.com; rental per hr €17)* rents kayaks and SUPs. You can also water ski, wakeboard or surf the waves of a latest-generation speedboat here.

 EATING AROUND LAKE ANNECY: OUR PICKS

Boulangerie du Lac: Five-star baguette sandwiches, pastries and picnic fare at Duignt's artisanal bakery, one of the Alps' best. *6am-7.30pm Thu-Tue* €

Les Jardins du Taillefer: It doesn't get more bucolic than lunch at this farm (p519) near Doussard; strictly homemade and veggie. *noon-2pm & 7-10pm Fri-Sun* €

Le Roc: One of two foodie musts by celebrity chef Yoann Conte in his iconic Maison Bleue, on the lakeshore in Veyrier-du-Lac. *noon-2pm & 7-8.30pm Fri-Tue* €€€

Auberge de Montmin: All-local produce, wild flowers and herbs govern Florian Favario's kitchen at this twin-starred Michelin address on the Col de la Forclaz €€€

Beyond Lake Annecy

With some of the cleanest lake waters in Europe sustaining a masterpiece tableau of lush green surrounds, it's only natural that Lake Annecy residents are an overwhelmingly outdoorsy bunch.

Winter skiers, summer walkers and four-season bikers are spoilt for choice with a flush of mountain resorts no more than an hour by car or bus.

East in the Chaîne des Aravis is fiercely French La Clusaz, with 125km of downhill runs for intermediate skiers, and smaller but ski-scenic Le Grand Bornand. Cross-country skiers gravitate to low-octane Semnoz in the wooded Massif des Bauges. In nearby Le Sambuy, a warming climate closed the last chairlift back in 2023, but its gentle hiking trails remain as hot as ever with weekending families.

North of Annecy, spectacular highs characterise Les Portes du Soleil (PDS), France's second-largest ski area with cross-border skiing (no passport or ID required) and world-class mountain-biking.

Places
Les Portes du Soleil p521
Vallée des Aravis p523

Les Portes du Soleil

TIME FROM ANNECY: 1HR

Ski two countries in snow-sure Avoriaz

Mogul fiends won't find bigger or better than white-knuckle **Le Mur Suisse** (the Swiss Wall) mogul run. It's accessible from the French ski resort of **Avoriaz** *(avoriaz.com)*, purpose-built in 1966 atop a mountain edge at 1800m. Once you've dared launch yourself down the icy headwall, which reaches a treacherous angle of 35 degrees to 40 degrees at the top, you're in Switzerland. Giant moguls, some the size of small cars, rip the entire piste – classified orange (that's tougher than black) and officially called Le Pas de Chavanette.

Should moguls not rock your boat, this is one of the few ski runs where it's acceptable for skiers to ride a chairlift *down* the piste. At the top of the run, hop on the Chavanette chairlift to Swiss **Champéry**, if only to marvel at the monstrous Swiss Wall moguls and ant-sized skiers falling like rag dolls. Before taking the chairlift back up Avoriaz (PDS ski pass required), grab a delicious taste of Switzerland aka a puddle of warm gooey raclette cheese, a 26 Switzerland craft beer and shot of *abricotine* (apricot liqueur) at no-frills wooden hut **Buvette Chavanette**.

GETTING AROUND

Private minibuses and shared taxis link Geneva airport with Les Portes du Soleil; Altibus *(altibus.com)* runs bus shuttles from **Thonon-les-Bains train station**. The latter also runs shuttles from Annecy train station to La Clusaz. Reserve weeks in advance.

Beyond these main ski resorts, your own car is indispensable for getting around. Let cheese be your guide: craft your own driving or cycling itinerary along the **Route des Fromages de Savoie** *(fromagesdesavoie.fr).*

FAMILY FUN IN LES PORTES DU SOLEIL

Snow Park de la Chapelle: Freestyle skiers congregate in this unmatched snow park, one of four in Avoriaz. Sunset from the terrace is legendary.

Avokart: Winter or summer, 'sledging' in Avoriaz means hurtling down a 3.2km descent in a three-wheel go-kart *(skipass-avoriaz.com/avokart)*.

Alta Lumina: Take a night walk though an enchanted forest in Les Gets filled with fantastical illuminations *(altalumina.com)*.

Luge 4 Saisons: Turbo-boost family fun in Les Gets with a descent on the resort's '4 season' luge *(lesgets.com/luge-4-saisons)*.

Les Landarets: Is there anything nicer than an ice cream on a summer's day and mountain goats to pet and snap pics of?

Morzine

Ice dive in Lac de Montriond

Contrary to common perception, you don't need any experience or diving license to ice dive. Plunging beneath the frozen surface of **Lac de Montriond** with a diving instructor from **École de Plongée Aquaventure** *(plongeesousglace-montriond.com; day/night dive €110/150, ice floating €55/65)*, expect to stay toasty warm, oddly vertical and completely blown away by the deeply profound silence and beauty of an extraordinary underwater world.

Bar the magnified sound of your own raspy breathing, a piercing stillness cloaks each dive. Daylight filters in through pinpricks in the ice and hypnotic bubbles dance like quicksilver beneath the frozen crust. Actual time spent underwater is no more than 20 minutes, but count 1½ hours to don the cumbersome dry suit, walk to/from dive holes cut in the ice pulling your kit-loaded sled, and wait by the water's edge while others in the small group dive. Dives typically happen from late December until early March; the ice must be at least 8cm – at 15cm a bus could apparently cross the frozen lake.

Wear thermal underwear and devour a wedge of *tarte de myrtilles* (blueberry tart) afterwards at **L'Auberge**

EATING IN LES GETS & MORZINE: LUNCH ON THE SLOPES

Le Wetzet: Savoury crepes and salads on a sun-bathed terrace, heartier dining in a tiny all-wood interior in Les Gets. *9am-4.30pm late Dec-early Apr, Jul & Aug* €

La Terrasse des Lindarets: Kick back in Les Lindarets' 'goat village' over top-drawer cheese fondue, music and an après-ski party vibe. *9am-5pm mid-Dec-mid-Apr & mid-Jun-mid-Sep* €€

Chez Nannon: Cheese rules the rustic roost at this traditional Savoyard kitchen in Morzine. *9.30am-5pm late Dec-early Apr, Jul & Aug* €€

La Païka: Lunch on steaks fire-grilled in the outside kitchen and famously lavish desserts on this sunny terrace in Les Gets. *9am-4.30pm late Dec-early Apr* €€€

(leboutdulac.com), a quaint chalet restaurant with a spectacular mountain-peak view the other end of the lake.

Embrace the Wild in Party-Loving Morzine

Après-ski doesn't get wilder than party-loving **Morzine** *(morzine-avoriaz.com)*, a Brit-packed resort with ample slopes for beginners, intermediates and families, and boozy pubs in spades. Prize for best 'in the wild' experience is shared between the vertiginous panorama from the 15m-long glass walkway **Le Pas de l'Aigle** *(the Eagle's Step; free)* suspended atop lofty **Pointe de Nyon** (2019m) – access via the Pointe de Nyon chairlift – and the ski resort's unique falconry experiences.

During the ski season, you can watch free **falconry shows** on Plateau de Nyon, ski with eagles *(€25)* or hold three birds of prey during a 40-minute falconry workshop *(€75)*. From April to September, an eye-opening afternoon at the birds' home, breeding and research centre **Les Aigles du Léman** *(lesaiglesduleman.com; adult/child €15/13)*, a 45-minute drive away on the shore of Lake Geneva, is time well-spent. Eighty white-tailed eagles will have been reintroduced from here into the wild in the Lake Geneva area by 2030.

Vallée des Aravis

TIME FROM ANNECY: **35MIN**

Backstage in a Cheese Ripener's Cellar

To understand the ancestral *savoir-faire* or 'know-how' behind *Reblochon* – the holy grail of Savoyard cheeses – join a backstage tour at family-run **Fromagerie Paccard** *(reblochon-paccard.fr; adult/child €10/7; tours 2.30pm Tue & Thu)*, tucked away in the Vallée des Aravis near the foodie hamlet of Manigod.

As an *artisan affineur* (artisan ripener), Paccard buys fresh cheese from 30-odd farm producers in Haute-Savoie. Each cheese – soft and hard, cow, goat or sheep – is meticulously washed, rubbed and ripened in subterranean red-brick cellars to create a perfect finished cheese. Visits climax with tastings of four or five cheeses, including soft and creamy *Reblochon*, Abondance (the secret to a *fondue Savoyard*), *Tomme de Savoie* and *raclette de Savoie*. If the Paccard boutique has blue-veined Bleu de Termignon in stock, buy a chunk – it's impossible to find outside Haute-Savoie.

CHEESY SAVOYARD SPECIALITIES

Fondue Savoyard: In Savoie equal parts of grated Comté, gruyere and Beaufort cheese are melted with white wine in a garlic-smeared pot. Dip chunks of crusty bread into the pot with a skewer.

Tartiflette: *Reblochon* is sliced and layered between sliced potatoes, diced bacon, cream and nutmeg in this classic oven-baked dish.

Raclette: Melted *raclette* – occasionally smoked or peppered – is scraped from a standing grill onto boiled potatoes. *Cornichons* (gherkins), charcuterie and green salad are essentials.

Berthoud: Slices of Abondance cheese are oven-baked with Savioe white wine, sweet Madeira wine, nutmeg and pepper until bubbling, crisp and golden.

Gratin de crozets: Savoyard 'pasta' squares are oven baked with Beaufort or *Reblochon* to create a gooey, crisp-crust gratin (oven bake).

 DRINKING IN LES PORTES DU SOLEIL: PARTY ICONS

Le Tremplin: This Morzine institution, a 1936 vintage, is the place to drink, dance to DJ beats and live bands on Pleney. *4-8pm mid-Dec–mid-Apr & mid-Jun–Aug*

La Folie Douce: Aerial cabaret shows, DJs and dancing on tables in Avoriaz, conveniently within walking-rolling distance of the Prodains Express cable car. *noon–6pm mid-Dec–mid-Apr*

Cavern Bar: Catch the best international bands on the Alps' circuit on stage at Morzine's much-loved music venue. *4pm–2am late Dec–early Apr*

Igloo Chalet Club: Les Gets' only nightclub, from 1938, lays claim to being the oldest in the French Alps. Expect rock, pop and a mixed-bag set. *midnight–5am late Dec–early Apr*

Chambéry

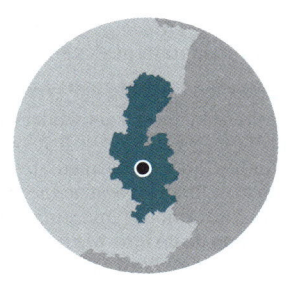

MOUNTAIN VIBE | CHEESE | HISTORY & CULTURE

GETTING AROUND

Chambéry is eminently walkable. Bus lines A, C and D operated by **Synchro Mobilités** *(synchro.grandchambery.fr; €1.40)* link the **train station** with the chateau, otherwise it's a 15-minute walk or five-minute cycle using one of the city's public-sharing bikes. Classic and electric wheels can be accessed at Synchro Vélostations bike stations *(synchro.grandchambery.fr/velo/; rental per hour from €2)* all over town.

From the backstage labyrinth of enigmatic *allées* (alleys) to the elegant Italianate arcades of 19th-century rue de Boigne and bistros cooking up aromatic *diots au vin blanc* (Savoyard pork sausages simmered in local white wine), there is no doubt where you are. Sandwiched between the appealingly low-key mountain ranges of Massif de la Chartreuse and Massif des Bauges, this small town plunges visitors into the heart and soul of Savoie (Savoy).

Snowheads transferring from Lyon or Geneva airports to alpine ski resorts typically know Chambéry as a toll booth on the *autoroute* (highway). But taking time to dip into this largely unsung town and explore its evocative tangle of streets is a waltz through regional history. Chambéry was capital of the powerful Duchy of Savoy from the 13th century until 1563 (when the Dukes moved to Turin across the border in Piedmont, Italy) and, as with the rest of Savoie, only became part of France in 1860.

Elephants, Alleys & Chateau Views

Old town *flânerie*

Rush through Chambéry's **Ville Ancienne** (old town), with 19th-century **theatre** nicknamed 'Petit Scala' for its sumptuous interior inspired by Milan's opera house, and you risk missing its most unique treasures. Adopt the traditional slow, observant pace of a French *flâneur,* beginning by the towering **Fontaine des Éléphants** on place des Éléphants. Four elephants sprouting from the base of the whimsical fountain celebrate the adventurous exploits of local lad Général de Boigne (1751–1830), who made his fortune in India and was honoured posthumously for bestowing some of his wealth on his home town. Locals lovingly refer to the elephants – whose front halves sprout from the statue – as the *quatre sans cul* (the rear-less four).

For a handsome perspective in every direction, stand at the intersection of arcaded **rue de Boigne** and long, handsome

☑ TOP TIP

Themed walking tours organised by Chambéry **tourist office** *(chamberymontagnes.com)* provide an alternative perspective to the town; reserve online.

CHAMBÉRY

HIGHLIGHTS
1. Château des Ducs de Savoie
2. Musée Savoisien
3. Place St-Léger
4. Sainte-Chapelle
5. Ville Ancienne

SIGHTS
6. Allée Chiron
7. Allée Henri Planche
8. Cathédrale St-François de Sales
9. Fontaine des Éléphants
10. Hôtel Castagnery du Châteauneuf
11. Passage Jean Planche

SLEEPING
12. Petit Hôtel Confidentiel

EATING
13. Bloomy Brunch & Coffee
14. Le Bistrot
15. Le Sporting
16. Les Halles

DRINKING & NIGHTLIFE
17. L'Arbre à Bières
18. Le 29
19. Le Corsaire
20. O'Cardinal's

ENTERTAINMENT
21. Théâtre Charles-Dullin

INFORMATION
22. Tourist Office

---

place St-Léger. The main square once had a river flowing through it (now paved over). Cafe terraces bask in the sun and 16th-century *hôtels particuliers* (mansions) built for aristocrats keep sentinel over the old town's emblematic *allées*.

Lose yourself in the atmospheric, old-world maze they form: **Passage Jean Planche** (zig-zagging between rue de Boigne and rue de la Metropole); **Allée Henri Planche** (one of several plunging south from place St-Léger) and **Allée Chiron** (tumbling onto Chambéry's oldest street, honey-hued **rue Basse du Château**, and out at the foot of the chateau's massive walls).

ALLÉES V TRABOULES

Continue the thrill of ducking and diving down dank, dimly lit alleys and passageways to unearth bijou courtyards and the occasional spiral staircase festooned in a romantic round tower with a *traboule* (secret underground passage) tour in Lyon (p458).

Fontaine des Éléphants (p524)

SHOWTIME

You can buy the album online, but nothing beats catching Chambéry's Grand Carillon ring out *Frère Jacques, Le Temps du Muguet* and other French classics in situ – for free. Bells in Sainte-Chapelle's belfry have spun tunes since 1938, but it's the current 69-bell ensemble – cast in bronze in 1993 by illustrious bell foundry Fonderie Paccard near Annecy – that turns heads. The world's fourth-largest carillon, it weighs 41 tonnes and scales six octaves. The smallest bell is 9kg, the biggest 5 tonnes. Listen to the carillon ring out in concert for 30 minutes at 5.30pm on the first and third Saturday of each month, and every Saturday in July and August.

Grandiose home to the Savoie *département* administration since 1860, the 11th- to 18th-century **Château des Ducs de Savoie** is not open to the public. Its one small history museum, inside the first gate, is closed for renovation work until 2026. Enjoy particularly fine views of the imposing chateau from the rose-draped courtyard of 17th-century mansion **Hôtel Castagnery du Châteauneuf**, with intricate wrought-iron grilles.

Optical Illusions

Trompe l'oeil art in the Franciscan cathedral and chateau

All is not what it seems inside Chambéry's 15th-century **Cathédrale St-François de Sales** *(free)*, decorated with 6000 dazzling sq metres of trompe l'oeil paintings. The largest such feature in any building in Europe, the ornamentation – created in 1810 by Milan-born artist Fabrizio Sevesi and 1834–5 by Piedmontese trompe l'oeil maestro Casimir Vicario – deceive the eyes into seeing Gothic vaults, an ornate carved ceiling and a mystical labyrinth that leads believers to Jerusalem.

Equally spellbinding is Vicario's spectacular, flamboyant Gothic 'vaulted' ceiling, painted inside the Savoy dukes' private

EATING IN CHAMBÉRY: OUR PICKS

Bloomy Brunch & Coffee: Just that (including awesome French toast with pistachio cream and black-bun burgers), on a picturesque street. *10am-5pm Wed-Sat, 9am-4pm Sun* €

Le Sporting: Traditional Savoyard fare and daily market-fuelled specials, in a fairy-light lit garden with cathedral view. *noon-2pm & 7-10pm* €€

Les Halles: Top-drawer regional cuisine served on a pretty terrace (not to be confused with the equally tasty market around the corner). *noon-2pm & 7-10pm Tue-Sat* €€

Le Bistrot: The pavement terrace at this retro bistro on old-world rue du Théâtre is a delight. Cuisine is traditional French. *noon-2.30pm & 7-10.30pm Tue-Sat* €€

Sainte-Chapelle *(guided visit only; adult/child €18/free)* in 1836 next to their chateau. His two evangelist statues behind the altar are also an illusion. The Gothic chapel was built to house the Holy Shroud, the linen cloth purported to be the burial cloth of Jesus Christ, transferred to Turin in 1578. Monthly guided visits of the chapel are run by the tourist office.

A Rich Romp Through Savoie's Past
Centuries of history, culture and monastical tradition at Musée Savoisien

There is good reason why Chambéry's landmark **Musée Savoisien** *(musee-savoisien.fr; free; closed Tue)* took eight years to renovate. An unparalleled showcase of Savoie's turbulent history, culture and diverse ethnography, this rich heritage museum has languished inside the Gothic cloister of Chambéry's 13th-century Franciscan convent since 1913 – the Zen location alone is a delight.

The 100,000-piece collection spans the gambit of Savoyard history and culture, from Palaeolithic relics and a Carolingian pirogue to bright orange 'eggs' used in surrounding ski resorts in the 1970s. Exhibitions are notably curated creatively by theme (population and environment, food, habitat, faith and beliefs, fashion etc) – allowing you to fully appreciate, for example, the evolution of cheesemaking utensils or the different garb winter-sports enthusiasts have worn on the slopes over the decades.

Playful children's *ateliers (workshops; from €2 to €50)* are in French, but many – such as dressing up in medieval costumes, pottery and 30-minute 'touch-and-feel' tours – also work for non-French speakers. Avoid Tuesday when the museum is closed.

> **ROUSSEAU'S PARADISE**
>
> A key figure of the Enlightenment and the French Revolution, Jean-Jacques Rousseau (1712–78) spent some happy years in Chambéry. Between 1736 and 1742, the Geneva-born philosopher, composer and writer enjoyed bucolic country living in a stone house with his older lover Madame de Warens (1699–1762). Rousseau met the Swiss heiress and libertine when he was 15 and she was his tutor. He described their alpine home – now the enchanting house-museum and summer concert venue **Les Charmettes** *(free)*, 2km uphill from the town centre – in *Confessions* and *Rêveries du promeneur solitaire* (Reveries of the Solitary Walker). After his death the house and surrounding garden became a place of literary pilgrimage for then-aspiring writers like George Sand and Alphonse de Lamartine. It is closed on Mondays.

 DRINKING IN CHAMBÉRY: BEST SUMMER TIPPLES

Le Corsaire: Kick back on this rooftop bar with a chilled Mont Blanc–brewed beer, cheesy Savoyard tacos or charcuterie board. *5pm-1.30am Tue-Sat, to 12.45am Sun & Mon*

L'Arbre à Bières: You can't beat the choice of 'Made in Savoie' craft beer at the Beer Tree. Homemade *flammenküches* (bacon, onion and cream tart) cover dinner. *5pm-12.30am Tue-Sat*

O'Cardinal's: The most French 'Irish pub' you'll ever find, crouching cheekily beneath the western facade of the cathedral. *11-1am Tue-Fri, from 10am Sat & Sun*

Le 29: Embrace summer's party vibe over expertly mixed cocktails, Savoie wines and DJ sets into the wee hours. *6pm-1.30am Tue-Sun*

Beyond Chambéry

Exploring the rich green tapestry around the veteran Savoyard capital is a journey through ancestral pride, alpine tradition and spirited hijinks.

Places

Massif de la Chartreuse p528

Vallée de la Tarentaise p531

Parc National de la Vanoise p532

Vallée des Belleville p533

GETTING AROUND

Having your own summertime wheels – car, camper van or e-bike – plus hiking boots will enhance your travel experience dramatically.

Winter skiers are well-served with long-distance transport: **Altibus** *(altibus.com)* operates coach shuttles from Geneva and Lyon airports to ski resorts in Les Trois Vallées and Paradiski; reserve your seat online well in advance. Moûtiers is the main **train station**, linked to Lyon and Paris by high-speed TGV and by **Transdev Savoie** *(savoie.transdev.com)* buses to local resorts.

With world-class skiing, accommodation and dining, the winter ski areas of Les Trois Vallées, Paradiski (La Plagne and Les Arcs, connected by the Vanoise Express cable car), glacier-capped Tignes and Val d'Isère are skiing icons. Yet it's the less-familiar valleys and mountain hamlets, where crowds pile out of church on Sunday morning and men still sport black Savoyard berets, that shine light on all that Savoyards hold dear: France's largest ibex colony in the country's oldest national park (Vanoise); the June transhumance when red Abondance cows around Beaufort are shepherded to higher pastures for their milk to becomes wheels of Chalet d'Alpage cheese; madcap tales of silent monks opening their door one day a year to take in 24,000 tonnes of flowers, herbs and roots. Dig out the stories.

Massif de la Chartreuse TIME FROM CHAMBÉRY: 1HR

The spirited story of green Chartreuse

Over the centuries medieval monks to modern mixologists have been seduced by Chartreuse, a shockingly acid-green herbal liqueur borne out of a 69%-proof medicinal elixir still available in French pharmacies. The liqueur's secret recipe is closely guarded by just three Carthusian monks, which makes a guided museum tour – with tastings – of **Caves de la Chartreuse** *(chartreuse.fr; adult/child €12/free; online advance reservation obligatory)* in small-town Voiron all the more intriguing.

Tours of the former production site, replaced by a modern out-of-town site in 2018, evoke the spirited story of this otherworldly liqueur. Contrary to the belief that Chartreuse is essentially 'the Alps bottled', the original liqueur was concocted by Carthusian monks in Paris in the 17th century with medicinal plants grown in their urban garden. Find out how monks in the Massif de la Chartreuse became distillers; smell cinnamon, star anise, wild thyme and some of the other 130 mystery herbs, plants and roots that go in the drink; and tour centurion cellars where the liqueur ages in 2.5m-high oak barrels. End with a fiery shot of Green Chartreuse (55% alcohol) and sweeter Yellow Chartreuse (40% alcohol).

Cirque de Saint-Même waterfall

Close the story amid cow-specked fields and forest-cloaked cliffs, 25km east near St-Pierre de Chartreuse, at the isolated **Monastère de la Grande Chartreuse** where some 25 monks live in silence. Ponder monastical life in the 'day in the life of a monk' at nearby **Musée de la Grande Chartreuse** *(mu see-grande-chartreuse.fr; adult/child €10/4.50)*, then walk 2km along a tree-lined alley – a clearly signposted *'Zone de Silence'* – to take in the magnificent, hushed and strangely moving, walled monastery from afar.

Hiking to the source

For spectacular waterfalls and wild swimming, hike to **Cirque de Saint-Même** – an enthralling amphitheatre of 400m-high limestone cliffs, spangled with the crash and thunder of four spectacular waterfalls from which the Guiers Vif River springs to life.

From the Pont Dugey car park in St-Même d'en Haut, 4.4km southeast of St-Pierre d'Entremont village along the sinuous D45c, the **Sentier du Fond du Cirque** trail (green markers, 30 minutes) meanders through forest to the lowest Pisse du Guiers waterfall. The **Sentier des Cascades** (red markers, 1½ hours, elevation gain 195m), a 3km loop to the Grande

BEST LOCAL TIPPLES

Chartreuse swizzle: Shake a Chartreuse Swizzle or another Chartreuse cocktail during a mixology class at **Caves de la Chartreuse**'s cocktail bar.

Seasonal gin: Look for locally distilled gin by Les Sauvagesses – Distillerie du Grand Som. Botanicals and bottle labels change each season.

Craft beer: Cool down with La Marmotte Masquée craft beer, brewed in St-Pierre de Chartreuse.

Kir au saffron: Toast unforgettable garden dining at St-Pierre de Chartreuse's saffron farm with this white wine-and-saffron liqueur apéritif.

Elixir végétale de la Grande Chartreuse: The monk's recipe for this 69%-alcohol 'elixir for life', distilled from 130 plants, has not changed since 1764.

 EATING & DRINKING IN CHARTREUSE: OUR PICKS

La Cabine: Hipster cafe-bar in St-Hugues en Chartreuse serving local craft beers and spirits. Taste a beer by Microbrasserie Noisigottery. *Santé! 11.30am-10pm Wed-Sun*

L'Herbe Tendre: Perched above the river makes alfresco summer dining at this friendly spot in St-Pierre d'Entremont effortlessly cool. Sublime fondue. *noon-2pm & 7-9pm Wed-Sun* €

Ferme de Brévardière: Home cooking perfumed with local saffron at this saffron farm; reservations essential (brevardiere.fr). *hours vary* €

La Peche à la Truite: Fish your own trout at this lakeside restaurant near St-Pierre d'Entremon, then have it grilled to enjoy alfresco. *10am-7pm Fri-Sun* €€

La Plagne

BEST ALTERNATIVE MOUNTAIN THRILLS

Moon-biking snowy trails in Courchevel astride a silent, electric snow bike with front sled blade and rear caterpillar track.

Fat biking at speed down on snow bicycles with ultra-fat tyres in La Plagne.

Acro-speleology (mixing climbing and canyoning) with a guide at the Grottes de St-Christophe caves in Massif des Chartreuse.

Electric mountain-biking along the Via 3 Vallées, a 34km cycling itinerary linking Courchevel, Méribel, Les Menuires and Val Thorens.

Mushing with American Eskimo, Greenland or Alaskan dogs through a snow globe of sugar-dusted firs, in several ski resorts. Sleds can fly at 50km/h.

Cascade, is more exciting. Steep, rocky and not for families with young children, the path climbs through thick beech forest. The Herculean roar of water is omnipresent and a rocky precipice halfway up provides dress-circle fall views. Twenty bat species live in caves here and golden eagles nest in the cliffs.

Picnic by the bridge beneath **Grande Cascade**. Stock up in St-Pierre d'Entremont on cheese from **Fromagerie Arpin** and air-dried *saucissons* (sausages), trout smoked over Chartreuse wood and meaty rissoles from **Boucherie Guerre**, family-run since 1830. Serious foodies can order online the day before and pick up organic nut bread, sourdough and chunky chocolate-hazelnut cookies from artisanal bakery **Les Champs du Pain** (*champsdupain.coop-pains.fr*) in St-Même d'en Bas's old school house.

Crossing the bridge, the return trail weaves downhill through pine forest. Don't miss the signposted fork on the right ducking down to **Cascade Isolée**, another majestic waterfall with a couple of tranquil pools suitable for swimming.

Under the Tooth of the Bear

Inject an e-burst of adrenalin into traditional two-wheeling along the 14km-long **Sous la Dent de l'Ours** e-bike trail (elevation gain 470m; two to three hours) in the Réserve Naturelle des Hauts de Chartreuse. Grab trail maps at the **tourist office** (*chartreuse-tourisme.com*) in **St-Pierre d'Entremont** and rent electric-assisted mountain- and fat-bikes to ride 'Along the Tooth of the Bear' at sports shop-cafe **Entre Monts Vélos** (*entre-monts-velos.fr; half/full day from €39/42*).

Climb 5.5km south to **St-Philbert**, stopping in **Le Villard** to buy a round of *labérou cendré* (goat's cheese dusted with vegetal charcoal made from maritime pine) at organic goat farm **Ferme de Labérou**

FAMILY SKIING

Keep teens out of mischief on the slopes at April's Enduro 3 Vallées ski-race event. Form a family team and race around every resort in Les Trois Vallées. Each stop poses a timed challenge: biathlon, freeride, slalom, super G, ski mountaineering. For family fun in Les Portes du Soleil, see p522.

(ferme-de-laberou.fr). Looping back north along the D102b, admire **Dent de l'Ours** ('Tooth of the Bear', 1820m) east and the twin summits of **Les Lances de Malissard** (2045m) and **Mont de Granier** (1933m) to the west. The latter's knife-edge north face was carved by a fatal landslide in 1248 that buried five villages alive. Enjoy more majestic views from the evocative ruins of 14th-century **Château de Montbel** *(free)* before pedalling back to St-Pierre.

Vallée de la Tarentaise   TIME FROM CHAMBÉRY: 1HR

Live the Olympic dream in La Plagne
With its 425km of gloriously wide intermediate slopes, purpose-built **La Plagne** *(en.la-plagne.com)* is a family hit. But it's the 11-village ski resort's scare-yourself-silly bobsled run that really raises the bar. A legacy of the 1992 Albertville Winter Olympics, and you can hurtle down the ice track solo in a self-braking bob *(€135)* or with a pro driver in a four-seater *(€55)*. You'll hit a speed of 120km/h on bend No 10 and flying around the 19 bends in all takes less than one minute. Advance reservations are essential.

Snowshoeing and summer safaris in Death Valley
Running wild in the curious 'ups and downs' of La Plagne's 12-hectare **La Cembraie** nature reserve is a rare rendezvous with centurion Swiss pines, saplings unwittingly planted by spotted nutcrackers storing seeds for winter and a diabolical rollercoaster of conical gypsum rocks. In this so-called Vallée de la Mort (Death Valley), grab a pair of snowshoes to track mountain hare and fox prints in fresh snow, and ponder French resistance heroes who hid between trees here during WWII.

In Plagne Centre, rent snowshoes at **Intersport** *(centre.laplagne-intersport.com)* and most other sports shops. At the **Bureau Montagne de la Plagne** *(la-plagne.com; half-/full-day snowshoeing from €35/65)*, hook up with local mountain guides offering small-group snowshoe safaris and igloo-building expeditions in winter. In summer they lead guided mountain hikes and survival camps with bivouac overnights.

Around the shores of Lac de Roselend
The southern approach to **Lac de Roselend** – across the 1968m-high mountain pass of **Cormet de Roselend** (open May to October) – is as spectacular as the turquoise-blue lake views that reward anyone (mainly cyclists and classic-car tourers)

SKIING LES TROIS VALLÉES

The world's largest ski area connects three valleys with 600km of pistes and 200 lifts. Key resorts:
Méribel: (1450m) Oh-so-British resort, best for intermediate skiers, with 150km of blue and red runs, two snow parks and a wild après-ski scene. Linked by gondola to budget Brides-les-Bains (600m). *meribel.net*
Courchevel: (1850m) Tree-fringed playground for the super rich and Moët-at-five brigade; La Tania (1400m) lower down is less flash. *courchevel.com*
Val Thorens: (2300m) Europe's highest ski resort, meaning the longest snow-sure season (usually late November to mid-May). *valthorens.com*
St-Martin de Belleville: (1450m) The traditional village option, with chic accommodation and gourmet mountain-hut to Michelin-star dining. *st-martin-belleville.com*

 EATING & DRINKING IN LA PLAGNE: OUR PICKS

Le Chalet du Plan Bois: Feeding ravenous skiers and summertime picnic lovers is what this family-run chalet in Montchavin does best. *hours vary Dec-Apr, Jul & Aug.* €€

Expédition: Hit Aime 2000 for sassy cocktails and food pairings bursting with regional produce at this wildly popular, new-gen address. *noon-2pm & 7-10pm* €€

Il Ristorante Alpina: Upmarket Italian alpine food to make you weep (black truffles!) in pretty Champagny-en-Vanoise. *noon-2.30pm & 7-10pm mid-Dec-Apr, Tue-Sun Jul & Aug* €€€

Le Brix: Join local riders for an après-ski craft beer or fiery shot of beer eau de vie at this longstanding, down-to-earth fave in Plagne Centre. *4pm-late mid-Dec-Apr, Jul & Aug*

RETHINKING CABLE CARS

Heated seats, USB ports, integrated wi-fi: as cable cars increase in comfort and strive to emulate the tech wizardry and convenience of transport on dry land, cable-car engineers in the mountain resort of **La Plagne** are adopting a radically different approach. Considered by some to be up there with the world's scariest cable-car rides, accessible during ski season and again in summer, **Aérolive** *(skipass-laplagne.com/fr/aerolive; per person €29)* transports six people at a time from 2739m to the resort's highest point at 3080m – in a bare-bones, cabin with no sides. Passengers are harnessed to ensure they don't fall out, and the ice-cold air at 3080m only heightens the discomfort and/or thrill.

who makes it to this handsome wedge of Beaufortain. The alpine pass and D925 skirting the lake's northern shore are part of the iconic **Route des Grandes Alpes** driving itinerary, created in 1937 to link the fashionable Côte d'Azur with Lake Geneva by way of 17 *cols* in the French Alps.

Park by **Chapelle de Roselend** and admire the twin-bell chapel, rebuilt to mirror the 13th- to 17th-century original submerged in 1960 – along with the hamlet of Roselend – by the construction of Roselend's hydroelectric dam. A walking trail climbs from lakefront **Bar-Restaurant Les Lanches**, through fields of bell-clanging cows, to smaller **Lac de Gittaz** (5km, 1½ hours). North looms the craggy peak of **Roc du Vent** (2360m).

Linger lakefront over a lunchtime *tartiflette* (oven-baked potatoes, *Reblochon* cheese and bacon) at restaurant-hotel **Chalet de Roselend** *(chaletderoselend.fr),* open late May to September, then continue 14km north to the small town of **Beaufort** where creamy milk from red Tarentaise cows fuels AOP Beaufort, *Tomme des Bauges* and *Reblochon* cheese. Watch a film showing how cheese is made and reserve online to visit the ripening cellar at **Coopérative Laitière de Beaufortain** *(cooperative-de-beaufort.com; exhibition free, cellar €3).* If it's shut, buy cheese from its vending machine outside.

Parc National de la Vanoise

TIME FROM CHAMBÉRY: 1½HR

Walking across Lac des Vaches

Cows graze on **Lac des Vaches** ('Lake of Cows'), cradled at 2318m in an amphitheatre of mountain peaks, glaciers and slate-grey moraine in the wild Massif de la Vanoise. Giant stone slabs form a 210m-long walkway across the lake which, when dry in August and September, doubles as pasture.

Pick up maps in Pralognan-la-Vanoise at the national park office **Maison de la Vanoise** *(vanoise-parcnational.fr)* and the nearby trailhead by the **Génepi chairlift** in Les Fontanettes. Entering the park, the trail piggy-backs the GR55 and is an alternative leg on the GR5. On Plateau de la Glière, dry-stone walls trace part of the historic Route du Sel (Salt Road). Passing abandoned shepherds' huts at Chalets de la Glière, follow wooden poles planted in the 1830s to guide early alpinists up to Lac des Vaches (5km, two hours) and 2.5km (45 minutes) beyond to panoramic Col de la Vanoise (2516m).

DRINKING IN LES TROIS VALLÉES: APRÈS-SKI PICKS

Le Rond Point: Méribel's veteran party central, aka 'le Ronnie', delivering crowd surfing, dancing and toffee shots in spades. *9am-7pm mid-Dec-Apr*

Bar 360: Live music and world-class DJs on the slopes – Val Thorens' dance-bar party that never stops, at a giddy 2368m. *11am-6pm mid-Dec–early May*

Trait d'Union – Refuge du Danchet: Chill at 1725m in low-key St-Martin de Belleville. Think post-slopes sauna, hot tub, Savoie wine and mountain views. Rooms too. *hours vary*

Les Caves de Courchevel: The 'it' address among rich circles in one of the Alps' most monied resorts to club the night away. Dress up. *11pm-5am*

GR5 trail, Parc National de la Vanoise

Vallée des Belleville
TIME FROM CHAMBÉRY: 1½HR

Wildlife encounters in Val Thorens & Les Menuires

Once the snow melts in the country's highest ski resort – the last to close in May – observe ibex and chamois around the summit of Grand Perron des Encombres (2824m) with a guide from Val Thorens' **Bureau des Guides** *(guides-belleville.com; half-/full-day group hike €25/40)*. Lower down in Les Menuires, join guides from **Maison de la Montagne** at 5.30am to observe spectacular summertime fauna on a sunrise hike.

At the **Maison de l'Abeille Noire et de la Nature** near Lac de Bruyères, Friday-morning workshops with beekeeper Kelly Duqueine introduce bee fans to the threatened Savoie bee *(abeille noire* or black bee) and the apiary where 500-odd queens are bred each year. Two kilometres south, pastoral tradition thrives at 1950s goat farm **Chez Pepé Nicolas** *(chezpepenicolas.com)*. Milk goats, buy *chèvre frais* (fresh goat cheese) and feast on cheese fondue and fresh produce from the farm's permaculture garden.

ROUTE DU SEL

The **Col de la Vanoise** has been a vital link between the high-altitude Maurienne and Tarentaise valleys since the Bronze Age. The Romans used it to flit between Rome and Lyon, and in the 11th century the Dukes of Savoy travelled across it from Chambéry to Turin. In the 18th century, mules laboured across the high mountain pass, carrying salt from the Royal Salt Works in nearby Moûtiers to Piedmont, Italy; they returned laden with spices and fabrics. Local Beaufort cheese, tanned leathers and mountain honey were likewise exchanged for potatoes, rice and corn on this strategic trade route.

 EATING IN VANOISE: BEST MOUNTAIN GRUB

Refuge du Col de la Vanoise: Dorms, grub and unparalleled views in a mountain hut from 1902, ecologically rebuilt with solar panels. *Mar-late Sep* €

Refuge des Barmettes: Feast and sleep like a Savoyard at this chairlift-accessible refuge above Pralognan-la-Vanoise. *late Dec-Mar & Jun-Sep* €

Refuge de la Femma: Sizeable mountain refuge-restaurant, with chickens, a donkey and wild marmots near Termignon-la-Vanoise. *mid-Mar-mid-May & Jun-Sep* €

La Bergerie – Refuge Le Repoju: *Raclette au feu de bois* (melted over the fire) is the sensational speciality at this rustic sheepfold in Le Prioux. *Dec-Apr, Thu-Sun May-Sep* €€

Grenoble

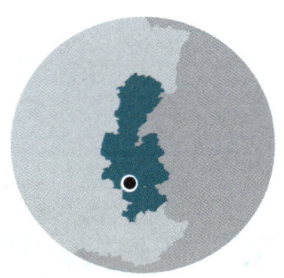

OUTDOOR ACTION | MUSEUMS | DRINKING & NIGHTLIFE

☑ TOP TIP
Most city museums offer free admission, so calculate if you'll get your money's worth before buying a **G-Pass** (grenoblepass. com; 24/72hr €24/32), either online or at Grenoble's well-organised tourist office. The latter runs some superb guided walking tours or you can go with a **Grenoble Greeter** (greeters.fr/grenoble).

Striding around in hiking boots or motoring through town with a bike trailer is the norm in France's self-styled 'Capital of the Alps'. Urban, green and fizzing with natural adrenalin, this is an unpretentious city where it's second-nature for locals to trail-run before work ('jog' is too lame a word for the popular hill run up to La Bastille) and every road leading out of town brushes a different regional nature park.

While France's self-styled 'Capital of the Alps' signature halo of breathtaking alpine peaks demands closer inspection, there's plenty to entertain in downtown Grenoble. The historic quarter of St-Laurent is a charm to stroll and, come summer, paddling by torchlight along the Isère River in a canoe or sunset-lounging with a bottle of wine and some of the city's 65,000-odd students on wooden decks built into the river banks is *de rigueur*. Embrace the moment.

Trails & Zip-Wires On An Urban Mountain
Scaling heady heights around Fort de la Bastille

One of Europe's few urban cable cars, the **Téléphérique de Grenoble–Bastille** *(bastille-grenoble.fr; single/return adult €6.50/9.60, child €3.60/5)* glides up from its riverside lower station to Grenoble's iconic hilltop fort in six minutes. The transparent *'bulles'* ('bubbles'), which run until midnight,

GETTING AROUND

The main sights are highly walkable – or brilliantly runnable along marked trail itineraries in hilltop La Bastille; the **tourist office** *(grenoble-tourisme.com)* has maps.
Eco-friendly tram lines and buses are run by **M** *(reso-m.fr/);* download the app to check timetables and routes, and buy tickets (€2).

Urban cyclists spin along 320km of cycling lanes: access an interactive route map at pass. mobilites-m.fr and rent shared wheels at a **Mvélo+** *(veloplus-m.fr)* bike-sharing station. Use the **Dott app** to locate free-floating e-bikes and e-scooters.

GRENOBLE

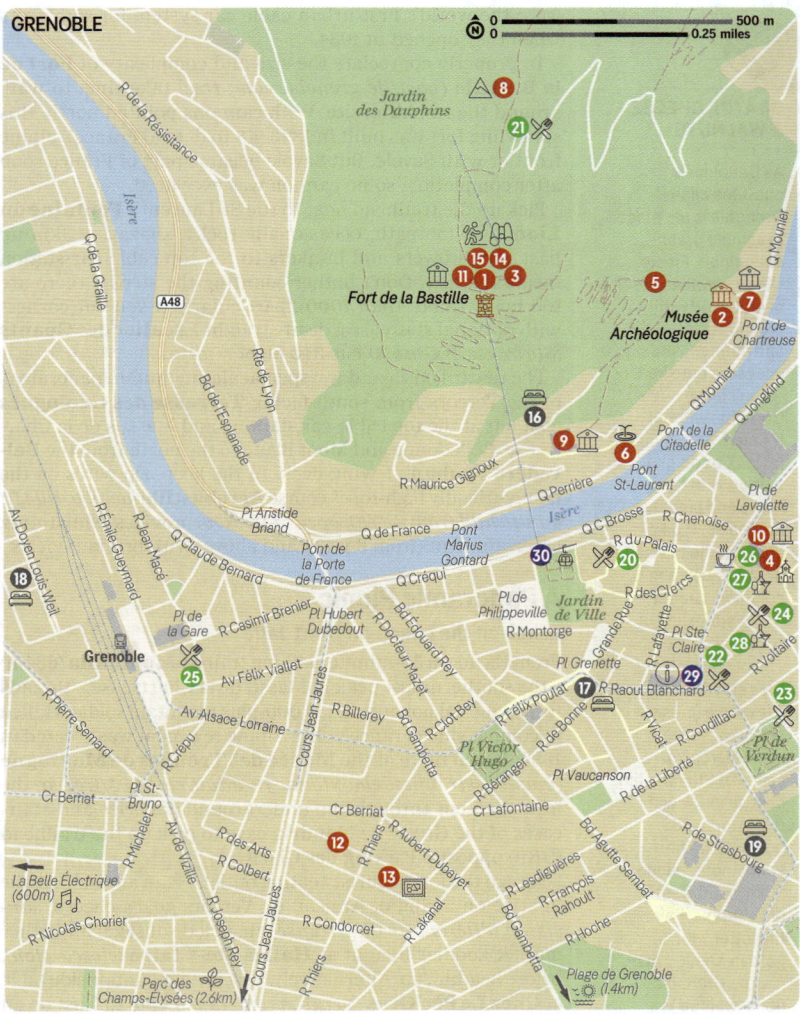

HIGHLIGHTS
1 Fort de la Bastille
2 Musée Archéologique

SIGHTS
3 Belvédère Vauban
4 Cathédrale Notre-Dame
5 Escalier des Géants
6 Fontaine du Lion
7 La Casemate
8 Mont Jalla
9 Musée Dauphinois
10 Musée de l'Ancien Évêché
11 Musée des Troupes de Montagne
12 rue Génissieu
13 Spacejunk Arts Centre
14 Terrasse des Géologues

ACTIVITIES
15 Acrobastille

SLEEPING
16 Babel Community
17 Hôtel de l'Europe
18 Le Hüb
19 RockyPop Grenoble

EATING
20 Café de la Table Ronde
21 Chez Le Pèr'Gras
22 Halles Ste-Claire
23 La Maison Fantin Latour
24 Le Dauphinoix
25 L'Inattendu

DRINKING & NIGHTLIFE
26 Le 1900
27 Le 365
28 Le Zinc

INFORMATION
29 Tourist Office

TRANSPORT
30 Téléphérique Grenoble-Bastille

GRATIN, CHEESE & WALNUTS

As Dauphiné's one-time capital, Grenoble is *the* place to sample *gratin dauphinois*. Finely sliced potatoes are oven-baked with cream, butter, garlic and nutmeg. Adding cheese is pure heresy.

Don't leave Grenoble without trying *ravioles* (mini ravioli), traditionally stuffed with fresh herbs and creamy *faisselle* (a type of cottage cheese made from raw cow's milk, commonly eaten with a sprinkling of sugar for dessert). The pasta cushions are served with *sauce à la crème* (cream sauce) or *sauce au St-Marcellin* – a sauce of St-Marcellin cheese made with unpasteurised goat milk in the eponymous village 50km southwest of Grenoble. Pair the latter with golden-shelled AOP *noix de Grenoble* (local walnuts) to enter epicurean nirvana.

---

were the world's first urban cable car system for sightseers when they opened in 1934.

To properly appreciate the size and complexity of **Fort de la Bastille** *(bastille-grenoble.com; free)* take time to walk around the rambling site. With cannons pointed north, this sprawling fort was built in 1823–48 to defend France's alpine frontier with Savoie. But Savoie became part of France soon after completion, so no cannon was ever fired.

Pick up the trailhead next to rue St-Laurent's **Fontaine du Lion**. The footpath, occasionally rocky, zig-zags 2.3km up past watchtowers and bunkers to the top cable-car station inside the fort. Don't bother counting the steps – there are too many (more than 1000), particularly if you cut corners with optional staircases; dead-straight **Escalier des Géants** *(Staircase of Giants)* has 340 alone.

The reward on clear days: spectacular mountain panoramas of the Vercors from south-facing **Terrasse des Géologues** (exit left at the top cable-car station), and Massifs de la Chartreuse, Belledonne and Mont Blanc to the north from the **Belvédère Vauban** viewing deck. In the keep, zip wires on the family-friendly high-ropes course **Acrobastille** *(acrobastille.fr; adult/child from €15/10; open Mar–Nov)* provides exhilarating entertainment (from 3 years and above) with brilliant views.

A Panoramic Picnic

Lunch on the cheap on Mont Jalla

From the fort a 30-minute walking trail on **Mont Jalla** (634m) – the southernmost peak in Massif de la Chartreuse – threads to a memorial honouring 150,000-plus mountain soldiers killed in combat since France's elite Alpine regiment was created in 1888. Learn more at the **Musée des Troupes de Montagne** *(museedestroupesdemontagne.fr; adult/child €3/free)* in the fort, then cut through the underground galleries and staircases of the Grotte de Mandrin cave to pick up the trailhead (GR9) opposite Parking des Glacis.

Forego the fort's touristy eating outlets. Plan ahead to picnic in style on a ring of Anneau du Vercors goat's cheese, *saucisson d'Hérens de Chartreuse* (air-dried sausage) and other market goodies bought at **Halles Ste-Claire** *(closed Mon)*, before heading up. Alternatively, reserve a mountainside table at **Chez Le Pèr'Gras** *(pergras.com; lunch €36)* to feast on an excellent-value *menu du marché* (fixed price 'market menu') and priceless alpine vistas. For dessert, order farm-made *faisselle* with honey from hives on La Bastille.

 EATING IN GRENOBLE: DAUPHINOIS CUISINE

Café de la Table Ronde: Locals reckon the *gratin dauphinois* served at Grenoble's oldest dining establishment (1793) is unbeatable. *noon-2.30pm & 7-10.30pm* €

Le Dauphinoix: Trout from France's oldest trout farm and a tip-top *gratin dauphinois*; one of several eating options on rue Bayard. *noon-2pm & 7-9.30pm Tue-Sat* €€

L'Inattendu: Local produce is the star of elaborate dishes served in the surprise menu at this wildly popular bistro. *10.30am-2.30pm & 7-10pm Mon-Fri* €€

La Maison Fantin Latour: Modern brasserie lunches and Michelin-starred evening dining in a mansion museum-turned-restaurant. *noon-1.30pm & 7-8.15pm Tue-Sat* €€€

Medieval Sarcophagi to Modern Snow Sports
Unearthing Grenoble's backstory

Open Grenoble's storybook inside the rose-brick rib vaults of the 13th-century **Cathédrale Notre-Dame** *(cathedraledegrenoble.fr; free)*, built on the site of a 4th-century church. At the **Musée de l'Ancien Évêché** *(ancien-eveche-isere.fr; free)* in the nearby Bishops' Palace, admire remains of the city's 3rd-century Roman walls and walk across metal grating exposing excavated ruins of a medieval baptistery.

Continue the Middle Ages chapter at the spellbinding **Musée Archéologique** *(musee-archeologique-grenoble.fr; free; closed Tue)* across the river in St-Laurent's 12th-century parish church. Self-guided visits, accompanied by sacred chants and video projections, peel away the bewitching layers of history buried beneath the church. Skeletons embedded in glass walkways and strewn in sarcophagi from a vast 4th-century mausoleum are just the beginning.

At **Musée Dauphinois** *(musee-dauphinois.fr; free)* the rise of winter snow sports, the 1968 Winter Olympics and alpine life come alive, alongside temporary exhibitions focusing on modern themes. Access it via the staircase next to rue St-Laurent's **Fontaine du Lion**. The fountain's entangled lion and serpent sculpted in 1843 symbolise the two tempestuous lifeblood rivers flowing through Grenoble.

Street Art Anarchy
Sprint from mural to mural at the Street Art Fest

Grenoble's street-art scene takes you into 'hoods you wouldn't otherwise explore. In Championnet, mural-hot **rue Génissieu** is a good spot to start. Grab a map at **Spacejunk Arts Centre** *(facebook.com/spacejunkgrenoble; free)*, open afternoons Tuesday to Saturday at No 19, and get the lowdown on recent art works created during Grenoble's annual **Street Art Fest** *(streetartfest.org)* in June; don't miss the 10km street art run!

BEST FAMILY FUN

Plage de Grenoble: Hit trucked-in golden sand, with beach volleyball courts, sun loungers and summer pop-ups galore *(plagedegrenoble.com)*.

Parc des Champs-Élysées: Not quite Paris ilk, but an attractive city park with sprawling lawns, children's playgrounds, statues, fountains and a lake.

Cabaret Frappé: Music-loving teens: this free festival raises the curtain on outdoor concerts (rock, pop) in 18th-century garden Jardin de Ville *(cabaret-frappe.com)*.

La Casemate: Inspire young minds with interactive science exhibitions and workshops *(lacasemate.fr)*.

Yes We Canyon: Rope up older kids for canyoning, speleology and rock-climbing *(www.yes-we-canyon.com)*. In town, canoe along the Isère.

 DRINKING IN GRENOBLE: TOP TERRACES

Le 1900	Le 365	Le Zinc	La Belle Électrique
Le 1900: A coffee or *pression* (draught beer) at this local institution on place du Notre-Dame is the epitome of French cafe terrace life. *7-2am Mon-Sat*	**Le 365**: Good-humoured mixologists preside over a fabulous cocktail list at this chic bar on busy rue Bayard. *6pm-2am Wed-Sat*	**Le Zinc**: Enjoy local and organic wines at this popular bar, with retro interior evoking an old-timey train station. *6-10.30pm Mon, to 11.30pm Tue & Wed, to 1am Thu-Sat*	**La Belle Électrique**: A cocktail or craft beer alfresco is as electrifying as the live music that rips through this striking, wood-and-glass venue. *10-1am Wed-Sat*

Beyond Grenoble

France's second-largest national park and mainland France's largest nature reserve reward those who venture beyond Dauphiné's historic capital.

Places

Alpe d'Huez p538
Parc Naturel Régional du Vercors p540

GETTING AROUND

December to April, **Transaltitude** (transaltitude.fr) runs buses and coach day-trips from Grenoble **bus station** to more than a dozen ski resorts, including Chamrousse, and Alpe d'Huez and Les Deux Alpes further afield; the bus company's excellent-value Skiligne deals include ski pass and same-day return bus fare.

Once the snow melts, you'll need a car to properly explore the Vercors and Écrins parks. E-bikes are popular – Grenoble **tourist office** (p534) has info on marked e-bike itineraries or search isere-tourism.com/cycling.

Spin the wheel and wherever the needle falls, you win. Outdoor adventure around Grenoble knows no limits: it extends 360 degrees. From the cluster of little-known and hot-shot Oisans ski resorts melting into the glacier-carved Parc National des Écrins (east), to the rugged gorges and serrated peaks of Parc Naturel Régional du Vercors barely a few kilometres southwest of the city, every compass point unleashes thrills and spills in spades.

This is where winter skiers chase powder beneath shark-toothed summits; where wilderness seekers hike in summer to unearth waterfalls, beech forests and ancient footpaths blazed by shepherds and smugglers centuries before. Skiing, snowshoeing, hiking, canyoning, flying down the world's longest pylon zip wire – it's all here.

Alpe d'Huez

TIME FROM GRENOBLE: 1¾HR

Fly Down Europe's Longest Black Run

Winter or summer, in the ski town of Alpe d'Huez, riding the two legs of the **Télépherique du Pic Blanc** (skipass.alpedhuez.com) up to **Lac Blanc** (2700m) and beyond to **Pic Blanc** (3330m) is dizzying. Prepare for bitter cold on the wind-whipped glacier – frequently -20°C in winter and -10°C on a sun-scorched spring day. Orientation tables highlight what's what in the epic sweep of French, Italian and Swiss peaks: Roche de la Muzelle (3465m), Grand Pic (3982m) and Le Doigt de Dieu (Finger of God, 3973m) in the Massif des Écrins, even Mont Blanc on a clear day.

Summit swooning done, a spectacular ski-swoosh down to Alpe d'Huez beckons – on Europe's longest black run, 16km-long **La Sarenne** with a 2km vertical drop. Except for a handful of steep, ungroomed segments polka-dotted with moguls, the snowy descent is more like a wide, rollercoaster red with a maddeningly long green at the end. Skip the final 'flat' by cutting off at Pont du Gua to take the Chalvet chairlift up, then ski the red Campanules down. To admire Pic Blanc and its glacier in an alternative, magical light, ski La Sarenne at sunrise with a *pisteur* (ski patroller) or after sunset by headtorch with a guide; book at the **tourist office** (alpedhuez.com) on Place Joseph Paganon.

Alpe d'Huez

Non-skiers fly down Europe's longest black run on two wheels during April's **Sarenne Snowbike** (*skipass.alpedhuez.com/hiver/sarenne-snowbike*) and in July when thousands of intrepid bikers rip down ice, slush and rocks at speeds of up to 100km/h during **Megavalanche**, the world's longest downhill mountain-bike event.

Trailing Tour de France Cyclists

No ascent is so hallowed or hated among road cyclists as Alpe d'Huez's legendary '21' – the killer of a mountain road (the D211) linking Le Bourg d'Oisans (717m) in Oisans' Vallée de la Romanche with purpose-built ski resort Alpe d'Huez (1840m). During the 1995 Tour de France, Italian pro rider Marco Pantani (1970–2004) took a record-breaking 37 minutes and 35 seconds to get up it. But you should count a good hour or two – more with stops – to bag the 21 hairpin bends and average 7.9% gradient (maximum 15%) on the brutal 14.45km climb.

Each *virage* (switchback) is numbered and named after a past winner of the Tour de France's most gruelling stage. The first bend, No 21, at 806m honours the first-ever Alpe d'Huez winner in 1952 (Italian rider Fausto Coppi) and, ironically, seven-time Tour winner Lance Armstrong, who bagged this

BEST SKIING IN OISANS

High altitudes, reliable snow cover and 250km of pistes for all ski levels: there's a reason **Alpe d'Huez**, king of Oisans ski resorts, is unflaggingly popular. It forms part off the Alpe d'Huez Grand Domaine ski area with family-friendly villages Auris-en-Oisans, Huez-en-Oisans, Oz-en-Oisans and Villard Reculas.

Vaujany: (1250m) Farming village-turned-insider hot spot to flee the Alpe d'Huez crowd; direct link via the Alpette cable car.

Les Deux Alpes: (1650m) France's second-oldest ski resort, with functional architecture, a legendary snow park and summer skiing for the pros.

La Grave: (1500m) Mountain village dominated by craggy La Meija; seriously steep free-riding and off-piste skiing from the top of the Téléphérique de la Grave-La Meija cable car.

 EATING & DRINKING IN ALPE D'HUEZ: OUR PICKS

Café Alpin: Italian coffee, hot chocolate with whipped cream and deckchairs around a mobile baby-blue Piaggio Ape; *hours vary Dec-Apr*

La Bergerie: An open fire and cheese fondues welcome skiers at this chalet on the slopes in Villard-Reculas. *9am-5pm mid-Dec–Apr, 9.30am-7.30pm Jul & Aug* €€

Au Grenier: Air-dried beef, Grenoble trout and partridge confit are refined local treats at this outstanding family-run restaurant. *noon-2.30pm & 7-9.30pm* €€

Underground Bar: Downtown spot for drinks and live music, run by Brits Adam and Gareth who came for a season in 1993 and never left. *4pm-2am Dec-mid-Apr, Jul & Aug*

TWO-WHEELING AROUND: TIPS & RESOURCES

Oisans Col Series: Pedal in peace on Tuesday morning in July and August when a different *col* (mountain pass) is closed to cars. Tourist offices have the schedule.

E-bike Rental: To tackle Alpe d'Huez's 21 bends with electric assistance, try **Bike Store 21** *(be21.store; per day from €62)* in Le Bourg d'Oisans.

Recharge e-bikes: Free in shops and restaurants displaying an 'E-Bike Service' sign.

Cyclo en Oisans: An 84-page booklet detailing 20 mapped cycling itineraries, free at Alpe d'Huez and Le Bourg d'Oisans tourist offices.

bike-oisans.com: Ultimate online resource for cyclists: bike parks, routes, rental shops, festivals.

individual stage in 2001 and 2004 (only to be stripped of all his titles in 2012).

Pit stop in **La Garde d'Oisans** at cafe-bar **Le Virage 16**, between bends 16 and 15. Or labour up to bend 7 where benches, toilets and a water fountain peer down on the Gorges de Sarenne, up to the Massif des Grandes Rousses, and across the street to **Église St-Ferréol** with 11th-century stone steeple. Another 500m slog uphill brings you to the original village of **Huez** (1455m) – a steep huddle of stone houses stacked around the church, pétanque court and cafe-bar-grocery **Maison d'Huez**. From here, the **Huez Express gondola** *(skipass.alpedhuez.com; free)* whisk winter skiers and summer hikers up to Alpe d'Huez.

The mythical climb ends on main drag **ave du Rif-Nel** in Alpe d'Huez; a bronze banner overhead marks the Tour's official finishing line. Die-hards can continue 5.5km uphill along Route des Lacs for sensational alpine views and a well-deserved flop on the shore of crystalline **Lac Besson** (2060m).

Parc Naturel Régional du Vercors

TIME FROM GRENOBLE: 1¾HR

On the Trail of Eagles, Orchids & Vercors Blue

The pickings are rich in the thick oak forests, plateaux and peaks of **Parc Naturel Régional du Vercors** *(parc-du-vercors.fr)*. Within these 2062 sq km of pristine nature rambling southwest of Grenoble, chamois and ibex perch on cliffs, wild tulips pop out of rocks, golden eagles wheel overhead and 75 types of orchids blaze show-stopping pinks and purple.

The park's prized heart is protected by mainland France's largest natural reserve, the **Réserve Naturelle des Hauts Plateaux**. To heighten your chances of spotting a bearded vulture, black grouse or family of tumbling marmots, join a themed hike led by a naturalist or mountain guide from **Curieux de Vercors** *(curieux2vercors.fr; adult/child from €22/15)* in **Autrans-Méaudre**.

Picnic fare? Fresh bread and a chunk of farm-made, AOC Bleu du Vercors-Sassenage cheese – the secret behind gooey *Vercouline* (the Vercors version of classic cheese-and-potato *tartiflette*). Buy at a village market (the morning **market** in **La Chapelle-en-Vercors** is a fave) or from one of the park's many dairy farms *(fermes-du-vercors.com)*.

CANYONING CAPERS

Canyoning with **Vercors Aventure** *(vercors-aventure.com)* plunges you into the gushing white-water heart of the Vercors' spectacular Gorges du Furon (pass through the limestone gorges on the southbound D531 from Grenoble, just before Lans-en-Vercors). The Ardèche (p467) is another canyoning spot.

Jura Mountains

CROWD DETOX | CHEESE & WINE | PRETTY VILLAGES

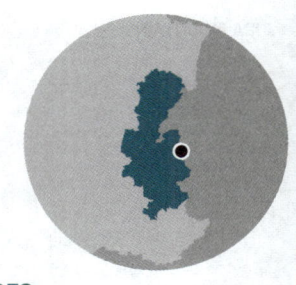

Catch your breath in the rural Jura, a tapestry of brooding mountain landscapes, sparsely populated plains and whisper-quiet villages. Extending along the Franco-Swiss border from Lake Geneva northeast to Belfort, these sub-alpine mountains lent their name to the Jurassic period in geology, when they formed. Rising highest is Crêt de la Neige (1720m), in the pristine Parc Naturel Régional du Haut-Jura, where skiers on cross-country trails leave the French Alps crowd for dust. In summer, walkers can ramble here all day without crossing a soul, pausing at lunchtime for Comté (cheese) tasting in a *fruitière* (cheese dairy) and a nip of the region's legendary *vin jaune*.

With only a few days to spare, base yourself in Besançon, folded in a bend in the Doubs River. Unsung Belfort, 95km north, is famed among music-festival fans for three-day Les Eurockéennes and is otherwise a convenient stopover for motorists driving from Alsace to Burgundy or the Alps. *Bonne route!*

> ☑ **TOP TIP**
>
> Gen up on the Jura's small but rich collection of wines before you arrive: consider getting a copy of Wink Lorch's **Jura Wines** *(winetravelmedia.com)*, the definitive bible.

Vauban's Military Might in Besançon
Get to grips with history and biodiversity inside Citadelle de Besançon

There is no lovelier – or mightier – spot to soak up commanding city views of the Doubs *département* capital and eponymous serpentine river than from UNESCO-listed 17th-century

---

GETTING AROUND

Direct trains link Besançon with historic and cultural destinations such as Arbois (50 minutes) and Belfort (1¼ hours). To venture beyond into rural Jura and visit wineries, you need wheels – motorised or e-powered.

Pick your trail: the **Grandes Traversées du Jura** (www.gtj.asso.fr/en) are long-distance summer routes that can be tackled on foot, mountain or road bike, e-bike or horse. If wine is your vice, motor through six *appellations* and past dozens of tasting cellars along the 80km Route des Vins du Jura (en.montagnes-du-jura.fr) driving itinerary.

JURA MOUNTAINS

★ HIGHLIGHTS
1. Cirque de Baume-les-Messieurs
2. Citadelle de Besançon

● SIGHTS
3. Abbaye Impériale
see 1 Cascade des Tufs
4. Domaine Dugois
5. Église St-Just
6. Maison de Victor Hugo
7. Musée de la Vigne et du Vin du Jura
8. Musée des Beaux-Arts et d'Archéologie
9. Musée du Temps
10. Saline Royale

● ACTIVITIES
11. Chemin de Vignes
see 1 Grottes de Baume

● SLEEPING
12. Auberge du Château de Vaite
13. Hôtel de Paris
14. Hôtel Regina

● EATING
15. Bistrot des Claquets
16. Circus
17. La Table du Grapiot
18. Le Bistronôme Lisa/Jerôme
19. Le Bistrot de la Tournelle
20. Le Poker d'As
21. Le St-Cerf
22. Les Caudalies
see 8 L'Oiseau du Temps
23. Marché Beaux-Arts

● DRINKING & NIGHTLIFE
24. Chez Le Père
see 13 Le Bouillon du Commerce
25. Le Privé
26. Titty Twister

● INFORMATION
27. Tourist Office

Citadelle de Besançon (*citadelle.com; adult/child from €5.80/9.50*). Perched up high on Mt St-Etienne, more than 100 vertical metres above Besançon's handsome old town, poking around the 12-hectare citadel is one way to suddenly feel very, *very* small.

Count on spending a full morning or afternoon at least at the fortress, which packs a punch with huge grounds and a trio of museums. Morph your visit into a family-fun fun game of riddle-solving with the citadel's playful 'Curse of the Centuries' self-guided tour *(two hours, €4.20)*. Or go old-school with independent meandering assisted by handy themed itineraries, games and a quiz for kids on the free MaCitadelle app – download it before you arrive. Don't miss the vertiginous Chemin de Ronde walk along a 600m section of the panoramic ramparts, or the **outdoor cinema** that screens movies beneath the stars on Thursday evenings in July and August.

Kick off your DIY tour in **Chapelle St-Etienne** with an engaging, multimedia introduction to the citadel's impressive military architecture – this is, after all, one of 11 defensive forts in France designed by star architect Vauban (1603–1707). Move onto the **Musée Comtois** showcasing local life in the region in centuries past, then **Le Muséum** which deep-dives into biodiversity with a captivating insectarium, aquarium and noctarium crawling with nocturnal dormice and voles. Final port of call, not suitable for children under 10: one of France's most in-depth WWII museums, the **Musée de al Résistance et de la Déportation**. During WWII, the Germans imprisoned British civilians in the citadel, and German firing squads executed about 100 resistance fighters here.

Freedom, Dignity, Time & Art in Besançon
Meet Victor Hugo at home

Join the dots between 19th-century activism and modern-day struggles for social justice at Besançon's compelling **Maison de Victor Hugo** (*maisonvictorhugo.besancon.fr; adult/child €3.20/free; closed Tue*), in the old town on main street Grande Rue where Victor Hugo, France's greatest novelist (1802–85) was born. An audioguide whirls French literature buffs and aficionados of *Les Misérables* through three floors of exhibits dedicated to freedom, dignity and equality – the deep-rooted principles that drove both Hugo's literary output and the work of modern NGOs like Amnesty International and UNICEF.

Admission is free on Sunday. Or consider a combo ticket *(adult/child €9/free)* to couple Victor Hugo with literal and

THE LION OF BELFORT

French sculptor Frédéric Auguste Bartholdi (1834–1904) didn't only design New York's Statue of Liberty. In 1875 he began work on what became, 15 years later, France's largest stone sculpture, the Lion du Belfort: a gargantuan red-sandstone lion, 22m long and almost 11m tall, that scowls down on a checkerboard of brick towers and ochre and rose-pink houses in Belfort from its majestic perch atop the town's citadel. The emblematic, sphinx-like statue commemorates the French army's tenacious spirit and resistance during the Franco-Prussian War (1870–71). The besieged French town, wedged between the Vosges and Jura mountains, held out to attacking Prussian forces for 103 days, thanks to which the town and surrounds escape being annexed to Prussia (unlike Alsace) and remained French.

EATING IN BESANÇON: MARKET PICKS

Marché Beaux-Arts: The town's food market showcases Jurassien cheese, charcuterie, fruit and veg. *7am-2pm Tue-Thu, to 6.30pm Fri & Sat, 8am-1pm Sun* €

Le St-Cerf: Market-sourced, zero-kilometre produce inspires the top-drawer modern cuisine at this bistro. *noon-2.30pm Mon-Fri, 7.30pm-midnight Thu & Fri* €€

Le Poker d'As: A locally revered staple since 1959, this family kitchen mixes creative flair with good, honest, French cooking. *noon-1.30pm & 7.30-9pm Tue-Sat* €€

L'Oiseau du Temps: Order the chef's *poulet au vin jaune* (chicken in yellow wine) and devour beneath vaults in an 18th-century granary. *noon-1.15pm & 7.15-9pm Tue-Sat* €€

HOT BOX, JÉSUS & CHRISTMAS TREE LIQUEUR

It's hot, soft and packed in a box. Vacherin du Haut Doubs is made with *lait cru* (unpasteurised milk) and derives its unique grassy taste from the spruce bark in which it's wrapped. Connoisseurs poke a hole in the soft-rinded cheese, sprinkle in garlic and white wine, and bake it to create a gooey *boîte chaude* (hot box), served with potatoes. Its meaty counterpart, *jésus de Morteau*, is a small, fat Morteau sausage, smoked with pinewood sawdust in a traditional *tuyé* (mountain hut).

Other culinary standouts are *liqueur de sapin* (fir-tree liqueur), crafted in Mouthe, 15km of Métabief, and *glace au sirop de sapin* (fir-tree ice cream). Sampling either is like ingesting a Christmas tree.

figurative interpretations at Besançon's thought-provoking **Musée du Temps** *(mdt.besancon.fr; closed Mon)* and with France's oldest public art collection, magnificently displayed in the town's former corn exchange, at the peerless **Musée des Beaux-Arts et d'Archéologie** *(mbaa.besancon.fr; closed Tue).*

Marvel at an 'Ideal City'

Learn how salt made the Jura rich at Saline Royal

Through modern eyes, the Jura's UNESCO World Heritage-listed masterpiece of 18th-century industrial design has a sinister side: radiating out from a central columned hall, the semi-circular shape of **Saline Royal** *(salineroyale.com; adult/child €10/15 incl digital guide)* ensured no worker could ever escape the beady eye of their watchful supervisor's eyes – not even for one moment.

Architect Claude-Nicolas Ledoux designed the royal saltworks and its outbuildings, in Arc-et-Senans, 35km southwest of Besançon, to be an 'ideal city'. And although his plans never really came to fruition, the wondrously symmetrical half-moon of elegant columns and neoclassical archways of his early-Industrial Age complex became UNESCO heritage listed in 1982 for their visionary composition and architectural mastery. Permanent exhibitions break down the design concept, Ledoux's life and the history of salt. Dazzling sound-and-light shows in the **Centre des Lumières** (Centre of Lights) brings other UNESCO world treasures to life through digital art, and 30 themed gardens – Zen, Wind, Time, Edible Forest, Ancient Grains – elaborately lacing the perimeter of this uniquely circular site sprawling 13 hectares to ensure you linger the best part of a day.

Unearth An Abbey, Waterfall & Bat-Filled Caves

Hiking the Cirque de Baume-les-Messieurs

The thickly forested Jura is known for its *cirques* – steep-head or blind valleys, formed 200 million years ago by glacial erosion – and **Cirque de Baume-les-Messieurs** is the finest specimen. Explore its vertiginous limestone cliffs and horseshoe brow on a circular day walk from the famously picture-postcard village of Baume-les-Messieurs, 1½ hour's drive south from Besançon.

Park next to Baume's emblematic **Abbaye Impériale** *(baumelesmessieurs.fr; adult/child €8.50/4),* open to visitors daily

DRINKING IN BESANÇON: OUR PICKS

Le Bouillon du Commerce: Brood beneath a chandelier, over a jug of Côtes du Jura, at this art nouveau watering hole, established 1873. *noon-10pm*

Titty Twister: Live rock and metal, cheap beer on tap and a great people-watching terrace on riverside quai Vauban. *3pm-2am Tue-Sat to midnight Sun*

Chez Le Père: Pick your spirit, then your cocktail at this sassy bar. Sublime homemade syrups and craft beer from Brasserie La Rouget de Lisle. *5pm-1am Wed-Sat, 2.30-10pm Sun*

Le Privé: Drink and dance until dawn at Besançon's wildly popular gay nightclub; €10 admission usually includes one drink. *midnight-5am Fri & Sat*

April to September, and wander through honey-stone lanes from the medieval abbey to the trailhead. Break from the intense summer heat with a one-hour guided tour of **Grottes de Baumes** *(adult/child €10/7),* Jurassic-era caves where niphargus (blind white cave shrimps with no eyes) swim in a cave lake and 5000 bats hibernate for six months in winter. Watching 800-odd resident summer bats circle wildly overhead is a highlight.

Picnic afterwards in the grounds of **Cascade des Tufs**, a massive mushroom-shaped waterfall where the Dard River dramatically crashes down over bulbous tuff beds.

Drink in Liquid Gold
Winemaking in Arbois and Pupillin

Legend says *vin jaune* ('yellow wine') was cooked up when a winemaker stumbled upon a forgotten barrel, six years and three months after he'd filled it, only to find its contents had become liquid gold. Sort fact from fiction in **Arbois**, 40km southwest of Besançon, where the slowly fermented golden wine is made. Arbois wines were France's first to gain an AOC in 1936.

Amid a tangle of honey-coloured stone houses framed by the Cuisance River and vineyards, head to the **Musée de la Vigne et du Vin du Jura** *(arbois.fr; adult/child €4/free).* Inside a turreted 13th- to 18th-century chateau, the wine museum unravels viticultural history and tradition. Vines planted in the garden illustrate grape varietals, including savagnin, unique to *vin jaune.* After six years and three months in oak barrels, 100L of grape juice become just 62L of *vin jaune,* bottled in chubby glass 0.62L *clavelin* bottles.

Pick up the **Chemin de Vignes** (2.5km) footpath through vineyards, at the top of the steps next to the chateau. Or head south along main street rue de l'Hôtel de Ville to **Église St-Just**. The **tourist office** *(coeurdujura-tourisme.com),* opposite the church, has walking maps. Follow the signposted *'Sentier pédestre'* past the cemetery, along the river and up through vines to Freddy Wood's eye-catching wrought-iron mesh **sculpture** of a glass and 6m-long bottle of *vin jaune.* Vineyard views continue all the way to **Pupillin**, a cute yellow winemakers' village 2.5km south, with a few *caves* (cellars) offering tasting. **La Table du Grapiot** *(legrapiot.com; menus from €60)* is the spot to lunch local and well, in the charmed company of the grandest Jura wines.

WHERE TO LEARN ABOUT JURA WINE

Wink Lorch *(winetravelmedia. com),* wine writer and author of award-winning books *Jura Wine* and *Wines of the French Alps,* shares three insider addresses.

With quintessential zinc bar, **Bistrot des Claquets** in Arbois is a gathering place for local *vignerons*. Pick up the local gossip over a simple home-cooked set lunch, or just come for a glass or bottle from a range of well-priced, natural Jura wines.

Domaine Dugois is a small family-owned winery in Les Arsures near Arbois. Make an appointment to taste an excellent, organic range of Jura wines in a traditional cellar.

Wrap up warm for **Pressée du Vin de Paille**, a joyous winter festival celebrating St-Vincent, patron saint of wine. Held the third Sunday in January in Arlay.

 EATING IN ARBOIS: BEST WINE-FOOD PAIRINGS

| **Le Bistrot de la Tournelle**: Sip estate wines by the river at the dreamy summer 'pop-up' of winemakers from Domaine de la Tournelle. *noon-9pm Jun-Aug* € | **Circus**: Nature and season decides what's cooking at this grassroots bistro. The wine list is appropriately biodynamic. *noon-1.30pm Fri & Sat, 7.30-9pm Tue-Sat* €€ | **Le Bistronôme Lisa/ Jerôme**: Modern gastronomic bistronomy paired with river views, and biodynamic or organic Jura wines. *12.15-1.30pm & 7.15-8.30pm Tue-Sat* €€€ | **Les Caudalies**: You can't beat the food-wine pairings here by chef-sommelier Philippe Troussard. Refined dining and tastings in a vaulted cellar. *noon-2pm Tue-Fri, 7-10pm Fri & Sat* €€€ |

HELP ME PICK:

Alpine Skiing

With skiing in France split across seven massifs and 300-plus different ski resorts, choosing where to fly down corduroy through a breathtaking kaleidoscope of bewitching mountain views can be tricky. On the plus side, the Alps sport *une station de ski* (ski resort) to suit every mood and moment. From a multi-generational ski trip with gran and the kids to a first time with friends or hardcore adventure, the French Alps has you covered.

Where to go if you love

Pow & Knarly Blacks

With Europe's loftiest mountain holding sentry here at 4805m, it's little wonder the French Alps cradle some of Europe's most challenging downhill skiing. Ski-expert resorts with legendary 'black' slopes – steep verticals, often ungroomed and pocked with moguls the size of small cars – include **Avoriaz** (the Wall), **Alpe d'Huez** (the 'Champagne Run'), Val d'Isère's **Espace Killy** (La Face) and **Courchevel** (p531) (the Corridor).

Extreme off-piste skiing in Oisans' **La Grave** (p539) is iconic, as is Chamonix' **La Vallée Blanche** (p500). It is also from Chamonix that powder-hounds drop into Italy and ski back (heli-skiing has been illegal in France since 1995).

Beginner Slopes

Most resorts have at least one or two 'green' slopes for debutants to tumble like marmots and hone snow ploughs. Faithful favourites for notable ease of slope access and mountains of family fun off-piste include **Les Gets, La Clusaz** and all-rounder **Alpe d'Huez** (with 49km of green pistes and 54km blue). **Les Deux Alpes** (p539) has the advantage of a sizeable nursery ski area (one of four) at a snow-sure 2200m.

Iconic Après-Ski

To dance on tables in ski boots before the last run home, hit **La Folie Douce** (*lafoliedouce.com*). Champion of French Alps' après-ski, the first Folie Douce opened on **Val d'Isère** slopes in 1974, mixing live music with cabaret acts and an intoxicating party vibe. Younger siblings in **Val Thorens, Courchevel-Méribel, Alpe d'Huez, Avoriaz** (p523) and **Chamonix** (p508) are equally wild.

Some brilliant music festivals bookend the ski season. Concerts kick off on the slopes mid-afternoon and provide endless dancing in the snow. Headline acts include **Rock The Pistes** (Les Portes du Soleil; *en.rockthepistes.com*), **Snowboxx** (Avoriaz; *snowboxx.com*) and **Tomorrowland** (Alpe d'Huez; *winter.tomorrowland.com*).

Pretty Alpine Villages

Purpose-built ski resorts that popped up at high altitudes in the late 1960s and '70s (looking at you Flaine, Les Arcs and Tignes) are breathtakingly functional, but soulless for skiers after alpine charm. Storybook 'village resorts' stitched from centuries-old farmsteads, wooden chalets and an ubiquitous *boulangerie* (bakery), include Parisian-chic **Megève** (pictured), overwhelmingly family-friendly **Le Grand Bornand**, and good-value **Combloux, Vallorcine** and **Saint-Nicolas de Véroce** in the Mont Blanc Massif. **St-Martin de Belleville** (p531) might lie low at 1450m, but it's foodie nirvana. Few have even heard of impossibly pretty **St-Sorlin-d'Arves** in Les Sybelles, France's fourth-largest ski area.

FORNAXSTOCK/SHUTTERSTOCK

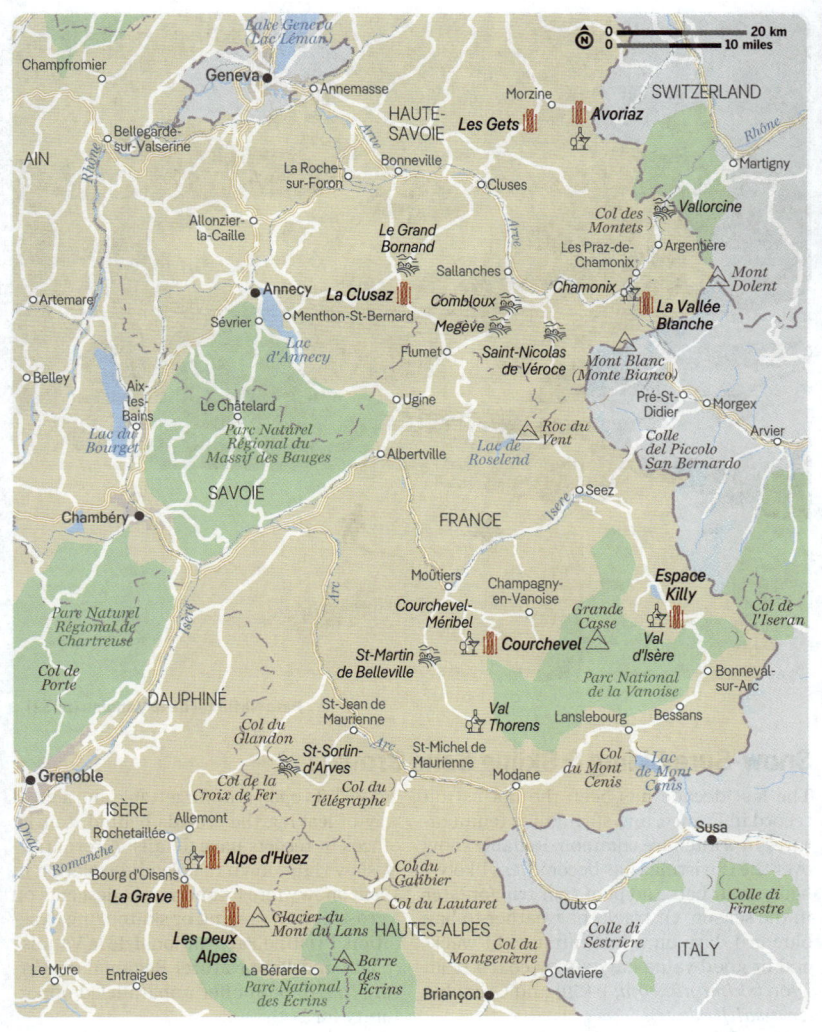

HOW TO

When to go January is cold but quiet. Conditions are tip-top in March, but afternoon slopes get slushy in late-March as temperatures rise.

Book ahead Bus transfers and pricier minibus shuttles from Lyon, Grenoble and Geneva airports require booking, preferably weeks ahead. Ditto for ski lessons during the holidays

Budget Count €35 to €85 per day for a ski pass; buying online can be cheaper. Watch for one-day Saturday deals. Hire ski equipment online and rent ski clothing to save cash.

Insurance Check your travel insurance policy covers winter sports. If not, add Carré Neige *assurance* (carreneige.com) to your ski pass; €3.30 a day is a snip of the price of mountain rescue.

Parc National de la Vanoise (p532)

Snow-Sure Skiing & Skiing Sans Crowds

The last decade has been the hottest on record in France, and spring-like temperatures in winter are common. Reliable snow over the Christmas has become less likely – hedge your bets and plan your trip for later in the season. Or track the weather to bag bluebird days on a last-minute ski weekend or good-value day-trip by coach from Lyon (*skimania.com;* p459) and Grenoble *(transaltitude.fr).*

High-altitude resorts above 2000m such as Val Thorens, Avoriaz and Tignes are snow-sure but can be busy. Don't be discouraged by thin snow cover in lower-altitude resorts. Rigorous snow management ensure resorts do an impressive job of making snow and maintaining pistes. Joining piste controllers for a 'first tracks' razz around on skis before lifts open is unforgettable and a great way of leaving the crowds behind; tourist offices in resorts have details. Alternatively, slow right down in splendid isolation in silent snowy forests and virgin descents on a cross-country skiing or ski-touring expedition. Pristine Parc National de la Vanoise (p532) and Parc Naturel Régional du Vercors (p540) both offer unparalleled opportunity for both.

Do your bit to keep greening ski resorts snow-sure by ditching air travel. Several lift companies and hotels offer discounts on ski passes and nightly rates to skiers who arrive by train. Favour resorts awarded the Flocon Vert label (flocon-vert.org) for sustainable commitment and environmentally responsible practice.

Places We Love to Stay

€ Budget €€ Midrange €€€ Top End

Chamonix MAP p502

Le Chamoniard Volant € Veteran favourite of climbers and ski bums on a budget, with bunk dorms and communal kitchen in a self-catering chalet.

Hôtel Richemond € Third-generation family hotel, with old-school rooms in a grand old building from 1914; exceptional value.

La Folie Douce €€ The iconic après-ski brand's only hotel (p508) parties hard inside a monumental Belle Époque palace.

Refuge du Montenvers €€ Mourn France's longest but fast-melting glacier at this elegant *grand dame* (p507), an 1880 vintage hotel with chic retro-styled rooms, restaurant and summer terrace above Mer de Glace.

Beyond Chamonix

Camping Les Dômes de Miage € Mont Blanc is your wake-up call at this campground with tent pitches in wooded hills, south of St-Gervais. First-rate facilities.

Le 1828 €€ Authentic Savoyard *mazot* (miniature wooden chalet) from 1828 near St-Gervais. Its luxury interior sleeps two and sports a tiny kitchen and bathroom inside, sun loungers and hot tub outside.

Le Coeur des Neiges €€ Unusually, this family-run hotel, with 15 alpine-chic rooms and spa in the heart of St-Gervais village, is open year-round.

Armencette €€€ Luxurious chalet-hotel with heated spa pool alfresco (swim in the snow!) in the enchanting hamlet of St-Nicolas de Véroce. Choice of dining and the hotel's village *boulangerie* bakes fresh bread for breakfast, cakes for tea.

Annecy MAP p516

Hôtel de Savoie € Two-star bargain, with an entrance tucked Venice-style in the monumental white facade of an Italianate Baroque church.

Hôtel du Château €€ Family-run hotel with panoramic breakfast terrace and free parking, on a hill across from the château's imposing gatehouse.

Le Boutik €€€ Twelve designer rooms and an enchanting garden cabin, each with a different theme and palette, in an old convent annexe.

Imperial Palace €€€ Edwardian *grand dame,* in the biz since 1913, with four-star rooms and glittering lake views.

Chambéry & Beyond MAP p525

L'Ancienne École du Villard € Sleep sweetly in a former school-turned-enchanting B&B with 1960s charm, in a sleepy hamlet near St-Pierre d'Entremont.

Cabanes Chartreuse Insolite € Overnight in a treehouse; in winter it's only accessible on skis or 40 minutes on foot with snowshoes from St-Pierre de Chartreuse.

Petit Hôtel Confidentiel €€€ Lux out in a five-star, family-run boutique hotel in a 15th-century building near the château. Design-sharp doubles are midnight-black or Scandi-themed.

Grenoble MAP p535

Le Hüb € Modern and design driven, the Hub has both hostel-esque pods, apartment-style studios with kitchenette and bedrooms.

Babel Community € Exceptional-value hotel-apartments in a modern co-living/working hub at the foot of La Bastide. Onsite rooftop bar Ciel is a fantastic bonus.

Hôtel de l'Europe €€ Grenoble's oldest hotel bristles with two centuries of history. It's dead-central, with vintage wrought-iron balconies and 39 modern white rooms.

RockyPop Grenoble €€ Games room, cocktail bar, brasserie dining on a sun-spangled patio garden and bike shop make this lifestyle hangout a fave for everyone. Also in Chamonix and Flaine.

Jura Mountains MAP p542

Hôtel Regina € Family-run *maison d'hôtes* (B&B) on Besançon's Grande Rue; some rooms open directly onto the walled garden.

Hôtel de Paris €€ Sleep in the same 18th-century coaching inn in Besançon as French novelists George Sand and Colette. Rooms fuse antique glamour with modern design.

Auberge du Château de Vaite €€€ Besançon's out-of-town choice: a château with rooms, glorious gardens and the Jura's signature *poulet au vin jaune*.

Above: Grande Plage (p589), Biarritz; Right: *Huîtres* (oysters), Bordeaux (p556)

Researched by
Nicola Williams

Bordeaux to Biarritz

WINE, SEA AND SURF

With roads through vine-striped hills and wild stretches of coastal sand, dunes and islands cascading into the Atlantic, this is where France returns to nature.

This stretch of coast in the southwest lives well – think French *art de vivre* bottled into an easily navigable road trip mixing seaside resorts and Pyrenean peaks, historic châteaux and vineyards, hipster beach bars, open-air markets and stunning food and wine.

It's hard to believe that main city Bordeaux fell under British rule for 300 years (from 1152 when Henry of Aquitaine was crowned King Henry II of England). Ferociously Bordelais to the last breath, France's sixth-largest city and dynamic student hub screams local pride and creative sass. This is where urbanites cycle to work on bicycles kitted out with wooden wine crates as bike baskets, or grab a dozen *huîtres à la Bordelaise* (fresh oysters with hot *crépinettes* sausages) and a glass of Entre-deux-Mers for lunch. Be it hobnobbing with coopers in a fifth-generation workshop or with the cool crowd on a fashionista rooftop, shopping for sustainable trainers made from grape seeds and artisan gins crafted from vine blossoms, liberal-thinker Bordeaux is game.

South of the city, the Côte d'Argent ('Silver Coast') takes centre stage with endless shimmering-gold beaches backed by dark-green pine forests. Surfers catch waves in the French surfing heartland of Hossegor and incredible sunsets over surf or rooftop spritz in celebrity Biarritz. When the glitz overwhelms, down-to-earth pilgrim towns and hilltop villages in rural Pays Basque (French Basque Country) near Spain beckon.

THE MAIN AREAS

BORDEAUX
Cultural capital and culinary hub.
p556

LA ROCHELLE
Portside panache and island springboard.
p573

BAYONNE
Heart of French Basque Country.
p583

ST-JEAN-PIED-DE-PORT
The final stop before Spain. **p594**

BORDEAUX TO BIARRITZ

THE GUIDE

Find Your Way

The Atlantic Coast romps along sandy shores from the Loire estuary, 200km north of La Rochelle, to the Spanish border. Decent public transport and roads make light work of navigating this approximately 650km-long coastline.

CAR

A car isn't vital along the coast, but it's needed in rural areas and those with poor public transport such as the northern part of the Médoc and the Basque hinterland. Some of the most idyllic *chambres d'hôte* (B&Bs) can only be accessed by car.

BICYCLE

Within towns, cities and along much of the coast, two wheels – regular or electric-assisted, widespread to rent – are a practical and exhilarating means of covering shorter stretches. Bike-packers can cover the entire coast along the long-distance cycling itinerary La Vélodyssée (p570).

TRAIN

It's easy to travel to the coast's main transport hubs by train. High-speed TGVs service Bordeaux, La Rochelle, Biarritz and Bayonne (four hours direct from Paris Montparnasse). Calculate itineraries and search for schedules, fares and traffic information on transports. nouvelle-aquitaine.fr.

La Rochelle, p573

North of Bordeaux, this old-world port on the Atlantic Coast is a summer cocktail of beaches, cycling trails and chic island escapes – a faithful French-family favourite.

Plan Your Time

Take it slowly to savour both the high-octane and hidden delights of this stretch of Atlantic Coast, one wine or Cognac sip at a time: from urban Bordeaux to unexplored Basque country.

Église Monolithique (p567), St-Émilion

If You Only Do One Thing

● Explore **Bordeaux** (p556) to understand just how well this coast does cities and culture. Pick your lens – wine, history, street art – through which to explore elegant streets and squares beaded with 18th-century architecture. In old-world **Chartrons** (p556) stroll leafy avenues lined with *hôtels particuliers* (mansions) built for wine merchants and watch local life roll by riverside. Lunch on traditional *lamproie à la bordelaise* (eel stew) at **La Tupina** (p561). Enjoy a tourist-office guided tour or river cruise in the afternoon (reserve), or go rogue with alternative art and a head-spinning silo climb at **VertiGina** (p563) in industrial wet dock 'hood Bassins à Flot. Savour sunset cocktails with rooftop views at **Tchanqué** (p563) and dinner at **Les Récoltants** (p560) or **Symbiose** (p562). Dance afloat at **iBoat** (p562).

Seasonal Highlights

This region's signature coastal nature makes it an obvious summer-holiday destination, but outside of high season there's buckets to entertain.

APRIL
Warm days. Seasonal beach restaurants and bars, snack shacks on coastal footpaths and bike trails emerge from winter hibernation. Bayonne celebrates its four-day **Foire au Jambon** (p586).

MAY
Cycling paths through *marais salants* (salt marshes) on Île de Ré blaze yellow with wild black mustard in bloom. Wild flowers colour Basque foothill hiking trails.

JUNE
Bordeaux celebrates wine with tastings, workshops, markets, music and fireworks during a four-day wine festival. Salt workers on **Île de Ré** (p580) harvest the first of the summer's 'white gold' (until September).

A Long Weekend

● After a few hours in Bordeaux, head by train to France's oldest wine region, **St-Émilion** (p566), or in a rental car to prestigious **Médoc** (p568). Think ahead: lunch or dinner at bucolic **Les Belles Perdrix** (p566) overlooking vines at Château Troplong-Mondot and Pauillac's local foodie secret **Nomade** (p568) both require an advance table reservation. Day two, follow in the footsteps of 19th-century Bordeaux bourgeoisie to seaside town **Arcachon** (p569). Rent an old-school bicycle to spin along the coast to Europe's highest sand dune, **Dune du Pilat** (p570). Dip in the sea and dine with A-listers around the pool at **La Co(o)rniche** (p570). Next morning, sail across the bay for another day of cycling on the chic, oyster-harvesting peninsula of **Cap Ferret** (p571).

More Than a Week

● Dive into the maritime fortifications, beaches and independent shopping scene of seafaring **La Rochelle** (p573). Paddle in a kayak to **Fort Bayard** (p577) or pedal to island idyll **Île de Ré** (p580). Its bird-rich salt pans and marshes, cycling trails, oyster farms and whitewashed villages are seductive.

● **Bordeaux** (p556) isn't the only wine party in town. With a full week, you have time to discover **Cognac** (p578). Book a distillery tour to learn about and taste a drink so heavenly even angels partake. Or go-slow hiking, medieval-town meandering and village hopping around **St-Jean-Pied-de-Port** (p594). En route, don't miss Basque capital **Bayonne** (p583) where a visit to chocolate maker **Monsieur Txokola** (p585) and fine art at the recently reopened **Musée Bonnat-Helleu** (p585) are absolute musts.

JULY
Temperatures sizzle on busy beaches. Enjoy festivals galore. Embrace the wild street party and living lesson in Basque culture during Bayonne's exuberant **Fêtes de Bayonne** (p585).

AUGUST
Bordeaux empties as urbanites head to the sea. Espelette farmers pick the first chilli peppers. Live jazz fills the open-air theatre beneath Île de Ré's lighthouse during **Jazz au Phare** (p581).

SEPTEMBER
The surf (until March) doesn't get any better than this. Grapes are harvested and the Médoc vineyards welcome road trippers and **wine-loving marathon runners**.

OCTOBER
Locals stroll empty beaches and button up the hatches in the Basque hinterland. Watch international artists at work during Bayonne's street-art festival **Points de Vue** (p587).

Bordeaux

WINE | GASTRONOMY | ART & ARCHITECTURE

☑ TOP TIP

The portfolio of themed guided tours – including wine-tasting tours to surrounding chateaux – offered by Bordeaux **tourist office** *(visiter-bordeaux.com)* is exceptional; reserve in advance online. One city tour is included in the **Bordeaux CityPass** *(bordeauxcitypass.com; 24/48/72 hours €37/47/55)*, covering admission to major museums and sights, and unlimited use of public transport.

Bordeaux's mood board hasn't changed since French novelist Victor Hugo (1802–85) visited in 1839, waxing lyrical in letters to his wife back in Paris about the city's elegant squares and quaysides, fountains and monumental theatre that reminded him of Versailles. He wrote 'and you will love Bordeaux, even if you only drink water'.

Bordeaux's heady cocktail of old and new – not to mention its legendary wine cellars, bistros, *bars à vin* and restaurants bursting with prestigious vintages – is as intoxicating as ever. From this Gallo-Roman city's golden past as medieval wine trader and key port in Europe during the Age of Enlightenment, to iconic vineyards, a spirited student population and a buoyant undercurrent of creativity, France's sixth largest city brims with surprising and enthralling stories worthy of a postcard home at every turn. Paired with an exceptional dining scene and captivating river life, there is no tastier marriage.

The Epic Story of Bordeaux Wine
Learn and taste in city museums

Bordeaux's intoxicating wine story begins in the ancient trading district of riverside **Chartrons**, named after medieval Carthusian monks. The city's life-blood wine trade originates

---

GETTING AROUND

Tram line A is the cheapest, quickest way to get into town – count 45 minutes – from **Aéroport de Bordeaux** *(bordeaux.aeroport.fr)* in Merignac, 10km west. The same tickets *(single/10-ticket card €1.90/15)* are valid on Bat3 river boats, likewise run by public-transport company TBM *(infotbm.com)*.

With its handsome architecture, wide avenues and monumental squares, Bordeaux is made for walking. To get from A to B quickly, TBM's public bike-sharing scheme Le Vélo has bike stations with classic and electric wheels all over town. Free-floating electric scooters by Pony *(getapony.com)* and Dott *(ridedott.com)* fill the gaps.

Musée du Vin et du Négoce

here. Discover the role of *négociants* (merchant traders) in the 18th and 19th centuries at the **Musée du Vin et du Négoce** *(museeduvinbordeaux.com; adult/child €12/free)*, in an Irish merchant's house from 1720. Visits end with a tasting.

Nearby, viticultural merriment morphs Chartrons' quaint main street, rue Notre Dame, into a street-party zone during October's two-day **Fête du Vin Nouveau et de la Brocante**. The wine trail continues at **La Cité du Vin** *(laciteduvin.com; adult/child €22/9)*, Bordeaux's emblematic 'Guggenheim of wine' in a curvaceous building resembling a wine decanter. Inside, spectacular cathedral spaces embrace every aspect of wine. Immersive exhibits (lots of sniffing and smelling – it's great!) end with a glass of *vin* or grape juice in 8th-floor bar Le Belvédère. April to October, taste while you tour on a one-hour Via Sensoria tour *(adult/child €22/9)* led by an English-speaking sommelier, with four wine-and-season pairings.

Back in the old-town quarter of St-Pierre, indulge in a wine aperitif at the hallowed **Bar à Vin** *(baravin.bordeaux.com; glass of wine from €2.50)* inside the Maison du Vin de Bordeaux. Art works from the 1950s, including tapestries and stained glass, further illustrate Bordeaux's epic wine story. End with dinner at **Soif** *(soif-bordeaux.com; 7-11pm Fri-Mon, plus 12.30-2pm Sat & Sun)*, a five-minute walk away on rue du Cancera, to dine in the company of organic, natural wines by brilliant boutique winemakers you've never heard of.

WHERE TO TASTE WINE IN BORDEAUX

Jane Anson, Bordeaux wine critic and author of *Inside Bordeaux: The Châteaux, The Wines and the Terroir*, shares her recommendations. @jane.anson

Start with the **Mémoires et Partages** *(memoiresetpartages.com)* walking tour about colonial trade. It has lots of wine links and you'll learn an important part of Bordeaux history not often talked about.

Visit restaurants with the best wine lists: **L'Univerre** and **Le Point Rouge** are very good, and **Ressources** is one of my favourites. Some great wine bars not to miss include **Wine More Time**, **Aux Quatre Coins du Vins** and **Le Bar à Vin** at the Conseil Interprofessionnel du Vin de Bordeaux (CIVB).

EATING IN BORDEAUX: FAVOURITE TERRACES

Magasin Général: All-day dining in France's largest organic restaurant, with vintage sofas and ping-pong tables in Darwin. *8am-7.30pm Mon-Fri, from 9am Sat & Sun, to 11.30pm Fri & Sat* €

Bar de la Marine: Nothing beats the €20 three-course lunch served in a summer flower garden in Bacalan. Funky 1950s memorabilia too. *9am-5pm Mon-Fri* €

Chiocchio: Tasty Franco-Tuscan fare on an urban terrace, foxy street art and prime people-watching on cafe-beaded place du Palais. *noon-3pm & 7-11.30pm Mon-Sat* €€

Le Pavilion des Boulevards: Seasonal gastronomy on a delightful terracotta-paved patio perfumed with magnolia. *noon-2pm Wed, noon-2pm & 8-10pm Tue & Thu-Sat* €€€

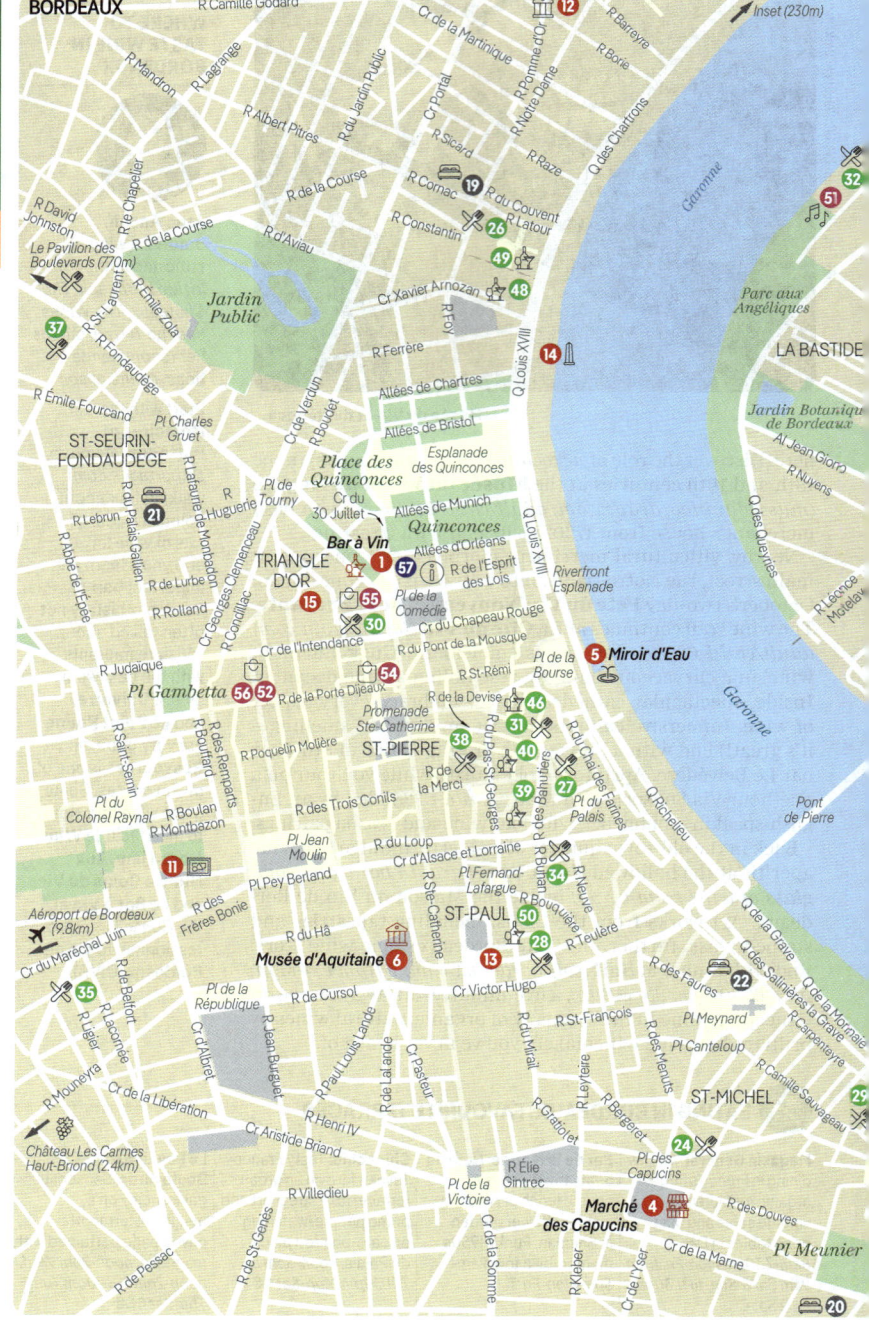

Meet One of France's First Female Artists

Rosa Bonheur at the Fine Arts Museum

Entering the Landscapes & Animal Painting room in the North Wing of Bordeaux's **Musée des Beaux-Arts** *(Fine Arts Museum; musba-bordeaux.fr; adult/child €6/free)*, inside the 1770s-built Hôtel de Ville, it's impossible not to be blown away by the monumental painting of white Camargue horses. This – *La foulaison du blé en Camargue* (Treading Wheat in the Camargue; 1899) – was the last (unfinished) painting by Bordelaise painter Rosa Bonheur (1822–99), one of France's earliest and most celebrated female artists, who dared wear trousers when she worked. Don't miss the portrait of Bordeaux's original rebel in her studio in 1893, showing her doing just this.

Trading Enslaved People in 18th-Century Bordeaux

Confronting history at the Musée d'Aquitaine

Spanning Gallo-Roman times to the present day, the evocative **Musée d'Aquitaine** *(musee-aquitaine-bordeaux.fr; adult/child €4.50/free)*, closed Monday, is a captivating waltz through urban history. But it's not all swashbuckling heroics and viticultural swag. Bordeaux's backstory gets grim on the 2nd floor where chronological exhibits move into 18th-century Bordeaux and its pivotal role in transatlantic trade and the trade of enslaved people. A hotly contested issue in times past, this period of history is presented with candour and uncomfortable detail. During the 480 'triangle' expeditions organised from Bordeaux between 1672 and 1837, some 130,000 to 150,000 Africans were 'purchased' in exchange for goods and later sold on as enslaved persons in the Americas.

The wealth that Bordeaux ship owners and traders amassed from this booming trade is only too evident in the exhibits, all donated by local families, in the **Musée de l'Histoire Maritime** *(museehistoiremaritimedebordeaux.fr; adult/child €10/free)*, to reopen in 2026 after renovation, a 30-minute walk north along the riverfront to Chartrons.

En route, pay your respects to the emotive **statue of Marthe Testas** (1765–1870) gazing out at the river on quai Louis XVIII. This young East African girl was purchased at the age of 16 by Bordelais traders Pierre and François Testas some time

---

TRIANGULAR TRADE

Trade was initially two-way in the thriving port of 17th-century Bordeaux. Merchant ships laden with Bordeaux wine, oil, silks and other local products sailed to the West Indies and Caribbean. Ships returned with coffee, cocoa, cotton, spices, sugar and tobacco.

But all too soon the commercial temptations of triangular trade proved too lucrative to resist. Merchandise from all over Europe was shipped from Bordeaux to ports on the east African coast where it was traded for African people. The ships then continued to the Caribbean where Africans were enslaved and sold, often to work on sugar plantations. Ships then returned back to Bordeaux stuffed with colonial goods. The entire voyage took 18 months.

Don't skimp on dessert

EATING IN BORDEAUX: GOOD-VALUE LOCAVORE DINING

Les Halles de Bacalan: Grab a gourmet bite from two dozen-odd producer and chef stalls in this contemporary food hall. *8am-11pm Tue-Sat, to 4pm Sun* €

Casa Gaïa: Veggie bowls and zero-km cuisine on a bijou patio at an organic bistro in Chartrons. Fab weekend brunch. *noon-2.15pm & 7-10.15pm Tue-Sat, noon-3pm Sun* €

Bistro Poulette: Finger-licking *moules-frites* (mussels and fries) are a highlight at this boisterous local legend, inside Marché des Capucins. *6am-3pm Tue-Sat, 5.30am-3pm Sun* €€

Les Récoltants: The ancient tomatoes, flower petals and buxom veg cooked up in lunch dishes at this farm-shop bistro zing with taste. *noon-3.30pm Mon & Tue, to 10.30pm Thu-Sat* €

Chez Jean Mi

between 1778 and 1781. She was subsequently enslaved by François Testas on his plantation in St-Dominique and bore two of his children. Upon his death in 1795, she was freed and inherited his estate. She later married a fellow freed enslaved person and died aged 105.

Market Shopping & Scoffing

Breakfast at Marché des Capucins

Mingle with Bordeaux's grassroots soul over a morning mooch and *petit déj* at Capucins' covered market. Stalls piled with fruit, veg, cheese, charcuterie, wine, tripe, fish, flowers and all sorts fill **Marché des Capucins** (marchedescapucins.com) – a modern rendition of a 19th-century, iron-and-glass gallery built using cast-offs from Paris' 1878 Universal Exhibition. Avoid Monday when the morning market, open from 5.30am or 6am until 2.30pm, is shut.

The cacophony of hawkers screeching, shoppers in raptures over the season's fresh bounty and *bons vivants* having a good time is electrifying. Stalls spill onto place des Capucins. Buy a *puits d'amour* ('Well of Love' choux-pastry tartlet filled with caramelised pastry cream and meringue) from **Maison Seguin**. Linger over oysters and white wine – yes, a cheeky tipple at 7am is perfectly respectable – at **Chez Jean Mi**.

LAMPROIE À LA BORDELAISE

Local myth claims that when enslaved people in Burdigala (Roman Bordeaux) fell out of favour, the Romans fed them to the lampreys. A sucker fish practically prehistoric in appearance, lampreys attach themselves to the bellies of other fish to feed on their blood. These eel-like creatures are still fished in abundance in the nearby Gironde Estuary and continue to star in Bordeaux's most emblematic, devilishly unique, dish: *lamproie à la bordelaise*. Chefs chop slippery lampreys into small chunks and simmer them with leeks and spiced red wine for three days. The resultant stew is traditionally conserved in jars, stored in the larder and eaten months later – in the honourable company of a medium-aged St-Émilion or Pomerol red of course.

 EATING IN BORDEAUX: TRADITIONAL BORDELAISE

Au Bistro: Timeless ode to traditional market cuisine and seasonal produce close to its source, Marché des Capucins. *noon-2.30pm & 7-11pm Wed-Sun* €€

Le Petit Commerce: Classic cooking, including top-drawer seafood and fish fresh from Arcachon and sinful pudding. The street terrace buzzes in summer. *noon-11pm* €€

Le Bordeaux: Cap Ferret oysters, duck, sweetbreads in Cognac sauce at the more affordable brasserie of double-Michelin-starred chef Gordon Ramsay. *noon-2.30pm & 7am-9.45pm* €€

La Tupina: Succulent milk-fed lamb, tripe, goose wings and other traditional southwest dishes at this iconic 1960s *auberge*. *noon-2pm & 7-11pm Tue-Sun* €€€

Palais de la Bourse

The World's Largest Reflecting Pool
Dance barefoot in the Miroir d'Eau

Cool down on hot days in Bordeaux's iconic water pool. Covering an area of 3450 sq metres of black granite on the quayside opposite the **Palais de la Bourse** and its harem of elegant 18th-century palaces, the sensational **Miroir d'Eau** or 'water mirror' provides hours of entertainment on warm sunny days when the reflections in its thin slick of water – drained and refilled every half hour – are stunning. To add to the fun (and photo ops), a fog-like vapour is ejected for three minutes above the water pool every 23 minutes. Don't be shy.

Garages, Gardens & WWII Relics
Experimental art in edgy Bacalan

Mingle with Bacalan eco-creatives. Immersive sound-and-light shows at **Bassins des Lumières** *(bassins-lumieres.com; adult/child €16/9)* are dazzling, but it's the play of digital colour with eyesore WWII architecture – Germans built the submarine base in 1941–43 to protect its U-boats from aerial attack – that hits the hardest. A museum explains the transformation.

A block north of Bacalan's Bassins à Flot (wet docks), what began as mechanics fixing cars is now a thriving community hub: **Le Garage Moderne** *(legaragemoderne.org)* hosts recycling workshops, concerts and cultural happenings. While its rue des Étrangers site is under renovation, find its lunchtime

BEST RIVER PARTIES

iBoat: Dance until dawn year-round on an upcycled ferry. Blonde Venus, its pop-up summer *plage* (beach) and bar on dry land, is equally on-trend.

Chez Alriq: Everyone's favourite *guinguette* (open-air dance 'hall') for craft beer and live jazz, swing and pop.

Les Chantiers de la Garonne: Toast summer nights with mussels and seafood platters around shared tables on the sand, by a boat hangar in La Bastide.

Effet Mer: Summer-only DJs, dancing and sunset cocktails by the Base Sous-Marin.

La Dame: Weekend clubbing, midnight until 5.30am, afloat a *péniche* (river boat) in the Bassins à Flot.

 DRINKING IN BORDEAUX: COCKTAIL & FOOD PAIRINGS

Symbiose: Modern cuisine and cocktails laced with homemade syrups and 'forgotten' ingredients on quai des Chartrons. *noon-2.30pm Mon, noon-2.30pm & 7pm-1am Tue-Sat*

Frida: Clandestine and colourful restaurant-cocktail bar in medieval St-Pierre, with a Mediterranean patio garden. *6pm-midnight Sun-Wed, to 2am Thu-Sat*

Mazal: Franco-Lebanese food and cocktails oozing local spirits, including truffle-laced Lillet and Maison Mounicq gin aged in red-wine barrels. *7.30pm-2am Wed-Sat*

A Cocktail Collective: Smoked jasmine tea, beetroot wine, horseradish soda: anything flies in the creative cocktails shaken at this St-Pierre speakeasy. *6pm-2am Thu-Sat, to 1am Tue & Wed*

canteen and after-work cultural action in a hangar at upcoming cultural complex **La Cité Bleue** *(cite-bleue.fr)* where sugar was refined in the 19th and 20th centuries.

Green energy fuels tree-shaded gardens at artists' residency **Les Vivres de l'Art** *(lesvivresdelart.org; free to €12)*. Craft markets, films, music concerts, DJ sets, LGBTIQ+ soirées, drag and dance shows enliven its beer garden, strewn with fantastical creatures, tables and chairs recycled from scrap metal. Check its Facebook page for events.

Made in Bordeaux
Eco-shopping in the city

Be it mooching boutiques on old-world **rue St-James**, fashion houses in the **Triangle d'Or**, or outlet and new-concept stores in riverside hangars at **Bord'eau Village** *(bord-eau-village.com)*, shopping is characterful.

For wine, spiral up the celebrity staircase at **L'Intendant** *(intendant.com)* or buy from the source at 16th-century **Château Les Carmes Haut-Briond** *(les-carmes-haut-brion.com; guided visits with tasting from €55)*, Bordeaux's only urban château (tram line A from Hôtel de Ville) with a beautiful walled vineyard. Whisky fiends: tour, taste and shop at artisanal distillery **Moon Harbour** *(moonharbour.fr; €20)*. Bookworms: browse 18km of bookshelves at France's largest independent bookshop **Mollat** *(mollat.com)*, a riveting 1896 vintage.

To blend in with the Bordelais crowd, add an embroidered French Disorder sweatshirt (from **Galeries Lafayette**, in an Art Nouveau building) and vegan Zèta trainers in grape leather (from eco-concept store **Altermundi**) to your 'made in Bordeaux' wardrobe.

Scaling New Heights
Climb up an industrial grain silo at VertiGina

Mid-April to early November, flex your muscles on France's urban highest climbing wall **VertiGina** *(vertigina.com; adult/child €25/13)* – spectacularly clinging to the concrete facades of two (of eight) 1950s silos, built in 1958 at the industrial wet docks as storage for oil mills operating here. Routes rated 4a to 7c cover all levels, scale heights from 8m to 33m, and reward with spectacular city views. Shoes, harness and helmet are available onsite *(each €4)* and guided one-hour *créneaux d'initiation* (initiation sessions; €31 including admission) are obligatory for beginners; reserve by email.

WHY I LOVE BORDEAUX

Nicola Williams, Lonely Planet writer

Bordeaux's artistic energy and commitment to living well makes my heart sing. Each time I cross the river to **Darwin** *(darwin. camp)* on right-bank La Bastide, the military barracks-turned-artsy eco-complex has a new wall mural or art installation to contemplate. Even the city's traditional neoclassical theatre flips tradition on its head, with *table d'hôte* dining around a shared table in the theatre restaurant's vaulted cellar. Bordeaux's groundbreaking **Pont Simone-Veil**, named after the French activist, is my latest *coup de cœur*. Crossed by 2000 cyclists and as many pedestrians daily, the half-kilometre-long modular catwalk with nine lanes and an esplanade for cultural happenings is so much more than 'just another bridge'.

 DRINKING IN BORDEAUX: BEST ROOFTOPS

Shasha sur le Toit: Cocktails, DJs and a bird's-eye view of the Garonne and Pont Chaban Delmas glistening below. *6pm-midnight Mon-Fri, from 3pm Sat & Sun*

Rooftop – Le Grand Hôtel: The timeless classic, sadly not as grand as its location atop Bordeaux's historic luxury hotel on place de la Comédie. *3pm-midnight Mon-Thu, from noon Fri-Sun*

Gina: An Italianate bar date with la dolce vita on the 9th floor of Bassins à Flot's striking Hôtel Renaissance. Drink, eat, dance to DJ sets beneath the stars. *5pm-midnight*

Tchanqué: Ocean vibes at Bassin d'Arcachon inspire the summery decor of this Chartons rooftop bar-restaurant. Champagne Sunday brunch is a hot date. *7am-midnight*

Catching the Wave

This wave-thrashed, wind-lashed stretch of golden sand on France's Basque and Atlantic coasts sports some of Europe's best surf. The concentration of wave varieties is unmatched – as is Biarritz' vintage 'basco cool' surf spirit that pulsates well beyond the beach today. All along the coast, eco-conscious surf hostels and hotels work with local chapters of **Surfrider Foundation Europe** (*surfrider.eu*) to clean up and protect the ocean.

Ironically it was an American film crew, on the Basque coast in summer 1956 to shoot a movie adaptation of Ernest Hemingway's 1926 novel *The Sun Also Rises,* that spawned the French surf scene. By the early 1960s, homegrown surf pioneers – nicknamed *'les tontons'* – were riding high on Biarritz' **Plage de la Côte des Basques**, cruising to the beach in open-top Cadillacs. Local French surf legend Jo Moraïz created the country's first surf club in Biarritz in 1963 and three years later was offering lessons and board rental from his beachfront trailer; his son Christopher runs France's first surf school (jomoraiz.com) today. At the time boards bobbing in the lineups waiting for *la plus belle vague* (the most beautiful wave) numbered no more than 15; today it's tenfold that at least.

How to

Autumn is prime surf time, with warm(ish) water temperatures, consistently good conditions on the water and a smaller, local crowd. Surf schools open for the season in April and close some time in October and December. Check conditions at fr.surf-forecast.com.

Book lessons ahead online to avoid disappointment. Outside of July and August, you can get away with dropping by the day before (or even same day) to arrange a 90-minute surf lesson (small group/private €45/100, including wetsuit, board and insurance). Multi-day courses comprising 90 minutes on the water each day run from two to 10 days. Several surf schools operate out of beach huts by the **Maison du Surf** overlooking Biarritz' **Plage de la Côte des Basques** and on Anglet's 4km sweep of sand.

ATLANTIC OCEAN

3 Seignosse
When the surf or huge crowds on Plage des Estagnots get too gnarly, retreat to hipster La Cabane des Estagnots for cocktails on the sand. Sunset's sensational.

6 Anglet
Some 4km of surf beach, for intermediates and experts. On the beachfront, on Anglet Surf Avenue, walk in the board-stance footprints of celebrated riders from 1930 to present.

8 Bidart
Beautiful views of Spain's Bay of Biscay and thrilling tubes on family-friendly Plage du Centre; for beginners and experts alike.

9 Hendaye
Beginners' paradise, with plenty of whitewash to warm up shaky surf legs. Mingle with surfers at concept store, surf shop and cafe Kooks Club or rooftop Jimba.

San Sebastián

SPAIN

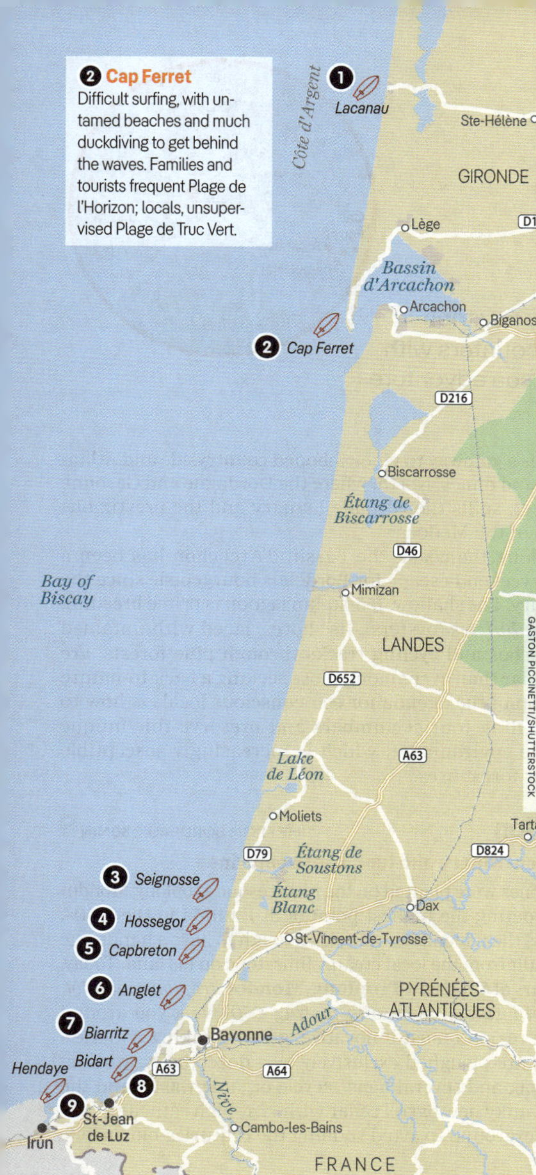

2 Cap Ferret
Difficult surfing, with untamed beaches and much duckdiving to get behind the waves. Families and tourists frequent Plage de l'Horizon; locals, unsupervised Plage de Truc Vert.

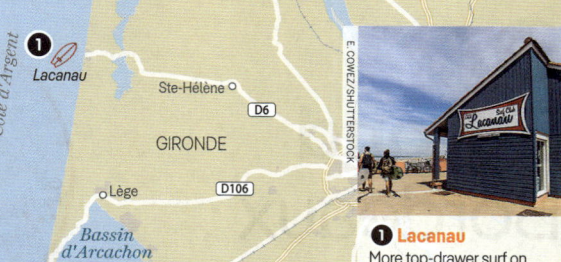

E. COWEZ/SHUTTERSTOCK

1 Lacanau
More top-drawer surf on sand beaches backed by pine forest and surf schools aplenty. Busy La Centrale is beginner central.

4 Hossegor
Watch pros battle it out for world-title points in the World Surf League in Europe's 'surf capital', awash with breathtaking emerald-green barrels and an achingly cool crowd.

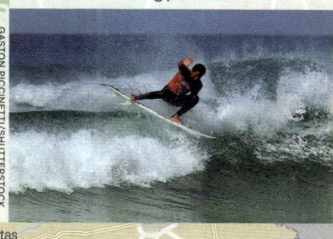

GASTON PICCINETTI/SHUTTERSTOCK

5 Capbreton
World-class surf to rival Hossegor, with crumbling WWII beach bunkers and a Pyrenees view for extra effect. Tamer summer waves suit intermediates.

7 Biarritz
The city's 1950s surf spirit lives on Joël Roux's sculpture Aux Tontons Surfeurs 957 (2007) that keeps sentry over surf-hot Plage des Côté Basques – beginner brilliant.

JEANLUCICHARD/SHUTTERSTOCK

GEAR UP

All the necessary kit, including neoprene boots on colder days, is usually included in group-lesson rates. Bring along a towel, sunscreen and water. Otherwise, surf shops in every surf town rent wetsuits and boards; expect to spend €15 per item/day.

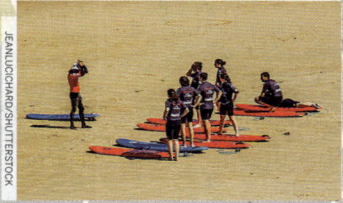

Beyond Bordeaux

An unmatched sensory feast, day trips beyond Bordeaux deliver encounters with natural landscapes, go-slow sea adventure and France's finest wine.

Places
St-Émilion p566
Arcachon p569
Pyla-sur-Mer p570
Cap Ferret p571

Bordeaux is a gateway to vine-ribboned countryside and Atlantic Coast sand dunes. North, where the Dordogne and Garonne Rivers meet, spills the Gironde Estuary and the prestigious vineyards of the Médoc.

South along the coast, the Bassin d'Arcachon has been a favourite weekend escape for Bordelais bourgeoisie since the 19th century. The shallow, 155-sq-km lagoon is prime breeding ground for *huîtres* (oysters). Its shores, laced with untamed sandy beaches and cycling tracks through pine forests, are more popular than ever among those seeking a back-to-nature retreat. Top of the agenda for eco-conscious locals is how to juggle swelling tourist numbers and preserve this unique and fragile environment, which is increasingly susceptible to summer forest fires.

GETTING AROUND

Heed the call of local environmentalists: with the exception of Médoc wine country, ditch the car. Mix train, bus, boat, bicycle and e-bike to get around.
  Arcachon has several bike-rental shops; **Dingo Vélos** *(dingovelos.bike)* near the seafront and **Beach Bikes** *(beachbikes.fr)* are recommended. On Cap Ferret, try **Ginette** *(ginetteveloscapferret. com)* or **Western Flyer** *(westernflyer. fr)*. Reserve well in advance online for summer wheels; the half/day rate for a classic bike is from €11/15.

St-Émilion

TIME FROM BORDEAUX: **30MIN**

Visit an eco-winery and lunch between vines

The first vines were planted on the picturesque Troplong Mondot estate carpeting the highest point of St-Émilion in the 1700s, and by 1745 the winemaker was rich enough to have a handsome château built from the local creamy limestone on his land. Today, guided tours of **Château Troplong-Mondot** *(troplong-mondot. com; 90min guided tour with tasting €50)* walk you around one of the region's most innovative, green-thinking wineries. Vineyards are ploughed exclusively by a dozen hefty working horses; a pig and several hens recycle organic waste; and the estate's swanky new barrel cellar with 12m-high cathedral ceiling is underground to avoid spoiling the centuries-old bucolic landscape.

Tours end with tastings of two vintages and there's a swish boutique where you can buy the *premier grand cru* wines. Alternatively, reserve a table at the château's Michelin-starred restaurant **Les Belles Perdrix** *(weekday lunch/dinner menus from €50/85),* overlooking vines, to indulge in outstanding modern French cuisine and perfect pairings. Count 20 minutes (2km) on foot from St-Émilion village to Troplong-Mondot.

EXPLORING ST-ÉMILION'S UNESCO-LISTED OLD TOWN

Framed by vineyards producing some of France's best full-bodied red wines, medieval St-Émilion is a gorgeous day trip by train from Bordeaux.

START	END	LENGTH
place du Clocher	La Tour du Roy	500m; 2-3hr

Arriving in the UNESCO-listed village, a 1.6km walk from its train station, grab a cold drink on a cafe terrace on main square ❶ **place du Clocher**. The panoramic terrace here proffers handsome views of the village's original market square and ochre-to-golden rooftops. At the ❷ **tourist office**, in the refectory of an 15th-century monastery on the same square, ask for the key to ❸ **Clocher de l'Église Monolithe**. Scale 196 steps inside the 12th- to 15th-century bell tower. Spot Bordeaux from the top. Duck through the archway by the tourist office into the romantic cloister of ❹ **Église Collégiale**. Cross it to access the church, with domed Romanesque 12th-century nave. Stumble out of the dimly lit church and into ❺ **Maison du Vin de St-Émilion** where you can gen up on St-Émilion's *appellations* and taste three *Grands Crus Classés* (€29). Continue the oenological lesson over *lamproie à la bordelaise* (lamprey simmered in red wine) and wine at celebrated vintage bistro ❻ **L'Envers du Décor**. Post-lunch, mooch up and down St-Émilion's signature *tertres* (steep, narrow, stone-paved streets) to ❼ **place de l'Église Monolithique**. Admire the exposed limestone rock of subterranean **Église Monolithique** from a cafe terrace on the square. End atop 13th-century tower ❽ **Tour du Roy**. The panorama – of St-Émilion rooftops, pea-green vineyards, the nearby Dordogne River and its bucolic valley – is sublime.

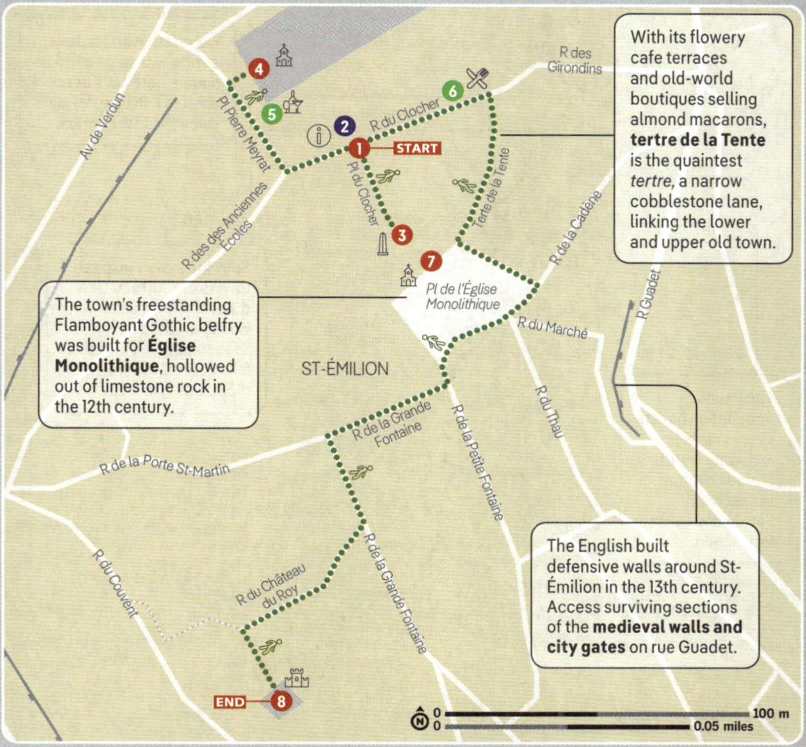

With its flowery cafe terraces and old-world boutiques selling almond macarons, **tertre de la Tente** is the quaintest *tertre*, a narrow cobblestone lane, linking the lower and upper old town.

The town's freestanding Flamboyant Gothic belfry was built for **Église Monolithique**, hollowed out of limestone rock in the 12th century.

The English built defensive walls around St-Émilion in the 13th century. Access surviving sections of the **medieval walls and city gates** on rue Guadet.

ROAD TRIP THROUGH THE MÉDOC VINEYARDS

Swirl, sip and scoot around one of Bordeaux's most prestigious yet youngest wine-growing areas.

START	END	LENGTH
Bages	Labarde	45km; 1 day

Begin 50km north of Bordeaux (1½ hour drive) in the wealthy hamlet of ❶ **Bages**, home to the Cazes family. Wines from their revered estate, **Château Lynch-Bages**, were among the 18 prestigious Cinquièmes Crus classified for the first time in 1855. Learn about local winemaking's evolution on a 90-minute guided tour *(lynchbages.com; €25 with tasting, by reservation only)* of the sleek winemaking facilities designed in 2022. Take your pick of 120-odd wines afterwards over a classic bistro lunch at the family's **Café Lavinal**, with idyllic terrace overlooking the village square. Motor 2km northeast to ❷ **Pauillac**. Stretch your legs along the waterfront, lined with 19th-century winegrowers' mansions. Meet Médoc *viticulteurs* (grape farmers) at the informative **Maison du Tourisme et du Vin** in July and August. Continue 9km north to ❸ **St-Estèphe** via Leyssac along the inland, chateau-beaded D2. The Médoc's most complex and powerful reds, good to drink after a half-century, come from 1250 hectares of vineyards here. Return south along the ❹ **Gironde Estuary's left bank** (the D2E4) to savour the line-up of *carrelets* (traditional fishing huts on stilts) along the mellow waterfront – impossibly romantic at sunset. Final port of call: the former teeny train station in ❺ **Labarde** for a gourmet symphony of surprise courses fusing modern French and world cuisine by Pauillac-born chef Thibault Guiet at **Nomade** *(restaurant-nomade.fr; reservations essential).*

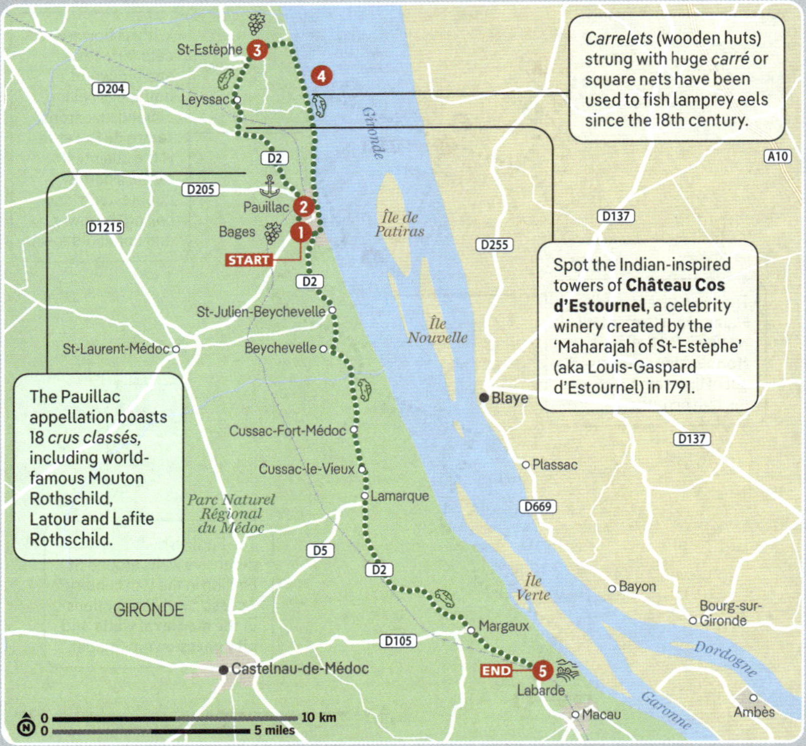

Carrelets (wooden huts) strung with huge *carré* or square nets have been used to fish lamprey eels since the 18th century.

The Pauillac appellation boasts 18 *crus classés*, including world-famous Mouton Rothschild, Latour and Lafite Rothschild.

Spot the Indian-inspired towers of **Château Cos d'Estournel**, a celebrity winery created by the 'Maharajah of St-Estèphe' (aka Louis-Gaspard d'Estournel) in 1791.

Ville d'Hiver

Arcachon

TIME FROM BORDEAUX: 1HR

A seaside 'hood for every season

From seafront carousel to cherry-red benches gazing out to sea, white sandy beaches and bicycle-packed boats bobbing in the bay, Arcachon delivers old-school seaside charm in spades. Bordelaise bourgeoisie flocked here to hobnob in its elegant cafes and casino in the 19th century, and the oft-whimsical villas they had built in Arcachon's Ville d'Hiver (Winter Quarter) – one of four quarters, each romantically named after a season – proffer an evocative walk down memory lane.

Architecture in the **Ville d'Hiver** (1860–90), on a hillside inland from beach-fringed **Ville d'Été** (Summer Quarter), is an eclectic mix of 'neo' styles (Gothic, Renaissance, Moorish) from the 19th century. Delicate wood tracery decorates some villas and many mix limestone, red brick and 'witch hat' slate roofs. Grab a map or reserve a spot on a 90-minute guided tour at the **tourist office** *(arcachon.com; adult/child €14.50/ free),* between the train station and the seafront at 22 bd du Général Leclerc.

Kayak to Île aux Oiseaux

Immerse yourself in the natural peace and beauty of triangular Bassin d'Arcachon on a guided kayaking expedition

ESCAPE TO PARADISE

At low tide, the chameleon 'bird island' of Île aux Oiseaux embraces as much as 1700 hectares of shifting sands, mudflats and salt meadows – which swiftly shrinks to anything from 100 to 260 hectares when the tide rises. From the 1840s until 1950s, local oyster farmers overnighted in wooden shacks on stilts here while working their oyster beds.

Today, the 33 remaining cabins – no running water or electricity – are prime real estate for off-grid escapes. Managed by the Conservatoire du Littoral, huts are leased for seven years at a time and occupants must prove a commitment to preserving the unique heritage and natural environment of the protected island.

Bag a table in the greenery-shaded courtyard

EATING IN ST-ÉMILION: OUR PICKS

La Petite Perdrix: Big windows at this bakery mean you can watch chefs baking baguettes and sensational breads. Sandwiches to go. *7am-7pm Tue-Sun* €

Lard et Bouchon: Excellent value, traditional French cuisine with wine galore in an atmospheric cellar. *noon-2pm & 7-8.30pm Tue-Sat, noon-2pm Sun* €€

L'Huitrier Pie: The gastronomic, creative cuisine bursts with flavour and style at this longstanding favourite. *noon-2pm & 7.15-9.30pm Thu-Mon* €€

La Terrasse Rouge: Knowing foodies adore this spectacular vineyard restaurant, 5km north of the village. *noon-2.30pm daily, 7.30-9.30pm Fri & Sat* €€€

– solo or *en duo* – from Arcachon's pleasure port to **Île aux Oiseaux** (Island of Birds).

Arriving on the uninhabited island, lug your vessel onto dry land and climb the wooden staircases of the island's emblematic **Cabanes Tchanquées** – wooden cabins on stilts. One was built for an oyster farmer in 1883, rebuilt after a storm in 1943 and again in 2007; the other dates of 1945 (a Swiss carpenter built it, hence the red shutters perhaps) and was restored in 2024. The surrounding wetland is paradise for little egrets, grey herons, brant geese, cormorants and abundant waterfowl. Observe migratory birds from the sea-facing terraces in September. Occasional outdoor music concerts are of once-in-a-lifetime ilk.

Half-day guided trips with **Arcachon Kayak** (*arcachonkayak.com; per person €35*) depart from the Centre Nautique Pierre Mallet at Arcachon's Port de Plaisance (pleasure port). Wind and current depending, count around one hour to paddle 5km from port to island. Advance reservations essential.

Pyla-sur-Mer
TIME FROM BORDEAUX: 1HR 30MIN 🚌 + 🚴

Climb europe's largest sand dune

Breathtakingly cold in winter and as hot as burning coals in the height of summer it might be, but barefoot is the most thrilling way to romp around the golden sands of Europe's largest dune. Local lore claims the shifting **Dune du Pilat**, 10km south from Arcachon, has swallowed trees, a road junction, even a hotel. What is certain is the spectacular panorama from the top. Looking west, see sandy shoals at the mouth of the Bassin d'Arcachon, Cap Ferret and bird-rich Banc d'Arguin. Facing east, dead black trees killed by forest fires polkadot rich green forest.

April to November, a staircase – around 150 steps – is built on the dune's eastern slope to help tourists stagger breathlessly to the top. Otherwise, use the locals' 'secret' shortcut to arrive midway up the dune: uphill past fashionista lunch hangout **La Co(o)rniche** on av Louis Gaume, then right onto the unmarked footpath between the bike stand and No 31 on av des Dunes.

To understand the fragility and diversity of Pilat's vulnerable sand scape, join a guided nature walk, sunrise or sunset hike, telescope workshop or storytelling sessions organised by the **Espace Accueil** (*ladunedupilat.com*) at the dune entrance. Snack bars and eco-boutiques here only sell local artisan fare.

Arriving by train in Arcachon, take bus line 3 (*busbaia.fr; single/day ticket €1/2, summer €2/4*) or pick up a

---

SPINNING ALONG LA VÉLODYSSÉE

As wonderful as its evocative name suggests, La Vélodyssée (*cycling-lavelodyssee.com*) is a coastal odyssey by *vélo* (bike) along France's Atlantic Coast linking Roscoff in Brittany with Hendaye on the French-Spanish border, 1270km away in Pays Basque.

The scenic Gironde stretch is 81km (four hours) from the tip of the Médoc south to Lacanau, just north of the Bassin d'Arcachon. Flat and reasonably unchallenging, the well-marked cycling itinerary kicks off with ethereal sea and Cordouan lighthouse views from Pointe de Grave (it's 108 steps up the cape's own, 28m-tall Phare de Grave lighthouse) before plunging through pine forests and past sand dunes, beaches, lake and lagoon on its stunningly beautiful route 7.5km south to Soulac-sur-Mer and beyond.

 EATING & DRINKING IN ARCACHON: OUR PICKS

La Pâtisserie de Ma Fille: Gourmet breakfasts, brunch, crêpes and cakes like art on market square place des Marquises. *8am-7pm Mon-Thu, to 10pm Fri-Sun* €€

Café de la Plage – Chez Pierre: A Mira craft beer brewed next door in La Teste-de-Buch or lavish shellfish platter: this timeless seafront duo delivers. *8am-2am* €€

Coquille: All-day ceviche, burgers, bowls, salads and meat/fish mains in a cosy, sea-inspired bistro near the market. *9am-midnight Tue-Sat, to 4pm Sun* €€

Club Plage Pereire: Sunset-smooch over oysters, seafood, cocktails and a great gin made from Cognac vine blossoms at this hipster pop-up on Plage Pereire. *10am-midnight Apr-Sep* €€

Dune du Pilat

OYSTER VILLAGES

Oysters taste better at the source. On Cap Ferret this translates as a ramshackle *village ostréicole* (oyster village) stitched from oyster-shell footpaths and wooden huts on stilts above the water, built a century ago from strawberry and pine trees. Nine protected villages on the peninsula provide an ungentrified lens on the hard graft of local *ostréiculteurs* (oyster farmers). Oysters take four years to produce: larvae stick to terracotta half-pipes in shallow waters near the shore and mature in deeper-water oyster banks. Shacks offering tastings are plentiful in Cap Ferret and L'Herbe's *villages ostréicoles*, but it's worth cycling 3km north from L'Herbe to off-grid 'wild west' **Piraillan,** home to two fishermen and a handful of oyster farmers. Track down weathered **Cabane 57** *(lacabane57.com)* with rough-cut tables above the water.

well-signposted cycling path (10km one way) with a stop en route at Le Moulleau's **La Maison du Glacier** for some of the country's finest organic ice cream.

Cap Ferret

TIME FROM BORDEAUX: 1HR 30MIN

Cycle to the lighthouse

Pedalling to Cap Ferret's red-and-white lighthouse is a highlight of this exclusive peninsula, a French-chic mash-up of sand dunes and oyster farms under canopies of pine trees.

Most people day-trip it here by boat from Arcachon *(bateliers-arcachon.com; 30min; adult/child oneway €10/8, day return €16/12)*. Rent wheels by **Jetée Bélisaire** where boats arrive, and spin through Cap Ferret's eponymous tiny main town to 53m-tall **Phare du Cap Ferret** *(phareducapferret.com; adult/child €7/4)*. At the ceramic-tiled beacon, built in 1947 to replace the original dynamited during WWII, spiral up 258 steps to a spellbinding panorama of Cap Ferret, the Bassin d'Arcachon and sand-white hump of Dune du Pilat. A ground-floor museum explains maritime navigation. Only 19 people at a time can scale the actual lighthouse; expect to queue.

 EATING ON CAP FERRET: OUR PICKS

This icon in L'Herbe covers all tastes

Marché du Cap Ferret: Shop for picnic fare and tuck into tapas and chit-chat at the market's Bistro de Peyo. *8am-1pm Wed-Sun mid-Jun–mid-Sep, shorter hrs rest yr* €

L'Auberge du Bassin: Sea urchins, baked oysters, confit lamb shoulder: chef Mélanie Serre thrills foodies by the sea in Claouey. *7-10pm Mon, Tue, noon-2pm & 7-10pm Thu-Sun* €€€

Mayzou: Gourmet shared plates – lots of veggie choices – oozing local produce, world flavours and unlimited creativity in Cap Ferret. *7pm-2am Thu-Sun* €€

Hôtel de la Plage: Grab cape-roasted coffee and cookies to go, slurp lunchtime oysters or devour burgers after dark (p572). *noon-3pm & 7-11pm Wed-Sun* €

Cap Ferret oysters

BEST SHOPPING ON CAP FERRET

Chez Pascal, Grand Piquey: Bakery famed for its *dunes* (choux puffs filled with flavoured cream), *chocolatines*, specialist breads and baguette sandwiches.

Tutti Frutti, Cap Ferret: Cap Ferret's oldest surf shop, in the biz since 1986.

Fumette, Le Grand Crohot: Taste and buy smoked mullet, trout and other fish at this artisanal smoker's.

Miche Coffee, Le Grand Crohot: Mel ditched a tech career in LA for coffee on Cap Ferret. Visit her roastery and buy ethically sourced, single-origin beans.

Pharmacie du Cap Ferret, Cap Ferret: Spoil yourself with organic oils, serums and other bodycare products by Océopin, crafted from the peninsula pine seeds.

Follow bike-path signs afterwards for 3.5km to **La Pointe**, the spit's southern tip, to gorge on more spectacular sea-and-sand views – this said, on cloudy days, I find the play of clouds casting shadows on Dune du Pilat across the water spellbinding. La Pointe is also a perfect spot to pick up the **Sentier de l'Abécédaire**, a 6km-long walking trail through dunes and pine forest showcasing the A to Z of Cap Ferret's fragile flora and fauna.

Lunch on oysters on the seashore

The simplicity of a traditional Cap Ferret lunch – freshly shucked oysters in an oyster farmer's seafaring backyard – is gold. At **La Cabane d'Hortense** *(lacabanedhortense.com)* and **Chez Boulan** *(chezboulan.fr)* in Cap Ferret's **Village Ostréicole** (also signposted 'Village des Pêcheurs'), 2km south of the jetty where Arcachon boats arrive, menus mirror every shack: *huîtres* from the family farm, *bulots* (whelks), Madagascar prawns, black pork pâté as a concession to non-shellfish eaters, white wine and mineral water.

In July and August, cycle 20 minutes north through pine forest to less-crowded **L'Herbe**. Admire neo-Moorish **Chapelle Ste-Marie du Cap** (1865), stroll the hamlet's single shack-lined street and savour a dozen oysters at **Le Ponton**, a farm overlooking a tiny golden-sand beach. Break for drinks at achingly cool cafe-bar-restaurant **Hôtel de la Plage** *(hotel delaplage-cap-ferret.fr)*, built in the 1860s to accommodate the first pine resin workers who settled Cap Ferret.

DRINKING ON CAP FERRET: OUR PICKS

Frédélian: Afternoon tea, ice cream, cakes and meals served beneath a candy-striped canopy or rooftop at Cap Ferret's 1939 icon. *8am-7pm Wed-Sun*

Le Vintage: With an outside sofa overlooking bd de la Plage, this wine and cocktail bar is a relaxed place for people-watching on Cap Ferret's main street. *10.30am-midnight Tue-Sun*

Le Sail Fish: The chic spot near the sea to sip sunset cocktails, hobnob with the glam set, dine well and dance to DJ sets. Reserve. *8pm-2am Apr-Sep*

Le Guinguette de Copains: Chill over drinks beneath the stars in a garden near Plage de l'Horizon. Think mythical ice-cream parlour in the 1950s, disco in the '80s. *5pm-late Jul & Aug, Fri & Sat Apr-Jun & Sep*

La Rochelle

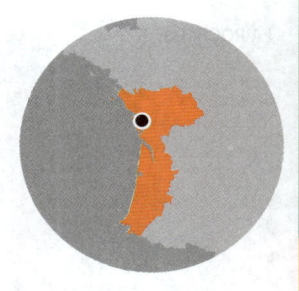

CYCLING | SEAFOOD | BOATING

An Atlantic Coast family favourite, the heritage port of La Rochelle mixes seafaring tradition with story-book adventure, urban beach life and seafood. The town's marketing slogan *'belle et rebelle'* (beautiful and rebellious) feels just right.

In few places does the wave-stirred ocean feel so close: 70km of coastline belongs to La Rochelle, a seaside town known for its high tides and peppering of islands and forts. As a key port from the 14th to 17th centuries, French settlers of Canada set sail from La Rochelle for a *nouveau monde* (new world) in the 17th century. Later, Parisians seeking new horizons arrived by train in La Rochelle to board steamers bound for South America and Africa.

The ocean, its biodiversity and health steer local dialogue today: by 2024 this green-thinking town, nicknamed 'La Ville Blanche' (The White City) after limestone facades that shimmer pearl-white in the sun, wants to be France's first zero-carbon urban coastal strip; a notable €82 million is invested in the project.

☑ TOP TIP

April to October, La Rochelle is a launchpad for boat trips to surrounding islands: tiny crescent-shaped Île d'Aix with sandy beaches and windswept walks, fortress-island Fort Bayard and larger Île d'Oléron. **Inter-Îles** *(inter-iles.com)* is one of several boat companies at the Vieux Port with kiosks on the Cour de Dames quay.

GETTING AROUND

Yélo bus D5 *(yelo.agglo-larochelle.fr)* links La Rochelle train station with **La Rochelle-Île de Ré airport** *(larochelle.aeroport.fr; €1.50; 12 mins)*. Buses use the bus station behind the train station: access it via the modern ramp in front of the château-like 1920s station, gleaming after a €38 million renovation project. (Spot 103 stone-sculpted shells in its facade and, on hot days, cool off in misters embedded in the square in front.)

Get a map showing 230km of bike lanes at the **tourist office** *(larochelle-tourisme.com)* and download the free Loopi app for cycling itineraries. Yélo public-sharing bike stations are abundant, but for longer spins you're better off with tailored wheels from a rental shop such as **Greenbike** *(location-greenbike.com; half/full day from €11/15)*.

Tickets for the Vieux Port's two silent, solar-powered bus boats – cross-port **Le Passeur** *(yelo-larochelle.fr; €1.50; three mins)* and marina-bound **Le Bus de Mer** *(€3; 20 mins)* – are sold on board. Both depart from the quayside by Tour de la Chaîne.

LA ROCHELLE

✪ HIGHLIGHTS
1 La Belle du Gabut
2 Musée Maritime
3 Vieux Port

● SIGHTS
4 Le Gabut
5 Tour de la Chaîne
6 Tour de la Lanterne
7 Tour St-Nicolas

● ACTIVITIES
8 Aquarium La Rochelle
9 Croisières Inter-Îles

● SLEEPING
10 Hôtel François 1er
11 La Fabrique
12 Le Yachtsman

● EATING
see 20 À la Gerbe de Blé
13 André
14 Annette
15 Aperta
16 Au Chabrot
17 Chez Loé
18 La Yole de Chris
19 Le Panier de Crabes
20 Marché Central

● DRINKING & NIGHTLIFE
21 Café Bletterie
22 Cave de la Guignette
23 La Terrasse de la Chaine
24 L'Echo

● SHOPPING
25 Aglaé
26 Espritvoiles
27 Studio Brocoli

● INFORMATION
28 Tourist Office

● TRANSPORT
29 Greenbike
30 Le Passeur

Medieval Towers & Candlelit Lanterns
Soak up maritime history at the Vieux Port

With a picturesque sickle of defensive towers cradling the old port since the 15th century, time travel to medieval La Rochelle is unavoidable. The cream-stone tower of 70m-high **Tour de la Lanterne** (tours-la-rochelle.fr; adult/under 26yrs €9.50/free) is often mistaken for a church spire. It was actually built between 1445 and 1476 as a lighthouse, lit by an enormous candle placed inside its conical, glazed-stone lantern. Later it became a prison. Spiral up 158 stone steps inside to enjoy panoramic sea views. Catch your breath on five different floors: walls are decorated with nautical or militaristic pictures and English-language graffiti carved by English privateers held here during the 18th century. Spot a backgammon board carved by a prisoner in wooden floorboards in room No 4.

Five minutes' walk along the ramparts (aka rue Sur Les Murs), the same ticket gets you into **Tour de la Chaîne**, built to protect the harbour entrance in the 14th century. In times of war an enormous chain was raised between Chain Tower and its counterpart across the water, 37m-high pentagonal stone tower **Tour St-Nicolas** (1376). Yes, the latter does lean Pisa-style. The tower has been shut for urgent renovation work since 2024, but you can admire its slant (and locals playing boules) from the grassy quays by the town's pétanque pitch on rue de l'Armide. To get here circle the picture-postcard Vieux Port on foot or zip across the water in three minutes from Cour des Dames aboard the solar-powered cross-port boat **Le Passeur** (p573).

Village Vibes in St-Nicolas
Follow the after-work crowd to La Guignette

For a taste of 1930s La Rochelle, hit **Cave de la Guignette** (la-guignette.fr) in the historic maritime quarter of St-Nicolas. Little has changed at this rough-cut wine bar since it opened in a blacksmith's yard in 1933. Vintage photos and posters evoke yesteryears when fishers and sailors flocked here from the rowdy port next door.

La Guignette – a fruity and fizzy, wine-based drink unique to this Rochelaise institution – is the drink to order by the glass, pitcher or bottle. Pick from vanilla, apple, red fruit or citrus fruit. On warm days, sit around oak-barrel tables outside and watch after-work shoppers flit between independent boutiques on St-Nicolas' quaint, village-like main street rue St-Nicolas.

LE GABUT

The cheery red, blue, green and mustard-yellow facades of waterfront **Le Gabut** – named after an Italianate *'gabbione'* or bastion built in medieval La Rochelle's southern city wall in 1568 (since demolished) – are a 1989 creation. This Scandi-chic quarter of colourful wooden houses toasts the port town's long trading history with Scandinavia and the Hanseatic League. Boisterous cafe life and wine-fuelled revelry until midnight at **L'Echo** and summer *guinguette* **La Belle du Gabut** – with pop-up bars, street food and live music in the street art-festooned courtyard of the former shipyard – keep the 'hood's traditional sailor spirit burning. Merriment reaches fever pitch during **La Dimancherie** (ladimancherie.fr; May-Aug), four Sundays of crowd-packed outdoor gigs, concerts and DJ sets on Esplanade du Gabet.

 EATING IN LA ROCHELLE: OUR SEAFOOD PICKS

À la Gerbe de Blé	Le Panier de Crabes	La Yole de Chris	André
Buy oysters at the covered market and eat them at this lively cafe-bar, tucked in the market's outer wall. *8am-10pm* €	Oysters, whelks and lavish seafood platters beneath St-Nicolas' emblematic paulownia tree on its 'village' square. *noon-2pm & 7-11pm* €€	Pina colada ceviche, lobster rigatoni, monkfish: refined fish dishes in triple Michelin-starred chef Christopher Coutanceau's beachfront bistro. *noon-2.30pm & 7-11pm* €€€	Mussels in sweet Pineau des Charentes wine, sauerkraut with razor clams, oysters…seafood rules at La Rochelle's iconic 1947 brasserie. *noon-2.30pm & 7-11pm* €€€

Musée Maritime

Fishy Family Fun
All aboard the Bassin des Chalutiers

By the mid-19th century the Vieux Port could no longer accommodate merchant ships and fishing trawlers sailing into port, so a new harbour – Bassin des Chalutiers – was built outside the city fortifications. Unravel port history at the **Musée Maritime** (*museemaritimelarochelle.fr; adult/child €8/free*). Kids love the model ships and short films, but the real entertainment is the line-up of retired boats moored here which you can freely clamber around: a *chalutier* (fishing trawler), a tug and meteorological research ship *France 1* with tapas bar and restaurant aboard – grab lunch afloat or come back later for sunset vibes.

Descending in a 'submarine' to the ocean floor at La Rochelle's state-of-the-art **aquarium** (*aquarium-larochelle.com; adult/child €18.50/12.50*), open until 8pm, to eyeball North Atlantic pouting fish and dancing seahorses is La Rochelle's other family highlight. Count at least two hours to spot the 12,000 marine animals and 600 different species swimming around here.

MORE FORTIFIED ROCKS

Fort Bayard isn't France's only fortress-island to inspire modern adventurers. Further south along the Charente coast, Fort Enet and Fort Louvois can both be reached on foot at low tide with a guide. To sea-kayak to France's best-known fortress on an island see p253.

EATING IN LA ROCHELLE: FAVE CAFES & BISTROS

Chez Loé: Sofas, soft jazz and savoury tarts, salads, cakes and cookies just like *chez vous (*or better!) on rue St-Nicolas. *10.30am-6pm Mon-Sat* €

Au Chabrot: Devour salads, *tartines* (open sandwiches) and *croques* (toasted sandwiches) at St-Nicolas' stylish cheese-and-wine spot. *9am-10pm Tue-Sat, 10am-3pm Sun* €

Annette: Smoked mashed potato, hake gravlax in a ginger broth, chocolate mousse with caramelised peanuts: this modern bistro stuns. *noon-1.30pm & 7-9.30pm Tue-Sat* €€

Aperta: Inventive shared plates are paired with small-producer wines at this market-fuelled bistro. *noon-2pm & 7-11pm Wed & Sat, 7-11pm Tue, Thu & Fri* €€

Summon Your Inner Sea Adventurer
Paddle to Fort Bayard

The cinematic 'stone ship' might be closed to visitors but kayaking around Fort Bayard's 20m-high walls on a half-day guided expedition with **Antioche Kayak** (antioche-kayak.com; €89) is the stuff of movies. The iceberg of a fortress was conceived in the 1700s to defend the Bay of Rochefort against the English, yet construction only began in 1804 and took more than 50 years. Since 1990 the French TV game show *Fort Boyard* has been filmed here.

If sea kayaking doesn't rock your boat, hop aboard a two-hour boat cruise (inter-iles.com; adult/child from €23/15) instead at the Vieux Port; sunset tours are best in July and August.

Sea Views Unlimited & Unlimited Seafood
Beach-hop by bike along the Sentier Littoral

You only need to glance at the wayside digital counters clocking the thousands of cyclists spinning along La Rochelle's cycling lanes to realise how big biking is here. Take your cue from local riders: cycle to the beach.

Golden-sand **Plage des Minimes** is a 15-minute cycle (3.6km) south from the Vieux Port past La Rochelle's sprawling marina. Out at sea admire **Phare du Bout du Monde**, a 16-sided wooden lighthouse built in 1999 to replicate the Cap Horn original featured in Jules Verne's adventure story *Lighthouse at the End of the World* (1905). Lunch on fish and chips at **Le Merluchon** (€14) and La Rochelle's best artisan ice cream – try grilled pistachio, crème brûlée or apricot and rosemary – at **Tonton Maboule** (tontonmaboule.fr; 1/2/3 scoops €3.80/4.90/5.90).

A half-hour cycle (5km) west along a mix of *sentier littoral* (coastal path), two-way bike lane and gravel track brings you to sandy **Plage de Chef de Baie**, popular for its safe accessible swimming (even at low tide). Next door at La Rochelle's industrial fishing port, seafood aficionados flock to **Tonton Louis** (tontonlouis.fr; buffet de la mer €40.90), with 7th-generation mussel farmer Bernard Bouyé at the helm. The restaurant's all-you-can-eat seafood buffet is legendary. In July and August sunrise tours of the wholesale fish market at **Port de Pêche de Chef de Baie** (port-peche-larochelle.com) reveal how the morning's catch travels from ocean to plate.

BEST SHOPPING: MADE IN LA ROCHELLE

Espritvoiles: Beach bags, deck chairs and accessories crafted from acrylic cloth used to make boat sails since 1931.

Studio Brocoli: Meet local *createurs* and buy their paintings, prints, jewellery and accessories at this rue St-Nicolas boutique.

Soöruz: Buy eco-responsible wetsuits made from recycled oyster shells at this surf brand's outlet shop. Invest in a 'Made in Rochelle' Black Local board to complete the ensemble.

Marché Central: Stock up on zero-kilometre picnic fare at La Rochelle's 19th-century covered market, open mornings until 1pm.

Aglaé: Watch Clara and Valentin sculpt exquisite perfumed candles. La Rochelaise – with bergamot, white tea and sandalwood notes – is the local favourite. Candle-making workshops (€50).

Its 180-degree ocean view is unparalleled

 DRINKING IN LA ROCHELLE: SUMMER TERRACES

| **La Terrasse de la Chaine:** Savour boozy sunsets at this spectacular rooftop bar, hidden atop the port's emblematic 'Chain Tower'. *2pm or 3pm-midnight May-Oct* | **Octopus:** Party with A-listers in the company of cool city views at this waterside bar-restaurant with rooftop, at the pleasure port. *10-2am* | **La Gueule du Loup:** Bands, DJs and dancing until midnight on summer nights enliven this wooden shack of an outdoor bar on the coastal path. *noon-late Tue-Sat Apr-Sep* | **Café Bletterie:** Lounge between shops over a pumpkin latte and cinnamon roll on the laidback pavement terrace of this fashionable coffee shop. *11am-6pm Tue-Sat* |

Beyond La Rochelle

Heading out of town, port-side panache melts into a heady cocktail of island beaches, scenic bike rides and grassroots gastronomy.

Places

Cognac p578
Île de Ré p580

Outside of France, few know Charente-Maritime, a *département* stitched from oyster beds, salt marshes and buckets of untouched golden-sand beaches. Feasting on an ancestral *éclade* – mussels arranged in a circle, covered with pine needles and cooked on a fire – at a village fête is magic. Ditto for a dozen Marennes-Oléron oysters with a dribble of Maison Bouteville smoked vinegar or an inland meander along the Charente River to medieval Cognac.

From La Rochelle a toll bridge takes you to Île de Ré, an island idyll that morphs from tranquil escape into high-octane microcosm of Paris in summer. Consider carefully when you go: this desirable sliver of Atlantic land is just 30km long and 5km at its widest point.

GETTING AROUND

Slow travel is à la mode. Visit atlantic-cognac.com for cycling routes, river cruises and donkey treks.

From La Rochelle you can drive across the 2.9km-long toll bridge **Pont de Ré** *(pont-iledere.fr; €4-16)* to Île de Ré, but once on the island, your car is redundant – rent a bike or use free electric bus shuttles. For a flat €2.50/4.50 single/return fare, bus line 150 links La Rochelle's bus station and airport with all the island's villages.

Cognac

TIME FROM LA ROCHELLE: 1¾–2HR

Smell the Angel's Share

From Cognac's old town of half-timbered 15th- to 17th-century houses, 1km nouth of the train station, walk downhill towards the river. Duck through fortified Porte St-Jacques, named after medieval pilgrims bound for Santiago de Compostela in Spain, to the forboding hulk of **Château de Cognac** *(chateaudecognac.com; guided tours adult/child from €24/14)*. It is here, in the medieval castle where François I (r 1515–47) was born in 1494, that any tour of the town's world-famous Cognac houses should rightly begin.

The château stuns – not for architectural beauty, but for its shocking black interior. The devilish doing of *'la part des anges'* ('the angels' share'), symbiotic sooty-black fungus clings to every stone surface that hasn't been recently cleaned. Home to the Cognac cellars of Baron Otard and the Cognac house's youthful offspring D'Ussé, guided tours take you into the château bowels. In the ageing cellars at river level, the heady smell of the angel's share – the evaporating alcohol that seeps through oak barrels in which the grape *eaux-de-vie* is aged – heightens the drama.

Further along the quay, dramatically different but equally spirited tours at sleek, eighth-generation Cognac house **Hennessy** *(lesvisites.hennessy.com; adult/child from €29/15)* divulge distiller secrets: the floral bouquet laid on oak casks to celebrate the cellar hand who lays his first perfectly stacked

Hennessy Cognac barrel

row; the skilled calligraphers who still write with chalk on the barrels; the inner sanctum or *paradis* ('paradise') where the rarest *eaux-de-vie* – some from 1800 – are safeguarded in wicket-encased, glass demijohns with no contact to air or light; the tasting committee and master blender who meet daily at 11am when their palate is sharpest. Two-hour 'immersive initiation' tours begin with a boat trip to Hennessy's cellar across the river and end with tastings (spittoon provided): neat, on the rocks and as a cocktail.

Cognac Cocktail Crawl

Cognac is so much more than a traditional after-dinner *digestif* – mixologists are shaking up the drinks scene. Learn more at an afternoon cocktail class at **Bar 1858** *(chaismon nethotel.com; cocktails €15)*, with 330-odd different Cognacs to choose from and a summer rooftop.

Reserve dinner at **Origins** *(origins.bar; cocktails €9-13)*, a trendy concept bar where cocktails are paired with zero-kilometre cuisine. Many ingredients come fresh from neighbouring market **Les Halles** on place d'Armes, a weekend staple for indulgent oyster breakfasts with beret-clad Michel at Huîtres Cocollos.

Finish the night beneath stars with Cognac cocktails and intoxicating city-vineyard views at **Indigo by Martell** *(mar tell.com; cocktails €9-13)*, the summer pop-up sky bar of 18th-century, Cognac-house heavyweight Martell.

BOUTIQUE COGNAC HOUSES

Exploring Cognac vineyards on foot, by car or bike raises the curtain on smaller Cognac houses too. **Téo Ferrini**, head bartender at Chais Monnet, shares his favourite boutique *maisons*. @teoferrini

Les Frères Moine: Two brothers run this very small Cognac house in Chassors. Call ahead for tastings. It's also a gallery with art works made with wood from old barrels. *moinefreres.fr*

Fanny Fougerat: Fanny makes the Cognacs herself and names each after the flower, plant or tree she tastes. *cognac-fannyfougerat.fr*

Château de Montifaud: This small family *maison* in Jarnac-Champagne produces some beautiful products including 50- and 150-year-aged Cognacs in hand-blown glass bottles. *chateaumonti faud.com*

 EATING ON ÎLE DE RÉ: OUR PICKS

Le Jardin du Marché: Veg-powered cuisine in a whimsical flower garden with driftwood and fruit sculptures; Ars-en-Ré. *noon-2pm & 7-10pm Fri & Sat, noon-2pm Sun-Tue & Thu* €

La Tour du Sénéchal: Every dish sizzles with grassroots flavours at this *épicerie*-bistro on Ars-en-Ré's church square. *9am-2pm Tue-Thu & Sun, to 8pm Fri & Sat* €€

Bistrot du Marin: St-Martin de Ré's decades-old 'go to' address for classic bistro fare, good vibes, waterfront terrace and funky interior. *8-2am* €€

La Cible: Oyster apéritifs, cocktails and fishy meals at St-Martin de Ré's fashionista beach restaurant on the sand. *9am-1.45am Apr-Sep* €€€

Phare des Baleines

TOP EXPERIENCE
Île de Ré

The call of the wild harks back centuries on this island of whitewashed villages with soft green and eggshell-blue accents. Chic Parisians fill it to bursting in summer, but traditional roots run deep: salt is harvested from ancestral salt pans, farmers work potato fields and oyster beds, and distillers craft gin and vodka from seaweed foraged on the seashore. Grab a bicycle and enjoy the ride – out of season if you can.

> **DON'T MISS**
>
> St-Martin de Ré
>
> Bike ride to Ars-en-Ré
>
> Oyster lunch at Ré Ostréa
>
> The view from Phare des Baleines
>
> Réserve Naturelle Lilleau des Niges

St-Martin de Ré

Graceful 17th-century star-shaped fortifications and a Vauban-designed citadel frame the island's quaint fishing port and romantic main town. Get your bearings from above atop the **bell tower** *(adult/child €2.25/1.25)* of 14th-century fortified Église St-Martin. Expensive fashion boutiques, art galleries and terraced cottages bejewel its manicured car-free streets, and fishermen sell the morning's catch from boats bobbing in the tiny port. Lose yourself in island history and art at the

PRACTICALITIES
- St-Martin's **tourist office** *(iledere.com)*, by the Vieux Port, organises themed walking tours and oyster-farm visits.

Musée Ernest Cognacq (musee-ernest-cognacq.fr; adult/child €5/3), opposite the tourist office, and join the queue for an unusual-flavoured ice cream at waterfront **La Martinière** (la-martiniere.fr; 1/2 scoops from €3.20/4). Try oyster, *praliné* seaweed, violet and blueberry or mango-ginger-mint.

Cycle to Ars-en-Ré

Spurn St-Martin's mass of touristy port-side restaurants and pick up the cycling path to Ars-en-Ré – on foot or by bike. Within seconds of hitting the coast, the path brushes oyster-farmer *cabanes* (huts). Kick back over island oysters, whelks, crab and langoustines on a bar stool facing the sea at **Ré Ostréa** (12 oysters from €14). At low tide, watch oyster farmer Didier tend his beds by tractor. Check the notice board for riveting guided farm visits (April to October).

A scenic 14km trail (one hour by bike) continues west along the coast, past more oyster farms, before crossing the island through ancient salt pans to pretty Ars-en-Ré. Buy coarse salt, *fleur de sel* and *salicorne* (samphire) from the island's salt-producers cooperative **Les Sauniers de l'Île de Ré** (facebook.com/sauniersiledere) on the village fringe. Taste it over lunch at gourmet bistro La Tour du Sénéchal (p579) by Ars' landmark church. In the 15th century its white-painted steeple with black tip doubled as 'lighthouse' beacon; call 07 67 50 88 16 to arrange a guided visit.

A Pair of Lighthouses

Cycle 7km from Ars-en-Ré to the island's scarlet-tipped **Phare des Baleines** (pharedesbaleines.com; adult/child €4.80/3.10) built in 1854 on its northwestern tip. Tackling the 257-step spiral staircase inside the 57m-tall lighthouse rewards with a bird's-eye panorama of the coast and mass of souvenir shops, cafes and ice-cream shops below. Live jazz fills the open-air theatre here during August's Jazz au Phare fest (jazzauphare.com).

Visit its neighbouring predecessor from 1672 – 30m-tall **Tour Vauban** (adult/child €6/4, with museum €10.60/5.50) – and soak up lighthouse history in the museum. Descend to the beach to admire both beacons. The centuries-old dry-stone walls on the sand here were built to break the swell and protect fishing waters; no more than a dozen of the original 140-plus remain.

Birding in Réserve Naturelle Lilleau des Niges

From the lighthouses, a 5km bike ride alongside Plage de la Conche and through pine forest brings you to **Maison du Fier** (maisondufier.fr; adult/child €4/free). Rent binoculars (€5) to spot kestrels, red shanks and blue throats along the nature centre's family-friendly nature trail (2km). The cycle ride back to Ars-en-Ré *'par le marais'* (via the salt marshes) in the stunning Réserve Naturelle Lilleau des Niges is probably

TOP TIPS

● Hotels and self-catering options are limited and expensive – camp or day-trip by bus from La Rochelle.

● Rent old-school wheels to get around (the island is flat, meaning no real need for electric bikes); reserve ahead in July and August.

● At beach and village entrances respect *'Cyclistes, pied à terre!'* signs ('Cyclists, get off your bike and walk!') Rent wheels at **Beach Bikes** (beachbikes.fr), with outlets island-wide.

● Picnic-shop at St-Martin's **covered market** at the Vieux Port or buy sandwiches at Ars-en-Ré's church-square bakery **Le Fournil**.

● Bring cash to buy island *fleur de sel* (delicate salt crystals) and refined salt from unmanned stands on cycling paths; pay in the honesty box.

> **BEACH TALK**
>
> Île de Ré's wilder southern shoreline cradles the island's best golden-sand beaches, including surfing and sailing hub **Plage de Gros Jonc** in Le Bois-Plage-en-Ré, and unofficial naturist beaches in Rivedoux Plage and La Couarde-sur-Mer. The island's longest beach (3km), dune- and forest-backed **Plage de la Conche**, unfolds like a seemingly endless ribbon of sun-scorched gold, at the island's western tip around Phare des Baleines.

the island's most scenic trail. Up to 35,000 migratory birds winter here.

Paddling in Fier d'Ars

May to October, naturalists from the Maison du Fier join canoeists at **Balade en Canoë** *(iledecanoe.com; adult/child €39/33)* to lead two-hour explorative forays in the Fier d'Ars, 4.5km east of Ars-en-Ré. No paddling experience is required to experience the bay's extraordinary peace, tranquility and privileged birdlife encounters afloat on the water. It's hard to decide which is more fun: disembarking on islets of squelchy muddy reeds to spot spoonbills and common terns with binoculars, zig-zagging along narrow channels fringed with wild mustard and alexanders, or flipping jumping *mulets* (mullets) back into the water when they leap into your canoe.

Réserve Naturelle Lilleau des Niges (p581)

Bayonne

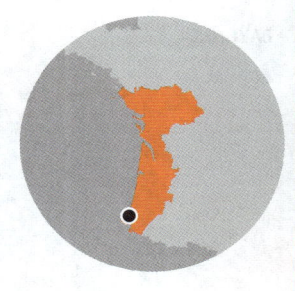

BASQUE CULTURE | FOOD | CAFE LIFE |

Edged by the Atlantic's brilliant blue Bay of Biscay and craggy foothills of the Pyrenees mountains, Pays Basque (French Basque Country) feels one step removed from the rest of France. This is a place with its own culture, history, flag, language (Euskara, spoken by about a million Basques) and capital city: small town Bayonne.

Wrapped around the confluence of the Adour and Nive Rivers, Bayonne bares its beauty along a bounty of riverbanks. It has been a strategic stronghold since medieval times, and ramparts remain visible around the outskirts of old town Grand Bayonne. Both here, and across the water in student-bolstered Petit Bayonne, colourful half-timbered buildings, riverside terrace restaurants, and backstreets loaded with boutiques and artisan workshops are made for languid mooching. Chocolate-making, street art and the much-anticipated opening of the town's top-drawer art museum after a 15-year hiatus make the Basque capital one of France's most exciting places to be right now.

GETTING AROUND

Bayonne was made for walking – count 10 minutes from the train station, across the Adour River, to the cathedral and covered market in Grand Bayonne. Foot bridges link the latter with old-world Petit Bayonne on the right bank of the Nive River.

Learn About Traditional Basque Culture
Local customs at Musée Basque et l'Histoire de Bayonne

Funerary rites, fishing, folklore, pastoral life and *pelota*: Petit Bayonne's riverfront **Musée Basque et de l'Histoire de Bayonne** *(musee-basque.com; adult/under 26yrs €8/free)* has brought Basque history, culture and crafts vividly to life since 1924. Its 20 rooms fill a 17th-century warehouse, built on the wharf by a merchant to store his goods once offloaded from the ship. Allow a couple of hours to absorb it all, avoiding Thursday morning and Monday when the museum is shut. Tickets are valid all day: break over a thick artisanal hot chocolate next door at **Chocolat Pascal** *(chocolat-pascal.fr)* on quai Galuperie.

Get orientated with a scale model of Bayonne port in 1805, showing **Grand Bayonne**, which the Romans founded on a

☑ TOP TIP

In high season or during Bayonne's madcap Fêtes de Bayonne (p585), when the sudden need for peace and quiet strikes, make a beeline for the **Jardin Botanique**. These lush, clandestine, botanical gardens (free) are squirrelled away 7m high, in a 17th-century Vauban bastion above the city ramparts.

BAYONNE

⭐ HIGHLIGHTS
1 Musée Basque et de l'Histoire de Bayonne
2 Musée Bonnat-Helleu

● SIGHTS
3 Cathédrale Ste-Marie
4 Cloister
5 Didam
6 Jardin Botanique
7 Pont St-Esprit
8 Quai des Lesseps
9 Tour St-Jean
10 Trinquet St-André

● SLEEPING
11 Hôtel Côte Basque
12 Hôtel des Arceaux
13 Hôtel des Basses Pyrénées
14 Péniche Djébelle

● EATING
15 Basa
16 Bistrot Pépite
17 Cantine du Musée
18 Cazenave
19 Chez Les Poulettes
20 Cidrerie Ttipia
21 Le P'tit Creux
22 Les Halles
23 Noisette Pâtisserie

● DRINKING & NIGHTLIFE
24 Chocolat Pascal
25 Coffee Muxu
26 Guinguette Kulunka
27 Kubata
28 L'Atalante
29 Le Comptoir
30 Puyodebat

● SHOPPING
31 Bayona
32 L'Atelier 53
33 Les Bâtons de Xab
34 Les Fromages de Laetitia
35 Monsieur Txokola
36 Napperon
37 Pierre Ibaïalde
38 Rollande

hill between the town's two rivers, and **Petit Bayonne** on the Nive's opposite riverbank, which flourished as a trading and shipbuilding hub from the 12th century. Spot the Gothic twin spires – one now clean-cream, the other dirty dark-grey – of 13th-century **Cathédrale Ste-Marie** *(free)* and its peaceful **cloister** *(free)* on place Louis Pasteur, and the 17th-century ramparts encircling the city.

Don't miss the rooms dedicated to *pelote Basque* (*pelota*) – the catch-all name for more than a dozen traditional Basque ball games, including *main nue* (played bare-handed) and *jaï alaï* (the most high-octane variant). Art, short films and players' kit shine light on the rules, the *fronton* (*pelota*) court), how to use the scoop-like basket called a *chistera*, etc. Post-museum, pass by **Trinquet St-André**, a 17th-century covered *jeu de paume* court on rue du Jeu de Paume, later adapted for *pelota*. Enjoy a drink in its bar-brasserie from 1943 and catch a game in action. It can be breathtakingly fast.

Admire World-Class Art
Renaissance at Musée Bonnat-Helleu and Didam

No fine-arts museum opening has been more anticipated than Petit Bayonne's venerable **Musée Bonnat-Helleu** *(mbh.bayonne.fr)*, reopening in November 2025 after a 15-year closure and renovation to the gargantuan tune of €35 million. Now doubled in size, the museum's 7000-piece collection includes works by Michelangelo, Van Dyck, Leonardo de Vinci, Raphaël, Rubens and Rembrandt. In 2028 the museum will jointly celebrate the bicentenary of the death of Spanish painter Francisco de Goya with its prestigious patron, Paris' Louvre.

Bayonne's artistic renaissance began a decade ago with the opening of contemporary-art centre **Didam** *(didam.bayonne.fr; free)* in the once-thriving dock area of St-Esprit. The beautiful sculpted art deco facade of the 1930s maritime building on quai de Lesseps is a masterpiece in itself.

Bayonne's Modern Chocolate Story
Watch chocolate being made at Monsieur Txokola

A pioneering duo, Ronan Lagadec and Cyril Pouil, market Monsieur Txokola as an *'alchimiste du cacao'* and the two inventive master chocolatiers have a point. Ever since they opened their modern chocolate kitchen-boutique **Monsieur**

FÊTES DE BAYONNE

Thousands of revellers fill Bayonne to bursting for five days during July's **Fêtes de Bayonne** *(fetes.bayonne.fr)*. White with a red sash and neck-scarf is the non-negotiable dress code. The street revelry starts on the last Wednesday in July or first in August with the traditional throwing of the city keys, literally, from the balcony of Bayonne's town hall. Fireworks and a *bal* (dance) follow. Brass bands, DJs and choirs perform all over town and there's folk dancing, *pelota*, omelette championships, espadrille throwing, tugs-of-war and stone lifting in *festivals de force basque* (strength competitions). Thursday's Journée des Enfants is packed with kids' activities. Less savoury are the Basque *courses des vaches* ('running of the bulls' but with horned cows) and *corridas* (bullfights).

 EATING IN BAYONNE: GOOD-VALUE DINING

Bistrot Pépite: Modern bistro fare and natural wines around '60s Formica tables: duck hearts with porto, curried mussels, veggie beignets. *7.30-9.30pm Tue-Fri, noon-1.30pm & 7.30-9.30pm Sat* €

Cantine du Musée: Laurent and Guillaume's excellent-value bistro serves seasonal Basque fare with lashings of *'bonne humeur'*. *12.15-1.30pm Tue, 12.15-1.30pm & 7.30-9.30pm Wed-Sat* €€

Cidrerie Ttipia: A juicy *txuleta* (beef steak) for two, fries, salad and a glass of cider is the thing at this rustic, noisy cider hall. *noon-2pm & 7-11pm Tue-Sat. noon-2pm Sun* €€

Basa: Good-value lunch *menus* in a contemporary brasserie with peaceful garden patio. Try smoked octopus with beetroot and caramelised dill. *noon-10pm Mon-Sat, to 2pm Sun* €€

BEST BASQUE PINTXOS

Jambon de Bayonne: The region's dry-cured ham, salted for days, dried for weeks, hung for a year, and served wafer-thin like prosciutto. Taste and tour drying rooms at ham shop **Pierre d'Ibaïalde**. April's **Foire au Jambon** has been a foodie 'don't miss' since 1462.

Chipirons à la plancha: Pan-fried baby squid, breaded or battered; *rabas* are regular deep-fried squid rings or strips.

Tortilla de patatas: Omelette with potatoes, sometimes spiked with fiery padron or Espelette peppers.

Txistorra: Garlicky Basque sausage, similar to chorizo; dried or semi-dried, served in warm pan-fried chunks.

Tripotx à la piperade: Sheep *boudin* (blood sausage) in red pepper, onion and tomato sauce.

Les Halles

Txokola *(monsieurtxokola.fr)* on the same street at Petit Bayonne's landmark fine-arts museum, they've turned heads with their artisan methods and ethical stance.

Unusually, cocoa beans sourced directly from farmers arrive in woven sacks, fermented and partially dried – for Monsieur Txokola to further dry, roast, winnow, grind and conch to produce scandalously moreish chocolate bars. Glass walls allow you to watch the entire process from the boutique, where shelves brim with highly sensible 500g chocolate bars, sachets of crushed cocoa beans, and tins of *sour au cacao* beer made in collaboration with the Azimut microbrewery in Bordeaux.

Bayonne's chocolate tradition stems from the Spanish Inquisition when Jewish chocolate-makers, fleeing persecution in their Spanish homeland, fled across the border to Bayonne. By 1870, Bayonne had 130 chocolatiers. Around a dozen remain.

Oysters, Walking Sticks & Striped Basque Shirts

A market-day shopping spree

Meet farmers and watch artisans craft at Bayonne's Saturday open-air market *(8am-1pm)*. Stalls overflowing with fresh produce fill the square in front of 19th-century covered market

DRINKING IN BAYONNE: FAVOURITE TERRACES

L'Atalante: From late afternoon onwards, the riverside terrace of this cinema bistro in edgy St-Esprit is the place to be. *1.30-10pm*

Le Comptoir: The locally loved choice on quai Galuperie for a Eguzki craft beer, iced sangria or gin cocktail in the late afternoon sun. *5pm-2am Thu-Mon*

Guinguette Kulunka: Perch on a stool facing the water or flop in a deckchair on the grass at this trendy riverfront spot in a wood-clad container; tapas too. *8.30am-10pm*

Kubata: Cocktails rule the roost at this wildly popular tapas bar, with sun-soaked terrace by the river in Petit Bayonne. *2pm-2am Mon-Fri, from 11am Sat*

Les Halles (rebuilt in 1944) and along the quays between Pont du Génie and Pont Pannecau. Buy artisan Ossau-Iraty AOP cheese at **Les Fromages de Laetitia** *(facebook.com/lesfromagesdelaetitia)*.

Across the water in Petit Bayonne, craft stalls dot quai Augustin Chaho. Look for Xavier, sculpting walking sticks from hazelnut or medlar wood, at **Les Bâtons de Xab** *(facebook.com/lesbatonsdexab)*. Shop for espadrilles and a kaleidoscope of traditional striped Basque fabrics.

Tuck into a punnet of *chipirons à la plancha* (squid) dunked in chorizo sauce from a food stall. Or head back to Les Halles to share *pintxos* (Basque tapas) and a dozen Cap Ferret or Île d'Oléron oysters on a cafe terrace. End with coffee and a signature, crunchy 'n' gooey *entremets noisette* (hazelnut cake) at designer Basque pâtisserie **Noisette Pâtisserie** *(instagram.com/maison.noisette.patisserie)*.

Unearth Basque Pride

Track down Exist, Invader and other street artists

Tune into Pays Basque's independent spirit and fiery heart through street art. The angular faces with Basque berets, by local artist **Exist**, peppering Petit Bayonne leave you in no doubt as to where in France you are. A favourite emblazons the metal shutter after-hours at Le Comptoir.

Iconic Paris artist **Invader** 'invaded' Pays Basque in November 2024, leaving 60 mosaics – each meticulously researched to reflect the significance of its location – in his wake. Start your search for Basque crests, wine, space invaders in red berets, the flag of Bayonne's Aviron Bayonnais rugby team, and all sorts on mosaic-clad **Pont St-Esprit**. Invader's 'Rock N' Roll' mosaic by 12th-century **Tour St-Jean** is hard to miss; it references the region's underground 'Radical Rock' music scene in the 1980s.

Watch artists at work and new works blossoming during October's month-long street-art festival **Points de Vue** *(pointsdevue.eus)*. Recently rejuvenated **Quai des Lesseps** in St-Esprit is a much-loved canvas.

BEST HANDMADE BUYS

Rollande: Sailing ropes, fabrics and leather marry seamlessly in Lucie's handcrafted wallets and bags. Hands-on leatherwork workshops too.

Napperon: Upcycled doesn't get sexier or more fun: lingerie and boxers stitched from placemats, curtains and lacy tablecloths at Julie Debove's rue d'Espagne atelier.

Bayona: Basque espadrilles in every colour and style, crafted in nearby St-Jean de Luz since 1890.

Puyodebat: Ganache-filled chocolates and hot chocolate served in a *tasse à moustache* – a china tea cup, typical of the 1800s, with a bridge across the top to protect drenching one's moustache.

L'Atelier 53: Watch painter Vincent Tessier at work and browse a succession of rooms packed with canvases incorporating upcycled newspaper, musical scores, wood, even bank notes.

 EATING & DRINKING IN BAYONNE: BEST COFFEE, BRUNCH & GOÛTER

Chez Les Poulettes: Themed brunches at this cool Basque bistro, with retro interior and cobbled-alley seating, fill up fast. *9.30am-6.30pm Tue & Wed, to 8pm Thu-Sat €*

Coffee Muxu: The Bordeaux-roasted Piha coffee, cakes (with a dollop of thick Muxu cream), breakfasts and brunch hit the spot. *9am-6pm Mon-Sat, to 5pm Sun €*

Le P'tit Creux: Pair a cathedral visit with brunch, lunch or a cuppa at this *salon de thé*, with enchanting terrace beneath trees. *8am-6pm Mon-Sat €€*

Cazenave: Indulge in a hot chocolate, hand-whipped like it's 1854 (order *'le mousseaux'*) at this 19th-century chocolate shop on rue Pont Neuf. *9.15am-noon & 2-7pm Tue-Sat €€*

Beyond Bayonne

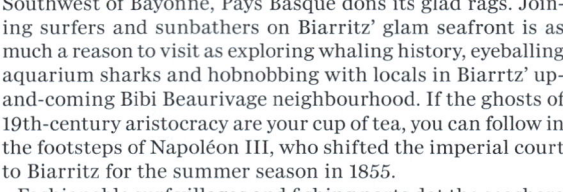

A cocktail of Basque history and contemporary cool, beyond Bayonne means beaches, bon vivant lifestyle and wave-whipped outdoor action.

Places
Biarritz p588
Bidart p591

Southwest of Bayonne, Pays Basque dons its glad rags. Joining surfers and sunbathers on Biarritz' glam seafront is as much a reason to visit as exploring whaling history, eyeballing aquarium sharks and hobnobbing with locals in Biarrtz' up-and-coming Bibi Beaurivage neighbourhood. If the ghosts of 19th-century aristocracy are your cup of tea, you can follow in the footsteps of Napoléon III, who shifted the imperial court to Biarritz for the summer season in 1855.

Fashionable surf villages and fishing ports dot the seashore south of Biarritz. Ruins of medieval ovens once used to melt whale blubber rub shoulders with trendy beach bars, bodegas and eco-boutiques. Walk the coastal Sentier du Littoral (the 25km stretch between Bidart and Hendaye is gorgeous) or bike the Basque section of La Vélodyssée (p570).

GETTING AROUND

Use Txiktxak buses *(txiktxak.fr; €1.30)* to get between downtown Biarritz and its out-of-town train station, its airport *(biarritz.aeroport.fr)* and south along the coast to St-Jean de Luz. Buy tickets from the driver or swipe your phone on the onboard ticket reader to pay with ApplePay or contactless card. Train run along the coast.

Rent classic and e-bikes in Biarritz at **Takamaka** *(biarritz.takamaka.fr; half/full day from €12/18),* near the **tourist office** *(destination-biarritz.fr).*

Biarritz

TIME FROM BAYONNE: **40MIN**

Exploring Biarritz' whaling past

The blubber was boiled down to become lighting fuel, the meat was eaten and the tongue – a delicacy – was saved for the church. So say the history annals about whaling, practised on the Basque coast from the 11th to 16th centuries. Initially a practical means of ridding sandy shores of beached whales, harpooning whales quickly morphed into a big business for Basque whalers. The last whale was hauled onto Biarritz' Plage de Port Vieux in 1686.

Learn more about Basque whaling history, subsequent cod fishing and 19th-century sea bathing – in the 1880s many local fishing folk ditched their dwindling trade to become *guides baigneurs* (bathing guides) instead, accompanying the first sea bathers into the water – at Biarritz' **Musée d'Histoire** *(musee-historique-biarritz.fr; adult/child €8/5),* open Tuesday to Saturday inside Église Saint Andrew. The sober Gothic church was built for the town's sizeable English community in 1878 and consecrated by the Bishop of London the same year.

Biarritz' landmark **Aquarium** *(aquariumbiarritz.com; adult/child €17/12),* a 1933 art deco edifice facing the sea on Esplanade du Rocher de la Vierge, celebrates whale life in its Galerie des Cétacés (Cetacean Gallery). Reconstructed models

Grande Plage, Biarritz

and skeletons of dolphins, porpoises, beaked and killer whales – fins, jaws et al – delight. To join a VR shark-study expedition underwater or catch cetaceans in 4D, join the crowds at sea-themed theme park **Cité de l'Ocean** *(citedelocean.com; adult/child €15/11)*, south along the coast. Save cents with a combo ticket *(€28/20)* covering both.

Lunch cheap on oysters and white wine

Pintxos, *poissons* and paella at Biarritz' iconic bistro-bodega **Bar Jean** *(barjean-biarritz.fr)* has been a Biarrot rite of passage since 1930. The round-the-clock festive vibe on the street terrace alone is memorable (unusually, food is served non-stop from 10.30am to 1am).

To keep things cheap dive into **Les Halles** *(halles-biarritz. fr; 6/12 oysters with glass of wine €8/14)* opposite. Swimming with the day's catch from 7.30am to 2pm daily, the fish hall buzzes with vendors flogging crab claws, whelks, seasonal sea urchins and an ocean of fish. Oyster farmers shuck variously sized *huîtres* for seafood lovers to devour standing up or slurp around shared tables on a no-frills mezzanine upstairs.

A sunset bar crawl

Biarritz sunsets seem bigger, bolder and more beautiful than elsewhere. Watch the magic unfurl over cocktails with done-in

BEST BIARROT BEACHES

Grande Plage: Biarritz' main golden-sand beach, much-loved since the days of Napoléon II and Eugénie.

Plage de la Côte des Basques: Long golden sand beach with trendy bars. A surfers' and sunset lovers' favourite.

Plage d'Ilbarritz: Another strip of powder-soft sand, enlivened with the summer terrace of beach bar Blue Cargo, a dance floor after dark.

Plage de l'Océan: Fringed by protected sand dunes and a golf green, this is wildest of Anglet's back-to-back swathe of sand beaches. Sunset drinks at beach bar Ozeanoa are a must.

Plage des Sables d'Or: Cafes, surf shops and several sandy beach-volley courts in Anglet.

 EATING IN BIARRITZ: BEST BREAKFAST & BRUNCH

Coffee Ekia: Pair dirty chai latte or devilwood-flower kombucha with pancakes, avocado toast and eggs. Ekia means 'sunshine' in Basque. *8am or 9am-6pm* €

Noisette Pâtisserie: Toasted egg-and-cheese muffins, designer pastries and a killer chocolate-hazelnut *roulé* near Plage du Port Vieux. *8.30am-6pm* €

Hungry Belly: Sweet creations of Bordelaise pastry chef Léa Villafafila (many gluten-free) are hard to resist. Artisan coffee and veggie lunches. *9.30am-5pm Tue-Sat* €

Hôtel du Palais: The lavish *'Impérial'* Sunday brunch inside Biarritz' sumptuous historic hotel is the stuff of legends. Reservation essential. *12.15pm-late Sun* €€€

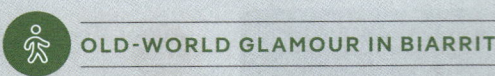

OLD-WORLD GLAMOUR IN BIARRITZ

Discover Biarritz' sights and coastal delights with this downtown stroll. Bring towel and trunks or bikini in case you fancy a dip.

START	END	LENGTH
Le Bellevue	Grande Plage	5.5km; 3 hours

Start on the esplanade in front of Biarritz' original casino ❶ **Le Bellevue** (1858). Enjoy the view over coffee at tea room ❷ **Miremont** (1872). Queen Victoria loved its caramels and Paris-Biarritz cakes. Zig-zag through gardens down to bd du Général de Gaulle. Walk west to admire the neo-Gothic facade of ❸ **Église Ste-Eugénie** (1864).

Mooch the old town to sandy ❹ **Plage du Port Vieux**. Follow Esplanade de la Vierge to ❺ **Rocher de la Vierge**. The virgin-and-child statue, atop a rock since 1865 and lit at night, is accessed via a footbridge. Ocean views melt into the mountains of the Spanish Basque Country.

Walk up the staircase next to the Art Deco Musée de la Mer (now the aquarium, p588) to ❻ **Jardins de l'Atalaye** and wind around the cape to ❼ **Port des Pêcheurs** (1870). This is Biarritz' old port, with *crampottes* (fishers' shacks) and fish restaurants. Lunch at **Chez Albert**.

Continue along the coast, admiring the panorama from ❽ **Rocher de Basta**, an islet reached by a bridge over the sand. It's 15 minutes to ❾ **Chapelle Impériale** (1864), an eclectic mix of Byzantine and Moorish styles.

Walk another 15 minutes to ❿ **Phare de Biarritz**. Coil up the lighthouse's 258 steps. Backtrack past Belle Époque hotel beauty ⓫ **Regina Experimental** (p601) and down staircase ⓬ **Descente de l'Océan** to end on golden main beach ⓭ **Grande Plage** (p589).

Napoléon III and his empress summered at Villa Eugénie, now luxurious palace-hotel **Hôtel du Palais**.

Biarritz buzzed with the cream of European society in the 1880s; Russian aristocrats had their own **Église Orthodoxe** (1887).

Spot the mosaic of playing cards by **French street artist Invader** on the back side of the seafront's 1929 casino.

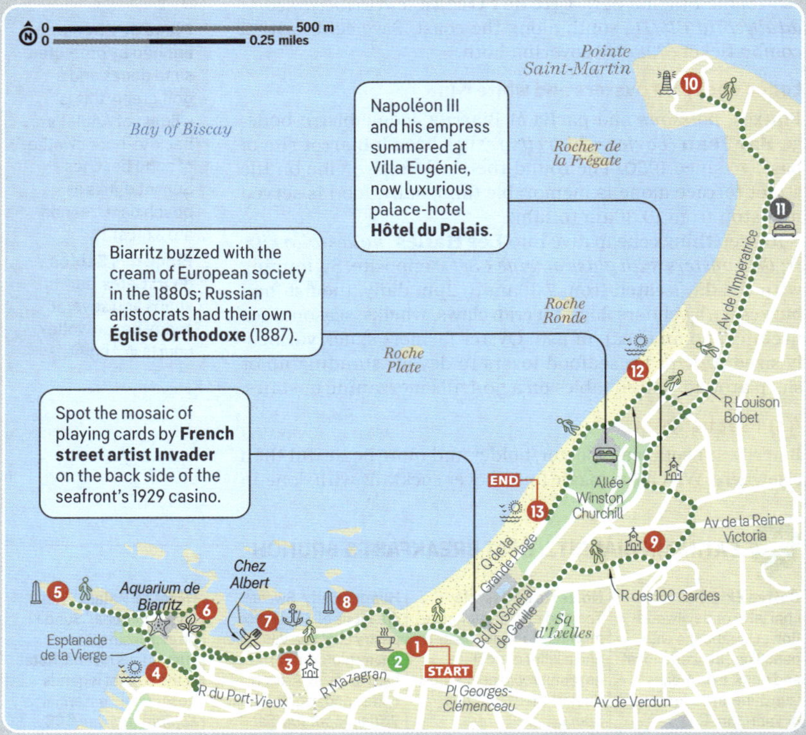

surfers and diehard groupies at **Carlos** *(instagram.com/ carlosbiarritz)* or neighbouring **Les Bains** *(lesbains-biar ritz.com),* in old art deco baths on the seafront at surf beach **Plage de la Côte des Basques**. Sun sunk, move upstairs to rooftop **Epic** for DJ tunes and a more boisterous, party vibe. Or hike up the 218 steps – don't miss the fantastic mosaic by French street artist Invader here – from the beach to the high road above for a star-topped nightcap at alfresco **Etxola Bibi** *(etxolabibi.com).*

In the old town, by bijou Plage de la Port Vieux, bathe in sunset's glow on the terrace of **Eden Rock Café** *(edenrock cafebiarritz.fr),* on a rocky terrace above the sand with sultry views of the mystical silhouette of the **Rocher de la Vierge** beyond. End the night at festive **Jack the Cockerel** *(jackthe cockerel.com),* with terrace peeping down on Grande Plage and dancing until 1am.

Bidart

TIME FROM BAYONNE: **30MIN**

Sustainable Arts & Seashore Crafts

Filling the fountain-pierced square in front of the covered market, Biarritz' morning **Marché des Créateurs** is an interesting spot to shop for 'Made in Biarritz' crafts, jewellery, sun hats and homewares until 1.30pm. The sea has inspired dazzling ceramic art pieces at **Cazaux** *(cazauxbiarritz.com),* since 1893.

To wrap your shopping spree around people- and *pelota*-watching on a village square, head 10km south to tiny **Bidart**. Browse Atlantik body products crafted from seaweed and Nynybird jewellery incorporating seashells at **Ama Lurta** *(ate lier-amalurra.com).* In July and August, artisans sell jewellery, espadrilles, cosmetics, striped Basque linens, sun hats etc at Bidart's **Marché Nocturne** *(place du Village, 6-11pm Thu).*

BEST SHOPPING: BIARRITZ BRANDS

Sowe: Invest in a eco-sleek bikini inspired by Basque beach life and heritage at this rue Mazagran boutique; mix 'n' match tops and bottoms.

Maison Chistera: Timeless Basque espadrilles in every colour and size, plus espadrille-esque shoes and sandals.

Galerie Sylvain Cazenauve: Wave-themed canvases by Biarritz' iconic, 1960s surf photographer in his studio on rue Gambetta.

Maison Adam: This celebrated Biarrot *pâtissier-chocolatier* has baked chewy almond macarons since 1660; €6.60 for a sachet of six.

BTZ: The last word in cool street 'n' surf-wear, shades and accessories by Biarritz' legendary clothing store.

Its 180-degree ocean view is unparalleled

 EATING IN BIARRITZ: HIP PICKS IN BIBI BEAURIVAGE

Bleach: Lunch with sassy locals over homemade food in a retro, '50s-styled cafe in Biarritz' coolest no-tourists 'hood. *9am-3pm Mon-Fri €*

Chéri Bibi: Off-grid modern neighbourhood bistro: expertly curated local produce with natural wines on a wooden people-watching deck. *7pm-midnight Thu-Sun €€*

Restaurant Hernani: Spend an evening in the Spanish Basque country at this lively bodega. The sangria flows. *7.30-11pm Tue-Sat €€*

Club Sandwich: Chicken burgers, truffle clubs, falafel salad by day. Vinyl nights, DJ sets, club nights come dark. *noon-3pm & 7pm-midnight Tue-Sat, noon-3pm Sun €*

CYCLING TRIP

Biarritz to Guethary by E-Bike

Freewheeling south from Biarritz, gear up for a scintillating coastal mash-up of one-time whaling stations, untamed sand coves, hillside chapels and pretty seaside villages with Basque-red woodwork and, as tradition demands, the village *fronton* (*pelota* court) filling one wall of the church or school. This tour is only 25km back and forth, but it's hilly – go electric. Few riders wear helmets but all rental shops stock them; you'll just need to ask for one.

❶ Plage d'Ilbarritz

A 10-minute spin (2.5km) from Biarritz' bike-rental outlet **Sobilo** (*location-velo-scooter-biarritz.com*) along a well-signposted cycling path ushers in this sweep of golden sand. Unusually this family-friendly beach with surf school and restaurants is also accessible at high tide.

The Ride: Admire Château d'Illbarritz on the hill. Approaching your next stop 3.5km away, pause at the *belvédère* (viewpoint) at the southern end of chemin Tutilenia.

❷ Espace Naturel Sensible d'Erretegia

This nature reserve protects 65 hectares of grey dunes, coastal meadows, cliffs and the trailhead for the 54km-long Sentier du Littoral (coastal footpath) to San Sebastián in Spain. Seaweed and driftwood on coarse-sand cove beach **Plage d'Erretegia** are not cleared to preserve the natural ecosystem.

The Ride: Wind downhill, padlocking your bike to a rack in the reserve's car park 250m from the water.

❸ Kanttu

Tuck into razor clams, *cassolette de chipirons* (squid stew) and *rabas* (fried squid) over lunch alfresco at this isolated shack overlooking Plage d'Erretegia. Local produce, including funky Olatu fruit juices and La Clique craft beer brewed in Bidart, fuel **Kanttu's** short menu. The tranquillity and sea views are heaven on earth.

The Ride: Pedal uphill to rejoin the cycling path and 10 minutes (1.2km) of big-blue views along Corniche de la Falaise.

Bidart

4 Chapelle Ste-Madeleine

Spain-bound pilgrims paid their respects at this weeny hilltop chapel, built to protect fisher folk, since medieval times. Take a pew on the grassy esplanade and soak in the coast-and-Pyrenees panorama. A dusty footpath to the left unveils La Rhune (910m) and the Spanish headland of Mont Jaizkibel (543m) sliding into the sea.

The Ride: Cycle two minutes along rue de la Madeleine to Bidart's pedestrian main square, place du Village.

5 Bidart

Linger over coffee on the people-watching terrace of **Bar du Fronton**, an 1869 vintage in front of Bidart's oldest *pelota* court. Lap up the square's ensemble of traditional Basque-red, half-timbered architecture. Consider an eco-shopping spree (p591).

The Ride: Fly down rue de l'Uhabia and up a short section of the D810 on a dedicated cycling track. After **Plage de l'Uhabia**, it's hard to miss Villa Emak Bakea, where Man Ray filmed the eponymous film in 1926.

6 Plage de Parlementia

On the glorious golden sands and crashing surf of Parlementia Beach, spy cliff-top Tour de Koskenia, a medieval staircase tower – restored and white today. Straw torches were lit here to alert fishers to whale sightings. Enjoy drinks and snacks at beachfront hut **Bahia Beach**.

The Ride: Ride up the hill, across the railway tracks in Guéthary village centre, and down super-steep chemin du Port.

7 Port de Guéthary

Time-worn fishing boats pepper the quaint old port of this one-time whaling station, now a gentrified seaside village with Paris price tags. Sunset drinks, a fishy meal and unmatched sea views at trendy **Hétéroclito** (*heteroclito.fr*) are always a good idea; reservations essential.

St-Jean-Pied-de-Port

HISTORY | WALKING | BASQUE CULTURE

GETTING AROUND

From St-Jean's toy-sized station, served by TER trains to/from Bayonne *(one hour; €12)*, it's a 10-minute walk along ave Renaud to the walled city. Those with babies should bring a sling – St-Jean's main street is one big hill, with bone-rattling cobblestones to boot.

It's difficult not to feel delightfully close to Spain in this good-looking, disarmingly charming town. Its name alone, meaning 'St John at the Foot of the Pass', rouses enchanting images of last-frontier musketeers straight off the pages of an old-school adventure story. Cradled at the foot of the Pyrenees, for centuries St-Jean-Pied-de-Port has been the last stop in France for pilgrims heading across the Spanish border, 8km south, and on to Santiago de Compostela.

The tiny, steeply pitched old town remains a popular waypoint for walkers. Some are pilgrims, but many are simply here to savour the rich Basque vibe with a spin at *pelota* on the village *fronton*, cream-filled *gateaux basques* and chilli-fired *tripotx* (blood sausage), and dips into the Pyrenean foothills on shorter day hikes. November to March, when snow blocks the 1337m-high Col de Bentarte mountain pass into Spain, the town quite literally shuts down.

Shell to Shell: Travel Back In Time

Old town meanderings

On foot, like a 12th-century pilgrim, is the only way to explore St-Jean. In medieval times the entire town was enclosed by defensive ramparts guarding France's southwestern corner against incursions from Spain, and its four original *portes* (city gates) still stand.

Begin at **Porte Navarre.** Walk up the staircase inside the city gate to access **Chemin de Ronde**, a walkway atop the ramparts with kaleidoscopic glimpses into the bijou back gardens of local inhabitants and St-Jean's 17th-century citadel ahead.

Emerge 15 minutes later inside **Porte St-Jacques**, the traditional point of entry for arriving pilgrims, at the northern (top) end of steep cobbled main street rue de la Citadelle. If you can face the climb, it's a 10-minute walk from here up to the hilltop **citadel** (closed to the public), with spectacular panorama of rolling hills and sloping Irouleguy vineyards. The fort was constructed in 1628, and rebuilt around 1680 by military engineers of the Vauban school.

✓ TOP TIP

Let cheese be your guide. To sample local AOP Ossau-Iraty cheese on farms where it's made, follow the Route du Fromage *(Cheese Route; ossau-iraty.fr)*.

ST-JEAN PIED DE PORT

★ HIGHLIGHTS
1. Camino de Santiago de Compostela
2. Pont d'Eyheraberry
3. Walled Town

● SIGHTS
4. Église Notre Dame du Bout du Pont
5. La Citadelle
6. Porte d'Espagne
7. Porte Navarre
8. Porte Notre-Dame
9. Porte St-Jacques
10. Prison des Évêques

● ACTIVITIES
11. Bureau des Pélerins

● SLEEPING
12. Hôtel Ramuntcho

13. Le Lièvre et la Tortue
14. Maison Mâje
15. Villa Esponida

● EATING
16. Arrambide
17. Café de la Paix
18. Café Ttipia
19. Chez Odette
20. Le Chat Perché
21. Maison Berthold

● SHOPPING
22. Crèmerie de Garazi
23. Elizaldia Merkatua
24. Les Halles

● INFORMATION
25. Tourist Office

Back at Porte St-Jacques, pootle through the gorgeous **walled town**, downhill along **rue de la Citadelle**, lined with 16th-century houses. Spot motifs of the scallop shell, the traditional symbol of the Santiago de Compostela. Pilgrims wait in line to receive their pilgrim's pass and a shell to dangle from their rucksack outside the **Bureau des Pélerins** (compostelle.fr) at No 39 – a record 58,450 passed through here in 2024.

Lower down the hill, seasonal exhibitions brighten 14th-century **Prison des Évêques** (Bishops' Prison) where deserters caught fleeing to nominally neutral Spain during WWII were interned. At the bottom of rue de la Citadelle, **Porte Notre-Dame** stands sentry over 14th-century **Église Notre Dame du Bout du Pont**, another key stop for faithful walkers.

SIGNS YOU'RE IN PAYS BASQUE

Hemen Euskara emaiten dugu ('Basque spoken here'): Euskara, the Basque language, is unrelated to any other tongue and is southwestern Europe's only language to have withstood the onslaught of Latin and its derivatives.

Lauburu: Basque culture's most visible symbol, the *lauburu* or curvaceous Basque cross, evocative of a four-leaf clover, symbolises prosperity. It also signifies life and death.

Ikurriña: The Basque flag flies high in Pays Basque. Look for a red field, white vertical cross and green diagonal cross.

EuskoPay: Pays Basque's local currency was launched in 2013 and locals will tell you it's 'Europe's most powerful independent currency'. Shops accepting contactless payment by eusko display a green Euskopay sign; download the app.

Ossau-Iraty cheese

A Bucolic Riverside Stroll
The short loop to Pont d'Eyheraberry

From Porte Notre-Dame (p595), a scenic 1km walk, loops peacefully along both banks of the River Nive. Before striding out, grab a farm-made ice cream from nearby **Chez Odette** (*1/2/3 scoops €3/5/7*), at the bottom of rue de la Citadelle, to sweeten the half-hour stroll. Fresh milk from cows at Ferme Baïlia goes into the creamy ice creams, made in Bardos village, 50km from St-Jean. Try salted butter caramel or go for a fruity sorbet like lime, raspberry and Espelette pepper.

Exiting the city gate, bear left along **Allée d'Eyheraberry** and cross the wooden bridge to the river's south bank. Follow the footpath for 10 minutes along the grassy banks – perfect for sunbathing, river paddling and skimming pebbles – to **Pont d'Eyheraberry**. This graceful stone-arched bridge has been a favourite with local youths who leap from the bridge into the icy water below (do not try it – swimming is forbidden) since 1720. Picnic tables encourage bucolic riverside lounging. Return via the upper, northern-bank footpath.

Stride Out in Pilgrim Footsteps
Walk one leg of the Camino de Santiago de Compostela

Even if you're not up for the 791km-long hike from St-Jean-Pied-de-Port to Santiago de Compostela, mellow St-Jean makes

EATING IN ST-JEAN-PIED-DE-PORT: OUR PICKS

Café de la Paix: Iraty trout, local pork and *brebis* cheeses at this bustling neighbourhood HQ – a beloved drinking-dining hybrid. *7.30am–11pm Wed-Mon* €

Café Ttipia: Lunch on a shady terrace with plane trees and gorgeous river view. Local charcuterie and well-done classics like *steak-frites*. *7.30am–11pm* €

Le Chat Perché: Walk through this tiny eatery on rue de la Citadelle into its secret garden out back. *noon-2pm & 7-9pm Tue-Sat, noon-2pm Sun* €€

Arrambide: Savour classic French cuisine in St-Jean's only refined, fine-dining restaurant. *12.15-1.30pm & 7.45-8.45pm Wed-Sun* €€€

a great base for hiking. Two long-distance GR *(grande randonnée)* hiking trails pass through town: the trans-Pyrenean **GR10** from the Atlantic to the Med, and the **GR65** covering the French leg (Chemin de St-Jacques) of the pilgrim route.

Shorter sections of each make for fabulous day hikes; St-Jean's efficient **tourist office** *(en-pays-basque.fr)* has information and maps. If you fancy joining Spain-bound pilgrims on the next (challenging) leg to Roncesvalles (seven hours; 26km), check the weather forecast to decide your route. The classic **Voie de Puy** crosses the Pyrenees over the dramatic Col de Bentarte (a stiff climb of 1365m), while the alternative *voie hiver* or 'bad weather' trail remains at lower altitudes.

Both trails are clearly signposted in St-Jean-Pied-de-Port at the intersection of route de St-Michel (D301) and chemin de Mayorga (D381). A sign here also says is the *col* (mountain pass) is *ouvert* (open) or *fermé* (closed). To stride out, exit the walled city through the aptly named **Porte d'Espagne**, picking up cheese at Crèmerie de Garazi for a picnic en route.

Basque Spirits

Shop fresh and local at Les Halles

Farmers from the Basque hills pile into St-Jean on Monday morning to sell their produce at market. On Thursday morning, June to September, they're joined by artisans who set up craft stalls in the indoor section of **Les Halles**.

Shop for nutty ewe-milk cheeses; AOP Ossau-Iraty cheeses marry beautifully with fruit jams made in nearby **Itxassou**, a village famed for its juicy black cherries. Buy air-dried ham, *gateaux basques* (cake layered with cream or cherry jam), yellow and green Izarra herbal liqueur, chutneys spiced with Espelette chilli pepper, and forest honeys crafted from linden, acacia and hawthorn in Les Landes. Pick up Euskola (the Basque version of cola) and *ketxup basque* (Basque ketchup) blending Aquitaine tomatoes with Basque peppers and Espelette chillis.

Winemakers craft Irouléguy wines from Ispoure vineyards on south-facing slopes north of St-Jean. Brana *(brana.fr)* also produces Espelette pepper-infused gin and *liqueur cacao* combining Bayonne chocolate with pear brandy at its out-of-town distillery in the **Village d'Artisans Ortzaize**. A one-stop shop for local crafts (pottery, ceramics, espadrilles) and farm produce, find it 11km north on the D918 towards Ossès and Bayonne.

UNDERWATER WINE

Alongside thirst-quenching *sagardoa* (apple cider), fizzy sangria, craft beers and Euskola (local cola) in Pays Basque's varied drinks cabinet, one artisan tipple stands out: Egiategis wines fermented at sea. Since 2007 pioneering Basque winemaker Emmanuel Poirmeur has been fermenting reds, whites and rosés for several months in underwater tanks submerged 15m deep in the Baie de St-Jean-de-Luz. Vineyards cloak clifftops along the coast and the wine is bottled in his **Egiategis** *(boutique-egiategia. com)* winery, in a 17th-century building overlooking Plage de Socoa in Ciboure. Fermenting wines at sea, stirred by the ocean in darkness and at a constant temperature, graces them with a subtle sparkle and fresh oceanic aromas. Expect to pay €40 a bottle.

 EATING IN ST-JEAN-PIED-DE-PORT: BEST PICNICS

Chez Odette: Baguette sandwiches filled with cheese and cherry jam or Basque pâté, Basque beer and farm ice cream; bottom of rue de la Citadelle. *10am-9pm Apr-Oct* €

Maison Berthold: Enjoy Basque *cannelés* (one-bite cakes) in different flavours from this pastry shop on rue d'Espagne. *10am-7pm* €

Crèmerie de Garazi: Pick up local farm cheeses at Pantxika's artisan dairy on rue d'Espagne. *9am-12.30pm & 3-7pm Mon & Wed-Sat, 9am-12.30pm Sun* €€

Elizaldia Merkatua: Enticing shop near the market selling air-dried hams from its farm, 10km north in Gamarthe. *8am-1pm & 3-7pm Mon-Sat, 8am-1pm Sun* €€

Beyond St-Jean-Pied-de-Port

St-Jean's mighty Pyrenean surrounds are an invitation to don walking shoes and an appetite for one of Pays Basque's best culinary treasures.

Places
Espelette p598
Sare p600
St-Étienne de Baïgorry p600

Befitting an ancient through-town where pilgrims coming from Paris, Vézelay and Le Puy-en-Velay gathered before making the same arduous crossing on foot over the Pyrenees into Spain, outdoor exploration is part of this area's DNA. Planted at the base of the Pyrenees, St-Jean-Pied-de-Port is the trailhead for day trips to traditional chilli-pepper farms, remote hilltop villages, pea-green vineyards in hills and thick beech forest that blaze fire-orange in autumn. An abundance of walking trails encourages zen exploration and eco-conscious chefs keep the Basque kitchen local and down-to-earth – literally in the case of Espelette's Michelin-starred Clément Guillemot, whose menu is a slow and deliberate culinary walk from the Basque mountains up to the coast.

Espelette
TIME FROM ST-JEAN-PIED-DE-PORT: **35MIN**
Feel the Heat

Basques say it requires a powerful throat formed by the hot southern sun to eat Espelette chillies. They're right. Spend the day in the Basque village of Espelette and you could encounter chilli-pepper blessings, October's ennoblement of the *chevalier du piment* (chilli knight) or whitewashed houses covered in dark-red chillis hung up to dry. Whatever the time of year, a visit to Espelette, 40km northwest of St-Jean-Pied-de-Port, is a rich gourmet treat.

On main square place du Marché, learn about the only French spice to have its own quality-branded AOP at the discovery centre, **Extea Centre d'Interprétation de l'AOP Piment d'Espelette** *(pimentdespelette.com; free).* Watch a 20-minute film on the history of the pepper, grown by local farmers since the 1650s. About 200 farms cultivate 275 hectares around the village today, producing 227 tonnes of the dried, fiery-red chilli powder a year.

Visit a Pepper Plantation

On the edge of the village, farm shop **L'Atelier du Piment** *(atelier-du-piment-espelette.fr; free)* overflows with chilli-pepper

GETTING AROUND

Your own wheels are essential for exploring the rural Basque hinterland. A handful of daily buses *(txiktxak.fr;* line No 45) link St-Jean-de-Luz train station with the Col de St-Ignace, the starting depot for the Petit Train de la Rhune.

Drying chillies, Espelette

products. During chilli pepper season (mid-May to late November), its outdoor discovery trail leads curios through the various stages of production, from seed to spice jar. Better still, plan ahead and book a guided visit of the shop's pepper plantation.

See seeds being sown during mid-March's **Fête de la St-Joseph**. The plants are moved to open fields in May or June. Stringent AOP rules mean they're planted 40cm apart, in rows 60cm apart. Flowers turn fields white from late June, and the first peppers are hand-harvested once they turn dark red in August. Some are sold fresh – in a hand-sewn *corde* or string of 20 peppers – and the rest are dried and crushed to become chilli powder.

Star-Spangled Gastronomy

When hunger beckons, cross the river to savour *piment d'Espelette* in the grassroots, modern-Basque cuisine of Michelin-starred chef Clément at **Choko Ona** *(choko-ona.fr; lunch/dinner menus from €39/67)*. Tables inside the traditional 18th-century Basque house overlook the chef's organic vegetable garden and every dish sizzles with seasonal flavour. 'Choko ona' is Basque for '*le bon coin*' or 'cosy corner'.

Espelette's new-gen brasserie is Basque gold

BEST OFF-GRID BASQUE VILLAGES

St-Étienne de Baïgorry: Picture-postcard village on the banks of River Nive, stitched from hiking routes, trail-run itineraries and vineyards in the quiet Vallée de Baïgorry.

Itxassou: This hilltop village is famous for its cherries and scenic surroundings.

La Bastide-Clairence: With whitewashed houses brushed in lipstick red, this is arguably the most beautiful of all Basque mountain villages.

Bidarray: A pretty riverside village famed for its whitewater rafting action.

Larressore: The *makhila* (Basque walking stick) workshop of the Anciart Bergara family, next to the village *fronton* (*pelota* court), is at the heart of this traditional village, 6km north of Espelette.

 EATING IN & AROUND ESPELETTE: OUR PICKS

Etchehandia: Savour burnt-red woodwork, exposed stone and classics like milk-fed Pyrenean lamb on the menu. *noon-2.30pm Tue-Sun, 7-9.30pm Fri & Sat* €€

Aintzina: Order *axoa de veau* (minced lamb and Espelette pepper) at this Espelette stalwart. *noon-2pm & 7-9pm Mon, Tue, Fri & Sat, noon-2pm Wed & Sun* €€

Choko Ona: Espelette's top dining spot sparkles with a Michelin star and eco-green clover. Natural wine pairings. *12.15-1.30pm & 8-9.30pm Tue-Sat* €€€

Ithurria: Michelin-starred modern Basque cuisine in a farmhouse by Ainhoa's *pelota* court; 10 minutes' drive from Espelette. *noon-1.30pm & 7.30-9pm Fri-Mon, 7.30-9pm Tue & Thu* €€€

Sare

TIME FROM ST-JEAN-PIED-DE-PORT: **50MIN** 🚗

Ride the Mythical Rhune Rack Railway

Hardest of hearts: get set to be shed a tear. The soul-soaring panorama of pea-green French Basque Country melting into the glittering blue Atlantic Ocean from the top of La Rhune is spectacular and unmatched. April to early November, the charming little **Train de la Rhune** *(rhune.com; adult/child return €25.50/17)* clanks slowly up the mountainside to the 905m-high summit that traditionally marks the start of the Pyrenees. The ginger wooden train first made the 35-minute journey in 1924 and has enchanted visitors ever since. At the top keep your eyes peeled for stocky little *pottok* (mountain ponies) grazing on the hillside.

Trains depart every 40 minutes between 8.50am and 5.30pm in July and August, and around nine daily other months. To avoid excessive crowding on the summit, you can only purchase a return ticket with fixed train times – allowing 1¼ hours at the summit (2½ hours complete round-trip).

Explore Prehistoric Caves

Who knows what the first inhabitants of the **Grottes de Sare** *(grottesdesare.fr; adult/child €10/6),* some 20,000 years ago, would make of today's whizz-bang technology that now lights up the Stygian gloom in these stunning subterranean caves? Multilingual 45-minute guided tours take you through a gaping entrance via narrow passages to a huge central cavern, where impressive shows of holograms and laser lights are staged. Wear sturdy shoes (lots of steps) and bring a sweater: the caves are 14°C year-round.

Cave admission includes free roaming around the surrounding tree-shaded park, peppered with reconstructions of prehistoric funerary monuments spanning 30 millennia. Evidence suggests the first monoliths appeared in Pays Basque during the Neolithic age between 4500 to 2800 BCE. Cremation and other death rituals are explored in the on-site museum.

Book tours well in advance in July and August – numbers are limited and places fill fast. To get to the caves, follow the D306 for 6km south from Sare village.

St-Étienne de Baïgorry

TIME FROM ST-JEAN-PIED-DE-PORT: **15MIN** 🚗

Buy Ham from a Fourth-Generation Butcher

Like so many Basque villages, picture-postcard St-Étienne de Baïgorry has two focal points: its unique church and *fronton* (*pelota* court), next to each other on the same square. By the fairytale old-stone Pont Romain crossing the river at the eastern end of the village, it's impossible to miss the *jambons* (hams) hanging in colourful striped Basque fabric bags on the first-floor balcony of **Maison Petricorena** *(petricorena. com).* Inside, the celebrated fourth-generation butcher and *épicerie* bursts with gourmet Basque goodies: local saffron, ham and chorizo, cherries, *brebis* (sheep's cheese) and its famous Sakari sauce.

WHERE TO FEEL THE BASQUE PULSE

Surf photographer and Biarritz gallerist **Sylvain Cazenave** reveals his favourite Basque places. @ *galeriesylvaincazenave*

Ferme Agerria, St-Martin d'Arberoue: Bernadette and Jean-Claude breed sheep, goats and black pigs on their farm *(agerria.fr)* and share their passion on year-round tours.

Arcé, St-Étienne de Baïgorry: I love to go here on Sundays. Pascal, the chef, cooks trout fresh from the river below. After lunch I hike to Col de l'Ispeguy, with views of the French and Spanish Pyrenees.

Rue de la Madeleine, Bidart: I like to sit on a bench on top of the cliff and watch Parlementia, my favourite wave, which I surfed for the first time in 1971. Parlementia is the closest in shape and power to waves found in Hawaï on Oahu's north shore.

Places We Love to Stay

€ Budget €€ Midrange €€€ Top End

Bordeaux
MAP p558

Jost € Only Bordeaux could do it: a new-gen lifestyle hostel with a Spritz-fuelled bar around a rooftop pool (guests only). Tip-top Italian tapas too.

Chez Dupont €€ B&B-style rooms decorated with vintage furniture and curiosities, on Chartrons' old-world main street.

Lola Hôtel & Bar €€ Bordeaux's newest boutique kid on the block, a welcome addition to village-like St-Michel. Sister hotel Rosa by Gare St-Jean is equally amenable.

La Maison du Lierre €€ As serene as its name, the House of Ivy has quaint boutique rooms and serves breakfast in a vine-draped garden.

Moxy Bordeaux €€ Good-value lifestyle digs at Bassins à Flot, with an open-plan buzzing cafe-bar doubling as work station and chit-chat hub.

Hôtel La Zoologie €€€ Four-star luxury in Bordeaux's historic Institute of Zoology, a glorious 1903 mashup of brick, stone and glass.

La Rochelle
MAP p574

La Fabrique € Last-minute deals at this former rope factory-turned-contemporary hotel are an exceptional steal. A pebble throw from the water.

Hôtel François 1er €€ Dazzling white rooms contrast with original street art and mesmerising rock memorabilia in public spaces at music-themed François I. Love it or hate it.

Le Yachtsman €€€ The four-star address at the Vieux Port to lay down your hat and kick back by the outdoor pool.

Cognac

Quai des Pontis € Bucolic riverside living in hotel rooms, wooden cabins on stilts or romantic vintage-styled *roulettes* (caravans).

La Nauve €€€ Boutique luxury in a wealthy distiller's riverside mansion, with sublime gardens, row boats and gastronomic dining to die for.

Île de Ré

Hôtel Le Martray € Excellent-value hotel-restaurant between salt marshes, a sandy beach and the cycling path to Ars-en-Ré; it rents wheels.

Le Sénéchal €€ This fashionable, 22-room boutique hotel languishes in several traditional old-stone *maisons de village* on Ars-en-Ré's church square. Tip-top bistro.

Bayonne
MAP p584

Hôtel Côte Basque € Bargain rooms in an 18th-century townhouse hotel by the train station. Triples and quads are family-perfect.

Hôtel des Arceaux € Colourful, no-frills rooms slumber inside this atmospheric, two-star hotel on Bayonne's prettiest arcaded street.

Péniche Djébelle €€ Two-room houseboat afloat the Adour, with cathedral-spire view and breakfast served on deck; closed Oct-Apr.

Hôtel des Basses Pyrénées €€ Grand Bayonne's most atmospheric joint, with tranquil fairy light-lit terrace tucked in the ramparts.

Okko €€ Superb deals can be had at this four-star hotel, with 9th-floor lounge and roof terrace facing the river; 10 minutes' walk into town.

Biarritz

Surf Hostel Biarritz € Small, fun-packed hostel, at home in a clifftop villa overlooking the sea; 20 mins walk into town.

Hôtel Marbella € Excellent-value rooms in the old town, several with balcony, a pebble's throw from Plage du Port Vieux.

Hôtel Palmito €€ Dorm, double or rooftop suite near Plage de la Vieux Port; world-food with festive vibe.

Regina Experimental €€€ Fashionista address by the lighthouse, in a 1907 clifftop villa reinvented by Parisian designer Dorothée Meilichzon.

Villa Magnan €€€ Six country-chic rooms on an out-of-town family estate, with bucolic summer dining.

St-Jean-Pied-de-Port
MAP p594

Hôtel Ramuntcho € Old-world address in the walled city, with fourth-generation charm and old town-Pyrenean-foothill views.

Le Lièvre et la Tortue € The Hare and Tortoise welcomes all corners in a six-bed dorm, quad and double. Fun vibe and tasty communal dinners.

Maison Mâje € The stylish pilgrims' choice in an old-world cottage with garden tucked in the ramparts. Dorm beds or 'posh' en-suite double. Look for the pea-green door.

Villa Esponida €€ Doubles, family rooms and apartments with kitchenette in an 1896 villa. Walkers can use its 'donkey service' (€8/bag) to have luggage transported.

Researched by
Chrissie McClatchie

Dordogne, Lot & Limousin

RIVERS, CHÂTEAUX, PREHISTORIC CAVES, FOOD AND WINE

Gentle countryside, lazy rivers, delightful medieval villages, astonishing prehistoric cave art, fairy-tale châteaux and superb cuisine: this part of France has the lot.

The Loire's castles, Provence's magazine-worthy villages, the Côte d'Azur's artistic footprint, Lyon's food scene. What if we told you that you could find a rival to every one of these global reputations in the southwestern triangle that is the Dordogne-Lot-Limousin?

The Dordogne is the land of 1001 castles, most in the medieval style of childhood fairy tales, while so enchanting are the villages scattered across this countryside that St-Cirq-Lapopie, in the Lot, was elected by the French as their favourite in the entire country. The impressionists were captivated by rural Limousin, but it's the prehistoric artists who, millennia before them, used caves as canvases, that have gifted the region its most magnificent artistic treasures. Local cuisine, from foie gras to truffles, beef and everything duck, fills the plates of global gourmands — and that tableware may well have been fired in Limoges. Plus, the Lot gave Argentina the malbec grape.

What about a lack of beaches, you may counter? Aha! This is where you learn that the glorious rivers that crisscross the landscape are made for swimming, canoeing and kayaking.

It's easy to see why the French and British fought over this region during the Hundred Years' War. And why it's still so beloved by the British today. But therein lies a great paradox. So prevalent are British second homeowners and tourists that it's affectionately nicknamed the Dordogne-shire. Yet, for much of the rest of the world, the area is hardly known. It's time for that to change.

THE MAIN AREAS

PÉRIGUEUX
Cafe culture, fine food and an excellent cathedral.
p610

VÉZÈRE VALLEY
Prehistoric caves, photogenic villages and river fun.
p622

CAHORS
Relaxed riverside living, medieval architecture and rich red wines. **p628**

LIMOGES
Lively university town with an Arts and Crafts heritage.
p639

For places to stay in Dordogne, Lot & Limousin, see p647

THE GUIDE

DORDOGNE, LOT & LIMOUSIN

Left: Great Hall of Bulls, Lascaux II (p625); Above: Château de Beynac (p620), Dordogne Valley

Find Your Way

At 9000 sq km, the Dordogne is mainland France's third-largest *département* and sits in the southwest near Bordeaux. Limoges, in the neighbouring Haute-Vienne, is a gateway to the vast landscapes of the Limousin, while, to the south, we venture along the Lot River.

Limoges, p639
With its fine museums, proud porcelain heritage, tasty food scene and market brimming with unique produce, Limoges is the regional highlight you least expected.

Périgueux, p610
Stylish Périgueux is the gateway to the Dordogne with an addictive cafe culture, impressive Roman ruins and the most remarkable cathedral in the region.

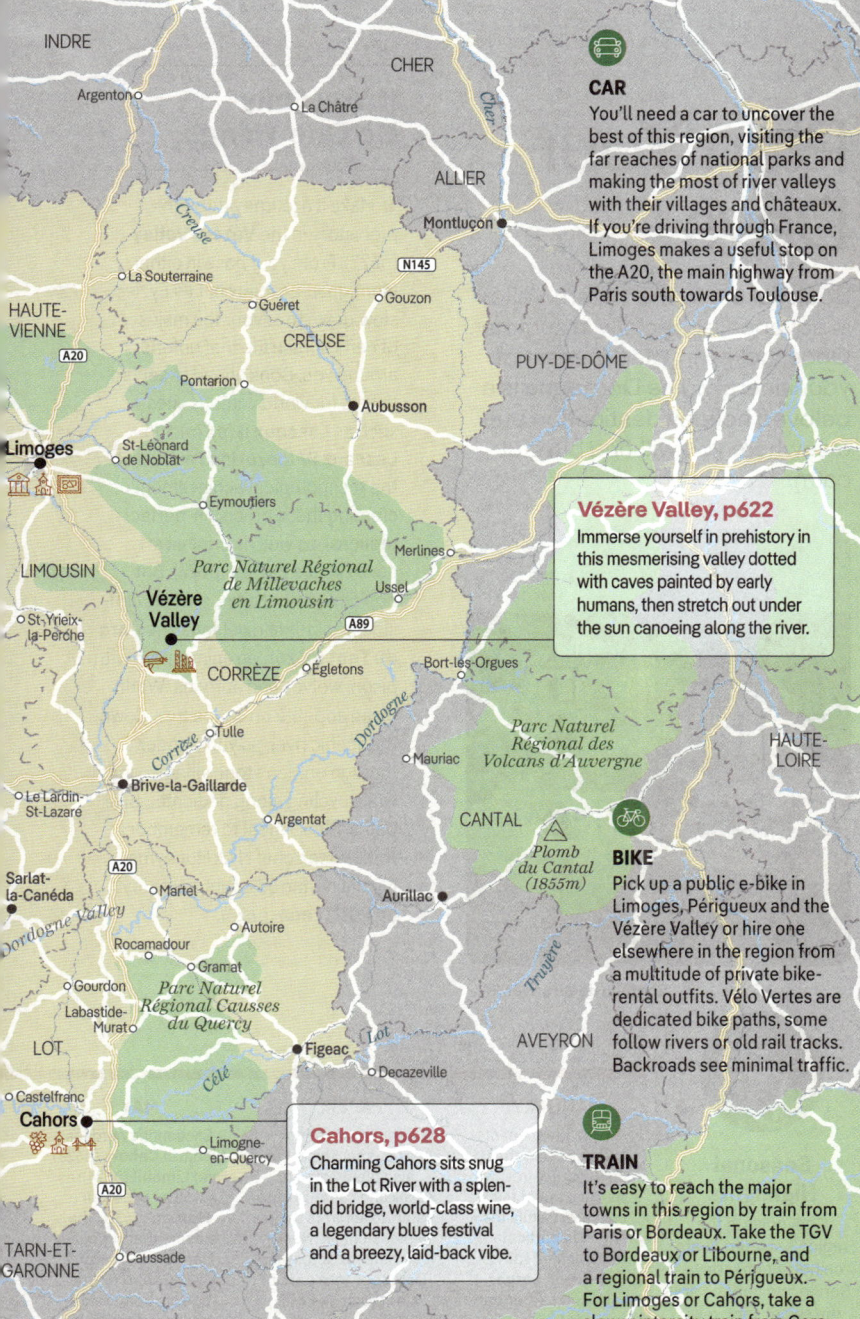

CAR

You'll need a car to uncover the best of this region, visiting the far reaches of national parks and making the most of river valleys with their villages and châteaux. If you're driving through France, Limoges makes a useful stop on the A20, the main highway from Paris south towards Toulouse.

Vézère Valley, p622

Immerse yourself in prehistory in this mesmerising valley dotted with caves painted by early humans, then stretch out under the sun canoeing along the river.

BIKE

Pick up a public e-bike in Limoges, Périgueux and the Vézère Valley or hire one elsewhere in the region from a multitude of private bike-rental outfits. Vélo Vertes are dedicated bike paths, some follow rivers or old rail tracks. Backroads see minimal traffic.

Cahors, p628

Charming Cahors sits snug in the Lot River with a splendid bridge, world-class wine, a legendary blues festival and a breezy, laid-back vibe.

TRAIN

It's easy to reach the major towns in this region by train from Paris or Bordeaux. Take the TGV to Bordeaux or Libourne, and a regional train to Périgueux. For Limoges or Cahors, take a slower intercity train from Gare d'Austerlitz in Paris.

Plan Your Days

Book tickets to the Vézère Valley in advance, especially in summer. Once locked in, plan the rest of your itinerary. The Dordogne is a beloved holiday destination but elsewhere you will find blissful calm.

Château de Biron (p618)

If You Only Do One Thing...

● Make it a journey through prehistory in the **Vézère Valley** (p622). From your base in either Montignac-Lascaux or Les Eyzies, slow down to savour the majesty of early human life that unfurls around you. Book ahead to secure tickets for world-famous sites such as **Lascaux II** (p626) and **Lascaux IV** (p626) (and marvel at the technological achievement of creating these precision-perfect replicas), as well as original art caves in **Les Eyzies** (p627). But don't miss other sites, such as cliffside troglodyte dwellings and **Parc du Thot** (p626), an animal parc with bison, wolves and aurochs. Work up an appetite on canoe trips down the scenic river, as you wander through golden stone villages and while cycling along dedicated bike paths. Plan a meal to remember at Antipodean chef Nick Honeyman's Michelin-starred countryside idyll, **Le Pétit Leon** (p624).

Seasonal Highlights

Cool down in the region's shaded rivers on hot summer days. Spring and autumn are the sweet spot: mild weather, fewer crowds and glorious gardens.

JANUARY

The heady scent of nugget-like truffes du Périgord, freshly snuffled out of thick oak forests, fills the winter air, particularly at dedicated truffle markets in **Sorges** (p616) and **Lalbenque** (p635).

APRIL

Spring can bring glorious sunshine, but also plenty of rain. Kayak and canoe outfits start to stir from their winter slumber. Nearly 100 châteaux across the Dordogne take part in **Châteaux en Fête**.

MAY

Enchanting gardens bloom in **Cahors** (p628) and **Limeuil** (p624); as well as at **Latour-Marliac** (p638), the nursery that supplied Monet with his water lilies. *Gabarres* (flat-bottom boats) start seasonal sightseeing cruises.

Five Days to Travel Around

- Dedicate two days to the **Vézère Valley** (p622) and a third day châteaux-hopping along one of the most scenic stretches of river in the world: the bends between Beynac-et-Cazenac and Domme in the **Dordogne Valley** (p620). From there, you have two choices: either continue along the river to **Bergerac** (p617), perhaps making a detour via the bastide town of **Monpazier** (p617), before finishing up in stylish **Périgueux** (p610) in time for cocktails with cathedral views at **La Cantina** (p613), or push into the neighbouring Lot at the deeply spiritual site of **Rocamadour** (p633), before sweeping in a loop across the Parc national régional et Géoparc Causses de Quercy through one of France's favourite villages, **St-Cirq-Lapopie** (p636), towards **Cahors** (p628), with its grand red wine and majestic medieval footbridge.

More than a Week

- With more than a week you can cover all corners of the region. Start along the Lot River, in water lily gardens that inspired Claude Monet in **Le Temple-sur-Lot** (p638) and the village with a funny name, **Montcuq** (p637), before winding up past Cahors and Rocamadour towards the golden market town of **Sarlat-la-Canéda** (p618). Prebook visits in the Vézère then dip along the Dordogne River to Périgueux. From there, push north into the Périgueux vert at too-pretty-to-be-true **Brantôme** (p614) before entering the Limousin region at sombre WWII martyr village, **Oradour-sur-Glane** (p643). Overnight in lively **Limoges** (p639), the biggest city covered in this chapter, before finishing up where we started, in landscapes along the river (this time the Creuse) that roused Monet (alongside other artists) in **Fresselines** (p644) and **Crozant** (p644).

JUNE
The region grooves till late for summer solstice (21 June). Fête de la Musique is France-wide but a university crowd makes it loud in **Limoges** (p639). The Creuse (p645) remains gloriously sleepy as summer season kicks off elsewhere.

JULY
The Tour de France can mean road closures – but also a lot of fun. The Lot grooves to the sound of moody blues at the **Cahors Blues Festival** (p630). Fireworks and music everywhere on Bastille Day (14 July).

AUGUST
Summer passes in a haze of *guinguettes* (outdoor taverns) and night markets, such as **Périgueux**'s buzzy food *fêtes* (p612). Head to swim spots along the river to cool down (p608). **Limoges' historic steam train** (p641) is back in action.

SEPTEMBER
Rocamadour Hot Air Balloon Festival (p634) floats high in the Lot skies. Less competition for tickets to **Lascaux II and IV** (p626) and the grottoes of **Les Eyzies** (p627). Harvest time for vineyards near **Bergerac** (p617) and **Cahors** (p628).

HELP ME PICK:

River Activities

With five navigable rivers in the Dordogne alone, you're never too far from the fresh breeze that swirls around water, a lifeline as the thermostat climbs higher in summer. Canoes and kayaks combine sightseeing and sport, while river beaches and inland lakes are just as laid-back and relaxing as their coastal alternatives. Each river in the region has its own identity. Pick the one that most matches your travel style, or get to know them all. Just don't forget your sunscreen.

Where to get wet if you like...

Canoes and kayaks

Dordogne River Classic stretch with more castles than river bends between Carsac and Envaux. Plenty of hire outfits; go the distance with **Canoë Détente** (canoe-detente.fr) in Envaux, where the longest circuit from Carsac passes seven castles and takes 10 hours.

PVINCE73/SHUTTERSTOCK

Dronne River The stretch between Brantôme and Bourdeilles (p614) is pure cinema; or start upstream at Fontaine de l'Amour for a shorter 4km journey with **Brantôme Canoë** (brantomecanoe.com).

Vézère River Canoes and caves are the perfect match. From Les Eyzies, **Canoës Les Trois Drapeaux** (p623) set you on an adventure passing prehistoric and medieval shelters carved into cliff-faces.

Lot River Puy-l'Évêque is canoe HQ on the Lot. **Copeyre**'s (gabare-copeyre.com) energetic canoe-bike combo has you paddling 5km downstream to Vire-sur-Lot, then hopping on bikes to return through vineyards along an old trainline converted into a dedicated bike path.

Creuse River Hire a kayak from **Hôtel Restaurant du Lac** (p646); after 6km, you arrive at the confluence so beloved by Monet.

River beaches

Plage Pont de Vicq Sandy beach and picnic area on the Dordogne at Le-Buisson-de-Cadouin with canoeing, stand-up paddleboarding and fishing. No lifeguards.

Gluges Plage Dramatic cliffs face this sandy beach near Martel on the Dordogne River. Lifeguard afternoons in July and August.

Plage du Limeuil At the confluence of the Dordogne and Vézère rivers there's a wide pebble beach (pictured), shallow waters and great views.

Plage de St-Cirq-Lapopie Swim spot in the Lot shaded by France's first favourite village. Grass not sand.

Lovely lakes

Lac de Pombonne Bergerac's local lake is surrounded by sand, with a cafe, walks and shady spots. Daily lifeguard (11.30am-6.30pm) July and August.

Lac de Montcuq Obstacle course for ages 6+ inflates in summer on Montcuq's popular lake in the southern Lot. Lifeguards (noon-6pm) July and August.

Étang de Tamniès Between Sarlat, Montignac-Lascaux and Les Eyzies with a crescent of sand, picnic tables and inflatables. Lifeguards (11am-7pm) and some accessible features (toilet and floating wheelchair).

HOW TO

Take note of the season Rivers are higher and the current is faster in early spring. Summer is the gentlest time to paddle, but also the most popular.

Transport The shuttles from the canoe base to your starting point or from your arrival point are included in the price.

Children As a rule of thumb, children must be at least five years old and able to swim to the bank unsupported. Life jackets must be worn.

Price Some operators fix the price by itinerary, others by the hour. Most will also offer a multiday rate. Call in advance to book.

Which River?

Dordogne River Shallow course of the river makes it beginner friendly, although, around places like Bergerac and La Roque-Gageac, be prepared to share the water with *gabarres*.

Vézère River Compared to its bigger sibling, the Dordogne, the Vézère River is more wild in landscape, the current stronger and the river narrower, so you'll stay closer to the bank as you paddle.

Isle River A river of marked fluctuations; can be very low in summer. Only between Corgnac and Montpon-Ménestérol is navigable. Périgueux is the hub.

Dronne River Flows through Périgueux Vert. Smaller river, so fewer people, although expect the odd boat. Shorter itineraries, most under 12km.

Lot River The Lot flows fast at the start of the season, and the water level is high. It's forbidden to canoe through a lock, so jump out of the water and drag the canoe to the other side instead.

Creuse River Untouched landscapes and mesmerising rock formations. No passing the Barrage d'Éguzon dam at the other end of the d'Éguzon. Also no return shuttles.

Périgueux

LAYERS OF HISTORY | SHADED SQUARES | FRAGRANT MARKETS

GETTING AROUND

Most of Périgueux's sights are concentrated in its pedestrianised historic centre, Puy St-Front, so park up at the edge of the neighbourhood and get around on foot if you're travelling by car. The streets around the centre can get clogged, especially during commuter hours. Périvélo (*perivelolibreservice. ecovelo.mobi/#/ welcome*) is the city's public shared e-bike scheme with hire fixed at €1/hr, although it requires a deposit of €150 to use.

☑ TOP TIP

Périgueux must be one of the more generous cities in France when it comes to parking — the first three hours are offered free on its street parking meters!

It's almost a relief to find that Périgueux is a fitting capital of the Dordogne — anything less for the gateway to such a glorious *département* would be an incredible letdown. You might assume the city is located on the mighty Dordogne River, but the city is actually set to the north, on the smaller Isle River. With a historic core of half-timbered buildings that cascade down to the riverbank, Périgueux has oodles of charm and you will be hard-pressed to remain immune to its atmospheric squares, busy restaurant and bar scene, fragrant produce markets and wonderfully unique cathedral. Think of Périgueux as the provincial city that prefers chic labels and sparkly accessories to vintage finds (if the latter is more your style, check out Cahors, p628). It's a vibe that's hardly new, if the pretty jewellery and other tokens of daily life unearthed in Vesunna, the city's grand villa complex from Roman times, are anything to go by.

Shout from the Rooftops
Be surprised by Périgueux's inspiring cathedral

Périgueux's grand Byzantine-inspired **Cathédrale St-Front** (*boutique.destination-perigueux.fr/les-toits-de-la-cathedrale*) comes as a bit of a surprise: a great, creamy white building with five majestic domes, even more turrets and a broad, 60m-high bell tower. Screw your eyes up and imagine a minaret in place of the steeple, and you can see why writer Victor Hugo called it 'the great mosque of Périgueux'. Its current look is thanks to an 1852 restoration by architect Paul Abadie, who would go on to design Sacré-Cœur in Paris. For the best views of it, head to nearby **Pont des Barris** and look up. For the best views from it, climb up to its roof for a close-up of those domes and sweeping views across town and the river. The **Tourist Office** organises one-hour guided tours (*adult/child €7/free*) almost daily. Booking in advance essential.

PÉRIGUEUX

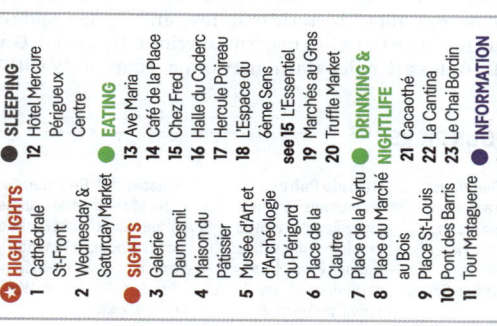

HIGHLIGHTS
1. Cathédrale St-Front
2. Wednesday & Saturday Market

SIGHTS
3. Galerie Daumesnil
4. Maison du Pâtissier
5. Musée d'Art et d'Archéologie du Périgord
6. Place de la Clautre
7. Place de la Vertu
8. Place du Marché au Bois
9. Place St-Louis
10. Pont des Barris
11. Tour Mataguerre

SLEEPING
12. Hôtel Mercure Périgueux Centre

EATING
13. Ave Maria
14. Café de la Place
15. Chez Fred
16. Halle du Coderc
17. Hercule Poireau
18. L'Espace du 6ème Sens
    see 15 L'Essentiel
19. Marchés au Gras
20. Truffle Market

DRINKING & NIGHTLIFE
21. Cacaothé
22. La Cantina
23. Le Chai Bordin

INFORMATION
24. Tourist Office

THE GUIDE

DORDOGNE, LOT & LIMOUSIN PÉRIGUEUX

Musée d'Art et d'Archéologie du Périgord

MARKET DAYS IN PÉRIGUEUX

Wednesday & Saturday Market: The produce market overtakes place de la Clautre on Wednesday morning and extends to place du Codere, place de l'Ancienne Hôtel de Ville and rue de Taillefer on Saturday mornings.

Truffle Market: Maison du Pâtissier fills with fresh truffles on Saturday mornings between December and February, production dependent. Fête de la Truffe is celebrated in January.

Marché au Gras: Between November and mid-March a foie gras market pops up on Saturday mornings on Place St-Louis.

Les Nuits Gourmands: On Thursday nights in July and August, Périgueux's historic core transforms into one big open-air restaurant.

Lazy Days in Leafy Squares
Embrace the city's café culture

All the cute shaded squares in Périgueux's Puy St-Front neighbourhood are just made for lingering over coffee, so it's no surprise that the city's cafe culture is superb, particularly on market days and Sunday mornings. **Place de la Clautre** is the largest; terrace tables provide cathedral views with your croissant and cappuccino. Surrounding **Halle du Coderc**, the city's market hall, place Coderc feels much smaller and intimate and is shaded by two towering linden trees. Some start to buzz as the sun sets, such as restaurant-lined **Place St-Louis** and **Place du Marché au Bois**. Others are where you want to pause right away, lest it prove impossible to find again. We're looking at you, serene **Place de la Vertu**.

Test Your Sense of Direction
Wander Périgueux's narrow streets

Full of narrow alleys, historic buildings and shaded squares, Périgueux is something of a magical labyrinth. Try to find: **Galerie Daumesnil**, a delightful network of courtyards within

EATING IN PÉRIGUEUX: OUR PICKS

Café de la Place: Bistrot fare with a fabulous side serve of people-watching in this classic brasserie. *8am-1pm Mon-Sat, 9am-5pm Sun* €

Chez Fred: Generous portions and a market fresh 3-course menu with a front-row view of Cathédrale St-Front. *9am-2pm & 7-10pm Tue-Sat, to 2pm Sun* €€

Hercule Poireau: Traditional Périgord ingredients revisited, providing innovative options in an old-town setting. *noon-1pm & 7.30-9pm Thu-Mon* €€

L'Essentiel: Périgueux's sole Michelin-star address plates up little artworks of local produce crammed with flavour. *noon-1.15pm Tue-Sat, 7-9pm Tue, Wed, Fri, Sat* €€€

15th- to 17th-century town houses. The entrance is near rue Limogeanne, a narrow street of ancient houses with boutiques reflecting modern tastes. On rue de la Sagesse, paving stones sport beautiful lines of poetry. Somewhere among the scene is **Maison du Pâtissier**, an impressive 14th-century Renaissance building on place St-Louis. Perhaps easiest to pinpoint is the 15th-century **Tour Mataguerre**, the only of the 28 towers that once encircled Puy St-Front still standing.

Step into Périgueux's Ancient Past
Walk through Gallo-Roman remains

Enclosing the vestiges of a 1st-century Roman *domus* (urban villa) uncovered in 1959, the sleek glass design of **Musée Gallo-Romain Vesunna** *(perigueux-vesunna.fr; adult/child €6/4)* stands out against Périgueux's heavy tome of Medieval architectural heritage. Set in gardens southwest of the historic centre in a meandering curve of the Isle, this excellent museum reveals the secrets of life 2000 years ago in Vesunna, as the city was known during Roman times. After viewing the site from a lofty mezzanine, the visit unfurls along wide walkways at the same level as the excavations. As it was back then, a fountain and its supporting pillars are the centrepiece. Objects unearthed from the 2400-sq-metre site are also on display. Combined tickets are available with the Musée d'Art et Archéologie and the museum is closed on Tuesdays. Don't leave without visiting the **Tour de Vésone** in the museum gardens. The tower is all that remains of a 2nd-century temple dedicated to local goddess Vesunna.

The Dordogne's First Museum
A display of prehistory and art

The **Musée d'Art et d'Archéologie du Périgord** *(perigueux-maap.fr; adult/child €6/4)*, occupying a grand building at the edge of the old town since 1835, has an eclectic collection split into four themes: prehistory, Middle Ages, beauxarts from the 16th century onwards, and an assortment of artefacts from outside of Europe. There is also a display of stonework from Cathédrale St-Front showcased in the cloister. English audioguide costs €1 extra and the museum is closed on Tuesdays.

WHEN FOIE GRAS MET BLACK TRUFFLE

It doesn't take long for Francis Delpey to reveal the secret code for Paté de Périgueux to visitors to his restaurant, **L'Espace du 6ème Sens**: 3 + 40 + 57. In order, that's the percentage of truffle, foie gras and stuffing (grain-fed pork). The recipe has been made in Périgueux since the 15th century, although maybe we should be happy it's no longer fashioned from pastry stuffed with whatever leftover fish and meat was to hand. As head of the Confrérie du Pâté de Périgueux, Delpey is part of a sacred brotherhood bringing the dish back to Périgueux's tables. To try it, a 200g tin (nothing bigger, nothing smaller, demand the Confrérie) eaten on Delpey's shaded restaurant terrace will set you back €38. For more about foie gras, see p619.

DRINKING IN PÉRIGUEUX: OUR PICKS

La Cantina: The spot on the riverfront for cool cocktails, tapas, DJs, dancing and cathedral views. *7pm-midnight Wed, to 2am Thu-Sat.*

Le Chai Bordin: Classic French hole-in-the-wall wine bar with tables made from old wine boxes. Buzzy vibe. *6-10pm Tue-Fri, from 9.30am Sat*

Cacaothé: Baristas that know the difference between a flat white and a latté. Brunch menu and a games corner. *8am-6pm Wed-Sun, to 3pm Mon*

Ave Maria: Sip on gins from around the world in a leafy courtyard hidden back from the street. Also does food. *6pm-midnight Tue-Sat*

Beyond Périgueux

Canoe down rivers past 800-year-old castles, feast on freshly plucked truffles, enjoy atmospheric night markets.

Places

Brantôme & Bourdeilles p614
Corgnac-sur-l'Isle p615
Sorges p616
Bergerac p617
Monpazier p617
Issigeac p618
Sarlat-la-Canéda p618

Beyond Périgueux and the vast landscapes of the Périgord, as the Dordogne was historically called, have been split into a quartet of colours. Radiating out from the city is the Périgord blanc (white), a nod to the creamy limestone plateaus that house the region's truffle HQ, Sorges. Villages Brantôme and Bourdeilles are a vision of lush nature in the Périgord vert (green) at the north of the *département*. To the south, around the hub of Bergerac on the Dordogne River, the Périgord *pourpre* (purple) is named for the grapes that thrive in its dry soils. While golden Sarlat-la-Canéda is the epicentre of the Périgord noir (black), with its dense oak forests and mind-boggling concentration of riverside medieval châteaux.

Brantôme & Bourdeilles

TIME FROM PÉRIGUEUX: **30MIN**

The Dordogne's Little Venice

If legends are to be believed, Charlemagne is among those to have fallen for the Brantôme's ample charm: it is said the 'Father of Europe', as the ruler is known, built the **Abbaye de Brantôme** *(perigord-dronne-belle.fr/abbaye-brantome-perigord)* in 769. Enquire at the **Tourist Office** to see if there are guided visits of its bell tower planned *(adult/child €8.50/6.50)*. Added on in the 11th century, the bell tower's access is tricky; you will have to tuck through narrow passages and scamper across the rooftop to climb – and it gets a little rickety at the top – but the views are stupendous. Carved into the cliffs behind the abbey is the dimly-lit **Grotte du Jugement Dernier** *(adult/child €5/4)* cave, where religious hermits once lived. It newly reopened in summer 2025 after works to secure the site, so you can once again see the star attraction here: a 15th-century frieze carved out of rock of the Last Judgement. Entirely surrounded by a picturesque loop of the Dronne River, Brantôme is called the Venice of the Périgord; even as pretty as the village is, it does feel like a case of wishful thinking.

Two châteaux for the price of one

A medieval fortress and renaissance residence standing side by side, **Château de Bourdeilles** *(chateau-bourdeilles.fr; adult/*

GETTING AROUND

Your own transport, whether two or four wheels, is the best way to reach all corners of the Dordogne, one of France's largest regions. The *réseau* TER Nouvelle-Aquitaine train service connects Périgueux with Le Buisson; and from there, a direct track links Bergerac with Sarlat along the Dordogne River. Reach Brantôme and Sorges by bus from Périgueux, Issigeac by bus from Bergerac.

Château de Bridoire

child €9.70/6.40) is a one-stop destination to compare building styles from two distinctly different eras. The 13th-century castle's thick walls kept people out, while the 16th-century castle was an opulent display of social stature for the world to see. The latter was also designed by a woman considered to be France's first architect: Jacquette de Montbron. A virtual medieval escape game (€20pp) is an experience everyone in the family will enjoy reliving long after you leave — that's what we found, in any case. Bourdeilles itself will keep you snap-happy, with its medieval bridge, watermills and weeping willows creating the most quintessential of bucolic river landscapes.

Corgnac-sur-l'Isle

TIME FROM PÉRIGUEUX: **35MIN**

Pedal the Vélorail du Périgord

The **Vélorail du Périgord Vert** *(veloraildefrance.com/24 -velorail-du-perigord-vert-minisite; per 2-5 people €45)* is huge fun for all the family (aged over three): a metal cart that runs on an old railway line through shady woodland and over a viaduct, powered by bicycle pedals. Each cart takes up to five people, two of whom pedal. The first 35 minutes is uphill from Corgnac-sur-l'Isle to Thiviers, so pedallers need to be fairly fit (though electric assistance is available). There's

BEST OF THE REST: DORDOGNE CHÂTEAUX

Château de Jumilhac: Most fairy-tale-like castle, with multi-turreted roof. *chateaudejumilhac. com*

Château de Hautefort: A mini Versailles north of Montignac-Lascaux, with formal gardens. *chateau-hautefort. com*

Château de Bridoire: Known as the castle of games, with a labyrinth (July and August) and over 100 medieval games. *chateaudebridoire. com*

Château de Puymartin: Home of the Dordogne's most famous ghost, the 'White Lady', believed to haunt its north tower. *chateau-puymartin. com*

Château de Fenelon: Birthplace of François Fénelon, influential archbishop and writer of the Louis XIV era. *chateau-fenelon.fr*

EATING & DRINKING IN BRANTÔME & BOURDEILLES: OUR PICKS

Bocaux de Liens: Takeaway meals prepared from zero-km produce served in jars you return once you're finished. *10am-4pm, Mon-Sat* €

La Table d'Emilie: Bright and convivial joint in Brantôme with a bistro menu, plenty of duck and some tasty cocktails. *noon-1.15pm Tue-Sun, 7-8pm Tue, Thu-Sat* €€

Le Troquet de Bimbillou: Riverside summer *guinguette* inside a troglodyte theme park. *10am-8pm Mon-Sun, to 11pm Wed & Fri* €

Nommad's: An eclectic menu of world flavours served up in the shadow of Château de Bourdeilles. *noon-1.30pm & 7-8.30pm Fri-Tue* €

Château de Monbazillac

FACT OR FICTION?

Climbing the hill from Quai Cyrano are the tiny lanes of Bergerac's medieval core, with place de la Mirpe and place Pelissière particular hubs of local life. Both squares sport statues of the town's favourite son, Cyrano de Bergerac, the large-nosed and unlucky-in-love character immortalised around the world in Edmond Rostand's 1897 eponymous play who, most-likely, never set foot in Bergerac. Wherever the truth lies, it's still an excuse for the interactive **Expérience Cyrano** *(quai-cyrano.com/un-lieu-unique/experience-cyrano; adult/child €8/4)* inside Quai Cyrano, where you follow fictional actor Antoine as he auditions, rehearses and steps on stage in the lead role of the play of Cyrano's life.

a 30-minute wait in the garden while the carts are turned around, followed by a 20-minute coast downhill. Take drinks for halfway and a picnic to enjoy by the riverside on your return. Bookings are by phone only *(05 53 52 42 93)* and you need to have the correct amount in cash for payment. Closed December and January.

Sorges

TIME FROM PÉRIGUEUX: **25MIN**

Truffle HQ

If truffles are your gastronomic fantasy, you will be on cloud nine in the Dordogne, the spiritual home of the globally worshipped Tuber melanosporum, or Truffe du Périgord. Deep in the Périgord Vert, the village of Sorges is considered the region's truffle HQ and can welcome up to 10,000 visitors for its Sunday morning truffle market in December and January, particularly over the three days it celebrates the annual **Fête de la Truffe**. For total immersion in the world of these prized black diamonds, head to the **Ecomusée de la Truffe** *(ecomuseedelatruffe.com; adult/child €6/free)*. The top floor is a smartly laid-out museum, while the bottom floor sells truffles and truffle creams, oils, mustards, honeys – even a truffle aperitif – from local producers. Stock up for a picnic under the trees along the delightful truffle walking route that begins 2km away from the museum – pick up a map from the ticket desk.

EATING IN BERGERAC: OUR PICKS

L'Imparfait: Long-running local favourite serving up inventive French cuisine. *noon-1.30pm & 7-9pm Mon-Sun* €€

Villa Laetitia: Périgord classics and market-inspired dishes served on a pretty cobblestone square. *noon-2pm & 7-8.30pm Tue-Sat* €€

Restaurant Bellevue: Riverfront address with a menu of French bistro staples enhanced by rich sauces. *9.30am-11pm Mon-Sun* €€

Halle de Bergerac: Pick up picnic supplies from Bergerac's small covered market. Brunch first Sunday of the month. *8am-2pm & 4-7pm Tue-Sat* €

Bergerac

TIME FROM PÉRIGUEUX: **45MIN**

Winetasting at Quai Cyrano
For a teaser of Bergerac's reputed wine scene, make your way to **Quai Cyrano** *(quai-cyrano.com)*, a wonderful riverfront space that serves as **tourist office**, tasting room, exhibition area (see Experience Cyrano) – oh, and even manages to deliver an atmospheric 17th-century cloister, Cloître des Récollets, to the mix, too. Each week, a new selection of wines to taste free of charge is uncorked in the 1st-floor wine lounge. Once you have found your favourite, order a glass *(from €4)* to savour on the terrace, which has to be the best spot for a drink in town. In summer, you can meet local winemakers or stay into the evening for a theatre performance or live music.

Bergerac's tobacco crop
If the tobacco barns typical of the southwest French countryside haven't gone unnoticed, a visit to the **Musée du Tabac** *(bergerac.fr/directory/musee-du-tabac €5/free)* might answer some questions. Housed in a beautifully-restored 17th-century townhouse, exhibits trace 3000 years of the crop's history and include vintage machinery and an extensive collection of pipes. Signage is in French with a leaflet in English available. Closed on Mondays.

A boat trip down the Dordogne
A boat ride on the flat-bottomed **Gabarres de Bergerac** *(gabarresdebergerac.fr; adult/child €12/9)* is a real highlight here. On a 50-minute guided trip, glide along an s-bend of the river, learning about the town's important historical role as well as its flora, fauna and beloved vineyards. There's a minimum of four daily departures between April to October from outside Quai Cyrano – two longer *(1hr 30min adult/child €15/10, 3hr 30min adult/child €20/15)* itineraries include a winetasting.

Monpazier

TIME FROM PÉRIGUEUX: **1HR 15MIN**

The perfect bastide?
Fun fact: it was an English king (Edward I) who founded Monpazier in 1284. One of 10 Dordogne villages to hold the *Plus Beaux Village de France* crown, Monpazier is considered the perfect specimen of a *bastide* town, or a medieval fortified town with grid-pattern streets. Its central square, place des Cornières, is the hub of local life and is framed by arcades with distinctive tipped arches, or *cornières*, to create an incredibly photogenic scene. A market has been held here on Thursday since the Middle Ages – in fact the grain measures under the timber-framed market hall have been standing in place since medieval times. The village is also a hub of arts, with stained-glass workshops and glassblowers among the crafts at home here.

Medieval fun and games
Set inside a 17th-century former convent, **Bastideum** *(bastideum.fr; adult/child €6/4)* is now an interactive museum near place des Cornières dedicated to the history of Monpazier and

---

BEST VINEYARDS NEAR BERGERAC

Château de Monbazillac: Fairy tale castle and emblematic *domaine* of the Monbazillac appellation, the region's prestigious sweet white wines. *chateau-monbazillac.com*

Château Feely: It's the classic tale: couple swap corporate gigs in a big city for the French vineyard dream. Biodynamic wines and a suite of wine tourism activities. *chateaufeely.com*

Château de Fayolle: Great set-up for all the family: wander the grounds, visit the *brocante,* tour the property by 4WD, picnic with paddleboats by the lake. *chateaufayolle.com*

Château de la Jaubertie: Organic vineyard on an estate that once served as Henri IV's hunting lodge. *chateau-jaubertie.com*

PILGRIMAGE ROUTES ACROSS THE DORDOGNE & THE LOT

Pilgrims on their way to Santiago de Compostela in Spain have been traversing this region for centuries en route to St-Jean-Pied-de-Port to connect with the Camino Frances. The two routes:

Voie de Vézelay: Also known as Via Lemovicensis or GR654, this 1100km long, 54-day route begins in Vézelay and visits Limoges, Sorges and Périgueux. A variant passes through Bergerac.

Voie du Puy: Also known as the Via Podiensis or GR65, this 750km-long route begins in Le Puy and passes through the Lot at Figeac, Cahors and Montcuq.

The Voie de Rocamadour, or GR652, is a variant, passing by Collonges-la-Rouge.

---

the other *bastide* towns scattered south of Bergerac. Between April and early November, Wednesdays are a particularly smart day for families to plan a visit, as its garden transforms into a playground of medieval children's games.

The traitor's castle

The combination of a photogenic hilltop setting, a largely intact interior and (just perhaps) the gunpowder stains on the castle walls, has made **Château de Biron** *(chateau-biron.com; adult/child €9.70/6.40)* a coveted film and TV set; most recently as the host of the French version of the popular reality show *The Traitors*. The château stands tall for its blend of architectural styles, thanks to the Gontaut-Biron family's insatiable appetite for DIY across the eight centuries they resided here. For four nights in August, the central courtyard becomes the stage for the atmospheric Les Villégiatures music festival *(lesvilleglatures.com)*.

Issigeac
TIME FROM PÉRIGUEUX: **1HR**

Experience a magical market

Unlike nearby Monpazier's network of perfectly parallel streets, Issigeac's narrow alleys are wound tight like a snail around its Gothic-style Église Saint-Félicien d'Issigeac. For six days of the week, it's a sleepy spot, but you wouldn't know that on a Sunday morning when it comes alive for its weekly produce (and a bit of everything else) market that seeps through every one of its streets. It's one of the most reputed markets in the whole of France.

Sarlat-la-Canéda
TIME FROM PÉRIGUEUX: **1HR 10MIN**

A fine flâneur

Much of the joy of golden-hued Sarlat-la-Canéda comes from embracing the French concept of *flâner*, or the simple art of wandering around while pausing for a drink on a terrace or a bite to eat in one of its many restaurants tucked down pretty side streets, in shaded courtyards or under vaulted cellars. The **Tourist Office** organises tours in English on Thursdays at 2pm, or pick up a guide *(50c)* that points out some of the main sights to take in on foot yourself, including the intriguing, pointed round tower of the 12th-century **Lanterne des Morts**; the stately **Manoir de Gisson** *(manoirdegisson.com; adult/child €9.90/4.80)* for a peek at how the bourgeoisie lived in the

---

EATING & DRINKING IN MONPAZIER & ISSIGEAC: OUR PICKS

The outdoor garden is a delight.

Bière de la Bastide: British-run microbrewery in Monpazier. Home-cooked Sunday lunches are accompanied by live music. *11am-11pm Wed-Sat, noon-10pm Sun* €

Le Croquant: Monpazier locals swear by this cosy lunch spot for great-value cuisine that changes up according to the season. *noon-1.30pm Thu-Tue* €

La Brucelière: Chef Anthony Hardy swapped a Michelin-starred kitchen in Brittany for his own restaurant in Issigeac. *noon-1.15pm & 7-9pm Wed-Sat, noon-1.15pm Sun* €€

Andy's Bar: Is Guinness the best medicine? Find out at this sweet Irish bar in Issigeac that occupies a former pharmacy. *11-10pm Tue-Fri, 6-10pm Sat, 8am-8pm Sun*

Sarlat market

17th century; and the **Ascenseur Panoramique** *(adult/child €5/1)*, a glass lift inside the bell tower of the deconsecrated Église Ste-Marie that takes you to an observation deck 35m high. The views from the top are stupendous.

Sarlat's must-visit markets

Pack your appetite for Sarlat: where the Dordogne meets the Lot, the best local specialities fill its markets, including Périgord strawberries, chestnuts and walnuts. Under the vaulted arches of the **Église Ste-Marie**, Sarlat's *marché couvert* (covered market) is the day-in, day-out workhorse: between April and October, it opens daily from 8.30am until 1pm at the earliest. Stallholders peddle fresh produce and picnic items, but don't forget to take in your surroundings, too: this deconsecrated church was designed by architect Jean Nouvel, who, among his other works, designed the Institut du Monde Arabe in Paris. The pièce de resistance is the sleek metal doors rising 15m high that swing open to reveal the colourful scene. On Wednesday mornings, the produce market spills onto the streets. The scene is repeated on Saturdays, except, alongside food, you can shop for souvenirs, clothes and artisanal wares. In winter, add foie gras and truffles into the mix.

FOIE GRAS EXPLAINED

Despite the controversy around *gavage* (force-feeding) of ducks and geese, there's no escaping foie gras in the Dordogne and Lot, with 90% of all producers in France found along the Dordogne Valley. Blocks of foie gras are sold whole, often *mi-cuit* (lightly cooked) and the dish is also eaten as a mousse, pâté or parfait. Traditionally, foie gras is served cold with a sprinkling of sea salt flakes and a wrist-flick of black pepper on walnut bread with fig jam or onion confit and a glass of sweet white wine such as Monbazillac. If you visit Sarlat-la-Canéda in early March for the annual two-day Fest'Oie, you will see geese running in the streets. Birds raised by artisan farmers are better treated than those farmed industrially.

 EATING & DRINKING IN SARLAT: OUR PICKS

La Chèvre et Le Chou: A vegetarian restaurant in the capital of canard and foie gras! Also vegan and gluten-free choices. *noon-2pm Tue-Sat, 7-9pm Wed-Sat* €

Brasserie La Lanterne: Unpretentious spot in same courtyard as La Chèvre et Le Chou. Bistro classics that don't disappoint. *noon-2pm Tue-Sun, 7-9pm Tue-Sat* €€

Le Bouchon: Sweet little tapas and wine bar with tables spilling into a side street. Cheese and charcuterie platters are huge. *noon-2.30pm & 7pm-1.30am Wed-Sat* €

Le Pub Sarlat: Sundowners on place de la Liberté can become late nights dancing to live music at this spirited bar near the covered market. *9am-midnight Mon-Sat*

ROAD TRIP

Château of the Dordogne Valley

In the Dordogne Valley, towering defensive fortresses that growled at each other during the Hundred Years' War now guide you along one of the world's most glorious stretches of river. Beyond the dramatic castles, this itinerary calls at gracious gardens and photogenic river's-edge villages. It's a short driving tour in terms of distance, but one jampacked with the region's unmissable highlights.

1 Château de Beynac

Begin at **Château de Beynac** (chateau-beynac.com; adult/child €11.50/free), Richard the Lionheart's 12th-century fortress presiding over the river. Climb up to the tower for views of arch nemesis: Castelnaud.

The Drive: After descending from the top of Beynac village to the river, pick up the D49 heading southeast. You'll coast the 5km to the next stop.

2 Jardins de Marqueyssac

It's hard not to be impressed by the **Jardins de Marqueyssac** (marqueyssac.com; adult/child €12.90/6.50) and its *Alice in Wonderland* vibes. Over 150,000 boxwoods are pruned by hand to ensure a picture-perfect aesthetic. A via ferrata course 200m above the river is included as part of the ticket. Open every day in July and August.

The Drive: Back on the road that hugs the river heading east, traffic can get backed up towards the end of the 4km journey to La Roque-Gageac.

Jardins de Marqueyssac

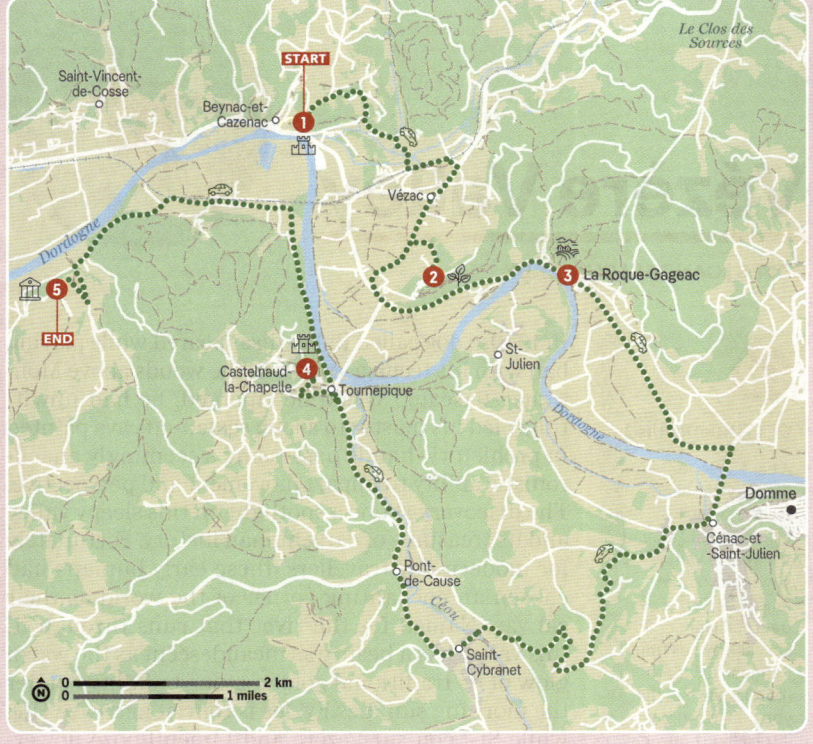

③ La Roque-Gageac

There's something almost unreal about the strip of golden-stone riverfront dwellings that form La Roque-Gageac, although the secret is definitely out. The medieval **Troglodyte Fort** (fortdelaroquegageac.com; adult/child €7/4.50) etched into the cliff above the village can once again be visited after shuttering for years, accessed by a vertiginous staircase. **Gabarres Caminade** and **Gabarres Norbert** share river cruise duties.

The Drive: Cross the Dordogne River, potentially detouring at the village of Domme. Wind through the forested hinterland on a 30-minute drive (window down).

④ Château de Castelnaud

The 12th-century **Château de Castelnaud** (castelnaud.com; adult/child €12.90/6.50) still fiercely guards its prime position on a rocky outcrop facing Château de Beynac – and maintains a penchant for warfare centuries after the Hundred Years' War concluded. Inside its Musée de la Guerre au Moyen Age, learn about trebuchet firing, watch a blacksmith at work and admire weapons and armour.

The Drive: Back driving parallel to the river, it's a gentle 7km to the last stop on a narrow, shaded road.

⑤ Château et Jardins des Milandes

Although built in the 15th century, **Château et Jardins des Milandes**' (milandes.com; adult/child €14/9) most famous owner, American-born performer Josephine Baker, found her dream 'sleeping beauty' castle to raise her 12 adopted children during the 1930s. Listen to her songs while browsing the display of photos and costumes that tell her incredible story. Also daily birds of prey shows between April and November.

Vézère Valley

CAVES | CANOES | CHÂTEAUX

GETTING AROUND
A car allows the mobility you need to visit the many historic sights around the Vézère Valley, although you can reach Les Eyzies by train and Montignac-Lascaux by bus from Périgueux. Sarlat (p618) is the hub that you transfer through if travelling between Les Eyzies and Montignac-Lascaux via bus, unless you are visiting in July and August when there is a direct line, 339. Line 320 connects Montignac-Lascaux and St-Leon-sur-Vézère. Public e-bikes can be unlocked in Montignac-Lascaux and Les Eyzies with La Vézère à Vélo.

In 1940, a dog called Robot disappeared while playing ball with his teenage owner in the woods above Montignac-Lascaux. When he emerged, he had unwittingly led his master to a long sealed-off cave painted in prehistoric hands possessing a seemingly anachronistic ability to impart movement and perspective. The discovery shone a spotlight on this sleepy valley and its treasures of early human history. Fortunately for modern-day travellers, these early humans had chosen an enchanting corner of the world as their canvas. Named for the river that runs through it, this valley has a beauty as incandescent as the warm glow of its traditional golden-stone buildings under the morning sun. Les Eyzies is tourist and cave HQ, while St-Léon-sur-Vézère and Limeuil ooze flower-box-pretty village charm. Montignac-Lascaux warrants time beyond its remarkable caves. This is a part of Dordogne to enjoy above ground, too — through canoeing and cycling and châteaux and cuisine.

Bike Through Prehistory
Pedal power
A gentle 22.3km Voie Verte, or bike lane, hugs the river from Les Eyzies to Limeuil. The **La Vézère à Vélo** station in the centre of Les Eyzies is where you can both sign up and unlock a public e-bike in under five minutes *(per hr €2)*. Leaving the village, you ride through grassy pastures before emerging at the pretty village of Le Bugue snug in the bend of the river. On Tuesday and Saturday mornings the scene is the setting for the weekly produce market. Push on a further 4.5km to Limeuil, with its splendid hilltop garden. Most of the route is along a dedicated path, except for when you cross through Le Bugue. The ride should take about 45 minutes each way, without stops.

☑ TOP TIP
If there's a part of France to map out your travels in advance and book tickets early, it's the prehistoric sites of the Vézère Valley.

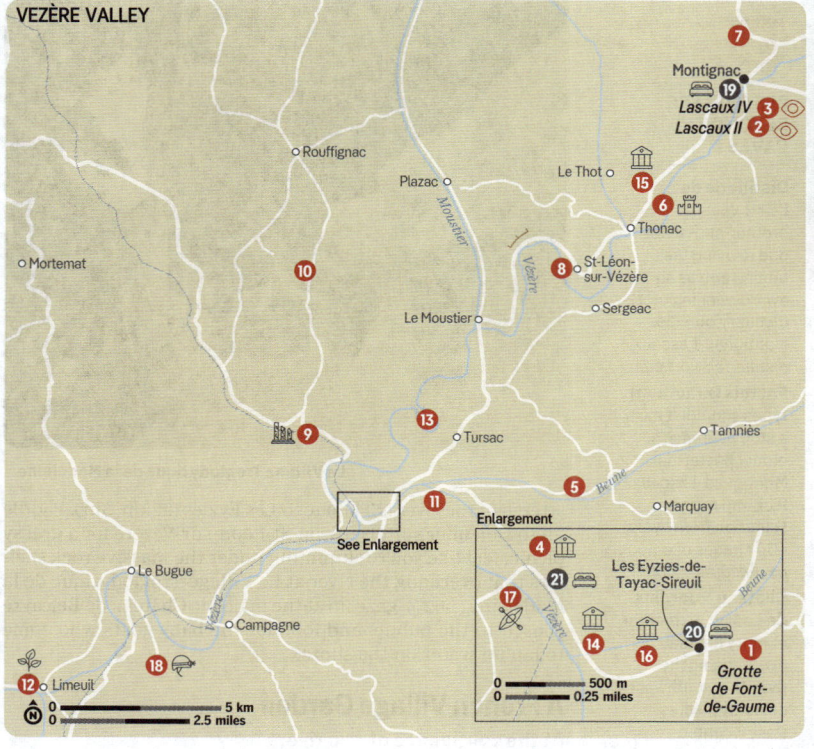

VEZÈRE VALLEY

HIGHLIGHTS
1. Grotte de Font-de-Gaume
2. Lascaux II
3. Lascaux IV

SIGHTS
4. Abri Cro-Magnon
5. Abri de Cap Blanc
6. Château & Jardins de Losse
7. Distillerie de l'Ort
8. Donjon et Manoir de la Salle
9. Gisement du Moustier
10. Grotte de Rouffignac
11. Grotte des Combarelles
12. Jardins Panoramiques de Limeuil
13. Le Village Troglodytique de la Madeleine
14. Musée National de Préhistoire
15. Parc du Thot
16. Pôle d'Interprétation de la Préhistoire

ACTIVITIES
17. Canoës Les Trois Drapeaux
18. Gouffre de Proumeyssac

SLEEPING
19. Hôtel de Bouilhac
20. Hôtel des Roches
21. Hôtel Le Cro-Magnon

EATING
- see 14 La Maison
- see 8 Le Déjeuner sur l'Herbe
- see 8 Le Petit Léon
- see 19 ro.bo

SHOPPING
- see 19 Pastels Girault

TRANSPORT
- see 14 La Vézère à Vélo

Canoe the Vézère

A nautical playground

There is no shortage of canoe and kayak outfits in the Vézère Valley. **Canoës Les Trois Drapeaux** in Les Eyzies *(canoes-3drapeaux.fr; adult/child from €20/10)* proposes a range of suggested itineraries – from the 9km journey between Tursac and Les Eyzies (2hr), as far as the mighty 30km stretch of river from Montignac-Lascaux to Les Eyzies (7hr), shuttle included. In terms of sightseeing, the most concentrated

BEST VÉZÈRE BEYOND THE CAVES

Distillerie de l'Ort: Visit the brother-and-sister duo reviving the family farm as an award-winning craft distillery outside Montignac-Lascaux. *distilleriedelort.com*

Pastels Girault: Arty types shouldn't miss a stop at France's oldest pastel maker in Montignac-Lascaux. Pick and mix your selection from over 400 shades of colour. *pastelsgirault.com*

Château & Jardins de Losse: Sixteenth-century château overhanging the river 6km southwest of Montignac. Rose-scented gardens with tearoom and restaurant. *chateaudelosse.com*

Donjon et Manoir de la Salle: Gleaming medieval estate in St-Leon-sur-Vézère comprising a manor, tower and romantic garden. *manoirsaintleon.com*

Le Village Troglodytique de la Madeleine

stretch of the river is Thonac to Les Eyzies (22km, 5hr). Paddle up to Dejeuner sur l'Herbe at St-Leon-sur-Vézère for a grassy picnic, feel like you're skimming under the massive rock shelters that overhang the river at Le Village Troglodytique de la Madeleine (p627), gaze up at the majestic Château de Belcayre (closed to the public) and look for the baby goats who come to lap up water on the shore.

A French Village Garden
At the confluence of two rivers

Limeuil has an important position at the confluence of the Vézère and the Dordogne. Stand facing the rivers at the entrance to the village: will you follow the flow of the Dordogne towards its clifftop châteaux or the Vézère and its caves and grottoes? But first, take a walk into the immaculately conditioned pedestrian streets that ascend towards the **Jardins Panoramiques de Limeuil** (*jardins-panoramiques-limeuil.com; adult/child €9.80/6.80*), a haven of botanic serenity atop the village.

Chef Nick Honeyman forages daily with his two young daughters.

 EATING IN THE VÉZÈRE VALLEY: OUR PICKS

Le Déjeuner sur l'Herbe: Riverside bolthole where light snacks and salads are enjoyed by the water in St-Leon-sur-Vézère. *10am-7pm Sun-Thu* €

La Maison: Périgord ingredients and global flavours served in an eclectically styled dining room in Les Eyzies. *7.30-10pm Mon-Sun* €€

Le Petit Léon: Michelin-starred venue from Antipodean chef in St-Leon-sur-Vézère is a culinary highlight. *noon-4pm Thu-Sat, 7.30-9pm Tue-Sat Apr-Oct* €€€

ro.bo: If you can't get a table at Le Petit Léon, Honeyman's second address is elevating the Montignac-Lascaux dining scene. *noon-4pm Thu-Sat, 7.30-9pm Tue-Sat* €€€

Lascaux IV

TOP EXPERIENCE

Vézère Caves & Grottoes

Prepare to be awestruck: the Vézère Valley has been occupied by humankind for 400,000 years. Here you'll find caves decorated by the hand of early humans, and rock shelters carved out from cliffs along the valley, alongside two museums to put everything you've seen into context. Tickets to certain sites are limited – so booking well before you visit is highly recommended.

Lascaux II & IV – Which One?

The actual Lascaux cave, known as Lascaux I, sniffed out by Robot in the woods behind Montignac-Lascaux was shut off to the public in 1963 to preserve the site. Today, you can visit Lascaux II, within sight of the original cave, and Lascaux IV, a low-slung modern building poking out of the hillside a few hundred metres away in the village of Montignac-Lascaux itself. Both are precision-perfect replicas of the original cave and its artistic highlights, such as the Great Hall of Bulls and the Frieze of Small Horses, and there are tours in English.

PRACTICALITIES

- Lascaux II & IV: ticketsdordogne.com/en ● Les Eyzies Grottoes: tickets.monuments-nationaux.fr

> **DON'T MISS**
>
> Lascaux – either IV or II, you decide
>
> Grotte de Font-de-Gaume
>
> Grotte des Combarelles
>
> Musée National de Préhistoire
>
> Parc du Thot

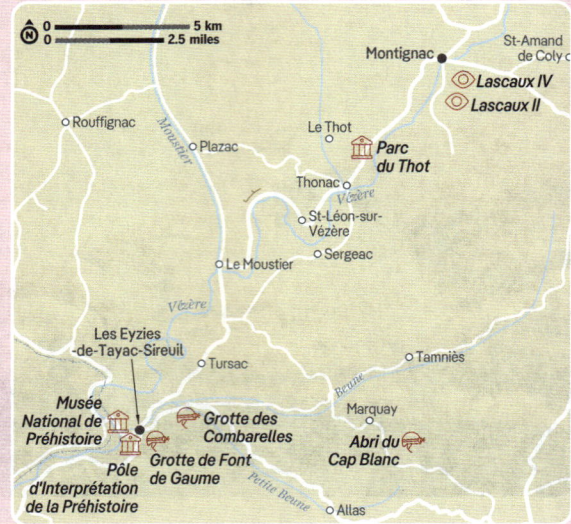

PARC DU THOT

Parc du Thot *(parc-thot.fr; adult/child €10.50/7.20)* is an animal park with a twist between Montignac-Lascaux and Les Eyzies, with large enclosures for descendants of some of the animals early humans hunted and painted, including bison, wolves, deer, aurochs and Przewalski's horses and more. Much of the information presented is in French, yet this is a smart place to break up a day of cave visits for families. Combined tickets with Lascaux II and IV possible.

You don't have to visit both – although, if you do, a combined ticket can be purchased on the ticketing site. The newer Lascaux IV, with its sprawling visitor centre and car park, is by far the more popular choice.

Lascaux IV

Lascaux IV *(lascaux.fr; adult/child €23/15)* opened in 2016. It is a supremely modern museum replicating the entire cave network. The first hour of the visit is with a guide through the replica cave. After that, you are handed a tablet to work through the exciting cutting-edge installations, 3D replicas and interactive screens in the adjoining Lascaux Studio. Plan for your site visit to take a minimum of two hours overall. Tours 12.30-1.40pm are self-guided only.

Lascaux II

Shaded by towering oak trees, **Lascaux II** *(lascaux.fr; adult/child €16/10.50)* opened in 1983 and replicates only 40m of the actual gallery but 90% of the original paintings, as well as the original cave's natural, woodland setting. In small groups, you are guided down into the subterranean space for an hour-long visit. Before leading you through to the cave itself by torchlight, your guide will take some time talking about Lascaux, its discovery, the theories around the identity of the artists as well as the tools they used in a small exhibition space that feels its 40-plus age. It's chilly, dimly lit and a bit damp, but you'll be mesmerised once you're inside the replica cave with its art-filled walls closing in around you. Open from April to November, not wheelchair-friendly.

Les Eyzies Grottoes

Grotte de Font-de-Gaume and Grotte des Combarelles, located close to each other in Les Eyzies, are two of the few original caves in France still open to the public to visit, although numbers are strictly limited – and both sites are closed on Saturday. **Grotte de Font-de-Gaume** *(sites-les-eyzies.fr; adult/child €13/free)*, 1km north of the centre of Les Eyzies, welcomes just 80 people a day on hour-long guided tours (two per day in English, at 11.30am and 1.30pm). Access to the cave is via a steep, narrow path around 400m long, but the rewards are worth it: a majestic gallery of bison, reindeer, horse and mammoth paintings in colour. Parking and the entrance to the **Grotte des Combarelles** *(sites-les-eyzies.fr; adult/child €13/free)* is a further 1.5km east along the road. Rather than paintings, it's the animal engravings carved out of the walls that make this long, narrow cave so enchanting. Only 40 tickets per day are available. Note the official website to buy tickets to both sites is *tickets.monuments-nationaux.fr*.

Les Eyzies Museums

The **Musée National de Préhistoire** *(musee-prehistoire-eyzies.fr; adult/child €6/free)* in Les Eyzies is an excellent starting point to appreciate the history of this valley, with a collection of artefacts, such as animal skeletons, Stone Age tools and a serious amount of teeth, guaranteed to incite wonder in curious children. Nearby, the modern **Pôle d'Interprétation de la Préhistoire** *(pole-prehistoire.com)* has the same objective, but the delivery is more interactive, using films and touchscreens and is free for all visitors.

Know Your Vézère Vocab

Abri Shelter, as in the **Abri Cro-Magnon**, the cave where the first Cro-Magnon remains were found in Les Eyzies. Closed at the time of updating this guide, the site may reopen in 2026.

Grotte Caves where art has been found on the walls, as in the **Grotte de Rouffignac** *(grottederouffignac.fr)* which is visited, in part, on an electric train.

Villages Troglodytiques Prehistoric and medieval living spaces carved into cliff-faces, such as **Le Village Troglodytique de la Madeleine** *(la-madeleine-perigord.com)*.

Gisement An archaeological site where prehistoric evidence has been uncovered, as in the **Gisement du Moustier** *(sites-les-eyzies.fr)*.

Gouffre A cavern or chasm, like the **Gouffre de Proumeyssac** *(gouffre-proumeyssac.com)* outside Le Bugue, with its famed crystal cathedral of stalactites.

ABRI DE CAP BLANC

If you're struggling for tickets to the caves, try the **Abri de Cap Blanc** *(sites-les-eyzies.fr/decouvrir/abri-du-cap-blanc; adult/child €9/free)*, 7.5km east of Les Eyzies. Ths 13m-long frieze of horses and bison sculpted 15,000 years ago showcases further skills of the prehistoric artists. As a lesser-known site, it doesn't book up as quickly, and same-day tickets are often available online. Tours at 1pm are in English.

TOP TIPS

- Make reservations as early as you can, before you even leave for France. Tickets for Grotte de Font-de-Gaume and Grotte des Combarelles sell out online three to four weeks in advance.

- There is a slim chance of picking up a same-day single ticket for either site at the ticket office at Grotte de Font-de-Gaume if you are there before it opens at 9.30am, but don't rely on it.

- If tickets say to arrive in advance, ensure you do. At Grotte de Font-de-Gaume, you must arrive 30 minutes early. Travellers often report being refused entry for turning up closer to their actual tour time.

Cahors

RIVER BREEZE | MEDIEVAL ARCHITECTURE | CLASSY WINES

GETTING AROUND

Cahors is well-served by train from Paris (5 hours) and Toulouse (1 hour), although these are slow, old-school services that call at many stations en route, not the modern TGV lines that make short work of large distances. Snug in a horseshoe bend of the Lot River, the town is compact and flat, with its share of pedestrianised streets, so park up at the edge of the town centre and use your feet to get around.

☑ TOP TIP

If you're planning on visiting some vineyard tasting rooms, best practice is to phone in advance to let them know you're coming.

You might not have heard of Cahors, but the capital of the Lot has given the world malbec wine, has one of the most photogenic bridges on the planet and was the birthplace of Léon Gambetta, the French statesperson whose name adorns a major street in every city in France. History is layered here like the fragrant notes of black fruits and spice that unfurl as you ease into a glass of the inky-coloured, full-bodied red wines that are produced in its soils. First there were the Romans, followed by the medieval moneylenders who propelled the town into a glorious golden age. The name Cahors may no longer echo throughout the known world, but we doubt the Cadurciens, as locals are called, are complaining. Life here is simple and good: fine dining in the shadow of half-timber houses and lazy days by the river. Just ask the Danish royal family, who spend every summer in their grand Château de Cayx (p631) just down the road.

Cahors' UNESCO Treasures

A remarkable bridge and cathedral

Cahors' emblematic bridge, **Pont Valéntré**, built in the 14th century and fully pedestrianised, spans 172m across the river on the western side of town and is particularly pleasing for the pinpoint symmetry of its design. As you walk across it, look out for a small sculpted devil figure scurrying up one of the three defensive towers. According to legend, a pact was made with him to finish the construction. For special events, such as 14 July Bastille Day celebrations, New Year's Eve and St Patrick's Day, the bridge illuminates in colours or is the setting for a stunning firework display.

The town's other UNESCO-listed monument is its 12th-century **Cathédrale St-Étienne**. Don't let first impressions put you off. Despite its grubby exterior, inside overflows with treasures, from two 32m-high domes (the largest built in the Middle Ages, after Hagia Sophia in Istanbul) to its peaceful

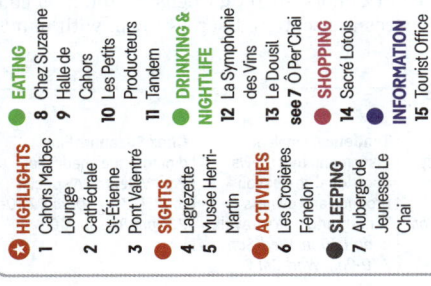

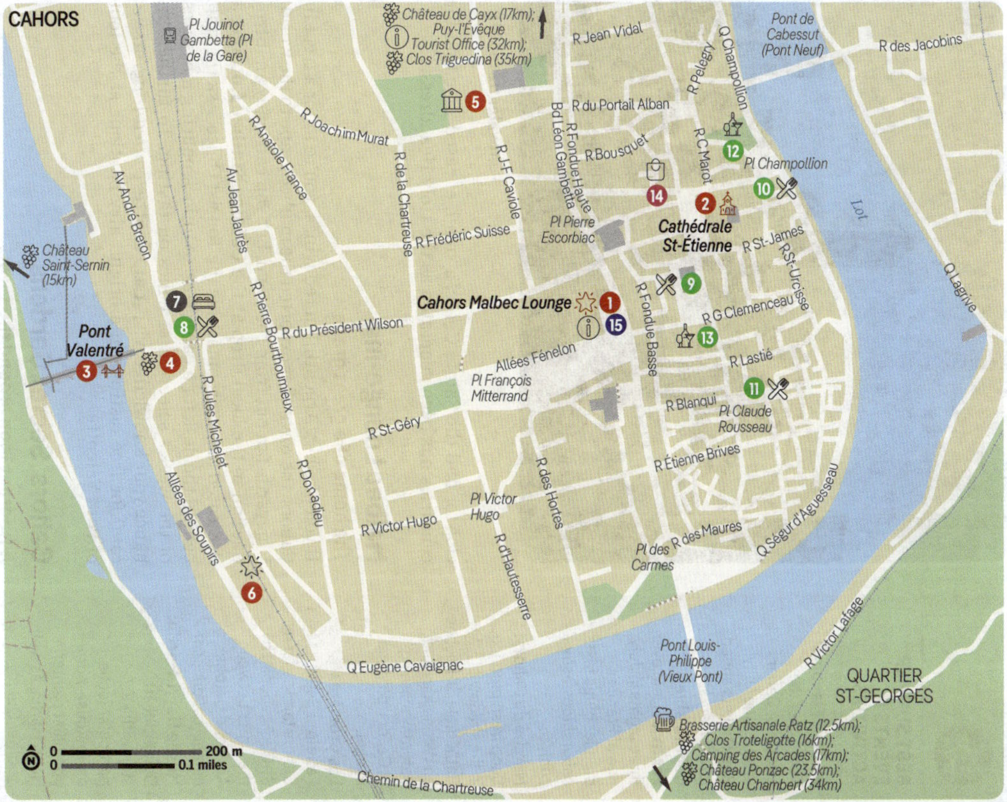

CAHORS

HIGHLIGHTS
1. Cahors Malbec Lounge
2. Cathédrale St-Étienne
3. Pont Valentré

SIGHTS
4. Lagrézette
5. Musée Henri-Martin

ACTIVITIES
6. Les Crosières Fénelon

SLEEPING
7. Auberge de Jeunesse Le Chai

EATING
8. Chez Suzanne
9. Halle de Cahors
10. Les Petits Producteurs
11. Tandem

DRINKING & NIGHTLIFE
12. La Symphonie des Vins
13. Le Dousil
    see 7 Ô Per'Chai

SHOPPING
14. Sacré Lotois

INFORMATION
15. Tourist Office

Pont Valéntré (p629)

BEST SUMMER EVENTS & ACTIVITIES

A Lot of Flavour: Takes over the streets of Cahors in late June/July. Book tickets ahead. *lotofsaveurs.fr*

Cahors Blues Festival: Held over three nights in July; one of France's premier blues fests. *cahorsbluesfestival.com*

Marché de Cahors: Shop fresh produce in the shadow of Cathédrale St-Étienne on Wednesday and Saturday morning at Cahors' produce market.

Les Crosières Fénelon: See Cahors (and as far as St-Cirq-Lapopie) by the water between April and October. *bateau-cahors.com*

Musée Henri-Martin: Delightful art stop with a particular focus on Toulouse-born pointillist painter Henri Martin, as well as other Quercy artists. Open year-round. *musee henrimartin.fr*

cloister and the Sainte Coiffe, a small, encased relic that for centuries has been venerated as the Holy Headdress.

Malbec Lounge-ing
The home of a great grape

If you like big, Argentinian red wines, you're in for a treat in Cahors, the town that exported the malbec grape to the world. Vineyards fan out from the town, but you can enjoy an introduction to the local drop at the **Cahors Malbec Lounge**, a dedicated tasting room inside the Tourist Office. Ask the staff behind the desk for a card *(free)* to unlock pouring measures of the week's selection of wines on tasting. To further enhance your knowledge, visit **Lagrézette** *(chateau-lagrezette.com)* for free tastings in a bright, airy boutique at the foot of Pont Valentré.

Cahors' Secret Gardens
A fragrant loop around the town

While you're at the **Tourist Office**, pick up a free map and set off in search of Cahors' secret gardens. In total, 25 concealed green spaces are scattered across town, with names

EATING IN CAHORS: OUR PICKS

Halle de Cahors: Cahors' covered market particularly buzzes on market days. The Bistrot des Halles has terrace tables. *7.30am-1.30pm & 3.30-7.30pm* €

Les Petits Producteurs: Enjoy the best of Quercy on a pretty square near the cathedral. Also a delicatessen. *9.30am-7pm Mon-Sun* €

Tandem: A small but tasty menu that draws upon local, in-season produce and owners' Tanguy and Lisa's travels. *noon-1.30pm Wed-Sun, 7.30-9pm Wed-Sat* €

Chez Suzanne: Fine dining in the shadow of Pont Valentré. A special treat. *12.30-1.30pm & 7.30-9.30pm Tue-Sat* €€

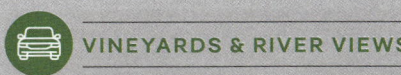

VINEYARDS & RIVER VIEWS

Taste your way along the Lot River with this driving tour through the vineyards of the Cahors AOC.

START	END	LENGTH
Cahors	Cahors	104km, 2hrs

Leaving Cahors from the south, it's a 20-minute drive along the D620/D653 to ❶ **Clos Troteligotte**, where biodynamic wines with poppy names like K-Or and K-Pot can be tasted in an airy barn space. Back on the D653, take the next major right turn onto the D656 towards Sauzet. Stay on the road, heading west past Sauzet, until the D45 appears on your right after about 3km. Not far down it is ❷ **Château Ponzac**, where the rustic tasting room has gorgeous valley views. Back on the D656, head west until the next major turnoff on the right, this time onto the D28 towards Floressas. There's a short, windy incline just before you reach ❸ **Château Chambert**, one of the renowned malbec producers in the region, with a sleek tasting room. If you time your visit for lunch, its fine-dining restaurant, Holodeck, is worth the splurge. Next stop is down near the river, reached along the D58/D5 from Floressas, at ❹ **Clos Triguedina** in Vire-sur-Lot. You can drop in for a free tasting, or book in advance from a program of paying wine-tourism activities, including e-bike itineraries through the vines. Once finished, cross the river on the D44 at Puy-l'Évêque and join the D811/D9 for a 25-minute drive (mostly) along the riverbank to ❺ **Château de Cayx**, the riverfront vineyard of the Danish royal family. Drop into the on-site boutique, before continuing on the D145, the main road, back to Cahors.

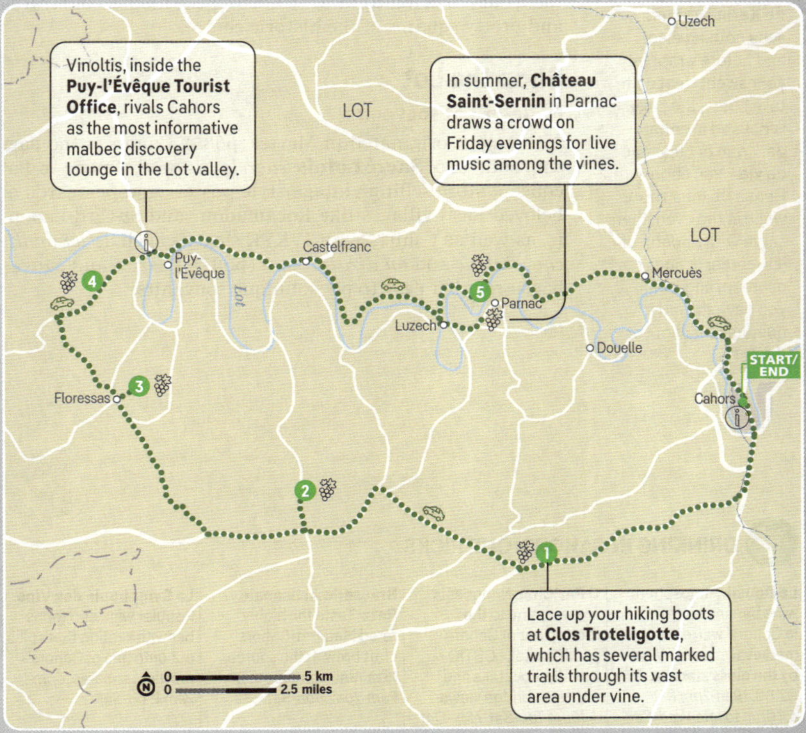

Vinoltis, inside the **Puy-l'Évêque Tourist Office**, rivals Cahors as the most informative malbec discovery lounge in the Lot valley.

In summer, **Château Saint-Sernin** in Parnac draws a crowd on Friday evenings for live music among the vines.

Lace up your hiking boots at **Clos Troteligotte**, which has several marked trails through its vast area under vine.

FRANCE'S OTHER PASTIS

Say the name pastis and you're immediately transported to Marseille and the clear aniseed liqueur that turns cloudy once mixed with water. It's the drink favoured by tanned locals as they play pétanque. But pastis has an altogether different meaning in the Lot, where pastis is a rustic cake made from ultrathin pastry and apples. At Cahors' twice-weekly produce markets, **Le Pastis de Karina**'s stand sells nothing else, and before wrapping your sweet treat up to take home, the cake is doused in either dark rum or clear eau de vie – you choose. Heat it up for a short while in the oven, then serve with a scoop of ice-cream or squirt of cream and, *voilà*, you have the most quintessential of Lot desserts!

Malbec barrels (p630)

like the Garden of Drunkenness and the Garden of the Witch and Dragon. Even if they are not in spring bloom, searching them out is a delightful way to uncover the hidden courtyards and pretty squares of the historic centre.

Shop the Lot

Made-in-Lot souvenirs

Although it originated in Martel (p635), Cahors is the flagship address of **Sacré Lotois** *(sacrelotois.com)*, a made-in-Lot concept store selling vintage-style posters and postcards of beloved local villages like Rocamadour and St-Cirq-Lapopie, as well as t-shirts with IYKYK slogans such as *ici on dit chocolatine* and *on dirait le sud* (p637). Puzzles and canvas bags are other easy to pack, unique souvenirs.

DRINKING IN CAHORS: OUR PICKS

Le Dousil: Atmospheric wine bar and bistro in Cahors' warren of medieval streets. Wine by the glass starts at €2.80. *11am-2pm & 6.30pm to late Wed-Sun*

Ô Per'Chai: Nonguests are welcome to the rooftop bar of Cahors' youth hostel. LGBTIQ+- friendly, cocktails and oh, those bridge views. *3-10pm Tue-Sat, May-Oct*

Brasserie Artisanale Ratz: Taste the highly rated Made-in-Cahors craft brew at the source, 15 minutes outside town. *9am-7pm Mon-Sat*

La Symphonie des Vins: Popular wine and tapas bar with seating that spills out onto one of Cahors' prettiest squares. *6pm-2am Wed-Sat*

Beyond Cahors

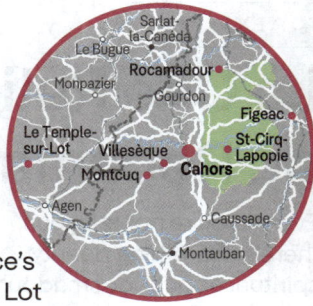

Sacred sites, funny town names and France's first favourite village. There's a whole lotta Lot to see.

The Lot doesn't enjoy the same renown as its neighbour, the Dordogne, but that's a win for those who do traverse its wide, lavender-coated plateaux, through its deep, carved out gorges and along its noble, eponymous river. Historically a part of the long-dissolved French region of Quercy – an identity it still proudly clings to – the Lot is the only *département* covered in this chapter to fall into the region of Occitanie, and leans much more towards Toulouse as its closest big city and the Mediterranean coast than across to Bordeaux and the Atlantic. Not to be confused with it is the Lot-et-Garonne, which cradles both the Lot and the Dordogne. This is rural France, at its bucolic best – but, ssshhh, can you keep it a secret?

Places
Figeac p633
Rocamadour p633
St-Cirq-Lapopie p636
Villesèque p637
Montcuq p637
Le Temple-sur-Lot p638

Figeac
TIME FROM CAHORS: **1HR 15MIN**
Cracking the code

Egyptologist and linguist Jean-François Champollion (1790–1832) has been credited with cracking the Rosetta stone, so it's only fitting that his birth home has transformed into the excellent **Musée Champollion** *(musee-champollion.fr; adult/child €6/free)* dedicated to the written word. Over four floors, the history of writing is traced through some startling artefacts, including Egyptian mummies and cuneiform tablets. The ground floor is a backlit space that slowly unravels Champollion's trials and errors as he attempted to decipher Egyptian hieroglyphics, although his actual breakthrough is scantily covered, which feels frustrating. The building's contemporary façade, an enormous sheet of copper pierced with scripts, is a wonderful juxtaposition with the historic feel of Figeac and its arcades, timestamped windows and upper-storey '*soleilhos*', or open-air galleries. Tucked behind the museum, the place d'Ecritures is inlaid with a massive reproduction of the Rosetta stone. The museum is closed Mondays outside of July and August.

Rocamadour
TIME FROM CAHORS: **1HR**
Rocamadour's other religion

Sacred in the Christian world, the name Rocamadour is also sacred in food circles, revered as one of the finest goat's cheeses

GETTING AROUND

Ideally, you will have your own car (or bike), although the liO public transport network *(lio-occitanie.fr)* does connect Cahors with many major towns and villages of the region, even if departures are often infrequent. The most important services are 889 for Figeac (1hr, 35min) and Bouziès for St-Cirq-Lapopie (30min, plus 5km on foot), 878 direct to St-Cirq-Lapopie (45min) in summer and 882 for Montcuq (45min). Line 876 links Figeac with Rocamadour between early June and late September.

TOP EXPERIENCE

La Cité Religieuse de Rocamadour

Even if you're not religious, there's something deeply spiritual about Rocamadour, one of the four most important pilgrimage sites of medieval Christendom. A huddle of buildings and chapels stuck to a sheer cliff overlooking the Alzou Gorge surrounded by only nature's greens, Rocamadour's very existence feels like one of the miracles granted by its revered Vierge Noire (Black Madonna).

TOP TIPS

- Crowds thin in late afternoon/evening and the village is angled away from the sun.

- View the scene from a hot-air balloon ride with Rocamadour Aérostat (rocamadour-montgolfieres.fr).

- Rocamadour Hot-Air Balloon Festival, last weekend of September, is a visual smorgasbord.

PRACTICALITIES

- sanctuairerocamadour.com ● 7am-10pm Jul-Aug; 8am-8pm May, Jun, Sep; 8am-7pm Apr & Oct; 8.30am-6.30pm Nov-Mar ● free

Sanctuaires

Some pilgrims still climb the 216 steps of the Great Staircase on their knees to reach the Sanctuaires, a complex of seven chapels huddled around a central courtyard. Tucked in the Chapelle Notre Dame, they come to pray for divine intervention before the Vierge Noire (Black Madonna), a modest walnut statue with the *Mona Lisa* effect: despite her diminutive size, you feel her gaze upon you.

La Cité & Le Château

Beneath the Sanctuaires, La Cité is a thin row of golden-hued houses along a pedestrianised street full of restaurants, shops and hotels. Atop the cliff is the 14th-century **Château** (adult/child; €2) that defended the town. The ramparts have excellent views.

Access

Drive down to the bottom of Rocamadour via a twisty road from l'Hospitalet, the neighbourhood at the top of the gorge, and park close to La Cité, or park in l'Hospitalet itself and take the funicular (one way/return €4.40/2.80, every 3 min 9am-7pm) from near the Château to the Sanctuaires. A lift connects the Sanctuaires to La Cité (one way/return €2.30/3.30, under 8 free). The classic footpath from l'Hospitalet is the Chemin de Croix (Stations of the Cross).

Rocamadour goat cheese (p633)

in France. It even has its own Appellation d'Origine Contrôlée (AOC). Follow your nose to **La Borie d'Imbert** *(fermelaboried-imbert.com; free)* a working goat's cheese farm five minutes away from La Cité Religieuse on a high plateau with gorgeous views across the Causses de Quercy. The farm is incredibly well set-up for free self-guided visits to watch the stages of production and walk through the various animal enclosures, even if the smell can be overwhelming at times. Those with young children may prefer to time their arrival to 5–6.30pm to see the goats being fed. An on-site shop does a roaring trade selling cheese, charcuterie and other gourmet delights for a pick-and-mix lunch in a shaded picnic area across the road from the farm.

A subterranean delight

The pioneer of caving, Édouard-Alfred Martel rappelled down the interior of the **Gouffre de Padirac** *(gouffre-de-padirac. com; adult/child €23/18)* chasm in 1889. Fortunately, we don't have to be quite so intrepid today. Descend the 75m-deep opening via a trio of lifts or stairs to the path that flows towards a magical subterranean river that is traversed on a flat-bottom boat. With nothing more than soft spotlights illuminating the walls of the cavern and turquoise water beneath you, it's easy to imagine that, like Martel, you're one of the first people to set eyes on this magnificent cave system. At the

BEST OF THE REST: LOT VILLAGES

Albas-la-Jolie: Lives up to its name, Albas the Pretty. Hooked into the bend of the river, hire canoes from Copeyre *(gabare-copeyre. com)*.

Puy-l'Évêque: A cascade of creamy Quercy stone buildings tumbling down to the water, this postcard-pretty riverside village is in the heart of the Cahors AOC.

Martel: The village of seven towers brims with cool independent boutiques and is the departure point for the historic Train à Vapeur de Martel steam train *(traindu hautquercy.info)*.

Lalbenque: Lights up in winter when connoisseurs from around the country flock here for its famous truffle markets.

Autoire: A gaggle of manors and châteaux have earned this charming spot the nickname Petit Versailles.

 EATING & DRINKING IN FIGEAC & ROCAMADOUR: OUR PICKS

Château de la Treyne: Michelin dining on clifftop overlooking the Dordogne, 20 minutes northeast of Rocamadour. *12.15-1.45pm Sat & 7.15-8.45pm Thu-Tue* €€€

Les Goûts et Les Couleurs: Working farm doubles as an ice-cream shop on the road to Rocamadour. *2-7pm Wed-Mon* €

Barbares: Hip spot in Figeac: local beers, refreshing cocktails, oodles of wine and colourful plates to share – or keep to yourself. *7-10pm Mon-Sun* €

La Racine et La Moelle: Market-fresh modern cuisine and a delightful patio in Figeac's side streets. Book ahead. *noon-2pm & 7.30-10pm Tue & Thu-Sat* €€

St-Cirq-Lapopie

ST-CIRQ-LAPOPIE: GETTING THERE & AWAY

Five car parks surround St-Cirq-Lapopie, with three of them at the top of the village and two more down near the river, requiring a more strenuous walk. Arrive as early as possible to avoid the crowds. A flat fee of €7 applies, although the first 30 minutes are free, as are the hours between 7pm and 8am. Alternatively, you can park 5km away in the riverside hamlet of Bouziès and walk the delightful Chemin de Halage de Ganil, an old towpath that connects the two villages. Almost 1km of the route is carved out of the rockface to create a tunnel effect. In summer, liO bus 878 links Cahors with St-Cirq-Lapopie; year-round, catch 889 to Bouziès to connect with the riverside towpath.

other end, galleries heavy with stalactites lead to a pair of underground lakes and a cathedral that rises 94m high. The classic self-guided visit takes 90 minutes and booking online is recommended, although groups enter the chasm every 15 minutes and you can buy tickets for the next available slot on-site. The ground inside is moist, and there are a lot of stairs, so sturdy shoes are a must, as is a jacket, as the temperature hovers at a steady 13°C and 98% humidity. This also means the cave system is fairly handy for ageing wine, and every year a stash of bottles from Cahors' **Clos Triguedina** (p631) is left underground. Pick up a bottle on-site, or book the ultimate wine experience deep in a subterranean tasting room. Deep pockets are required, too: the price for this VIP wine experience is €500 for a group of one to four people.

St-Cirq-Lapopie

TIME FROM CAHORS: **35MIN**

France's first favourite village

East of Cahors, the small village of St-Cirq-Lapopie with its narrow, cobbled lanes that brim with flower boxes, hugs the cliff side 100m above the Lot. An important defensive town with several fortresses, it featured in the Albigensian crusades, the Hundred Years' War and the Wars of Religion. Today, tourism is its main preoccupation. Looking like something straight out of a Disney fairy tale, it's one of the most beloved villages in France. So much so, the French voted it the inaugural winner of a popular annual contest to name *Le Village Préféré des Français* (The Favourite Village of the French) in 2012. Soak up the medieval atmosphere and browse cute shops – pottery and leatherwork are village specialities. While its fortress is in ruins, the views from the **Castle Ruins** into the valley below are superb.

OTHER FAVOURITE VILLAGES OF THE FRENCH

Since St-Cirq-Lapopie's s victory in 2012, a new favourite village has been elected every summer, including Rochefort-en-Terre (p304) in Brittany in 2016, Hunspach (p338) in Alsace in 2020, and Collioure (p694) in the Languedoc-Roussillon in 2024.

Take a flat-bottom boat trip

The region's traditional wooden flat-bottom boats once ploughed this section of the river, loaded with Cahors wine and tobacco for Bordeaux. Departing daily from Bouziès between April and October, **Les Croisères de St-Cirq-Lapopie** *(croisieres-saint-cirq-lapopie.com)* sail a replica fleet along the river, taking in St-Cirq-Lapopie from the water along with other riverside sights, including the Château des Anglais: a fort squeezed into a crack between two cliffs in Bouziès. Besides its classic '7 Wonders' cruise *(1hr, 10mins)*, you can also embark on a family-friendly pirate adventure to uncover the Lot's hidden treasures in July and August *(1hr)* or opt for a cruise–hike combo to arrive in St-Cirq by boat and return along the Chemin de Halage de Ganil towpath (see 'Getting There & Away' sidebar) by foot.

Villesèque

TIME FROM CAHORS: **20MIN**

The Lot's lavender fields

Although Provence has become world famous for its lavender, the plant also thrives in the Quercy's dry, calcareous soils. So much so, that, at one point, the region grew a tenth of France's total crop. While nowhere near the scale of Valensole, the Lot's lavender fields are still fragrant scenes of beauty – without busloads of tourists jostling for the perfect photo. Just south of Cahors, **Mas de l'Essentiel** *(lemasdelessentiel.fr)* offers more than just a pretty field to frolic in, with a smart QR code set up to guide you through the family-run lavender farm and learn how the plant is grown, harvested and distilled *(free)*. Kids will also love the backpack full of intrepid tools to unlock a series of enigmas around the property *(adult/child €12/8)*. Swirly soaps, among other products, are made on-site, too. If you fancy making some scented souvenirs to take home, book onto one of the soap-making workshops *(€35)*.

Montcuq

TIME FROM CAHORS: **30MIN**

A tiny village with a funny name

Tell anyone French that you're going to Montcuq and wait a beat for their giggle: because this speck of a village south of Cahors has a name that sounds very close to *mon cul* in French (to put as politely as possible, my arse). It's one of the country's favourite village names. If you want to bottle the charm of small town, southwest French life, you could do much worse than spending a day here, particularly on a Sunday morning for its lively and large farmers' market that attracts a crowd from miles; and popular swim spot, the **Lac de Montcuq** (p608).

NINO FERRER'S LE SUD

If you're putting together a playlist for your southern French road trip, Nino Ferrer's *Le Sud* is *the* classic to have on it. The song, which evokes carefree summer days, was released in 1975 but its chorus *'on dirait le sud'* ('we call it the south', as Ferrer croons in the English version) is still guaranteed to bring your French friends together in an all-singing, all-swaying, group huddle. Ferrer, who was born in Genoa, Italy, made the Montcuq countryside his home, where he sadly took his life in 1998. An accomplished artist as well as singer-songwriter, his canvases are on permanent display inside the Tour de Montcuq, the historic tower in the centre of the village.

 EATING & DRINKING ALONG THE LOT: OUR PICKS

Guinguette d'Albas: Casual summer drinking spot opposite the canoe hire in Albas. Live music on Wednesday eve. *11am-late Sun-Mon, 5pm-late Wed-Sat*

Restaurant Le 6: A tapas bar run by an Irishman in Montcuq. Very buzzy on Sunday morning market days. *10am-1.45pm & 5.30-10pm Wed-Sat, 10am-3pm Sun* €

La Tonnelle: Salads, meats, platters all with some form of duck. In St-Cirq-Lapopie. Book ahead. *noon-2pm & 7-9pm Mon-Sun, Jul & Aug* €

Le Gourmet Quercynois: Classic dishes, local wines served on top floor of gorgeous St-Cirq-Lapopie stone building. *noon-1.30pm & 7-8.30pm Mon-Sun* €€

BEST OF THE LOT-ET-GARONNE

Château de Bonaguil: Fairy-tale 15th-century fortress set amid forest is largely ruined yet worth visiting. *chateau-bonaguil.com*

Villeneuve-sur-Lot: France's oldest organic market has taken place every Wednesday morning since 1975 on place d'Aquitaine. *marchebiovsl.fr*

Monflanquin: Superb hilltop *bastide* 45km south of Bergerac.

Penne-d'Agenais: Hilltop village crowned by Basilique Notre-Dame de Peyragude with a zinc dome that can be seen for miles.

Les Folies de Sophie: The Lot-et-Garonne is France's plum garden, thanks to families like Sophie Billat's, who are sixth generation fruit farmers. Visits, tastings, plus treehouses to stay the night. *lesfoliesdesophie.com*

Truffles, all year-round

The treasures uncovered from Jean-Paul Bataille's **Truffes Noires de Montcuq** *(truffesnoiresdemontcuq.com; adult/child €10/5)*, a 500-tree oak grove in a picturesque lavender valley five minutes' drive from the village, are snapped up by fine-dining chefs as far away as Luxembourg. They might get bragging rights to the best produce, but they definitely miss out on the theatre of how they are uncovered: by an overexcitable Lagotto Romagnolo (aka Italian truffle dog) called U2 – yes, after the band – who sniffs out Tuber melanosporum in winter and Tuber aestivum in summer. Over two hours, Jean-Paul and U2 offer a full immersion into the world of truffle farming in French, although handy English reference cards translate much of the detailed content Jean-Paul shares about his passion. Plus, watching U2 sniff out truffles is a joy that translates into any language! For an extra €3, Jean-Paul serves up a plate of truffle shavings on slices of baguette, accompanied by a glass of crisp white wine. You are also welcome to BYO picnic to enjoy among the oak trees.

Le Temple-sur-Lot

TIME FROM CAHORS: **1HR 25MIN**

Monet's water lily supplier

If, like us, you have wondered where Monet sourced his beloved water lilies from, the answer is hiding along the Lot River in the Lot-et-Garonne *département*. Had local horticulturalist Joseph Bory Latour-Marliac not found a way to hybridise white water lilies into a rainbow of warm colours, the world's first water lily nursery would never have sprung into life in 1875 – and Monet would never have become a customer in 1899. This history is traced in a small museum on-site at **Latour-Marliac** *(shop. latour-marliac.com; adult/child €9/free)* which, as well as still supplying water lilies to Giverny (and now Dior), is classified as one of France's remarkable gardens. An afternoon spent browsing over 250 varieties of water lilies growing in rows of deep basins popping with frogs is simply enchanting. Light lunches are served under vines at the on-site cafe. Open 1 May to 30 September, and at its best from June when the tropical water lilies and lotus come into bloom.

A time capsule, opened

Not long after Latour-Marliac died in 1911, his family home five minutes away was sealed off like a time capsule. In 2024, it opened for the first time to the public, as the **Maison-Musée Latour-Marliac** *(nympheas.info; €8/free)*. An easy walk from the nursery, it still preserves much of its turn-of-the-century feel. The property's new owner, landscape architect Thierry Huau, hails from Monet's hometown, Giverny, and has styled each room as a whimsical cabinet of curiosities that traces the influence of plants on art. Cutting-edge visual technologies capture your attention when you least expect it, as mirrors turn into screens, and tables spring to life with dining settings. The mix of old and new is captivating and immersive and you won't want to move onto the next room until you're sure to have uncovered every nugget of information the current one holds.

Limoges

ARTS & CRAFTS | SHOPPING | INTRIGUING FOODS

The biggest city of the Dordogne-Lot-Limousin region, Limoges is also its most gritty, lively, artsy – and interesting. Think buzzy dining and drinking precincts, with a vibe even on weeknights, small boutique shopping and global cuisine. Plus, delightfully historic streets that bring you face-to-face with slumped half-timber houses which, in a city founded by the Romans in 10 BCE, are in fact verging on modern.

Limoges is built on crafts, porcelain to be precise, and is ordained a UNESCO Creative City, so it brims with cool, artistic types. While mid-to-late 20th century town planning hasn't been kind to the city, with the outskirts marred by uninspiring concrete residential blocks, discard them like layers of an onion until you get to the core and you will find that this is a destination definitely worth the detour. So resist the temptation to drive on by.

> ### ✅ TOP TIP
> A lot closes in the city – and the region – on a Tuesday, including the city's outstanding museums and many restaurants. If at all possible, time your visit for another day of the week.

Limoges' Precious Porcelain
A fine craft heritage

The discovery of kaolin, a key ingredient in porcelain fabrication, near Limoges in the 18th century changed the course of the city's history and made it a name to be revered inside France's royal palaces. Limoges porcelain still graces legendary addresses like the Ritz hotel in Paris. The city's world-class

GETTING AROUND

Limoges' two historic districts, the Château quarter and La Cité, are mainly pedestrianised, so best navigated by foot. Street parking is free for the first 30 minutes. There's also a large open-air car park near Gare des Bénédictins train station and Musée National Adrien Dubouché. Free electric shuttles *(limoges.fr/pratique/des-navettes-electriques-en-centre-ville)* run every eight minutes (10am–6:30pm, Wednesday–Saturday) on loop, connecting some of the most popular attractions. The city also has a fleet of Pony *(getapony.com)* public e-bikes.

LIMOGES

★ HIGHLIGHTS
1. Cathédrale St-Étienne
2. Musée des Beaux Arts
3. Musée National Adrien Dubouché

● SIGHTS
4. Chapelle St-Aurélien
5. Conservatoire Ferroviaire Territoires Limousin Périgord
6. Cour du Temple
7. Frac-Artothèque Nouvelle-Aquitaine

see 5 Gare des Bénédictins

8. Jardin de l'Évêché
9. Musée de la Résistance
10. Pavillon du Verdurier
11. Rue de la Boucherie

● SLEEPING
12. Hôtel de Paris

● EATING
13. Chez Alphonse
14. Halles Centrales
15. La Cuisine du Cloître
16. Le Bouillon Limousin
17. Les Petits Ventres

● INFORMATION
18. Tourist Office

Musée National Adrien Dubouché (*musee-adriendubouche. fr; adult/child €7/free*) is dedicated to the material, with tall, almost floor-to-ceiling, shelves full of precious artefacts displayed chronologically, starting with pottery from Ancient Greece, followed by early pieces from China and then Europe. As you climb the four floors of the museum, designs change to reflect the fashions of the era. The war porcelains fired during WWI are especially sobering. One of the oldest porcelain manufacturers, Royal Limoges (*royal-limoges.fr*), has a city centre location with an outlet store and its own museum, the **Four des Casseaux** (*museedescasseaux.com; adult/child €4.50/free*), where the standout feature is a 2-storey brick kiln that you can walk inside.

The Pre-Porcelain Cité
A hub of Roman and medieval history

Of course, Limoges has a rich pre-porcelain story to tell, too, and La Cité, a neighbourhood that dates from the 4th century, is the place to learn it. First up, the **Cathédrale St-Étienne** (*cathedrale-limoges.fr*), the city's enormous cathedral. The first foundation stones were laid in 1273, yet it wasn't completed until 1888. Facing it, the **Musée des Beaux Arts** (*beauxarts. limoges.fr; adult/child €5/free*) is a must-visit attraction that traces Limoges' Roman foundation, when it was known as Augustoritum, through to its absolute mastery of enamel work in the Middle Ages. The museum's fine art collection is also top class. Surrounding both sites is the **Jardin de l'Évêché**, a delightful public garden with terraced flower beds overlooking the river and shaded spots for a tranquil picnic.

Dare to Try Market Specialities
Test your stomach

Limoges' **Halles Centrales** covered markets open at 7am, but that might be a little too early to sample some of the local delicacies, particularly *grillons limousins*, a pâté-like regional speciality fashioned out of seasoned pork fat, or the various cuts of tongues, testicles and feet that comprise the city's culinary cookbook. The other typically Limousin snacks you can find here are less polarising: *pâté aux pommes de terre* (a potato pie), or sweet cherry and apple clafoutis. You can also pick up picnic favourites: wedges of cheese, rotisserie chicken and freshly harvested fruits and vegetables.

BEST UNDER-THE-RADAR ATTRACTIONS

Musée de la Résistance: Trace the history of Limoges' resistance against Nazi occupation in WWII through wartime memorabilia. *resistance.limoges.fr*

Frac-Artothèque Nouvelle-Aquitaine: Old industrial building in the centre of town revived as a hip space for contemporary art in 2025. *fracartotheq uenouvelleaquitaine.fr*

Underground Tours: Check with Tourist Office for availability of its guided forays into secret galleries and vaulted cellars underneath the city. *destination-limoges. com*

Limoges Greeters: Free walking tour with a local. *greeters.fr/ limoges-metropole*

Conservatoire Ferroviaire Territoires Limousin Périgord: Visit the Limousin countryside on a steam train. Departures in July and August. *trainvapeur.com*

 EATING IN LIMOGES: OUR PICKS

Le Bouillon Limousin: A taste of Paris' cheap and cheerful *bouillons* in the provinces. Book ahead. *9am-1.30pm Tue-Sat & 7-8.30pm Thu-Sat* €

La Cuisine du Cloître: Chef Guy Queroix lists the season's ingredients but little else on his daily menu. *noon-1.45pm Wed-Sun & 8-9.45pm Wed-Sat* €€€

Chez Alphonse: Quintessential French bistro next to Halles Centrales with dishes like *pied de cochon* (pigs trotter). *noon-2pm Mon-Sun & 7.30-10.30pm Mon-Sat* €

Les Petits Ventres: Limousin cuisine served up in a half-timber dining room on rue de la Boucherie. *noon-2pm & 7-9.30pm Tue-Sat* €€

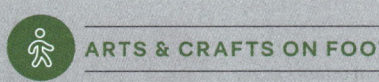

ARTS & CRAFTS ON FOOT

View the historic centre of Limoges through an Arts and Crafts lens. The city overflows with artistic detail in places least expected.

START	END	LENGTH
Gare des Bénédictins	Rue de la Boucherie	2km, 45min

A big question to start this walking tour of Limoges: do you agree with those who say that ❶ **Gare des Bénédictins** is the most beautiful train station in Europe? Whatever you think, there are worse first impressions to a city. The ❷ **Tourist Office**, almost diagonally southwest of the station, is stocked with some of the city's porcelain treasures. It's a good stop to see who, among the current crop of artisans, appeal to your tastes. Just around the corner, on rue du Collège, the ❸ **Pavillon du Verdurier** is an octagonal building dating from 1919 covered in shimmering gold, green and blue tiles in the middle of a busy street. Nearby, as you head into the historic heart of the city ❹ **Cour du Temple**, a hidden courtyard framed by 16th-century half-timber façades tucked between rue du Temple and rue du Consulate. From there, it's a couple of minutes to the ❺ **Halles Centrales** (p641) on place de la Motte. Even if the city's market is closed, you can still admire the intricate tile detailing around the upper edges. Nearby, ❻ **Rue de la Boucherie** is one of Limoges' most atmospheric streets and the hub of the Boucherie district. Home to a cluster of butchers' shops in the Middle Ages, it now brims with trendy bars and restaurants – and plenty of half-timbered houses angled like the Leaning Tower of Pisa.

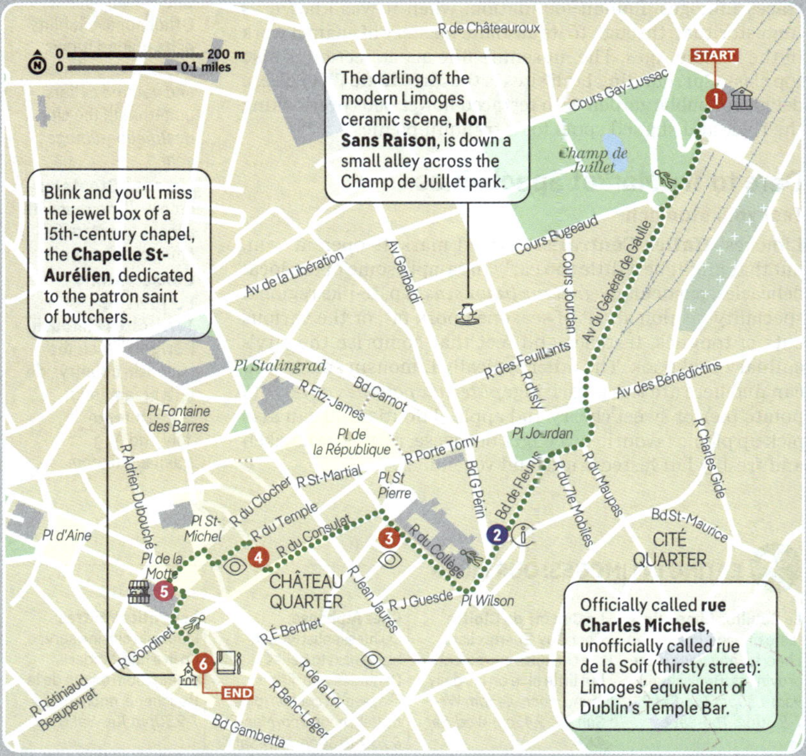

Beyond Limoges

The rewards of some of France's least-visited corners: artists' landscapes, moving history and villages the earth has stained red.

The little-known, seldom-visited *départements* of the Creuse and Corrèze in the Limousin are a time-capsule of life from decades ago. Even the mobile network drops out as you move through its sleepy country roads. Claude Monet lucked out here in search of the rural idyll to immortalise on canvas. One can only wonder what he and his artist friends would have made of the red village of Collonges-la-Rouge, had they just ventured a little further south. Closer to Limoges and the region's important place at the crossroads of history is everywhere you look, none more emotive than Oradour-sur-Glane, a village frozen in time the day the Germans invaded in 1944. Do you dare to get off-the-beaten-track, even for a few hours?

Places
Oradour-sur-Glane p643
Crozant & Fresselines p644
Collonges-la-Rouge p646

Oradour-sur-Glane
TIME FROM LIMOGES: **20MIN**

Terror frozen in time

More than 80 years on, the terror that ripped through Oradour-sur-Glane on 10 June 1944 is still palpable. The effect of walking along real streets framed by charred, crumbling buildings with rusting 1930s automobiles parked in the very spot their owners left them all those years ago is a far greater lesson on the horrors of war than any history book or war drama.

Access to the **Martyr Village**, as the ruined town is known, is free and through the **Centre de la Mémoire** *(oradour.org; adult/child €7.80/free)*. You can pass through the centre directly to the village, although it is highly recommended to pay the entrance fee to the unmissable and, at times, confronting historical background on display about the massacre, including heartbreaking mementos such as the last class photos ever taken at Oradour's schools and the tokens of daily life that have been salvaged from the ruins.

The detail still doesn't prepare you for the sombre air that hangs over the crumbling town. Signs explaining what service stood in each building, whether a bakery, doctor's surgery or restaurant, show just how vibrant life here was and contrast with the moving memorials outside the buildings where the people were executed. Etched into the main road are tram tracks that once connected Oradour with Limoges and now go nowhere, a metaphor for the hundreds of lives cut short that day.

GETTING AROUND

This is deep in what the French call the *diagonale du vide*, which falls from right to left across France like a beauty queen's sash, through a swathe of vastly underpopulated regions. Fortunately, the A20, one of the country's most important road arteries, cuts straight through rural Limousin. Your own wheels are essential.

Martyr Village (p643), Oradour-sur-Glane

THE HORRORS OF WAR

On the afternoon of Saturday 10 June 1944, lorries of Germany's SS 'Das Reich' Division surrounded Oradour-sur-Glane. It was market day, so the village was busier than normal, full of chattering visitors and children playing. The men were herded into barns, where they were machinegunned before the structures were set alight. Several hundred women and children were hurried into the church, which was also set on fire. In total 642 people, including 193 children, were killed. Only one woman and five men who were in the town that day survived the massacre. Rather than reconstruct it, Charles de Gaulle vowed to leave the site untouched as a reminder of the horrors of war. A new town has risen alongside it.

In 2017, a wall of photos of the victims was erected, and their faces form an emotional guard of honour as you enter and exit the village. Expect a heavy presence of school groups on weekdays – but rather than being annoyed, be thankful that such atrocities are far from being forgotten. The Centre is closed from mid-December to mid-January annually.

Crozant & Fresselines

TIME FROM LIMOGES: **1HR 10MIN**

The grandest ruin

If it wasn't ruined, the **Forteresse Médiévale de Crozant** (*forteresse-crozant.com; adult/child €4.50/free*) would surely be one of France's grandest sites. Even in its crumbling state, it's obvious this fortress, which occupies a finger-thin promontory with sublime views of the confluence of the Creuse and Sédelle rivers, was an absolute tour de force in the Middle Ages. At its apogee, it spanned 380m and encompassed 10 towers! This alone makes the contrast with how forgotten these ruins, and the Creuse in general, are today even more striking. Over a dozen information panels placed around the site help you picture how lively it must have been in its medieval heyday. It's a place to scramble around, so wear sturdy footwear – and don't be surprised if you have the site all to yourself.

Discover the École de Crozant

Monet never made it to Crozant, too busy was he painting river scenes in nearby Fresselines, but plenty of other artists did: in fact, so much did the local landscape capture the rural idyll for landscape painters that a whole artistic movement arose from the village: the École de Crozant. Learn their names and see some of the original works of art they painted at the **Musée Hôtel Lepinant** (*hotel-lepinat.com; adult/child €6.50/3*). Once the *auberge du jour* to rest their heads, it's now

MONET'S RURAL IDYLL

Retrace Claude Monet's footsteps along the banks of the Creuse River in Fresselines: so idyllic is the setting, he painted it 23 times.

START	END	LENGTH
Espace Monet Rollinat	Espace Monet Rollinat	3.2km, 1hr

Start this bucolic walk through artists' country outside ❶ **Espace Monet Rollinat**. With the building on your right, walk down towards the Creuse. The road is steep; just after it curves around to the right, you will see the grass trail that cuts down towards the river. As you come out on the road below, you'll see the first of Monet's paintings bookmarked: ❷ **Le Pont de Vervy** (you may remember driving over it to reach the village). From there, head back up the road. It's a bit of a climb but it flattens out just before the water tower. Turn left here onto ❸ **Chemin de Confolent** and pass a small car park on your right. Continue straight ahead, cutting through a field where cows silently graze on a path that leads towards the river. After about five minutes, and two more signposted scenes Monet painted, you emerge at the ❹ **Confluent des Deux Creuses**, the Petite Creuse and the Grande Creuse, where he stood to paint his series 'Les Eaux Semblantes'. The stretch between here and the *passerelle* to cross to the other side of the river is glorious, particularly around the spot where he captured ❺ **Torrent de la Petite Creuse à Fresselines**. Two more artistic bookmarks follow on the other riverbank, before the path crosses back across the river on the sturdy ❻ **Pont du Bois** and loops back up into town.

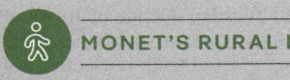

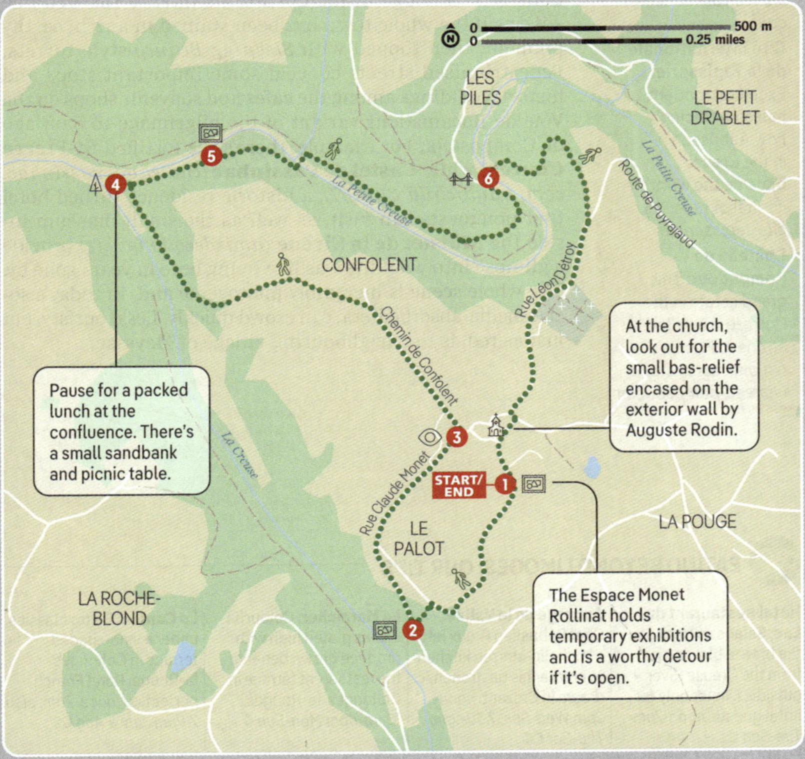

0 500 m
0 0.25 miles
LES PILES
LE PETIT DRABLET
La Petite Creuse
Route de Puyrajaud
CONFOLENT
Rue Léon Détroy
Chemin de Confolent
Rue Claude Monet
START/END
LE PALOT
LA POUGE
LA ROCHE-BLOND
La Creuse
Pause for a packed lunch at the confluence. There's a small sandbank and picnic table.
At the church, look out for the small bas-relief encased on the exterior wall by Auguste Rodin.
The Espace Monet Rollinat holds temporary exhibitions and is a worthy detour if it's open.

BEST MUSEUMS & MORE BEYOND LIMOGES

Château de Châlus-Chabrol: Feels more like a dusty bric-a-brac store than the storied location south of Limoges where Richard the Lionheart died.

Musée Départemental d'Art Contemporain Chateau De Rochechouart: 45km west of Limoges, this château houses over 1300 works of contemporary art. *musee-rochechouart.com*

Cité Internationale de la Tapisserie: Excellent modern museum tracing how Aubusson in the Creuse became the world capital of tapestry. *cite-tapisserie.fr*

Château de Pompadour: This grand estate in the Corrèze is reputed as one of France's national horse studs. *chateau-pompadour.fr*

a museum (closed Monday and Tuesday outside of July and August). Afterwards, set off on foot to see the spots where they once placed their easels on a signposted trail, Le Sentier des Peintres, that leaves from the village. The route is outlined outside the museum, or ask at the front desk for a map. The fairly gentle 4km path takes a little over an hour to complete and passes by millhouses and fields of French broom and is punctuated with signs showing who painted what where.

Trains, boats and canoes

The charming waterfront **Hôtel Restaurant du Lac** *(hoteldulac-crozant.com)* is a bit of an unexpected tourist hub in low-key Crozant and runs 70-minute-long river cruises *(adult/child €15/9; reserve in advance)* between mid-April and late September, as well as canoe and kayak hire *(per hr from €7)* from its front desk. The hotel even operates the mini-train *(petittrain-crozant.com; adult/child €10/5)* that leaves from outside the Musée Hôtel Lepinant. The property shutters on Mondays.

Collonges-la-Rouge TIME FROM LIMOGES: 1HR 20MIN
The red village

The presence of iron oxide in the local stone is what gives Collonges-la-Rouge in the Corrèze its intense rust-red hue – it's as if the whole town has been stained in a rich, earthy pigment, then topped with *Sleeping Beauty*-style turrets. Pedestrianised streets conceal some important stops and historic buildings among the cafes and souvenir shops on the Voie de Rocamadour variant of the pilgrimage to Santiago de Compostela. For example, there's the fortified **St-Pierre Church**; while **Castel de Vassinhac** *(chateaudevassinhac.com; adult/child €8.50/7)*, a historic residence turned hotel that nonguests can visit, as well as the small museum inside the **Maison de la Sirène** *(amisdecollonges.fr)* provide a glimpse into what life was like living here in years gone by. The whole scene is incredibly photogenic and, in today's social-media-absorbed-era, can crowd quickly. Less touristy, but just as red, is the neighbouring village of Meyssac.

EATING BEYOND LIMOGES: OUR TIPS

Hôtel Restaurant du Lac: Salads as fresh as the breeze blowing in from the Creuse River outside. Dinner only for hotel guests. *noon-2pm Tue-Sun* €

Auberge de la Vallée: Chef Sébastien Proux left a Michelin-starred kitchen to create this gastronomic dream in Crozant. *noon-2pm Wed-Sun, 7.30-9pm Thu-Sat* €€

Le Maraîcher: Colourful dishes plated high with produce grown beneath the restaurant terrace in Collonges-la-Rouges. *10am-11pm Mon-Sun* €

Le Cantou: Bistro classics under a vine-shaded terrace in Collonges-la-Rouge. Rural French perfection. *noon-2pm, also 7-9pm July & Aug* €€

Places We Love to Stay

€ Budget €€ Midrange €€€ Top End

Périgueux & Around — MAP p611

Villa Medicis € Stéphanie and Pascal's cosy Brantôme B&B is a five-minute walk from town. Three rooms ooze rustic charm, as do chickens in their large garden.

Hostellerie Les Griffons €€ A storybook setting on the Dronne River in Bourdeilles. Ten rooms with river views and antique fireplaces, as well as a gastronomic restaurant.

Hôtel Mercure Périgueux Centre €€ Périgueux is crying out for some stylish boutique city-centre options. Until that happens, this brand name is clean and modern, with a great location.

Bergerac & Around

La Brucelière € Five rustic yet quaint rooms, completely refreshed in 2024, above the restaurant of the same name in Issigeac.

Hôtel de Bordeaux € Like Périgueux, accommodation choices are limited in the centre of Bergerac. This is a clean and comfortable, if not generic, choice. Pool is a bonus.

Hôtel Edward 1er €€ Chic bolthole in a turreted château at the edge of Monpazier. Pool loungers are the place to be in summer.

Dordogne Valley

Auberge de Jeunesse Cadouin € Unique opportunity to stay in a UNESCO-listed Cistercian abbey. Some dorms have direct cloister views.

Camping le Capeyrou € Large riverside pitches with stunning views of Château de Beynac.

La Lanterne €€ Guesthouse in Sarlat's historic centre that oozes period character. Five rooms and one self-catered apartment. Breakfast is wonderful.

Vézère Valley — MAP p623

Hôtel des Roches € Rooms are a bit dated but the price is right and there's on-site parking, a big garden for kids to run off energy and a swimming pool. Les Eyzies.

Hôtel Le Cro-Magnon € The charming choice in Les Eyzies with a wisteria-clad façade and part of the building carved into the cliff.

Hôtel de Bouilhac €€ Dreamy stone residence originally owned by Louis XV's doctor in Montignac. The interior decor is inspired by the era. On-site restaurant, ro.bo (p624) is a big plus.

Cahors — MAP p629

Auberge de Jeunesse Le Chai € Bright and airy youth hostel in a sleek and modern building, with close-up views of Pont Valentré from its rooftop terrace.

Camping des Arcades € Delightful family run campsite set around an old Quercy stone watermill near Villesèque's lavender fields.

Beyond Cahors

Camping de Floiras € Dutch couple Susan and Erik have been running this sweet riverside campsite for 35 years. Large grassy plots for tents, caravans and motorhomes. Dedicated space for cyclists.

Hôtel Le Quatorze € Shaded spot on the edge of Figeac's old-town with a garden, lift and, as of 2025, air-con in every room. Breakfast is a smorgasbord of local produce.

Hotel les Esclargies €€ Sixteen rooms, many with balconies in Rocamadour, in shaded parkland close to La Cité. Parking is a real plus.

Château de la Treyne €€€ The most legendary inn in the region, this turreted castle clings to the clifftop above the Dordogne River. Utter magic.

Limoges & Beyond — MAP p640

Hôtel de Paris € Longstanding Limoges favourite close to the train station and the historic centre, with some wonderful period features and cuddly resident cats.

Hôtel Restaurant du Lac € Sunny rooms in a riverside inn just outside Crozant. The setting – like you've stepped out of the modern world – is the real selling point.

Le Nid des 2 Creuse € Motorbike-friendly B&B in Fresselines with the most gorgeous breakfast room we encountered during our research.

Above: Petit Train Jaune (Little Yellow Train; p692); Right: *Cassoulet* (p685), Carcassonne

Researched by
Paul Stafford

Languedoc-Roussillon

ARTISTIC INSPIRATION AND CULINARY DIVERSITY

Bas (Lower) Languedoc's coastal cities, Haut (Upper) Languedoc's natural beauty and the Catalonia-France-Spain mélange of Roussillon provide a heady mix of cuisines, cultures and architectural landmarks.

Languedoc-Roussillon is an individualistic and proud region of France, whose well-preserved past coexists with debonair modern living.

Thin, sandy bars span most of the coastline, separating the Mediterranean from a series of salt pans and *étangs* (lagoons) that teem with wildlife. The historic cities in this region are relatively flat, accessible, and packed with fabulous architecture and youthful energy.

Away from the sea, the land begins to crumple like crepe paper, first into gentle escarpments covered in vineyards and olive groves, and then into jagged peaks and deep gorges. This sparsely populated, little-visited region epitomises the magic of travel, where formidable Cathar castles crumble on inhospitable mountaintops, thrilling roads probe the many wild recesses and, when the tarmac runs out, rivers and trails galore are perfectly suited to the whims of thrill seekers and outdoors enthusiasts.

Take a magnifying glass to Languedoc-Roussillon and it fragments even further: when the Cévennes mountain range evolves into the Pyrenees further south, so too do the languages, customs and cuisines, as the frontiers of France, Spain and Catalonia begin to merge.

One consistent note throughout is the top-quality food and drink, including crisp white wines and oysters on the coast, spicy sausage, olives and tomatoes on the borders of Spain, rich stews around Carcassonne, and pungent blue cheeses, such as Roquefort, from the limestone caves of the Causses' plateaux.

THE MAIN AREAS

NÎMES
Foodie credentials and Roman relics.
p654

MONTPELLIER
Art galleries and nightlife.
p663

CAUSSES ET CÉVENNES
Gorges and mountains.
p675

CARCASSONNE
Fairy-tale castles and sparkling wine.
p682

PERPIGNAN
A taste of Catalan culture.
p686

Find Your Way

Whether seeking sweeping beaches or hilly hinterlands, you're likely to base yourself in one of the well-connected lowland cities. Each one displays its distinct personality in fascinating ways through history, cuisine and culture.

Carcassonne, p682
Explore the historic crenellations of a vast fairy-tale citadel, sample Languedoc wines on a guided tour and get to know the Canal du Midi.

CAR

The joy of exploring Languedoc-Roussillon is in the unexpected discoveries. Practically every town and village has its own medieval church, tumbledown fortress or abbey. To experience the best sides of this destination, your own transport is essential. Much of the Haut Languedoc and Pyrenees regions are otherwise inaccessible.

BUS

There are decent bus routes from main cities radiating out to surrounding towns, particularly further south. Look for the red regional buses run by liO. Flixbus and Blablacar Bus operate most of the intercity services.

TRAIN

Bas Languedoc's coastal cities and Carcassonne are well served by regular, efficient local (TER) and national (TGV and Intercités) trains, all operated by SNCF. Montpellier is the main regional hub, with sizeable stations at Nîmes and Perpignan. Regular onward trains head to Paris, Toulouse, Marseille and Barcelona.

Perpignan, p686
Experience the crossroads of French, Catalonian and Spanish cultures through food, wine and spirits, plus visit the hangouts of top fauvist and cubist luminaries.

Causses et Cévennes, p675

Remote traditional villages contrast with vertiginous mountains grooved with gaping gorges and webs of hiking trails in this must-see destination for nature lovers.

Nîmes, p654

Catch a show in the Roman amphitheatre, taste the city's burgeoning food revolution and kayak beneath a UNESCO World Heritage Site.

Montpellier, p663

The regional capital is abuzz with youthful energy. Experience the nightlife, kick back on an uncrowded beach and seek form's perfection in a major art gallery.

Plan Your Time

Explore some of the finest landmarks in Languedoc-Roussillon over a few neatly planned days or find your ideal pace for delving deeper into Roman ruins, wine tours and rugged hiking trails.

Canoeing, Gorges du Tarn (p675)

Short Stay, Big Sights

● **Nîmes** (p654) embodies many of Occitania's finest qualities. Start with a wander through the city centre, where Roman ruins such as **Les Arènes** (p654) and the **Maison Carrée** (p657) temple are among the world's best preserved. Spend the afternoon ambling around the **Jardins de la Fontaine** (p657) or take a bus to the **Pont du Gard** (p660), a three-tiered Roman aqueduct.

● The next day, head southwest to **Carcassonne** (p682) to explore the **Cité Médiévale** (p682) and its 3km of ramparts with 52 towers. To slow things down a little, cycle along the **Canal du Midi** (p670) and hire a car for a couple of days to drive the thrilling road through the precipitous **Gorges du Tarn** (p675).

Seasonal Highlights

Spring and autumn are the ideal seasons for many outdoor experiences. Beaches fill up in summer, but the mountains offer a cooler escape.

MARCH
Spring's onset brings beautiful blossoms to the cherry trees around **Céret** (p692) and meadow flowers to the mountain plateaux of the **Grands Causses** (p675).

APRIL
Trails in the **Cévennes** (p675) begin to fill with people attempting long-distance treks such as the Stevenson Trail in optimal hiking conditions.

APRIL/MAY
The Roman Days of Nîmes, aka **Les Grands Jeux Romains** (p655), fill the streets with gladiatorial duels, Roman encampments and raucous parades for three days.

A Week-Long Sojourn

● A seven-day itinerary allows time for short hops between the coastal cities. Start in **Montpellier** (p663), where you'll find world-class art galleries such as **Musée Fabre** (p663), then sample local produce such as juicy oysters and crisp Picpoul de Pinet white wine in **Sète** (p673). Next, head to **Béziers**, where the **Cathédrale St-Nazaire** (p671) sits above the Orb River.

● Nearing the Spanish border, discover the North Catalonian region of Roussillon and the former Majorcan kingdom's main seat, the **Palais des Rois de Majorque** (p687), in **Perpignan** (p686). Art was forever changed in Roussillon, where luminaries such as Pablo Picasso and Henri Matisse honed their singular forms of artistic expression. Discover how along the **Chemin du Fauvisme** (p694) in **Collioure** and at the **Musée d'Art Moderne** (p692) in **Céret**.

Four Wheels, 14 Days

● Delve inland to explore Haut Languedoc's little-visited bounty of charming villages and mountain scenery. Start at **St-Guilhem-le-Désert** (p669), with the **Abbaye de Gellone** (p669) at its core. Continue to **Cirque de Navacelles** (p679) for its impeccable wilderness vistas. Hiking is in the marrow of the Cévennes. Tackle its myriad of short- and long-distance routes, such as the **Stevenson Trail** (p678; officially the GR70).

● On week two, head south into the Grands Causses, stopping at **Roquefort** (p678) for a cheese tasting at **Roquefort Société** (p678). Spot vultures at **Maison des Vautours** (p677) in Gorges de la Jonte and ride along the river with **Les Bateliers** (p677) in the **Gorges du Tarn** (p675), before looping back to Nîmes via **Uzès** (p661), with its endearing Renaissance core.

JUNE
As temperatures rise, flocks of flamingos fill the coastline *étangs*, and the time is ripe to enjoy the beaches without the summer holiday crowds.

JULY
Each year on **Bastille Day** (14 July) evening, **Carcassonne** (p682) holds one of France's great fireworks displays from the castle's ramparts.

AUGUST
In the coastal town of **Sète** the **St Louis Festival** (p673) provides a novel way to cool off with les Joutes Nautiques (nautical jousting).

AUGUST–DECEMBER
Graffiti and street art are front and centre at the annual **L'Expo de Ouf** (p659) in the Gambetta and Richelieu neighbourhoods in Nîmes, which diversifies and brightens the streets.

Nîmes

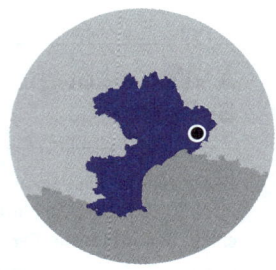

ROMAN LEGACY | REGIONAL CUISINE | STREET ART

☑ TOP TIP

If you plan to visit many, or all, of the Roman attractions in Nîmes, save money with the **Pass Romanité** *(museedelaromanite.fr/en/ discovery-pass-2; adult/ child €20.50/9.50)*. Valid for three days, it allows an admission to the Musée de la Romanité, Les Arènes, the Maison Carrée and the Tour Magne.

Nîmes (pronounced 'neem') unfurls like an open-air museum. The scale and quality of its Roman amphitheatre and temple draw comparisons with those in Rome, while a wealth of historic artefacts is reverentially preserved in the modern Musée de la Romanité (p656). Founded beside a natural spring along the Via Domitia (the Roman road linking the Mediterranean coastline to Italy), Nîmes became an important settlement in Roman Gaul. Today, some of its impeccably preserved ruins still function as places of public gathering, beyond their historic and touristic context.

This ancient heritage seamlessly complements Nîmes' pleasant, largely pedestrianised centre. Its tangle of medieval streets and palm-shaded squares is the focal point for one of France's fastest-growing food scenes, where local flavours are served by a host of energetic young restauranteurs keen to make their mark with fresh ingredients and even fresher ideas. Meanwhile, muralists are reimagining the northern neighbourhoods with some beguiling street art.

A Gladiator's Office

Two thousand years of bloody entertainment

The main Roman relic in Nîmes is **Les Arènes** *(arenes-nimes. com; adult/child €11/5.50)*, a magnificent two-tier amphitheatre which is so well preserved it still hosts music concerts.

 GETTING AROUND

Nîmes city centre's flat, broad boulevards and public spaces make exploring on foot the preferred way to get around; it takes roughly 15 minutes to walk from Les Arènes on the south side to the Jardins de la Fontaine on the north side at an amble. North of the centre, the land rapidly steepens and it's worth bringing a bottle of water with you if you plan to visit Tour Magne on a hot day. Driving in the city is best avoided where possible, as the one way system often complicates what seems like a straightforward route. If arriving by car, your hotel might be the best option for finding parking.

NÎMES

⭐ HIGHLIGHTS
1. Les Arènes
2. Les Halles de Nîmes

● SIGHTS
3. Carré d'Art
4. Jardins de la Fontaine
5. Mairie de Nîmes
6. Maison Carrée
7. Musée de la Romanité
8. Musée des Beaux-Arts
9. Musée du Vieux Nîmes
see 6 Place de la Maison Carrée
10. Place des Arènes
11. Place du Marché
12. Porte d'Auguste
13. Temple de Diane
14. Tour Magne

● SLEEPING
15. Appart'City Collection Nîmes Arènes
16. Hostel Flamingo
17. Royal Hôtel

● EATING
18. À la Végétale
19. Cali Kitchen
see 2 Fromagerie Vergne
see 2 La Pie Qui Couette
20. Le Pétrin Nîmois
see 18 Léone
21. L'Imprév'
see 2 Maison BOSC
22. Restaurant Skab
23. Textures
24. The Bird

● ENTERTAINMENT
25. Le Spot

Although some features were lost or damaged when it was commandeered by locals for use as housing during the Middle Ages, the structure remains in fine condition. You can explore vast sections of Les Arènes – built around 100 BCE – including *vomitoria* (corridors), stairways and some of the 34 terraces that hold up to 24,000 spectators (the space is still used for music concerts). Use the audio guides included in your ticket (requires a form of photo ID as deposit) to learn about the history and the forms of gladiatorial combat that once took place here. You can watch a live recreation of these events during **Les Grands Jeux Romains** (The Roman Days of Nîmes) in late April or early May.

Les Arènes (p654)

The Story of Nîmes
Trace the city's Roman past

Looking like it's wrapped in a shimmering toga, the **Musée de la Romanité** *(museedelaromanite.fr; entry €9)* is a state-of-the-art home for the Roman riches of Nîmes. Designed by architect Elizabeth de Portzamparc, it may be 2000 years younger than its neighbour, Les Arènes, but it's a worthy accompaniment. Inside, Nîmes' origin story is told using thousands of artefacts – statues, frescoes, coins and some exquisite mosaics – starting around 800 BCE through the Roman occupation and the Middle Ages. A well-marked route leads through the airy interior. Highlights include the mosaic floor of Pentheus Nîmes from 20 CE featuring images of Dionysus and animals, and a cache of weapons and skulls, which demonstrate a custom in the 4th and 3rd centuries BCE of Gaulish soldiers cutting off enemy heads and bringing them home to put on display. To top things off, there are engaging exhibits, interactive panels and an AI camera that dresses you in Roman clothing.

ROAMING ROMANS

Memories of the Roman empire's ingenuity and heritage can be found throughout France. Notable landmarks within easy reach of Nîmes include the Théâtre Antique (p776) in Orange and Les Arènes (p765) in Arles.

EATING IN NÎMES: BEST RESTAURANTS

Léone: The chefs at this cosy bistro perform exquisite feats with celery roots and artichoke hearts. One of the most exciting restaurants in the region. *noon-3pm & 7-11pm Wed-Sat* €€

The Bird: Reliable, homemade French cuisine with an emphasis on beef, served in an intimate bistro setting. Dishes use regional produce such as Auvergne veal. *7-11pm* €€

Restaurant Skab: Don't let the name put you off, this Michelin-starred restaurant uses only the best fresh ingredients for its creative tasting menus. *7.30-9pm Tue-Sat* €€€

L'Imprév': Mediterranean influences abound, from risotto to Iberian pork, via a foie gras terrine. One of the better spots in town for vegetarians, too. *noon-2pm & 7-10pm Thu-Mon* €€

EXPLORING ROMAN NÎMES ON FOOT

Discover the spiritual, defensive and recreational sides of Roman Nîmes on this amble through the compact city centre.

START	END	LENGTH
Place des Arènes	Tour Magne	2.7km; 3 hours

Start in the pedestrianised ❶ **Place des Arènes**. This is the best spot to get photos of the Les Arènes amphitheatre. From here, head northeast, past Fontaine Pradier, to ❷ **Porte d'Auguste**, one of the city's main gates. Next, follow rue Nationale west and make your way to ❸ **Place de la Maison Carrée**. At its core, the impressive ❹ **Maison Carrée** – a limestone temple in the Ancient Greek vein completed in 130 CE – gleams like polished bone. The small museum within details the building's history. Visit the ❺ **Carré d'Art** (p658) gallery across the road for avant garde and contemporary art exhibitions. From here, head north on bd Alphonse Daudet for three blocks then turn left onto quai de la Fontaine, following the northern side of the canal. Soon you'll see the Champagne-coloured balustrades, bridges and sculptures of the 17th-century ❻ **Jardins de la Fontaine**, so named for its natural spring, a key reason why the Romans established Nîmes here. Beside it is the ❼ **Temple de Diane**, dedicated to the Roman goddess of hunting. Follow the paths that zigzag up through parkland to ❽ **Tour Magne**, an octagonal structure built around 15 BCE atop Mont Cavalier. It formed part of the wall of Nîmes built around the same time. Climb the 140 steps within for scenic city views.

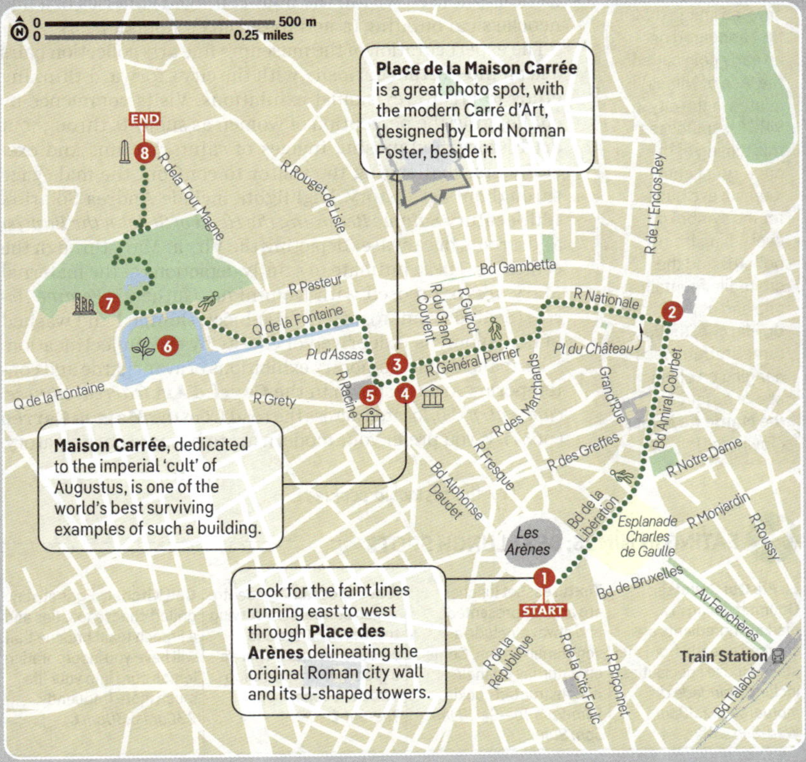

Place de la Maison Carrée is a great photo spot, with the modern Carré d'Art, designed by Lord Norman Foster, beside it.

Maison Carrée, dedicated to the imperial 'cult' of Augustus, is one of the world's best surviving examples of such a building.

Look for the faint lines running east to west through **Place des Arènes** delineating the original Roman city wall and its U-shaped towers.

Blue Jeans de Nîmes
Home of the original double denim

As the denim industry grew in Nîmes in the 17th century, a twilled cloth called Serge de Nîmes was invented. Eventually it was picked up by Levi Strauss & Company, who used it to create what would become known as blue jeans. The **Musée du Vieux Nîmes** *(nimes.fr; adult/child €5/3)* dedicates most of its exhibition space to exploring the city's textile industry, which produced all sorts of fabrics, most notably denim. There's a large denim loom as well as some elegant armoires with Biblical stories depicted on their carved wooden panels, made by Huguenot artisans who turned to the craft after religious persecution deprived them of regular work in the late 17th century. The museum is closed on Mondays, as are most museums in Languedoc-Roussillon.

The Art of Participation
Interact with art history

Much like the city's major landmarks, the art galleries of Nîmes provide a window onto art history while creating space for contemporary artistic expression. Opened in 1907, the **Musée des Beaux-Arts'** *(nimes.fr; adult/child €5/3)* permanent collection is housed within the high-ceilinged galleries of a fine neoclassical building (a nod to the city's Roman past).

The expert curation of the museum's fine arts collection pairs a keen intellectual curiosity with the city's forward-thinking ethos to create revisionist exhibitions. Visits commence by challenging the perception of women as subjects throughout art history, juxtaposing images of saints, victims and executioners, challenging the visitor to confront the male gaze throughout art history. Highlights include Andrea Solario's 16th-century *Salome Receiving the Head of St John the Baptist* and a room of canvases depicting the Virgin Mary through the centuries. These intimate to saintly depictions of the maternal Mary are juxtaposed with Dominique Gutherz's *Femme Assise* (Seated Woman), of a tired subject, slumped and washed of her colour, as if deprived of energy by the subjectification.

Permanent and temporary exhibitions of avant garde and contemporary art are shown in the **Carré d'Art** *(carreartmusee.com; entry €8)*, located across the road from the **Maison Carrée** (p657). If you prefer your modern art to be more participatory,

---

THE NÎMES CROCODILE

Nîmes' delightfully bizarre symbol, which you'll see all over the city, is a crocodile chained to a palm tree. Around the time the Roman colony of Nîmes was founded (28 BCE), Octavian (aka Gaius Julius Caesar Augustus, who would soon become the first Roman emperor) had recently defeated Anthony at the Battle of Actium, adding Egypt to Rome's empire. The chained croc, an image that first appeared on an early coin called the 'Ace of Nîmes', minted in the city in 9 BCE, symbolises this taming of this once-great empire. Keep an eye out for the symbol on everything from bollards and the crocodile fountain at one end of the **Place du Marché**, to the three stuffed crocs hanging on chains above a staircase in the **Mairie de Nîmes** (Town Hall).

EATING IN NÎMES: BEST LUNCH SPOTS

Try the pistachio cookies

La Pie Qui Couette: Gourmet dining in a market. Ingredients are sourced directly from the stalls. House specialities include *brandade de morue*. *8am-2.30pm Wed-Sun* €€€

Textures: Set lunches are artfully presented and always include a vegetarian option. Come on Saturday for their deconstructed cookie. *9am-9pm Tue-Sat, 11am-5pm Sun* €

À la Végétale: City-centre vegan coffee shop serving top-notch coffee and creative pastries. There's a great health food shop attached. *10am-6pm Tue-Sat* €

Cali Kitchen: Eggs all day, grilled cheese toasties and a French toast brioche that will have you incorporating lemon curd into your life much more frequently. *9.30am-3.30pm* €

Fougasse **(similar to focaccia)**

head over to the western edge of the city, where free afternoon *ateliers* (workshops) are held every other Wednesday at the **Centre d'Art Contemporain de Nîmes** *(CACN; cacncentre-dart.com; free)* in conjunction with the current exhibition. To visit the gallery (Wednesday to Saturday), take the T2 tram bus from rue de la République, on the south side of Les Arènes.

Urban Canvas
Discover the city's best street art

Some of the best modern artists use building façades as their canvas. In the last five months of the year, **L'Expo de Ouf** sees street artists creating new works in the Gambetta and Richelieu neighbourhoods, north of the city centre. These fresh works complement those from previous years. To take a self-guided street art tour of these areas, head first to the friendly cultural centre **Le Spot** *(lespotnimes.com)* in the afternoon from Thursday to Saturday and ask for their free street art map, known as the Carte d'Expo de Ouf, which pinpoints all the works. The orange dots represent the latest works, while the clusters of yellow dots are works from previous years, such as the huge, multicoloured crocodile mural, symbol of Nîmes, smoking a pipe at the corner of rue Rangueil and rue de Bourgogne.

La Cuisine Nîmoise
Local delicacies in Les Halles

Nîmes is steadily gaining traction as a destination for food lovers, thanks to the abundance and diversity of local produce from the Cévennes mountains and the Mediterranean, plus from nearby Camargue and Provence. That has given rise to a number of specialities unique to the city. You can sample them for yourself in **Les Halles de Nîmes** *(leshallesdenimes.fr)*, such as goat's milk Pélardon from the Cévennes at **Fromagerie Vergne**. Then pull up a stool at the gourmet market counter of **La Pie Qui Couette** for a lunch made exclusively with food from the market's produce.

WHAT TO EAT IN NÎMES

Céline Gomez, owner of The Food Tour in Nîmes, guides visitors to the city's signature flavours. @nimesfoodtour

Brandade de morue is a garlic salt cod dish and the signature dish of Nîmes. In most French people's minds, *brandade* is like a fish pie with potato, but in Nîmes it is unique, typically without potatoes and usually served cold. Also, truffle *brandade* is great in the wintertime, during black truffle season around Uzès.

Petit pâté Nîmois is a small (and cute) pork and veal pie. The best ones are from **Maison BOSC** in **Les Halles**.

Fougasse is like a bread, but most bakers use puff pastry. Shaped like a a leaf, it usually contains *grattons* (pork crackling), olives, or herbs and cheese. Try it from **Le Pétrin Nîmois** (just outside Les Halles).

Beyond Nîmes

Discover medieval settlements, a UNESCO World Heritage Site and a town encapsulated by mighty battlements beside the salt pans.

Places
Vers-Pont-du-Gard p660
Collias p661
Uzès p661
Aigues-Mortes p662

When the natural spring in Nîmes became insufficient to sustain the city's burgeoning population in the 1st century CE, the Romans built an aqueduct. Sections of it remain, including the extraordinary Pont du Gard. Both this and the historic town of Uzès, where the aqueduct begins, make for great day trips from Nîmes. Uzès is particularly notable for its Renaissance-era town centre, a ramble through which is tantamount to stepping back six centuries. Down towards the Mediterranean coastline, the land fragments into a patchwork of ponds and salt flats, coloured a range of hues from spring green to rose pink like the flamingos that flock to the region. It is here that the fortified *bastide* town of Aigues-Mortes stands like a proud sentry.

GETTING AROUND

Aigues-Mortes may be geographically closer to Montpellier, but it's only connected by direct trains to Nîmes, running at least three times a day. You can reach Uzès in 40 minutes on the 152 bus departing from the southeastern side of Nîmes station. Bus 121 departs from the same place, taking roughly an hour to reach the Pont du Gard and Collias. Get off at the Vers-Pont-du-Gard stop and follow the signs on foot for roughly 1km to the Roman bridge.

Vers-Pont-du-Gard

TIME FROM NÎMES: **1HR**

Moving Water Over Water

Roman engineering at its very finest is on show over a leafy stretch of the Gard River. The **Pont du Gard** (*pontdugard.fr; adult/child €8/free, tours €15/6*) is the architectural highlight of a 50km-long aqueduct transporting water from Uzès to Nîmes, built around 50 CE to handle water requirements for the rapidly growing city, while also fuelling thermal baths, fountains and other lifestyle benefits. The existence and endurance of this remarkable three-tiered bridge is even more impressive when you consider that each block of stone, weighing around 5 tonnes, had to be hand-carved and transported from nearby quarries.

Take the guided tour to walk across the bridge, including access to the upper level. General access provides entry to the trails, best viewpoints and an interactive and immersive museum exploring how exactly the Romans managed to commandeer the world around them so effectively without modern machinery or scientific insight.

Also included is access to the 1.4km **Mémoires de Garrigue** walking trail, created and curated to explore the impact of humanity on the landscape, particularly before the 19th century. The trail encounters further remnants of the Roman aqueduct above ground, set amid traditional farm terraces and other dry stone features such as igloo-shaped huts used as shelters by shepherds called bories.

Rock climbing with Bureau des Moniteurs du Gard, Collias

Collias
TIME FROM NÎMES: **40MIN**

Kayaking Down the Gard River
The village of Collias, 7km upriver from the Pont du Gard, is packed with adventure opportunities. But the main reason to visit is for the kayaking (p662). You'll see the tutti-frutti–coloured craft all along this gentle stretch of river, which barely registers more than a ripple or two, making it a great beginner route.

Follow the 8km stretch of languid river through the valley, passing beneath the Pont du Gard and ending at a pickup point, where staff will drive you back to the start point. Rates start at around €27 and the trip takes around two hours, or longer if you stop at a shaded riverbank spot for a picnic along the way. Life jackets and a dry container for valuables are provided.

Visit in spring or autumn to kayak along the Gard; the water level at other times is either too high or too low.

Connect With the Wild
Collias is a gateway to various other adventure and wildlife experiences including a via ferrata (a climbing route using steel cables drilled into the rock) and rock climbing organised through the various tour companies around the village, such as **Bureau des Moniteurs du Gard** (p662). For families, the information (in French and English) at **Maison du Castor** (gorgesdugardon.fr; adult/child €6/4) about the beavers that live nearby is a worthwhile stop and will help you to identify other wildlife living in the Gorges du Gard.

Uzès
TIME FROM NÎMES: **35MIN**

Medieval Towers & Gardens
With its Champagne-brick buildings lining a warren of old cobbled streets, the town centre of Uzès is among the most

---

THE GENIUS OF ROMAN HYDROLOGY

As the Roman Empire grew, so did the challenges of sustaining the growing populations of its cities, the driving force of the empire's success. To ensure that Nîmes' residents had enough water throughout the year, the Romans located a plentiful, higher-altitude source 50km away in water-rich Uzès and began constructing an aqueduct. Although gravity was not a concept at that time, the Romans understood that a gradual and consistent gradient ensured water continued to flow steadily downhill to Nîmes. Most aqueducts were channelled underground, but occasionally, natural barriers such as river gorges meant the aqueduct was forced to pass over the obstacle in order to maintain that steady gradient. The Pont du Gard is an elegant example of that understanding in action.

BEST ADVENTURE TOUR COMPANIES BEYOND NÎMES

Bureau des Moniteurs du Gard: A Collias favourite offering the usual kayaking trips plus access to the via ferrata and climbing near the Gard gorge.

Canöe Collias: Kayaks and canoes, plus an excellent pickup operation for self-guided trips beneath the Pont du Gard. March to October.

Happy Tour Camargue: Just north of Aigues-Mortes, these popular e-bike tours explore the marshy Camargue, seeking out local wildlife.

Kayak Vert: Offers a half-day combined canoeing and e-bike tour, plus longer kayaking trips of up to 30km.

Location Vélos Uzès: Rents out bicycles and e-bikes, providing detailed information about 12 different cycle trails of varying difficulty around Uzès.

---

handsome in the region. The top sights are all medieval in origin, such as the **Jardin Médiéval** *(jardinmedievaluzes.com; entry €7)*, a botanical collection put to various uses across food and medicine. It is laid out as it likely was during the Middle Ages, but with every plant neatly labelled. At its heart is the imposing **Tour du l'Évêque** (Bishop's Tower), built in 1493. Next to it, **Tour du Roi** (King's Tower) has an art exhibition spread over various floors and a panoramic viewpoint at the top. The two towers here were largely used by local bishops as living quarters, as a prison and as a seat of justice.

Next door is the bulky **Duché** *(Château Ducal; uzes.com; entry €22)*, which looks like a cross between a castle and a palace, depending on where you stand. Access by guided tour (French only) takes in the 800-year-old cellars, fortified keep and richly appointed rooms. It is arguably just as impressive when viewed from the outside, where its 16th-century façade blends various neoclassical designs with other Revivalist architectural elements, including Corinthian columns.

Aigues-Mortes

TIME FROM NÎMES: **1HR**

Salt Flats & Waterfront Fortress

Aigues-Mortes is an excellent example of a 13th-century bastide (fortified town), whose intact, 1640m-long **Tours et Remparts** *(Towers and Ramparts; aigues-mortes-monument.fr; €9)*, complete with five towers and 10 gates or posterns, holds a commanding presence over the surrounding wetlands. The town within, much of it pedestrianised, retains its medieval layout. Access the ramparts from the northwest corner. The most impressive view is from the parade grounds outside the southern wall.

Built on the western fringe of the Camargue wetlands, Aigues-Mortes was used by the Capetian dynasty monarchs, starting with Louis IX (who would become the globally ubiquitous St Louis after his death in Carthage in 1270), as an important Mediterranean stronghold and the launching base for the Seventh Crusade in 1248. Although the Latin origin of Aigues-Mortes translates to 'dead waters', the surrounding salt pans have a thriving ecology, capped by scores of fascinating flamingos. Wooden boardwalks and paths lead along the edge of the magenta-tinted **Étang de la Ville**, which are easily reached from the **Porte de la Marine** (Navy Gate).

Montpellier

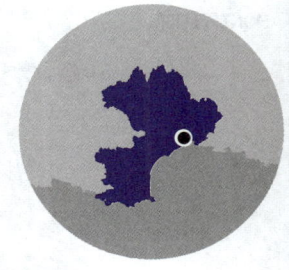

CULTURAL BASTION | GREEN SPACES | LIVELY NIGHTLIFE

Founded in the 10th century, Montpellier is a young city compared to its Roman, ruin-kissed neighbours. Despite that, it easily claims the title of Languedoc-Roussillon's capital and is second only to Toulouse in the Occitania region. It's also one of France's most enigmatic cities, both energetic and laid-back, creative and yet careful to conserve its character and history. While its lauded *hôtels particuliers* remain largely out of bounds to visitors, its art galleries, such as Musée Fabre, showcase some of the finest collections in southern France. Other historic buildings are repurposed as modern art museums, and the oldest botanical garden in France, the Jardin des Plantes, continues to thrive. This neat balance of old and new is largely thanks to the sizeable student population, who make up roughly a third of the city's inhabitants. Seemingly around every cloistered corner, the hum of life swells up from alfresco diners or groups of friends socialising over an *apéro*.

> ☑ **TOP TIP**
>
> The **Montpellier City Card** *(montpellier-france.com/traveller-information/city-card)* offers lots of benefits, including entry to the Fabre and MO.CO. museums, a range of guided tour options and access to the city's trams. Passes are available for one, two or three days. Available online.

Musée Fabre's Vast Collection
Art from Renaissance to contemporary

When neoclassical painter François-Xavier Fabre founded **Musée Fabre** *(museefabre.fr; entry €9)* in 1825, it was to display a modest collection of fine art to the public. Today it is one of southern France's finest collections. While primarily

---

GETTING AROUND

Vélomagg, the local bikeshare scheme with 57 bike stations across Montpellier, is easy to use and can be accessed via the M'Ticket app. You can also buy local bus and tram tickets there. The latter criss-crosses the centre of the city along four separate routes. The Line 620 bus is the only public transport route to and from Montpellier airport. It departs from place de l'Europe roughly every 30 minutes from 8am to 8pm and hourly for an hour or two either side of that. On-street parking can be difficult to find in the centre, but there are plenty of large multistorey car parks around the train station.

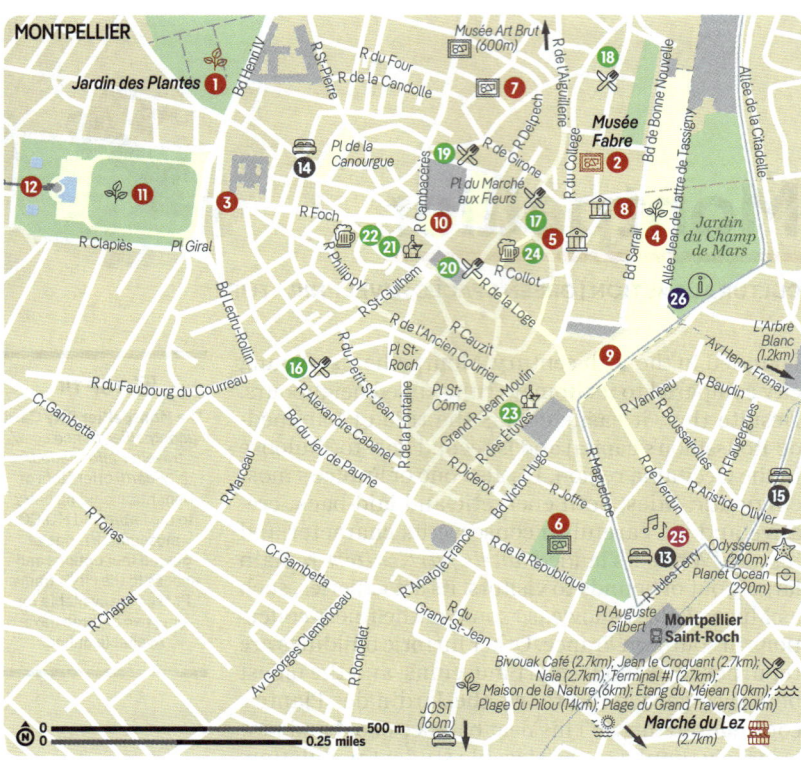

MONTPELLIER

- ★ **HIGHLIGHTS**
  1. Jardin des Plantes
  2. Musée Fabre
- ● **SIGHTS**
  3. Arc de Triomphe
  4. Esplanade Charles de Gaulle
  5. Hôtel de Varennes
  6. MO.CO.
  7. MO.CO. Panacée
  8. Musée Sabatier d'Espeyran
  9. Place de la Comédie
  10. Place Martyrs de la Résistance
  11. Promenade du Peyrou
  12. St-Clémont Aqueduct
- ● **SLEEPING**
  13. EKLO Montpellier
  14. Hôtel du Palais
  15. Privilege Hôtel Eurociel Centre Comédie
- ● **EATING**
  16. Bistro Urbain
  17. Céna
  18. Ébullition
  19. Green Lab
  20. Halles Castellane
- ● **DRINKING & NIGHTLIFE**
  21. Bar Foch
  22. Le Rebuffy
  23. Pousse Pas Mémé Dans La Vigne
  24. The Shakespeare
- ● **ENTERTAINMENT**
  25. Rockstore
- ● **INFORMATION**
  26. Tourist Office

comprised of Renaissance works, around 600 years of art history are charted, and in particular the French eminence in the arts from the 17th to the 20th centuries.

Highlights include: paintings by Peter Paul Rubens and Pieter Brueghel (Salle 3); Jan Steen's *Comme les Vieux Chantent, les Enfants Piaillent* (Salle 5); the mesmerisingly brutal *Chasse au Sanglier* by Abraham Hondius (Salle 7), of an attack by a pack of rabid dogs on a terrified wild boar; while neoclassicist works by Fabre himself hang in Salle 22.

Gustave Courbet's *Bonjour Monsieur Corbet* in Salle 37 is a fine example of French Realism; Salle 39 explores the

Musée Fabre (p663)

emergence of Impressionism through Edgar Degas and especially the works of Montpellier native Frédéric Bazille, such as his 1868 painting *Vue de Village*. You'll also find Édouard Manet's portrait of Antonin Proust here. In Salles 41 and 42, you see the emergence of Fauvism and other steps in the transition from Impressionism to Modernism, including Sonia Delaunay's *Philomène* and works by Henri Matisse.

Brut Force
Making modern art accessible

Montpellier is a major hub for all forms of modern art. Among the slew of fascinating galleries is the **Musée Art Brut** *(musee-artbrut-montpellier.com; entry €8)*, in the former family home of non-conformist artist Fernand Michel, whose works (mostly made with zinc) are also on display. It's refreshing to hear laughter in an art gallery. Not at the naivety of the art on show, but due to the charming and surprising turns the creative mind can make when not bound by thoughts of form or art history.

Art Brut is the term given to the work of autodidacts who create purely out of elementary inspiration, without a deeper understanding of art history. For example, the joyful human and animal forms of Jean-Joseph Sanfourche are a highlight; wonderfully absurd and almost childlike, they remain rooted in a deeper understanding of the world's complexities.

PIERRE MAGNOL & BOTANICAL ORDER

You'd be forgiven for not having heard of the 1689 scientific paper *Prodromus Historiae Generalis Plantarum*. Indeed, today it will seem outdated even to ardent botanists. You may not have heard of the botanist who penned it, either, but Pierre Magnol was born in Montpellier and, in addition to serving as director of the Royal Botanic Garden (Jardin des Plantes), he was the first to group plants with similar attributes into families. This was a crucial advancement in taxonomy, which is central to our understanding and ordering of the natural world today. He laid the foundation for later botanists to develop the modern taxonomic system. You will likely have heard of magnolias, the genus of large flowering plants subsequently named in honour of Magnol.

DRINKING IN MONTPELLIER: BEST NIGHTLIFE

Pousse Pas Mémé Dans La Vigne: Start the evening with an *apéro* at this debonair wine bar. The rarest bottles are kept in an old bank vault downstairs. *9.30am-1am*

Le Rebuffy: Together with **Bar Foch** next door, Le Rebuffy is the cool place to hang out. And the cheap drinks mean it's for unostentatious reasons. *noon-1am*

Rockstore: Club nights and live bands most nights of the week, with a couple of different bars. Enter below half a red Cadillac. *hours vary*

The Shakespeare: Predating the Bard himself, the 14th-century building hosting The Shakespeare is a good place to find whisky and British beers beneath a vaulted ceiling. *hours vary*

EXPLORING HISTORIC MONTPELLIER ON FOOT

Encounter Montpellier's historic charm through pleasant urban spaces and medieval heritage buildings on this easy walking tour.

START	END	LENGTH
Place de la Comédie	St-Clémont Aqueduct	1.6 km; 2 hours

Locals call the ❶ **Place de la Comédie** 'l'Oeuf' (the egg) because of its shape. Its central fountain, created by Étienne Dantoine in 1790, features the three Graces representing youth, humour and elegance, which epitomise the city to this day. Wander northeast along the ❷ **Esplanade Charles de Gaulle**, with its stout regiments of plane trees to ❸ **Musée Sabatier d'Espeyran**, an adjunct of the nearby Musée Fabre. Next, head west onto rue Montpellieret, into the old town labyrinth. Wiggle your way to the ❹ **Hôtel de Varennes**, one of the few *hôtels particuliers* partly open to the public. Visitors can wander through the entrance hall, with its ribbed vaulted ceilings, and courtyard. Continue west, through the ❺ **Place Martyrs de la Résistance**, dominated by the main administrative building for the Hérault prefecture, and onto rue Foch. This 300m-long, tree-lined boulevard is reminiscent of those seen in Paris and approaches Montpellier's very own ❻ **Arc de Triomphe**. This veritable, late-17th-century chunk of absolutism is flanked by the showy neoclassical Court of Appeal and frames a statue of King Louis XIV, to whom the arch is dedicated, riding on horseback. Wander through to ❼ **Promenade du Peyrou**, reaching a water tower at the western edge of the square, which marks one end of the 18th-century ❽ **St-Clémont Aqueduct**.

Montpellier's *hôtels particuliers* are actually private mansions, built by wealthy merchants from the 17th century onwards, usually exhibiting some fine architecture.

With views towards nearby mountains such as Pic St-Loup, **Promenade du Peyrou** is an excellent spot for a photo.

The **Musée Sabatier d'Espeyran** building, typical of the 19th-century houses in this part of the city, now exhibits period furnishings, antiques and sculptures.

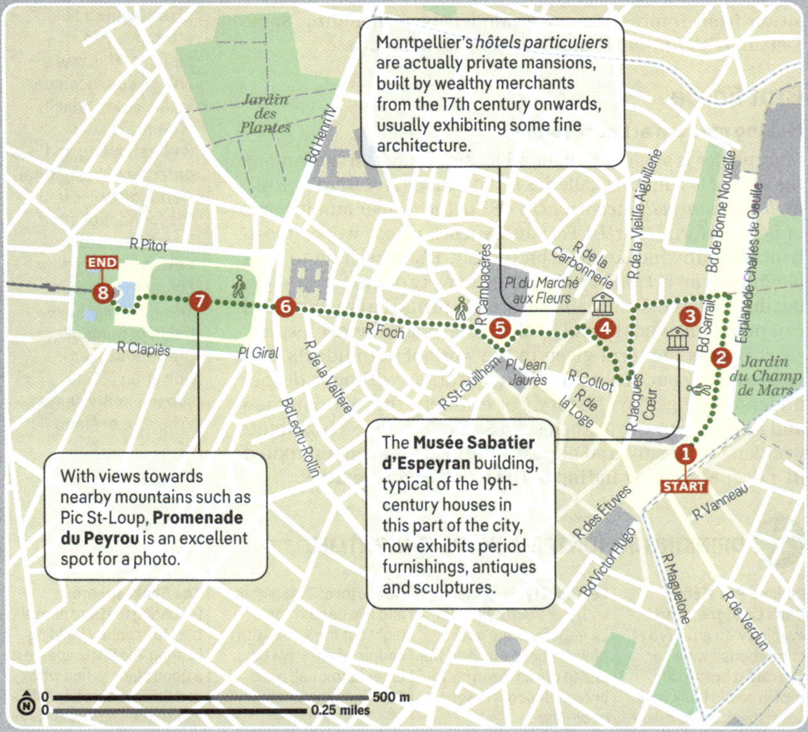

Montpellier's foremost modern art institution – comprising two art museums and the city's main school of fine arts – is **MO.CO.** *(moco.art; entry €8)*. The main gallery (with its watering can fountain) on rue de la République occupies the former Hôtel Montcalm, with displays of public and private collections. Its revolutionary and thought-provoking temporary exhibitions examine the frictions of modern existence and have included works from an array of eminent artists, including Berlinde de Bruyckere and Eduardo Paolozzi. **MO.CO. Panacée** *(moco.art; free)* focuses more on local artists. Check the website for exhibition dates. The downstairs cafe at Panacée, with its large courtyard garden, usually remains open, and is a popular meeting place.

A Botanical Oasis
Shaded paths and rare trees

Henry IV of France created the **Jardin des Plantes** *(facmedecine.umontpellier.fr/jardin-des-plantes; free)* in 1593, making it the country's oldest botanical garden. It was here that Pierre Magnol devised an early system of botanical order in the 17th century (see box). When the mercury climbs higher during the day, it's a serene and shaded refuge in the heart of the city, where the series of paths through plantations of bamboo, conifers and flower beds invites you to explore. A 19th-century orangery in the centre occasionally hosts an exhibition of local art.

Wine, Cheese & Regional Delicacies
Tasting Montpellier's local produce

The city centre's **Halles Castellane** are Montpellier's main central market, where you can try a number of local ingredients that showcase the region's unique gastronomy. Taste Mediterranean influences, such as olive tapenade and nutty oysters, creamy goat cheeses from the Cévennes, and spicy, dark fruit-laden red wines from the local Grés de Montpellier AOP.

Embracing the city's youthful energy, **Marché du Lez** *(marchedulez.com)*, 3km southeast of the city centre, is a hipster haven where terms like 'upcycled old warehouse,' 'post-industrial' and 'vintage VW campervan' readily apply. You'll find a host of much-loved food stalls and innovative restaurants clustered here, plus plenty of bars with sundeck seating.

> **EASY ACCESS MONTPELLIER**
>
> **James Turiel**, accessible tourism expert at Montpellier Méditerranée Métropole **Tourist Office**, recommends his favourite landmarks for people with restricted mobility.
>
> **Place de la Comédie:** As a wheelchair user, I can say that Montpellier is a wonderfully inclusive city that is improving a lot in terms of access. Place de la Comédie is the heart of the city.
>
> **Antigone:** A flat district and therefore easy to move around, whether you use a manual or electric wheelchair. Enjoy the neo-Greek architecture with statues and fountains, and along the banks of the Lez you'll find interesting contemporary buildings, like **L'Arbre Blanc** by Sou Fujimoto.
>
> **Odysseum:** The tram network has 174 priority stops, made accessible to people with reduced mobility. The Odysseum district includes the unmissable **Planet Ocean**.

 EATING IN MONTPELLIER: BEST EATS AT MARCHÉ DU LEZ

Terminal #1: The Pourcel brothers imbue regional ingredients with touches of global influence at this Michelin Guide–listed restaurant. *noon-2pm & 8-11pm Tue-Sat* €€€

Bivouak Café: Step around the old Land Rover to reach your seat and don't miss the tuna ceviche. Good set brunch menus on Sundays. *10am-midnight* €€€

Naïa: French (beef tartare) and Mediterranean (sautéed shrimp) classics alongside must-try cocktails (including some great non-alcoholic ones). *11am-2pm & 7pm-midnight* €€

Jean le Croquant: This yellow street-food van dishes out next-level croque monsieurs (try the Segun with goat cheese and fig jam). Perfect with a cold beer in the sun. *hours vary* €

Palavas les Flots

Shore Leave
Sandy beaches and wild wetlands

Technically located a good 12km south of the city centre, the Mediterranean shoreline near Montpellier is underscored with a largely unbroken strip of sand. In the summer, much of it is lost beneath sunbathers and families escaping the heat of the city, particularly where resort towns such as **Palavas les Flots** are concerned. Escape all of this at the far quieter and prettier pebble-strewn **Plage du Pilou** to the south (a free mini land train takes people to the beach from the car park during peak months), or for a quieter beach with somewhere to grab a drink nearby, try **Plage du Grand Travers** to the north.

Often, you will see the quirky silhouettes of flamingos tracing across the sky above you. They're likely heading to the series of wetlands and ponds cradled between the beaches and the mainland. To get a closer look, walk the excellent series of boardwalks and paths to **Étang du Méjean** from the **Maison de la Nature** *(ville-lattes.fr; free)*, near the satellite town of **Lattes**. Common sightings include storks, flamingos and a non-native, beaver-like rodent called a nutria, as well as of a variety of flora.

EATING IN MONTPELLIER: OUR PICKS

Céna: Creative modern bistro in a medieval building. The daily, changing menu promotes seasonal, fresh ingredients sourced locally. *noon-2pm & 8-9.30pm Thu-Mon* €€€

Bistro Urbain: Up-and-coming eatery offering creative tasting menus, with a vegetarian option. The rum baba cakes are a popular mainstay. *1-3pm & 7.30-9pm Wed-Sat, 1-3pm Tue* €€

Ébullition: Creative haute cuisine tasting menus and spectacular wines inside a low-lit, bare-brick space. Awarded a coveted Michelin star in 2025. *noon-1pm & 7.30-8.30pm Tue-Fri* €€€

Green Lab: Vegetarians and vegans can breathe a sigh of relief; Green Lab serves healthy falafel bowls and salads, plus great Alaryk beer from Béziers. *noon-10pm* €

Beyond Montpellier

Leave the city behind to explore quaint villages, sample the region's exquisite produce and discover life along Languedoc's Mediterranean shore.

The land west of Montpellier gradually climbs up away from the Mediterranean. Vineyards and olive groves are replaced with verdant valleys with orchards and stone villages perched on mountainsides. Nature's paintbrush used particularly dramatic licence when constructing the land around Mourèze and St-Guilhem-le-Désert, which are further enhanced by the churches and villages constructed there in harmony with their surroundings. Further south, Sète and the Étang de Thau region offer a welcome dose of seaside glamour through art and oysters. Meanwhile, Sète turns raucous in August, when teams of rowers compete in Joutes Nautiques (nautical jousting) tournaments. Inland, pretty Béziers is a key waystation along the Canal du Midi and Pézenas retains the 17th-century charm that kept Molière enthralled.

Places
Cazevieille p669
St-Guilhem-le-Désert p669
Mourèze p670
Béziers p670
Pézenas p671
Pinet p672
Bouzigues p672
Sète p673

Cazevieille
TIME FROM MONTPELLIER: **30MIN**
Hiking Pic St-Loup
The well-marked trail and mountaintop vistas over the city make **Pic St-Loup** a popular hiking spot for Montpellier citizens, thanks to its proximity, 23km away. At the top sits a hermitage dedicated to St Loup, a metal cross, and a battered old weather station that rattles in the wind. The peak stands at 658m, requiring an ascent of 370m from the **Pic St-Loup trailhead** in the car park outside Cazevieille. The 6km path (there and back again via the same route) to the top is of moderate difficulty, largely owing to the jagged rocks along its much of its length. Wear appropriate footwear and bring water.

St-Guilhem-le-Désert
TIME FROM MONTPELLIER: **45MIN**
Pilgrimage to the Romanesque Abbey
Beautifying the craggy edges of the rough-hewn Gorges de l'Hérault is the chocolate-box village of St-Guilhem-le-Désert. Its narrow lanes and historic cottages parade uphill to the sound of gurgling water from the local springs until you reach the **Abbaye de Gellone** (saint-guilhem-le-desert.com; free),

GETTING AROUND

Béziers is well connected by train to the rest of the region's cities. There are car parks near the station, as well as close to Pont-Vieux and the 9 Écluses. Sète is also connected to Montpellier by train, while Bouzigues can be reached on yellow bus 23 from Sète or the 604 bus from Montpellier's Sabines bus station, which is in turn connected to the city centre by the tram. For everywhere else, you'll need your own form of transport.

BUILDING THE 9 ÉCLUSES & CANAL DU MIDI

Connecting the Étang de Thau and Sète on the Mediterranean, the Canal du Midi, built between 1666 and 1681, runs for over 240km to Toulouse, where it joins the Canal de Garonne, heading towards the Atlantic. Designed and overseen by Pierre-Paul Riquet, the Canal du Midi was a remarkable feat of engineering (Britain's Bridgewater Canal would open 80 years later), originally incorporating 86 locks and over 100 bridges. The most famous section is reserved for Riquet's home town of Béziers, where the **9 Écluses de Fonseranes** – a nine-lock staircase dropping 21.5m – were a response to the challenge of bringing the canal into the Orb River valley on the southwestern edge of Béziers. Since 1996, the canal has been inscribed on the UNESCO World Heritage List.

which stands like a fortification fronted by gardens of roses, olives and grape vines. The abbey is said to contain a piece of the original cross on which Jesus was crucified. Although the one on display is a replica, the abbey became a key station along one branch of France's Santiago de Compostela pilgrimage route. Today it enjoys UNESCO World Heritage Site status, along with **Pont du Diable**, a Roman bridge 3km south of St-Guilhem-le-Désert.

The abbey is Romanesque and mostly dates to the 12th century, although construction began around 804 CE, when the eponymous Guilhem's cousin Charlemagne bequeathed the piece of original cross to him. Place de la Liberté in front of the abbey is lined with cafes and shaded by a single mighty sycamore tree planted in 1855.

Mourèze
TIME FROM MONTPELLIER: **55MIN**
Dolomite Monolith Formations

The pretty village of Mourèze clambers up a steep protrusion overlooking a series of remarkable dolomite rock chimneys of up to 500m tall. A brilliant, simple hike through the heart of this **Cirque de Mourèze** and its surrounding oak forest runs for around 2km, or there's a longer route of around 7km. Yellow markers point you in the right direction. Look out for a turning to Le Belvédère close to the tourist centre. This slight detour through a narrow ravine to a lookout provides a fantastic overview of Mourèze and the site you're about to explore.

Béziers
TIME FROM MONTPELLIER: **45MIN**
Riverside Vistas & Engineering Marvels

Béziers will have you constantly reaching for your camera. The classic view of the city is down by the Orb River, in **Jardin Emile Ain**. From here, the 241m-long, 12th-century pedestrian footbridge, **Pont Vieux**, leads to the foot of a hill which displays the city's historic wares, including Cathédrale St-Nazaire, like a market stall.

Footpaths along the Orb turn southwest to follow the **Canal du Midi** to the **9 Écluses de Fonseranes**, a series of nine canal locks that gradually step canal barges up and down a hill. For much of the year the locks are in use. You can pass through them on a canal barge, with **Cap au Sud** (*capausud.eu; adult/child from €13/8*) offering English tours. **Les Bateaux du Soleil** (*les-bateaux-du-soleil.fr; adult/child from*

 EATING IN BÉZIERS & PÉZENAS: OUR PICKS

L'Orangerie: Modern takes on French classics such as tuna tataki or beef tartare. Try the egg parfait with porcini mushroom cream. Béziers. *hours vary Tue-Sat* €€

La Maison de Petit Pierre: French bistro with three-, four- and six-course tasting menus and good regional wines. Béziers. *hours vary Mon, Tue & Thu-Sat* €€€

Restaurant Chez Paul: Cosy setting for meats, such as Aubrac entrecôte with bone marrow, or juicy burgers if you're feeling less adventurous. Pézenas. *hours vary Mon-Sat* €€

Le Pré Saint Jean: Beautiful gastronomic inventions, such as monkfish stuffed with squid fricassee. Obscenely good value for its Michelin star. Pézenas. *hours vary Tue-Sun* €€

Cirque de Mourèze

€16/11) runs cheery canal barge tours with the odd singalong, and **Les Bateaux du Midi** *(lesbateauxdumidi.com; from €45)* runs dinner cruises. The Midi then crosses above the Orb River via **Pont Canal**.

For a view in the opposite direction towards the Pont Canal and Pont Vieux, head back up to the **Cathédrale St-Nazaire** *(free)* where you can climb the bell tower's 165 claustrophobic, occasionally crowded, steps.

Pézenas

TIME FROM MONTPELLIER: 55MIN

Walk in Molière's Footsteps

The medieval town of Pézenas is Molière mad. In **Place Molière** there's a bust of the great French playwright, overlooking **Le Grand Hôtel Molière**. Nearby, his legacy also lives on in **Brasserie Molière**. Although it's best, and most appropriately preserved at the number of theatres around town, such as **Théâtre de Pézenas**. Although turned into a theatre only in the mid-1800s, the building, built in 1635, served as chapel of the Brotherhood of the Black Penitents while Molière was in town.

The narrow streets of Pézenas' historic centre are little-changed in the four centuries since. Start at the 14th-century **Porte Faugères**, heading through this original remnant of the medieval town, through the old **Jewish Quarter** (13th to 14th centuries) to **Place Gambetta**. This focal point is where the barber shop, which Molière frequented to observe local characters for inspiration, now serves as **Musée Boby Lapointe** *(bobylapointe.fr; adult/child €2.50/1)*, dedicated to the popular 20th-century French singer and actor, also from Pézenas. Just downhill from it is **Hôtel de Lacoste** *(free)*, the 16th-century home of the Lords of Lacoste, which Molière likely passed many a time, best known for its ornamental 1638 staircase and vaulted ceiling. There are few tangible remains

MOLIÈRE IN PÉZENAS

Arguably France's greatest playwright, Molière (1622–73) lived as dramatic a life off the stage as he did on it. He spent time in prison for failing to repay debts (hence his later peregrinations), married the supposed daughter of his lover and business partner, and collapsed on stage, before continuing the show and dying hours later.

Following his release from prison, Molière moved steadily south, eventually reaching Pézenas in 1650, where he would live, on and off until 1656, during the years that the Prince of Conti, Armand de Bourbon, maintained patronage to his theatre troupe, 'The Illustrious Theatre',

Molière studied Pézenas' citizens as they visited his friend Guillaume Gély's barber shop, drawing inspiration from them for his comedies, such as *Tartuffe* and *Le Misanthrope* (both of which he penned while in Pézenas). They remain popular in global culture to this day, while Molière's legacy and the love of theatre remain steadfast in Pézenas.

THE BEST WAY TO EAT OYSTERS

Sebastian Reynolds and **Irene Salas**, owners of **Le Cercle des Huîtres** *(lecercledeshuitres. fr)*, advise on the best way to eat oysters.

The special oysters (which are removed from the water for 24 hours once every week to make them bigger) are sweet and taste a bit like hazelnut. First, cut underneath the oyster to detach the flesh from the muscle that attaches it to the shell. You can eat this muscle, too. Next, add three drops of lemon, and it's tradition in France to have raw oysters with a glass of white wine. Having them with bread and butter is very French, too. Then tip the oyster directly from the shell into your mouth. You can chew the oysters a few times slowly; you don't need to swallow them whole.

of Molière and his life, beyond his plays, but the **Musée de Vulliod St-Germain** *(entry €4)* contains an ornate walnut wood armchair used by Molière while in town.

Pinet
TIME FROM MONTPELLIER: **45MIN**
Picpoul Wine Tastings

Crisp, citrusy Picpoul de Pinet AOP white wines hail from a small region hugging the western banks of the Étang de Thau lagoon, where Picpoul and Terret grapes thrive. The regimental lines of vines spread out like sunrays from the production centre, Pinet, a small town that's big on wine tastings. Of the town's producers that offer tastings in English (which are usually free), **D'omaine Gaujal** *(gaujal.fr)* is a highlight. Their Ludovic Gaujal is a fantastic wine with notes of pear and lemon, while the 1744, aged in acacia wood barrels, pairs well with lots of dishes. Other good tasting options are **Cave de l'Ormarine** *(cave-ormarine.com)*, which sits on the edge of Pinet town, while **Montpellier Wine Tours** *(montpellierwinetours.com)* run guided trips to the area, visiting two wineries.

Bouzigues
TIME FROM MONTPELLIER: **40MIN**
Gastronomic Pearls

The surface of the **Étang de Thau** between Bouzigues and Mèze is covered in squadrons of oyster baskets. These local delicacies form the perfect accompaniment to a glass of Picpoul de Pinet, as though the natural world decided to gift visitors to the region not one, but two gastronomic delights.

The reality, however, is that although oyster farming dates back to at least the 2nd century BCE, oysters weren't cultivated in Bouzigues until 1908. This, and everything you wanted to know about oyster farming, plus plenty you never thought you'd need to know (for example, female oysters are capable of producing a million eggs at ovulation) is presented at the **Musée de l'Étang de Thau** *(patrimoine.agglopole.fr; adult/ child €5/3.50)*. Learn how the lagoon's conditions are ideal for oysters through French, English and German descriptions, interactive exhibits and a full-size *nacelle de l'Étang de Thau* (flat-bottom skiff typical of this lake). If you enjoy tasting fine food and wine at its source, most of the oyster farms immediately to the south of Bouzigues haul the molluscs out of the water and straight onto your plate in their lagoon-side tasting rooms.

 EATING AROUND BOUZIGUES: BEST OYSTERS

Le Cercle des Huîtres: Family-run oyster farm with upcycled dining furniture and exceptional oysters. Their Godzilla oysters are huge. *noon-2pm Sun-Fri* €€

L'Huître d'Oc: A larger-scale oyster farm where you can watch, and even participate in, the harvesting process. Try their seafood platters. *10am-3pm* €€

Chez La Tchepe: Restaurant with some of the best-value oysters in town beyond the farms. One of the few that opens early for coffee. *9am-6pm Tue-Sun* €€

La Noisette d'Oc: Pull up a seat on their terrace above the water and try their home-grown oysters and mussels. Also offers overnight camper van parking. *hours vary* €€

Sète

Sète

TIME FROM MONTPELLIER: **30MIN**

On the Waterfront

With the **Étang de Thau** lagoon on one side and the Mediterranean on the other, plus the Canal du Midi making the final stop on its 240km course, the former trading port of Sète is a town at ease with the water. **Sète Croisières** (sete-croisieres.com; adult/child from €10/6) runs three main types of boat tour: a Mediterranean coastline cruise, a canal explorer and a glass-bottom boat trip into the Étang de Thau to view the mussel and oyster farms. If the idea of self-propulsion is more appealing, then **KayakMed** (kayakmed.com) have rental points for kayaks and SUPs on both the lagoon- and sea-facing sides of town.

The main exhibition at the **Musée de la Mer** (icisete.fr; free) explores the **Joutes Nautiques**, including videos, costumes and replicas of the jousting poles and shields used. Although most explanation is in French, there's a decent visual section detailing the region's boat building, including some good models of the distinctive wooden fishing boats called *bateaux-bœufs* (ox boats), common between here and Catalonia.

NAUTICAL JOUSTING

Each year from mid-June to August, the St Louis Festival (in honour of the town's patron saint) is Sète's main event, involving competitions, music and firework displays. The main events see participants clamber into wooden boats, dressed in traditional sailors' costumes and carrying wooden jousts and shields, in an attempt to jab one another into the water. These week-long **Joutes Nautiques** (nautical jousting) tournaments, which began in 1966 but have roots that go back much earlier, are a great time to visit, although hotel accommodation is usually scarce in the weeks around 25 August, the festival's main day. During the event, the Royal Canal that runs through the heart of Sète is draped in the French tricolore and its banks are lined with spectators.

EATING IN SÈTE: BEST SEAFOOD

La Maison de la Méditerranée: One of the best places in town to try local dishes, such as the *tielle Sètoise* (p674). A decent place to try oysters, too. *hours vary* €€

Fleur de Sel: Behind the unassuming façade, chefs concoct some of Sète's finest dishes, such as *bourride Sètoise* fish soup. Reservations essential. *noon-2.30 & 7.30-10pm Mon-Sat* €€€

Au Bout d'la Rue: Escape the clamour (and prices) of the waterfront restaurants at this cosy wine bar with tasty cheese boards and seafood tapas. *10am-1am* €

La Coquerie: Six-course tasting menus are the only option at this bistronomic fish restaurant with a fantastic sea view. Exceptional wine list. *hours vary Thu-Sun* €€€

Musée International des Arts Modestes

PAUL VALÉRY: FAMOUS SON OF SÈTE

Although he never won the Nobel Prize in Literature, Paul Valéry (1871–1945) was nominated 12 times, primarily for his symbolist poetry, but he also wrote essays and literary criticism. In fact, Sète's most notable resident was a polymath with broad interests that led him away from writing for many years until, in his mid-40s, he gained recognition for *La Jeune Parque*, a collection of poetry he'd intended to be his last. He is buried in Sète at the **Cimetière Marin**, which lies slightly down the slope towards the sea beneath **Musée Paul Valéry**. The cemetery, which Valéry wrote a poem about in 1946, also holds the grave of Jean Vilar, the playwright and director who once ran the Théâtre National Populaire.

There's still an active fishing community in **La Pointe Courte** neighbourhood, northwest of the train station. An evening stroll here gives a good sense of what the whole town used to be like decades ago. Unsurprisingly, Sète has its own culinary style, the pan-Mediterranean, seafood-centric '*cuisine Sètoise*', with a highlight being *tielle Sètoise* (octopus pie).

Water Colours

The sea is a recurrent theme in the works on display at the **Musée Paul Valéry** (*museepaulvalery-sete.fr; adult/child €10/5.50*), dedicated to the eponymous Sète-born writer and featuring a couple of his own drawings. Among the ground floor's 19th- and 20th-century works are the nautical-themed Fauvist works of Gabriel Couderc, and a seascape by the Realist Gustave Courbet. The basement floor, with its blue carpet and white walls, includes a beautiful, anonymous oil painting from 1869–80, which elegantly depicts 19th-century Sète.

Art takes on a much less grandiose role in the **Musée International des Arts Modestes** (*MIAM; miam.org; entry €5.60*), where temporary installations explore the overlooked spaces in art, which has included anything from a collection of historical individual citrus fruit wrappers to the art found on shopping bags.

Causses et Cévennes

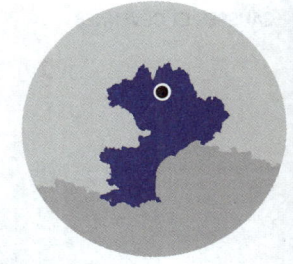

BUCOLIC CHARM | PUNGENT CHEESES | DRAMATIC GORGES

France's Massif Central saves its most dramatic act for its southernmost reaches. Meet the Causses et Cévennes, a biodiverse region of shifting mountainscapes. You can be cruising over an open plateau one minute, plunging through dense forests of oak and chestnut the next, before emerging in a yawning gorge, its precipitous walls thick with nesting vultures. It is punctuated by pretty rural hamlets of stone cottages with wooden shutters. No wonder the region was designated a UNESCO World Heritage Site.

The name Languedoc, or *langue d'Oc*, refers to the vernacular language of the Occitania (pronounced ock-si-*tan*-ee-a) region, to which Languedoc-Roussillon belongs. The mountainous interior was once cut off from the rest of France. Perfect, then for the persecuted Cathars and Protestant Huguenots, keen to hold onto their way of life. These days it's not quite so non-conformist, but the unique combination of its history and its natural beauty make the Parc National des Cévennes, and the Parc Naturel Régional des Grands Causses which blends into it, so alluring.

> ### ☑ TOP TIP
> IGN Top25 maps offer the best coverage. Tourism offices (the main one, **Maison du Tourisme**, is in Florac) provide maps and detailed hiking routes. *Cévennes and Grands Causses* by Dirk Hilbers is a great nature guide. Harder to find are Cicerone Guides' out-of-print *Walking in the Cévennes* and *Walks in the Cévennes* by the French Ramblers Association.

Adrenaline in the Gorges du Tarn
Thrilling drive and boating trips

One of France's most thrilling natural wonders is found in the zone where the Cévennes becomes the Causses: the Gorges du Tarn. If you have a car, prepare for one of the country's truly

GETTING AROUND

Aside from the steam train between Anduze and St-Jean-du-Gard (from which you can pick up various multiday hiking trails), very little headway was ever made into the Causses et Cévennes region by public transport. For many people, that is the reason it remains so unspoiled. It also means driving is required to appreciate the region. The Stevenson alternative is to hike (preferably not while forcing a poor donkey to go along with you).

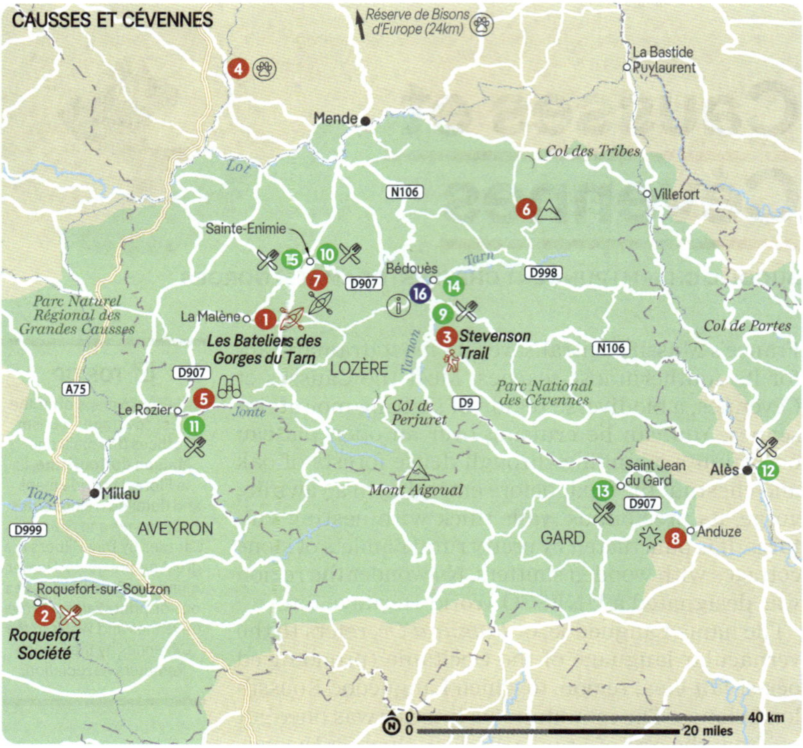

CAUSSES ET CÉVENNES

HIGHLIGHTS
1. Les Bateliers des Gorges du Tarn
2. Roquefort Société
3. Stevenson Trail

SIGHTS
4. Les Loups du Gévaudan
5. Maison des Vautours
6. Mont Lozère

ACTIVITIES
see 1 Canoë 2000
see 1 Canoe au Moulin de la Malène
7. Canoë Méjean

8. Train à Vapeur des Cévennes

EATING
9. Auberge Cévenole
10. Auberge du Moulin
11. Capluc Kfé
12. Épices et Tout
13. Gîte le Pré de Modestine
14. La Lozerette
see 11 L'Alicanta
15. Le Petit Paris

INFORMATION
16. Maison du Tourisme

spectacular, and slightly unnerving, drives. The gorge runs for around 50km, but a good entry point is the pretty village of **Ste-Énimie** (aka Gorges du Tarn Causses). From here, the D907 balcony road scrapes its way past vertiginous cliffs, which occasionally hang right over the road. When you can't

EATING IN GORGES DU TARN: BEST RESTAURANTS

L'Alicanta: Seasonal ingredients (often linked to beef, pork or lamb) with good-value set menus in Le Rozier. The Michelin Guide is paying close attention. *7-8.30pm* €€

Le Petit Paris: A great place to try regional dishes, such as *aligot* (delightfully cheesy mashed potato served with sausage) in Ste-Énimie. *hours vary Fri-Tue* €€

Capluc Kfé: The charcuterie and cheese boards, river trout and *aligot* with pork sausages dripping in onion gravy are hearty fare at this Le Rozier favourite. *hours vary* €€

Auberge du Moulin: Terrace dining in Ste-Énimie, overlooking the gorge, with French cuisine staples such as roast leg of lamb with vegetables. *Thu-Tue Apr-Oct* €€

slip by it, the road tunnels through, narrowing, in parts, to a single lane. Every twist and turn affords a fresh perspective on the gorge as the turquoise river trundles along beside you.

Midway along is the stunning **La Malène** village, the best point to get out of the car and into a boat. **Les Bateliers des Gorges du Tarn** (gorgesdutarn.com; €26), the revered local boaters, steer you down the river in a green wooden boat. Kayaking and canoeing are popular alternatives, and the river is safer here than Ste-Énimie for beginners. **Canoë 2000** (canoe-kayak-gorgesdutarn.com) and **Canoe au Moulin de la Malène** (canoeblanc.com) rent all the necessary equipment and drive you back to the village at the end. In Ste-Énimie, try **Canoë Méjean** (canoe-mejean.com). Back on the road, at **Le Rozier** you can turn east into Gorges de la Jonte, which has another stunning gorge drive on wider, less crowded roads.

Telescopic Raptors
Observing vultures in their natural habitat

Although once native to the Causses et Cévennes, vultures were hunted or poisoned to local extinction by the early 20th century. Today, at the fantastic **Maison des Vautours** (maisondesvautours.fr; adult/child €8/5), you can learn how they made a comeback, starting in 1966 with a reintroduction programme. While the early releases were failures, by 1986, 58 vultures were back in the wild. Today, four species of vulture – griffon, black, bearded (aka lammergeiers) and Egyptian – call the Gorges de la Jonte home, together numbering more than 2700 birds, most of which are griffon vultures.

The museum uses a combination of interactive displays, video presentations and informative panels about their unique evolution, lifestyles and feeding habits, to engage different age groups. The highlight is the rooftop belvedere, where a dozen telescopes are trained on the vulture nests high up the sides of the gorge. The view on its own is magnificent, but watching the vultures in their natural habitat makes this a special experience.

Old Ways Through The Valleys
Hiking the Stevenson Trail

Robert Louis Stevenson, the Scottish writer of *Treasure Island* fame, is worshipped in these parts. That's because in 1879, he wrote *Travels with a Donkey in the Cévennes*, a nonfiction account of his weeks-long hike along the region's shepherd

TOP CAUSSES & CÉVENNES HIKING TRAILS

For more information, see gr-infos.com.

GR67: Considered the ultimate guide to the Cévennes on foot, the 130km GR67 is a loop hike that begins and ends in Anduze, summiting Mt Aigoual.

GR68: The GR68, aka the Mont Lozère loop, never actually climbs the mountain, rather using it as the axle around which the 115km hike revolves.

GR736: From Albi to Villefort, this 317km route encompasses the entire Causses et Cévennes.

GR4: Passes through the Causses et Cévennes on its way from the Atlantic to the Mediterranean.

GR700: Essentially a longer version of the GR70, the Regordane Way, as it's known, continues to Nîmes and beyond.

EATING ON THE STEVENSON TRAIL: OUR PICKS

Auberge Cévenole: Just outside Florac, this rustic restaurant does fantastic Cévennes cuisine, such as *aligot* with mushrooms and chestnuts. *hours vary Wed-Sun* €€

Épices et Tout: Celebrate the end (or beginning) of your hike with an excellent-value gourmet set menu in Alès. The salmon tartare is recommended. *hours vary Mon-Sat* €€

Gîte le Pré de Modestine: Brick farmhouse with donkeys and hearty meals. Ideal place for a good feed continuing along the GR70 from St-Jean-du-Gard. *hours vary* €

La Lozerette: This fine dining establishment in Cocurès village, midway along the GR70, offers an incredible cheese board and 300 wines. *hours vary Apr-Oct* €€€

WILDLIFE IN THE LOZÈRE & CÉVENNES

The vulture reintroduction programme is part of a wider rewilding project attempting to restore crucial lost links in the natural order. But while educating people about the benefits of vultures opened the door to their return, larger mammals face a much trickier return. **Les Loups du Gévaudan** is an enclosed space where wolves are able to roam, however a widespread misunderstanding-based fear of wolves is the ultimate barrier to any significant release programme in the near future. Further north, **Réserve de Bisons d'Europe** sees European bison spread over a much wider, yet still controlled area. Successful wild reintroduction programmes have returned beavers and Przewalski's horses to these lands, joining wild boar, deer, otters and badgers, among other wild mammals in the region.

trails. The route he took is known today as the **Stevenson Trail** *(Chemin de Stevenson; officially the GR70; gr-infos.com/en/gr70.htm)* and its 268km is completed by thousands of hikers every year. Much like the Camino, there are many wonderful *gîtes* to stay in along the way. To follow the route as Stevenson did it, start in Le-Puy-en-Velay (p480) and finish in St-Jean-du-Gard (p677), or continue a little further to Alès. The route climbs **Mont Lozère** (1699m), the highest peak in the Cévennes.

Steam-Powered Cévennes
Old locomotives through the hills

The **Train à Vapeur des Cévennes** *(trainavapeur.com; adult/child from €13.50/11)*, puffing along since 1909, throws out palls of steam as it chugs through a valley between Anduze and St-Jean-du-Gard beneath the foothills of the Cévennes. The fleet of gleaming black locomotive engines, the youngest built in 1949, are in fine fettle. Many of the carriages – gaily painted with murals of local wildlife and of the villages visited during the 40-minute journey – are open sided. Trains do not depart every day but when they do run, it's usually three times daily in either direction. Most people spend a few hours in either Anduze or St-Jean-du-Gard before jumping on the return train.

Caves, Penicillin & Sheep Farms
A taste of Roquefort's cheese tours

Surrounded by high cliffs in the Grand Causses lies the town of Roquefort, where some of the world's finest blue cheese is made. With a special AOP *(Appellation d'Origine Protegée)* protection that limits production to this region only, just a handful of companies can legally make this creamy, salty blue cheese and call it Roquefort. Milk must come from Lacaune sheep within a 100km perimeter of town, where the ripening also has to take place.

Seven companies make Roquefort. Among them is **Roquefort Société** *(roquefort-societe.com; tours from €7.50)*, whose cave tours allow an up-close look at how this unique cheese is made and aged. Blue cheese was invented by mistake. Shepherds would often shelter in the surrounding caves and the most likely story is that one left behind some curds from their sheep's milk and much later discovered that it had grown some marbled blue veins. Biology and geology work hand in hand: rockfalls created fissures in the limestone known as *fleurines*, which allow air to flow into the caves, bringing moisture with it, providing a natural climate control favoured by Penicillium roqueforti fungus, which exists naturally in the caves. The presence of the curds did the rest.

TOO MUCH CHEESE?

The answer is, of course, that there's no such thing. For other cheesy tours, you can watch **reblochon** (p523) being made in the Haute-Savoie region of eastern France and visit the **Musée du Camembert** (p244) in Normandy.

Beyond Causses et Cévennes

Cathar strongholds, chocolate-box villages and spectacular countryside beguile and surprise in these out-of-the-way nooks of southern France.

Places
Navacelles p679
Mende p680
Lastours p680

The foothills around the Causses and Cévennes continue the themes of the UNESCO World Heritage zone. That means more natural beauty, quaint villages and time-stamped pastoral heritage, plus delicious local foods such as the blue cheeses of the Aubrac region and the cheesy, stringy local mashed potato dish, *aligot*. When it comes to natural geological features, the remarkable Cirque de Navacelles is one of the most captivating sights in Languedoc-Roussillon. In Mende, Lozère's regional capital, the Musée du Gévaudan (p680) explores regional history. The city is a great base for exploring, or using as a stopover between the Cévennes and L'Aubrac, whose pretty plateau pastures sit above the upper Lot Valley, home to some of southern France's prettiest villages.

Navacelles
TIME FROM GORGES DU TARN: 2HR 30MIN

Natural Amphitheatre & Historic Mills

Sitting at the bottom of a natural amphitheatre, the **Cirque de Navacelles**, dug out of the limestone by a meander of the Vis River, is the exquisitely poised Navacelles village (not to be confused with Navacelles town near Alès), ringed by a dried-up oxbow of the river. The best viewpoint is from **Belvédère de la Baume Auriol**. Not only is the car park here free (overnight parking not allowed), but at 615m high, it offers sweeping spurs and meanders of the valley. Above the river, terraced olive groves grace the lower slopes and there's a 2km walk along the **Sentier du Facteur**, which drops about 300m down to Navacelles.

The chocolate-box village is alive with bearded iris and wisteria in spring, while below the stone buildings, the languid Vis River passes beneath an historic old stone bridge, **Pont Vieux en Pierre**, culminating in a magnificent waterfall. Another way to Navacelles is via the narrow, hairpin road (unsuitable for some camper vans) from the belvedere.

Hiking to the Old Watermills

From Navacelles village you can pick up the 5km trail through the valley to a series of cascades, straddled by **Les Moulins**

GETTING AROUND

Mende is connected to other cities in the region by public transport. The 280 bus travels once a day from Montpellier, with two daily trains direct to Nîmes. From Mende there are plenty of good cycling routes into the Cévennes. But travel by car is still the only effective method of exploration throughout the region; towns such as Lastours are difficult to reach without your own transportation, unless you take a guided tour from Montpellier or Carcassonne.

BURONS

As you drive through L'Aubrac, you'll likely notice the squat, wood and stone cabins known as *burons*. These buildings (called 'oil' in the local Occitan language) served as summertime homes away from home for transhumant shepherds, when they brought their flocks up to graze the plateau pastures for months on end. The interiors would often be cosy, with sleeping quarters, a dairy and cheese making station, and a makeshift cellar where cheeses were matured. Many surviving burons were converted into restaurants, where dining is done communally at long wooden tables. **Buron de l'Aubrac**, **Le Buron de Born** and **Buron du Ché** are culinary highlights of the region. *Aligot* (a little like cheesy mashed potato) served with pork sausages is the most popular regional dish.

de la Foux *(free)*, two watermills, which were abandoned after a flood in 1907. Alternatively, drive west of the village to the Moulins roadside parking, from which a 1.1km **trail** (the closest any road comes to these buildings) leads down through slopes clad in a mix of cedar, buckthorn and fig. When you hear the roar of the water tumbling through the ravine, you're close to the Moulins de la Foux. For much of the year, the river rages down in an angry white torrent, passing directly beneath the empty mill buildings, which are accessible to visitors, their hefty millstones still in place.

Mende

TIME FROM GORGES DU TARN: 1HR

Rocks, Dinosaurs & a Mythical Beast

Capital of the Gévaudan region until the 18th century, Mende is now the administrative capital of Lozère. The **Musée du Gévaudan** *(musee-du-gevaudan.fr; free)* touches on aspects of the geology, social history, natural history (including ichthyosaurus fossils) and archaeology of the region. An entire room is dedicated to the mythical Bête du Gévaudan (Beast of Gévaudan), which is rumoured to have eaten people during the late 18th century. The museum also contains paintings by local artists, such as Jeanne Bourrillon-Tournay and Victorin Galière.

Lastours

TIME FROM GORGES DU TARN: 3HR

Towers in the Wilderness

Rising up a haggard mountain spine above the valley-bottom village of Lastours is not one, but four Cathar castles. With their tight cylindrical forts standing like fortified kitchen rolls on the most unsurpassable rocky outcrops, whose slopes are awash in birdsong coming from the Italian cypress trees, **Les 4 Châteaux de Lastours** *(lastourisme.fr; adult/child €9/from €4.50)* are a magnificent sight.

It's a steep, rocky walk up from the entrance (follow the riverside walkway, rather than the road, to find it). The full walk loop takes about two hours, first reaching **Quertinheux** castle, isolated on its own peak and offering a magnificent view of the other three. The trail then continues to **Tour Régine** (Queen's Tower) and **Cabaret**, named after the Lords of Cabaret, who were rulers of these Cathar-friendly lands until the Albigensian Crusade in 1211. You can climb this tower's narrow circular steps but will need your phone's torch. End at **Surdespine** castle.

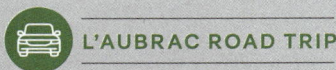

L'AUBRAC ROAD TRIP

Many visitors hike through the hilly L'Aubrac region of France's Aveyron department, but this one-day road trip is a great alternative.

START	END	LENGTH
St Geniez d'Olt et d'Aubrac	Aubrac	64km; 7 hours

One branch of the Camino de Santiago passes over the Aubrac plateau and down into the upper valley of the Lot River, where you'll encounter a string of beautiful villages. Start in ① **St Geniez d'Olt et d'Aubrac** where a 14th-century Augustinian monastery sits at the heart of town. Follow the D988 west for 2km to ② **Ste-Eulalie-d'Olt**, a medieval, flower-filled commune. A further 20km along the D6 is ③ **St-Côme-d'Olt**, whose church has a twisted spire and where hikers flow along this branch of the Camino. The 14km drive to stunning ④ **Estaing**, the pick of the pretty litter, is a simple one along D987 and then D920 on the north side of the river. A 16th-century Gothic bridge spans the river, while the **Château d'Estaing** presides over the whole valley. Pull yourself away to drive back to St-Côme-d'Olt, then follow the D987 northwards for another 21km, up and out of the valley and onto the plateau that defines L'Aubrac. The eponymous settlement, ⑤ **Aubrac**, is a cattle farming village on the high plains at the heart of the region, although from May to October you'll see as many Camino hikers as you do cows. **Maison de l'Aubrac** has a tourist centre, cafe and a small, well-curated museum about local life. Close the loop from Aubrac to St Geniez or continue on to your next destination.

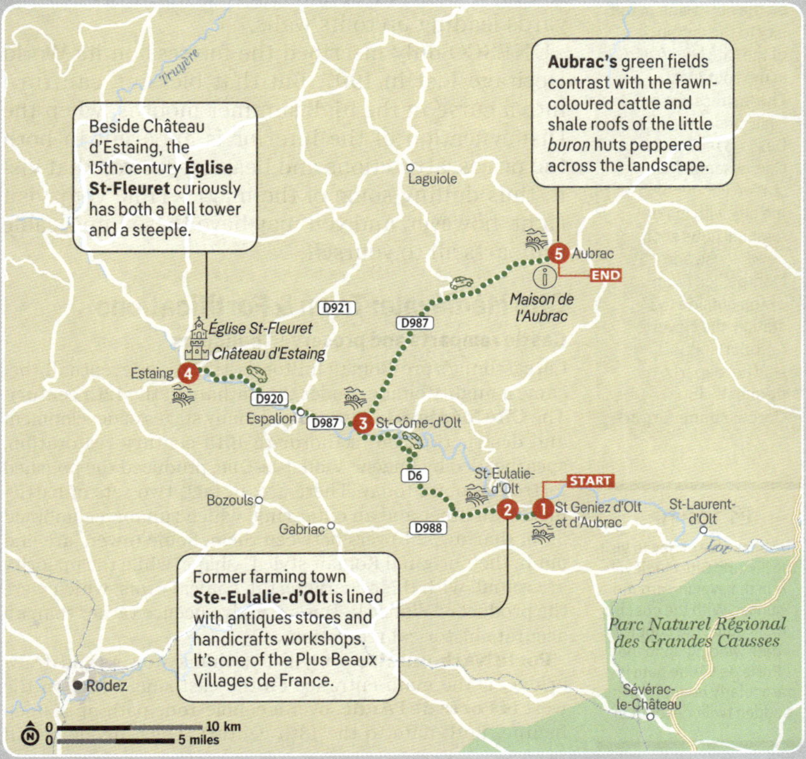

> Beside Château d'Estaing, the 15th-century **Église St-Fleuret** curiously has both a bell tower and a steeple.

> **Aubrac's** green fields contrast with the fawn-coloured cattle and shale roofs of the little *buron* huts peppered across the landscape.

> Former farming town **Ste-Eulalie-d'Olt** is lined with antiques stores and handicrafts workshops. It's one of the Plus Beaux Villages de France.

Carcassonne

CATHAR CASTLES | SPARKLING WINES | HEARTY STEWS

GETTING AROUND

Although split into two halves, Carcassonne remains a fairly small city. It's a 2km walk from the **train station** on the north side of the city to the entrance of the Cité Médiévale in the southeast. The fortress sits on a hill, although Ville Basse is fairly flat. Carcassonne train station connects the city with major regional hubs such as Toulouse and Montpellier. From a stop outside the station, the Navette Aéroport (airport shuttle) departs frequently for **Carcassonne Airport**.

☑ TOP TIP

The best time of day to visit the historic Cité Médiévale is in the evening around sunset. With the coach tours gone, the cobbled path winding up to the Porte de l'Aude gate is particularly beautiful in its sudden twilit desolation.

Brimming with whimsy from its ice-cream cone turrets to the crenellated battlements undulating over contours of a hill, Carcassonne's medieval citadel looks like something only Disney could conjure up. It is among the best preserved fortified cities in Europe, and so carefully cared for that much of the newer part of the city, known as the Ville Basse (or La Bastide St-Louis) sprawls away from, rather than around it, so that in some directions there is nothing but vineyards leading up to its walls.

UNESCO duly inscribed the fortress on its World Heritage List in 1997. But that blessing can turn into a curse in the high summer months, when the Disneyfication of the interior is apparent in both the prices, attractions and heaving crowds that visit, thus dulling some of the magic. Time your visit right, however, and you may have these impeccable ramparts all to yourself.

Cité Médiévale: Town & Fortifications

Castle ramparts and preserved buildings

Carcassonne's pre-Roman hilltop fortifications eventually became a mighty citadel under the Cathars in the 12th century. The **Cité Médiévale** experienced many stages of development and destruction, but a thorough 19th-century restoration, spearheaded by Eugène Viollet-le-Duc, produced the polished fortress you see today. There are, in fact, two sets of battlements, an inner and an outer ring, which run for a combined 3km, sharing 52 towers between them. Some towers are laid out in their original Roman-style U-shape, while the majority are round, with their characterful, conical roofs, which were the product of Viollet-le-Duc's creative licence rather than an accurate historical recreation.

Porte Narbonnaise, with its two chunky towers and drawbridge, is the main entrance on the east side, while on the west is **Porte de l'Aude**, over a cobblestone path up a steep incline. Both date to the 13th century. Once inside, you'll

HIGHLIGHTS
1 Château et Remparts
2 Cité Médiévale

SIGHTS
3 Basilique St-Nazaire
4 Cathédrale St-Michel
5 Musée des Beaux-Arts de Carcassonne
6 Pont Neuf
7 Pont Vieux
8 Porte de l'Aude
9 Porte Narbonnaise
10 Vins & Vinos

ACTIVITIES
11 Carcassonne Croisières

SLEEPING
12 Hôtel de la Cité

EATING
13 Adélaïde
14 Agapé Carcassonne
15 Au Lard et au Cochon
16 Barrière Truffes
17 Brasserie à Quatre Temps
18 La Marquière

TRANSPORT
19 Le Petit Cyclo
20 Train Station

discover a tangle of streets lined with tourist-oriented shops and attractions, most of which detract from the majesty of the place, although there are some fine restaurants within.

Access the **Château et Remparts** (remparts-carcassonne.fr; adult/child from €14/free, prices are 50% higher in summer) to walk sections of the wall and discover the 12th-century castle, built for the city's viscounts. Buy a timed-entry ticket online in advance to skip the long queues. The museum within displays artefacts from the original building. Exit the château beside the city's Gothic cathedral, **Basilique St-Nazaire**, with its exquisite stained glass; a key stop for Camino de Santiago pilgrims.

BEST WINERY TOURS NEAR CARCASSONNE

For visits of the following, advanced reservations are often necessary.

Domaine de Baronarques: Guided tours of this elegant 17th-century property and terroir. The seven-wine Heritage Tour includes tastings of four vintages.

Domaine La Louvière: Tuesday morning vineyard tours from May to September and year-round tastings of this winery's blanquette de Limoux.

Château de Brasse: Over 300 years of winemaking history at this stunning château with cellar tours and riverside terrace tastings.

Maison Guinot: Located in the heart of Limoux town. A great option for a driving-free day trip by train from Carcassonne.

Boutique Sieur d'Arques: Located just outside Limoux, this wine cellar has its own first-floor museum about blanquette and local history.

Cité Médiévale (p682)

Ville Basse Culture
Art and religion

Carcassonne's Ville Basse (La Bastide St-Louis) sits across the Aude River from the medieval fortress. The most enjoyable route across is via the **Pont Vieux** footbridge, although the best views back toward the fortress (particularly at sunset) are from the **Pont Neuf**, just to the north, which incorporate the older bridge's honey-coloured stone arches. Ville Basse was first started in 1240 and has a distinct personality to its revered older cousin. It has its own cathedral, **Cathédrale St-Michel** *(tourisme-carcassonne.fr; free)*, built in the 13th century, plus a collection of local and regional art at **Musée des Beaux-Arts de Carcassonne** *(carcassonne.org/lieux/musee-des-beaux-arts; free)*.

 EATING IN CARCASSONNE: BEST FINE DINING

Reserve ahead, it has two Michelin stars

Agapé Carcassonne: Family-run fine-dining restaurant where the high-concept, seven-course tasting menu poses the best value in Languedoc. Reserve in advance. noon-2.30 & 7-10pm Mon-Fri €€

Le Jardin en Ville: Dishes at this neo-rustic spot are made with ingredients grown in the restaurant garden. There's usually a decent vegetarian option. *hours vary Mon-Sat* €€

La Table de Franck Putelat: Chef Putelat's 'classic-fiction' approach to cuisine reinvents old favourites with homegrown garden produce. *hours vary Tue-Sat* €€€

Barrière Truffes: Tastings of foie gras, oysters, carpaccio and goat cheese, all covered in grated truffle, paired with biodynamic wines, define this gourmand haven. *hours vary Tue-Sun* €€€

Canal Du Midi Journeys
Cruises and cycling

Slow things down to an ambling place with a cruise along the canal. Boat tours with **Carcassonne Croisières** *(carcassonne-navigationcroisiere.com; adult/child from €10/7.50)* pass through locks on the Canal du Midi. The journey is not particularly photogenic, and most people come for the live commentary (in English and French) about the history of the Canal du Midi along the way. To explore the canal at your own pace, follow the towpath on foot or by wheel. Hire bicycles from **Le Petit Cyclo** *(le-petit-cyclo.com)* near the train station, with e-bikes offering a fun alternative.

Take a Limoux AOP Wine Tour
Vineyards, tastings and fizzy wine

The Languedoc is the country's largest wine-producing region by volume. So ubiquitous are the vineyards that they even touch the very walls of the Cité Médiévale. Carcassonne sits in the Malepère AOP region and immediately south is the lauded Limoux AOP, whose pedigree is reinforced by the fact that sparkling wine was invented, quite by accident, by monks at **Abbaye de St-Hilaire** *(saint-hilaire-aude.fr; adult/child €6/2)* in 1531. Similar to many religious buildings in the region, the abbey has fortifications, such as a double portcullis gateway, a prison where the abbot was in charge of administering justice and, crucially, wine cellars.

Limoux town is the epicentre of this sparkling blanquette de Limoux wine production. Commonly grown grapes in this region include syrah and carignan. Winery tours with English-speaking guides are available from Carcassonne's Ville Basse via **Vins & Vinos** *(carcassonnewineshop.com)*, which also runs in-house wine tastings.

FEELING BUBBLY?
Fizzy white wine went on to finer and better things in Champagne and is now the very definition of success. Tours of famed **Champagne houses** (p314) are an unmatched way to sample it at the source.

 EATING IN CARCASSONNE: BEST PLACES FOR CASSOULET

La Marquière: Given its Cité Médiévale location, La Marquière's price-to-quality ratio defies expectation. Its clay pot *cassoulet* uses delightfully tender meat. *hours vary Tue-Sat* €€€

Au Lard et au Cochon: Specialises in *cassoulet*, although the *magret de canard* (duck breast with mushroom sauce) is worthy. *noon-2pm & 7-9pm Tue-Sat* €€€

Adélaïde: Another good shout for *cassoulet* in the Cité Médiévale and at prices more in line with the less touristy parts of the city. *noon-2.30pm & 7-9.30pm* €€

Brasserie à Quatre Temps: Ville Basse *cassoulet* served in an earthenware dish alongside an extensive wine list of regional and national bottles. *8am-10.30pm* €€

Perpignan

MEDIEVAL HISTORY | BAROQUE ART | CATALAN CUISINE

☑ TOP TIP

Ask for a **Pass Découvertes** booklet at the first ticketed place you visit and get it stamped on the back page. Present it from your second entry onwards at practically every museum and attraction across the Pyrénées-Orientales and you will receive discounted entry.

If arriving in Perpignan by train, then welcome to the centre of the universe; at least according to Salvador Dalí. Typical of many frontier zones, allegiances and borderlines blend here, with French, Spanish and Catalonian interests vying for the hearts and minds of local people. To further complicate history, Perpignan was once the capital of the former Kingdom of Majorca and its remnants remain the best sights in the city.

Capital of the 'Roussillon' of Languedoc-Roussillon, these days referred to as Pyrénées-Orientales, this is a region where the French tricolore is often joined by the red and yellow stripes of Catalonia. Catalan is frequently heard spoken in the streets and road signs are in both languages. It is a rare side of France that admits outside influence, although rugby, much more a French than a Spanish sport, is followed with a fervour that matches the rest of southern France. Many museums are closed on Sundays and Mondays (and occasionally Tuesdays) in French Catalonia.

Kingdom of Majorca Relics
Palaces, towers and a cathedral

The Kingdom of Majorca is one of those many little European empires that pales in comparison to its larger neighbours like France and the Crown of Aragon. Nevertheless, for a brief spell from around 1276 to 1349 – after a succession dispute between the sons of King Jaume I of Aragon led to Jaume II

GETTING AROUND

Bus coverage in the Pyrénées-Orientales is typically better than other parts of the region, with the red liO buses plying multiple routes around Perpignan and out to the satellite towns beyond, although service is patchy at best on Sundays. Perpignan is the last major train station in southern France en route to Spain, with connections to practically every major city in Occitania, Toulouse and its surroundings. But the city centre itself is compact and easy enough to explore on foot.

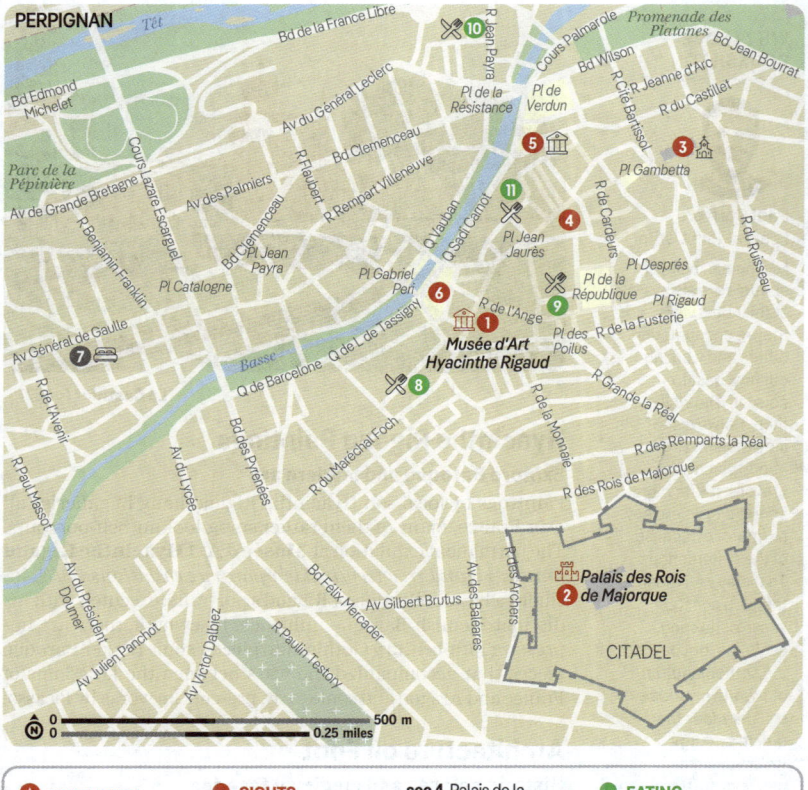

HIGHLIGHTS
1. Musée d'Art Hyacinthe Rigaud
2. Palais des Rois de Majorque

SIGHTS
3. Basilique-Cathédrale de St-Jean-Baptiste
4. Hôtel de Ville
5. Le Castillet

see 4 Loge de Mer
see 4 Palais de la Députation
6. Place Arago
see 4 Place de la Loge

SLEEPING
7. Nyx Boutique

EATING
8. Crêperie Foch
9. La Famille
10. La Galinette
11. Le Divil

breaking from the kingdom – this little empire burned brightly. Consisting of Spain's Balearic Islands and the lands around Perpignan, almost as far up as Montpellier for a while, Jaume II began to build the **Palais des Rois de Majorque** (*Palace of the Kings of Majorca; ledepartement66.fr; adult/child €9/ free*) as a worthy seat for a successful king. It remains the most impressive building in the city.

Basilique-Cathédrale de St-Jean-Baptiste (*cathedrale perpignan.fr; free*) was also started during the reign of the Majorcan monarchs, on the site of a 10th-century church. The empire's collapse halted construction but it was eventually completed in the 15th century. Meanwhile, the emblem of Perpignan, a stocky main gate to the city called **Le Castillet** (*mairie-perpignan.fr; adult/child €2/free*), was built in 1368, soon after the city returned to Aragon's control. Climb to the top for views over the city.

WHY I LOVE ROUSSILLON

Paul Stafford, Lonely Planet writer

Like human beings, cultures are always at their best when they're encountering others and working out how best to coexist. And while there's always the inevitable wrangling about which one prevails, it's far more interesting when they all improve because of their interactions. That may well mean there's a constant sense of flux and evolution, but beyond the settlements, an old-world mystique still pervades the region's craggy valleys, where medieval fortresses cling relentlessly to existence, hinting at the determination it took to build them, let alone live there. This cauldron of conflict, compromise and coexistence in Roussillon never gets old. No wonder the region inspires so much great art.

Le Castillet (p687)

Hyacinthe Rigaud Paintings

Explore Baroque and modern art

Paintings by local son Hyacinthe Rigaud hang in galleries all over France, many of them rather smug-looking self-portraits. The permanent exhibition at **Musée d'Art Hyacinthe Rigaud** *(musee-rigaud.fr; entry/incl temporary exhibitions €8/11)* includes a large collection of Rigaud's portraits, executed with his distinct Flemish Baroque influence. Elsewhere, there are impressive 15th-century Gothic altarpieces, some darker Baroque pieces that accompanied the wars between the kingdoms of France and Aragon and some early, pre-cubism works by Picasso.

Architecture on Foot

Historic palaces and medieval façades

Perpignan's low-traffic historic core is packed with historic flourishes, particularly between **Place Arago**, the main cafe-lined square beside the Basse canal, and the chic, boutiques-lined streets around **Place de la Loge**. This area contains the main bulk of the old town, which was once the city's nucleus. The southern side of Place de la Loge is lined with historic palaces, such as the stone and brick-patterned façades of the **Hôtel de Ville** (Town Hall; 16th century), **Palais de la Députation** (Courthouse; 15th century) and the Gothic **Loge de Mer** (Sea Lodge; built between the 14th and 16th centuries), which now houses the city's tourism office.

 EATING IN PERPIGNAN: OUR PICKS

Le Divil: Give in to temptation at this matured meat steak restaurant with an old-world brick and wood interior and a 300-bottle wine list. *hours vary Tue-Sat* €€€

Crêperie Foch: Friendly spot with an old car in the middle, serving sweet crêpes and savoury *galettes*. Try the walnut and Roquefort salad. *hours vary Tue-Sat* €

La Famille: The innovative set lunch menus change regularly, but the inventiveness, artistic presentation and exceptional value are constant. *hours vary Mon-Sat* €€

La Galinette: Inventive dishes, all with natural ingredients from chef Christophe Comes' garden. Two Michelin stars (one regular, one green). *hours vary Wed-Sat* €€€

Beyond Perpignan

Influential art communities, undulating coastline, Pyrenean mountainscapes and windswept castles await the intrepid explorer in this diverse, yet overlooked, region.

Snowy Pyrenean peaks crowd the skyline wherever you are in Pyrénées-Orientales (aka Roussillon) but they are at their most impressive in the west of the region. The imposing mountain you see in Perpignan (the perfect base for exploring the region), often capped with snow, is Mont Canigou. Pushing southwest from Perpignan, the Têt Valley draws people from the city to the great outdoors, while Villefranche-de-Conflent's fortifications suggest a battle-strewn past. Although they have more in common with Carcassonne than Catalonia, the main cluster of Cathar fortresses that punctuate the remote borderlands between Languedoc and Roussillon are best visited on a road trip from Perpignan. Further north, the Romans make a reappearance around Narbonne, while Céret and Collioure's creative communities forever changed art as we know it.

Places

Narbonne p689

Gruissan p691

Abbaye de Fontfroide p691

Villefranche-de-Conflent p691

Thuir p692

Ille-sur-Têt p692

Céret p692

Collioure p694

Paulilles p694

Narbonne

TIME FROM PERPIGNAN: **45MIN**

Doing Things the Narbonne Way

Roman Narbonne lies 65km north of Perpignan. Striking the visitor immediately at **Musée Narbo Via** *(narbovia.fr; entry/incl 3 Roman sites €9/15)* is the 'Stone Wall', a lofty, wide array of blocks taken from various temples and ruins around Narbonne and preserved from the elements. Explore the deities, floral motifs, ceremonial scenes and funerary rituals depicted among the array using the interactive panels, which allow you to select blocks and learn more about their history and provenance, as well as offering detailed notes about the carvings.

 GETTING AROUND

Buses are much better in this region than in Languedoc. Céret, Thuir, Villefranche-de-Conflent and Collioure are all linked to Perpignan by red liO buses. Most routes run daily, although some of the more provincial routes are unreliable on Sundays. The coastal towns and Narbonne enjoy good regional train links. To visit the Pays Cathare's castles, you'll almost certainly need your own transportation and a good pair of walking boots. The same goes for the mountains.

BEYOND PERPIGNAN LANGUEDOC-ROUSSILLON

THE BEST BEACHES IN PYRÉNÉES ORIENTALES

The southern reaches of Languedoc-Roussillon have some excellent beaches, including:

Plage Centrale: The region's best beach is a long, gently shelving stretch of blond sand in Argelès-sur-Mer, ideal for taking a dip or sunbathing.

Plage de Collioure: Shingle beach with stunning views of the surrounding mountains and Château Royal de Collioure.

Plage de Paulilles: Secluded sweep of sand and shingle, backed by pine forest near a former dynamite factory.

Plage de l'Ouille: Picturesque cove beach, hemmed in by rocky escarpments midway between Argelès-sur-Mer and Collioure.

Plage de Canet: Flat, wide sandy beach and with a small amusement park and carousel.

Abbaye de Fontfroide

The best-preserved artefacts are saved for the galleries in the museum beyond, where detailed descriptions are provided in English, French and Spanish. Quiet and provincial compared to its brasher neighbours, Narbonne was once Narbo Martius, a bustling Roman port and a key city, founded in 118 BCE, along the Via Domitia in their Gaul empire. Bas relief stone carvings of ships being loaded from the 1st century CE highlight Narbonne's importance, before the Aude silted up, cutting off its sea access.

A joint ticket also provides access to **L'Horreum**, a former Roman granary beneath Narbonne city centre, and **Amphoralis**, 15km to the north of the city, where clay amphorae were made to transport wine.

Exploring the Cathedral & Palace Complex

Central Narbonne is dominated by the 13th-century **Palais des Archevêques** *(narbonne.fr; entry €8)*, a former archbishops' palace. The interior holds a disconnected collection of exhibitions. Climb a spiral staircase up the donjon for views over the city and **Cathédrale St-Just**, built between 1272 and 1340, which is connected to the palace. What looks like an elaborate western entrance is actually an unfinished transept. A series of 14th-century calamities, including the Black

 EATING BEYOND PERPIGNAN: BEST CATALAN CUISINE

Les Clos de Paulilles: Run by winegrowers with vines everywhere. Traditional recipes like poached monkfish, adorned with unusual ingredients like sea lettuce. *hours vary Wed-Sun* €€€

Vigatane: Fine Catalan cuisine done with all the regional specials including *cargolade* (snails) and some phenomenal seafood platters. Canet-en-Roussillon. *hours vary* €€

Les Loges du Jardin d'Aymeric: Ingredients sourced from the kitchen gardens, keeping recipes traditional, such as beef fillet with wine sauce and artichokes. *hours vary Tue-Sun* €€€

Le Fanal: Catalan-centric tasting menus with a seafood focus. Think anchovies pickled in Banyuls-sur-Mer vinegar and smoked hake brandade. *hours vary* €€€

Death, put an end to construction on what would have been one of the region's largest cathedrals.

The palace also holds the **Parcours d'Art gallery**, atop an 88-step grand staircase. The collection is mostly of Renaissance art, including works by Pieter Breughel and Tintoretto, with Baroque ceiling frescoes. The commissioning archbishop intriguingly chose the nine muses, heralding back to Ancient Greece, as the subject, rather than drawing inspiration from the sacred texts.

Gruissan
TIME FROM PERPIGNAN: 1HR

Pink Lakes & Wetland Boardwalks

The coastline around Narbonne is particularly rewarding for nature lovers. At **La Salin de Gruissan** (*lesalindegruissan.fr; tours from €12*), guided tours of the pink rectangular salt flats known as *salines* run from two to five times a day depending on the season. The rest of the time you can buy various salt products in the shop and visit the free museum. A loftier perspective is afforded from the **Tour Barberousse** (*free*), built to defend the coast from pirate raids, in the centre of Gruissan town.

Nearby at **Peyriac-de-Mer**, the salt flats may not have the same pink hue, but there are usually flamingos here throughout the year. Get closer to these quirky birds by following the wooden **Promenade des Pontons** (*free*) boardwalk and various shoreline paths that circumvent the *étang* (lagoon).

Abbaye de Fontfroide
TIME FROM PERPIGNAN: 1HR

Middle Ages Abbey Architecture

Cavernous Romanesque halls and dormitories have a curiously empty feel at **Abbaye de Fontfroide** (*fontfroide.com; from €14*), once home to Benedictine, followed by Cistercian, monks. This is evident in the lack of decorative features, reflecting the Cistercian ban on depicting animals or humans. Some of the finest architecture is found in the cloisters, which feature robust Gothic stonework, marble columns and vast round oculi (eyes) in the tympani that let in lots of light. Around the back is a devoutly tended garden, steeped in the scents of rose and lavender. Paths here lead to terraces studded with oak, cypress and bay trees.

Villefranche-de-Conflent
TIME FROM PERPIGNAN: 50MIN

Mighty Keep & Fortified Village

Deep in the Vallée de la Têt (Têt Valley), surrounded by precipitous slopes, is Villefranche-de-Conflent. Listed as one of the Plus Beaux Villages de France, this tiny village encased in protective walls draws people primarily to visit **Fort Libéria** (*fort-liberia.com; adult/under-11 €8/4.50*), a much sturdier fortress overlooking the village. Take the shuttle bus to the top if climbing the 844 steps (and many more once you reach the fort) sounds unappealing. Unlike the Cathar castles, this is a more modern fortress, built in the 17th century and improved under Napoleon III.

LAND OF THE WIND

Most people visiting the Roussillon region for the first time are quick to notice the wind, thinking it to be an unusually windy day. Gusts can be particularly strong on exposed ridges and hilltops. But particularly along the coast between Narbonne and the Spanish border, wind is a way of life, with strong, persistent wind on most days of the year. Locals call it *'le pays du vent'*, or land of the wind, and the winds from different directions even have their own names. The main culprit is the Tramontane from the northwest. The trade-off is that, despite being by far France's windiest region, it is also among the sunniest. These conditions are also ideal for windsurfing and sailing.

CATALAN CUISINE

Dining out around the Pyrénées-Orientales region brings with it a unique set of flavours and ingredients, distinct in their combination from anywhere else in France. Peppers and spicy sausage make an appearance as the food begins to take on a Spanish and Catalonian flair. The mountains and the Mediterranean each contribute fresh ingredients, including goat's cheese and figs, sardines and citrus. Then there are uniquely northern Catalonian dishes, such as *cargolade*, which often involves hundreds of snails stuffed with parsley, paprika and garlic butter, then grilled over hot coals. During winter and early spring, whole bushels of barbecued *calçots*, a type of green onion, are polished off, while *crema catalana* and *rousquille* biscuits, which look like doughnuts and taste like Christmas, are unmissable local dessert treats.

Les Petits Trains

Departing from Villefranche-de-Conflent's station, the **Petit Train Jaune** (*Little Yellow Train; ter.sncf.com/occitanie; late May to early Dec*) is a much-loved engine that chugs along a 63km route through the Pyrenees to Latour-de-Carol-Enveitg on the Spanish border. Trains running the entire route depart roughly six times a day, running through the core of **Parc Naturel Régional des Pyrénées Catalanes**. The oft-overlooked **Petit Train Rouge** (*Little Red Train; letrainrouge.fr; late Apr to Oct*) charts a 60km route from **Rivesaltes**, just north of Perpignan, loosely following the D117 through Cathar country eastwards to **Axat**. In both cases, it's possible to travel out and back in a day, with a few hours to explore at the terminus.

Thuir
TIME FROM PERPIGNAN: **50MIN**

Time for an Apéro

Byrrh (pronounced 'beer') is an apéritif made in Thuir, 16km southwest of Perpignan. The aromatic fortified wine is made with Muscat grapes, adding quinine, coffee, cinchona bark, cinnamon, orange peel and elderberry to taste. At Thuir's **Caves Byrrh** (*caves-byrrh.fr; adult/child €6.50/3.50*) where it is made, audio guides automatically play the relevant information based on where you are stood. The highlight is wandering through the vast cellar, which is crowded with scores of giant oak vats, each holding up to 89,000L. A byrrh tasting (for the adults) cherry-tops the end of your visit.

Ille-sur-Têt
TIME FROM PERPIGNAN: **25MIN**

Encountering the Orgues Monoliths

A series of intriguing sandstone formations, known as **Les Orgues d'Ille-sur-Têt** (*orgues.netinfo.pro; adult/child €5/ from €3.50*), lie 27km west of Perpignan. Formed by wind and water erosion over millions of years, these 'fairy chimneys' stand at around 10m to 12m high and as the name Les Orgues (the organs) suggests, they look like the pipes of a church organ from certain angles. Others look like mushrooms, cloaked figures and, depending on your imagination, various appendages of the human body.

Céret
TIME FROM PERPIGNAN: **35MIN**

Hanging with Picasso, Miró & Dalí

The **Musée d'Art Moderne** (*musee-ceret.com; adult/child €10/free*) sits at the leafy, cafe-dotted core of Céret, a town also known for its cherry and melon orchards. Between the 1910s and 1950s, Céret was the unofficial centre of the art world. Showcasing works from this era of unbridled creative exploration, upon entry you are immediately confronted with works by Jean Marchand and ceramics by Pablo Picasso. Many works on display were either painted in Céret, or in nearby Collioure – including some of those by Chagall and Miró. Salvador Dalí donated some fascinating photo-based artworks to the museum.

CATHAR CASTLE COUNTRY ROAD TRIP

Explore the remote wildernesses that allowed the Cathars to endure for centuries on this thrilling driving tour.

START	END	LENGTH
Château de Puilaurens	Château de Quéribus	158km; 10 hours

Remote Pays Cathare was the last stronghold of the Gnostic group the Cathars, during the Middle Ages, who were brutally persecuted by the Catholic Church. On this road trip from Perpignan, the first leg is the longest, following the D117 west for 60km, through vineyard- and orchard-studded countryside.

Turn left at Lapradelle, following the signs up to ❶ **Château de Puilaurens**. A steep zigzag path from the ticket kiosk leads to this mini version of Carcassonne's citadel.

Head back east along the D117 for around 16km until St-Paul-de-Fenouillet. From here, a quick detour north into the ❷ **Gorges de Galamus** takes you down a thrilling road to stop above a deep ravine, cradling ❸ **Ermitage St-Antoine de Galamus**, a rock-cut church. You can reach it via a 1.5km walk from the car park.

Head back to St-Paul-de-Fenouillet then continue east along the D117 to Maury, where you'll turn north onto the D19. From here, drive 16km to ❹ **Château de Peyrepertuse**, a once-mighty fortress with spectacular views that juts above the ridge like the prow of a stricken ship. The surface area within its walls is similar to that of Carcassonne castle.

Head back south on the same road and take a left to ❺ **Château de Quéribus**. This 14th-century building, the youngest and wildest of the castles, is a lofty, emaciated keep on a jagged mountaintop.

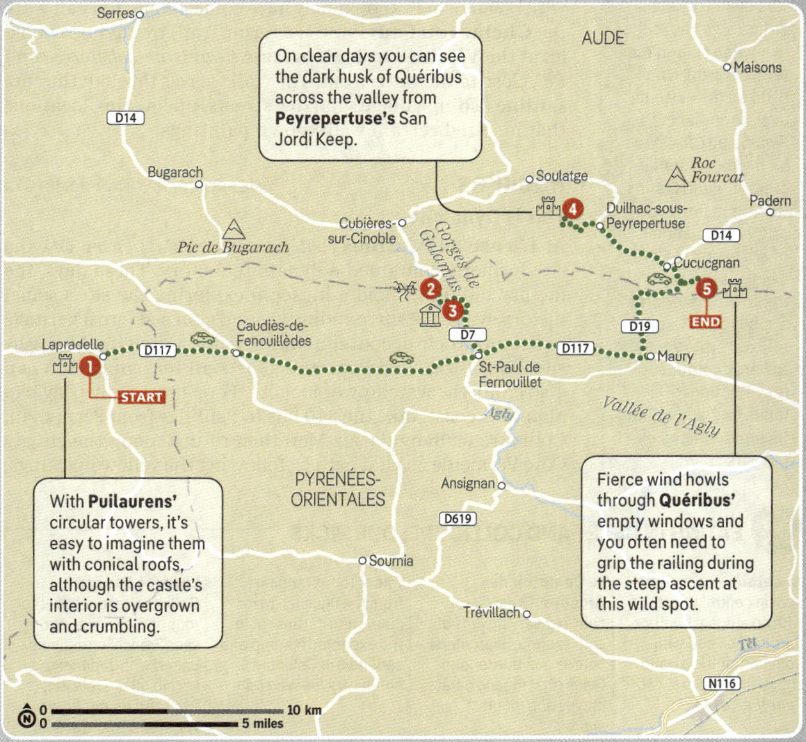

WILD BEASTS

In the 20th century's first few decades, two pretty little French towns close to the Spanish border – Céret and Collioure – would become the art world's nucleus. In Collioure in 1904, artists began letting pure colour play the role of translator of the painter's emotions. The Fauves (meaning Wild Beasts), as the painters of Fauvism became known, was intended as a derogatory term. It was coined by art critic Louis Vauxcelles (who also coined the term cubism), who disliked the extreme uses of colour in *La Femme au Chapeau* by the movement's creator, Henri Matisse. But it transformed art. By the summer of 1911 in pretty Céret, Georges Braque and Pablo Picasso were applying Fauvism's relaxed attitude towards colour and reevaluating form itself, bringing about the abstractions of cubism.

Collioure

Collioure
TIME FROM PERPIGNAN: **30MIN**

Stroll the Chemin du Fauvisme
Look out at the pastel seafront cottages and gaily painted traditional boats along the shores of Collioure (30km south of Perpignan) and you can imagine how the use of colour for which Fauvism is known may have come about. You can walk the **Chemin du Fauvisme** (Fauvism Trail) by buying a booklet at the **Vitrine sur le Fauvisme** *(tourisme-collioure.com; €6)*, close to the waterfront. The trail weaves through the cute sardine fishing village's narrow streets, uncovering locations that inspired certain well-known paintings.

Paulilles
TIME FROM PERPIGNAN: **30MIN**

This is Dynamite
At **L'Anse de Paulilles** *(ledepartement66.fr; entry €4)*, the site formerly contained a dynamite factory. These days, the factory buildings hold a museum exploring the site's social history, while the surrounding grounds, turned into a heritage park since their decontamination, enjoy a growing biodiversity, with owls, wild boar and genets all returning. You can also climb the watchtower lookout. For a more active day trip along the coast, take the 540 bus to Paulilles from Perpignan, Collioure or Banyuls-sur-Mer, then return along the craggy Côte Vermeille coastal path by following the yellow markings.

EATING IN CÉRET AND COLLIOURE: OUR PICKS

Al Català: Cheery little spot in central Céret with an elegant bamboo garden. The cod with honeyed aioli is a good shout. *noon-2pm & 7.30-9pm Tue-Sat* €€

Le Comptoir des Arcades: Great Céret cafe-bar serving jugs of cold sangria, charcuterie boards and borderland tapas (that means patatas bravas *and* moules). *7am-1am* €€

Paco: Tapas ranging from the unusual (razor clams and cuttlefish) to the expected (shrimp and sardines) in Collioure. *hours vary Fri-Wed* €€

Le 5ème Péché: Collioure's most adventurous haute cuisine spot sees French ingredients paired with Japanese sensibilities. Delicate, fishy and foamy. *hours vary Tue & Thu-Sat* €€€

Places We Love to Stay

€ Budget €€ Midrange €€€ Top End

Nîmes MAP p655

Royal Hôtel € Quirky hotel that takes an eclectic approach to decor. It's surrounded by restaurants in view of the Maison Carrée.

Hostel Flamingo € Dorms and private rooms next to the train station. The rooftop terrace is ideal for meeting fellow travellers.

Appart'City Collection Nîmes Arènes €€ Just near Les Arènes, this suave hotel has spacious rooms, some with Juliet balconies.

Beyond Nîmes

La Maison d'Uzès €€€ Beautiful rooms spread between three 17th-century houses in the heart of Uzès. If that's not elegant enough, the hotel's restaurant has one Michelin star.

Le Vieux Castillon €€€ Contemporary comfort in the old rooms of a Renaissance building in Castillon.

Montpellier MAP p664

EKLO Montpellier € A dorm spirit, but with tiny, yet well-appointed basic-boutique private rooms in an excellent location.

JOST € Modern hotel with a penchant for displaying old LP records everywhere. Great views from the rooftop terrace bar.

Hôtel du Palais €€ Welcoming guests since 1870, this hotel has touches of historic elegance laced throughout.

Privilege Hôtel Eurociel Centre Comédie €€ Large, cosy rooms and free parking, minutes from the city centre.

Beyond Montpellier

Auberge de Val Mourèze €€ Mini resort with a pool and wellness centre minutes from the Cirque du Mourèze.

Hôtel le XIX €€ Set on Béziers' place Jean Jaurès in a 19th-century building. Rooms are elegant and modern with parquet flooring.

Château du Parc €€€ Luxury apartments in a 16th-century castle near Pézenas. Ask for a lower-floor room if you struggle with old staircases.

Georges Hostel & Café € Beds with isolation curtains in spacious dorms and private rooms, plus a cafe-bar for meeting fellow travellers in Sète.

Florac

Les Copains à Bord € A stunning farm with a few goats, located in a forested valley near Florac. Private rooms, plus cabin and glamping options.

Millau

Couvent de la Salette €€€ Rooms in a 19th-century former convent outside Millau where original bare-brick walls overlook plush rooms with freestanding bathtubs.

Gorges du Tarn

Hôtel Burlatis €€ Rooms in Ste-Énimie with gorge views and good proximity to the amenities of the village. Closed in winter.

Hôtel de la Muse €€ Great riverside location near Le Rozier with an outdoor pool. Rooms are modern and some have balconies.

Château de la Caze €€€ Possibly the most unique hotel experience in Languedoc is a stay at this 15th-century stone castle in the gorge.

Carcassonne MAP p683

Hôtel du Pont Vieux €€ At the foot of the old town, this hotel has a courtyard garden, terrace and some rooms with castle views.

Good Knight €€ Modern accommodation moments from the Narbonnaise Gate with a lovely castle-facing garden.

Hôtel de la Cité €€€ Five-star, palatial residence in the heart of the Cité Médiévale with a pool, hammam and restaurant.

Perpignan MAP p686

Nyx Boutique €€ Quirky modern-art-filled hotel midway between the train station and city centre. Some rooms have a balcony.

Beyond Perpignan

Maison Le S €€ Lovely rustic-chic rooms with modern furnishings in a calm, warm setting at the heart of Argelès-sur-Mer.

Les Roches Brunes €€€ Upscale seaside charm in Collioure. Most rooms have a view of the castle and Mediterranean.

Hôtel Le Mas Trilles €€ Set in a 14th-century stone farmhouse, 3km from Céret, rooms have terraces and access to the pool.

Researched by
Paul Stafford

Toulouse & the Pyrenees

RURAL IDYLLS AND MOUNTAIN ADVENTURES

From the rose-tinted cultural bastion of Toulouse to the snow-capped Pyrenean wildernesses, the western half of Occitania is top prize in the intrepid traveller's lottery.

Undulating farmland and ungainly peaks, fortified medieval villages and high-tech industry, adrenaline-coursing pistes and leisurely feasts. These are just a few of the unlikely juxtapositions you'll encounter in Toulouse and the Pyrenees.

The region – formerly known as Midi-Pyrénées – merged with Languedoc-Roussillon to form Occitania in 2016. But this western half of the administrative region was shaped by very different forces.

During the 14th century's Hundred Years War, the English advance was halted in the lands to the north and west of Toulouse. Scores of castles, thick-walled churches and fortified settlements (known as *bastides*) sprang up to guard this crucial frontier's fertile plains and river valleys. As the threat ebbed, a staunchly French spirit and culture remained, centred around an agrarian economy that still produces versatile Gaillac wines and plummy Armagnacs at elegant châteaux today.

Amid these rural climes lies mighty Toulouse, a cutting-edge citadel of aeronautics and culture, buoyed by its energetic university scene. Although it's on the pulse of humanity's modern achievements, there remains a rich vein of tradition, rooted in its pivotal religious and historic landmarks.

Indeed, history and religion remain important to locals, from the windswept mountaintop Cathar castles to the neatly tended abbeys and Lourdes' pilgrim hordes. To the south, the mountains of adventure-centric Parc National des Pyrénées and family-friendly Parc Naturel Régional des Pyrénées Ariégeoises are a formidable wall of rock and ice, scored by pistes and trails, pierced by caves, and striated by dramatic valleys.

THE MAIN AREAS

TOULOUSE
Magnificent machines and cultural cachet.
p702

PARC NATUREL RÉGIONAL DES PYRÉNÉES ARIÉGEOISES
Subterranean treasures and mountaintop castles. **p721**

PARC NATIONAL DES PYRÉNÉES
Dramatic scenery, pilgrims and outdoors activities. **p727**

For places to stay in Toulouse & the Pyrenees, see p739

Left: Pic du Midi de Bigorre trail (p733), Parc National des Pyrénées; Above: Gaillac vineyards (p709)

Find Your Way

All roads lead to Toulouse, France's fourth-largest city. The land beyond its suburbs is loosely divided into two types: rolling countryside, dotted with historic towns and small cities, and the high mountains along the France–Spain–Andorra border.

Parc National des Pyrénées, p727

Strung along the Spanish border, this national park's karst landscape inspires outdoor adventure with its hiking, skiing and wildlife spotting opportunities, with thermal baths the day's-end reward.

Parc Naturel Régional des Pyrénées Ariégeoises, p721

Prehistoric cave paintings, subterranean rivers and medieval castles pepper the snow-capped mountains of this picturesque natural park bordering Spain and Andorra.

Toulouse, p702

Occitania's enigmatic capital is home to Europe's largest aeronautics industry, along with an architecturally and spiritually rich old town, vibrant nightlife and gastronomic treasures aplenty.

THE GUIDE

TOULOUSE & THE PYRENEES

CAR

For trips beyond the major towns and cities, having your own transportation is essential. The wine regions, medieval towns and plethora of caves, mountains, hiking trails and valleys cannot be accessed without one. You'll be rewarded with some fantastic scenic driving on quiet, well-paved roads.

METRO

Toulouse metro operates two lines – A (red) and B (yellow) – which run regularly (averaging every five minutes peak and 20 minutes off-peak) through the city centre. Trains run until 3am on Friday and Saturday and until midnight Sunday to Thursday. Line C (green) is slated to open in 2029.

TRAIN & BUS

Separate train lines branch out from Toulouse to Carcassonne, Castres, Albi, Montauban, Auch, Lourdes, Bagnères-de-Luchon and Foix regionally, many continuing further afield from there. Buses are much less ubiquitous. Local liO buses (lio-occitanie.fr) connect Auch to Montauban (route 933) and Castres to Toulouse (route 760).

Plan Your Time

Forming the bulk of Occitania, the Midi-Pyrénées is the mainland's largest region. Getting around this vast swathe of southwest France isn't always fast, but you'll want to slow down anyway. Much is closed in summer.

Escalier Monumental and Cathédrale Ste-Marie (p719), Auch

A Flying Visit

● To make the most of a brief stay, **Toulouse** (p702) is the most rewarding destination. Spend day one getting to know the old town, walking from **Pont Neuf** (p707) to the **Place du Capitole** (p703), stopping in at the **Couvent des Jacobins** (p706), where the Dominican Order was founded.

● On your second day, head to the northern suburbs to feel dwarfed by an A380 in **Aeroscopia's** (p710) impressive plane hangar. Next, visit **Stade Ernest-Wallon** (p710), home stadium of Toulouse's revered rugby union team Toulousain.

● With a third day, hop on a train to **Albi** (p714) to visit the art-filled palace of **Musée Toulouse-Lautrec** (p715) and admire the fresco-lined interior of **Cathédrale Ste-Cécile** (p715). If you have time, stop at **Château Lastours** (p716) for a Gaillac AOC wine tasting.

Seasonal Highlights

The countryside is best in spring and autumn. Summer is festival season and winter is ski season in the Pyrenees.

JANUARY
Ski season peaks in the latter half of winter at resorts throughout the Pyrenees, including **Luchon-Superbagnères** (p732), **Cauterets-Le Lys** (p732) and **Ax 3 Domaines** (p726). For a fun alternative, try snowshoeing in **Payolle** (p733).

APRIL
Pilgrimages to the **Grotte de Massabielle** (p736) and **Basilique Notre-Dame-du-Rosaire** (p734) in Lourdes begin around Holy Week and Easter, when this sacred site is vibrant with processions and special services.

JUNE
Snow melts in the upper reaches of the Pyrenees, opening roads and trails. The **Le Nouveau Printemps** (visual arts), **Rio Loco** (music and arts) and **Tangopostale** (dance) festivals (p706) kick off Toulouse's busy events calendar.

A Week or More to Explore

- Add dinner at one of the restaurants above **Marché Victor-Hugo** (p703), made with fresh market produce, to your Toulouse itinerary. Using the city as your base from which discover the surrounding countryside, take a train to discover **Montauban's** (p718) sculpture collection at **Musée Ingres Bourdelle** (p718). Next day, head west to Gascony's historic capital, **Auch** (p719), where you can climb the elegant **Escalier Monumental** (p719) up from the Gers River to **Cathédrale Ste-Marie** (p719).

- Hire a car for a few days. Hike the mysterious, boulder-strewn forests of **Le Sidobre** (p714) and brave the 140m-long gorge-spanning footbridge at **Mazamet** (p712), then road trip around the medieval *bastide* towns of northern Tarn, exploring the **Forteresse de Penne** (p717) and **Bruniquel's Village Médiéval** (p717).

A Mountain-Minded Fortnight

- Use mountain town **Foix**, with its medieval-recreation **château** (p722) as a base for taking a cave boat tour of **Rivière Souterraine de Labouiche** (p723) and discovering the prehistoric cave paintings at **Grotte de Niaux** (p723).

- Next, spend a day or two driving the mountain roads through **Parc Naturel Régional des Pyrénées Ariégeoises** (p721), stopping to visit caves such as **Grotte du Mas d'Azil** (p724) and go canyoning with **Vertikarst** (p725) in **Auzat**. Continue towards **Parc National des Pyrénées** (p727), crossing scenic mountain passes such as **Col du Tourmalet** (p731) and visiting the **Pic du Midi de Bigorre** (p733) for its observatory and mountain views, then ride **Le Petit Train d'Artouste** (p730) near **Laruns**.

- Finally, visit the sacred **Grotte de Massabielle** (p736) pilgrimage site in Lourdes.

JULY
Roadsides fill with spectators cheering on the **Tour de France** cyclists attempting some of the race's most challenging climbs and summit finishes. Routes change annually but always include a couple of stages in the Pyrenees (p731).

AUGUST
Although most French people are on holiday, there's music in Toulouse, with EDM at **Fabulous Festival** and the **Toulouse d'Été** series, including jazz and the **Halle Summer Long** concert series at **Halle de la Machine** (p711).

OCTOBER
Toulouse les Orgues celebrates all things church organ-related, with music concerts and displays of the capabilities of great instruments, particularly the organ at **Cathédrale St-Étienne** (p708), given over two weeks.

NOVEMBER
With the autumn foliage painting the countryside in warm tones throughout the region, **Armagnac** (p720) celebrates the distillation of its namesake spirit a few months after the grape harvest in the Fête de la Flamme.

Toulouse

MARVELLOUS MACHINES | GAME-CHANGING CHURCHES | CULTURAL KERNEL

☑ TOP TIP

If you're in Toulouse for two full days or more and plan to visit lots of sights, it's worth taking a look at the **Pass Tourisme** (toulouse-tourisme.com/en/what-to-see-and-do/pass-tourisme; with/without public transport €36/26), which offers free entry to most attractions along with discounts at Aeroscopia and Cité de l'Espace.

Toulouse – France's fourth-largest city and the capital of Occitania – is steeped in history, architecture, arts and science. Originally called Tolosa, the city, nicknamed La Ville Rose (The Pink City) for its signature rose-tinted terracotta bricks, dates back to the 2nd century BCE and served as the first Visigoth capital from 418–507 CE.

For centuries, Toulouse played a crucial role in the regional power of Christianity, as evidenced by the cathedral and various spectacular churches around the city. But it's the city's hyper-modern achievements that generate the most excitement; Toulouse is a hub for the manufacture of airplanes and rockets, with many global companies, such as Airbus, located in the city. Aeroscopia and Cité de l'Espace let visitors clamber aboard some of humankind's finest inventions. Add to that Europe's pre-eminent rugby union team and a penchant for a rip-roaring festival and you have a city that will linger long in the memory.

A Capitole Idea

An introduction to Toulouse

Toulouse's city hall, the **Capitole** *(free)*, demonstrates many facets of the city's cultural character. With its rose terracotta and white brick neoclassical façade, complete with eight pink and cream marble Corinthian columns, it is one of Toulouse's

GETTING AROUND

The AERO shuttle bus connects **Toulouse-Blagnac Airport** to **Gare Matabiau** (Toulouse's train station) via the city centre roughly every 15 minutes. Trains connect to the rest of France and into Spain from here. Toulouse's city centre is flat and traffic-light. While this means driving is less than ideal and parking scarce, it's perfect for exploring on foot or wheel. Miles of leafy paths line the banks of the Garonne and Canal du Midi, which meets the Canal de Garonne here. Toulouse also has two metro lines, A (red) and B (yellow), plus two tram lines (T1 and T2).

Marché Victor-Hugo

signature buildings. The exterior's architectural display is balanced by the interior's impressive frescos and paintings, which decorate the chambers and halls.

Enter from the **Place du Capitole**, the city's social focal point, whose perimeter arcades are packed with patrons of its Belle Époque bistros and brasseries. Inside, follow the entry signs through security. Once through, climb the elegant main staircase, overlooked by Renaissance-style murals. At the top, local artist Henri Martin's huge post-impressionist canvases fill Salle Henri-Martin, while painted scenes from Toulouse's history decorate the Salle des Illustres (Hall of the Illustrious).

The southern end of the building hosts the **Théâtre du Capitole** *(opera.toulouse.fr)*, where the city's ballet and opera companies perform regularly. If you're lucky, you might be able to catch one of the occasional €5 lunchtime recitals (book in advance).

Sociable Dining in Toulouse

Local flavours with the locals

Three blocks northeast of the Capitole, you'll encounter the nucleus of the Toulouse dining scene: **Marché Victor-Hugo** *(marche-victor-hugo.fr)*. Its stalls are decadently laid out like

continued on p706

DOMINICANS & THE FRENCH INQUISITION

The Dominican Order was founded at a time of religious upheaval. In the first decades of the 13th century, Toulouse was embroiled in the deadly Albigensian Crusade, with the French Crown dead-set on destroying the Cathars on behalf of the Catholic Church. The new convent duly received a papal bull from Pope Honorius III – a seal of approval known as 'of pontifical right' in 1216 – further confirming Toulouse as an important religious hub. But by 1234, deep in the fog of holy absolutism, the Dominicans spearheaded a French Inquisition that would last well into the 17th century, making Toulouse and nearby Albi its central hub. At least 560 people are documented to have been executed, with many more tortured, imprisoned or forcibly converted.

 EATING IN TOULOUSE: OUR PICKS

Chez Tran: Playful neon lighting and paper lanterns. Try their signature bo buns. On rue Pargaminières, known as the 'street food half-mile'. *hours vary* €

Au Bon Graillou: Try the excellent-value seasonal three-course lunch menu, which makes best use of the fresh ingredients from Marché Victor Hugo downstairs. *noon-3pm Tue-Sun* €€

L'Oncle Pom: Sagely takes a potato-forward approach: first, select your preparation (gratin, French fries etc) before choosing a meat or fish to accompany. *hours vary* €€

Restaurant Emile: Michelin Guide–level *cassoulet* served in clay bowls. The *magret de canard* (duck breast) is a great alternative. Book ahead for terrace seating. *noon-1.30pm & 7.30-9.30pm* €€€

TOULOUSE'S BEST CULTURAL FESTIVALS

Music, dance and cuisine are elevated to celebrated status at a plethora of festivals and special events in Toulouse.

Flash Festival: (May; music) Relative newcomer to the city's festival scene showcasing local up-and-coming musical acts.

Rio Loco Festival: (June; world music and arts) A celebration of diversity in the rejuvenated St-Cyprien neighbourhood.

Le Nouveau Printemps: (June; culture) Events and exhibitions across the visual arts spectrum, including cinema and architecture.

Tangopostale: (June-July; tango music and dance) Tango dancing and concerts in Carlos Gardel's birth city.

Toulouse d'Été: (July-August) This loose collection of smaller music festivals includes a summer concert series at Halle de la Machine.

Fabulous Festival: (August; electronic music and gastronomy) Transforms the grounds of Château de la Garrigue, 35km north of Toulouse.

---

continued from 703

an old-timey store, with racks of wines from the Fronton and Gaillac AOCs, walls of cheeses touching the ceiling and fresh local produce around the market's edge. Must-try items are the *pavé Toulousain* cheese from **Xavier**, facing the market, and **Maison Garcia's** *saucisse de Toulouse* (a garlic, red wine and pork sausage). Visit on Sunday morning for the best *dégustations* (tastings). Similar to most museums in the region, the market is closed on Mondays.

A raft of restaurants on the second floor, such as **Le Louchebem** and **Au Bon Graillou** (p703) make excellent use of these products, and you'll find plenty of seasonal dishes alongside regional classic dishes such as *cassoulet* (bean, pork and duck stew) and *aligot* (cheesy potatoes). Seating is largely communal and it's customary to pull up a free chair and greet others at the table with a simple '*bonjour*'. Two excellent food tours explore the market's gourmet delights in greater depth: Jessica Hammer's **Taste of Toulouse** *(tasteoftoulouse.com)* and Chef Alejandro's **Toulouse Gourmet Tours** *(toulousegourmettours.com)*.

Travel at its Most Creative
Experiencing Toulouse through sketching

As you stroll through some of the most picturesque streets on a clear day, you'll often see artists and amateurs sitting with a sketchpad in lap. There's nothing stopping you from joining them. The global artist community **Urban Sketchers** has an active Toulouse branch *(facebook.com/groups/urbansketcherstoulouse)* who meet once a month, each time in a different part of the city. Some of the more experienced members are on hand to help you capture the city's beautiful buildings, gardens and canal views.

Find Some Religious Order
Discovering the city's holy legacy

From the moment that Christian emissary St Saturnin was tied to a bull by pagan priests and dragged to his death through the streets of Toulouse in 257 CE, it was clear religion was going to play a significant role in the city's lore. **Basilique St-Sernin** *(basilique-saint-sernin.fr; free)*, built over an original 4th-century basilica in 1070, houses the tombs of both St Saturnin (aka St Sernin) and St Honoratus. Its octagonal Romanesque-Gothic, five-tiered tower is a cherished emblem of Toulouse. This, along with its formidable collection of relics, places it among the most important stops along the Chemins de St-Jacques-de-Compostelle.

The Dominican Order was established in Toulouse in 1215. You'll occasionally see visiting friars, wandering the streets in their bone-coloured tunics, near the order's imposing mother church, the **Couvent des Jacobins** *(jacobins.toulouse.fr; adult/child €5/3)*. Entry is through the **Église des Jacobins** *(free)*, which was deconsecrated following the French Revolution in 1789. Within, palm-vaulted columns prop the lofty

TOULOUSE'S OLD TOWN ARCHITECTURE ON FOOT

Discover the eclectic blend of Romanesque, Gothic and Renaissance architecture on this walk through streets, squares and riverside paths.

START	END	LENGTH
Place du Capitole	Place St-Pierre	3.3km; 3 hours

Toulouse's genteel charm is in its design. Head east from the neoclassical ❶ **Place du Capitole** (p703) to the tree- and fountain-filled ❷ **Place Wilson**, then south to the Romanesque ❸ **Cathédrale St-Étienne** (p708), which sports some 13th-century Gothic additions. Wander east to the Gothic ❹ **Musée des Augustins** (p709), which houses Romanesque sculptures and artworks from around Occitania. Continue down towards the river, stopping at the 16th-century Hôtel d'Assézat, a fine example of a French Renaissance mansion, now housing ❺ **Fondation Bemberg's** (p709) art collection.

Slalom through the back streets to neoclassical ❻ **Basilique Notre-Dame de la Daurade**, which was built in the 19th century on the site of a Roman temple dedicated to Apollo. Head south along the Garonne riverfront and cross the stone ❼ **Pont Neuf**, a bridge completed in 1632. The tower at the other side is ❽ **Château d'Eau**, a former water tower now holding temporary exhibitions.

Turning back north into the trendy St-Cyprien neighbourhood, the impressive building overlooking the river is a former hospital, the ❾ **Hôtel-Dieu St-Jacques**, founded in the 12th century. Continue north and cross the river again over ❿ **Pont St-Pierre** to end at ⓫ **Place St-Pierre** with an *apéro* at one of the riverfront *guinguettes*, looking across the river at the mint green dome of baroque Chapelle St-Joseph de la Grave.

Basilique Notre-Dame de la Daurade holds the **Black Madonna**, a highly revered, 19th-century icon. The 15th-century original was stolen.

The statue in **Place Wilson** is of poet Pierre Goudouli, whose main work *Ramelet Moundi* was written in the local Occitan language.

The **Hôtel-Dieu St-Jacques'** pretty gardens and two small medicine-related history museums are open to the public.

Cathédrale St-Étienne

ceiling above capacious stained-glass windows, flooding the space with light. In the centre lie the sacred relics of the eminent theologian-philosopher St Thomas Aquinas (1225–74), whose work greatly impacted western philosophy and exemplified how the Dominicans tended to eschew hard labour for devoted study.

HOLY STROLLERS

The Camino de Santiago is called the Chemins de St-Jacques-de-Compostelle in France. Those making the pilgrimage are called Jacquets. Other key stops along some of the multiple branches heading towards Spain include Cathédrale Notre-Dame (p477) in Le Puy-en-Velay and Abbaye St-Pierre (p718) in Moissac.

Tubular Knells
Attending an organ show

Construction on **Cathédrale St-Étienne** *(paroissescathedraletoulouse.fr; free)* started in 1075, but the majority of the work took place in the first half of the 13th century. The result is a rather haphazard layout in a mix of Romanesque and Gothic styles, whereby the choir is roughly twice the width of its nave. A grand organ, built in 1612, overhangs the choir, comprising 3060 pipes, four keyboards and 47 stops (which, when pulled out, create a louder, fuller sound, hence the phrase 'pulling out all the stops').

The best chance to see it in action outside church service hours is at **Toulouse les Orgues** *(toulouse-les-orgues.org)* in October, an organ festival that includes powerful recitals

The dessert station is excellent

EATING IN TOULOUSE: BEST VEGAN & VEGETARIAN RESTAURANTS

La Faim des Haricots: Eat a rainbow of healthy, delicious food at this bustling veggie buffet. Cheaper between 3pm and 5pm. *noon-10pm* €

Peacock: Try the homemade pecan cookies. The Saturday brunches bring the best ambience to this chic café's vaulted ceiling space. *9am-6pm Wed-Sun* €

Café Brûlé: Minimalist-modern eatery serving creative vegan brunches, such as savoury scrambled tofu pancakes with tonkatsu sauce and fried onions. *hours vary Wed-Sun* €

Sixta: Great value vegetarian set lunch menus given the gourmet treatment with artful presentation. The chefs work magic with aubergines and courgettes. *noon-6pm Mon-Sat* €

throughout the city. An additional programme sees performances in July and August. At other times, organ concerts are sporadic. Ask at the **tourist office** (inside the Donjon du Capitole) about the latest schedules.

On Top Form
Medieval and contemporary art

Toulouse hosts a number of fabulous, well-curated art collections. Reopened following a seven-year remodelling starting in 2018, Toulouse's main art museum, the **Musée des Augustins** (augustins.org; entry €5), has been showcasing a collection of Romanesque sculptures and fine arts since soon after the French Revolution. Housed in a former 14th-century Augustinian monastery, it gives a great overview of Occitan creative expression since the Middle Ages.

Nearby, **Fondation Bemberg** (fondation-bemberg.fr ; adult/child €18/12) occupies the first and second floors of Hôtel d'Assézat, an urban palace built in the 16th century. The collection includes a room of sketches by Toulouse-Lautrec and Picasso, with works by the Venetian masters such as Titian, Fauvist Henri Matisse and more. Picasso is also on show in the modern and contemporary art museum **Les Abattoirs** (lesabattoirs.org; entry €5), with his huge 1936 work *The Remains of the Minotaur in a Harlequin Costume*.

Two other excellent collections to check out include the exquisite horology (antique clocks) displayed at **Musée Paul-Dupuy** (museepauldupuy.toulouse.fr; adult/child €5/3), and the Roman sculptures and ecclesiastical art at **Musée St-Raymond** (saintraymond.toulouse.fr; adult/child €5/3).

Towpath Adventures
Boating and biking the waterways

The **Canal de Garonne** runs east from the Atlantic; the **Canal du Midi** runs west from the Mediterranean. They meet in Toulouse, forming one continuous, navigable coast-to-coast waterway. Exploring the towpaths, which are shaded by regimented parades of plane trees, can be as simple as a leisurely stroll or a day-long cycling trip. For the latter, rentals are available from the city's 400 bike stations using the **vélôToulouse** (velotoulouse.tisseo.fr) bike-sharing app.

A more substantial waterway, the Garonne River, cleaves its way through the heart of the city. Get onto the water with **Les Bateaux Toulousains** (bateaux-toulousains.com; from

THE TOP TASTES OF TOULOUSE

Cassoulet: With its white bean stew base, Toulouse's iteration of the region's official dish uses liberal amounts of duck confit alongside Toulouse sausage.

L'alicuit de canard: Those poor ducks can't catch a break. This Gascon favourite stews duck wings, neck and offal with white wine, carrots, onions and potatoes.

Cheeses: Raw cow's milk and a distinctive cube shape signify *pavé Toulousain*, the main local cheese. A creamier alternative is *Tomme des Pyrénées*.

Fronton and Gaillac wines: Berry and currant-forward reds produced with négrette grapes are Fronton's primary output, while Gaillac's orchard-crisp whites go well with fish.

Fénétra: Apricot jam, candied lemons and almond *dacquoise* topping make up this irresistible tart with Roman-era origins.

 EATING & DRINKING IN TOULOUSE: BEST COFFEE & BREAKFAST

Salon Cacao'T: Exceptional *kouign amann* cakes with a crunchy exterior and soft buttery heart. Caramel butter flavour is a good place to start. *8am-7pm Tue-Sun* €

Café Papiche: Cute cafe making excellent coffee alongside a delicious cardamom *babka*. Try the set brunch menu on weekends. *hours vary Wed-Sun* €

Ekylibre Saint-Georges: Healthy açaí and Buddha bowls, bougie avocado toast and pancakes heaped with fruit in lovely place St-Georges. *hours vary Mon-Sat* €

L'Estaminot: Typical Toulousain *salon de thé* (tea house) with a quirky bookshop vibe in the up-and-coming St-Cyprien neighbourhood. *9.30am-7pm* €

TOULOUSE'S AEROSPACE INDUSTRY

From Clément Ader's early attempts to fly in 1890 through to the rapid, war-fuelled aircraft development during the two world wars, Toulouse emerged as one of the world's foremost sites of industrial aircraft production. The first aeronautical factory was built by Pierre-Georges Latécoère in 1917. Then, with the emergence of Airbus (a consortium of European manufacturers that has since settled primarily in Toulouse) in 1970, it became the city where boundaries were pushed, creating Concorde and the Airbus A380 (the largest civilian aircraft ever commercially built), capable of taking more than 550 passengers. Today, aeronautics and aerospace are the city's main industry, although you'd never know it in the historic city centre, where even the road traffic is kept to a minimum.

€8), with their 30-minute cruises from July to October. The same boats are used for canal cruises from March to June.

Temple of the Oval Ball
Catch a Toulousain rugby union match

Rugby union is big business in southwestern France. At the time of research, half the teams in the Top 14, France's premier professional league, came from the region. While regional rivals Bordeaux, Perpignan and Montpellier have seen success in the past, no team is as decorated as **Stade Toulousain** *(stadetoulousain.fr)*. Winners of the European Rugby Champions Cup an impressive six times (two more than the next best team, Leinster), Stade Toulousain play home league games at **Stade Ernest-Wallon**, a perfect place to tap into the city's sporting spirit. Seasons usually run from September to June. Toulousain's European Rugby Champions Cup games are usually played at **Stadium de Toulouse**, south of the centre.

Conquering the Skies
Wander through a Concorde

Toulouse has long been seen as the world capital of aeronautics. And aviation, space and technology enthusiasts have not one, but four major landmarks in store. Of them, the most impressive is **Aeroscopia** *(aeroscopia.fr; adult/child €15/12)*, which brings together scores of planes, among them some of the world's largest. Passing through an entry tunnel to emerge into a giant hangar packed with planes. A tiny French Bleriot XI and a Mignet HM 293 Pou-du-Ciel dangle like mosquitos beside a hulking great SGT 201 Super Guppy, built to transport sections of rocket for NASA.

You can walk through a Concorde (its 1970s style seats and complex control panels preserved in place behind Perspex) and an Airbus A380 on the tarmac outside, where parts of the fuselage and flooring are stripped back to expose the complicated wiring. The lower level of the main hangar delves deeper into the specific workings of modern aeronautical engineering, stripping back jet engines, fighter plans and some of the more unusual designs, such as the canard wing configuration.

Nearby, **Ailes Anciennes Toulouse** *(Old Wings Toulouse; aatlse.org; entry €7)*, open only a few days a week, holds a fine collection of 47 heritage planes, including a French Dassault Mirage, British De Havilland Vampire T11, and a US Lockheed T-33 Shooting Star.

 DRINKING IN TOULOUSE: BEST PLACES FOR AN APÉRO

Chez Tonton: Come for the 7-9pm happy hour deals (eg two for one pastis), stay for the spectacular sunsets over the Garonne River. *hours vary*

Au Père Louis: Traditional French wine bar opened in 1889, known for its *quinquina* (aromatised wines), such as Byrrh, and its tasty tapas. *noon-2pm & 6pm-late Tue-Sat*

Le Petit Voisin: Student favourite, which means shooters and cheap cocktails above apéritifs. There's also foosball. *9am-midnight*

Pêcheurs de Sable: Fantastic *guinguette* (open-air cafe) by the riverside with some good craft beers and ciders in pretty Port de la Daurade. *10am-10pm*

Aeroscopia

Let's Visit Airbus (*manatour.fr; adult/child €16/13*) runs tours of the Airbus Factory. Book in advance for either the A350 Tour or the Kid's Tour, both available in French or English, to get a sense of what it takes to assemble such complex aircraft.

Nothing martials humanity's scientific advances like the exploration of space. Toulouse's contribution to our airborne feats beyond the stratosphere are celebrated at the vast **Cité de l'Espace** (*cite-espace.com; adult/child €29/22.50*) space museum. Highlights include boarding a Mir space station, riding the Apollo mission simulator and seeing real pieces of moon rock.

Fantastic Mechanical Beasts

Meet the Minotaur

Engineering takes an artistic turn at **Halle de la Machine** (*halledelamachine.fr; adult/child €12/9; closed Jan to mid-Feb*) where visitors are greeted by a 14m-high Minotaur. Within lies an assembly of whimsical machines in humanoid and animal form, including a fossil-limbed spider, which are so big that they can carry a dozen or more people. The fantastical moving sculptures are brought to life by teams operating an ingenious array of levers and controls.

CITY OF VIOLETS

It is dubbed the Rose City but Toulouse is also a city of violets. Specifically, the flowers, which are cultivated locally in winter and used to make *liqueur de violette* – a popular ace up the sleeve with local mixologists – *violettes de Toulouse* candies, and Paris-Toulouse pastries, consisting of hazelnut praline and violet-infused Chantilly cream. If used well, violet flowers create a subtle fragrant note, rather than the soapy flavour you might expect. To buy violet products, check out **La Maison de la Violette**, a shop in a canal barge. In a nod to this violet heritage, the local football team, Ligue 1's Toulouse FC, play in purple and even released a third kit in the 2024–25 season emblazoned with violet flowers.

DRINKING IN TOULOUSE: BEST NIGHTLIFE

La Tireuse: Ciders, wines and 20 craft beers on tap. Live music (anything from Baroque to Irish folk to rock) from local music school's prodigies. *5pm-late Mon-Sat*

Fat Cat: Low-lit cocktail lounge a minute from place du Capitole concocting inventive bespoke cocktails. Visit on Wednesdays for live jazz. *7pm-2am Tue-Sat*

Le 5 Wine Bar: Try a bottle of Braucol Rouge from nearby Gaillac, using the self-pour stations or ask the in-house sommeliers for their expert recommendations. *6pm-midnight Tue-Sat*

Le Bikini: This legendary club and live music venue, located on the southeastern edge of the city, is one of the city's best nightlife spots. *hours vary Tue-Sat*

Beyond Toulouse

Toulouse is a gateway to fortified medieval towns, vineyard-clad hills and dramatic river valleys, plus the majestic monuments of Albi.

Places
Mazamet p712
Castres p713
Lacrouzette p714
Albi p714
Cordes-sur-Ciel p715
Montauban p718
Moissac p718
Auch p719
Condom p720

Head in any direction from Toulouse and you're guaranteed to discover natural beauty, elegant wine country road trips and historic towns packed with culture and art. To the east is Tarn, where the fringes of Parc Naturel Régional du Haut-Languedoc fragment into dramatic gorges and mysterious, boulder-strewn woodland. Capital Albi's historic episcopal core enjoys UNESCO World Heritage status. North of Toulouse, where Tarn becomes Tarn-et-Garonne, a wild expanse of vineyard tasting rooms and medieval *bastides* clinging to defensible hillsides, such as Cordes-sur-Ciel, make for the ideal road trip. To the west lie the heartlands of Gascony (now the Gers *département*), centred around former capital, Auch, with the Armagnac region presenting more opportunities for tastings.

GETTING AROUND

Castres, Mazamet, Albi, Montauban and Auch are well connected by regular trains to Toulouse, ideal for day trips from the Occitan capital. For the myriad attractions that lie in between, you'll need your own transport. Away from the city, roads are in excellent condition and generally low in traffic. Alternatively, you might join the Chemin de St-Jacques hikers to reach Moissac, a key stop on the trail towards Spain.

Mazamet
TIME FROM TOULOUSE: **1HR 45MIN**

Braving the Bridge

Mazamet's fantastic 140m-long **Passerelle de Mazamet** *(free)* suspension footbridge quivers above the deep Arnette River gorge. Sturdy as it is, it's still a pretty unnerving walk. The best way to reach it is to hike the 500m trail up through the forest from the **Parking Passerelle** car park *(parking €3)* on the southern edge of Mazamet. Follow the 'Accès Passerelle' signs.

After crossing the bridge, the trail continues up to the medieval village of **Hautpoul**, which decorates the mountain ridge. The ruined **Château de Hautpoul** at its lower reaches was built on the orders of Simon de Montfort in 1212 after having defeated Cathar ruler Roger Trencavel following a siege during the crusade against the Cathars.

It's another steep walk up through the village, passing a medieval herb garden to the **Rocher de la Vierge**, where a statue of the Virgin Mary and baby Jesus hold a commanding view of Mazamet, the bridge and the surrounding valley. Reward yourself with a Nutella crêpe at **La Fringale** after the hike. Back down in Mazamet town, you can learn more about Catharism at the **Musée du Catharisme de Mazamet** *(museeducatharisme.fr; entry €6)*, a rather dry but informative display with some English and Spanish translations available.

Jardin de l'Évêché

Castres

TIME FROM TOULOUSE: 1HR

The Art of Display

The wealth of Castres was made off the back of the wool and textiles industries. Today that history can still be seen beside the Agout river in the form of ornate craftsman houses, whose wooden upper storeys – complete with balconies or window boxes – overhang the water. The best view of them is from **Pont Neuf**. The finest relic of this past wealth is the city's **Mairie de Castres** (town hall) and its ornate **Jardin de l'Évêché** gardens created by André Le Nôtre, the landscape architect responsible for Versailles.

Wander from the garden into the town hall to find the entrance to **Musée Goya** (museegoya.fr; adult/child €9/6), with its fantastic collection of Spanish art. Salle (room) 11 introduces us to Goya through a timeline of his life, revealing how his going deaf at age 47 in large part contributed to the darkness that crept into his work. Salle 12 holds the museum's three huge Goya canvasses, two portraits (one a self-portrait, the other of artist Francisco del Mazo) and the huge *The Junta of the Philippines* (1815), Goya's largest painting, to which a great heaviness and unease clings.

Other highlights include 17th-century golden age paintings by Francisco Pacheco and Diego Velazquez in Salle 3, Murillo's *Our Lady of the Rosary* (1650) in Salle 6, and an exploration of the ugliness of mortality through Pedro Anastasio Bocanegra's *Allegory of the Plague* and El Greco's *St Francis of Assisi and Brother Leon Meditating on Death* in Salle 9. Salle 18 contains some abstract portraits by Carlos Pradal, a late cubist work, *Bust of Man Writing* (1971) by Picasso, and a Joan Miró piece.

GREAT MINDS & CHALLENGING IDEAS

The moniker 'father of French Socialism' given to Jean Jaurès from Castres doesn't do him justice. In principle, he rejected orthodox ideology, seeking instead to reconcile society's conflicting viewpoints. His principles remain popular in France today, hence the prevalence of squares and streets named after him. There's a small museum (only in French) dedicated to the leader, who was assassinated in 1914, at the **Centre National et Musée Jean Jaurès** in Castres.

Significant advances in analytic geometry and number theory were made by mathematician Pierre de Fermat. He rarely provided proof for his theorems, but most were proved following his death in 1665. Except for one. It wasn't until 1994 that Andrew Wiles proved the so-called Fermat's Last Theorem. The great mathematician's birthplace in Beaumont-de-Lomagne is now the **Musée Fermat**.

HENRI DE TOULOUSE-LAUTREC

Born with a number of ailments in Albi in 1864 to the wealthy aristocratic Toulouse-Lautrec family, Henri de Toulouse-Lautrec (1864–1901), whose parents were first cousins, broke both legs on separate occasions as a teenager. By adulthood, his disabilities and stunted height of under 5ft profoundly shaped his world view, which he brought into his artwork. He is most associated with his paintings from 1891–95 of sex workers in the Parisian brothel scene and, notably, his humanity around the works, avoiding the degradation or moral judgement cast by most of his contemporaries. The portraits are sharp and intangible, dark and light, with a sense of his fragile psychological state poking through. Toulouse-Lautrec summed them up when he said: 'everywhere and always ugliness has its beautiful aspects'.

Cathédrale Ste-Cécile ceiling, Albi

Lacrouzette

TIME FROM TOULOUSE: **1HR 30MIN**

Nature's Rock Sculptures

Le Sidobre *(free)* is a broad forest-clad region of western **Parque Naturel Regional du Haut Languedoc**, where a series of mysterious granite boulders cut unusual shapes across the countryside. They're the product of millions of years of erosion of the granite plateau, whereby the subsoil and granite's natural fissures are worn down by the elements. Among the most fascinating boulders left by this process are **Peyro Clabado**, near Lacrouzette village, a 780-tonne boulder seeming to rest on a tiny pedestal. Like many of the rocks, it's reached via a short *sentier* (trail) from a car park. The road east passes through deep forest, where giant, moss-cloaked boulders line the road. From Crémaussel, the well-marked 1.6km (1-mile) **Sentier des Merveilles** trail visits Le Sidobre's best-known formations, including **Les Trois Fromages** (Three Cheeses) and **Le Roc de l'Oie** (Goose Rock). Maison du Sidobre tourist centre also has a short sculpture trail and some interactive exhibits showing how locals mine the granite.

Albi

TIME FROM TOULOUSE: **1HR 15MIN**

Majesty of the Episcopal City

Albi is an advert for medieval French Gothic architecture. The UNESCO-listed Episcopal City's streets retain most of their

---

 EATING IN ALBI: OUR PICKS

Le Lautrec: Opposite Toulouse-Lautrec's birthplace, this backstreet gourmet gem does wonderful, lightly smoky *cassoulets* and great-value set menus. *noon-2pm & 7.30-9.30pm Tue-Sat* €€

L'Épicurien: The presentation is so artful at this French brasserie that you'll feel guilty for eating it. Great grilled sea bream and asparagus salad. *noon-2pm & 7-10pm Mon-Fri* €€

Sérès Café Hôtel de Ville: Healthy veggie lunch bowls, such as beluga lentils with cardamom yogurt, not-so-healthy brownies and great coffee all day. *10am-6pm Tue-Sat* €

Bruit en Cuisine: Terrace views of Cathédrale Ste-Cécile make this an iconic spot for classic French dishes, such as the excellent veggie goat cheese gratin. *noon-2pm & 7-10pm* €€

original features, with many structures – built in a burnt-orange brick – dating back to the 10th and 11th centuries, such as **Pont Vieux**. Refurbished in 2025, the bridge was initially built in 1040.

At its core lies **Cathédrale Ste-Cécile** (*cathedrale-albi.com; entry to nave/choir & treasury free/€6*). This sacred behemoth, built from 1282–1390, is the world's largest brick-built cathedral. Its austere exterior blends the sensibilities of castle and cathedral, a purposeful design to counter the Albigensian Cathars, who claimed the Catholic Church was too ostentatious. However, the flamboyant South Portal and the entire interior, is the exact opposite: an overt ostentation of sacred enlivenment, which sees every inch covered in carved wood, stone or lively fresco.

An impressive fresco of The Last Judgement emblazons the base of two rounded towers, beyond which lies the cathedral's main chapel. A huge organ sits above it. In the eastern side of the cathedral, an intricately carved limestone rood screen separates the nave from the exquisite Choir of the Canons. St Cécile is patron saint of the cathedral and also of musicians, hence the reverence given to the choir, whose 120 stalls are overlooked by sculptures the Virgin Mary flanked by the 12 Apostles and two angels. There's a treasury up the stairs on the north side of the choir.

Spending Time with Toulouse-Lautrec

Albi's archbishops and bishops once lived in the **Palais de la Berbie**, which strikes an imposing presence over the Tarn River. Today it is occupied by the **Musée Toulouse-Lautrec** (*musee-toulouse-lautrec.com; adult/child €10/free*) providing ample space for the sizeable collection of Henri de Toulouse-Lautrec's paintings, along with works by some of his contemporaries. The collection spans his entire career, from early portraiture through to his final work *Examination at the Faculty of Medicine*, painted shortly before his death in 1901. It includes a good selection of his Paris brothel paintings – *In the Salon at the Rue des Moulins* is a highlight – rendered with real humanity and exploring the quotidian lives of the sex workers, rather than sliding into the bawdy or lurid.

Allow yourself at least two hours to explore the galleries. At the end, don't miss Palais de la Berbie's elegant **Jardin du Palais** (*free*), consisting of a flower and topiary centrepiece fringed with fragrant bay trees and white roses. This is overlooked by vine-strewn gallery walkways atop the building's curtain wall. The silty Tarn River sits down below.

Cordes-sur-Ciel
TIME FROM TOULOUSE: 1HR 15MIN

Artisans & Time Portals

Cordes-sur-Ciel is considered by many to be the Tarn region's quintessential medieval hilltop settlement. From afar, you could half-expect to see dragons wheeling above the ridgetop town. It's a gruelling plod up the cobbled rue de l'Horloge to the fortified **Porte de l'Horloge** and into the old town. But the artisan craft workshops are a fine distraction. Ceramicists,

---

TARN'S TOP ATTRACTIONS

Patricia Golin and **Philippe Dunand**, owners of L'Orée du Ciel bed and breakfast, recommend their favourite experiences. @oreeduciel.

Forteresse de Penne: The site is magnificent and the people who undertook the rehabilitation of it made it look very pretty (p717).

La Cité Episcopal d'Albi: Inside the cathedral, there's a part that you have to pay to visit and in that area, you'll find a medieval mappa mundi of the Mediterranean from the 8th century. One of the oldest maps in the world.

Domaine Gayrard: A Gaillac wine producer run by the same family since the 15th century.

Abbaye de Beaulieu-en-Rouergue: It's a former Cistercian abbey that was bought by a Parisian couple and turned into an excellent contemporary art gallery.

ROAD TRIP

Tarn Wine & Bastides Drive

This leisurely countryside drive starts amid the poppy-lined vineyards of Gaillac and ends in Penne, a dramatic clifftop settlement. Beyond the hills, you'll discover, historic walled villages overlooking dramatic river gorges, windswept castles and plenty of enticement to slow things down with a glass of crisp white wine, before returning to the comparatively lively Cordes-sur-Ciel. What's more, the view from the car is never dull.

❶ Château Lastours

As one of the oldest wine producing regions of France, the Gaillac AOC has plenty of sites where oenophiles can also get their history fix. Elegant Château Lastours, perched on the Tarn riverbank, is a family estate spanning more than four centuries. Full vine-to-glass tours are available. Reserve in advance.

The Drive: Head into Gaillac, then north on the D964 for 11km.

❷ Castelnau-de-Montmiral

Typical of the medieval villages throughout the region, Castelnau-de-Montmiral crowns the highest spot of land, not that you'll see much beyond the warren of exciting passageways and cobbled streets in its pristine centre. The main attraction is its arcaded square, overhung by half-timbered buildings – the ideal spot for an *apéro*.

The Drive: Continue west along the D964 for 12.5km, then take a slight right onto D8 up a forested hillside to the town.

❸ Puycelci

Proper castle walls with deep arrow slits and rounded towers protect medieval Puycelci. When the walls stop, it's because the steep rocky outcrop on top of which the town sits, plunges straight down. Unusually, the Benedictine Église St Corneille's

Forteresse de Penne

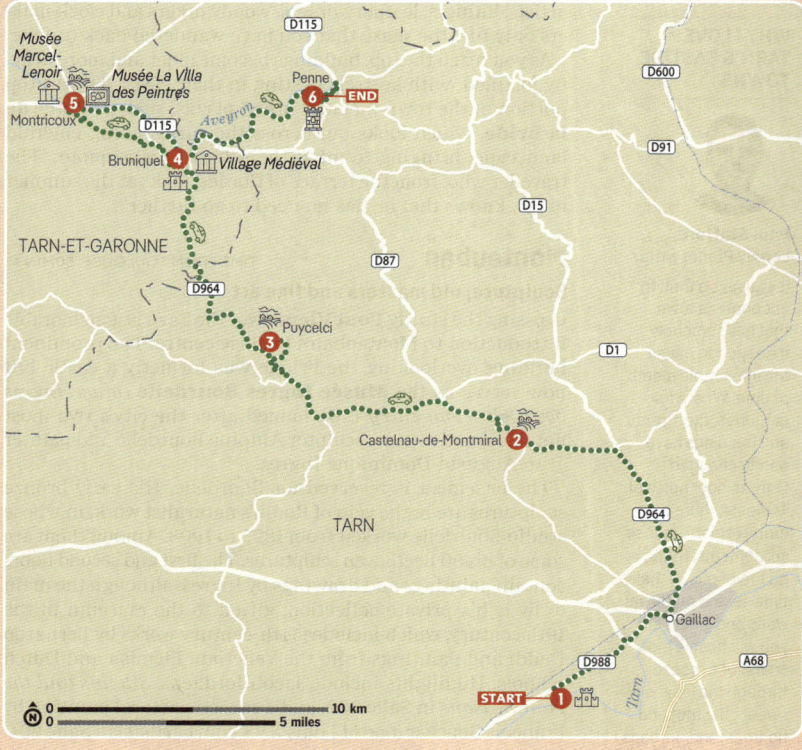

spire sits directly above an arched passage, which also acts as the entrance to maximise the limited space.

The Drive: Return back down to the D964 and head northwest, through increasingly picturesque countryside for 12km.

❹ Châteaux de Bruniquel

The 12th-century Châteaux de Bruniquel keep a formidable defensive watch over the deep Aveyron River. Below, a delightful hillside ramble of cobbled streets and stone steps wind around the **Village Médiéval's** stone houses. The town is large enough that you'll feel intrepid but small enough that you'll never actually get lost.

The Drive: Rejoin our old friend the D964 for just 6km.

❺ Montricoux

Pretty, half-timbered buildings with crooked wood and brick frames overhang the narrow streets, giving Montricoux a rustic, open-air museum feeling. Artist Marcel-Lenoir retired to the town and there are two museums dedicated to his work: **Musée Marcel-Lenoir** is housed in a castle built by the Knights Templar, which includes an original fresco on the chapel ceiling. Art collector Diego Lara exhibits his private Marcel-Lenoir collection at **Musée La Villa des Peintres** nearby.

The Drive: Head east, following the Aveyron river gorge on the D115 for 13.5km.

❻ Forteresse de Penne

Forteresse de Penne is among the most dramatically poised in all of France, hanging above the valley like a structurally unsound game of Jenga. The castle was thoroughly revamped using medieval techniques similar to the original building methods. The museum inside on of the towers holds a collection of coins, 12th- to 14th-century swords and everyday items used by the soldiers.

WHY I LOVE TARN'S BASTIDE TOWNS

Paul Stafford, Lonely Planet writer

It's always a thrill to encounter a town that has somehow managed to pause the inexorable march of time. Where for centuries, the streets and buildings have barely changed. Only an hour north of Toulouse there is an entire region of these settlements. Stand on top of one of their time-tested medieval walls and listen; all you will hear is the sound of a breeze through the leaves of sweet chestnut and fig trees, and perhaps the cuckoo's call in the summer. Places like this are as close as you'll come to feeling intrepid, particularly in a country like France, whose every inch seems known to the whole world. The fact that you can break the illusion and rejoin the modern world in Toulouse whenever you like makes it all the sweeter.

---

artists, luthiers, leatherworkers, woodworkers and clock-makers only fuel the sense that you have wandered back in time.

As you reach the top, buildings become older and more heavily fortified, with kestrels nesting in their eaves. The hilltop portion of the town includes broad plazas, such as **Place de la Bride**, which looks out across the surrounding emerald landscape, bringing to mind the Albert Camus quote: 'The traveller who, from the terrace of Cordes, looks at the summer night, knows that he has no need to go further'.

Montauban

TIME FROM TOULOUSE: **50MIN**

Sculpture, old masters and fine art

Crossing the sturdy **Pont Vieux** over the Tarn is a memorable introduction to Montauban's historic centre. The prominent building overlooking the bridge was formerly a castle but now serves as the **Musée Ingres Bourdelle** (*museeingresbourdelle.com; entry €10*), named after the city's two most notable creative sons: sculptor Antoine Bourdelle and painter Jean-Auguste-Dominique Ingres.

The basement is reserved for Bourdelle. His early bronze sculptures are in the vein of Rodin's naturalist work, in whose studio Bourdelle worked from 1893 to 1908. Among them are some of his 80 Beethoven sculptures. The first and second floors contain paintings and drawings by Ingres, although the main draw is his private collection, gifted to the museum in the 19th century, which includes 14th-century works by Bernardo Daddi and paintings from the Venetian, Flemish and Dutch schools. Highlights include Jacob Jordaens' *Silenus and the Four Seasons* in Salle 202, and a rococo pastoral painting by François Boucher (one of Louis XV's court artists) in Salle 204.

Moissac

TIME FROM TOULOUSE: **1HR**

A hiker's retreat

You'll see plenty of scallop shells attached to backpacks in Moissac. They signify hikers walking the Chemin de St-Jacques de Compostelle, who flock this town near the Tarn River confluence with the Garonne to visit the **Abbaye St-Pierre** (*free*). The Gothic church's southern portal yawns like the mouth of a basking shark, swallowing up penitents and hikers into its 15th-century Gothic interior. Pause to observe the entrance's superbly carved Romanesque tympanum (worth the trip alone), depicting the second coming of Jesus during the Apocalypse. Head round to the northwest side of the

---

 EATING IN MONTAUBAN & AUCH: OUR PICKS

Nous: Creative local ingredient-based dishes, with everything made in-house. So good they don't even need to open for dinner. Montauban. *noon-1.30pm Mon-Sat* €€

Du Bruit en Cuisine: Tapas-style dishes and mains given a gourmet makeover, such as pork tenderloin with rosemary jus. Montauban. *10am-3pm & 6-11pm Tue-Sat* €€

La Grande Salle: Great Pyrenean trout, served with smoked potato and coriander oil. In an elegant dining room of the Hôtel de France, Auch. *hours vary Wed-Sun* €€€

Le Marceau: Tucked away down an alley in Auch, this is a great place to try *magret de canard* (duck breast), served in a citrus sauce. *hours vary Wed-Sun* €€

Abbaye St-Pierre tympanum, Moissac

church to access the 11th-century **Cloître** *(abbayemoissac. com; adult/under-12 €7/free)*, which features more carved stories in its pillars and capitals.

Auch

TIME FROM TOULOUSE: 1HR 30MIN

Taking monumental steps

Gascony's capital, Auch (pronounced like 'gauche' without the 'g') has Roman roots and a strong Renaissance-era character in its champagne-coloured brick and duck egg blue wooden window shutters. Wandering the historic core reveals some wonderful half-timbered buildings, such as **Maison Henri IV**. The highlight is the **Escalier Monumental**, an Italian Renaissance–style staircase of 374 broad steps leading 35m up from the Gers River to the trickle of fountains, occasionally widening to a balcony. At the top sits **Cathédrale Ste-Marie** *(free)*, which features some fine Gothic touches, such as the cross-ribbed vaulting and an elegant round-petalled rose window.

Romans, Egyptians and the Inca

Auch hosts France's largest collection of pre-Columbian art, outside of Paris. It is housed – together with some Ancient Egyptian artefacts and Roman relics – at the **Musée des Amériques-Auch** *(aka Musée des Jacobins; adult/child €6/free)* in the city centre. Roman, prehistoric and medieval artefacts found in archaeological digs around Gascony dot the first floor, including a statue of the Roman god Jupiter.

The first floor features ceramics from the Americas – including Inca religious iconography and some fascinating Peruvian portrait vases – and an Ancient Egyptian wooden sarcophagus, still retaining much of its original design, from the 4th century BCE. It's an exquisite collection of beautifully presented items.

HOW IS ARMAGNAC MADE?

Patrick Giacosa, local winegrower, Armagnac producer and owner of **Château Le Courrejot**. *@armagnac_lecourrejot*

We're in the region called Armagnac-Ténarèze, which sits between Bas-Armagnac and Haut-Armagnac. Together, the three form the Armagnac region. The soil here is calcareous clay, which is good for growing ugni blanc grapes. We harvest in early September and leave them to ferment between six weeks and two months. We then pass this wine through an alembic still. The distillation process is crucial and work takes place 24 hours a day for about 10 days. To age the clear, colourless *eau de vie* we obtain from distilling the wine, we only use barrels made of oak. Over the years, the alcohol evaporates, which we call *la part des anges* (the angels' share). We lose between 3–6% per year, which adds up because we age our Armagnac at least 10 years.

BEST SIGHTS AROUND CONDOM

All around Condom (candidate for France's funniest place name), you will find pretty abbeys, bulky *bastides* and a handful of Plus Beaux Villages.

Larressingle: Alluring little castle village enclosed by 13th-century ramparts, with seven towers and a drawbridge entrance over a moat.

Abbaye de Flaran: Beautiful gardens and, surprisingly, an excellent art gallery containing Dalí and Rodin sculptures, a Toulouse-Lautrec portrait sketch, and Monet, Renoir and Courbet paintings.

La Romieu: Flower-kissed Plus Beaux Village with the fortress-like **Collégiale St-Pierre** (completed in 1318) church and cloisters at its heart.

Fourcès: Yet another Plus Beaux Village of half-timbered houses built in a circle around a central square.

Montréal: Plus Beaux Village whose **Villa Gallo-Romaine de Séviac** hints at the settlement's long history.

Armagnac ingredients, Château de Cassaigne

Condom

TIME FROM TOULOUSE: 1HR 50MIN

Armagnac distillery tastings

Famed for its eponymous tipple, Armagnac is the oldest form of brandy and is produced extensively across the region. Many of the vineyards and distilleries are located at fabulous châteaux, although some of the most authentic tastings take place at small family-run farms. Taste the complex notes of prune, vanilla and dried apricot for yourself at **Château de Cassaigne** *(chateaudecassaigne.com; self-guided tour €2.50)*, where deer and vineyards fill the surrounding grounds of the chateau, which is entwined with a surrounding village.

It's only at 10 years that Armagnac is considered mature, when the colour darkens to amber. Getting darker with time, 20- to 30-year-old Armagnacs are considered to be of the highest quality. Other great tasting spots are the small-batch Armagnacs at **Château Le Courrejot** *(chateaulecourrejot.fr)*, **Chateau de Mons** *(chateaumons.com)* and **Château de Gensac** *(gensac.com)*, all set amid rolling, vine-clad countryside freckled with brick *pigeonniers* (dovecotes). Tastings are available year-round and, while advance reservations are not essential, they are preferred, especially for larger groups.

Parc Naturel Régional des Pyrénées Ariégeoises

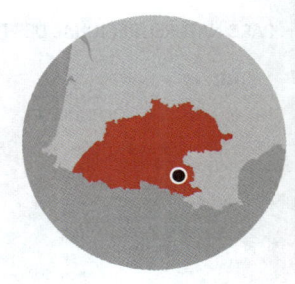

SUBTERRANEAN ADVENTURES | FORMIDABLE FORTRESSES | FAMILY FUN

They may lack the majesty of the Alps, but the Pyrenees mountains are packed with drama, much of it ensconced beneath the surface. This is particularly true of the Parc Naturel Régional des Pyrénées Ariégeoises, where elaborate cave networks are sometimes so extensive that they contain navigable subterranean rivers and some of the world's oldest, most exquisite ancient cave paintings.

The park's main point of access is along the N20, which connects Paris, via Toulouse, towards Andorra and Spain. Castle-capped regional capital Foix and the laid-back Tarascon-sur-Ariège are the main two towns. Between them they provide access to a host of thrilling experiences – including the family-friendly museums of Les Forges de Pyrène and Parc de la Préhistoire – and a variety of outdoor activities from cycling and via ferrata in summer to skiing in winter. Artisanal workshops and *dégustations* reveal glimpses into the Pyrenean way of life, while foodie highlights include traditional *aligot* (cheesy potatoes), Pyrenean fondue and sweet Jurançon wines.

☑ TOP TIP

The French alternative to Britain's OS Maps are the blue and white IGN maps. Look for map numbers IGN 2147ET and IGN 2047ET for hikes using Foix or Tarascon-sur-Ariège as a base. Alternatively, download the free IGNrando' app, which also shows certain cycle routes.

GETTING AROUND

There are regular trains between Toulouse and Ax-les-Thermes via Foix and Tarascon-sur-Ariège. Beyond that, there's little in the way of public transport and renting a car is by far the easiest way to experience the best of the Ariège Pyrénées region. There is some fantastic driving to be had in this area. The alternative is to cycle the quiet roads or hike in along one of the many trails that crisscross the region.

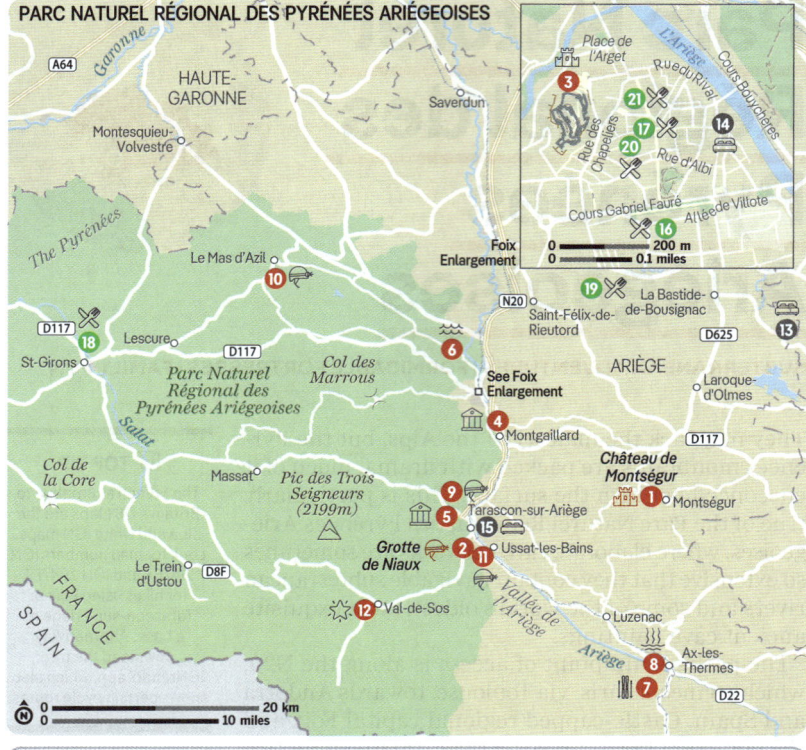

PARC NATUREL RÉGIONAL DES PYRÉNÉES ARIÉGEOISES

- ★ **HIGHLIGHTS**
  1 Château de Montségur
  2 Grotte de Niaux

- ● **SIGHTS**
  3 Château de Foix
  4 Les Forges de Pyrène
  see 1 Musée Archéologique de Montségur
  5 Parc de la Préhistoire
  6 Rivière Souterraine de Labouiche

- ● **ACTIVITIES**
  7 Ax 3 Domaines
  8 Bassin des Ladres
  9 Grotte de Bédeilhac
  see 2 Grotte de la Vache
  10 Grotte du Mas d'Azil
  11 Grotte Lombrives
  see 8 Les Bains du Couloubret
  see 2 Spéléo Canyon Ariège
  12 Vertikarst

- ● **SLEEPING**
  13 Abbaye de Camon
  14 Hôtel Lons
  15 Logis Hôtel le Manoir d'Agnès

- ● **EATING**
  16 Bistro Régent
  17 Guarana
  see 12 La Table de l'Orriégeoise
  18 Le Carré de l'Ange
  19 Le Clos Saint Martin
  20 Le Jeu de l'Oie
  21 Noï
  see 15 Pizza de Peppo

Trebuchets & Donjons
See a castle come to life

Foix, capital of the Ariège *département*, has long been a regional seat of power for notable counts such as 14th-century Gaston Fébus, self-styled 'Prince of the Pyrenees'. It's no surprise then, that the **Château de Foix** (*sites-touristiques-ariege.fr/en/chateau-de-foix; adult/child €12.50/9*), with its two sturdy donjons and a third, round tower are an unmissable display of defensive prowess.

It's possible to clamber up all three towers and the castle is brought to life with era-approximate furniture and

CASTAWAY CASTLES

Foix castle was once a Cathar stronghold, fighting the Catholic Church for the right to worship in their own way. Eventually pushed underground, the Cathars built their castles in increasingly remote spots, such as the ones at Lastours (p716) and Peyrepertuse (p693).

artisanal craft and weapons demonstrations made by people in period costume. The most exciting is the life-size trebuchet (sans the giant building-crushing rock). Geared more toward families, with a somewhat kitschy museum that paints a biased account of history, it is nevertheless an impeccably preserved castle.

Ancient Beasts & Traditional Trades
Museums for the family

Continuing the living history theme set at Château de Foix, traditional craft trades such as blacksmithing, tanning and thatching are brought to life at **Les Forges de Pyrène** (forges-de-pyrene.com; adult/child €11.50/8), 4km south of Foix. Visitors get the chance to give some of the crafts a try and see a 15th-century hammer forge in action.

Further south, in the laidback town of Tarascon-sur-Ariège, you can see life-sized replicas of some of the ancient beasts that once roamed the valley at **Parc de la Préhistoire** (sites-touristiques-ariege.fr/parc-de-la-prehistoire; €12.50/9). There are real skeletons of a cave bear and a woolly mammoth, plus an audiovisual suite exploring how the first humans came to settle in the area and leave their art in the nearby caves.

Flowing Deeper Underground
Navigate a subterranean river

Europe's longest navigable underground river can be found just 6km northwest of Foix. Hop into one of the specially designed barges at **Rivière Souterraine de Labouiche** (labouiche.com; adult/child €16.50/14), manoeuvred by a pulling a rope (done by your guide) along a 1.5km stretch of this underground waterway, it's a great way to explore the caves that are legion in this part of the Pyrenees. Tours end at **Cascade Salette**, an underground waterfall.

History Written in Primitive Paint
Visiting prehistoric cave art

One of the great experiences in southwestern France is visiting cave paintings made by our predecessors at **Grotte de Niaux** (sites-touristiques-ariege.fr/grotte-de-niaux; adult/child €16/12). Radiocarbon dating places these rare and magnificent works – made using black manganese dioxide and red hematite as paints – to between 17,234 and 14,881 years old.

BEST FOIX CONCERTS & FESTIVALS

Foix is the cultural centre of the Ariège Pyrénées.

Concert dans la Grotte de Bédeilhac: Every year since 1929, a chamber orchestra transforms the caves with a concert that benefits from their natural acoustics. *Jun*

Festival Résistances: A Foix festival of film sharing rarely seen works that cover themes linked to contemporary social issues. *Jul*

Jazz à Foix: Popular jazz festival with performances from a range of jazz traditions, such as classical and African jazz. *Jul*

Apéritif at Gaston: For three Tuesday evenings a year during the summer holidays, feast like a medieval knight in Château de Foix's banquet hall. *Jul-Aug*

Festivale Ingeniouse Afrique: Foix is transformed by the art, dance and music of African cultures in August with free concerts. *Aug*

 EATING IN FOIX: OUR PICKS

Le Jeu de l'Oie: Best known for its duck dishes, but there are a couple of good vegetarian options, too. Dishes are presented with elegance. *noon-1.30pm & 7-9pm Tue-Sat* €€

Guarana: Octopus carpaccio, tender porcini mushroom ravioli and a superb aubergine à la parmigiana are highlights at this much-loved Italian restaurant. *noon-2pm & 7-9pm Tue-Sat* €€

Bistro Régent: Precisely what you'd expect from a French bistro: quality meat, doused in tasty sauce, with giant heaps of *frites* on the side. *noon-2.30pm & 7-9.30pm* €

Noï: Tucked away down a little alley, Noï does dishes rooted in the Mediterranean but influenced by the world. Veggie options available. *hours vary, daily* €€

All visits are via guided tour, with multiple daily tours in French and usually one a day in English. This is one of the rare remaining sites where you can actually visit the original paintings in situ. Trips begin with a steady descent into the huge gaping limestone cavern, using only the torches provided to light the way. It is a long, unpaved walk over uneven ground, so a certain degree of fitness and agility is needed.

The paintings don't start until 600m deep inside the caves and it's a genuinely moving experience to consider that somebody who stood on the same spot millennia ago is communicating with us in the present. The art focuses not only on animals, such as horses, bison, aurochs, deer and ibex, all of which once commonly roamed these lands, but also geometric patterns using dots and lines. The meaning of these patterns is open to interpretation. It could have been spiritual or may have functioned like a map.

In total there are 70 prehistoric paintings in these caves, although the tours only unveil around 20. There is one access-all-areas tour per month; it's only in French and must be booked at least six months in advance. For regular tours, book at least a month in advance for summer visits.

Cave Stories

Natural cave art

For most of the caves in Parc Naturel Régional des Pyrénées Ariégeoises, nature's slow calciferous processes are the art. Of the many caves you can visit, four in particular offer some spectacular sights. **Grotte de la Vache** *(sites-touristiques-ariege.fr/grotte-de-la-vache; adult/child €9.50/6)*, in the same valley as **Grotte de Niaux** (p723), has been the source of fascinating archaeological discoveries, including primitive tools, weapons and decorated objects dating back 15,000 years.

Grotte de Bédeilhac *(sites-touristiques-ariege.fr/grotte-de-bedeilhac; adult/child €11.50/7.50)* contains some spectacular chambers where rock formations have taken millions of years to develop. There's also a couple of prehistoric hand prints. But nothing beats **Grotte du Mas d'Azil** *(sites-touristiques-ariege.fr/grotte-du-mas-dazil; adult/child €11.50/7.50)* for scale: it's so large that it's possible to drive through it.

Finally, **Grotte Lombrives** *(grottedelombrives.com; adult/child €12/10)* is the most beautifully lit, making it possible to better appreciate the stalactite and stalagmite formations inside one of Europe's largest cave systems.

Long-Distance Pyrenees

Tackle a multi-day hiking or biking trail

Most long-distance hiking trails through the Pyrenees are accessible from late spring to autumn, while most roads are kept open year-round. It's worth noting, however, that the Pyrenees pose some of the most challenging cycling stages, even to professional cyclists.

One excellent long-distance cycling route is the 650-km V81, aka the **Vélosud**, which sticks to the northern foothills of the

NIAUX'S PAINTERS & BEASTS THAT ONCE ROAMED

It's hard to imagine what southern France would have looked like 17,000 years ago. The climate would have been around 6°C cooler, as the planet was going through the most recent Ice Age. At the time, prehistoric humans roved these lands. Known as the Magdalenian people, they were directly descended from Cro-Magnons (the first modern humans). Most archaeological evidence we have on the Magdalenian people was found in modern-day France. They were semi-nomadic hunter-gatherers (farming wouldn't be developed for another 8000 years) who made tools and weapons, interacting with mammals that are long gone from France's wilds, such as aurochs. The animals they painted in the caves of the Pyrenees – horses, bison, ibex and even a weasel – may have had symbolic or spiritual meaning.

Bison cave painting, Grotte de Niaux (p723)

Pyrenees, bypassing the worst of the climbs. See francevelotourisme.com for an in-depth overview.

One of the most challenging long-distance hikes in France is the **GR10**, which parallels the coast-to-coast border of France and Spain. Known as the Great Traverse of the Pyrenees, the 900km trail largely keeps to the northern fringe of the highest parts of the mountain range.

Rarely leaving the wilderness but crossing paths with some spectacular, remote castles is the **Sentier Cathare** (GR367) from Foix all the way to the Mediterranean. For some basic information and maps, gr-infos.com is a good starting point.

The Cave Less Travelled
Caving and canyoning around Auzat

If you've ever wanted to go caving or canyoning, Parc Naturel Régional des Pyrénées Ariégeoises is the perfect place to do it. Auzat-based canyoning company **Vertikarst** (vertikarst.fr) runs trips in the surrounding wilderness, such as Canyon de l'Artigue and in to the Grotte de Vicdessos cave near Val-de-Sos, seeking out underground rivers and stunning rock formations that can only be accessed with specialist gear and guidance. Another good tour provider running a similarly

VISITING ANDORRA & SPAIN FROM FRANCE

Ariège shares a border with both Spain and Andorra. For most visitors, separate visas for Spain won't be necessary if you already have a Schengen visa for France (always check your government's travel advice before travelling). For entry to Andorra, there are no visa requirements for nationals of most countries. Head to Andorra's capital, Andorra La Vella, for beautiful views across the Pyrenees from Parc Central and to explore the Barri Antic (Old Town). You can continue south into Spain from here. Alternatively, for a quirk of territorial treaty history, you can visit Llívia, a Spanish exclave territory to the east of Andorra. It is completely surrounded by France, adrift from the rest of Spain, which lies 1.5km away.

EATING IN ARIÈGE: OUR PICKS

Le Clos Saint Martin: In the countryside between Mirepoix and Pamiers, this *haute cuisine* restaurant pairs artistry with bold flavours and excellent wine pairings. *hours vary Fri-Tue* €€€

Le Carré de l'Ange: The terrace seating with Pyrenean views is hard to beat. Same applies to the set menus (including a vegetarian option). St-Lizier village. *hours vary Thu-Tue* €€

Pizza de Peppo: Sourdough pizzas cooked in a wood-fired oven and a decent tiramisu for dessert. Try to grab a riverside table. Tarascon-sur-Ariège. *6-9.30pm Wed-Sun* €

La Table de l'Orriégeoise: Dishes are simple and well-defined, just like the menu – which gives you three options, changing by the season. Auzat. *hours vary Thu-Sun* €€

Château de Montségur

WHO WERE THE CATHARS?

The Cathars claimed to live holy lives, similar to those of Jesus' apostles, praying regularly, observing anti-materialism, chastity and vegetarianism, and scorning all cults, statuary and relics that were common to the Catholic Church. They focused on the New Testament and the idea of Jesus being the Messiah who could not die, rather than on eternal punishment and crucifixion in the way that often gripped Catholicism.

Naturally, the Catholic ruling class in medieval France took umbrage, denouncing the Cathars as Albigensian heretics and dissidents. In 1209, Pope Innocent III announced the Albigensian Crusade to eliminate Catharism. This ushered in an Inquisition, with torture being legalised in 1252 in order to smoke out Catharism. Gradually pushed to the fringes of society, only their castles remain today.

intrepid array of canyoning and caving trips near Grotte de Niaux is **Spéléo Canyon Ariège** *(speleo-canyon-ariege.com).*

Powder & Steam
Skiing in the Ariège

With so many mountains, it's fair to expect some good skiing in winter and the Pyrenees don't disappoint. The best pistes around Vallée de l'Ariège, especially for beginner and intermediate skiers, is at **Ax 3 Domaines** *(ax.ski)* near Ax-les-Thermes. The three areas in question are Saquet's exposed mountaintop runs, more challenging black and red pistes of Les Campels, and the wide blue and green runs through the forest of Bonascre.

When you're unclipped from board or ski, head back down to Ax-les-Thermes, where you'll find the **Bassin des Ladres**, a hot spring in a town centre square designed for dangling your feet on. For a more comprehensive soak, try the natural thermal baths at **Les Bains du Couloubret** *(boutique.bains-couloubret.com; adult/child from €25/17).*

Cathar Stronghold
Hiking up to Montségur's castle

Sitting like a jaunty hat on a steep-sided mountaintop, **Château de Montségur's** *(montsegur.fr/chateau-et-musee; adult/child €6/3)* formidable natural defences made it the ideal spot for a beleaguered group of religious outcasts to set up camp. So steep that it makes roads impossible, visitors must hike the hairpin trail for around 30 minutes, to the sound of redstarts and cow bells clanging in the valley below, to the castrum (a fortified village). In 1243, 3000 crusader soldiers laid siege for 11 months, before the Cathars were finally forced to surrender. While the castle's empty shell does little to convey what life would have been like, the views all around are exceptional. Tickets include entry to the **Musée Archéologique de Montségur**, located back down in Montségur village.

Parc National des Pyrénées

SNOW SPORTS | WILD ENCOUNTERS | SCENIC HIKES

The Parc National des Pyrénées has some of France's most colourful, contrasting and mesmerising landscapes. The park's saw-toothed skyline, which includes the Pyrénées-Atlantiques and Hautes-Pyrénées, divides France and Spain for roughly 120km (although the mountains continue well beyond that in either direction). The regions of true wilderness in this stretch of the Pyrénées create a formidable photogenic playground for lovers of the great outdoors, with plenty of waterfalls, mountain trails and skiing pistes, plus the multitude of ways humans have devised to traverse them and spike the adrenaline at the same time.

The observatory-capped Pic du Midi de Bigorre (p733) offers some of the finest views in southern France. Elsewhere, spectacular natural amphitheatres such as the Cirque de Gavarnie are part of a natural landscape teeming with flora and fauna, including 70 species of mammal and 2500 plant species. This is the backdrop for goat farms and artisans who open their doors to visitors as the weather warms.

☑ TOP TIP

For hiking trail information, French-only caminaspe.fr is a fantastic resource. *Trekking the GR10* and *Walks and Climbs in the Pyrenees,* published by the ever-dependable Cicerone, feature a number of up-to-date hikes in Parc National des Pyrénées. IGN Maps (hard copies or the app) are also handy. Weatherwise, meteoblue.com provides crucial, localised forecasts.

Get Your Boots On

Hiking the GR10 from Lescun

Located 11km south of the closest train station (Bedous), the charming hillside village of **Lescun** is a springboard to some

GETTING AROUND

Trains from Pau run around four times a day to Bedous. With the exception of **Le Petit Train d'Artouste** (p730), which isn't connected to the broader rail network, this is the only train servicing the national park. Driving is a top experience in its own right here – which is a good thing because it's largely necessary: accessing much of Parc National des Pyrénées is tricky without some form of motorised transportation. If you're planning to enter via one of the long-distance trails, hiking is best from late spring to early autumn.

PARC NATIONAL DES PYRÉNÉES

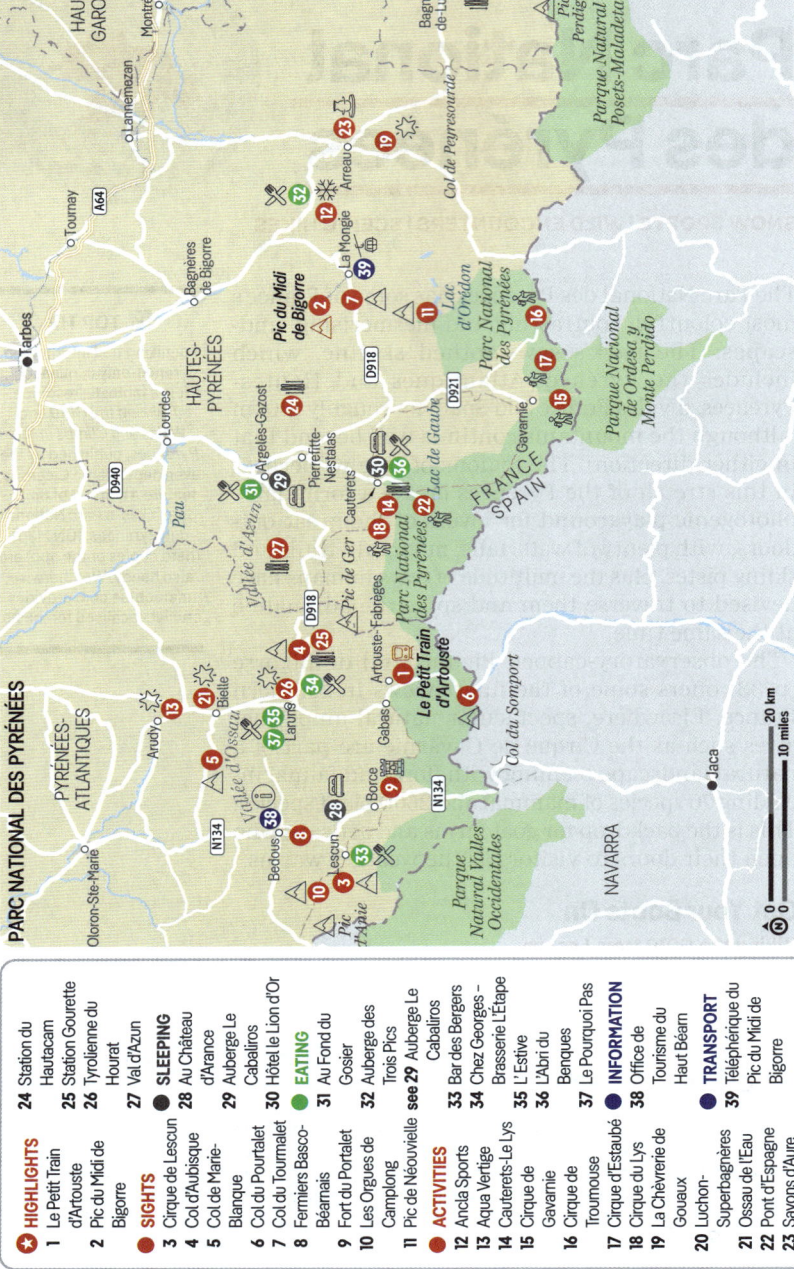

PARC NATIONAL DES PYRÉNÉES

★ HIGHLIGHTS
1. Le Petit Train d'Artouste
2. Pic du Midi de Bigorre

● SIGHTS
3. Cirque de Lescun
4. Col d'Aubisque
5. Col de Marie-Blanque
6. Col du Pourtalet
7. Col du Tourmalet
8. Fermiers Basco-Béarnais
9. Fort du Portalet
10. Les Orgues de Camplong
11. Pic de Néouvielle

● ACTIVITIES
12. Ancla Sports
13. Aqua Vertige
14. Cauterets-Le Lys
15. Cirque de Gavarnie
16. Cirque de Troumouse
17. Cirque d'Estaubé
18. Cirque du Lys
19. La Chèvrerie de Gouaux
20. Luchon-Superbagnères
21. Ossau de l'Eau
22. Pont d'Espagne
23. Savons d'Aure
24. Station du Hautacam
25. Station Gourette
26. Tyrolienne du Hourat
27. Val d'Azun

● SLEEPING
28. Au Château d'Arance
29. Auberge Le Cabaliros
30. Hôtel le Lion d'Or

● EATING
31. Au Fond du Gosier
32. Auberge des Trois Pics
see 29 Auberge Le Cabaliros
33. Bar des Bergers
34. Chez Georges – Brasserie L'Étape
35. L'Estive
36. L'Abri du Benques
37. Le Pourquoi Pas

● INFORMATION
38. Office de Tourisme du Haut Béarn

● TRANSPORT
39. Téléphérique du Pic du Midi de Bigorre

of the best hiking in the Pyrenees. Nearby, the natural serrated limestone forms a natural amphitheatre called the **Cirque de Lescun**, with Pic d'Anie (2507m) towering above it. To reach Lescun without a car, take the irregular local bus from Bedous to Pont de Lescun, then hike the remaining 5km.

Heading west from Lescun along a particularly impressive stage of the GR10 will take you past the Cirque de Lescun. You'll also pass **Les Orgues de Camplong**, a dramatic rock escarpment, on the way to Refuge Jeandel. Bedous' **Office de Tourisme du Haut Béarn** sells copies of a local hiking guidebooks and local IGN maps. Many trails in this area are high-altitude and susceptible to rapid changes in weather.

Alternatively, heading east along the GR10 takes you deeper into Parc National des Pyrénées to **Etsaut**. Keep following the GR10 trail for another day and you'll head south to the 19th-century **Fort du Portalet** *(pyrenees-bearnaises.com; adult/child €13/8)*, which is partially cut into the mountainside. It is possible to get buses onwards to Oloron-Ste-Marie from Borce or Urdos.

Cheese, Glorious Cheese
See how goat cheese is made

Across the world mountains are seen as good places for raising sheep and goats. The Pyrenees are no different and cheese production is widespread, from the dedicated mountain cabins of transhumant sheep herders to small farmsteads with a few goats. The result is some excellent local cheese, including pungent goat cheese, creamy *Tomme,* and the nutty Ossau-Iraty cheese produced by the **Fermiers Basco-Béarnais** *(fermiers-basco-bearnais.fr)* fromagerie and sold at their cooperative farm shop 2.5km south of Bedous. It pairs perfectly with a hunk of homemade bread and some sour cherry jam.

Many local sheep and goat farms now open their doors to visitors in a bid to channel some of the tourism euro, to varied results. One sure-fire bet is a trip to **La Chèvrerie de Gouaux** *(lachevreriedegouaux.fr; free)*, who run daily tours of their goat farm at 5.30pm (January to September). There's a chance to pet the goats and watch as they're taken through the milking process. At the end you can try and buy the resultant goat cheese.

Vulture Culture
Seeking wildlife in the Vallée d'Ossau

Part of Parc National des Pyrénées' charm is its expanses of true wilderness. These difficult-to-access spots have become a last refuge for wildlife due simply to the absence of humans. But you don't have to hike for days to have meaningful encounters with the natural world. As one of the quieter valleys running through the mountains, Vallée d'Ossau has become a haven for griffon vultures, particularly between Aste-Béon and Castet. With a good pair of binoculars, you'll likely be able to spot them nesting in the cliffs above the village.

BEST MOUNTAIN ROAD PASSES

There's a lot of spectacular drives (or cycles if you're fit enough) throughout Parc National des Pyrénées. These mountain passes are often closed in winter.

Col du Tourmalet: Legendary stage in the Tour de France, featured in more than 75% of the races. At 2115m, it is the highest mountain pass in the Hautes-Pyrénées.

Col d'Aubisque: Popular stage on the Tour de France in the high mountains. Beware of sheep and horses in the road.

Col du Pourtalet: Among the world's most spectacular border crossings, passing mountain peaks presiding over the switch from France to Spain.

Col de Marie-Blanque: Peaceful, winding drive through the forest, climbing above the 1000m mark. Has also been a Tour de France stage.

CHEESY GOODNESS

Nowhere does a cheese tour and tasting quite like France. Numerous farms open their doors for tastings in Munster (p344), while among Auvergne's numerous excellent cheeses, time-ripened Cantal (p484) has no shortage of producers happy to open their doors to visitors.

Over on the east side of the park, on the slopes of **Pic de Néouvielle**, you'll have a good chance of spotting marmots and chamois, elusive capercaillies and crossbills around the series of reservoirs. Ultra-cute, endangered Pyrenean desmans live along the banks of the many rivers that feed them.

Jumping Down Waterfalls
Spelunking debunked

If simply observing nature is not enough, Vallée d'Ossau is also a beautiful place to engage with it. A couple of excellent canyoning tour providers operate from the villages of Castet and Laruns. **Ossau de l'Eau** *(ossaudeleau.fr; from €45)* does river descents for absolute beginners as well as more experienced spelunkers. The emphasis is always on pushing your boundaries without abandoning the bounds of safety. The routes take you into otherwise inaccessible Vallée d'Ossau canyons. **Aqua Vertige** *(aqua-vertige.com; adult/child from €50/45)* conquers canyons but also explores local caves.

Soaring Over Canyons
Ziplining in Laruns

At the foot of the **Col d'Aubisque**, the **Tyrolienne du Hourat** *(larunsaventures.com; adult/child €23/17)* in Laruns is a series of 22 ziplines and three narrow foot bridges that breach the gaps between plunging gorges and craggy cliff faces, above rushing waterfalls and over sparkling turquoise water. It's a thrilling mix of stirring views and sheer adrenaline as you work your way along the rushing Gave d'Ossau River's course.

The Mile-High Chug
Riding the nosebleed express

One novel way to take in the Pyrenean views is by riding **Le Petit Train d'Artouste** *(artouste.fr; adult/child from €27/19)*. At 1940m above sea level, it is one of Europe's highest railways. Trips start from Artouste-Fabrèges ski resort, south of Laruns. To reach the train station you have to first take a cable car up the side of up the Pic de la Sagette. The toy train chugs through the mountains for 10km, often following rails cut into the side of a steep peak. The hour-long trip ends at an outlook point above the Lac d'Artouste. Unless

THE TRANSHUMANCE

Every year in late May, large flocks of sheep are herded up onto the high pastures to graze for the summer, then down to lower levels in October to see out the winter snows. The transhumance, as it's called, is a tradition dating back around 1000 years in the Pyrenees. A diet of fragrant grasses is said to enhance the flavour of sheep's milk, and therefore the cheeses made from it. Look for the phrase *'fromage d'estive'* on packaging to denote cheeses made with this summer pasture milk. Pays Toy is the main area where sheep are herded for their summer pastures within Parc National des Pyrénées. There are many wooden huts on these slopes where shepherds stay with their flocks throughout the summer, making fresh cheeses and other dairy products in situ.

Try the regional garbure stew

EATING IN OSSAU & ASPE VALLEYS: OUR PICKS

L' Estive: Undisputed champions of melted cheese-based dishes, with top-notch fondue and *raclette*. Partially tucked behind a building in central Laruns. *hours vary Thu-Mon* €€

Le Pourquoi Pas: Why not indeed! Especially given how good the local trout is here. They do a fantastic roasted Camembert, too. Laruns. *noon-1.30pm & 7-8.30pm Fri-Tue* €€

Chez Georges – Brasserie L'Étape: Old-school French, where most dishes involve *frites* accompanying slabs of meat. Lunch only. Eaux-Bonnes. *9am-3pm Thu-Tue* €

Bar des Bergers: Hearty dishes, including duck confit and *garbure* (p733), but it's the desserts that make it worth stopping for. Vegan-friendly spot in Lascun. *hours vary* €€

Col du Tourmalet

you're planning some serious hiking, you have to return the way you came in. Tickets including the return trip and cable car rides. The train runs throughout early May until early October. Phone connection is patchy in the Pyrenees so if you have booked in advance, print your tickets or download them before you travel.

Cycling Magnificent Cols & Valleys
Join the Tour de France: the Tourmalet Stage

Ordinarily, the Pyrenees are a peaceful slice of rural French charm, but that all changes when the Tour de France rolls through. Although the sporting world's favourite bike race changes its course every year, some stages are just too good to pass over for long. And many of those stages – lauded for their combination of natural beauty and technical difficulty – are in the Pyrenees. Most popular is the **Col du Tourmalet** – known as *l'incontournable* (the unavoidable) – whenever it is featured (and it has been included more than any other stage). Roadsides fill with spectators as the cyclists battle with gravity and there's no better way to experience it than to attend in person. Unless, of course, you like a challenge. To follow in the Tour's wheel tracks, take part in the annual **Montée du Géant du Tourmalet** in early June, riding up at your own pace for a summit carnival atmosphere.

UNESCO-Approved Beauty
Hiking in superlative countryside

Snug with the Spanish border, the village of **Gavarnie** is the gateway to arguably the prettiest site in the Pyrenees. Sticking to the objective truth, UNESCO deemed the natural, glacier-cut amphitheatre called **Cirque de Gavarnie** a World

RETURN OF THE BROWN BEAR

Once a common sight in the Pyrenees, native brown bears were hunted to extinction in France by 2004, when the last one was shot by a hunter in 'self-defence'. The loss of the bear, who was named Cannelle (French for cinnamon) by French conservationists, predictably led to a public outcry, a couple of bears too late. Although the native population is now extinct, a reintroduction programme had already begun in the 1990s, bringing in captured brown bears from Slovenia. Their numbers have subsequently flourished and the French Office for Biodiversity (OFB) announced in 2025 that they detected around 96 brown bears throughout the French Pyrenees. Their conservation is not always popular with landowners, but for now they are making a rebound.

BEST PYRENEES SKIING SPOTS

Cauterets-Le Lys: A natural amphitheatre carved by a glacier becomes a snowy playground in winter, with slopes for all abilities.

Station du Hautacam: Smaller family-oriented ski resort with mostly easier green trails among a majority of wider blue runs and just one or two harder pistes.

Station Gourette: Neatly laid out to keep beginner slopes sheltered from intermediate and above. Has a couple of good snowshoeing trails as well.

Val d'Azun: Best known for cross-country skiing (also known as Nordic skiing) along trails that usually also lend themselves well to snowshoeing.

Luchon-Superbagnères: Extensive ski resort with a range of pistes for intermediate and advanced skiiers, as well as some easier slopes.

Pic du Midi de Bigorre views

Heritage Site (part of the Mont Perdu massif, most of which lies in Spain). The three-hour return hike up the valley from the village is a fairly accessible (by Pyrenean standards) and uncomplicated hike – so much so that it can get quite busy on the trail.

But it doesn't stand alone. Immediately to the east are two more *cirques* (natural amphitheatres): **Cirque d'Estaubé**, which can only be reached after a half-day hike, and **Cirque de Troumouse**, which can be reached in summer via a drive, followed by a *petit train* ride. Both are usually much quieter than Gavarnie.

Two Feet or Two Skis

Hiking and skiing in Cauterets

More top-class hiking can be found at **Pont d'Espagne** in summer. A huge chunk of forest has been cleared to build a vast car park, such is the beauty of this part of the Pyrenees. The best hike is southwest into the wild Vallée du Marcadau. The more popular route from Pont d'Espagne is the trail to Lac de Gaube, to the south. In the winter, Cauterets reveals

EATING IN THE EASTERN HALF OF PARC NATIONAL DES PYRÉNÉES

Auberge Le Cabaliros: Great Pyrenean trout with saffron risotto. Their Friday Pyrenean Garbure Bigourdane, including *garbure* and pork confit, is popular. Arcizans-Avant. *12.30-1.30pm & 7.30-8.30pm* €€

Au Fond du Gosier: *Haute cuisine* in Argelès-Gazost. They do all the Pyrenean classics to perfection. The set lunch menus are excellent value. *hours vary Tue-Sat* €€

L'Abri du Benques: Directly overlooking the Cascade de Lutour, this modern-bucolic fine dining spot, hidden away from the road, does French classics with a gourmet makeover. *10am-7pm* €€

Auberge des Trois Pics: Good value Pyrenean classics including braised trout and an excellent *garbure*. Good views of the Pic du Midi. Payolle. *hours vary Tue-Sun* €€

its original raison d'être as a ski resort, with many miles of trails, making good use of the **Cirque du Lys** natural amphitheatre at the **Cauterets-Le Lys** *(cauterets.com)* ski resort.

Walking on Snow
Snowshoeing in Payolle

Roughly 40km of winter trails run from the little village of Payolle, whose surrounding topography is much gentler than the Pyrenean mountains closer to the Spanish border. While cross-country skiing and sledding are popular ways to access this landscape, snowshoeing (known in French as *raquettes*) is an excellent alternative, the wide attachments for your boots making it much easier to move across the show. Try **Ancla Sports** *(ancla-sports.com)* for snowshoe rentals and advice on the best routes.

Funicular to the Observatory
The ultimate Pyrenees view

For the best views in the Parc National des Pyrénées, you only need to look for where scientists decided the best place to site an observatory would be. That happens to be on the summit of **Pic du Midi de Bigorre** *(2877m; picdumidi.com; €53)*, which sits on the northern side of the Col du Tourmalet. Tickets are cheaper when booked in advance online and include the price of a ride on the **Téléphérique du Pic du Midi de Bigorre**, starting from La Mongie, almost 1000m below. At the top, there are various panoramic viewpoints which, on a clear day, provide spectacular vistas. The clearest skies are generally in the evening and early morning. There is also an exhibition about the mountain's history and a planetary science room. For additional fees, you can visit the planetarium and observatory.

A Good Lather
Attend a traditional craft demonstration

Artisanal crafts and agrarian traditions developed over the centuries in the fertile valleys of Parc National des Pyrénées still endure. Brewers, *fromageries,* confectioners, ebonists and soapmakers occasionally open their doors, especially during the summer, to let visitors discover the Pyrenees beyond the tourist track. Every Tuesday at 3.30pm during the summer, **Savons d'Aure** *(savonsdaure.com)* in Arreau holds a cold process soap-making demonstration. You'll have the chance to select essential oils for the smell you're after, then learn how the soap is made using all-natural ingredients and processes so that you can carry a piece of the Pyrenees home with you.

BEST PYRENEES LOCAL FLAVOURS

The Pyrenees mountains are rich in jams, honeys, meats and cheeses. Here are some flavours unique to the region.

Garbure: A satisfying soup based around goose confit and cabbage. Originally regarded as a peasants' soup. Today it's a speciality.

Brown trout: Thriving in the Aragnouet region, brown trout are often served with wild garlic, peppers and local tarbais beans.

Béarnaise sauce: Béarnaise sauce is this region's variation on hollandaise. You'll commonly find it served with *steak-frites*.

Chestnuts: Readily available in autumn, chestnuts are versatile. Look out for the seasonal *velouté de châtaigne* (chestnut broth) and chestnut cakes.

Porc noir de Bigorre: Free-range black pigs feast on chestnuts and acorns and are prized for the delicacy and flavour of their meat.

Beyond Parc National des Pyrénées

Life is still dictated by topography in the lands around Parc National des Pyrénées. Expect skiing, pasture-fed sheep's cheese and castles.

Places
Lourdes p734
Gan p737
Pau p737

Mountains continue to rise and fall beyond the east and west edges of Parc National des Pyrénées. Although not as severe as those protected by the park, the peaks present myriad opportunities for outdoor expeditions, foraging trips and funicular rides. Further north, as the mountains calm to an undulating simmer of hills, you'll find the pilgrim-popping town of Lourdes, where tales of a real-life miracle have cast a veil of sacred awe over every nook and cranny that was ever touched by Bernadette Soubirous (St Bernadette). Pau, meanwhile, is a pilgrimage site for the sweet-toothed, with its array of chocolatiers, while lower altitudes open the door for Jurançon AOC's winemakers to strut their stuff.

GETTING AROUND

Pau and Lourdes both sit on the main rail line from Toulouse to Bayonne, with half a dozen daily trains in either direction. A more regular service connects Pau, Lourdes and Tarbes. Direct trains to Paris run twice daily. There's also a train from Pau to Bedous in the Pyrenees. After a long closure, the Montréjeau-Luchon line reopened in summer 2025, connecting the skiing hub with the rest of France. Beyond these hubs, you'll need your own transport.

Lourdes   TIME FROM PARC NATIONAL DES PYRÉNÉES: 15MIN

Torchlight in a holy town

The traditional **Procession aux Flambeaux** *(lourdes-info-tourisme.com)*, also called the Marian Torchlight Procession, in Lourdes usually features thousands of participants, including locals, visitors and pilgrims. The group wanders through the streets with flaming torches while singing hymns from the Grotte de Massabielle (p736; also called the Grotte des Apparitions) to the esplanade in front of the **Basilique Notre-Dame-du-Rosaire**. It's the perfect time to witness the powerful reverence at the heart of the sanctuary that forms the holiest place in the Catholic world outside Rome and the biblical cities. While Easter is the most fervent, and busiest, time to do it, the event takes place every evening at 9pm between April and October.

Visiting the Bernadette homes

Bernadette's family were forced to move around as their financial woes deepened. Today, every place Bernadette is known to have lived is immortalised as a museum and extension of the pilgrimage route. The main two are **Le Cachot** *(lourdes-info-tourisme.com; free)* a former jail cell in a cellar where her whole family lived, and **Maison Paternelle de Ste-Bernadette**

Basilique Notre-Dame-du-Rosaire, Lourdes

(maisonpaternelledesaintebernadette.com; entry €2.50), a house purchased for the family by the local bishop following the apparitions. More than anything, they are windows into the way many people lived during the 19th century.

Pyrenean towns in miniature

Visiting Lourdes today and experiencing the religious theme park-like quality it has taken on, it's easy to forget that the town has a history before the apparitions. But the town was locally important enough, even in the Roman era, for there to be a fortification on the town's high ground. **Château Fort Musée Pyrénéen** *(chateaufort-lourdes.fr; entry €8)* now houses a local folk and social history museum, set in pretty gardens that contain a veritable model village of regional architecture. Its old battlements offer fantastic vistas over the city towards the Sanctuaire.

Hiking around Lourdes

On the south side of town, the metal cross-topped **Pic du Jer** *(picdujer.com; funicular adult/child €13.50/10.50)* is a popular hiking spot. It's a 550m ascent if you want to do the whole trip on foot. You'll likely be sharing the route with mountain

BERNADETTE SOUBIROUS & THE APPARITION

Long before the apparitions that made her and Lourdes famous in the Catholic world, Bernadette Soubirous was a miller's daughter, suffering from the ill-effects of the cholera she contracted as a baby. She was one of nine children, and her family, having fallen on hard times, were living in **Le Cachot**, a basement that had once been a jail. It is believed that, while out gathering firewood one day, she stopped at a grotto when the first apparition is said to have occurred. Over the coming days, more apparitions followed, whereby Bernadette and the Virgin Mary formed a bond, leading to Mary conveying a message through Bernadette, encouraging Christians to make a pilgrimage to reaffirm their faith. Bernadette died, aged 35, in 1879. Pope Pius XI made her a saint in 1933.

EATING IN LOURDES: OUR PICKS

L'Ami Toulousain: Great-value Pyrenean cuisine. Their *garbure* set menu is served with a leg of duck and stewed pork. Less than 200m from Porte St-Michel. *hours vary* €

Le Majorelle: Fine dining in art nouveau surroundings and lofty dishes, such as monkfish with carrot ginger purée. There's a dress code, naturally. *noon-2pm & 7-9pm* €€

Les Perséides: Rustic-chic setting for multi-course set menus that almost always use the unexpected (think wood pigeon). In Lézignan, 3km east of Lourdes. *hours vary* €€€

O Piment Rouge: Traditional French Basque cuisine such as baby squid in garlic sauce and desserts made with Espelette pepper. *noon-1.30pm & 7-9.30pm Thu-Mon* €€

TOP EXPERIENCE

Sanctuaire Notre-Dame de Lourdes

On 11 February 1858, the Virgin Mary is believed to have appeared before a 14-year-old Bernadette Soubirous in an underground grotto in Lourdes. Over the course of six months, Bernadette received 17 more apparitions. Practically every place the apparitions occurred are today treated with great reverence. Catholics come from around the world to retrace those moments.

Grotte de Massabielle

TOP TIPS

● It gets crowded during holidays and important dates on the Christian calendar. Avoid queues by visiting early in the morning or late at night.

● It is permitted to touch the stone walls of the Grotte de Massabielle lightly with your fingertips.

PRACTICALITIES

● lourdes-france.com
● 6am-1am ● free

Approach Along the Esplanade

After entering the site via the Porte St-Michel, wander west along the broad Esplanade du Sanctuaire towards the slim spires and gilded mosaics of Basilique Notre-Dame-du-Rosaire (p734), behind which is the Gothic **Basilique Supérieure**, casting a commanding presence across the town.

Follow the Pilgrims

Basilique Supérieure sits above the sanctuary's sacred core: **Grotte de Massabielle**, where all 18 apparitions took place. You'll likely need to queue, sometimes for hours, for a chance to enter the grotto, touch the rock – which has become smooth and polished from the ritual – and, if you're a believer, pray and light votive candles.

Something in the Water?

Great significance is placed on the natural spring water that comes from the Sanctuary. So much so, that you will see people bottling it in whatever containers they can find to take home. That's because, during the ninth apparition, the Virgin Mary told Bernadette to drink and wash in the spring. Drinking the water or, if you prefer, immersing yourself in one of the holy baths, is known as the 'water gesture'.

bikers. Allow between an hour and 90 minutes. Otherwise, the kilometre-long ride on the **Funiculaire du Pic du Jer** takes only eight minutes. Starting from av Francis Lagardère, the ride gives incredible views of Lourdes and the surrounding mountains. You can then walk the remaining 1km or so through broom and purple bellflowers.

The **Chemin de Croix** *(Way of the Cross; free)* is another popular hike from Lourdes. The 1.5km route weaves up and around Espélugues Hill, immediately to the south of the grotto, with 15 'stations' where you'll find statues of different moments from the Passion of the Christ.

Gan
TIME FROM PARC NATIONAL DES PYRÉNÉES: **30MIN**

Taste Jurançon whites
The sweet and dry white wines of the Jurançon AOC region around Gan are noted for their tropical fruit notes, such as mango. The sweets are particularly popular, with the petit manseng grapes growing well in the Pyrenean foothills. You can learn more about the wines at **La Cave de Jurançon's** *(cavedejurancon.com; free)* delightfully presented cellars and tasting room. The informative tour includes the chance to see some original Gallo-Roman mosaics. You'll learn about the different stages through which grapes are turned into wine, as well as the regional cooperative status of the vineyards. *Dégustations* of both sweet and dry Jurançons follow, including a chance to compare the differing floral and honey notes.

Take a veggie cooking class
French cuisine is inseparable from meat and the country has long had difficulty opening its heart to more plant-based living. As such, French cooking classes don't usually tend to be veggie- and vegan-friendly. That's where the folks at **La Carotte Sauvage** *(lacarottesauvage64@gmail.com)*, who run the Jardin de Plumes organic farm, come in. From spring to autumn, their Veggie Kitchen Workshops take place on working farms around the region, sometimes incorporating some foraging for the various edible wild herbs and plants, like poppies, mallow, fennel and nettles, found locally. Afterwards you'll enjoy an *apéro* with the light meal you've created. You can also have the recipe and instructions emailed to you.

Pau
TIME FROM PARC NATIONAL DES PYRÉNÉES: **35MIN**

Renaissance châteaux an Brits
The **Château de Pau** *(chateau-pau.fr; adult/child €7/5.50)* is perhaps best known for being the birthplace of Henri IV (known as Henri de Navarre prior to his coronation). You'll find a turtle's shell inside the 16th-century Renaissance castle (which replaced an older building), where he was supposedly placed soon after birth, in lieu of a cradle. The rooms remain furnished with items from a 12,000-piece collection that includes some stunning 17th- and 18th-century tapestries. Outside the summer months, the château can only be accessed on guided tours. Book ahead for English-language tours.

TRIBUTE OF THE THREE COWS CEREMONY

World leaders could learn a thing or two from two small frontier villages on the France-Spain border. Every year on 13 July, people living in the Vallée de Barétous in France and Valle del Roncal in Spain meet at the Col de la Pierre St Martin, right on the border. Those on the French side hand over three cows to those on the Spanish side in what is known as the Tribute of the Three Cows. They have been doing this since before 1375 as part of a treaty between the two sides, with the exception of a couple of suspensions to allow for various wars. These days, the event is an excuse for people from either side of an imaginary line to come together and celebrate unity.

Château de Pau (p737)

CHOCOLATIERS IN PAU

If you have a sweet tooth, the ubiquity of artisanal chocolatiers in Pau is as good a reason as any to visit.

Boutique Xavier Berger: Slick, modern Boutique Xavier Berger is the Prada of chocolatiers, with national accolades to prove it.

Maison Constanti: Primarily a patisserie, but they make lovely chocolate pralines called *bérets,* shaped like the hat.

Les Biscuits de Mr Laurent Pau: Chocolate biscuits and cookies, as well as their fantastic Coup de Barre box, containing six imaginative chocolate bars.

Chocolaterie de la Couronne: Traditional wooden shop front. Pralines, stacked high, are the main focus of La Couronne.

Maison Francis Miot: Fantastic little cafe making *coucougnettes,* a delightful marzipan and chocolate confectionery.

Pau's historic core spreads out east from the château. The majority of the vestiges hail from the 19th century, a time when British tourists flooded the town (these days, very few travellers know anything about Pau) which was seen as a pretty sanatorium. By the end of the century, locals were calling it *'la ville anglaise'* and **St Andrew's Anglican Church** remains open on Sunday mornings. To enter the town much like the 19th-century visitors would have, ride the **Funiculaire de Pau** *(tourismepau.com; free)* up from the train station.

Grand masters

Pau's small yet significant collection of fine arts is on show at the **Musée des Beaux-Arts** *(mba-pau.opacweb.fr; free).* Alongside temporary exhibitions (charges apply) the permanent collection includes four main sections: Northern European painters such as Jan Brueghel, with the highlight being *Thetis Receiving Achilles' Arms from Vulcan* by Peter Paul Rubens; Italian and Spanish masters, with works by El Greco and Eugenio Lucas Velázquez; 19th- and 20th-century modernism, with the impressionist work *Pasie Sewing in Bougival's Garden* by Berthe Morisot.

EATING IN PAU: OUR PICKS

Omnivore: Wood panelled interiors, quasi–art deco lighting and a menu that always keeps French classics – lamb, duck, beef – classy. *hours vary Tue-Sat* €€

jumo&co: There are lots of fancy dishes with elegant preparation at this city centre culinary bolthole, but their burger is what hits the high notes. *hours vary* €€

L'Ossau: Best known for the *poule au pot,* a chicken and vegetable stew that's especially good on a cold day. Their veggie lasagne is a great alternative. *noon-1.30pm & 7.30-9.30pm Mon-Fri* €€

Maynats: Food so artfully presented that you'll feel a tinge of guilt for eating it. Ingredients are just as elegant, such as mahi-mahi with lobster bisque. *hours vary Tue-Sat* €€€

Places We Love to Stay

€ Budget €€ Midrange €€€ Top End

Toulouse MAP p704

La Petite Auberge de St-Sernin € Hostel located close to the Basilique, with straightforward, affordable dorms.

Hôtel des Beaux Arts €€ This hotel is moments away from Pont Neuf in the Carmes district, a hub for coffee shops and Belle Époque mansions.

Le Grand Balcon €€ Elegant modern rooms just a minute's walk from place du Capitole. There's an on-site cocktail bar.

The Social Hub Toulouse €€ Rooms for the tech-savvy contemporary traveller with nothing overlooked. You'd never believe that it's also a hall for students.

Grand Hôtel de l'Opéra €€€ High-end hotel with classical art throughout and some rooms facing onto the place du Capitole.

Villa du Taur €€€ Classy boutique hotel with exceptionally well-designed rooms in a traffic-free street beside Basilique St-Sernin.

Lacrouzette

L'Orée des Bois € Simple budget accommodation with large common spaces. The sun-dappled terrace and log fire common room have you covered whatever the weather.

Albi

Villa Caroline €€ Tasteful rooms in an antique house with plenty of common space, including a lounge-kitchen and a rooftop terrace with fine views of Albi cathedral.

Alchimy €€€ City centre townhouse hotel with an art deco design motif and easy access to the Episcopal City.

Cordes-sur-Ciel & Around

L'Orée du Ciel €€ This note-perfect bed and breakfast (they even make their own granola) will leave you wanting for nothing. Modernity with classy touches of history throughout.

Hotel Raymond VII €€ Slightly faded hotel but the location, in a 13th-century building in the heart of Cordes-sur-Ciel's old town, cannot be beaten.

Montauban

Abbaye des Capucins € Spend the night in a 17th-century abbey with a pool-centric courtyard and dining options in the old wine cellar. Good value.

Armagnac

Château de Mons $$ Rather basic rooms but you'll forgive them for the exceptional Armagnac in a pretty château (p720).

Parc Naturel Régional des Pyrénées Ariégeoises MAP p722

Hôtel Lons € A bit old-fashioned, but this remains one of the best hotels in Foix. The dining room balcony overlooking the river is a treat.

Abbaye de Camon €€ A converted Benedictine monastery, surrounded by spectacular views, in the countryside north of Montségur.

Logis Hôtel le Manoir d'Agnès €€ Cosy rooms in a beautiful old mansion in Tarascon-sur-Ariège. The artwork and tapestries around the place add a little whimsy.

Parc National des Pyrénées MAP p728

Au Château d'Arance €€ Parts of this castle property date back to the 13th century, a turreted wonder that is further enhanced by the steep slopes all around.

Auberge Le Cabaliros €€ Good base for exploring the national park in various directions. The attached restaurant serves fantastic food.

Hôtel le Lion d'Or €€ Characterful hotel in Cauterets with easy access to the thermal baths and a restaurant serving Pyrenean cuisine.

Beyond Parc National des Pyrénées

Chambres d'Hôte l'Oustal € Welcoming *chambres d'hôte* in Oloron-Ste-Marie with traditional food and local cheese *dégustations*.

Hotel Spa Gasquet € Relaxing location in Bagnères-de-Luchon for incredible snowy views. Spa access and treatments cost extra.

Les Perséides €€ Pretty guest house in a serene patch of countryside just east of Lourdes, with luxury furnishings and views of the distant Pyrenees (p735).

Above: Gorges du Verdon (p790); Right: Market produce, Aix-en-Provence (p758)

Researched by
Michael Frankel and Ashley Parsons

Provence

THE EPITOME OF THE FRENCH COUNTRY DREAM

A region that veers from wildly enthralling city life to tranquil village idyll – complete with fine wine, lavender fields and coastal castaway coves.

When you find yourself awash in Provence's famous light, it becomes clear why so many artists have been magnetically drawn here for centuries, seeking to unlock something bigger than themselves. This land epitomises springtime, having inspired great post-impressionist painters Cézanne and Van Gogh to create their seminal works.

As the mistral wind howls down the Rhône Valley toward the sea, slamming the wooden shutters of homes throughout the night and clearing the skies for what feels like endless sunshine, it creates a climate that is not only inviting for travellers but also ideal for farming. Sampling the fresh produce nurtured here is an essential part of the journey, especially in the bustling markets and endless stretches of vineyards.

The region's palpitating heart is Marseille, France's second-largest city, with its vibrant cultural energy. Beyond the urban landscape are breathtaking *calanques* (coves) and the timeless beauty of the Camargue wetlands. Inland you'll find the still-thriving Roman towns of Aix-en-Provence and Arles, as well as Avignon, a city once home to the papacy. In the distance? That's Mont Ventoux, a dream challenge for many cyclists; the Luberon, where chic villas and innovative restaurants sit below ruined châteaux; and the Gorges du Verdon, the region's wild side.

Whether you'd rather be stretched out by the sea, driving quiet countryside roads or lost in nature, you'll find Provence – the *départements* of the Bouches-du-Rhône, Vaucluse and the Alpes-de-Haute Provence – is a sensuous Mediterranean experience waiting to be discovered.

THE MAIN AREAS

MARSEILLE
Cosmopolitan urban sprawl meets unspoilt beaches. **p746**

ARLES
Roman ruins and modern art. **p762**

AVIGNON
Dense medieval city with a flair for the stage. **p769**

LUBERON
Perched villages, vineyards and idyllic landscapes. **p781**

GORGES DU VERDON
Iconic gorges and dreamy lavender. **p790**

Find Your Way

Marseille, Aix-en-Provence and Avignon are transport hubs for the region; plan to pick up a rental car to set off on quiet backroads towards inland villages, lavender plains and adventure hot spots. Lots of options for cycling trips too.

Avignon, p769
With the world's best theatre festival, the streets come alive each summer, on and off stage. Discover the history of the popes and the role of the Rhône in this medieval city.

Arles, p762
A slow-paced Roman city with a preserved grandness that goes back centuries. Food, drink and nightlife reflect the untamed soul of Camargue life.

Marseille, p748
A cutting-edge city transforming itself for a new generation. As historic as it is fun, and home to some of the most unspoiled coastline in France.

Luberon, p781
Part wild and full of mystery, part chic holiday destination, the Luberon's hilltop villages, ochre cliffs, and food and wine scene will reel you in.

CAR
Driving in this region can be a joy, even if parking can sometimes be a pain. To be able to spontaneously stop in tiny villages, wind your way to far-flung vineyards or park up at many of the perfectly remote beaches is a luxury.

BICYCLE
Provence is one of the best cycling areas in France thanks to its endless backroad options. Many villages now have a local bike rental shop with a selection of mountain, road and e-bikes for day rentals or longer.

BUS
The comprehensive ZOU! bus service runs lines all around the region. Great for connecting villages and sights, but, with infrequent services, it's not so great if you want to dine at a restaurant outside of town or have booked accommodation in the countryside.

Gorges du Verdon p790
Lavender plains, dramatic scenery and a heart of adventure, from cliff hikes to gorges that are on the bucket list of every traveller.

Plan Your Time

Provence is a vast and diverse region where coastal resorts give way to bucolic countryside and pure nature as you venture inland. Here's how to plan your time in France's second-largest city and three of Provence's loveliest *départements*.

Gordes (p784)

Pressed for Time

● Using **Marseille** (p748) as your base makes sense if you are on a flying visit. For a taste of true Mediterranean life, the city delivers across-the-board urban life of achingly hip restaurants and bars with grab-and-go street food on every corner. Use one day to sail out on a **captained boat** into the Med (p752), or escape the city to the **Îles du Frioul** (p754), only 20 minutes away.

● With an extra day, take a trip to soak up the art history and cafe culture of **Aix-en-Provence** (p758) or dive head-first into **Arles** (p762), a town that swings from a host of historical wonders to a small village in a matter of moments.

Seasonal Highlights

Winters are mild, but a mistral wind can change that. Spring is blissful for the great outdoors; summers are hot and autumn seems to last forever.

FEBRUARY
Peak truffle season. Visit the **Marché aux Truffes** (p775) in Carpentras to spot traders dealing in the black gold. Seafood lovers flock to Carry-le-Rouet for its sea urchin feast, **Oursinades** (p757).

APRIL
Early spring harvests fill stalls around the region, with local produce on display on market days. Wild asparagus makes its way onto restaurant menus in the **Luberon** (p781).

MAY
France's Roma people pour into **Stes-Maries-de-la-Mer** (p767) on 24 May, ending their annual pilgrimage. Warmer temperatures mean hiking, cycling and climbing are at their best.

Six Days to Travel Around

- With more time, spend a couple of days in and around Marseille and its splendid coastal **Calanques** (p755) before heading north to **Aix-en-Provence** (p758). Push on to **Avignon** (p769) to visit the **Palais de Papes** (p772). The drive to **L'Isle-sur-la-Sorgue** (p778) and its antique markets is an easy side trip, before moving into the **Luberon** (p781), the Provence of Hollywood dreams. Wake up early for a sunrise visit to **Gordes** (p784) and the **Abbaye Notre-Dame du Sénanque** (p784), hidden away in a small canyon. Rent a bike and cycle around photogenic hill villages like **Bonnieux** (p787) and **Ménerbes** (p786) on your last day and mark the end of the trip with a splashy meal in chic **Lourmarin** (p788).

More than a Week

- A longer itinerary allows you to reach all corners of the region. Soak up the vibe on a walking tour of **Marseille** (p748) before making a beeline for the windswept **Camargue** (p766) wetlands. Take your time travelling through the landscape that inspired Van Gogh around **Les Alpilles** (p760) and travel further back in time during a day trip to Roman **Orange** (p776).

- Base yourself in a pretty **Luberon hilltop village** (p781) for a few days. Don't leave without an adventure fix at the **Gorges du Verdon** (p790), France's answer to the Grand Canyon. If you're touring in June or July, tack on a detour to the purple-hued **Plateau de Valensole's** (p795) lavender fields.

JUNE
Lavender is everywhere – for a photoshoot that makes your friends swoon, visit the **Plateau de Valensole** – responsibly – (p795) or swerve the crowds in **Sault** (p779).

JULY
In the city of popes, theatre is in full swing for the **Festival d'Avignon** (p771). **Les Rencontres d'Arles** (p763) is an internationally renowned annual photography festival held throughout the city.

SEPTEMBER
Cooler temperatures at the end of summer make cycling the villages of the **Luberon** (p781) a dream. Meanwhile the *vendange*, or grape harvest, begins.

DECEMBER
After the olive harvest wraps up in November, locals get ready for a Provençal Christmas with the famous 13 desserts. The cutest **Christmas market** (p789) in the region gets underway at Cucuran.

Marseille

BOATING | CUTTING-EDGE CULTURE | MEDITERRANEAN CUISINE

☑ TOP TIP

'This is a city where we like to joke with everyone,' said JC, manager of **Le Trois Quarts** bistro in the Camas. 'It's what we call *t'emboucaner*. If we make fun of you, it's to make you feel at home. Don't take yourself too seriously here and you'll do well.'

Marseille has an edge. France's second-largest city puts its arms around you as a drunken friend would – passionately and deliriously. It is a city that revels in its status as France's underdog. As you explore its hidden corners it will reveal a beauty that is difficult to capture in photographs: an urban sprawl interspersed with pockets of inspiring nature that must be experienced in person. Since it was founded by the Greeks in 600 BCE the tremendous influx of migration to this port city has never ceased. In Marseille, North and West Africans live shoulder to shoulder with a vast Corsican community, and it's within easy reach of northern Italy and Spanish Catalonia.

Greater Marseille is divided into 16 *arrondissements*, which are often indicated in addresses. The city's main thoroughfare, La Canebière, stretches eastwards from the Vieux Port towards the train station, a 10-minute walk away. Just uphill is Le Panier, the oldest neighbourhood in the city.

Soak up Marseille's Lively Squares
Mix with the locals

Sooner or later, you'll end up on the **cours Julien** (known locally as 'le cours Ju') for a drink, and for good reason. As a pedestrian area slathered with street art and bohemian

---

 GETTING AROUND

Marseille has two metro lines (Métro 1 and Métro 2), two tram lines (yellow and green) and an extensive bus network. Bus, metro or tram tickets are available from machines in the metro, at tram stops and on buses. In general, however, Marseille is a delight to explore on foot.

From April to the end of September, the maritime shuttle crossings from the Vieux Port can also take you to the extremities of L'Estaque and Pointe-Rouge.

Sign up to the Levélo public e-bike network to navigate the city by bike. Download the app *(levelo.ampmetropole.fr; €1 for 30 min, then €0.05/min)*, find a bike, unlock the bike and off you go.

Noailles

yearnings, this is the home of some great bars and restaurants, which remain open day and night. Wander the narrow side streets, packed with bookshops, galleries and tattoo parlours, until you reach the noisy and elongated main square, a destination for a solid night out, and a microcosm of the city itself. You are likely to hear boom boxes blasting, guitars strummed and African drums pounding as soon as the sun comes out.

Place Jean-Jaurès, also known as La Plaine, is another vast square surrounded by bars and restaurants. For years it has been the battleground for left-wing militants and artists. Closed for urban renewal before the pandemic, it reopened to mixed emotions in 2021, with some claiming the square had become too controlled and sanitised. Unlike many public areas worldwide, however, it has been redesigned with skateboarders in mind, with long smooth runs and no anti-skate guards in sight. Buzzing day and night in the spring and summer months, it remains a beating heart for locals escaping the tourist traps, whether in the bars or in the public seating areas beneath the trees. La Plaine is only a 10-minute walk east from cours Julien.

African Food in Noailles

Travel your taste buds

Like Naples in Italy, Marseille is an anomaly in Europe: the poorest residents live in the centre of town, rather than on

continued on p750

LOCAL TIPS FOR NOAILLES

Sadia Chellah, Algerian-born owner of **Le Bar du Peuple**, is passionate about her neighbourhood. As she describes it, 'Noailles is the place where people arrive. I love that we now have flower shops in the neighbourhood and tourism.' She shares some of her favourite local spots.

OM Boutique: There is only one team in this city: Olympique de Marseille (p750). Get your shirts here.

Maison Empereur: This hardware and homewares store was founded in 1827; it's one of the oldest in France. A great place for anything your kitchen would need.

Jiji la Palme d'Or: Enough North African bowls, baskets and rugs to make your home feel loved.

Baussens Emmanuel: The only place you can buy pork in the whole neighbourhood. It's been there a long time.

EATING IN NOAILLES: BEST AFRICAN RESTAURANTS

Chez Yassine: No-nonsense Tunisian restaurant with long lunch queues – for good reason. *11.30am-9pm Tue-Sun* €€

La Jungle: Serves massive plates of Cameroonian food. It's as much a party as it is a restaurant on weekends. *noon-midnight* €€

Mama Ghana: West African food prepared with love. Also a great spot to watch televised sports events *noon-11pm Wed-Sun, noon-9pm Mon & Tue* €€

Restaurant Le Fémina: Eat couscous prepared by an all-female kitchen staff. An Anthony Bourdain favourite. *noon-2.30pm & 7-11pm Tue-Sat, noon-2.30pm Sun* €€

MARSEILLE

Enlargement

- ⭐ **HIGHLIGHTS**
  1. Musée des Civilisations de l'Europe et de la Méditerranée

- 🔴 **SIGHTS**
  2. Cathédrale de la Major
  3. Cours Julien
  4. Palais Longchamp
  5. Place Jean-Jaurès
  6. Plage des Catalans

- 🟢 **ACTIVITIES**
  7. Capitaine Coco
  8. Eco-Calanques
  9. Le Bateau Jaune
  10. Les Barquettes

- ⚫ **SLEEPING**
  11. Hôtel Belle-Vue
  12. Hotel Peron
  13. La Relève
  14. Le Ryad
  15. Les Appartements du Vieux Port
  16. Les Bords de la Mer
  17. Mama Shelter

- 🟢 **EATING**
  18. Baussens Emmanuel
  19. Belleville/Mer
  20. Chez Yassine

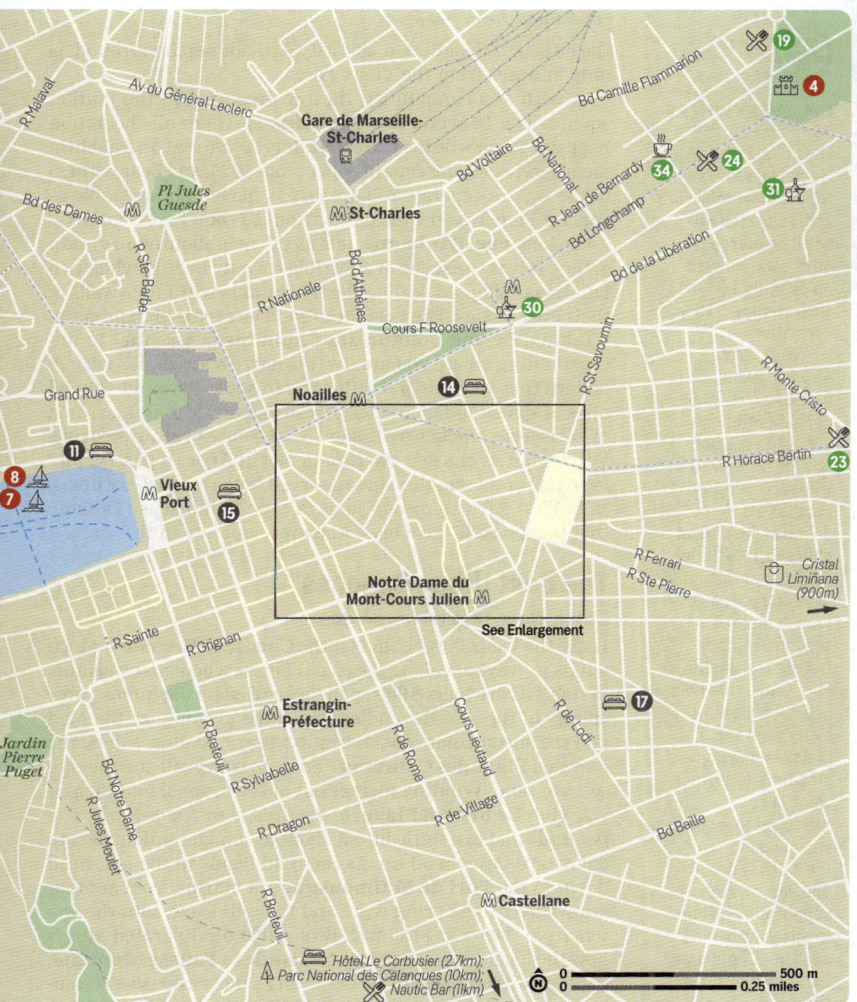

21 La Jungle	● DRINKING & NIGHTLIFE	32 Le Bar du Peuple	37 Cinésud
22 Le Bistrot Plage		33 PMU le blabla	38 Jiji la Palme d'Or
23 Le Trois Quarts	28 Bar des Maraîchers	34 Pollux	39 Maison Empereur
24 Les Babines de Mars	29 Cafe Prinder	● ENTERTAINMENT	40 Marché des Capucins
25 Mama Ghana	30 Grand Bar du Chapitre	35 OM Boutique	41 Savonnerie Marseillaise de la Licorne
26 Restaurant Le Fémina	31 Ivresse	● SHOPPING	
27 Vanille Noire	see 13 La Relève	36 Bière de la Plaine	

continued from p747

the outskirts. Noailles, a majority African neighbourhood, is only minutes from the Vieux Port.

As with any community, life revolves around the market square. The **Marché des Capucins** is where all the action happens. Sit outside the **Cafe Prinder** *(6am-6pm)*, an establishment serving strong cups of coffee since 1925, and bear witness to the square's energy. You are just as likely to hear Arabic as you are French as the locals come out to shop for essentials.

The long **rue d'Aubagne** acts as the neighbourhood's main artery. It was the scene of a terrible tragedy in 2019 when two buildings collapsed, killing the inhabitants within the walls of their own homes. The neighbourhood has refused to forget it.

Taking the **rue Longue des Capucins** is essential to understanding where you are. In this narrow street, it's easy to believe that you're in a North African souk. Pyramid-shaped piles of spices, halal butchers, fresh fish on ice and the aroma of rotisserie chicken will send your senses into overdrive. Vegetarian or chicken *pastilla* (a North African pastry) and *kesra* (a round semolina bread served hot) are must-try items, as is West African *bissap* juice (a type of hibiscus). Do note that pickpockets have been known to operate in this area.

The Best Urban Beaches

Catch some rays on *les plages*

Leave the Vieux Port behind for the **Corniche Kennedy**, which winds its way east along the coast. This is where many visitors first fall under Marseille's spell, bedazzled by the intense, raw energy of the sea, the endless sunshine glinting off the Med and the spectacular coastal beauty. Your first stop will be the crowded **Plage des Catalans** – home to volleyball and the rare sight of sand. Winding further out of town, you'll find the private club **Le Bistrot Plage** *(bistrot-plage.fr; 10am-10pm; €25 per day)*, and can settle into its famous orange sunloungers to enjoy tapas as you oil up. As the road bends to the left, head down to the **Port de Malmousque** – a marina from another era where people bring wine and then glide out into the waters from the rocks at sunset. Bronzed and exhilarated: this is how the locals do it. Next is the **Anse de la Fausse Monnaie**, situated directly below one of the city's most exclusive restaurants, **Le Petit Nice** *(passedat.fr/fr/le-petit-nice; noon-9.30pm Tue-Sat)*. This is where the best-looking, tattooed and nearly naked go to show themselves off and admire each other while pretending to read books on philosophy. It's hot. For a more

OM, EVERYWHERE

Olympique de Marseille is the only top-level football club in the city. You will see it emblazoned on chests, sprayed up on walls, in shop windows: OM, everywhere.

To experience a sports event fuelled by the kind of ear-shatteringly unbridled passion you are unlikely to witness again, book your tickets (from €15) online at the official club site, billetterie.om.fr, way in advance of your trip. The French football season begins in August and ends in May. Games are held in the league almost every weekend, played at the home stadium every other week or so.

It is best to request seats around the halfway line. The fierce Ultra supporters position themselves behind each goal, lighting flares as their cries fill the air.

EATING & DRINKING AROUND MARSEILLE: COASTAL BARS WITH A VIEW

Le Cabanon de Paulette: Sunbathers retire to flirt and dance on this terrace overhanging the Med. *10.30am-11.30pm in summer*

Sunset Bar: A simple bar on the corniche, perfect for a drink after a swim at sunset. Get a pastis and a tan. *6.30-8.30pm Mon-Sat*

Restaurant La Baie des Singes: There's better food to be found in Les Goudes, but these views can't be beaten. *noon-9pm in summer* €€

Nautic Bar: Staring into the Calanque de Morgiou with a glass in hand, you will not want to go back to the city in a hurry. *noon-10pm Tue-Sun* €€

LE PANIER ON FOOT

Discover the oldest and some of the most charming parts of the city founded by the Phoenicians in 600 BCE.

START	END	LENGTH
Hôtel Belle-Vue	Place de Lenche	2.5km, 1 hour

The Vieux Port, all boats and bars, is Marseille's central point, where you begin beneath the historic ❶ **Hôtel Belle-Vue** (p796).

Walking away from town, turn right at ❷ **passage Pentecontore**, taking the steps up through the arch. This is a great spot to sample ice cream from ❸ **Vanille Noire**, renowned for its charcoal-coloured vanilla flavour.

Not far from here is the steep, narrow corridor of steps of ❹ **rue Beauregard** and rue des Moulins, now emblazoned with street art. These lead to ❺ **place des Moulins**, home to windmills in the 17th century. Today, it offers serenity no matter the time of year.

Descending the ❻ **rue des Muettes** and ❼ **rue du Refuge** takes you into the heart of Le Panier. 'The Basket' is Marseille's oldest quarter, the site of the original Greek settlement and nicknamed for its steep streets and buildings.

Make your way along ❽ **rue des Pistoles** and ❾ **rue du Petit Puits** via rue Antoine Becker, to come to the ❿ **Cathédrale de la Major**.

If you time this walk for sunset the square will deliver a blazing view. Below on ⓫ **bd Jacques Saade** are a line of tapas bars, another perfect sunset stop before you settle for an evening in the buzzy ⓬ **place de Lenche**.

DISCOVER THE HISTORY OF PASTIS

The apéritif pastis is easy to spot: a milky-looking concoction served in a tall glass that adorns outdoor tables across Provence. In 1932 in Marseille, Paul Ricard developed his aniseed-and-liquorice-based liqueur (*pastís* means 'mix' in Occitan) after absinthe was banned in France out of fear that it caused hallucinations and madness. Since then, it has become a drink that is synonymous with the city. Ricard may now be part of a multinational conglomerate based in Lille, but there are still independent producers in Marseille where you can arrange a visit, including **Cristal Limiñana** (cristal-liminana.com) and the independent brewery **Bière de la Plaine** (*Distillerie de la Plaine; instagram.com/distillerie_de_la_plaine*).

Plage des Catalans (p750)

standard beach, but much further, you can always head to the vast **Plages du Prado**. It's family orientated, has a famous skate park and yes, there's sand.

Eco-Friendly Cruises on the Med
Take to the water

There is no more joyful escape than to take to the waters around Marseille.

At the Vieux Port you can find Fanny's *barquettes* at **Capitaine Coco** (*capitainecoco.fr; from €80 per person*) to experience the immediacy of the sea on a 1960s Provençal leisure vessel. You will help run up the sails, learn about biodiversity and enjoy a vegetarian lunch. It is an intimate and hands-on affair that can be geared towards educating children. She will meet you at the port at the end of rue de la Prison.

The **Eco-Calanques** (*eco-calanques.com; €125 per person*) eco-trawler is partly solar-powered, and local guide Thibault will entertain passengers with stories about the city's history as he takes you out to the most tranquil bays. While the Mediterranean is blessed with calm, warm waters in summer, the mistral wind may postpone excursions in winter. The price includes lunch and the use of masks and snorkels to splash about in the *calanques*.

DRINKING IN MARSEILLE: BEST PASTIS BARS

Bar des Maraîchers: Listen to '80s radio hits with owner, Serge, who features in his own hilarious fresco of the Last Supper. *3pm-2am*

Grand Bar du Chapitre: A young crowd in a leafy square at the top of the main thoroughfare, La Canebière. *10am-12.30am*

PMU le blabla: Super cheap and one of the best sun traps protected from the wind in the city. *6.30am-9pm*

La Relève: In the Endoume neighbourhood. Pastis can still be fancy and here it's served with great food and music. *8am-10pm Mon-Sat, 9am-5pm Sun*

Based near the **Musée des Civilisations de l'Europe et de la Méditerranée** (Mucem) museum, **Les Barquettes** (lesbarquettes.com; €110 per person) also has a traditional 1970s fisherman's boat converted into a pleasure vessel, but its pride and joy is its sailing boat, a replica of a historical ship from 1903. It holds 20 people and the 3½-hour sunset tour includes an apéritif too. They will pick you up at an allotted time right alongside Mucem.

Dive into Les Goudes

Seafood at the end of the world

A common insult in Marseille is 'Go throw yourself in the Goudes', but Les Goudes is easily one of the area's highlights: a tiny fishing village locked in time, with access to spectacularly rugged coastlines. Its proximity to the **Parc National des Calanques** (p755) means the village is afforded the same legal protection; thus, there has been little development here. For now, the bygone era remains.

There has been a shift since **Tuba Club** arrived, a hotel so exclusive it's almost impossible to book one of its only eight rooms. It is possible to make reservations to have a drink on the rocks after 5pm. In the heart of the village is **L'Esplaï du Grand Bar des Goudes**, a rowdy seafood restaurant and bar. As you rub shoulders with those who grew up in these narrow streets, eating fish that has practically leapt out of the ocean and onto your plate, you'll be face to face with all the local pride you can take.

The walk to the **Baie des Singes**, an old smuggling cove, is a surreal sun-beaten experience – don't miss it. The restaurant has sunloungers at €25 for the day. It's beyond picturesque.

Bus 19 and then 20 will get you close to Les Goudes year-round. From the end of April to September, boats leave from the Vieux Port – you will need to switch ferries in Pointe-Rouge.

Escape to the Château d'If

Island life

For a quick and easy trip out to sea, hop on the Frioul-If ferry to Marseille's closest islands: the Île d'If (for historians) and the Îles du Frioul (for nature lovers).

Commanding access to Marseille's Vieux Port, the **Château d'If** (chateau-if.fr; adult/child €7/free) was immortalised by Alexandre Dumas in his classic 1844 novel, *The Count of*

A MAN OF THE PEOPLE

Eric Signoret is one of the most recognisable faces of Les Goudes and has been the owner of the only convenience store for kilometres around for nearly 40 years.

I prefer to say 'no comment' when I am asked about how life is changing in Les Goudes. We feel that we are being pushed to the side of our own lives, not by tourism – tourists have always been welcome here – but by politicians. They tow our cars and make changes they do not fully understand. Visit Les Goudes from town, but do so on foot, by bike, boat or bus and avoid using an app to rent a house here. We welcome you to visit us.

🍴 EATING IN LES GOUDES: OUR PICKS

Chez Paul: Serves seafood right in the heart of the village and is where those who know will choose for a sit-down meal. *noon-2pm Wed-Sun, 7.45-10pm Mon-Fri, 8pm-10pm Sat & Sun* €€

La Grotte: Incredibly refined settings in the Port de Callelongue just outside the village. *noon-2.30pm & 7.30-11pm Mon-Thu & Sat, noon-3pm & 7.30-10.30pm Sun* €€

Gelateria des Goudes: An Italian family business serious about their 1950s-style ice cream and a new addition to the village. A brioche ice cream sandwich is the one. *11am-8pm* €

Au Bord de l'Eau: In the small port of Madrague Montredon, the perfect spot to watch the fishermen deliver your lunch. *noon-2pm Mon-Wed, noon-3pm & 7pm-10pm Thu-Sat, noon-3pm Sun* €€€

CLEANLINESS IS CLOSE TO GODLINESS

Following the cholera outbreaks of the early 1830s, which claimed thousands of lives in the city, a plan was devised to improve public health by channelling water from the Durance River in the Alps. By 1869, the Palais Longchamp was opened to the public as a 'hymn to water', celebrating this remarkable engineering achievement.

Marseille's iconic soap (Savon de Marseille) also played a significant role in reducing infant mortality and the spread of contagious diseases during the 19th century. Originally made with olive oil and free of colouring and perfume, it now comes in various shapes and smells. The **Savonnerie Marseillaise de la Licorne** on cours Julien is an excellent place to purchase this soap, and it offers free daily tours of its factory.

Monte Cristo. At the 16th-century island prison with three towers, one giving a great view across the bay, you can wander unaccompanied or visit with an audio or guided tour; the contrast between the cells for the wealthy and the dungeon pit strikes a tone. This is the ferry's first stop; it's 20 minutes from the Vieux Port.

It's another 15 minutes to the next stop, the Port du Frioul, your entry point to two of the **Îles du Frioul**, Pomègues and Ratonneau, which are connected by a dam.

Attacking the unspoiled jagged rock of **Pomègues** is liberating. Following the seawall after you dock will lead to the Fort de Caveaux, leaving you lost at sea on an uninhabited island, revisiting ghosts in the bunkers of WWII. Finding a spot to feel utterly alone with the swooping seabirds is easiest in spring.

The island of **Ratonneau** has a few small shops and restaurants and is popular for its beaches and tiny village. There's a chapel that resembles a Greek temple and the ruins of the Hôpital Caroline, which once housed quarantined travellers, but the highlight is the St-Estève beach, where you can swim safely, protected from the wind.

The ticket pier for **lebateau** ferries *(lebateau-frioul-if.fr; one/two islands return €11.10/16.70)* is at the Vieux Port. When facing the port, get in line at their large booth on the left. The Château d'If is closed on Mondays.

Another way to get here is with the **Le Bateau Jaune** *(lebateaujaune.com; adult/child from €40/35)* in the Vieux Port, which organises snorkelling and diving trips around the islands.

A Palace & its Museums
Marseille's most chic neighbourhood

The centre point of Marseille's chic Longchamp neighbourhood is the sublime **Palais Longchamp**, an outrageous 19th-century palace with monumental fountains gushing in celebration of fertility and the arrival of water to the city. Its green and pleasant gardens host an international jazz festival every summer and are perfect for lazing around in. This magnificent building also houses the **Musée des Beaux-Arts** (home to 17th- and 18th-century art), the **Muséum d'Histoire Naturelle** and an observatory, all free to enter.

EATING & DRINKING IN LONGCHAMP: OUR PICKS — *Fancy brunch, too!*

Ivresse: Easily the hottest candlelit date spot in town. Small food plates, natural wine and the perfect service. *6pm-11pm Mon-Sat €€*

Belleville/Mer: Simple, no-frills dishes with the local crowd on the patio. A friendly spot that is the place to be on Sundays. *8am-10.30pm Wed-Sun €€*

Pollux: Coffee lovers unite. Choose anything from a rare bean espresso to a Vietnamese iced coffee. *8.30am-5pm Mon-Fri, 9.30am-3pm Sat & Sun €€*

Les Babines de Mars: A dedication to working with local products and fish from the port has helped Les Babines settle straight in. *11am-11pm Mon-Fri €€*

Beyond Marseille

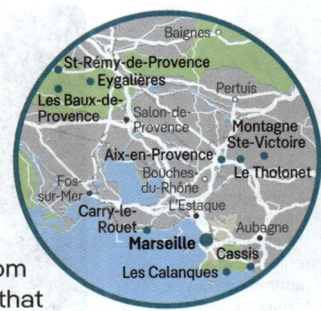

To truly appreciate Marseille, cut loose from its intense energy and explore the nature that surrounds it.

Leaving Marseille, the sudden bursts of birdsong or the light breaking through the pine trees in spring will have you breathing easier. Head inland to the Provençal countryside, famous for its idyllic charm, or cut yourself off from the world on far-flung beaches on the savage and yet increasingly fashionable coastline that extends in both directions from the city.

In Aix-en-Provence, the sun magically lights up centuries-old mansions while fountains gurgle in small squares and locals stare at you from stylish cafe terraces, coolly sipping espresso. Ancient villages, winding mountain climbs offering views to the valleys below and landscapes that have inspired countless artists are everything you dreamed Provence could deliver.

Places
Les Calanques p755
La Côte Bleue p757
Aix-en-Provence p758
Le Tholonet p759
Les Alpilles p760

Les Calanques
TIME FROM MARSEILLE: 1½HR 🚌 1HR 🚴

Outdoor Adventures in the Parc National des Calanques

It feels like a miracle to find a refuge like the **Parc National des Calanques** only a short distance from Marseille. In parts of this diminutive 85-sq-km patch of scrubby promontories, it's easy to believe you're miles from civilisation. Then a twist in a pine-clad gully reveals the entirety of France's second metropolis spread out within apparent touching distance; the *calanques* appear almost as its uninhabited suburbs.

But with their light-shifting geometry, rich plant and animal life and idyllic hidden coves, Les Calanques are so much more than that. They are beloved of the Marseillais, who come for the sun and to hike over pine-strewn promontories, mess about in boats and generally refresh their souls.

Of the many *calanques* along the coastline, the most easily accessible are **Calanque de Sormiou** and **Calanque de Morgiou**. Remote inlets such as **Calanque d'En-Vau** and **Calanque de Port-Miou** take dedication and time to reach, either on foot or by kayak. Note that overland access is often limited from June to September due to fire danger; always check first on the app: *calanques-parcnational.fr/fr/application-mobile-officielle-mes-calanques*. The app is also excellent for up-to-date info on the park and activities.

There is also reservation system in place for two of the most popular *calanques* in summer: **Calanques de Sugiton** and **Calanque des Pierres Tombées**. See *calanques-parcnational.fr*.

GETTING AROUND

Without a boat, you'll have to drive, cycle or take public transport to visit Cassis and the nearby *calanques*. Be warned that roads are rough, parking scarce and the going slow. In peak summer season, the municipality recommends arriving by bus. In the other direction, the train along the Côte Bleue is cheap and allows you to drink wine with your lunch. Regular ZOU! trains and Lecar buses connect Marseille with Aix. As a general rule, although exploring by car is the most practical, there is a real cycling culture in these parts.

Calanque d'En-Vau

WHAT IS A CALANQUE?

Calanques are coastal geological features typical of the Mediterranean region. These picturesque coves, formed in limestone and famously located between Marseille and Cassis, are characterised by steep cliffs rising above vibrant turquoise waters. When the sun shines, the small beaches within these narrow bays, made up of either pebbles or fine sand, attract crowds. Escaping to them has become a way of life for city dwellers, leading to various regulations protecting the natural sites. Access to the *calanques* by car can be challenging, and most routes are closed between June and October as the arid conditions during this period place the parks at a high chance of wildfires. The strong mistral winds that can sweep through the area further intensify the risks.

There's no shortage of outdoor activities here: hiking, kayaking, stand-up paddleboarding, swimming, diving and rock climbing are all incredible. You'll find guides and gear rental in both Marseille and Cassis. From October to June, hiking trails lead through the maquis (scrub). Marseille's **tourist office** leads guided walks and has an excellent hiking map of the various *calanques*, as does Cassis' **tourist office**.

For access by public transport take bus 19 from Marseille's Castellane bus station down the coast to its terminus at La Madrague, then switch to bus 20 to Callelongue. Note that the road to Callelongue is only open to cars on weekdays from mid-April to May and closed entirely from June to September.

Clambering Down to Paradise

The small port of **Cassis** has lost some of its charm over the years, but the coastline beyond is another story. The village is the perfect staging point for approaching the stunning **Calanque d'En-Vau** from the east, rather than Marseille to the west. From Cassis, make your way to the **Calanque de Port-Miou** on foot (30 minutes) or, alternatively, park in the Presqu'île car park. This is the start of a difficult, unshaded

Eat with the locals

 EATING IN CASSIS: BEST POST-BEACH RESTAURANTS

Le Poisson Rouge: Modern creative cuisine that has its focus on local winemakers and a good time. *7.30pm-11pm Tue-Sat* €€

La Maison de Jo et Gaby: Friendly wine cellar. The charcuterie plates reflect just what the Med has to offer. *10am-1pm & 5-11.45pm Tue-Sun* €€

La Presqu'île: Come here for crisp white tablecloths and a Michelin star paired with great bay views. Reserve. *9.30am-11pm Tue-Sun* €€€

Chez Poulette: Fried seafood fresh from the sea or subtle Asian fusion served by the owner. *noon-2.30pm Wed, Thu, Sat, Sun, 7-10pm Thu-Sat* €€

hike, but it's worth every stretch of sinew. Expect it to take a solid 1½ hours from here.

The first stop is the **Calanque de Port-Pin** for a quick dip. It takes at least 20 minutes to get here as you keep the water to your left and the boats below. From Port-Pin, there are two paths to the Calanque d'En-Vau. Take the blue-coded coastal path, which is longer (around one hour) but more rewarding. Arriving at the cliffs, you'll be glad you made the effort.

Clambering down to the beach is tricky for newbies; you can easily tell who's local, as they look like mountain goats when scampering down the cliffs. If you arrive with good footwear and take your time the descent is fine, though if you suffer from vertigo, this is not for you. Ideally, plan on arriving by late morning and bring enough water and food for the day.

Cassis is 30km east of Marseille and is best reached by car in low season. At other times of year, taking the train (30 minutes) is advised as you may not be able to find a parking spot. From the Cassis train station, take the M1 bus to the centre of town (15 minutes).

La Côte Bleue

TIME FROM MARSEILLE: **15-30MIN**

Coastal Walks of Carry-le-Rouet

Only 30km west of Marseille, **Carry-le-Rouet** is another pearl on the Côte Bleue rail line, with its charming port, fragrant pine trees and perfectly rough-hewn inlets. The train from Gare de Marseille St-Charles is around €6, and the 35-minute sea-view trip passes in the blink of an eye.

However, renting a car allows more freedom to stop in places along the way. You can drive along roads where limestone rises all around you, and long-horned goats nibble on scrub, although parking will never be easy. The first three Sundays of February are the subject of a grand celebration, when seafood fanatics descend into the port for the **Oursinades**, a tasting festival offering an abundance of sea urchins considered the best in the Med. If you're not crazy about urchins, everything else pulled from the ocean, including shellfish, is also available.

At any time of the year, the jaggy promenade from the port to Sausset-les-Pins is the perfect coastal stroll, with no shortage of places to stop and take it all in. The beaches are more pebbly than sandy, but the waters are transparent. Every summer during July and August, the Parc Marin Côte Bleue *(parc marincotebleue.fr)* organises free guided tours on the Plage du Cap Rousset, including a wetsuit, snorkel and mask. To book, see en.otcarrylerouet.fr.

RIDE LA CÔTE BLEUE RAILWAY

Heading west from **Gare de Marseille St-Charles** is the spectacular **Côte Bleue** (Blue Coast) railway. A 15-minute journey (€3) takes passengers to **L'Estaque**; the views from the train window are the same as the ones that once inspired the impressionists. From L'Estaque's train station it's only a 10-minute walk to the port.

Another 15 minutes on the train past L'Estaque brings you to **Niolon**, a pretty Provençal village. Follow the crowd to make your way along the rocky path to the **Calanque du Jonquier** and swim in the shadow of the spectacular arched viaduct as you gaze across the calm waters back towards the city. Pretty unbeatable.

 EATING AROUND CARRY-LE-ROUET: OUR PICKS

Rest'o Cap Rousset: The sound of sun-worshippers flinging themselves into the *calanque* below as the ice cubes clink in your glass. *8am-9.30pm* €€

La Cale: Stop for great pizza if you are gently trekking between Carry and Sausset-les-Pins. Stunning views out to the Calanque de la Tuilière. *10am-10.30pm* €€

MyPitchu: Relaxed beach bar on the sand in Sausset-les-Pins serving fish fresh from the sea. Reach it along the coastal path from Carry. *9am-11.45pm Mon-Sat, 9am-5pm Sun* €€

La Villa Arena: For a gastronomic experience rather than fish and chips, this 17th-century mansion restaurant will serve food for your eyes. *noon-9.30pm Tue-Sat* €€€

Aix-en-Provence TIME FROM MARSEILLE: 40MIN 45MIN

Celebrate Cézanne

Paul Cézanne's post-impressionism significantly influenced contemporary art of the 19th and 20th centuries. Born in the city and having studied in the Musée d'Aix, now known as the **Musée Granet** *(museegranet-aixenprovence.fr/accueil; adult/child €6.50/free)*, he struggled for recognition for most of his career. Today, his paintings, capturing its landscapes and its people, have become synonymous with the city itself.

Aix celebrated its famous artist and his legacy in 2025 with a busy calendar of events, especially around the reopening of the renovated **Bastide du Jas de Bouffan** *(cezanne2025.com/en/cezanne-sites/jas-de-bouffan-mansion-cezannes-family-home; adult/child €9.50/free)*, his family home, and his final studio, the **Atelier des Lauves** *(cezanne2025.com/en/cezanne-sites/cezannes-studio-the-artists-last-workshop; adult/child €9.50/free)*, also renovated.

To be in his studio is like snooping into someone's life. As luminous sunlight pours through the windows, painting tools and still-life models are positioned as if the artist has just left, and his hat is still hanging on a hook. He produced iconic paintings of Montagne Ste-Victoire from this studio until his death – views you can enjoy for yourself from the peaceful gardens outside. From there, as the birds coo and the breeze shakes the leaves in the trees, it is easy to understand that it is not only nature that inspires but that tranquillity is essential to the creative process itself.

For more, check out the self-guided app In the Footsteps of Cézanne *(cezanne-en-provence.com/en/app-cezanne)*.

Gourmet Picnics

The market in **place Richelme**, open from early morning until lunch Monday to Saturday, is the town's premier spot for quality local produce: you'll find fresh bread, speciality *saucissons* (sausages), the usual cavalcade of hard and soft cheeses, plus vibrantly coloured fruit and vegetables, jams and tapenades. In short, it has everything you would expect from a Provençal market and is the perfect spot to find picnic inspiration. For regional wines, try **La Cave du Félibrige**: the folks here are experts in natural and biodynamic wine. It's only a short walk from the market and like all French *cavistes*, they are more than happy to educate you on the stuff.

THE OPTICAL ILLUSIONS OF VICTOR VASARELY

While Cézanne inspired modern movements including cubism and was called by Picasso the 'father of us all', Aix is also home to the undisputed father of op art: Victor Vasarely.

Just 4km west of the city is the **Fondation Victor Vasarely** *(fondationvasarely.org; adult/child €15/9)*, a cavernous 1970s hyper-contemporary building of glass and metallic geometric blocks. An architectural masterpiece, it has 16 interconnecting, hexagonal galleries purpose-built to display and reflect the patterning of this Hungarian-French artist's 44 acid-trip-ready, floor-to-ceiling geometric artworks.

It is a world of anamorphic patterns within seven galleries, each containing six works of art. This is a place where art can lead to transcendental meditation in what he described as a 'laboratory of ideas'.

 EATING IN AIX-EN-PROVENCE: OUR PICKS

Café Caumont: For refined tea and cakes looking over the gardens of the Caumont Centre d'Art in the Mazarin district. *10am-6pm Oct-Apr, 10am-7pm May-Sep* €€

Le Coude à Coude: Fancy little plates for young lovers in a candlelit cave that goes way beyond intimate. *noon-midnight Tue-Sat* €€

Brasserie de L'Archevêché: Around the corner from Aix's IEP university, the lunchtime terrace buzzes with students under the shade of plane trees. *8am-11pm Mon-Sat* €€€

Drôle d'Endroit: Those who know head for a narrow alleyway in the heart of Aix for a great twist on regional produce, including vegan. *noon-2pm Tue & Thu-Sat; 7pm-9pm Tue-Sat* €€

Montagne Ste-Victoire

For green spaces that turn bright orange in autumn, the **Promenade de la Torse** is a wide-open space a half-hour's walk to the southeast of the main artery, **cours Mirabeau**. Wooden bridges pass over a lively stream inhabited by ducks and herons. The grounds of the **Pavillon Vendôme**, only 10 minutes from Aix's iconic **Fontaine de la Rotonde**, are everything you would expect Aix-en-Provence to be: manicured gardens in the shadow of historical opulence built by a love-sick Duke. It's as regal a setting as you could wish for for what is now an art museum. **Parc Jourdan** is a city park the locals are likelier to use to play boules and where many workers and university students eat sandwiches at lunchtime. What it lacks in beauty is made up for with local authenticity.

Le Tholonet

TIME FROM MARSEILLE: **40MIN**

Hiking Through Cézanne's Landscapes

Provence is a hiker's dream. Climbing to the summit of **Montagne Ste-Victoire** seems like the obvious trek as it rises in the distance, but it can be excruciating – especially in the heat. A great alternative, especially for lovers of art and nature, is a ramble in Cézanne country. A 3½-hour hike from Le Tholonet with an expert guide can be booked at Aix's tourist office or online (*aixenprovencetourism.com; adult/child €29/19*).

REGIONAL HERITAGE

The tradition of olive oil production in Salon-de-Provence, less than an hour's drive northwest of Aix, has also played a crucial role in Salon's manufacturing of soap. The famous Savon de Marseille would not exist without it. The **Savonnerie Marius Fabre** (*marius-fabre.com; free*) has been toiling away for over 120 years and welcomes you to follow the soap-making process before visiting its boutique. It has managed to survive despite cataclysmic events including WWII and the shift from shopping local to blindly purchasing mass-produced goods in supermarkets. What is most illuminating is realising that what comes from the earth creates the culture, something that's increasingly lost on many of us living in cities.

 EATING AROUND MONTAGNE STE-VICTOIRE: OUR PICKS

Le Relais de Saint Ser: Panoramic views at sunset from this hotel restaurant as you dig into delicious rabbit. *10am-5pm Wed & Thu, 10am-11pm Fri & Sat, 10am-6pm Sun* €€€

La Table du Boucher: Huge slabs of oozing beef or charcuterie plates to devour with a cocktail in hand. Carnivores only! *hours vary* €€€

Le Relais Cézanne: Perfect spot to relax before or after a hike up to the Bibemus quarries. The patio across the street gets lively on weekends. *10am-11pm* €€

Ancora Pizza: Where the Aixois drive out for pizza, even when they're already spoiled for choice in town. *noon-10pm Mon-Sat* €€

Monastère St-Paul de Mausole

NOSTRADAMUS' BIRTHPLACE

A plaque on 6 rue Hoche in St-Rémy commemorates where the famous prophet Nostradamus lived with his family. Born into a Jewish family forced to convert to Catholicism to escape the Inquisition, Michel de Nostredame's life in St-Rémy de Provence began to take shape when he was expelled from medical school. He chose to practise as a physician regardless.

Profound grief from having tragically lost his wife and children to one of the many plagues of his era led him to write grim predictions that would befall the earth, drawing on ancient Jewish mysticism and astrology.

The first book of prophecies was published in 1555. Some consider them vague noodlings and others divine foreseeings. He is said to have predicted wars, natural disasters and global upheaval for 2025.

Le Tholonet provides the perfect starting point with its waterfalls, windmills, cafes and restaurants. Here, you are at the mountain's base, with the hike eventually taking you through the right angles of the **Carrières de Bibemus** (cezanne-en-provence.com; guided tours from €17) and beneath the pine trees. This is the rock that Aix and its monuments were carved from, and the place where Cézanne had a stone house built so that he could immerse himself in his work. As you climb the terrain of dark earth and loose stones, the views take you into the shapes and colours of his paintings. The summer treks that set off at 6pm offer magical light.

Reaching the plateau offers the panoramic vistas that Cézanne made famous in his oil paintings and watercolours. You'll need plenty of water, especially in the arid summer months when forest access may be restricted to protect the region from fires. Check before you set out on risque-prevention-incendie.fr/bouches-du-rhone.

Les Alpilles

TIME FROM MARSEILLE: **1H10MIN**

St-Rémy Dreams in the Hills

In 1889, Vincent Van Gogh arrived in St-Rémy-de-Provence to commit himself to the Monastère St-Paul de Mausole, a psychiatric asylum, where he lived for a year.

His arguably most haunting work, *Starry Night*, a psychedelic and disturbing portrayal of the night swirling out of control, was one of over 150 paintings produced while battling with his mental health following his tragic act of self-mutilation.

The free, self-guided walk from **Musée Estrine** (musee-estrine.fr; adult/child €9/free) in the centre of St-Rémy, signposted to St-Paul, includes reproductions of his works and snatches of his letters to friends and loved ones.

Arriving at the **Monastère St-Paul de Mausole** *(saint pauldemausole.fr; adult/child €9/free)*, which retains an all-female art-therapy wing, one can imagine how an artist could be as prolific as Van Gogh in a haven such as this, resting between wild countryside and order. The intricate gardens at the right moment command a stillness and contemplation that one would expect from a Romanesque cloister.

The re-creation of his room on the first floor would be more moving if it were possible to experience it alone, and it is best to avoid visiting at all during the high season.

From Les Baux-de-Provence to Eygalières

Les Baux-de-Provence is the destination for views for days over the mountain range of Les Alpilles, although, with its fortified castle and hordes of tourists, you may wonder if you've made your way to a Mediterranean Disneyland. To escape the crowds in the best possible way, take a hike. The **Val d'Enfer** hike is a 2½-hour loop that leads you past limestone caves – the remnants of troglodyte homes from the Neolithic era – and the **Carrières de Lumières** *(carrieres-lumieres.com; adult/child €16.50/14)* – a stone quarry that was turned into a cultural centre in the late '70s, an outstanding cavernous chamber where music and spellbinding light projections have replaced the sounds of clacking rock.

Only half an hour's drive northeast will take you to **Eygalières**, a limestone village poking out from the top of a hill where calm is the order of the day. With the sweet smell of Mediterranean flora in the air, this is a place to wander to the sound of cicadas and gurgling fountains and to appreciate the soft-shoed rhythm of village life. On Friday mornings, the local market gives Eygalières a gentle buzz, with all the local cheeses, meats and wines you would expect on display, as does the antique market on the last Sunday of the month.

For great panoramic views and sacred energy, take the 2km walk to the **Chapelle St-Sixte**, painted by Van Gogh when he stayed in the asylum in nearby St-Rémy. The cypress trees can't help but remind you that this was once the site of an ancient Roman temple.

VILLAGES IN LES ALPILLES

The mountain range of the Alpilles is an understated destination where old French writers passed on to the next life and Hollywood stars still come wanting the semblance of a normal life. It could be the shady squares when spring has sprung, the colourful shutters of the homes or the treks into nature that make you stop and stare over and over again. Time slows down in this collection of unique villages – from Maillane to Le Paradou to Mouriès – with their customs and history that all reflect the generosity of Provence in bloom. For those who want a quiet life, you won't find much better than this.

EATING IN LES ALPILLES: OUR PICKS

Restaurant de la Reine Jeanne: The most stunning vista in town. Go for the slow-cooked lamb above a tremendous drop. *8am-6pm Sun-Thu, 8am-11pm Fri & Sat* €€

Restaurant Le Mas d'Aigret: The ancient interior of a troglodyte dining room and a charming patio with knock-out surroundings. *noon-1.30pm & 7-8.45pm* €€

Le Café de la Place: Busy bar that has been the centre of village life in Eygalières for a good and a long time. Grab oysters and wine. *hours vary* €€

Restaurant L'Opale: Go on a sunny day to eat gently layered plates on a terrace among the trees in Eygalières. *noon-2pm & 7-9pm Tue-Sat, 11am-2pm Sun* €€€

Arles

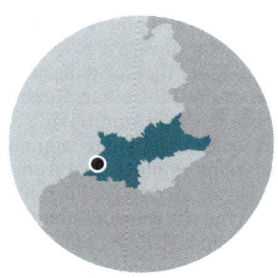

ROMAN HISTORY | MODERN ART | PEACEFUL SQUARES

GETTING AROUND

Arles is well connected by train to Avignon, Marseille and Nîmes. Buses leave for Stes-Marie-de-la-Mer and St-Rémy de Provence. Getting around town is easy on foot and bicycle.

Your arrival in Arles is bound to be rocked by its historic legacy. The power of Rome lies beneath your feet, and there is a glory to this town that belies its village intimacy. Indeed, Arles backed Julius Caesar when he wrestled for power and defeated its ancient coastal rival, Pompey's Marseille.

And then there is its place in the history of art. Writers have flocked to the city to write in the shade, and some of Van Gogh's finest works were conceived here. Nearly a century and a half later, the contemporary art world continues to boldly uphold the French ideal of straddling both the future and the ancient past at the same time. Art and refinement effortlessly go hand in hand. It seeps into your whole experience as you wander the city, with history spiralling out before you at its own pace; a bastion in the vast, wet flatlands of the Camargue.

Capital of Art

Steel, glass and amphitheatres

Frank Gehry and Maja Hoffmann's **Luma Arles** *(luma.org/en/arles.html; adult/child €15/free)* is a towering steel-and-glass testament to contemporary art and a billionaire-funded funhouse. As a statement, it demands we consign Van Gogh and Gauguin to the past, ushering in a spangly new future in its cutting-edge studios, galleries and performance spaces.

The **Fondation Vincent Van Gogh** *(fondation-vincentvangogh-arles.org; adult/child €10/free)* does more than pay homage to one of the great masters by showcasing some of the most famous work that he produced while living in the city. By staging temporary exhibitions and seminars and keeping a contemporary eye on what has come before, it puts Van Gogh's time in the city into context.

To return to the 1st century CE, visit the **Museon Arlaten** *(museonarlaten.fr; adult/child €8/5)*, a 15th-century mansion, which was built around the remains of the Roman forum and displays Provence's arts and crafts from across time.

☑ TOP TIP

Set your alarm to before the city comes to life. Wandering the narrow alleys and ancient Roman vestiges at dawn is a form of time travel.

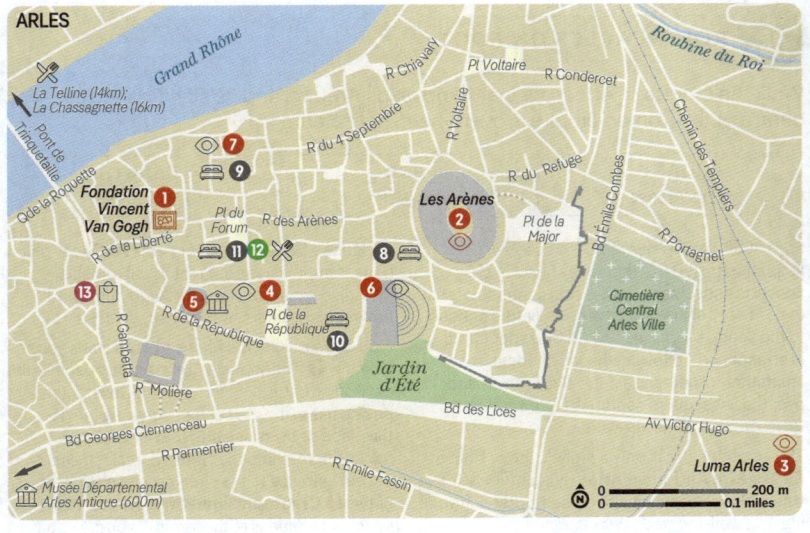

ARLES

HIGHLIGHTS
1 Fondation Vincent Van Gogh
2 Les Arènes
3 Luma Arles

SIGHTS
4 Cryptoportiques
5 Museon Arlaten
6 Théâtre Antique
7 Thermes de Constantin

SLEEPING
8 Hôtel de l'Amphithéâtre
9 L'Arlatan
10 Le Cloître
11 Le Nord-Pinus

EATING
12 Le Tambourin

SHOPPING
13 Maison Genin

Each year the city welcomes **Les Rencontres d'Arles** (July to September), an annual photography festival that began in the mid-'60s. It celebrates the big names, discovers new talent and has the art world out until dawn on the festival's big 'Night of the Year' – a raucous international gathering that brings up to 150,000 people to the city.

Life of a Bull

The symbol of the Camargue

Unlike in Spain, here it is the name of the bull on the arena posters, not the bullfighter *(le raseteur)*. The bulls (known here as *les bious*) stamp and snort as the stars of the **Course Camarguaise** *(ffcc.info)*, a bloodless competition held in arenas around the city from July to October. The Cocarde

EATING AROUND ARLES: WHERE TO EAT BULL

La Chassagnette: If you're going to splurge on a special meal in the region, it should be at this Michelin-starred former sheepfold. *noon-1.30pm Thu-Mon, 8-9pm Sat & Sun €€€*

Maison Genin: Arles' outstanding artisanal butcher and deli since 1877. Cold cuts and *saucisson* served with a big smile. *9am-12.30pm & 3.30pm-7pm Tue-Fri, 9am-1pm Sat €€*

Le Tambourin: More authentic than you might think, with many locals eating beneath the mounted bull heads all year-round. *8am-midnight Mon-Sat €€*

La Telline: Eat like a cowboy in what feels like a family home: a deep, rich stew and more than a few glasses of heavy red wine. *noon-1.30pm Fri-Sun, 7.30-9pm Thu-Mon €€*

ROMAN ARLES ON FOOT

Walk the streets of Arles, originally known as Arelate, and its significance as centre of the Roman empire is overwhelmingly clear.

START	END	LENGTH
Les Arènes	Cryptoportiques	3km, 30min

Start at ❶ **Les Arènes**, a well-preserved amphitheatre (90 CE) that today hosts huge concerts and regional bull-racing competitions. It once hosted chariot races and gladiators fighting to the death, with as many as 21,000 spectators in attendance. Following the fall of Rome, the amphitheatre became a defensive fortress and over the subsequent centuries a 'town within a town' grew up within its walls.

The amphitheatre is only a stone's throw from the ❷ **Théâtre Antique d'Arles** (1st century BCE), which also remains part of contemporary cultural life as a well-curated concert venue.

Walk 20 minutes across town, passing through the grounds of the ancient circus, for the ❸ **Musée Départemental Arles Antique**, which houses impressive archaeological remains, including a marble statue of Augustus found between the pillars of the theatre in 1750.

A quiet walk along the Rhône's banks leads you past the ❹ **Thermes de Constantin**; peek into the old Roman baths built for Emperor Constantine's private use in the 4th century. As you return to the place de la Forum, the Nord Pinus hotel's facade merges into the almost unreal remains of the old entrance to the underground chambers of the ❺ **Cryptoportiques**, which once made up the foundations of the forum. If you are into subterranean chambers, have a look around – or choose a spot in the square above them for a drink.

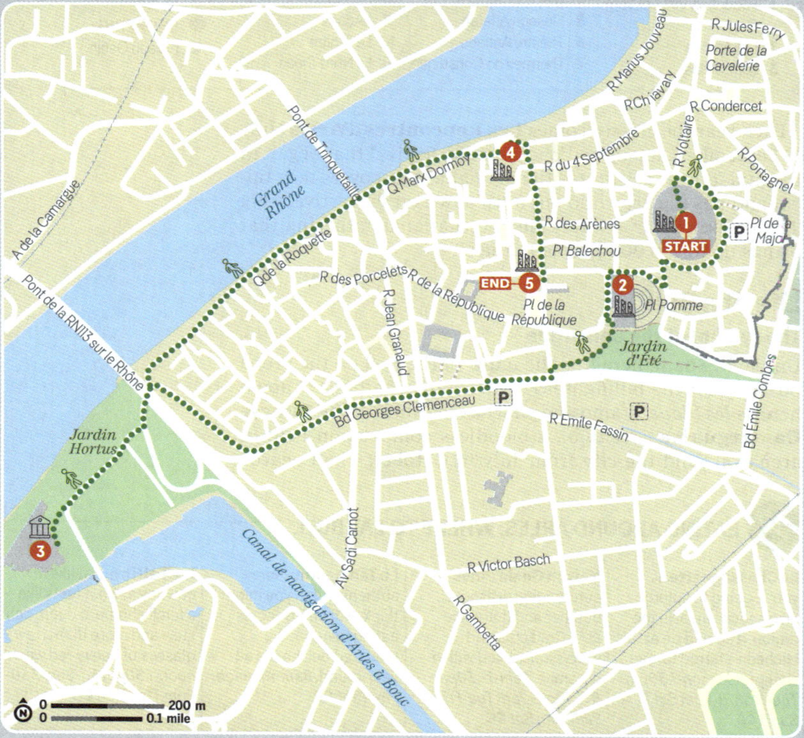

Les Arènes

d'Or, in **Les Arènes** *(arenes-arles.com adult/child €11/free)*, is the main event.

The bull spends 20 minutes in the arena as the *raseteurs* show off by dodging and ducking it (rather than attempting to harm it). The following three months are spent grazing in the fields.

In summer the villages of the region come alive to celebrate the bull as king by throwing joyous parties known as *abrivados,* historically the occasion when the strongest and fiercest bulls would be transported from their fields to the arenas.

Although the bulls are not harmed in the competition, many argue that the animals still suffer stress and that the spectacle should be avoided.

COWBOYS OF THE CAMARGUE

Gardians, the Camargue cowboys, are herders of semi-feral cattle and horses in the Camargue's wetlands who dream that their bulls will bring them honour. Bulls are selected by temperament at three years of age; the rest are sent to the abattoir to be butchered. Those chosen may have a career in the ring lasting up to 15 years before a peaceful retirement. After their death, they are buried in an almost sacred ritual facing the sea. Bulls that do not have bronze statues to commemorate their greatness in the ring are likely to end up as part of the regional cuisine: *gardiane de taureau* is Provençal bull stew, a slow-cooked, comforting dish made with red wine and enjoyed in the winter months with Camargue rice.

Beyond Arles

To venture into the Camargue is to immerse yourself in another world that is distinct from modern France.

Places

Salin de Giraud p766
Stes-Maries-de-la-Mer p767

The Camargue arises where the Petit Rhône and Grand Rhône meet the Mediterranean: 930 sq km of salt flats, saltwater lakes and marshlands, where the sea and the earth become one. The world here feels completely isolated: it is slow-go country, a timeless wetland chequered with salt pans and rice paddies. It is a land of ancient customs that go back so far that it's easy to suspect the Romans encountered a similar landscape to the one that still exists today. The Camargue is an adventure that extends to music and food. Its beating hub is Stes-Maries-de-la-Mer, a town wrapped up in its own mysticism, rendering it much more than just another Mediterranean beach resort.

Salin de Giraud

TIME FROM ARLES: **50MIN**

Wild Beaches

Les Plages d'Arles are savage, windswept beaches that are atypical for the south of France. To get here, drive south out of Arles to Salin de Giraud, which is about 40km south of Arles and is your last chance to purchase water or provisions.

Following the D36D out of Salin to the route de la Mer, don't miss the car park on your right, where you'll find the **points d'observation des salins**, lookouts with views of the pink salt pans and a chance to see all manner of birdlife in their natural habitat as they feast upon various tiny creatures – a perfect stop for photos.

From here, the dusty drive to the **Plage de Piémanson** beach gets narrower to the point that you may doubt the road beneath you, but it's worth it. On arrival, the beach gives little indication nowadays of its Burning Man–style past when unlicensed parties lasted for days, unpoliced on the edge of the world. Part of the beach on the eastern side is still famously dedicated to nudists. There is only a lifeguard station in the summer months.

Another way to get off the beaten track is to get back on it to another off-the-grid beach at the end of a potholed road. The kitesurfer's paradise of **Plage de Beauduc** makes the most of the ravaging embrace of the mistral winds, drawing in lovers of the sport from across the globe. More difficult to get to but somehow more populated, it rates highly as a place to lay down a towel with no phone signal for kilometres around.

GETTING AROUND

Touring the tiny roads criss-crossing this flat, wild region is best done by car or bicycle. Cycling from Arles into the Camargue requires long sleeves, long trousers, closed shoes and mosquito repellent. Rent bikes at VéloCarles (velocarles.fr). Envia (tout-envia.com) runs the A50 bus, which takes less than an hour from Arles to Stes-Maries-de-la-Mer for €1.

Horse Riding in the Camargue

Livestock in the Camargue has a reputation for being at least half-wild, but riding the horses of the **Domaine de la Palissade** (*palissade.fr adult/child from €5/free*) at the right time of day can be one of the most peaceful and authentic experiences you could find in the region.

Riding through the wetlands with the region's iconic flamingos swooping in low patterns all around you, you'll be left with the impression that this is how the Camargue has looked for centuries. Time disappears as you go deeper into the marshes along the trails, especially when the early evening sky glows red.

The local guides are well informed and enthusiastic, and more than patient with first-timers. Do not be wary if you've never ridden a horse, but note children must be at least eight years old. On the three-hour trips down to the Plage de Piémanson *(€70)*, more experienced riders will finally get to cut loose and gallop ecstatically down the hot sands.

Your guide's English is enough to keep you safe, but you will need a relatively good command of French to learn more about the local culture, flowers and fauna. There are more English-friendly schools near Stes-Maries-de-la-Mer but the terrain does not compare.

For English speakers, it is easiest to book through instagram.com/domainedelapalissade. Remember to bring mosquito repellent and wear long trousers and closed shoes.

Stes-Maries-de-la-Mer   TIME FROM ARLES: 50MIN

A Pilgrimage to Notre-Dame-de-la-Mer

Stes-Maries-de-la-Mer has evolved from a fishing village to a town that revolves around its 12th-century Romanesque church, **Notre-Dame-de-la-Mer**, part holy site and part coastal fortress. Climb to the rooftop terrace for tremendous views. Even as a tourist destination, the church remains significant to the small community here and is likely the first site of Christianity in the Camargue.

In the crypt at the back and to the right, in a host of vivid-coloured materials draped across her form and bedecked in prayer beads, jewellery and a silver crown, is the statue of the patron saint of the Roma people, St Sara. According to local legend, she was the servant of Mary Magdalene, who landed here with Lazarus, Marie-Salomé and Marie-Jacobé after fleeing persecution in the Holy Land in 45 CE; they were all canonised after spreading the gospel. Sara-la-Kâli,

WHITE WONDERS

The famous white horses of the Camargue are the first things that catch your eye as you drive into the flatlands. With short necks and thick manes, they are one of the oldest breeds of horses and the most visible of the glorious triumvirate of the Camargue's postcard-friendly animals (horses, bulls and flamingos). They have been bred to do a specific job, and to be brave, spirited and powerful. Living as semi-wild creatures, they also possess a sharp instinct for survival.

At the **Fête des Gardians** in Arles on 1 May, the day ends at the town's Roman amphitheatre, where the *gardians* demonstrate how they use their horses to round up bulls, displaying the dynamic grace of these iconic animals.

 DRINKING BEYOND ARLES: BEST REGIONAL VINEYARDS

| **Domaine Mas de Rey**: A farmhouse dating back to the 12th century is the setting for a tasting that feels as much like an education. *10am-12.30pm & 2-6pm Mon-Fri* | **Mas de Valériole**: A real sense of family with lots of bull meat *saucisson* and regional cheese to accompany a very friendly tasting. *9am-noon & 3-7pm Mon-Fri, 3-7pm Sat* | **Domaine de Beaujeu**: Organic wines and rice from where the river meets the sea. It is impossible to leave its *épicerie* empty-handed. *9am-noon & 3-7pm Mon-Fri, 3-7pm Sat* | **Domaine Isle St-Pierre**: This winery is also a great base for a popular hike on the opposite banks of the Rhône. Fantastic reds! *9am-noon & 2-6pm Mon-Sat, 9am-noon Sun* |

or Sara the Black, is adored by her community of Romanies, Manouches, Tziganes and Gitans, who amass here together for their springtime pilgrimage, the **Pèlerinage des Gitans,** on 24 May.

This is a time for reunions, and the town comes alive with many people camping out on the streets and the beach – there was even a time when pilgrims slept next to the saint in the crypt, playing violins and singing into the night. Before the telephone, these disparate nomadic communities, who had no other way to stay in touch, would return to Stes-Maries each year to keep up with each other's lives. Their newborn children would also be baptised in the church in intense and noisy candlelit ceremonies that have changed little over the centuries. When there are so many candles burning there is barely any oxygen in the crypt left to breathe as the *gitans* kiss the hem of her dress and hold their babies up to plant a kiss upon her face.

Bird-Watching in the Parc Ornithologique

If you're not a bird lover, a trip to the **Parc Ornithologique du Pont de Gau** *(parcornithologique.com; adult/child €8/5, binocular rental €5)* might turn you into one.

This nature reserve, 4km north of Stes-Maries-de-la-Mer on the D570, encompasses 60 hectares of wetland beauty and is home to over 200 species of migratory birds year-round. Explore the 7km of trails on foot and make use of the bird hides that allow you to approach the birds as if you're participating in a real-life wildlife documentary. Admiring the unreal beauty of flamingos swooping overhead or flocking together on the waters from your observatory or from deep grass is wondrous. Your ticket is for the day, so it's worth packing a picnic.

The park was devised as an almost artificial utopia for Camargue wildlife – some birds have given up migrating and live here full-time in inlets repopulated with the ideal flora and fauna to ensure they thrive. It is also a place that focuses on educating visitors to understand the fragile balance of the ecosystem, and is a good family excursion.

For the finest photographs, arrive late afternoon to avoid the glare. In early autumn, you will be blessed with pastel sunsets and flamingos at their pinkest, making for an unforgettable sight.

THE FUTURE OF THE RHÔNE DELTA

The Rhône Delta, where the river meets the sea, is the largest delta in western Europe. But as the summers grow hotter and sea levels rise, life in the Camargue's marshes and lagoons faces an existential threat. An even more pressing problem than coastline erosion is that droughts have allowed the sea to push inland, destroying pastures and leaving the wetlands infertile.

Tourism has also played its part. Until 2012, these beaches acted as wild, overcrowded campsites that raged all summer. There are now more restrictions against pitching tents overnight. In the national park, the **Musée de la Camargue** has a great permanent exhibition highlighting how pressing the region's ecological issues have become.

EATING IN STES-MARIES-DE-LA-MER: OUR PICKS

La Casita: Authentic family restaurant that serves catch of the day *à la plancha* (grilled) a stone's throw from the bullring. *noon-2.30pm Tue-Sun, 7.30-10.30pm Tue-Sat* €€

Restaurant Chante Clair: Modern, popular choice: from *filet de taureau* and spaghetti in squid ink to huge vegetarian plates. *noon-3pm & 6-11pm Thu-Tue Apr-Nov* €€

La Bohème by JF: Well-established brunch spot serving great eggs and coffee that wouldn't look out of place in any major city. *11.30am-4.30pm Fri-Mon, to 2.30pm Tue* €€

Boho Beach: Fresh modern tapas with your feet in the sand in Stes-Maries' best beach bar. *hours vary, summer* €€

Avignon

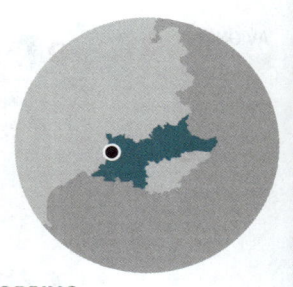

PAPAL PALACES | PEOPLE-WATCHING | MUSEUM HOPPING

Perched on the banks of the Rhône, Avignon is the key to understanding Provence. Inside the rampart-ringed old town, visitors can learn about the story of Avignon as a papal city, visit the numerous Provençal gardens or people-watch from one of the pedestrian-zone cafes and leafy squares. Many restaurants blend the French pastime of eating *en terrasse* with seasonal menus that flaunt flavours from the rich agricultural plains alongside the Rhône and the Durance rivers. And don't discount Avignon's museum scene: with half a dozen museums with world-class Provençal and Italian painting collections, as well as contemporary museums and galleries, Avignon is for lovers of the arts. In July, the city fills to bursting for the Festival d'Avignon. With theatre troupes walking the narrow streets in costume to promote their plays, the whole city feels like a stage.

> ☑ **TOP TIP**
>
> Need somewhere to stay during peak times? If there's not much on offer inside the walls of Avignon, don't turn up your nose at staying in Villeneuve-lès-Avignon, just on the other side of the Rhône. There are regular shuttles, and the city's bike-rental service Vélopop' has stations in Villeneuve.

Art in Avignon
From the Gauls to the digital age

Stay cool in the dog days of summer with a visit to one, or several, of Avignon's superb collection of museums. They are all within easy walking distance of one another. At the top of the list is the **Musée du Petit Palais** *(free)*, which was the archbishops' palace during the 14th and 15th centuries. Inside you'll find outstanding collections of primitive, 13th- to 16th-century Italian religious paintings by Old Masters. The most famous is Botticelli's *La Vierge et l'Enfant* (1470).

 GETTING AROUND

Avignon is pretty straightforward to navigate, especially the centre, which is very walkable. Many areas of the city centre are car-free, so best to park outside the city in a free lot like the **Parking de l'Île Piot** and grab a free shuttle into town. There are paid lots too, like the **Parking Palais des Papes**. Around the *rocade*, or walls of the city, is a tramway, which stops at the main station. A bike-sharing service called Vélopop' has nearly 30 e-bike hubs around the city and in nearby Villeneuve-lès-Avignon. Inside the city walls, a free electric shuttle connects the main squares.

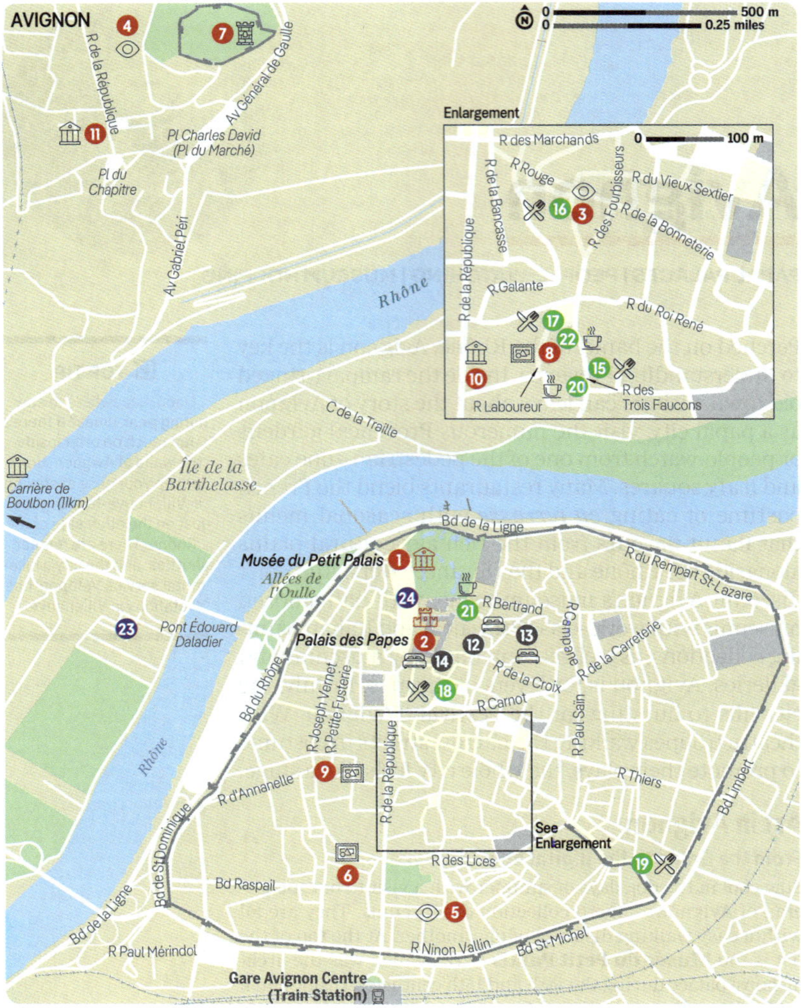

AVIGNON

★ HIGHLIGHTS
1. Musée du Petit Palais
2. Palais des Papes

● SIGHTS
3. Chapelle des Pénitents Blancs
4. Chartreuse du Val de Bénédiction
5. Cloître des Célestins
6. Collection Lambert
7. Fort St-André
8. Musée Angladon
9. Musée Calvet
10. Musée Lapidaire
11. Musée Pierre de Luxembourg

● SLEEPING
12. La Banasterie
13. La Divine Comédie
14. La Mirande

● EATING
15. Fou de Fafa
16. Graines de Piment
17. Grand Café Barretta
18. L'Épicerie
19. Numéro 75

● DRINKING & NIGHTLIFE
20. Buna Café
21. Café Roma
22. Tulipe Café

● TRANSPORT
23. Parking de l'Île Piot
24. Parking Palais des Papes

Tiny **Musée Angladon** *(angladon.com; adult/child €8/3)* harbours an impressive collection of realist, impressionist and expressionist treasures, including works by Cézanne, Sisley, Manet, Modigliani, Degas and Picasso – but the star piece is Van Gogh's *Railway Wagons*. Impress your friends by pointing out that the 'earth' isn't actually paint, but bare canvas.

The elegant Hôtel de Villeneuve-Martignan (built 1741–54) provides a fitting backdrop for Avignon's fine-arts museum, the **Musée Calvet**, *(institutcalvet.fr/en; free)* with 16th- to 20th-century oil paintings, compelling prehistoric pieces, 15th-century wrought iron, and the elongated landscapes of Avignonnais artist Joseph Vernet.

The **Musée Lapidaire** *(free)* is housed inside the town's striking Jesuit Chapel and is the archaeological collection of the Musée Calvet. There's a good display of Greek, Etruscan and Roman artefacts, but it's the Gaulish pieces that really draw the eye – including some grotesque masks and deeply strange figurines.

Finally, the **Collection Lambert** *(collectionlambert.fr; adult/child €12/5)* is Avignon's contemporary-arts museum. It focuses on works from the 1960s to the present. Works span from minimalist and conceptual to video and photography – in stark contrast to the classic 18th-century mansion housing it.

In or Off: The Festival d'Avignon Unlocked

The play's the thing

The **Festival d'Avignon** is among the largest and most renowned festivals in the world for the performing arts. For three weeks in July, the otherwise calm and sometimes sleepy city of Avignon becomes a hive for the theatre world – shows are mostly in French, but some are in other languages or non-verbal.

The official festival, **Avignon In** *(festival-avignon.com)*, takes place across the city, with its epicentre in the UNESCO-listed old town. Tickets go on sale in April and sell out fast, although resale tickets are advertised on a noticeboard at the box office in Cloître St-Louis. The unofficial fringe festival, **Avignon Off** *(festivaloffavignon.com)*, runs during the same period. The difference between the two lies in the selection and promotion of performances: the In festival's selection is done by a jury. The Off festival is more bootstrappy – troupes are responsible for signing up their piece for the festival, renting a theatre space and promoting their show. Want to see an acclaimed play? Check out the In. Want to see something more alternative? Go for the Off.

AVIGNON FESTIVAL VENUES

Setting the stage is key in performance, and Avignon has no lack of creative settings. Take the **Carrière de Boulbon**, located in a former limestone quarry outside the city, which is absolutely worth the trip if you can get tickets. But the most emblematic stages of the festival have to be those in former papal and abbey courtyards.

Wherever the popes went, vast construction projects followed. During their 100-year reign in Avignon, the popes commissioned the courtyards, gardens and chapels that are now home to some of the Festival d'Avignon's most unique theatres. Try to catch a play at the **Palais des Papes'** (p772) Cour d'Honneur, the **Chapelle des Pénitents Blancs** or the **Cloître des Célestins**.

EATING IN AVIGNON: BEST RESTAURANTS

Numéro 75: Chic restaurant in a *hôtel particulier* with a private courtyard, excellent Mediterranean menu and a stellar wine list. *noon-2.30pm & 7-10pm Mon-Fri* €€€

Graines de Piment: Affordable, tasty bistro on place de la Principale that gives disadvantaged youth a chance to gain work experience. *12.15-1.30pm Mon-Fri* €

Fou de Fafa: Four-course dinners at this Avignon staple, drawing on Mediterranean and Provençal cuisines. Reserve. *7-11pm Thu-Mon* €€

L'Épicerie: Classic French bistro with rustic decor in the heart of old Avignon. Plenty of hearty meat-based dishes; vegan options too. *noon-2.15pm & 7-10pm Thu-Mon* €€

TOP EXPERIENCE

Palais des Papes

The vast rooms and shady arcades of this 14th-century palace offer a glimpse into medieval times, when Avignon was the centre of the Catholic world. A visit is supported by tablets (available in multiple languages) that digitally restore lost frescoes and furniture. It's a surprising example of tech that genuinely deepens the experience, bringing rooms to life with audiovisual storytelling and changing art installations.

Frescoes

TOP TIPS

● Buy tickets online to save time at the entrance, especially during the busy summer season and July theatre festival.

● Don't miss the Jardins du Palais, designed in the English style and accessible from the former apartments of the Pope – his place for wandering reflection.

PRACTICALITIES

● palais-des-papes.com
● Mar-Oct 9am-7pm, rest of year 10am-5pm ● adult/child €12/€6.50

Rooms that Speak

From the moment you step into the echoing stone corridors of the palace, you're drawn into a journey that unfolds gradually. Each space reveals something different – a shift in light, a change in scale, a surprising view across the rooftops. Guided by the tablet, the experience brings to life vast halls like the Grand Tinel and more intimate cloisters and private chapels. The Great Chapel represents the largest covered space in the palace. Construction began in 1348 but was slowed by the Black Death pandemic. In the 14th century, the windows were of stained glass, the floors were carpeted and walls covered with drapery dominated by green tones.

Fragments of Colour & Life

Tapestries and frescoes reigned as decor during the papal period in Avignon. In the Stag Room, delicate frescoes depict a papal hunting scene – a glimpse into the world of the Avignon popes. This was a court with its own rituals: scholars and scribes in heated debate, cardinals processing in crimson robes, feasts unfolding by candlelight in echoing halls. Elsewhere, such as the papal chambers, fragments of wall paintings and digital reconstructions suggest a setting once filled with pattern, fabric, ceremony and scent. Your imagination will have to fill in the rest.

Fort St-André

A Stone's Throw Away

On the other side of the river, explore Villeneuve-lès-Avignon

Begin your visit by getting a lay of the land. The climb to **Fort St-André** *(fort-saint-andre.fr; adult/under 26 €7/free)*, a 14th-century fortress atop Mont Andaon, isn't too difficult. Commissioned by King Philippe le Bel, this imposing structure was designed to assert French dominance when facing the papal Avignon – yes, it's a little petty! But as you walk through its well-preserved ramparts and towers, you'll be rewarded with views of Avignon, the Rhône Valley, and even Mont Ventoux.

Indoors, visit the **Musée Pierre de Luxembourg** *(adult/child €4.50/3.50)*, inside a beautiful 17th-century *hôtel particulier*. Home to two notable works featuring the Virgin Mary dating from the 14th and 15th centuries, this small museum also holds an impressive collection of Baroque paintings from the 16th and 17th centuries.

Today an active artists' and playwrights' residence, **La Chartreuse du Val de Bénédiction** *(chartreuse.org; adult/under 26 €8/6.50)* is one of France's largest Carthusian monasteries. Founded in the 14th century by Pope Innocent VI, the complex encompasses serene cloisters, chapels and the pope's mausoleum. Throughout the year, La Chartreuse offers a diverse cultural programme, including performances, readings and exhibitions. It's almost certain there will be something on but if not, a walk through the monastery and to the gardens is worth the visit.

THE GREAT SCHISM

Avignon first gained its ramparts – and reputation for arts and culture – during the 14th century, when Pope Clement V fled political turmoil in Rome. From 1309 to 1377, seven French-born popes invested huge sums in the papal palace and offered asylum to Jews and political dissidents. Pope Gregory XI left Avignon in 1376, but his death two years later led to the Great Schism (1378–1417), during which rival popes (up to three at one time) resided at Rome and Avignon, denouncing and excommunicating one another. Even after the matter was settled and an impartial pope, Martin V, established himself in Rome, Avignon remained under papal rule. Avignon and Comtat Venaissin (now the Vaucluse *département*) were ruled by papal legates until 1791.

 DRINKING IN AVIGNON: BEST CAFES FOR PEOPLE-WATCHING

Tulipe Café: This small coffee, brunch and lunch spot has the best coffee in Avignon. Attached to the concept store and yoga studio Nid. *9am-5.30pm Tue-Sat, to 3pm Mon* €€

Café Roma: Just behind the Palais des Papes, grab a seat in the shade and people-watch. *noon-2pm & 7-10pm Tue-Sat, noon-2.30pm Sun* €

Grand Café Barretta: In the same building as Avignon's first cafe is this sprawling terrace under a large plane tree. *8am-10.30pm* €

Buna Café: Not much for outdoor seating, though there are a few tables and chairs. This is one of the best spots for good coffee in Avignon. *8.30am-7pm Tue-Sat, 9am-3pm Sun* €

Beyond Avignon

Reconstruct the stories of the Gallo-Romain empire in Orange, hunt out antique treasures in L'Isle-sur-la-Sorgue or tackle the holy grail of cycling, Mont Ventoux.

Places

Châteauneuf-du-Pape p774
Carpentras p774
Orange p776
Vaison-la-Romaine p777
L'Isle-sur-la-Sorgue p778
Fontaine de Vaucluse p778
Mont Ventoux p779

From Avignon, the Vaucluse *département* fans out eastwards into Provence. To the north, Orange brims with grand Roman vestiges, including one of only three preserved Roman theatres in the world. To the northeast, rich red wines flow through the vineyards of Châteauneuf-du-Pape, Gigondas and Vacqueyras. Below them, Carpentras warms up in winter to the smell of its world-famous truffle market, while to the east, L'Isle-sur-la-Sorgue's famous canals are flanked by antique boutiques. Overlooking the scene is the 'Giant of Provence', Mont Ventoux, a favourite destination for cyclists, whether on e-bikes or road bikes. The area surrounding Mont Ventoux is a paradise for outdoor enthusiasts, boasting an impressive landscape of rolling hills, towering mountains, canyons, rocky riverbeds and quiet backroads.

GETTING AROUND

The easiest way to explore beyond Avignon is by car, especially if you want to spend time in villages, visit vineyards, or hit multiple stops in a day. E-bikes make the hills more accessible, and rental shops are easy to find. Public transport is limited but possible, with frequent trains from Avignon's central station to Orange, Carpentras and L'Isle-sur-la-Sorgue. There are also ZOU! buses for inter-village travel.

Châteauneuf-du-Pape   TIME FROM AVIGNON: 30MIN
Wines with the Papal Seal of Approval

In the world of fine wines, Châteauneuf-du-Pape retains a special cachet, prized by oenophiles the world over. As its name hints, the hilltop château after which the wine is named was originally built as a summer residence for Avignon's popes in the 14th century, but it's little more than a ruin now – plundered for stone after the Revolution and bombed by Germany in WWII for good measure. Nonetheless, the village itself is a perfect day trip for honeymooners to pick out a few bottles to take home and enjoy on anniversaries – this is a wine that keeps for a long time. To immerse completely while staying in the village, visit the **Musée du Vin Brotte** *(museeduvinbrotte.com, from €8)*, which follows the history of a family's vineyard while giving a good insight into this prestigious wine.

Carpentras   TIME FROM AVIGNON: 30MIN, 45MIN
Capital of La Truffe

Have a truffle lover in the family? Then a visit to the Carpentras truffle markets is a must. The Vaucluse region produces an estimated 70% of the black truffles in France.

Châteauneuf-du-Pape vineyard

Taking place from November to March, the Friday-morning **Marché aux Truffes** on place Aristide Briand is far from the typically busy and buzzing markets of Provence. Here, secrecy and mystery reign as chefs and wholesalers haggle for the best deals of this rare mushroom.

Summer truffles are less sought-after but still have their fan club. From May to September, try summer truffles grated over salads, atop omelettes or sliced, drizzled with olive oil and enjoyed on toast.

Winetasting in the Vaucluse

You could spend a lifetime discovering the nuances of the world-renowned Côtes du Rhône wine. But it'd be a shame to die without ever tasting a glass of Gigondas, Châteauneuf-du-Pape, Vacqueyras or Beaumes-de-Venise wine!

All four of these appellations grow within a short drive of Carpentras (10–20km), making it the perfect city to start a wine tour. Growing in the limestone and ochre hills to the west, these are sun-drenched grapes that rely on water from the Rhône Valley. At the **Clos de Caveau** *(closdecaveau.com; free)* vineyard, go for a walk along the marked nature trail to learn more about the geology and climate of the vineyards

WHAT MAKES CHÂTEAUNEUF-DU-PAPE SPECIAL?

The wine blends up to 13 varieties of grape: grenache, syrah, mourvèdre, cinsault, muscardin, counoise, vaccarèse, picpoul, terret noir, clairette, bourboulenc, roussane and picardon. Most other wines, even in France, are less complex.

Each winemaker has their recipe. Each hectare parcel cannot produce more than 35L of wine; therefore, the grapes are all sorted and only the finest selected to use to make the wine. And, like other Côtes du Rhône grapes, the Châteauneuf-du-Pape grapes are grown along the Rhône River, in clay soil topped with river rock, which absorbs the sunlight during the day and diffuses it at night, providing the roots with a constant temperature.

 DRINKING AROUND AVIGNON: VINEYARDS TO VISIT

Château Mont-Redon: Three kilometres from Châteauneuf-du-Pape, Mont-Redon is gorgeously placed among sweeping vineyards. *9am-7pm Mon-Fri, from 9.30 Sat & Sun*

Maison Ogier: Organic wines with lots of personality and freshness, which comes from the large proportion of grenache in the blend. *9.30am-6pm Mon-Sat, closed noon-2pm*

Domaine Usseglio Raymond & Fils: Biodynamic family vineyard with a good selection of wines and a friendly welcome (reservation required). *9am-noon & 1.30-5pm Mon, Tue & Thu, to 4pm Fri*

Bouachon: Pavillon des Vins: Get in on the action and blend your own wine. Reservations required but possible from only two people at €45/person. *10am-12.30pm & 2-7pm Tue-Sat, 10am-12.30pm Sun*

JEWISH HERITAGE IN PROVENCE

During the papal reign in Avignon in the 14th century, Provence's Jewish community found protection in the Vaucluse but, by the 17th century, they were forced into ghettos in Avignon, Carpentras, Cavaillon and L'Isle-sur-la-Sorgue. The **Carpentras Synagogue** *(synagoguede-carpentras.fr; €7),* in the centre of town, is the oldest synagogue (1367) still in use in France. Take a peek into medieval Jewish life in the subterranean level, where you'll see baths, a kosher abattoir and bread ovens. Visit Monday to Friday for self-guided tours, or arrange a guided tour through the tourism office. The synagogue's wood-panelled main level was rebuilt in the 18th century and is still a place of worship.

Théâtre Antique, Orange

below the sharp folds of the Dentelles de Montmirail, and then stop to taste the aromatic and powerful Vacqueyras wine in the cellar. In Gigondas, the **Caveau du Gigondas** *(gigondas-vin.com)* represents 100 small producers and offers free tastings.

Most vineyards also host tastings, but some go above and beyond to guide the senses: try **Domaine de Longue Toque** *(gabriel-meffre.fr; from €10)* for a detailed and personalised wine-tasting session. Wine lovers who've seen it all will love the organic and natural wine tastings at the **Domaine de Ferme St-Martin** *(fermesaintmartin.com; €15)* on the terraces above the village of Suzette. Accompanied by a sommelier, visitors are guided to a state of bliss before beginning a tasting of one of the finest wines in the region: Beaumes-de-Venise, famous for its *or blanc* (white gold) – sweet muscat wines, best drunk young and cold.

Orange

TIME FROM AVIGNON: **30–45MIN**

Living Roman Heritage

Ancient art and culture lovers shouldn't skip Orange. The UNESCO-protected **Théâtre Antique** *(theatre-antique.com; adult/child €11.50/9.50),* one of only three intact Roman

EATING IN ORANGE: OUR PICKS

La Cantina: Eat inside a natural cave near the Roman theatre. Generous portions for a fair price. *noon-2pm & 7.30-9pm Mon-Wed, noon-2pm Thu, noon-2pm & 6.10-10pm Fri, 6.10-10pm Sat* €€

La Grotte d'Auguste: Also near the theatre, another cave restaurant. Has three-course menus starting around €25. *noon-2.30pm & 7pm-1am Tue-Sat* €€

La Guinguette de la Colline: Typical French fare at this laid-back outdoor restaurant, on the hill above the theatre. *7.30pm-1.30am Tue-Sat, 5-10.30pm Sun* €

Au Petit Patio: Gastropub fare with a Provençal spin; try sweet potato tataki or a chocolate dessert with porcini mushrooms. *noon-1.30pm & 7-9.30pm Mon, Tue, Fri Sat, noon-1.30pm Wed, Thu* €€

amphitheatres left in the world (the others are in Syria and Turkey), is worth the visit alone. Its sheer size is awe-inspiring: designed to seat 10,000 spectators, it has a stage wall 37m high, 103m wide and 1.8m thick.

You don't have to imagine how performances might have been in this theatre; the first two weeks of July, the **Chorégies d'Orange** opera festival takes place on stage. The rest of the year, book ahead for an Odyssée Sonore, an immersive light-and-sound performance that travels back in time to meet the gods and celebrities of mythology.

In the amphitheatre's **Musée d'Art et d'Histoire**, don't miss the 3rd-century mosaic *Aux Amphorettes*, either.

Orange's **Arc de Triomphe** lies less than 1km from the theatre. Once the entrance to the city of Arausio, as Orange was known in 35 BCE, the monument is so ornately decorated that scholars consider it to be an exemplary example of Roman art. Film fans might recognise it from *The Da Vinci Code*.

Vaison-la-Romaine

TIME FROM AVIGNON: 1HR

Immersion in Antiquity

While Orange and Arles have the monumental Roman sites, Vaison-la-Romaine unveils more of the day-to-day Roman lifestyle. The modern city sits atop the old Gallo-Roman city of Vasio Vocontiorum, only parts of which have been excavated.

Visitor passes to the **Sites Antiques de Vaison-la-Romaine** *(provenceromaine.com; adult/child incl all ancient sites, museum & cathedral €9/4)* are sold for a 24-hour period, which is just the right amount of time to travel back to Roman days and follow the city's story through the Middle Ages. For younger visitors up to age 12, two of the main sites (Puymin and the Théo Desplans museum) are part of a grand treasure hunt – the game booklet is available for free at the museum.

Start at the ancient **Puymin** site, a former neighbourhood, where a hive of activity once buzzed in the shops and public squares. Also here is the huge **Maison à l'Apollon Lauré** – a manor with a feasting room, kitchen, private baths and more. Next, hit the **Musée Archéologique Théo Desplans** to admire a rich collection of marble statues and other objects. Imagine the sparks of joy and entertainment visitors must have experienced in the nearby 6000-seat theatre. Check online to see if your visit coincides with one of the regular concerts put on by the city.

No more daylight? Wander up to the spectacular walled, hilltop **Cité Médiévale** – one of Provence's most magical ancient

NO TICKET, NO PROBLEM

Budget-friendly ways to explore Vaison-la-Romaine.

Window-shop on the cour Henri Fabre: Local pottery, Provençal linens and small galleries line this shady court in the new town.

Sip coffee on place Montfort: Cafe chairs sprawl beneath leafy plane trees on this mellow square for people-watching.

Cross the Ouvèze at sunset: The Roman bridge glows golden, with the medieval *cité* rising dramatically behind it.

Pick up picnic fare at the Tuesday market: Come early for strawberries, goat cheese, and just-baked *fougasse* (focaccia).

Wander rue des Fours at dusk: This narrow, stepped street catches the last of the day's light and there's often no one else at all.

 EATING IN VAISON-LA-ROMAINE: GOURMET STOPS

La Caillette: Delicious daily specials and local beers up in the medieval town. *10.30am-4pm* €

L'Arbre à Vins: Specialising in wines from the Rhône region, it serves homemade focaccia in the centre of the lower town. *10am-1pm & 3.30-11pm Tue-Sat* €

Bistro du'O: Tidy design, private terrace and seasonal dishes put local ingredients and traditions in the spotlight. Reservations suggested. *lunch & dinner Tue-Sat* €€

Léone Artisan Glacier: Step back into town to try a scoop of homemade verbena ice cream. *12.30-6.30pm Wed-Sun* €

'DROWN THE DOG' BOATS?

In Provençal, the name of traditional fishing boats, *négo chin*, means 'drown the dog', due to their inherent wobbliness. Adapted to the shallow, clear waters of the Sorgue, they are manœuvred with a long oar. Today, traditional net fishing is forbidden and the boats are used for pleasure.

But each year in mid-July, the Confrérie di Pescaîre Lilen, the local fishing guild that dates back to 1593, hosts La **Pêche d'Antan festival**, featuring these boats, with traditional fishing-method demonstrations, races through the city's canals, boat rides and a floating market. Occasionally, other floating markets pop up during the year – check the town calendar online (*islesurlasorgue-tourisme.com*) or at the town hall. It's a cumulation and celebration of river culture.

villages – for dinner before starting fresh the next morning with a sunrise visit to the 12th-century castle overlooking the valley. If possible, take a guided tour of the **Site Antique de la Villasse**, where local guides are adept at bringing back to life the daily routines of residents.

L'Isle-sur-la-Sorgue

TIME FROM AVIGNON: **45MIN** 🚗, **1½HR** 🚲

Vintage Finds Await

If your manor house needs that perfect Louis XV chandelier, don't miss L'Isle-sur-la-Sorgue on weekends. It's home to one of the largest and most famous flea markets in France, with most of the antique dealers open Friday to Monday, with Sunday being the biggest day. Twice a year, at Easter and in August, the city hosts an international Art, Antiques and Flea Fair, which attracts thousands of visitors.

You can find five main antiques villages along the canals of the Sorgue River. **Quai de la Gare**, located on av de la Libération, is home to galleries like Frédéric Bousquet and Cabanon Design. **Le Village des Antiquaires de la Gare**, located at 2 bis av de l'Egalité, is another great spot to browse. **Dongier Antiquités**, located at 15 esplanade Robert-Vasse, is a must-visit for antique lovers. **L'Ile aux Brocantes**, located at 7 av des Quatre Otages, is home to shops like l'Art et la Manière and Françoise Aillaud. And last but not least, **Rives de Bechard**, located at 38 av Jean-Charmasson, is another great option to explore for contemporary finds.

There are also a number of independent antique dealers scattered throughout town. **Objets de Hasard** is worth checking out.

Fontaine de Vaucluse

TIME FROM AVIGNON: **50MIN** 🚗, **1HR 45MIN** 🚲

Day Trip to Fontaine de Vaucluse

The village of Fontaine de Vaucluse is known for its spring, also called **La Fontaine de Vaucluse**, which gushes out of a chasm at more than 90 cu metres per second, making it France's largest karst spring and the fifth-largest on the planet.

Consider this itinerary: starting off the day at 9am, head to cute waterside cafe **Lou Fanou** to kick-start the day with a delicious cup of coffee. After that, hike up to the top of the

EATING IN L'ISLE-SUR-LA-SORGUE: TOP RESTAURANTS

Maison Moga: Sommeliers and cheese experts pair gourmet platters of cheese or charcuterie with the appropriate wine. *hours vary* €€

Le 17 Place aux Vins: Incredible local wine list and inventive tapas such as shrimp hot dogs, burrata with confit tomatoes or polenta with pulled pork. *hours vary Tue-Sun* €€

Les Coulisses: New bistro and wine bar with live music on weekends and classic French *planches*, or charcuterie boards. *8.30am-midnight Tue-Sun* €

La Prévôté: Upscale gastronomic restaurant in the old town. You might enjoy guineafowl with gnocchi or chestnuts with blackcurrant and smoked milk. *dinner Wed-Fri, lunch & dinner Sat & Sun* €€€

Fontaine de Vaucluse

cliffs from the Font de l'Oule. The hike is of medium difficulty and takes about an hour to reach the top. Once at the top of the cliffs, celebrate with a picnic or snack and enjoy the view. Bring plenty of water, as the weather can be quite hot in the summer months.

Afterwards, wander back to Fontaine de Vaucluse and hike 1km up to the source. The hike is a bit steep, but the view of the clear water is soothing and the chasm impressive. After the hike, head down to the river near the Aire des Vergnes for a refreshing swim in the cold water. The water temperature hovers around 14°C year-round. Time for an apéritif: sip on a cocktail before moving to **La Figuier** for dinner. It's the best place in town!

Mont Ventoux

TIME FROM AVIGNON: 1½HR

Cycling Mont Ventoux from Sault

Ready to take on the challenge of reaching the summit of Mont Ventoux (1910m) without putting a foot down? This legendary mountain, which is often a part of the Tour de France, is a must-visit destination for cyclists. **Albion Cycles** (albioncycles.com) just outside the centre of Sault rents both road bikes and e-bikes. The best time to cycle is in spring or autumn when the weather is mild. Winter can be chilly and windy, and summer can be extremely hot. Consider making a day of it – its about a 50km round trip but steep enough to slow you down during the climb. Pack a picnic lunch with a sandwich from the bakery **Aux Saveurs du Ventoux** next to the bike shop. Don't hesitate to add a homemade pastry to the picnic from the same shop – they're divine, and the sugar boost might help you reach the top.

The 25.7km route climbs 1152m in elevation and is the easiest of the three standard ascents of the mountain, taking cyclists through stunning lavender fields before the real work begins.

LAVENDER TOP TIP

The Plateau de Valensole is the top of many travellers' lists for lavender photos, but Sault and the plateau nearby is a hot spot for lavender too, without the crowds. For a family stroll, follow the Chemin des Lavandes, just below the village, in the direction of Mont Ventoux. The 5.3km lavender-strewn trail is well marked, and information panels periodically share the botanical properties, cultivation, harvesting and distilling techniques of the region's 'blue gold'. To level up your lavender expertise, visit **La Ferme aux Lavandes** (la-ferme-aux-lavandes.com; adult/child €2.50/1.50), a working lavender and beekeeping farm with a charming outdoor cafe and relaxation area or **Aroma Plantes** (distillerie-aromaplantes.com) with a plant library, gallery and lavender discovery room.

PICNIC PANTRIES

Sault's weekly Wednesday Provençal market has been running since the 16th century. Other not-to-be-missed markets in the region are in **L'Isle-sur-la-Sorgue** (p778), **Arles** (p762) and **Aix-en-Provence** (p758).

It's a climb for sure, but if you need a distraction, just look around and see if you can spot a local bird of prey or a wild boar. Many portions of the road easily lend themselves to becoming an impromptu picnic spot.

Once you reach Chalet Reynard, you'll have completed two-thirds of the climb. Smile for the freelance photographers just before arrival and grab their card to purchase a copy of the shot. At the top, drink a local beer, get comfy on your bike and check your brakes – the descent goes fast!

Note that you can also ascend by car year-round, but you cannot traverse the summit from 15 November to 15 April, or in the case of lingering snow or dangerously high winds.

Cycling Mont Ventoux from Bédoin

On Mont Ventoux' southwestern flanks, Bédoin is a typical Provençal village that serves as the perfect starting point for cyclists climbing the peak. Rent a bike from **Bédoin Location** *(bedoin-location.fr)* in the village, from €25 per half-day. From here, the route to the peak is 21.3km, with an elevation gain of 1589m. The climbing grade is more consistent than the Malaucène route and the sights are more varied: it begins in the fields, climbs through forests, and then tops out in the moonscape of the wind-shorn summit.

Be sure to check the weather before departure – if the mistral wind is in the forecast, reconsider. This fierce wind, which sometimes reaches speeds of 250km/h, will definitely knock you off your bike. Bédoin is 30km west of Sault.

Cycling Mont Ventoux from Malaucène

Malaucène, 45km northwest of Sault, has deceptively lovely plane tree–lined streets, which hide the challenge that awaits: ascending Mont Ventoux along this northwestern route is considered to be the hardest route to the summit. To tackle this climb, rent a bike from **Provence Cycles** *(provence-cycles.com)*, from €49 per half-day. If you've decided on this route because it's the shortest (21.2km), don't think you're off the hook. You'll climb 1535m in elevation, passing a few strenuously steep sections that will put your endurance to the test. There are relatively few flat sections to give you a break.

The landscape on the northwest side of the mountain, which faces the Drôme region, is different from the other routes. Conifer forests clothe the mountain slopes, and there is usually less vehicle traffic. Join the hundreds of cyclists who dream of cycling Ventoux three times – once from each direction.

WHY I LOVE MONT VENTOUX

Ashley Parsons, Lonely Planet writer

I think of Mont Ventoux as a choose-your-own-adventure bike ride. There are three possible routes: from Sault, Bédoin and Malaucène. Each one is different, and each one presents its own challenge. Something about the difficulty of the climb and the encouraging applause from other cyclists at the top keeps me coming back. My favourite is from Bédoin – it's the classic way up, and the village has embraced the popularity of the ride. I find the Malaucène route to be the hardest, because the climb is inconsistent and it's harder to get a rhythm. No matter what, my number one don't-forget-to-pack item is a windbreaker for the ride back down – even in summer!

Luberon

HIDDEN HERITAGE | FARMHOUSE LUXURY | MARKET MORNINGS

No one comes to the Luberon, the mountain range that offers up the most quintessential of French landscapes, to stay in the big towns at its edges. Why would you, when you've got the most beautiful village in the world (seriously, it won the prize), Gordes, shining bright like the jewel in Provence's crown? From the hilltop settlements with their rich pastoral traditions to the ochre cliffs on the plain the north Luberon is wild and full of mystery. The south Luberon is epicurean, chic and sundrenched. Come here for the fine dining, wine tasting and a lively summer scene. Even if you lived in the Luberon, it would be hard to do it all. But here are the best parts.

All around Apt

Prehistory and preserved fruit

For those interested in the prehistory of the Luberon region, start in Apt. The **Musée d'Apt** *(apt.fr/le-musee-de-l-aventure.html; adult/child €5/3)*, located in a former 18th-century mansion built on the remains of an ancient theatre, has a special collection on antiquity in the Annex Apta Julia, where the archaeological treasures of the region are presented.

Apt has long been an important market town, dating back to the Middle Ages. The town's strategic location at the crossroads of several trade routes made it a centre of commerce and a destination for merchants from all over the region. Today, the product everyone is after is *fruits confits* (candied fruits). The fruit is preserved in sugar syrup and then dried, creating a delicious and long-lasting treat. Apt is considered the largest producer of candied fruit in the world, and you'll find a wide variety of flavours at the market, from apricots to figs to oranges.

A visit to **La Maison du Fruit Confit** *(lesfleurons-apt.com)* unveils the process; the shop is the best place to buy fruit confit. The oldest shop in town is the **Confiserie Marcel Richaud**, which is the only remaining shop to prepare the fruit by hand – its not glamorous or glitzy but it's great candied fruit at an unbeatable price.

GETTING AROUND

Driving is the easiest way to get around, although there are many secure cycling lanes in the region, and with an e-bike, there is hardly anywhere you can't go. ZOU! bus 909 connects Apt with Aix-en-Provence via Bonnieux, Lourmarin and Cadenet, 914 connects Apt with L'Isle-sur-la-Sorgue via Bonnieux and Goult, and certain 917 services connect Apt with Cavaillon via Roussillon and Gordes. Buses are infrequent.

☑ TOP TIP

Obtaining restaurant reservations is a local sport in the Luberon. If you want to go to a trendy restaurant, no matter its price point, book a table well in advance.

LUBERON

HIGHLIGHTS
1. Abbaye Notre-Dame de Sénanque
2. Colorado Provençal
3. Sentier des Ocres

SIGHTS
4. Cave de Bonnieux
5. Cave du Luberon
6. Château de Saignon
7. Château du Grand Pré
8. Église Notre-Dame de Pitié
9. Mines de Bruoux
10. Musée d'Apt
11. OKHRA – Écomusée de l'Ocre

ACTIVITIES
12. Mind Climbing

SLEEPING
13. Auberge des Seguins
14. Aux Deux Fontaines
15. Camping Les Chênes Verts
16. Domaine de Fontenille
17. Domaine Les Martins
18. Gîte d'Étape de Murs
see 7 Gîte d'Étape de Vitrolles en Luberon
19. L'Auberge La Fenière
20. Les Milles Roches
21. Un Patio en Luberon

EATING
see 19 Auberge La Fenière
22. Café du Cours

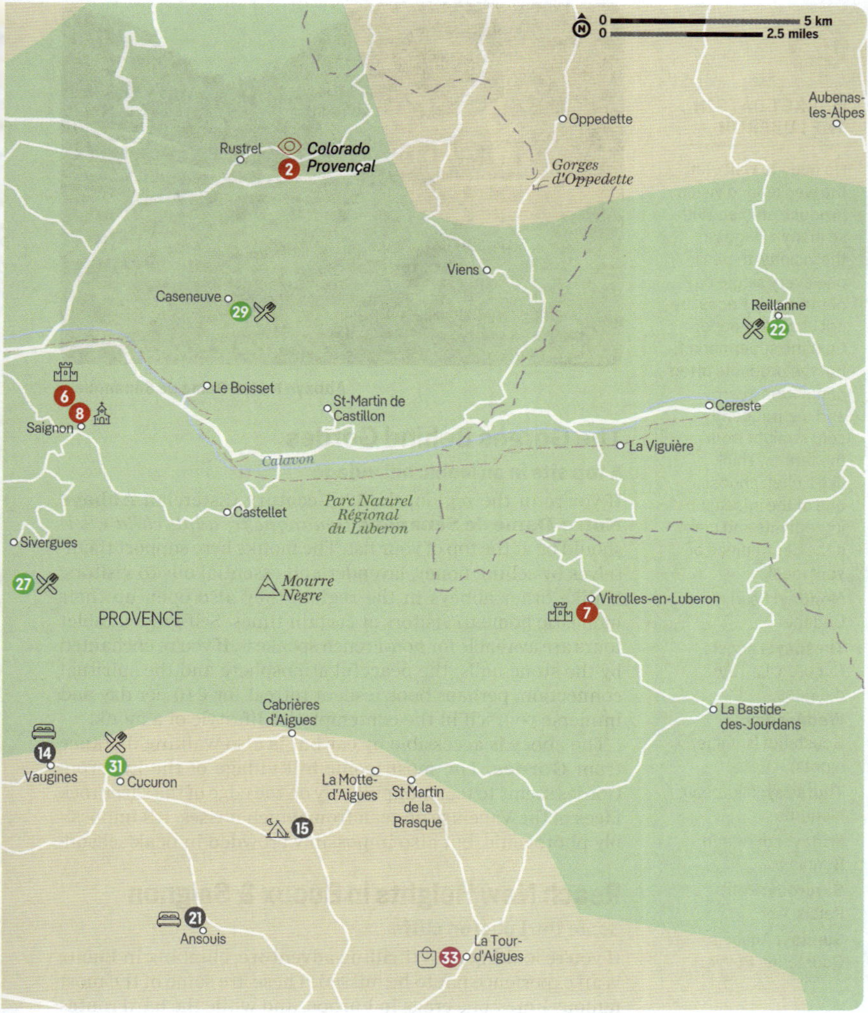

23 Café La Félicità	**28** La Table des Amis
24 Chez Lulu	**see 25** La Trinquette
25 Clover Gordes by Jean-François Piège	**see 13** L'Auberge des Seguins
26 Glacier Crêperie Le Tinel	**see 25** Le Mas des Romarins
see 26 JU Maison de Cuisine	**29** Le Sanglier Paresseux
27 La Table 1720	**see 25** Le Tigrr
	see 7 Le Vieux Presbytère
30 L'Intramuros	**35** La Maison du Fruit Confit
31 Matcha Restaurant	
see 31 Moris Restaurant	● **INFORMATION**
see 22 Multiverres	**36** Maison du Parc du Luberon
32 Vin te Voilà	
● **SHOPPING**	● **TRANSPORT**
33 À l'Ombre de l'Olivier	**37** Luberon Bike Rental
34 Confiserie Marcel Richaud	

MARKET DAYS IN THE LUBERON

No need to wait until the weekend to visit a produce market. With so many villages in the vicinity, there is one every single day of the week. Prices are not always cheaper than the supermarket, but the products often come from nearby and are frequently sold straight from the farmer. Think like a chef: choose one of the in-season ingredients and make it the centrepiece of your meal.

Monday: Lauris, Cadenet

Tuesday: Lacoste, Cucuron, La Tour d'Aigues

Wednesday: Coustellet (summer nights)

Thursday: Mirabeau, Ménerbes

Friday: Lourmarin, Bonnieux

Saturday: Petit Palais, Apt

Sunday: Ansouis, Coustellet, Puyvert

Abbaye Notre-Dame de Sénanque

The Gorges Behind Gordes
A top site in an iconic hill village

If you're in the region, the 12th-century Cistercian **Abbaye Notre-Dame de Sénanque** *(senanque.fr; adult/child €8/4)* should be at the top of your list. The monks here support themselves by selling honey, lavender and essential oils to visitors. Unlike other abbeys in the region, they also open up their monastic home to visitors at certain times. Self-guided tablet tours are available for non-French speakers. If you're enchanted by the stone halls, the peaceful atmosphere and the spiritual connection, perhaps book a silent retreat for €40 per day and immerse yourself in the contemplative lifestyle of a monk.

The abbey is accessible by car but is also walking distance from **Gordes**. The most iconic hill village of the Luberon, Gordes seems to teeter improbably on the edge of the sheer rock faces of the Vaucluse plateau from which it rises. It's impossibly photogenic, but also impossibly crowded in peak season.

Reach New Heights in Buoux & Saignon
Scale the Luberon cliffs

If you're looking for a thrilling adventure, climbing in Buoux is an experience not to be missed. These are some of the most famous limestone crags in Europe, and while the hard routes are *really* hard, beginners can get in on the action as well. It's not for the faint of heart, though – the area is known for

EATING IN APT: OUR PICKS

Café La Félicità: Two mains per day: a Japanese dish, like minced beef *à la japonaise*, and an Italian one, like sautéed gnocchi with peppers. *10am-6pm, Tue-Fri, 9am-4pm Sat* €

Le Sanglier Paresseux: An established classic. Seasonal mains might include sea bass tartare with cauliflower pickles or duck stuffed with dried fruits. *lunch & dinner Fri-Mon, dinner Thu* €€

L'Intramuros: Calling the bar's rum and gin menu extensive is an understatement. Colourful vintage decor, with rotating daily specials. *lunch & dinner Tue-Sat* €€

Vin te Voilà: Small wine bar with a great local wine selection and hearty, seasonal appetisers, with lots of veggie options. *6-11pm* €€

its single-pitch sport climbs, with a lot of overhanging and sustained routes. **Mind Climbing** *(mind-climbing.com)* runs guided sessions for climbers of all levels. The best seasons to go are spring and autumn, when temperatures are cooler and the crowds are thinner.

Above Apt, the village of Saignon oversees the valley. It was once an important centre for the production of wool and silk (many of the buildings in the village date back to this time period), but today Saignon residents live a peaceful routine, and the whole village oozes relaxation.

Wander up the streets to visit the **Château de Saignon**, a ruined medieval castle that sits at the top of the hill overlooking the village. Then weave back down to visit the cool interior of the **Église Notre-Dame de Pitié**. Built in the 12th century, the church features stunning Romanesque architecture and fading frescoes.

Small Village, Big Heart
Music and markets in Reillanne

Don't let the intimate size of Reillanne, a small village in the Luberon Oriental, diminish its character and soul. Reillanne is a vibrant hub of social activity, largely thanks to the **Café du Cours** *(@cafeducoursdereillanne)*. This cool cafe situated above the main square is a popular hangout for locals and visitors of all ages. The cafe's Friday night concerts have become the centrepiece of the village's social scene, showcasing the musical talent of both established and up-and-coming artists.

The good news is that the village's music scene has expanded. A group of friends who frequent the Café du Cours have purchased the old Café de la Place nearby and transformed it into the **Multiverres** *(multiverres.fr)*, which hosts live music concerts every Saturday night. So, if you're a music lover, a weekend in Reillanne is all you'll need to get your fix. Come and experience the soul of the village through its music, food and friendly vibe.

After the music and dancing, shake off the Sunday morning blues with the **Grand Marché de Reillanne**. You can't miss it – the stands take over the centre of town. It's one of the most authentic places to buy local olive oil, lavender essence and farm-fresh eggs and chickpeas. Many of the vendors are producers themselves. Don't expect everything to look perfect, but do expect a great selection of organic and biodynamic produce. The beefsteak tomatoes are always full of flavour, which should be reason enough to make a stop here.

LUBERON WINE

The Luberon was historically a region full of small vineyard operations, and its communities came together at the end of WWI to create co-operatives that have endured, and grown, over the years. The wine produced by these co-operatives is still delicious, and the sale price is often lower. The oldest wine co-operative in the Vaucluse region is the **Cave de Bonnieux** *(cave-bonnieux.com)*, which includes Bonnieux, Goult, Roussillon, Lacoste and Gordes. The second-largest co-operative in the area is nearby: the **Cave du Luberon** *(caveduluberon.fr)*. It celebrated its 100th anniversary in 2023 and offers one of the best affordable white wines in the region, Les Bories, a Ventoux that's perfect for a light apéritif under the trees while snacking on local tapenade.

EATING IN GORDES: OUR PICKS

Clover Gordes by Jean-François Piège: You may recognise the stunning backdrop from *Emily in Paris*. The cuisine is a homage to braised dishes. *lunch & dinner in summer* €€€

La Trinquette: As stunning a view as you can order. Regulars on the summer menu include Provençal aïoli and vegetable platters with chickpea sauce. *dinner Thu-Mon* €€

Le Tigrr: The more relaxed alternative to the renowned St-Tropez restaurant, this Asian-inspired restaurant puts flavours like ginger, basil and lime in the spotlight. *dinner in summer* €€

Le Mas des Romarins: Small snacking menu at this breezy hotel restaurant. Extremely affordable for the quality. Try a home-cooked pizza or a rabbit terrine. *afternoons & evenings in summer* €

CYCLING TRIP

Pedalling the Luberon

With backroads galore, a wink to the agricultural fertility of the valley and twisty switchback turns to reach perched villages, cycling around the north side of the Luberon is the best way to experience what makes this region hum. It isn't just the chirping of the cicadas, but the constant movement of the entire ecosystem in tune with the seasons: from the farmers to the holidaymakers to the wildlife.

❶ Coustellet

Forty years ago, the village of Coustellet was simply a crossroads, but today it's a commercial hub for the hilltop villages flanking it to the north and south. There are a few bike rental shops, such as **Luberon Bike Rental** *(luberon-bike-rental.com)*, where visitors can get equipped to hit the road.

The Ride: Follow the Calavon greenway east out of town. At Les Beaumettes (km 5), turn right onto route des Écoles to climb up to Ménerbes.

❷ Ménerbes

It was a sleepy farming village at the foot of the Luberon range until Peter Mayle's bestselling *A Year in Provence* brought fame and new blood to the town.

The Ride: Head east out of town on the route de Bonnieux. After km 14, turn left onto route de la Valmasque and pedal up to the top of the hill, which leads down to Lacoste.

❸ Lacoste

Perched on the east side of the hill, the village of Lacoste has been well restored

Ménerbes

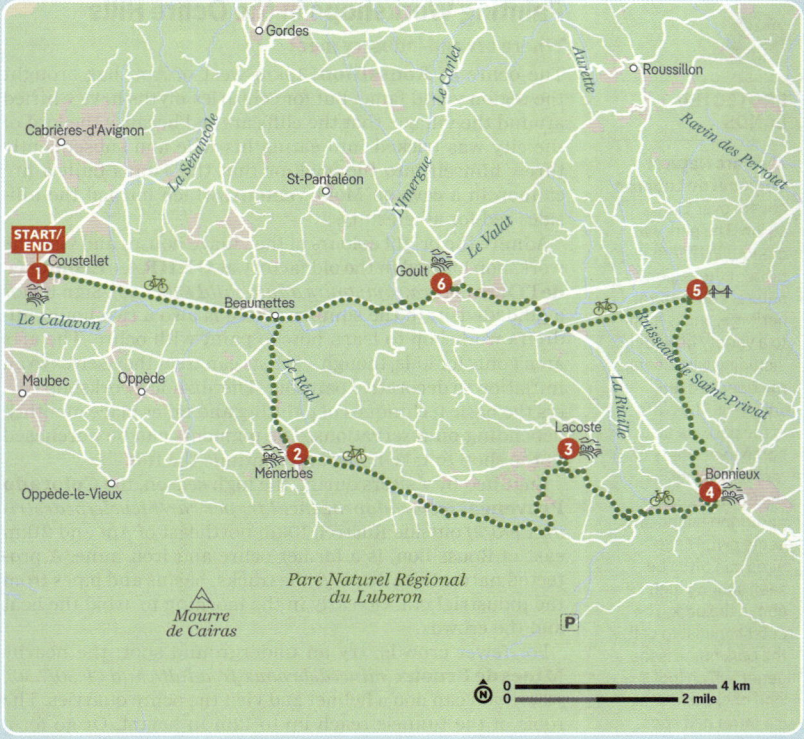

thanks to a certain French billionaire (Pierre Cardin). An American art school has a satellite here and outdoor exhibitions sometimes decorate the town.

The Ride: Hold the course on route de Bonnieux. It's a short descent through cherry and olive groves, followed by another climb up to Bonnieux.

4 Bonnieux

This rival hill village is a bit more lively than Lacoste. Stop for a house-made ice cream at **Glacier Crêperie Le Tinel**.

The Ride: Leave Bonnieux from the north and pick up the chemin de Gargas until it hits the D36. Turn right and then take the first left onto an unnamed road. On a map the road runs more or less parallel to the larger route du Pont Julien.

5 Pont Julien

This Roman bridge (3 BCE) is part of the Via Domitia, an important trade route linking Narbonne and Turin. Until 2005, cars were allowed to use the bridge, but today it is pedestrians or cyclists only.

The Ride: Pedal over the bridge and back, because to return you'll need to follow the Calavon greenway for a spell. Turn right on the D36, cross the river and the D900 roundabout to reach Goult.

6 Goult

A medieval village tucked behind a hill, Goult has loads of character and a tradition of fine dining. It's difficult to choose a restaurant, but try the cool garden and market menu at La Gaudina for a lunch fit for a cyclist.

The Ride: Leave Goult taking the direction 'Lumières', and then follow the Calavon greenway for the last 6km of the journey, taking you back to Coustellet.

Painting Workshops in the Ochre Hills
Where art and industry meet

The ochre of **Roussillon**, 13km west of Apt, has brought the region world fame. But for centuries myths have whirled around the village: that the cliffs are red because the lord of the city was tricked into eating his wife and subsequently threw himself into the void, or that the Titans built a fire cannon in a cave on Mont Ventoux, which burned the hillsides red for all eternity.

Admire the bright colours of the village houses and visit the workshop located in the old factory at **OKHRA – Écomusée de l'Ocre** (okhra.com; tours adult/child €10/7.50). Sign up for a guided visit; in the summer, there is also a two-hour children's workshop to learn how to paint with ochre. The arts aren't only for kids, though – artists can treat themselves to an initiation to decorative painting. The six-hour workshop covers the basic techniques of painting and takes place monthly, depending on reservations. The pigments can be purchased in the shop to take home and continue the fun.

Engulfed by visitors during the high season, the **Colorado Provençal** (coloradoprovencal.fr; per car/bicycle/pedestrian €8/3/2) outside Rustrel, 10km northeast of Apt and 21km east of Roussillon, is a former ochre and iron mine. A protected natural site displays the tracks, basins and pipes from the industrial era. Go early in the morning to avoid the heat and the crowds.

For fewer crowds, try an underground spot: the nearby **Mines de Bruoux** (minesdebruoux.fr; adult/child €9.50/7.50), where you can don a helmet and visit the ochre quarries. The roofs of the tunnels reach up to 12m in height. Or go for a short hike on the **Sentier des Ocres** in Roussillon, to see the ochre cliffs dotted with bright green pine trees.

Road Trip Through the Hills
Queue up your Provence playlist

Just have one day in the South Luberon? Rent a vintage car and hit the road to discover the châteaux of the area and the unique character traits of each village. Start in chic **Lourmarin** – you can't choose a bad cafe as long as it's in the centre with good people-watching. Get the car in gear and make for **Ansouis**. The part-fortified village's elegant history is still felt in the air today – Ansouis was previously a

---

PROTECTED LANDS

The **Parc Naturel Régional du Luberon** covers over 2500 sq km. The park was created in 1977 to protect the region's natural and cultural heritage, and is home to a variety of wildlife, including wild boars, roe deer and red squirrels. The cliffs in the park are also home to a variety of rare birds, such as the Bonelli's eagle, peregrine falcon and eagle owl. These birds can often be seen soaring high above the park. The cutest animal to call the park home is the genet, which looks kind of like a ferret... if a ferret had spots like a leopard and a mask like a racoon. Sightings are rare. The **Maison du Parc** (visitor centre) is in Apt.

 EATING IN THE NORTH LUBERON: COUNTRYSIDE EATS

| **L'Auberge des Seguins**: The restaurant of this country-chic Buoux hotel serves simple lunches during the season: hearty salads and homemade desserts. *lunch hours vary Apr-Nov* €€ | **La Table 1720**: In Sivergues, fixed-price menu, with plates to share and mains that are microseasonal and locally sourced. Goat cheese and vegetables from the garden. *lunch & dinner* €€ | **La Table des Amis**: With two Michelin stars, this Bonnieux restaurant is not cheap (€245) but it's unforgettable and brings technical finesse to Provençal ingredients. *dinner* €€€ | **JU Maison de Cuisine**: At Bonnieux's new Michelin-starred restaurant, you might enjoy a trout from the Sorgue or dessert infused with basil. *lunch & dinner Fri-Tue* €€ |

Sentier des Ocres

summer residence for the nobility of Aix-en-Provence. Ramparts, watchtowers and gateways ring the village's old centre, and it's also home to one of the rare Luberon châteaux that's open to the public (chateauansouis.fr; adult/child €13/10); reservations are required.

Next on the route is **La Tour d'Aigues** and its Renaissance château, which today houses a *faience* (clay pottery) museum. Pick up local olive oil nearby at **À l'Ombre de l'Olivier** boutique. Nearby **Mirabeau** has a fascinating fortress, but it's more famous as the backdrop for the cult film *Jean de Florette* (1986). If you watch one French film before or during your trip to Provence, this is the one. It's based on the novel *L'Eau des Collines* (1963) by local writer Marcel Pagnol. In the centre of town sits a statue of protagonist Manon on the edge of the fountain.

You'll have to head northwards and inwards to reach **Vitrolles-en-Luberon**, last on the list, and less celebrated than other villages on this route. The château from the period of Louis XVI here is under renovation, but it's already possible to visit parts of **Château du Grand Pré** (chateaudugrandpre.com; €12). The view of Montagne Ste-Victoire from the château is beautiful. The fact that it's being renovated by a passionate couple whom you might run into makes the experience all the more personal. Need a refreshment afterwards? There is a sweet hikers' B&B named **Le Vieux Presbytère** that serves simple fare and cool drinks in this small village, with a quiet terrace.

BEST ANNUAL EVENTS

Summer is the busy season here but you'll find something happening all year long – check with the local tourism offices.

Festival Vins & Passions: In late July, an elegant afternoon of wine tasting, small-plate dining and wellness workshops, celebrating viticultural heritage (passion-luberon.com).

Fête de la Musique: This takes place across France on 21 June but Lourmarin does a great job: open-air concerts, street performances and a bubbling atmosphere.

Marché de Noël: In Cucuran, the central pond and square are illuminated by the Christmas market, one of the cutest in the region. Just don't expect much snow.

Le Fascinant Weekend: At the end of the October, vineyards across the Vaucluse set up events for one last hurrah before winter. Expect anything – concerts, workshops, hikes and dinners.

 EATING IN SOUTH LUBERON: ECO-RESPONSIBLE RESTAURANTS

Moris Restaurant: A top table in Cucuron. Dine on the cool patio where daily specials might include sole fish with sweet potatoes and passionfruit. *lunch & dinner Tue-Sat, lunch Sun* €€€

L'Auberge La Fenière: In Lourmarin, vegetarian and gluten-free dishes, with chef Sammut using ingredients from the restaurant's garden. *lunch Wed-Sun, dinner Thu-Sun* €€€

Matcha Restaurant: Cucuron's modern health-oriented restaurant: the *plat du jour* might be vegetable Wellington or a homemade hot dog. *lunch Tue & Wed, lunch & dinner Thu-Sat* €€

Chez Lulu: Enjoy a local fish of the day with roasted chard and fennel confit in this Lauris restaurant. *lunch & dinner Fri-Tue, lunch Wed* €€

Gorges du Verdon

ADVENTURE HUB | LAVENDER FIELDS | ARTISANAL WARES

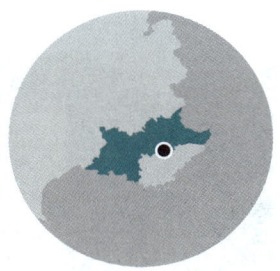

GETTING AROUND

Traffic gets crazy in the Verdon during high season. Best to park your car as soon as possible in Moustiers-Ste-Marie or La Palud and get around by bike, foot or raft. Bus 450 runs from Moustiers-Ste-Marie through La Palud to the departure point of many hikes, and on to Castellane. Hikers can reserve the Navette Blanc-Martel *(navette. parcduverdon.fr)* for drop-off and pick-up at the start and exit points of the famous hike of the same name.

If you love the great outdoors, the Alpes-de-Haute-Provence, one of France's largest, yet least known, *départements*, is the Provence for you. In the adventure-rich Gorges du Verdon, a majestic river canyon carved out over millions of years and the country's answer to the Grand Canyon, hikers can tackle riverbank trails, cyclists can challenge themselves with steep climbs on scenic roads and adventure seekers will get their thrills canyoning or rafting.

For every canyon and mountain, however, there's a vast, open field like those of the Plateau de Valensole, where the lavender blooms light up summer landscapes, while the laid-back village of Moustiers-Ste-Marie, considered one of the most beautiful villages in France, vies with its Luberon neighbours in the French country style stakes. Long celebrated for its fine faience pottery, the town is a photographer's dream, snug in the base of towering limestone cliffs. Wherever you tread, however, you'll feel the proud mountain tradition. Welcome to Provence's rural, wild interior.

Moustiers-Ste-Marie from Above

The ultimate sunset spot

Suspended between the cliff walls above Moustiers-Ste-Marie is a golden star. Legend says the original was hung by a knight in 1210 in honour of the Virgin Mary. Climb above the village to get a better view of the star and the Gorges du Verdon in the distance. There are two ways to reach the path (the Sentier de la Chaîne): on foot or by electric mountain bike.

On foot from the centre of town, pick up the trail at the Parking Haut, which leads to the **Chemin de Courchon** (the old Roman road). After 1.5km, pick up the Sentier de la Chaîne until you reach the star. This is a steep hike; not recommended for young children.

☑ TOP TIP

Sunset and sunrise are the least crowded and coolest times to visit the Plateau de Valensole. Harvest can start as early as 1 July, so to be safe, plan to come mid to late June.

continued on p794

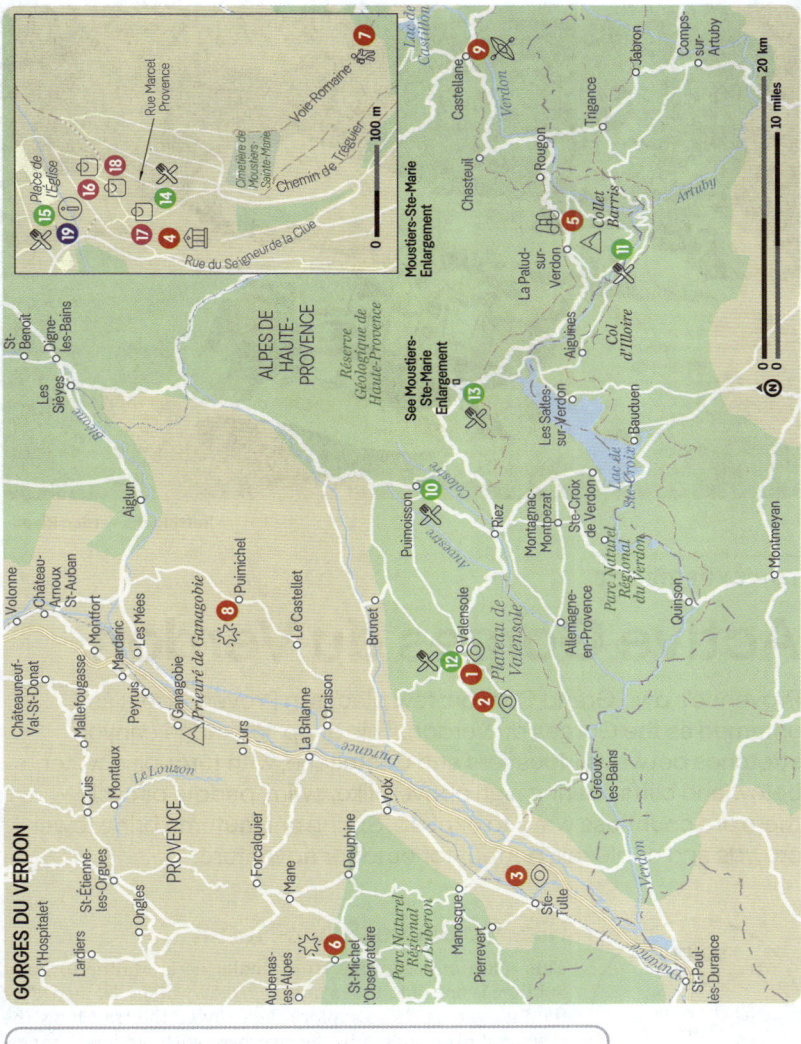

GORGES DU VERDON

SIGHTS
1. La Ferme du Riou
2. Lavandes Angelvin
3. Les Lavandes d'Isabelle et Sébastien
4. Musée de la Faïence
5. Route des Crêtes

see 2 Terraroma

ACTIVITIES
6. Centre d'Astronomie de St-Michel l'Observatoire
7. Chemin de Courchon
8. Observatoire Astronomique de Puimichel
9. Yeti Rafting

EATING
10. Café des Arts
11. Chalet de la Maline
12. Comptoir de Valérie
13. La Ferme Ste-Cécile
14. La Grignotière

see 12 Le Jardin de Celina

15. Les Tables du Cloître

see 12 Maison de Marius

SHOPPING
16. Atelier Bondil
17. Atelier Serrailler
18. Atelier Soleil

see 12 Lavande Bio Berenger

INFORMATION
19. Moustiers Ste-Marie Tourist Office

Rafting the Verdon River

TOP EXPERIENCE

Active Gorges du Verdon

Provence's own Grand Canyon: few places in Provence feel as untamed as the Gorges du Verdon. This deep limestone canyon stretches between Moustiers and Castellane, with turquoise water below and cliffs soaring high above. Hike, swim, paddle or cycle – there are countless ways to explore. Spring and autumn bring fewer crowds and cooler air, perfect for outdoor adventure.

DON'T MISS

Sentier Blanc-Martel

Route des Crêtes

River rafting

Canyoning tours

Le Palud-sur-Verdon

Birdwatching

Hike the Sentier Blanc-Martel

This 16km one-way trek from Chalet de la Maline to Point Sublime is one of France's most legendary hikes. Named after the first geologists to explore the canyon, the trail hugs the cliffs and drops down to the riverbed, with ladders, tunnels and dizzying views along the way. It's demanding but not extreme – suitable for fit beginners with proper footwear. Book the **Navette Blanc-Martel** *(navette.parcduverdon.fr)* in advance for transport to the trailhead and pickup at the end. Hikers should carry plenty of water, snacks and a torch for the tunnel. Get an early start to avoid the heat and crowds.

PRACTICALITIES

● Avoid visiting in winter – trails close and roads can be icy. In summer, use e-bikes or shuttle buses to dodge traffic.

Cycle the Route des Crêtes

This 24km balcony road loops out from La Palud-sur-Verdon, rising over 650m in elevation and offering heart-stopping views straight into the canyon. Originally designed for motorised day-trippers, parts of the **Route des Crêtes** are now restricted or closed to vehicles on select days, giving cyclists a stretch of silence and space. The ride is challenging but manageable with an e-bike – rentals are available in La Palud. Spring and autumn are the best times to ride, with cool weather and lighter traffic. Stop at *belvédères* (lookouts) along the way, where vultures and climbers share the same dizzying vertical playground. A helmet, water and good brakes are essential.

Raft the Verdon River

From April to June, when the river is flowing strong, rafting the Verdon is a wild, splashy ride through limestone corridors and rolling rapids. Most trips depart from Castellane, on the gorge's eastern end. Rapids range from easygoing to intense (Class I to IV), making this a good fit for both beginners and adrenaline junkies. Book ahead with a certified company such as **Yeti Rafting** *(verdon-rafting.net; from €40/person)* – gear and guides are included. Minimum age varies by route (usually seven to 16), and all participants must be able to swim. It's a half-day adventure that takes you deep into the canyon, with moments of calm water to catch your breath between the thrills.

Try Canyoning in the Gorge

Canyoning in the Verdon means jumping, sliding and rappelling through chutes of clear river water, surrounded by towering cliffs. It's a full-sensory way to explore the gorge – part obstacle course, part wilderness immersion. You'll need to swim and scramble over rocks, but no experience is required. Outings depart from Moustiers-Ste-Marie and La Palud, with gear provided: wetsuits, harnesses, helmets and ropes. All you need are grippy shoes and a sense of adventure. For non-French speakers, it's easiest to book through the **tourist office** in Moustiers-Ste-Marie.

LOOK UP

The Gorges du Verdon is home to one of France's most impressive bird populations, including griffon, cinereous and Egyptian vultures. These massive birds ride the thermals above the cliffs, often visible from Route des Crêtes or trail lookouts. Bring binoculars and look for their broad wingspans and slow, soaring flight – especially active on warm afternoons with rising air currents.

TOP TIPS

- Go early, stay late. Morning light is best for photography; late afternoon brings fewer crowds and golden cliff glow.

- Skip weekends in summer. The roads clog fast – aim for midweek if you're visiting in July or August.

- Rent an e-bike. A game-changer for the Route des Crêtes, especially if you're not a seasoned cyclist.

- Wear real shoes. Trails can be rocky and slippery; sandals are a mistake.

- Buy the hiking map. Tourist offices stock the best Verdon trail maps in English.

- Picnic at Point Sublime. It's popular, but for good reason – the views really are.

STARGAZING IN PROVENCE

Clear skies and low light pollution combine to make the Alpes-de-Haute-Provence a destination for stargazing. One of the best places to observe the distant galaxies is at the **Centre d'Astronomie de St-Michel L'Observatoire** *(centre-astro.com; adult/child €7/4.50)* outside the village of St-Michel-l'Observatoire, a scientific research centre that is open to the public. Here, you can join guided tours and peer at the stars through telescopes with the help of experienced astronomers. English-speaking nights are held in the summer. Another option is to visit the **Observatoire Astronomique de Puimichel** *(adult/child €20/10)* in Puimichel, where you can learn about the workings of the observatory as well as explore the night sky with telescopes. Reservations need to be made at the Manosque tourist office.

Lavender fields, Plateau de Valensole

continued from p790

By electric mountain bike, take the main road out of town towards Puimoisson. Turn right towards En Naups and Le Castillon. The route passes above Le Castillon and hugs the hill until it comes back around nearly full circle to Moustiers-Ste-Marie, just on the other side of the hill. After the campground, turn on the bike's motor to help you climb up to the top of the hill via the old Roman road. It's marked with yellow-and-white VTT (mountain bike) trail signs.

Ceramics in Moustiers-Ste-Marie
From royal households to your table

A craft practised in Moustiers-Ste-Marie since the Middle Ages, the decorative faience (glazed earthenware) made here once graced the dining tables of Europe's most aristocratic houses. Typical decoration of faience pieces includes scenes in shades of blue; *aux guirlandes*, which is usually a single scene in the centre of the dish, surrounded by garlands; and

---

EATING IN MOUSTIERS-STE-MARIE: OUR PICKS

Les Tables du Cloitre: The restaurant to reserve. Stone interior with a local, rustic menu of dishes like rabbit or wild mushrooms. *noon-2pm Wed-Sun, 7-8.30pm Sat & Sun* €€

La Grignotière: Trendy breakfast and brunch place in the centre of Moustiers with a laid-back shady terrace. *9am-6pm Wed-Sun* €€

La Ferme Ste-Cécile: Enjoy country specialities by chef Patrick Crespin between Moustiers and the Gorges du Verdon (not vegetarian-friendly). *noon-1pm & 7-8pm Tue-Sat, noon-1pm Sun* €€

Chalet de la Maline: Restaurant attached to the Club Alpin Français, with a terrace overlooking the Gorges du Verdon plus local beer. *hours vary* €

grotesques, which usually incorporate animal or even some fantasy figures. Seven workshops still sell ceramics today, including **Atelier Serrailler**, **Atelier Soleil** and **Atelier Bondil**. For antique masterpieces, visit the small **Musée de la Faïence** *(musee-moustiers.fr; adult/child €5/free)* adjacent to the town hall.

Sustainable Lavender Visits

Lavender is the new green

Dive into the new face of ecologically responsible lavender production by visiting an organic lavender farm on the **Plateau de Valensole**. To start with, look for the lavender fields that have let golden grass grow up between the rows of purple – these farms are doing their part to preserve the soil for the next generation. Many farms are open year-round to guests, but run special tours during the harvest season. And no visit would be complete without trying some lavender-based products straight from the source, such as essential oils, soaps and perfumes produced on-site using sustainable methods.

The lavender fields of Valensole are usually the highlight of a photography tour of Provence. Visit in late June or early July, but no later. During this time, the fields are alive with colour and fragrance, providing a stunning backdrop for your photos. To get the perfect shot, you'll have to get up early – sunrise has the longest 'soft-light' period, which reduces shadows and harsh glare. Don't go tramping in the fields, but tread carefully between rows – these are precious crops for local farmers. What to wear? Consider colours that will complement the lavender fields. Soft pastels, earthy tones and neutral colours work well in this setting. Avoid wearing bright colours that may clash with the lavender or draw too much attention away from the landscape's natural beauty.

LAVENDER FARMS ON THE PLATEAU DE VALENSOLE

La Ferme du Riou: This organic farm runs distillery visits during the harvest season and farm visits year-round.

Lavande Bio Berenger: Organic producer with a cabin in the fields during harvest season. Otherwise, stop into the shop in Valensole.

Lavandes Angelvin: Runs distillery visits during high season and guided visits on Tuesdays at 3pm.

Terraroma: Very photogenic lavender and almond farm, with a few sunflower fields to complete the mosaic.

Les Lavandes d'Isabelle et Sébastien: Technically off the plateau and closer to Manosque, this little family lavender farm is less crowded and has a small boutique to find your favourite products.

 EATING IN VALENSOLE: OUR PICKS

Le Jardin de Celina: In a chic farmhouse setting, this standout table pairs creative Provençal cuisine with serious wine and a cosy garden. *hours vary seasonally* €€

Comptoir de Valérie: Good bistro to grab summer dishes like a tomato and burrata salad or local melon with cured ham. *noon-2pm Tue-Sun, 7.30-9pm Fri & Sat* €

Maison de Marius: Homemade from start to finish, this charming spot is also an *épicerie* (gourmet grocer) where you can stock up on local treats. *8.30am-12.30pm & 3.30-6pm Mon-Sat, 9am-12.30pm Sun* €€

Café des Arts: On the other side of the Plateau de Valensole is the much less crowded Puimoisson and its surprisingly good Café des Arts. *7am-3pm Sun-Tue, 7am-10.30pm Thu-Sat* €

Places We Love to Stay

€ Budget €€ Midrange €€€ Top End

Marseille   MAP p748

Mama Shelter € Budget with some style. This hotel can turn into a party with live music and a raucous bar on the weekend.

Hôtel Belle-Vue € Incredible views of the Vieux Port and a famous historical restaurant that turns into a jazz venue on Sundays. Great value.

Les Appartements du Vieux Port €€ Large, calm apartments with balconies, close to the Vieux Port. When you prefer to have a modern home-from-home.

La Relève €€ There are only four rooms, so book in advance for this '50s-inspired guest house that is attached to a very cool bar in the 7eme.

Hôtel Le Corbusier €€ A little out of the way, but this is a unique and historic monument to urban planning. Great pool on the roof.

Hotel Peron €€ Wes Anderson–style hotel with views of the corniche and beyond. Art deco from every angle and a friendly reception.

Le Ryad €€ North African–inspired hotel that has a sanctuary of a garden to drink fresh mint tea in after a long day.

Les Bords de la Mer €€€ Modern architectural lines that make it all about the views of the Plage des Catalans as you have breakfast. A statement option.

Aix-en-Provence

Hôtel Escaletto €€ Friendly, modern spot close to the Roman baths with a rooftop cocktail bar that goes late into the night.

Hôtel des Augustins €€ Incredible location just off cours Mirabeau with plenty of old-school Aixois ambience.

Domaine Gaogaïa €€ One for summer. Cocktails in the garden, and only 10 minutes from town but feels like a world away.

Le Relais de Saint Ser €€ At the foot of Montagne Ste-Victoire – the views from the restaurant are the best for miles around. Incredible food too (p759).

Bastide de Ganay €€€ Quiet Provençal luxury with a saltwater pool in manicured gardens. Only a 15-minute drive into the centre of Aix.

Arles   MAP p763

Hôtel de l'Amphithéâtre € Quaint sleeper in the heart of the city. No frills but plenty of character.

Le Nord-Pinus €€ Sleep where Hemingway once did. This is a historic triumph of a hotel in the centre of town.

Le Cloître €€ Tasteful remodelling of a grand building, with a great summer roof bar and restaurant.

L'Arlatan €€€ An abundance of style and substance. The attention to each design detail is mind-boggling.

Stes-Maries-de-la-Mer

Hôtel Casa Marina € A short hop from the sands and beach bars of Stes-Maries. Friendly and sparkly clean.

Hotel Le Neptune en Camargue € Small hotel that delivers charm, warmth and a huge breakfast.

Hôtel Les Arnelles €€€ A comfortably authentic experience in the wilds of the Camargue. Make the most of its stable to go for a horse ride at sunset.

Avignon   MAP p769

La Banasterie €€ In the centre of Avignon, find yourself in one of those old, upscale hotels you see in films – excellent service, interesting guests and tasteful design.

La Mirande €€€ Easily the most upscale hotel in Avignon; you can pretend you're royalty here amid the luxurious 19th-century decor.

La Divine Comédie €€€ Theatre fans coming for the festival in Avignon can get a feel for old-world luxe in this private B&B.

Carpentras

Metafort €€ Can't hype this place up enough. Book the tiny house in the cave – you won't regret it. And order breakfast to enjoy on the terrace.

Hôtel le Blason de Provence €€ A 15-minute drive from Carpentras, on the edge of the charming village of Monteux.

Château Martinay €€€ Spend a luxurious night in this castle on the western outskirts of Carpentras.

Orange

Château du Mourre du Tendre €€ This guesthouse in the garden of the castle grounds is surrounded by Châteauneuf-du-Pape vines; there's pool access too. Don't miss organising a wine tasting of one of the five *appellations* made by this vineyard.

Grand Hôtel d'Orange €€
Pretty and modern hotel in the centre of Orange. You can feel like royalty without the price tag.

Mont Ventoux & Around

Aurel Inattendu €
Comfortable, no-frills wooden *roulotte* (caravan), overlooking lavender fields.

La Bastide de la Loge €€
House rental a few kilometres outside Sault on the plain below Mont Ventoux.

Maison Leonard du Ventoux €€
In the centre of Sault, a large B&B of five rooms with great linens and a private garden and just two steps from shops and cafes.

L'Isle-sur-la-Sorgue

La Magnanerie de l'Isle €€
Character-filled guesthouse in a former industrial building in the heart of the historic centre.

Mas la Vitalis €€
Magali's B&B consists of two inviting bedrooms in a calm, restored farmhouse near town.

La Maison sur la Sorgue €€€
Historic boutique hotel with sumptuous suites and a hidden garden with a small stone pool.

Luberon MAP p782

Gite d'Étape de Murs €
Simple dorm-style lodging, from €30 without dinner (€51 with dinner).

Gite d'Étape de Vitrolles en Luberon €
A great budget option for families or groups, this homestay offers half-board and a quiet stopover.

Camping Les Chênes Verts €
Small lakeside campground near the Étang de la Bonde; it's basic but not expensive and it's kid-friendly.

Les Milles Roches €€
Trendy, artsy guest house in Gordes. Rooms or a home for up to six people, designed with light, simplicity and style.

Auberge des Seguins €€
Secluded B&B with a pool and view of the cliffs of Buoux. Restaurant and cafe onsite.

Aux Deux Fontaines €€
A favourite spot – Provençal chic in Vaugines with great decor and an attentive but not overbearing host. Get the breakfast for homemade jams.

Un Patio en Luberon €€
In the centre of Ansouis, a beautiful stone B&B with spacious beds and bathrooms.

Domaine Les Martins €€€
Quiet guest house with lovely gardens near Gordes. It's an expensive area but a good deal for the calm and beauty.

Domaine de Fontenille €€€
Bathed in decadence, with a touch of well-being. Friday nights are for barbecues in the garden. About 2km northwest of Lauris.

L'Auberge La Fenière €€€
Comfortable rural hotel near Lourmarin linked to the Michelin-starred restaurant and farm of chef Nadia Sammut.

Moustiers-Ste-Marie

Camping à la Ferme de la Graou €
Stellar views over the Verdon and shady sites. There's no electricity or hot water, but it's a great, close-to-nature budget option.

Camping à la Ferme du Maunard €
Right on the lake, this is a clean, calm, family-friendly campground.

Hôtel Le Colombier €€
Set among olive trees and lavender fields, this charming hotel offers modern rooms with private terraces, a heated pool and tennis courts, all within a short walk of the village centre.

La Ferme Rose €€
This boutique hotel, set in a former farmhouse, boasts uniquely decorated rooms filled with vintage artefacts, lush gardens and a relaxed ambience, perfect for a serene getaway.

Le Jardin de Celina €€€
Stylish yet relaxed, this boutique guesthouse has a pool, spa, and restaurant – with lavender fields just beyond your terrace. A serene base for exploring the plateau.

La Mirande, Avignon

Researched by
Chrissie McClatchie & Alexis Averbuck

Côte d'Azur & Monaco

WHERE THE MOUNTAINS MEET THE MEDITERRANEAN

A world-famous coastline, entrancing hilltop villages and an emerging hinterland scene: the Côte d'Azur and Monaco are eternally chic, but there are new surprises waiting.

What's in a name? In 1887, the French writer Stéphen Liégeard set off on a journey across France's eastern Mediterranean coastline, chronicling his experiences in the book *La Côte d'Azur*. Until just a few decades before, this corner of the country had acted as little more than a stopover point for intrepid travellers en route to Italy, but that was changing as a new train line unfurled from the north, bringing with it foreigners waving doctors' prescriptions for a healthy dose of the region's winter sun. Nobility, artists and royalty soon followed, ready to flaunt their best dress on waterfront promenades and in the black-tie casinos. Liégeard's 'Azure Coast' cast a wide net from Marseille to Genoa, but the name he coined stuck.

There's still no hard-and-fast starting and finishing point. For some, the Côte d'Azur is defined as stretching from Menton, at the Italian border, to Cannes, both towns in the Alpes-Maritimes, the *département* tucked into the southeastern nook of France. For others, the French Riviera, as it is interchangeably called, extends beyond St-Tropez and deeper into the neighbouring Var (as it does in this chapter). What's not debated is that this is France's glittering blue coast. Princely Monaco lies in its embrace. The Côte d'Azur maintains its glorious long-time allure with its intoxicating mix of sun, sea, culture, food and wine, and the green mountain interior beckoning today's batch of adventure travellers.

VIOLETTE FRANCHI FOR LONELY PLANET

THE MAIN AREAS

NICE
Beaches, architecture and a blossoming foodie scene. **p806**

CANNES
Flashy festivals and refreshingly quiet spaces. **p823**

ST-TROPEZ
The Côte d'Azur's capital of glitz. **p835**

MONACO
Small in size, big in glamour. **p850**

For places to stay in Côte d'Azur & Monaco, see p858

Left: Cours Saleya (p813), Nice; Above: Vieux Port (p835), St-Tropez

Find Your Way

In France's southeastern corner, lively resort towns along the coast quickly give way to perched inland villages. Behind them, vast national parks stretch across mountain landscapes.

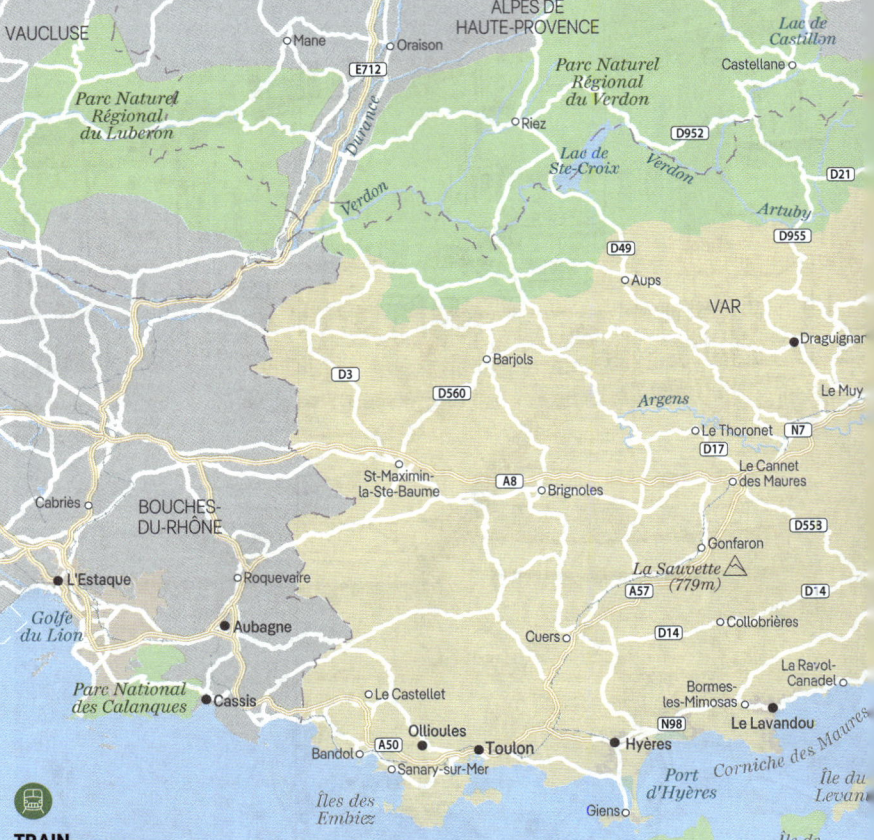

TRAIN

The scenic TER Sud Provence-Alpes-Côte-d'Azur train line connects the region's seafront destinations between Hyères and Menton (including Monaco, but not St-Tropez) and beats taking the car every time. A train service also links Grasse to the coast.

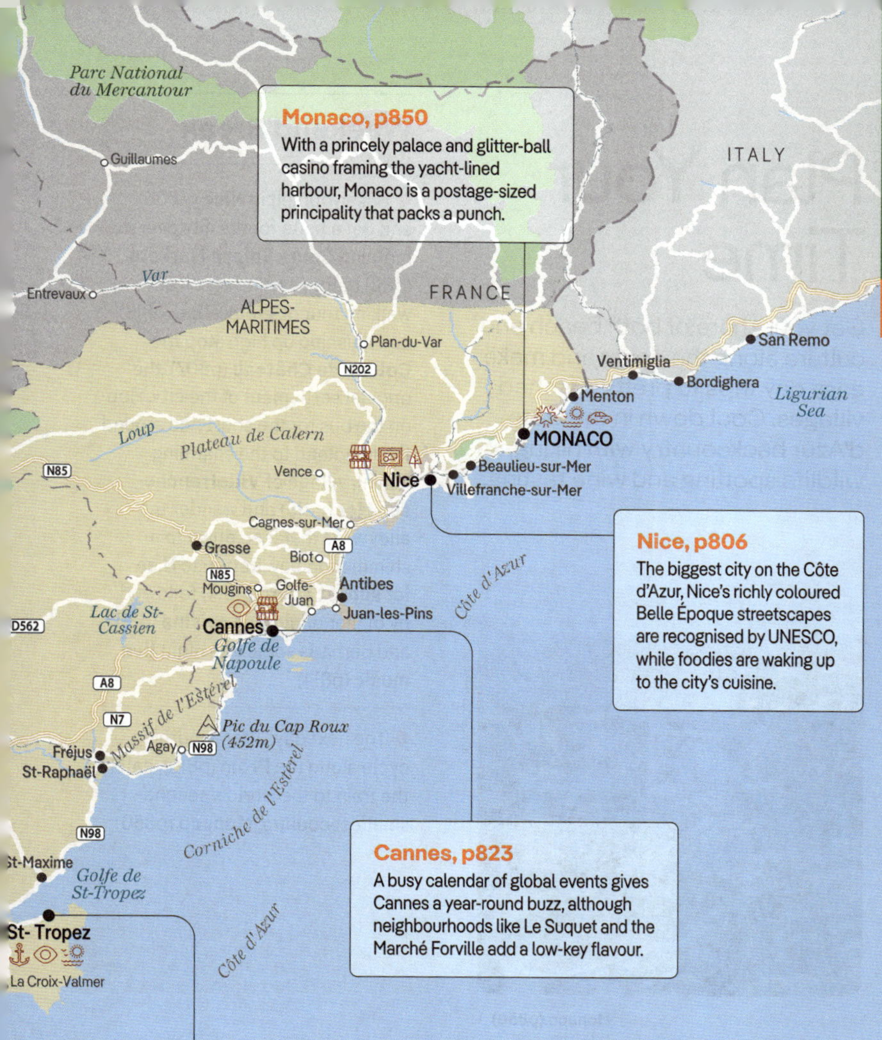

Monaco, p850

With a princely palace and glitter-ball casino framing the yacht-lined harbour, Monaco is a postage-sized principality that packs a punch.

Nice, p806

The biggest city on the Côte d'Azur, Nice's richly coloured Belle Époque streetscapes are recognised by UNESCO, while foodies are waking up to the city's cuisine.

Cannes, p823

A busy calendar of global events gives Cannes a year-round buzz, although neighbourhoods like Le Suquet and the Marché Forville add a low-key flavour.

St-Tropez, p835

The capital of hot summer nights; come here to live out your French Riviera dreams, beach or harbourside.

CAR

Driving is a hassle in Nice, Cannes, Monaco and especially St-Tropez, and parking can be pricey, but your own transport is the best way to see the Côte d'Azur that exists beyond these busy destinations.

BUS

Cheap and comprehensive, the ZOU! intercity bus network links St-Tropez, Cannes and Nice with smaller towns both along the coast and further inland, although expect longer travel times than the train when faced with a choice between the two.

Plan Your Time

Get your share of both beach and culture along the coast and make easy day trips to pretty perched villages. Cool down in the Côte d'Azur backcountry with hiking, wildlife spotting and wine tasting.

Monaco (p850)

Weekend Break

● Base yourself in **Nice** (p806) and get a taste for the city over its morning **Cours Saleya Markets**, (p811) before setting off on a walking tour of **Vieux Nice** (p813) and finishing up high atop the **Colline du Château** (p807), the original settlement of the city. Hop on the bus for the short ride around the headland to the charming fishing village of **Villefranche-sur-Mer** (p815) and wander the alleyways that lead down to a shimmering bay. Return to Nice for **sunset apéro** (p814) followed by dinner of **niçoise cuisine** (p811) and perhaps some late night **live music** (p814).

● The next day, after a morning cycle along the **Prom** (p810), catch the train to the world's second-smallest country, **Monaco** (p850).

Seasonal Highlights

The Côte d'Azur's winters are sunny and mild and the heat of summer is punctuated by refreshing sea breezes.

JANUARY

The **Route du Mimosa** (p833) bursts into bloom around Bormes-les-Mimosas and along the Corniche d'Or. The soils of **Aups** (p847) conceal precious truffles, celebrated during the annual Fête de la Truffe Noire.

FEBRUARY

A frenzy of festivals including the **Carnaval de Nice** (p812) and the **Fête du Citron** (p820) in Menton light up the last days of winter. Menton's famous lemon trees are heavy with golden fruit.

MAY

A mammoth month of public holidays. The red carpet rolls out for the **Festival de Cannes** (p823), while **Grasse's** famous rose gardens (p831) are awash with pastel-pink flowers ready to be picked for perfume houses.

Five Days to Travel Around

● Still based in Nice for the first few days, you can learn more about its newly minted **UNESCO status** (p806) and marvel at **masterful art** (p811). Day trips allow you to extend your reach towards lemon-scented **Menton** (p820) on the Italian border, towards cinematic **Cannes** (p823) or the artist's villages of **St-Paul de Vence** (p832), **Antibes** (p829) or **Mougins** (p831).

● Swap Nice for **St-Tropez** (p835) for the last couple of days, arriving in style by **ferry** (p835). Spend one morning exploring **the harbour and old town** (p835), then go for lunch at a club on **Plage de Pampelonne** (p840). Dance till dawn at one of St-Tropez' **bars or clubs** (p841). Sleep off the night on a lounger or a **catamaran** (p841), then hit St-Tropez' **fashion boutiques** (p838).

Longer Than a Week

● With more than a week, you have enough time to linger over long lunches like the locals do. Base yourself in either arty **Nice** (p806) or glamorous **Cannes** (p823) and take a day to drive the spellbinding coastal **Route du Mimosa** (p833), hop on the short ferry ride to **Île Ste-Marguerite** (p826), play in **St-Tropez** (p835) and loop up towards perfumed **Grasse** (p831).

● In the Var, you can connect with nature in the chestnut groves of **Monastère de la Verne** (p844) and **Collobrières** (p844) before going **wine tasting** (p847) to find your favourite rosé. Then dine and sleep below the cliffs of **Cotignac** (p846).

● Finish up at under-rated coastal hotspot **Hyères** (p845), planning at least a day hiking, cycling and swimming around the photogenic spread that is the **Île de Porquerolles** (p848).

JUNE
In 2026 the **Monaco Formula One Grand Prix** (p850) officially moves to the first week in June. The summer solstice is celebrated in style: **La Fête de la Musique** is a France-wide affair on 21 June but particularly rocks in Nice.

JULY
Every weekend buzzes with an outdoor event: fireworks, music, cinema. The region is packed, especially around **Bastille Day** (14 July). Markets brim with strawberries and tomatoes; pair with rosé for charming beach picnics.

SEPTEMBER
Dreamy backcountry hiking, particularly alongside alpine fauna near **St-Martin-Vésubie** (p821) and deep into the **Vallée des Merveilles** (p822). Boat shows and regattas mean accommodation fills up fast in Cannes, Monaco and St-Tropez.

DECEMBER
First flurries of snow and first mugs of mulled wine at **Christmas markets,** particularly in Nice, Antibes and Monaco. Shops shut early on 24 December, although it's back to business from 26 December.

HELP ME PICK:
Côte d'Azur Beaches

It can almost feel like the whole of France has decamped south to the Côte d'Azur in the warmer months, so swarming are its main beaches with bodies. That said, there are ways to ensure a relaxing, rather than harried, experience: arrive early in the morning and be gone before lunch, fork out for a sunlounger at a private beach, or make the effort to access out-of-the-way local haunts. As soon as you slip into the refreshing Mediterranean Sea, you won't want to leave it.

Where to Swim if You Love...

Loungers & Cocktails

Baia Bella France's first carbon-neutral private beach, according to Allcot, uses organic ingredients, solar panels to heat water and rainwater to water plants. In Beaulieu-sur-Mer. *baiabella.com*

Plage Keller On Cap d'Antibes' legendary Plage de la Garoupe, once the playground of Hemingway, Picasso and Fitzgerald. *plagekeller.com*

Castel Plage Nice's oldest private beach is LGBTIQ+-friendly and catches the day's last rays of sunshine. *castelplage.com*

La Guérite The only way to access this beach club on the Île Ste-Marguerite is by boat. Expect a glam crowd, with the odd celeb mixed in. *restaurantlaguerite.com/cannes*

Le Club 55 (p840) *The* beachclub that started it all on St-Tropez' buttercream Plage de Pampelonne. Prime celeb spotting. *club55.fr*

Public & Free

Plage des Sablettes Menton's beloved beachfront strip, where the sand is fringed by restaurant terraces, a playground and a wide, smooth footpath for rollerblading and scooters.

Plage des Marinières (pictured left) Finer pebbles than Nice and a train station just footsteps away make Villefranche-sur-Mer's public beach prime real estate on summer days.

Plage Publique de l'Opéra Play volleyball by day or lay out a picnic with friends at night on this popular, pebbly stretch of public beach across from Vieux Nice.

Plage de Pampelonne (p840) Yes, this iconic beach has plenty of public spots to sunbathe for free. Sand is soft and the water is superb. Perfect for all the family.

Shh...Locals Only

Crique des Pêcheurs This hidden cove at the foot of Monaco-Ville is bliss for a refreshing dip at low tide.

Coco Beach It's not your classic beach, but the translucent water at Nice's craggy eastern edge is ideal for snorkelling.

Plage de la Darse Pebbly beach sheltered from the cruise-ship crowds near the port of Villefranche-sur-Mer. Also great for snorkelling.

Calanque de Maubois (p833) Hidden cove along the Corniche d'Or with crystalline waters and red pebbles that match the ochre-red Esterel mountains that frame it. Accessed by steep steps.

Plage des Sablettes

HOW TO

When to go Private beaches dust off their sunloungers for another season from around April. By October, everything is packed neatly back away until next summer.

Book ahead Beach loungers fill up, particularly in July and August, so make sure you phone in advance to guarantee your space.

Budget The cost of a sunlounger is inching ever higher: be prepared to pay anywhere upwards of €25 for a day.

Another tip Expect to shell out more if you want prime front-row placement. Most private beaches also offer half-day bookings, too.

Pebbles or Sand?

Rather than soft sand, Nice's beach strip is covered in smooth pebbles, some as big as the palm of your hand. Intriguingly, the city trucks in whole container loads to cover the beach afresh every March! Their official name is *galets* (one of the private beaches is named for them). These *galets* aren't particularly comfortable to walk on, nor, to be honest, to lie on, which is why a pair of jelly shoes and a thick straw beach mat are smart investments before your summer vacation to the city. Further towards Italy, especially around Villefranche-sur-Mer and Beaulieu-sur-Mer, the *galets* make way for smaller, softer stones. If you find any sand, such as along Monaco's **Plage du Larvotto**, it's safe to assume that it's been imported.

If your holiday dreams hinge on buttercream sandy beaches, the best bet is to base yourself somewhere west of Antibes. Fluffy fine sand can be found in Antibes, Juan-les-Pins and Golfe-Juan, Cannes and all along the Var coastline. So beautiful is **Plage de Notre Dame** (p849) on the Île de Porquerolles that it's widely cited as a slice of the Caribbean in the Mediterranean.

One more tip: it can be frustratingly hard to find sunscreen in supermarkets before April, so pack some in your suitcase if warm weather is on the horizon.

Nice

BEACHES | ART | FOOD

☑ TOP TIP

The tram from Nice Côte d'Azur Airport to the centre is a flat €10 return fare. If you're travelling light, consider walking the 6km along the Promenade des Anglais. The wide, beachfront pedestrian promenade is a delightful introduction to Nice's outdoor lifestyle. There's also a bike lane – pick up a shared e-bike (p810) at the airport.

The capital of the Côte d'Azur, Nice has undergone a complete refresh in the last decade or so, with investments in a smart tram network, upgraded civic areas and new hotels – and the pace of change doesn't look like it's going to slow down anytime soon. Don't be surprised to find certain landmarks from past visits closed for renovation, or even torn down, as concrete makes way for greenery in France's fifth-largest city.

As the UNESCO Winter Resort Town of the Riviera, the city has a new purpose and swagger. Nice is no longer living off its reputation for beaches, palm trees and sunshine. An exciting food scene is simmering, bringing local produce and traditional cuisine to the fore, alongside cool wine bars and independent boutiques in trendy yet local neighbourhoods such as the Port and Libération. Visit today and you'll realise that Nice is finally growing into its nickname, Nissa la Bella.

Soak up Nice's Protected History

A UNESCO World Heritage Site

Nice's UNESCO heritage can be seen in around 800 buildings across the city, and their art deco detailing and Belle Époque

GETTING AROUND

Ditch the car on your visit to Nice. Driving in the centre is a frustrating experience as streets have been dug up and replaced by leafy bike lanes, and street parking has become the hottest commodity in town. Many of the main highlights can be navigated on foot – although Ligne d'Azur's tram line and extensive bus network are also blessings for weary feet. Tickets (€1.70 single fare) are paperless, so be prepared to fork out an extra €2 on your first trip for the city's transport card, La Carte, available at ticket machines and booths (Android users can download a card directly on the Ligne d'Azur app). From the airport, the tram fare is €10 return. Near the airport, the Grand Arénas has emerged as the main transport hub, where most intercity bus lines begin. Gare de Nice St-Augustin-Aéroport is also on the site for trains to Cannes and Menton, and the stations in between.

View from Colline du Château

flourishes can be admired from the street. The excellent Explore Nice Côte d'Azur app *(explorenicecotedazur.com/en/discover-the-unesco-heritage-routes)* organises some of the most noteworthy sites into a series of self-guided neighbourhood walks, complete with a pop-up historical outline of each building listed. You can also deep dive into this protected heritage at the **Musée Massena** *(massena-nice.org; adult/child €10/free)* on the Promenade des Anglais. Much of the permanent collection is dedicated to the history of Nice; the 19th-century romantic landscapes of the city and its surrounds painted by the trio of Trachel brothers are particularly worthy of contemplation.

Nice's First Settlement

Ruins with a view

The Ancient Greeks didn't set up base on the **Colline du Château** for the sea views, but the site of Nice's original settlement offers up the best panorama of the city. The rocky outcrop that sits snuggly between Vieux Nice and Port Lympia has witnessed every era of the city; during the Middle Ages, it was the fortified settlement at the base of which today's *vieille*

continued on p810

WHEN WINTER WAS THE HIGH SEASON

Before the Côte d'Azur became the place to sun yourself in summer, this stretch of the Mediterranean coast was the winter destination du jour for royalty, politicians, aristocrats and artists from Britain, northern Europe and Russia, who flocked here for its mild climate and winter sun and to stroll in their glad rags along the newly paved Promenade des Anglais (English Promenade). The most famous visitor was Britain's Queen Victoria; so beloved were her sejourns here that, on her deathbed in England, she apparently remarked, 'If only I was in Nice, I should recover'. The rich architectural legacy from this period (1760–1940) saw Nice inscribed on the UNESCO World Heritage list in 2021 as the Winter Resort Town of the Riviera.

You'll want to return for the comfort of the chicken pie alone!

 EATING IN NICE: OUR PICKS

Lavomatique: Trendy bistro in Vieux Nice where shared plates are cooked in an open kitchen and washed down with natural wines. *noon-1.45pm & 7-10pm Tue-Fri, 7-10pm Mon* €€

Babel Babel: Cuisine from around the Mediterranean, served right across from the Mediterranean. Don't miss the panisse with homemade za'atar. *10am-midnight Mon, Thu & Sun, to 2am Fri & Sat* €€

Le Bistrot de Jan: More casual sibling to the Michelin-starred Jan next door. The decor is straight from a design magazine. *noon-3pm & 7pm-12.30am Tue-Sat, 11am-3pm Sun* €€

Le Canon: Unpretentious neighbourhood favourite with a hyper-local focus: each farmer is named on the menu. *noon-2pm Mon, Tue, Thu & Fri, 7.30-11.30pm Mon-Fri* €€

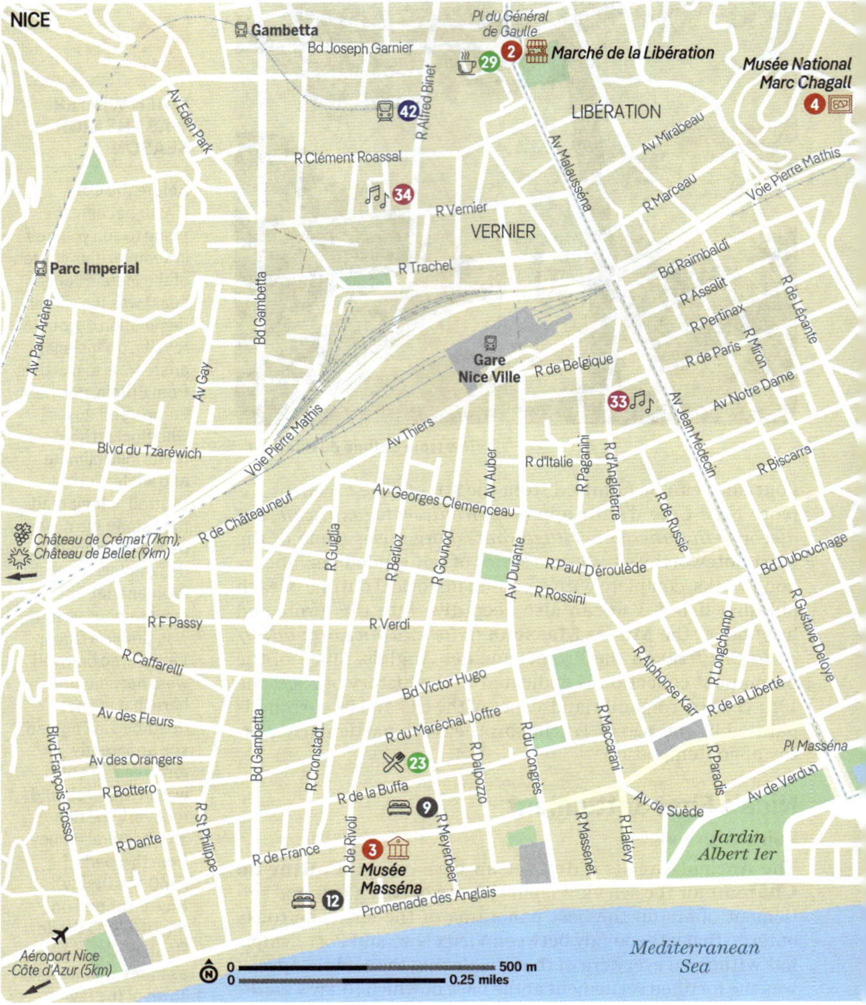

HIGHLIGHTS
1. Colline du Château
2. Marché de la Libération
3. Musée Masséna
4. Musée National Marc Chagall

SIGHTS
5. La Tour Bellanda
6. Musée d'Art Moderne et d'Art Contemporain
7. Palais Caïs de Pierlas
8. Palais Lascaris

SLEEPING
9. Hostel Meyerbeer Beach
10. Hôtel La Pérouse
11. Hôtel Rossetti
12. Le Negresco

EATING
13. Acchiardo
14. Babel Babel
15. Café Paulette
16. Chez Pipo
17. Chez René Socca
18. Chez Thérésa
19. Kalös
20. La Merenda
21. Lavomatique
22. Le Bistrot de Jan
23. Le Canon

	DRINKING & NIGHTLIFE	29 L'Altra Casa	35 Opéra de Nice		TRANSPORT
		30 Le Café des Chineurs	36 Shapko		41 Colline du Château Lift
24	Cave Bianchi	31 Rouge	● SHOPPING	42	Gare de Nice-CF de Provence
25	Cave de la Tour	see 26 SuperBar	37 Cours Saleya Flea Market		
26	Comptoir Central Électrique	32 Wayne's Bar	38 Maison Auer		
27	La Civette du Cours	● ENTERTAINMENT	39 Nicolas Alziari		
28	La Part des Anges	33 La Cave Romagnan	40 Pêche Locale		
		34 La Zonmé			

LIME VS PONY

You'll notice two different brands of shared bikes being pedalled around: Lime *(li.me)* and Pony *(getapony.com)*. Both are unlocked and locked via their own apps, which also show the closest available bikes to you. Both bikes come with a convenient saddle at the back, should you need to carry a passenger. Pay per ride: for e-bikes, the rate is set at €1 to unlock and between €0.23 and €0.26 per minute. Pony's option to privatise a bike for four hours for €19.99 or 24 hours for €29.99 is a good choice. Save for the colour, there's little discernible difference between either the quality of the bikes or their availability at designated pick-up and drop-off spots, so download one app and stick with it.

Promenade des Anglais

continued from p807

ville (old town) sprung up. Louis XIV ordered the castle destroyed in the early 18th century, and it became a park at the end of the 19th century.

The site reveals its secrets as you follow its shaded pathways towards a grassy plateau that is a favourite picnic spot for locals; think centuries-old stone walls covered by climbers, as well as the occasional excavation site. The views over the terracotta-red rooftops of the city are what steal the show, particularly from **La Tour Bellanda** viewpoint. Plenty of staircases sprout from the back alleys of Vieux Nice to the hilltop; there's also the free **Colline du Château Lift**, operating 10am to 5.25pm. It's also from here that Nice's midday cannon (read: a firework) is set off at noon every day!

Cycling the Prom

Take Nice's public e-bikes for a ride

The combo of Nice's public e-bike fleet and the dedicated, flat bike lane that extends the entire 6km length of the Promenade des Anglais (and then some) is one of the city's best pairings. The Prom is scattered with bike pick-up and drop-off points. Propelled by the battery and the fresh sea air, you'll

DRINKING IN NICE: BEST WINE BARS

Rouge: Sleek spot just back from Port Lympia serving up stylish, modern tapas plates, washed down with organic wines. *noon-10.30pm*

Cave de la Tour: A soundtrack of 1940s jazz, an interior that has hardly changed since then and Nice wine by the glass. A Vieux Nice institution. *8am-2.30pm & 6-8.30pm Tue-Sat, 8am-12.30pm Sun*

La Part des Anges: A treasure trove of natural and organic wines in the city centre voted best wine bar in France in 2020. *10am-8.30pm Mon-Sat*

Cave Bianchi: History seeps out of every nook of this atmospheric Vieux Nice wine shop and bar across from the Opera. *9.30am-7.30pm, to 10.30pm Fri & Sat*

reach **Aéroport Nice-Côte d'Azur** in less than 20 minutes (if starting out at the eastern end opposite the arcades of Vieux Nice), but you can easily stop along the way and lock your bike on the app until you're ready to get cycling again. If you're in the groove, push further west on the same path for pretty beachside towns St-Laurent du Var or Cagnes-sur-Mer. In fact, you can pedal all the way to Antibes (p829) – a total distance of 20km.

Chagall & Matisse in Nice
Two masters and their museums

It is a truth universally acknowledged that the light on the Côte d'Azur has an allure unlike anywhere else in the world. Countless artists have been drawn to the region in search of it: two in particular have left their mark (or, perhaps it's the other way around?): Marc Chagall and Henri Matisse. Dedicated museums to both artists occupy sprawling grounds in Cimiez, the leafy residential neighbourhood in the north of Nice, and can be visited on the same day. Start at the **Musée National Marc Chagall** (musees-nationaux-alpesmaritimes .fr/chagall; adult/child €10/free), where the most extensive public collection of the Belarusian artist's work hangs. The 12 monumental canvases depicting scenes from the Old Testament are spellbinding in colour and detail and will linger in your memory long after you've left. A further 20 minutes' walk (or Ligne d'Azur bus 5) and you'll arrive at the **Musée Matisse** (musee-matisse-nice.org; adult/child €10/free). The array of paintings, sculptures, drawings and prints trace the artist's love affair with Nice. The setting, in a coral-red Genoese villa dating from the 17th century, is magic, with olive groves and ancient ruins. Matisse is buried in the **Monastère Notre Dame de Cimiez** at the eastern end of the parkland. The serene monastery gardens are worth a detour, too. Both museums are closed Tuesdays.

Morning Markets
Antiques and fresh produce

Bright and bustling, Nice's morning markets are worth waking up early for. On Mondays, the **Cours Saleya Flea Market** takes over Vieux Nice's busy restaurant-lined thoroughfare, filling every corner with antique stands peddling vintage posters, tableware and other curios. Don't be afraid to bargain

WHAT IS NIÇOISE CUISINE?

Nice's street-food culture, including classic snacks like chickpea-based *socca* and panisse, *pan bagnat* (salade niçoise in a bread roll) and *pissaladière,* an onion-topped dough, is based on the colourful vegetables and legumes that thrive in the poor, water-deprived soils of the Mediterranean coastline. It feels closer to Italy in nature and flavour than the heavier, sauce-based cuisine of northern France. The city brims with cheap and cheerful street-food stops, as well as more classic local bistros. If you see the Cuisine Nissarde sticker displayed proudly at a restaurant's entrance, you know their dishes respect local culinary traditions. Beyond the traditional addresses, a new wave of trendy chefs is putting a fine-dining twist on local dishes, elevating them to a semi-gastronomic standing.

Despite the name, merda de can is simply green gnocchi!

 EATING IN NICE: BEST NIÇOISE ADDRESSES

Chez Pipo: The point of reference for fresh-from-the-oven *socca* in Nice for over 100 years. *11.30am-2.30pm & 5.30-10pm Wed-Sun* €

Chez René Socca: This cheap and cheerful Vieux Nice institution is the classic Niçois street-food stop. *9am-9pm Tue-Sun* €

Acchiardo: Atmospheric, family-run favourite in the heart of the old town with local specialities like *merda de can* on the menu. *noon-2pm & 7-10pm Mon-Fri* €

La Merenda: Wonderfully rustic dining room with only 24 seats and a blackboard of Niçois specialities. Book: lamerenda.net or @lamerendanice. *noon-1.45pm & 7-9pm Tue-Fri* €

BEST EVENTS IN NICE

Carnaval de Nice: For two weeks in late February and early March, floats and flower battles take over the streets. One of Europe's brightest carnivals, running since the Middle Ages.

Lou Queernaval: France's first queer carnival runs adjacent to the Carnaval de Nice; expect glitter, dazzling floats and drag queens.

Nice Jazz Festival: Jam-packed four-night calendar of performances in Jardin Albert Ier and fringe concerts popping up all around town.

Pink Parade (Pride): Crowds swarm Nice's main streets for July's Pink Parade (Pride); the afterparty lasts all night.

Noël à Nice: Sip bubbles with fresh oysters and ride on a giant Ferris wheel: Nice lights up in festive delight during December.

– strongly – if something takes your fancy. From Tuesday to Sunday, the *brocante* is swept away, replaced by baskets brimming with fresh fruit, veg and flowers. Do like the locals and shop according to the season, so sweet pears in autumn and juicy tomatoes in summer. These prices, however, are fixed. For the city's quintessential market experience, make a beeline for the **Marché de la Libération** in the Libération neighbourhood in the north of Nice. Long considered the city's best because it serves locals every day but Monday, no matter the season. All markets start around 7am and are packed away just before 1pm.

The Coolest Street in Town

Bars, restaurants and the LGBTIQ+ scene

The strip and the surrounding streets around **rue Bonaparte** are Nice's hip LGBTIQ+ district, having earned the nicknamed *le petit Marais*, a nod to Paris' famous bohemian gay quarter. A part of the road is painted in blue, à la San Francisco's Castro District, and the stretch between place Garibaldi and place du Pin is now fully pedestrianised. This is where you should head if you are looking for a guaranteed evening buzz, as new bars or restaurants are always opening – just remember that you're still in the provinces, and even the most lively bars shutter by 1am, particularly out of season.

Taste Nice Wine

Nice's hidden vineyards

Interspersed between the Provençal villas of Nice's western flank are nine boutique vineyards that form the Bellet AOC. Not only is this postage-stamp-sized appellation – with just 50 hectares of vines – one of France's smallest, but it's also the only one in the country to fall within city limits. Two grape varieties grown here – folle noire and braquet – don't grow anywhere else in the world. These aren't the sprawling estates you'll find in major wine regions, and many still have a *'vin de garage'* feel.

The two largest producers offer a delightful perspective of the city's history alongside a comprehensive visitor experience. **Château de Bellet** *(chateaudebellet.com)* is the oldest of the Bellet vineyards, and 45-minute tours in English run daily (€20, including three wines, book ahead) and start from an intimate private chapel built by the Barons of Bellet in 1873. **Château de Crémat** *(chateaucremat.com)* is housed in a

EATING & DRINKING IN NICE: RUE BONAPARTE PICKS

Comptoir Central Électrique: With its bohemian vibe, exposed walls and mismatched seating, this is the bar that started it all on rue Bonaparte. *9am-12.30am*

SuperBar: Super-stylish newbie with a cocktail menu that goes well beyond the tried and tested. *5pm-1am*

Kalōs: Soak up the buzz on the cheap at this Mediterranean street-food eatery specialising in oh-so tasty pitas. *11.45am-2.45pm & 6.30-10.30pm, closed Sun* €

Café Paulette: Perennial favourite, partly because it's whatever you need it to be: cool cafe, lively lunch spot or chic wine bar. *8am-12.30am Tue-Sat, 9.30am-5pm Sun* €€

A COLOURFUL MEANDER THROUGH VIEUX NICE ON FOOT

A wander through the pastel-pretty Vieux Nice, the city's pedestrian old town, on foot is one of the highlights of any trip to the Côte d'Azur.

START	END	LENGTH
14 rue St-François de Paule	place St-Augustin	1km, 30mins

This colourful meander through Nice's charming old town starts outside the warm yellow façade of ❶ **Nicolas Alziari**, a local olive-oil producer whose distinctive blue tins grace the region's top restaurant tables. The flat stretch of street surrounding the grand 19th-century ❷ **Opéra de Nice** is home to some speciality shops worth browsing for a local souvenir. Continue straight ahead to the ❸ **cours Saleya**, the city's lively restaurant-lined strip and setting for fragrant fresh produce and flower markets and an **antique market** (p811). Take a left turn to head deeper into the busy, labyrinth-like alleyways. On rue Doite, the wood-fired oven at ❹ **Chez Thérésa** has been baking *socca* since 1925 (fresh platters are also cycled down to a stand at the cours Saleya markets). The gentle rise is barely noticeable as you continue towards ❺ **Palais Lascaris**, a fresco-adorned 17th-century noble house turned museum and wonderfully preserved example of Baroque architecture. At the next corner, another history lesson awaits, if you can spot it. The heavy ❻ **cannonball** attached to the wall was fired by Turkish forces in 1543 during the Siege of Nice. The city managed to repel the forces and history has turned a local washerwoman called Catherine Ségurane into the heroine of the victory. In ❼ **place St-Augustin**, after a slight uphill stretch, you'll find a plaque in her honour.

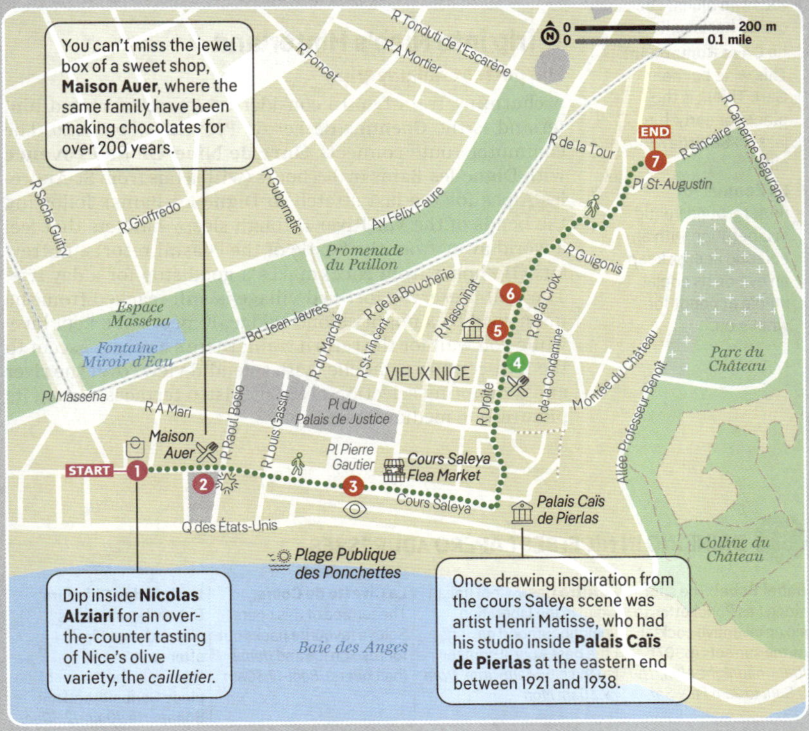

You can't miss the jewel box of a sweet shop, **Maison Auer**, where the same family have been making chocolates for over 200 years.

Dip inside **Nicolas Alziari** for an over-the-counter tasting of Nice's olive variety, the *cailletier*.

Once drawing inspiration from the cours Saleya scene was artist Henri Matisse, who had his studio inside **Palais Caïs de Pierlas** at the eastern end between 1921 and 1938.

towering, terracotta-red, faux-medieval fortress dating from 1906. Its interlocking C's motif is said to have inspired the logo of Coco Chanel, who is known to have spent glamorous evenings on its vast terrace during the Roaring Twenties. You can decide if the tale is fact or fiction, but the possibility does make a fascinating theme for the 1½-hour-long tour through the property. The visit concludes with a tasting – how many wines dictates the price of the tour (three for €30, six for €35).

Happy Hour
Sunset drinks in the city

Come 5pm, under the glow of the late afternoon sun, Nice's residents flock to the nearest terrace for an *apéro*, as the pre-dinner apéritif is more colloquially known. It's an easy habit to slip into during your visit. Prime *apéro* spots can be broken down into four main areas. Along the **cours Saleya** in Vieux Nice, chilled rosé and thirst-quenching pints are served with a side of people-watching, particularly in the cluster of cafes and restaurants at the eastern end. Just outside, along **Les Ponchettes**, a series of beachfront bars have balconies positioned perfectly to catch the last of the afternoon sun: many people find nothing beats a DIY *apéro* on the beach. For a local vibe, head to the **Libération** neighbourhood above the main train station.

A Trip into Nice's Hinterland
The perfect rail day trip

A charming train trip to consider into Nice's forested hinterland is the Chemins de Fer de Provence *(cpzou.fr)*. The commuter route connects **Gare de Nice-CF de Provence** with Digne-les-Bains in 3½ hours (with a bus from St-André-les-Alpes for the last stretch to Digne-les-Bains), following the bends of the Var River through sleepy hamlets that feel a world away from the bustle of the coastal resorts. Entrevaux (1½ hours from Nice) makes a good stop for a day trip. The well-preserved fortified village is still reached from the main road by a mighty stone bridge. Expect to be kept busy while you wait for the return train: there's a sporty ascent to the 17th-century Citadelle, with splendid views over the river and a tempting selection of shady bistro terraces among its picturesque medieval streets.

LIVE MUSIC IN NICE

Did Kwo is a local guitarist and songwriter who has played in bars and restaurants across the city. He shares his top spots for live music in Nice.

Wayne's Bar: This fun English pub in Vieux Nice is the spot to find cover bands playing favourite party songs to get people dancing on the tables.

Shapko: A great late-night bet in Vieux Nice for jazz, soul, R&B and blues. The crowd here is all ages.

La Cave Romagnan: This wine bar near Gare Thiers is the place for early-bird jazz on Saturday night.

La Zonmé: An underground venue in Libération with an eclectic lineup; keep an eye on its social media account for what's on.

 DRINKING IN NICE: BEST APÉRO ADDRESSES

Babel Babel: The spot along Les Ponchettes to sip an inventive cocktail as the sun sets (p807). *10am-midnight, Mon, Thu & Sun, to 2am Fri & Sat*

L'Altra Casa: Cool Italian joint in the Libération neighbourhood mixing the best Aperol spritzes in the city. *6am-11pm, from 9.30am Mon*

La Civette du Cours: The terrace of this cours Saleya favourite packs out for rosé on ice and *demis* (half beers). *8am-12.30am*

Le Café des Chineurs: Boho vibe and tapas plates draw a hip after-work crowd to this bar at the corner of place Garibaldi and rue Bonaparte. *10am-12.30am*

Beyond Nice

Nice's surrounds brim with postcard-pretty resort towns, eagle's-nest villages, energising hiking trails and unexpected alpine experiences.

You don't have to travel too far from Nice to feel like you've left the big city behind; in fact, the pace turns down a few notches as soon as you arrive in Villefranche-sur-Mer, a charming fishing village joined to Nice at its eastern hip. The trio of sublime corniches, or coastal roads, layered between Nice and Monaco weave through Belle Époque coastal resorts, pass eagle's-nest villages and open onto lush hiking trails. They merge together in Italianate Menton, the last huff of France before the Italian border. Nice's backcountry destinations like St-Martin-Vésubie and the dramatic pre-alpine landscapes of the Parc National du Mercantour are having a moment, too.

Places

Villefranche-sur-Mer p815

St-Jean-Cap-Ferrat p816

Èze p817

Roquebrune-Cap-Martin p820

Menton p820

St-Martin-Vésubie p821

Vallée de la Roya p822

Villefranche-sur-Mer

TIME FROM NICE: **20MIN**

La Flânerie in Villefranche-sur-Mer

Irresistibly photogenic Villefranche-sur-Mer starts at Nice's eastern edge but is a world away from the buzz of the big city. This is small village life, where locals catch up on gossip at the Wednesday and Saturday morning produce markets or play pétanque in the shadow of the high-walled 16th-century **Citadelle St-Elme**. The pedestrian streets of Villefranche's old town are ideal to awaken your inner *flâneur* – someone who strolls in a leisurely manner.

Start by admiring the green thumbs of residents along rue Volti and rue Baron de Brès, who have turned their pastel-palette façades into delightful street gardens that have become impromptu settings for social media shoots. Staircases down to the water frame views of the glistening sea. Just before the waterfront, rue de Poilu is a hub of activity with restaurants and small, lavender-fragranced boutiques selling floaty dresses and wide-brimmed straw hats. One street down, **rue Obscure** is a 130m-long vaulted alley that offers a shadowy glimpse into the village's medieval past. The whimsical brushstrokes of Jean Cocteau cover the walls and ceilings of the must-see **Chapelle St-Pierre**, telling the story of Villefranche's fishing traditions.

GETTING AROUND

When the train runs to timetable, the TER Sud line makes small work of travel times between Nice and coastal stops and takes a supremely scenic track built right on the coast. The bus network is the best bet for St-Martin-Vésubie. To really dive deep into the sublime lower alpine landscapes of the Côte d'Azur, you'll need your own transport; whether car or bike is up to you.

BIKE CLUB

For serious road cyclists, the mountain passes behind Nice are bucket-list rides. The most mythical of all is the 925m Col de la Madone, made famous as Lance Armstrong's pre-Tour de France fitness test. *Café-vélos*, or cyclist cafes, are popping up across France as places not only for good coffee, but also to connect with others who are passionate about the sport and to participate in scheduled rides. In Nice's **Café du Cycliste** *(cafeducycliste.com)*, join in on a weekly group ride or set off on your own on an itinerary that starts from its doorstep into the hinterland. Road and gravel bikes are available to hire. It also sells its own branded sportswear.

Villa Ephrussi de Rothschild

St-Jean-Cap-Ferrat

TIME FROM NICE: **30MIN**

Belle of the Belle Époque

There's nowhere better to appreciate the ornate Belle Époque beauty of the Côte d'Azur than at **Villa Ephrussi de Rothschild** *(villa-ephrussi.com; adult/child €18/12)*, one of the great architectural treasures of the coast. As soon as you set foot inside the pink-and-white villa, sitting high atop the leafy – and incredibly wealthy – peninsula of Cap-Ferrat, which juts out into the Mediterranean with the bays of Villefranche-sur-Mer and Beaulieu-sur-Mer on either side, you'll be swept back to a time when Louis XVI furniture and Fragonard paintings were the height of fashion. Commissioned by socialite and art collector Baroness Béatrice Ephrussi de Rothschild and completed in 1912, the elaborate two-storey residence is frozen in time with original furnishings and decorations, which a free audio guide provided at the entrance explains in detail. Don't rush the nine themed gardens that fan out from the villa, an enchanting landscape of sweeping stone staircases, rose-covered pergolas and even a theatrical fountain. The sea views framed by crumbling stone pillars and olive groves are sublime.

 EATING IN VILLEFRANCHE-SUR-MER: OUR PICKS

La Voile Bleue: This simple shack on the beach serves some of the best *pan bagnat* on the coast from April to early autumn. *9am-10.30pm, to 7.30pm Sun & Mon* €

Lou Bantry: Of the water's-edge restaurants, Lou Bantry stands out for its menu of Niçois classics and reasonable prices. *8am-6pm, to 7pm Sat & Sun* €€

Bistro de l'Étoile: A village favourite set back from the waterfront with a sunny terrace and a fresh menu of home-cooked treats. *noon-2pm & 7-10pm Tue-Sat* €€

Achill's: Good grub, but the real star here is the rooftop terrace that grooves till early in the morning on hot summer nights. *9am-1.30am* €€

See the Sea

Plenty of boat rental and excursion outfits can get you out on the water beyond Nice, but few and far between are those that offer the opportunity to sail up to 35km off the coast on board a replica 16th-century wooden Mediterranean trading boat – and help safeguard the ocean along the way. For over three decades, local association **SOS Grand Bleu** (*sosgrandbleu.asso.fr*) has fought for the protection of dolphins and whales in the Mediterranean. In 2005, it took possession of the 23m *Santo Sospir* sailing yacht. For €65 per person (€45 for children under 12), you can jump on board this beautiful vessel for a full-day group outing (maximum 20 passengers) in search of these majestic marine animals. Pack your own picnic lunch, sunglasses, hat, sunscreen and swimming costume. April to November only.

Èze

TIME FROM NICE: **30MIN**

Exotic Flowers

Although you'll increasingly need to swerve around selfie-stick-wielding visitors as you meander through it, the **Jardin Exotique d'Èze** (*jardinexotique-eze.fr*; adult/child €5/free) is still one of the region's most delightful experiences. Around the ruined 12th-century château above the terracotta rooftops of the village, a peaceful cactus garden grows: it's more than worth the entry fee for the sweeping sea views that extend beyond Cannes alone.

Hike the Nietzsche Trail

You can drive the three corniches (p818), or you can scramble up them on foot on the **Sentier Nietzsche**, an old mule track connecting Èze-bord-de-Mer and Èze Village. Named for German philosopher Friedrich Nietzsche, who found inspiration to complete the third part of *Thus Spoke Zarathustra* while walking it, the 3.8km trail can be tackled from top down, but the classic departure point is across the road from the Èze train station on the Basse Corniche. BYO water: it's a steep ascent from the coast on a well-defined yet rocky path that winds through Mediterranean shrub and feels far from civilisation.

After about 45 minutes, you'll emerge at the base of medieval Èze Village on the Moyenne Corniche. To return, either hike back down to the train station or catch the Ligne d'Azur bus 82 back to Nice from Èze Village, bearing in mind that this is probably the busiest bus stop along the whole of the Côte d'Azur.

BEST PERCHED VILLAGES

Gorbio: Shaded by a 300-year-old elm tree in the main square, Gorbio is a classically beautiful Provençal village.

Castillon: Quirky artists' village rebuilt on a new site in the 1950s after it was destroyed first by an earthquake and then war. A rock-climbing paradise.

Ste-Agnès: Soaring 800m above Menton, Ste-Agnès claims to be the highest coastal village in Europe. Showstopping views and a sweet medieval garden crowning the scene.

Peillon: Half the adventure is getting to Peillon, in the Nice hinterland, on a twisty mountain road. Book ahead for lunch at **Auberge de la Madone**.

Roquebrune: A splash of orange buildings and terracotta rooftops seemingly stuck to the cliffside. Views to Monaco – and France's oldest tree.

 EATING IN ÈZE & CAP FERRAT: OUR PICKS

Le Cabanon Cap Ferrat: Among all the mansions is this no-frills kiosk on the coastal path in St-Jean-Cap-Ferrat. Light bites and fresh ceviche. Summer only. *10am-7pm* €

Deli' Èze Village: Atmospheric al-fresco salad bar near the entrance to the Jardin Exotique d'Èze. Walk-ins only; be prepared for a short wait for a lunch table. *9am-6pm* €

Château Eza: Michelin-starred modern French cuisine and jaw-dropping views. *The* special occasion spot on the Côte. *noon-2pm & 7.30-9.30pm* €€€

Restaurant Béatrice: The original dining room of the Villa Ephrussi de Rothschild is delightful for a light lunch or afternoon tea. *11am-5.30pm, to 6.30pm Jul & Aug* €€

ROAD TRIP

Driving the Three Corniches

Three corniches (coastal roads) cling to the cliffs between Nice and Monaco: the Basse, Moyenne and Grande Corniche (in order, the lowest, middle and highest). With a new favourite vista around every bend, the views of the Mediterranean can be a distraction, but thankfully there are plenty of lookout points. You could drive this route without stopping in under an hour, but that would mean skipping many of the Côte d'Azur's crown jewels.

❶ Mont Boron

Begin at Nice's wooded eastern fringe, the **Parc Forestier du Mont Boron**. This urban forest is a hikers' favourite, but you can park close to the 16th-century Fort du Mont Alban for scene-stealing views across the bay of Villefranche-sur-Mer – a taster for the road ahead.

The Drive: This fairly flat 5km stretch of the Basse Corniche hugs the coast. Stop for photos at the Mémorial Princesse Grace viewpoint at the entrance to Villefranche-sur-Mer.

❷ Villefranche-sur-Mer

Villefranche-sur-Mer's **Citadelle St-Elme** (p815) looms tall at the entrance to the small harbour, but don't let the immense walls scare you off: inside, a charming sculpture garden blooms under the nurturing touch of the Mediterranean sea breeze.

The Drive: Continue along the low road for a further kilometre, before turning left onto av Léopold II, a narrow road that winds up to the Moyenne Corniche. Settle in for a scenic 5km stretch to Èze.

Jardin Exotique d'Èze

3 Èze

Parking can be tricky but this isn't a stop to miss: snuggled into a rocky nest nearly 500m above the sea, Èze is a Côte d'Azur sparkler where the narrow medieval streets all lead to one place, the **Jardin Exotique d'Èze** (p817), a multi-level garden that sprouts among the ruins of the old château.

The Drive: Not long after leaving the village, turn left onto the route de la Turbie to head even higher above the sea. At the top, merge onto the Grande Corniche and La Turbie will appear around the first bend.

4 La Turbie

So high is La Turbie that the village often sits in a soft cloud. When it clears, you can clearly make out three countries from the **Tête du Chien** viewpoint: France, Monaco and Italy. You can't miss the **Trophée d'Auguste**, a victory monument raised for Roman emperor Augustus. Even better: the buttery croissants at **Ma Première Boulangerie**, some of the best in the region.

The Drive: Staying on the Grande Corniche, the road twists and turns for 5km as you sweep around Monaco.

5 Roquebrune-Cap-Martin

A huddle of rich red and warm yellow buildings clinging to the cliffside, Roquebrune-Cap-Martin's medieval village is another of the Côte d'Azur's most charming perched sites, just without the hordes of tourists like Èze. Park up at the entrance then head off on foot to explore the warren of alleyways: look out for the signs leading to the 10th-century **Château de Roquebrune** (and France's oldest tree!).

Roquebrune-Cap-Martin

TIME FROM NICE: **30MIN**

Le Corbusier's Château

Le Corbusier called it his Château on the Côte d'Azur: a small 14 sq metre pinewood cabin at the water's edge in Cap Martin. Now a UNESCO World Heritage Site, the **Cabanon Le Corbusier**, as it's known, remains the only structure that the Swiss-born architect designed for himself. It was built as his summer residence in 1952 on a strip of land adjacent to **Villa E-1027**; the latter was designed by his friends, Irish interior decorator Eileen Gray and Romanian-born architect Jean Badovici. An early example of modernist architecture, the villa dates from 1929 and has been meticulously restored to Gray's original vision, down to a faithful replica of the door handles. The ensemble of the site – including the Étoile de Mer, the neighbouring bar shack owned by Thomas Rebutat, and its five holiday cabins designed by Le Corbusier – now goes by the name of **Cap Moderne** *(capmoderne.monuments-nationaux.fr; adult/child €19/10)*. An excellent two-hour guided tour of the four buildings departs on foot daily at 10am and 2pm from a hangar at the Gare Cap-Martin-Roquebrune train station between April and October. Arrive 15 minutes early to have a chance to browse the informative exhibition inside. Booking well in advance is encouraged; make sure you select the English-language visit. Le Corbusier had a heart attack swimming off the rocks outside his cabin in 1965 and is buried in the cemetery in medieval Roquebrune village, 300m above his beloved 'castle' on the coast.

Menton

TIME FROM NICE: **40MIN**

A Day at the Lemon Farms

Arguably the most delightful way to whittle away a day on the Côte d'Azur is by visiting **La Ferme des Citrons** *(lafermedescitrons.fr; adult/child €39/25)* citrus farm, where the warm golden yellows of the sun and the fruit set against the bright blues of the sky and the sea are a superb, all-natural mood enhancer. The excursion starts at a central meeting point in Menton in the morning, where a 4WD awaits you for a short yet steep drive to the farm. After an hour-long guided tour through avocado trees, olive groves and, of course, lots of lemon trees, you are allowed ample time to relax on a sunny terrace with a shaded children's play area and nature's best views. A tasty Niçoise lunch is included in the price of the

---

MENTON'S PRECIOUS LEMONS

There's something about the mountains-meets-sea microclimate of Menton, the last curve of France before the Italian border, that encourages lemon trees to thrive. Historically a mainstay of the town's economy, a combination of factors saw the decline of production in recent years. Happily the crop is undergoing a renaissance and today the *citron de Menton* is feted anew for its sweet taste and impressive size. During February's annual **Fête du Citron** celebrations, the streets around the waterfront light up yellow and orange. Tickets are required for the street parades of floats and flamboyantly dressed dancers, but you won't need to pay a cent to admire the giant citrus displays sculpted to a different theme every year in the central Jardins Biovès.

 EATING HIGH ABOVE THE COAST: OUR PICKS

Le Righi: The terrace views from this Ste-Agnès institution might be the best of any restaurant on the Côte d'Azur. Best for big plates of fresh pasta. *9am-6pm Thu-Tue* €

L'HarTmonie: This *bistrot de pays* in Castillon supports employment for people with disabilities. Emphasis on regional cuisine. *9am-4pm Wed-Sun, 6-10pm Sat* €

Le Beauséjour: Local fare in a dining room straight out of a French country magazine, overlooking Gorbio's beloved elm tree. *noon-2.30pm Thu-Tue Mar-Oct, dinner Jul-Aug* €€

La Grotte & l'Olivier: Prince Albert of Monaco is known to frequent this friendly bistro built into a rock in Roquebrune's medieval village. *10am-11pm Wed-Mon, closed Wed lunch* €€

Citrus sculpture, Fête du Citron

visit, before your 4WD transfer back to town mid-afternoon. Request an English-speaking guide when booking.

Enchanting Gardens

Considered the green lung of the Côte d'Azur, Menton dazzles with its remarkable gardens. Those with evergreen opening hours include **Jardin Botanique du Val Rahmeh** *(jardin botaniquevalrahmehmenton.fr; adult/child €8/6),* just back from the beach towards the Italian border, where over 1700 different species bloom in this 120-year-old terraced garden, originally designed for British general Sir Percy Radcliffe (closed on Tuesdays). From the waterfront, a narrow road snakes towards the entrance to **Jardin Serre de la Madone** *(serredelamadone.fr; adult/child €15/11)* on the road to Gorbio. Ponds, pergolas and plenty of statues decorate this charming garden that dates to 1924, when Anglo-American Laurence Johnston started planting flora here collected from his world travels (closed Mondays). A handful of other delightful gardens are open sporadically and for guided visits only – visit Menton's **tourist office** for up-to-date programming and availabilities.

St-Martin-Vésubie

TIME FROM NICE: **1HR 10MIN**

Indoor & Outdoor Adventure

The coastline and the sea blues might steal the limelight, yet over 80% of the Alpes-Maritimes, the French *département* which lies in the Côte d'Azur's embrace, is actually mountain

NICE'S ALPINE SIDE

If you only have time to visit one village in Nice's alpine hinterland, make it St-Martin-Vésubie, also known as *La Suisse Niçoise* (Nice's Switzerland) for its green setting and pretty wooden chalets situated 1000m above sea level north of Nice. In 2020, lives were lost and buildings and bridges washed away when Storm Alex struck the Vallée de la Vésubie and the neighbouring Vallée de la Roya. The scars are still very evident, as you will notice by the boulder-scattered landscape and presence of bulldozers and other construction equipment, but the community is showing its mountain spirit as it rebuilds after the devastation. Your support and spend is an enormous boost to their efforts – but you'll get something back, too.

EATING IN MENTON: OUR PICKS

Le Mirazur: A mere 20m from the Italian border, Mauro Colagreco's three-Michelin-star address is farm-to-table perfection – priced accordingly. *12.15-2pm Thu-Sun, 7.15-10pm Wed-Sun* €€€

Halles Municipales: Pick up a feast of seasonal fare at Menton's covered food market near the seafront. *8am-1pm* €

Le Bistrot des Jardins: *Bistronomique* (fine dining in a bistro setting) address with a delightful patio garden and fresh, seasonal flavours. *noon-2.15pm & 7-9.30pm Tue-Sat, noon-2.30pm Sun* €€

Mitron: Colagreco's organic bakery is bringing France's forgotten flours back to the bakehouse; a divine lemon tart is another speciality. *8am-7pm Tue-Sat, to 3pm Sun* €

terrrain. Pretty St-Martin-Vésubie is a hiking haven and a great jumping-off point into the Côte d'Azur's alpine interior. From here, you can pick up numerous trails through the flora- and fauna-rich valleys of the **Parc National du Mercantour**, a magnificent national park that encompasses 679 sq km, stretching from the Côte d'Azur into Haute-Provence. In the company of friendly English-speaking guides from **Guides06** *(guides06rando.com)*, you'll uncover the best mountain paths to get up close to majestic chamois and whistling marmots. The village is also home to the excellent **Vésubia Mountain Park** *(puremontagne.fr/en/to-see/vesubia-mountain-park; prices vary depending on activity)* an indoor adventure-sports centre where kids and adults scale climbing walls, kit up for canyoning or tackle the rooftop adventure course. Consider reserving tickets online in advance during summer months.

Vallée de la Roya

TIME FROM NICE: 1HR 30MIN

Valleys of Wonder

Tens of thousands of engravings, some of horned animals and others of humans, dating from the Neolithic and Bronze Age are carved into stone in two mysterious valleys around 2000m above sea level north of Nice: the **Vallée des Merveilles** and **Vallée de Fontanalba**. These smooth rock canvases are framed by a majestic landscape of mirror lakes and rocky slopes. It's a setting that gives the name the Valley of Wonders a dual meaning. The carvings can be visited from the end of May to the beginning of October and are reached after two (Fontanalba) to four hours (Merveilles) of walking from car parks in Les Mesches or Casterino near Tende in the Vallée de la Roya. Plan and book ahead to stay overnight at the **Refuge de Merveilles** *(refugedesmerveilles.ffcam.fr)* and **Fontanalba** *(refugedefontanalbe.com)*. You can hike two marked discovery trails independently, although to really experience the full scope of the whole site, including engravings not on the hiking routes, arrange a registered guide *(vallee-merveilles.com)*. In Tende, don't miss **Musée des Merveilles** *(museedesmerveilles.departement06.fr; free)* just across from the train station, with its large visual displays and artefacts that trace the history of these valleys.

France's Sistine Chapel

A 20-minute drive from Tende, just outside the village of La Brigue, the **Sanctuaire Notre-Dame-des-Fontaines** *(adult/child €4/free)* is an astonishing 15th-century church nestled in nature that has been dubbed the Sistine Chapel of the Southern Alps for the detailed frescoes that cover every inch of the 220 sq metre interior. There's no electricity or lighting, which only adds to the ethereal atmosphere inside the intimate chapel – although you also need to time your visit before daylight starts to fade. Visits must be reserved in advance with **La Brigue Tourist Office** *(menton-riviera-merveilles.fr)* so someone can be on site to meet you. From the tennis court in the village, a marked walking trail leads to the chapel if approaching on foot. Plan for 1½ hours each way from the village.

TRAIN DES MERVEILLES

The commuter train that connects Nice with the communities of the Vallée de la Roya is known as the Train des Merveilles (Train of Wonders), and for good reason. The route carves a dazzling course through deep gorges, pine forests and rushing cascades, and feats of engineering include dizzying viaducts, plenty of tunnels and spiral loops. Completed in 1928, the track once connected Nice with Italy, but now French trains only go as far as Tende. In late 2024 the line closed for maintenance; while replacement buses are running, they don't compare with the beauty of the train line, which should be operational again in mid 2026. When it is, here's hoping the live commentary in both French and English (daily June to September, weekends only in April and October) also returns.

Cannes

ISLANDS | CINEMA | BEACHES

Cannes is the host with the most; not content to hold just one world-leading industry affair a year – yes, Cannes Film Festival, we're looking at you – the conference and event schedule is so busy that dates spill out from the calendar most months. It's a place that always feels on and dressed in its global party best, pushing local traditions and experiences into the wings as a consequence.

Yet despite first impressions, including superyachts crowding the bay and luxury cars double-parked outside the designer boutiques of the town's iconic waterfront boulevard La Croisette, Cannes is an old Provençal soul, as the traditional fishing boats bobbing in the harbour or the battered courgette flowers cooked fresh in the Marché Forville bear witness. And, in a world now celebrating what makes each destination unique, this understudy is starting to shine.

GETTING AROUND

The centre of Cannes is mostly flat and, with La Croisette as a point of reference, easily walkable – although the landscape does get a little hilly around Le Suquet. If you're driving, don't rely on street parking. Follow signposts to central parking stations, including **Parking Palais**.

Festival Fever

Roll out the red carpet

For two weeks every May, Cannes rolls out the red carpet for a galaxy of stars during the annual **Festival de Cannes** (the Cannes Film Festival). The harbourfront **Palais des Festivals et des Congrès** is the epicentre. For the remainder of the year, the gloss barely fades. Follow the trail of over 400 stars who have cast their handprints in stainless steel along the **Chemin des Étoiles** (path of stars) outside the Palais. Dates for tours *(adult/child €6/3)* inside the Palais are only scheduled six weeks in advance by the **tourist office** (conveniently housed in the building), depending on the upcoming event calendar, and are only in French. When visits do run, you're given a 1½-hour behind-the-scenes insight into one of cinema's most legendary venues.

☑ TOP TIP

Over 140 annual festivals and events, including June's Cannes Lions International Festival of Creativity and the MIPs (MIPCOM, MIPIM and MIPTV), mean accommodation books up early and hotel prices often rise sky high. If there's an event on during your visit, consider staying outside of town.

CANNES CÔTE D'AZUR & MONACO

CANNES

★ HIGHLIGHTS
1. La Croisette
2. Marché Forville

SIGHTS
3. Église Notre-Dame de l'Espérance
4. La Malmaison
5. Le Suquet des Artistes
6. Musée des Explorations du Monde
7. Palais des Festivals et des Congrès

SLEEPING
8. Banana's Camp
9. Hôtel de Provence
10. Hôtel Le Mistral

EATING
see 2 Dr Mezze
11. Le Pompon
12. Poissonnerie Forville
see 2 Rotisserie de Forville
see 2 Socca'nnes
see 2 Soupe Poisson Forville

DRINKING & NIGHTLIFE
13. Bar Fouquet's
14. Maison Grenache

INFORMATION
15. Tourist Office

TRANSPORT
16. Horizon Ferries
17. Parking Palais
see 16 Planaria Ferries
see 16 Trans Côte d'Azur Ferries

Le Suquet

A Village in a Town

Art and viewpoints

Meaning 'summit' in Provençal, Le Suquet is Cannes' oldest neighbourhood and relaxes with its sleepy charm. Feel the crowds and the big-name bling of La Croisette fade into the distance as you wander the quiet streets stretching up from the western edge of Le Vieux Port. Loops of colourful village houses with floral balconies are crowned by a cluster of historic attractions, including the medieval castle of the monks of the Îles de Lérins that now, as the **Musée des Explorations du Monde** *(cannes.com; adult/child €6.50/free)*, harbours treasures from all four corners of the world. Outside the entrance, the Cannes selfie sign is deliberately angled to capture a stunning view of the bay, although you can go one better by scaling what's left of the castle ramparts in front of the 17th-century **Église Notre-Dame de l'Espérance** around the corner.

LA CROISETTE, RENEWED

The scaffolding is coming down in autumn 2026 on **La Croisette**, after the iconic waterfront strip completes its biggest renovation since the 1960s. The trendy (and pricey) beach bars and designer boutiques haven't changed, nor have the quick and easy food kiosks and the public chess boards. New features to watch out for as you stroll the palm-shaded strip include public benches in the form of waves, much more greenery and a new event space, Le Théâtre de la Mer. Look down at the ground: the all-new pavers reflect the rich red of the Massif de l'Esterel mountains that frame Cannes' western edge.

EATING & DRINKING IN CANNES: OUR PICKS

Poissonnerie Forville: Bustling fish counter outside Marché Forville serving fresh-from-the-sea treats such as oysters and sea urchins (in season). *7am-2.30pm Tue-Sun* €€

Le Pompon: A menu of creative small plates that changes daily with the season. Colourful ingredients and beautiful presentation. *lunch & dinner Tue-Sat* €€

Bar Fouquet's: Many a business deal is done at the Hôtel Barrière Le Majestic over an artful cocktail where homemade bitters, jellies, even edible perfumes, are standard. *10am-midnight*

Maison Grenache: Atmospheric wine bar next to the Marché Forville with ultra-knowledgeable owners. *9am-5pm, to 10.30pm Fri & Sat*

Abbaye de Lérins

TOP EXPERIENCE

Îles de Lérins

When you're shoulder-to-shoulder with crowds on La Croisette, it's hard to believe that a pocket of Cannes exists where the buzz of doing business is replaced by the sweet smell of pine and the gentle sound of waves. Yet such a spot exists and, if you look up and out to sea, you'll spot it: the Îles de Lérins, the two islands off the mainland.

DON'T MISS

Fort Royal

Musée du Masque de Fer et du Fort Royal

Écomusée Sous-Marin de Cannes

Abbaye de Lérins

Vineyards of Île St-Honorat

Forteresse de St-Honorat

Action-Packed Île Ste-Marguerite

Of the duo, Île Ste-Marguerite feels more action-packed, and that's not only because it's inside the 17th-century **Fort Royal** where the mysterious man in the iron mask was incarcerated under the orders of King Louis XIV. You can stand inside the exact cell – and learn about the island's strategic importance – when you visit the Musée du Masque de Fer et du Fort Royal, which is an easy walk from the ferry pier. The island is much bigger than its monastic neighbour; the coastal loop is 9km long, although wide pine-scented alleys cut through its centre, too. The best swim spots are on the southern side, facing Île St-Honorat. Weekends are particularly popular with families

PRACTICALITIES

- cannes-france.com/decouvrir-visiter/iles-de-lerins/sainte-marguerite ● cannes-ilesdelerins.com/fr ● Accessible year-round

and groups of friends making the crossing from Cannes to picnic and swim in shallow waters.

Underwater Museum
At depths of 3m to 5m below sea level, an underwater gallery of seafloor sculptures by Jason deCaires Taylor sits off the southern coastline of the Île Ste-Marguerite. The six submerged statues of the **Écomusée Sous-Marin de Cannes** stand 2m high and depict the faces of residents of the city. The renowned British underwater sculptor has chiselled their profiles out of pH-neutral marine-grade cement, a textured material on which marine life can set up home. Located between 84m and 132m from the shore, the site can be accessed for free from the island. BYO mask and snorkel.

Serene Île St-Honorat
By contrast, peaceful Île St-Honorat is privately owned by a community of monks. A group of 25 work and pray away from prying eyes and, although much of the 19th-century Abbaye de Lérins is closed to the public, you are allowed into the church and to participate in Mass (11.25am Tuesday to Saturday and 9.50am Sunday). Plan about an hour to complete the shady, eucalyptus-fringed loop that skims the circumference of the island, passing small chapels scattered amid the woodland and even two furnaces built at the command of Napoléon Bonaparte to heat cannonballs. After extensive renovations, the **Monastère Fortifié**, what remains of the original monastery, was set to reopen in summer 2025 (at the time of research). Jutting protectively into the sea at the southern edge of the island, it dates from the 11th century.

Holy Wines
Unlike on its bigger neighbour, vines thrive in St-Honorat's soil. Once a month, you can learn why during a short vineyard tour and tasting of two wines. Book your tickets for this **Journée Vignes-Vins** *(cannes-ilesdelerins.com; €25)* in advance on the website. The price includes the return ferry.

Getting There & Away
Boats leave Cannes from the western side of the harbour and take 15 to 20 minutes. Due to construction works, the three ferry operators are based in temporary structures on quai St Pierre just opposite the Canopy by Hilton Cannes hotel. **Trans Côte d'Azur** and **Horizon** run ferries to Île Ste-Marguerite *(adult/child €18.50/12.50)*, while **Planaria** *(cannes-ilesdelerins.com; adult/child €22/14)* shuttles back and forth from Île St-Honorat. Ferry times vary depending on the season; check the websites for latest timetables. Frustratingly, there's no inter-island ferry, so to visit the pair of them, you have to return to Cannes first.

SLEEPING & EATING ON THE ISLANDS

Centre International de Séjour Îles de Lérins: This hostel inside Île Ste-Marguerite's fort is mainly for school groups although the general public can reserve a bunk on weekends from April to early November.

La Tonnelle: The only restaurant on Île St-Honorat. The feet-in-the-sand setting comes with fine-dining prices. Reserve in advance (there's also a snack bar inside for takeaway paninis and drinks).

TOP TIPS

Book online Horizon and Planaria offer cheaper tickets (a euro or so less) if brought in advance online.

Take your rubbish with you Neither island has any rubbish bins, so be prepared to leave with everything you came with.

Limited food outside of the season Apart from a small snack bar on Île Ste-Marguerite, most food outlets shutter over winter, so pick up a picnic from Marché Forville before you board the ferry.

Kayak If you prefer to tackle the 1.3km that separates Île Ste-Marguerite from Cannes' Palm Beach yourself, **Sea First Kayak** *(seafirst.fr)* rents out kayaks. A full day's hire costs €35.

Shop like a Local

Cannes' covered market

Skip the supermarket and make your way instead to **Marché Forville**, behind Le Vieux Port. Open Tuesday to Sunday from 7.30am to 1pm, Cannes' covered produce markets are an explosion of juicy fruit, plump vegetables and food stalls serving up cuisine from around the world, although upgrades currently underway mean half the space is cordoned off. Seasonality rules, so depending on the time of year, fill your basket to the brim with ruby-red strawberries from nearby Carros or pungent black truffles snuffled out from the neighbouring Var – or grab lunch to take away. On Mondays, the space brims with curios for the weekly Marché de Brocante flea markets.

Watersports HQ

Zippy Zodiac excursions and water toy hire

A cluster of boat tour and watersport operators emerge from their off-season hibernation at the start of April around **Port du Béal**, on the sandy stretch of beach heading west out of Cannes. Think of the small marina as your adrenalin HQ. For parasailing adventures and to play captain for the day by taking out a small boat *sans permis* (without a licence) – even as far as the **Îles de Lérins** (p826), there's BoatEvasion *(location-bateaux-cannes.com/port-du-beal)*; for superhero-inspired eFoils, head to eFoil Côte d'Azur *(efoilcotedazur.fr, €150/hour)*. Most fun for all the family are Black Tenders' 12-seater semi-rigid Zodiacs that zip in and out of the secluded rust-red coves along the Corniche d'Or on a 1½-hour excursion *(blacktenders.fr; €45)* stopping along the way for refreshing swims in peacock-coloured waters. Departures are late afternoon and early evening to avoid the heat of the summer sun.

BEST ARTS EXPERIENCES & EVENTS

Festival d'Art Pyrotechnique: Countries from around the world compete to win the best firework show crown. Six nights in summer.

Les Plages Électroniques: Epic three-day dance festival on the beach with eight stages and over 50,000 festivalgoers. In August.

Musée Bonnard: Neo-impressionist painter Pierre Bonnard (1867-1947) was known as the Painter of Happiness, and Le Cannet, at Cannes' northern fringes, was his happy place.

La Malmaison: A showcase of contemporary art in a historic, recently renovated building on La Croisette.

Le Suquet des Artistes: A small but avant-garde exhibition space in the ex-city morgue that brings local artists to the fore, with four in workshops on site.

 EATING IN CANNES: MARCHÉ FORVILLE FAVOURITES

| **Rotisserie de Forville**: Between March and late October, courgette flowers are battered and deep-fried in front of your eyes. *7.30am-1pm Tue-Sun* € | **Soupe Poisson Forville**: Alexandre Serre starts cooking big pots of fish stew before sunrise to be ready for the morning trade (pre-order bouillabaisse). *7.30am-1pm Tue-Sun* € | **Socca'nnes**: Panisse – either *au nature* (plain) or infused with flavours such as truffle, *herbes de Provence* and green olives – is the speciality here. *7.30am-1pm Tue-Sun* € | **Dr Mezze**: Aussayd Mando escaped war in Syria to build a life in Cannes. He's brought recipes from home; his fried eggplant sandwich is incredible. *7.30am-1pm Tue-Sun* € |

Beyond Cannes

Let Cannes be your springboard into perfumed villages bathed in a light that has inspired generations of artists.

The coastal roads out of Cannes lead either towards the mimosa-scented Mandelieu-La Napoule, which once exported these floaty yellow flowers to the furthest corners of Europe, or Antibes and Juan-les-Pins, neighbouring resort towns that groove to the smooth beats of jazz come summer. The pine-shaded landscapes of this coastal stretch have long been a magnet for artistic types, and this heritage can still be felt in irresistibly pretty inland villages such as Mougins, muse for Picasso, or St-Paul-de-Vence and Vence where Matisse and Chagall have left an imprint. Rising up behind them, Grasse's flower fragrances sold around the world, while the landscapes of the Gorges du Loup are simply out of this world.

Places
Antibes p829
Vallauris p830
Mougins p831
Grasse p831
Gorges du Loup p832
St-Paul de Vence p832
Vence p834

Antibes
TIME FROM CANNES: **15MIN**

Markets & Megayachts

Antibes is the quintessential Riviera resort town and mixes traditional village charm with flashy wealth: its marina, Port Vauban, is Europe's largest. You can spend a fabulous day simply pottering about in **Vieil Antibes'** colourful pedestrian streets and sampling what is arguably the Côte d'Azur's best coffee scene. The **Marché Provençal** beckons for a DIY lunch; juicy olives, garlicky tapenades (olive spreads), gooey cheeses and Corsican charcuterie are just some of the produce to tempt your taste buds (Tuesday to Sunday, daily in July and August). A walk along the ramparts offers up sublime snowcapped peaks-meets-Mediterranean sea views and leads around to the harbour. Barriers separate mere mortals from the gigayachts

---

GETTING AROUND

The train connects Cannes and Mandelieu-La Napoule, with multiple departures every hour; for Vallauris, hop on Palm Bus 9 from outside **Gare Cannes** train station. Despite its proximity, public transport between Cannes and Mougins Vieux Village is surprisingly weak; a rideshare service such as Uber should set you back around €20 each way. The train ride between Cannes and Grasse takes just half an hour; rest up as it's a 15-minute walk uphill to the perfumeries. Heading west from Cannes, the train is also the best option for Antibes and the pairing of St-Paul-de-Vence and Vence (change at Cagnes-sur-Mer for ZOU! bus 655). For the Gorges du Loup and beyond, your own wheels are recommended.

TENDER IS THE NIGHT

A century ago, before it became the postcode of choice for the world's elite, Cap d'Antibes was a playground for the Lost Generation of American writers including Ernest Hemingway and F Scott Fitzgerald. They whittled away days at **Plage de la Garoupe**, the starting point for the fabulous 5km coastal footpath, the **Sentier de Tirepoil**. The Cap's legendary five-star **Hôtel du Cap-Eden-Roc**, immortalised as the Hôtel des Étrangers in Fitzgerald's *Tender is the Night*, was another favourite hang. Fitzgerald's tome was actually written in a waterfront villa in Juan-les-Pins, which would become another five-star lodging: **Hôtel Belles Rives**. Inside the art deco stunner, the street-level Bar Fitzgerald is still furnished with some original pieces from the era.

on the appropriately named Quai des Milliardaires (Billionaires Quay), but if you are in the mood for some yacht spotting, you can ogle them from the **Bastion St-Jaume**. Here, the 8m-tall *Nomade* (2010) sculpture of a figure looking out to sea is just as attention-grabbing as the shiny boats below.

Picasso in Antibes

'If you want to see the Picassos from Antibes, you must come to Antibes to see them,' the great Spanish artist famously quipped, so do as he instructed. Picasso set up his studio inside the imposing 14th-century Château Grimaldi in the old town in 1946; it became the **Musée Picasso** *(antibesjuanlespins.com/en/discover/the-must-sees/picasso-museum; adult/child €12/free)* in 1966. The mesmerising *Ulysses and Siren*s is the headline act, although a series of still lifes depicting platters of octopus, cuttlefish and sea urchins are a charming insight into the memorable meals he enjoyed on the coast. The museum is closed on Mondays.

A Spotlight on the Sea

The all-new **Posidonia – Espace Mer et Littoral** *(antibes.fr/posidonia; adult/child €12/6)* at the tip of Cap d'Antibes is difficult to label. Part exhibition space, part aquarium, part pine forest, the common thread is the marine habitat and what we can do to better protect it. As the name suggests, the star of the show is *Posidonia* (seagrass), a vital ingredient in the Mediterranean ecosystem. It's designed to appeal to all ages: young kids will enjoy the interactive exhibits and coral-filled aquarium, and the 10-plus group will get the biggest buzz from the virtual diving experience *(€3 extra)*. Between June and September, you can also set off on guided kayak and snorkelling tours from the site; book in advance on the website.

Vallauris

TIME FROM CANNES: **40MIN**

Picasso's Purple Patch

There are prettier spots on the Côte d'Azur, but Vallauris is a worthwhile stop to browse local ceramic studios. So intertwined is the name Vallauris with ceramics that many of the street name signs are *petit* works of art. The town's most famous disciple is...you guessed it...Picasso, who came here to learn about the craft. After an hour inside the **Musée National Picasso 'La Guerre et la Paix'** *(musees-nationaux-alpesmaritimes.fr/picasso; adult/child €6/free)*, you emerge with an understanding of just how much of a natural the artist

EATING & DRINKING IN ANTIBES: OUR PICKS

Lilian Bonnefoi: Hip, child-friendly brunch spot next to the ramparts with photogenic plates. *hours vary Wed-Sun* €

Le Zinc: Small, stylish wine bar and bistro just steps from the Marché Provençal. A small menu of market favourites. *7-10pm Mon-Sun, 10.30am-2pm Wed-Sun* €€

Absinthe Bar: Put on a funny hat and sip the green fairy at this dimly lit cellar bar, an Antibes institution. Live music on weekends. *9am-2am*

Le Bistrot de Curé: Lunch on salads and Niçois classics at this garden bistro next to the Phare de la Garoupe lighthouse. *9am-5pm Tue-Sun* €

was with clay, firing more than 4000 pieces. The entrance ticket grants access to three museums in one and, while ceramics is the medium most celebrated, the most moving work is his immense *Chapelle La Guerre et la Paix* (War and Peace Chapel), a small, windowless 12th-century chapel with an incredible mural he painted covering every surface but the floor.

Mougins

TIME FROM CANNES: **20MIN**

Fine Dining & Fine Art

Wound as tightly as the swirl on a snail shell, Mougins' hilltop old town is a photographer's delight for snapping dreamy Provençal scenes. This sunny spot is the place for art and gastronomy, so plan enough time to indulge in both – and bring a little extra cash, as fine dining here doesn't come cheap. The polished-to-perfection medieval alleys brim with galleries and studios; the one to bookmark is **FAMM** (Female Artists of the Mougins Museum) *(famm.com; adult/child €16/5)*. The four floors are an incredible visual journey celebrating pioneering women in art. Standout canvases include the impressionist works by Monet's step-daughter and daughter-in-law Blanche Hoschedé-Monet.

Grasse

TIME FROM CANNES: **35MIN**

Follow Your Nose in Grasse

Grasse's status as the world capital of perfume was cemented with the awarding of UNESCO's Intangible Cultural Heritage status in 2018. A trio of local fragrance houses dominate this sprawling town stretched out high in the hills above Cannes. With its historic factory at the entrance to the pedestrianised old quarter, **Fragonard's Usine Historique & Musée du Parfum** *(fragonard.com)* is the most visible. See original extraction and distilling equipment up close during the free 20-minute guided visits of the factory floor, while the two upper levels of the building are given over to a gorgeous boutique and small self-guided perfume museum. An easy 10-minute walk away on bd Victor Hugo, the cherry-red *bastide* (country house) of **Molinard** *(molinard.com)* features a glass roof constructed by Gustave Eiffel and a similar complimentary tour. Heading out of town, the **Galimard** *(galimard.com)* factory along the route de Cannes also offers free guided visits. Hands-on experiences are the real highlight when in Grasse, allowing you the chance to play perfumer for anywhere between 20 minutes to an hour. You can reserve workshops at

GRASSE'S PERFUMED GARDENS

Grasse's garden of perfume flowers includes the rose de Mai, the base of the most iconic of scents, Chanel N°5. Jasmine grandiflorum is the other emblematic flower of Grasse's perfume industry and is hand-harvested at dawn to capture its powerful yet sweet fragrance. Grown higher up in the plateaus and mountains behind Grasse, lavender's herby hints are a highly prized addition to many scents, while the intensely fragrant, sensual white bell-shaped tuberose is said to have been a particular favourite in the court of the Sun King, Louis XIV. The world's greatest perfume flowers grow a 20-minute drive from Grasse in the enchanting **Jardins du MIP** *(jardinsdumip. museesdegrasse. com; adult/child €4/ free)* in Mouans-Sartoux.

EATING & DRINKING IN MOUGINS: OUR PICKS

Le Petit Fouet: Frogs' legs, terrines, foie gras and duck: classic French in a relaxed setting. Also popular for breakfast. *9am-1.45pm & 6.30-9.45pm, Fri-Tue* €€

Resto des Arts: Artsy restaurant serving up cool cocktails and modern-French cuisine. *7-10pm Mon-Sun, noon-12pm Sat & Sun* €€

La Cave de Mougins: Chic wine bar with a sunny terrace at the entrance to the village; tasting boards to nibble on. *11am-late, from 6pm Wed* €

Bohème: Fabulous fine dining at the entrance to the village. Fine cuts of beef cooked on embers are a speciality. *noon-2pm & 7-10pm Tue-Sat* €€

CANYONING IN THE GORGES DU LOUP

Lionel Richard is a climbing and canyoning guide with Bureau des Guides LesGeckos *(lesgeckos.eu)*. Here's why he says the Gorges du Loup is paradise for outdoor sports.

Le Pont du Loup is the launching pad for incredible hiking, swimming, rock climbing and canyoning adventures. Most of the rock-climbing sites are for experienced climbers, although the Belvédère site is suitable for beginners. Canyoning is our most popular activity during summer. On a half-day excursion, we begin at the bottom of the Courmes waterfall and abseil into the gorge, followed by plenty of jumps and slides – at one point, you get to plunge 8m into the water below! Our half-day tours take about three hours and are for ages eight and up.

all three perfume houses online; Molinard's setting is particularly atmospheric. In a high-ceiling, monochrome-tiled room, you'll mix and match dozens of top, middle and base notes to create a custom scent to take home. A short *Petit Parfumer* experience *(ages 4 to 8, €32)* offers children an introduction to the wonder of scent.

Gorges du Loup

TIME FROM CANNES: **50MIN**

Scenic Villages along the Loup River

From the mountain plains high above Cannes, the Loup River runs all the way down to the Mediterranean and is at its most dramatic northeast of Grasse, snaking through a landscape of plunging cliffs, perched villages, refreshing waterfalls and thick forest, an area known as the Gorges du Loup. Meaning 'wolf' in English, the Loup has given its name to a cluster of delightful villages, starting with sun-kissed Le Bar-sur-Loup, which has a rich tradition of cultivating bitter oranges. The next wolf along, Le Pont du Loup, is more hamlet than village, but the craft beer brewed at **Bacho Brewery** *(bachobrewery.com)* attracts a crowd from Nice and beyond. Set among a terrace of orange trees lit by fairy lights, this atmospheric microbrewery is the place for a quiet drink or a party night, depending on your mood. Just down the road, you can learn how clementines, rose petals and violets are crystalised and candied during a short tour at the Côte d'Azur's equivalent of Willy Wonka, **Confiserie Florian** *(confiserieflorian.com; free)*. Tourrettes-sur-Loup, closer to Vence (p834), is known as the village of violets, particularly when the flower blooms between October and March. Find out why at the charming **Bastide aux Violettes** *(tourrettessurloup.com/la-bastide-aux-violettes-horaires-visites, adult/child €2/free)*, 10 minutes' walk from the centre of town.

St-Paul de Vence

TIME FROM CANNES: **50MIN**

Walking Walls & Ramparts

Nestled in the Côte d'Azur hinterland, the artists' village of St-Paul de Vence is another of Provence's almost-too-pretty-to-be-true hilltop villages – but this magazine-spread perfection means it's also a particular magnet for tour buses. Dodge the crowds inside the walls by following the **Sentier des Fortifications Henri Layet**, a 30-minute walk around the base of the western ramparts that tells of the village's history as

EATING IN GRASSE: OUR PICKS

Les Délicatesses de Grasse: Part-restaurant, part-deli on place aux Aires with gorgeous tasting boards of cheese, charcuterie and tapenade. *10am-10pm* €

Taverne de l'Oratoire: So smart is the idea of a medieval-themed tavern in Grasse's old town that it's a wonder no one has done it sooner. Menu is meat heavy. *6pm-midnight Mon-Sun, noon-3pm Fri-Sun* €

Auberge du Vieux Château: With your own wheels, this classic address in nearby Cabris is wholly worth the detour. Location, views and French classics. *noon-2pm Wed-Sun, 7-9pm Tue-Sat* €€€

L'Imprévu: Conveniently opposite the Musée International de la Parfumerie with something for everyone and a sunny rooftop terrace. *11am-4pm Mon-Fri, 10.30am-5pm Sat & Sun* €

DRIVING THE ROUTE DU MIMOSA

Drive sweeping coastal curves through the striking, ochre-red Massif de l'Esterel on this classic Côte d'Azur road trip that shines gold with mimosa in winter and sunshine in summer.

START	END	LENGTH
Château de la Napoule	Bormes-les-Mimosas	123km; 5 hours

Start this drive along the Corniche de l'Estérel (also known as the Corniche d'Or) at ❶ **Château de la Napoule**, a medieval fortress turned art foundation in Mandelieu-La Napoule, just west of Cannes. Continue west; the road lights up in gold in winter. Depending on traffic, you'll reach pretty Théoule-sur-Mer in a handful of minutes. The soft sand of the public ❷ **Plage du Suveret** beckons for a refreshing swim, although parking is a lottery in the height of summer. Pushing on, the landscape transforms as you enter the Massif de l'Esterel, the mountain range that frames the eastern edge of the Alpes-Maritimes. The road cuts through the rich red rocks that cascade into the translucent sea below. Many of the sparkling *calanques* (small coves) are only accessible by boat, although the sheltered ❸ **Calanque de Maubois** has a small car park and a steep staircase down to the water. Park along the cheerful ❹ **Agay** beachfront strip for lunch and a quick dip. At St-Raphaël the road becomes the D559 as it winds along the coast to ❺ **Domaine du Rayol** (p843), where you can descend through its abundant gardens. Just inland is the quaint village of ❻ **Bormes-les-Mimosas** (p843), where the large nursery has 90 varieties of mimosas, especially resplendent from January to March when mimosas bloom.

The gardens of the **Château de la Napoule** (lnaf.org; adult/child €4/free) open from April to September (closed Mondays).

The strange pink building in Théoule-sur-Mer is the **Palais Bulles**, a bubble house once owned by Pierre Cardin (closed to the public).

Ferries ply the waters between Ste-Maxime or St-Raphaël and St-Tropez, a convenient way to spend a few hours in the lovely village, without a car.

BEST ART EXPERIENCES IN ST-PAUL DE VENCE & VENCE

La Colombe d'Or: You have to book a table or a room to admire the art at this five-star inn, where Picasso and Matisse once paid their bills with canvases.

Chapelle Folon: This intimate chapel glimmers in gold and pastel mosaic, the last work of Belgian artist Jean-Michel Folon.

Fondation Maeght: Find a who's-who of 20th-century artists inside this gallery. The avant-garde building and sculpture gardens are a delight.

Chemin Ste-Claire: Artists once took this delightful short path to the Fondation Maeght: a handful of tiny chapels break up the walk.

Chapelle du Rosaire: Matisse viewed this chapel in Vence as his masterpiece. The museum traces its creation through sketches, photos and texts.

---

both a military stronghold and an agricultural heartland. Cast your gaze down the flanks and you'll notice neat rows of vines. Further along, an orchard bursts with bitter orange trees while birdcalls fills the fragrant air. The path ends at the southern part of the thick medieval walls. From there, you can head into the village – but before you do, pay your respects to Marc Chagall, who is buried in the local cemetery.

Boutique Wine

Those vines you saw as you walked the base of the fortification? It's a teeny vineyard, cultivated by Domaine des Claus, a boutique biodynamic winery whose grapes are mainly grown in nearby Tourrettes-sur-Loup. While this particular parcel is not open for visitors, you can taste them, or souvenir a bottle, at **La Cave de Saint-Paul** *(cavesaintpaul.com)* inside the village. If only the walls of this subterranean cavern could talk: dating from the 14th century, it once housed the local lords' wine stash. Pull up a stool to swirl and sip a trio of the village wines for €20 (or €9 for a single glass). No reservations for this tasting necessary, but be aware this small space fills up quickly.

Vence

TIME FROM CANNES: **50MIN**

Vence Walking Tour

Unlike nearby St-Paul de Vence, tourists don't overwhelm Vence: the fact that there's no space for tour buses to park is deliberate, explains local Steve Wilkerson *(steveandcaroleinvence.com)*. During Wilkerson's 90-minute walking tours inside the walls of the old city *(adult/child €10/free)*, you'll quickly understand why the American has fallen under the charm of this well-preserved walled town: although more lived-in than its Disney-perfect neighbour, there are centuries of history on every corner, a lively market most mornings (particularly Friday and Saturday) and an impressive concentration of foodie addresses for its size, many spilling out onto atmospheric squares. Along with pinpointing the blink-and-you'll-miss-it details, such as Roman columns, medieval doorways and even the historic 'Hell' neighbourhood, Wilkerson also introduces you the **Cathédrale Notre-Dame de la Nativité** *(vence-tourisme.com/cathedrale-notre-dame-de-la-nativite; free)*, France's smallest cathedral, and many of Vence's 20 fountains. So reputed is the pure water from the local spring, La Foux, that it was nearly bottled in the early 1900s. Had that happened, the name Vence just might be as globally known as Évian.

EATING IN ST-PAUL DE VENCE & VENCE: OUR PICKS

Le Tilleul: A shady terrace and a menu of fresh flavours beckon you to settle in for a long lunch on the ramparts of St-Paul. *noon-2.30pm & 7-11pm* €€

La Colombe d'Or: Considering the artwork on display in the dining room, if this isn't worth a once-in-a-lifetime splurge, little else is. *12.30-1.30pm & 7.30-9.30pm* €€€

Les Petits Tabliers: Rustic-chic wine bar and bistro in Vence. Menu changes weekly, with local produce, including fish. Shaded rear terrace. *9.30am-10.30pm Tue-Sat* €€

Le Michel Ange: Long-standing Vence favourite serving up Niçois classics on a fountain-clad square. *noon-2pm Tue-Sun, 7-9.30pm Fri & Sat* €€

St-Tropez

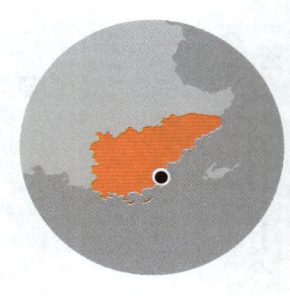

GORGEOUS TOWN | HOT BEACHES | GLAMOUR

Sexy St-Tropez might be the most desired destination on the Côte d'Azur and a byword for lithe, tanned bodies dancing on tables at trendy beach bars along buttercream Plage de Pampelonne, but it hasn't always been the jet-set magnet it is today. The sleepy fishing village was thrust into the global spotlight in the 1950s, when a young Brigitte Bardot filmed *And God Created Woman* here. It was as if a switch had been flicked. Now, is it even a St-Tropez summer without gleaming yachts, glitzy restaurants and designer shopping?

If bling isn't your thing, that doesn't mean you should bypass St-Tropez. Meander cobbled lanes in the old fishing quarter of La Ponche, watch games of pétanque beneath plane trees on place des Lices, fill your picnic basket at its produce market (don't forget a bottle of local rosé), or hike along the coast from beach to beach on the Presqu'île de Saint-Tropez peninsula. Just be aware: in summer, every inch of space is jam-packed.

> ☑ **TOP TIP**
>
> Bike or take a shuttle to the beaches – don't drive. *The year-round shuttle (saint-tropez.fr; ticket €0.50)* from place des Lices serves **Plage de la Bouillabaisse** (p840) and **Plage des Salins** (p840). From May to October, one route includes Pampelonne.

Stroll Central St-Tropez
Soak up the history and glamour

Start your visit by promenading along the quays at the richly charming **Vieux Port** (old port), where yachts line the harbour and denizens sip coffees or cocktails from waterfront cafes.

continued on p838

 GETTING AROUND

During high season, those in the know avoid horrendous four-hour traffic bottlenecks on the one road into St-Tropez (and €40 scarce parking) by parking in nearby Port Grimaud, Ste-Maxime or Cavalaire and taking a **Les Bateaux Verts** (p841) shuttle boat. **Les Bateaux Bleus** serve St-Raphaël, Fréjus and Agay. **Trans Côte d'Azur** has ferries to Nice and Cannes. Pricey **sea taxis** *(taxi-boat-saint-tropez.com)* serve the gulf. By train, the most convenient station is St-Raphaël.

St-Tropez Enlargement

- 28 Chez Camille
- 29 Gourd'l Saint-Tropez
- 30 La Petite Plage
- 31 La Ramade
- 32 La Tarte Tropézienne
- 33 Le Sporting
- 34 Le Traiteur de l'Auberge des Maures

● **DRINKING & NIGHTLIFE**
- 35 Gaio
- see 4 Hôtel Bar Le Sube
- 36 La Cabane Méditerranée
- 37 Le IO51
- 38 Le Club 55
- see 24 Le Tigrr
- see 23 Les Caves du Roy
- 39 Sanctum
- 40 Sénéquier

● **SHOPPING**
- 41 K.Jacques
- 42 La Pause Douceur
- 43 La Vieille Mer
- 44 Le Dépôt
- 45 Les Galeries Tropéziennes
- 46 Les Maîtres Vignerons de la Presqu'île de St-Tropez
- 47 Place des Lices Market
- 48 Rondini

● **INFORMATION**
- 49 Tourist Office

● **TRANSPORT**
- 50 Les Bateaux Bleus
- 51 Trans Côte d'Azur

continued from p835

Sable-coloured townhouses glow in the sun, and the **Bailli de Suffren statue** of a 17th-century naval hero, cast from a 19th-century cannon, peers out to sea.

Once you've snapped all the pics you want, shrug off the harbour's buzz and wander back into St-Tropez' historic fishing quarter, **La Ponche**, to the northeast. Place Garrezio sprawls east from 10th-century Tour Suffren to place de l'Hôtel de Ville. From here, rue Guichard leads southeast to sweet-chiming **Église de St-Tropez**, a quintessential St-Tropez landmark. Building began in Italian Baroque style in the 17th century and was completed in 1784. Inside, look for the bust of St Torpes, namesake and patron of the city.

Follow rue du Portail Neuf south to the 1645 **Chapelle de la Miséricorde** and continue on to St-Tropez' legendary, charming central square, **place des Lices**, studded with plane trees and cafes. Linger and watch the pétanque players, and jostle with the crowds at the twice-weekly **market** *(8am-1pm Tue & Sat)*, jampacked with everything from fruit and veg to antique mirrors and sandals.

St-Tropez Fashion Spree

Indulge in stylish elegance

Most global luxury brands have a boutique somewhere in the narrow streets of St-Tropez. But look past the flashy names and you'll discover some unmissable shopping spots. As in Capri and Menorca, St-Tropez has its own signature sandal: **Rondini** *(rondini.fr)*. For over 80 years, the Rondini family has been crafting high-quality leather sandals. Their flagship model, the gladiator, is available in both low-cut and ankle-wrap versions and is exclusively made-to-measure.

It's a good alternative to **K Jacques** *(kjacques.com)*, handcrafting sandals since 1933 for such clients as Picasso and Brigitte Bardot.

Les Galeries Tropéziennes *(galeriestropeziennes.com)* has been a mainstay in St-Tropez shopping life since 1903. On one side, a practical space brings together everyday accessories (haberdashery, metre fabrics, brushes, household linen), the other side is an emblem of St-Tropez elegance (swimsuits, espadrilles, cashmere sweaters, straw hats and tableware). Bargain hunters should visit **Le Dépôt** *(ledepot-saint-tropez.com)*, a chic boutique of secondhand and vintage designer clothes and accessories.

EXPLORE RIVIERA ART

Art lovers will easily find inspiration throughout the village. Whet your appetite at **Musée de l'Annonciade** *(saint-tropez.fr; adult/child €6/free)* which showcases an impressive collection of modern art infused with that legendary Côte d'Azur light. In a gracefully converted 16th-century chapel you can browse the collection, from pointillist Paul Signac to Cubists Georges Braque and Picasso, and Fauvist artists including Derain and Matisse. If marine nostalgia is more your vibe, delve into La Ponche's narrow lanes to reach **La Vieille Mer** *(06 74 07 91 46)*, a cavern of treasures from the sea. Ships' lanterns, wheels, telescopes, clocks and all forms of marine memorabilia are on display. Generally, art shops and galleries are open April to October.

 EATING & DRINKING IN ST-TROPEZ: WITHOUT BREAKING THE BANK

Au Caprice des Deux: Traditional *maison de village* (stone townhouse) is a local fave, with award-winning chef Stéphane Avelin. *7.30pm-midnight Wed-Mon* €€

Gourd'I Saint-Tropez: Friendly Italian *épicerie* (grocery), where daily pasta specials and charcuterie platters are always delish. *9am-10.30pm* €€

La Ramade: Old-fashioned Provençal hospitality at this terraced bistro with great French service. *noon-3pm & 7pm-1am Tue & Sat, 7-9pm Mon, Wed-Fri & Sun* €€

Le Sporting: There's a bit of everything on the menu at this always-packed bar-bistro, and it's one of St-Tropez' more reasonably priced spots. *7am-2am* €

Tarte Tropézienne (orange-blossom sponge cake)

Stock Your Picnic Basket
Delectable delicacies

St-Tropez' twice-weekly **market** is a must, but don't leave town without sampling *tarte Tropézienne*, an orange-blossom-flavoured double sponge cake filled with thick cream, created by Polish baker A Mickla in 1955. His smart, lively cafe-bakery **La Tarte Tropézienne** (*latartetropezienne.fr*) is the originator, and you'll see branches all over the region. For a more rarefied experience, visit **La Pause Douceur** (*instagram.com/la_pause_douceur_st.tropez*), run by a local family. This irresistible little shop sells delicious homemade chocolates, biscuits and sweet treats. To stock your picnic basket with more than just sweets, pop over to **Le Traiteur de l'Auberge des Maures** (*instagram.com/le.traiteur.de.lauberge*), where you can browse the homemade takeaway meals, from charcuterie to potatoes *gratin* and buy by the kilo.

A Guide to St-Tropez Beach Clubs
Get your toes in the sand

Beach clubs first took off in St-Tropez in the 1950s, when a 22-year-old Brigitte Bardot turned the town into a popular

ROSÉ AT THE SOURCE

Mas de Pampelonne: Excellent, crisp rosé from 15 hectares of the verdant St-Tropez Peninsula. Find it a few hundred metres inland from Plage de Pampelonne. *masdepampelonne.com*

Château de Chausse: Another superb rosé producer, near La Croix-Valmer. *chateaudechausse.fr*

Vignobles de Ramatuelle: Modern tasting room in the heart of St-Tropez wine country, also specialising in rosé. *vignoblesderamatuelle.com*

Château Minuty: Family-run winery with a warm welcome, just north of Gassin. *minuty.com*

Les Maîtres Vignerons de la Presqu'île de St-Tropez: Not a tasting opportunity, but a shopping roundup of regional vineyards, near roundabouts west of St-Tropez. *vignerons-saint-tropez.com*

 EATING & DRINKING AROUND ST-TROPEZ: DINING WITH THE IN-CROWD

La Vague d'Or: Triple-starred gastronomic temple from chef Arnaud Donckele at Cheval Blanc St-Tropez. *7.30-9.30pm Thu-Tue May-Sep* €€€	**Chez Camille:** Former 1913 fishing cottage turned beachside restaurant famous for wood-grilled fish/bouillabaisse. *noon-2.30pm & 7-10pm Apr-Sep* €€€	**La Petite Plage:** Luxurious, cool dishes, an oyster bar and caviar in boho-chic style, smack on the harbourfront. *noon-2.30pm & 7pm-3am* €€€	**Hôtel Bar Le Sube:** Nab a table on the balcony overlooking the harbour to see the swishy action while sipping a sunset *apéro*. *8am-1am*

Plage de Gigaro

BEACHES OF PRESQU'ÎLE DE ST-TROPEZ

Plage de Pampelonne: Luxurious, long white-sanded beach lined with celebrity-rich beach clubs.

Plage des Salins: A 600m-wide pine-fringed beach at the southern foot of Cap des Salins; served by a shuttle year-round.

Plage de Tahiti: Famous nudist beach, also a naturally magnificent sandy stretch, 4km southeast of St-Tropez.

Plage de Gigaro: Local favourite for unscripted beach days on the southern edge of the peninsula.

Plage de la Bouillabaisse: Just west of town, it can get busy, but it's convenient and kid-friendly.

Plage de La Ponche & Plage de la Fontanette: More for views than swimming; start of Sentier du Littoral.

destination for the rich and famous. Since then, there's been no turning back. This seaside scene revolves around sandy clubs and restaurants, all with their own style. Most are open May to September, and advance bookings are highly recommended. Beaches also have public areas where you can lay down your towel.

The 5km-long, celebrity-studded **Plage de Pampelonne** is the most famous of the beaches and has the largest selection of exclusive clubs and restaurants. It's the place to see and be seen – you'll want to reserve a lounger and lunch. Lined with clubs, it's about as 'hot European summer' as you can get, with neat rows of picture-perfect parasols and chairs lining the coast. Atmosphere? Indulgence, glitz and relaxation. **Le Club 55** (leclub55.fr) is the longest-running Pampelonne club, originally the crew canteen during *And God Created Woman* and still catering to incognito celebs. Nikki Beach (nikkibeach.com/sttropez) is favoured by dance-on-the-bar glitterati, and those who just want to be seen. For a more chill vibe, try **Le 1051** (le1051.com), one of the newer clubs (2018) and popular for some of the best food on the strip.

Looking for a quieter beach experience without sacrificing luxury? Book ahead for **La Cabane Méditerranée** (lacabanemediterranee.com; loungers from €30), on the edge of

 DRINKING IN ST-TROPEZ: SUNSET COCKTAILS

Pearl Beach: Keep things classic with an Apérol spritz at this chic Plage de la Bouillabaisse bar, perfect for a sunset drink. *10am-4pm*

La Cabane Méditerranée: Try a Cabana spritz with curaçao, lime and prosecco; Plage d'Héraclée near Gigaro. *10.30am-7pm, to 9.30pm Fri & Sat*

Hôtel Cheval Blanc: Pricey cocktails but a once-in-a-lifestyle mixology experience, with a rarified sunset view. Plage de la Bouillabaisse. *9am-late*

Le Tigrr: Escape the crowds at laid-back Ermitage Hotel, with enchanting views of the rooftops of old St-Tropez and the sea. *5pm-midnight Apr-Oct*

Plage d'Héraclée. About 10km further south from St-Tropez, the beach is wilder than Pampelonne, and the club is tucked into the edge of a rock.

Hit the Open Seas

Set sail at sunset

Get out on the water to take in the gorgeous coast. It can be as easy as taking a ride on **Les Bateaux Verts**, with boat excursions throughout the region. Or opt for a water-skimming catamaran on Golfe de St-Tropez at sunset with **Sport Decouverte** *(sport-decouverte.com; €40)*, where you can sip an *apéro* suspended in the nets of the catamaran, sandwiched between the blues of the sea and the sparkling sky.

Coastal Walks

Amble the Sentier du Littoral to Gigaro

For a more active holiday, embark on the spectacular coastal path, **Sentier du Littoral**, as it wends past rocky outcrops and hidden bays 35km south from St-Tropez, around the peninsula to the beach at **Cavalaire-sur-Mer**. In St-Tropez, the yellow-flagged path starts at **La Ponche** (p838), immediately east of Tour du Portalet, and curves around Port des Pêcheurs, past the citadel. It then leads past the walled Cimitière Marin, Plage des Graniers and more lovely, less-crowded beaches. The **tourist office** has maps with distances and walking times (Plage des Salins is 8.5km or around 2½ hours' walk).

You can also pick it up in **Gigaro**, on the southeastern coast of the Presqu'île de St-Tropez near La Croix Valmer (17km south of St-Tropez). This seaside hamlet harbours a sandy beach, some lovely eating and sleeping options, and a watersports school. From the far end of the beach, a board maps the portion of the Sentier du Littoral that works its way around the coast to Cap Lardier (4.7km, 1½ hours) and past Cap Taillat to L'Escalet (9km, 2¾ hours).

ST-TROPEZ SUNSETS

At sunset, St-Tropez transitions from lazy beach days to wild nights. Plan the sunset moment in advance so you'll have the best seat in the house. **Plage de Gigaro** is hands-down the best sunset beach. In town, **Plage de la Bouillabaisse** is convenient for a sunset cocktail before heading home to change for dinner. But since beach bars here are usually packed, you'll only get a spot if you've been here all day. **Plage de La Ponche** and **Plage de la Fontanette** make for easy town-based views. And, for the more adventurous sunset spotters, bring your own snack and bottle to the historic **Cap Camarat** lighthouse, perched on the edge of the peninsula, a one-hour walk from Pampelonne on the Sentier du Littoral.

DRINKING AROUND ST-TROPEZ: BARS AFTER THE BEACH CLUB

Gaïo: Since 1958, the stars have come here to hit the dance floor. Order Nikkei cuisine from the kitchen if you need extra fuel. *8pm-5am*

Les Caves du Roy: Bar at legendary Hôtel Byblos is champion of St-Tropez nightclubs. Dress to impress. *11pm-5am Fri & Sat Apr-Oct, daily Jul & Aug*

Sanctum: Can't stumble back to town? Stay on Plage de Pampelonne in July and August when resident DJs take it all night long. *midnight-6am*

Sénéquier: Lounge in the iconic red chairs, harbourside, day and night, with pricey drinks and white-linen service at this St-Tropez classic. *8am-1am*

Beyond St-Tropez

Coast through flower-rich villages and gardens before diving inland into chestnut and truffle forests or offshore into vibrant marine landscapes.

Places
Fréjus & St-Raphaël p842
Corniche des Maures p843
Massif des Maures p844
Hyères p845
Cotignac p846
Aups p847
Haut-Var p847

GETTING AROUND

ZOU! buses connect St-Tropez to many nearby Var towns, including St-Raphaël and Hyères, while coastal trains serve Gare de Hyères and Gare de Saint-Raphaël Valescure. Central Hyères is best on foot while Fréjus blends into St-Raphaël and the centres are walkable. Further afield, a car is simplest, but if you're staying in a village for a few days, renting an e-bike (from €35 per day) is a great ecofriendly option.

A wild range of wooded hills, Massif des Maures is a pocket of wilderness a few miles from the coastal hustle. Around the village Bormes-les-Mimosas, the region's gardens and winter mimosa blooms are unrivalled. St-Raphaël and Fréjus are good matches for families and budget-conscious travellers, while Hyères, once a rightly acknowledged gem of the Var, is under-appreciated in the glamour-seeking mind of today's Riviera sun-chaser. Odd, when you consider its rich history and a sparkling beach scene, not to mention the fantastic Îles d'Hyères. North of the A8 autoroute is vastly different; peaceful hilltop villages like Cotignac are within easy reach of the wild Gorges du Verdon (p790). A slower pace of life, lush vineyards and earthy black truffles await.

Fréjus & St-Raphaël
TIME FROM ST-TROPEZ: 1HR
Coastal City Vibes with Beaches

Fréjus and St-Raphaël are two beach towns merging into one another 37km east of St-Tropez. Easygoing, they're worth a day's exploration.

Founded by Julius Caesar in 49 BCE, Fréjus is dotted with Roman ruins, including an amphitheatre, **Les Arènes** *(frejus.fr; free),* and aqueduct, well explored at its **Musée Archéologique** *(ville-frejus.fr; adult/child €3/free).* Visitors can also walk the town's medieval quarter, where narrow streets and picturesque buildings include 13th-century Gothic **Cloître de la Cathédrale de Fréjus** *(cloitre-frejus.fr; adult/child €7/free),* housing a unique collection of medieval ceiling frescoes. Fréjus is particularly worth a visit on Wednesday and Saturday morning, when the old-town market is in full swing. **Plage de St-Aygulf** is a popular spot for swimming and sunbathing, while **Plage de Port-Fréjus** is super central, with calm waters, sandy shores and views of St-Raphaël.

St-Raphaël briefly flourished as a Jazz-Age hangout during the 1920s and '30s, but urban sprawl has somewhat obscured its charm. It's a handy base for exploring Massif de l'Estérel – and a lot cheaper than Cannes. Take a break in the town's lively marina area or on its long stretch of sandy **Plage Beaurivage**, perfect for swimming, sunbathing and watersports. And not

Bormes-les-Mimosas

to be outdone, it has its own good **Musée Archéologique de St-Raphaël** (*ville-saintraphael.fr; admission free*). St-Raphaël's train station is the most convenient for the region, and **Les Bateaux Bleus** runs boats to/from St-Tropez.

Corniche des Maures TIME FROM ST-TROPEZ: **45MIN**

Bormes-les-Mimosas, the 12th-Century Floral Village

The Corniche des Maures (D559) unwinds beautifully southwest from La Croix-Valmer to Le Lavandou along a shoreline trimmed with sandy beaches ideal for swimming, sunbathing and windsurfing. Slightly inland, **Bormes-les-Mimosas** is the jewel in its crown. It's named after the 100-plus species of mimosa growing here, which bloom between January and March, filling the town and surrounding countryside with bursts of vibrant yellow colour. Every February, **Le Corso Fleuri Festival** celebrates the flower with bloom-covered floats.

The town's love affair with the mimosa began in the 19th century when the flower was introduced from Australia and local businesses use the flower in products such as perfumes, soaps and candles. Explore the cobbled streets of this 12th-century village to find boutiques selling these, like **Savonnerie de Bormes** (*savonnerie-bormes.com*).

Botanical World Tour at Domaine du Rayol

Spend a few hours in **Domaine du Rayol** (*domainedurayol. org; adult/child €14/10*), a unique botanical garden started in

TIPS FOR HIKING & MOUNTAIN BIKING MASSIF DE L'ESTÉREL

Local tourist offices have leaflets detailing popular walks of **Massif de l'Estérel** (*circuits.esterel-cote-dazur.com*), including Pic de l'Ours (496m) and Pic du Cap Roux (452m) and mountain-bike rides. Buy IGN's *Carte de Randonnée* (1:25,000) No 3544ET *Fréjus, Saint-Raphaël & Corniche de l'Estérel* for more serious walks. For a more informed hike, sign up for a three-hour guided walk with a forest ranger at **St-Raphaël tourist office** (*saint-raphael. com*). Access to the range is prohibited on windy or particularly hot days because of fire risks; check with the tourist office before setting off. The waterfront Corniche de l'Estérel also has a **Sentier du Littoral**.

 EATING & DRINKING AROUND ST-RAPHAËL: OUR PICKS

| **Chez Gaston**: Pavement tables, a wall of wines and hearty dishes (steak *Béarnaise*; fish soup). St-Raphaël. *11.30am-2pm Tue-Fri, 7-9.30pm Tue-Sat* €€ | **L'Entrée des Artistes**: Brothers run this intimate bistro with a front terrace overlooking a square in the historic centre. Fréjus. *noon-2pm & 7-9pm Tue-Sat* € | **Le Palais du Fromager**: Friendly cheesemongers sell great cheeses and prepare charcuterie platters on street-side tables. Fréjus. *9am-7pm Tue-Sat* € | **Villa Matuzia**: Provençal house serving elaborate Mediterranean cuisine, some of the best on the Estérel coast road. Agay. *noon-1.30pm & 7-9.30pm Wed-Sun* €€ |

CORNICHE DES MAURES BEACHES

Plage de Cavalière: As the D559 hugs the coast, you'll reach the beautiful beach at **Cavalière** (not to be confused with Cavalaire-sur-Mer).

Plage du Layet: Rocky point Layet has its own minute sandy arc hidden from view.

Plage du Rayol: Tiny, particularly enchanting beach backed by pine trees, with a restaurant on the sand.

Cap de Brégançon: Scenic peninsula with imposing 11th-century **Fort de Brégançon** *(bormeslesmimosas. com; adult/child €12/10; reserve 72 hours ahead)*.

Plage du Lavandou: Small but intact old town **Le Lavandou** has 12km of golden sand backed by family-oriented beach resorts. Boats sail to Îles des Hyères.

Vieille Ville, Hyères

1910 that showcases the landscapes of the world with a climate similar to the Mediterranean. The dense flora cascades down the hillside to the sea, and while the flowers are at their best in April and May, it's always worth a visit.

In July and August, a free shuttle runs from the nearby town of Rayol-Canadel-sur-Mer.

Massif des Maures

TIME FROM ST-TROPEZ: 1HR

Chestnut Tasting at Collobrières

Hidden in the Massif des Maures forests, roughly an hour and change from St-Tropez, the leafy village of **Collobrières** is *the* place to sample chestnuts. Local producer **Confiserie Azuréenne** *(confiserieazureenne.com)* has a well-stocked shop of *marrons glacés* (candied chestnuts), chestnut ice cream, *crème de marrons* (chestnut cream) and chestnut liqueur. There's also a small, free museum showing how chestnuts are processed.

Across the 11th-century bridge, the **tourist office** *(mpm tourisme.com)* can help you join the October chestnut harvest, celebrated with the **Fête de la Châtaigne**, or join a guided forest walk. And one of the best Provençal markets takes place in the centre on Thursday and Sunday mornings.

Retreat to a Dreamy Monastery

Don't miss the majestic 12th-century Carthusian **Monastère de la Verne** *(bethleem.org; adult/child €7/5)* perched on a

 EATING & DRINKING IN MASSIF DES MAURES: OUR PICKS

La Petite Fontaine, Collobrières: Book ahead for wild boar stew and lamb with candied vegetables. For dessert: famed chestnut ice cream. *noon-2pm Tue-Sun* €€

La Farigoulette, Collobrières: Local produce, especially chestnuts, feature at this small, welcoming restaurant. *noon-2pm Thu-Mon* €€

Ferme de Peïgros: Farm restaurant 1.8km along a gravel track from top of Col de Babaou (8km from Collobrières). *noon-2pm Sun, Mon, Thu & Fri, 7-9pm Fri* €€

Auberge de la Môle, La Môle: No-frills village inn, with legendary terrines, pâtés and feisty pickles. *9.30am-1.30pm & 7.30-10pm Tue-Sat, 9.30am-2pm Sun* €€

forested ridge 15km east of Collobrières. You'll see it rising like an island of honeyed stone in a carpet of green, with views to the sea. It was founded in 1170 and has been ravaged by fire and rebuilt several times – a 20-minute video details the restoration. The monastery now houses a community of approximately 30 Sisters of Bethlehem. You'll get to visit their austere Romanesque church, the prior's cell (with small formal garden and workshop), the bakery and the olive mill.

The nuns live partially off the shop, which sells honey, leatherwork and brilliant ceramics they've made. Trails lead from the monastery through ancient *châtaigneraies* (chestnut groves), and when you alight at the car park, you'll walk the final 700m on an unpaved road.

Meet the Hermann's Tortoise

The western Hermann's tortoise *(Testudo hermanni hermanni)* is an endangered species found in small pockets of the Mediterranean coast: it mainly lives in Italy, Sardinia and Corsica, but you can still find a number of them living in the Var. The tortoise is fairly small – they only grow 7cm to 18cm long – but the distinct black-and-yellow pattern on its shell makes them easy to recognise (assuming they're not camouflaged in the underbrush). Want to get to know them better? Visit the tortoise sanctuary, **Village des Tortues** *(tortupole.fr)* in Carnoules.

Hyères

TIME FROM ST-TROPEZ: 1HR

Soak up Hyères on Foot

Begin by exploring the **Vieille Ville** (old centre), packed with picturesque streets, colourful facades, monuments and historical sites. Enter on the western side of place Georges Clemenceau through the 13th-century **Porte Massillon** and walk rue des Porches, with its polished flagstones and shady arcades.

Ascend beyond the **Tour des Templiers** *(free)*, originally built by the Knights Templar, where you can check to see if there's a temporary exhibit. Continue up beyond the **Vieux Lavoir** (old washhouse; *free*) to **Collégiale St-Paul** *(free)*, where you should duck inside to see its moving collection of ex votos, paintings made in thanks for miracles and cures rendered.

Climb to the 10th-century **Château d'Hyères**, on the heights of Castéou Hill, before descending back to **Parc Castel Ste-Claire** *(provencemed.com; free)* with its superb neo-Romanesque mansion built on the foundations of an old convent by Olivier Voutier, a naval officer who discovered the *Venus de Milo*. It was later home to American writer Edith Wharton.

DRIVING THE ROUTE DES CRÊTES

For breathtaking views of sea, islands and forests, follow **Route des Crêtes** as it winds through maquis-covered hills some 400m above the water. From Bormes-les-Mimosas, follow the D41 uphill (in the direction of Collobrières) past the Chapelle St-François and, 1.5km north of the village centre, turn immediately right after the sign for Col de Caguo-Ven (237m).

You can take a break at **Relais du Vieux Sauvaire**, a restaurant and pool with dreamy 180-degree views. Past the restaurant, rte des Crêtes joins the final leg of the panoramic **Col du Canadel** road. On the *col* (mountain pass), turn left to descend into the heart of the forested Massif des Maures, or right to the sea and the coastal Corniche des Maures (D559).

EATING & DRINKING IN HYÈRES: CASUAL & CREATIVE

Au Fil de l'Eau: Book ahead for refined seafood (good catch-of-the-day selections) in the *vieille ville*. *noon-2pm Tue-Thu, 7-11pm Tue & Wed* €€

La Cabane: Fun small bistro near Porte Massillon serving inventive French with a distinct Mediterranean twist. *noon-2pm & 7-10pm Tue-Sat* €

La Salle: French fare with Asian highlights in a charming restaurant that doubles as a *brocante* (vintage shop). *noon-2pm & 7-10pm, closed Sun & Wed* €€

Vola Cafe: Local favourite up by Collégiale St-Paul, with a leafy terrace. *9am-2pm & 5-9pm Mon, Thu & Fri, 10am-10pm Sat & Sun* €

BLACK GOLD

If truffles are divine, then **Chez Bruno** in Lorgues is their high temple on an 18th-century estate. For other heavenly truffle experiences, see Carpentras (p774) in the Luberon.

Wrap up at the cubist **Villa Noailles** *(villanoailles-hyeres.com; free)*, a national art centre.

Creativity from Ateliers to Markets

One of the treats of Hyères is the mass of creative artists and craftspeople who work here. They have banded together in the Parcours des Arts *(provencemed.com)*, mapping out the myriad studios and shops you can visit. Some examples include **Artdanh** *(artdanh.com)* with edgy art and accessories. **Sous les Palmiers** *(souslespalmiers.net)* features upcycled arts and crafts. For ceramics, visit **L'Atelier d'Aurélia** *(instagram.com/aureliabelnetpoterie)* and **Valeria Tarroni Créatures en Terre** *(valeria-tarroni.com)*. Nearby, **Vévédentelles** *(instagram.com/vevedentelles)* feels like a flashback, with all the detailed needlework. For African textile fashion, **Diweye Créations** *(diweyecreations.fr)* is the place. Pop across the street where **Atypique Provence** *(atypiqueprovence.com)* produces natural soaps and unguents. Still want more? The large **Tuesday and Saturday Market** fills the city centre from 6am to 1pm, bringing abundant food to the mix.

Beach Days on the Presqu'île de Giens

Presqu'île de Giens is the promontory due south of Hyères, facing Île de Porquerolles (p848). The peninsula is home to stunning but low-key beaches and historic **Salin des Presquiers**, where saltpans are used to harvest sea salt.

Windsurfers and kitesurfers flock to **Plage de l'Almanarre** – the western shore of the 'leg' connecting to the peninsula's foot. With white sand and shallow water, this beach is also safe for swimming.

Plage du Pradeau, near the peninsula's heel, is only accessible on foot or by boat, and it's sheltered from the wind. From here you can walk the coastal path to 17th-century **Fort du Pradeau** *(portcros-parcnational.fr; adult/child €6/3)*, renovated in 2022 to contain a **Parc National de Port-Cros** (p848) interpretation centre, tipping the promontory at **La Tour Fondue**.

Handiplage at **Plage de la Bergerie**, along the eastern shore, is a wheelchair-accessible beach equipped during summer with amphibious wheelchairs, assistance for entering the water and adapted restroom facilities.

PRESQU'ÎLE DE GIENS ACTIVITIES

Hyères Windsurf Organisation: Windsurf and wind-foil rentals and lessons.

Flyboard Hyères: Zoom on a Flyboard above the water. *flyboard-hyeres.com*

MF Kitesurf: Rent equipment or learn to kitesurf. *mfkite.com*

Sentier du Littoral (Coastal Path): Trail along the south of the peninsula.

Bird-watching: Flamingos dot **Salin des Presquiers**. Hyères tourist office *(provencemed.com)* guides bird walks.

Route du Sel (Salt Rd): Spectacular western sandbar road (May-Oct).

Cycling: À Vélo 83 *(avelo83.com)* and **À Motos & Vélos** *(amotos.fr)* hire out standard and e-bikes.

Cotignac

TIME FROM ST-TROPEZ: **1H30**

Cliff-Face Dwellings

Sheltered beautifully under a towering 400m-long sienna tufa cliff-face, the stone village of Cotignac is a real picture. The Cassole River and tree- and bistro-lined promenade cours Gambetta run through its heart, but above are **Grottes Troglodytes de Cotignac** *(adult/child €2.50/free):* dwellings cut directly into the rockface. The **Tuesday-morning market** is lively, and the tourist office has maps of area walks, including to **Shrine of Our Lady of Graces**, a minor place of pilgrimage. After you've explored, pop into **Les Vignerons de Cotignac** *(vigneronsdecotignac.com)* collective to taste and buy local rosé.

Aups

TIME FROM ST-TROPEZ: **1H40**

Dig into Aups' Famous Truffles

Amber-hued Aups, a gateway to the Gorges du Verdon (p790) to the north, has a history older than even its quaint streets suggest, having been a Celtic *oppidum* (fortified settlement), Roman town and a Moorish stronghold. Now it's best known for precious black gold: Tuber melanosporum (black truffles). From November to late February they mature beneath the area's frigid ground and you can see them (and buy them) at the Thursday-morning **truffle market** on the central plane-tree-studded square. It generally runs 9am to noon (closing earlier if they sell out), from late November to late March; but check the website, as markets end when that year's harvest ends.

Maison de la Truffe (*maisondelatruffe-verdon.fr; Truffle Adventure adult/child €2.50/1.50*), attached to **Aups tourist office** (*aups-tourisme.com*) sells truffles in various forms (whole, in pastes and pastas). It's also home to Truffle Adventure, an interactive space exploring the precious fungus, its history and gastronomy. Check online for truffle-hunting and other activities.

Want a truffle-enhanced meal? Reserve at **Restaurant des Gourmets** (*restaurantdesgourmets.com*), one of the best places in Aups to try them, even in the form of truffle ice cream.

Tastings and truffle-hunting demonstrations lure a crowd on the fourth Sunday in January during the annual **Fête de la Truffe Noire**.

Haut-Var

TIME FROM ST-TROPEZ: **45MIN–1½HR**

Rosé All Day

Don't miss sampling Var rosés, a staple at lunch tables across Provence. Choosing from more than 300 regional vineyards may leave you feeling overwhelmed, but here's a start...

If your time is short, just go to **Maison des Vins Côtes de Provence** (*maison-des-vins.fr*), 2.5km southwest of Les Arcs-sur-Argens. It's a one-stop shop: learn about and buy (at producers' prices) Côtes de Provence wines, including those made at local cooperatives. Each week 16 of the 800 wines from 250 wine estates are selected for tasting (for free!).

Just south, begin with **Domaine des Beaucas** (*domainedesbeaucas.com; tasting from €10*), a chance to drive the vineyard-carpeted valley beyond the thundering **Cascades de l'Aille**. Jaunting 23.5km west of the falls, history, art and fine wine merge at the certified organic vineyard **Commanderie de Peyrassol** (*peyrassol.com; tastings from €20*). Our choice? A bottle of Le Clos Peyrassol Rosé over a light lunch at its bistro. Reserve ahead for a Thursday evening concert in July and August.

Travelling with family? Push on and reserve a *visite ludique* (*adult/under 10 €20/free*) at **Château Nestuby** (*nestuby.com; tastings from €6*), 24km north, which includes a treasure hunt in the vineyard. You can stay over, too, or head into nearby Cotignac.

VAR VILLAGE MARKET DAYS

Most Var villages hold a weekly market; a window into local life, and the best way to build a picnic. Markets usually set up from 7am and pack up noon/1pm.

Monday: Bormes-les-Mimosas

Tuesday: Bandol, Callas, Cotignac, Fayence, Hyères, Lorgues

Wednesday: Aups, Bormes-les-Mimosas, La Garde Freinet, Salernes, Sanary-sur-Mer, Tourtour

Thursday: Aups (truffles, in winter), Bargemon, Callas, Collobrières (July and August), Fayence, Hyères, Ramatuelle

Friday: Entrecasteaux, La Motte

Saturday: Aups, Carcès, Claviers, Cogolin, Draguignan, Fayence, Hyères, Tourtour

Sunday: Ampus, Cavalière, Collobrières, Gassin (April to October), La Garde Freinet, Ramatuelle, Salernes, Vidauban

Île de Porquerolles

TOP EXPERIENCE

Îles d'Hyères

The Îles d'Hyères are also known as Îles d'Or (Islands of Gold) – not only for their mica-rich rock but also for golden beaches fringing their forested hinterland. Just a short ferry ride from Hyères, Île de Porquerolles is the largest, and a paradise for outdoor enthusiasts. For a more adventurous experience, nearby Île de Port-Cros offers fantastic snorkelling and some of the best hiking in the region. No cars allowed!

DON'T MISS

Cycling Porquerolles

Hiking Port-Cros

Plage de Notre Dame

Calanque de Brégançonnet

Domaine de la Courtade

Villa Carmignac

Île de Porquerolles

Paradise with Bikes & Bathing Suits Only

With its own chilled-out personality, **Île de Porquerolles** is a magnet for families and nature lovers, despite the huge influx of summer day trippers. Two-thirds of its sandy white beaches, pine woods, maquis and eucalyptus are protected by **Parc National de Port-Cros** *(portcros-parcnational.fr)*, and a wide variety of indigenous and tropical flora thrive. Pottering along the island's rough unpaved trails on foot or by bicycle, breaking with a picnic lunch on the beach and a dip in crystal-clear turquoise water, is heavenly. The southern

PRACTICALITIES

● provencemed.com/hyeres-porquerolles/porquerolles ● Accessible year-round

edge of the island is the most dramatic and uncluttered, but the inland vineyards and olive groves have a magic of their own, as do the gorgeous beaches of the northern coast.

Snorkel Crystalline Waters

Founded in 1963, the Parc National de Port-Cros is also France's first marine national park with exceptional marine fauna and flora, which makes it a snorkelling paradise. **Calanque de Brégançonnet** is easily accessible if you have gear and want to go on your own. Otherwise, book a boat and a guide with **Iléo Porquerolles** (*ileo-porquerolles.fr; €45*) and spend several hours discovering the vibrant and delicate underwater ecosystem off the coast. Most frequently spotted fish include tiny blenny fish, shiny mendoles and the large black-headed sea bass.

Sip Local Wines

Domaine de la Courtade (*lacourtade.com; tours/tastings from €15/5*) offers tastings of its island rosés if you book ahead online. Or if you're in town, **Domaine de l'Île** (*domainedelile.com*) offers tastings by appointment in its town-based **boutique** and restaurant.

Modern Art Mansion & Sculpture Garden

Art lovers should check out what's on at dazzling **Villa Carmignac** (*fondationcarmignac.com; adult/child €16/free*), from May to November. Not only will you get to see cutting-edge art, but you can get inside the bespoke home, with an aquatic ceiling, of Fondation Carmignac and its elaborate sculpture gardens. It's a 15-minute walk or five-minute cycle east of town.

Best Beaches

Many say that **Plage de Notre Dame** is one of Europe's most beautiful beaches. But it's not the only one of Porquerolles' best beaches. **Plage de la Courtade** is a gorgeous crescent of sand with watersports, while **Plage d'Argent** is popular with families for its summer beachside cafe, lifeguards and toilets.

Île de Port-Cros

Hike the Pristine Île de Port-Cros

When you arrive at **Port-Cros port**, pick up a map at **Maison du Parc** (*portcros-parcnational.fr*) of the island's hiking routes. The national park doesn't even allow bicycles on the well-marked trails of this undeveloped little island, so strap on your boots and bring a towel and swimsuit for great swims along the way. Add a picnic, water and sunblock (bring it all from the mainland) and you're good to go.

Swim an Underwater Guided Path

Swim a **Sentier Sous-Marin** a 35-minute underwater circuit offshore at **Plage de la Palud**. Fishing is prohibited on the island, and the bay is home to 180 species, plus 500 types of algae. The *sentier* is marked by buoys with explanatory panels, and Maison du Parc at the port sells a waterproof leaflet (€5). Rent equipment from portside **Sun Plongée** (*sun-plongee.com; dives from €48*).

GETTING THERE & AWAY

Transport Littoral Varois (*tlv-tvm.com*) runs year-round ferries from **La Tour Fondue** (p846) to Île de Porquerolles (*return €24 May-Sep, reduced rest of year; 20 minutes*) and less-frequent services from Port d'Hyères to Île de Port-Cros (*return €29; one hour*). There's also a summer, two-island day-trip (*return €30*) to Port-Cros and Le Levant. Bringing a bike costs extra (*adult/child €17/14.50*).

TOP TIPS

● On Île de Porquerolles, visitors are capped at 6000 per day in July and August. Reserve your ferry crossing well in advance.

● Pick up maps or book guided tours at Parc National de Port-Cros Maison du Parc (*portcros-parcnational.fr*).

● Plenty of bike and e-bike hire outfits in town vie for your custom and prices are pretty uniform (*adult/child €19/15 per day; e-bike €45*).

● April and May are the best months to spot some of the 114 bird species.

● The third of the Îles d'Hyères, Île du Levant, is part military camp part nudist colony, Heliopolis (*iledulevant.com.fr*). Baring all is not obligatory except on beaches.

Monaco

GLITZ | MOTORSPORTS | ROYALTY

☑ TOP TIP

Although still considered pricey compared to most other destinations, Monaco's high-end restaurant menus that veer towards exorbitant for dinner are often more wallet-friendly for weekday lunch, when restaurants are out to court the business crowd. Expect to pay around €30 per person for a set lunch menu with a glass of wine – a price that wouldn't cover the main course come sunset.

Monaco is constantly evolving. Towering cranes are as ubiquitous as superyachts and sports cars as the principality stretches up and out to sea to maximise every inch of its limited space. Nowhere else on the Côte d'Azur feels so built up, but in fact over 20% of Monaco's territory is made up of gardens. Spearheaded by HSH Prince Albert II, the principality harbours even greater green ambitions with a goal of carbon neutrality by 2050.

'Green is glam' (as Monaco's sustainable push with a luxury twist is known) is the latest chapter in the Hollywood history of the world's second-smallest country, whose reputation was built on a lavish Belle Époque casino and sealed with the marriage of a Grimaldi prince, Rainier III, to a silver-screen princess, Grace Kelly. The glitz is as pervasive as ever, but is now balanced out by local experiences – and flavours – that add another side to Monaco's real identity and culture.

Racing Weekends

Fast cars, three ways

For the Monaco **Formula One Grand Prix**, 2026 is a marquee year: the traditional late-May race weekend has been

continued on p854

GETTING AROUND

On foot is the best way to get around Monaco with no distances longer than an hour's walk, but the terrain can be very steep. Skip the stairs – and catch your breath – in one of the principality's 79 public lifts or 35 escalators. The Compagnie Autobus de Monaco operates six bus lines that serve all corners of the principality; tickets can be purchased on board the bus (cash or card) for €2; you can purchase up to six tickets with one credit/debit card. MonaBike is Monaco's excellent electric bike-sharing scheme; register in advance on the Monapass app. If driving, avoid commuter hours as traffic coming into the principality is bumper to bumper. Public parking fills up fast and can be pricey during daytime hours, although the hourly rate drops significantly come evening.

TOP EXPERIENCE

Casino de Monte-Carlo

Built on an arid plateau where citrus trees once prospered, the Casino de Monte-Carlo is the ornate Belle Époque marvel that put the principality on the map for Europe's high rollers when it first opened in the 1860s. Yet this gilded address is so much more than a spot for a flutter – in fact, it's one of the region's architectural treasures.

More than a Gambling Den

In the morning, you can ogle the ornate marble and gold-leaf-clad *salons privés* without risking a cent on a self-guided tour through the gaming rooms. Take your time and admire the intricate styling of each of the 10 rooms you pass. An audio guide, included in the entrance fee, weaves in history and entertaining anecdotes while pointing out the incredible decorative detail. Even the fittings and fixtures are works of art. In Salle Europe, the oldest gaming room, roulette wheels spin underneath eight dazzling Bohemian crystal chandeliers, weighing 150kg each. Salle Blanche, a private den, sparkles with mosaic detailing and caryatids. The Empire-style Salle Médecin, where the casino's original high rollers played away from prying eyes, is also a silver-screen star, with two Bond movies, *Golden Eye* and *Never Say Never Again*, shot here.

Fancy Flutter

Fun fact: Monaco nationals are not allowed to gamble. For all other nationalities, you must be at least 18 years and have a photo ID to enter the gaming rooms after 2pm. There's a strict dress code: think smart attire rather than shorts, sportswear and flip-flops.

TOP TIPS

● Between October and March the group visits thin out.

● Don't miss the back of the building: the sea-facing rear facade is wonderfully elaborate, too.

● Fancy a flutter? The minimum bet in the Salle Europe is €5 for roulette.

PRACTICALITIES

● montecarlosbm.com/en/casino-monaco/casino-monte-carlo ● adult/child €19/free ● 10am-1pm; last entrance at 12.15pm (for visits). Gaming starts at 2pm.

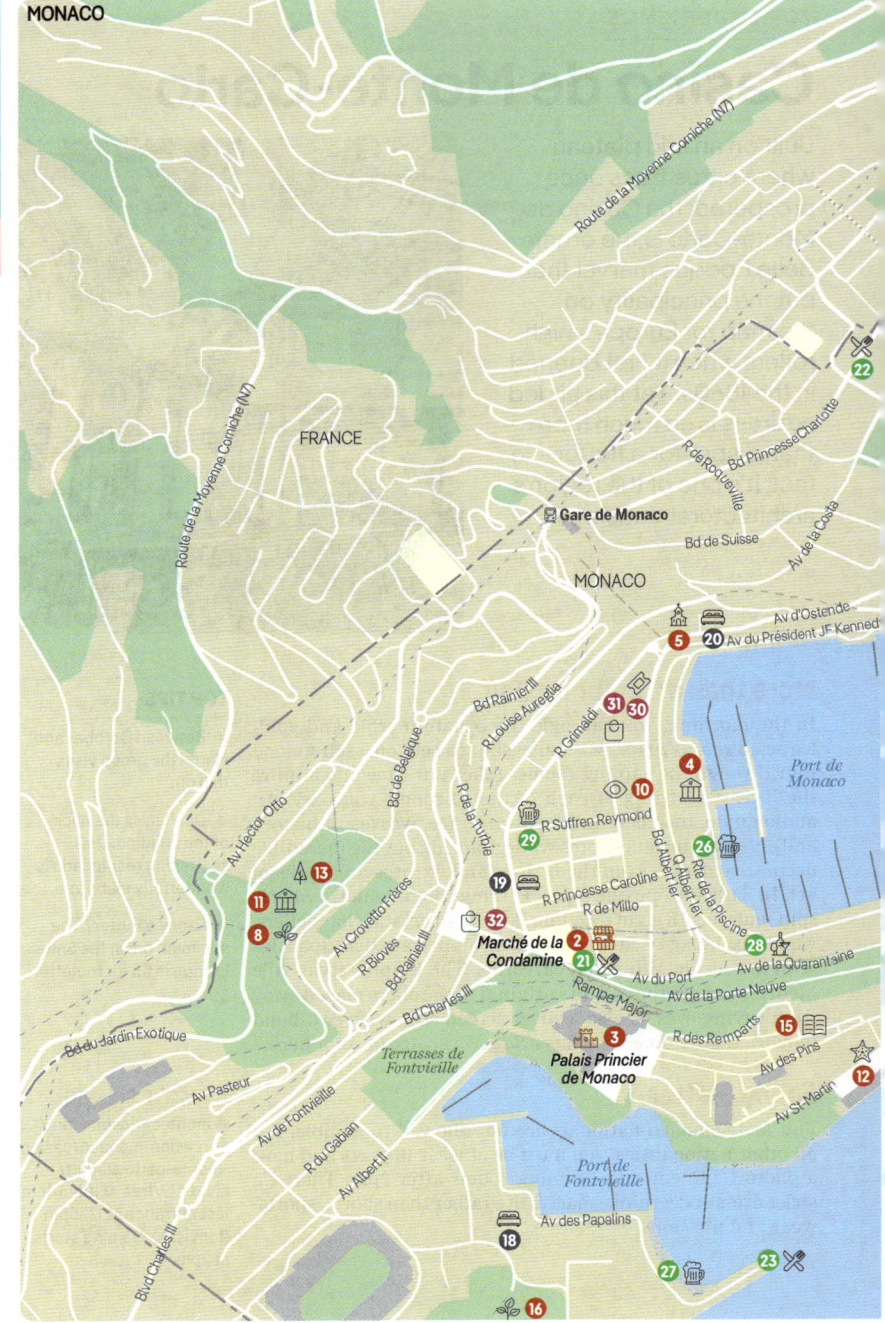

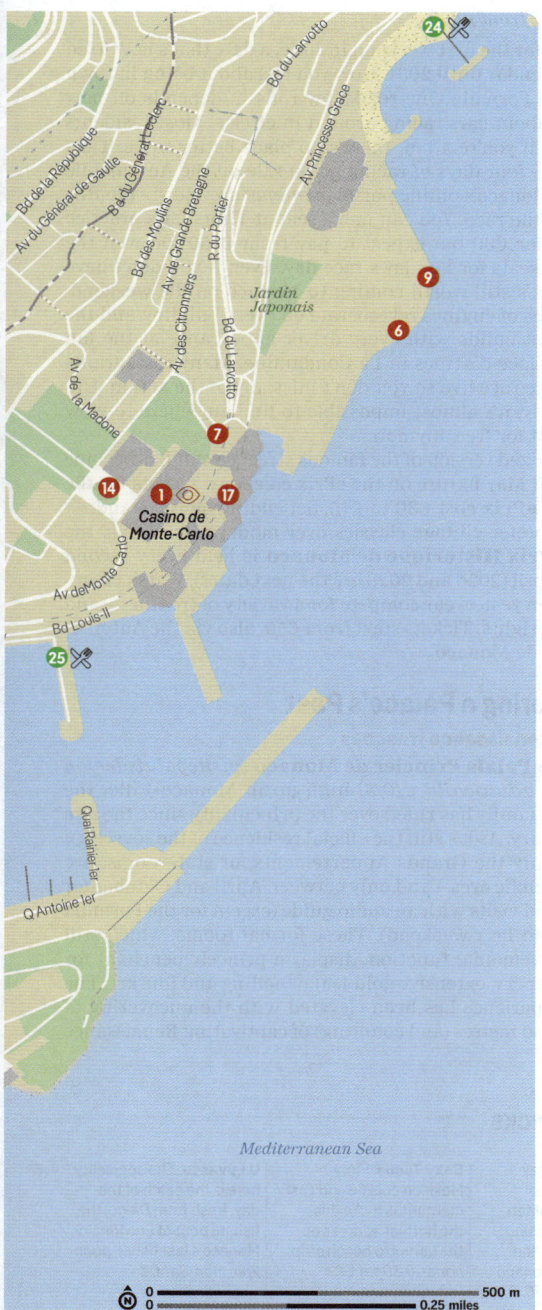

★ HIGHLIGHTS
1. Casino de Monte-Carlo
2. Marché de la Condamine
3. Palais Princier de Monaco

● SIGHTS
4. Collection de Voitures de SAS le Prince de Monaco
5. Église Ste-Dévote
6. Espace de Méditation
7. Fairmont Hairpin
8. Jardin Exotique
9. La Grotte Bleue
10. Monaco Grand Prix Starting Grid
11. Musée d'Anthropologie Préhistorique de Monaco
12. Musée Océanographique de Monaco
13. Parc Princesse Antoinette
14. Place du Casino
15. Princess Grace Irish Library
16. Roseraie Princesse Grace
17. Tunnel Louis II

● SLEEPING
18. Columbus Monte-Carlo
19. Hôtel de France
20. Hotel Miramar

● EATING
see 2 A Roca
21. Chez Roger
22. Il Terrazzino
23. Les Perles de Monte-Carlo
see 21 Maison des Pâtes
see 2 Mitron Bakery
24. Sexy Tacos
25. U Luvassu

● DRINKING & NIGHTLIFE
26. Brasserie de Monaco
27. Gerhard's Café
28. La Rascasse
29. Slammer's

● ENTERTAINMENT
30. Automobile Club de Monaco

● SHOPPING
31. La Boutique de l'Automobile Club de Monaco
32. La Distillerie de Monaco

JARDIN EXOTIQUE REOPENING

After five years of extensive renovations and safety upgrades, Monaco's cliffside **Jardin Exotique** (exotic garden) is set to reopen in the second half of 2025 – although at the time of researching this guide, no firm date had been provided. Before it shuttered, it was one of the principality's most popular sites; over 150,000 visitors a year passed through its gates to roam among the 30,000 species of plants sprouting in a rocky setting carved into a cliff face high above Port Hercules. There's no doubt that when it does open, it will once again be worth tackling the ascent to the tip of the principality to visit. Keep an eye on the website for updates: jardin-exotique.mc.

continued from p850

swapped for the first weekend in June, a date that's now fixed in the calendar until 2031. How you feel about being in town when the Formula One roadshow rolls in depends on how you feel about cars racing around in circles. Most residents leave but if you're a fan, there's no place better to be. Tickets for the four days of racing go on sale on the Automobile Club de Monaco's online portal *(acm.mc)* around six months ahead of the race. You can nab a seat at Thursday's practice sessions for €30 but expect to pay from €550 for even the cheapest seats for Sunday's race day. Even if you don't have a ticket, it's still worth coming to Monaco on the weekend. The echoes of engines reverberate off every building and the excitement builds with every driver appearance at the fan zone on place d'Armes in La Condamine. Many restaurants stream the race live so you don't miss any of the action. Unfortunately, it's almost impossible to find anywhere to view the circuit for free anymore.

An abridged version of the famous street circuit has become an annual May fixture on the ePrix calendar. Tickets for the **Monaco ePrix** cost €30 to €45, depending on the stand.

If you prefer vintage classics over modern iterations, the **Grand Prix Historique de Monaco** is held every second year in April (2026 and 2028 are the next dates). Watch champions from yesteryear compete for a variety of trophies – and bragging rights. Tickets start from €50, also via the Automobile Club de Monaco.

Uncovering a Palace's Past

Hidden Renaissance frescoes

From the **Palais Princier de Monaco** *(visitepalaisdemonaco.com; adult/child €10/5)* high up in Monaco-Ville, the Grimaldi family has ruled over the principality since the late 13th century. As it's still the official residence of the sovereign family, only the Grands Appartements, or staterooms, are open to public eyes – and only between April and October for self-guided visits with an audio guide (except for the Formula One Grand Prix weekend). These formal rooms, which still have a ceremonial function, display a princely penchant for heavy drapery, extensive gold-leaf panelling and fine art. The entire experience has been elevated with the uncovering of over 600 sq metres (and counting) of captivating Renaissance

EATING IN MONACO: OUR PICKS

Les Perles de Monte-Carlo: Tuck into oysters reared on site at this marine research centre turned seafood counter in Fontvieille. *noon-2.30pm Mon-Sat, 7-10pm Wed-Fri* €€

Il Terrazzino: Buzzy business lunch spot serving up Neapolitan favourites near Casino Square. A taste of the Amalfi Coast in Monaco. *noon-2.30pm & 7-10.30pm Tue-Sat* €

Sexy Tacos: Fiery Mexican cuisine and zesty margaritas make this the hottest address on the Larvotto beach strip. *noon-10.30pm* €€

U Luvassu: The speciality here is the catch of the day, fresh from *Diego*, the fishing boat of Eric Rinaldi, Monaco's last fisher. *noon-2pm Mon-Sat* €€

MONACO F1 ON FOOT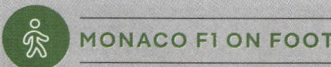

Visiting outside of race day? Set the pace on a walking tour of the legendary street circuit – and familiarise yourself with many of Monaco's sights along the way.

START	END	LENGTH
Port Hercules	Port Hercules	3.4km; 1½ hours

Begin this tour in pole position, literally, at 17 bd Albert Ier on Port Hercules, aka the ❶ **Monaco Grand Prix starting grid**. A few doors down at number 23 is race organiser the ❷ **Automobile Club de Monaco** (ACM); it's a members-only address, but you can browse the memorabilia on display in the windows. The Ste Dévote bend is named after the ornate ❸ **Église Ste-Dévote**, a church so small compared to the apartment blocks around it that it looks like a decorative figurine.

You'll next start the climb towards ❹ **Place du Casino**, the world's glitziest car park for supercars, before descending to the ❺ **Fairmont Hairpin**, the slowest corner of any F1 circuit. Follow the footpath down to ❻ **Tunnel Louis II**. Once you have walked through it, you'll emerge at the ultra-exclusive Yacht Club de Monaco. The rest of the route is flat, following the harbourfront.

Next stop is the ❼ **Collection de Voitures de SAS le Prince de Monaco**, Prince Rainier III's shiny automotive stockpile, including vintage F1 and rally racers. In F1 terms, ❽ **La Rascasse** (p856) is the tight corner just before the pit lane entrance, but in Monaco it's also the name of the popular bar in the same place. Happy hour runs from 6pm to 8.30pm. You're so close to the finish you could call it a day here, or sweep back around to the starting line to close the loop.

MONACO WITH KIDS

Musée Océanographique de Monaco: This world-class marine museum on Le Rocher includes an aquarium and floor-to-ceiling multimedia shows.

Parc Princesse Antoinette: A multitude of play areas suitable for kids of all ages. Play mini golf at the small snack bar on site.

Musée d'Anthropologie Préhistorique de Monaco: Small anthropology museum with enough rows of bugs, butterflies and beetles in glass cases, plus a mammoth skeleton, to spark curious minds.

Roseraie Princesse Grace: A pastel-pretty English-style garden in Fontvieille where 6000 rose bushes burst into bloom in spring. Inside the Parc Paysager de Fontvieille.

Princess Grace Irish Library: Guardians of Grace Kelly's tomes of Irish literature on Le Rocher. The kids' corner on rainy days is a welcome shelter.

Palais Princier de Monaco (p854)

frescoes that depict three heroes from antiquity – Hercules, Odysseus and Europa – hidden for centuries under layers of paint. The work is ongoing, as the metres of scaffolding attest, using natural solvents and environmentally friendly solutions to gradually restore walls and ceilings to their original decoration. It's a project those at the palace believe will last the lifetime of the current sovereign, His Serene Highness, Prince Albert II. Time your visit around the changing of the guards, daily at 11.55am.

Morning, Mareterra!
A new neighbourhood rises from the sea

Although primarily residential, Mareterra, Monaco's newest neighbourhood, is still worth a mosey, if anything to appreciate the marvels of land reclamation. You can't access all corners, but you get sensational views across to Italy along a smooth, 500m-long seafront promenade that connects with the Larvotto beachfront at the eastern end. Look out for two unmarked doors along the way that open onto a couple of the Principality's most curious attractions: a cavern of pink crystals styled as an **Espace de Méditation**, or public meditation space, and **La Grotte Bleue**, a sliver of the 26m-high

Happy hour runs from 6-8pm

 DRINKING IN MONACO: LOCAL HAUNTS

La Rascasse: Legendary bar on the F1 corner of the same name. Chilled happy hours, loud late-night parties. *4.30pm-3.30am Tue-Thu, 6.30pm-4.30am Fri & Sat*

Slammer's: Small pub with big sports screens and a reputation for atmosphere, especially on Grand Prix weekend. *4pm-1am*

Gerhard's Café: Long-running German pub on Fontvieille's bar and restaurant strip with a laid-back atmosphere and friendly vibe. *8am-3am, from 11am Sun*

Brasserie de Monaco: Boisterous microbrewery on Port Hercules pours organic pale ales and wheat beers brewed on site, alongside typical pub grub. *noon-2am*

foundations left exposed for public viewing. It's a nice idea, but the room is unlit and little more than a concrete railing separates you from the drop into the sea, so the whole experience ends up eerie rather than engaging.

Made in Monaco Drinks
Taste the local spirit

Agriculture was the lifeblood of Monaco's economy until the mid-19th century when the Grimaldi family ceded 95% of its territory to France. Today, if you look closely enough, there are still clues to this heritage, such as the 600 bitter orange trees that line some of the principality's main boulevards. **La Distillerie de Monaco** *(distilleriedemonaco.com)* transforms this tangy citrus into a punchy orange liqueur, called L'Orangeraie, and also makes a seven citrus gin and a velvety chocolate liqueur made from Monaco's national tree, the carob. Swing by the distillery to buy a bottle, but reach out ahead to book a 15-minute tasting *(€9)* or a 25-minute tour and tasting *(€27)* – much of the price difference comes down to how many miniatures you are gifted to take home (one versus three).

Where the Locals Lunch
A small square and big market

Despite its glitzy image, the good news is that you don't have to take out a loan to eat well in Monaco. You can find a hub of cheap and cheerful eats inside the bustling **Marché de la Condamine** on place d'Armes. This lively square, just back from Port Hercules in La Condamine neighbourhood, bursts with fresh flowers and colourful fruit and vegetables from just across the border in Italy. The covered market rises early to cater to the breakfast trade, although the real buzz is at lunch when workers from nearby offices flood in to tuck into plates piled high with fresh pasta and other tasty, quick eats. Note that the food hall was set to shutter in January 2026 for an extensive 13-month upgrade that La Condamine residents hoped won't strip away the market's charm. While the works are underway, you'll find the stallholders installed in temporary chalets on the square.

GET TO KNOW MONACO'S NEIGHBOURHOODS

Despite being used interchangeably with Monaco, Monte Carlo is just one of the principality's neighbourhoods, albeit its most famous, with sites such as the **Casino de Monte-Carlo** (p851). La Condamine, around Port Hercules, has a distinctly local flavour and hosts the place d'Armes market. A huddle of colourful buildings above the port, Monaco-Ville, also known as Le Rocher, is Monaco's historic heart, with narrow streets fanning out from the **Palais Princier de Monaco** (p854). Like Mareterra, Monaco's newest neighbourhood, Fontvieille has risen out of the sea at the western edge. The Larvotto beachfront strip is one of the most expensive slices of real estate in the world, while **Jardin Exotique** (p854) teeters at its highest tip. Les Moneghetti and St-Roman are predominately residential.

 EATING IN MONACO: BUDGET BITES AT MARCHÉ DE LA CONDAMINE

Mitron Bakery: Monaco outpost of Mauro Colagreco's organic bakery in Menton. Freshly baked breads and sweet lemon tarts. *7.30am-1.30pm Tue-Sun* €

Chez Roger: So renowned is the *socca* and *pissaladière* at Chez Roger that there's little need to sell anything else. *9.45am-1.30pm Tue-Sat* €

Maison des Pâtes: The lunch crowd flock with good reason to this pasta spot for strings of fresh tagliatelle or pouches of ravioli. *7am-3.30pm Mon-Sun, 6-9.30pm Tue-Sat* €

A Roca: The spot for *barbajuans*, tasty fried ravioli considered the principality's national dish. *8.30am-2.50pm Tue-Sat, 8am-1pm Sun* €

# Places We Love to Stay

€ Budget €€ Midrange €€€ Top End

Nice
MAP p808

Hostel Meyerbeer Beach € Friendly hostel with a cracking city-centre location, just three minutes from the beach. Dorms are mixed.

Le Saint Paul €€ Across from the breakwater in Port Lympia, this church-run choice has the best-value seafront rooms in Nice.

Hôtel Rossetti €€ Charming three-star boutique hotel with seven rooms in the shadow of Cathédrale Ste-Réparate in Vieux Nice. The hidden terrace is lovely.

Hôtel La Pérouse €€€ Clinging to the Colline du Château with a hidden pool and sea views, this delightful four-star hotel is one of Nice's finest.

Le Negresco €€€ The grande dame of Nice's hotels set across from the beach. Each room is unique and styled to a theme. The art collection is priceless.

Villefranche-sur-Mer & Èze

La Régence – Chez Betty € Top-value find in the centre of Villefranche-sur-Mer with charming, Provençal-styled rooms, a family feel and a bar where you'll get chatting to locals.

Hôtel de la Darse €€ Basic but smart two-star choice across from the water in Villefranche's quiet port neighbourhood. Sea-view rooms with sunny balconies.

Château Eza €€€ Fourteen rooms scattered throughout Èze's atmospheric alleys, many with sublime sea and coast views. If you're looking to propose, few settings are more memorable.

Menton

Hôtel Lemon € Comfortable rooms shaded the colours of Menton near the train station. The citrus garden and organic breakfast are highlights.

La Fabrique à Poupées €€ Three rooms and one apartment in a clay-red villa that, until 2002, produced folkloric dolls for souvenir shops. Stylish with a great location.

St-Paul de Vence & Vence

Camping Pinèdes € Shaded pitches and mobile homes, with a swimming pool and wild river swimming on the doorstep. Ten minutes' drive from St-Paul de Vence.

Hôtel Les Messugues €€ Dreamy Provençal *mas* (stone house), surrounded by olive groves of the Fondation Maeght in St-Paul. Quirk: doors have come from prison cells.

Orion Treehouses €€ Four cedarwood treehouses around a wild swimming pool. An utterly enchanting and unique setting at the base of St-Paul de Vence. Reservations Saturday to Saturday in summer.

La Maison du Frêne €€ A real *coup de cœur* for this richly decorated B&B in the centre of Vence that reflects the passion of the owners, Thierry and Guy, for Baroque and pop art.

Cannes
MAP p824

Banana's Camp € Clean and bright mixed and female dorms in a buttermilk-yellow villa less than 10 minutes' walk from the train station.

Hôtel de Provence €€ This leafy oasis in central Cannes is a real find, but fills up fast. Opt for room 12, 14 or 15.

Hôtel Le Mistral €€ The friendliness of owner Jean-Michel and the nightly price makes up for some dated decor. Unbeatable location near the Palais des Festivals et des Congrès.

Antibes

Le Relais du Postillon €€ Three-star hotel on a popular square at the edge of the old town. Rooms are snug but full of Provençal charm.

Hôtel Josse €€ For a more summer vibe, this low-slung, whitewashed, 27-room hotel just across from the beach is a top choice.

Grasse

Auberge les Arômes € Simple yet spacious rooms, on-site parking, a delicious Greco-Armenian restaurant and a family touch lacking in most hotels nowadays.

Domaine de la Cascade Parfumée €€€ Romantic suites with luxe trimmings in a canary-yellow *bastide* (country house) behind Grasse, fully renovated in 2024.

Monaco
MAP p852

Hôtel de France € Cheapest hotel in Monaco with 26 well-appointed rooms and airy high ceilings. There's no lift.

Columbus Monte-Carlo €€€ This stylish three-star hotel in Fontvieille punches above its weight with a pool and great views.

Hôtel Miramar €€€ Boutique hotel with a superb location opposite Port Hercules, a chic nautical theme and a cool rooftop bar. Watch out for last-minute discounted rates.

St-Tropez
MAP p836

Hôtel Le Colombier €€ Immaculately clean converted house, five minutes' walk from place des Lices.

B Lodge Hôtel €€ Muted tones and rooms with balconies and Citadelle views are fabulous.

Hôtel Ermitage €€ Self-consciously retro, with sweeping views over town.

Hôtel Lou Cagnard €€€ Lovely jasmine-scented garden patios and welcoming feel. Open year-round.

Hôtel Byblos €€€ Perennial favourite among Hollywood A-listers, it's also got a nightclub and Michelin-star restaurant.

Presqu'île de St-Tropez

La Vigneraie 1860 € Tents and caravans camp off Plage de Pampelonne, surrounded by vineyards. Basic apartments, too.

Le Refuge €€ Rustic house off Plage de Gigaro. Humble rooms and studios open onto terraces.

Around Bormes-les-Mimosas

Hôtel California € Vintage hotel in Le Lavendou, with clean rooms for travellers on a budget.

La Villa Thalassa €€ Comfortable B&B with three bedrooms, plus a cute wooden caravan. Pool with sunset view.

Le Relais des Maures €€ This inn, tucked just off the D559, has homely guest rooms, some with sea views.

Fréjus & St-Raphaël

Hôtel Les Calanques € Family-run three-star on the rocks above its own quiet cove in Les Issambres.

Hôtel L'Aréna € Provençal decor, with garden, pool and restaurant in Fréjus. Duplexes for families.

Hôtel le 21 €€ Small, plain hotel in St-Raphaël; handy for both the train station and town centre.

Hyères

Lilou €€ In the city centre, comfortable with a restaurant, small pool and parking, handy for families.

Hôtel Les Orangers €€ Casual, clean hotel around a shady courtyard and convenient to the centre.

Presqu'île de Giens

Hôtel Le Méditerranée € Pleasant little hotel abutting Hyères' racing track. Short walk to the beach and port.

Camping à la Ferme le Pradeau € Small campground with direct access to Plage du Pradeau.

Hôtel Bor €€ Right beside Plage Bona, this Scandi-tinged, palm-fringed hotel is a stylish place to stay.

Le Lodge des Îles d'Or €€€ Luxe resort back from Plage de la Bergerie with light-filled rooms.

Île de Porquerolles

Villa Ste-Anne €€ Inn on the square with fun restaurant terrace overlooking the pétanque pitch.

Les Mèdes €€ Traditional rooms and self-catering apartments, with terraced garden and pool.

Le Mas du Langoustier €€€ Splashy inn with its own private beach; Michelin-starred restaurant.

Cotignac

Hotel La Falaise € A bright, clean and spacious hotel right in the heart of the village.

Mas de l'Olivette €€ Lovely proprietors welcome you so warmly to their tiny B&B that it feels like home.

Hotel Lou Calen €€€ Swank vintage-modern guest rooms, abundant gardens and a pool, with warm service.

Le Negresco, Nice

Above: Citadel (p868), Bastia; Right: Canyoning, Canyon de Purcaraccia (p865)

Researched by
Jean-Bernard Carillet

Corsica

AN ISLAND OF BEAUTY, MARVELS AND SURPRISES

Explore the powerful contrasts between maquis-cloaked mountains, crystalline turquoise seas fringed by world-class beaches, hilltop villages and elegant Italianate towns, on the Mediterranean's fourth biggest island.

It's not known as the *Île de Beauté* (Island of Beauty) for nothing. Jutting from the foaming Mediterranean like an impregnable fortress, Corsica combines vast expanses of shorelines with the powerful beauty of the mountains. Within half an hour's drive, the landscape ranges from glittering bays, vibrant coastal cities and fabulous beaches lapped by transparent turquoise waters to sawtooth mountain ridges, remote valleys, majestic forests and superb stone villages clutching improbably to rocky outposts. Driving is a joy – the scenery that unfurls along the island's super scenic small roads will have you stopping at every other lay-by to whip out your smartphone.

Corsica is the ideal outdoors destination for adventurers, photographers, road-trippers and beach bums. From April to late October you can trek, hike, cycle, swim, snorkel, dive, rock-climb, sail, kayak and canyon. Food lovers will sample local delicacies in trendy *paillotes* (beach restaurants) and snug eateries. For culture buffs, prehistoric sites, a few great museums and plenty of heritage buildings await.

Though Corsica's been officially part of France for over 200 years, it does feel different from the mainland in everything from customs, cuisine, language and character, and that's part of its appeal. Locals love to explain their Corsican identity, so plenty of engaging evenings await, especially if food, wine and traditional Corsican chants are involved.

In all, it's hard to find a better combination of nature, culture and leisure.

ANTONEE/SHUTTERSTOCK

THE MAIN AREAS

BASTIA
Dynamic city with an urban vibe.
p866

CALVI & LA BALAGNE
Awesome setting by the beach.
p873

CORTE
Sporty, mountainous, intimate. **p879**

AJACCIO
Stylish official capital that Napoléon chose.
p884

BONIFACIO
Spectacular clifftop town and beaches. **p892**

Find Your Way

Corsica has four airports. The two most convenient are Ajaccio and Bastia. By sea, the island can be reached from the ports of Nice, Marseille and Toulon in mainland France.

Calvi & La Balagne, p873
Seaside town with a gorgeous beach, water sports and a hinterland peppered with villages that ooze character.

Bastia, p866
Age-old Corsica, medieval Genoa and modern France interweave harmoniously in this pastel-colourel city. Great base for exploring the Cap Corse.

Corte, p879
15th-century fortress keeping watch over this pleasant town. Good base for exploring the west coast and spectacular inland gorges.

Ajaccio, p884
Curved around a bay, this stylish city is slow-paced and laid-back. Gateway to maritime reserves, world heritage landscapes and beaches.

Bonifacio, p892
Must-see town whose ancient houses teeter on the edge of 100m-high limestone cliffs. Beaches and prehistoric sites nearby.

CAR
Measure in time not distance. Roads are frequently narrow, generally twisty. You're likely to drive in second gear most of the time! There are no motorways, so no tolls to pay.

TRAIN
Corsica has two lines. The main line runs between Bastia and Ajaccio. From Ponte Leccia, between Bastia and Corte, a spur runs to L'île-Rousse and Calvi. A little train also shuttles back and forth between Calvi and L'Île-Rousse.

Bastia (p866)

Plan Your Time

There's so much to discover in Corsica. It's a Mediterranean island and also a high mountain range, so allow some time for outdoor activities.

A Week in Haute-Corse

- If you have a week, starting in **Bastia** (p866), drive around the **Cap Corse** (p870) and recharge the batteries in **L'Île-Rousse** (p876) or **Calvi** (p873) in the Balagne. Drive down the spectacular D81 to the **Golfe de Porto** (p888) and take a boat tour in the **Réserve Naturelle de Scandola** (p890). Continue south to **Ajaccio** (p884) before returning to Bastia via **Corte** (p879).

Two Weeks Covers it All

- Extend the route by continuing south to the **Golfe du Valinco** (p889), blessed with scenic landscapes, before heading east to **Bonifacio** (p892) perched atop 100m-high limestone cliffs. Take a boat ride to the **Lavezzi islands** (p894) and flop on on paradisiacal **Plage de Palombaggia** (p895). Spend a day around the **Alta Rocca** (p896) before driving quickly up the flat eastern shore back to Bastia.

Seasonal Highlights

SPRING
The maquis is in full flower, locals are relaxed, no crowds, prices are reasonable. Too cold for swimming but ideal for hiking.

SUMMER
Too hot to trek but lovely to swim. Avoid mid-July to mid-August when it's seriously overcrowded, hot and expensive.

AUTUMN
Prices drop, the sea is warm enough for swimming, and the mountains are cloaked in gold, russet and red.

WINTER
Many hotels and restaurants close from early November to late March. The best season to experience the other Corsica!

HELP ME PICK:

Walking in Corsica

Corsica's a walker's paradise. It's a real pleasure to get off the roads and into nature on foot. Some of the most inspirational hiking trails in Europe are here, passing through scenery of bewildering beauty. And it's simple to enjoy it. Walking options range from the most challenging, long-distance hike, such as the iconic GR20, to an easy afternoon stroll along the coast. There is something for all tastes and all abilities.

Where to go if you like...

Challenging Treks

Corsica's most famous and challenging trek is the 200km-long **GR20** that traverses from Calenzana in the northwest to Conca in the southeast, mostly along mountain ridges. It's split into 16 segments (6.5km to 16km) each of which an experienced trekker can cover in an average of 4½ to eight hours a day, spending every night in a *refuge* (mountain hut). The northern section, from Calenzana to Vizzavona, is the hardest as the path can be steep and rocky.

Intermediate Treks

Much easier (and shorter) than the GR20 and almost as rewarding are the three **Mare a Mare** (Sea to Sea) paths that link the west and east coasts via the central mountains.

Other fairly easy alternatives are the **Mare e Monti Nord** (from Calenzana to Cargèse; 135km, 10 segments each four to seven hours, accessible all year), and the **Mare e Monti Sud** (74km, five segments each four to six hours) that runs between the bay of Porticcio and the bay of Propriano (passable year-round). Unlike the GR20, which stays away from settlements, these routes pass through villages. They offer considerable comfort with good sleeping options every night.

In the Cap Corse, the **Sentier des Douaniers** (24km, seven hours; pictured left) is a fantastic coastal path between Macinaggio and Centuri, that can be divided into small segments.

Other Walks

There are tons of easy walks of a day or less. Favourites include the **Capu Rossu** (7.8km, 3½ hours) walk in the Golfe de Porto and the **Gorges de la Spelunca** (2.5km, 1½ hours), also in the Porto area, but inland. Don't miss short walks in Les Calanques de Piana, including **Château Fort trail** (2km, one hour). Inland from Ajaccio, **Lac de Creno** (6km, 2½ hours) is another stunning hike to a glacial lake. In the south, the walk to **Cap Pertusato** (5km, 2½ hours) from Bonifacio, along towering cliffs, is absolutely memorable. In the Alta Rocca, there are excellent hiking options in the vicinity of the **Col de Bavella**, including the walk to **Trou de la Bombe** (5km, 2½ hours) the hollow eye of a rocky needle southeast of the *col*.

Hiking the GR20

HOW TO

Before you go Camping gear is strongly recommended in high season, as there are only a limited number of places available in refuges along the way.

When to go Coastal walks can be done year-round, while the GR20 can only be undertaken between June and the end of September.

Book ahead In July and August, it's necessary to book refuges on the GR20 (*pnr-resa.corsica*). *Gîtes* (mountain lodges) can also be booked online.

Budget As a general rule, you'll need between €18 (if you bring your own food) and about €45 per day if you eat and sleep in *refuges*.

Canyoning

Offering another dizzying approach to Corsica's mountains, canyoning is a must-do for thrill seekers. It's a mix of hiking, climbing, abseiling, swimming and some serious jumping or plunging down water-polished chutes in natural pools, river gorges and waterfalls. It's increasingly popular in Corsica due to the perfect terrain. The Massif de Bavella is the mother of all canyoning experiences on the island, with two iconic canyons: **La Vacca** and **La Purcaraccia**, which are set in some of the most grandiose scenery in Corsica. Both are suitable for all levels. For families, the easy **Canyon de Pulischellu** gets our vote. In the Vallée du Niolo, **Canyon de la Ruda** and **Canyon de Frascaghju** are the main hot spots.

Canyon du Bas-Vecchio, near Corte, is also suitable for beginners and kids. In the Propriano area, make a beeline for **Canyon du Baracci**.

Experience is not usually necessary. Adventure centres that offer canyoning provide wetsuits, helmets, harnesses and qualified instructors. Based in Corte, **Altipiani** (*altipiani-corse.com*) organises all sorts of guided tours, including trekking and canyoning. Other reputable operators include Canyon Corse (*canyon-corse.com*) and **Corsica Madness** (*corsicamadness.fr*), which run guided walks in the Massif de Bavella. A half day's canyoning will set you back around €50. Bring a picnic and spare clothes.

Bastia

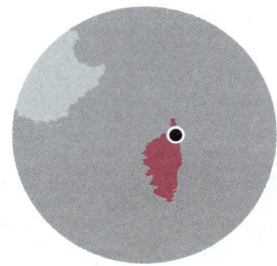

URBAN ATMOSPHERE | FINE DINING | GREAT MONUMENTS

☑ TOP TIP

Leave your vehicle all day for the price of a beer at the **place St-Nicolas** parking, just 500m from the ferry port exit. From here it's a pleasant walk south through Terra Vecchia to the citadel either down the pedestrianised rue Napoléon or the elegant bd Paoli.

Filled with heart, soul and character, the lively passenger port of Bastia is a pleasant surprise. Sure, it might not have the relaxed charm of its long-term rival Ajaccio, but it oozes a raw magnetism that's irresistible. Don't be put off by its hectic traffic, peeling paintwork and ramshackle tenement blocks. Bastia is a more authentic snapshot of modern-day Corsica, a lived-in city that's resisted the urge to polish up its image just to please the tourists. Most mornings you'll see businesspeople walking purposefully to appointments, busy construction workers, cafe staff laying tables and parents urging children to hurry for school. It's certainly more than a gateway to the island and deserves more than a fleeting glance after you've disembarked from the ferry. Linger a little to take in the city's seething old port, great restaurants, cafes, interesting museums and dramatic citadel.

People-Watch on Place St-Nicolas
Bastia's animated focal point

The vast place St-Nicolas, nearly 300m long and one of France's largest squares, sprawls from the ferry port towards the old harbour. Shaded by palms and plane trees, it's the focus of everyday life of Bastia. Throughout summer it's enlivened by free concerts. It's bordered by a string of attractive terrace cafes along its western edge. Our favourite spot for people-watching is the **Palais des Glaces** *(lepalaisdesglaces.com)*,

GETTING AROUND

Feet are best! Park your vehicle and walk as Bastia is a town designed for pedestrians. Both Terra Vecchia and the citadel are small so you can easily explore them thoroughly on foot. For people with reduced mobility, use the little tourist train (adult/child €8/3.5) that leaves from the place St-Nicolas to access the citadel. Frequent shuttles (€10, 25 minutes) operate between **Aéroport Bastia-Poretta**, 20km south of the city, and the centre. The ferry terminal is right in the centre and can be accessed on foot.

BASTIA

★ HIGHLIGHTS
1. Terra Vecchia
2. Vieux Port

● SIGHTS
3. Cathédrale Ste-Marie
4. Chapelle de l'Immaculée Conception
5. Église Ste-Croix
6. Église St-Jean-Baptiste
7. Jardin Romieu
8. Palais des Gouverneurs
9. Place du Marché
10. Place St-Nicolas

● SLEEPING
11. Hôtel des Gouverneurs
12. Hôtel Les Voyageurs

● EATING
13. Le Bistrot du Marché
14. Le Petit Vincent
15. L'Epica
16. Les Affranchis
17. Palais des Glaces

see 15 Ô Sud

● SHOPPING
18. A Biscutteria
19. A Campagna
20. Cap Corse Mattei
21. Chez Mireille
22. U Muntagnolu
23. U Paese

● DRINKING & NIGHTLIFE
see 15 Café Wha!

BASTIA'S BEST PRODUCE SHOPS

U Paese: Sells top-quality local charcuterie as well as cheeses, jams, liqueurs and about 200 Corsican wines.

U Muntagnolu: Sells charcuterie from 30 producers, olive oil, honey and a vast selection of wines.

Cap Corse Mattei: This iconic boutique has the look and feel of a grocer from the 1900s. It sells Mattei's signature aperitif, Cap Corse.

Chez Mireille: The place to head to for *canistrelli* (biscuits) and *fiadone* (a cheesecake made with local ricotta).

A Campagna: Come here for carefully selected jams, biscuits, cheeses and terrines.

A Biscutteria: Sells to-die-for *migliacciu*, a salty dough stuffed with fresh cheese, as well as crunchy, sweet *cuggliulelle* (pastry) made with olive oil and white wine.

a brasserie with a marble-floored dining room and attractive terrace tables.

Sip a Cold One By the Harbour
Bastia's most photogenic part of town

Bastia's **Vieux Port** (old harbour) is a crowded harbour ringed by towering 19th-century tenements. The lively waterfront is lined with tempting terrace restaurants and bars, the ideal spot for an evening refreshment – opt for a Pietra beer at the Mexican-themed **Café Wha!** or a fresh fruit cocktail at neighbouring **Ô Sud**.

Bracketing the ancient fishing port, narrow streets invite exploration. This is **Terra Vecchia**, Bastia's heart and soul. Use the near-identical pinky-beige bell-towers of **Église St-Jean-Baptiste** as beacons to guide you as they rise above the sea of pastel and grey buildings at its feet. Walk around the right of the church into **place du Marché** (also known as place de l'Hôtel de Ville) where a busy market opens 8am to 1pm on Saturdays and Sundays. It's much loved by *Bastiais* (residents of Bastia) who meet after their shopping for a chat and a drink at one of the atmospheric cafes around the square. One block west, **Chapelle de l'Immaculée Conception** is well worth a peek for its rich wooden panelling and elaborately painted barrel-vaulted ceiling.

Climb to the Citadel
Striking buildings and fantastic views

From the southern side of the old port take the beautiful imperial staircase to **Jardin Romieu**, a pleasant little garden. Another flight of steep stone steps lead up to rue St-Michel, where you turn right into place du Donjon. You're now in the upper part of the city, called **Terra Vecchia**, from where you can enjoy stunning views over the old port and the city. Looming over this cobbled square is the **Palais des Gouverneurs**, a Genoese citadel built in 1530. Walk along narrow rue Notre-Dame to reach elegant **Cathédrale Ste-Marie**. Skirting the side of the cathedral, you come to the rococo **Église Ste-Croix**, which features gilded ceilings and a mysterious black-oak crucifix.

EATING IN BASTIA: BEST MEDITERRANEAN CUISINE

Le Bistrot du Marché: This café, brasserie and wine bar has a wide selection of fish and meat dishes as well as salads. *7am-11pm* €

L'Epica: Fine Corsican cuisine is served at this lovely spot by the Vieux-Port. If available, try the sardines with Brocciu cheese. *noon-2pm & 7-10pm Tue-Sat* €

Les Affranchis: Bastia's best venture for innovative Mediterranean-inspired cuisine made of seasonal ingredients. In the citadel. *noon-2pm & 7-9pm Tue-Sat* €€

Le Petit Vincent: Up in the citadel, here's known for its grilled fish and meat dishes and delightful desserts. *7-9.30pm Tue-Sun, noon-2pm Sat & Sun* €€

Beyond Bastia

From Bastia, you can head to the Nebbio, to the west. It's home to stylish St-Florent and the vineyards of Patrimonio.

Approximately 20km west of Bastia, past the Col de Teghime (536m), lies the Nebbio, a relatively lightly travelled area. It's something of a buffer zone, squeezed between Bastia and Cap Corse to its north and La Balagne to the south. Chic St-Florent will tempt you with its hedonistic delights and trendy atmosphere. The Nebbio's also one of the island's prime wine-producing areas. The vineyards in and around Patrimonio produces some of the island's finest vintages – allow plenty of time for wine cellar visits and tastings. West of St-Florent the wild coastline is fringed with scenic expanses of white sand lapped by turquoise, shallow waters – paradise!

Places
St-Florent p869
Patrimonio p872

St-Florent

TIME FROM BASTIA: **40MIN**

Relax in the St-Tropez of Corsica

If you believe the locals, the chic resort of St-Florent ('St-Flo') is a kind of St-Tropez in miniature – and indeed, if you stroll alongside the marina where luxury yachts are moored, you'll see what they're driving at. Join the crowds for the early-evening ritual of strolling along the harbour, then head to **place Doria**, the cool and shady heart of old St-Florent, with its tinkling central fountain. Both locals and tourists meet here for a drink or a chat.

Take a Boat Trip to Sumptuous Beaches

There are two fabulous beaches west of St-Florent. The picture-postcard **Plage du Lotu** is a superb stretch of fine white sand fringing a shallow bay of scintillating turquoise water. It's a beautiful spot for swimming and sunbathing, and the shallow water is safe for children to play in. The beach is completely undeveloped – no hotels, no snack bars, no deckchairs – so bring a picnic and plenty of water, and some form of shade.

Just a few kilometres west of Plage du Lotu lies the bigger **Plage de Saleccia**, a 1km-long strand of dazzling white sand backed by scented grove of Corsican pine.

Both beaches are hard to get to by land. The easiest way to get there – a 20-minute boat trip from St-Florent harbour – is also the most enjoyable. From May to September, **Le Popeye** (lepopeye.com) runs regular trips to Plage du Lotu (round-trip adult/child €15/20) and Plage de Saleccia (round trip €35).

GETTING AROUND

Driving is a great way to explore the hilly region surrounding Bastia and the Nebbio, especially if you are planning to take advantage of the many landscape photo opportunities found in the rural areas and visit the various wineries around Patrimonio. Pick up a rental car at Bastia **train station**. Bike rental is also available in St-Florent; with an e-bike, it's a relatively easy ride to Patrimonio, about 8km to the northeast. Contact **Costa E-Bike** (ebikecosta.wixsite .com/ebikecosta; from €43).

ROAD TRIP

Around the Cap Corse

Although the Cap Corse peninsula, north of Bastia, is only 40km long and 10km wide, the narrow road that runs around its coast claims in 120km of switchback curves and stunning scenery. A wild and rugged region, it's often described as 'an island within an island'. Allow at least two days if you want to chill out and make the most of its cute fishing villages and seductive beaches.

❶ Erbalunga

North of Bastia, the coast road winds past small beaches to reach this harbour village after 9km. As tiny as it is picturesque, Erbalunga squeezes onto a pocket-sized promontory and centres on a cute seafront square, strewn with well-worn fishing boats and tempting restaurants. Narrow alleys lead to a romantic and crumbling Genoese tower by the water.

The Drive: Follow the D80 to the north. The stretch between Sisco and Santa Severa offers spectacular vistas. The road also passes by several massive Genoese towers.

❷ Macinaggio

The hub of the eastern cape, Macinaggio has a pleasant little harbour. With a range of activities, including boat excursions to Îles Finocchiarola, diving and walking, the town makes a good base for exploring the northern reaches of the peninsula. For sunbathing and swimming, nothing can beat **Plage de Tamarone**, north of Macinaggio.

Erbalunga

The Drive: The coastal road now swings inland until Botticella (Ersa), where the D253 branches off to the north.

3 Barcaggio

Corsica's northernmost village, Barcaggio feels like the end of the world. There's a spectacular, uncrowded beach. Walkers can tackle the **Sentier des Douaniers** (p864), a trail that hugs the shoreline, until Tollare (45 minutes).

The Drive: Drive back to the D80 following the D153. Pause at **Col de Serra** for the stunning views of the rugged west coast.

4 Centuri

The tiny harbour of Centuri is easily the most photogenic in Cap Corse. It's also famous for its seafood restaurants that cluster tightly round the harbour. If you order crayfish, make sure it's taken from the *vivier* (live tank). There's no proper beach in Centuri, but diving is available.

The Drive: In several places, minor roads lead off the D80 and corkscrew down to bijou bays, including **Marine de Scalu**, **Marine de Giottani**, **Marine de Canelle** and **Marine d'Albo**.

5 Nonza

Cap Corse's most ravishing village, Nonza clings to the flanks of a rocky pinnacle topped with a stone tower, 150m above a black-sand beach. Beside the main road in the heart of the village is the red-and-yellow 16th-century Église Ste-Julie. Opposite the church, follow the steep alley that leads up to the 18th-century Tour de Nonza (tower of Nonza). Come sunset, stop for a drink or a snack at **La Sassa** (*castalibre.com/lasassa*), which has a clifftop terrace nestled among the rock outcrops below the tower, and savour the extraordinary views over the Mediterranean.

CORSICAN WINES

The third-largest wine producing island in the Mediterranean after Sicily and Sardinia, Corsica has nine AOC regions, including Patrimonio, Ajaccio, Calvi, Figari and Sartène. Local wines are produced mainly from three Corsican *cépages* (grape varieties). The Vermentinu produces fine, dry, zesty white wines (great for seafood). The Niellucciu yields a pungent, earthy red similar to the best Tuscan chiantis. It's usually blended with the indigenous Sciaccarellu, which brings a ruby tint and bright, vivid flavours of maquis flowers to the final wine.

Wine buffs can pick up the list of local domaines at any local tourist office. Most welcome visitors and offer tastings, when you can sample their range of whites, reds and rosés. More on vinsdecorse.com

Plage du Lotu (p869), St-Florent

If you're fit, you can also get there by **kayak** from St-Florent – count on 1½ hours to Plage du Lotu and 2½ hours to Plage de Saleccia. **Agriates Kayak** (*agriateskayak.com*) in St-Florent rents kayaks *(half day from €30)*.

The best way to enjoy both beaches in a day is to follow the **Sentier du Littoral** that links Plage du Lotu and Plage de Saleccia. It's a pretty easy walk (4km, about one hour) near the shore – expect sensational vistas.

Patrimonio

TIME FROM BASTIA: **30MIN**

Discover the Fine Wines of the Nebbio

The Patrimonio area was the first in Corsica to to be granted an AOC seal of quality; the region's vineyards are small, the vines are picked by hand and almost all wines – crisp dry whites, rosés more golden than pink, robust reds – are organic. There are about 40 winemakers. Most of the wineries welcome visitors for tastings without appointment. Some of our favourites include **Domaine Orenga de Gaffory** (*orengadegaffory.com*), which is famous for its Cuvée des Gouverneurs, **Domaine Devichi Mlle D** (*mlledevichi.com*), founded in the 18th-century, and **Domaine Arena** (*domainearena.com*), which produces a creative white, the Morta Maio.

EATING IN THE NEBBIU: BEST RESTAURANTS

Mamo La Tablée: In St-Florent, this waterfront favourite is renowned for its exquisitely presented Mediterranean dishes. *noon-2pm & 6.30-9.30pm* €€

Libertalia Bistro Tropical: Locavore restaurant with good vibes, tempting dishes (wood-fired pizzas), shady terrace and live music. In Patrimonio. *7-10pm* €€

Poppa: The tables of this enticing Corsican/Italian restaurant overlook the marina in St-Flo. Their chalkboard specials are not to be missed. *noon-2pm & 7-9.30pm* €€

La Gaffe: A stylish option in St-Florent, with top-notch seafood and meat dishes served in elegant surrounds. *noon-2pm & 7-9.30pm Thu-Mon* €€€

Calvi & La Balagne

VIBRANT CULTURE | GOURMET RESTAURANTS | STUNNING SEASCAPES

Northwest of Corsica, the striking region known as La Balagne blends history, culture and beach, with a healthy dash of Mediterranean glam to seal the deal. Basking between the fiery orange bastions of its medieval citadel and a glittering moon-shaped bay, Calvi is easy on the eye. Since the 1920s, Calvi has been a tourist hot spot, to the point where it now has the feel – and, in high season, the crowds and prices – of a chichi French Riviera resort. Palatial yachts jostle in its marina, overlooked by upmarket brasseries, while higher up, the citadel watchtowers stand aloof. Apart from its scenic setting, Calvi offers several kilometres of sandy beach backed by a dark ribbon of pines – great for swimming and sunbathing. L'Île-Rousse is another coastal town that offers *la dolce vita*. Venture inland to explore La Balagne's spectacular hinterland, where you'll come across cute-as-can-be villages hidden among valleys and spurs.

Explore the Citadel
History and wraparound views

Crowning a rocky headland, Calvi's massive citadel was fortified by Corsica's Genoese rulers from the 12th century onwards, and has fended off everyone from Franco-Turkish raiders to Anglo-Corsican besiegers. While it holds little commercial activity to match the modern town below, a scenic hour-long stroll is rewarded with superb views from its five bastions.

Relax on Calvi's Beach
Time to chill

Sun-worshippers don't have far to stroll. Backed by a grove of pine trees, Calvi's stellar white-sand beach curves eastwards for 4.5km around the Golfe de Calvi from the marina. If you fancy something more strenuous than pressing a beach towel, **Calvi Nautique Club** *(calvi-nautique-club.com)* rents kayaks, paddleboards and windsurfing boards *(one hour €10 to €20)*.

GETTING AROUND

Aéroport Calvi Ste-Catherine, about 7km to the south, can be reached by taxi *(from €18)* with Ecolimousine *(ecolimousine.fr)*. In summer, it's hard to find a parking place in town, so come prepared. Calvi is easily negotiable on foot. If you want to explore the surroundings or get to a less-crowded section of the beach, consider renting a bike or an e-bike – contact **Wild Machja** *(wildmachja.com)*. You can also rent a scooter with **Tramare e Monti** *(tramare-monti.com)*.

☑ TOP TIP

Expect traffic jams in summer. Your best bet to avoid them is to arrive early (before 9am) and leave in the evening.

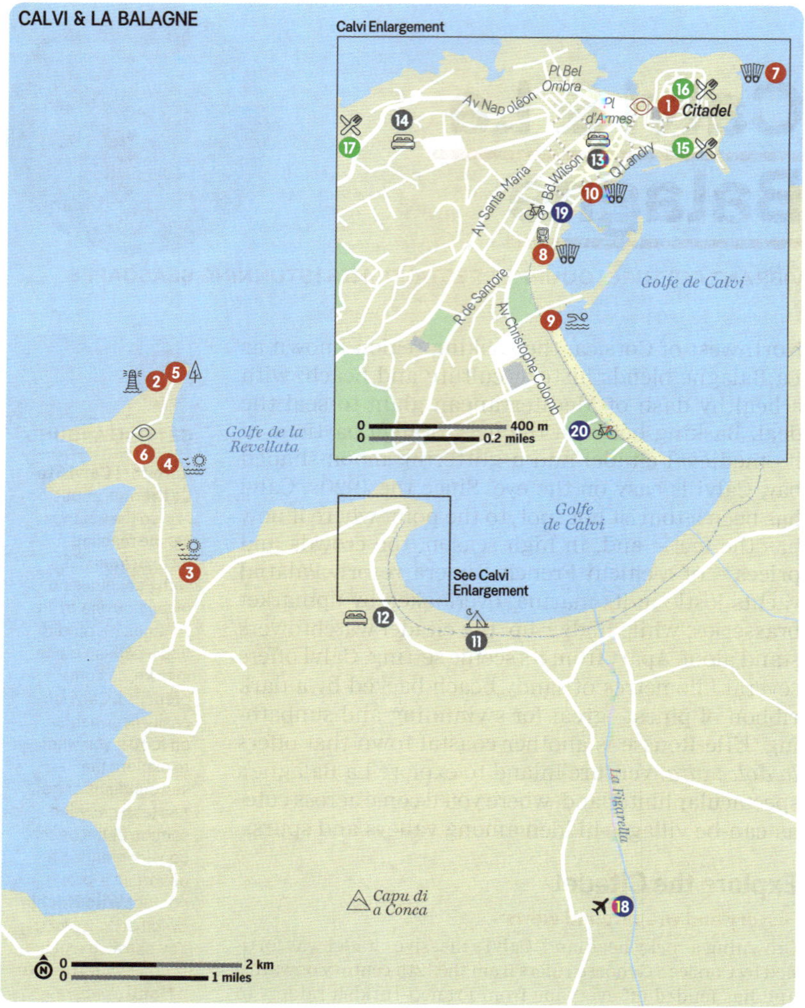

CALVI & LA BALAGNE

● HIGHLIGHTS
1. Citadel

● SIGHTS
2. Lighthouse
3. Plage de l'Alga
4. Plage de l'Oscelluccia
5. Pointe de la Revellata
6. Pointe de la Revellata

● ACTIVITIES
7. B-17
8. Calvi Epic Plongée
9. Calvi Nautique Club
10. Plongée Castille

● SLEEPING
11. Camping La Pinède
12. Campo di Fiori
13. Hôtel Le Magnolia
14. Hôtel Saint-Érasme

● EATING
15. Le Chalet
16. Ô Fao
17. U Fanale

● TRANSPORT
18. Aéroport Calvi Ste-Catherine
19. Tramare e Monti
20. Wild Machja

Walk Around Pointe de la Revellata
Scenic seascapes and secret beaches

Thrill your senses with a short scenic drive west along the coastal D81B (signposted 'Route de Porto – bord de mer' from just below Calvi's citadel) to Pointe de la Revellata, the nearest point on Corsica to the French mainland. Suddenly, after 4km, the majestic cape pops into view, with a toy-like white **lighthouse** at its tip. Park in the lay-by and head off to explore the network of dusty walking trails etched in ginger. Allow two to three hours to complete the relatively easy round trip walk. Bring plenty of water, a hat and sunscreen.

Fancy a dip? We suggest you stop at **Plage de l'Alga** or **Plage de l'Oscelluccia**, two hidden coves lapped by azure waters that locals would love to keep for themselves. Shhh...

Aquatic Wonders
Below the waterline

Calvi is one of Corsica's great diving destinations, with a range of dive sites suitable for all levels (beginners are welcome). The shoreline around Pointe de la Revellata, to the west, is extraordinary, with an abundance of fish species and a spectacular seascape – think canyons, boulders and small valleys. If, like us, you're a wreck buff, be sure to dive the sensational **B-17**, which features the wreck of a WWII B-17 bomber in a good state of preservation (maximum depth 27m). Recommended dive operators include **Calvi Epic Plongée** (epic-plongee.com; single dive €50) and **Plongée Castille** (plongeecastille.com; single dive €60). They also offer snorkelling trips to Pointe de la Revellata.

Attend Iconic Festivals
Festive mood and live music

Calvi is big on festivals, mostly held during summer months. Let's start with **Jazz in Calvi** (calvifunspirit.com), held in late June, with open-air and indoor concerts plus a range of jam sessions. Then comes **Calvi on the Rocks** (calviontherocks.com) in early July, which features three days of electronic and experimental music. In mid-September, don't miss **Rencontres de Chants Polyphoniques** (rencontrespolyphoniques.com), a festival of traditional Corsican chants staged in various locations within Calvi's citadel – a great and poignant way to immerse yourself in Corsican culture.

POLYPHONIC SINGING

'A voice from the depths of the earth, a song from the dawn of time.' So wrote UK writer Dorothy Carrington on first hearing Corsica's unique polyphonic singing. You're bound to hear it, wafting out of cafes and restaurants or played over the speakers sotto voce as you inspect supermarket shelves or sit waiting at a bus station. But for uninterrupted pleasure and time to appreciate its haunting refrains, you need to attend a recital, often held in the local parish church. It's singing typically in a trio or small chorus, where each participant takes a different melody, and without musical accompaniment. In summer, several ensembles, including A Filetta and Chœur de Sartène, tour the island and any tourist office can give you details of upcoming events.

EATING IN CALVI: TOP CORSICAN FOOD

A Piazzetta: Tuck into home-cooked pasta dishes at this cosy den with a shady terrace. Cash only. *noon-2pm & 7-9.30pm Tue-Sun* €

Ô Fao: One of the few eating options within the citadel, intimate Ô Fao serves charcuterie and cheese platters as well as tempting specials. *10am-4pm Wed-Mon* €

Le Chalet: A colourful hole-in-the-wall specialising in grilled meat. Also serves salads and pasta. *noon-2pm & 7-9.30pm* €€

U Fanale: A well-established venue on the road to La Revellata. The classically Corsican menu revolves around fresh local meats, fish and vegetables. *7-10pm* €€

Beyond Calvi

Explore L'Île-Rousse, Calvi's little sister, and spare the time to head up and inland to discover scenic forests and valleys, far from the crowds.

Places
L'Île-Rousse p876
Forêt de Bonifatu p876
Vallée du Fangu p877

Sure, it's tempting to spend a whole week in vibrant Calvi, but that would be a shame to restrict yourself to La Balagne's main resort. About 22km east of Calvi, the attractive little beach town of L'Île-Rousse straddles a long, sandy curve of coastline that is backed by maquis-cloaked mountains. Unlike Calvi, it has a more laid-back holiday feel even out of season. After indulging in seaside pleasures, grab the steering wheel to venture inland. Hidden among the valleys and spurs of La Balagne's spectacular hinterland, even on the hillsides lining the coast, you'll come across cute-as-can-be villages, scenic roads, wild valleys, natural pools and dense forests.

L'Île-Rousse

TIME FROM CALVI: **45MIN**

Wander Amid the Old Town

L'Île-Rousse's delightful **old town** centres on tree-shaded **place Paoli**. Dodge the pétanque players on the square to shop in the open-air Grecian temple of a market where you can fill your basket with Corsican charcuterie and cheese. In the late afternoon take a stroll along the town's **Promenade de la Marinella** that hugs the beach – it doesn't get more relaxed than this.

Hop on the Coastal Train

You may well tremble as the *petit train des plages* (little beach train) – the affectionate nickname for the dinky little coastal train *(cf-corse.corsica; from €2)* between Calvi and L'Île-Rousse – trundles along its sand-covered tracks. Running at least six times daily, and calling at 14 intermediate stations by request only, it's the easiest way to access numerous hidden coves and beaches. Hop off at one of the stops between Calvi and l'Île-Rousse for a quiet rocky cove or, for sand, leave the train at **Lumiu-L'Arinella**, **Algajola** or **Plage de Bodri**.

Forêt de Bonifatu

TIME FROM CALVI: **30MIN**

Immerse Yourself in a Scenic Forest

Accessed by a lightly trafficked road, the forest of Bonifatu spreads over 3000 hectares and ranges in elevation from 300m to 2000m. It's a mix of maritime and *laricio* pines, green oaks

GETTING AROUND

You can comfortably survive on the coast without a vehicle, taking the **petit train des plages** between Calvi, L'Île-Rousse and intermediate stations. But to head southward or to experience the seductive inland delights of La Balagne, a vehicle of your own is the only way. If you just want to get around L'Île-Rousse, e-bike rental is available in town. The **train station** is at the inland end of the causeway to the ferry port.

Forêt de Bonifatu

LOCAL PRODUCE

When it comes to *produits du terroir* (local produce), Corsica has a lot to offer. First, charcuterie. Corsica is famous for its flavoursome cured meats, made from free-range pigs that feed on chestnuts and acorns. Make sure you purchase it in reputable speciality shops. Cheese has also been elevated to an art form in Corsica. Ah Brocciu! Mild, crumbly and white, not a million miles from ricotta, it's made from the *petit-lait* (whey) of either goat's or ewe's milk. Corsican olive oil is also sought afer because it's extremely aromatic. The main olive oil-producing regions are the Balagne and the Alta Rocca. A number of local producers also sell delicious homemade jams (made with clementines, figs, chestnuts etc) as well as fragrant honey.

and other broad-leafed trees. On the upper slopes, outcrops of granite, pink, beige or grey according to the ambient light, poke through. Should you fall in love in the place, consider staying at the **Auberge de la Forêt** *(auberge-foret-bonifatu. com)*, at the road's end. It's a great base for hikes both easy and demanding (the warden can advise you). You'll also find plenty of idyllic spots for a picnic along the river Figarella, as well as transparent green natural pools in which you can swim.

Vallée du Fangu

TIME FROM CALVI: **40MIN**

Discover a Little-Travelled Valley

For a riverside picnic and a refreshing dip, the valley of the river Fangu offers perfect conditions. About 1km beyond the hamlet of Fangu, clear pools glisten beneath **Ponte Vecchiu**, a steeply arched Genoese bridge. If the best spots have been taken, there are several other opportunities upstream beside steep, yet shallow, gorges.

Downstream, the **Delta du Fangu** *(delta-du-fangu.com; rental per hr from €8)* is a wild estuary that you can explore by kayaking.

EATING IN L'ÎLE-ROUSSE: OUR PICKS

A Casa Corsa: This wine bar does a brisk trade in salads, tartines (open-faced sandwiches), cheese and charcuterie platters. Prime location on place Paoli. *10am-11pm* €

L'Osteria: Combines modern renditions of Corsican staples with pan-Mediterranean classics. *noon-2pm & 7-10pm Mon-Sat* €

A Siesta: Overlooking the beach, A Siesta receives great reviews for its wholesome fish dishes served with fresh seasonal vegetables. *noon-2pm & 7-10pm* €€

L'Escale: On the waterfront, this restaurant serves up the town's best seafood, including tuna, swordfish and octopus. *noon-2.30pm & 6.30-10pm* €€

LA BALAGNE'S INLAND TREASURES

Clunk on your safety belt and brave the twisting minor roads of La Balagne to reach scattered hilltop villages that are a world away from the seaside towns.

START	END	LENGTH
L'Île-Rousse	L'Île-Rousse	95km; three hours

Head eastward from ❶ **L'Île-Rousse** along the T30 and, after 7km, turn right for ❷ **Belgodère**, a typical Balagne village with its square, fountain, church and a couple of cafes. Continue along the RT301 and the D963 via Olmi-Cappella to ❸ **Col de Battaglia** (1099m). From the terrace of the **A Merendella** restaurant and bar, you'll enjoy sensational views of the long sweep of coastline. A steep, twisting descent brings you to ❹ **Speloncato** (600m), which owes its charm to the little streets densely packed with stone houses. Continue on the D71 before forking right onto the D151 for the oh-so-photogenic hilltop village of ❺ **Sant'Antonino** (490m). Climb to the top of the cobbled streets, bordered by souvenir shops, for ever-more impressive views. Back at the car park, stop by the vaulted cellar of **Clos Antonini**, noted as much for its citrus juices as its wines, and relish a refreshing glass of freshly squeezed lemon juice trickled over ice. Back on the D151, head to ❻ **Aregno**, where the Église de la Trinité, built in the two-tone Pisan Romanesque style, stands out. Then comes the bijou village of ❼ **Pigna**. Wandering along the village's steep cobbled alleys, you'll come across the workshops of various craftspeople. Find the finest Corsican produce, sourced from small-scale producers, at **Casa Savelli** before returning to L'Île-Rousse.

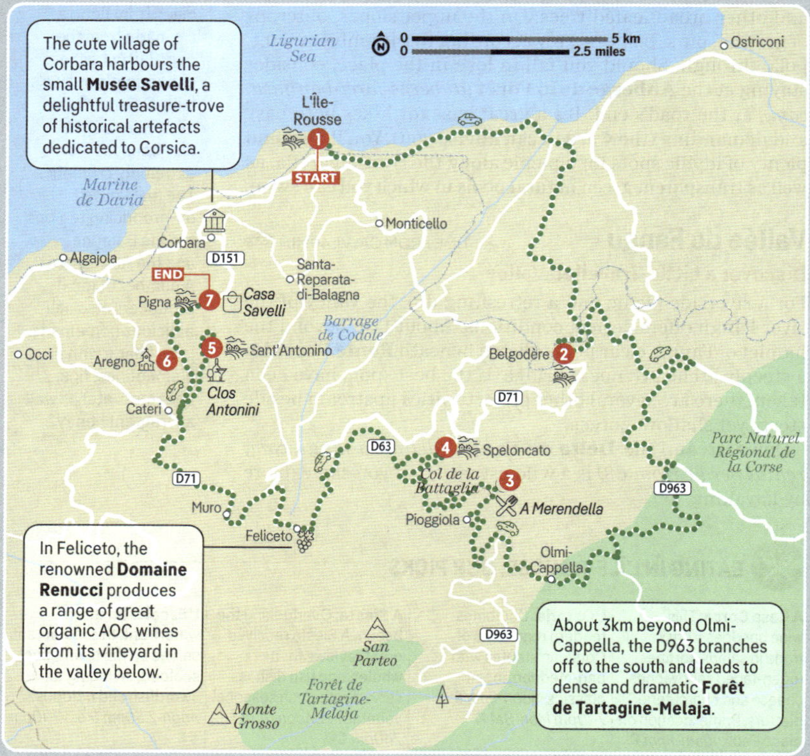

The cute village of Corbara harbours the small **Musée Savelli**, a delightful treasure-trove of historical artefacts dedicated to Corsica.

In Feliceto, the renowned **Domaine Renucci** produces a range of great organic AOC wines from its vineyard in the valley below.

About 3km beyond Olmi-Cappella, the D963 branches off to the south and leads to dense and dramatic **Forêt de Tartagine-Melaja**.

Corte

CORSICAN CULTURE | OUTDOORS | SPECTACULAR SCENERY

Secretive. Inward looking. Staunchly Corsican. In many ways, Corte, the biggest town in Corsica's interior, feels different. Roughly midway between Bastia and Ajaccio, this is the beating heart of the island, in a fabulous setting. The fairy-tale sight of the citadel atop a craggy mount that bursts forth from the valley is sensational. Centring on this towering pinnacle that's been fortified for over 2000 years, Corte has been at the centre of the island's fortunes since Pasquale Paoli made it the capital of his short-lived Corsican republic in 1755. Despite its isolation, the town is full of atmosphere. It is home to the island's only university, so it is lively with students during the academic year. From April to October, many visitors make their base here, eager to explore the Restonica and Tavignano valleys, just on the outskirts of town, as well as lesser-explored areas further in the interior.

GETTING AROUND

Corte's **train station** is across the Tavignanu River 800m below the town centre. If you're driving, be aware that traffic congestion is common in Corte in summer, and it's not easy to find a space to park your car in the centre. Corte is small enough to be navigated on foot. The main street in Corte's old town is the Cours Paoli that runs on a north–south axis and is lined with shops and restaurants.

Statue of Pascal Paoli (p881)

☑ TOP TIP

It's not a bad idea to reach Corte by train from either Bastia or Ajaccio, as the ride is superscenic and traverses some of the island's most spectacular landscapes.

HIGHLIGHTS
1 Citadelle

SIGHTS
2 Belvédère
3 Cours Paoli
4 Église de l'Annonciation
5 Musée de la Corse
6 Place Gaffory
7 Statue of Pascal Paoli

SLEEPING
8 Le Duc de Padoue

EATING
9 A Casa di l'Orsu
10 La Trattoria
11 Le 24
12 Pâtisserie Casanova

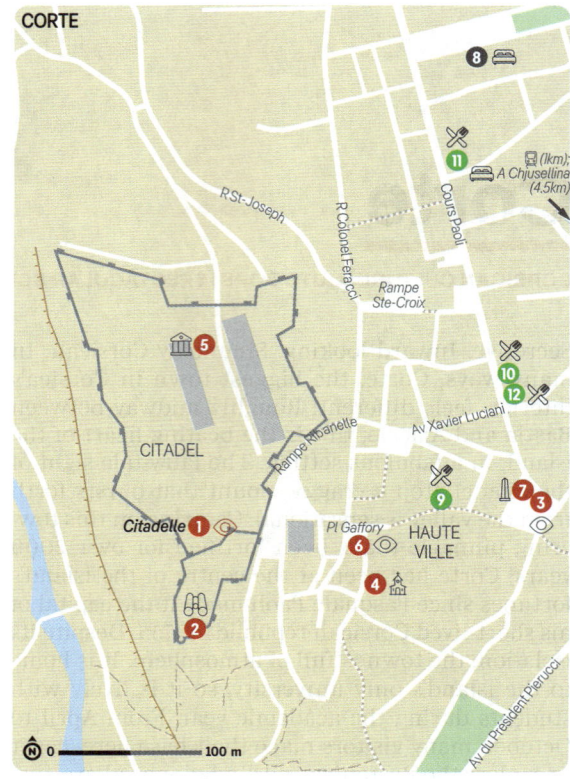

Explore the Citadel

History and superb panoramas

For a bird's-eye view of Corte, haul your way up to the **Citadelle** *(closed Mon)*, which occupies a stark rocky crag above the valley. The citadel itself was built in 1419, while the two buildings facing one another past the gate, the Caserne Padoue (Padoue Barracks) and Caserne Serrurier (Serrurier Barracks), were added in the 19th century. The latter houses the **Musée de la Corse** *(musee-corse.com; adult/child incl citadel €5.50/3; closed Mon)*, the island's principal museum of Corsican history and anthropology; well worth a visit if you want to get the lowdown on Corsica's past and culture (add an extra €2 for the English audioguide). To reach the upper level of the Citadelle (and enjoy the views), you have to pass through the museum. To sample just as prodigious a panorama for free, follow signs to the **Belvédère**, a free-access viewing platform.

Below the citadel, **place Gaffory** is a lively little square that's dominated by the 15th-century **Église de l'Annonciation**.

Citadelle

See the bullet holes that pockmark nearby houses? They date from Corsica's war of independence in 1755.

Stroll Down Cours Paoli
Feel the pulse of central Corte

Ready to experience a miniature version of an Italian *passegiata* (stroll)? At aperitif time, ramble along **Cours Paoli**, Corte's main thoroughfare. Start from place Paoli, the city's focal point, which is dominated by a **statue of Pascal Paoli**, and stroll down the *cours* (street). There are plenty of reasons to linger – think atmospheric terrace restaurants and bars. Will you be able to resist the tantalising display of sweet treats at **Pâtisserie Casanova** *(patisserie-casanova1887. fr)*? Hmmm, their *falculella* (a Corsican dessert made with Brocciu cheese and chestnut flour) lingers long on the palate.

WHO WAS PASQUALE PAOLI?

General Pasquale Paoli (1725–1807) is the Father of Corsica (U Babbu). Born near Morosaglia (40km northeast of Corte) and educated in Naples, he led the Corsican insurrection against Genoa in 1755. Under his leadership, independent Corsica was blessed with one of the world's first democratic constitutions, its own currency, a flag and a university in Corte. Independence lasted 14 years until his defeat by the French at the Battle of Ponte-Novo on 8 May 1769. Exiled, he left for London seeking help from the British. Following a naval attack in January 1794 led by, then Captain, Horatio Nelson, an Anglo-Corsican kingdom was declared. It lasted two years. Paoli was exiled again on 14 October 1795 and died in London on 5 February 1807.

 EATING IN CORTE: OUR PICKS

La Trattoria: This snug place dishes up classic Mediterranean cuisine, with everything from salads to meat dishes and pasta. *noon-2pm & 7.30-10pm Mon-Sat* €

A Casa di l'Orsu: Tasty modern Corsican food made from carefully chosen ingredients. Also has vegetarian options. *noon-2pm & 7-10pm* €

Le 24: Besides tapas and great wines, this cool hangout serves a full array of meat and fish mains, with Corsican- and seafood-themed menus. *noon-2pm & 7-10pm* €€

A Chjusellina: Meals served at this farm south of Corte use products straight from the property. Dinner by reservation. *7pm Mon-Sat* €€

Beyond Corte

Pristine valleys with *vasques* (natural pools), cool forests, great walks, tucked-away villages and breathtaking panoramas – you can't go wrong when exploring the mountainous area around Corte.

Places

Vallée de la Restonica p882

Vallée du Tavignanu p883

Vallée du Niolu p883

Corte makes a perfect central point from which to explore Corsica's mountainous heart, where you'll find fresh mountain air, deep forests, picturesque valleys, abundant hiking trails and sweet swimming spots in gin-clear rivers. You come here to enjoy the scenery and rejuvenate mind and body in a pristine environment. You don't really need to travel far to find such conditions. Right on Corte's doorstep, the wooded Vallée de la Restonica beckons, while the nearby, car-free Vallée du Tavignano, whose former mule track leads deep into the mountains, is a dream come true for nature lovers and photographers. Further north, the easily overlooked Vallée du Niolu was for centuries all but cut off from the rest of the island and retains a special character.

GETTING AROUND

The region is traversed by the relatively lightly trafficked T20 road linking Ajaccio and Bastia. The pressure can be intense driving in the Vallée de la Restonica, which has a large number of tight bends and few passing opportunities. Navigation is easy in the little-travelled Vallée du Niolu. If you're keen on slow-travel style, some villages around Corte can be reached from Bastia or Ajaccio by Corsica's single-track railway, which runs through forests and around mountains.

Vallée de la Restonica

TIME FROM CORTE: **5MIN**

Refresh Yourself in Natural Pools

Crashing down from the grey-green mountains southwest of Corte, the Restonica River has carved a gorgeous pine-forested valley that extends right to the edge of town. From Corte, the narrow D623 winds its way for 15km to a dead end.

Apart from the majestic landscape, the Vallée de la Restonica's main attraction is the river itself, which in summer presents a series of languid, sparkling green *vasques* (pools) fringed with granite slabs, ideal for picnicking and sunbathing. Come early to find your own pool. Hint: the best swimming spots can be found between **Auberge de la Restonica** and the **Point Information** (information kiosk), about 4km along the Restonica gorge from Corte.

Due to significant storm damages in 2023, access to the high valley is now restricted to private vehicles. You can drive until **Camping de Tuani**. Past the camping, you'll have to walk. Your best bet is to take the shuttle from Corte railway station (€4 return), which goes up to near the dead end. Book online using the app M-Ticket Via Corsica Restonica.

If you're fit, we suggest you walk to **Lac de Melu** (1711m) and **Lac de Capitellu** (1930m), two picture-pretty glacial lakes.

The path starts from the **Chalet Chez Theo** at the end of the D623. Allow two hours (return) for Lac de Melu and 3½ hours (return) for Lac de Capitellu. Back to Chez Theo, treat yourself to a well-deserved *omelette au Brocciu*.

Vallée du Tavignanu
TIME FROM CORTE: **5MIN**
Wander Along a Quiet Valley

If you feel overwhelmed by the vehicles in the Vallée de la Restonica, car-free Vallée du Tavignanu is for you. This deep gorge is only accessible on foot and sees few visitors, despite being on Corte's doorstep. From Corte, the signposted track heads through the maquis, hugging the river as it climbs deep into the mountains. We suggest that you walk until **Passerelle de Rossolinu** footbridge, reached after 2½ hours. This is an idyllic spot for a picnic and a swim in one of the many transparent green *vasques* near the bridge.

The Vallée du Tavignanu can also be explored on horseback – contact **L'Albadu** *(hebergement-albadu.fr; 2hr €50)* in Corte, which can arrange horse-riding excursions.

Vallée du Niolu
TIME FROM CORTE: **25MIN**
Explore the Heart of Corsica

Nowhere guards the secrets of traditional Corsica better than this remote and utterly photogenic valley. Relatively isolated from the rest of the island, it's well worth a few days of exploration. From Corte, head north along the T20 as far as Francardo and turn west onto the D84. Now the adventure begins. The narrow road winds its way for about 20km through a vertiginous ravine known as **Scala di Santa Regina**, one of the island's most dramatic landscapes. Then the road reaches **Calacuccia**, the 'capital' of the Niolu. Other villages to visit include **Albertacce**, **Lozzi**, **Casamaccioli** and **Calasima**, which, at 1100m, lays claim to being Corsica's highest village. The iconic Monte Cinto (2706m), the Paglia Orba (2525m) and the distinctive jagged peaks of I Cinque Frati form a heart-stopping backdrop.

The **Association Sportive du Niolu** *(haute-montagne-corse.com; canyoning trips from €50)* offers guided hiking, climbing, canyon descents and, in winter, cross-country ski treks throughout the valley. Most outings are suitable for all levels.

Sporty types can climb Paglia Orba, one of Corsica's most scenic hikes. Allow at least six hours (return) from Calasima.

If you're around in early September, make sure you attend the **Santa di u Niolu**, in Casamaccioli. This is a fantastic opportunity to immerse yourself in one of Corsica's most venerated religious festivals, which attracts thousands of pilgrims. A gaudy statue of the Madonna is proudly paraded through the village, and you can attend competitions of polyphonic singing.

MAQUIS

Covering 40% of Corsica, the maquis is a dense concentration of 78 varieties of endemic flowers, 42 species of orchids, aromatic plants, olive-trees, cork and holm oaks. If you're in Corsica in spring or early summer, be prepared for a sensory overload, when the maquis bursts with sweet-smelling, flowering plants and herbs. Typically scrubby and short, the maquis is tough enough to survive summer's intense heat, burns quickly – a carelessly extinguished cigarette butt or discarded broken glass can cause dramatic wildfires – but grows rapidly, too. It provides a safe-haven for most of Corsica's 40 kinds of orchid and pungent herbs such as rosemary, lavender and the tiny blue-violet flowering Corsican mint with its summertime aroma.

Ajaccio

HISTORY | URBAN VIBES | BOAT EXCURSIONS

✅ TOP TIP
Don't overlook **Pointe de la Parata** (p887) and the **Îles Sanguinaires** (p886), west of Ajaccio – allow a day to explore both.

Commanding a lovely sweep of bay, the handsome city of Ajaccio has the self-confidence that comes with a starring role in world history. In summer, there's more than a whiff of the Côte d'Azur to its pastel-toned, cafe-filled historic core and the trendy waterfront promenade that stretches west – buzzing with beachgoers by day and party people later on. But it's in the tangled old-town lanes that the spectre of Napoléon Bonaparte looms largest. He's everywhere, in street names and museums, and watching mournfully over the pétanques players from atop his pedestal in the place d'Austerlitz. With ferries from mainland France mooring right alongside, Ajaccio's always bustling with activity. Everyone from solo travellers to romance-seeking couples and families will love moseying around the buzzing centre, replete with historic buildings and buzzing cafes – not to mention its vast marina and the route des Sanguinaires area, a few kilometres to the west.

Walk in Napoléon's Footsteps
Napoleonic heritage

Corsica's major art institution, **Palais Fesch – Musée des Beaux-Arts** *(musee-fesch.com; adult/child €10/free)* exhibits works collected by Cardinal Joseph Fesch, Napoléon's maternal uncle. It is the most important collection of Italian paintings

GETTING AROUND

Finding parking in the centre of Ajaccio is a nightmare and few hotels have their own facilities. Leave the car at a paying car park and explore Ajaccio on foot. There are large car parks at the **train station**, near the **ferry terminal**, beneath place de Gaulle (parking du Diamant) and northeast of place Foch. The

Aéroport d'Ajaccio Napoléon Bonaparte is 6km east of the town centre around the bay, It's linked by the half-hourly Muvistrada bus 8 (€10, 30 minutes) to Ajaccio's train station. There are ferry services to the French mainland ports of Marseille, Nice and Toulon.

AJACCIO

🟠 **HIGHLIGHTS**	**11** Le Roi de Rome
1 Palais Fesch – Musée des Beaux-Arts	🔵 **TRANSPORT**
🔴 **SIGHTS**	**12** Charles-Ornano
2 Chapelle Impériale	**13** Gare Maritime
3 Maison Bonaparte	**14** Train Station
🔴 **ACTIVITIES**	
4 Nave Va	
⚫ **SLEEPING**	
5 Hôtel Napoléon	
🟢 **EATING**	
6 A Calata	
7 A Merendella Citadina	
8 A Nepita	
9 Le 20123	
10 Le Grand Café Napoléon	

885

Fêtes Napoléoniennes

NAPOLÉON, SON OF CORSICA?

Despite Ajaccio's endless Napoléonic connections, *le petit caporal*'s attitude to his home island was rather ambivalent, if not condescending or hostile to it. Born to an Italian father and a Corsican mother, and largely educated in France, Napoléon actually spent relatively little time on the island, and never returned following his coronation as Emperor of France in 1804. In 1814, the year of his first definitive defeat, the people of Ajaccio threw a bust of the emperor into the sea. Corsican resentment, however, seems to have passed with time and, by the 19th-century, the house in Ajaccio where Napoléon was born had become almost a place of pilgrimage. Ultimately Napoléon was lionised as the homeboy who brought the island fame.

in France outside the Louvre in Paris. If you're short of time, go straight to the basement where there's a small but lovely collection of Corsican landscapes and lively portraits, and look at the collection of Napoléonic memorabilia on the ground floor.

The **Chapelle Impériale**, across the courtyard from the Palais Fesch, holds the tombs of Napoléon's parents and several other relatives. Don't expect to find the man himself, though – he's buried in Les Invalides in Paris.

A five-minute walk from there will bring you to **Maison Bonaparte** *(musees-nationaux-malmaison.fr; adult/child €7/free; closed Mon)* where Napoléon was born on 15 August 1769. Napoléon only lived here until he was nine, so don't expect to learn much about him here: the museum is more about Corsica and the house.

Ajaccio's biggest event is **Fêtes Napoléoniennes**, which celebrates Napoléon's birthday on 15 August. Expect military-themed parades, street spectacles and a huge fireworks display.

Explore the Golfe d'Ajaccio
A gentle boat trip to offshore islets

Enjoy a half-day sailing trip to the **Îles Sanguinaires** (Bloody Islands) with **Nave Va** *(naveva.com: adult/child from €34/19)*.

EATING IN AJACCIO: BEST RESTAURANTS

A Merendella Citadina: The stone-arched cellar is a bit noisy but the food's delicious, using fresh, local ingredients. *7-10pm Tue-Sat* €€

A Nepita: With modern French cuisine and elegant setting, here's a nice change from traditional Corsican. *noon-1.30pm & 7.30-9.30pm Tue-Sat* €€

Le Roi de Rome: This buzzy venue is half wine bar, half convivial neighbourhood restaurant. Meats are the house speciality. *6-10pm Tue-Sun* €€

Le 20123: Feast on a seasonal five-course menu that's rich in meaty traditional cuisine. *noon-2pm & 7-10pm Mon-Sat, 7-10pm Sun* €€

These tiny, uninhabited islands, named for their vivid crimson colours at sunset, lie off Pointe de la Parata, at the northern end of Golfe d'Ajaccio. They're a haven for seabirds. Boat trips include a one-hour stop (and swim) at Mezzu Mare, the largest of the islands.

Wander along Pointe de la Parata
Pristine nature and sensational views

The slender promontory of Pointe de la Parata, 12km west of Ajaccio, is a magnet for walkers. An easy-to-follow trail around the cape rewards with great sea views and tantalising close-ups of the four islets of the Îles Sanguinaires. Count on one hour for the loop. You can get there by car (there's a paying car park) or by bus 5 (€1, 30 minutes), which runs to the trailhead from just west of Ajaccio's place de Gaulle.

Dive the Golfe d'Ajaccio
Dramatic seascape and fish life in abundance

The Golfe d'Ajaccio is a diver's treat, with a good balance of scenic seascapes and dense marine life. The most spectacular dive sites are found along the southern and northern sections of the gulf. A few favourites include **Le Tabernacle**, with a plateau sloping gently to below 22m, and **Sette Nave**, with lots of nooks and crannies in the rock formations.

Contact **Isula Plongée** (isula-plongee.com; single dive €56), a reputable dive centre.

Experience Ajaccio's Dynamic Nightlife Scene
Lively bars and festive mood

Ajaccio's most atmospheric bars tend to be concentrated along bd Pascal Rossini by the western waterfront, and rue Roi du Rome up in the old town. Look around the chichi port **Charles-Ornano**, at the marina, too. In high summer, the centre of pleasurable gravity shifts west to the rte des Sanguinaires, which is lined with trendy *paillotes* (beachside venues), including **Le Scudo** (lescudo.fr), that organise *soirées à thème* (themed nights).

GENOESE TOWERS

Somewhere or another you'll have seen that classic photo of a stately Genoese tower silhouetted on a rocky promontory at sunset. Around 60 of these iconic fortified structures are dotted along the coastline, a reminder of centuries of Genoese presence on the island. Sited all around the coastline so that each was visible from the next, the towers formed a vast surveillance network. Mostly round but occasionally square, they are about 15m high. Dating from the 16th century, they stand today in various states of repair; some of them have been wonderfully restored, while others are crumbling away.

The most stunning Genoese towers can be found around Cap Corse, Golfe de Porto, Golfe d'Ajaccio and Golfe du Valinco.

EATING IN AJACCIO: OUR PICKS

Le Grand Café Napoléon: This Ajaccio institution has a menu featuring elegantly presented fish and meat dishes. *noon-2pm & 7-9.30pm Mon-Sat* €

Le Bistrot Gourmand: This cosy place is noted for its excellent market-driven fare. *noon-2pm & 7.30-10pm Tue-Sat* €€

A Calata: Has an eclectic menu, with an assortment of fish and meat dishes, as well as frondy salads. *noon-2pm & 7-10pm Tue-Sat, noon-2pm Sun* €€

La Crique: Delicate seafood dishes using local, seasonal products. Fine sea views on rte des Sanguinaires. *noon-2pm & 7.30-9.30pm Tue-Sat, noon-2pm Sun* €€

Beyond
Ajaccio

Head north to Les Calanques de Piana for some unforgettable landscapes and south to the Golfe du Valinco for beaches and outdoor activities.

Places
Calanques de Piana p888
Golfe du Valinco p889

There's a good mix of hedonistic, cultural and adrenaline-fuelled experiences beyond Ajaccio. North of Ajaccio, the plunging cliffs of Les Calanques offer the most spectacular panoramas of the island (and that's saying a lot). They are part of a UNESCO World Heritage site and are unmissable. South of Ajaccio, the Golfe du Valinco, shaped like a huge bite chomped out of the fretted coastline, is another stunner. At the eastern end of the bay is Propriano, a lively holiday centre in summer. There are also two smaller coastal pleasures on each side of the bay, Porto Pollo and Campomoro, both blessed with magnetic beaches lapped by lapis lazuli waters. Allow at least five days to explore the wonders around Ajaccio.

Calanques de Piana

TIME FROM AJACCIO: 1½HR

Be Awed by Unique Geological Formations

No amount of praise can do justice to the astonishing beauty of **Les Calanques**. These sculpted cliffs, more than 400m high, rear above the Golfe de Porto in staggering scarlet pillars, teetering columns and irregularly shaped outcrops of pink, ochre and ginger. This giant granite jumble was formed by the erosion of wind and sea.

There are several ways to discover the Calanques. You can drive the 10km stretch of the D81 between the villages of Piana and Porto. As you sway around switchback after switchback along the rock-riddled road, one mesmerising vista piggybacks on another. But we prefer renting an e-bike with **Porto Location Vélo** *(04 95 26 10 13; per day €45)* in Porto, which makes it much easier to stop by the roadside to take pictures. Another sustainable option is to don your walking shoes and follow the Château Fort trail (p864). Park near the Tête de Chien, a rock that's signposted on a large bend in the D81, 3.5km east of Piana. After about 20 minutes, you'll reach a platform known as the **Château Fort** (Fortress), from where the view over the Golfe de Porto and the inlets of Les Calanques is unsurpassable. For a sea-level perspective, take a boat tour from Porto (p890).

Tip for photographers: come late afternoon, when the rocks are flaming red in the sunlight. Afterwards, flop on the sand

GETTING AROUND

Destinations such as Propriano and Piana cannot be easily accessed from Ajaccio using public transport. A car is essential for exploring the beaches around the Golfe du Valinco and getting to Les Calanques de Piana. The meandering country roads make for a memorable road trip. Be sure to rent a small vehicle as most roads are quite narrow. Be warned that in summer the road through the *calanques* (rocky inlets and cliffs) is nose-to-tail busy.

D81, Les Calanques

on the idyllic beaches of **Ficajola** or **Arone**, 5km north and 12km southwest of Piana respectively.

Golfe du Valinco
TIME FROM AJACCIO: 1¼HR

Explore the Wonders of a Scenic Gulf
Our favourite beach is 7km south of Propriano on the road to Campomoro – **Plage de Portigliolo**, an incredible 4km long stretch of fine, white sand. We also love the secluded **Plage de Cupabia**, north of Campomoro, with its long, wide expanse of brilliant-white sand and azure waters. It's also a playground for all things watersports: paddleboarding, kayaking and surfing. Contact **Waterplay** (waterplay.fr; 1hr rental paddleboard/kayak €15/10).

In Campomoro, at the southern tip of the gulf, **Sud Nautik** (sudnautik.com) rents out kayaks (from €12 per hour) and can organise guided kayak outings (half-day adult/child €39/20) to access some secret coves along the coast.

Diving's more your thing? Check out the best dive sites of the gulf, including **Les Aiguilles** and **Les Cathédrales**, all within easy reach of Porto Pollo. For beginners there are sheltered inlets that offer safe conditions for introductory dives. **3P Porto Pollo Plongée** (portopollo-plongee.fr; single dive €72) has good credentials.

RURAL GEMS IN THE AJACCIO HINTERLAND

Céline Bellini works for the cinema industry. She's of Corsican descent and spends all her holidays in her family home near Ajaccio. She names her favourite Corsican villages. @bettyoooops

My roots are in this tiny village of **Carbuccia**, hidden in the Gravona valley. It's a great place if you want to lose track of the days. This is rural Corsica at its best.

I love getting to **Bocognano** to shop for local produce, whether it be charcuterie, cheese, jams or honey. There's also a little cafe that's great to mingle with locals.

Reaching the village of **Pastricciola** is bit of an adventure. From the D4, a secondary road traverses a majestic pine forest. There are plenty of walking options in a very wild environment.

 EATING BEYOND AJACCIO: OUR PICKS

Auberge Kallisté: Enjoy refined meals of locally sourced meat and organic vegetables at this reputable restaurant in Porto Pollo. 7-9.30pm Mon-Sat €€

Le Café de la Plage: This *paillote* specialising in fish dishes has a delightful vine-shaded terrace that opens onto Plage d'Arone. 11.30am-2pm & 7-9pm €€

Les Roches Bleues: On the D81, the restaurant clings onto the cliff edge with the *calanques* as a backdrop. noon-2pm & 7-9pm €€

Les Roches Rouges: Savour inventive cuisine, magnificent decor and exceptional views of the Golfe de Porto. noon-2pm & 7-9pm Tue-Sun €€€

Réserve Naturelle de Scandola

TOP EXPERIENCE

Golfe de Porto

Plunging flame-red cliffs, staggering views, golden beaches, aquamarine waters and a protected natural reserve – no amount of praise can do justice to the bewildering beauty of the Golfe de Porto. A UNESCO World Heritage site, it offers a wide variety of experiences, both on land and at sea, which allow visitors to make the most of its dazzling splendour.

DON'T MISS

Réserve Naturelle de Scandola

Girolata

Punta Mucchilina dive site

Porto's Genoese Tower

Plage de Gradelle

Réserve Naturelle de Scandola

Created in 1975, the **Réserve Naturelle de Scandola** at the northern end of the Golfe de Porto extends both above and below the water. It's home to a large variety of plant and animal species, including osprey, cormorant, puffin, dolphins, coral and various types of seaweed. With no road or trail access, you can only explore this majestic wilderness by boat.

Several Porto-based **boat operators** run half-day excursions (adult/child from €40/20) into the reserve, in some cases combining it with a visit to Girolata (adult/child €65/45). Opt for

PRACTICALITIES

● ouestcorsica.com ● best season: April–October ● main access roads: D81 & D84

smaller boats with hybrid engines, as they can nudge into coves and caves and have lesser impact on the environment.

Porto

The crowning glory of the west coast, the seaside town of Porto sprawls at the base of a thickly forested valley trammelled on either side by crimson peaks. Crowded in season and practically deserted in winter, it's a fantastic spot for exploring the shimmering seas around the Golfe de Porto and the rugged interior.

The village is split by a promontory, topped by a restored **Genoese tower**, erected in the 16th century to protect the gulf from Barbary incursions. From the bustling marina, an arched footbridge crosses the estuary to a eucalyptus grove and Porto's pebbly patch of beach.

For a sterling sunset view of the harbour and tower, nothing beats the tight little terrace of **Le Palmier** (lepalmierporto.com) – oh, and their ice-creams are devilish.

Girolata

On the fringe of the Réserve Naturelle de Scandola, the tiny hamlet of Girolata is a definite must-see. It's only accessible by boat from Porto or on foot from **Col de la Croix** (four hours return), 23km north of Porto on the D81.

From a distance, Girolata, set within a horseshoe-shaped bay and guarded by a well-preserved Genoese fort, is stunning. In high season, it can be overcrowded during the day because of the numerous sightseeing boats that disgorge their passengers. If you get there on foot, start very early as shade is limited.

The most straightforward way to reach Girolata is by taxi boat with **Yaka Bateau Taxi** (06 01 00 53 71; yaka.girolata@gmail.com; per person €20).

Diving

You can enjoy some of Corsica's finest diving around the Golfe de Porto, which drops to 800m at its deepest. Fear not, there are sites suitable to all levels. Porto's outfits can take you to the best spots just outside the Scandola reserve. Our favourite dive site is **Punta Mucchilina**, which has tons of fish and a superb contoured terrain.

Contact **Bleu Marine Plongée** (bleumarineplongee.com; single dive €62), which also runs snorkelling trips (from €36).

Plage de Gradelle

From Porto, it takes about 40 minutes by car to reach **Plage de Gradelle**, about 26km northwest. Sure, this gently curving beach facing the dramatic backdrop of the southern side of the gulf is coarsely pebbled, but you're guaranteed to find a quiet spot even in high season. Bonus: there's a good restaurant on the beach that also rents kayaks (per hour €12).

EXPLORE THE GULF AT YOUR OWN PACE

Renting a four-seater motor boat (no licence required) is the best way to experience the pristine coastline of the gulf and reach otherwise inaccessible coves (no crowds!). **Patrick & Toussaint** (patrickettoussaint.com; motor boat 1 day from €120) is a reputable outfit. It also rents kayaks (per hour €10). A map of the gulf with suggested itineraries is provided. Bring snorkelling gear and a picnic.

TOP TIPS

● If you want to avoid the crowds in Girolata, spend the night in one in the two simple *gîtes* in the village so that you'll have the place practically to yourself late afternoon and early morning.

● Bring binoculars if you want to see ospreys in the Réserve Naturelle de Scandola.

● All activities are weather-dependent and may be cancelled if the prevailing wind, the *libecciu*, is too strong (which regularly happens in summer).

● There's no fast or easy way to reach Porto – come prepared. Whether you're driving the coastal D81 from Calvi (75km north) or Ajaccio (80km south), you can expect two hours of switchbacks.

Bonifacio

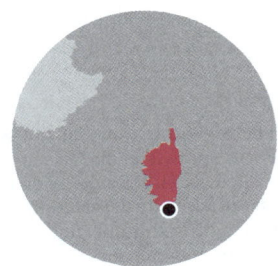

AWESOME SETTING | FANTASTIC PANORAMAS | BOAT EXCURSIONS

GETTING AROUND

In Bonifacio a car is useless as the town is tiny and mostly pedestrian (and atop a cliff!) but if you want to reach some of the beaches that are a bit far to walk to then you'll need your own wheels. Your best bet is to find an accommodation that provides a parking space. A little road train departs from the port to the old town every half hour.

What a stunning setting! Nothing prepares you for your first glimpse of Bonifacio. Protected by vast smooth walls, the town itself stretches along a narrow, top-heavy promontory, undercut by creamy-white limestone cliffs hollowed out by centuries of ceaseless waves. Down below, connected by steep footpaths and a single winding road, and lapped by cornflower-blue waters, its harbour and modern marina shelter at the landward end of a snaking fjord-like inlet. It's down by the port where much of Bonifacio's tourist trade is concentrated, including ferries across to nearby Sardinia, boat tours to Corsica's southerly beaches and the Îles Lavezzi, and a busy clutch of bars, restaurants and brasseries along the quayside. The old city, though, is what truly lingers in the mind, a ravishingly romantic web of alleyways lined by ramshackle medieval houses and chapels with faded pastel plasterwork. Such a beauty couldn't stay ignored – Bonifacio is very crowded in high season.

Wander Amid the Streets of the Haute Ville
Loads of atmosphere and mesmerising vistas

Much of Bonifacio's charm comes from strolling the citadel's shady streets, soaking up the architecture and the atmosphere. The paved steps of **montée du Rastello** and **montée St-Roch** lead up from the marina to its old gateway, the Porte de Gênes, complete with an original 16th-century drawbridge. Immediately inside, the **Bastion de l'Étendard** (bonifacio.fr/visite-decouverte/bastion-de-letendard; adult/child €3.50/1) was the main stronghold of the fortified town. Built to hold heavy artillery, it now houses a small museum and provides access to the ramparts, which offer jaw-dropping views. To the south of the bastion are place du Marché and place de la Manichella, with their superb views over the limestone cliffs to the east. On the southern side of the citadel, the **Escalier du Roi d'Aragon** cuts down the cliff-face.

We love walking beyond the old core to the west, past Gothic **Église St-Dominique**, until the eerily quiet **marine**

TOP TIP

Avoid July and August when Bonifacio gets extremely crowded. If you must visit then, either plan to overnight or arrive before 10am, otherwise you'll find nowhere to park your car.

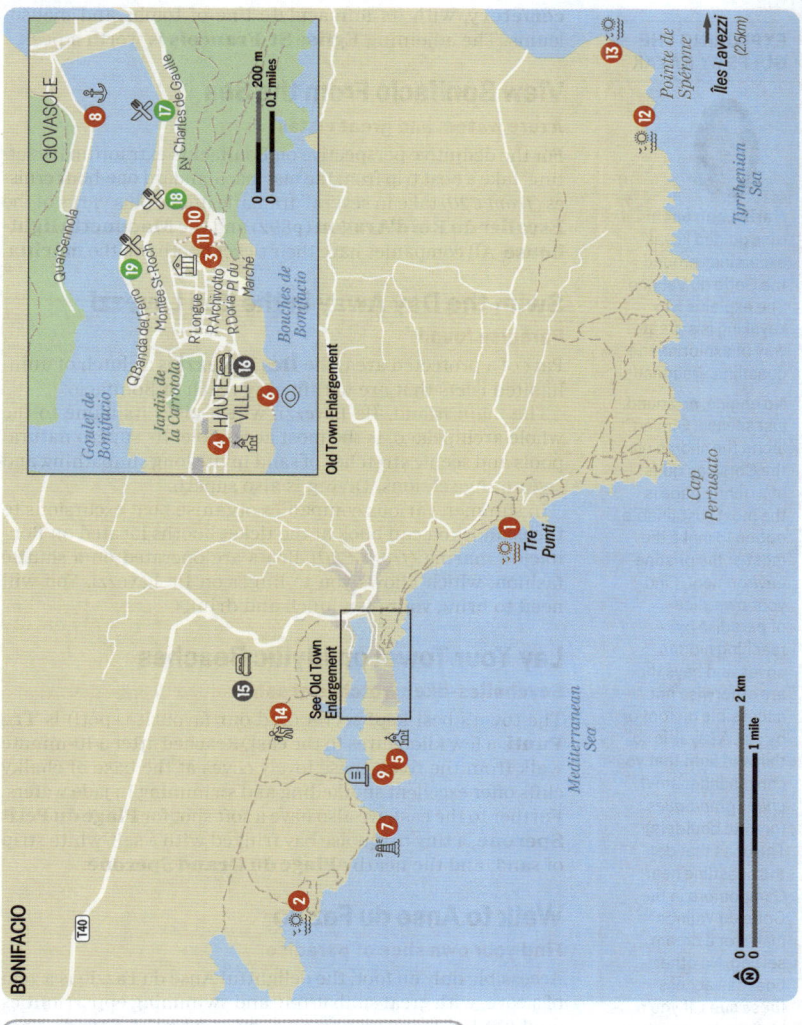

EXPLORING THE GULFS BY KAYAK

Marie Lanfranchi runs guided kayak excursions around the Golfe du Valinco. She explains why kayaking is a great way of exploring the coastline. @sudnautik

No engine, no sound, just silence. Gliding along the shores of the Corsican gulfs at a gentle pace is the most sustainable option to make the most of the pristine environment. Find your own slice of paradise by reaching hidden coves and bays that are otherwise not accessible on foot or by car. A kayak is so thin and light that you can meander amid *chaos granitiques* (granite boulders). The ones that dot the coastline near Campomoro in the Golfe du Valinco make for a dream setting. No other boat can access these sites. If you're lucky, you may spot dolphins.

cemetery, with its immaculate line of tombs and mausoleums. The adjoining **Église St-François** is worth a peek.

View Bonifacio From the Sea
Azure waters and great vistas

For the definitive perspective on Bonifacio's extraordinary setting, take a boat trip from the marina. Standard one-hour cruises *(from €20)* take in several dramatic inlets, plus views of the **Escalier du Roi d'Aragon** (p892) and the **Madonetta lighthouse**. All companies have their ticket booths on the **marina**.

Swim the Day Away in the Îles Lavezzi
Paradise found

Part of a protected area, the **Îles Lavezzi** is a clutch of uninhabited islets that are within easy reach of Bonifacio.

The main island, Île Lavezzi, which gives its name to the whole archipelago, is the most accessible. Its superb natural pools and scenic stretches of sand invite long sunbathing and swimming sessions. Diving is also superb.

In summer, various companies organise boat excursions to the island; you can book at the ticket booths located on Bonifacio's marina *(from €30)*. Boats are operated on a shuttle fashion, which allows you to linger on Île Lavezzi. You will need to bring your own lunch and drinks.

Lay Your Towel on Idyllic Beaches
Seychelles-like stretches of sand

The town's best-kept secret (and our favourite spot!) is **Tre Punti**, a few kilometres to the east. Reached after a 10-minute walk from the road, these lovely coves at the base of chalky cliffs offer excellent snorkelling and swimming in jade waters. Further to the east, we also have a soft spot for **Plage du Petit Sperone**, a tiny turquoise bay fringed with a salt-white strip of sand, and the nearby **Plage du Grand Sperone**.

Walk to Anse du Fazzio
Find your own slice of paradise

Accessible only on foot, the delightful Anse du Fazzio is a gem of a cove, with great sunbathing and swimming opportunities (and not too many visitors). Follow the trail **A Strada Vecchia** that starts about 100m south of Camping de l'Araguina, to the west. It's an easy one-hour walk across the maquis.

 EATING IN BONIFACIO: HARBOURFRONT DINING

D'Amore: This high-calibre Italian venture serves delightful dishes, including risotto with saffron and octopus. *noon-2pm & 7-10pm* €€

Les 4 Vents: Surveying the harbour through giant windows, the 'Four Winds' offers delicious shellfish and fresh catch. *noon-2pm & 7-9.30pm Tue-Sun* €€

L'An Faim: Fusion-flavoured modern restaurant preparing seasonally changing specials using market-sourced produce. *noon-2pm & 7-10pm Wed-Mon* €€

Finestra: For an unforgettable meal, head to Bonifacio's first Michelin-starred restaurant for dishes that burst with creative, Mediterranean flavours. *7.30-10pm* €€€

Beyond Bonifacio

After sampling la dolce vita in Porto-Vecchio and the nearby beaches, head inland for some great surprises.

The region around Bonifacio is blessed with an embarrassment of riches. For starters, it's hard not to but be dazzled by chic Porto-Vecchio. Despite growing urban development, it's an an essential stop on everyone's Corsican itinerary. Although there is no beach by the town proper, the coastline nearby is studded with dozens of heart-palpitatingly gorgeous expanses of sand, including the iconic Plage de Palombaggia. What about culture? The regions musters up a handful of megalithic vestiges that are well worth the detour. And if you want to see a slice of rural Corsica, head to the rustic Alta Rocca, a world away from the bling and bustle of the coast.

Places

Porto-Vecchio p895

Plage de Palombaggia & Around p895

Cauria p897

Tizzano p897

Porto-Vecchio

TIME FROM BONIFACIO: 35MIN

Explore the Haute Ville

Sitting in a marvellous bay, Porto-Vecchio is fairly short on sights but the Haute Ville, within an old Genoese citadel, has charm in spades. Its picturesque backstreets lined with restaurant terraces and designer shops are well worth a stroll. If you want to chill out with a drink in hand, head to place de la République.

Plage de Palombaggia & Around

TIME FROM BONIFACIO: 40MIN

Work on Your Suntan on Scenic Expanses of Sand

Immense, crystalline and glossy, the east-facing Plage de Palombaggia is a treat for swimmers and snorkellers who dabble in its gorgeous, lucent depths. Of course, its appeal is no secret – expect it to be saturated in summer. South of Plage de Palombaggia, **Plage de Tamaricciu** (also known as Plage de la Folacca) is no less spectacular, but we prefer the nearby **Plage d'Acciaghju** because it's a bit less frequented. If you're after more seclusion, make a beeline for **Plage de Carrataghju**, which is often overlooked by visitors because getting there involves a 20-minute walk through the maquis. The trailhead starts near Ranch Campo Palombaggia; ask for directions as it's not signposted.

Most beaches in this area have private paying car parks (about €5). You can also try parking for free along the roadside, but arrive early in the morning.

GETTING AROUND

Porto-Vecchio can be reached by bus from Bonifacio (about 30 minutes). Outside of Porto-Vecchio, bus services are infrequent. It's best to have your own transport to get around. The T40 (towards Sartène) and the RT10 (to Porto-Vecchio) are in very good condition. Be mindful that finding a parking spot along the most popular beaches can be difficult in summer. Arrive early in the morning. In the villages, you'll have less trouble finding parking spaces.

WHEELING AROUND THE ALTA ROCCA

After too much time spent on the beach it's time to shake off the towel and head inland to explore the Alta Rocca, north of Porto-Vecchio.

START	END	LENGTH
Porto-Vecchio	Cucuruzzu & Capula Archaeological Site	92km; four hours

Leave ❶ **Porto-Vecchio** by the winding D368, which will take you to the calm surroundings of ❷ **L'Ospédale**, at an altitude of about 1000m. The village is close to the Forêt de L'Ospédale, which offers excellent walking opportunities and tranquil picnic spots. Follow signs to ❸ **Zonza**, a quintessential mountain village with the soaring Aiguilles de Bavella as a backdrop.

From Zonza, it's a short drive to the ❹ **Col de Bavella** (p864) (Bavella Pass; 1218m), from where you can marvel at the iconic Aiguilles de Bavella (Bavella Needles). Jabbing the skyline at an altitude of more than 1600m, these granite pinnacles resemble giant shark's jaws and are, unsurprisingly, an all-time photographic favourite.

Backtrack to Zonza and follow the D420 to ❺ **Quenza**, another little charmer. It's cradled by thickly wooded mountains and the Aiguilles de Bavella loom on the horizon. West of Quenza, turn onto the narrow D20 and head to ❻ **Ste-Lucie de Tallano**. This lovely village has a few monuments worthy of interest, including the well-proportioned Église Ste-Lucie and the Renaissance-style Couvent St-François, an imposing building scenically positioned at the edge of the village. Next stop is ❼ **Cucuruzzu & Capula**, a lovely archaeological site with impressive megalithic vestiges amid grandiose scenery. The site is signposted off the D268, about 5km east of Ste-Lucie de Tallano. Here you can get a feel for what life was like in ancient times in Corsica.

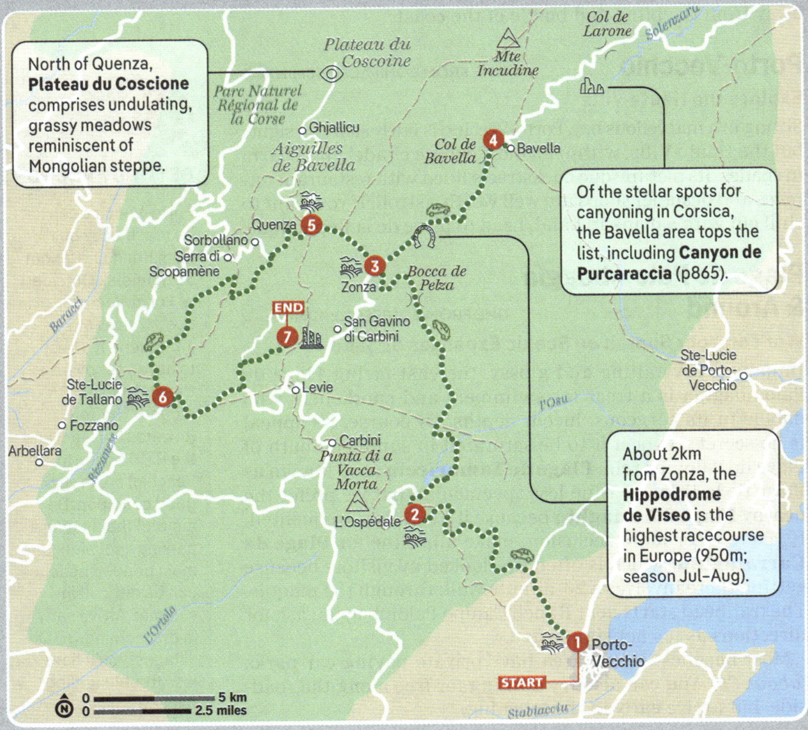

North of Quenza, **Plateau du Coscione** comprises undulating, grassy meadows reminiscent of Mongolian steppe.

Of the stellar spots for canyoning in Corsica, the Bavella area tops the list, including **Canyon de Purcaraccia** (p865).

About 2km from Zonza, the **Hippodrome de Viseo** is the highest racecourse in Europe (950m; season Jul–Aug).

Alignement de I Stantari, Cauria Plateau

Cauria

TIME FROM BONIFACIO: 1¼HR

Wander Amid Prehistoric Sites

Off the winding D48, the beautiful Cauria Plateau is home to three megalithic curiosities that can be visited along the one-hour loop trail (no entrance fee). The Alignement de I Stantari consists of 23 vertical stones, some representing faces with their mouths open in muted cry. The Alignement de Renaghju is larger and 300m further on, at the edge of a little wood. From there, a path leads to Funtanaccia dolmen, about 400m away. According to archaeologists, the dolmen marks a burial chamber.

Tizzano

TIME FROM BONIFACIO: 1¼HR

Discover a Laid-Back Hamlet

At the end of the D48, which peels off the T40 about 17km to the north, Tizzano appears like a mirage. This charming little cove is an enchanted place that has escaped development due its relative isolation. Tizzano has a cute beach, **Cala di l'Avena**, but the 2km-long golden-sand **Plage de Tra Licettu**, 6km to the southeast and accessible by a dirt track, is well worth the bumpy ride.

WHY I LOVE THE BONIFACIO AREA

Jean-Bernard Carillet, Lonely Planet writer

The Bonifacio area is one of my favourites in Corsica, especially in spring and autumn, when it's almost crowd-free. When arriving in Bonif', the views of the imposing ramparts and fortifications always leave me in awe. Moseying around the old town labyrinth of paved streets is also supremely enjoyable – I feel like I'm in Italy. What's more, Bonifacio is emerging as a gourmet destination, with a couple of reputable restaurants (not a mean feat in such a touristy place). I also love the nearby bays and beaches, with plenty of options for sunbathing and watersports, including top-notch diving around the Îles Lavezzi. And if I really want to get away from it all, the rustic Alta Rocca is not that far.

EATING BEYOND BONIFACIO: SMART SPOTS

Tamaricciu: Chic beach restaurant, on the Palombaggia sands, with first-class views and beautifully presented Mediterranean cuisine. *noon-2pm & 7-9.30pm* €€

L'Acciaro: A top spot on Acciaghju beach. The food tends to be modern Corsican/Mediterranean, with excellent seasonal products. *noon-2pm & 7-9.30pm* €€

Costa Marina: Overlooking Plage de Palombaggia, this trendy restaurant is renowned for Mediterranean-influenced cuisine with local ingredients. *7-10pm* €€

Le Bellagio: An easy-going crowd comes to this cheerful restaurant in Porto-Vecchio to eat excellent Mediterranean food with a fusion twist. *noon-2pm & 7-10pm* €€

Places We Love to Stay

€ Budget €€ Midrange €€€ Top end

Bastia   MAP p867

Sud Hôtel-Restaurant € About 3km south of the city centre in a renovated building with a nice roof garden and a free car park. The restaurant uses organic produce from the garden.

Hôtel les Voyageurs € Historic, family-friendly hotel with spacious rooms and a private car park very close to the port.

Hôtel des Gouverneurs €€ The only hotel within Bastia's hilltop citadel is a stylish contemporary venue, with peaceful, spacious rooms and tremendous views.

Patrimonio

Hôtel du Vignoble € Features simple, well-kept and colourful rooms in the centre of Patrimonio.

Casa Eva Maria € This B&B is a welcoming port of call if you want to visit the wineries in Patrimonio. Rooms are bright, crisp and discreetly decorated.

St-Florent

La Dimora Hôtel & Spa €€ Soak up the tranquil atmosphere of this little charmer set in a renovated 18th-century farm south of town. Bonuses: a spa and restaurant.

Basgi Basgi €€ St-Florent's most recent and eco-friendly option occupies a former wine cellar, and sports fresh, contemporary rooms with a boutique feel.

Cap Corse

Casa Maria € A great retreat in a coolly refurbished 18th-century mansion in the heart of Nonza.

Casa di Babbo € A lovely B&B surrounded by fruit trees on the hillside 1km south of Macinaggio.

Castel Brando €€ Housed in a stately, mid-19th-century mansion in Erbalunga, this historic hotel offers soothing rustic-chic rooms set around a shady courtyard.

Misincu €€€ Entirely refurbished in 2025, Misincu is the only luxury venture in the Cap Corse. It has green credentials and harbours a reputable restaurant.

Calvi   MAP p874

Camping La Pinède € Large campground with excellent facilities, close to the main beach 2km southeast of the town centre,

Hôtel Le Magnolia €€ Right by the church in the heart of town, this attractive mansion sits in a beautiful high-walled courtyard garden adorned by a handsome magnolia tree.

Hôtel Saint-Érasme €€ A good find west of the centre, with top views of the Pointe de la Revellata.

Campo di Fiori €€ A cool property with lovingly decorated *maisons de charme* (charming houses), a short walk from the beach. Great pool and a flowery garden.

La Balagne   MAP p874

Casa Musicale €€ Two village houses in Pigna hold 14 simple but quirky rooms blessed with fabulous valley views.

Le Niobel €€ In Belgodère, Le Niobel has a family atmosphere, tidy rooms and a restaurant.

Cas'Anna Lidia €€ This refined cocoon in Feliceto offers eight artfully designed and sensitively furnished rooms with top valley views.

L'Île-Rousse

Le Grillon € Affordable two-star venture with space-efficient rooms, straightforward decor and neat bathrooms.

Hôtel Perla Rossa €€€ This boutique option offers 10 rooms decorated in a soothing cream-and-orange palette.

Corte   MAP p880

Le Duc de Padoue € Upstairs in a large townhouse, Le Duc de Padoue has a central location and well-kept rooms.

A Chjusellina € This attractive *ferme-auberge* (farm-inn) south of Corte has five light-filled rooms. Meals use products from the farm (p881).

Ajaccio   MAP p885

Hôtel Marengo € A 15-minute walk from the city centre, this haven of peace close to the beach offers excellent value for money.

Hôtel Napoléon €€ A prime location on a side street in the heart of town makes the Napoléon an excellent midrange choice.

Les Mouettes €€€ Nestled right at the water's edge, 1.5km west of the old town, this colonnaded, peach-coloured 19th-century mansion is a dream.

Beyond Ajaccio

Camping Funtana a l'Ora € The pick of Porto's campsites, with lots of pleasant sites sheltering under olive trees and green oak. Also rents chalets and mobile-homes.

Les Roches Rouges €€ Step back in time in this historic hotel in Piana with a spectacular dining room and some superb sea-facing rooms with balconies (p889).

Bonifacio   MAP p893

Hôtel Colomba €€ Occupying a tastefully renovated 14th-century building, this hotel enjoys a prime location on a picturesque (steep) street, bang in the heart of the old town.

Hôtel Cala di Greco €€€ Offers outstanding views of the citadel. Each bungalow has its own little front garden and terrace.

Beyond Bonifacio

Pozzo di Mastri €€ A well-run venture with 22 rooms and four renovated *bergeries* (shepherd's huts) on a huge property near Figari.

Hôtel Moderne €€ Right in the centre of Porto-Vecchio, this perky little hotel offers 15 muted coloured, tasteful rooms.

Hôtel Son de Mar €€ This modern building has neat, well-organised rooms, a two-minute walk away from the beach in San Cipriano.

U Capu Biancu €€€ A haven of peace, this chic, boutique-style hotel about 10km east of Bonifacio has ravishing sea views, a gleaming pool, a gastronomic restaurant, a *paillote* (beachside restaurant; open to all) and 29 tastefully decorated rooms.

A Mandria di Murtoli €€€ Exclusive and intimate, this peach of a place, opened in 2025, features a couple of *bergeries* that were turned into gleaming, luxurious accommodation nestled in an immense property in the foothills near Cauria.

Hameau de Saparale €€€ Surrounded by vineyards, this far-flung eco-lodge off the D50 in Vallée de l'Ortolo was opened in 2025. It consists of 16 luxurious rooms and suites that ooze charm and character. Great onsite restaurant, too.

Alta Rocca

A Pignata €€€ Hidden in a peaceful property, this boutique-style inn offers superb rooms and splendid suites that are decorated with a contemporary twist. There's a great restaurant, too.

Le Mouflon d'Or €€€ Opened in 2025, this boutique-style establishment occupies a gorgeously restored granite building in Zonza. Also offers luxury *bergeries* and a top-notch restaurant.

Les Mouettes, Ajaccio

TOOLKIT

Produce market, Provence (p740)
FLEGERE/SHUTTERSTOCK

TOOLKIT

The chapters in this section cover the most important topics you'll need to know about in France. They're full of nuts-and-bolts information and valuable insights to help you understand and navigate France and get the most out of your trip.

Arriving p902

Getting Around p903

Money p904

Accommodation p905

Family Travel p906

Health & Safe Travel p907

Food, Drink & Nightlife p908

Responsible Travel p910

LGBTIQ+ Travellers p912

Accessible Travel p913

How to Shop at the Food Market p914

Nuts & Bolts p915

Language p916

Arriving

For many, touchdown in Paris, at Charles de Gaulle or Orly, is their first taste of France. For others, it is international airports south in Lyon-St-Exupéry, Marseille-Provence or Nice-Côte d'Azur. FlixBus links Paris' Bercy Seine bus station and major French cities with continental Europe, as do high-speed rail services. Book Eurostar tickets to/from London St Pancras well in advance to ensure best rates.

Land Borders
France is part of Schengen, so there are no border formalities with its European neighbours. Always travel with your ID card or passport – by law in France, you must prove your identity if asked.

Visas
EU nationals don't need a visa. Arrivals from the UK, Canada, New Zealand and the US can stay up to 90 days within a 180-day period without a visa. Keep updated with schengenvisainfo.com.

SIM Cards
The cheapest way to use your phone is to buy a prepaid French SIM (*carte prépayée*), online or at *tabacs* (newsagents) and phone shops at the airport and in towns. Data-only eSIMs also work.

Wi-fi
Free wi-fi is available at airports, hotels and many eating and drinking venues. In remote mountainous areas (and in châteaux and older buildings with thick walls) the signal can be patchy or nonexistent.

Airport to City Centre

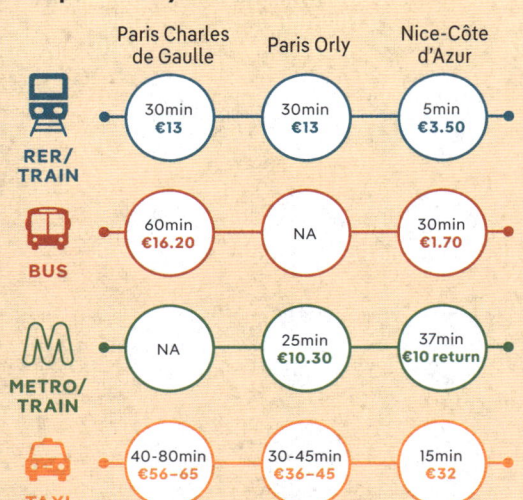

	Paris Charles de Gaulle	Paris Orly	Nice-Côte d'Azur
RER/TRAIN	30min €13	30min €13	5min €3.50
BUS	60min €16.20	NA	30min €1.70
METRO/TRAIN	NA	25min €10.30	37min €10 return
TAXI	40-80min €56-65	30-45min €36-45	15min €32

ETIAS

By the end of 2026, it is anticipated that arrivals from the UK, US, Canada and New Zealand, among others, will have to fill in a pre-arrival, online form to meet the European Union's new electronic vetting system. ETIAS – European Travel Information and Authorisation System – aims to prescreen arrivals from non-EU visa-exempt countries. Once approved, ETIAS will be valid for three years and will cover multiple entry into Schengen's 27-country zone. It will cost €7 (free for under-18s and over-70s), payable online via the official ETIAS website or mobile app. For updated information, see etiasvisa.com.

Getting Around

Excellent public transport joins the dots between towns and cities. But such is the beauty of the open road, particularly in rural France, that you'll also want your own wheels to explore deeper.

TRAVEL COSTS

Car rental
from €30/day

Petrol
approx €1.72/L

Bike hire
€15–40/day

Train Paris to Bordeaux
from €39

Train & Bus

France's reliable SNCF rail network is first class, with affordable fares and frequent services (both high-speed TGVs and regional TER trains). Principal rail lines radiate out from Paris like wheel spokes, making services between towns on different spokes slow or nonexistent. Bus services are reduced on weekends and during school holidays.

Bicycle & e-Bike

Dedicated cycling paths are widespread; many skirt canal towpaths or retired railway lines (*voies verts* or greenways). Long-distance itineraries like La Vélodyssée (p570) and ViaRhôna (p465) favour roads with light traffic and are ideal for bike-packing. Bike rental – road and mountain bikes, regular and electric-assisted – is widespread.

TIP

Make the journey the destination afloat the **Canal du Midi**, a ferry to Corsica or a boat to an offshore island.

PRIORITY TO THE RIGHT

Under France's *priorité à droite* (priority to the right) rule, any car entering an intersection (including a T-junction) from a road (including a tiny village backstreet) on your right has the right of way unless street signs indicate otherwise. Locals will assume every driver knows this.

DRIVING ESSENTIALS

Drive on the right

Speed limit is 50kmh in urban areas, 80–110kmh on secondary roads, and 130kmh motorways. When raining, count 10kmh less on fast roads.

Blood alcohol limit is 0.5g/l, reduced to 0.2g/l for under-21s.

Hiring a Car

Driving is a delight in backstage France, but a car is a liability in traffic-plagued city centres. Find rental agencies at airports and by train stations; many offer electric cars. Some cities have a public car-sharing scheme, ideal for an out-of-town day flit. Consider car-sharing platforms *oiucar.fr* and *fr.getaround.com*.

Using Motorways

Motorways (*autoroutes*) command tolls (*péages*). Most spit out a ticket on entering and you pay when exiting. Cash payers: drive into a toll booth displaying a green arrow – booths showing a white card symbol only accept cards. Check traffic conditions, motorway services etc on *bison-fute.gouv.fr*.

Ridesharing

Covoiturage (ridesharing) in France is a national institution. BlaBlaCar (*blablacar.fr*) is the most popular app, connecting passengers with drivers. In towns and cities, hitchhikers can stand in front of an 'Arrêt sur le pouce' sign to be picked up by a vetted driver in the Rézo Pouce network (*rezopouce.fr*).

 Money

CURRENCY: EURO (€)

Credit & Debit Cards

Payment by card is widespread and can be contactless up to €50; smaller shops can impose a minimum payment (€10 or €15). In rural France and Corsica, many B&Bs, *fermes auberges,* produce markets and taxi drivers don't accept cards. You cannot hire a car without a credit card.

ATMs

ATMs – *points d'argent* or *distributeurs automatiques de billets* in French – are the cheapest and most convenient way to get euros, usually offering the best exchange rates. Cashpoints connected to Visa/MasterCard/Cirrus/Maestro networks are situated in all cities and towns, on central squares, outside banks on main streets and inside large supermarkets.

Taxes & Refunds

A 20% value-added tax known in French as TVA *(taxe sur la valeur ajoutée)* is included in the price of most goods and services. Non-EU residents aged over 16 who spend more than €100 in a shop displaying a 'Tax Free' sign can claim a refund when leaving France.

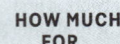

HOW MUCH FOR...

a metro ticket
€1.90–2.50

a cinema ticket
€7–12

beach lounger & parasol rental
€15–50

museum admission
free–€22

HOW TO... Save Euros

City tourist cards Discounts on museums, tours etc.
Public transport Purchase a multi-journey ticket or day pass.
First Sunday of month Many state museums are free.
Markets Buy picnic supplies at the morning food market (p914).
Supermarkets Shop cheap. Prevent waste with *toogoodtogo.com*.
Drinking water Fill bottles at public fountains spouting *eau potable* (drinking water); some are even sparkling.
Dining out Order the *formule* (two-course lunch deal) and *une carafe d'eau* (free jug of tap water).

LOCAL TIP

A pocketful of small change is handy for paying for public toilets, metered street parking, restaurant tips, a trolley for your supermarket shop or a crêpe on a Paris street corner.

BUDGET TRAVEL

Paris ranks in the world's top 10 priciest capital cities, but budget travel around the country is possible with savvy planning. Favour less touristed regions; pick rural over urban. Visit during shoulder and low seasons, and choose low-tech exploits in the great outdoors over hi-tech theme parks, and sights and activities commanding high admission fees. Consider ridesharing. Buy train tickets in advance to bag lower fares; book at least three months ahead to get score SNCF's heavily discounted Prem's ticket. Check *ouigo.com* for last-minute deals.

Accommodation

Chambres d'Hôte

Provençal oil mill or *mas* (farmhouse), seaside surf shack or sophisticated *hôtel particulier* (private mansion): for French charm, a heartfelt *bienvenue* (welcome) and solid home cooking, little beats a privately run B&B – rife in the countryside. Breakfast is included in the nightly rate and the property, by law, has a maximum of five rooms. Mention any dietary requirements in advance.

Châteaux

Sweet dreams come true in *la belle France*. Waking up in a fairy-tale castle with turrets and centurion maze as sentry is perfectly achievable in France without breaking the bank. In the châteaux-strewn Loire Valley and Dordogne, in particular, plenty of midrange B&Bs shack up in châteaux; wi-fi can be shaky. Countrywide, luxurious hotels slumber in historic castles.

Farms & Wineries

Many countryside farms and *domaines* (wine-producing estates) have B&B rooms in the main house, treehouses, tent pitches, and converted outbuildings to rent to self-caterers. Most feature on *bienvenue-a-la-ferme.com*. Eco-responsible, energy self-sufficient cabins in the Parcel Tiny House network (*parceltinyhouse.com*) are always on a producer's land, encourage slow living and promise insight into agricultural life.

Refuges & Gîtes d'Étape

Refuges (mountain huts) offer dorm beds in basic huts along walking trails in uninhabited mountainous areas like the Alps and Pyrenees. Most close in winter; others stay open with minimal service, ie no guardian to cook, clean and share tips. Reservations are essential; see *ffcam.fr*. More comfortable *gîtes d'étape* are usually proper buildings with showers in a village.

HOW MUCH FOR A NIGHT IN...

a B&B in chambre d'hôte
€75–350

a dorm bed in mountain refuge
€20–45

a double in château hotel
€120–500+

Gîtes

Bijou cottage, villa with pool, palatial mansion or mountain chalet – they're all *gîtes*, aka self-catering holiday homes, available to rent by the week or out-of-season short stay. Gîtes de France (*gites-de-france.com*) lists thousands of properties all over France; those with a WWF-approved Gîtes Panda label are in nature reserves and national parks. Bed linen and end-of-stay cleaning usually cost extra.

AIRBNB

As France is the world's most visited country, with some 100 million tourists annually, it's no surprise that Airbnb rental is a booming business; it has an estimated 930,000 rentals in France, with some 90,000 (or 45.7 per 1000 inhabitants) in Paris alone. In a bid to keep the quotidian fabric of local neighbourhoods intact, French residents are only allowed to rent out their primary home for a maximum of 120 days in a calendar year.

Family Travel

France spoils families with its incredibly rich mix of cultural and historical sights, outdoor activities, festivals and entertainment for children of all ages. With advance planning savvy parents will find creative kid appeal in almost every museum and monument in France, blockbuster must-sees included.

Hotel Rooms

Most hotels have cots (free) and extra beds (€30–50). Interconnecting or family rooms are most common in cities and coastal areas. Breakfast (€7–35) is rarely included in room rates.

Chain hotels such as Ibis Budget and Formule 1, on the outskirts of most large towns, have family rooms and make a convenient overnight stops for motorists driving from continental Europe or the UK (Troyes in Champagne is popular for Brits en route to the Alps).

Discounts

Most attractions offer discounted admission for children. In general, kids under five don't pay and many sights are free to under-18s. Some museums offer family tickets for two adults and two kids.

Children under four travel for free on French trains or, if they need their own seat, pay €9 with a *forfait bambin* to any destination (€5/8 on any classic/high-speed Ouigo). Children aged four to 11 travel for half price.

Baby & Tot Essentials

Cobbled streets, metro stairs and hilltop villages are not pushchair-friendly, so bring a sling. Children under 10 years or less than 1.4m in height must be strapped in an appropriate car seat, available from rental companies but at extortionate rates. Bring your own to save euros.

Sightseeing

Many Paris museums organise creative *ateliers* (workshops) for children aged seven to 14, parent-accompanied or solo. Countrywide, when buying tickets at museums and monuments, ask about children's activity sheets – most have something to appeal to kids. Familiscope (familiscope.fr) is the definitive family-holiday planner (in French).

KID-FRIENDLY PICKS

Jardin du Luxembourg (p162)
Chase 1920s toy sailboats around a lake in Paris' most elegant park.

Dune du Pilat (p570)
Europe's biggest sand dune mesmerises; join a guided nature tour.

Brittany (p267)
Beaches, boats, lighthouses and pirate islands – old-fashioned outdoor fun in spades.

Corsica (p861)
Island life is gold for active teens: sail, kayak and snorkel clear turquoise water.

Lake Annecy (p514)
Cycle, swim, sail, SUP or paraglide with birds over Europe's cleanest lake.

EATING OUT

Most restaurants offer a *menu enfant* (children's meal with a soft drink at a fixed price, usually up to 12 years), although kids in France might soon tire of the ubiquitous *spaghetti bolognaise* or *steak haché* (beef burger minus the bun) and *frites* (fries) and ice cream. Asking for a half-portion of an adult main is acceptable. For fussy or very young eaters, order *pâtes au beurre* (pasta with butter, pictured).

Free bread accompanies every meal; teething babies love the *quignon* (knobbly end bit) of a baguette. Skip the pricey fizzy drinks for a free *carafe d'eau* (jug of tap water) or *un sirop* (fruit syrup diluted with water – grenadine and mint are favourites).

Health & Safe Travel

INSURANCE

Insurance is not required when visiting France, but a comprehensive travel policy covering theft, loss and medical treatment is highly recommended. Check the fine print if you intend to do any high-risk activities such as scuba diving, motorcycling, skiing or hiking at high altitude. EU citizens get a free European Health Insurance Card (EHIC), which covers emergency medical care without charge.

Health Care

Health care is readily available throughout France. Pharmacies – look for an illuminated green cross outside indicating a pharmacy is open – are extremely helpful and sell a wide range of medicines without prescription (*ordonnance*). Details of the closest *pharmacie de garde* open at night and on Sundays are displayed in pharmacy windows. Call 118 or Europe-wide 112 for an ambulance.

Drinking Water

Bring your own bottle to fill with tap water – drinkable countrywide, including in restaurants where you simply ask for *une carafe d'eau*. Fountains in some villages and towns also spout drinking water (*eau potable*; undrinkable is '*non potable*'). In Paris, seek out dark green, cast-iron Wallace fountains, financed by Englishman Richard Wallace in the 1800s; some spout sparkling water. Find a map at wallacefountains.org.

SEASONAL MENACES

In rural areas, avoid woods with any sign of hunting activity from September to February. When walking in woodlands, forests and long grass in May and June, cover up – ticks, some causing Lyme disease, are increasingly rife.

SWIM SAFELY

Green flag
Safe to swim

Yellow flag
Swim with caution; be vigilant

Red flag
Danger; swimming is forbidden

Purple flag
Danger; water pollution

Red and yellow stripes
Supervised by lifeguards within the flagged zone

Black and white chequered
Swim with caution; water sports are allowed

Theft

Pickpockets are typically active in crowded touristy areas, on Paris and Marseille metros and on airport shuttles. Don't leave wallets or phones on cafe tables or back pockets to tempt snatchers. In cities, if you're uncomfortable using public transport after dark, play safe with a taxi or rideshare. By the beach, empty your car of valuables to avoid someone else doing it for you.

MOUNTAIN EXTREMES

In the Alps and Pyrenees, check the weather forecast and avalanche report (meteofrance.com) – conditions are unpredictable. Many *cols* (mountain passes) are shut in winter. In mountainous areas, cars must be fitted with snow tyres from 1 November to 31 March.

Summer storms can be sudden and violent, with hailstones and rockfall. In June 2024 a landslide destroyed the village of La Bérarde in Les Écrins. Stay vigilant and don't underestimate the summer heat.

Food, Drink & Nightlife

When to Eat

Petit déjeuner: (7am to 10am) Breakfast is traditionally coffee and a croissant or *tartine* (buttered baguette with jam).

Déjeuner: (noon to 2.30pm) Lunch swings between a salad and a three-course meal with wine.

Goûter: (4pm) The sweet childhood treat that lives on.

Apéritif: (5pm to 8pm) A pre-meal drink with friends, preferably on a terrace.

Dîner: (8pm to 11pm) Dinner, with several courses, can last hours.

Where to Eat

Auberge: Country inn.

Ferme auberge: Farm restaurant.

Bistro: (bistrot) Small casual restaurant.

Bouillon: Traditional budget diner from the 19th century; all the rage in Paris.

Neobistro: Contemporary bistro.

Brasserie: Casual eatery serving all-day meals and drinks.

Guingette: Pop-up summer eatery, with drinks and food alfresco.

Crêperie: Pancake restaurant.

Salon de thé: Tearoom, also serving light lunches.

Table d'hôte: Homemade meal served around a shared table in a B&B.

Winstub: Cosy wine tavern in Alsace.

Estaminet: Flemish-style eatery of Flanders and *le nord*.

MENU DECODER

Carte: Menu, as in the written list of what dishes are available to order.

Menu: A two- or three-course meal at a fixed price.

À la carte: Order random dishes from the menu (rather than a fixed *menu*).

Formule: A cheaper lunchtime option to a *menu*: main course plus starter or dessert.

Plat du jour: Dish of the day.

Menu enfant: Two- or three-course kids' meal with a soft drink at a fixed price.

Menu dégustation: Fixed-price tasting menu served in many top-end restaurants; five to seven modestly sized courses.

Entrée: Starter, appetiser.

Plat: Main course.

Fromage: Cheese, accompanied with fresh bread (never crackers and no butter except in formal gastronomic restaurants); always served before dessert.

Dessert: Just that, served after cheese.

HOW TO... Order

Bread If a basket of complimentary bread is not automatically brought to the table after ordering, ask for some. Butter is a standard accompaniment with oysters and seafood (*demi-sel* or salted), and in top-end gastronomic restaurants (*doux* or unsalted). Except in top-end places, don't expect a side plate – simply put the bread on the table. And yes, mopping up sauce on your plate with a bread chunk is acceptable.

Coffee Order *un café* (espresso). Never end a meal with a cappuccino, *café au lait* (long milky coffee) or cup of tea, which, incidentally, never comes with milk in France. *Une tisane* (a herbal infusion) like mint or verbena is also acceptable.

The bill *L'addition* is only brought to the table when you ask for it. By law the bill includes a 15% service charge; assuming you're happy with the service, tipping 5% to 10% of the bill is not expected but is much appreciated.

HOW MUCH FOR...

an espresso
€2–4

a baguette
€1–€1.30

steak-frites
€15–20

a dozen market oysters
€15–20

a *barbajuan* (savoury pasty) in Monaco
€1.50

a bistro lunch
€15–30

a Michelin-starred dinner
€50 and above

a glass of wine
€6–12

HOW TO... Prepare the Perfect French Picnic

A French *pique-nique* on a mountain hike or cycle between vines is in a class of its own. Here are some hamper ideas.

Baguette Buy a *baguette* or skinnier *ficelle* from the *boulangerie* (bakery), and fill it with Camembert or pâté and *cornichons* (mini gherkins). *Un jambon-beurre* (butter and ham) and *jambon-fromage* (ham and a hard cheese) are classics. The sweet-toothed can go French kid-style – a slab of milk chocolate inside.

Noir de Bigorre It's a delicacy, but the Pyrenees' chestnut- and acorn-fed pigs are said to produce some of the country's finest ham.

Macarons The sweet end to a picnic, famously from Ladurée and Pierre Hermé.

Kouign amann Breton butter cake or another succulent Breton pastry (p299).

Fruit The further south, the juicier the choice: black cherries from Apt and peaches, apricots and tomatoes from the Rhône Valley, Provence and the Riviera.

Provençal olives or peppers Marinated, often stuffed, and sold in buckets at market stalls.

Champagne Toast your good fortune with bubbles and *biscuits roses* (pink ladyfinger sponge biscuits) from Reims.

Country produce Pâté, walnuts and foie gras from the Dordogne; or Limousin's pâté-like *grillons limousins* made from seasoned pork fat.

Cheesy Facts
The French don't pre-slice cheese – pack a cheese chunk or round and a pocket knife in your picnic, to cut in situ. Purists: slice like a pie or in horizontal slices depending on the cheese shape.

GOING OUT

A French night out begins one way: with an early-evening apéritif on a street terrace, fashionable rooftop or beach. The point is not to get drunk; rather, it is to spend a convivial moment with friends, family or colleagues in a relaxed, attractive setting. Upon arrival, greet everyone at the table with *la bise* (a cheek-skimming kiss, two to four depending where in France you are).

In cafes and bars, complimentary peanuts might accompany a *kir* (white wine with blackcurrant liqueur), glass of rosé, beer, cocktail or mocktail – anything goes these days. Favour the *apéritif maison* (house apéritif), any locally made apéritif, or a spirit distilled in the region. In Burgundy, order *gougères* (cheesy pastry puffs) to graze on.

Around 8pm (6.30pm or 7pm in northern France) move to a cafe, bistro or restaurant for dinner. Outside tables are prime real estate. Meals can be one course or 10, and last a quick hour to until midnight or later. It all depends on the occasion.

After a casual dinner, city clubbers head to *la before* – drinks in a trendy bar with DJ – until around 1am, when they hit a club for *la soirée*. Occasionally the party continues past dawn with *l'after*. In summer, parks and river quays hum with urbanites lounging over late-night BYO picnics, drinks and music. *Santé!*

Responsible Travel

Climate Change & Travel

It's impossible to ignore the impact we have when travelling; Lonely Planet urges all travellers to engage with their travel carbon footprint, which will mainly come from air travel. While there often isn't an alternative, travellers can look to minimise the number of flights they take, opt for newer aircrafts and use cleaner ground transport, such as trains. One proposed solution – purchasing carbon offsets – unfortunately does not cancel out the impact of individual flights. While most destinations will depend on air travel for the foreseeable future, for now, pursuing ground-based travel where possible is the best course of action.

The **UN Carbon Offset Calculator** shows how flying impacts a household's emissions

The **ICAO's carbon emissions calculator** allows visitors to analyse the CO2 generated by point-to-point journeys

Sleep Green

Verfiy eco-credentials of hotels, campsites and B&Bs – France's Clé Verte (Green Key; *laclefverte.org*), the European Ecolabel and Green Globe are common green labels. Search by 'gîte panda' to find green self-catering accommodation on *gites-de-france.com*.

Harness Wind Power

Ditch the ferry to Corsica for sailing ship – from St-Raphaël to Calvi in 15 to 24 hours wind-dependant with Sailcoop *(sailcoop.fr)*. Other fun low-impact voyages: Metz by solar-powered boat (p361) and sand-yachting on the Côte d'Opale (p216).

Favour Fast Food With A Conscience

Ditch global fast-food chains for smart local initiatives like Bocaux de Liens (p615) in Brantôme. Takeaway meals are prepared from zero-kilometre produce and served in returnable *bocaux* (glass jars).

Discover the lesser-known. Swap over-touristed celebs (identified with an 'Expect Overcrowding' badge in this guide) like Paris' Louvre, Provence's St-Paul-de-Vence, Mont St-Michel, Corsican superstar Bonifacio or Normandy's Étretat cliffs with quieter, backstage abbeys and natural wonders (p20).

Support low-tech music festivals powered by renewable energy such as Paris' electro-pop fest We Love Green in Bois de Vincennes. In Bordeaux catch events by Low Tech Bordeaux; April's SlowFest celebrates energy-saving ways to share music.

DINE ON LOCAL INGREDIENTS

Choose restaurants working with local seasonal products; several in Paris get fruit and veg from rooftop farm Nature Urbaine *(nu-paris.com)*. Look for eateries with a menu du marché (market-sourced menu) or their own kitchen garden.

SHOP SECOND-HAND

Save money and reduce your environmental impact. Every town has a *friperie*, *brocante* or *dépôt-vente* selling second-hand fashion, homewares and knickknacks (p274). Monumental flea markets: Paris' Puces de St-Ouen, Lyon's Les Puces du Canal and Lille's spectacular annual Braderie.

Support Wildlife Projects
Acquaint yourself with some of the Alps' oldest natural inhabitants during a falconry workshop on Morzine's ski slopes. Learn how white-tailed eagles are being reintroduced into the wild at Les Aigles du Léman (p523).

Buy Your Own Nostalgic Heirloom
Recreate the romance of a Norman farmhouse back home: visit fourth-generation linen farm La Maison Embrin (p235), romp through flax fields, and order a traditional quilted bed cover featuring your favourite Côte d'Albâtre beach.

Shop at the Source
Buy Provençal olive oil direct from the *moulin à l'huile* (mill), wine from the château or estate, oysters direct from Cap Ferret and Cancale farmers, and picnic supplies at *marchés des producteurs* (farmers markets).

Respect Beach Rules
On beaches and dunes, check signs outlining local fishing and foraging rules: seaweed is limited to 2kg countrywide and no, you can't take a pebble from Nice's Promenade des Anglais to paint back home.

In cities, walk and use public-sharing bikes. Plot regional itineraries around the rail network and mapped e-bike routes.

Join an urban Greeter (greeters.fr) on a free walking tour to see their city through a local lens.

31%
Forests cover 31% of the country and summer fires are common in Provence, Côte d'Azur, on the Atlantic Coast and in Corsica. June to September, high-risk trails close, campfires (and often barbecues) are forbidden and smoking in and near forests is illegal.

TOOLKIT — RESPONSIBLE TRAVEL

RESOURCES

bienvenue-a-la-ferme.com
Campsites, B&Bs and self-catering cottages on farms.

fairbnb.coop
Community-powered accommodation-rental platform in Paris and Marseille.

bistrotdepays.com
Support restaurateurs in rural communities; eat at a *bistrot de pays*.

CLOCKWISE FROM TOP LEFT: OLENA BORONCHUK/SHUTTERSTOCK, PAGE FREDERIQUE/SHUTTERSTOCK

LGBTIQ+ Travellers

The rainbow flag flies high in France, a country that allowed its LGBTIQ+ citizens out of the closet long before many of its European neighbours. 'Laissez-faire' perfectly sums up France's liberal attitude towards homosexuality and people's private lives in general, in part because of a long tradition of public tolerance towards different lifestyles.

Gay Paris

Gay Paris lives up to its name. It's so open that there's less of a defined 'scene' here than in other French cities where it's more underground. Le Marais is the nightlife hub, but you'll find LGBTIQ+ venues attracting a mixed crowd city-wide.

Paris was the first European capital to vote in an openly gay mayor (Bertrand Delanoë, in office 2001–14). Same-sex couples commonly display affection in public and checking into a hotel room together is unlikely to raise eyebrows.

MARCHE DES FIERTÉS

Gay Pride in June is the biggest and most colourful event on the French gay and lesbian calendar, attracting crowds of thousands. An annual Marche des Fiertés (Gay Pride March) parades through Paris, Lyon, Marseille, Bordeaux, Rouen, Caen and dozens of cites all over France in an exuberant spectacle of music and entertainment. Parties flesh out the six-day *semaine des fiertés* (Pride Week).

Fédération LGBTI+

Countrywide, 23 gay and lesbian associations are members of the national Fédération LGBTI+ *(federation-lgbti.org)*. Regional and city centres provide LGBTIQ+ information, and organise drop-in support centres and a rainbow of gay-orientated social events. Key *Centres LGBTI* include Paris, Lyon, Côte d'Azur (Nice), Normandy, Touraine and Bordeaux.

RIVIERA PARTY QUEEN

Historic French Riviera queen Nice is the hub of the Med's LGBTIQ+ scene, known for its welcoming attitude and inclusive party vibe. Rue Bonaparte is the seaside city's hip LGBTIQ+ strip. Lou Queernaval – France's first queer carnival – showers Nice in glitter and confetti in February, as does July's Pink Parade (Pride). Hello Dolly! – a street party when everyone wears white – is the annual highlight of Nice's loud, proud gay festivities.

Gay-Led Tours

Paris Gay Village *(parisgayvillage.com)* leads themed tours in Paris exploring homosexuality in the city from the 17th century onwards: Left Bank Lesbians, Secrets of Le Gay Marais and a tour of the graves of famous gays like Rosa Bonheur, Oscar Wilde, Gertrude Stein and Marcel Proust are some themes.

RESOURCES

Gay Sejour *(gay-sejour.com)* LGBTIQ+-friendly listings guide, covering hotels, bars, restaurant and entertainment.

Gay France *(gay-france.net)* Just that.

Les Mots à la Bouche *(motsbouche.com)* Based in Paris' IIe arrondissement, one of France's oldest gay and lesbian bookshops was founded in 1980.

Gay & Lesbian *(parisjetaime.com)* Paris' tourist office provides a solid overview of the scene and provides key addresses.

Accessible Travel

France presents constant challenges for *visiteurs à mobilité réduite* (visitors with reduced mobility) and *visiteurs handicapés* (visitors with disabilities), but inroads are being made into increasing accessibility.

Cobbles, Hills & Pavements

Cobbled streets in historic old towns make wheelchair navigation tricky. Ditto for steep, pavement-less roads in hilltop villages. Cafe terraces sometimes spill across pavements, making them impassable by wheelchair.

Airports

Paris' airports lend wheelchairs to passengers. A Service Assistance Mobilité assists getting passengers to the gate and on/off planes. Contact the service 48 hours in advance (call 3950, *parisaeroport.fr* or download the Paris Aéroport app.

Accommodation

Hotels are required to have a room with wider doorways and accessible bathrooms adapted to a *personne à mobilité réduit* (person with reduced mobility or PMR). Adapted rooms can be harder to find in rural France.

RESOURCES

Association Tourisme & Handicaps (tourisme-handicaps.org) has comprehensive information in English.

SNCF's **Accèss Plus** and **Accès TER** services (accessibilite.sncf.com) provide assistance to train travellers.

Rent an adaptive car through car-sharing service **Wheeliz** (wheeliz.com).

Find hotels, restaurants and more adapted for travellers with disabilities on **accessible.net**.

Visiting Paris? Download the invaluable **Accessible Paris** guide from parisjetaime.com.

Accessibility filters on the **Jaccede app** (jaccede.com) allow you to search 100,000 accessible addresses in France.

PARIS METRO

The Paris metro is not good for accessibility. Line 14 was built with lifts to be wheelchair-accessible, but remains challenging to navigate in a wheelchair – unlike Paris buses, which are 100% accessible.

Outdoors

Countrywide, landscapes are criss-crossed with adapted paths; use accessibility filters on *cirkwi.com* to locate hiking trails navigable by wheelchair (two/three-wheel, electric, off-road). Some nature reserves and beaches – like Lake Annecy's Réserve Naturelle du Bout-du-Monde (p519), parts of Dune du Pilat (p570) and Arcachon's long sandy beachfront (p569) – sport wooden boardwalks. In Brittany, St-Malo's city walls (p279) have accessibility ramps.

ALPINE SKIING

Wheelchair skiing is popular, with most ski resorts sporting adaptive ski lifts, reduced lift passes and ESF schools offering ski sessions with a qualified *moniteur handiski*. Tignes, host to the 1992 Winter Paralympics, is particularly well equipped.

Some public beaches, such as Nice's Plage du Centenaire and Plage de Carras, have ramps into the water, amphibious wheelchairs and dedicated parking and restroom facilities for disabled visitors.

Above: Les Halles Centrales (p424), Dijon; Below: Melons

HOW TO... Shop at the Food Market

As chefs spin gastronomic menus from the day's fresh produce, shopping at *le marché* has never been so in vogue. Yet the unspoken rules and rhythms of this humble, time-worn institution don't change. Market food shopping is not cheaper than a supermarket, but it offers greater value in terms of quality, seasonality and origin. Markets also give you the chance to mingle with farmers and chefs and taste regional dishes hard to find elsewhere.

Market Days

Every village, town and city neighbourhood has an outdoor street market – at least weekly and in the morning, from around 7am to 1pm.

In addition to the weekly market mixing food stalls with clothing, homewares and more, many towns host a *marché des producteurs* (farmers market). At these markets you buy direct from the farmer or producer; find a local one at marches-producteurs.com. If a market is bio, produce is organic.

Covered food markets, often called *les halles,* open five or six days a week – mornings or all day – and tout stalls with lunchtime tables. Most fill the historic market hall, often a 19th-century ensemble of iron, glass and red-brick. Markets in Cannes, Bordeaux, Dijon, Bayonne, Toulouse, Metz, Montpellier, Reims, Lille, Limoges and Sarlat-la-Canéda (actually a church redesigned by star French architect Jean Nouvel) are covered favourites.

Etiquette

Resist the temptation to touch that shiny, luscious fruit and veg – wait for the vendor to serve you. Some distribute plastic bowls for you to pick your own.

Bring a bag – a woven basket bag or pull-along bag on wheels differentiates locals from tourists. If stuck, use a sturdy, reusable shopping bag (€1.50) from any French supermarket.

When buying cheese (or any other food), don't be shy in asking the vendor – invariably the maker – for recipe ideas and cooking tips.

Bargaining is a no-go, and bring cash to pay; most stalls don't accept cards.

Seasonal Specialist Markets

Don't miss markets specialising in a single food product – invariably an epicurean delicacy and pristine reflection of the season. Think fresh garlic in Marseille (June), sun-spun melons in Cavaillon (May to September) and oysters in Cancale year round. Winter (November to March) celebrates decadent black truffles in Provence and the Dordogne, and every imaginable duck part and product known to humankind at Dordogne's raucous *marchés au gras.*

SUMMER NIGHT MARKETS

Marchés de nuit or *marchés nocturnes* unfurl alfresco from around 5pm to 11pm in July and August. They all have food stalls, but the star attraction is the portfolio of *créateurs* – regional artists and artisans, showcasing and selling their work. Street entertainment, concerts and food trucks turn the market into a memorable evening out. Summer night markets are particularly plentiful in Provence, the Dordogne (Périgueux in July) and coastal areas (don't miss Bidart in Pays Basque).

Nuts & Bolts

OPENING HOURS

In many towns and villages, shops close on Monday.

Banks 9am–noon and 2pm–5pm Monday to Friday or Tuesday to Saturday

Bars 7pm–1am

Cafes 7am–11pm

Clubs 10pm–3am, 4am or 5am Thursday to Saturday

Restaurants Noon–2.30pm and 7pm–9pm or later six days a week

Shops 10am–noon and 2pm–7pm Monday to Saturday

Smoking

Illegal in indoor public spaces, summer forests and – since July 2025 – in public parks and gardens, beaches, bus shelters, sports facilities and outdoor spaces around schools.

Weights & Measures

France uses the metric system.

Drugs

Importing, possessing, selling or buying drugs risks 10 years' imprisonment and a €500,000 fine.

GOOD TO KNOW

Time zone
GMT+1

Country code
33

Emergency number
112

Population
68 million

Electricity 230V/50hz

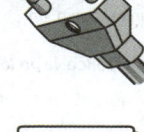

Type C
220V/50Hz

Type E
220V/50Hz

PUBLIC HOLIDAYS

Countrywide the following *jours fériés* are celebrated. Good Friday and Boxing Day (26 December) are public holidays in Alsace and the Moselle *département* of Lorraine.

New Year's Day 1 January

Easter Sunday & Monday Late March/April

May Day 1 May

WWII Victory Day 8 May

Ascension Thursday May; 40th day after Easter

Pentecost & Whit Monday Mid-May to mid-June; 7th Sunday after Easter

Bastille Day (Fête Nationale) 14 July

Assumption Day 15 August

All Saints' Day 1 November

Remembrance Day 11 November

Christmas Day 25 December

Language

Standard French is taught and spoken throughout France. This said, regional accents and dialects are an important part of identity in certain regions, but you'll have no trouble being understood anywhere if you stick to standard French.

Basics

Hello. Bonjour. *bon·zhoor*
Goodbye. Au revoir. *o·rer·vwa*
Yes. Oui. *wee*
No. Non. *non*
Please. S'il vous plaît. *seel voo play*
Thank you. Merci. *mair·see*
Excuse me. Excusez-moi. *ek·skew·zay·mwa*
Sorry. Pardon. *par·don*
What's your name? Comment vous appelez-vous? *ko·mon voo·za·play voo*
My name is ... Je m'appelle ... *zher ma·pel ...*
Do you speak English? Parlez-vous anglais? *par·lay·voo ong·glay*
I don't understand. Je ne comprends pas. *zher ner kom·pron pa*

Directions

Where's ...?
Où est ...? *oo ay ...*
What's the address?
Quelle est l'adresse? *kel ay la·dres*
Could you write the address, please? Est-ce que vous pourriez écrire l'adresse, s'il vous plaît? *es·ker voo poo·ryay ay·kreer la·dres seel voo play*
Can you show me (on the map)?
Pouvez-vous m'indiquer (sur la carte)? *poo·vay·voo mun·dee·kay (sewr la kart)*

Signs

Entrée Entrance
Fermé Closed
Ouvert Open
Sortie Exit
Toilettes/WC Toilets

Time

What time is it? Quelle heure est-il? *kel er ay til*
It's (8) o'clock. Il est (huit) heures. *il ay (weet) er*
Half past (10). Il est (dix) heures et demie. *il ay (deez) er ay day·mee*
Morning matin. *ma·tun*
Afternoon après-midi. *a·pray·mee·dee*
Evening soir. *swar*
Yesterday hier. *yair*
Today aujourd'hui. *o·zhoor·dwee*
Tomorrow demain. *der·mun*

Emergencies

Help! Au secours! *o skoor*
Leave me alone! Fichez-moi la paix! *fee·shay·mwa la pay*
I'm ill. Je suis malade. *zher swee ma·lad*
Call ... Appelez ... *a·play*
  a doctor un médecin. *un mayd·sun*
  the police la police. *la po·lees*

Eating & Drinking

What would you recommend?
Qu'est-ce que vous conseillez? *kes·ker voo kon·say·yay*
Cheers! Santé! *son·tay*
That was delicious.
C'était délicieux! *say·tay day·lee·syer*

NUMBERS

1 un *un*
2 deux *der*
3 trois *trwa*
4 quatre *ka·trer*
5 cinq *sungk*
6 six *sees*
7 sept *set*
8 huit *weet*
9 neuf *nerf*
10 dix *dees*

DISTINCTIVE SOUNDS

Throaty r, silent h, nasal vowels (pronounced as if you're trying to force the sound 'through the nose').

Street Talk

What's up? Quoi de neuf?
Drop it/nevermind! Laisse-tomber!
I can't be bothered/am feeling lazy J'ai la flemme
Enjoy your meal! Bon app!
No way! C'est pas vrai!
Let's go/do it! C'est parti!
Perfect! It's good! Nickel
Oh god! La vache! (literally 'the cow')
Good luck/break a leg Merde
There you go/there you have it Et voilà

And if you want to swear French-style (or express your joy at a gobsmackingly gorgeous view, amazement or disbelief at something... the word is used in many different ways), simply say *Putain!*

DONATIONS TO ENGLISH

Numerous – thanks to the Norman invasion of England in the 11th century, some estimate that three-fifths of everyday English vocabulary arrived via French. You may recognise café, déjà vu, bon vivant, cliché...

Must-Know Grammar

French has a formal and informal word for 'you' (*vous* and *tu* respectively); it distinguishes between masculine and feminine forms of words, eg *beau/belle* (beautiful).

Language Family

Romance (developed from the Latin spoken by the Romans during their conquest of the 1st century BCE). Close relatives include Italian, Spanish, Portuguese and Romanian.

False Friends

Warning: many French words look like English words but have a different meaning altogether, eg menu is a set lunch, not a menu (which is carte in French).

Just Be Nice

Forget the age-old stereotype about the French being rude. Say 'Bonjour' (Hello) when entering shops, restaurants, hotels etc; make an effort to speak a few words of French; and you'll be treated with politeness, friendliness and enthusiasm.

WHO SPEAKS FRENCH?

French is an official language of 29 countries, including France, Belgium, Canada, Democratic Republic of the Congo and Vanuatu.

TOOLKIT LANGUAGE

STORYBOOK

STORYBOOK

Our writers delve deep into different aspects of French life

History of France in 15 Places
Mass migration, Roman subjugation and civilisation, the rise of nobility.
Nicola Williams
p920

Meet the French
The French don't actually wear berets, but they love a good strike as much as their food and wine.
Daphné Leprince-Ringuet
p924

How to Make a French Girl
Becoming a mother allowed me to see how the French are formed through childhood.
Cyrena Lee
p926

Pavement Politics
The French are champions when it comes to striking, but they've had plenty of time to practice.
Anna Richards
p929

Who Owns the Côte d'Or? The Cost of Continuity
Burgundy's Côte d'Or is a sticky story of fracture passed down through generations.
Madeleine Rothery
p932

A HISTORY OF FRANCE IN
15 PLACES

Mass migration, Roman subjugation and civilisation, the rise of nobility: early French history mirrors that of much of Europe. Yet nowhere else would such a strongly independent church continue to coexist under a powerful central authority. Such secularism or *laïcité* drives France's action-packed story. By Writer Name

FRENCH HISTORY BURSTS with drama and punchy characters: virgin warriors and wine-mad popes, bombastic kings and bloody-minded queens, Louis XVI's consort who alienated every segment of society and the 1920s cabaret star who lovingly adopted 12 children from around the world as 'an experiment in brotherhood' and a nod to France's enduring national motto *Liberté, Egalité, Fraternité* ('liberty, equality, fraternity').

Celtic Gauls first settled French lands. Roman France bequeathed the south with amphitheatres, aqueducts and public baths. Building on the Greek's dabbling in viticulture, the Romans planted vineyards in Burgundy and Bordeaux, and crafted techniques to process wine. They introduced the newfangled faith of Christianity. France got its first king – and name – with Frankish leader Clovis I (r 481–511), and the coronation of Hugh Capet in 987 spawned a dynasty that ruled France for eight centuries. Art and culture blossomed during the reign of Renaissance king François I (r 1515–47), sowing the seeds for France's thoroughly well-deserved modern reputation as a centre of avant-garde.

Long and bloody wars pitted the French against the English (Hundred Years War; 1337–1453) and Catholics against Protestants (Wars of Religion; 1562–98), forging inextricable rivalries that never quite died out. Napoléon Bonaparte's 19th-century Napoléonic Code notably granted freedom of religion and a century later, the Dreyfus Affair and Catholic Church interference forced the promulgation of *laïcité* (secularism) in France. It's been a hot potato ever since.

1. Vézère Valley
EUROPE'S FIRST ART

In a Europe covered by vast ice sheets that periodically expanded and retreated, people lived a hunter-gatherer lifestyle in what is now France, using the mouths of natural caves as temporary shelters while they followed the migration routes of their prey. Using flint stones some 30,000 years ago and later charcoal and red pigments (after 17,000 BCE), these early Palaeolithic people etched and painted a bestiary of bisons, reindeers, horses, mammoths and now-extinct megaloceros on cave walls in Lascaux and 20-plus other caves in the Dordogne's Vézère Valley to create Europe's very first art.

To visit replicas of Dordogne's UNESCO-protected caves – or two astonishing originals in Les Eyzies – see p625.

2. Carnac Alignments
OLDER THAN STONEHENGE

Historians remained baffled by the world's largest concentration of monumental menhirs and dolmens in Brittany, erected by Neolithic people during the New Stone Age from 7000 BCE. In and around Carnac, some 3000 standing stones, some 8m tall, mushroomed between 5000 and 3500 BCE, but no one knows how or why. It's thought the 20m-tall Er Grah was broken into four gigantesque chunks 700 years after it was erected in 4700 BCE. Burial mounds or tumulus – passage graves with chambers, covered in dry stone – from the same period likewise beg a thousand questions.

To walk around the Carnac alignments and less-crowded sister stones in south Morbihan, see p303.

3. Les Journées Romaines
ROMAN OLYMPICS

Centuries of conflict between the Gauls and the Romans ended in 52 BCE when Julius Caesar's legions crushed a revolt by many Gallic tribes led by Celtic Arverni tribe chief Vercingétorix at Gergovia, near present-day Clermont-Ferrand. Relive the drama and bloodshed of this momentous point in history with theatrical shows, gladiatorial duels and Olympian-esque games during the raucous three-day Les Journées Romaines festival in Nîmes. It was for this Roman city that the Pont du Gard aqueduct was constructed in 60 CE.

To immerse yourself in Roman Nîmes, see p654.

4. Musée de la Tapisserie de Bayeux
COMIC STRIP BATTLES

The tale of how William the Conqueror and his forces mounted a successful invasion of England from their base in Normandy in 1066 is told on the Bayeux Tapestry, showcased inside Bayeux's Musée de la Tapisserie. In 1152 Eleanor of Aquitaine wed Henry of Anjou, bringing another third of France under the control of the English crown. The subsequent rivalry between France and England for control of Aquitaine and the vast English territories in France lasted three centuries, degenerating in 1337 into the Hundred Years War.

To learn more about Bayeux in Normandy and its storytelling heritage, see p251.

5. Historial Jeanne d'Arc
THE VIRGIN WARRIOR

Divine revelations prompted 16-year-old peasant girl Jeanne d'Arc, or Joan of Arc, to flee her home village in 1428, expel the English from France and facilitate the coronation of French Charles VII in Reims cathedral. In 1429, armed with sword, horse and army, she stormed Orléans and smashed English forces who'd occupied the Loire Valley city for seven months. She was subsequently captured by the Burgundians, sold to the English, convicted for witchcraft and heresy by a tribunal of French ecclesiastics in Rouen's archbishops' palace (today Rouen's Historial Jeanne d'Arc museum) in 1431, and burned at the stake.

To trace the final footsteps of France's patron saint, canonised in 1920, see p225.

6. Château de Chambord
RENAISSANCE SPLENDOUR

With the arrival of Italian Renaissance during the reign of François I (r 1515–47), secular matters assumed new importance over religious life. Reflecting the splendour of the monarchy, fast moving towards absolutism, François I had a weekend hunting retreat built in Chambord. Mixing classical components with the rich decoration of Flamboyant Gothic style, the Loire Valley château of monstrous proportion showcased his wealth and ancestry. Its 426 rooms, 282 fireplaces and 77 staircases were arranged on five floors around a central axis, ensuring easy circulation in an edifice that many deem to be France's first modern building.

To visit Château de Chambord and its forested estate, see p381.

Château de Chambord (p381), the Loire

7. Palais du Parlement de Bretagne
BRETON TO THE LAST BREATH

Wedged between two powerful kingdoms, Brittany was hotly contested by both France and England until 1532, when a series of strategic royal weddings finally brought an end to *la Guerre Folle* ('the Mad War') between France and Brittany. The latter was incorporated under the French crown, but Brittany retained its fierce independent spirit, distinct identity and its own doggedly rebellious parliament – at home in a gilded palace in Breton capital Rennes.

To take a guided tour of Palais du Parlement de Bretagne and learn more about Breton history, see p274.

8. Château de Versailles
SUN KING MEGALOMANIA

Louis XIV (r 1643–1715), better known as Le Roi Soleil (the Sun King), ascended the throne aged five. Bolstered by claims of divine right, he involved the kingdom of France in a series of costly wars with Holland, Austria and England. Taxation to refill the state coffers caused widespread poverty and vagrancy, but didn't stop Louis XIV from building the most extravagant palace on French earth at Versailles in 1663. The king forced his 6000 courtiers to compete with each other for royal favour, thus quashing the feuding aristocracy and creating the first centralised French state.

To be razzle-dazzled by the French monarchy at the height of its glory, see p184.

9. MuCEM
THE KINDEST CUT

Hanging, drawing and quartering – roping the victim's limbs to four oxen or horses, which then ran in four directions – was once the favoured method of publicly executing commoners. To make public executions more humane, French physician Joseph-Ignace Guillotin (1738–1814) invented the guillotine. During the Reign of Terror (September 1793 to July 1794) in Paris, some 17,000 had their head sliced off by the 2m-odd falling blade. By 1977 when the time the last person in France was guillotined (not in public), the contraption could slice off a head in 2/100 of a second.

A Real McCoy guillotine is among the historical cultural objects displayed at Marseille's MuCEM; see p753.

10. Îles Sanguinaires
AN EMPEROR FROM CORSICA

Local lore says Napoléon Bonaparte (1769–1821) acquired his taste of war as a child watching soldiers from Ajaccio's garrison practice manoeuvres on place du Général de Gaulle, dominated by an equestrian statue of the Corsican general who overthrew France's First Republic in 1799 to become emperor of France. During his 16 years of despotic rule, Napoléon instituted key reforms, including the Code Napoléon (the basis of the French legal system). In Ajaccio he tackled public health by building a lazaret – to quarantine Corsican fishermen returning from months-long fishing expeditions in North Africa – on the flame-red rocks of the Îles Sanguinaires.

To lap up Napoléonic vibes in Ajaccio, see p884.

11. Musée Massena
UNE TRÈS BELLE ÉPOQUE

It was fashionable *hivernants* (winter tourists) that first shone light on the Côte d'Azur, or French Riviera, as the place to be. Attracted by its mild Mediterranean climate and restorative seaside air, these early tourists followed in the footsteps of England's Queen Victoria from 1882 to wintertime Nice. They arrived by train aboard the world's first night train, the luxurious blue-and-gold *Train Bleu* (1886) linking Calais with Menton further along the coast, and spent their days strolling Promenade des Anglais, hobnobbing over afternoon tea and risking all in Monte Carlo Casino.

Explore UNESCO's 'Winter Resort Town of the Riviera' on p807.

12. Route des Crêtes
MOUNTAIN WARFARE DURING WWI

No more than a few kilometres from the border with Germany in eastern France, Alsace's low-lying Massif des Vosges was fiercely fought over from December 1914 until armistice in November 1918 during WWI. The bloodiest battles were at Vieil Armand (956m), a strategic rocky spur overlooking the Alsace plain and Rhine Valley. It was nicknamed 'man-eating mountain'. Some 90km of trenches were dug in the mountain – many remain – and the Route des Crêtes (Ridge Road) through the Vosges *ballons* (bald, round-

The Panthéon (p152), Paris

ed mountain peaks) was built to get supplies to troops.

For a driving tour along the Route des Crêtes to a memorial remembering 7000 fallen soldiers, see p347.

13. Le Grand Bunker – Musée du Mur de l'Atlantique
LEST WE FORGET

Thirteen million cubic metres of concrete and the lives of 10,000 Allied soldiers went into the construction of the Atlantic Wall, or Mur de l'Atlantique, in France – coastal fortifications built by the Germans between 1942 and 1944 to defend 4000km of coastline from Norway to southern France. From a telemetry post inside a blockhouse (open to visitors as Le Grand Bunker – Musée du Mur de l'Atlantique) in the small Norman fishing port of Ouistreham, Germans surveyed Normandy's coastline fringed by golden sand beaches where Allied soldiers would land on D-Day.

To ponder the infamy of WWII D-Day landing beaches and battle scars close-up, see p246.

14. Cité de l'Architecture et du Patrimoine
GRANDS PROJETS IN PARIS

Just as the megalomaniac 'Sun King' flaunted his power at Versailles, so French political leaders in the 1970s and 1980s sought to immortalise themselves through *grands projets* – huge public edifices. Architects behind Paris' Centre Pompidou stuck the cause célèbre's functional 'insides' on the outside to create a Parisian icon. The thrust of the current gargantuan renovation project (from 2026 until 2030): to reconnect the building with its 'original utopian vision'. The idea of transforming Gare d'Orsay train station into an art museum was considered equally preposterous in 1986. François Mitterrand's clocked up a €4.6-billion taxpayers' bill with his architectural landmarks with attitude. Emmanuel Macron's Pompidou bill: an estimated €262 million.

Track Paris architecture through the ages at the Cité de l'Architecture et du Patrimoine on p71.

15. The Panthéon
LIBERTY, EQUALITY, FRATERNITY

Voltaire, Rousseau, Victor Hugo and Marie Curie lie beneath the stately neoclassical dome of Paris' Panthéon. In 2021 they were joined in their time-honoured resting place of France's 'greatest' by Josephine Baker (1906–75). The American-born music-hall star, French Resistance fighter and civil-rights activist arrived in Paris during les *Années folles* (the 'crazy years' of the 1920s) – a magnet for US performers facing racial segregation in their homeland. Her risqué cabaret shows thrilled Paris. Of the 80 luminaries buried in the Panthéon since 1791, only six are women. Baker is the first performing artist, American and Black woman.

For more on the Panthéon, see p152.

MEET THE FRENCH

The French don't actually wear berets, but they love a good strike as much as their food and wine. Daphné Leprince-Ringuet introduces her people.

DO AN ONLINE search for a map showing, across France, how many *bises* (kisses on the cheek) are appropriate to greet your friends, and you will see how difficult it is to encapsulate the French in just a few paragraphs. Etiquette changes from one square kilometre to the next and typically no one agrees on the right way to do things.

For a country so attached to its identity, France is indeed a curious melting pot. Stand on the coast of Brittany: you could be looking over Cornish cliffs in southern England. Visit Strasbourg's Christmas market and you will be savouring Germanic-sounding delicacies. In the streets of Corsican villages, you will inevitably overhear greetings like *bonghjornu* and *avvèdeci* tinged with a similar melodic rhythm to the Italian language.

That's only a taster of France's huge variety of accents and dialects, landscapes and gastronomies, without mentioning the one most important rule across the country – if you are travelling in the southwest, do not ask your local bakery for a *pain au chocolat*. Down there it is called a *chocolatine*, and it is not a matter taken lightly.

Of course, France is more than an amalgam of bastions with their own peculiarities. There are many things that draw the French together and perhaps topping that list is an enduring inclination for protesting – and as a natural continuation of that, for striking (p929). France is no exception in its readiness to take to the streets to do and undo political action, but somehow it is where the cliché has stuck the strongest. And it is not entirely without basis: from pension reforms to fuel prices through same-sex marriage and #MeToo marches, all causes warrant some street action.

But it's not all about politics. Another great French unifier – and another cliché living up to its reputation – is food. Wherever you are staying in France, the UNESCO-protected 'gastronomic meal of the French', referring to large family meals celebrating togetherness for special events such as birthdays or weddings, is still very much a reality. And perhaps even more universal is its little sister, *apéro*, which derives from apéritif and describes the hour or so before a meal spent coming together with a drink and a snack. *Apéro's* versatility has made it an essential part of French life. It can be taken with family, friends, colleagues or strangers you just met at the cafe. It can be a civilised affair, opening a fancy meal, or a casual drink with friends that escalated to end in the early hours of the morning. It's about munching on crisps and *saucisson* with a beer or savouring smoked salmon with a glass of champagne. Pretty much anything goes, as long as you're having a great time. *Alors, on prend l'apéro?*

The French in Numbers

France has a population of 68.6 million and its diversity is ever-growing. Immigrants represent over 10.7% of the population, more than twice what it was in 1946. The majority come from Algeria and Morocco, followed by Portugal, Tunisia and Italy.

Pictured clockwise from top left: Christmas market, Strasbourg (p334); Lyon restaurant (p458); Pension reforms protest (p929); Paris; Calvi (p873), Corsica

ATYPICALLY BILINGUAL

I spoke English from a young age with my mother, who is half Scottish, and was lucky to receive an international education. But this is not the most typical profile in France. The French have a reputation for being pretty average speakers of English, ranking nearly last in Europe for English proficiency according to censuses. Things are changing, especially among younger generations, with polls showing that 48% of 18- to 24-year-olds understand English, as opposed to 15% of those over 65 years old. And while France has one of the lowest emigration rates in the OECD, top expat destinations include English-speaking countries like the USA, Canada and the UK. In fact, an ongoing debate exists as to whether London, with its estimated 150,000 French residents, ranks among France's largest cities. Regardless, play it safe and learn a few basic words – it's always much appreciated.

Cyrena's daughter Kiko

HOW TO MAKE A FRENCH GIRL

Becoming a mother allowed me to see, in real-time, how the French are formed through childhood. By Cyrena Lee

IN THE HAZE of giving birth to my first child in the 12th arrondissement of Paris, I was handed a medical report on her vital statistics. Amid a blur of numbers listing her weight and measurements, a line jumped out at me: skin colour, pink.

'Her race is... pink?' I stifled a confused laugh, pointing out the word rose to my very pale French husband. Her newborn skin did have a flush of red tone, in sharp contrast to my olive skin.

'No, silly.' My husband patted my shoulder. 'It's just a medical report. This is France, not America.'

Data collection on ethnicity, race and religion in France was banned in 1978. Emphasis on racial identity is discouraged in favour of assimilation – namely, to adopt the French ways of speaking, being and thinking. I was aware of this from my preparations to apply for citizenship, which include learning French history, the language and the values of the Republic.

French Assimilation vs American Integration

As a first-time, millennial parent, I want to get things right. Therefore, I overanalyse, Google everything and read countless books on parenting. My parents, Taiwanese immigrants to suburban New Jersey, imparted bits of their culture as best they could: Chinese school took over Saturdays, I ate congee and beef noodle soup at home, and shared Lunar New Year traditions with my classmates in line with America's updated 'salad bowl' cultural theory – that new citizens and first-generation Americans can maintain their unique culture while integrating. I speak English fluently, love nothing more than a New York slice, and would never miss an annual Thanksgiving meal.

Yet I couldn't count the number of times I've been made to feel other in America. Strangely, in France, where I'd first studied abroad in 2009 and mastered the language, I didn't feel that constant pressure. Civil rights activist and writer James Baldwin escaped to France in 1948 to dodge the rampant racism stateside, though I, too, find that the dominant assimilation policy flattens racism and rewards doing as the French do (though there is plenty of debate around this point). And the French do things in very particular ways.

Sounds of French Childhood

'*Et boum!*' Two 11-month-olds are crawling and attempting to walk in my kitchen. My neighbour, who has a son about a week younger than my daughter, adds this

STORYBOOK

inexplicable onomatopoeia as my daughter, Kiko, falls onto the floor. I watch this scene curiously. As she helps her up, she adds *'et hup!'*

The French love to echo the sounds of everyday life in their daily discourse. Test this theory: watch any French person pick up an object. Invariably, they will add the sound 'hup' like they are in a cartoon show. Verbalising *'tac'* is used for objects being thrown or set down, or liberally sprinkled in speech when an action is accomplished.

The summer she turned two, we were on a long stretch of Normandy beach on the Cotentin peninsula, enjoying the tidal changes on a summer day. Kiko stood before the crashing shoreline. *'Allez,'* she screamed in a mini-sumo squat, before running into the cold water and breaking into a fit of giggles. Her older cousin showed her how to pat sand into a bucket, and as she did so, she pronounced a 'tap tap tap' for every tap. Kiko followed along accordingly because making weird noises with your mouth is fun.

One day, I pulled my daughter aside. 'You can just pick things up without saying hup,' I explained. In return, my child looked at me and made that *je-ne-sais-pas* mouth-fart sound the French use to indicate that they have no response worthy of words.

Cultural Values in Nursery Rhymes

'If you're happy and you know it, clap your hands, CLAP CLAP!' This refrain of scream-screaming and clapping has been going on loop for nearly 20 minutes. My daughter is giggling and shrieking, each scream accentuating my headache.

This misery is of my own making: to compensate for the dominance of the French language, I resolved to play only English language nursery songs and stories. But the decision has me full of regret: the nursery rhymes are repetitive, loud and downright irritating. How many times can the wheels on a bus go round? Then I realise, perhaps this is the Sapir–Whorf hypothesis on a new level: language influences not only how we perceive the world, but how we act in it. These songs are much like Americans, a bit loud and proud: see the teapot, short and stout, hear it shout!

Admittedly, I now prefer French children's songs, which are more sophisticated, romantic and poetic. *À la Claire Fontaine* evokes images of bathing in a spring while reminiscing over a past love. Kiko loves listening to Guy Prunier's elegant vocal stylings of stories and garden tours. She sings lines from *Fais dodo, Colas, mon p'tit frère*: *'Maman est en haut / Qui fait du gâteau / Papa est en bas / Qui fait du chocolat'*. The popular lullaby's emphasis on parents lovingly making sweets and pastries reflects France's love of savoir-faire and *le goûter*, an afternoon sweet snack, whereas *Hush Little Baby* unabashedly hints at America's love of buying things and capitalism.

Toddler Wisdom

Presented as a way to tackle inequality, as mostly poorer, immigrant and non-francophone communities were not enrolling their youngest, Macron passed a law in 2018 that made school mandatory starting at age three. My daughter is off to school this fall, and I worry that'll make it even harder to impart a sense of American or Chinese identity on her. I fret that she's too young, and as I anguished over this aloud, my daughter patted me on the back. *'Oh la la, maman,'* she tried to comfort me. *'Ce n'est pas grave.'*

I smiled at her in return. 'Just don't forget, you are also American. And Chinese!' But perhaps all of my worry and overanalysing of what it means to be French or any other nationality is a silly, adult concern – missing the forest for the trees. Perhaps the most important thing is that she maintains a sense of herself. Too young to have any notion of identity politics, she looked at me squarely in the eyes and shook her head. 'No,' she said sagely, 'I am Kiko.'

PAVEMENT POLITICS

The French are champions when it comes to striking, but they've had plenty of time to practice. By Anna Richards

ANYONE WHO HAS spent more than a smattering of time in France is likely to have coincided with a strike or protest. It's a national pastime, and one the French hone through regular practice. The SNCF alone is responsible for some 5 million work days lost to strikes in just 20 years – but at least they're consistent. There has been at least one SNCF strike every year since 1947. If striking were an Olympic sport, France would be on the podium every time. This is a country where rebellion forms the very fabric of the tricolore (literally, since it was officially adopted as France's flag post-Revolution in 1794), but France's penchant for a protest long predates the French Revolution.

Wine Wars

The first strike on record was over 500 years earlier, and began as a pub brawl. The fight broke out in a Parisian tavern on Faubourg St-Marcel in 1229. Students, at the heart of strikes from the get-go, were thirsty for a bargain even then. Outraged by the increasing price of wine, students from the University of Paris began to cause a scene. Locals called upon *'sergents royaux'*, officers tasked with enforcing royal justice. The repercussions were severe and students were beaten, killed and thrown into the Seine, with some sources saying hundreds were killed. What's sure is that it sparked a mass protest, with professors and students alike walking out, and many going into exile at foreign universities like Oxford and Bologna. Two years later, Pope Gregory IX declared the University of Paris independent of secular authorities, and officially granted its professors and students the right to strike under certain circumstances – namely if a student or professor was harmed or their privileges violated. And strike they did, every few years subsequently.

One of the first labour strikes for better pay took place in Lyon in the 1500s. A major player in the printing business, Lyon had 181 printing houses at the turn of the 16th century, and many of the workers formed *confréries,* or brotherhoods. A little like a workers' union, Lyonnais printers walked out en masse on 25 April 1539 in a strike that lasted over three months and became known as *'le Grand Tric'* (a 16th-century local word for a strike). There's little information on whether the printers got the pay rise they'd striked for, but François I banned brotherhoods linked to jobs in the months that followed.

STORYBOOK

The First Trade Union

The first of the Révoltes des Canuts (silk workers' strikes) in the 19th century, also in Lyon in 1831, has been described as the 'first example of a workers' uprising'. Economic downturns were affecting the silk industry and manufacturers paying less and less for weavers' work, leading to the *canuts* demanding a fixed minimum wage. Thousands took to the streets to protest, before being repressed by the military. The second *canuts*' strike, in 1834, was much bloodier. Thousands of *canuts* were arrested and hundreds more killed in a week that became known as *semaine sanglante* (bloody week). Although the struggles of the *canuts* sowed the seeds for the legalisation of trade unions in 1884, they reaped none of the rewards at the time. Minimum hourly wage took much longer, and wasn't officially introduced in France until 1950.

One of the largest strikes in France happened in 1968 and finished by mobilising almost two-thirds of the French workforce. What began as a student protest escalated nationwide to involve some 10 million people. Authoritarianism in universities, police repression of student protests and outdated curriculums were the catalysts, but as the strikes spread to the wider population they rapidly expanded to include grievances such as stagnant wages and poor working conditions. This particular strike was a success. Minimum wage increased by 35% in the space of just a few years, among other breakthroughs, and it became a global symbol of youth rebellion.

On The Picket Line Today

Walk past the Hôtel de Ville in any major French city and there's often a gaggle of protesters with placards. The right to strike has been enshrined in the French constitution since 1946, and employers are forbidden from discriminating against their employees for exercising their right to strike.

It's only intensified this side of the millennium. The world watched in fascination as the *gilets jaunes* (yellow vests) took to the streets in 2018 to oppose a proposed green initiative to raise taxes on diesel and petrol, donning the hi-vis jackets French motorists are obliged to keep in their vehicles. Many of the protests turned violent, and the movement largely petered out with the outbreak of the COVID-19 pandemic.

In early 2023, president Emmanuel Macron's plan to raise the retirement age from 62 to 64 years old sparked widespread outrage. Although still among the lowest retirement ages in Europe, at least a million people protested. Fearful that the bill wouldn't pass, Macron invoked Article 49.3, a provision in the Constitution to push through a law without voting on it at the Assemblée Nationale – fuel to the flames for angry protesters.

Evidence of *manifs* (slang for protests) is everywhere in France. Often it's in the form of political graffiti: like *'non à 49.3'* in spidery black writing above a shop. In the wake of a big protest it can be smashed windows, generally those belonging to large corporations like banks, or in the lingering acrid smell of firecrackers in the air. Sometimes it's in quiet acts of civil disobedience. Driving around rural France, it's now almost as common to see road signs with village names upside down as the right way up. Local farmers are behind this one, part of the widespread protests around the precarity of the farming industry, and high overheads for low remuneration. Several large protests have also seen farmers block major motorways with tractors and hay bales.

Arriving at the train station only to see a long list of *annulés* (cancelled trains) can be frustrating, but console yourself with the fact that you're experiencing an integral part of French culture.

> **ONE OF THE LARGEST STRIKES IN FRANCE HAPPENED IN 1968 AND FINISHED BY MOBILISING ALMOST TWO-THIRDS OF THE FRENCH WORKFORCE. WHAT BEGAN AS A STUDENT PROTEST ESCALATED NATIONWIDE TO INVOLVE SOME 10 MILLION PEOPLE.**

'Bloquons Tout' ('block everything') protests

WHO OWNS THE CÔTE D'OR? THE COST OF CONTINUITY

Mapped, memorised and revered across centuries, few landscapes carry the weight of prestige and myth quite like the vineyards of Burgundy's Côte d'Or – literally, the 'coast of gold'. But behind that veneer of order lies something far more precarious: a sticky story of fracture passed down through generations. By Madeleine Rothery

SHAPED BY GENEALOGY as much as geology, centuries of tradition have cultivated not just the region's vines, but a kind of spectral ownership – something held as much in memory as in matter. Parcels of vineyard, once measured in fields, now change hands in fractions, as families cling to the region's prestige row by row, and at an incredible cost.

The splintering of Burgundy's vineyards was legislated in idealism: after the French Revolution, the Napoleonic Code decreed that all children must receive an equal share in inheritance – a move designed to dismantle the rusty rule of primogeniture. Under this very specific, very French law, if you have two children, at least half your estate must be divided equally between them; if you have three, two-thirds must be shared in equal parts, and so on. But with the law in place for over two centuries, vineyard holdings are now sliced finer than ever, producing an increasingly surreal geometry: siblings owning alternating rows within the same vineyard, cousins cultivating adjoining vines under competing labels.

Stormy Inheritance

Consider the case of the illustrious Clos de Vougeot, a château and vineyard tucked between the villages of Vougeot and Chambolle-Musigny on the Côte d'Or. Today, more than 80 owners tend to fragments of what was once a single monastic plot. Even the most mythic domaine in the region, Romanée-Conti, is the product of shared inheritance, co-owned by the de Villaine and Leroy/Roch families, whose alternating stewardship speaks not only to the fragility of such legacies, but also to the diplomatic interdependence they require to survive.

In theory, inheriting vines in Burgundy is a privilege. In practice, it can feel more like a financial curse with France's steep inheritance taxes (which can climb upwards of 50%). Some families are forced to sell, while others restructure. Even valuable domaines like Leflaive have turned to *groupements fonciers agricoles* (GFAs) – corporate shelters that convert soil into shareholding structures, built less for cultivation than for continuity. Yet no clever contract can protect against grief or the slow-burn politics of family. It's not uncommon for a court to force the sale of a vineyard when heirs can't come to an agreement – and after decades, sometimes even centuries, of division, that disagreement can implicate dozens, even hundreds, of family members.

To speak of inheritance in Burgundy is to consider a sentiment closer to ritual than to simple real estate or a battle of legalese. After all, this is the region from which the famously esoteric term *terroir* is derived: the 'somewhereness,' the essence of a particular vineyard. Among vignerons, there is often a reluctance to describe themselves as proprietors; they are instead guardians, stewards or servants of the land. To inherit land here is to inherit a story – one that binds the body to the earth and the self to a larger, older whole. The idea that *terroir* can be passed from parent to child is not just poetic, but foundational to the Burgundian imagination. To many, this is the true cost of losing land: the vanishing of a voice in a centuries-long conversation.

The Price of Prestige

But when legacy begins to splinter, some family members see an opportunity for liquidation rather than preservation. In recent decades, as parcels passed through generation after generation – growing smaller and more fraught with each handover – a different kind of heir has begun to arrive. Global investors, drawn by the region's mythic prestige and the security of fine wine as a luxury asset, have started acquiring slivers of Burgundy's most storied vineyards.

In 2017, French billionaire François Pinault purchased Clos de Tart, a 7.5-hectare *grand cru monopole* in Morey-Saint-Denis. The sale, reportedly worth just under €200 million, made headlines not just for its price, but for its symbolism: Pinault is only the fourth owner in nearly nine centuries. His acquisition lands in a broader trend that has seen major estates – including Clos des Lambrays and Bonneau du Martray – sold to luxury conglomerates and ultra-high-net-worth individuals, many of whom live far from the Côte d'Or. Scarcity, prestige and the promise of long-term value have drawn in collectors and corporations seeking both cultural capital and financial security.

This wave of foreign investment has prompted ambivalence among locals: some welcome the resources and renewed prestige, while others mourn what feels like the slow unmooring of Burgundy's soul. The tension is not only economic, but metaphysical: if *terroir* is defined by the lived relationship between land and labour, then what happens when the hands that own the vines no longer speak the language of the soil?

Holding onto History

Nowhere is this collision of heritage and capital more sharply felt than in the story of the Château de Gevrey-Chambertin. Once a noble estate, it had fallen into disrepair and stood empty for years. But in 2012, Chinese billionaire Louis Ng purchased the château for €8 million, outbidding a coalition of local winegrowers who had hoped to preserve it as part of the region's cultural *patrimoine*. The sale sparked national debate with Jean-Michel Guillon, head of the local winemakers' union declaring: 'It is a despoliation. Our heritage is going out of the window.' Restoration is now underway, but the château's new role – and its place in the village's emotional landscape – remains uncertain.

Burgundy remains, for now, a place where the old stories are still told – of monks and soil, of family lines and lunar cycles – but those stories are being translated, their meanings diluted, their audiences altered. To inherit in Burgundy has always been to bear a contradiction: between continuity and change, memory and ambition, devotion and survival. That tension is no longer local, it is global. But the vines, at least, are still making good wine.

INDEX

9 Écluses de Fonseranes 670-1

A

Abbaye de Fontfroide 691
accessible travel 913
accommodation 38, 905, 910
activities, see outdoor activities
Aigues-Mortes 662
Aiguille du Midi 504-5
airports 902
Aix-en-Provence 35, 796
Ajaccio 884-7, **885**
 accommodation 898
 beyond Ajaccio 888-91
 food 886, 887
 nightlife 887
 travel within 884
Albert 205
Albi 714-15, 739
Alpe d'Huez 538-40
Alsace 331-53
 itineraries 333
 navigation 332, **332**
 travel seasons 333
 travel within 332
Alta Rocca 896, 899, **896**
Amiens 202-4, **203**
 accommodation 217
 beyond Amiens 205-11
 drinking 203
 food 203
 travel within 202
Annecy 33, 549
Antibes 829-30, 858
Apt 781
aquariums
 Aquarium Biarritz 588-9
 Aquarium La Rochelle 576

Aquarium Tropical 137
Nausicaá 213
Arcachon 31, 569-70
Arc de Triomphe 78-9
architecture, see also chateaux, churches, cathedrals & basilicas, Roman sites
 art deco 72, 260-2, 316-17, 72
 art nouveau 72, 367, 368, 72, 368
 French-Gothic 714-15
 medieval 149, 153, 688
 Middle Ages 691
 museums 71, 166-7, 923
 post-WW II 236, 236
 walking tours 72, 157, 236, 368, 707, 72, 157, 236, 368, 707
 Wilhelmian 361
Arles 29, 762-3
 accommodation 796
 beyond Arles 766-8
 food 763
 walking tour 764, **764**
Armagnac 719, 720, 739
Arras 201, 217
Arromanches-es-Bains 246
art 16-17, see also art galleries & museums, street art
art galleries & museums
 Atelier Sainte Croix des Arts 361
 Bourse de Commerce 93-4
 Centre Pompidou 95
 Centre Pompidou-Metz 360
 Cité Internationale de la Tapisserie 646
 Collection Lambert 771
 Dalí Museum 96, 100
 Entre Tissu et Papier 245
 FAMM 831
 Fondation Bemberg 709
 Fondation Cartier pour l'Art Contemporain 93
 Fondation Henri Cartier-Bresson 121
 Fondation Victor Vasarely 758

Fondation Vincent Van Gogh 762
Frac-Artothèque Nouvelle-Aquitaine 641
Galerie de l'Arsenal 361
Galerie Emmanuel Perrotin 121
Galerie Modulab 361
Galerie Octave Cowbell 361
Galerie PJ 361
Galeries Bartoux Normandy 245
Grand Palais 80
Jeu de Paume 89-90
La Flèche d'Or 135
La Galerie des Arts du Feu 227
Lafayette Anticipations 121
Les Abattoirs 709
Les Jardins des Sculptures 230
Luma Arles 762
MAIF Social Club 121
Maison Européenne de la Photographie 121
Musée Angladon 771
Musée Art Brut 665, 667
Musée Bonnard 828
Musée Bonnat-Helleu 585
Musée Calvet 771
Musée Bourdelle 183
Musée d'Art Hyacinthe Rigaud 691
Musée d'Art Moderne de Paris 71
Musée d'Art Moderne (Céret) 692
Musée d'Art Moderne (Troyes) 325
Musée de Flandre 200-1
Musée de l'Annonciade 838
Musée de l'Orangerie 89-90
Musée Départemental d'Art Contemporain Chateau De Rochechouart 646
Musée des Augustins 709
Musée des Arts Décoratifs 89-90

Musée des Beaux-Arts (Bordeaux) 560
Musée des Beaux-Arts (Dijon) 424
Musée des Beaux Arts (Limoges) 641
Musée des Beaux-Arts (Marseille) 754
Musée des Beaux-Arts (Nancy) 367
Musée des Beaux-Arts (Nîmes) 658
Musée des Beaux-Arts (Pau) 738
Musée des Beaux-Arts (Rouen) 226
Musée des Beaux-Arts de Caen 252
Musée des Confluences 462
Musée d'Orsay 166-7
Musée du Louvre 86-7
Musée du Petit Palais 769
Musée du Quai Branly - Jacques Chirac 73
Musée Fabre 663-5
Musée Goya 713
Musée Hôtel Lepinant 644, 646
Musée Ingres Bourdelle 718
Musée Lapidaire 771
Musée Marmottan Monet 63, 70
Musée Matisse 811
Musée National Adrien Dubouché 641
Musée National des Arts Asiatiques Guimet 73
Musée National Marc Chagall 811
Musée National Picasso 'La Guerre et la Paix 830-1
Musée National Picasso-Paris 115
Musée Paul Valéry 674
Musée Picasso 830
Musée Pierre de Luxembourg 773
Musée Rodin 172-3
Musée Toulouse-Lautrec 715

Map Pages **000**

934

Museon Arlaten 762
Palais de Tokyo 70-1
Palais des Beaux Arts 196-7
Palais Fesch - Musée des Beaux-Arts 884, 886
Petit Palais 79
Polka Galerie 121
ATMs 904
Auch 719
Aups 847
Auray 302
Auteuil 62-3
Auvergne 449-93
  itineraries 452-3
  navigation 450-1, **450-1**
  travel seasons 452-3
  travel within 450-1
Auxerre 442-4, **443**
  accommodation 447
  beyond Auxerre 445-6
  drinking 444
  food 443
  travel within 442
Avenue de Champagne 319, 322
Avenue des Champs-Élysées 76
Avignon 769-73, **770**
  accommodation 796
  beyond Avignon 774-80
  drinking 773
  food 771
  travel within 769
Avranches 257-8
Aÿ 329

bagadoù 290
Balazuc 472
Balzac, Honoré de 70
Barfleur 263
basilicas, *see* churches, cathedrals & basilicas
Basilique du Sacré-Cœur 97
Bastia 866-8, **867**
  accommodation 898
  beyond Bastia 869-72
  drinking 868
  food 868
  travel within 866
Basque culture 598-600
bastides 14, 716-17, **717**
batteries
  Batterie d'Azeville 250
  Batterie de Crisbecq 250
Battle of the Somme 207
Bayeux 246-52, **248-9**
  accommodation 265
  food 251
  travel within 246
Bayeux Tapestry 251, 921

Bayonne 31, 583-7, **584**
  accommodation 601
  beyond Bayonne 588-93
  drinking 586, 587
  food 585, 586, 587
  shopping 587
  travel within 583
beaches 19
  Biarritz 589
  Bonifacio 894
  Calvi 873
  Corniche des Maures 844
  Côte d'Azur 804-5
  Dordogne 608-9, **609**
  Fréjus 842
  Golfe du Valinco 889
  Île de Porquerolles 849
  Île de Ré 582
  Îles Lavezzi 894
  La Rochelle 577
  Lake Annecy 520
  Les Calanques 755-7
  Marseille 750, 752
  Montpellier 668
  Plage de Palombaggia 895
  Pointe de la Torche 294
  Presqu'île de Giens 846
  Pyrénées Orientales 690
  Quiberon Peninsula 306
  Rennes 275
  Rhuys Peninsula 303
  safety 907
  Salin de Giraud 766
  St-Florent 869
  St-Gildas-de-Rhuys 303
  St-Malo 281, 283
  St-Raphaël 842-3
  St-Tropez 839-40
  Vannes 299
bears 731
Beaujolais 463
  accommodation 492
  road trip 464, **464**
Beaune 430-5, 440, **431**
  accommodation 447
  beyond Beaune 436-41
  drinking 432, 433
  food 434, 435
  travel within 430
beer 230
Belle Île 36
Belle-Île-en-Mer 305, 307
Bergerac 617, 647
Betschdorf 338
Béziers 670-1
Biarritz 588-91, 601, **590**
bicycle travel, *see* cycling, mountain biking
Bidarray 599
Bidart 591
birdwatching
  Causses et Cévennes 677
  Île de Ré 581-2

Lac Kir 427
Mont St-Michel 255-6
Parc National des Pyrénées 729-30
Parc Ornithologique du Pont de Gau 768
Blois 28
boat travel
  Canal St-Martin 105
  Crozon Peninsula 292
  Marseille 752-3
  Seine river 69
  Strasbourg 337
Bois de Boulogne 74-5
Bois de Vincennes 138-9
Bois-Guilbert 230
Bonaparte, Napoléon 172, 884, 886
Bonifacio 892-4, **893**
  accommodation 899
  beyond Bonifacio 895-7
  food 894
  travel within 892
books 41
Bordeaux 31, 551, 556-65, **558-9**
  accommodation 601
  beyond Bordeaux 566-72
  drinking 562, 563
  food 557, 560, 561
  itineraries 554
  shopping 563
  travel within 556
Bordeaux to Biarritz 551-601
  itineraries 554-5
  navigation 552-3, **552-3**
  travel seasons 554-5
  travel within 552-3
border crossings 725, 902
Bormes-les-Mimosas 34, 843
Boulogne-sur-Mer 212-13, **213**
  accommodation 217
  beyond Boulogne-sur-Mer 214-16
  food 213
  travel within 212
bouquinistes 158
Bourdeilles 614-15
Bouzigues 672
Brantôme 614-15
Brazier, Eugénie 458
bridges
  Pont Alexandre III 78
  Pont Neuf 147
Brittany 267-307
  itineraries 270-1
  navigation 268-9, **268-9**
  travel seasons 270-1
  travel within 268-9
budget 17, *see also* costs
Bullecourt 210

Burgundy 414-47
  itineraries 418-19
  navigation 416-17, **416-17**
  travel seasons 418-19
  travel within 416-17
bus travel 903
business hours 915
Bussy-Le-Grand 429

cabarets 100, 102
Cabourg 37
Cadet Roussel 444
Caen 246-52, **248-9**
  accommodation 265
  drinking 252
  travel within 246
cafes 18
Cahors 628-32, **629**
  accommodation 647
  beyond Cahors 633-8
  drinking 632
  food 630
  road trip 631, **631**
  shopping 632
Calais 32, 214-15
Calanques de Piana 888-9
calvados 244
Calvi 873-5, **874**
  accommodation 898
  beyond Calvi 876-8
  food 875
  travel within 873
Cambrai 210
Camino de Santiago 477-8
Camino de Santiago de Compostela 596-7
Canal du Midi 670-1, 685, 709
Canal St-Martin 104-5
Cancale 286
Cannes 823-8, **824**
  accommodation 858
  beyond Cannes 829-34
  drinking 825
  food 825, 828
  shopping 828
  travel within 823
canoeing
  Dordogne 608-9, **609**
  Vézère Valley 623-4
Cantal 486-7, **486**
canyoning 725-6, 730, 793, 865
Cap Corse 870-1, 898, **871**
Cap Ferret 571-2
Cap Fréhel 284
car travel 903
Carcassonne 28, 682-5, **683**
  accommodation 695
  drinking 684
  food 684, 685
  travel within 682

Carnac 36, 303-4, 920-1
Carpentras 774-6, 796
Casino de Monte-Carlo 851
Cassel 200-1, 217
Cassis 756-7
Castillon 817
castles, *see* châteaux
Castres 713
Catalan cuisine 692
Cathars 693, 726, **693**
cathedrals, *see* churches, cathedrals & basilicas
Cauria 897
Causses et Cévennes 675-8, **676**
 beyond Causses et Cévennes 679-81
 food 676, 677
 travel within 675
cave paintings
 Abri de Cap Blanc 627
 Grotte Chauvet 2 467
 Grotte de Bédeilhac 724
 Grotte de la Vache 724
 Grotte de Niaux 723-4
 Grotte du Mas d'Azil 724
 Grotte Lombrives 724
 Lascaux II 625-7
 Lascaux IV 625-7
caves
 Grotte Aven d'Orgnac 469, 472
 Grotte Chauvet 2 467
 Grotte de Bédeilhac 724
 Grotte de Font-de-Gaume 627
 Grotte de la Vache 724
 Grotte de Niaux 723-4
 Grotte des Combarelles 627
 Grotte du Mas d'Azil 724
 Grotte Lombrives 724
 Grotte St-Marcel 468
 Grottes de Sare 600
 Grottes Troglodytes de Cotignac 846
 Lascaux II 625-7
 Lascaux IV 625-7
 Vézère caves 625-7, **626**
caving 725-6
Cazevieille 669
celtic dance circles 290
cemeteries
 Ayette Indian & Chinese Cemetery 209

Cimetière Allemand 210
Cimetière de Passy 62-3
Cimetière du Père Lachaise 124-5
Commonwealth cemeteries 210
Flatiron Copse Cemetery 208
ceramics 251-2, 289-90, 338, 437
Céret 692
Cézanne, Paul 758
Chablis 446, 447
Chagall, Marc 811
Chaîne des Puys 482-8, **483**, **487**
 beyond Chaîne des Puys 489-91
 drinking 488
 food 484, 485
 travel within 482
Chambéry 524-7, **525**
 accommodation 549
 beyond Chambéry 528-33
 drinking 527
 food 526
 travel within 524
Chambres d'Hôte 905
Chamonix 500-9, **502**
 accommodation 549
 drinking 503, 508
 food 501, 503, 508
 shopping 509
 travel within 500
Champagne 308-29
 itineraries 311
 navigation 310, **310**
 travel seasons 311
 travel within 310
Champagne (wine) 314-15
 Atelier 1834: Champagne Boizel 322
 Avenue de Champagne 319, 322
 Champagne A Bergère 322
 Champagne De Castellane 322
 Champagne Leclerc Briant 322
 Champagne Mercier 322
 Champagne Perrier-Jouët 322
 Champagne Pommery 317
 Champagne Taittinger 317
 Maison Ruinart 317
 Moët & Chandon 322
 Veuve Clicquot 317
Chanel, Coco 481
Chartreuse 528-9
Château de Fontainebleau 186-7

Château de Versailles 184-5, 922
Châteauneuf-du-Pape 774
châteaux 14-15
 accommodation 905
 Cabanon Le Corbusier 820
 Château & Jardins de Losse 624
 Château de Beynac 620
 Château de Biron 618
 Château de Bonaguil 638
 Château de Bourdeilles 614-15
 Château de Bridoire 615
 Château de Bussy-Rabutin 429
 Château de Caen 252
 Château de Castelnaud 621
 Château de Châlus-Chabrol 646
 Château de Chambord 921
 Château de Cognac 578-9
 Château de Foix 722-3
 Château de Fontainebleau 186-7
 Château de Fougères 278
 Château de Hautefort 615
 Château de Jumilhac 615
 Château de Montségur 726
 Château de Roquebrune 819
 Château de Val 485, 488
 Château de Vascœuil 230-1
 Château de Versailles 184-5, 922
 Château de Vincennes 139
 Château de Vitré 278
 Chateau d'If 753-4
 Château du Champ de Bataille 229-31
 Château et Jardins des Milandes 621
 Château et Remparts 683
 Châteaux de Bruniquel 717
 Clos de Vougeot 427-8
 Le Palais Idéal du Facteur Cheval 466
 Palais des Papes 772
 Palais des Rois de Majorque 687
 Palais du Parlement de Bretagne 274, 922
 Palais Longchamp 754
 Palais Princier de Monaco 854, 856
cheese
 AOP 244, 678
 Bleu d'Auvergne 484

Camembert 244
Cantal 484
 dishes 523
Fourme d'Ambert 484
goat 231, 633, 635, 729
Livarot 244
 making 231
Munster 344
Neufchâtel 244
PDO 484
Pont-l'Évêque 244
road trip 244, 244
Salers 484
St-Nectaire 484
Roquefort 678
Cherbourg 260-4, **261**
 accommodation 265
 drinking 264
 travel within 260
chestnuts 844
children, travel with 51, 906
chocolate 170, 585-6, 738
churches, cathedrals & basilicas
 Abbaye de Fontfroide 691
 Abbaye de Gellone 669-70
 Abbaye du Mont St-Michel 253
 Abbaye Notre-Dame de Sénanque 784
 Abbaye St-Germain 442-3
 Abbaye St-Pierre 718
 Basilica Notre-Dame de Fourvière 459
 Basilique du Sacré-Cœur 97
 Basilique Notre-Dame de Brebières 205
 Basilique St-Rémi 317
 Basilique St-Sernin 706
 Basilique-Cathédrale de St-Jean-Baptiste 687
 Cathédrale Notre-Dame (Amiens) 202
 Cathédrale Notre-Dame (Reims) 312, 316
 Cathédrale Notre Dame (Rouen) 225
 Cathédrale Notre-Dame (Strasbourg) 334, 336
 Cathédrale Notre Dame de Paris 142-5
 Cathédrale Notre-Dame-de-l'Assomption 490-1
 Cathédrale St-Corentin 287
 Cathédrale Ste-Cécile 715
 Cathédrale St-Étienne (Auxerre) 443
 Cathédrale St-Étienne (Cahors) 628, 630

Cathédrale St-Étienne (Metz) 358, 360
Cathédrale St-Étienne (Toulouse) 708
Cathédrale St-François de Sales 526-7
Cathédrale St-Front 610
Cathédrale St-Pierre et St-Paul 323
Chapelle St-Michel d'Aiguilhe 476-7
Couvent des Jacobins 706, 708
Église Abbatiale de St-Robert 481
Église de Plateau d'Assy 513
Église Notre Dame de l'Assomption 510
Église Saint-Pierre de Saint-Gilles 317
Église St-Étienne du Mont 149, 153
Église St-Germain-des-Prés 169
Église St-Sulpice 169-70
Notre-Dame-de-la-Mer 767-8
Sainte-Chapelle 140, 146
Saint-Jean-Baptiste de Belleville 126
Sanctuaire Notre Dame dee Lourdes 736
Sanctuaire Notre-Dame-des-Fontaines 822
Savigny-sur-Ardres 317
cider 231, 244
Cimetière du Père Lachaise 124-5
Cité de l'Architecture et du Patrimoine 923
Clermont-Ferrand 489-91, 493
climate change 910
climbing 50
clothes 40
Cognac 578-9, 601
Collias 661
Collioure 694
Collonges-la-Rouge 646
Colmar 341-3, **342**
 accommodation 353
 beyond Colmar 344-52
 food 343
 travel within 341
Combloux 513
Compiègne 211
concentration camp 346
Conciergerie 146-7
Condom 720
Cordes-sur-Ciel 715, 718, 739
Corgnac-sur-l'Isle 615-16
Corniche des Maures 843-4

Corsica 861-99
 itineraries 863
 navigation 862
 travel seasons 863
 travel within 862
Corte 879-81, **880**
 accommodation 898
 beyond Corte 882-3
 food 881
costs 904, 905, 909
Côte d'Albâtre 232-8, **233**
 accommodation 265
 food 235, 237
 travel within 232
Côte d'Azur 798-859
 itineraries 802-3
 navigation 800-1, **800-1**
 road trips 818-19, 833, **819, 833**
 travel seasons 802-3
 travel within 800-1
Côte de Nuits 438-9
Côte d'Opale 32, 215
Côte d'Or 932-3
Côte Fleurie 238-43, **240-1**
 accommodation 265
 food 242, 245
 road trip 244, **244**
 shopping 242
 travel within 238
Cotentin 260-4, **261**
 accommodation 265
 drinking 264
 travel within 260
Cotignac 846, 859
credit cards 904
Crozant 644, 646
Crozon Peninsula 291-2, 307
culture 924-5, 926-8
currency 904
cycling 44-5, 50-1, 903
 Alpe d'Huez 539-40
 Beaujolais 463
 Biarritz to Guethary 592-3, **593**
 Cap Ferret 571-2
 Chaîne des Puys 482, 484
 Deûle River 198-9, **199**
 Dolce Via 475
 Île de Ré 581
 La Rochelle 577
 La Vélodyssée 570
 Lake Annecy 518-19, **519**
 Luberon 786-7, **787**
 Massif de la Chartreuse 530-1
 Meuse Valley, the 362
 Mont Ventoux 779-80
 Nice 816
 Parc National des Pyrénées 731
 Parc Naturel Régional des Pyrénées Ariégeoises 724-5

planning 44-5
Rennes 275
Route of the Vines 440-1, **441**
Toulouse 709-10
Tour de France 539-40, 731
Vallée de la Rance 284-5
Vélorail du Périgord Vert 615-16
Vézère Valley 622
ViaRhôna 465-6

dangers 907
D-Day Landing Beaches 246-52, **248-9**
 accommodation 265
 food 247
 travel within 246
de Pas, Jean-Marc 230
Deauville 245
Dijon 33, 420-5, **421**
 accommodation 447
 beyond Dijon 426-9
 drinking 422, 425
 food 423, 424, 425
 travel within 420
Dinan 285, 307
disabilities, travellers with 913
distilleries
 Monaco 857
 Vézère Valley 624
diving 891
Domaine de la Palissade 767
Dôme des Invalides 172
Dordogne 602-47
 itineraries 606-7
 navigation 604-5, **604-5**
 travel seasons 606-7
 travel within 604-5
Dordogne Valley 620-1, 647, **620**
drinking 908-9
driving 903, see also road trips
Drôme Provençale 475
drugs 915
druids 296
Dune du Pilat 570-1
Dunkirk 214

Eiffel Tower 66-9
electricity 915
enslaved people 560-1
Épernay 318-22, **319**
 accommodation 329
 drinking 322

food 322
travel within 318
Espelette 598-9
Essoyes 327-8, 329
Étretat 232
events, see festivals & events
Eygalières 761
Èze 817, 819, 858

F

family travel 51, 906
fat biking 51
festivals & events 39
 A Lot of Flavour 630
 Avignon In 771
 Avignon Off 771
 Beaujolais Wine Marathon 465
 Braderie de Lille 47, 197
 Cabourg Mon Amour Festival 239
 Cahors Blues Festival 630
 Calvi on the Rocks 875
 Carnaval de Dunkerque 215
 Carnaval de Nice 812
 Chinese New Year 180
 Chorégies d'Orange 777
 Concert dans la Grotte de Bédeilhac 723
 Course Camarguaise 763, 765
 Dîner sur la Digue 239
 Festival d'Art Pyrotechnique 828
 Festival d'Avignon 39, 771
 Festival de Cannes 823
 Festival de Cornouaille 39, 288-9
 Festival Résistances 723
 Festival Vins & Passions 789
 Fête de la Coquille et de la Pêche 47, 233
 Fête de la Musique 39, 132, 789
 Fête de la Renaissance 472
 Fête de la Transhumance 39
 Fête de la Truffe 47, 616
 Fête des Fraises 47
 Fête des Marins 239
 Fête du Citron 39, 820
 Fête du Vin Nouveau et de la Brocante 557
 Fêtes de Bayonne 39, 585
 Fêtes Napoléoniennes 886
 Flash Festival 706
 Formula One Grand Prix 850, 854

festivals & events
continued
French Open 75
Géants 39
Jazz à Foix 723
Jazz à Vienne 39, 463, 465
Jazz in Calvi 875
Joutes Nautiques 673
La Fête des Lumières 461
La Fête du Roi de l'Oiseau 478
La Fête du Vin Bourru 438
Le Festival de St-Vincent Tournante 437
Le Nouveau Printemps 706
Les Castagnades 474
Les Plages Électroniques 828
Les Rencontres d'Arles 763
Lou Queernaval 812
Lyon Street Food Festival 47, 461
Marché de Noël 789
Marche des Fiertés 121, 912
Nice Jazz Festival 812
Noël à Nice 812
Nuits de Fourvière 461
Nuits Sonores 461
Peinture Fraîche 461
Pink Parade (Pride) 812
Procession aux Flambeaux 734
Rencontres de Chants Polyphoniques 875
Rio Loco Festival 706
Sacred Music Festival 481
Toulouse les Orgues 708-9
Tour de France 539-40, 731
Trans Musicales 275
Tribute of the Three Cows 737
Vin et Hip Hop 47
We Love Green 139
Figeac 633
films 41
Flamel, Nicolas 119
Flanders 191-217
  itineraries 193
  navigation 192, **192**

Map Pages **000**

travel seasons 193
travel within 192
Florac 695
Fontaine de Vaucluse 778-9
Fontaine-d'Ouche 426-7
food 46-9, 908-9, *see also* cheese, chestnuts, chocolate, lampreys, lemons, oysters, truffles
football 750
Forêt de Bonifatu 876-7
Forêt de Paimpont 276-7
forts
  Citadelle de Besançon 541, 543
  Fort de Douaumont 362
  Fort de Vaux 362
  Fort Libéria 691
  Fort National 280-1
  Fort Royal 826
  Fort St-André 773
  Forteresse de Penne 717
  Forteresse Médiévale de Crozant 644
  La Roque-Gageac 621
  Neuf-Brisach 345
Fougères 278
Fréjus 842-3, 859
French Alps 494-549
  itineraries 498-9
  navigation 496-7, **496-7**
  travel seasons 498-9
  travel within 496-7
French Revolution 129, 131
Fresselines 644-6, **645**

Gainsbourg, Serge 168-9
Gan 737
Garcia, Jacques 229-31
gardens, *see* parks & gardens
Gardians 765
gay travellers 912
  Nice 812
  Paris 120
Gérardmer 369-70
gin 512-13
Girolata 891
gîtes d'étape 905
gîtes 905
Giverny 224-8, **228**
  accommodation 265
  beyond Giverny 229-31
  food 228
  travel within 224
Golfe de Porto 890-1
Gorbio 817
Gorges de l'Ardèche 467-72, **468**
  accommodation 492
  beyond Gorges de l'Ardèche 473-5

food 469
travel within 467
Gorges du Loup 832
Gorges du Tarn 675-7, 695
Gorges du Verdon 35, 790-5, **791**
  food 794, 795
  travel within 790
Goya, Francisco 713
Grand Balcon Nord 506-7, **507**
Granville 258
Grasse 831-2, 858
Great Schism 773
Grenoble 534-7, **535**
  accommodation 549
  beyond Grenoble 538-40
  drinking 537
  food 536
  travel within 534
Gruissan 691
guinguettes 400

Haute-Loire 493
Hauterives 466
Hautes-Côtes de Beaune 436-7
Hautes-Vosges 371
Haut-Var 847
health 907
Hermann's tortoise 845
highlights 14-27
hiking 50
  Aiguille du Midi 504-5
  Camino de Santiago 477-8
  Camino de Santiago de Compostela 596-7
  Cantal 488
  Causses et Cévennes 677
  Chaîne des Puys 484-5
  Corsica 864-5
  Côte d'Emeraude 284
  Crozon Peninsula 291-2
  Étretat 232-3
  Gérardmer 370
  Gorges du Verdon 792, 793
  GR10 727, 729
  GR34 291-2
  Grand Balcon Nord 506-7, **507**
  Grenoble 534, 536
  Île de Port-Cros 849
  Jura Mountains 544-5
  Lac Blanc 508-9
  Le Tholonet 759-60
  Les Baux-de-Provence 761
  Lourdes 735, 737
  Massif de la Chartreuse 529-30

Massif de l'Estérel 843
Moissac 718
Navacelles 679-80
Nietzsche Trail 817
Parc Naturel Régional des Pyrénées Ariégeoises 724-5
Pic St-Loup 669
Pointe de la Varde 283
Route des Crêtes 793
Stevenson Trail 480, 677-8
Voie de Vézelay 618
Voie du Puy 618
history 920-3
holidays 915
Honfleur 243, 245
horse riding 767
Hôtel de Ville 114-15
Hugo, Victor 543-4
Hunspach 338, 340
Hyères 845-6, 859

ice diving 522-3
Île de Porquerolles 848-9, 859
Île de Ré 580-2, 601
Île-aux-Moines 301-2
Île Ste-Marguerite 826-7
Île St-Honorat 827
Îles de Lérins 826-7
Îles d'Hyères 848-9
Îles Sanguinaires 922
Ille-sur-Têt 692
insurance 907
internet access 902
Issigeac 618
itineraries 28-37, **29**, **31**, **33**, **37**, *see also individual locations*
Itxassou 599

Jardin des Plantes (Paris) 154-5
Jardin du Luxembourg 162
Jaurès, Jean 713
Jeanne d'Arc 921
Jewish Paris 116
Joan of Arc 921
Jura 494-549
  itineraries 498-9
  navigation 496-7, **496-7**
  travel seasons 498-9
  travel within 496-7
Jura Mountains 541-5, **542**
  accommodation 549
  drinking 544
  food 543, 545
  travel within 541

kayaking 51
  Arcachon 569-70
  Collias 661
  Côte d'Albâtre 234
  Dordogne 608-9, **609**
  Gorges de l'Ardèche 470-1, **471**
  La Rochelle 577
  Sète 673-4
King Arthur 276, 277
Kingdom of Majorca 686-7

La Balagne 873-5, **874**
  accommodation 898
  road trip 878, **878**
  travel within 873
La Bastide-Clairence 599
La Butte aux Cailles 174, 178
La Chaise-Dieu 480-1
La Cité Religieuse de Rocamadour 634
La Côte Bleue 757
La Hague 264
La Rochelle 30, 573-7, **574**
  accommodation 601
  beyond La Rochelle 578-82
  drinking 577
  food 575, 576
  nightlife 575
  shopping 577
  travel within 573-7
La Vallée Blanche 500-2
Labeaume 472
Lac Blanc 508-9
Lac de Montriond 522-3
Lac de Roselend 531-2
Lac des Vaches 532
Lac Kir 426
Lac Pavin 485
lacemaking 251
Lacrouzette 714, 739
Lake Annecy 514-20, **516-17**
  beyond Lake Annecy 521-3
  food 515, 520
  shopping 515
  travel within 514
lampreys 561
Langres 328, 329
language 41, 908, 916-17
  Alsatian 340
Languedoc-Roussillon 649-95
  itineraries 652-3
  navigation 650-1, **650-1**
  travel seasons 652-3
  travel within 650-1
Larressore 599

Lascaux II 625-7
Lascaux IV 625-7
Lastours 680
L'Aubrac 681, **681**
lavender
  Drôme Provençale 475
  Plateau de Valensole 795
  Villesèque 637
Le Bout du Monde 436
Le Corbusier 820
Le Crotoy 216
Le Guilvinec 293-4
Le Havre 232-8, **233, 234**
  accommodation 265
  travel within 232
  walking tour 236, **236**
Le Monastier-sur-Gazeille 480
Le Puy-en-Velay 476-8, **477**
  accommodation 492
  beyond Le Puy-en-Velay 479-81
  food 478
  shopping 478
  travel within 476
Le Temple-sur-Lot 638
Le Tholonet 759-60
lemons 820-1
Les Alpilles 760-1
Les Arènes 654-6
Les Baux-de-Provence 761
Les Bourgeois de Calais 214-15
Les Calanques 755-7
Les Catacombes 176
Les Goudes 753
Les Portes du Soleil 521-3
LGBTIQ+ travellers 912
  Nice 812
  Paris 120
libraries
  Bibliothèque Humaniste 340
  Bibliothèque Mazarine 160-1
  Les Franciscaines 238-9
L'Île-Rousse 876, 898
Lille 194-9, **195**
  accommodation 217
  beyond Lille 200-1
  cycling tour 198-9, **199**
  drinking 196, 197
  food 197
  shopping 196
  travel within 194
Limoges 639-42, **640**
  accommodation 647
  beyond Limoges 643-6
  food 641
  travel within 639
  walking tour 642, **642**
Limousin 602-47
  itineraries 606-7

navigation 604-5, **604-5**
travel seasons 606-7
travel within 604-5
Lion du Belfort 543
L'Isle-sur-la-Sorgue 778, 797
Locronan 296
Longueval 207
Lorraine 354-71
  itineraries 357
  navigation 356, **356**
  road trip 363, **363**
  travel seasons 357
  travel within 356
Lot 602-47
  itineraries 606-7
  navigation 604-5, **604-5**
  travel seasons 606-7
  travel within 604-5
Lourdes 734-7
Luberon 781-9, **782-3**
  accommodation 797
  food 784, 785, 788, 789
  travel within 781
Lyon 449, 454-62, **456-7**
  accommodation 492
  beyond Lyon 463-6
  drinking 458, 461, 462
  food 455, 459
  itineraries 452
  travel within 454
  walking tour 458
Lyons-La-Forêt 231

maquis 883
Marché aux Puces de St-Ouen 108-9
markets 914
  Antibes 829-30
  Arras 201
  Bayonne 586-7
  Beaune 434
  Bidart 591
  Bordeaux 561
  Cahors 630
  Dijon 424
  Grenoble 536
  Hyères 846
  Lille 197
  Limoges 641
  Luberon 784
  Lyon 462
  Montpellier 667
  Nice 811-12
  Nîmes 659
  Paris 62, 71, 73, 108-9, 117, 134, 148, 153, 160
  Périgueux 612
  Rennes 272
  Sarlat-la-Canéda 619
  St-Tropez 838
  Toulouse 703, 706

Vannes 297
Var villages 847
Marseille 29, 746-54, **748-9**
  accommodation 796
  beyond Marseille 755-61
  drinking 750, 752, 754
  food 747, 750, 753, 754
  travel within 746
  walking tour 751, **751**
Massif de la Chartreuse 528-31
Massif des Maures 844-5
Matisse, Henri 811
Mazamet 712
measures 915
Médoc 568, **568**
megaliths 303-4
Megève 513
Mende 680
Menton 34, 820-1, 858
Metz 358-61, **359**
  accommodation 371
  beyond Metz 362-4
  food 360, 361
  travel within 358
Meuse Valley, the 362, 364, 371
Millau 695
millinery 242
Moissac 718
Molière 671
Monaco 850-7, **852-3**
  accommodation 858-9
  drinking 856, 857
  food 854, 857
  travel within 850
  walking tour 855, **855**
monasteries
  La Chartreuse du Val de Bénédiction 773
  Monastère de la Verne 844-5
  Monastère Fortifié 827
Monet, Claude 63, 227-8, 638, 645
money 904
monoliths
  Cauria Plateau 897
  Les Orgues d'Ille-sur-Têt 692
  Mourèze 670
Monpazier 617-18
Mont Jalla 536
Mont St-Michel 37, 253-6, **254**
  accommodation 265
  beyond Mont St-Michel 257-9
  food 255, 256
  shopping 255
  travel within 253
Montauban 718, 739
Montcuq 637-8

939

Montpellier 663-8, **664**
  accommodation 695
  beyond Montpellier 669-74
  drinking 665
  food 667, 668
  nightlife 665
  travel within 663
Monts de l'Ardèche 473-5, 492
Mont Ventoux 779-80, 797
Morzine 523
mosques 156, 158
Mougins 831
Moulin Rouge 100, 102
mountain biking 50-1, 370, 843
mountain climbing 784-5
Mourèze 670
Moustiers-Ste-Marie 790, 794-5, 797
Mulhouse 344-5
Munster 344
Musée d'Orsay 166-7
Musée du Louvre 86-7
museums
  Aeroscopia 710
  Ailes Anciennes Toulouse 710
  Airborne Museum 250
  Bastide du Jas de Bouffan 758
  Bastideum 617-18
  Cambrai Tank 1917 210
  Centre des Lumières 544
  Centre National et Musée Jean Jaurès 713
  Château Fort Musée Pyrénéen 735
  Cité de la Mer 260
  Cité des Sciences et de l'Industrie 107
  Dead Man's Corner Museum 250
  Écomusée Sous-Marin de Cannes 827
  Fisheries Museum 235, 237
  Fragonard's Usine Historique & Musée du Parfum 831
  Galerie de Géologie et de Minéralogie 155
  Gallery of Paleontology & Comparative Anatomy 155
  Grande Galerie de l'Évolution 155
  Historial de la Grande Guerre 206-7
  Historial Jeanne d'Arc 225
  Hôtel de la Marine 79
  Hôtel des Invalides 170
  Hôtel-Dieu des Hospices Civils de Beaune 430-2
  Institut du Monde Arabe 158-9
  Jean & Denise Letaille Bullecourt 1917 Museum 210
  La Demeure du Chaos 461
  La Piscine - Musée d'Art et d'Industrie 197
  Latour-Marliac 638
  Le Cassissium 429
  Le Grand Bunker – Musée du Mur de l'Atlantique 923
  Le Redoutable 260
  Les Forges de Pyrène 723
  Les Franciscaines 238-9
  M Musée du Vin 63
  Maison Bonaparte 886
  Maison de Balzac 70
  Maison de l'Outil et de la Pensée Ouvrière 325
  Maison de Victor Hugo (Besançon) 543-4
  Maison de Victor Hugo (Paris) 115
  Maison et Jardins de Claude Monet 227-8
  Maison Gainsbourg 169
  Maison-Musée Latour-Marliac 638
  Mémorial de Caen 252
  Memorial Museum of Omaha Beach 250
  MuCEM 922
  Musée Archéologique 537
  Musée Archéologique Théo Desplans 777
  Musée Basque et de l'Histoire de Bayonne 583
  Musée Carnavalet 115
  Musée Champollion 633
  Musée Cinéma et Miniature 461
  Musée Cognacq-Jay 115
  Musée d'Anthropologie Préhistorique de Monaco 856
  Musée d'Apt 781
  Musée d'Aquitaine 560
  Musée d'Art et d'Archéologie du Périgord 613
  Musée d'Art et d'Industrie 479
  Musée Dauphinois 537
  Musée de Bretagne 274
  Musée de Cluny - Musée national du Moyen Âge 159
  Musée de la Bataille de Fromelles 211
  Musée de la BNF (Bibliothèque Nationale de France) 90
  Musée de la Chasse et de la Nature 115
  Musée de la Corse 880
  Musée de la Cour d'Or 360
  Musée de la Mine 479
  Musée de la Libération 262
  Musée de la Résistance 641
  Musée de la Romanité 656
  Musée de la Tapisserie de Bayeux 921
  Musée de l'Ancien Évêché 537
  Musée de L'Armée 170, 172
  Musée de l'Étang de Thau 672
  Musée de l'Histoire de l'Immigration 135
  Musée de l'Histoire Maritime 560
  Musée de Normandie 252
  Musée Départemental Breton 287-8
  Musée des Amériques-Auch 719
  Musée des Arts et Métiers 115, 117
  Musée des Cristaux 503
  Musée des Explorations du Monde 825
  Musée des Troupes de Montagne 536
  Musée des Verts 479-80
  Musée d'Histoire 588
  Musée du Debarquement 246
  Musée du Gévaudan 680
  Musée du Louvre-Lens 201
  Musée du Quai Branly - Jacques Chirac 73
  Musée du Vieux Nîmes 658
  Musée du Vin de Champagne et D'Archéologie Régionale 319, 322
  Musée du Vin et du Négoce 557
  Musée et Sites Archéologiques de St Romain-en-Gal 465
  Musée Gallo-Romain de Fourvière 455
  Musée Gallo-Romain Vesunna 613
  Musée Lumière 460
  Musée Maritime 576
  Musée Massena 807, 922
  Musée Narbo Via 689-90
  Musée National de l'Automobile 344-5
  Musée National de Préhistoire 627
  Musée National Eugène Delacroix 173
  Musée Océanographique de Monaco 856
  Musée Savoisien 527
  Musée Unterlinden 343
  Museum Dunkerque 1940 214
  Overlord Museum 250
  Palais des Archevêques 690-1
  Palais Rohan 336
  Parc de la Préhistoire 723
  Parc du Haut-Fourneau U4 364
  Parc Explor Wendel 364
  Pôle d'Interprétation de la Préhistoire 627
  Posidonia - Espace Mer et Littoral 830
  Radar Museum 1944 250
  Saline Royal 544
  Sir John Monash Centre 206
  Somme 1916 Museum 205
  Thiepval Museum 207
  Utah Beach Landing Museum 250
  Villa du Temps Retrouv 243
  Vulcania 485

Nancy 365-8, **366**
  accommodation 371
  beyond Nancy 369-70
  food 367
  shopping 367
  travel within 365
  walking tour 368, **368**
Nantes 30
Napoléon I (Bonaparte) 172, 884, 886
Napoléon III 87
Narbonne 689-91
national parks
  Parc National de la Vanoise 532
  Parc National de Port-Cros 848-9

Parc National des Calanques 755-7
Parc National des Pyrénées 727-33, **728**
Parc National du Mercantour 822
natural & regional parks
  Illwald 340
  La Cembraie 531
  Parc Naturel Régional des Pyrénées Ariégeoises 721-6, **722**
  Parc Naturel Régional des Vosges du Nord 339, 339
  Parc Naturel Régional du Luberon 788
  Parc Naturel Régional du Vercors 540
  Parque Naturel Regional du Haut Languedoc 714
  Réserve Naturelle de Scandola 890-1
Natzweiler-Struthof 346
Navacelles 679-80
Neuf-Brisach 345
Nice 34, 806-14, **808-9**
  accommodation 858
  beyond Nice 815-22
  drinking 810, 812, 814
  food 807, 811, 812
  LGBTIQ+ 812
  travel within 806
  walking tour 813, **813**
  nightlife 908-9
Nîmes 654-9, 921, **655**
  accommodation 695
  beyond Nîmes 660-2
  food 656, 658
  travel within 654
  walking tour 657, **657**
Nîmes Crocodile 658
Normandy 218-65
  itineraries 222-3
  navigation 220-1, **220-1**
  travel seasons 222-3
  travel within 220-1
Nostradamus 760
Notre Dame 142-5
Noyers-Sur-Serein 445-6, 447

olive oil 759
Olympic Winter Games 503
opening hours 915
Oradour-sur-Glane 643-4
Orange 776-7, 796-7
outdoor activities 24-5, 50-3, **52-3**, see also individual activities
oysters 286, 571

paddleboarding 520
Palais des Papes 772
Palais du Parlement de Bretagne 274, 922
Panthéon 152, 923
Paoli, Pascuale 881
paragliding 50
  Lake Annecy 515, 520
  Mont St-Michel 255-6
Parc de la Combe à la Serpent 427
Parc National des Pyrénées 727-33, **728**
  accommodation 739
  beyond Parc National des Pyrénées 734-8
  food 730, 732, 733
  travel within 727
Parc Naturel Régional des Pyrénées Ariégeoises 721-6, **722**
  accommodation 739
  food 723, 725
  travel within 721
Paris 28, 56-189
  accommodation 188-9
  Bastille 129-39, **130**
  Belleville 122-8, **123**, **127**
  Champs-Élysées 76-81, **77**
  drinking 79, 107, 114, 117, 121, 132, 134, 137, 156, 164, 168, 170, 182
  eastern Paris 129-39, **136**
  Eiffel Tower 62-75, **64-5**
  entertainment 131-2
  food 63, 70, 78, 80, 81, 88, 89, 90-1, 93, 94, 95, 100, 102, 107, 115, 120, 128, 131, 134, 135, 146, 147, 153, 158, 163, 169, 170, 178, 180, 183
  Grands Boulevards 76-81, **77**
  Islands, the 140-8, **141**
  itineraries 60-1
  Latin Quarter 149-59, **150-1**, **157**
  Le Marais 110-21, **111**, **112-13**, **116**, **119**
  Les Halles 82-95, **83**, **92**
  Les Invalides 160-73, **165**
  LGBTIQ+ 120
  Louvre 82-95, **83**
  Ménilmontant 122-8, **123**
  Montmartre 96-109, **98-9**, **101**
  Montparnasse 174-83, **175**
  navigation 58-9, **58-9**
  nightlife 95, 100, 102, 104, 120, 122, 134, 170, 182
  northern Paris 96-109, **98-9**, **103**, **106**
  shopping 81, 84-5, 89, 90, 90-1, 115, 117, 120, 153, 156, 163-4
  southern Paris 174-83, **175**, **181**
  St-Germain 160-73, **161**
  travel within 58-9, 62, 76, 82, 96, 110, 122, 140, 149, 160, 174
  walking tours 72, 84-5, 101, 116, 118-19, 126-7, 133, 157, 171, 177, 179, **72**, **85**, **101**, **116**, **119**, **127**, **133**, **157**, **171**, **177**, **179**
  Western Paris 62-75, **64-5**
parks & gardens
  Bois de Boulogne 74-5
  Bois de Vincennes 138-9
  Domaine du Rayol 843-4
  Jardin Botanique du Val Rahmeh 821
  Jardin Catherine-Labouré 168
  Jardin des Plantes (Montpellier) 667
  Jardin des Plantes (Paris) 154-5
  Jardin des Tuileries 88-9
  Jardin du Luxembourg 162
  Jardin du Palais 715
  Jardin du Palais Royal 82-3, 88
  Jardin Exotique 854
  Jardin Exotique d'Èze 817
  Jardin Serre de la Madone 821
  Jardins de Marqueyssac 620
  Jardins Panoramiques de Limeuil 624
  Les Jardins des Sculptures 230
  Les Jardins Suspendus 237
  Parc de Bercy 137
  Parc de la Citadelle 198
  Parc de la Combe à la Serpent 427
  Parc de la Pépinière 367
  Parc de la Villette 107
  Parc des Buttes-Chaumont 128
  Parc du Champ de Mars 69
  Parc Princesse Antoinette 856
  Parlement de Bretagne 274, 922
  Passy 62
  Pastis 752
  Patrimonio 872, 898
  Pau 737-8
Paulilles 694
Pays Bigouden 294, 295, **295**
Pays d'Auge 37
people 924-5, 926-8
perfumeries
  Grasse 831-2
  Paris 120
Périgueux 610-13, **611**
  accommodation 647
  beyond Périgueux 614-21
  drinking 613
  food 612
  travel within 610
Péronne 206-7
Perpignan 686-8, **687**
  accommodation 695
  beyond Perpignan 689-94
  food 688
  travel within 686
Petite-Rosselle 364
Pézenas 671-2
Picasso, Pablo 115, 830
Pigalle 100
Pinet 672
place de la Bastille 129, 131
place de la Concorde 79
place de la République 114
place des Vosges 110
Plage de Palombaggia 895
planning
  clothes 40
  etiquette 40
  France basics 40-1
  shopping at food markets 914
Plateau de Valensole 795
podcast 41
Pointe de la Revellata 875
Pointe de la Torche 294
Pointe du Raz 292-3
politics 929-31
polyphonic singing 875
Pont Alexandre III 78
Pont d'Arc 470
Pont du Gard 29, 660
Pont-Aven 296
population 915
porcelain 639, 641
Porto 891
Porto-Vecchio 895
Presqu'île de Giens 859
Presqu'île de St-Tropez 859
protests 929-31
Proust, Marcel 243
Provence 741-97
  itineraries 744-5
  navigation 742-3
  travel seasons 744-5
  travel within 742-3
public holidays 915
puppet theatre 204
Puy-de-Dôme 484, 493

941

Pyla-sur-Mer 570-1
Pyrenees, the 696-739
  itineraries 700-1
  navigation 698-9, **698-9**
  travel seasons 700-1
  travel within 698-9

Quiberon Peninsula 306, 307
Quimper 287-90, **288**
  accommodation 307
  beyond Quimper 291-6
  drinking 290
  food 289
  travel within 287

radio 41
rafting 793
Randan 491
refuges 905
regional parks, see natural & regional parks
Reillanne 35, 785
Reims 32, 312-17, **313**
  accommodation 329
  drinking 317
  food 313, 316
  travel within 312
Rennes 272-5, **273**
  accommodation 307
  beyond Rennes 276-8
  drinking 275
  food 274
  nightlife 275
  shopping 274-5
  travel within 272
Renoir, Pierre-Auguste 327-8
responsible travel 910-11
Rhône Valley 449-93
  accommodation 492
  itineraries 452-3
  navigation 450-1, **450-1**
  travel seasons 452-3
  travel within 450-1
ridesharing 903
Rigaud, Hyacinthe 688
road trips 23
  Alta Rocca 896, **896**

Map Pages **000**

Beaujolais 464, **464**
Cahors 631, **631**
Cantal 486-7, **487**
Cap Corse 870-1, **871**
Cathar Castle Country 693, **693**
Château of the Dordogne Valley 620-1, **621**
Côte Fleurie 244, **244**
Four Countries 363, **363**
Gorges de l'Ardèche 469
La Balagne 878, **878**
L'Aubrac 681, **681**
Luberon 788-9
Médoc Vineyards 568, **568**
Meuse Valley, the 362
Parc National des Pyrénées 729
Parc Naturel Régional des Vosges du Nord 339, **339**
Route des Crêtes 347, 845, **347**
Route des Vins d'Alsace 349-52, **350**
Route du Mimosa 833, **833**
Tarn Wine & Bastides 716-17, **717**
Three Corniches 818-19, **819**
WWI 208-9, **209**
Rocamadour 633-6
Rochefort-en-Terre 304, 306
Rochemaure 472
rock climbing 473
Rodin, Auguste 172-3, 214-15
Roman sites
  Carcassonne 682-3
  Les Arènes 654-6
  Lyon 454-5
  Musée de la Cour d'Or 360
  Musée de la Romanité 656
Nîmes 657, **657**
Orange 776-7
Pont du Diable 670
Pont du Gard 660
Sites Antiques de Vaison-la-Romaine 777
Théâtre Antique 776-7
Vienne 465
Roquebrune-Cap-Martin 819, 820
Rouen 224-8, **225**
  accommodation 265
  beyond Rouen 229-31
  food 227
  shopping 226-7
  travel within 224

Rousseau, Jean-Jacques 527
Roussillon 788
Route de la Potasse 346, 348
Route des Crêtes 347, 845, 922-3, **347**
Route des Vins d'Alsace 349-52, 353, **350**
Route of the Vines 440-1, **441**
rugby 710

safe travel 907
sailing 51
Sainte-Chapelle 140, 146
Salavas 472
Salin de Giraud 766-7
sand yachting 263-4
Sare 600
Sarlat-la-Canéda 618-19
Sélestat 340
Sète 673-4
Shakespeare & Company 156
SIM cards 902
skiing 51
  Alpe d'Huez 538-9
  Avoriaz 521
  Chaîne des Puys 488
  Chamonix 500-2
  French Alps 546-8, **547**
  Les Trois Vallées 531
  Lyon 459-60
  Oisans 539
  Parc National des Pyrénées 732
  Parc Naturel Régional des Pyrénées Ariégeoises 726
  Vallée de la Tarentaise 531
  Vallorcine 511
smoking 915
snorkelling 50, 849
snowboarding 51
snowshoeing 531, 733
Somme, the 191-217
  itineraries 193
  navigation 192, **192**
  travel seasons 193
  travel within 192
Sorges 616
Soubirous, Bernadette 734-5, 736
Soufflenheim 338
spas 473
sports venues
  Stade Ernest-Wallon 710
  Stade Roland Garros 75
  Stadium de Toulouse 710
stargazing 794

St-Armel 302-3
St-Cirq-Lapopie 636-7
Ste-Agnès 817
St-Émilion 566-7, **567**
Stes-Maries-de-la-Mer 767-8, 796
St-Étienne 479-80, 493
St-Étienne de Baïgorry 599, 600
St-Florent 869, 872, 898
St-Gervais-les-Bains 512-13
St-Gildas-de-Rhuys 303
St-Guilhem-le-Désert 669-70
St-Jean-Cap-Ferrat 816-17
St-Jean-Pied-de-Port 594-7, **595**
  accommodation 601
  beyond St-Jean-Pied-de-Port 598-600
  drinking 597
  food 596, 597
  travel within 594
St-Malo 36, 279-83, **280**
  accommodation 307
  beyond St-Malo 284-6
  food 281, 283
  travel within 279
  walking tour 282, **282**
St-Martin-Vésubie 821-2
St-Paul de Vence 832, 834, 858
St-Raphaël 842-3, 859
Strasbourg 334-7, **335**
  accommodation 353
  beyond Strasbourg 338-40
  food 336, 337
  shopping 337
  travel within 334
street art 337, 537, 659
strikes 929-31
St-Tropez 34, 835-41, **836-7**
  accommodation 859
  beyond St-Tropez 842-9
  drinking 838, 839, 840, 841
  food 838, 839
  shopping 838
  travel within 835
St-Vaast-la-Hougue 262
St-Valery-sur-Somme 216, 217
Sundgau, the 345-6
surfing
  Bordeaux 564-5, **564-5**
  Lake Annecy 520
synagogues
  Agoudas Hakehilos Synagogue 116
  Carpentras Synagogue 776
  Rashi House & Synagogue 326

Tarn 715, 716-17, 718, **717**
taxes 904
thalassotherapy 239, 242
theatres
　Comédie Française 89
　Great Palais Garnier 80-1
　Moulin Rouge 100, 102
　Opéra Bastille 131-2
　Théâtre de l'Odéon 158
theft 907
Thiepval 207
Thuir 692
time zone 915
Tizzano 897
Toulois, the 369, 371
Toulouse 702-11, **704-5**
　accommodation 739
　beyond Toulouse 712-20
　drinking 709, 710, 711
　food 703, 708, 709
　travel within 702
　walking tour 707, **707**
Toulouse-Lautrec, Henri de 714, 715
trains 903
　Côte Bleue railway 757
　Le Petit Train d'Artouste 730-1
　Petit Train Jaune 692
　Train à Vapeur des Cévennes 678
　Train de la Rhune 600
　Train des Merveilles 822
　Tramway du Mont Blanc 512
travel to/from France 902
travel within France 903
travel seasons 38-9, see also individual locations
trekking, see hiking
Troyes 33, 323-6, **324**
　accommodation 329
　beyond Troyes 327-8
　drinking 325
　food 325
　travel within 323
　walking tour 326, **326**
truffles 774-5, 847

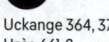

Uckange 364, 371
Uzès 661-2

Vaison-la-Romaine 777-8
Valéry, Paul 674
Vallauris 830-1
Vallée de la Rance 284-5
Vallée de la Restonica 882-3
Vallée de la Roya 822
Vallée de la Tarentaise 531-2
Vallée des Aravis 523
Vallée des Belleville 533
Vallée du Fangu 877
Vallée du Niolu 883
Vallée du Tavignanu 883
Vallorcine 510-11
Van Gogh, Vincent 760-1, 762
Vannes 297-300, **298**
　accommodation 307
　beyond Vannes 301-6
　drinking 300
　eating 300
　food 297, 299
　travel within 297
Vasarely, Victor 758
Vascœuil 230-1
vegan travellers 48, 336
vegetarian travellers 48
Vence 834, 858
Verdun 364
Versailles 184-5, 922
Vers-Pont-du-Gard 660
Veules-les-Roses 235
Vézère caves 625-7, **626**
Vézère Valley 28, 622-7, 920, **623**, **626**
　accommodation 647
　travel within 622
Vienne 463, 465
Villedieu-les-Poêles 258-9
Villefranche-de-Conflent 691-2
Villefranche-sur-Mer 815, 818, 858
Villeneuve-lès-Avignon 773
Villers-Bretonneux 206
Villesèque 637
Vimy 210-11
visas 902
Vitré 278
Vogüé 472
Volvic 491
Vougeot 427-8
vultures 677, 729-30

walking 50, see also hiking
　Corsica 864-5
walking tours
　Arles 764, **764**
　Biarritz 590, **590**
　Fresselines 645, **645**
　Le Havre 236, **236**
　Limoges 642, **642**
　Lyon 458
　Marseille 751, **751**
　Monaco 855, **855**
　Nancy 368, **368**
　Nice 813, **813**
　Nîmes 657, **657**
　Paris 72, 84-5, 101, 116, 118-19, 126-7, 133, 157, 171, 177, 179, **72**, **85**, **101**, **116**, **119**, **127**, **133**, **157**, **171**, **177**, **179**
　Pays Bigouden 295, **295**
　St-Émilion 567, **567**
　St-Malo 282, **282**
　Toulouse 707, **707**
　Troyes 326, **326**
weather 38-9
weights 915
wine 42-3, see also Champagne (wine)
　Bordeaux 556-7
　Malbec 630
　Picpoul de Pinet 672
　reds 42-3
　rosés 43, 839, 847
　tasting 42-3
　whites 43
wineries
　accommodation 905
　Beaujolais 463
　Beaujolais Nouveau 465
　Beaune 433
　Bergerac 617
　Cahors 631
　Carcassonne 684
　Carpentras 775-6
　Chablis 446
　Champagne 314-15
　Châteauneuf-du-Pape 774
　Côte de Nuits 438-9
　Côte d'Or 932-3
　Gaillac 716-17
　Île St-Honorat 827
　Jura Mountains 545
　Jurançon 737
　Limoux 685
　Luberon 785
　Médoc Vineyards 568, **568**
　Nice 812, 814
　Patrimonio 872
　Pinet 672
　Route des Vins d'Alsace 349-52, **350**
　Route of the Vines 440-1, **441**
　St-Émilion 566
St-Jean-Pied-de-Port 597
St-Paul de Vence 834
St-Tropez 839
Toulois, the 369
World's Fairs 71
WWI
　38th Welsh Division Memorial 208
　Australian National War Memorial 206
　Battle of the Somme 207
　Beaumont-Hamel Newfoundland Memorial 209
　Canadian National Vimy Memorial 210
　Historial de la Grande Guerre 206-7
　Lochnagar Crater 208
　Mémorial de l'Armistice 211
　Mémorial Sud-Africain Delville Wood 207
　Meuse Valley, the 362
　Musée de la Bataille de Fromelles 211
　Ring of Remembrance 211
　road trip 208-9, **209**
　Sir John Monash Centre 206
　Thiepval Memorial 207
　Verdun 364
WWII
　Batterie de Crisbecq 250
　D-Day Experience 247, 250
　D-Day Landing Beaches 246-52
　Mémorial de l'Internement et de la Déportation - Camp de Royallieu 211
　Musée de la Libération 262
　Musée du Debarquement 246
　Museum Dunkerque 1940 214
　Natzweiler-Struthof 346
　Oradour-sur-Glane 643-4
　St-Malo 283

ziplining 730
zoos
　Ménagerie 155
　Parc Zoologique de Paris 139

"The fog was so thick at Puy Mary (p485) that to start off with I climbed the wrong volcano. The clouds suddenly lifted and I realised my mistake."

ANNA RICHARDS

"That time I visited the Cirque de Navacelles (p679) at dawn and had it all to myself, aside from a company of vultures."

PAUL STAFFORD

"Nothing compares to your first sight of the Chartres Cathedral rising in splendor above endless agricultural fields – I was a teen and it's still engrained in my brain."

MARY WINSTON NICKLIN

All rights reserved. No part of this publication may be copied, stored in a retrieval system, or transmitted in any form by any means, electronic, mechanical, recording or otherwise, except brief extracts for the purpose of review, and no part of this publication may be sold or hired, without the written permission of the publisher. Lonely Planet and the Lonely Planet logo are trademarks of Lonely Planet and are registered in the US Patent and Trademark Office and in other countries. Lonely Planet does not allow its name or logo to be appropriated by commercial establishments, such as retailers, restaurants or hotels. Please let us know of any misuses: lonelyplanet.com/legal/intellectual-property.

Mapping data sources:
© Lonely Planet
© OpenStreetMap http://openstreetmap.org/copyright

THIS BOOK

Destination Editor
Annemarie McCarthy

Production Editor
Kathryn Rowan

Book Designer
Virginia Moreno

Cartographer
David Connolly

Coordinating Editor
Anita Isalska

Assisting Editors
Liana Cafolla, Sally Davies, Kevin Ebbutt, Trent Holden, Kate Mathews, Karyn Noble, Charlotte Orr, Maja Vatrić

Cover Researcher
Katelyn Perry

Paper in this book is certified against the Forest Stewardship Council™ standards. FSC™ promotes environmentally responsible, socially beneficial and economically viable management of the world's forests.

Published by Lonely Planet Global Limited
CRN 554153
16th edition – March 2026
ISBN 978 1 83869 780 8
© Lonely Planet 2026
10 9 8 7 6 5 4 3 2 1
Printed in China